'Michael Morales has marshalled a breathtaking spectrum of Jewish, Christian and critical perspectives unprecedented in commentary to Numbers – or to any book of the Hebrew Bible. His attention to the ways in which structure, themes and vocabulary create a unified whole within chapters and across the book makes this an indispensable resource.'
Joshua Berman, Bar-Ilan University, Israel, and author of *Inconsistency in the Torah: Ancient Literary Convention and the Limits of Source Criticism*

'With close attention to the text, and deeply informed by classical and modern sources, Michael Morales offers a theologically rich and informative reading of Numbers. By highlighting the importance of Israel's Camp he demonstrates the literary integrity of the book. Far from Numbers being the junk room of the priestly material, he demonstrates that it is a coherent work. This substantial commentary will therefore be a key point of reference for all future work on Numbers.'
David G. Firth, Trinity College Bristol

'Michael Morales's work on Numbers is a breathtaking achievement. It is a rare thing for a work of this scale (or any scale) to marry depth of scholarship, breadth of reading, clarity of expression and an evident commitment to the gospel of Christ, but this book has it all. It's worth having for the introduction alone, which brilliantly outlines a theological approach to Numbers that is both dramatically fresh and yet historically rooted, particularly in the rich Jewish tradition of reading the book as a keystone of the Pentateuch. Morales's careful and thoughtful exegesis is married with a profound commitment to biblical theology. Judicious insights and stimulating suggestions are presented with a beautiful lightness of touch. This deserves to be the standard evangelical work on Numbers for many years to come, and will repay careful study by pastors, scholars and students alike.'
J. Gary Millar, Principal, Queensland Theological College, Brisbane, Australia

'Page-turner and game-changer! I never expected to say that of a book about Numbers. Michael Morales's commentary on Numbers changes everything. No commentary or study opens up Numbers more richly than these two volumes – from the census of the first generation to the second ruling about the inheritance of the daughters of Zelophehad. Every page of Morales's interpretation leads me to re-study Numbers as though I have never read it before. The exciting engagement with rich Judaic interpretative traditions sets every part of Numbers within the entire book and the entire Torah as well as within all of the Christian Scriptures. Pastors, students and scholars will want to set aside the latest paperback in order to take to the beach or to the park Morales's

page-turner of a commentary and find out what's next. Morales invites all of us back into the wilderness sojourn of Numbers as though for the very first time.'
Gary Edward Schnittjer, Distinguished Professor of Old Testament, Cairn University, Philadelphia, and author of the award-winning *Old Testament Use of Old Testament: A Book-by-Book Guide*

APOLLOS OLD TESTAMENT
COMMENTARY
4b

NUMBERS 20 – 36

TITLES IN THIS SERIES

EXODUS, T. Desmond Alexander
LEVITICUS, Nobuyoshi Kiuchi
NUMBERS 1 – 19, L. Michael Morales
NUMBERS 20 – 36, L. Michael Morales
DEUTERONOMY, J. G. McConville
JOSHUA, Pekka M. A. Pitkänen
RUTH, L. Daniel Hawk
1 & 2 SAMUEL, David G. Firth
1 & 2 KINGS, Lissa Wray Beal
PROVERBS, Paul Overland
ECCLESIASTES & THE SONG OF SONGS,
Daniel C. Fredericks and Daniel J. Estes
DANIEL, Ernest C. Lucas
HOSEA, Joshua N. Moon
OBADIAH, JONAH & MICAH, Elaine A. Phillips
HAGGAI, ZECHARIAH & MALACHI,
Anthony R. Petterson

SERIES EDITORS

Gordon J. Wenham, 2002–23
David W. Baker, 2002–
Beth M. Stovell, 2023–

Apollos Old Testament
Commentary
4b

NUMBERS
20 – 36

Series Editors
David W. Baker and Beth M. Stovell

L. MICHAEL MORALES

Apollos,
London, England

APOLLOS (an imprint of Inter-Varsity Press)
SPCK Group, Studio 101, The Record Hall, 16–16A Baldwin's Gardens, London
EC1N 7RJ, England
Email: ivp@ivpbooks.com
Website: www.ivpbooks.com

© L. Michael Morales, 2024

L. Michael Morales has asserted his right under the Copyright, Designs and Patents Act 1988 to be identified as Author of this work.

All rights reserved. No part of this publication may be reproduced, stored in a retrieval system or transmitted, in any form or by any means, electronic, mechanical, photocopying, recording or otherwise, without the prior permission of the publisher or the Copyright Licensing Agency.

Unless otherwise noted, Scripture quotations are the author's own translation.

First published 2024

British Library Cataloguing-in-Publication Data
A catalogue record for this book is available from the British Library.

ISBN: 978–1–78974–555–9
eBook ISBN: 978–1–78974–520–7

Typeset in Great Britain by Fakenham Prepress Solutions, Fakenham, Norfolk
Printed in Great Britain by Clays Ltd, Elcograf S.p.A.

Produced on paper from sustainable sources

Inter-Varsity Press publishes Christian books that are true to the Bible and that communicate the gospel, develop discipleship and strengthen the church for its mission in the world.

IVP originated within the Inter-Varsity Fellowship, now the Universities and Colleges Christian Fellowship, a student movement connecting Christian Unions in universities and colleges throughout Great Britain, and a member movement of the International Fellowship of Evangelical Students. Website: www.uccf.org.uk. That historic association is maintained, and all senior IVP staff and committee members subscribe to the UCCF Basis of Faith.

CONTENTS

Illustrations	vii
Abbreviations	ix
Text and Commentary	**1**
Bibliography	497
Index of Scripture references and ancient sources	575
Index of modern authors	633
Index of subjects	672

The bibliography and indexes apply to both volumes

ILLUSTRATIONS

FIGURES

1. Numbers 20 as bridge between generations	5
2. First generation wilderness sojourn	7
3. Balaam's vision	182
4. Promised Land, Numbers 34	457
5. Levitical cities and cities of refuge	480

TABLES

1. Complaint patterns	8
2. Numbers 21 – from Egypt to the land of Canaan	86
3. Balaam story: blessing versus curse inclusio	96
4. YHWH overrules Balak's attempt to curse Israel through Balaam, and blesses his people	98
5. Divination versus prophecy	108
6. 'Divination' and 'enchantment' usage	123
7. Act 1, scene 3	139
8. Curse and blessing in the first parable	153
9. Balaam's first parable, 23:7–10	154
10. Balaam's second parable, 23:18–24	161
11. Balaam's third parable, 24:3–9	175
12. Balaam's third parable: Israel in the land	176
13. From divination to prophecy	177
14. The blessing of Judah	186
15. Nachmanides' chronological reading of Balaam's oracles	191
16. Balaam's fourth parable, 24:15–19	192
17. Baal Peor and the golden calf	249
18. Baal Peor and the strayed wife	253
19. Census tallies: a comparison	267
20. Moses' prayer for a new shepherd	283
21. Whole burnt offerings in Numbers 28 – 29	345
22. Numbers 30: structure	353
23. Numbers 31: structure	375
24. Battle with Midian as culmination	376
25. The five kings of Midian	382
26. Numbers 31 and the Tabernacle offerings	393

27. Numbers 32: tribal lands east of the Jordan River	402
28. Arabah – Plains of Moab road	434
29. YHWH's final speeches	438
30. Ten tribal leaders	459

ABBREVIATIONS

TEXTUAL

1Q3	1QpalaeoLev-Num
1QM	*War Scroll*
4Q365	4QReworked Pentateuch
4QMMT	*Halakhic Letter*
4QNum[b]	Numbers text from Qumran, Cave 4 (4Q27)
11Q19, 11QT[a]	*Temple Scroll*
AgBem	*Aggadah Bemidbar*
Aq	Aquila
Ar.	Arachin
Av.	Avot
b.	Babylonian Talmud
B. Qam.	*Bava Qamma*
Bav. Bat.	*Bava Batra*
Bek.	*Bekhorot*
Ber.	*Berakhot*
CD	Cairo Damascus Document/Rule
Deut.	*Deuteronomy*
DSS	Dead Sea Scrolls
Exod. Rab.	*Exodus Rabbah*
Frg. Tg.	*Fragment Targum(s)*
Gen. Rab.	*Genesis Rabbah*
Gk	Greek (texts)
HB	Hebrew Bible
Hebr.	Hebrew
Ḥuk.	*Ḥukkat*
Ḥul.	*Ḥullin*
Jub.	*Jubilees*
K	Kethibh (the written Hebrew text)
Kel.	*Kelim*
Ket.	*Ketubot*
Leg. Alleg.	Philo, *Legum Allegoriae* (Allegorical Interpretation)
Lev. Rab.	*Leviticus Rabbah*
LXX	Septuagint
m.	*Mishnah*
Mak.	*Makkot*
Meg.	*Megillah*

Meil.	Meilah
MekhI	Mekhilta deRabbi Ishmael
MekhSh	Mekhilta deRabbi Shimon ben Yohai
Men.	Menaḥot
Mid.	Middot
MQ	Moʻed Qatan
MS(S)	manuscript(s)
MT	Masoretic Text
Naz.	Nazir
Ned.	Nedarim
Num. Rab.	Numbers Rabbah
Par.	Parah
Pes.	Pesaḥim
PesRab.	Pesiqta Rabbati
PesRK	Pesiqta de-Rav Kahana
Pirk. Av.	Pirkei Avot
Q	Qere (the Hebrew text to be read out)
Rosh HaSh.	Rosh HaShannah
SamP	Samaritan Pentateuch
Sanh.	Sanhedrin
Shab.	Shabbat
Shem.	Shemot
Shev.	Shevuʻot
Sif.	Sifre
Sif. Deut.	Sifre Deuteronomy
Sif. Num.	Sifre Numbers
Sif. Zut.	Sifre Zuta
Sot.	Sotah
Spec. Laws	Philo, *Special Laws*
Suk.	Sukkah
Sym	Symmachus
Syr	Syriac Peshitta
T	Tosefta
t.	tractate
T. Ab.	Testament of Abraham
T. Levi	Testament of Levi
T. Naph.	Testament of Naphtali
Taʻan.	Taʻanit
Tam.	Tamid
Tan.	Tanḥuma
Tg(s)	Targum(s)
TgNeof	Targum Neofiti
TgO	Targum Onqelos
TgPal	Palestinian Targum
TgPs-J	Targum Pseudo-Jonathan

Theo	Theodotion
Tos.	*Tosafot*
VetLat	The Old Latin
Vg	Vulgate
Yalk. Reuv.	*Yalkut Reuveni*
Yalk. Shim.	*Yalkut Shim'oni*
Yev.	*Yevamot*
Yom.	*Yoma*
Zeb.	*Zebachim*

HEBREW GRAMMAR

abs.	absolute
adj.	adjective, adjectival
art.	article
cohort.	cohortative
conj.	conjunction
const.	construct
def. art.	definite article
f.	feminine
gen.	genitive
hiph.	hiphil
hith.	hithpael
hithpal.	hithpalel
hoph.	hophal
imp.	imperative
impf.	imperfect
inf.	infinitive
juss.	jussive
m.	masculine
niph.	niphal
pi.	piel
pl.	plural
pr.	pronoun/pronominal
prep.	preposition
ptc.	participle, participial
pu.	pual
sg.	singular
suff.	suffix

MISCELLANEOUS

ad loc.	at the place (passage of a commentary where citation may be found)
Ag. Ap.	Josephus, *Against Apion*
ANE	ancient Near East(ern)
Ant.	Josephus, *Antiquities of the Jews*
ASV	American Standard Version
AV	Authorized (King James) Version
Barn.	*Barnabas*
c.	circa
Creation	Philo, *On the Creation*
ESV	English Standard Version
Gig.	Philo, *De Gigantibus*
Gk	Greek (texts)
GNT	Good News Translation
JPS	Jewish Publication Society translation
J. W.	Josephus, *Jewish War*
LAB	Pseudo-Philo, *Liber Antiquitatum Biblicarum*
lit.	literally
Mir. S.S.	Augustine, *De Mirabilibus Sacrae Scripturae*
MishT	Maimonides, *Mishneh Torah*
Moses	Philo, *Life of Moses*
NAB	New American Bible
NEB	New English Bible
NET	New English Translation (2005 ed.)
NIV	New International Version (1984 ed.)
NJPS	New Jewish Publication Society translation
NKJV	New King James Version
NRSV	New Revised Standard Version
NT	New Testament
PG	Patrologiae graeca
PL	Patrologiae latina
Quaest. in Num.	Augustine, *Quaestiones in Numeri* (Questions on Numbers)
Quaest.in Oct.	Theodoret, *Quaestiones in Octateuchum* (Question on the Octateuch)
SamP	Samaritan Pentateuch
Sir.	Ben Sira, *Sirach* (Ecclesiasticus)
TEV	Today's English Version
tr.	translated by / translation

JOURNALS, REFERENCE WORKS, SERIES

AB	Anchor Bible
ABD	D. N. Freedman (ed.), *Anchor Bible Dictionary*, 6 vols., New York: Doubleday, 1992
ABG	Arbeiten zur Bibel und ihrer Geschichte
ABR	*Australian Biblical Review*
ACCS: OT	Ancient Christian Commentary on Scripture, Old Testament
AJSLL	*The American Journal of Semitic Languages and Literatures*
AJT	*American Journal of Theology*
AnBib	Analecta Biblica
AnOr	Analecta Orientalia
AOAT	Alter Orient und Altes Testament
AOTC	Apollos Old Testament Commentary
ArBib	The Aramaic Bible
ATANT	Abhandlungen zur Theologie des Alten und Neuen Testaments
AThR	*Anglican Theological Review*
AUSS	*Andrews University Seminary Studies*
BA	*Biblical Archaeologist*
BAR	*Biblical Archaeology Review*
BASOR	*Bulletin of the American Schools of Oriental Research*
BBR	*Bulletin for Biblical Research*
BBRS	Bulletin for Biblical Research Supplement
BDB	F. Brown, S. R. Driver and C. A. Briggs, *The Brown-Driver-Briggs Hebrew and English Lexicon, with an Appendix Containing the Biblical Aramaic*, Boston: Houghton, Mifflin, 1906; repr. Peabody: Hendrickson, 2012
BETL	Bibliotheca ephemeridum theologicarum lovaniensium
BGBE	Beiträge zur Geschichte der biblischen Exegese
BHS	K. Elliger and W. Rudolph (eds.), *Biblia Hebraica Stuttgartensia*, Stuttgart: Deutsche Bibelgesellschaft, 1983
Bib	*Biblica*
BibInt	*Biblical Interpretation*
BJS	Brown Judaic Studies
BKAT	Biblischer Kommentar, Altes Testament
BN	*Biblische Notizen*
BR	*Biblical Research*
BRev	*Bible Review*

BSac	*Bibliotheca Sacra*
BSC	Bible Student's Commentary
BST	The Bible Speaks Today
BT	*The Bible Translator*
BTB	*Biblical Theology Bulletin*
BZ	*Biblische Zeitschrift*
BZAW	Beihefte zur Zeitschrift für die alttestamentliche Wissenschaft
BZGBE	*Beiträge zur Geschichte der biblischen Exegese*
CAL	Comprehensive Aramaic Lexicon
CBQ	*Catholic Biblical Quarterly*
COT	Commentar op het Oude Testament
CTQ	*Concordia Theological Quarterly*
CurTM	*Currents in Theology and Mission*
CV	*Communio viatorum*
DATD	*Das Alte Testament Deutsch*
DOP	*Dumbarton Oaks Papers*
DOTP	T. D. Alexander and D. W. Baker (eds.), *Dictionary of the Old Testament: Pentateuch*, Downers Grove: InterVarsity Press; Leicester: Inter-Varsity Press, 2003
DSB	Daily Study Bible
DSD	*Dead Sea Discoveries*
EBC	Expositor's Bible Commentary
ECC	Eerdmans Critical Commentary
ETL	*Ephemerides theologicae lovanienses*
EvQ	*Evangelical Quarterly*
ExpTim	*Expository Times*
FAT	Forschungen zum Alten Testament
GKC	*Gesenius Hebrew Grammar*
HALOT	L. Koehler, W. Baumgartner and J. J. Stamm, *The Hebrew and Aramaic Lexicon of the Old Testament*, tr. and ed. under supervision of M. E. J. Richardson, 2 vols., Leiden: Brill, 2001
HAT	Handbuch zum Alten Testament
HBT	*Horizons in Biblical Theology*
HS	Hebrew Studies
HSM	Harvard Semitic Monographs
HTR	*Harvard Theological Review*
HUCA	Hebrew Union College Annual
IBC	Interpretation: A Bible Commentary for Teaching and Preaching
ICC	International Critical Commentary
IDB	G. A. Buttrick (ed.), *Interpreter's Dictionary of the Bible*, 4 vols., Nashville: Abingdon, 1962

IDBSup	G. A. Buttrick (ed.), *Interpreter's Dictionary of the Bible*, Supplement vol., Nashville: Abingdon, 1976
IEJ	*Israel Exploration Journal*
Int	*Interpretation*
JAGNES	*Journal of the Association of Graduate Near Eastern Students*
JANEBL	*Journal for Ancient Near Eastern and Biblical Law*
JANES	*Journal of the Ancient Near Eastern Society*
JAOS	*Journal of the American Oriental Society*
JBL	*Journal of Biblical Literature*
JBQ	*Jewish Bible Quarterly*
JETS	*Journal of the Evangelical Theological Society*
JJS	*Journal of Jewish Studies*
JPT	*Journal of Pentecostal Theology*
JPTSup	*Journal of Pentecostal Theology Supplement*
JQR	*Jewish Quarterly Review*
JSJ	*Journal for the Study of Judaism in the Persian, Hellenistic, and Roman Period*
JSOT	*Journal for the Study of the Old Testament*
JSOTSup	*Journal for the Study of the Old Testament: Supplement*
JSQ	*Jewish Studies Quarterly*
LHBOTS	Library of Hebrew Bible / Old Testament Studies
MTZ	*Münchener theologische Zeitschrift*
NAC	The New American Commentary
NCBC	New Century Bible Commentary
NICNT	New International Commentary on the New Testament
NICOT	New International Commentary on the Old Testament
NIDOTTE	W. A. VanGemeren (ed.), *New International Dictionary of Old Testament Theology and Exegesis*, 5 vols., Grand Rapids: Zondervan, 1997
NIGTC	New International Greek Testament Commentary
NIVAC	New International Version Application Commentary
NovT	*Novum Testamentum*
NSBT	New Studies in Biblical Theology
NSKAT	Neuer Stuttgarter Kommentar, Altes Testament
OBO	Orbis biblicus et orientalis
OBT	Overtures to Biblical Theology
Or	*Orientalia*
OTE	*Old Testament Essays*
OTG	Old Testament Guides
OTL	Old Testament Library

OtSt	*Oudtestamentische Studiën*
PAAJR	*Proceedings of the American Academy for Jewish Research*
PBM	Paternoster Biblical Monographs
PEQ	*Palestine Exploration Quarterly*
Presb	*Presbyterion*
RB	*Revue biblique*
ResQ	*Restoration Quarterly*
RevExp	*Review and Expositor*
RTR	*Reformed Theological Review*
SANT	Old Testament Library
SBJT	*Southern Baptist Journal of Theology*
SBL	Society of Biblical Literature
SBLDS	Society of Biblical Literature Dissertation Series
Sem	*Semitica*
SFSHJ	South Florida Studies in the History of Judaism
SJLA	Studies in Judaism in Late Antiquity
SJOT	*Scandinavian Journal of the Old Testament*
SJT	*Scottish Journal of Theology*
SOTSMS	Society for Old Testament Studies Monograph Series
SSN	*Studia semitica neerlandica*
ST	*Studia theologica*
StOr	Studies in Oriental Religions
TBL	Themes in Biblical Narrative
TDOT	G. J. Botterweck and H. Ringgren (eds.), *Theological Dictionary of the Old Testament*, tr. J. T. Willis, G. W. Bromiley and D. E. Green, 8 vols., Grand Rapids, 1974–
THAT	E. Jenni and C. Westermann (eds.), *Theologisches Handwörterbuch zum Alten Testament*, 2 vols., Munich, 1971–1976
TLOT	E. Jenni (ed.), with assistance from C. Westermann, tr. M. E. Biddle, *Theological Lexicon of the Old Testament*, 3 vols., Peabody, 1997
TOTC	Tyndale Old Testament Commentaries
TWOT	R. L. Harris, G. L. Archer Jr. and B. K. Waltke (eds.), *Theological Wordbook of the Old Testament*, 2 vols., Chicago: Moody, 1980; repr. as one vol. 2003
TynB	*Tyndale Bulletin*
TZ	*Theologische Zeitschrift*
UF	*Ugarit-Forschungen*
VT	*Vetus Testamentum*
VTSup	Vetus Testamentum Supplements

WBC	Word Biblical Commentary
WTJ	*Westminster Theological Journal*
ZABR	*Zeitschrift für altorientalische und biblische Rechtgeschichte*
ZAH	*Zeitschrift für Althebräistik*
ZAW	*Zeitschrift für die alttestamentliche Wissenschaft*
ZBK	Zürcher Bibelkommentare

TEXT AND COMMENTARY

NUMBERS 20: THE FAILURE OF THE FIRST GENERATION LEADERS

Translation

20:1Now the sons of Israel, the whole community, came to the wilderness of Zin on the first month, and the people dwelled in Kadesh; and there Miriam died and there she was buried. ²But there was no water for the community, and they assembled against Moses and against Aaron. ³And the people contended with Moses and they said, saying, 'If only we had perished when our brothers had perished before YHWH. ⁴Why have you brought the assembly of YHWH to this wilderness so that we and our beasts should die there? ⁵Why did you make us ascend out of Egypt to bring us to this evil place? – not a place of seed or fig or vine or pomegranate, nor is there water to drink!' ⁶And Moses came, and Aaron, from the presence of the assembly to the door of the Tent of Meeting, and they fell on their faces, and the glory of YHWH appeared to them.
⁷And YHWH spoke to Moses, saying, ⁸'Take the staff, and assemble the community, you and Aaron your brother, and speak to the rock before their eyes, and it will give its waters, so you will bring forth for them water from the rock, and cause the community and their beasts to drink.' ⁹And Moses took the staff from before YHWH, just as he had commanded him. ¹⁰And Moses and Aaron assembled the assembly before the rock, and he said to them, 'Hear now, rebels: from this rock shall we bring forth for you water?' ¹¹And Moses raised his hand

and he struck the rock with his staff twice, and many waters poured forth, and the community drank, and their beasts.'

¹²And YHWH said to Moses and to Aaron, 'Because you did not trust in me to sanctify me before the eyes of the sons of Israel; therefore, you will not bring this assembly into the land that I have given them.' ¹³These are the waters of Meribah (contention), in which the sons of Israel contended with YHWH, and he was sanctified through them.

¹⁴And Moses sent messengers from Kadesh to the king of Edom, 'Thus says your brother Israel: "You yourself know all the hardship which has met us. ¹⁵Our fathers descended into Egypt, and we have dwelled in Egypt many days, and the Egyptians did evil to us, and to our fathers. ¹⁶And we cried out to YHWH and he heard our voice, and he sent a Messenger, and he brought us forth out from Egypt, and – look! – we are in Kadesh, a city on the outskirts of your border. ¹⁷Let us pass, please, through your land, we will not pass through in field and in vineyard, and we will not drink waters of a well; we will go along the Way of the King and not stretch out to our right hand or left until we have passed through your border."' ¹⁸And Edom said to them, 'You will not pass through me, lest with the sword I go forth to encounter you.' ¹⁹And the sons of Israel said to him, 'We will ascend by the highway, and if I and my livestock drink from your water, I will give their payment – I will only pass through with my feet, nothing else.' ²⁰And he said, 'You will not pass through.' And Edom went forth to encounter him with a weight of people and with a strong hand. ²¹And Edom refused to give Israel passage through his border, and Israel stretched away from him.

²²And they journeyed from Kadesh, and the sons of Israel, the whole community, came to Mount Hor. ²³And YHWH said to Moses and to Aaron in Mount Hor, by the border of the land of Edom, saying, ²⁴"Aaron will be gathered to his people, for he will not enter into the land which I have given the sons of Israel, since you rebelled against my word at the waters of Meribah. ²⁵Take Aaron and Eleazar his son, cause them to ascend Mount Hor. ²⁶And strip Aaron of his garments, and clothe Eleazar his son, but Aaron will be gathered – there he will die.' ²⁷And Moses did just as YHWH had commanded, and they ascended to Mount Hor before the eyes of the whole community. ²⁸And Moses stripped Aaron of his garments, and clothed Eleazar his son with them, and there Aaron died on the summit of the Mount, and Moses descended, along with Eleazar, from the Mount. ²⁹And when the whole community saw that Aaron had perished, they wept for Aaron thirty days – the whole house of Israel.

Notes on the text

3. 'with Moses': There is weak attestation for adding 'and with Aaron' (Syr and one MS), harmonizing with pl. verbs in vv. 4–5.

4. 'that we . . . should die there': LXX has *apokteinai* (to kill us).

5. 'seed': LXX has 'not sown' (*ou speiretai*).

8. 'you will bring forth . . . cause to drink': MT has sg. form for these last two verbs; LXX has pl. 'Speak' is isolated as pl., inclusive of Aaron.
11. 'his staff': LXX has 'the staff'(*tē rhabdō*).
12. 'in me': lacking in LXX and Vg.
13. SamP adds material from Deut. 3:24–28 (minus 26a).

Form and structure

Chapter 20 has three sections, connected by the Kadesh locale (vv. 1, 14, 16, 22) and the 'sons of Israel' (vv. 1, 12, 13, 19, 22, 24), and thematically by the deaths of the first generation's leaders (vv. 1, 12, 28–29) and the desire to progress into the land (vv. 5, 17, 19):

1–13 The second generation's lack of water and the sin of Moses and Aaron
14–21 Edom's refusal to allow Israel to pass through his border
22–29 The transition to Eleazar as high priest with Aaron's death, mourned by Israel.

The death of Aaron alludes directly to the sin of Moses and Aaron (v. 24; cf. v. 12), forming a frame around the Edom passage, creating an intercalation whereby 'the middle story nearly always provides the key to the theological purpose' (Edwards 1989: 196; cf. Kee 1977: 54–56). Beginning with the chronological marker 'the first month' (of the fortieth year in the wilderness), chapter 20 is Janus-faced (facing backwards and forwards): capping the larger section pervaded by the death of the first generation with the death and/or judgement of its leaders (chs. 16–20), even as the second generation has emerged, eager to inherit the land.

The chapter's first section, Numbers 20:1–13, is divided in MT into three paragraphs related to the crisis of lack of water for the second generation (vv. 1–6), YHWH's proposed solution, along with Moses and Aaron's deviation from his instructions (vv. 7–11), and YHWH's judgement of Moses and Aaron, along with a summary statement (vv. 12–13). The narrative employs multiple uses of 'face' (*pānîm*): 'before' YHWH (v. 3), going from the 'presence' of the assembly (v. 6), falling on 'their faces' (v. 6), taking the staff from 'before' YHWH (v. 9), gathering the assembly 'before' the rock (v. 10) (W. W. Lee 2003a: 231). The root for 'assemble' (*q-h-l*) occurs seven times (vv. 2, 4, 6, 8, 10 [twice], 12). Features such as the designation 'community' (*'ēdāh*), the appearance of YHWH's glory, the centrality of the Tent of Meeting, and the presence of Aaron have led many to trace the story, if containing pre-literary traditions, to the P source (e.g. Kohata 1977; Baden 2014), perhaps with traces of JE (cf. Wellhausen 1889: 109–110), a heterogeneous composition with several stages of literary growth (Garton 2017: 202–235; e.g. Hölscher 1927). Since there is little consensus on details, Holzinger, for example, assigning Miriam's death to E (1903: 84), Noth to J (1981: 32; Budd 1984: 216–217; Burns 1987: 120), Propp to P (1988: 25), and Sturdy to a later redactor (1976: 139), such analysis is manifestly inconclusive.

Numbers 20:1–13 contains rich resonances with other portions of Numbers and the Torah, especially with the water from the rock incident in Exodus 17. Similarities include both structure and parallel or verbatim wording (K. Brown 2020: 103–104): in both 'the whole congregation' of 'the sons of Israel' are in or near 'the desert of Sin/Zin' where there is no water (Exod. 17:1; Num. 20:1–2a); 'the people quarrel with Moses' (Exod. 17:2a; Num. 20:3a) and ask, 'Why did you bring us up from Egypt?' (Exod. 17:3c; Num. 20:5a); Moses is told to 'take the staff' (Exod. 17:5c; Num. 20:8a) and he strikes the rock and water pours out (Exod. 17:6; Num. 20:11); and both refer to Meribah, concluding that 'the Israelites quarrelled with YHWH' (Exod. 17:7b; Num. 20:13b). While Numbers 20:1–13 is usually assigned to the Priestly source, Exodus 17:1–7 is typically assigned to the Yahwistic and/or Elohistic source(s) (e.g. Baden 2009: 173–179, 259–261; Specht 2013: 273–313). Rather than seeing these texts as contradictory traditions related to the same event (Noth 1968: 146–147; Römer 2013: 79–80), the two episodes, balanced within the Torah's compositional structure, display narrative progression rhetorically anchored not only in similarities but in patent differences. These 'water from the rock' episodes form an inclusio, bracketing Israel's wilderness period (cf. Currid 2009: 275), and are part of a larger mirrored structure connecting Exodus, Leviticus and Numbers (Schart 1990: 52).

Numbers 20, a narrative more about Moses and Aaron's failure than of a parallel water miracle (Specht 2013: 308), also shares similarities with Numbers 12, which likewise involves Miriam, Aaron and Moses together, along with the theme of sin among leaders (see Boorer 2015). Both stories result in exclusion, of Miriam from the Camp (12:15), and of Moses and Aaron from the land (20:12); turn on the notion of 'speaking' (12:1, 2, 8; 20:8; cf. Ps. 106:33); relate Moses to YHWH's 'mouth' (12:8; 20:24). While Moses is 'faithful' (*'āman*) in YHWH's house (12:7), here he is not 'trusting' or 'faithful' (*'āman*) to YHWH (20:12). There are also structural correspondences between Numbers 20:1–12 and both Exodus 16 and Numbers 13 – 14 that cause significant differences to emerge (Boorer 2012): Moses and Aaron's behaviour in chapter 20, failing to give the people a knowledge of YHWH, forms a reversal of their behaviour in Exodus 16; and while chapters 13–14 focus on the failure and demise of the people, chapter 20 focuses on the failure and demise of the leaders Moses and Aaron.

Numbers 20 closes the account of the first generation in the wilderness (chs. 11–20) by recounting the death of its leaders, even while opening the story of Israel's second generation, and serves as the cap for the subsection of chapters 16–20, reflecting thematic and lexical similarities with Korah's rebellion as well (chs. 16–17), with its focus on Aaron's staff as an admonitory sign for 'rebels' (*mārāh*, 17:10; 20:10), Moses' saying 'Hear now' (*šim'û-nā'*, 16:8; 20:10), and the subject of 'perishing' (*gāwa'*, 17:12, 13; 20:3, 29). Ending with the transition from Aaron to Eleazar, chapters 16–20 focus on the office of priesthood, even as chapters 11–15 focus on Moses' prophetic office. The central section on Edom's refusal to grant Israel passage (vv. 14–21) functions in a twofold manner. It serves as commentary on the sin of Moses (and Aaron), and by similar terminology and themes anticipates the next subjection (see Figure 1), given to Israel's encounters with the nations surrounding Canaan (chs. 21–25): 'messenger(s)' (vv. 14, 16; 21:21; 22:5, 22, 23, 24, 25, 26, 27, 31, 32, 34, 35; 24:12), 'in field and in vineyard' (v. 17; 12:20, 22, 23, 24), 'stretch' (vv. 17, 21; 21:15, 22; 22:23, 26, 33; 24:6), 'right or left' (v. 17; 22:26), 'sword' (v. 19; 21:24; 22:23, 29, 31; cf. 31:8), 'encounter' (vv. 18, 20; 21:23, 33; 22:5, 20, 34, 36, 37; 23:3; 24:1) and 'feet' (v. 19; 21:32; 22:25, 28, 32, 33).

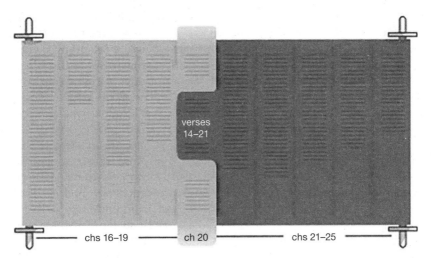

Figure 1: Numbers 20 as bridge between generations

Comment

20:1–13

The account of the sin of Moses and Aaron has been described as 'one of the most veiled sections of the Torah' (Nahshoni 1989: 4:1076) and 'one of the more difficult in the Pentateuch' (Margaliot 1983: 200), with

Moses' failure to lead the people into the land considered one of the book's central tragedies (Helfgot 1993: 51). While ambiguities and gaps are present, such features characterize the Torah's style of storytelling in general; presuming redactors have deliberately obscured the nature of Moses' sin out of regard for him is unnecessary (as supposed by Cornhill 1891; G. B. Gray 1903: 258; Kapelrud 1957: 242; E. W. Davies 1995b: 205–206). The text is clear that Moses (and Aaron) not only deviated from YHWH's instructions but did so in rebellion, a tragic point that explains the justice of his exclusion from leading the second generation of Israel into the land. The chapter's focus on Miriam, Moses and Aaron, siblings within the tribe of Levi, is a reminder that Numbers has a special focus on Levites, which begins as early as the genealogy in 3:1–4. Within the context of death and judgement, moreover, the demise of these Levitical leaders, who were part of the first generation of Israel, forms a fitting conclusion to the subsection of the wilderness sojourn concerned with the inner camp of Levites and the priesthood (chs. 16–18). Since, however, YHWH's response to the inner camp's failure was already given in Numbers 18, with chapter 19 displaying the transition of generations, *chapter 20 should be read as related to the Camp's heart*, the central camp of the *Shekhinah* – this time narrating the failure of Moses and Aaron, who represent YHWH to his people. In this way, the wilderness sojourn's drama has progressed from the outer camp of twelve tribes (chs. 11–15) to the inner camp of Levites and priests (chs. 16–19) to the central camp of the *Shekhinah* (ch. 20), narrating the failure and usurping of divine prerogative, YHWH's kingship, by the leaders of each of the three concentric divisions of the covenant community (see Figure 2). Numbers 20 thus brings us to the narrative holy of holies, perhaps signalled by the sixfold use of the root *q-d-š*: 'Kadesh' as the locale for the incident (vv. 1, 14, 16, 22), and 'sanctify' as both the divine assessment for Moses and Aaron's failure as well as the story's summary point (vv. 12, 13). The supernatural gift of waters is, moreover, associated with the archetypal holy of holies, the garden of Eden (Gen. 2:10–14) and with the holiest place of the eschatological temple – YHWH's throne (Ezek. 47; Rev. 22:1–2). The supernatural gift of waters was divinely intended as a display of YHWH's benevolent kingship to Israel's newly emerged generation (on the supply of waters as a sign of kingship, see Anthonioz 2014). By contrast, a lack of waters was a sign of divine abandonment (see Exod. 17:7; Sabo 2014: 432).

1–2. Four wayyiqtol verbs present the narrative context for the story, with two actions related to the sons of Israel and two related to Miriam: the sons of Israel *came* (to the wilderness of Zin in the first month) and the people *stayed* in Kadesh; then the focus narrows: there (in Kadesh) Miriam died, and there Miriam was buried.

The 'sons of Israel, the whole community' (*kol-hā'ēdāh*), come to dwell in Kadesh in the wilderness of Zin, a region described as 'barren,

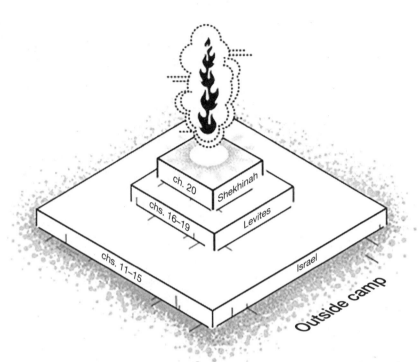

Figure 2: First generation wilderness sojourn

rugged, and waterless' (Beck 2003: 138; cf. Aharoni 1979: 31). The unusual phraseology of 'sons of Israel, the whole community' (vv. 1, 22), a unique designation in the Torah, may signal the emergence of Israel's second generation. Of 'the whole community', Rashi writes that 'those who were to die in the wilderness had already died, and these who composed the assembly were set apart, for life' (1997: 4:236), a key observation, especially in relation to Moses' failure (cf. Litke 2011: 33–34), and which resonates with the placement of the red heifer ritual (ch. 19). Hirsch similarly observed that the judgement decreed on Israel had been fulfilled so that all who entered the wilderness of Zin were the community 'before whom a new future had now opened up' (2007a: 442), and a comparison with Deuteronomy 1:46 – 3:17 leads to the same conclusion (cf. Dozeman 1998: 158). The sages of the Midrash grasped this significance, explaining that the 'whole community' relates to 'The complete community, the community that will enter the land, since those who had come out from Egypt had died' (*Tan.*, *Ḥuk.* 37). The point is crucial (Samet 2014e: 258–259; emphasis original):

> The key to understanding the story is its timing – it takes place at the beginning of the *fortieth year*. The nation that complains here

is a generation that has never known slavery. They have grown up in the desert as free people, their gaze turned towards the Promised Land, and now – with the beginning of the fortieth year – they begin anxiously awaiting the moment of finally entering it . . . They do not wish to return to Egypt; they want to go into *Eretz Yisrael*.

Whether there are still some remaining survivors of the first generation yet to die, the congregation may now be identified as the second generation. 'The water-story in Numbers is the first episode recorded after the generation of the Exodus has passed from the scene,' writes Helfgot (1993: 54); 'it is the first narrative of the new generation'. The death of Aaron the high priest fully and finally closes off the story of the first generation, whom he represents, and the installation of Aaron's son Eleazar as the next high priest marks the transition of generations as well, *in terms of leadership*. The form of the complaint narrative also argues for the subjects being the second generation of Israel. Childs, attending to the larger framework within which murmuring language is found, discerned two distinct patterns, which may be charted as in Table 1 (2004: 258–261; cf. Sanchez 2000: 37–64).

Table 1: Complaint patterns

Pattern I		*Pattern II*	
1. Initial need	Exod. 15:22, 23; 17:1; Num. 20:2	1. Initial complaint	Num. 11:1; 16:41; 21:5
2. Complaint	Exod. 15:24; 17:2; Num. 20:3	2. God's anger and punishment	Num. 11:1; 16:45; 21:6
3. Intercession by Moses	Exod. 15:25; 17:4; Num. 20:6	3. Intercession by Moses	Num. 11:2; 16:45; 21:7
4. Need met by God's miraculous intervention	Exod. 15:25; 17:6f; Num. 20:11	4. Reprieve of punishment	Num. 11:2; 16:50; 21:9

That Numbers 20 fits 'Pattern I' not only positions the complaint narrative within the context of a genuine need, the first since the original water-from-rock story in Exodus 17, but also aligns the second generation's first complaint with the first of the previous generation (Exod. 15:22) – the narrative has come full circle. Indeed, this is part of Moses' problem: while the people of Israel, like the narrative, have started afresh, he has not. Seebass, who discerns the generational transition rightly, describes the younger generation as 'struggling to life from 20:1–13 onwards (water in the desert), willing to learn though not totally without guilt (25:1–15)', and also, therefore, perceives the true nature of the sin of Moses, who was 'dismissed as Israel's leader because he missed utterly Yahweh's willingness to respect the new generation by the gift of water in the desert' (2010: 267).

The chronology notice 'in the first month' is clarified in the travelogue of Numbers 33:36–39, where Aaron's death is reported as occurring 'in the fortieth year', and justifies the narrative progress. The first generation has died in the wilderness under YHWH's judgement, and now this stark chapter recounts the death of that generation's leaders: it begins with the death of Miriam, ends with the death of Aaron and portends the death of Moses in the middle (v. 12), all within the context of a younger, newly emerged Israel ready to inherit the land. Presuming the action of chapters 15–18 took place shortly after YHWH's judgement on the first generation in Numbers 14, then thirty-eight years of biding time in the wilderness have been omitted completely – the story resumes only when the second generation, newly risen to comprise the community, are ready to progress into the land. Shamah reads 'on the first new moon' as in 'the first day of the first month', remarking that YHWH was eager, on the earliest day possible, to reconnect with Israel and bring them into the land (2011: 788). Within the narrative progression whereby chapter 19 signifies the transition of generations, with the new generation being cleansed from the death and judgement of the old generation, 'first month' also symbolizes the new start for Israel. According to the pattern of the Nazirite vow, when one who was consecrated as a Nazir becomes defiled by corpse pollution, he or she must be cleansed and then start the period of separation over again, since the 'former days will fall' (6:12) – just as the former generation 'would fall in the wilderness' (14:29, 32). On this reading 'first month' not only refers to the first month of the fortieth year chronologically, but to the first month after Israel's cleansing – to the fresh start of the second generation whereby their wilderness sojourn is seen through the prism of a Nazir's period of separation. The phrase 'in the first month' (*baḥōdeš hāri'šôn*) occurs four times in Numbers, with each of the other three occurrences being related to Passover (9:1; 28:16; 33:3), an association founded on the original legislation (Exod. 12:2). The exodus out of Egypt had established Abib as the first month of Israel's liturgical calendar (Exod. 12:2; cf. Exod. 13:4; 23:15; 34:18), so the phrase 'first month' occurs regularly with reference to Passover (Lev. 23:15; Num. 9:1; 28:16; cf. Deut. 16:1) (Tervanotko 2016: 93–94). In Numbers 9, we noted that the Passover legislation, which makes allowance for those defiled by a corpse to celebrate the feast on a second occasion after their cleansing, not only followed the paradigm for the Nazirite's cleansing and restart (6:9–12) but also adumbrated YHWH's provision for the second generation's emergence. Miriam's New Year's death, LeFebvre writes (2019: 63), signifies the 'generational transition', calling every ensuing generation to celebrate New Year's Day by leaving behind the rebellions of the wilderness generation. Fittingly, Israel's new life begins in synch with the liturgical calendar. Within an implicit

Passover context, 'Miriam' here possibly forms a play on 'bitter (herbs)' (*mĕrōrîm*) in that legislation (cf. 9:11). The second generation has emerged, restless for the land, and complains that 'this wilderness' was not the goal of the exodus (v. 5).

The place designation 'Kadesh' (*qādēš*) that unites the chapter (vv. 1, 14, 16, 22) is built on the root for 'holy' (*q-d-š*), linking it thematically with Moses and Aaron's failure to 'sanctify' (*lĕhaqdîšēnî*) YHWH (v. 12), and the summary statement that YHWH was nevertheless 'sanctified' (*wayyiqqādēš*) among them (v. 13), thus serving as an inclusio for the story. Numbers 20 thus combines the notion of holiness with YHWH's provision of water, as chapter 19 does with the waters of purification. Equally significant, Kadesh functions as a reminder of the first generation's failure and judgement in Numbers 14 (cf. Emmrich 2003: 55), paralleling the failure and judgement of that generation's leaders in Numbers 20. Rather than using the word for 'encampment' (*ḥānāh*), as when Israel begins to make progress toward the land in the next chapter (21:10, 11, 12, 13; 22:1), here the people are said to 'stay' (*yāšab*) in Kadesh. That Miriam's death and burial took place in Kadesh is emphasized with a twofold use of 'there' (*šām*). The last mention of Miriam had been in Numbers 12, the only other episode in Numbers featuring all three siblings together, where she had been struck with leprosy 'as one dead' (*mēt*, 12:12). The emphasis on Miriam's death and burial at Kadesh may recall the previous chapter's focus on the need for cleansing from corpse pollution (19:11, etc.). This possibility is strengthened with verse 2's opening phrase 'But there was no water for the community'. Miriam's death has been connected to her sin of slandering Moses in Numbers 12 (cf. e.g. Stubbs 2009: 157–158), and, alternatively, for her presumed participation in the first generation's revolt after the scouts' report in Numbers 14 (Burnside 2016: 140). Possibly the notice in 12:15 that 'the people did not journey until Miriam *was gathered* ('*āsap* in niph.)' foreshadowed her death, hinting at the idiom of being gathered to one's people (see Gen. 25:8, 17; 35:29; 49:29, 33; Num. 20:24, 26; 27:13; 31:2; Deut. 32:50). Her death sets the context for the chapter and augurs YHWH's judgement on Moses and Aaron for their rebellion. The brief notice of her death may even be intended to elucidate the behaviour of Moses and Aaron, mitigating their failure to comfort the people amid an urgent need of water by opening with their own personal grief (J. M. Cohen 1984: 158; cf. Ginzberg 1967: 3:317–318; Reiss 2010: 188). The final three stops of Israel's wilderness journey will see the deaths of its three leaders (Burns 1987: 119–120): Miriam at Kadesh (20:1), Aaron at Mount Hor (20:22–29) and Moses at the plains of Moab (27:12–23; Deut. 34:1–8).

Another possible connection with the episode of Numbers 12 may explain the function of Miriam's death in the present chapter. It may well be that all three leaders – Miriam, Aaron and Moses – represent their (first) generation of Israel in different ways. Aaron represents Israel, for example, as the people's high priest, and Moses as their primary leader. Recalling that in Numbers 11 – 15 the focus is specifically on the failure of the twelve tribes, the outer camp and that this failure is in relation to the prophetic ministry, there may be significance to the fact that Miriam had taken the lead role in defaming Moses' unique prophetic status (cf. 12:1, 10–15): perhaps Miriam especially represents the nation of Israel, the outer camp (later, the daughters of Zelophehad will symbolize the new generation). Just as the sojourn progressed from the outer camp's failure and judgement (chs. 11–15) to that of the inner camp of Levites (chs. 16–18), the present chapter moves from the death of their respective leaders, of Miriam (representing the nation of Israel) and of Aaron (the Levites). In considering Miriam and Aaron's accusations of Moses in Numbers 12, moreover, scholars commonly observe that Miriam represents the prophets, while Aaron represents the priests (e.g. Römer 2007: 439), categories that align her with the prophetic emphasis of the outer camp (chs. 11–15) and Aaron with the priestly emphasis of the inner camp (chs. 16–19). Leveen's observation that the opening verse refers to Israel in three different forms ('sons of Israel', 'the whole community' and 'the people') within the context of Miriam's death is significant (2013: 266): 'Such emphasis on the collective in the same verse in which Miriam dies hints at a deep connection between Miriam and the people.' While Aaron's death confirms the death of the old generation whom he represented as high priest, Numbers 20 may allow for a finer distinction: Miriam's death seals the passing of the former generation of Israel, while Aaron's not only accomplishes the same but signals the transition for the Levitical and priestly generation even as Eleazar descends Mount Hor, donned with high priestly garments. Moses, who represents YHWH's central *Shekhinah* presence, is judged (precisely for misrepresenting YHWH), but will continue until the journey's end. Aside from being juxtaposed, the stories of Miriam's leprosy and the scouts are linked through reference to the wilderness of Paran (Waxman 2017; see 10:12; 12:16; 13:3, 26). As Miriam had slandered Moses, Israel slandered the land – the first garnered doubt for YHWH's mouthpiece; the second, for his promises uttered through that mouthpiece. M. Douglas, too, asks whether Miriam may feature as a rhetorical symbol, observing that even the strange story of her defilement by leprosy (Num. 12) 'makes more sense if she is representing the people of Israel' (2001: 197). She strengthens this reading by noting how in the Bible 'a woman is often a metaphor for Israel', with the prophets commonly presenting Israel 'as the erring wife who has betrayed her husband', and pointing out how this principle is already at work within Numbers itself, in relation to the strayed woman law (5:11–31) and the vows of women (ch. 30) (2001: 199). As Moses' sister, Miriam is marked out 'as a major symbol of Israel's broken faith', being punished with leprosy 'not because she is a woman, but because she is Israel' (2001: 203). Such a proposition, if correct, yields a twofold clarification. First, it explains the priority of Miriam in Numbers 12, and positions her judgement of death-like disease and expulsion from the Camp for seven days as prefiguring the judgement against Israel and the nation's exclusion from the land. Given the analogy between the Camp and the land, Miriam's being sent out for disparaging the medium of God's prophetic word forms a foreshadowing of Israel's failure to enter the land. Second, connecting Miriam with Israel also unfolds the logic of her death-notice in 20:1, coordinated as it is with 'the first month' and the reference to 'Kadesh', which together recall YHWH's judgement on the first generation even while announcing the end of the forty-year period – her death and burial forms the grave marker of the old generation.

The connection between Miriam's death and the lack of water was acknowledged whimsically in Jewish lore by the idea of Miriam's well, the rock that followed Israel throughout the wilderness journeys and which is said to have run dry with her death (see *TgNeof* Num. 12.16; 21:1; *TgPs-J* Num. 12.12, 16; 20:1–2; *Mekhl.* 4.5; 16.35; *Seder Olam* 9–10; *T, Suk.* 3.11–13; Pseudo-Philo, *LAB* 10.7; 11.15). To be sure, Miriam is often connected with water in the Torah, integral to the narrative of infant Moses' deliverance in the Nile (Exod. 2:1–10), rejoicing with her tambourine at the sea crossing (Exod. 15:20–21), followed by the lack of water and the 'bitter' (*mārar*) water story (Exod. 15:22–26; cf. Num. 5:18). As there had been no more complaints about water since the rock incident in Exodus 17, it is believed the rock's waters continued to flow miraculously by the merits of Miriam – and so with her death ran dry. Expressing the significant transition from the miraculous era of the wilderness sojourn to the mundane experience of life in the land, Jewish traditions tell of three divine gifts that came with Israel's original leaders, ceasing with their deaths: the manna with Moses, the glory Cloud with Aaron and the water supply with Miriam (cf. Pseudo-Philo, *LAB* 20.8). While her death notice is terse compared with that of Aaron's, the fact that she is noted is a testimony to her role and honoured place in Israel's tradition (cf. Tervanotko 2016: 90–92). Josephus nevertheless fills the gap, elaborating the account with a lavish funeral, burial atop a mountain and thirty days of mourning, and then explains the red heifer ritual, reversing the order of the two accounts, as the purification ceremony for those Israelites who participated in her funeral rites (*Ant.* 4.78–79). The interpretative challenge remains to understand how Miriam's death and the lack of water – however connected together – function to introduce the ensuing narrative. Clearly, YHWH responds to the people's need with a supply of water, but what is the relevance of Miriam's death? Sweeney suggests that Moses and Aaron, as Miriam's closest relatives, would have been responsible for her burial; their subsequent fault lay in coming before YHWH without having first purified themselves (2017: 85; 2019). While his view incorporates the context of the red heifer ritual, the text itself offers other specific faults more explicitly. At the least, the lack of water aligns the second generation's opening wilderness experience with that of the first (Exod. 17), even as Miriam's death signals the passing away of the first generation.

The community 'assembles (*wayyiqqāhălû*) against Moses and against Aaron', a statement recalling Korah's rebellion verbatim (see 16:3), one of several connections to that section, including use of Aaron's staff and the term 'rebel' (17:10). This assembling together is explained as the result of there being 'no water for the community' (cf. Exod. 17:1). Significantly, it is the narrator who supplies this notice as background information, which adds a measure of sympathy, especially given the phraseology that there was 'no water *for the community*'. Indeed, verses 2–5 are framed by the narrator's remark and the people's complaint that there is 'no water' (*lō'-hāyāh mayim . . . mayim 'ayin*), so that the latter's assessment matches the contextual reality. While the people's 'contentiousness' (*rîb*) is blameworthy, the text nevertheless communicates a legitimate basis, justifying their concern. Exodus 17:1 reads specifically that there was no water for the people 'to drink' (*lištōt*), omitted here, although the people's complaint concludes with lack of water to drink (v. 5), and YHWH's response also focuses on their drinking (vv. 8, 11). Looking at patterns of complaint in the Pentateuch, Numbers 20, concerning a legitimate need, conforms to the type not seen since Exodus 15:22–27, 16:1–36 and 17:1–7, each of which deals with the need for water or food. YHWH, in this early relationship with the second generation, wanted Israel to know that he was more than willing and fully able to supply their needs as their sovereign Shepherd (Sanchez 2000: 37–40).

3–5. 'And the people contended with Moses, and said' parallels Exodus 17:2 verbatim. While they contend specifically with Moses, their accusations, using 2nd m. pl., include Aaron. Nevertheless the narrative focus of the episode is on Moses (cf. Sakenfeld 1985). The range of meaning for 'contend' (*rîb*) includes strife, dispute, complaint, public hostility and a legal claim (BDB 936). In Exodus 17, *rîb* combines with *nāsāh*, 'to test' (17:2, 7), portraying the people's behaviour more negatively as rebellion (Margaliot 1983: 217 n. 66). The complaint includes an exclamation (3b), two accusing questions (4, 5a) and a negative assessment (5b). Repeated use of *rîb* (vv. 3, 13) forms a frame around the narrative (cf. Zeelander 2015: 338). The exclamation with its twofold use of 'perish' (*gāwa'*) recalls another twofold use of the same term by which the Korah episode had concluded (Num. 16:12–13), four of the five uses of *gāwa'* in Numbers (cf. 20:29) – 'our brethren', then, likely refers to the immediate deaths of chapter 16 as opposed to the generation's forty-year death in the wilderness, signalled by Miriam's death. Her death pressed the question as to whether the community would remain in the wilderness after all, remain without anyone to lead them into the land. Their remark about dying in this wilderness 'to die there' (*lāmût šām*, v. 4) parallels Miriam's death there (*wattāmāt šām*, v. 1).

While use of 'our brothers' has led some to identify the 'community' here as the first generation (as with 'make us ascend out of Egypt', v. 5), other factors favour the traditional Jewish reading that the community refers to the second generation (see also Emmrich 2003: 59–60). First, YHWH tells Moses and Aaron that they will not bring 'this assembly' (*haqqāhāl hazzeh*) into the land he is giving them (v. 12). Second, this chapter marks the first progress toward the land (vv. 14–21) since YHWH's previous judgement on the first generation (14:25, 45) – only as a new generation does Israel's sojourn resume. Third, Israel will experience battle victory at Hormah (21:1–3), another indication the narrative entails the second generation's progress into the land. The point has significant interpretative implications: Aaron's death marks the end of the first generation whom he had represented, and in large measure Moses' sinful reaction to the people, accruing to them the sins of the former generation, will display that a new leader is needed for the second generation (cf. Shamah 2011: 792). Here, the parallels with Exodus 17 are relevant: Numbers 20 represents a similar event of thirst in the wilderness but for the second generation. Israel's story has started over and YHWH, in whose sight 'a thousand years is as yesterday when it is past' (Ps. 90:4, a psalm of Moses), deals graciously with the people's legitimate need of water, as he had done with the first generation (Exod. 17), without rebuking them. But Moses, who had endured nearly forty years in the wilderness, having suffered long with the first generation's complaints, threats and rebellions, and now faced with the loss of his sister, proves unable to handle the risen generation with a fresh supply of tender patience. Perhaps it was even their use of 'our brothers' (as 'our brethren'), claiming solidarity with the previous generation, that so 'embittered' (*mārāh*) Moses' spirit (in Ps. 106:32–33).

Propp notes how the people's complaint moves backward through time: would that we had died with Korah, why are we in this desert, why did you bring us out of Egypt at all, even as the description of lack of water grows ever more graphic: no water for people (v. 2), none for cattle (v. 4), none for vegetation (v. 5), closing with 'no water to drink' (v. 5), echoing verse 2 (1987: 92 n. 156; 1988: 21 n. 15). The focus, nevertheless, remains on their present situation in the wilderness versus their desire to be in the land. The two accusatory questions resonate with the first generation's question in Exodus 17:3: 'Why this that you (sg.) made us ascend out of Egypt to kill us and our sons and our cattle with thirst?' (cf. Exod. 14:11–12; 16:3). Both questions here, however, use a m. pl., bringing Aaron closer within the story's purview, a critical distinction as Aaron will be judged for his complicity. As in Exodus 17:3, the people leave God out, not crediting him with the exodus deliverance, whereas in his negotiations with Edom, Moses renders the glory to YHWH for the exodus (v. 16). By contrast to many of the complaints recorded for the first generation, in which one finds a 'return to Egypt' motif, the second generation's complaint expresses an urgent desire to be in the land – *instead of* the wilderness – as the goal of the exodus out of Egypt. Having never lived in Egypt, they have no memory of its culinary offerings, unlike the previous generation (see Exod. 16:3; Num. 11:5). Rather than a yearning for the 'fleshpots of Egypt' (Exod. 16:3) or the 'fish . . . cucumbers, melons, leeks, onions and garlic' of Egypt (Num. 11:5), the second generation lists the promised fertility and produce of the Promised Land: 'a place of seed, fig, vine, pomegranate and water to drink' in contrast to 'this wilderness . . . this evil place'. In Numbers 13:23, the land's fertility was illustrated with just these specimens: a cluster of grapes, and with pomegranates and figs. The same language is reflected in Deuteronomy (8:7–8), where Israel is told that YHWH God is

> bringing you into a good land, a land of brooks of water, of fountains and deep waters that spring out of valleys and hills; a land of wheat and barley, and vines and fig, and pomegranates; a land of olive oil and honey.

The new Israel's complaint is forward-looking rather than backward-looking (so, too, P. Kahn 2007b: 87, 91; Samet 2014e: 260), zealously longing for, however impatiently, life in the land of Canaan. Even when the second generation sins, writes Samet (1997), 'they appear quite different from their fathers. They long not for Egypt, but for Canaan.' The sons of Israel, having risen to become 'the community' over the past thirty-eight years, are ready to inherit the land. They refer to the dissonance between the land as the goal of the exodus and the prospect of their dying in the wilderness, along with their beasts, and mention the lack of water almost as an afterthought (cf. Helfgot 1993: 52). Such a reality does not excuse the sinfulness of Israel's contending with Moses and Aaron, and ultimately with YHWH, yet that their complaint is for a legitimate need and driven by a desire to inherit the land explains some of the dynamics at play in the narrative, including their character. The focus on place – 'this evil place' (*hammāqôm hārā' hazzeh*) – underscores Israel's desire to be in the land.

The complaint ends emphatically on the lack of water, with the particle of negation (*'ayin*) peculiarly standing after the object denied, water, and, forming an inclusio with the opening of verse 2 (enveloping vv. 2–5), 'enhances the severity of the lack of water' (W. W. Lee 2003a: 226). Moreover, the people's remark about dying 'before YHWH' and the accusation that Moses and Aaron ('you' pl.) brought YHWH's assembly into the wilderness, assumes a disjuncture between Moses' will and that of YHWH, that Moses has acted contrary to YHWH's intention for his people. While readers understand that nothing could be further from the truth, the accusation sets up the narrative's shocking turn where Moses does in fact misrepresent YHWH's will.

6. Given the sg. 'came', Moses initiated the departure from the presence of the assembly to the door of the Tent of Meeting, an act often read as a panicked fleeing (see Ibn Ezra 1999: 158). Moses' movement 'from the presence' of the assembly images the gap that separates him from the second generation, and in every other instance where the collocation *min* + *pānê* is found in Numbers, it is set against a perceived hostile threat (see 10:35; 22:3, 33; 32:17, 21; 33:8, 52, 55). Moses and Aaron fall on their faces, a gesture they have made several times already (see 15:5; 16:22, 45; cf. 16:4), as a plea for YHWH's help and intervention. In response, the glory of YHWH (*kĕbôd-yhwh*) appears to them, the fourth occurrence in Numbers (see 14:10; 16:19, 42). In each of the three earlier contexts, the glory of YHWH appears in defence of Moses and Aaron, and is followed immediately by a divine declaration of judgement on the people (14:11–12; 16:20, 44–45). This appearance of YHWH's glory, the central axis of the story (Samet 2014e: 254), forms the first such instance within the context of the second generation of Israel. S. Klein makes two observations in accord with the idea that YHWH treats the second generation differently (2015a). First, YHWH's glory is revealed to Moses and Aaron, but not to the rest of the people, and, second, this is the last such appearance in Numbers – after this point, no further mention is made of the Cloud and fire, even in contexts where one would expect to find them (e.g. 25:1–4, 5–9). In preparation for the 'mundane' life of faithfulness in the land, he weans Israel from the supernatural existence of the wilderness sojourn. The transition of generations, with its implicit move from slavery to liberty, and from the miraculous life of the wilderness to the mundane life in the land meant the second generation 'would no longer require the use of Moshe's *staff*; rather, Moshe's *word* would suffice for finding the path of life and salvation' (Hirsch 2007a: 562–563; emphases original). The observation is relevant inasmuch as it may explain the difference in YHWH's approach, by contrast with Exodus 17, that Moses was to *speak to*, rather than strike, the rock. The episodes and battles found in Numbers 21 are fitting examples of his gradual resort to natural means – Israel experiences victory by trusting and obeying YHWH. Moses and Aaron, however, function in the present narrative not only as mediators, but as the only remaining vestiges (aside from Joshua and Caleb) of the former generation – YHWH's glory appears *to them*.

7–8. Rather than responding with exasperated judgement, YHWH responds to Israel's second generation in much the same way he had in the similarly early stage of his relationship with the first (Exod. 17:5–6): he gives Moses instructions for supplying the people water from the rock. The associations with the Horeb (Mount Sinai) pericope of Exodus 17 support understanding YHWH's intention in the present narrative as providing the newly risen generation of Israel with their own 'Sinai' experience, the significance of which is brought out by Propp (1987: 63): 'Horeb is described as a mountain on which Yahweh appears and as a mountain running with water. To the Israelite, this would conjure up . . . the image of the divine abode, whether Eden, Zion or all Canaan.' In spite of Moses, YHWH would indeed create a wondrous renewed Sinai experience, as waters pour forth from the rock in abundance (v. 11; cf. Exod. 17:6).

The prologue of the wilderness sojourn (11:1–3) offers a basic paradigm for complaint narratives, with the following typical sequence: (1) the people sin, (2) YHWH responds with judgement, (3) Moses intercedes for the sake of the people, (4) YHWH relents his judgement, and (5) the place is named to memorialize the event. In Numbers 20, the pattern is broken: YHWH does not respond in judgement, and Moses, rather than interceding on their behalf, seeks the people's punishment. The absence of any sign of disapproval over the people's genuine need in YHWH's response forms a sharp contrast to previous occasions where his fierce anger was kindled (11:1, 10), he was ready to destroy them completely (14:11–12), or he wrought a definitive judgement (16:31, 35) (cf. Sanchez 2000: 66–67). While YHWH neither expresses judgement against the people nor instructs Moses even to speak to them, Moses does judge them, addressing them as 'rebels' (cf. Boorer 2012: 59). That YHWH addresses Moses alone, highlighting his role as communicator, 'is consistent with the expression of the relationship between the two leaders [Moses and Aaron] in Exodus 4:15–16' and may be relevant for discerning Aaron's otherwise muted involvement in the ensuing transgression (Sakenfeld 1985: 141–142). The instruction is threefold, followed by an explanation and purpose clause. Moses is to (1) 'take the staff', (2) 'assemble the community' (the imperatives here are sg., with 'you and Aaron' added), and then both Moses and Aaron are to (3) 'speak to the rock' before the assembled people. YHWH then explains the result (4) that the rock 'will give its waters', so that Moses ('you' sg.) may 'bring forth (sg. verb) water from the rock'. The purpose clause indicates that (5) Moses will 'cause the community and their beasts to drink (again, sg. verb)'. Critically, four of the six verbs in verse 8 are directly related to providing water for the people and their animals, clearly demonstrating YHWH's desire to provide water in the wilderness for them (W. W. Lee 2003a: 229). Unlike previous complaint stories in Numbers, writes Samet (2014e: 257), YHWH here makes 'no mention of any punishment for the nation for quarreling with Moses', but, on the contrary, 'commands Moses to effect a great miracle, to bring forth water from a rock, and further commands him to water the nation and their flocks himself!' Evidently displeased with YHWH's response, Moses and Aaron's sin will relate to their denial and misrepresentation of God's intention.

The first command, 'to take' (*qaḥ*), uses a key word from Korah's rebellion (16:1, 6, 17, 18, 39, 46, 47; 17:2, 9), the last two uses related to the staffs that had been deposited 'before YHWH' whereby Aaron's staff had blossomed forth, yielding almonds – precisely 'the staff' Moses is now instructed to take 'from before YHWH' (v. 9). Rather than taking the staff of judgement, by which he had struck the Nile (Exod. 17:5), Moses is instructed to take a *tree of life*, the staff that had blossomed and produced almonds. The importance of Aaron's staff is demonstrated by its twofold reference (20:8, 9), and as the climax of Numbers 17, underscoring its importance as a sign ('*ôt*, 17:10), a critical point that removes any need to find the staff's relevance in the striking of the rock, which was likely done with Moses' staff. The staff, most generally, represents YHWH's authority, that Moses and Aaron are his emissaries, chosen and consecrated by him to represent his will to the people. Ironically, the demonstration of YHWH's provision of abundant waters from the crag, alongside the upheld staff of Aaron, was meant to vindicate both Moses and Aaron, that it had indeed been YHWH who brought the people into the wilderness of Zin, and that he was fully able to supply abundantly for all their needs, and that of their animals.

The second command, to assemble the community, demonstrates that offering the people water, far from a mundane occurrence, was intended by YHWH to be a corporate spiritual experience for the people who had been officially gathered by God through his mediator and high priest. Helfgot suggests the phraseology hearkens to the first generation's experience of Mount Sinai, dubbed 'the day of Assembly' throughout Deuteronomy (e.g. 9:7; 1993: 55). He further adds that 'the Torah seems to present the water crisis at *Mei Meriva* as a potential experience of receiving the Torah for the new generation' (Helfgot 2012a: 167–168).

The third command differs drastically from the scenario recounted in Exodus 17. Here Moses (with Aaron) is 'to speak' (*wĕdibbartem*) to the rock, whereas some forty years earlier Moses had been commanded 'to strike' (*wĕhikkîtā*) the rock with his staff (Exod. 17:6). Verse 8 presents the Torah's first use of *sela'*, which can be translated 'rock', 'crag' or even 'mountain', typically 'tall and ribbed with crevices', serving as 'a place of refuge or secure residence' (Propp 1987: 21–22). Understanding 'the rock' in terms of a mountain supports reading the divinely orchestrated event in terms of providing the second generation with their own Mount Sinai experience. The phrase 'and Aaron your brother' marks another significant difference from Exodus 17, where Moses alone appears, and looks to his inclusion in divine judgement (v. 12) and subsequent death and replacement by Eleazar (vv. 23–29). Aaron's presence is explained by the other fundamental difference with Exodus 17: *the use of his budded staff* rather than Moses' staff. Some understand the command as speaking 'concerning' or 'about' the rock (cf. Margaliot 1983: 205–206), but the case for such a reading is weak: the text clearly reads 'to' (*'el*) rather than 'concerning' (*'al*), and even when Ezekiel was called to prophesy 'concerning' the bones, he also prophesied 'to them' (37:4). Speaking to the rock is emphatic inasmuch as the instruction is unusual, presents a major deviation from YHWH's last instructions (in Exod. 17) and because, in the narrative's artistry, speech is largely absent: Moses and Aaron made no response to the assembly's accusing questions (vv. 2–5), and did not speak to YHWH, either to complain, seek his defence or to inform him of the people's need of water (cf. Lim 1997: 142). Apparently, YHWH's message to his people was intended to be communicated through the supernatural and abundant gift of waters in the wilderness, flowing out of the rock, with Moses' speech to the rock being overheard. The definiteness of 'the' rock, mentioned four times in the story, leads naturally to question which rock, and has fed the notion in Jewish lore that the rock of Exodus 17 had been following Israel supernaturally throughout the nation's sojourn in the wilderness. Inasmuch as 'speak' is 2nd m. pl., including Aaron, some exegetes suggest that Aaron functions here, in accord with his original calling (Exod. 4:14–16; 7:1–2), as Moses' interpreter (Margaliot 1983: 209; Propp 1988: 23). Given the singular form of the rest of the instructions, however, the plural here may merely serve as including Aaron's role within Moses' speech. Use of speech instead of striking the rock fits the transition in God's dealings with his people noted earlier, that YHWH's signs and wonders through Moses for the exodus generation, especially through the staff, were being replaced by YHWH's *word* through Moses, a gesture that fruitions with the book of Deuteronomy. Hirsch thus wrote that this miracle was 'meant to show that the *word* of Moshe [versus the striking of the staff] suffices to bring forth living water out of the rock' (2007a: 448).

Other differences abound between the two accounts, some of which help explain the nature of Moses and Aaron's failure. In Exodus 17, YHWH stands before Moses upon the rock (v. 6), whereas there is no hint of his doing anything similar in Numbers. Also the terms for 'the rock' are different in each account: *haṣṣûr* (Exod. 17:6) and *hassela'* (Num. 20:8). It is difficult to know how much to make of this diverse terminology since their ranges of meaning overlap, used in parallel (cf. Deut. 32:13; Pss 18:2, 31, 46; 71:3; 78:15–16; Isa. 2:21). In the Psalms, using *sela'*, YHWH is referred to as a 'rock' (18:2; 31:3; 42:9; 71:3), but, using *ṣûr*, he is also called 'rock' in Deuteronomy (32:4, 15, 18, 30, 31) and elsewhere (1 Sam. 2:2; 2 Sam. 22:3, 32, 47; 23:3; Pss 28:1; 31:2; 62:2, 6, 7; 78:35; 89:26; 92:15; 94:22; 95:1; 144:1; Isa. 17:10; 30:29; 44:8; Hab. 1:12). In recounting the water from the rock incidents, the Psalms use both terms (Ps. 78:15–16):

He cleaved rocks (*ṣurîm*) in the wilderness,
    and caused them to drink of the great deeps.

He brought forth streams from the rock (*sāla'*),
and caused waters to descend as rivers.

See also Nehemiah 9:15 for use of *sela'* in the water from the rock story, and Deuteronomy 8:15, Isaiah 48:21 and Psalms 78:20, 81:16, 105:41 and 114:8 for use of *ṣûr*. Propp cogently identifies *ṣûr* as Horeb, the mountain of God, translating the term as 'mountain', and *sela'* in Numbers 20 as 'crag' (1987: 59–61, 67–68; Beck's 2003 analysis is unconvincing and raises many questions). Exodus 17, then, portrays the holy mountain of Yahweh's running with water, an image of the divine abode shared with Eden and Zion (Propp 1987: 63), and the crag of Numbers 20, flowing with the cosmic 'many waters' (v. 11; see May 1955), is likely intended to conjure the same image. Within the wilderness, this 'evil place' with no water, the crag bursts forth with many waters, a life-yielding river of God. The abundant rivers of water, flowing amid the gathering of Israelites, also reflects the nature of the Camp gathered about the *Shekhinah*'s central Dwelling. That the event takes place in 'Kadesh' (Holy) resonates with the narrative focus on the camp of the *Shekhinah*, and, as other passages exhibit, a mountain flowing with supernatural rivers of waters reflects YHWH's throne and kingship (see Ezek. 47; Rev. 22:1–2).

Another difference between the accounts of Exodus 17 and Numbers 20 relates to the intended audience: the waters are drawn from the rock before the eyes of the elders of Israel in Exodus 17 (vv. 5, 6), but to be done before the eyes of the people, the assembled community, in Num. 20 (v. 8). In the present scenario, related to the second generation, YHWH had wanted to teach the whole people a lesson, a greater purpose sought than the stated one of causing the community and their beasts to drink. YHWH's instructions were aimed at sanctifying himself before the eyes of the sons of Israel – a purpose fulfilled in spite of his servants' failure (vv. 12, 13).

Returning to what is perhaps the critical distinction between Exodus 17 and Numbers 20, here Moses is to take the staff of Aaron (contra Margaliot 1983: 210–211; Lim 1997). In relation to the staff in Exodus 17, Moses had been instructed, 'your staff, with which you struck (*hikkîtā*) the Nile, take in your hand . . . and strike (*hikkîtā*) the rock' (vv. 5, 6), whereas now Moses is instructed to take 'the staff', and the last staff noted was Aaron's budded staff when it was deposited before YHWH's presence (17:10), for the express purpose of being kept as an admonitory sign for 'rebels' ('sons of rebellion', *běnê-merî*), precisely what Moses calls the people (v. 10): 'rebels' (*hammōrîm*). YHWH had devised the staff ordeal in order to rid himself of the people's 'complaints' (*tělunnôt*, 17:5), and Numbers 20 presents the first complaint since then, the first opportunity to use the staff in its emblematic function (cf. Amy-Dressler 1986; Propp 1988: 22; Sanchez 2000: 30), clarifying why

Moses was not instructed to strike the rock with the staff. The phrase 'his staff' in verse 11 may readily be explained either by the fact that Moses is holding the staff (thus regarded as his) or, more probable, that for this specific act Moses did use his own staff while Aaron was holding the budded staff as commanded by YHWH. These explanations suffice quite apart from pursuing either LXX's 'the staff' (*tē rhabdō*), removing any ambiguity, or the argument for emending MT (see Propp 1988: 22). Clearly, YHWH is doing something different with the second generation that has arisen in the wilderness, who are not shackled by a culture of slavery as their fathers had been. Rather than striking the rock with the staff of Moses, which had struck the Nile, the budded staff of Aaron is to be held as a sign, according to YHWH's explicit purpose for it. Indeed, it would have been odd for Aaron's staff *not* to make a later appearance within the book's horizon. One commonly touted question, then – 'Why is Moses commanded to take the staff if not to hit the rock?' (see Nachmanides 1975: 210–211; Cohen 1984: 153) – is soundly dismissed by the literary context: the staff, Aaron's staff, is to serve as a sign. As Propp observes (1988: 22), the Korah episode 'provides an adequate explanation of why Moses is commanded to take Aaron's rod', since it was 'to be preserved as a sign to potential rebels against Moses, Aaron, and Yahweh'. With this understanding, other features unfold: speaking to the rock makes sense since explanatory words may accompany a visual sign, and since striking the rock with the staff that had budded forth with blossoms and yielded ripe almonds would be inappropriate for – and perhaps destroy – its use as a visual sign. Aaron's staff was a life-out-of-death sign, demonstrating YHWH to be Israel's fountain of life, such life mediated to his people through the house of Aaron. Similarly, drawing rivers of water from the rock amid the act of speaking would also set forth YHWH God as the Maker of heavens and earth who spoke the world into existence, drawing out life from what was not, a word befitting obedience (see Rashi, ad loc.). Such emphasis on Moses' speaking and the life-giving power of YHWH was a necessary conviction for the generation of Israel that would inherit the land (cf. Deut. 32:44–47). If more tenuously, Edenic imagery is present: recalling that the Candelabra, a stylized tree of life, was an almond tree, then Aaron's budded staff, along with abundant waters flowing supernaturally from a large crag, creates a scene that resonates with the depiction of Eden (Gen. 2:8–14), portraying the Camp of Israel as a paradise in the wilderness (see Num. 24:5–7). Aaron's rod, in any case, had become a sign of life, whereas the 'exodus' rod of Moses, even in supplying water from the rock in Exodus 17 *by striking it*, carries the notion of judgement.

Finally, while both Exodus 17 and Numbers 20 use *šātâ* for 'drink', a singular exception occurs in 20:8, where YHWH's instructions culminate with the end result that Moses (sg.) causes the community and their beasts 'to drink', this time using *šāqâ*, a term used elsewhere in Numbers only for the strayed woman's drink, three times (5:24, 26, 27). It may be that YHWH's inclusion of 'beasts' in his instructions (v. 8), whereas 'people' only is used in Exodus 17:6 (cf. 'livestock', 17:3), has led to the choice of *šāqâ* which is used for watering animals, as well as irrigation generally (cf. Gen. 2:6, 10). Perhaps the term is a clue to how lavish a supply of water YHWH intended to provide or, more simply, it was used because *šātâ* never occurs in the causative hiph. in the Torah. In his instructions, YHWH was urging Moses that he himself water (*hišqîto*) the people, a duty he apparently baulked at (v. 10). Ironically, Moses' momentous transgression seems to recall the narratives of his early life, when he 'struck' (*nākâ*) an Egyptian (Exod. 2:12, 13; Num. 20:11) and 'watered' (*šāqâ*) the flocks of Midianite daughters, having rescued them (Exod. 2:17; Num. 20:8).

9. Moses took the staff from 'before YHWH' (*lipnê yhwh*), a phrase used with reference to Aaron's rod twice already in 17:7, 9, again marking the staff as the high priest's that had budded with blossoms and almonds. That the fulfilment formula 'just as he had commanded him' comes immediately after obedience to the *first* of three instructions functions in two ways. It confirms the role of Aaron's staff – whatever else Moses did or did not do in his failure to sanctify YHWH before the community, the staff of Aaron was involved – and, confirming Moses' obedience for the first act alone raises the question as to whether his ensuing acts conformed to YHWH's instructions and intention. Such an early confirmation raises suspicion, since the obedience formula is not offered as a summary of all his actions (cf. Olson 1996: 126; N. MacDonald 2012a: 130). At least some of Moses and Aaron's action after the obedience formula is disassociated from the divine will in the narration, as if to say, 'This far Moses obeyed and no more.' Given his consistent obedience throughout Numbers (see 1:19; 2:33; 3:42, 51; 4:37, 41, 45, 49; 8:4; 13:3; 20:27; 27:22), Moses' disobedience here is profoundly tragic (cf. Blum 1990: 274; Schart 1990: 104–105).

10–11. Moses and Aaron assembled the assembly before the rock ('toward the face of the rock', *'el-pĕnê hassalaʻ*), which also appears in accord with YHWH's instructions, although there is a difference in language: YHWH had said to assemble 'the community (*hā-ʻēdāh*', v. 8), while Moses is said to assemble 'the assembly' (*haqqāhāl*', v. 10). Although the designations may vary for stylistic purposes, Riskin, understanding *qāhāl* as an assemblage of individuals and *ʻēdāh* as a community with a purpose, functioning as a 'witness', suggests the terminology difference betrays Moses' changed mindset regarding YHWH's people (2009: 170–171). That Moses' obedience report comes *before* this act (v. 9), supports searching for meaning in any incongruity, even if overly subtle. When the people quarrel with Moses, their self-designation is the *qĕhal* of YHWH (v. 4).

The next phrase, 'and he said (*wayyōʾmer*) to them', may at first be construed as beginning the third and final act of obedience inasmuch as YHWH had instructed them 'to speak' to the rock. Moses appears to be the subject, whereas YHWH had instructed both Moses and Aaron to 'speak' (*wĕdibbartem*), again a subtle difference that perhaps merely implies Moses as speaking for both (Sakenfeld 1985: 143). That a variance is noted and must be explained may be an intended textual feature, creating a sense of uncertainty over Moses' actions. Similarly, while the object of Moses' speech, 'to them' (i.e. the assembly, versus 'the rock'), may be explained by the notion of Moses' speaking concerning the rock (to them) rather than speaking directly to the rock, the narrative fulfilment departs conspicuously from the language of YHWH's instructions and should probably be deemed 'significant' (Lim 1997: 146). Any uncertainty, however, dissipates with the report of Moses' speech: 'Hear now, rebels . . .' Contrary to his exasperation expressed against the first generation (see 14:26–27), here YHWH had shown nothing but a patient willingness to provide for his people's need of water in the wilderness. Jarringly, Moses – perhaps Jonah-like in anger over YHWH's incomparable forbearance – lashes out at the people, chiding them as rebels. To be sure, the purpose for Aaron's staff had been to serve as a sign against rebels (17:10), but Moses, by his words and actions, failed to represent YHWH faithfully to the community, arguably his leading role. His 'hear now' (*šimʿû-nāʾ*) echoes precisely the words of YHWH in Numbers 12 (cf. 16:8), when, ironically, he had defended Moses as 'faithful' (*ʾāman*) in all his house (12:6–7) – whereas YHWH will shortly accuse Moses and Aaron of not trusting or being faithful to him (20:12).

While some commentators have focused Moses' blameworthiness on the word 'we', in the sense that Moses (along with Aaron, presumably) sought to take credit for the miracle (Milgrom 1990: 451–452; Burnside 2016: 128), such self-seeking, aside from being utterly out of character, makes no sense at this point in the narrative. More significantly, Moses' words mark one of the few points of agreement with YHWH's instructions: 'so you will bring forth for them water from the rock' (v. 8). Indeed, the 'we' is not emphatic at all as there is no separate pr. (*ʾănāḥĕnû*) present – rather, 'for you' (*lākem*) receives focus, once more showing unjustified ill-will toward the people, which misrepresents YHWH. The *entire* chiding speech to the community was inappropriate, inserted between the gathering of the community (the second command) and Moses and Aaron's dealings with the rock (the third command). Whereas previously Moses had openly exclaimed over the burden of the people's complaints and rebellion only before the face of YHWH (see Exod. 17:4; Num. 11:11–15), even while speaking plainly to the people regarding their sin (see Exod. 32:30) or perhaps passing on to them YHWH's own castigation (Exod. 33:5), and never for the sake of their judgement (with the possible exception of Num. 16:15), here Moses

– quite apart from any vehemence displayed from YHWH – rebukes the people severely, calling them 'rebels' (*mōrîm*) instead of their objective status within the covenant, God's people. The irony that YHWH will accuse both Moses and Aaron of rebelling (*mĕrîtem*, v. 24; 27:14) underscores the wrongfulness of Moses' words. Outside Moses and Aaron's sin, the root for 'rebellion' (*mārāh*) occurs only at 17:10, related to the admonitory function of Aaron's blossomed staff, 'a sign for the sons of rebellion (*merî*)'. YHWH had called Moses to take precisely this sign, Aaron's budded staff, but did not charge him to berate the people as 'rebels'. In doing so Moses and Aaron 'rebelled' (*mĕrîtem*) against his word (20:24; 27:14), and will be excluded from life in the land.

What Moses calls the rebels to hear is a rhetorical question: 'From this rock shall we bring forth for you water?' His words may be taken in a variety of ways, Sakenfeld suggesting three (1985: 148; cf. Margaliot 1983: 213–214): (1) an open-ended question, perhaps luring the people to beg for water; (2) an interrogative expecting a negative answer, inviting unbelief; (3) a rhetorical question expressing an indignant refusal to supply water (Shall we indeed?! Why should we . . . ?). The first option appears irrelevant and petty, and Moses has experienced too much of YHWH's power and glory to assume he could have doubted God's ability now, making the second option unlikely. Rather, the whole tenor of his words and actions aligns only too well with the third scenario. His tone in addressing the people, as Arden puts it (1957: 52), 'is that of annoyance and condescension', 'a fit of indignation', 'a bitter denunciation'. Moses 'expressed anger and impatience' to the Israelites treats them 'like desensitized slaves' (Litke 2011: 33); that is, as if they were the first generation. Sanchez also reads the words of Moses as 'loaded with sarcasm', since he had wanted, contrary to YHWH, the people's judgement (2000: 33, 59–60). What makes the story so remarkable, writes Burnside (2016: 130), 'is precisely that Moses, here, abandons his vocation and speaks with his own authority'. The weight of this remarkable fact – the singular occasion when Moses abused his office by misrepresenting YHWH by his *own* attitude, words and act – must settle in sufficiently to perceive the gravity of his sin. However one approaches the rhetoric of Moses' question, he fundamentally changed YHWH's command into a question: YHWH's word that Moses will bring forth water from the rock *for them* (*lāhem*, v. 8), expressing mercy on the nation, is 'transformed by Moses into a harsh question, bursting forth from his anger' at these 'rebels': *for you* (*lākem*, v. 10) shall we bring forth water – are *you* deserving of divine mercy? (Samet 2014e: 261, quoting Moriel's analysis). Moses implies 'that the people do not deserve water', writes Waxman (2014b: 266): 'As far as he is concerned, they deserve to die.' The force of Moses' speech is underscored inasmuch as Moses has said nothing up to this point, and now expresses great anger (Bazak 2014b: 276–277).

If there were lingering doubts as to how to hear Moses' previous speech in terms of heatedness, of his being blind with rage (cf. Blum 1990: 271–278), his anger is shown plainly by his striking the rock twice. Given that the staff symbolized divine authorization (whichever staff was used), representing the power of YHWH himself, and given that it was wielded contrary to divine instruction in a violent act that misrepresented God, Moses' act was not only rebellious but a sacrilege. Having focused the people's attention on the rock, with 'from this rock' fronting the verb, he then strikes it repeatedly in anger. Glossing this act as a mindless repetition, as if by habit, of the commanded action in Exodus 17 nearly forty years previously, borders on the absurd and creates an artificial fog over the text's clarity. Of all figures in the Torah, no one understood the absolute need to follow YHWH's instruction carefully more than Moses. Seeking to mitigate his sin by asserting a general but flawed gesture of obedience only dishonours his character and undermines the magnitude of his greatness more deeply. Worse, it portrays YHWH himself, who responds with judgement, as a capricious perfectionist – whereas Moses himself appears frustrated precisely by YHWH's seemingly boundless patience. Rather, one both honours Moses' place and YHWH's character by embracing the text's presentation of Moses engaged in knowing rebellion against YHWH. Moses, I suggest, did not want to provide water for the community – rather than speaking to the rock, he struck it twice in anger, venting his frustration. The one who drew the people out of the waters (Exod. 2:10; Isa. 63:11) refused to draw the waters for them. From beginning to end, the drama of Moses' life turns on waters (see Sabo 2014).

Within the overarching observation of Moses' 'intention not to produce water' (W. W. Lee 2003a: 233), we may attend to the details of his action. First, he 'raised his hand' (*wayyārem . . . 'et-yādô*), distinct language not used throughout the exodus and wilderness narratives for his raising of the staff. Instead, use of both 'raise' (*rûm*) and 'hand' (*yād*) recalls their use in Numbers 15:30, describing the soul who sins with a 'raised hand' (*běyād rāmāh*), who sins defiantly, employed elsewhere to signify rebellion (see 1 Kgs 11:26, 27; Mic. 5:9). Whether out of angst against the people or YHWH himself, sadly, the description of Moses' raised hand portrays his act as one of defiance (cf. Wong 2008; Burnside 2016: 130–131). Next, he struck the rock with his staff twice. Not only did he strike the rock instead of speaking to it (cf. Holzinger 1903: 85; Buis 1974), but he repeated the smiting a second time – a bold act of rebelliousness. It is possible to read *paʻămāyim* as 'a second time' rather than 'twice', which, if an allusion to the first time in Exodus 17, would serve to reinforce his wrongdoing (Sakenfeld 1985: 149). If, somehow, the same 'rock' as in Exodus 17 is being assumed (using different Hebr. terms), then perhaps a 'second time' reinforces the inappropriateness of his action along these lines: having been struck once already, opening a fissure, only speaking was necessary now. Moses' striking of the rock was an act of defiance, 'venting out his anger and demonstrating his disgust for the people' (Lim 1997: 148; so also Koenig 1963: 168). If read independently, within the context of Numbers alone, there would be no notion whatsoever that the staff had to be implemented only by striking the rock, and Moses' transgression would appear remarkable. Within the context of Exodus 17, however, what stands out is the change in YHWH's instructions, underscoring Moses' rebellion. Not only does YHWH command Moses to strike the rock in Exodus, but there is also no narrative dramatization of his obedience: it is simply stated that 'Moses did so' (Exod. 17:6; cf. K. Brown 2020: 104), whereas here we are given a vivid description of Moses' action, underscoring his substantial departure from YHWH's instructions.

The identification of 'his staff' may be approached now within the larger context of taking Aaron's budded staff (vv. 8, 9). Either, still holding Aaron's staff (v. 9), Moses struck the rock with Aaron's staff ('his' inasmuch as Moses was holding it), or, more likely, while Aaron held the budded staff as an admonitory sign, Moses strikes the rock twice with his own staff. The latter option, whereby Moses strikes with his own staff, fits what the text says and helps explain how ambiguity arose in the text's reception. Others have discerned sacrilege inasmuch as the rock itself, struck twice in anger by Moses with either staff, might have symbolized YHWH or his presence (de Vaulx 1972: 226–227). The mere, deliberate misrepresentation of YHWH's will and character are enough to indict Moses: his 'words and behavior were tantamount to a most serious profanation and desecration of Y[HWH]'s Name and reputation' (Margaliot 1983: 215).

Many of the story's difficulties, such as why Moses is called to speak (rather than striking the rock), which rod is being referenced, and even Aaron's passive role in the matter, may be resolved by the structural key of Israel's Camp. Within the outer camp (chs. 11–15), Moses' singular role as prophet had been vindicated by YHWH, with whom he speaks mouth to mouth (12:6–8); then within the inner camp (chs. 16–18), Aaron's role as high priest was vindicated by YHWH through his budding staff (17:8). It is in the authority and aura of these vindicated roles that Moses and Aaron are called to stand before the rock amid the gathered assembly, and to uphold the kingship of YHWH (the central camp), vindicating his blessed rule and faithful guidance through the wilderness by the pouring forth of abundant waters. Parallels with Numbers 12 and 17 suggest that YHWH had planned to offer the newly risen generation of Israel the major lessons of the first generation's sojourn in one grand display of his own sovereign, gracious kingship. Yet, tragically, in their very offices as vindicated by YHWH against challenges and complaints, roles which represented their respective leadership over the outer and inner camps, they dishonoured YHWH and misrepresented him before the people. With this scenario in mind, certain details are clarified: Moses, therefore, had taken Aaron's rod 'from before YHWH' *for Aaron* to hold, signifying his office. Aaron's role in the event is to hold his staff as a sign – this is his communication before the people. Moses' taking the staff from the holiest place himself makes sense since he had put it there (17:10–11), and the high priest may only enter on the Day of Atonement. Moses, in demonstration of his office and of the significance of divine *torah*, was instructed only to speak; instead, he strikes the rock twice with his own staff, which he always had on hand.

The next detail, that 'many waters poured forth', should be read as the final unexpected wonder in a verse full of surprises: *despite* Moses and Aaron's rebellion, and arguably Moses' desire to impede YHWH's provision of water for the people, YHWH responds with an overabundance of many waters. Whereas the original divine instruction was to bring forth 'water', the fulfilment is of 'many waters'. Lest the people interpret Moses' ill-will as that of God's own character and disposition, YHWH, as Margaliot states (1983: 221), 'turns the profanation of his Name in the presence of all the people into a proof of His might and of His will to help his people by now giving them at once water "abundantly" from the rock – the strongest possible repudiation of Moses' words and action.' It was surely this language of 'many waters' (*mayim rabbîm*) that led to later descriptions of abundant streams in the wilderness, whether in the Psalms or in later Jewish depictions, for example, of twelve rivers flowing out of the rock (*t. Suk.* 3.11–13). In Psalm 78:15, YHWH watered his people out of the 'great depths' (*tĕhōmôt rabbā*), and Psalm 105 describes the waters 'gushing forth' (*yāzûbû*) 'like a river' (*nāhār*). Indeed, 'many waters' typically has cosmic associations in the HB (see May 2014), and the provision of abundant waters is a sign of kingship in both the HB and the ANE world (see Anthonioz 2014). In Balaam's third prophetic oracle, by the Spirit of God he proclaims a vision of Israel's encampment as supremely blessed in terms of a lush, well-watered garden – such is the message of blessedness YHWH desired to communicate to the risen generation in the wilderness (the only other use of 'many waters' in Numbers is in 24:7). The last clause, relating that the community and their beasts drank, with no mention of Moses, reflects a more impersonal form than YHWH's original instruction for *Moses* – 'you' – to cause the community and their beasts to 'drink' (*hišqîtā*, v. 8), likely indicating that the provision of water for them occurred in spite of Moses' intentions. Boorer, who notes that verse 11 is 'careful not to mention Moses causing them to drink', writes that the 'water is provided despite Moses and Aaron's disobedience', which would have otherwise served 'to block the knowledge of YHWH from the people' (2012: 51, 60). By contrast to YHWH's instructions for Moses to bring forth water and to water the congregation and their cattle, YHWH fulfils the command to bring forth water, and then Moses 'lets the nation manage on its own' (Samet 2014e: 262). Waxman similarly points out YHWH's instruction for Moses 'to water' (*šāqeh*, v. 8) the community and their beasts, a shepherding form of leadership Moses had displayed when he saved Jethro's daughters and watered their flocks (Exod. 2:17), and how the fulfilment, that the people 'drank' (*šātāh*, v. 11), portrays Moses as reluctant – not as their shepherd (2014b: 267). As a result, Moses will not bring this assembly into the land.

Recalling that the community had not been present for YHWH's instructions to Moses and Aaron as he revealed his compassionate intention to provide water straightway for the people and their beasts (vv. 6–7), Moses and Aaron's words and behaviour could not but be perceived as ill-will from YHWH – his not caring to meet their severe need for water in the wilderness. Thus, YHWH's abundant waters literally burst forth through their impediments and false representation of him, overturning and undoing – thwarting – their own ill intentions. W. W. Lee similarly argues that Moses struck the rock twice 'to prove that water would not come out', and that waters gushed forth 'not as a result of Moses' insolent action, but in spite of it', although his case for the adversative force of the conjunction ('*but* much water gushed out') has no basis and is not essential (2003a: 234). Vindication of YHWH's kingship, through use of *wayyēṣ'û*, matches the vindication of Aaron's priesthood, through *wayyōṣē'* – the rock bringing forth many waters, with the staff bringing forth buds, demonstrations of abundant life (17:8; 20:11).

One wonders how Moses responded inwardly when YHWH had explained his plan of an abundant provision of waters for his people; surely, no prolonged meditation was necessary to observe the depths of divine compassion for this complaining people. But rather than conforming to YHWH's character, submitting his own heart to the fashioning of divine will, Moses, as Jonah later would, stumbled on the expanse – seemingly unjust in its vastness – of the tender mercies of God. A mitigating factor in defence of YHWH's servant is that Moses' vision had been clouded by his long dealings with the first generation of Israelites, having become exasperated by their unbelief, depravity, relentless complaints, vicious accusations and rebellions, and having grown weary under the slow passage of their judgement, through thirty-eight heavily darkened years – all of which are by-passed swiftly by the reader with the mere turning of a page – until he could not separate the present generation, which had arisen steadily amid the toiling years, from the old one that had been buried in his sister's grave. Ultimately, Moses' 'you rebels' would be washed away by the roaring waves of YHWH's character as 'merciful and gracious, longsuffering, abounding in steadfast love and truth' (Exod. 34:6), and Moses' vision, wiped clear by YHWH's gentle hand of discipline, would see finally to Israel's only but sure hope (Deut. 30:1–10). His later words to the king of Edom (vv.

14–17) demonstrate a changed, more deeply compassionate perspective on God's people – the perspective of YHWH himself, who chose to meet his people's need both for water and for a demonstration of his abundant love for them, *before* dealing with the rebellion of his servants Moses and Aaron.

The language of Moses' 'smiting' (*wayyak*) 'the rock' (*'et-hassela'*) 'with his staff' (*bĕmaṭṭēhû*) will be echoed later as Balaam 'strikes' (*wayyak*) 'the donkey' (*'et-hā'ātôn*) 'with the rod' (*bammaqqēl*) (22:27; cf. 22:23). While the function of this parallel is open to argument, that Balaam was wrong to strike the donkey, and confronted twice for doing so (22:28, 32), would seem to colour further Moses' act as a transgression of YHWH's will.

12–13. YHWH's response to Moses and Aaron offers an unambiguous rationale for their judgement: 'because' (*ya'an*) they 'did not trust' (*lō'-he'ĕmantem*) in him 'to sanctify' (*lĕhaqdîšēnî*) him 'before the eyes of the sons of Israel'. The word 'trust' (*'āman*) includes the notion of confirming or supporting (BDB 52–53), of being 'loyal, steadfast, faithful, reliable, trustworthy' (Margaliot 1983: 222). Rather than being aligned with YHWH's will to provide abundant waters for the people and their animals, confirming that divine desire, they misrepresented his character by acting against his will. Cohen brings the causative sense of the hiph. into play: 'you did not *cause* trust' (1984: 160; emphasis original), a reading that accords well with the following line regarding the failure of Moses and Aaron to sanctify YHWH 'before the eyes of the sons of Israel', but the hiph. form of 'trust' occurs elsewhere in the Torah without a causative sense (Gen. 15:6; 45:26; Exod. 4:8; Deut. 9:23), making such a reading difficult to determine. Nevertheless, the broad idea that Moses and Aaron failed to impress upon the people YHWH's faithfulness to them as their covenant God is certainly true (Margaliot 1983: 222). Since the sons of Israel had no reason to suspect their insubordination (not having heard YHWH's instructions), Moses and Aaron grievously misrepresented YHWH to them, failing to sanctify him in their eyes – indeed, their attitude, words and actions have 'no reference point in YHWH' at all, or any 'indication that YHWH is behind this miracle' (Boorer 2012: 52, 59; similarly, Sanchez 2000: 71). Possibly, Moses and Aaron did not trust or believe YHWH that his *means* of being sanctified before the people; namely, through lavish mercy, was wise or just, wanting to rebuke them sternly instead and in accord with their own exasperation.

Failing to understand the seriousness of Moses' sin leads to sensing – and worse, asserting – injustice regarding YHWH's response, and is sometimes counterbalanced by maligning Moses' character elsewhere throughout Numbers, so that the present transgression merely portrays his culminating rebellion (e.g. Fairholm 2002). The seriousness of Moses' particular sin in Numbers 20, however, is offered by the text through

YHWH's own assessment. Attempts to reduce the failure to a single specific act alone, whether Moses' words, his not speaking to the rock, his act of striking the rock (at all, or twice instead of once) or Aaron's failure either to speak to Moses or to impede his behaviour fall short as false either/or options, and only muddy the waters (as do source-critical claims of a 'mutilated' story; e.g. G. B. Gray 1903: 262). Scriptural references to this account focus on different aspects of Moses' failure: Psalm 106 says the Israelites 'infuriated' (*qāṣap*) and 'provoked' or 'embittered' (from *mārāh*) Moses' spirit so that he spoke 'rashly' (*bāṭā'*) (vv. 32–33), while, before Aaron's death, YHWH says Moses and Aaron 'rebelled (*mārāh*) against my word' (Num. 20:24). Moses and Aaron disobeyed YHWH's instructions not simply by failing to speak to the rock, but by berating the people in anger, calling them rebels and, with a raised hand – defiantly – striking the rock twice, and this failure to sanctify YHWH was done 'before the eyes of Israel'.

In addition to other connections with Korah's rebellion (Num. 16 – 17), this Kadesh incident is also concerned with 'the relationship between Israel's leaders and Yahweh's holiness' (Mann 1987: 185), positioning Moses and Aaron's failure to sanctify YHWH in an especially negative light. What then does it mean to sanctify YHWH before the people? A clue comes from Leviticus: 'You will keep my commandments and do them – I am YHWH. But do not profane my holy Name, for I will be sanctified in the midst of the sons of Israel – I am YHWH, who sanctifies you' (22:31–32). Within a larger section oriented to Aaron's house (Lev. 22:1–2), YHWH underscores the obedience required of his mediators, so that his Name is sanctified rather than profaned in the midst of his people. The context includes mishandling sacred objects or approaching them while in a state of uncleanness. More broadly, disobedience profanes YHWH's holy Name and fails to sanctify him before his people. By misrepresenting him, Moses and Aaron had borne YHWH's Name in vain (Exod. 20:7; so, too, Maimonides, *Shemoneh Perakim* 4). After the deaths of Aaron's sons Nadab and Abihu, a sober judgement that casts a long shadow over Numbers, YHWH had declared – through Moses no less (Lev. 10:3):

By those who draw near I will be sanctified (*'eqqādēš*),
And before all the people I will be glorified.

Both Moses and Aaron qualify as 'those who draw near', and they failed to 'sanctify' YHWH 'before all the people'. Moses and Aaron were to impress on the people YHWH's faithfulness to them, within the context of his promises and self-imposed obligations within the covenant (see e.g. Margaliot 1983: 222–223; W. W. Lee 2003a: 235). Whatever else it means that they did not trust YHWH to sanctify him, the failure was aggravated because it was public, before the eyes of the gathered assembly, as YHWH reminds them (v. 12) – one of the key differences with the account in Exodus 17, where the miracle was performed only before the elders (vv. 5–6) (cf. Helfgot 1993: 53). In YHWH's rehearsal of the event in Deuteronomy 32:49, the public nature of the sin is underscored by describing it as 'amid the sons of Israel' twice (Anisfeld 2011: 216). YHWH himself had originally orchestrated his intended provision of abundant waters in the wilderness to display his glory before the sons of Israel (note 'before their eyes', v. 8), so Moses and Aaron not only missed an opportunity to demonstrate YHWH's ability, fostering the second generation's trust in him, but misrepresented YHWH's character and will. Nearly unbelievably, Moses sought to overturn YHWH's overture and demonstration of compassionate mercy within the solemn context of a sacred gathering and occasion, directed by YHWH God – his sin involves 'the spoiling of the sacred moment' (Sakenfeld 1985: 150; cf. Lohfink 1969; Helfgot 1993: 55), which would have sanctified YHWH (cf. Artus 1997: 237). Having once pleaded, 'Show me your glory' (Exod. 33:18), Moses here recoiled from its demonstration to Israel, the ocean of YHWH's mercy. Beyond providing for his flock's dire need of water in the wilderness, YHWH had gathered the community for a sacred event meant 'to glorify and hallow his Name in the eyes of the people'; but rather than causing the people to rejoice at the sight of abundant waters and in the knowledge that YHWH was with them, 'Moses, in a fit of indignation', turned the occasion 'into a bitter denunciation', cursing the people and smiting the rock – 'he destroys the hallowed moment that God had so clearly intended' (Arden 1957: 52). So, too, Margaliot writes that since it was YHWH's intention 'to impress His greatness upon the second generation at this event, the people were not to be reproved, but to be made personal witnesses of His might', to experience his readiness to help them (1983: 218). Rather than fostering 'the people's perception of God as the benevolent provider' (Anisfeld 2011: 215; cf. W. W. Lee 2003a: 223), Moses rebelled against his divine compassion and misrepresented him absolutely. The gatekeeper of divine revelation, Moses especially presented YHWH to the people – every utterance, act and disposition was to be taken by them as communicated by YHWH himself. In this way, YHWH's superabundant provision of waters, marked as it was by an overflowing compassion, can be seen only as a direct and powerful contradiction of his servants' mischaracterization. Accordingly, the failure to sanctify YHWH 'before the eyes of the sons of Israel' manifests a failure in their leadership of the sons of Israel – this illuminates the justice of their not being allowed to bring Israel into the land, explaining their deaths in the wilderness.

While it cannot be dealt with adequately here, in Deuteronomy Moses communicates that his entry to the land was barred due to the people's sin, with reference to the first generation in Numbers 13 – 14 (see Deut. 1:37; 3:23–29; 4:21–22). The difference in emphasis relates to the focus in Deuteronomy on the accountability of the people throughout, and it is possible that Moses understood his inclusion within the divine judgement passed on the entire first generation, since only Joshua and Caleb were explicitly excluded. On this reading, Moses had been forbidden to inherit and enjoy the land as an Israelite in Numbers 14, but was still, by his office, to lead Israel into the possession of the land, to conquer and inherit the tribal territories. As a result of his own sin as a leader in Numbers 20, however, that privileged duty of 'bringing' the people into the land was also stripped away – a consequence related separately (Deut. 32:48–52; cf. Num. 27:12–14). The issue in focus is the leadership of the second generation of Israel, to whom YHWH will give the land. As Sakenfeld observes (1985: 151), the question is not 'Why didn't Moses go into the land?' but, 'Why didn't Moses and Aaron lead the people into the land?' The nature of Moses and Aaron's behaviour underlines the second generation's need for new leadership, unjaded by the stains of the first generation and able to see *these* sons of Israel afresh and with sympathetic compassion (cf. Helfgot 1993: 55–56). While God understands the younger generation and shows them his mercy, Samet observes (1997), Moses and Aaron do not understand them, but regard them as a direct continuation of the previous generation, so that it 'becomes apparent, therefore, that Moses and Aaron are no longer able to continue leading this generation'.

As a chapter that concludes with the death and/or judgement of the first generation's highest leadership, Moses' sin, in distorting and even seeking to impede the grace of God from his people, is portrayed after the fashion of the first generation's tribal chieftains, the ten scouts who had maligned YHWH's gracious gift of the land. Among other parallels between Numbers 13 – 14 and 20 pointed out by Noonan, the following similarities correlate Moses and Aaron's sin with that of the first generation, which was excluded from the land (2020: 84): (1) both narratives are linked with a place called Kadesh (Num. 13:24; 20:1); (2) God accuses the guilty party of disbelief, using the same collocation of *lō'* + the hiph. of *'āman* + the object *bî* (14:11; 20:12; cf. Ps. 106:24); (3) disbelief is connected with rebellion against God (14:9; 20:24; cf. 27:14) and a failure to treat God properly: the Israelites treat him with contempt (14:11, 23), and Moses and Aaron fail to treat him as most holy (20:12); and (4) the divine punishment is disqualification from entering the land.

Later (v. 24), YHWH further declares that they rebelled against his word, terminology that 'regularly expresses violation of specific commands of the Lord' (S. R. Driver 1902: 22–23). As a result of their sin, Moses and Aaron will no longer bring the people into the land, a punishment that underscores the inappropriateness of their leadership over the second generation ('*this* community'; 'I have given *them*'). Also, and an extremely significant point in itself, whereas previously, even on the cusp of the land, YHWH had spoken of the land 'I am giving' (*nōtēn*) to the sons of Israel (13:2; 15:2), here he refers to the land 'I have given' (*nātattî*) to them (cf. also 20:24; 27:12), designating the second generation as those who will indeed possess the land. The second generation of God's people require a second generation of leaders, precisely how the chapter ends, with the transition from Aaron to his son Eleazar to serve as Israel's new high priest. Without excusing Moses' sin, it is apparent that he had become jaded by his inordinately prolonged tenure with the first generation in the wilderness and had, however momentarily, been unable to separate the risen generation from the first Israelites (an impulse perhaps fed by their use of 'our brothers', v. 3). That Moses remained a godly, selfless and faithful servant of YHWH, further humbled and shaped by YHWH's discipline, will become clear in Numbers 27:12–23.

The episode closes with a characteristic epilogue, naming the place according to what happened there. In this case the waters are labelled 'waters of contention' (*měrîbāh*) because the sons of Israel 'contended' (*rābû*) with YHWH. The label 'waters of contention' may be a wordplay with the 'waters of bitterness' (*mê hammārîm*) and 'waters that cause a curse' (*hammayim ham'ărărîm*) in Numbers 5:23 (cf. Burnside 2016: 142). Verse 3 had opened with the same terminology recounting how the people 'contended' (*wayyāreb*) with Moses, a point that may be lost amid the sin and judgement of Moses and Aaron. The divine judgement, however, does not pit their sin in contrast to the people's innocence or righteousness, but against YHWH's tenacious compassion for his people, the more magnified given their contentiousness, a compassion Moses and Aaron had misrepresented, obscured and opposed. There is some question as to the referent of the suff. in the closing words 'by/in/through/among them' (*bām*). YHWH 'sanctified himself', read reflexively rather than passively, by his judgement on Moses and Aaron (so Rashi), to be sure, but they are the least likely referent since they are not mentioned earlier in the epilogue. A more probable meaning is with the sons of Israel as the object – they contended against YHWH, but YHWH was sanctified *among* them as he had intended. Perhaps the strongest possibility is that YHWH sanctified himself through the waters; that is, *through* his abundant provision of them. This reading is persuasive, especially given the stress on the waters in the opening of the verse, along with language used elsewhere (Num. 27:14; Deut. 32:51) (Margaliot 1983: 226–227). Whichever reading, the narrative emphasis is on YHWH's intent that his provision of water be accomplished before the eyes of his assembled people (vv. 8, 10, 12), an astoundingly abundant gushing forth of waters that would sanctify him in the praise of his people for many generations afterward (Pss 78:15–16; 81:7; 105:41; 114:7–8; cf. Deut. 8:15; Job 28:9–10; Isa. 48:21). Chizkuni comments that it was as a result YHWH's being 'sanctified' that 'the name of this place henceforth was *Kadesh*, a sanctified location' (ben Manoach 2013: 4:965). As the locale where YHWH asserted his holiness and benevolent kingship, Kadesh is fitting for the narrative's focus on the camp of the *Shekhinah*.

Returning to YHWH's declaration about the land, a significant change is registered. As Frevel observes (2009: 115):

> From Num. 20:12 onwards the land which was promised to the fathers is given already on a text level, namely syntactically by the shift from *n-t-n yiqtol* to *n-t-n qatal*. Whereas this is merely stated by God in Num. 20:12, it is becoming to be accomplished from Num. 21:1 onwards. (See also 20:24; 27:12; 32:7, 9; 33:53.)

The closing verses round out the story by forming a inclusion with its beginning, based on the words 'contend' (*rîb*), 'holy' (*qādaš*) and 'sons of Israel' (*běnê-yiśrā'ēl*), and on the theme of death outside the land for Israel's leaders (cf. Samet 2014e: 253–255):

v. 1	'sons of Israel' (*běnê-yiśrā'ēl*)
v. 1	'Kadesh' (*qādēš*)
v. 3	'contended' (*wayyāreb*)
v. 1	Miriam dies outside the land
vv. 12–13	'sons of Israel' (*běnê yiśrā'ēl*), 'sons of Israel' (*běnê-yiśrā'ēl*)
vv. 12–13	'sanctify' (*lěhaqdîšēnî*), 'sanctified' (*wayyiqqādēš*)
v. 13	'waters of contention' (*měrîbāh*), 'contended' (*rābû*)
v. 12	Moses and Aaron, no longer allowed to lead the people in, will die outside the land

20:14–21: Edom refuses Israel to cross through its land

The central section of Numbers 20 serves two functions within its literary placement. First, it foreshadows the book's next subsection, chapters 21–25. The language of Israel's engagement with Sihon (21:21–25) and the Balaam narrative (chs. 22–24) has many similarities with this episode. Indeed, Edom's judgement will be announced by Balaam himself (see 24:18–19). Second, and more immediately, the refusal of Edom, violating all sense of kinship obligation, serves as a mirror and commentary on Moses' own behaviour toward the second generation of Israelites (vv. 1–13). No reason is given for Moses' leading of the people eastward – even after Edom's refusal to allow Israel passage, he leads the Camp south and then turns northward around Edom rather than attempting, as with the first generation, an ascent through the Negev (13:22). Some conjecture that Moses sought to avoid a repeat of the first generation's fear of giants in the mountainous region of Hebron (however, see comment on 21:1). Be that as it may, in Numbers 21:21–35 we learn that by this circuitous route Israel would conquer and possess land east of the Jordan, the kingdoms of Sihon and Og, allowing Moses a foretaste of the conquest of the land of Canaan (cf. Granot 2014c: 298–299).

Some commentators fault Moses in this episode, asserting that Edom's refusal is a result of Moses' 'acting on his own', apart from consulting YHWH. Moses, however, approaches Edom with a humble, brotherly appeal and magnifies YHWH's deliverance of Israel out of Egypt in the process, an episode completely in accord with YHWH's guidance (cf. Deut. 2). This is not to say the scene does not unfold within the sombre shadow of Moses' judgement. Edom's refusal of passage to Moses and the nation of Israel with him flows on the undercurrent of YHWH's refusal of entrance into the land for Moses and Aaron that frame the account (20:12, 23–24).

14. Moses sends messengers from Kadesh to the king of Edom with a diplomatic communiqué (on Edom, see Bartlett 1989; on the Israel–Edom kinship motif in the prophetic corpus, see B. A. Anderson 2012). His message follows typical protocol for ANE diplomatic correspondence: introduction, past relationship, historical setting and/or present circumstances, formal request, stipulations offered, and conclusion (see Cole 2009: 373). The term 'king' (*melek*) is the first mention of kingship in Numbers, arguably marking what will be a main theme in the next major subsection of the wilderness sojourn, chapters 21–25 – beginning with the present chapter's focus on YHWH's kingship, the camp of the *Shekhinah*. While Moses' prophetic office majored in chs. 11–15, and Aaron's priestly office in chs. 16–20, the next section will focus on Israel's relations with surrounding nations, through their kings, and in Balaam's oracles will yield prophecies concerning the rise of Davidic kingship, which culminates with the Messiah. With the prospect of life in the land, the subject of kingship arises naturally (see Deut. 17:14–20). The term 'messengers' anticipates chapters 21–25, where it will recur (21:21; 22:5; 24:12), just as Moses' mention of YHWH's 'messenger' (v. 16) anticipates the 'messenger of YHWH' who appears in the Balaam narrative (22:22, 23, 24, 25, 26, 27, 31, 32, 34, 35).

Mention of Edom, along with Moses' language of 'your brother' Israel, recalls the Genesis narrative of Jacob and Esau as a backdrop to the scene, especially Genesis 32, where Jacob encounters Esau on his return to the land:

> And Jacob sent (*wayyišlaḥ*) messengers (*mal'ākîm*) before him to Esau his brother (*'āḥîm*) to the land of Seir the country of Edom (*'ĕdôm*). (Gen. 32:3)

> And Moses sent (*wayyišlaḥ*) messengers (*mal'ākîm*) from Kadesh to the king of Edom (*'ĕdôm*), 'Thus says your brother (*'āḥîkā*) Israel . . .' (Num. 20:14)

Such a parallel highlights differences: whereas even Esau, who had once breathed out threats against his brother, and not without some justice (Gen. 27:36, 41–45), received him back with compassion and goodwill (Gen. 33:4), here the king of Edom will show little sympathy for all that Israel has suffered in Egypt and responds only with hostility. 'You yourself' (*'attā*), with which Moses addresses the king, indicates that word had surely spread concerning YHWH's deliverance of his people out of Egypt's cruel bondage (see e.g. Josh. 2:8–13). Edom's hostility, despite Moses' rhetoric of persuasion aimed at the king's sympathy, forms but one chapter in the story of Edom as Israel's archetypal enemy (heading the list in Ps. 83:6), a story that will end with Edom's utter destruction (Amos 1:11; Obad.), yet not completely devoid of hope (see Amos 9:12; Obad. 1:21).

While this overall section on Edom's refusal holds up a mirror to Moses' own lack of compassion toward Israel in the previous narrative, nevertheless the Midrash rightly underscores how Moses' sending of messengers to Edom reflects positively on his character, since he persevered with Israel's mission to inherit the land in spite of his own exclusion (*Num. Rab.* 19.7).

15–16. Moses offers a summary of the exodus, a gem that has received surprisingly little scholarly attention inasmuch as it rehearses the material found in Genesis 37 – 50 and Exodus 1 – 15. He recounts how the 'fathers' (the twelve patriarchal sons of Jacob) descended into Egypt and dwelled there many days. Along with 'Kadesh' (20:1, 14) and use of 'brother' (20:3, 14), several verbal and thematic links urge a reading of Israel's encounter with the king of Edom in the light of the previous story of Moses and Aaron's sin. The fathers' dwelling in Egypt uses the same term, *yāšab*, for Israel's 'dwelling' in Kadesh (v. 1), and 'many days' (*yāmîm rabbîm*) may recall the 'many waters' (*mayim rabbîm*, v. 11). The Egyptians 'did evil' (*rā'a'*) to us and to our fathers, Moses states truly, a reality that should have stirred some sense of brotherly understanding from Edom. The fact that Israel now stands as a thriving multitude near Edom's border is testimony to YHWH's own compassionate character and glory – for 'we cried out to YHWH and he heard our voice, and he sent a Messenger'. The Messenger (or 'Angel', *mal'ak*) of YHWH, who had appeared to the patriarchs (Gen. 16:7; 22:11, 15; 24:7, 40; 31:11; 48:16), first encountered Moses in a flame of fire in the midst of a bush (Exod. 3:2), later leading and accompanying the sons of Israel out of Egypt and through the wilderness toward the land (see Exod. 14:19), and is often understood by theologians as a manifestation of the pre-incarnate Son, given that he partakes of and is yet distinct within the Godhead (see Vos 1975: 72–76, 107–108), along with his role in being sent (e.g. John 13:20). The two distinct functions for this Messenger are indicated, 'as guide in the wilderness journey and as holy warrior in the promised land'

(Dozeman 2009: 556). YHWH had promised to send a Messenger to lead and keep his people, and to bring them into the land of Canaan, cutting off the Amorites, Hittites, Perizzites, Canaanites, Hivites and Jebusites (Exod. 23:20, 23; cf. 32:34; 33:2), a reality apparently forsaken by the faithless first generation of Israel. The Messenger of YHWH will have a significant role in the Balaam narrative (22:22–35), here foreshadowed. Whereas in the previous story the people had questioned Moses and Aaron, asking, 'Why did *you* make us ascend out of Egypt?' (v. 5), here Moses credits YHWH's Messenger as the One who 'brought us forth out from Egypt'. The function of his mention of the Messenger is debatable, and might have been intended as reflecting YHWH's pity on Israel, encouraging Edom to respond similarly, or perhaps as an underlying threat to Edom.

The evidence of their deliverance out of Egypt by YHWH is Israel's very presence on Edom's outskirts: look! – here we are (*'ănaḥnû*). The 'outskirts of your border', however, is taken as a menace by the king of Edom who distrusts Israel's assurances to the contrary, a grievous snub especially in the light of YHWH's firm instruction to Israel not to meddle with them (cf. Deut. 2:2–5). The term 'outskirts' (*qĕṣêh*) appears eight times in Numbers, referring to the outskirts of the Camp (11:1; 22:41; 23:13), Edom's border (20:16; 33:37), Moab's border (22:36), the border of the wilderness (33:6) and of the land (34:3). While fully acknowledging YHWH's deliverance, the stress weighs more upon Israel's weariness, and the afflictions they have endured, so as 'to rouse the sympathy of the Edomites for their "brother" Israel and to respond generously' (N. MacDonald 2012a: 131). Milgrom observes that the goal of Canaan is left out so as not to arouse Edom's envy (1990: 167). Nevertheless, Moses' rehearsal of the exodus serves rhetorically as a turning point of the wilderness journey (Frevel 2009: 124), and comes close to presenting a seamless movement from Egypt to Canaan (skipping over the first generation's failure, and the journey list in 33:1–49 arguably does as well).

17. As YHWH's judgement of death in the wilderness on the first generation has now given way to the promise of bringing the second generation into the land, there is an urgency and anticipation of arrival. Journeying through Edom being the most direct route to the land, Moses asks meekly ('please', *nā'*) for the king of Edom to allow Israel to pass through his land. While passing through Edom's land, Moses assures, they will not pass through field and vineyard and will not drink water from their wells; that is, they will not, like an army of locusts, deplete the land's resources as they make their way through. This was perhaps an unrealistic pledge, given the thousands of Israelites who would march through Edom, but Moses' language may amount to cultural hyperbole meant to assure goodwill, conveying what the sons of Israel would state more directly in verse 19. The terms 'fields and vineyards' (*śādeh wākārem*) were last mentioned in Numbers 16:14 in Dathan and Abiram's accusation of Moses, and are related thematically, along with the idea of drinking water, to the previous story (v. 5). Rather than pilfering the land, Israel, so Moses vouchsafes, will travel only along the main thoroughfare, the Way of the King highway, without 'stretching out to our right hand or left', language not only of keeping to the path but of refusing to clutch at Edom's resources. The Way of the King, used frequently by Egyptians in the Middle and Late Bronze Ages, was the major roadway that ran northward from the Gulf of Aqaba through the hill country of Transjordan, through Edom and Moab (Budd 1984: 212). Reaching the eastern border of the land across the Jordan by the most direct route, after some forty weary years in the inhospitable wilderness, is the goal – Israel simply wants to 'pass through your borders' (irony may be intended by contrast with v. 5).

The language in verse 17 of not passing through 'in field and vineyard' anticipates the next major subsection, chapters 21–25, with Israel's remarks to Sihon that they will 'not stretch in field or in vineyard' (21:22; cf. v. 20) and in the Balaam narrative as his donkey is forced out into the field (22:23) and the messenger of YHWH stations himself in the vineyard (22:24). Similarly, that Israel will 'not stretch out to our right hand or left' (v. 17) will be echoed as Balaam's donkey has nowhere to turn either 'to the right or left' (22:26). The term 'stretch' (or 'turn aside', *nāṭāh*) in verses 17, 21 recurs in the following chapters as well (21:15, 22; 22:23, 26, 33; 24:6).

18. Despite Moses' appeals to brotherly sympathy and overtures of goodwill, Edom responds with self-protecting animosity, forbidding Israel entry. Edom literally contradicts Moses' last words: 'until we have passed through your border' is countered by 'You will not pass through me.' The denial is backed by a military threat: 'lest with the sword I go forth to encounter you', which may reflect Isaac's pronouncement to Esau that 'by your sword you will live' (Gen. 27:40). Edom's refusal is recounted in Judges 11:17.

Edom's threat that he would go forth to encounter you with 'the sword' (v. 18) anticipates Israel's smiting of Sihon with the edge of 'the sword' (21:24), and of the messenger of YHWH's encountering Balaam 'with sword' (22:23, 31) and Balaam's ironic desire for a sword at hand (22:29), with his eventual slaying 'with the sword' (31:8) (cf. Frisch 2005: 108). Language of Edom's encountering (*l* + *qārā'*) Israel in verses 18, 20 also recurs, as Sihon encounters Israel (21:23), Og encounters Israel (21:33) and appears in the Balaam narrative (22:5, 20, 34, 36, 37; 23:3; 24:1).

19. Although Moses had begun the action (vv. 14–17), now the sons of Israel continue negotiations, displaying a new maturity in the nation. These sons of Israel probably comprise the delegation dubbed 'messengers' (v. 14), to whom the king of Edom responded ('them', v.

18). The sons of Israel will, they say, stay on the highway. It may be that to 'ascend' the 'highway' (*měsillā*) means they would no longer take the 'Way of the King', the more convenient road that passed through fields and vineyards and dug-out wells, but that they would now take the more difficult, meandering route over the mountains – and even pay for whatever natural sources of water they used along the way (Hirsch 2007a: 455–456). Edom's refusal in verse 20 may reflect this difference (Leibowitz 1982: 251): previously, he had said, 'you will not pass *through me*' (i.e. the Way of the King), but now he says, 'you will not pass through' (at all). They desire to pass through with 'my feet alone' – in other words, using neither hands nor weapons either to deplete Edom's resources or engage in hostility against its inhabitants. Their offer to pay for whatever water they and their livestock drink accords with YHWH's instructions later noted in Deuteronomy (2:6), and might have been intended as a lucrative motivation for allowing Israel passage – such payment would have boosted their economy. The phrase 'nothing else' (*'ên-dābār*) may also be rendered 'it is a small thing' or 'it is nothing', an attempt to persuade Edom that Israel was not requesting anything costly or outlandish – just to pass through. While vowing not to pillage and plunder as marauders, nevertheless since, as Ashley points out (1993: 391), Edom cannot be crossed in a day, one wonders how the Israelite thousands would supply themselves with food and water, and where they would stay, and so on – concerns that would surely have made Edomites anxious. Zakovitch suggests Edom's refusal, even after offer of payment, was revenge for Jacob's demanded payment for satisfying Esau's famished condition in Genesis 25:29–34 (2012: 25; see Milgrom 1990: 168).

20–21. Given the perseverance of the sons of Israel, who are eager for a direct eastward route to the land, Edom, threatened by such fervour, repeats his twofold response – (1) forbidding Israel to pass through his borders, (2) threatening military force – but this time with action, going forth against Israel with a 'weight' (*kābēd*) of people and a 'strong hand' (*yād ḥăzāqāh*). Within the Torah, 'strong hand' is exodus language, used repeatedly to describe YHWH's 'strong hand' by which he delivered Israel out of the bondage of Egypt's king (see Exod. 3:19; 6:1; 13:9; 32:11; Deut. 4:34; 5:15; 6:21; 7:8; 9:26; 26:8). Use of *kābēd*, whose root occurs thirty-seven times in Exodus (Pharaoh's 'hardened' heart, a 'severe' plague, YHWH's 'honour', the appearance of YHWH's 'glory', etc.) may function similarly, as part of the exodus motif running through chapters 20 and 21 as a whole. Such language, moreover, creates a bitter awareness that Israel *could* – given YHWH's 'glory' and 'strong hand' displayed in the exodus – pass through Edom, even conquering them if need be, yet *may not*, given their need under YHWH to respect brotherly relations (cf. Deut. 2:1–7). Israel is so close to the land and yet, with Edom's denial, so needlessly far away, a point that will lead to discouragement (21:4). With Edom's 'refusal' (*mā'ēn*), Israel must turn away southward to the Sea in order to skirt around the land of Edom. Within its ANE context, Edom's refusal is a grievous failure of hospitality. Intriguingly, the tension in Jacob and Esau's relationship originally began and developed through meals (Gen. 25:29–34; 27:1–42), so that, again, Edom's action may be perceived as revenge for an ancient grievance. Edom's refusal forms an ironic reversal of the last encounter of reconciliation between Jacob and Esau: whereas Esau did come out with a contingent of men upon Jacob's return to the land, as Edom does now against Israel, yet Jacob's fears of hostility had evaporated with Esau's embrace and kind reception (Gen. 32 – 33). Through the prophet Amos, YHWH would later proclaim judgement on Edom 'because he pursued his brother with the sword and cast off all pity' (1:11).

Certainly, given all that Israel had endured both under the affliction of bondage in Egypt and then with the severe hardships experienced in the wilderness as an entire generation died out, the reader's empathy with God's people marks Edom's hostile refusal, especially after Moses' appeals for brotherly compassion and Israel's assurances of goodwill, as harsh and unkind, a profound enmity worthy of divine retribution and judgement. Why is this story placed here? The fact that it simply 'happened' at this point historically disregards the narrative strategy whereby some events are in fact dischronologized while others may be left out completely for theological reasons. The lexical and thematic links shared with the previous story of the sin of Moses and Aaron (vv. 1–13), enables us to understand the depth of their sin from a clearer perspective. The history of Israel conveyed by Moses to the king of Edom, aimed at stirring brotherly sympathy, should surely have inspired some compassion in Israel's designated shepherds themselves. Edom's refusal to give Israel water from his wells, a topic broached in verses 17 and 19, discomfortingly reminds the reader of Moses' heated rebuke of YHWH's flock: 'Hear now, rebels, from this rock shall we bring forth for you water?' (v. 10). To be sure, Moses and Aaron had tasted their own share of hardship *because* of Israel's rebellions and complaints, and had recently buried their sister Miriam. Such mitigating factors aside, however, their response to the people demonstrated that new leaders were needed for a new generation. 'The sin of Moses and Aaron', writes S. Klein (2015b), 'is an expression of the gap that exists between the leadership and the generation that is about to enter the Land of Israel.' Nevertheless, Moses' tender recounting of Israel's hardships to the king of Edom display more than a rhetoric of persuasion: his words reveal that he had received YHWH's judgement and discipline with humility and was indeed shaped, corrected and sanctified by YHWH's discipline. The shadowed episode of Edom's refusal, far from displaying

Moses' ineffectiveness, might have been inserted as a counterbalance to the previous story, exhibiting how closely aligned he became with YHWH's own sympathetic view of Israel's new generation and how, despite his own exclusion from the land, he still yearned for the nation to receive its inheritance.

20:22–29: Death of Aaron and the installation of Eleazar as high priest

22–23. As with verse 1, God's people are designated 'the sons of Israel, the whole community', and their journey is recounted from Kadesh to Mount Hor ('Mountain of the Mountain' or 'Hor, the Mountain'). The designation may refer to a smaller mountain rising at the summit of another mountain (*Num. Rab.* 19.16). The locale, with its mention of Kadesh and the border of Edom, along with Aaron's death as a result of his sin, unifies the three stories of the chapter. Mount Hor is often identified with modern day Jebel Nebi Hârûn, some 50 miles south of the Dead Sea (Keel and Küchler 1982: 2:176; cf. Aharoni 1979: 201–202, as generally near Kadesh en route to Arad), a tradition noted by Josephus (*Ant.* 4.4.7). Aaron's death on Mount Hor is mentioned also in Deuteronomy 32:50.

The locale of YHWH's speech to Moses and Aaron is given with greater detail than the travelogue of the previous verse. He addresses them not only at Mount Hor, but 'by the border of the land of Edom', perhaps bringing into play the function of the Edom account, and lending gravity to YHWH's words.

24–26. YHWH announces that Aaron 'will be gathered to his people', language that, used for the peaceful deaths of the patriarchs (Abraham, Gen. 25:8; Isaac, 35:29; and Jacob, 49:29; of Ishmael, Gen. 25:17; and of Moses, Num. 27:13; 31:2; 32:50), differentiates his death from that of the rest of the first generation, whose carcasses fall in the wilderness (14:29, 32). Moreover, while YHWH had struck down in the wilderness thousands among the rebellious generation, he calls Aaron and then Moses 'up mountains to receive them to himself', honouring them 'even in their humiliation' (Gane 2004: 674). The idiom 'gathered to his people' possibly originated with the practice of burial in family tombs (cf. Ashley 1993: 395), although its usage in Scripture overflows that context, suggesting a greater spiritual reality. Despite dying outside the land, it is certain that Aaron will be gathered to his people, reflecting ancient Israel's 'conviction about life after death, that in *Sheol*, the place of the dead, people will be reunited with other members of their family' (G. J. Wenham 1981b: 172). Nevertheless, while Aaron is indeed elderly, his death, staged by YHWH, is set forth as a divine and judicial act: 'for' (*kî*) he will not enter into the land YHWH is giving to the sons of Israel, 'because' (*'al 'ăšer*) you rebelled against my word ('mouth', *pî*) at the waters of Meribah. Note the wordplay between 'you rebelled' (*mĕrîtem*) and waters of 'Contention' (*Mĕrîbāh*), as well as the ironic rebuke for having dubbed the people 'rebels' in 20:10. Although Aaron's death is in focus, YHWH speaks to both Moses and Aaron and his admonition 'you rebelled' is pl. Even in the midst of just consequences for rebellion, the land continues to be designated as that land 'which I have given (*nātattî*) the sons of Israel' (cf. v. 12). The nature of Aaron's involvement in the rebellion remains obscure, 'one of the most difficult Gordian knots' of the Pentateuch (Lim 2001: 127), especially since the focus of the story is on Moses, whose sin has also been dubbed a Gordian knot (Milgrom 1983a: 251). Nevertheless there is no distinction made between the gravity of Aaron's sin and that of Moses – and Aaron dies without glimpsing the land with Moses (cf. J. M. Cohen 1984: 153). Suggestions as to Aaron's failure include his total passivity (Asher 1989), neither speaking to the rock nor preventing Moses from striking it (Lim 2001) or his being complicit in Moses' rebellion by association (Sakenfeld 1985: 146; Propp 1988: 24), or that we are to assume his participation with Moses. As Miriam's death is shadowed by her previous sin (Num. 12), so Aaron's death is tainted by his involvement in the golden calf episode (Exod. 32); however, only his role in Numbers 20 is offered as an explicit reason for his not entering the land. YHWH includes him equally with Moses in rebellion (vv. 12, 24), in acting treacherously (Deut. 32:51). As noted earlier, Aaron's primary role was to hold up his budded staff as a sign. Seemingly passive, this was a significant gesture, and was contravened by his apparent complicity with Moses' rebellion. Although a difficult text, Deuteronomy 33:8b, recounting how 'Levi' 'strove' (*rîb*) with YHWH at the waters of Meribah, may be read as an indictment of Aaron. As a literary character, Aaron is quite weak, never acting on his own initiative, whether in the direst of scenarios (cf. 16:46), or even in his sin: he is complicit in Israel's apostasy with the golden calf (Exod. 32), complicit in Miriam's slander against Moses (Num. 12) and complicit in Moses' rebellion against YHWH (Num. 20:1–13). Israel will finally emerge out of the wilderness, by contrast, through a zealous young priest who takes decisive action for the honour of YHWH (Num. 25).

YHWH's instructions begin with 'take' (*qaḥ*), an unhappy reminder of his original instructions for providing water for the people out of the rock (v. 8; a key term in chs. 16–18). Moses is to take Aaron and Eleazar, leading them to ascend the summit of Mount Hor, wherein the office of high priest will transfer from Aaron to Eleazar before Aaron is gathered. Three times Eleazar's name is followed by 'his son' (*bĕnô*, vv. 25, 26, 28), underscoring not only that the priesthood is a family dynasty but the transition from the older to the younger generation. The death of Aaron, who as high priest represents Israel, closes the chapter on the first generation, even as it closes a subsection grappling with the problem of death (chs. 16–20). The transition from Aaron to Eleazar his son as high priest forms a microcosm of Israel in the wilderness, as the first generation dies out, giving way to the children who will inherit YHWH's gift of the land. That his garments are 'stripped' (*pāšaṭ*) by Moses before Aaron's death avoids their pollution by corpse impurity. The term 'to strip' possibly has negative connotations, a degrading of Aaron. 'Clothing' (*lābaš*) Eleazar with the garments forms an installation rite, recalling when Moses had first clothed Aaron as high priest, article by article, nearly forty years earlier (see Exod. 29:8; Lev. 8:7–9; cf. Gen. 3:21) – now Moses dons the same articles of clothing on Aaron's son. The priestly garments of Aaron are described in Exodus 28 and, again, were fitted upon him in Leviticus 8:7–9. YHWH's speech ends by contrasting Eleazar's induction as high priest with a second reminder that Aaron 'will be gathered' – for 'there' (*šām*) on Mount Hor he will 'die' (*mēt*). There may be a sense of compassion for Aaron implied since before his own death he is allowed 'to see himself living on in the person of his son' (Hirsch 2007a: 457).

27–29. The fulfilment formula, that Moses did just as YHWH had commanded, opens the recounting of Moses' obedience, step by step, using the precise language of YHWH's instructions: 'ascend' (*'ālāh*), 'strip' (*pāšaṭ*), 'clothe' (*lābaš*). The only difference between YHWH's instructions and Moses' fulfilment is the narratorial insertion that they ascended Mount Hor 'before the eyes' (*lĕʿênê*) of the whole community, a detail recalling that the sin of Moses and Aaron had also been 'before the eyes' of God's people. The detail also sets up the action of the closing verse, when the whole community 'saw' (*wayyir'û*) that Aaron had perished. 'Poignantly', writes Leveen (2002: 256), 'in order to take on the role of high priest, signified by the wearing of his father's clothing, Eleazar must first witness his dying'.

Aaron, Israel's founding high priest, 123 years old (Num. 33:39), is dead. As with the emphasis on Kadesh for Miriam's death, emphasis is here placed on the summit of Mount Hor as the locale of Aaron's death – 'there' (*šām*) he died (twice, vv. 26, 28; cf. 33:38–39). Tersely, without mention of burial, the text moves to the next wayyiqtol, narrating Moses' descent from the mountain with Eleazar, who will now represent God to his people. Significantly, however, the whole community, upon witnessing that Aaron had perished, weeps for him thirty days (as with Moses, Deut. 34:8). As the regular period for mourning was seven days (cf. Gen. 50:10; 1 Sam. 31:13; 1 Chr. 10:12), the thirty days designated for Aaron underscore the historically momentous event of the passing of Israel's original high priest; Aaron became the ancestor of a priestly lineage that would serve for many centuries at the Jerusalem temple. That Aaron's being gathered to his fathers is also described with both 'to die' (*mût*) and 'to perish' (*gāwaʿ*) recalls the question with which chapters 16–17 ended: 'Whoever draws near – even draws near – to the Dwelling of YHWH will die (*mût*)! Shall we end with perishing (*gāwaʿ*)?'

and forms an inclusion with the second generation's complaint (20:3). The word 'perish' likely carries a connotation of judgement, as with the flood (Gen. 6:17) and with Achan (Josh. 22:20) (cf. Milgrom 1990: 171). Outside Genesis, the Torah's only uses of g-w-ʿ occur in Numbers 17 (vv. 27–28) and 20 (vv. 3, 29), connecting the incidents, both of which position dying within the context of YHWH's holiness (Mann 1987: 185–186). That the 'whole house of Israel' is unified in mourning the loss of its first high priest offers a glimmer of hope when contrasted with the previous generation's challenge for the priesthood (16:3). Ordained with inscrutable wisdom, the sobering justice of God, wherein he sanctified himself as holy in the eyes of his people (v. 13), is intended for their lasting good and fruitfulness.

Explanation

Numbers 20, framed by the deaths of Miriam and Aaron, closes the story of the old generation by recounting the deaths of its leaders, along with the failure and judgement of Moses. These siblings die separately and in order of birth (Olson 1996: 132; cf. Budd 1984: 219). Through the prophet Micah, YHWH would later remind his people of the great blessing of having had the leaders he raised up for Israel: 'For I caused you to ascend from the land of Egypt and from the house of bondage, and I sent before you Moses, Aaron and Miriam' (6:4). Significantly, the rebellions of the first generation of Israel, along with their divine judgement of death in the wilderness, trace the pattern of the Camp's structure: judgement comes first to the fringes of the Camp (11:1) and Miriam's sin causes her to be shut outside the Camp's boundary (Num. 12); then the narrative recounts the sin of the twelve tribes led by their princes (chs. 13–14, the outer camp), followed by the sin of the Levites and chieftains related to Aaron's priesthood (chs. 16–17, the inner camp), and finally the death or judgement of that generation's leaders, including Moses, who misrepresented and maligned YHWH's kingship (the camp of the *Shekhinah*). Panning back, it appears that each group's failure was in relation to usurping the next level of authority: the princes, representing their respective tribes (the outer camp), attempted to usurp Moses' prophetic authority (chs. 13–14); the Levites (the inner camp) attempted to usurp Aaron's priestly authority (chs. 16–17); and, finally, Moses (the camp of the *Shekhinah*) attempted to usurp YHWH's authority directly. Ironically, it was in the gravity of their respective offices *as vindicated by YHWH*, and summing up the divine lessons of the outer and inner camps in the first generation's sojourn, that Moses and Aaron failed to uphold YHWH's kingship, the blessedness of the central camp.

More than the fountainhead of the prophets or the one who established the sacrificial cult, Moses represents the kingship of YHWH

God. With reason, Book Four of the Psalter, which centres on YHWH's kingship, begins with a psalm of Moses (Ps. 90). Every ensuing leader and king, who functioned as YHWH's 'son' (rather than as YHWH), would be measured by his adherence to the Torah of Moses (see Deut. 17:14–20; Josh. 1:7–9; 1 Kgs 2:1–4; Ps. 1), but not so Moses himself – he functioned as the *revelation* of YHWH's will and reign. Moses is not a paradigm for Israel's future monarchs, but their standard, the means by which they may coordinate their rule with YHWH's will, so as to reflect his reign. Moses was called not merely to reflect but to express the kingship of YHWH, a reality that intensified the gravity of his one rebellion against God's will. Accordingly, and fittingly given the locale of Kadesh (holy) and the image of many waters, Numbers 20 relates to the holy of holies and YHWH's kingship (cf. Gen. 2:10–14; Ezek. 47; Rev. 22:1–2). If the scouts episode recalled the Tree of Knowledge transgression (Gen. 3), and Korah's rebellion recalled Cain's murder of Abel (Gen. 4), the context for Moses and Aaron's failure is the river of life running through Eden's garden, branching out into four headwaters to water the four quadrants earth (Gen. 2:10–14), waters Moses sought to impede from the Camp of Israel.

In the 'first month' of the fortieth year, the assembly of YHWH, comprising the second generation of Israel, raised up in the wilderness and eager to inherit the land, arrives and stays in Kadesh. Restless and impatient, and lacking water, they contend with Moses, complaining that he and Aaron have brought YHWH's assembly into the wilderness to die. They express a preference for an instant death over against lingering in the wilderness, referring to Korah and his community as 'our brothers', a solidarity with the first generation that appears to have provoked Moses. YHWH, however, exhibits no stern wrath or intent to judge the people, instructing Moses along with Aaron to supply the people and their animals water by taking up Aaron's budded staff from his presence in the holiest, gathering the people, and speaking to the rock. In the magnificence and instructive nature of their divine offices, Moses was to speak to the rock while Aaron held up his budded staff, displaying and vindicating the beneficent kingship of YHWH. Incensed against the people, Moses and Aaron rebel against YHWH's intention, endeavouring to impede his merciful provision of water for them: Moses berates the people as 'rebels' and strikes the rock twice with his own staff. Rather than granting the people a knowledge of YHWH as their compassionate Shepherd in the wilderness, Moses and Aaron misrepresent him, abusing their offices, which YHWH had previously vindicated. In spite of their rebellion – overturning their efforts – YHWH supplies a superabundant flow of waters so the people and their cattle may drink. He also declares that Moses and Aaron will no longer lead this assembly into the land he is giving Israel, just retribution for usurping his kingship. The place-name Kadesh (holy) may function as a memorial to how YHWH sanctified himself among Israel through his supply of many waters, despite Moses and Aaron's failure to sanctify him before his people's eyes.

Luzzatto (1800–1865) lamented that while Moses had committed one sin, the commentators have loaded thirteen or more sins on him, since each invents a new one (cf. Luzzatto 2012: 3:1073). Yet the nature of Moses and Aaron's sin is described in a variety of ways in Scripture; and unsurprisingly so, given the multivalent nature of sin itself. Within Numbers, YHWH's own assessment is as follows:

> you did not trust in me to sanctify me before the eyes of the sons of Israel (20:12)

> you rebelled against my word (20:24)

> you rebelled against my word . . . to sanctify me in/through the waters before their eyes (27:14)

These references offer a rationale for their failure; namely, not 'trusting' (*'āman*) in YHWH; a result of their failure, not 'sanctifying' (*qādaš*) him before the eyes of Israel; and a characterization of their failure as a 'rebellion' (*mārāh*) against his word – not imprecision or a mistake, but rebellion, an insubordinate act of determined defiance against YHWH's manifest will. Similar terminology is used of the first generation of Israel in the wilderness, who refused 'to trust' (*'āman*) in YHWH, even after all his signs (14:11), and who 'rebelled' (*mārāh*) against the 'mouth' of YHWH (Deut. 1:26, 43; 9:23) (cf. Emmrich 2003: 57; Burnside 2016: 138–139). The retribution for their failure is that they will not 'bring' (*bô'*) the assembly into the land (20:12), which means, for Aaron, his premature death outside the land – he will not 'enter' (*bô'*) it (20:24). Although Moses will be allowed to see the land from the summit of Mount Abarim, he too must die outside (27:12–14). In Deuteronomy, YHWH describes their sin similarly as failing to sanctify him, but explains it further as an act of treachery, noting twice the public nature of the sin ('in the midst of the sons of Israel'): 'for you acted treacherously/unfaithfully (*māʿal*) against me in the midst of the sons of Israel . . . for you did not sanctify (*qādaš*) me in the midst of the sons of Israel' (32:51). In Numbers, treachery or unfaithfulness labels the sorts of sins dealt with in the purity laws, deemed unfitting for life in YHWH's Camp (5:6, 12, 27), as well as the heinous apostasy committed by the sons of Israel with the Midianite women, joining themselves to Baal (31:16). These examples accord with Levine's understanding that *māʿal* implies sacrilege and impurity, an apt term for the misappropriation of sanctuary property or the betrayal of trust involved in marital infidelity and in the worship of foreign gods (1989: 30). Their rebellion against YHWH's word and misrepresentation of his will and character means

Moses and Aaron were disloyal to YHWH himself, and betrayed the covenant (cf. Lim 1997: 154). Psalm 106:33 mentions Moses' speech: 'because they embittered his spirit, he spoke rashly (*bāṭā'*) with his lips'.

The focus on Moses' speech resonates with the parallel concern shared between Numbers 12 and 20, and the relationship between YHWH's and Moses' speech (12:7–8; 20:7–8, 10): Moses, the mouthpiece of God and prophet par excellence, whose words are the very words of YHWH, faithful in all his house, here faithlessly disobeys YHWH, usurping his role and misrepresenting him, precisely by the words he speaks (Boorer 2015: 128–131; so also Arden 1957; Margaliot 1983). Without being reduced to speech alone, Moses' harsh words may nevertheless serve as a summation of his rebellion, which includes his striking of the rock. The fountain of Moses' speech was his angry impatience with God's people and consequent attempt to defy YHWH's mercy to them. Maimonides underscores Moses' misrepresentation of YHWH God to Israel (quoted in Leibowitz 1982: 239):

> When they [Israel] saw him thus in anger, they must certainly have concluded that he was not displaying personal animus or pique but, on the contrary, had not God been angry with them at their demand for water, Moses would not have been provoked. Yet we do not find that God was angry or showed disapproval.

Again, YHWH's revelation through Moses' speech is precisely what YHWH had vindicated (Num. 12). In his anger, Moses rebelled against YHWH: he was 'unfaithful' to him – that is the final point for which he was punished (cf. Mann 1979: 483). In sum, Moses' sin against YHWH 'was astoundingly serious', a 'fundamental betrayal of their relationship' (Waxman 2014b: 264). Why did this otherwise meek and faithful servant of YHWH rebel against God? The justice of the punishment – that Moses and Aaron would not lead the assembly into the land – explains the nature of the rebellion: he could not relate to God's people with the sympathy needed to lead them (cf. Margaliot 1983: 204; Ron 2003: 193–194; Kahn 2007b; Samet 2014e: 262; Held 2017: 145–151). Lichtenstein similarly states that Moses' bitterness and anger betray the rift in relationship and lack of communication between him and the people – a generation gap (2014b: 290). In his rebellion, Moses (along with Aaron) bore the Name of YHWH in vain, for which he would not be held guiltless (Exod. 20:7). Moses' previous forbearance only serves to highlight the exception with regard to the new generation. As the foremost proponent of YHWH's steadfast love for his people, Moses' resemblance to Jonah here, becoming exasperated with the boundless mercy of YHWH, is as uncanny as it is tragic (cf. Boyce 2008: 190). Moses thus remains a man of the wilderness: his death 'leaves him betwixt and between, neither in Egypt nor the Promised Land' (Hendel

2001: 618) – he is 'permanently liminal' (S. Ackerman 2014: 113). Yet his greatness is only amplified in that he bore greater fruit of selfless love and humility after divine correction (Num. 27:12–23; Deut. 1:11), and, by his singular failure, Moses directs our gaze to the new Moses, whose first petition and deepest yearning would be for the hallowing of his Father's Name (Matt. 6:9).

The closing words of the episode, asserting that YHWH 'was sanctified among them' (v. 13), leaves the emphasis on the manifestation of God through his provision of abundant waters in the wilderness. While the wilderness has come to represent the place of death (Num. 14:29), the waters symbolize new life and cleansing. Chapter 19 set forth the pattern of transition from the impurity of corpse pollution, positioned in the wilderness, to the life-giving presence of YHWH within the Camp *through the waters of separation*. Chapter 20 marks the conclusion of the era of death by recounting the deaths of the first generation's leaders, even sealing the death of Moses while the second generation of Israel, in their first encounter with YHWH, experience his presence and kingship through his plentiful supply of rushing rivers out of a crag – and the next chapter continues the presentation of a 'new' Israel's being supplied with water in the wilderness (21:10–20). Isaiah will later describe the wonders of the new exodus with similar imagery, proclaiming that the wilderness of Zion 'will become a fruitful field' through the outpouring of the Spirit, who is linked closely with the image of water (32:15). Again, Isaiah says YHWH will make Zion's 'wilderness like Eden, and her desert like the garden of YHWH' (51:3; see also Isa. 41:17–20; 48:20–21), a garden known as being 'well-watered' (Gen. 13:10), since one of its leading features is a river flowing through it to water the land (Gen. 2:10–14). Given the analogy between the mountain of God and the temple, as an architectural divine mountain, Scripture speaks of waters flowing from either the Jerusalem mount (Zech. 12:10; 13:1; 14:8) or its Temple (Ezek. 47; Joel 3:18). God is the source of the river that makes glad his city (Ps. 46:4; cf. Rev. 22:1), for he is the fountain and wellspring of life. The Messiah would baptize his people with the Spirit, pouring out the renovating waters of life (John 1:32–33; cf. 3:3–5; 4:10–14; 6:63; 7:37–39). In Numbers 20, the abundant supply of many waters in the wilderness was a self-revelation of YHWH God, demonstrating to Israel that he and he alone is the source of his people's life – and that he is more than willing and able in his compassionate loving-kindness and mercy to supply them with such waters. The abundant water from the crag, divinely outpoured before the assembled Israelites, was to be like YHWH's Advent and Revelation at Mount Sinai for the second generation (cf. Exod. 19 – 24). Indeed, Mount Sinai, where the older generation had first embraced YHWH's kingship, is likely 'the rock in Horeb', the source of waters supplied for Israelites at Rephidim (Exod. 17:6), as well as the brook mentioned after the golden calf incident (Exod. 32:20), associating divine revelation, *torah*, with waters of life. Similarly, in preparation for the revelation of Sinai, YHWH's instruction, his 'statute and judgement', is associated with 'sweet water' in Exodus 15:22–27 (also, the root of 'showed' in v. 25 is the same for *torah*).

The next story relates further Israel's eagerness to reach the land by the shortest route, through Edom (vv. 14–21). Moses sends messengers to the king of Edom, rehearsing Israel's afflictions and requesting permission to pass through his territory, but is rebuffed and threatened. After the sons of Israel renew the request, avowing to pay for any water drunk by the people and their cattle, the king of Edom refuses passage through his border and brings out a militia, causing Israel to turn away. Beyond leading to Israel's frustration, which will surface in the next chapter (21:4–5), the narrative offers a fresh perspective on the character of Moses. On the one hand, Edom's lack of brotherly sympathy for Israel, refusing the people passage, with its focus on Edom's supply of water, enables readers to see Moses' previous lack of sympathy for God's people in a new light – revealing his lack of compassion for the Israelites who were weary and ready to leave the wilderness and inherit the land. On the other hand, Moses' moving description of Israel's plight to the king of Edom forms a stark contrast with his previous rhetoric ('you rebels'), and demonstrates that he had indeed been humbled under YHWH's heavy hand of discipline. The episode also anticipates chapters 21–25, which narrate Israel's encounters with the nations surrounding Canaan.

Affirming the transition to the next generation, especially as the high priestly office is transferred from Aaron to his son Eleazar (cf. W. W. Lee 2003b: 265), yet the chapter closes on the note that Aaron has 'perished', with Israel's mourning his loss. Aaron's death, however, also functions to underscore that the judgement on the first generation is complete (Moses excepted). As Numbers 35:25–32 instructs, the high priest's death forms his last act of atonement so that the manslayer may be liberated from the city of his refuge; just so, the death of Aaron, who as high priest had represented the first generation of Israelites before YHWH God, signals Israel's release from the wilderness and from God's judgement. The period of wandering is over and may now give way to Israel's purposeful journey to inherit the land. In this sense, hope may be found in Aaron's death (cf. also P. Guillaume 2009: 150). Within the broader canonical movement, the mere fact of Aaron's death casts a shadow over the entire Levitical priesthood, pointing us to another priesthood whose basis would be the indestructible life of resurrection, and to a high priest able to save to the uttermost precisely because he always lives – and this to make intercession for us (Heb. 7:23–25).

Broadening the view (chs. 11–20), N. MacDonald observes that 'death hovers' over the wilderness sojourn, beginning with the outskirts of the

Camp (11:2), penetrating to the whole people in the scouts episode (14:35), reaching the Levites with the rebellion of Korah and his community (16:31–35) and now, finally, engulfing Israel's leaders (2012a: 130). The narrative logic, whereby the first generation's demise is traced according to the structure and theology of Israel's Camp, is manifest: the failure of the outer camp of twelve tribes (chs. 11–15), the failure of the inner camp of Levites (chs. 16–18), the failure of Moses (and Aaron) in relation to the central camp of the *Shekhinah* (ch. 20, which begins in 'Kadesh' and ends with YHWH's being 'sanctified'). In the purity laws, YHWH's kingship was symbolized by his outpoured blessing, through the priestly benediction from the camp of the *Shekhinah* (6:22–27), precisely the theological dynamics at work in chapter 20. Ultimately, it is to YHWH himself, the Shepherd of Israel who is able and compassionately willing to supply his people's needs in the wilderness, that Israel must look. The apostle Paul, understanding the church to be in an analogous situation to that of Israel in the wilderness, and deploying a theological image of God as 'rock' (cf. Deut. 32; Pss 78; 95) for a Christological purpose, writes that 'the rock was Christ' (1 Cor. 10:4) (Fisk 2008; cf. Thiessen 2013), signalling that every divine provision for God's people in their sojourn to the blessed land of inheritance is supplied through his Son.

'Water gushing forth in Mesopotamia', writes Anthonioz (2014: 49, 66), 'is the image, *par excellence*, of divine life given to humanity through the king,' a literary motif that can be traced over millennia, including within the HB, for 'water becomes very plainly the sign of the kingship of YHWH'. The living waters that will flow from Jerusalem, as proclaimed by the prophet Zechariah, exhibit that 'YHWH will be king over all the earth' (14:8–9; Anthonioz 2014: 74). The Son's first act upon his exaltation to the right hand of the Majesty is to pour out the life-giving waters of the Spirit (Acts 2:33; cf. John 4:13–14; 7:37–39). Moses, Aaron and the abundant waters dimly adumbrate Scripture's closing Trinitarian vision of a river of living waters flowing from the Throne of God and the Lamb (Rev. 22:1; cf. Ezek. 47).

NUMBERS 21: THE SECOND GENERATION'S EXODUS, SOJOURN AND CONQUEST

Translation

[21:1]And the Canaanite, king of Arad, who was dwelling in the Negev, heard that Israel came by the way of the Atharim, and he fought against Israel, and captured from him captives. [2]And Israel vowed a vow to YHWH and said, 'If you will surely give this people into my hand I will utterly devote their cities.' [3]And YHWH heard the voice of Israel and he gave the Canaanites and they utterly devoted them and their cities, and he called the name of the place Hormah.

⁴And they journeyed from Mount Hor by way of the Sea of Suph to go around the land of Edom, and the soul of the people was impatient because of the way. ⁵And the people spoke against God and against Moses, 'Why did you cause us to ascend from Egypt to die in the wilderness, for there is no bread and there is no water? Our soul loathes this miserable bread!' ⁶And YHWH released fiery serpents among the people, and they bit the people and many people of Israel died. ⁷And the people came to Moses and said, 'We have sinned for we spoke against YHWH and against you. Pray to YHWH that he would cause the serpent to turn away from upon us.' And Moses prayed on behalf of the people. ⁸And YHWH said to Moses, 'Make for yourself a fiery (serpent), put it on an ensign, and it will happen that anyone who has been bitten, when he looks at it, will live.' ⁹And Moses made a serpent of bronze, and he set it on an ensign, and it happened that if the serpent had bitten a man and he observed the serpent of bronze he lived.

¹⁰And the sons of Israel journeyed and they encamped at Oboth. ¹¹And they journeyed from Oboth and encamped at Iye of the Abarim in the wilderness that faced Moab, toward the rising of the sun. ¹²From there they journeyed and encamped at the wadi of Zared. ¹³From there they journeyed and encamped across Arnon, which is in the wilderness that stretches forth from the border of the Amorite, for Arnon is the border of Moab, between Moab and the Amorite. ¹⁴Therefore it is said in the Book of the Battles of YHWH:

. . . Waheb in Suphah
and the wadis of Arnon
¹⁵and the stream of the wadis,
that stretches to the dwelling of Ar,
and leans to the border of Moab.

¹⁶And from there to Beer (Well), that is the well where YHWH said to Moses, 'Gather the people, and I will give them water.' ¹⁷Then Israel sang this song:

Spring up, O well! Sing out to it!
¹⁸The well dug out by princes!
Quarried by the nobles of the people!
With the scepter, with their rods!

And from the wilderness to Mattanah (Gift). ¹⁹And from Mattanah (Gift) to Nahaliel (Wadi of God), and from Nahaliel (Wadi of God) to Bamoth (The Heights). ²⁰And from Bamoth (The Heights) to the valley that is in the field of Moab, by the summit of the Pisgah, which looks out on the face of the wasteland.

²¹Now Israel sent messengers to Sihon, king of the Amorites, saying, ²²'Let me pass through your land. We will not stretch in field or in vineyard; we will not drink waters of a well – in the Way of the King we will walk until we pass through your border.' ²³But Sihon would not give Israel to pass through in his

border, and Sihon gathered all his people and he went forth to encounter Israel in the wilderness; and he came to Jahaz and battled against Israel. ²⁴And Israel struck him down with the edge of the sword, and possessed his land from Arnon as far as Jabbok, as far as the sons of Ammon, for strong was the border of the sons of Ammon. ²⁵And Israel took all these cities, and Israel dwelt in all the cities of the Amorites, in Heshbon and in all her daughters (villages). ²⁶For it, Heshbon, was the city of Sihon king of the Amorites, and he had battled against the former king of Moab and had taken all his land from his hand as far as Arnon. ²⁷Therefore, the parable-makers say:

Come to Heshbon!
May the city of Sihon be built and established!
²⁸For a fire has gone forth from Heshbon,
A flame from the town of Sihon,
Devouring Ar of Moab,
The lords of the heights of Arnon.
²⁹Woe to you, Moab!
You are destroyed, O people of Chemosh!
He has given his sons as fugitives,
And his daughters in captivity
To the king of the Amorites, Sihon.
³⁰We have shot at them,
Heshbon is destroyed as far as Dibon,
And we have laid them waste as far as Nophah,
Which is as far as Medeba.

³¹So Israel dwelt in the land of the Amorites. ³²And Moses sent to spy out Jazer, and they seized her daughters (villages), and he dispossessed the Amorites who were there.

³³And they turned and ascended the way of Bashan, and Og king of Bashan went forth to encounter them, he and all his people for battle at Edrei. ³⁴And YHWH said to Moses, 'Do not fear him, for into your hand I have given him and all his people and his land, and you will do to him just as you did to Sihon king of the Amorites who were dwelling in Heshbon.' ³⁵And they struck him down and his sons and all his people so that no survivor remained to him, and they possessed his land.

Notes on the text

1. 'king of Arad': Syr has 'king of Godar'. 'way of Atharim' is 'way of the explorers (*ḥattārîm*)' in Tg, Vg, Syr, Aq, Sym; cf. Num. 14:6.
   5. 'against God': LXX has 'to God'.
   11. SamP includes material from Deut. 2:9.
   12. SamP includes material from Deut. 2:17–19.

14. 'Waheb in Suphah': SamP has 'Waheb on the Sea of Reeds', LXX reads 'has set on fire Zoob and the brooks of Arnon' and Vg has 'what he did in the Red Sea'. There is no main verb apparent (Dentan 1962b), making the sense unintelligible (A. Ehrlich 1908: 2:190), but Steiner (2020) proposes that *'et* (preceding both 'Waheb' and 'the wadis') is an archaic apocopated imp. of *'-t-y*, meaning 'come!'

18. 'scepter' (*ḥōqēq*) derives from *ḥāqaq*, leading to the notion of a prescriber of laws or commander, then to a commander's staff (BDB 349; cf. Gen. 49:10)

'and from the wilderness to Mattanah' may be 'from the wilderness a gift'.

20. SamP includes material from Deut. 2:24–25.

21. 'Israel sent': LXX has 'Moses' (cf. 20:14). LXX and SamP also include 'with words of peace', from Deut. 2:27.

22. SamP includes material from Deut. 2:28–29.

23. SamP includes material from Deut. 2:31.

26. 'as far as Arnon': LXX reads 'from Aroer to Arnon'.

28. 'Ar of Moab': SamP and LXX read 'as far as' (*'ad*); BHS suggests 'cities of' (*'ārê*).

'the lords': LXX reads 'devoured', presuming *bālĕ'āh*, 'swallow up' (cf. Num. 16:30), creating a parallelism with the previous line.

30. 'We have shot at them': LXX reads 'their seed shall perish'.

'laid them waste': LXX reads 'and their women'.

'which': the MT has a *puncta extraordinaria* above the resh of *'ăšer*, signifying that the resh does not belong here, which accords with SamP and LXX readings of 'fire' (cf. Tov 2001: 56).

'Medeba': LXX reads 'Moab'; Syr has 'the desert'.

31. 'land': SamP and LXX read 'cities of'.

32. LXX clarifies that 'they took it (Jazer)' as well as its villages.

'dispossessed': reading hiph. with Q, along with SamP, LXX, Tg.

35. 'and his sons': omitted from SamP.

Form and structure

Making sense of Numbers 21, with its vignettes and fragments of ancient songs, has been a longstanding challenge in scholarship, in terms of the chapter's unity and role within the book. Noth confessed that traditional source criticism was a futile waste of effort on this chapter (1940: 178). Yet understanding the message and function of Numbers 21, acknowledged by Frevel and others as a transitional pivot and compositional joint within the book (2009; cf. Olson 1996: 133), remains a crucial goal. Milgrom correlates chapters 20–21 structurally, but, along with his including 21:1–3 as the end of chapter 20, the parallels are forced (1990: 463–467). He did correctly observe, however, that these chapters contrast the leaders (ch. 20) and the people, the new generation of Israel (ch. 21). While chapter 20 begins and ends with the death of the old generation's leaders, chapter 21 begins and ends with battle victories for Israel's new generation. The language of Moses' diplomatic communication with Edom (20:14–21) is paralleled especially in Israel's engagement with Sihon (21:21–26) and, again, manifests a significant contrast: whereas in chapter 20 Israel was rebuffed, in chapter 21 Israel conquers and takes possession of land. Without presuming to resolve the complex riddles pervading nearly every aspect of the material, we may nevertheless demonstrate that Numbers 21, through verbal and conceptual allusions, summarizes the second generation's sojourn in the wilderness as a reliving of the first generation's experience of redemption and sojourn to the land, but with a positive result that anticipates the conquest. Stringing together vignettes, Numbers 21 divides naturally into four sections:

1. Numbers 21:1–3: Prologue: Israel from captivity to conquest
2. Numbers 21:4–9: Israel's deliverance from the serpent
3. Numbers 21:10–20: Israel's journeys and the Song of the Well
4. Numbers 21:21–35: Israel's conquest and possession of lands

The opening verses (1–3), which narrate Israel's encounter with and complete destruction of the Canaanites, function as a prologue and microcosm of the chapter, with the remainder of the material breaking down into a threefold movement of deliverance (4–9), journey (10–20) and conquest (21–35).

I take 21:21–35 as one unit (cf. L. Schmidt 2004: 100–116), while subdividing the material with reference to Sihon (vv. 21–32) and Og (vv. 33–35). Others use this subdivision for a fivefold outline, frequently beginning the last unit at verse 32 (W. W. Lee 2003b: 157–166; Knierim and Coats 2005: 235–246; Frevel 2009: 123), and sometimes ending it with 22:1 (Seebass 1993: 2:305–367), and some begin the last subunit at verse 32. Regarding the latter modification, verse 32, with its mention of the Amorites, is better conceived as a conclusion to the previous unit. Even though Og of Bashan may be regarded as an Amorite (cf. Deut. 3:8–10; Amos 2:9), the text reserves this ascription for Sihon (21:21, 25, 31, 34). Moreover, there is an inclusio whereby verses 31–32 together repeat elements from verses 24b–25, and the larger section (21:21–32) begins and ends with Israel and Moses 'sending' (*šālaḥ*), respectively. That said, the division within the larger section of 21:21–35 is more practical than necessary and need not be pressed – Moses' sending of spies in verse 32 may also be seen as starting a new subsection, in parallel with Israel's sending in verse 21. Besides, the conquests of Sihon and Og are often listed together as a joint pair (cf. Num. 32:33; Deut. 1:4; 4:46–47; 29:7; 31:4; Josh. 2:10; 9:10; 1 Kgs 4:19; Pss 135:11; 136:19–20; Neh. 9:22), so any boundary between verses 31 and 32 is slender if not artificial.

As the section titles manifest, the chapter tracks the positive progress of the second generation of Israel. In the face of loss, Israel turns to YHWH and vows to him the utter devotion of the Canaanite cities, for which he grants them victory. Although they later speak against God and Moses, the Israelites, humbled by YHWH's judgement of fiery serpents, confess and repent, something never observed in the previous generation, marking the second generation's spiritual progress, even as their geographical progress is tracked. The chapter concludes with two victories, over Sihon and Og, and the possession of lands, a foretaste of Israel's possession of Canaan. Israel's progress is narrated, moreover, with an eightfold mention of Moab (21:11, 13 [twice], 15, 20, 26, 28, 29), setting up the story of the ensuing chapters as Balak king of Moab hires Balaam to curse Israel (chs. 22–24), and then many Israelites commit apostasy with Moabite (and Midianite) women (ch. 25) (cf. Frevel 2009: 118).

Interspersed amid Israel's journeys and battle victories, the chapter records three ancient songs: one about the border of Moab from the Book of the Battles of YHWH (vv. 14–15), a song about a well dug up by princes (vv. 17–18), and a 'parable' (*māšal*) of Sihon's victory and possession of Moabite lands (vv. 27–30).

Comment

21:1–3 Prologue: Israel from captivity to conquest

Comparable to Numbers 11:1–3, which functioned as a prologue for Israel's rebellions in the wilderness (chs. 11–20), this little story serves as a prologue to the second generation's journeys (chs. 21–25), establishing the paradigm that Israel will experience victory by turning to and relying on YHWH their God and King. Both prologues, moreover, resolve with an etiology, signalling a narrative movement through two generations of Israel, from YHWH's 'kindled fierce anger' against Israel ('Taberah', 11:3) to Israel's 'total destruction' of its enemy by YHWH's strength ('Hormah', 21:2). Within the compass of three verses, framed by Mount Hor (20:22–29; 21:4), the shift from military failure to success occurs (cf. Frevel 2009: 124). As such, this episode more narrowly forms a microcosm of the chapter, which ends with the conquest and possession of the strongholds and lands of the Amorites and Bashan so that 'no survivors remained' (v. 35), as with Hormah (v. 3) – both prologue and chapter conclude with Israel's victories. An exodus motif pervades the chapter with this prologue arguably portraying the movement from exodus to conquest *in nuce*. Although the second generation was already in view in Numbers 20, that chapter, capping the death of the old generation, focused on the death of the first generation's leaders; but now, with this stunning victory over the Canaanites, the advent of the new generation of Israelites is heralded (Levine 1993: 62). The favourable turn for the second generation of Israelites, significantly, follows on the death of Aaron the high priest and representative of the first generation of Israel (20:22–29) – the era of YHWH's judgement has ended, and the light of his uplifted countenance has dawned.

1. The subject is 'the Canaanite, the king of Arad, who was dwelling in the Negev', and the inciting action is that he 'heard' about Israel's progress, that 'Israel came'. Jewish interpretation presses the question as to what precisely the king heard, suggesting by context that he had heard of the death of Aaron, Israel's high priest, and the subsequent loss of the protective Cloud of glory, leaving the people vulnerable to attack (*TPs-J* ad loc.; *m. Yom.* 1.38b; *Num. Rab.* 19.20). The Canaanite is dubbed 'king' (*melek*), the first of thirteen occurrences of the term in chapters 21–24 (21:1, 21, 22, 26 [twice], 29, 33, 34; 22:4, 10; 23:7, 21; 24:7), a key word of this section, foreshadowed in Moses' interaction with Edom in the previous chapter (20:14, 17) – even for the remaining uses of 'king', each looks back to these chapters, including chapter 25 (see 31:8; 32:33; 33:40). While 'chieftain' is likely to be understood, language of kingship is used since YHWH's kingship in Israel and over the nations forms an underlying theme of chapters 21–25. As Milgrom suggests (1990: 172), it may be 'dwelling' (*yōšēb*) should be understood as 'ruling', that his realm was the entire Negev. Hirsch notes that while 'Arad' is generally taken as the name of a region, some sources (see *Gemara, Rosh HaSh.* 3a; *b. Bav. Bat.* 78b) take Arad as the king's name and link '*ărād* ('wild ass'; cf. Job 39:5; Dan. 5:21) with Sihon (young ass) (2007a: 460; cf. Vilensky 1978: 3:296). The suggestion is of interest inasmuch as, in the Balak narrative (chs. 22–24), Balaam will be lampooned as an ass. Other traditions identify the Canaanite king as Amalek (cf. *Tan., Ḥuk* 18; Nachmanides 1975: 233–234), rather than Sihon – although the text mentions only a Canaanite's ruling in the south.

As Israel nears the inheritance of YHWH's promise, the nations – far from helping them along their way – will oppose God's people, seeking vainly to thwart his purposes. As Budd observes (1984: 229), the 'way of Atharim' was read by Tg, Vg, Syr, Aq and Sym as the 'way of the explorers' (reading *hattārîm*, from the root *tûr*; cf. Num. 14:6), a possible derivation for the proper name. Rashi thus suggests that Moses had gone back to his original plan of leading Israel from the south through the Negev (1997: 4:249; cf. Num. 13:22); both Nachmanides and Ibn Ezra also understand 'way of the explorers' here (ad loc.). Almost certainly, Atharim, 'the gateway to the settled and populous region of southern Canaan', is the 'Athar', just south of Hebron, found in an ancient Egyptian topographical list of Ramesses III at Medinet Habu, and earlier in a map of Ramesses II (Krahmalkov 1994: 61). The Canaanite king's response to the news will be to 'do battle' (*lāḥem*) against Israel, a motif anticipated by Edom's earlier response (20:14–21) and duplicated in the responses of Sihon (21:21–32) and Og (21:33–35). The verb 'to fight, do battle' (*lāḥam*) is used only four times in Numbers, and never with Israel as the subject: the Canaanite king of Arad 'fought against Israel' (21:1), Sihon 'fought against Israel' (21:23), Sihon fought against the former king of Moab (21:26) and Balak king of Moab calls Balaam to curse Israel in order to 'overcome' them (22:11). As an initial result, the king of Arad 'captured captives' (*šābāh*, *šĕbî*) from among the Israelites. Presumably, as none are described as having been slain in battle, there was no loss of life experienced here, and Israel's defeat of the king of Arad likely involved the restoration of Israel's captives (cf. Nachmanides 1975: 234). Tellingly, the only losses among the second generation of Israelites will be, as with the former generation, in judgement from YHWH (21:6; 25:9), but none die in battle (cf. 31:49). The captivity of Israelites here serves as the background for Israel's response and YHWH's subsequent reply (vv. 2–3). By divine wisdom, Israel's well-being and battle victory were not automatic, but required their turning to YHWH for help.

Frevel suggests (2009: 125) that the taking of captives 'is the reversal of the liberation of the exodus', an insight in accord with other exodus echoes, although use of *šābāh/šĕbî* in Exodus is negligible (Exod. 12:29; 22:10). In keeping with the prologue nature of these verses, perhaps the whole exodus movement is given in summation – certainly, the notice that YHWH delivered up 'the Canaanites and they utterly devoted them and their cities' (v. 3) portrays the episode as a foreshadowing summary of the entire conquest. There seems to be a link, moreover, between this story and that of Abram's rescue of his nephew Lot, who had been 'taken captive' (*nišbā*) (Gen. 14:14). This link is strengthened as it is set within a chapter that mentions Moab – Lot's descendants – eight times, and which precedes a three-chapter narrative on Moab's attempt to curse Israel through Balaam (chs. 22–24), followed by Israel's sin with the daughters of Moab (ch. 25). Given the clear allusions to the Abrahamic blessing (Gen. 12:3) that somewhat frames the Balaam narrative (22:6; 24:9), it is likely that the Abraham and Lot stories of Genesis inform the Israel and Moab narratives of Numbers at a deep structural level. Just as the Camp's setting out from Sinai had alluded to the call of Abram (10:29–32), Israel's experience continues to retrace the patriarch's life.

Rather than the familiar designation 'sons of Israel', in Numbers 21 'Israel' recurs some eight times (cf. 20:21): 'Israel came' (v. 1), 'Israel vowed a vow' (v. 2), 'Israel sang' (v. 17), 'Israel sent messengers' (v. 21), 'Israel smote' (v. 24), 'Israel took', 'Israel dwelled' (v. 25), 'Israel dwelled' (v. 31). Using the name 'Israel' portrays the second generation as coming into their own, acting in unison and taking initiative. While Moses remains their needed mediator, especially with regard to his role of intercession (vv. 4–9), yet this new Israel has matured beyond the slave mentality of the previous generation, acting regularly apart from Moses.

2. What will Israel do when faced with such a setback at the hands of Canaanites – complain, give in to fear or despair, yearn for a return to Egypt or turn to YHWH God for help? Israel 'vowed a vow' (*wayyiddar neder*) to YHWH, saying that if YHWH would 'surely give' (*nātōn tittēn*) this people into Israel's hand, Israel would in turn 'devote' (*ḥāram*) their cities to YHWH by means of total destruction (or 'the ban'), a vow that could not be undone (see Lev. 27:28–29). Inasmuch as Israel, for the first time, addresses YHWH God directly, asking him for divine help, a spiritual and theological milestone has been reached – they even turn to him apart from the mediation of Moses, who is nowhere mentioned. Israel's reaction is, perhaps, intended to be read as the fruit of YHWH's magnificent display, having provided abundant streams of water from the rock in chapter 20 – having set before them his faithful character and abundant power to provide for them. Israel's response, further, manifests the second generation's zeal to possess the land: rather than being discouraged or cowering in fear they turn in faith to YHWH, trusting that he is surely able to grant them victory over their enemies. They understand that YHWH is the sovereign King, able to determine the outcome of battles by his sheer will alone.

Their vowing a vow calls to mind the earlier *torah* of the Nazirite vow (Num. 6:1–21, 'to vow a vow', *nědōr neder*), including the paradigm of resolving an initial setback. In that section, I argued the Nazirite vow was the exemplary path (versus that of the straying woman) set before the Camp of Israel before their journey through the wilderness to the land of Canaan. Israel was to approach the time in the wilderness as a Nazirite, willingly giving up life's pleasures in order to draw near to YHWH. Just as the Nazirite freely forsook grape products, death pollution even for close kin, and cutting his hair, so now Israel freely vows to forsake all the spoils of victory – gold, silver and bronze work, practical tools and implements, fine clothing, sheep, cattle and slave labour – devoting them all to YHWH. Such a vow 'represents an extreme form of self-denial', since a share in the spoils was a troop's only means of payment (Milgrom 1990: 172). Israel's vow indicates that the people are beginning to devote themselves to God, following the exemplary Nazirite path (cf. Stubbs 2009: 164).

As devoted to YHWH, the spoils are considered sanctified, set apart to him, and must be destroyed or dedicated to the sanctuary, preventing the possibility of profane use. The 'ban' or devotion of whole cities, involving the utter destruction of all life and material goods, is thus similar to the theology of consecration involved with the whole burnt offering (see Morales 2019a), and, more practically, ensured that war was not waged merely out of self-interest. More deeply, the destruction of the people was understood as divine judgement from YHWH God for their own continued defiance of him, expressed by their idolatry, sexual immorality, violence and injustice. YHWH had told Abraham that his descendants would not inherit the land for some 400 years, since he would not 'judge' (*dān*) the Amorites until their guilt had reached full measure (Gen. 15:14–16). In Deuteronomy, Moses reiterates that Israel was not inheriting the land because of their own righteousness, 'but because of the wickedness of these nations' (9:5). As YHWH's righteous judgement on the Canaanites, the conquest under Joshua involved devoting whole cities (see Josh. 6 – 8), although a variety of circumstances made possible the mitigation of utter destruction (cf. Josh. 6:17; 9). Apart from the destruction of the Canaanite nations, moreover, Israelites would be seduced to intermarrying with them and turning away to serve other gods, and thus be in danger of being destroyed by YHWH themselves (7:1–11; cf. Exod. 32:25–29), precisely what happens in Numbers 25.

3. Verses 1 and 3 begin with the same word in Hebr., 'And-he-heard' (*wayyišmaʿ*). The crisis began when the Canaanite heard that Israel had come, but is now resolved as YHWH heard the voice of Israel: he 'heeded' Israel's prayer and vow. Earlier, Moses had explained to the king of Edom how 'YHWH heard our voice' when Israel had cried to him under Egyptian oppression, and he sent his Messenger to bring them forth out of Egypt (20:16). The language of fulfilment mirrors Israel's plea in the previous verse: YHWH 'gave' (*wayyittēn*) the Canaanite, and then Israel 'devoted' (*wayyaḥărēm*) them and their cities. YHWH's giving of a people into one's hand is an idiom found throughout the HB, expressing his sovereign determination of battle (see e.g. 2 Chr. 36:17). The notice that he called the name of the place Hormah ('devoted', from *ḥāram*) typically has either YHWH or Moses as the implied subject, but in this case may refer to Israel, portrayed as a single character, with all verbs being 3rd m. sg. (note 'my hand' in v. 2). 'Hormah' recalls the first generation's sound defeat in 14:45 at the hands of the Amalekites and Canaanites, as Israel was routed 'as far as Hormah'. That had been an anachronistic use of the name, reflecting Israel's defeat, but now the name is revealed to have derived from the utter destruction of the Canaanites, who had attacked Israel – a rhetorical device that could not convey more dramatically the reversal of Israel's providence, although it required the transition of generations. This episode definitively reverses the refusal of the first generation to possess the land 'filled with giants' and their subsequent routing (Achenbach 2003b: 346), and serves as a fitting prologue to a chapter that culminates with Israel's smiting the house of Og, a legendary giant (Deut. 3:11). Whereas the former generation of Israelites had attempted to conquer the Canaanites on their own apart from YHWH (14:43–44), this new generation of Israelites recognizes the crucial need of his presence and help, that he is the one who sovereignly determines the outcome of battle. Since Moses is not in the story's view, the focus remains on *Israel's* trust and obedience of YHWH, triumphing by God's help (Pressler 2017: 189). The complete absence of

Moses from this account, aside from spotlighting the maturation of the second generation, may be due to YHWH's previous judgement in 20:12, forbidding Moses and Aaron from bringing the assembly into the land, for, in a way, this victory over the Canaanites functions as a sample of the conquest and, if YHWH had chosen to lead Israel along this southern route, would have stood as the beginning of the conquest, the first of many continual battles.

21:4–9: Israel's deliverance from the serpent

Structurally, this episode, which presents Israel's last complaint in the wilderness, mirrors the opening complaint of the journey from Sinai (11:1–3): the people complain, YHWH punishes them, the people plead with Moses to intercede, Moses prays, YHWH relieves the punishment. The wilderness journeys are thus framed by stories of Moses' intercession, underscoring his role in Israel's emergence out of the wilderness. There are a few lexical links between this episode of the bronze serpent and the Balaam narrative (chs. 22–25): the wordplay of 'serpent' (*nāḥāš*), 'bite' (*nāšak*) and 'bronze' (*nĕḥōšet*), the root occurring seven times (21:6, 7, 9 [five times]), is carried over in the Balaam story with the term 'enchantment' (or 'divination', *naḥaš*, 23:23; *nĕḥāšîm*, 24:1). Literary variety is displayed as the full designation *hannĕḥāšîm haśśĕrāpîm* (v. 6) is followed first by *hannāḥāš* (v. 7), and then by *śārāp* (v. 8). The word 'loathes' (*qāṣāh*) finds an echo in Moab's 'distress' (*yāqāṣ*, 22:23), which shares the same root (*qûṣ*), and in 'outskirts' (*qĕṣêh*, 22:36, 41; 23:13); and 'miserable' (*qĕlōqēl*) uses the root (*q-l-l*) for curse. Although the Balaam narrative does not use this designation for curse, Moses does in Deuteronomy 23:5, explaining that YHWH did not heed Balaam, but turned his 'curse' (*qĕlālāh*) into blessing. YHWH is able to deliver his people from the deathly bites of serpents as well as from the execrating lips of sorcerers.

Frevel observes how this narrative seems to be intended as a closing parenthesis of the murmuring tradition, composed in a way that relates to the other murmuring narratives in Numbers, linked in various ways especially to the beginning of the journey through the wilderness (chs. 11–12) (2009: 128–129; cf. L. Schmidt 2004: 102–103): (1) The term for 'short' (*qāṣar*), translated here as 'impatient' (v. 4) is used only one other time in Numbers, in 11:23 (is YHWH's hand 'shortened'?). (2) To 'speak against' (*dbr b-*), used twice here (vv. 5, 7), links to the only other instances when Miriam and Aaron 'spoke against' Moses (12:1, 8). (3) The phrase 'Why did you cause us to ascend from Egypt?' (v. 5) parallels the same phrase verbatim in 20:5, and links closely with a similar question in 11:20, which uses 'go forth' (*yāṣā'*) instead of 'ascend' (*'ālāh*). (4) The expression 'we loathe this miserable bread' (v. 5) resonates with the earlier rejection of manna and YHWH's subsequent judgement (11:6, 20). (5) The people's confession 'we have sinned' (*ḥāṭā'nû*, v. 7) parallels ironically the empty confession before the first generation's defeat at Hormah (14:40) and perhaps echoes Aaron's confession of sin in 12:11. (6) The hith. form 'to pray' is found only at 21:7 and 11:2, both with reference to Moses' interceding amid divine punishment.

4. Three statements combine to convey a sense of discouragement facing Israel on their journey: they journeyed from Mount Hor, the place where Aaron the high priest had died; their route was by 'way of the Sea of Suph' (*yam-sûp*), insinuating a lack of progress since the crossing of the *yam-sûp* some forty years earlier (Exod. 13:18; 15:4, 22) and recalling the original judgement to turn from Canaan (Num. 14:25) – the only two uses of this phrase in Numbers; and 'to go around the land of Edom' not only recalls the failed endeavour for a direct route to the land, but underscores that now a much longer journey was required. These reasons function rhetorically to foster some understanding and empathy when reading that the 'soul' (*nepeš*) of the people grew 'impatient' (*wattiqṣar*) on the way. The term *qāṣar* carries the notion of shortness (of patience) and discouragement. The second generation's strength, their desire to inherit the land, becomes their point of weakness, when the people's expectation and hope is deferred. Whereas the previous account (vv. 1–3) referred to God's people as 'Israel' consistently, this story uses 'the people' (*hā'ām*) consistently. The discouragement of Israel's reroute is given here, after the victory against king Arad and the Canaanites, rather than in 20:14–21 when Moses was rebuffed by the king of Edom. The opening story may be dischronologized to function as a prologue, but the narrative effect of its current placement still needs to be weighed. With the victory over the Canaanites just south of Hebron, Israel it seems was ready to proceed through the first generation's original route, but now YHWH has redirected them for an eventual eastern entry, across the Jordan. The plains of Moab would serve as an ideal locale for Moses' final speeches (Deuteronomy), whereas continuing the southern route would have, in effect, begun the conquest. Aside from needing to prepare the people through his final speeches, Moses had been forbidden to take part in Israel's entry and conquest of Canaan, a point that may explain the absence of his name in 21:1–3. That Israel experienced victory over the Canaanites at the southern entry point, a foretaste of conquering the land, only to turn around and pursue a lengthier journey, might have played some role in the people's discouragement.

Following Rashi's understanding, the people's discouragement was not 'on the way' but '*because* of the way' (*baddārek*), presumably referring to the 'way of the Sea of Suph', because of the long detour to skirt around Edom (1997: 4:251). Their ensuing complaints regarding food and water are not legitimate concerns, but merely a venting of their frustration.

5. Sinful speech springs up readily in the soil of discouragement and impatience. The people 'spoke against God and against Moses'. The construction 'speaking against' (*wayĕdabbēr b-*) has hostile undertones (cf. BDB 181). When they had first crossed the Sea of Suph, Israel had 'believed (*'āman*) in YHWH and in Moses his servant' (Exod. 14:31), quite a contrast (Milgrom 1990: 173). Why, the people ask, did you (pl., God and Moses) cause us to ascend from Egypt to die in the wilderness? The prologue appears to move from exodus (captivity) to conquest (21:1–3), summarizing the chapter. Here in the first story after the prologue, the exodus motif surfaces with the second generation's questioning of the ascent out of Egypt. As we will see, both YHWH's punishment and remedy, involving a serpent, also relate to the exodus motif and part of the chapter's overall movement from Egypt to Conquest. Israel will mature spiritually through YHWH's twofold response (releasing the serpents, and the uplifted bronze serpent) – this story presents the *last* time the nation will ever question the exodus out of Egypt.

As with chapter 20, a focal concern of their complaint appears to be their sustenance: there is no bread or water. However, even before a reader can ask, 'What about the manna?', the people say, 'Our soul loathes (*qāṣāh*) this miserable (*qĕlōqēl*) bread!' Gane suggests (2004: 679 n. 4) a chiastic relation between *qṣr nepeš* ('impatient/shortness of soul', v. 4) and *nepeš qwṣ* (our soul loathes) here, 'linking the people's impatience to their revulsion toward the manna'. The word 'loathe' or dread will show up in the Balaam narrative as the Moabites 'loathed' the presence of Israel (22:3). The second generation's sin is similar to that of the first generation in Numbers 11, when they complained, saying, 'Now our soul is dried up – there is nothing at all except this manna before our eyes!' (v. 6). In their discouragement, the people become discontented with YHWH's provision of manna. Given its root (*q-l-l*, 'curse'), the description 'miserable' (*qĕlōqēl*) is a strongly derisive term expressing contempt and implying an object's worthlessness (cf. BDB 886–887). As manna signifies divine provision for Israel's journeys *within the wilderness*, even this complaint occurs within the context of Israel's eagerness to possess the land. Nevertheless, speaking against God, Moses, and the manna, will generate a disciplinary response from YHWH. Not only is their complaint of 'no bread' undercut by the divine provision of manna, but their complaint of 'no water' is bracketed by stories of abundant water – the 'many waters' that gushed out of the rock (20:11), and YHWH's provision of water at Beer (21:16; note also the wadi of Zared, Arnon River, stream of the wadis and wadi of God, vv. 12–19). In every other complaint for water, moreover, the absence of water is noted by the narrator at the start of the story, then YHWH provides water through Moses, and there is no divine punishment of the people regardless of their sinful disposition since water is a legitimate need (Exod. 15:22, 25; 17:1, 5–6; Num. 20:2, 7–8); each of these three elements is lacking in this story, signalling the emptiness of their grievance (see Birkan 2005: 65).

There may be significance in that the speaking was 'against God' (*bē'lōhîm*), perhaps suggesting relational distance, whereas their repentant confession will acknowledge their having spoken against 'YHWH' (v. 7). The apostle Paul wrote to the church at Corinth, admonishing the saints not to 'test Christ, as some of them [Israelites in the wilderness] tested, and were destroyed by serpents', demonstrating the abiding relevance of this example for God's people today (1 Cor. 10:9; see Osburn 1981).

6. Just as YHWH is near in the Camp to hear his people's plea for help (v. 3), that same nearness means he hears their complaints as well (cf. 11:1; 12:2). Unlike other occasions where YHWH's act of judgement is preceded by a notice of his fierce anger being kindled (see 11:1, 10; 12:9), here his response is recounted simply: 'YHWH released fiery serpents (*hannĕḥāšîm haśśĕrāpîm*) among the people' – there is no indication that he has become angry or that his wrath has been kindled. The motif of sending ('sent', *šālaḥ*) unites chapters 21–25 with a tenfold use (21:6, 21, 32; 22:5, 10, 15, 37 [twice], 40; 24:12), and is also found in the Edom episode foreshadowing this section (20:14, 16). Nevertheless, there is an exegetical detail, rarely observed (exceptions include Leibowitz 1982: 261–262; Hirsch 2007a: 463), concerning *šālaḥ* here; namely, that it is in the pi. stem, often employed for the third meaning of *šālaḥ*: 'let loose' or 'set free'. In the qal stem, *šālaḥ* refers simply to sending, such as when Moses sends messengers to Edom (20:14), and as when Jacob sent messengers to Esau (Gen. 32:4) – these both use the qal *wayyišlaḥ*. However, occasions that carry the nuance of releasing or letting go, such as the release of the Israelites from Egypt (Exod. 5:1; 13:17), freeing slaves (Deut. 15:12), or when Noah released the raven and then the dove from the ark (Gen. 8:7, 8, 10; cf. Deut. 22:7), or even when simply allowing a guest to leave (Gen. 18:16; 24:54), these situations use the pi. as here in 21:6, which is best translated, 'YHWH *released* fiery serpents among the people.' Our text is the first example of this use in the *Theological Wordbook of the Old Testament* (1980: 928): 'This means that God removes his protective hand and unleashes various hostile forces (Num. 21:6; Jer. 9:16; Amos 4:10; etc.)' (cf. BDB 108–1019). Every use of the pi. form of *š-l-ḥ* in the Torah having an animal as its object means 'release' rather than 'send' (cf. Birkan 2005: 66). The implication is that the wilderness is a place of 'fiery serpents and scorpions', as Moses later recalls (Deut. 8:15), and that YHWH had been providentially restraining such threats from harming his people – as Leibowitz puts it (1982: 263): 'It was not therefore the attack of the serpents, but rather their absence during the whole of their wanderings till then, that constituted the miracle.' Now, when they speak against him, YHWH allows them to taste what life in the wilderness

apart from his sovereign presence would be – to realize afresh that he had been their faithful shepherd and protector all along. 'The sole purpose of the snake bites', Hirsch writes (2007a: 464),

> was to make the people see the dangers that lie in wait for them at every step in the wilderness, and to make them realize that it was only God's miraculous power that had kept these dangers away from them, so far away that they did not even have an idea of their existence.

Chizkuni preserves the tradition that it was the Cloud of glory that had protected the Israelites, burning up any snakes that had approached the Camp (an era that ended with Aaron's recent death; cf. ben Manoach 2013: 4:969–970).

A variety of ancient sources testify to the presence of numerous kinds of poisonous snakes in the wilderness; and in the modern era, Lawrence of Arabia's published recollections of his time in the desert – with its plague of horned vipers, puff-adders, cobras and black snakes, his guides killing some twenty serpents per day, so that the people feared every step – are often cited (see T. E. Lawrence 1927: 93). In the annals of Assyria, one of the military campaigns of Esarhaddon (681–669 BC) through the Sinai wilderness reports, '(there were) two-headed serpents [whose attack] (spelled) death – but I trampled (upon them) and marched on' (Pritchard 1969: 292; cf. Borger 1956: 56, 112). The theology of releasing the serpent is akin to excommunication (1 Cor. 5:5), causing one to taste life apart from the blessedness of being in the fold of the good Shepherd, in hope that the disciplined person will despise the miseries of the world and, repenting, flee to the refuge and fellowship of God among his people in a posture of humility and a heart of gratitude.

The descriptor 'fiery' derives from *śārap*, meaning 'to burn', often used for common burning (see 17:2, 4; 19:5, 6, 8, 17; 31:10); that is, burning which does not take place on the altar of whole burnt offering, but is also used of the angels dubbed 'burning ones' or *seraphim* in Isaiah (6:2, 6). Here fiery likely refers to the heat of the serpents' poisonous bite (or to their appearance, per Coats 1968: 117 n. 51). This fiery aspect of his judgement recalls earlier judgements on the first generation (see 11:1; 16:35; note use of *haśśěrupîm* in 16:39). It may be that *seraphim* were understood as flying serpents or to have wings (see Isa. 14:29; 30:6), which may rather reflect a cobra-like appearance (in the genus *Naja*, which produce 'hoods'). Lederman offers several accounts of flying serpents in the desert (2015): In the eighth century BC, Isaiah includes the 'fiery flying serpent' (*śārāp mě'ōpēp*) as among the dwellers of the Negev (30:6); in the seventh century BC, one of Esarhaddon's Assyrian campaigns against Egypt mentions 'snakes with deadly breath and yellow flying serpents' (Weinfeld 1991: 395); and in the fifth century BC, the Greek historian Herodotus wrote about flying serpents that inhabited the Arabian desert (*Histories* 3.107). Wiseman (1972) discounts these historical descriptions and suggests the Isaiah texts may be translated with 'poisonous' (with *mĕʿôpēp* denoting 'jab, prick') rather than 'flying'; in any case, Numbers does not include 'flying' as a descriptor. Fretheim observes how many readers ignore the Egyptian context of the story, pointing out that the winged *seraph* 'is probably to be identified with the Egyptian cobra' (1978: 267; cf. Joines 1974: 8). Currid, noting that *seraph* was originally an Egyptian word referring to serpents that spit fire or glow like fire, related in numerous Egyptian texts where such serpents protected Pharaoh and Egypt, says they were an emblem of ancient Egypt, sent by God as a plague among the Israelites, who, ironically, wanted to return to Egypt (2009: 296–297; see also *Exod. Rab.* 3.12; *Yalk. Shim. Vaʿera* 181). He dedicates an entire chapter – dubbed 'The Egyptian Complexion of the Bronze Serpent' (Currid 1997: 142–155) – to the Egyptian customs, iconography and motifs that lie at the heart of this story and are key for its proper understanding. One Old Kingdom (c. 2686–2160 BC) text, 'Spell 221', reads, 'Ho Fiery Serpent! Grant that the dread of me be like the dread of you; grant that the fear of me be like the fear of you' (Faulkner 1969: 49). In Egypt, Lederman further explains (2015), the cobra was often dubbed 'the flaming one', and the image of an upraised cobra (a *uraeus*) ready to strike was worn on every Pharaoh's headdress, symbolizing his supreme kingship and the protection of his patron cobra goddess, Wadjet (cf. Budge 1969: 2:377; Joines 1974: 47; Morenz 1992: 261; Myśliwiec 2000: 87–88). Illustrating her point by an inscription at Medinet Habu describing Ramesses III (1187–1156 BC) in battle – 'Dreadful is thy serpent-crest among them; / The war mace in thy right hand' – Birkan remarks that the cobra-crest, which was used in war through the twelfth century BC, served not only to protect the Pharaoh, but 'was a vessel he used to execute judgement against his enemies' (2005: 15). Invoked with 'O Magician, O Fiery Serpent!' the cobra-diadem was believed to be the source of the Pharaoh's powers (Birkan 2005: 16; see also Lesko 1991). Pyramid Text 396, as another example, reads, 'His *uraeus*-serpents are over his head. / The leading snake of Unas is at his forehead' (quoted in Currid 1997: 147). Further, by way of illustration, in an inscription celebrating Ramesses II's victory over the Hittites at Qadesh, Ramesses describes 'how he entered the fray and fought ferociously, with his '*uraeus*-serpent' beating back his enemies and spitting 'fiery flame' into the faces of his enemies' (Wells 2009: 190). Two- or four-winged serpent depictions recur in Egyptian iconography and plastic arts; a gold collar was found in Tut-ankh-Amon's tomb (New Kingdom, Eighteenth Dynasty) depicting the goddess Wadjet as an upraised cobra with outspread wings (Lederman 2015). Plainly, sculpted serpents were commonplace within Egyptian culture – such as the gilded wood cobra, the figure of Netjer-ankh, buried with Tut-ankh-Amon (1347–1339 BC), or the *uraeus*-crest on the same Tut-ankh-Amon's golden mask (cf. Keel 1974: 77; Birkan 2005: 12–13). In short (Swanson 2002: 464), 'In Egypt, the Uraeus was a very visible royal symbol, worn on the diadem of the pharaoh and some Egyptian deities, including the sun god Re.' It seems reasonable to suggest, then, that among the various natural means at YHWH's disposal, he released fiery serpents, an image that resonates as a ubiquitous emblem in Egypt, as a form of poetic justice. Stubbs similarly suggests 'the serpent likely symbolized Egypt and its gods', so that YHWH's punishment uses a symbol of Israel's desire, 'life back in Egypt under the rule of the snake, Pharaoh, and the gods of Egypt' (2009: 167). Currid ably demonstrates how this story 'mirrors Egypt far more strongly than has been previously recognized', bearing 'a strong Egyptian flavor historically and culturally', with Egypt being 'foundational to the story', poetic justice for Israel's desire to return to Egypt (1997: 146, 147, 154–155). However, one may press more deeply into the function of the story within the flow of the chapter, why this extraordinarily strong exodus motif here? *The serpent episode marks the second generation's experience of Egypt, both its bitter oppression and YHWH's sovereign deliverance out of Egypt.* Given that the winged *uraeus* is a symbol found on eighth-century seals in Judah, some scholars even read Hezekiah's destruction of Nechushtan, Moses' bronze serpent (2 Kgs 18:4), as his removal of Egyptian royal symbolism, demonstrating the nation's shift in political allegiance from Egypt to Assyria (see Swanson 2002; Shanks 2007; cf. Keel and Uehlinger 1998: 273). If, moreover, the serpents allude to the Egyptian *uraeus*, symbolizing kingship, then the episode coordinates with the general kingship theme that runs as an undercurrent throughout chapters 21–25.

The second generation of Israel experiences a crisis of death: the serpents 'bit' (*nāšak*) the people and 'many' (*rab*) of them died.

7. In response to YHWH's judgement, the people come to Moses and confess their sin. That the people understood the fiery serpents encountered in the wilderness as released by YHWH and then embraced their own guilt may demonstrate spiritual maturity, beyond any terror or desire for self-preservation: that divine discipline bears fruit among the second generation of Israel. Just as, in the previous story's confrontation with the king of Arad, Israel recognized YHWH's sovereign kingship over the outcome of battle, so now they acknowledge his control over their dilemma in the wilderness, including his control over serpents. We have 'sinned' (*ḥāṭā'nû*) they tell Moses and then they confess that sin specifically: 'we spoke against YHWH and against you'. This extremely rare corporate confession of sin sets apart the second generation from the first – indeed, 'this is the first time the sons of Israel recognize their sin and acknowledge it openly!' (Bazak 2014b: 277). Amid all the divine judgements experienced by the first generation in the wilderness and, aside from Aaron's confession (Num. 12:11), the only 'we have sinned' heard from their lips had been an act of defiance against YHWH's

word (cf. Num. 14:40). As with the prologue's use of 'Hormah', so the confession underscores the contrast between generations. Humbled and having been made to reflect on their need for Moses, the second generation of Israel calls for Moses to intercede – 'pray (hithpal.) to YHWH', that YHWH would cause 'the serpent' to turn away from them. This is also 'the first and only time that the people asked Moses to pray on their behalf' (Anisfeld 2011: 218). Their use of 'the serpent' may simply be an instance where the sg. represents the class (see R. J. Williams 2007: §87), but it may also function to unify the symbolic value of the punishment, with reference to Egypt. Moses' significant role as intercessor is underscored (cf. chs. 12, 14), as is the people's repentance and trust, replacing the 'monotone pattern of murmuring' (Frevel 2009: 130). Repentance to life is a gift worth obtaining whatever the affliction it costs.

More deeply, the paradigm of beseeching Moses to intercede on behalf of a people, to mitigate God's judgement, hearkens back to the exodus out of Egypt. After both the second and fourth plagues, Pharaoh called on Moses and Aaron to 'entreat' YHWH on his and Egypt's behalf (Exod. 8:8, 28). After the seventh plague, Pharaoh confesses, 'I have sinned,' and bids them to entreat YHWH (Exod. 9:27–28). Then, after the eighth plague, Pharaoh confesses, 'I have sinned (*ḥāṭā'tî*) against YHWH your God and against you,' and asks to be forgiven before calling on them to entreat YHWH to 'turn away from upon me (*wĕyāsēr mē'ālay*) only this death' (Exod. 10:16–17), using remarkably similar terminology.

The narrative does not recount any reprimand or scolding, or even a reply to the people from Moses, reporting rather his immediate compliance: 'And Moses prayed (*wayyitpallēl*) on behalf (*bĕ'ad*) of the people.' If the previous story recalled the instructions for the Nazirite vow, this account recalls YHWH's remedy for the one who has committed 'any sin (*ḥaṭṭō't*)', any unfaithfulness against YHWH: he or she 'shall confess (*wĕhitwaddû*) the sin (*ḥaṭṭā'tām*)' (5:6–7), another instance whereby the second generation is portrayed as conforming to the purity expectations for life with YHWH in the Camp.

8. That YHWH does not turn the serpents away, as the people wanted, seems to follow from the text's omission of any report of his doing so, especially in the light of their specific request. Rather, he responds to Moses' prayer with a healing remedy for anyone bitten and dying. As noted above (v. 6), the presence of fiery serpents was natural for this region of the wilderness, but YHWH had been shielding his people from them throughout Israel's journeys. It had been within the context of such divine protection and ease of danger that the people had been emboldened to complain. Now they cannot go back to how things were; presumably, the new normal for life in the wilderness would include fiery serpents. From another angle, one may suggest the people had *merely* requested a turning away of the snakes, but YHWH had (also?)

provided a healing remedy, saving alive those who had been bitten. There is no narrative closure in terms of storing away the bronze serpent or by naming the locale as a memorial to the event, which seems, on the whole, to leave open the ongoing use of the bronze serpent for the rest of Israel's journeys in the wilderness (so, too, Olson 1996: 136).

Focusing on the plain answer to Moses' intercessory prayer, YHWH would provide healing and life, a remedy for anyone bitten. In his wisdom, YHWH determined that regular salve for ongoing affliction was better for his people's spiritual maturity than to remove all affliction. In this way, Israel would look continually to him with gratitude for his daily mercies, fully appreciating their daily dependence on him. The reality of threatening serpents, a continual reminder of a potentially worse prospect, would also guard them from taking YHWH's faithful provision for granted and, therefore, from murmuring against him about their plight. With good reason, this is the last complaint story of the wilderness era. In Deuteronomy, Moses calls Israel to reflect on how YHWH had led them through 'that great and terrible wilderness with fiery serpents (*nāḥāš śārāp*) and scorpions, a parched land with no water' (8:15; 'no water', *'ên-māyim*, matches the people's complaint in Num. 21:5).

Moses is to make for himself a *śārāp*, a 'fiery' (serpent) and put it on a standard or 'ensign' (*nēs*). The verbal root for 'ensign' occurs with the sense of fleeing for refuge throughout Numbers (10:35; 16:34; 35:6, 11, 15, 25, 26, 32), related since an ensign is a rallying point to which one flees, and once with the meaning of 'sign' (of warning or judgement, 26:10), and then its twofold use here as an upheld standard (vv. 8, 9), clearly with the intent of Israel's looking upon it (*rā'āh 'ōtô*). The term first appears in the Torah after Israel's victory against an attack by Amalekites, as Moses builds an altar, calling it YHWH is 'my banner' (*nissî*, Exod. 17:15; for other similarities between Exod. 17 and Num. 21, see B. P. Robinson 1985: 17–18). The *nēs*, writes Birkan, 'is not a walking staff but a propping standard, which had a particular role in Egypt'; referencing reliefs depicting Egyptian kings (Usaphais, Snefru) with serpents on standards smiting their enemies, she explains that standards were symbols of power often brought on to the battlefield (2005: 7, 20–21). Egyptian standards, frequently depicted with a serpent on top, even served as something of a repository of the deities' power, imbued with divine force (Currid 1997: 151–152). Use of an ensign, then, contributes to the Egypt motif evident throughout the story. Perhaps, given that the serpent was a commonplace symbol in Egypt, the bronze serpent lifted on the pole was intended as a reminder of Israel's Egyptian bondage, represented by the dire affliction of fiery serpents in the wilderness. Looking at the bronze serpent, beyond recalling Israel's Egyptian bondage, would function to remind them that YHWH, who had redeemed the nation out of Egypt, would now deliver them from the deathly attack of serpents. In this way, the upraised standard bearing a copper serpent, represented blessing and healing for Israelites, since YHWH was sovereignly able to subjugate the serpent and heal his people, but it also represented a dire warning against any desire to turn back to Egypt, a land devastated under the hand of YHWH (cf. Currid 1997: 154).

That the manner for healing is extraordinary and unexpected is evident in YHWH's explanation of how it will work: 'and it will happen that'. All who have been bitten, who are under the serpent's sway of death; that is, 'the serpent-bitten-ones' (*hannāšûk*) are to look upon the fiery serpent ensign and they will live. It is perhaps relevant that looking upon 'it' (*'ōtô*) is similar in sound and consonants to the term for 'sign' (*'ôt*; cf. Num. 2:2; 14:11, 22; 17:3, 25). Some have proposed a medicinal notion whereby the remedy reflects the malady – having been bitten by a serpent, looking at the serpent is healing, or some other magical practice (see e.g. Fabry 1998, esp. 379; Levine 2000: 89; Hurowitz 2004), and others point to the Egyptian practice of wearing serpent-shaped amulets to ward off serpents (Joines 1968: 251–252). On the other hand, suggestions that the bronze serpent signified a dead or vanquished serpent on a pole appears to go beyond the text, apart from further historically contextual evidence – and, to be sure, most moulded creatures in the ANE, such as the upraised cobra in Egypt, were intended to represent living realities. Whatever the precise reasoning, and it is not altogether clear, the manner is not driven by magic but by YHWH's own will and power – which is not to say that it has no symbolic significance, such as YHWH's judgement and the people's guilt. Jewish sources provide ample instances of this sensible understanding: that as the Israelites gazed upwards at the bronze serpent, their hearts were subject to their heavenly Father (*m. Rosh HaSh.* 3.5), not being saved by the thing seen but by God, the Saviour of all (Wisdom of Solomon 16.5–7). Their looking up forms a divine test of trust in YHWH and obedience to his word – only those who heeded his instructions would be saved. As Fretheim underscores (1978: 270; emphasis original), the 'means provided are indeed effective, not because of some magical properties inherent in the means, but because of the *promise* that is given in conjunction with the means'. It is YHWH's promise of life for those who look; that is, YHWH himself, who has promised to heal anyone who trusts and obeys his word – which leads to life. The verse ends with authoritative hope: 'he will live' (*wāḥāy*). The next verse, the obedience report of Moses (v. 9), also ends with *wāḥāy*, yielding an emphasis on YHWH's provision of *life* in the midst of the death threat of fiery serpents in the wilderness. The remedy signals 'the role of Yahweh as Provider and Protector and Guide' (Boraas 1978: 277).

Just as the fiery serpents as a divine judgement appear to reflect an exodus motif, reflecting the harsh and bitter treatment of Israelites in

Egypt, so the remedy, a bronze serpent lifted on a pole, may signify YHWH's deliverance out of Egypt. Currid similarly interprets the standard as 'a symbol of Yahweh's vanquishing of Egypt . . . a sign of his conquering that nation' (1997: 149). To be sure, the first sign YHWH gave Moses, when the latter had insisted the Israelites in Egypt would not believe YHWH had sent him, was for Moses' staff to transform into a 'serpent' (*nāḥāš*) (Exod. 4:1–5). Later, as a preface to the first plague, Aaron casts his rod before Pharaoh and it becomes 'a serpent' (Exod. 7:8–13). Beyond authenticating Moses' divine mission (cf. Childs 2004: 151), these opening signs of a staff turning into a serpent were meant to convey YHWH's sovereign power over Egypt. Pharaoh may even be portrayed as a crocodile/serpent in the Exodus account (see P. Guillaume 2004; Morales 2020: 54–61; on the serpent-like Pharaoh in Ezekiel, see Carvalho 2014: 211–214). DeRouchie points to the parallel usages of 'put out (*šālaḥ*) the hand' through the Exodus narrative, as affirming a correlation between Pharaoh and the serpent sign (2020: 308; see Exod. 3:19–20; 4:2–3; 9:15–16). Before the exodus, 'the serpent' (*hannāḥāš*) is introduced as an embodiment of evil, who led the primal couple on the way of death and remains at enmity with God's people (Gen. 3:1–15; on the Eden serpent as dragon, see R. D. Miller 2018: 202–207). It is possible that the serpents released among the people in Israel's Camp, the covenant community having YHWH's Edenic Tent of Meeting in its midst (cf. 24:5–6), intends some allusion to the Eden narratives. Although not obvious, nevertheless, a common denominator throughout the history of Jewish and Christian interpretation is the connection of the bronze serpent episode to the serpent in the garden of Eden (cf. Ullmann 1995). Interestingly, given that the bronze serpent would be included in the collection of furnishings in the Tent and later Temple, which contain Edenic symbolism, the serpent – alongside the cherubim and the lampstand (as tree of life), also resonates with the story of Eden (on this, see Mazor 2002; Wénin 2008). The Midrash recalls the serpent of Genesis 3, assuming 'one serpent' (cf. 21:7), but only to observe that the serpent was the first to speak slander, so Israel should have learned the lesson and not spoken against God and Moses (*Num. Rab.* 19.22; see also *TgPs-J* and *TgNeof.*; cf. Slotki 1951: 6:771; one may also add that in both narratives, humanity was dissatisfied with God's provision of food). Philo also connects the serpent to the temptation of Eve allegorically, without any development (*Leg. Alleg.* 2.20.79–81). The root *n-ḥ-š* will resurface in the Balaam narrative as 'enchantment' (*naḥaš*, 23:23), leading Hepner to write (2011: 186 n. 6; cf. Savran 1994: 49–51): 'In an allusion to the *nāḥāš*, *serpent*, in the garden of Eden (Gen. 3:10), Moses demonstrates his power over *hannĕḥāšîm*, *the serpents* (Num. 21:6), immediately before Balaam explains his inability to curse Israel,' there being 'no enchantment' (*naḥaš*) against Israel (Num. 23:23). The connection is sound, although it is YHWH's power over the serpent that is demonstrated. The Bible ends with the Messiah's conquering 'the great dragon, that old serpent, called the Devil and Satan' (Rev. 12:9; cf. 20:2).

9. Moses' follow-through obedience and its result fulfils YHWH's word of life. Moses 'makes' a serpent of 'bronze' (*něḥōšet*), and 'puts it' on an 'ensign', 'and it happened' that any man 'bitten' by a serpent, when he observed the serpent of bronze 'he would live'. N. MacDonald, noting the definite article '*the* standard', entertains the possibility that the standard may refer to the rod that Moses held high to ensure Joshua's victory against the Amalekites (Exod. 17:8–17), an association made already by the rabbis (*m. Rosh HaSh.* 3.8; 2012a: 132). Adding tin to copper to make the latter in its alloy form (as bronze) for sculpting, was a technique well known throughout the ANE since the second millennium, and while an argument can be made that bronze would appear more 'fiery', it is anyone's guess whether the fashioned serpent was copper or bronze. The term *něḥōšet* is likely an Egyptian loanword, *teḥ(ḫ)ost*, for 'bronze' (see BDB 638), a detail that may add further to the Egypt motif. The only previous use of 'bronze' was for the bronze censers that were hammered out as a cover for the altar after YHWH's fire had consumed the 250 who dared approach him with incense (16:39). Later in Numbers we are told this judgement became a 'sign' (*nēs*; 26:10), so that Korah's rebellion and the brazen serpent episode share two rare terms. This association endows the bronze serpent as a symbol with an aspect of divine judgement and warning, even as submission to YHWH, in looking up to it, leads to life. In Egypt, the term *něḥōšet* 'often referred to the mountings on a flagpole or standard' (Currid 1997: 147), precisely the function here. 'By utilizing two prominent Egyptian symbols [the serpent and the ensign] for castigation,' writes Birkan, 'the narrative of Numbers 21 amplifies God's compassion' since 'the very symbol of punishment and judgement was used to provide healing' (2005: 72).

Two differences between YHWH's instruction and the fulfilment are, first, the designations for the serpent: 'fiery' (*śārāp*) versus 'serpent of bronze' (*něḥaš něḥōšet*); the latter use of bronze is likely in accord with its appearing 'fiery'; and, second, in the terms used for seeing: 'look' (*rā'āh*) versus 'observe' (*hibbîṭ*), which equally means to look and may be a stylistic change. Perhaps 'observe' is used with the nuance of 'pay attention' (cf. Isa. 22:8), indicating that healing came through an intentional act of trust and obedience, not by an inadvertent glimpse (cf. Ashley 1993: 406; Rashi 1997: 4:254). Although his punishment had been severe, the remedy in its sheer simplicity and ease demonstrates YHWH's abounding mercy and steadfast love: the bitten-ones need not weeks of slow healing and discomfort, or arduous means for procuring their remedy – they simply need to look in order to live, an instruction even the youngest child among them could follow. Healing thus accompanied a simple act of obedience: trusting YHWH's word (cf. Keil and Delitzsch 1973: 3:139). The divine remedy reminds us that while murmuring was a communal sin, yet that community was comprised of individuals who chose to speak against YHWH and Moses. In divine wisdom, YHWH's remedy is applied at the individual level whereby each Israelite needed to take his or her sin to heart, turning in confession and contrition to YHWH's gracious provision of mercy.

This area around Edom, the Timna Valley, has been mined for copper since the fifth millennium BC; it was an Egyptian copper-smelting site during the Late Bronze Age (thirteenth-twelfth century BC) (see Rothenberg 1972; Leonard 1989: 22), although copper-smelting activity here appears to have peaked in the early Iron Age (eleventh-ninth centuries BC) primarily under Edomite control (Ben-Yosef and Greener 2018). Archaeologists discovered a five-inch copper serpent at the Hathor temple, apparently from a later Midianite occupation (Cole 2009: 375). The travelogue of Numbers 33 mentions that Israel, while skirting around Edom, encamped at Punon (vv. 42–43), a centre for mining and smelting copper in antiquity (Milgrom 1990: 173). Journeying through this region, copper was plainly available to Moses.

When generations later Hezekiah began to reign as king of Judah, one of his accomplishments for which he is honoured as doing right in the eyes of YHWH was to remove from the land places and images of idolatry. Among his efforts at restoring the exclusive worship of YHWH, he 'crushed in pieces the bronze serpent that Moses had made because (kî) up until those days the sons of Israel were burning incense to it, and called it Nehushtan (něḥuštān, 2 Kgs 18:4; n-ḥ-š is a root for both 'copper' and 'serpent'). An image meant to reflect the people's guilt and just judgement, along with YHWH's merciful salvation, had become an object of idolatry. The Israelites were surrounded by three prominent ancient serpent deities of healing, each with its own temple (Ningishzida of the Sumerians, Asclepius of the Greeks and Eshmun in the Phoenician-Canaanite cults); this, along with increased Egyptian influence in the eighth century BC, likely influenced their drift into deifying the bronze serpent that had been fashioned by Moses at God's command (cf. Birkan 2005: 33).

21:10–20: Israel's journeys and the Song of the Well

This central section on Israel's journeys forms a transition from the wilderness to the conquest of the land, describing their route around Edom (cf. Frevel 2009: 131), a function that remains clear despite textual difficulties (on the latter, see e.g. Seebass 1997: 256–257) and the challenge of making geographical sense of the stations (see J. M. Miller 1989; cf. also Van Seters 1972; G. I. Davies 1983; Roskop 2011) along with the lack of uniformity among the three accounts of the journey: Numbers 21:10–20, Numbers 33:1–49, and Deuteronomy 2 (see Granot 2014c). Oboth and Iye of the Abarim are mentioned in the itinerary of 33:44; wadi of Zared and Arnon are noted in Deuteronomy 2:13–14, 24; and the last cluster of stations foreshadows the Balaam narratives: Bamoth (22:41), Pisgah (23:14), 'wasteland' or Jeshimon (23:28) and 'field of Moab' (cf. 22:1) (following Frevel 2009: 132). Israel is making progress to the land despite Edom's delay, the battle with Canaanites and the affliction of serpent bites. The Camp is back in the rhythm of journey and encampment, set up in early chapters (cf. 1:51–53; 2:1–2, 17, 34; 9:15–23). Moreover, en route YHWH continues to provide water for his people faithfully, using not only Moses but now also the chieftains of Israel. The poems here – a quote from the Book of the Battles of YHWH (21:14–15) and the well song (21:17–18) – along with the taunt song of Sihon in 21:27–30 lend the chapter coherence with the Balaam narrative with its poetic oracles (23:7–10, 18–24; 24:3–9, 15–19, 20, 21–22, 23–24). The 'seemingly achronological redaction' of the chapter whereby the song's 'sequential misplacement remains problematic' has been duly noted by scholars (Twersky 2022: 29), and may be the result of shaping the second generation's experience as a reliving of the first generation's exodus pattern. The exodus motif is present in Israel's 'Song of the Well' after crossing the Arnon River, akin to the 'Song of the Sea' sung by Israel after crossing the Sea (Exod. 15:1–21). Their experience mimics that of the first generation, in the chapter's ongoing comparison between Israel's first generation and the new community that will inherit the land. Careful attention to the function of the Arnon River, serving as a border between Moab and Amorites, serves to legitimate Israel's claims on the Transjordan, especially against Moabite disputes (cf. Levine 2000: 126–133).

The Midrash connects the well (v. 16) with Miriam's legendary well, apparently restored on the merit of Moses, offering an ideal, paradisal view of the Camp that, while fanciful, is still relevant theologically (cf. 24:5–6): the princes of each tribe stood by the well, drawing water with their staffs, making water channels between the standards of the tribal encampments and forming a river that encircled the Camp, so that ships were needed to travel between standards and a variety of trees and herbage sprang forth all about (see *Num. Rab.* 19.26).

10–15. It may be that some of the itinerary names (vv. 10–11, 18–20) should be translated, retaining their appellative character, with 'Oboth' referring to 'mediums' or 'necromancers', and 'Iye of the Abarim' reading 'the ruins on the other side' (J. M. Miller 1989: 581; Nowell 2011: 91). 'Toward the rising sun' (*mizraḥ haššāmeš*; cf. 25:4) recalls the 'eastward' (*mizrāḥ*) encampment of Judah (2:3), as well as Moses and the priesthood's encampment 'eastward' (*mizrāḥ*) of the Tent of Meeting (3:38). Generations earlier, Israel, the nation's patriarchal namesake, had returned limping toward the land with the rising of the sun (Gen. 32:31). The earlier idealistic portrayal of the Camp's journeys (Num. 9:15–23) is recalled in the fourfold use of both the terms 'journey' (*nāsaʻ*) and 'encamp' (*ḥānāh*) in verses 10–13 (cf. Cole 2000: 352). The second generation of Israel is pursuing YHWH in the wilderness faithfully.

Careful attention is given to Moab's border, likely in recognition of what Moses would declare in Deuteronomy: that YHWH would not give any Moabite land to Israel, for he had given that territory to Lot's descendants as a possession (2:9). The Arnon, a perennial tributary flowing westward into the Dead Sea and having a variety of wadies, is given special focus as it forms Moab's northern border, separating Moab from the Amorites (cf. Deut. 3:8, 16; Josh. 13:16). The land north of the Arnon 'was disputed territory in antiquity' (Currid 2009: 299), claimed alternatively by Moabites, Amorites and Ammonites, and would be settled by the tribes of Reuben and Gad (Num. 32). Aside from textual difficulties and ambiguities, the ancient song or poem quoted from the Book of the Battles of YHWH forms a proof-text that Arnon serves as Moab's border – note the introductory 'therefore' (*ʻal-kēn*) (for ancient songs serving as documentation, see Rabinowitz 1993; cf. Greenstein 2018: 13) and how the song is framed by references to the 'border of Moab' (vv. 13b, 15b). Border disputes and land possession were serious matters, especially in the light of a theology of divine grant (see Judg. 11:12–28). The most one can say regarding Ar (city) is that it was a city of prominence in Moab, associated with the Arnon or one of its tributaries (J. M. Miller 1989: 590–592; cf. Isa. 15:1). Ar may be the same as the 'city of Moab on the border of Arnon' in the Balaam narrative (22:36).

Understandably, much speculation has swirled around the now lost 'Book of the Battles of YHWH', which appears to have been an anthology of ancient songs of battle, akin to the other lost source, the Book of Jashar (Josh. 10:13; 2 Sam. 1:18). In Exodus, YHWH had bidden Moses to write of Israel's victory over Amalek 'in a book' (*bassēper*) as a memorial and to rehearse it in the ears of Joshua (17:14); if not equated with the same writing, the Book of YHWH's Battles might have served a similar purpose. Greenstein (2017) rightly cautions, however, that book titles in the ancient world were not descriptive, but rather mere quotations from the document's opening line, and suggests that all three poems of chapter 21, including the Song of the Well, may derive from the same source. The book is quoted as authoritatively affirming Arnon's function as a border between Moab and the Amorites, which looks to Israel's conquest of Sihon and the Amorites (21:21–32), justifying its claim to their land. The Targums understand 'the book' as the Torah, so that a separate book recounting YHWH's wars never existed, a position followed by a few scholars (cf. Seligsohn 1906), while von Rad had wondered if the Book of Wars was the origin for the Day of YHWH concept (1959: 108). The poetic excerpt is difficult textually, Albright regarding it as beyond reconstruction (1968: 44), and even delimiting the lines varies across textual traditions – LXX, for example, includes 'the war of the Lord' (*Polemos tou kyriou*) as part of the poem itself (as do the Aramaic Targums). With the wider tradition, taking 'the Book of YHWH's Battles' as the source for the following quotation, the excerpt appears to begin mid-sentence with a direct object marker, connected to *wāhēb*. Noting the verbal root *'th* (to come), which occurs only in poetry (cf. Deut. 33:2; Ps 68:32; Isa. 21:12), and emending *wāhēb* to the tetragrammaton while deleting occurrences of *'ăšer*, Christensen (1974) reads the song as describing YHWH, the divine warrior, marching forth in battle: '[YHWH] came in a whirlwind; / He came to the branch wadis of the Arnon. / He marched through the wadis; / He marched (or turned aside) to the seat of Ar. / He leaned toward the border of Moab.' Although his emendation and deletions are forced, the translation of *sûpāh* as 'whirlwind' or 'storm-wind' makes good sense, and would be in accord with a storm theophany – which was Nachmanides' translation as well (1975: 237–238). The LXX, moreover, translates *sûpāh* with *ephlogisen*, 'set on fire'. Steiner, while leaving the subject vague, also parses the object marker as a shortened form of the poetic verb *'-t-y*, 'Come to (Mount) Waheb (in the Desert of Kedemoth) during a storm,' noting how the Song of Heshbon (Num. 21:27–30) also begins with 'come', albeit using *bō'û*, and reads *sûpāh* similarly as 'storm' (2020: 566, 568–573). Such a defensible reading of *sûpāh*, along with the reference to YHWH's battles in the title (or first line) of the book, make it possible that a storm theophany is in view, but it is difficult to conclude anything definite. The fundamental purpose for citing the source, establishing the limit of Moab's territory, should not be obscured by any proposed reconstruction. Rashi, along with *TgO*, reads *wāhēb* as derived from the root *y-h-b* (to give), understanding, 'What was given at the Sea of Suph was also (given) at the streams that form the Arnon' (1997: 257; cf. Hirsch 2007a: 467–468), a reading that yields an exodus motif that appears true to the context, but that remains uncertain. Steiner, who suggests Waheb is the name of a mountain, takes the derivation ('giver, donor') to imply that during storms, the mountain supplied the gift of abundant water by the torrents of run-off and its collection into cavities as pools (2020: 572; cf. 20:11).

16–18. Israel's next stop was at Beer (well) – use of the *directional h* (*b'r-h*) signifying a place name. Propp associates Beer with the Massah-Meribah tradition (20:1–13), pointing to the similarities as YHWH commands Moses to gather the people to provide them water – the 'leaders' being analogous to Moses and their 'walking sticks' to his staff (1987: 51–52). Since *bĕ'ēr* means 'well', the locale might have been named afterward for the well dug out there by Israel's princes. Whereas previously a water shortage led to the people's complaint, exposing their lack of trust (20:2–5; 21:5), YHWH's guidance here precedes any want, calling for Moses to gather the people so that he, YHWH, might give them water. In Numbers 20:8, YHWH had called for *Moses* to give the people water ('you', 20:8). This time YHWH says, 'I will give them water.' Is this a subtle rebuke for Moses' 'Shall we bring forth water for you'? Other differences between the stories include 'assemble' (*qāhāl*) and 'the community' (*hā'ēdāh*) in 20:18, versus 'gather' (*'āsap*) and 'people' (*hā'ām*) here. The text suggests a closer relationship between YHWH and the people. Corporate 'gathering' often precedes YHWH's work among his people, and *'āsap* was a key word for chapters 11 and 12. YHWH's provision of the well is but one of three sources of water mentioned, including the wadi of Zared and the Arnon River, with its wadis, so the section brims with waters, promising an end to the wilderness era as Israel journeys closer to the land.

The provision of the well causes Israel to celebrate in song, the Song of the Well (on its archaic constructions, see D. N. Freedman 1960). The opening line of verse 17 echoes the Song at the Sea, one of the chapter's many allusions to the exodus:

Num. 21:17: *'āz yāšîr*   *yiśrā'ēl 'et-haššîrāh hazzō't*
Exod. 15:1: *'āz yāšîr-mōšeh ûbĕnê yiśrā'ēl 'et-haššîrāh hazzō't*

The second generation of Israel had recently crossed the Arnon River (21:13; cf. Deut. 2:24) and now, like the first generation after crossing the Sea, they sing a song. Rashi thus notes that just as God's people recounted the miracle of the Sea of Suph, so should they recount the miracles of the Arnon River (cf. Rashi 1997: 4:257). The difference with the Exodus reference, that Moses is not mentioned in Numbers 21:17, underscores the role of Israel (also, the Song at the Sea was a song of praise 'to YHWH', whereas the Song of the Well is a general, celebratory song over YHWH's provision of water). In recalling the Song at the Sea, which portrays YHWH as a 'man of war' (Exod. 15:3), that song's triumphant declaration that YHWH would stay their enemies, planting Israel in the land of inheritance (Exod. 15:16–18), a reality now dawning, is also reaffirmed (cf. Twersky 2022: 36).

While Moses still functions vitally as Israel's mediator (21:7) and is used by YHWH to provide for his people's needs (21:16), the present chapter demonstrates the second generation's maturity primarily through their initiative and participation, as with their vow in response to defeat (21:2) and here in their singing, along with their leaders' quarrying of the well (for subterranean streams in Moab, see Routledge 2004: 50). Apparently, in ancient custom the digging of a well was ceremoniously inaugurated by a sheikh or headman, which may be analogous to the role of Israel's leaders here, and to the function of the song (T. H. Gaster 1981: 302). Ibn Ezra refers to this well as 'a miracle' (or 'wonder') inasmuch as the water flowed forth as soon as the chieftains struck with their staffs (1999: 171) – rather than actual work implements and hard toil, water ushered forth by a ceremonial or symbolic digging (cf. Woods and Rogers 2006: 313). Perhaps this water-drawing serves to contrast ironically with Moses' twofold striking of the rock. Due to the song's brevity, some Jewish traditions suggest David removed the original song to the Psalter, identifying it with Psalm 136 (see Viezel 2015: 112–115; Farber 2021). Noting a strong resemblance to a Bedouin song ('Spring up, O well, / flow copiously. / Drink and disdain not, / with a staff we have dug it.'), however, Greenstein observes that Israel's song may well constitute the entire poem, rather than merely a fragment of a larger work (2018: 9). 'Spring up (or 'ascend', *ălî*) O well! Sing out to it!' presumably was sung by labourers as they dug out a well (cf. Eissfeldt 1965: 88), or it was simply a celebration song over a newfound or newly dug-out well; in either case, the next line names the 'princes' (*śārîm*) and 'nobles' (*nĕdîbê*) as those who led the effort, along with the use of their sceptres or rods. A beautiful harmony appears in this episode among YHWH, who says 'I will give them water', Moses, the mediator who gathers the people at YHWH's behest, and the people, who sing in celebration about the supply of water and of the initiative of their princes, who dug out the well. The well is a sign that the wilderness period is drawing to a close, that 'the gift of water will be available in the land they are approaching' (Nowell 2011: 91–92), even as it celebrates 'God's steadfast and unflinching devotion to Israel' (Twersky 2022: 35). The ceremony, beyond being merely celebratory, is likely also legal in nature, functioning as a witness to Israel's claim of ownership over the well and its water, and perhaps of the surrounding region as well (Steiner 2020: 576; cf. van Zyl 1960: 7).

The song, although distributed across two verses, is set apart in the MT by use of athnaks, excluding the last part of verse 18 from the song, 'and from the wilderness toward Mattanah (gift)', recommencing the itinerary as verse 19 makes clear. The phrase 'from the wilderness' is highly significant. As Dozeman explains (1998: 165), there is a theological purpose for this travel list, with its threefold mention of wilderness (vv. 10, 13, 18b), with the third reference marking Israel's departure out of the wilderness – the Camp is transitioning 'from Israel's wilderness wandering to its conquest of fertile land'. Others have understood this last section of the verse as still part of the song, celebrating God's 'gift' (of a well) in the 'wilderness', with the following verses (19, 20) forming a description of the well's abundant waters flowing down into valleys and ascending the heights (Nachmanides cites *TgO*; cf. 1975: 239).

19–20. The itinerary (including the end of v. 18) presents the fourfold progress of Israel to the 'field of Moab'. The place names are descriptive: Gift, Wadi of God, the Heights, making their identification all the more difficult. The terms for 'journeying out' and 'encamping' are absent, rendering the impression of Israel's progress toward the land as swift, despite the earlier delay in trekking around Edom. Alternatively, Cole explains the absence of journey verbs by proposing the itinerary continues the song (2000: 355). More recently, Steiner has made a strong case that verses 14–20 comprise the substance of the poetic excerpt from the Book of the Wars of YHWH, forming something of a poetic invitation to take a tour of inspiring sites, an exhortation to experience a taste of the wonders Israel had experienced during this period (2020: 566): thus, 'Come to Mount Waheb during a storm' (v. 14) continues with '(come) to the/a well – the well about which the Lord said to Moses' (v. 16), and onward to: 'And from (that well, named) Mattanah, (come) to Nahaliel (Mighty Canyons)' (v. 19), and '(come) to the valley (in front of Baal's temple on Mount Peor) in the open country of Moab, (and) to the top of Pisgah, overlooking the wasteland'. Such exhortations to relive the past, Steiner further observes (2020: 588), are a form of 'ancient tourism' found elsewhere in Scripture, as when YHWH says, 'Go to my place at Shiloh' (Jer. 7:12; see also 2:10), or 'Cross over to Calneh and see, go from there to Great Hamath, and go down to Gath of the Philistines: Are they better than these kingdoms?' (Amos 6:2; see also 4:4), and function as an admonition to 'Go (and) see the works of YHWH/God' (Pss 46:8; 66:5).

Within the context of Israel's progress, two significant points are conveyed. First, in a narrow sense Israel has journeyed out of the wilderness proper (v. 18), and are now in the 'conquest and possessing the land' phase even when in a 'wilderness' (cf. 21:23). Second, as with the song from the Book of YHWH's Battles (21:14–15), the last itinerary stop, the 'field of Moab', foreshadows the Balaam narrative while Israel is 'encamped in the plains of Moab' (22:1). The 'summit of Pisgah' (*rō'š happisgā*) will recur verbatim as Balak leads Balaam to the summit of Pisgah for a second attempt at cursing Israel (23:14) – it is also the summit from which Moses will behold the land before he dies (Deut. 3:27; 34:1). The 'wasteland', which may rather be a proper place name Jeshimon (*hayĕšîmōn*; cf. 1 Sam. 23:19, 24; 26:1, 3), also recurs in the Balaam narrative, another summit to which Balak takes Balaam (23:28). As Milgrom points out, Jeshimon refers to a particular wasteland 'north of the Dead Sea on both sides of the Jordan' (1990: 179). Thus Israel's itinerary 'ends with three locations which are all linked to the setting of the following stories of Balaam' (Frevel 2009: 132), and, as Twersky observes (2022: 32), Bamoth, the summit of Pisgah and the wasteland are even repeated in the same order in the Balaam narrative (22:41; 23:14; 23:28).

21:21–35: Israel's conquest and possession of the lands

This narrative explains how Israel came to possess the Transjordan, the land east of the Jordan river, culminating the chapter with Israel's outstanding victories by YHWH's help. The stories also 'set the stage for two upcoming stories', forming their background (Pressler 2017: 187): the king of Moab's hiring of Balaam to curse Israel (Num. 22 – 24), and the settling of the Transjordan by the tribes of Reuben and Gad and the half-tribe of Manasseh (Num. 32). Aside from a variety of references to the victories over both Sihon and Og (Josh. 2:10; Neh. 9:22; Pss 135:11; 136:19–20), the conquest of Sihon king of the Amorites is recounted three times in the Bible (Num. 21:21–32; Deut. 2:24–35; Judg. 11:9–22), underscoring its importance.

21–24. As the comparison demonstrates, 21:21–22 parallels 20:14, 17–18 closely:

21:21: And Israel sent messengers to Sihon king of the Amorites.
20:14: And Moses sent messengers . . . to the king of Edom.

21:22: Let me pass through your land. We will not stretch in field or in vineyard; we will not drink waters of well – in the way of the king we will walk until we pass through your border.
20:17: Let us pass, please, through your land. We will not pass through in field or vineyard, and we will not drink waters of well; in the way of the king we will walk . . . until we pass through your border.

21:23: But Sihon would not give Israel to pass through in his border . . . and went forth to encounter Israel.
20:21: But Edom refused to give Israel to pass through in his border . . . (20:18) I will go forth to encounter you.

While Edom had threatened to encounter Israel with the 'sword' (*ḥereb*) (20:18), Israel will strike down Sihon with the 'sword' (21:24). As argued previously, 20:14–21 anticipates chapter 21; here, Israel is presented as taking initiative, sending messengers, a role performed earlier by Moses. The second generation of Israelites, born in the wilderness, is much more proactive than their fathers, who had been slaves in Egypt. Absent from Israel's entreaty is Moses' rehearsal of Israel's hardships and the exodus (20:14b–16) as well as a softening 'please' (v. 17), reflecting that while Israel had reasons to hope for brotherly sympathy from Edom, no such kindred bonds existed with the Amorites.

Sihon battles Israel at Jahaz. Presented in the Mesha Stele (or 'Moabite Stone', 840 BC) as a city of some military standing, Jahaz is listed along with Heshbon in Isaiah (15:4; cf. Deut. 2:32; Judg. 11:20), and some have identified it with Khirbet el-Medeineh near the desert fringe (see Dearman 1984). Eventually, as reported by the Chronicler, Jahaz became one of the Levitical cities in the territory of Reuben (1 Chr. 6:78). As Edom had done (20:20–21), Sihon gathers his people to encounter Israel, but whereas Edom's forces had only blocked the land's borders defensively, Sihon 'battled' (*wayyillāḥem*) against Israel – and Israel, who had turned away from Edom (20:21), strikes down Sihon and possesses his land. YHWH had given the Edomites, descendants of Jacob's brother Esau, their land, so Israel was not to meddle with them (Deut. 2:2–6); the Amorites, by contrast, were now due YHWH's judgement over their iniquity (cf. Gen. 15:16; Amos 2:10). Another foretaste of the conquest under Joshua (as with 21:3), Israel 'possessed his [Sihon's] land', 'took all these cities' and 'dwelt in all the cities of the Amorites, in Heshbon and in all her villages'. The terms *yāraš* (dispossessed) and *yāšab* ('dwelt', v. 25) are highly significant (cf. Ska 2006: 35–38), bringing the chapter to its culmination with Israel's 'conquest' of land. The land of promise lies east of the Jordan River, but these lands of Sihon (and then of Og) will be 'annexed', as it were, to the land, possessed and dwelt in by the descendants of Gad, Reuben and by half of Manasseh's tribe (ch. 32). Moses, while barred from leading Israel in its conquest of the land, is divinely granted a foretaste in these victories and possessions of land.

Great care is taken once again (cf. 21:13–15) to delineate the borders of the land conquered by Israel: 'from Arnon as far as Jabbok, as far as the sons of Ammon, for strong was the border of the sons of Ammon' ('strong' may refer to the city of Jazer; see Budd 1984: 246). This detail documents that Israel possessed land belonging only to the Amorites, which was integral to YHWH's will, while scrupulously eluding the land of Ammon, the people descending from Lot, Abraham's nephew, and therefore enjoying a bond of kinship (cf. Gen. 11:31; 12:4; 19:30–38). In Deuteronomy, Moses asserts that YHWH had forbidden Israel to harass the Ammonites, for YHWH had given that land to Lot's descendants (2:19), and then rehearses that Israel 'did not go near the land of the sons of Ammon – anywhere along the bank of the torrent of Jabbok, or the cities of the mountain, or wherever YHWH our God had commanded us' (2:37). When, in Judges (11:12–28), an Ammonite king wars against Israel claiming that on coming out of Egypt the Israelites had taken his land, Jephthah sends messengers to the king, essentially recounting Numbers 20:14–21; 21:10–35.

25–32. Repeated use of the words 'took' (*lāqaḥ*), 'dwelt' (*yāšab*), 'Amorites' (*hā'ĕmōrî*), 'daughters (villages)' (*bat*) and '(dis)possess' (*yāraš*) in verses 24b–25 and 31–32 form an inclusio. The designation 'Amorites' is imprecise, used diversely in different times and places, and may serve as a generic label for the inhabitants of the Canaan region as a whole or for one of its indigenous ethnic groups (Michalowski 2000). Whereas Edom and Moab had kinship ties with Israel, through Esau and Lot, respectively, the Amorites were descended from Ham through his cursed son Canaan (see Gen. 9:18, 22, 25; 10:6, 15–18). Their judgement here, however, is due to the depth of their own wickedness (Gen. 15:16; Deut. 9:4–5). The general description of Israel's conquest and dispossession of the Amorites frames a portrait of Israel's victory over

Heshbon, the mother-city and capital of Sihon's domain, the outlying villages idiomatically referred to as Heshbon's 'daughters'.

Again the text is careful to explain the history of Heshbon in order to underscore that Israel had not transgressed YHWH's will related to the lands of Moab (for a historical review of Sihon's sweeping campaign over this territory, see Aharoni 1979: 184–192). Previously Moab had possessed land beyond the Arnon border (i.e. beyond the land YHWH had designated for Moab), but Sihon had battled against the former king of Moab, dispossessing them of it, including the great city of Heshbon. It may be that 'former' also refers to the 'first' chieftain, with Israel encountering a relatively recently established Moabite state (Milgrom 1990: 181). This historical note is backed by what was likely an old victory-taunt song, celebrating Sihon's victory over Moab – now used ironically to taunt the Amorites themselves in their defeat. Given that Balaam's oracles are each dubbed a *māšol* (Num. 23:7, 18; 24:3, 15), reference here to *hammōšlîm* ('poets' or 'proverb makers') led Jewish sages to assume the song was uttered by Balaam (Twersky 2022: 33; see *Num. Rab.* 19.30; *Tan.* 24; *AgBem* 21.30). The opening line calls for the Amorites to (re)build Heshbon as Sihon's city – after conquering and destroying it as a Moabite stronghold. If verse 30 comprises Israel's contribution, then Sihon's former taunt that he had 'destroyed' (*'ābad*) Moab (v. 29) now falls on his own head as Israel sings that Heshbon is 'destroyed' (*'ābad*) (v. 30) (so Currid 2009: 307; the verse has been reconstructed in a variety of ways; cf. P. D. Hanson 1968). The term 'parable-makers' (v. 27), from *māšāl*, will become a key word in the Balaam narrative (23:7, 18; 24:3, 15, 20, 21, 23). Quoting the ancient song accomplishes two other purposes, aside from serving as a proof-text, justifying Israel's claim to the land. First, along with the other poems (21:14–15, 17–18), the Song of Heshbon lends a celebratory character to the material; chapter 21 narrates Israel's victorious march toward the land with singing. Second, with Israel's progress the tension with Moab builds, especially in this section, anticipating the conflict and Moab's response recounted in chapters 22–25. Moabites are dubbed 'people of Chemosh', their national god, to whom Israelites would stray and consequently be exiled, with Solomon even building a high place for Chemosh, 'the abomination of Moab' (1 Kgs 11:7, 33; 2 Kgs 23:13; cf. Judg. 11:24; Jer. 48:7, 13, 46). Chemosh himself is said to have given his sons as fugitives and his daughters as captives to Sihon, king of the Amorites. That Israel has now conquered Sihon, the conqueror of Moab, will fill Moabites with dread (22:2–3). In his own prophecy against Moab, Jeremiah will quote from this taunt-song (see Jer. 48:45–46). The term 'captivity' (*šĕbî*, v. 29) was used twice in the chapter's opening verse, linking the beginning and closing victories of Israel, which frame the chapter (cf. also 24:22).

That Israel is said to 'dwell' (*yāšab*) in all the cities (v. 25) and in the land (v. 31) of the Amorites, signals a narrative end to Israel's wilderness journeys (though not officially so until the census of Num. 26), and serves as a foretaste of the conquest of Canaan. Moses sends 'to spy out' (*lĕraggēl*) Jazer. The term *rāgal* has a stronger connotation of spying and is different from the leading designation for Israel's original mission to 'scout' the land, and one can assume this mission of espionage was a smaller affair, perhaps two people, and carried none of the political display of the mission in chapter 13. Nevertheless, mention of the spy mission, seizing Jazer and her villages and dispossessing the Amorites serves as a reversal of the first generation's failure, and anticipates the full realization of the goal of the exodus. Jazer and its surrounding region will later be given to the tribe of Gad by Moses (see 32:34–35; cf. Josh. 13:25). As a hinge, verse 32 concludes the preceding section and segues into the next unit on the victory over Og king of Bashan.

33–35. With two successive wayyiqtol verb forms, '(they) turned, (they) ascended', Israel is portrayed as going from conquest to conquest victoriously and successively. Ascending the 'way of Bashan', Israel is immediately confronted by Og the king of Bashan who sets forth 'to encounter' them with 'all his people', using language that parallels the responses of Edom (20:20) and Sihon (21:23). Other biblical sources refer explicitly to two details left unspoken here, although perhaps assumed by the original audience (cf. Gane 2004: 681): that Og was a giant (Deut. 3:11; Josh. 12:4), and that his people were Amorites (Deut. 4:47; 31:4; Josh. 2:10; 9:10). Kosman, in addition to noting that the Amorites themselves are depicted as being tall and stout (Amos 2:9), makes two further observations that imply an understanding of Og's exceptional size (2002: 161–162): one may read between the lines that Moses was apprehensive about encountering Og, as evident in YHWH's encouragement 'Do not fear,' and the multitude of later biblical references to Israel's victory over Og demonstrate an appreciation that Og had been a uniquely mighty foe (Josh. 2:10; 9:10; 12:4; 13:12, 30–31; 1 Kgs 4:19; Neh. 9:22; Ps. 135:11–12; 136:20). Og gathers his forces for battle at Edrei. Located 60 miles south of Damascus at Der'ā, Edrei (along with Salecah) was 'a border city from where the king's army watched for an attack either from the south or the east' and was eventually 'assigned to the Machirites, a clan of the tribe of Manasseh (Josh. 13:31)' (Gregor 2000).

With Og's forces set for battle at Edrei, YHWH communicates to Moses, a divine act aimed at encouraging Israel's leader – for Israel's sake as well, but his speech employs second person sg. The admonition is simple: 'Do not fear him,' Og, the hostile enemy. Fear, to be sure, had betrayed the first generation's unbelief, and sprouted into rebellion and disobedience (13:31 – 14:4). Joshua and Caleb, the two faithful scouts, had twice charged Israel with the same command of not fearing (14:9). More, this word of encouragement not only culminates the chapter, but previews the leading instruction to Joshua for the whole conquest, stated positively as 'be strong and of good courage' (Josh. 1:6, 7, 9). Hardly a clearer contrast can be made between the first generation of Israelites and their children now than in their opposite responses to the charge to 'fear not' the enemy, a response that demands absolute trust in YHWH.

YHWH undergirds his words 'do not fear' with a justifying reason and a supporting proof. 'Because (*kî*) into your hand I have given him' – and not only him, but also 'all his people and his land'. YHWH is sovereign over history and the affairs of men: he alone determines the result of battles as he does the casting of lots (cf. Prov. 16:33). YHWH's initiative here, akin to his spontaneous provision of water in verse 16, marks a transition from the opening episode, from Israel's vow 'If you will give . . . ' (v. 2) to YHWH's unsolicited affirmation 'I have given . . . ' (v. 34). YHWH also encourages him with a supporting proof: you will 'do' (*'āśāh*) to him 'just as' (*ka'ăšer*) you 'did' (*'āśāh*) to Sihon in Heshbon. YHWH's recent faithfulness against Sihon proved that he was *with* Moses and Israel, versus the first generation's rebellious battle wherein YHWH was not among them (Num. 14:42). Under YHWH's sovereign ways and guiding hand, he not merely defends Israel against hostility, but turns the assaults of the nations into bountiful gifts for his people, victories that result in the possession of land. Similarly, Numbers 22 – 24 will demonstrate that YHWH does not simply protect his people against sorcery and cursing, but transforms curses into blessings for Israel. While verses 33 and 35 could be read successively without noticing any disorder, YHWH's central affirmation in verse 34 is the key for understanding the theology of Israel's conquest. However gigantic the king of Bashan was, there can be no shadow of a hint of comparison with Israel's King – with good reason, 'YHWH reigns for ever and ever' was Israel's confession after the sea crossing (Exod. 15:18). The account ends with a resounding victory: Israel struck him down and 'all his people' and possessed 'his land', just as YHWH had said he had given these into Moses' hand. The report adds 'and all his sons' to the smiting, and that 'no survivor remained to him', underscoring the profundity of Og's resounding defeat and demonstrating the majestic power of YHWH. His word is not fulfilled by measure, for he is superabundantly able to accomplish his purposes. It should be noted that not a single death in Israel is reported in the chapter, nor in the later battle against the Midianites (see 31:49).

This short addendum to the conquest of Sihon, relating the similar defeat of Og, functions to demonstrate that the victory over Sihon and possession of his lands established a paradigm for the rest of the conquest: Israel would be able 'to do to' the other nations in Canaan 'just as' they had done to Sihon king of the Amorites – by YHWH's help. Bashan was renowned for its rich and fertile pasturage east of the Sea of Galilee, apparently yielding portly cows (see Amos 4:1), and was inherited by the half-tribe of Manasseh (Deut. 3:13; cf. Num. 32).

Explanation

The role of Numbers 21 – 25, conveying the wilderness sojourn of the second generation, is crucial for understanding how Israel was matured by God and made ready for life in the land – even in spite of the apostasy at Baal Peor, a disastrous failure remedied through the young priest Phinehas. These chapters also deal with the responses of the nations to Israel's progress toward possessing the land, along with Israel's reaction in turn. Both the battles and the seductions to sexual immorality and idolatry would prove to be recurring threats to life in the land among the nations. The second generation's experience of conflicts, victories and failures in its engagement with the nations not only foreshadow the later history of Israel, but also underline YHWH's faithfulness as the key to their hope of triumph and blessing, forgiveness and healing. In terms of narrative movement, dramatic tension heightens as Israel approaches the land of inheritance, only to face the nations' hostility and opposition – even sorcery and seduction – at every turn. Will Israel ever make it out of the wilderness? These chapters present, as it were, the final test of Israel: when opposed by the powers of the world, God's people must mature in looking to YHWH for strength and help, trusting that his promises will indeed come to fruition.

After the largely stark section of chapters 16–20, pervaded by rebellion and death, Numbers 21 signals a new, more optimistic turn as the second generation of Israel grows in its relationship with and reliance on YHWH. As they journey ever closer to the land, Israel experiences the faithful shepherding of YHWH, who preserves his people by healing them, giving them water and granting them victory upon victory over hostile nations. Israel's two experiences of setbacks early in the chapter, with some being taken captive by the Canaanites in battle (2:1–3) and many being bitten by snakes in divine judgement (21:4–9), serve to mature the people in their trust of YHWH. Both hindrances become the backdrop to YHWH's provision of victory and preservation of life, bearing fruit in the rest of the chapter as Israel experiences victory over the attacks of the Amorite kings Sihon and Og, possessing their lands. By the third account (vv. 10–20), which forms a transition from wilderness to land, the setbacks and murmuring are past and YHWH leads Israel, providing for their needs (v. 16) and granting them victory and possession of land, completely apart from any response to his people's setback or complaints (vv. 24–25, 34–35). In Numbers 21, YHWH's kingship, especially as displayed in his sovereign control over life and death, is evident. Just as prophecy was a major theme for chapters 11–15, and priesthood for chapters 16–20, so kingship dominates the concern of chapters 21–25 – adumbrated in chapter 20's display of YHWH's kingship, and with the book's first use of the root *m-l-k* (20:14, 17), which occurs fourteen times in chapters 21–25 (21:1, 21, 22, 26 [twice],

29, 33, 34; 22:4, 10; 23:7, 21; 24:7 [twice]; cf. also 26:33, 45 [twice]; 27:1; 31:8 [twice]; 32:33 [four times]; 33:40; 36:11).

The four stories (21:1–3, 4–9, 10–20, 21–35), simply in terms of verse count, display an escalation in form (from 3 to 6 to 11 to 15 verses), matched by increasing optimism and blessing as Israel moves from an initial setback at the hands of Canaanites (v. 1) to the conquest of mighty Amorite strongholds and possession of their lands (vv. 33–35). Israel's vow and victory (vv. 1–3), a prologue and microcosm of the whole chapter, transitions from captivity to victory through Israel's dependence on YHWH. The story with the bronze serpent (vv. 4–9) marks a transition from rebellion and judgement to repentance and healing – to life, the last word being 'he lived' (*ḥāy*). Just as the 'captivity' of the prologue likely recalls Israel's Egyptian bondage, so the story of the brazen serpent is marked by an abundance of Egyptian motifs, and the second generation's deliverance from the deadly poison of serpents may be intended as their own experience of deliverance out of Egypt – never more is the question heard, 'Why did you cause us to ascend out of Egypt?' In the third section, on Israel's journeys (vv. 10–20), the transition from wilderness to land by the second generation is recorded, along with YHWH's unprompted provision of water as Israel's faithful shepherd. Here, Israel sings a song by the well, just as the first generation had done by the sea (Exod. 14). In Israel's conquest and possession of Amorite lands (vv. 21–35), YHWH grants Israel spectacular victories over mighty strongholds, and gives their lands for a possession, a foretaste of the conquest and possession of the land of Canaan. In Numbers 32 (cf. Deut. 3:12–20; Josh. 1:12–16; 12:6), these lands east of the Jordan will be granted to the tribes of Reuben and Gad, to the south in Sihon's former region, and to the half-tribe of Manasseh northward in Og's former territory. These conquests were long celebrated by future generations of Israel, praising God for his faithful love (see Pss 135:11; 136:19–20; cf. Neh. 9:22). The chapter, as tabulated in Table 2, forms a summary of Israel's movement from Egypt to the land of Canaan, from bondage to victory and possession of land, as the second generation – Israel *redivivus* – relives the experiences of the first generation, but with a successful end.

My own exegesis of Numbers 21 confirms the following general assessment by Helfgot concerning how the new generation of Israel is presented in the second half of Numbers (2012a: 169, 173):

> In effect, then, the entire process of the travels and travails of the desert, with, of course, the clear changes related to place and circumstances, are experienced by the second generation . . . The second generation re-experienced many of the seminal events of the first generation. Since the mission of the first generation had gone awry, the second generation now had to relive their history, overcome it, and continue . . . [T]hey confronted the major crisis-mistakes of the first generation . . . and were able to emerge victorious.

Table 2: Numbers 21 – from Egypt to the land of Canaan

Prologue / Microcosm	*From Captivity to Victory* – 'way of Atharim' – 'captives' – 'he gave the Canaanites . . . utterly devoted them and their cities' – 'Hormah'	vv. 1–3
(1)	*Deliverance out of Egypt* – 'Sea of Suph' – 'ascend from Egypt' – 'to die in the wilderness' – 'We have sinned . . . pray to YHWH that he take away' – 'serpent(s)' – *nēs* – from death to life	vv. 4–9
(2)	*Song by the Sea* – 'Israel journeyed and encamped' – 'Then Israel sang this song' – 'from wilderness to land'	vv. 10–20
(3)	*Victories and Possession of Land* – 'struck him down with edge of the sword' – 'sent to spy out' – 'Do not fear . . . into your hand I have given' – 'they possessed his land' – conquest and possession of Heshbon and surrounding lands of Sihon – conquest and possession of Bashan and lands of Og (the giant)	vv. 21–35

With God's people journeying ever closer to the land, chapters 21–25 are marked by Israel's encounters with the surrounding peoples – Edomites, Canaanites, Amorites, Moabites and Midianites – underscoring YHWH's faithful preservation of his people among the hostility of the nations (cf. Frevel 2009: 121), and serving as a preview of the continual threats and temptations Israel will face once in the land. After the sea crossing, Moses had led Israel to sing:

> Now the chiefs of Edom will be dismayed;
> the mighty rulers of Moab, trembling will take hold of them;
> all the inhabitants of Canaan will melt away.
> Terror and dread will fall upon them,
> by the greatness of your arm they will be still as a stone,

until your people cross over, O YHWH,
until your people cross over, whom you have purchased. (Exod. 15:15–16)

Now Israel begins to experience the fulfilment of those prophetic lines. In an eightfold manner, Israel's progress is tracked with particular reference to Moab: 'that faced Moab' (v. 11), 'border of Moab', 'between Moab and the Amorite' (v. 13), 'border of Moab' (v. 15), 'the field of Moab' (v. 20), 'the former king of Moab' (v. 26), 'Devouring Ar of Moab' (v. 28) and 'Woe to you, Moab!' (v. 29). The movement traces Israel's ever-increasing threat, from Moab's perspective, beginning with Israel's encampment 'that faced Moab' and ending with the dire warning 'Woe to you, Moab!' (vv. 11, 29). Although Israel was scrupulous to avoid Moab's borders, and we learn from Deuteronomy that YHWH had forbidden Moab's lands to Israel, commanding his people not to do battle with them (Deut. 2:9), Numbers 22 opens with Israel 'encamped' on the plains of Moab, causing the people of Moab great fear and distress (22:1–3). Aside from the other emphases of Numbers 21, then, the chapter functions to set up Moab's response to Israel's progress and nearness, yielding three chapters narrated largely from Moab's perspective.

The bronze serpent episode is known especially by the use Jesus made of it in John's Gospel, saying, 'Just as Moses lifted up the serpent in the wilderness, so the Son of Man must be lifted up, that everyone who trusts in him may have eternal life,' God's giving his only Son out of love for the world (John 3:14–16). Isaiah employs multiple uses of 'ensign' or 'standard' (*nēs*), often with verbs for 'lifting up' (*nāśā'*; see 5:26; 11:12; 13:2; 18:3; cf. 30:17) or 'exalting' (*rûm*, see 49:22; 62:10), and speaks of the Messiah as an 'ensign' (11:10) and as being 'exalted' and 'lifted up' very high (52:13, using *nāśā'* and *rûm*). These lines come together in John's Gospel, where 'lifted up' often has the sense of exalted, referring to Jesus' glory, not only as culminating with his resurrection and ascension but beginning with his crucifixion: 'And I, when I am lifted up from the earth, will draw all peoples to myself' (12:32). A Man of Sorrows, he who knew no sin was made to 'be sin' for us (2 Cor. 5:21), becoming our sacrifice (Rom. 8:3) and condemned for our law-breaking (Gal. 4:4–5), that we who lift our eyes to him in faith may live. Augustine explained the uplifted bronze serpent as a symbol of death, since death came through the means of the serpent in Eden, but which savingly signified the death of Jesus Christ, who endured the penalty of his people's sin (see *On the Trinity* 3.9; *On the Forgiveness of Sins and Baptism* 1.61; *On the Psalms 118*, Sermon 26.4; 'On the Lord's Appearance to Moses in the Burning Bush', in *Sermons on the Old Testament* 6.7; cf. Ullmann 1995: 179–181; Turnage 2008). Just as God, out of his infinite love, sent his Son for the eternal healing of the world, so he provided the remedy for Israel's serpent-bites out of love for them. What the Zohar says regarding the bronze serpent applies to the crucified Messiah: 'As soon as he (the victim) turns his eyes and sees the likeness of the serpent, he forthwith becomes filled with awe and prays to the Lord, knowing that this was the punishment that he deserved' (*Shelaḥ*, 175; quoted in Leibowitz 1982: 264). Significantly, this last of the complaint narratives concludes with the theme of YHWH as healer, which was highlighted in the first complaint narrative, where God had avowed that if Israel would give heed to his commands, he would not put on them the diseases he had brought upon the Egyptians, 'for I, even I, am YHWH your healer' (Exod. 15:26; similarly, Birkan 2005: 75).

As with the prologue (vv. 1–3), the chapter ends with Israel's victory over hostile nations who strive to halt Israel's inheritance of the land promised to the patriarchs. As stressed throughout the stories, Israel triumphs by the sovereign leadership of YHWH (cf. Pressler 2017: 188). In Joshua, in a section that summarizes the conquest of kings before recounting the distribution of land to the twelve tribes (11:16 – 12:23), there is a portion that recounts the kings and lands conquered 'on the other side of the Jordan' by Moses the servant of YHWH, who had given those lands as a possession to the Reubenites, Gadites and half the tribe of Manasseh (12:1–6; see also 13:8–33). Recounting the events of Numbers 21 at this place in Joshua promotes reading these victories under Moses as foretastes of the conquest under Joshua. While forbidden to enter the land (i.e. cross the Jordan), Moses was nevertheless enabled to experience a taste of the realization of the patriarchal promises, a gracious honour bestowed on him by YHWH. Numbers 21 as a whole, especially the three poems within it, underscore the themes of life-giving water, Israel's exalted leadership and Israel's military prowess, elements that will 'form the crux of Balaam's final blessing' (Twersky 2022: 33), making the chapter a fitting prelude to the Balaam narrative.

NUMBERS 22 – 24: YHWH CONFIRMS ISRAEL'S ELECTION AND VOCATION WITH BOUNTIFUL BLESSING

Translation

22:1 And the sons of Israel journeyed and they encamped in the plains of Moab, across the Jordan at Jericho.
²Now Balak the son of Zippor saw all that Israel had done to the Amorites. ³And Moab dreaded greatly the presence of the people for they were many, and Moab loathed the presence of the sons of Israel. ⁴And Moab said to the elders of Midian, 'Now the assembly will lick up all around us just like an ox licks

up the grass of the field,' and Balak son of Zippor was king of Moab at that time. ⁵And he sent messengers to Balaam son of Beor at Pethor, which was by the River, the land of the sons of his people to call him, saying, 'Look! A people has come forth from Egypt. Look! They cover the eye of the land, and they are dwelling over against me. ⁶So now, please, come curse this people for me for they are mightier than I – perhaps I will (then) be able to strike them down and drive them out from the land, for I know that whom you bless will be blessed and whom you curse will be cursed.'

⁷And the elders of Moab and the elders of Midian went with divinations in their hand, and they came to Balaam and spoke to him the words of Balak. ⁸And he said to them, 'Lodge here tonight and I will return you word just as YHWH speaks to me,' so the princes of Moab stayed with Balaam. ⁹And God came to Balaam, and he said, 'Who are these men with you?' ¹⁰And Balaam said to God, 'Balak son of Zippor king of Moab sent them to me: ¹¹Look! The people has come forth from Egypt, and they have covered the eye of the land. Now come, condemn him for me – perhaps I will be able to battle against him and drive him out.' ¹²And God said to Balaam, 'You will not go with them; you will not curse the people, for they are blessed.' ¹³And Balaam arose in the morning and he said to the princes of Balak, 'Go to your land, for YHWH refused to give me leave to go with you.' ¹⁴And the princes of Moab arose and came to Balak, and said, 'Balaam refused to go with us.'

¹⁵And yet again Balak sent princes many more and more honoured than these. ¹⁶And they came to Balaam, and said to him, 'Just so Balak son of Zippor says, "Let nothing, please, hinder you from coming to me, ¹⁷for I will surely honour you greatly, and all that you say to me I will do, so come, please, condemn this people for me."' ¹⁸And Balaam answered and said to the servants of Balak, 'If Balak gave me the fullness of his house, silver and gold, I would not be able to pass beyond the mouth of YHWH my God to do (anything) small or great. ¹⁹Now you also, please, stay this night, so I may know what more YHWH will speak to me.' ²⁰And God came to Balaam at night, and said to him, 'If the men come to call you to go, arise, go with them – but only the word which I will speak to you, that is what you will do.'

²¹And Balaam arose in the morning, and saddled his donkey, and went with the princes of Moab. ²²And the fierce anger of God was kindled because he was going, and the angel of YHWH stationed himself on the way to be an adversary against him. Now he was riding on his donkey and two of his servant lads were with him. ²³And the donkey saw the angel of YHWH stationed on the way, and his sword drawn in his hand, and the donkey turned away from the way and went into the field, and Balaam struck the donkey to turn her onto the way. ²⁴And the angel of YHWH stood in the furrow through the vineyards, a barrier on this side and a barrier on that side. ²⁵And the donkey saw the angel of YHWH and pressed toward the wall, and Balaam's foot pressed into the wall, and he struck her again. ²⁶And again the angel of YHWH passed over and stood in a narrow place where there was no way to turn aside to the right or left. ²⁷And the donkey saw the angel of YHWH, and she lay down under

Balaam, and the fierce anger of Balaam was kindled, and he struck the donkey with his rod. ²⁸And YHWH opened the mouth of the donkey, and she said to Balaam, 'What have I done to you that you have struck me these three times?' ²⁹And Balaam said to the donkey, 'Because you have taunted me – if only there were a sword in my hand, for I would slay you now!' ³⁰And the donkey said to Balaam, 'I, am I not your donkey on which you have ridden for so long till this day? Was it ever my habit to do so to you?' And he said, 'No.' ³¹And YHWH uncovered the eyes of Balaam, and he saw the angel of YHWH stationed on the way, and his sword in his hand, and he bowed and prostrated himself, to his brow. ³²And the angel of YHWH said to him, 'Why have you struck your donkey these three times? Look! I myself came forth as an adversary – indeed, the way hastened in front of me. ³³The donkey saw me and turned aside from my face these three times. If she had not turned aside from my face, then surely you I would have slain and her I would have left alive.' ³⁴And Balaam said to the angel of YHWH, 'I have sinned for I did not know that you were stationed to encounter me on the way, and now if it is evil in your eyes let me return.' ³⁵And the angel of YHWH said to Balaam, 'Go with the men, but only the word which I will speak to you, that is what you will speak.' And Balaam went with the princes of Balak.

³⁶And Balak heard that Balaam had come, and he went forth to encounter him, to the city of Moab which was on the border of Arnon, which was on the outskirts of the border. ³⁷And Balak said to Balaam, 'Did I not surely send for you to call for you – why did you not come to me? Truly, am I not able to honour you?' ³⁸And Balaam said to Balak, 'Look! I came to you. Now am I even able to speak anything? The word that God puts in my mouth, that is what I will speak.' ³⁹And Balaam went with Balak, and they came to Kiriath-Huzoth (Village of Courts). ⁴⁰And Balak sacrificed cattle and sheep, and he sent for Balaam and for the princes that were with him.

⁴¹And it came to pass in the morning, Balak took Balaam and they ascended the Heights of Baal, and from there he saw the outskirts of the people.

²³:¹And Balaam said to Balak, 'Build for me here seven altars, and prepare for me here seven bulls and seven rams.' ²And Balak did just as Balaam had spoken, and Balak with Balaam offered up a bull and a ram on each altar. ³And Balaam said to Balak, 'Station yourself by your whole burnt offering, and I will go; perhaps YHWH will meet to encounter me, and whatever word he will have me see I will report to you.' And he went to a bare height. ⁴And God met Balaam, and he said to him, 'Seven altars I have arranged, and have offered up a bull and a ram on each altar.' ⁵And YHWH put a word in the mouth of Balaam, and he said, 'Return to Balak, and just so you will speak.' ⁶And he returned to him, and look! He was stationed by his whole burnt offering, he and all the princes of Moab. ⁷And he took up his parable, and said:

> From Aram Balak has led me,
> The king of Moab from the mountains of the east:

Go, curse for me Jacob,
And go doom Israel!
⁸How shall I condemn whom El has not condemned?
Or how shall I doom whom YHWH has not doomed?
⁹For from the summit of rocky-crags I see him,
and from the hills I behold him
Look! A people dwelling alone,
And not reckoned among the nations.
¹⁰Who has counted the dust of Jacob?
Or numbered a fourth of Israel?
May my soul die the death of the upright,
And may my latter end be like his!

¹¹And Balak said to Balaam, 'What are you doing to me? It was to condemn my enemies that I took you, and, look, you have surely blessed them!' ¹²And he answered and said, 'Is it not what YHWH puts in my mouth, that I must keep to speak?' ¹³And Balak said to him, 'Go, please, with me to another place; from there you will see him – only his outskirts you will see; all of him you will not see – and curse him for me from there.' ¹⁴And he took him to the field of Zophim to the summit of Pisgah, and he built seven altars and offered up a bull and a ram on each altar. ¹⁵And he said to Balak, 'Station yourself here by your whole burnt offering, and I myself will seek-to-meet there.' ¹⁶And YHWH met Balaam, and he put a word in his mouth, and said, 'Return to Balak, and just so you will speak.' ¹⁷And he came to him, and, look, he was stationed by his whole burnt offering, and the princes of Moab with him. And Balak said to him, 'What has YHWH spoken?' ¹⁸And he took up his parable, and said:

Arise, Balak, and hear,
Give ear unto me, O son of Zippor!
¹⁹No man is El so as to lie,
Nor a son of a human so as to relent.
He himself has said, and will he not do,
Or has he spoken, and will he not fulfil?
²⁰Look! To bless I was taken,
He has blessed and I cannot revoke it.
²¹He has not observed iniquity in Jacob,
Nor has he seen trouble in Israel.
YHWH his God is with him,
The trumpet blast of a King is among them.
²²El brought them forth from Egypt,
He has the horn-strength of a wild ox.
²³For there is no enchantment against Jacob,
Nor divination against Israel;
At once it must be said to Jacob,

And to Israel, what El will do!
²⁴Look! A people like a king of beasts arises,
And like a lion lifts himself up.
He will not lie down until he devours the prey,
And drinks the blood of the slain!

²⁵And Balak said to Balaam, 'Neither condemn him at all, nor bless him at all!' ²⁶But Balaam answered and said to Balak, 'Is this not what I spoke to you, saying all that which YHWH speaks that I will do?'

²⁷And Balak said Balaam, 'Go, please; let me take you to another place; perhaps it will be right in the eyes of God, and you will condemn him for me from there.' ²⁸And Balak took Balaam to the summit of Peor, which looks out on the face of the wasteland. ²⁹And Balaam said to Balak, 'Build for me here seven altars, and prepare for me here seven bulls and seven rams.' ³⁰And Balak did just as Balaam had said, and he offered up a bull and a ram on each altar.

²⁴:¹When Balaam saw that it was good in the eyes of YHWH to bless Israel, he did not go as at other times to encounter by enchantments, but he set his face to the wilderness. ²And Balaam lifted up his eyes, and he saw Israel dwelling by his tribes, and it happened that the Spirit of God came upon him. ³And he took up his parable and said:

Oracle of Balaam son of Beor,
And oracle of the man whose eye is opened.
⁴Oracle of the one hearing the words of El,
Who envisioned a vision of Shaddai,
The one falling and his eyes uncovered:
⁵How goodly are your tents, O Jacob,
Your dwelling places, O Israel!
⁶Like palm groves they stretch forth,
Like gardens by the riverside,
Like aloes planted by YHWH,
Like cedars by the waterside.
⁷He will pour out waters from his buckets,
And his seed in many waters.
May his king be exalted above Agag,
And his kingdom lifted up!
⁸El brought him forth from Egypt,
He has the horn-strength of a wild ox,
He will devour the nations of his enemies,
And their bones he will crush,
And his arrows will shatter them!
⁹He crouched, he lay down as a lion,
And as a king of beasts, who will rouse him?
Who blesses you is blessed,
And who curses you is cursed!

¹⁰And the fierce anger of Balak was kindled against Balaam, and he struck his hands together, and Balak said to Balaam, 'To condemn my enemies I called you and, look, you have thoroughly blessed them these three times! ¹¹Now, flee for yourself to your place! I had said I would honour you greatly but, look, YHWH has withheld from you honour!' ¹²And Balaam said to Balak, 'Did I not speak to your messengers that you had sent to me, saying, ¹³"If Balak gives me the fullness of his house, silver and gold, I will not be able to pass over the mouth of YHWH to do good or evil from my own heart, since what YHWH speaks that is what I will speak? ¹⁴Now, look, I am going to my people. Go, I will guide you as to what this people will do to your people at the end of days."' ¹⁵And he took up his parable, and said:

Oracle of Balaam son of Beor,
And oracle of the man whose eye is opened.
¹⁶Oracle of the one hearing the words of El,
And who knows the knowledge of Elyon,
Who envisioned a vision of Shaddai,
The one falling and his eyes uncovered.
¹⁷I see him but not now,
I behold him, but not nearby.
A star treks forth from Jacob,
A scepter rises from Israel,
He will shatter the brow of Moab,
And pate of the sons of Sheth.
¹⁸And Edom will be dispossessed,
And Seir will be dispossessed by his enemies,
But Israel will do valiantly.
¹⁹And from Jacob he will exercise dominion,
And he will destroy survivors from the city.

²⁰And he saw Amalek, and he took up his parable and said:

The first of the nations was Amalek,
But his last end unto destruction!

²¹And he saw the Kenites, and took up his parable and said:

Firm is your dwelling place,
Set upon a crag your nest.
²²But Cain will be burned up,
How long until Ashur takes you captive?

²³And he took up his parable and said:

Alas, who will live when El sets to it?
²⁴And ships from the shore of Kittim,

They will afflict Ashur and afflict Eber,
And he also unto destruction!

²⁵And Balaam arose and went and returned to his place, and Balak also went his way.

Notes on the text

22:4. 'the assembly': SamP, LXX, Syr and Vg read with a demonstrative 'this assembly'.
5. 'the River': LXX and Vg have 'river of the land'.
'sons of his people': with LXX and Tgs; however, SamP, Syr and Vg read 'Ammon' (cf. Lust 1978), which works well as a counterpart to Moab and may be preferred; some translations render 'land of Amaw' (NAB, NRSV, TEV, NET, ESV) or Amavites (NEB) based on a fifteenth-century BC inscription from Alalakh that refers to the territory of Amau, between Aleppo and Carchemish. Another possibility is *Āmu* in northern Mesopotamia (see Yahuda 1945).
6. 'for me': LXX has pl. 'for us'.
10. Although MT and SamP lack 'saying', it is attested in LXX, Syr and Vg.
11. 'the people': SamP, LXX, Tg have 'a people' (cf. v. 5).
13. 'to your land': LXX reads 'to your lord'.
'YHWH': LXX has 'God', but MT is supported by SamP, Syr and Vg.
18. 'servants of Balak': LXX reads 'princes of Balak'.
20. 'God': SamP reads 'angel of God'.
22. 'of God': SamP and some Gk witnesses have 'YHWH'.
32. 'an adversary': SamP adds 'against you'.
'hastened': *yāraṭ* occurs only here and possibly in Job 16:11 and appears to mean 'to precipitate'; LXX has 'not beautiful/seemly' (*ouk asteia*); SamP has *hāra'* ('evil', adj.) while 4QNumᵇ list has *rā'āh* ('evil', noun).
'the way': SamP, LXX have 'your way'.
39. 'they came': SamP, Syr, Tg read 'and he led him' (hiph.).
23:2. 'offered up': the verb is sg., and LXX lacks 'Balak and Balaam' (my 'with' tr. preserves a sg. subject).
'each altar' (23:2, 4, 14, 30): a contextual translation of Hebr. 'on the altar'.
3. 'offering': SamP and Syr read pl. here (harmonizing with v. 1), LXX maintains sg.
'YHWH': SamP and LXX read 'God', but MT is preferred.
4. 'God': LXX has 'the angel of God'.
'met': SamP has 'found' (*māṣā'*).
5. 'YHWH': LXX has 'God', and SamP reads 'the angel of God'.

6. 'offering': LXX and Syr have this in pl.; LXX ends the verse with 'and the Spirit of God came upon him'.
10. 'Or numbered': *ûmispār* likely abbreviates 'Who has numbered' (see G. R. Driver 1960; Ginsburg 1966: 168).
'fourth' (*rōba'*); see Levine (2000: 176). LXX reads 'people' (*dēmous*); for 'dust-cloud', see Albright (1944: 213).
12. 'YHWH': LXX reads 'God'.
15. 'he': SamP and LXX read 'Balaam'.
'offering': SamP and LXX have this in pl.
'seek-to-meet': LXX reads 'enquire of God'; perhaps a clarifying gloss.
16. 'YHWH': LXX reads 'God'.
17. 'came': LXX and Vg read 'returned'.
'offering': SamP and Syr have this in pl.
20. 'I was taken': following vocalization of LXX, Syr and Vg.
'He has blessed': SamP and LXX read 'I have/will bless(ed)'.
26. 'YHWH': SamP, LXX and Vg read 'God'.
24:3. 'whose eye is opened': LXX reads 'who sees truly'.
4. 'Oracle of the one hearing the words of El': this clause is absent from SamP.
'vision of Shaddai': LXX has 'vision of God in sleep'.
7. LXX has a messianic reading: 'There shall come a man out of his seed, and he shall rule over many nations.'
'Agag': SamP, LXX, VetLat, Aq and Sym read 'Gog'.
8. 'brought him forth': SamP and LXX read 'guide'.
13. 'what YHWH speaks': LXX has 'God'.
14. 'my people': LXX reads 'to my place', and Syr has 'to my country'.
17. 'I see him': LXX has 'I will show him' as hiph.
'I behold him': LXX reads 'I bless him.'
'a scepter': LXX has 'a man', Syr 'a prince' and *TgO* 'an anointed one' – messianic interpretations.
'pate': following SamP, emending *wĕqarqar* (devastate) to *wĕqodqōd* (cf. the important parallel in Jer. 48:45) for a reading in parallel with 'brow' in the previous line (cf. e.g. Budd 1984: 253, 256; Brown et al. 2003: 903).
'Sheth': may derive from the root for 'tumult', reading 'sons of tumult'.
19. 'city': this may be the proper noun 'Ar'.
22. 'But Cain will be burned up': LXX reads 'and though Beor should have a skilfully contrived hiding place'.
23. While LXX reads 'Og' here, MT, SamP and Vg do not supply to whom the oracle is addressed.
'Alas, who . . .': Because the question (apparently) lacks a parallel line, some suggest a line has dropped out (de Vaulx 1972: 296).
24. 'ships': SamP and LXX read here the verb 'to go forth' (*yāṣā'*, *exeleusetai*).
'shore': literally 'hand'.
'Eber': LXX, Syr and Vg understand 'the Hebrews'.

Form and structure

The Balaam narrative, or 'Chronicle of Balaam' (Cox 1884), is considered by some scholars to be the apex of Numbers from a literary and theological perspective (especially the oracles; see e.g. Sturdy 1976: 158). The story revolves around the interplay of blessing and curse upon Israel (cf. Coats 1973: 23; Ward 2009: 53–56), as seen in the inclusio made by 22:6, Balak's original plea to Balaam, and 24:9, 10, Balaam's third blessing of Israel and Balak's reaction. (See Table 3.)

Table 3: Balaam story: blessing versus curse inclusio

Numbers 22:6	Numbers 24:9–10
So now, please, come **curse** this people for me for they are mightier than I – perhaps I will (then) be able to strike them down and drive them out from the land, for I know that whom you **bless** will be **blessed** and whom you **curse** will be **cursed**.	He crouched, he lay down as a lion, And as a king of beasts, who will rouse him? Who **blesses** you is **blessed**, And who **curses** you is **cursed**.
	And the fierce anger of Balak was kindled against Balaam, and he struck his hands together, and Balak said to Balaam, To **condemn** my enemies I called you, and, look, you have thoroughly **blessed** them these three times!

The climactic third prophetic utterance of Balaam ends with an ironic allusion to Balak's call, reversing his intended goal. An initial sense of closure is established with Balak's rehearsal ('To condemn my enemies I called you, and, look, you have thoroughly blessed them these three times!', v. 10) and with his summary dismissal of Balaam ('Now, flee for yourself to your place!', v. 11). As rooted in YHWH's promise to Abram 'I will bless those who bless you, and curse him who dishonours you; and in you all the families of the earth will be blessed' (Gen. 12:3), the question of whether Balaam will be able to curse God's people probes the very status and character of the covenant community, as well as the character of YHWH and the veracity of his word – can he be manipulated to turn his face of blessing away from Abraham's seed? More deeply, will God's plan of redemption, the divine agenda to bless the nations through Abraham's seed, be thwarted (Gen. 12:3; 22:18)?

As Alter observes (1981: 105), there is a 'curse–blessing opposition' that runs throughout the narrative: Balak calls for Balaam naively believing that 'whom you bless is blessed and whom you curse will be cursed' (22:6), an error refuted almost immediately by God, who instructs

Balaam, 'you will not curse the people, for they are blessed' (22:12), and proclaimed in Balaam's first utterance 'How shall I condemn whom God has not condemned?' (23:8), only to be repeated in the climactic third prophetic utterance, resonating with the original promise to Abraham 'Who blesses you is blessed, and who curses you is cursed!' (24:9; cf. Gen. 12:3). As YHWH lifts his face upon his people during Aaron's priesthood (6:22–27), blessedness is central to the nature of the Camp. The root 'to bless' (*bārāk*) occurs fourteen times in the Balaam narrative (Num. 22:6, 12; 23:11, 20, 25; 24:1, 9–10); the only other place where it is used is in the priestly blessing, three times (Num. 6:23, 24, 27), bringing these two texts into close relationship – with Balaam's threefold blessing likely forming an allusion to the former (cf. 24:10). Can sorcery and divination negate the upheld palms of the high priest? Through the very one hired to curse his people, YHWH will further establish their blessedness, and reveal greater splendours concerning the nature of his covenant community, Israel. The two roots for 'to curse' occur seventeen times: 'condemn' (*qābab*) ten times (Num. 22:11, 17; 23:8, 11, 13, 25, 27; 24:10) and 'curse' (*'arar*) seven times (Num. 22:6, 12; 23:7; 24:9); the only other use of either root in Numbers is *q-b-b* with reference to the 'tent-chamber' (*qubbāh*) where the Israelite man and Midianite woman enter brazenly, perhaps signifying that, despite YHWH's faithfulness, Israel would incur her covenantal curse by straying from him (cf. Lev. 26:14–39; Deut. 28:15–68).

'Seeing' (*rā'āh*), arguably the opening word of the Balaam story (22:2), forms a key word and, along with synonyms (and 'eyes', 22:5, 11, 31, 34; 23:27; 24:1, 2, 3, 4, 15, 16), is a key motif throughout the story (Alter 1981: 105; cf. Moyer 2009: 307–313; Ward 2009: 49–53). The plot begins when Balak 'saw' all that Israel had done to the Amorites (22:2), develops as Balaam's donkey 'saw' the angel of YHWH three times (22:23, 25, 27; cf. 22:33), ironically unseen by Balaam the supposed seer until YHWH opened his eyes and he 'saw' (22:31), continues as Balak brings Balaam to high places in order for him to 'see' the people and curse them (22:41; 23:13), and culminates with Balaam's visions, shown him by God, which include 'seeing' other nations and their future destruction (24:20, 21), but emphasize his 'seeing' Israel's blessedness (23:9; 24:2), that God has not 'seen' trouble in Israel (23:21); finally, when he 'saw' that it pleased YHWH to bless Israel (24:1), Balaam lifted his eyes and 'saw' the spiritual glory of the encampment as paradise (24:1–9).

These chapters also display a prominent use of questions that unifies the story's scenes, including the donkey episode, across its varied genres, including proverbs (22:9, 28, 30, 32, 37, 38; 23:10, 11, 12, 17, 19, 26; 24:9, 13, 22, 23). God, in a manner that hearkens back to the early Eden narratives of Genesis (Gen. 3:9, 11, 13; 4:6, 9, 10), comes to Balaam and asks, 'Who are these men with you?' (22:9). The she-ass turns to Balaam, with mouth opened by YHWH, to ask, 'What have I done to you that you have struck me these three times? . . . Am I not your donkey on which you have ridden till this day? Was it ever my habit to do so to you?' (22:28, 30); and the angel of YHWH also prods him, 'Why have you struck your donkey these three times?' (22:32). Upon arriving at Moab, Balaam is accosted by Balak's asking, 'What took you so long? Am I not able to honour you?' (22:37), to whom Balaam responds, 'Am I able to speak anything?' (22:38). Then, amid Balaam's prophetic utterances, we hear questions such as 'Who has counted the dust of Jacob, or numbered a fourth of Israel?' (23:10) and YHWH 'has spoken, and will he not fulfil?' (23:19; cf. 24:9, 21), along with Balak's increasingly frustrated replies 'What are you doing to me?' (23:11) and Balaam's standard excuse 'Did I not tell you I must speak what YHWH speaks?' (23:25; 24:13). The final question, uttered in the last and seventh proverb, has a ring of culmination: 'Alas, who will live when El sets to it?' (24:23).

Following G. J. Wenham's analysis, the use of threefold repetition is the clearest structural device in the narrative (1981b: 185): Balaam has three initial encounters with God before meeting up with Balak (22:9–12, 20, 31–35); the donkey attempts to avoid the angel of YHWH three times (22:23, 25, 27); Balaam beats his donkey three times (22:23, 25, 27), with 'three times' mentioned three times in the narrative (22:28, 32, 33); Balaam arranges three sets of sacrifices before each of his three attempts to curse Israel (23:1, 14, 29), and encounters God three times before pronouncing blessing on Israel (23:4, 16; 24:2). The drama thus falls into two cycles of three-scene acts, which can be outlined as in Table 4.

Table 4: YHWH overrules Balak's attempt to curse Israel through Balaam, and blesses his people

Act 1	Balaam called by Balak to curse Israel	22:1–35	Act 2	Balaam constrained by YHWH to bless Israel	22:36 – 24:25
Setting	Balak dreads Israel	22:1–6	Setting	Balak meets with Balaam	22:36–40
Scene 1	Balaam's first call	22:7–14	Scene 4	Balaam's first parable	22:41 – 23:12
Scene 2	Balaam's second call	22:15–20	Scene 5	Balaam's second parable	23:13–26
Scene 3	Balaam goes to Moab (confronted by angel)	22:21–35	Scene 6	Balaam's third parable (plus further parables)	23:27 – 24:25

Several observations emerge from this literary scheme (G. J. Wenham 1981b: 185–186): in every scene there is an emphasis on Balaam's speaking only what YHWH permits him to say (22:12, 20, 35; 23:3, 12, 17, 26; 24:2, 13). The first and second scenes are in parallel with the fourth and fifth scenes, as Balaam seeks YHWH on his own initiative (22:8, 19; 23:3, 15), and the considerably longer third and sixth scenes are also in parallel, as God encounters Balaam unbidden (22:22; 24:1–2). The story also makes use of telescoping: scene 3 entails a threefold journey of Balaam and his donkey to Moab (22:21–23, 24–25, 26–27), leading to three mentions of 'three times' (22:28, 32, 33); and in scene 6, Balaam's third parable of blessing (23:27–24:9) leads into a fourth parable about Israel's future king, who would conquer Moab and Edom (24:10–19), which leads to three parables against other nations (24:20–24), before Balaam's departure (24:25). There is, then, incremental intensification across the two acts, the first flowering into a triplet and the second into a quadruplet (cf. I. Clark 1982: 143). Finally, Balaam's threefold journey in scene 3 parallels the three scenes of Act 2, with Balaam and the donkey being analogous to Balak and Balaam, respectively, paralleling the donkey's role with that of Balaam (cf. Licht 1986: 69–74).

Finally, Balaam's prophetic utterances, when taken as a whole, display a steadily mounting note of exaltation (cf. Sturdy 1976: 157–158), and may even be understood as progressing through the history of Israel. Moreover, the poetic oracles are, as Twersky points out, unified by their outer narrative frame, which shares common themes and language, and so should be interpreted within their literary context (2022: 148): all three attempts at cursing Israel (1) begin with offering seven bulls and rams (23:1–2, 14, 29); (2) are introduced by the phrase *wayyiśśā' měšālô* and feature Balaam's referencing himself (23:7, 18; 24:3); (3) contain a description of the high place from which Balaam gazes on Israel (Num. 22:41; 23:14, 28); (4) make use of the concept of 'seeing', using a rich variety of terms, as well as within the poems, such as *rā'ô*, 'to see' (22:41; 23:3, 9, 13, 21; 24:1, 2, 17, 20), *šûr*, 'to behold, regard' (23:9), *ṣāpâ*, 'to look out' (23:14), *nābaṭ*, 'to look' (23:21), *šāqap*, 'look down' (23:28), *maḥăzê*, 'vision' (24:4), along with *gĕlûy 'ênāyim* (24:4) and *šĕtum hā'āyin* (24:3, 15) for 'open-eyed'.

While older critical scholarship assigned the Balaam narrative to the J and E sources, albeit with disagreement over precise divisions (G. B. Gray 1903: 309–310; Gross 1974; for an early critique, see Seraphim 1900), Wellhausen declared that the redactor had so thoroughly combined sources that the narrative appears to derive 'completely from a single source' (*ganz aus einem Guss*; Wellhausen 1889: 11; see Bewer 1905a: 238–240; cf. Mowinckel 1930). Milgrom similarly remarks that the editor's fusion of sources is 'so thoroughgoing and skillful that the original seams are no longer visible' (1990: 468; cf. von Pakozdy 1958: 164; Levine 2000: 137–138; Friedman 2003: 280). Relatedly, the narrative's use of divine names, a loadstar of source criticism, defies typical source-critical categories (cf. Lohr 1927: 86–87; Albright 1944: 207–208) and presents a 'serious problem' for this approach to the narrative (Powell 1982: 14; cf. Grundke 1995: 54). As W. H. Green pointed out (1895: 96–98), use of divine names in the Balaam story may be appreciated as part of the author's literary strategy and theological purpose; for example, while Balaam repeatedly tells of his relationship with 'YHWH', the narrator, especially early on, will undercut this claim by using 'Elohim' for Balaam's encounters with God. Since the story indeed flows as a unity, and its perceived tensions exhibit rhetorical purpose (cf. e.g. Darnov 2007), I will exegete and interpret the text as it stands. 'Textual difficulties disregarded,' Moriarty observes (1968: 95), 'few sections in the Pentateuch are more important theologically than this remarkable narrative. In a real sense the Balaam story may be said to summarize the revelation of God's purpose as it was communicated to Moses.' So, too, Allen justly dubs the Balaam narrative 'one of the most eloquent expositions of Yahweh's deep and abiding relationship with his people Israel' (1981: 84).

Finally, although there are connections with other sections of Numbers and the rest of the Torah, the Balaam story is narrated from a perspective outside Israel's Camp and appears to be a self-contained unit (Margaliot 1977: 279), which leads to a question of its provenance. Early Jewish tradition asks how Moses obtained this information – not only was he not involved in the narrative action, but his name is not even mentioned throughout its three chapters, an exceedingly unusual phenomenon. The rabbis acknowledged the uniqueness of the Balaam narrative when asserting that Moses wrote 'his book' (the Torah) *and* 'the portion of Balaam' (*b. Bav. Bat.* 14b; *y. Sot.* 5). Hengstenberg suggested that, wanting the monetary satisfaction denied by Balak, Balaam visited Israel's encampment and reported all to Moses; but Moses, perceiving his base nature, dismissed him so that Balaam responded by approaching the Midianites with his proposal against Israel (1848: 512–513). Keil, on a slightly different approach, proposed that Balaam, in the hope of bargaining for his life during the defeat of the Midianites, reported his oracles either to Israel's general or to Phinehas (Keil and Delitzsch 1973: 3:203), and Cox, understanding 'they slew with the sword' (31:8) as judicial execution, suggested the details of the Balaam narrative came out during his trial (1884: 14–16). Aalders thought the victorious Israelites might have found a written copy of the oracles on Balaam's corpse (1949: 157), and Harrison adds the possibilities of Balaam's story deriving from one of his disciples or through Moabite sources (2004: 620, 630), while Allis included the option of a direct revelation of God to Moses (1972: 127). Given the details found within the Torah, Spero (2013: 197) suggests that Balaam shared his experience while consorting with the Midianites and then Phinehas the priest, who led the campaign against them (31:8), learned of the details and then shared them with Moses. What most of these scenarios have in common is the fact that both Balaam and the Israelites overlapped in their contact with the Midianites, leaving open a variety of reasonable possibilities, aside from the general observation that news of political events spread readily throughout the ANE (e.g. Josh. 2:8–13).

BALAAM: DEVOUT PROPHET OR DEVIOUS SORCERER?

One of the narrative's interpretative challenges is understanding Balaam's character (see e.g. Moore 1990: 1, 116; for a reception history of Balaam, within Judaism, Christianity and Islam, see Allen 1973: 27–54; and the collection of essays in van Kooten and van Ruiten 2008), one in whom apparently both 'pagan magician and Israelite prophet are combined' (Kaufmann 1960: 84). Was he a saintly Gentile prophet or an evil sorcerer? Balaam has been dubbed 'one of the most perplexing problem characters in all literature' (Butzer 1953: 247; quoted in Ward 2009: 195). The perceived dichotomy of his character is so great, one scholar asserted two separate figures completely: the first a 'righteous prophet' of YHWH who, after blessing Israel, returned home, and the second, 'a soothsayer or oracle-monger of the Midianites who hated Israel' and tempted God's people to worship Chemosh (Black 1930: 67). Source-critical scholars, assuming conflicting traditions through diverse stages of history, resist harmonizing as futile and, beyond exacerbating the challenge of Balaam's character, further complicate his origin as well. G. B. Gray, for example, split verse 22:5, arguing that 'Pethor, which was by the River' was E, with the E narrative strand presenting Balaam as an Aramean, while 'sons of his people', which he read as 'sons of Ammon', was J, with the J source presenting Balaam as an Ammonite (1903: 309–313).

Sals captures the multifaceted nature of Balaam's character, writing (2008: 315–316):

> Balaam is a foreign prophet although in some odd ways kin to Israel. Just like Israel's ancestors he comes from the Euphrates (Num. 22:5; Josh. 24:2), from Aram respectively (Num. 23:7; Deut. 26:5), just like Moses he climbs the Pisgah seeing Israel the people (Num. 23:14) where Moses sees Israel the land (Deut. 34:1).

And one could add that he refers to God by the designations familiar to Israel: El, Elyon, Shaddai and YHWH. Do Balaam's repeated assertions that he can speak only what YHWH speaks (22:18, 38; 23:3, 12, 26; 24:13) reveal his devotion to YHWH's word and will, or rather his utter impotence against them? Coats, for example, reads Balaam as one who 'does only what Yahweh tells him to do' (1973: 24), as 'a saint' and 'paragon of a distinctive virtue' (1982b: 54). If so, then why does God need to warn and remind Balaam only to speak his word (22:20, 35; 23:5, 16)? Some understand Balaam as a convert to Yahwism, who, by a desire for gain, abandoned YHWH to scheme against Israel (e.g. Albright 1944; Kaiser 1996; on Balaam as a diviner of Asherah, see Lutzky 1999). Holding such a view, Margaliot describes Balaam as both prophet and mantic: originally he was a prophet of YHWH who, enticed by riches, chose to act as a mantic to curse Israel. Between Balak's offer of riches and honour and his prophetic duty before YHWH, writes Margaliot (1977: 283), the 'weakness of Balaam's character at once reveals itself: his inability to make a clear decision for the one or the other; by his artful procrastination, a continuous dramatic suspension is created'. Balaam's 'waverings, his thoughts and second thoughts at every turn of this narrative can only be realized by close analysis of the text', Margaliot continues (1977: 284), justly assessing the narrative as containing 'the elements of a great human drama, the struggle of a man's soul torn between the greatness and responsibility of his prophetical call, and his avidity to obtain honour and material wealth – the latter finally overpowering the former'. Margaliot's reading is compelling, and he is right that the thoroughly negative views of Balaam's character by the ancients are more correct than those of modern scholars 'who try to save Balaam's honour as true prophet of Y[HWH] by doubtful exegetical means' (1977: 284 n. 23). Vuilleumier (1996) also understands Balaam's character as deviating from good to bad to worse as the narrative progresses. By the offer of riches, YHWH had put him, his prophet of wavering loyalty, to the test, which Balaam in the end fails – even after finally renouncing his repeated attempts to curse Israel and blessing them as a prophet (ch. 24), he reverts to being a mantic, promoting Canaanite religious practices (ch. 25) to obtain the riches and honour that had so far eluded him, and thus becoming an 'apostate prophet' (cf. Deut. 13:2–4; 18:18–20; 1 Kgs 22:1–28; Jer. 23:9–40; Ezek. 13) (Margaliot 1977: 281, 283; see also Margaliot 1990). The ancient reception of Balaam as thoroughly negative, however, may be still more correct than the suggestion of a moral struggle within him; that is, all of Balaam's vacillation may just as easily be understood as the struggle between his desire for gain and his dread of YHWH's threatened punishment. Since his own words are the only indication of his loyalty to YHWH, and there is reason to suspect duplicity, tracing a narrative arc whereby Balaam falls from grace and becomes apostate remains open to challenge.

Reading Balaam's character as marked by avarice is in line with the New Testament's view (cf. 2 Peter 2:15; Rev. 2:14), and with Jewish tradition. The ancient rabbis regularly dubbed him 'Balaam the wicked (*rāšāʿ*)', his disciples conforming to his 'evil eye, proud spirit, and unrestrained appetite' (*m. Av.* 5:19), so that he is 'the Wicked Man *par excellence*' (Vermes 1961b: 174). Shenk agrees the understanding of later biblical interpreters that greed was 'Balaam's damning motivation' makes sense (e.g. 2 Peter 2:15–16; Judg. 11), especially since it 'is only upon Balak's sending of a more important emissary with greater promises of honour and his implicit offer of great wealth that Balaam actually makes the trip' (1993: 34). Anisfeld (2013), following Rashi, points to a number of textual features as evidence that Balaam is avaricious and haughty, traits that alone explain why he undertook the mission to curse Israel, although it was doomed to failure from the start. Perceiving Balaam's wicked obduracy throughout the narrative removes any wonder from his ensuing complicity in Israel's apostasy (Num. 25; 31:16) once he is freed from the Spirit's control and the threat of God's angelic messenger (Shenk 1993: 46), and also accords with God's earlier fierce anger against him (22:22) and later destruction of him (31:8).

Exploring the donkey episode (22:22–35), a 'masterpiece of ancient Israelite narrative art' (Noth 1968: 178), forms an integral part of assessing Balaam's character. Yet its clear negative portrayal of Balaam is often negated since critical scholars widely consider the tale a late insertion (Kalisch 1877: 26, 49–57; Noth 1968: 171–172, 178; Coats 1973: 22; Sturdy 1976: 161–165; Rofé 1979: 54–57), ascribed either to J (Rouillard 1980: 239 suggests multiple J layers) or to an independent document not affiliated with any of the classic documentary sources (Frisch 2005: 104). Several features have led to dubbing the donkey episode 'an erratic block in the Pentateuch' (Daube 1973: 16), including: unique vocabulary (e.g. 'angel of YHWH' appears only here within chs. 22–24 – but see 20:16), a perceived contradiction with God's anger at Balaam's journey (22:22; versus 22:20), and use of resumptive repetition (cf. Rofé 1979: 55–57), where we are told at the end of verse 35 that Balaam 'went with the princes of Balak', picking up where verse 21 had left off ('went with the princes of Moab'). Most significantly, it is asserted that apart from the donkey episode, which clearly lampoons Balaam, shaming him as a charlatan, the rest of the narrative presents him positively as a true and even righteous seer devoted to YHWH (see e.g. Coats 1973; L. Schmidt 1979; Moore 1990). The donkey tale, it is claimed, serves 'to *introduce* a negative interpretation of the non-Israelite diviner' (Dozeman 1998: 183 emphasis mine; cf. Marcus 1995: 31–41; Levine 2000: 154–155). Likewise, Milgrom writes that the goal of the ass episode is 'doubtless the humiliation of Balaam', who is depicted 'on a level lower than his ass' and who is 'in reality a fool, a caricature of a seer, one outwitted even by his dumb beast' (1990: 469). The argument is often developed further by tracing biblical references to Balaam, constructing a chronology whereby Balaam's character, received positively at first (Mic. 6:5; Num. 22 – 24, *excluding* the donkey episode), becomes more and more negative until he is perceived only as an evil, money-grubbing sorcerer for hire – with Numbers 31:8–16 and Deuteronomy 23:4–5 as the latest traditions, built on previous references,

Joshua 13:22 and 24:9–10 and Nehemiah 13:2 (see e.g. Donner 1977: 113; Rouillard 1980: 483–485; Van Seters 1997; Robker 2013; 2019: 266). Vermes asserted that it was – 'almost entirely' – the priestly supplement (Num. 31) that 'completely altered' the otherwise 'blameless' character of Balaam as a 'tragic hero' (1961b: 175–176).

Without question, the donkey episode lampoons Balaam, undermining his reputation as a seer. Even more may be said, as the donkey episode seems also to include a host of sexual innuendos, with 'unmistakably disparaging sexual jibes' aimed at casting Balaam as 'a charlatan and a fundamentally polluted character', already singling him out as 'the chief architect of the Baal Peor affair', exposing him as 'an oracular prostitute (Num. 22:18; 24:13)' and ultimately foreshadowing his 'downfall after the Baal Peor episode' (Twersky 2022: 156). That the rest of the Balaam narrative presents him as blameless, however, is questionable, as is the notion that biblical references evolve chronologically from positive to negative portrayals, especially since each text may be read simply as a consistent interpretation of Numbers 22 – 24. The Micah 6:5 reference is quite terse and exalts YHWH rather than Balaam, providing no explicitly positive remark on the latter (cf. Isbell 2002: 90). Assuming the Balaam narrative of Numbers as a whole, Balaam's 'answer' in Micah would be understood naturally in line with Nehemiah's explanation that 'our God turned the curse into a blessing' as Balaam spoke (13:2). A sound argument may be made, rather, for a consistently negative portrayal of Balaam throughout Scripture, including explicit renderings of him as greedy for the wages of unrighteousness (2 Peter 2:15; cf. Jude 11; Rev. 2:14). Nevertheless, the fact that Balaam is the only foreign prophet in Scripture to utter true prophecy and blessing (cf. M. Douglas 1993: 412) has naturally led to divergent opinions of him throughout the narrative's reception history, both in Jewish and Christian traditions (see Seerveld 2001). And yet, the very ambivalence of his character is a telling feature against Balaam. The whole narrative offers subtle clues that Balaam is *not* a pious Gentile prophet, and closer inspection of his actions evoke suspicion (cf. Held 2017: 159). Later scriptural assessment that Balaam 'loved the wages of unrighteousness' (2 Peter 2:15–16) refers in the first place to the narrative of chapters 22–24, without resort to Numbers 31:8, 16. Cutting the story apart and asserting two divergent accounts is only to label the problem one has created. Alternatively, by assuming literary artistry in the final composition, one may appreciate its rhetorical devices, including use of hidden motives and delayed information.

As it stands, the Balaam narrative reads as a unity, with the ass episode forming an indispensable part of the larger story (see e.g. Sutcliffe 1937; I. Clark 1982; J. S. Ackerman 1987; Shenk 1993; Grundke 1995; Hepner 2011; Moyer 2012). Rightly, Moberly pointed out (1999: 14) the structural link between the ass episode and its context; namely, the pattern of three plus one, missed by modern interpreters because of their genetic presuppositions and approach. Building on the work of Licht, who discerned two tripartite patterns in Numbers 22 (1986: 69–74), Moyer argues further that this sequence offers a twofold prefiguration of Balaam's experience in Numbers 23 – 24 (2012: 170), as suggested in my outline. Licht further points out *seven* unifying statements related to Balaam's obligation to do or speak only what YHWH instructs him (22:18, 20, 35, 38; 23:12, 26; 24:13), the first and last forming an inclusion, and two of which are found in the donkey episode (1986: 73; cf. Moyer 2012: 170–172; Margaliot 1990). Moreover, the discrepancy in Balaam's character between the negative interlude of the donkey episode and the presumably positive presentation of Balaam in the rest of the narrative has been exaggerated (e.g. Rofé 1979: 53; Marcus 1995: 41) – it is certainly possible to interpret a consistent portrayal of Balaam's character, including the negative report in chapter 31 (see e.g. Stebbins 1885; Frisch 2005). M. Douglas (1993: 415), as one example, argues that 'from the story itself it is perfectly clear that the character of Balaam is unequivocally bad'. There are more than a few aspects of the narrative before the donkey episode that may be interpreted as signalling Balaam's devious traits (22:1–21). Sharp (2009: 134–151), sensitive to the dynamic of what is said and not said in the story, is not convinced the narratives outside the donkey tale lionize Balaam, and she points out literary evidence demonstrating that Balaam's voice is presented as unreliable, with significant disjuncture between his self-presentation and the truth of his words, and how at crucial moments there are textual ambiguities that undermine his character. Moreover, the two references to magic (a negative practice in Israel's perspective) in the narrative fall outside the donkey episode: 'divinations' (*qesem*, 22:7) and 'enchantments' (*nāḥaš*, 24:1) – asserting that these are later insertions (e.g. Rofé 2019) is manifestly circular.

The donkey episode, to be clear, functions as an interlude or intercalation, providing a key for understanding the entire narrative. Rather than assuming intercalations are the work of later editors or redactors, the insertion of interludes appears to be a standard literary technique, which might have been employed by the original author. Moyer points out 'numerous alliterative, keyword, repetitive, and structural patterns that run the length of the pericope, whose force would be deeply undermined by the removal of the jenny episode from the narrative as a whole' (2009: 492). We have already observed its use in Numbers 20, where the Edom episode (20:14–21) is inserted between the failure of Moses and Aaron (20:1–13) and Aaron's consequent death (20:22–29) – resumptive repetition is no less an author's art as it is an editor's (cf. Barré 1997: 260; Sharp 2009: 140). In the light of the whole story, the donkey episode serves several functions, the first of which, as widely acknowledged, is to expose Balaam's unscrupulous character more vividly as well as his impotence as a seer (and that of all pagan sorcerers), underscoring YHWH's exclusive sovereignty.

Second, narrative tension is created as Balaam, much like the donkey, finds himself between the proverbial rock and hard place, between two competing aims: the allure of wealth and fame from Balak for cursing Israel, and the continual threat of death from YHWH. The final encounter with the angel of YHWH underscores for Balaam that he is continually under the threat of death, even when he cannot see YHWH's messenger – a further inducement to speak only YHWH's words. The angelic encounter adds humour to Balaam's repeated insistence to Balak that he can speak only YHWH's words, since the audience, through the lens of the donkey episode, can glimpse his self-preserving motive (cf. I. Clark 1982: 139, 142).

Third, precisely because YHWH will bless his people richly through the mouth of an unscrupulous pagan seer, the donkey episode establishes the point that YHWH is sovereign over speech: he who is able to open the donkey's mouth can also proclaim his determined will through Balaam – Israel need not doubt the divine oracles uttered by this Mesopotamian diviner. The interlude with the donkey, then, has exegetical and interpretative significance: it 'points ahead to this outcome' (Barré 1997: 264). As Augustine wrote, 'If God can make an ass speak, he can certainly make an ungodly man submit to the spirit of prophecy for a short time' (*De diversis quaestionibus ad Simplicianum* 2 [PL 40, cols. 129–130], quoted in Cathcart 1998: 517). Indeed, the blessings are now received as all the more glorious inasmuch as they are uttered through the devices of an enemy intent on cursing Israel. Fourth, the donkey episode serves as a bridge into act 2, building narrative tension, and, significantly, much of its characteristic humour is also on display in act 2, with Balak's mounting, caricatured anger (23:11, 25; 24:10). Much as Balaam's frustration with the donkey in act 1, scene 3 was crafted to delight the audience at the protagonist's expense, so Balak's frustration with Balaam's oracles is aimed at the audience's amusement in act 2. Balaam's journey to Moab on his donkey, then, is integral to the whole story at a profound level. Even those who advocate a 'long and complex compositional history' for Numbers 22 – 24, still avow that 'in its present form, it is a truly exquisite specimen of Hebr. narrative prose, on par in both plot and character development with the Joseph story, Esther, Jonah, or Ruth' (E. Schwartz 2020). One may go further, with Margaliot (1977: 279 n. 2), who wrote that the Balaam narrative, including the parables, constitutes a literary unit, which was not compiled from various sources – the 'difficulties created by various divine names, and by the complexity of Balaam's character' may be explained without resorting to a source-critical theory.

Related to pious or devious portrayals of Balaam, does the story regard him as a prophet or sorcerer? Milgrom argued that the story's tension is created by two forms of magic, along with their conflicting expectations: Balak wants a sorcerer, one who can curse or bless, while Balaam only functions as a diviner, one who foretells events but cannot affect them (1990: 471–473; cf. Moore 1990: 113–116), an approach in line with his own saintly view of Balaam (apart from the ass episode). The tension, however, appears to be found between the expectations of Balak and God, especially as Balaam never relays God's original message that Israel is blessed and not to be cursed (22:12), nor does he deny his international reputation as one whose blessings and curses are effectual – this is the very basis for his summons, hiring and journey to Moab (22:6). Cole writes that 'Balaam had apparently achieved international fame for his ability to carry out such activity [of cursing and blessing]' (2000: 381, 366–367) – Balaam, in other words, is introduced in the story as one renowned for sorcery. In an important study of parallels between Balaam's characterization and Babylonian rituals for the *bārū* (a 'seer' frequently consulted by the king), Daiches suggests that there are more magical elements in the Balaam story than previously realized, showing that 'Balaam was a sorcerer plain and simple' (1909: 60; followed by Albright 1944; Largement 1964). As Orlinsky explains (1969: 250), 'Soothsayers, seers, miracle workers; that is, priests who divined by magic formula, who gave out oracular utterances, who professed expertness in transmitting the supernatural – were a definite social group in the ancient civilizations of the Near East,' and Balaam fits well within this context. Moore, in a comprehensive study (1990: 98–109), argues that Balaam is presented as both a seer and an exorcist. Like a *bārū* priest, Balaam may be thought of as 'a kind of military medicine man' (Seerveld 2001: 49).

Wiggershaus (2021), moreover, convincingly argues that, in the light of the ANE system of divination, not only can Balaam be identified soundly as a diviner, but many of the narrative's perceived inconsistencies may be explained, yielding a unified reading. The following conventions of ANE praxis may be detected in the Balaam cycle (Wiggershaus 2021: 24–69, 198): a single investigation can be carried out through multiple modes, by numerous practitioners (often in competition and holding conflicting interpretations), before a variety of deities, and on repeated occasions, features that marked divination as inherently complex and unreliable, as reflected in its capacity to influence the divine will, the uncertainty with which military leaders deferred to it, the scepticism of its patrons and the safeguards employed by its practitioners. While Balaam's speeches may be dubbed 'oracles' broadly (cf. Knierim and Coats 2005: 250–251), it is possible to be more specific, and in a way that unfolds the narrative movement of the story. Balaam is never called a prophet in Scripture – he is, rather, 'the diviner' (*haqqôsēm*, Josh. 13:22). But in one of the dramatic turns of the story, YHWH sovereignly grants prophetic utterance to Balaam by his Spirit (cf. 24:2). As Wiggershaus shows (see Table 5), Balaam's first two oracles (23:7–10, 18–24) fit the divination report genre, while the second set of oracles (24:3–9, 15–24) fits the prophetic report genre (2021: 131–158).

Table 5: Divination versus prophecy

	Divination Report Oracle	Prophetic Report Oracle
Perspective	A human perspective, whose interpretation of omens is recounted.	A divine perspective, with the speech forming literally the utterance of the deity, or a visionary description of deity's message.
Initiative	Result of an initial query by a diviner on behalf of a patron; a diviner, as an earthly representative offered sacrifices, asking the heavenly court to convene, and thus appealed for divine judgement.	Spontaneously initiated by deity, not necessarily the result of enquiry.
Audience	The enquirer or patron is identified as audience	Audience marked out by use of vocative, since message was unexpected or unsolicited; the deity's relationship to the audience is detailed
Results	Signs and portents analysed and interpreted by diviners, who sometimes conferred with one another	Divine utterances or visions
Message	The findings of the diviner, usually containing the original query	Often include a summation of past divine support, and a pledge of future help or judgement (i.e. predictive)
Cataloguing	Recorded according to the enquirer or patron	Recorded with the name of the prophet, often included in a superscription

Accordingly, the differences between the oracles of Numbers 23 and 24, long noted by scholars who usually assign them to E and J, respectively (see Noth 1968: 171; Tosato 1979: 98; Chavalas 2003: 76), may be explained by their different genres *as appropriate to the narrative movement*. The oracles of chapter 23, Wiggershaus observes (2021: 159–178), were initiated by sacrifices, as customary within ANE divination practice (23:1–4, 13–15), are clearly written from Balaam's (first person) perspective ('From Aram Balak led me,' 23:7), address Balak directly as the patron ('Get up, Balak, and listen!', 23:18), never supply God's speech, make no future prediction and read as a response to or result of his enquiry ('Behold, "Bless" I received,' 23:20) – with 23:8 being key: 'What may I curse? El has not cursed! How may I condemn? YHWH has not condemned!' The oracles of chapter 24, by contrast, no longer call for a curse, do not involve the seeking of omens, include superscriptions identifying the speaker and making references to prophecy and visions ('The utterance of Balaam son of Beor... who sees the vision of the Almighty,' 24:3, 15), are more oriented to the future (e.g. 'His king will be higher than Agag,' 24:7), use the vocative to grip the recipient ('How good are your tents, O Jacob! How good are your homes, O Israel!', 24:5) and no longer address Balak directly (Wiggershaus 2021: 178–191). Wondrously, YHWH uses a diviner, hired by Balak to curse his people, sovereignly denies him omens of curse (ch. 23) and then, beyond this, unexpectedly sends his Spirit to utter the most profound and glorious prophecies through him, assuring Israel's future blessedness (ch. 24). Understanding ANE conventions of divination, then, enables a unified, sensible and even dramatic reading of the Balaam cycle in its present form.

Perhaps most conclusively, Balaam's character is seen especially negatively when compared with the great fountainhead of prophets in the HB, Moses. The Midrash waxes eloquent on the differences, stating that God 'raised up Moses for Israel and Balaam for the idolaters', and pointing out how, while Moses and the prophets warned Israel against transgressions, Balaam schemed the apostasy at Peor, seeking 'to uproot a nation for no crime!' (*Num. Rab.* 20.1; Slotki 1951: 6:786–787). Margaliot even refers to Balaam as an 'anti-Moses', arguing that the Balaam narrative presents an antithesis between false prophecy and true, between a disloyal, treacherous, criminal and a prophet who is loyal to his God and to his mission – a comparison whereby the greatness of Moses' personality and the significance of his prophetic mission gain additional dimensions, allowing for a fuller appreciation of his monumental achievement (1977: 285, 289–290; for parallels between the Balaam narrative and Exod. 3, Num. 12 and Deut. 13, 18, see Ward 2009: 74–75). Elsewhere he writes that the 'comparison between Balaam and Moses almost forces itself upon the reader' (Margaliot 1990: 82). Another midrashic tradition, noted by Rashi, underscored the implied contrast between Balaam and Moses by filling gaps in the scriptural account: it was because Moab and the elders of Midian perceived that the power of Moses 'is nothing but his mouth' that they decided to come against them with someone, Balaam, whose power was also in his mouth (*Tan.* 3; *Num. Rab.* 20.4; Rashi 1997: 4:271). Nachmanides also zealously points out the differences between Moses' superior access to YHWH, available whenever Moses wanted, versus Balaam's experience, where the Spirit would come on him momentarily and never at any other time (1975: 275–277). Balaam's 'personality', writes Allen (1973: 233), 'serves as a foil to demonstrate the excellence of the character of Moses'. Although the name 'Moses' does not even appear in the Balaam narrative, he stands behind the text as 'the unseen opponent of the soothsayer and interpreter of omens' – indeed, by the happy blessings of Israel spoken 'from the mouth of the heathen, the unsouled *nabi*, YHWH confirms what has been founded by his true emissary' (Buber 1946: 171). Unlike Moses, and every other true prophet throughout Israel's history, 'Balaam is not sent; God makes use of him, but does not commission him' (Buber 1946: 170). Whereas Moses' highest level of magnificence and prophecy are attained in his dialogues with YHWH, pursuing the divine will for Israel's blessedness, Balaam, who acts consciously and continually contrary to YHWH's will, possessing no goodwill toward Israel, shares no meaningful dialogue with YHWH (Margaliot 1977: 286). Hawk similarly argues that incongruities in the story are narrative devices aimed at portraying Balaam as a prophetic anti-type in contrast to Moses. He notes that both figures try to change YHWH's mind (Hawk 2017: 80): 'Balaam does so through ritual manipulation and with the idea that YHWH can be induced to curse what YHWH has blessed,' whereas Moses 'directly appeals to YHWH for mercy in response to a divine decree of destruction'. While Balaam endeavours to persuade YHWH to veer from his intention to bless Israel, Moses, who 'knows YHWH to be a deity who is not capricious but rather is compassionate and gracious, slow to anger and full of love and faithfulness (Exod. 34:6)', intercedes to persuade YHWH to remain loyal to his own character and ultimate intention to bless his people (Hawk 2017: 88). Unlike Moses, who took not even a donkey from the Israelites (Num. 16:15), Balaam accepts and desires monetary benefits for pronouncing a divine word, a recurring indictment of false prophets who 'take money for their divination' (Mic. 3:11; cf. Jer. 14:14; Ezek. 13:6–9, 23; 22:28) (Margaliot 1977: 287). Moses, who could not be bribed with gifts, was not honoured by Israel, yet bore their burden and led them faithfully, serving continually as an *advocate* (*Fürsprecher*) of the people before YHWH (Goldberg 1970: 106). In the light of these considerations, the Balaam narrative may be read as Balak's attempt to confront Moses' spiritual leadership on the prophetic level with Balaam's sorcery in a struggle for YHWH's power, in order to bring divine destruction on the heads of the Israelites. Such a reading gains force within the context of the last section's conclusion (chs. 16–20), on Moses' failure (20:1–13), which perhaps called into question the efficacy of his ministry. While Balaam foolishly endeavours to change YHWH's unchanging nature and determined will through the manipulation of sacrifices and sorcery, Moses struggles with YHWH only in order to magnify his nature and fulfil his own word, through his unique face-to-face relationship with YHWH as Israel's chosen mediator. Yet, because of the stark contrast between Moses and Balaam, the story of Balaam underscores the ḥesed of YHWH in a more breathtaking way – it is YHWH's faithful loving-kindness on display. Whereas Moses' mediation is often the instrument that causes YHWH to turn from his fierce anger and to continue his merciful ways with his people, the present story brims with the tension of Moses' absence and, consequently, his inability to intercede;

worse still, the protagonist Balaam craves the riches and honour due him for cursing Israel: with no one to advocate on Israel's behalf, how will YHWH respond?

Comment

22:1–35 Act 1: Balaam called by Balak to curse Israel

22:1–6 Setting: Balak and Moab in dread of Israel

1. This marks the last journey and encampment of Israel before the conquest led by Joshua (see also 33:49–50), with 'the plains of Moab across from (or 'by') the Jordan at Jericho' being the setting for the remainder of Numbers, especially prominent as a unifying feature in the book's third major section, chapters 26–36 (26:3, 63; 31:12; 33:48, 49, 50; 34:15; 35:1; 36:13), as well as the setting for Moses' farewell exhortations in Deuteronomy (Deut. 1:1, 5; 34:8). Concluding the journey motif, this hinge verse also provides the context for the Balaam narrative and the rest of the Torah (cf. Cole 2000: 377). Numbers 22:1 thus anticipates the book's final section (chs. 26–36), which concludes with 'the plains of Moab across from the Jordan at Jericho' as Israel's setting, but this topographical information here does not form a structural element, at least not at the highest level (contra García López 2008: 79). Especially after the building momentum of chapter 21, which had culminated with astounding victories over Sihon and Og, the second generation now faces two colossal threats to their inheritance of the land: the first, unbeknownst to the Camp, is Balaam's sorcery as commissioned by Balak of Moab (chs. 22–24), and the second is destruction at the hands of YHWH after many Israelites commit spiritual harlotry, seduced by the women of Moab and Midian (ch. 25). The two ploys, aggression and seduction, form Moab's response to Israel's encampment on the plains of Moab, and serve as an instructive paradigm for how nations will respond to the presence of God's people in the land.

2. As with 21:1, this verse marks a transition in perspective to that of Moab:

> The sudden transition from a point of view locked on Israel to events taking place outside of the encampment, presumably within Moab itself (although this is not explicit), signifies a dramatic shift from inside to outside, from centre to peripheral, from familiar to foreign. (Leson 2007: 156; see also Dijkstra 1995a)

As Israel draws ever nearer to inheriting the land, the surrounding nations feel threatened. In chapter 21, their response was military aggression (cf.

also 20:18, 20). Given Israel's decisive victories over the Amorite superpowers Sihon and Og, however, an alternative stratagem is desired – this is the point of the detail in verse 2: that Balak the son of Zippor 'saw all that Israel had done to the Amorites'. There was great reason for fear: Sihon had overpowered Moab, so Israel had proven even mightier than Moab's conquerors. Use of 'saw' (*rā'āh*) here, a key word throughout the narrative, will culminate when Balaam 'saw' that it pleased YHWH to bless Israel, and lifted his eyes and 'saw' Israel's encampment (24:1–2). Balak grasped the lesson Israel had recently learned (21:1–3), that Israel's God, YHWH, sovereignly controls the outcome of battle, regardless of military might. He therefore understands the need to turn divine favour away from them, as a prerequisite to battling Israel (v. 6). Not unreasonably, Rashi, along with the Midrash, surmises that as the great kings of the region, Sihon and Og, were paid by Canaanites and Moab to guard their lands, so that now, with their confidence broken, Moabites tremble in fear (see 1997: 4:270; *Num. Rab.* 20.2). Likely, the name 'Balak' would have been heard as 'Devastator' (BDB 118; cf. J. F. Ross 1962; Snaith 1967: 286), increasing the narrative tension, as the threat against Israel, encamped and completely unaware of the danger, begins to mount. Later generations of Israel would remember Balak's strivings with contempt (see Judg. 11:25). The name Zippor (sparrow) is the m. version of the name of Moses' Midianite wife, Zipporah (Exod. 2:21; 4:25; 18:2). The title *ben ṣippôr* may indicate that Balak's father was an augur (Way 2005: 684–685; Wiggershaus 2021: 85).

3. Two parallel statements in verse 3 describe Moab's response to the nearness of 'the people'/'the sons of Israel': *gûr*, 'dread or terror' – and this 'greatly' (*mĕ'ōd*), and *qûṣ*, 'loathing, abhorrence, sickening dread' (cf. BDB 158–159, 880–881). The reason for such dread, in addition to what Balak had heard Israel had done to the Amorites, is 'because they were many' (*kî rab-hû'*) and 'mighty' (*'āṣûm*, v. 6). Balak and Moab's reaction to YHWH's blessing of Israel, that the nation had increased abundantly, echoes the reaction of Pharaoh and Egypt, who 'loathed' (*qûṣ*, Exod. 1:12) the sons of Israel because they were 'many' (*rab*) and 'mighty' (*'āṣûm*) (Exod. 1:9) – indeed, Balak is something of a Pharaoh *redivivus* (J. S. Ackerman 1987: 86; Sherwood 2002: 174; Bazak 2014a: 309–311; for other parallels with Exodus, see Isbell 2002). In the Torah's literary structure, the threat posed by Pharaoh and his court magicians to Israel's deliverance out of Egypt is paralleled in the threat posed by Balak and Balaam to Israel's inheritance of the land. In both cases YHWH's utter sovereignty – his kingship – is on display.

After crossing the Sea, Moses had led the sons of Israel to sing of the fear that would lay hold of the inhabitants of the land, including the mighty rulers of Moab who would tremble with fear and dread – since 'YHWH will reign for ever and ever' (Exod. 15:14–18; cf. Josh.

2:9–10), the reality of which here begins to be fulfilled. Numbers 21 may be read as an introduction to the Balaam narrative inasmuch as Israel's encroachment on Moab surfaces throughout, first arriving at their border (21:13–15) and then by conquering lands that formerly belonged to Moab (21:26–30). It is even possible that the singing of the victory taunt song, with its 'Woe to you, Moab!' (21:29), triggered Moab's dread, leading to Balak's summoning of Balaam to curse Israel (cf. van Zyl 1960: 7; Allen 1981: 81). Moab's position, writes Geikie (1897: 112–113), was full of alarm: 'Already stripped of more than half its territory, it seemed now in danger of losing the rest,' with Balak's father Zippor ('bird' or 'sparrow'; cf. BDB 862) having lost his life in the battle with Sihon, which had cost him also the greater and richer part of his kingdom, and now, seeing 'the utter overthrow of the Amorites, the conquerors of his own people', Balak was indeed in sore distress. Seerveld captures the atmosphere of the story (2001: 48; emphasis original):

> There was something uncanny, supernatural, existence-threatening about this special folk (Israel) with an Almighty God – *total* victory over the Amorites and Og. Weaponry you could touch would not be strong enough for preserving Moab land, life, and possessions. Demonic powers would be needed, aid from the spirit world, an effective curse to break the spell of these Hebraic invaders from the wilderness.

He rightly likens the Balaam story to the dragon's attempt to swallow up the child born of the woman in Revelation 12, with the similar message that YHWH God delivers his people from the dire threat of the Evil One (Seerveld 2001: 53).

4. Moab turns to the elders of Midian, who share a mutual interest, to conspire against Israel. The Midianites were descendants of Abraham through Keturah who were sent away to the land of the east (Gen. 25:1–6; 1 Chr. 1:32) and so, like the Moabites, related to Israel; their general territory was north-east of the Gulf of Aqaba (cf. Phelps 2000). As with the Moabites (21:26), Midianites had been vassals of Sihon (Josh. 13:21). Midianites will be part of the delegation sent to call for Balaam (22:7) and will later take part in the ploy to seduce the sons of Israel (25:6, 14, 15), for which they will suffer YHWH's vengeance (31:1–9). The link between Numbers 22 and 25 is the more significant since Moab and Midian are rarely mentioned together (the only other instance is Gen. 36:35; Leson 2007: 201 n. 23), and Ibn Ezra even identified these elders with the five Midianite kings mentioned in 31:8 (Ibn Ezra 1999: 178). Nachmanides adds that they used to be kings until, conquered by Sihon, they were relegated to being elders, having become his tribute-bringing servants, a not implausible observation he supports by reference to a detail in Joshua 13:21, where the five chieftains of Midian are said to be 'princes of Sihon' (1975: 247). As traders and caravanners within Moabite-controlled land (see Gen. 36:35), Midianites would perceive the presence of Israelites more as an economic – rather than military – threat, competing 'for scarce resources, control of trade routes, and the like' (Moyer 2009: 376).

Ironically, as revealed in Deuteronomy, Moses had been instructed by YHWH not to harass or contend in battle with Moab since their land had been given as a possession to the descendants of Lot (Deut. 2:8–9), so Moab's fears were baseless. Although this information is not detailed in Numbers, Nachmanides points out that Moab had known Israel would not take their land since, later in Judges 11:17, it is made known that Israel had sent them the same message of peace as it had to Edom (20:17, 19) and to Sihon (21:21) – as such, their fears of Israel 'licking up the grass all around' were likely more economic in nature (1975: 245–246). Balak's antagonistic scheme is seen as more heinous in being committed against a nation that not only had no ill-intent but was scrupulous concerning Moab's boundaries (21:13–15, 24–26). If Israel's dealings with Edom recalled Jacob's dealings with his brother Esau (20:14–21), Israel's dealings with Moab recall Abraham's dealings with Lot. Originally, there had been strife between Abram and Lot's herdsmen since the land was not able to support the flocks and herds of both, a conflict that led to their separation and to YHWH's renewed promise of the land of Canaan to Abram (Gen. 13). So, too, the concern Moab spreads to the elders of Midian is over land and resources, that Israel 'will lick up all around us just like an ox licks up the grass of the field' (v. 4) – a fitting image since Israel had just conquered Bashan, well known for the fertile grazing provided for cattle and livestock (see Num. 32; Deut. 32:14; Ezek. 39:18; Ps. 22:12; Amos 4:1). The progress of Israel's journey to the land symbolically presses further back in time (from Jacob/Esau to Abram/Lot), as allusions to YHWH's promise to Abraham, an undercurrent throughout Numbers, increasingly surface. Balak refers to Israel as 'the assembly' (*haqqāhāl*), no doubt intended derogatorily in the sense of a 'mob' (cf. Levine 2000: 145).

Only at the end of verse 4 are we told that Balak is king of Moab. Some interpreters, appreciating the literal order as well as the phrase 'at that time', suggest Balak was now made king for the sake of dealing with the threat of Israel, this due to his shrewd observations of Israel (v. 2) and because of 'the exigencies of the hour' (*Num. Rab.* 20.4; cf. Slotki 1951: 6:789; Nachmanides 1975: 248), or he was made king after the defeat of Sihon (Ashley 1993: 444). Perhaps supporting a recent rise to kingship, the verse reads literally 'king to/for Moab' (*melek lĕmô'āb*) instead of the typical construction found in 22:10, 'king of Moab' (*melek mô'āb*). As king, he sends messengers to Balaam, a soothsayer apparently renowned throughout the ANE, to curse Israel as a prerequisite to smiting them in battle and driving them away. The Moabites and Midianites are desperate: 'The supernal or infernal powers, or both, must be invoked, and, if possible, at whatever cost enlisted in their behalf. The most prevailing of the diviners must be obtained to bring down calamity and ruin on the victorious host' (Stebbins 1885: 386).

5–6. The character of Balaam, son of Beor at Pethor, was likely known to the original audience of Israelites, although he has been an enigma in scholarship. Was he truly a devotee of YHWH, a righteous prophet among pagans who desired only to do YHWH's will? Was he a genuine diviner who was corrupted by the allure of wealth and fame, or was he already an avaricious soothsayer? The narrative's literary artistry, creating suspense and tension, spawns much deeper questions that yield a more consistent reading of Balaam as a diviner-for-hire, greedy for gain. While the fees of 'divination' (v. 7) portray Balaam as a diviner, one skilled in predicting the future, able to determine a deity's will by reading omens or practising rituals, Balaam is first introduced as a sorcerer, hired to execrate Israel. Balak, as Hawk observes (2017: 84), 'is not interested in knowing the future but in changing it', so he 'enlists Balaam as a sorcerer . . . who is able to wield transcendent power for good or ill'. Perhaps the severest flaw in studies of Balaam's character has been the omission of addressing his relation to Israel. How does his view of Israel compare with that of YHWH – does he really conform to YHWH's will regarding Israel? How does his role compare with that of Moses, again, in relation to Israel? As explored in the ensuing comments, part of the tension and play of the narrative is in the hemming in of Balaam: he cannot but plunge forward in his pursuit of wealth and prestige at the hands of Balak, but at the same time the threatening, sword-bearing hand of YHWH hovers before him, compelling him only to say precisely the reverse of what Balak has hired him to utter – he will, finally, be slain by the sword (31:8). And there is no escaping the dilemma, either by turning back from his journey, for YHWH himself will force him to complete what he has begun, or by plunging fully into the cursing of Israel, for the stranglehold of threatened death will not be released.

In 1967, at a site often identified as the biblical Sukkoth, a Dutch team of excavators discovered several fragments of inscriptions at Tell Deir 'Alla, written in a Canaanite form of Aramaic with ink on the smooth plaster of a wall in a room that might have been used for scribal training (for this paragraph, see Robker 2019: 271–305; cf. Franken 1967; Hoftijzer 1973; Hackett 1980; Weippert 1991; Dijkstra 1995b). Dated to around 800 BC, the fragments were found scattered about the floor, perhaps due to an earthquake, making the 760 BC quake referenced in Amos 1:1 a possibility. Of relevance to Numbers 22 – 24, the Tell Deir 'Alla inscription recounts 'The Admonitions of the Book of Balaam' whereby 'Balaam son of Beor', a 'man who saw the gods', is visited at night by the gods, also called *Shaddayin* (and the solar deity Shamash is also mentioned), who were sent by El with a message of doom and destruction presumably for Balaam's people, who find him fasting and weeping. Without further supplementation, the most that can be deduced from the inscription of relevance for Numbers 22 – 24, is that in the ninth to eighth centuries the figure of Balaam was (still) renowned as a mantic or seer who received messages from gods in night visions. Those responsible for the Deir 'Alla inscription were likely 'well acquainted with the Numbers 22–24 tradition' (Chavalas 2003: 77). The fact that Balak fervently sends for him implies that Balaam was well known to Moab and the elders of Midian as a soothsayer with power to influence gods – able to strike down Israel since whomever he cursed was cursed indeed (v. 6). In a narrative about perspective and vision, we learn of Balaam's character first through Balak, and the story will unfold in act 2 through Balak's perspective – a rhetorical device that leaves its audience in the suspense of Balak's own ignorance, and which also creates much of the section's humour.

The name 'Balaam' might have been heard by the original audience as signifying 'Destroyer (or 'Swallower up') of the people,' from *bālaʻ* ('swallow up, engulf' or 'destroy, annihilate') plus *ʻam* (people), and 'son of Beor' similarly meaning something like 'son of destruction', with Beor derived from *bāʻar* ('to burn, consume', BDB 129) (cf. Guyot 1940: 332; Keil and Delitzsch 1973: 3:159), a name perhaps designed to promote him 'as a dreaded charmer and conjuror' (Hengstenberg 1848: 352). Some scholars used to equate Balaam with 'Bela son of Beor' in Genesis 36:32 (Sayce 1904: 405–406; Mowinckel 1930: 237; Snaith 1967: 287), a proposal that has since been soundly rejected (see e.g. Albright 1944: 231). Ambiguity surrounds Balaam's homeplace – he has been dubbed an Aramean, an Edomite, a Moabite, an Ammonite, a Midianite, a Musrite, a Hittite and a North-Syrian (see Allen 1973: 151–163 and refs. in Layton 1992: 32–33). The location 'at Pethor, which is by the river' is identified by some as the city of Pitrû on the Euphrates (see G. B. Gray 1903: 325–326; Görg 1976; Delcor 1982), a reasonable association since 'River' regularly signifies the Euphrates River (see Gen. 31:21; Exod. 23:31; Josh. 24:2), and others understanding Pethor – with *pĕtôrāh* meaning 'seer' – as a folk etymology for 'visionary land' (Robker 2019: 309–310) or 'interpretation of dreams' (Albright 1915: 387–388; cf. Hengstenberg 1848: 364), a reading that may find some support in Joshua 13:22: 'Balaam son of Beor, the diviner (*haqqôsēm*)' (cf. Barré 1997: 256; Layton 1992: 38–39 also reads *pĕtôrāh* as a *nomen agentis* for 'diviner'). The further ascription 'the land of the sons of his people' may possibly refer to Balak's people, as suggested by the Midrash (*Num. Rab.* 20.7) and Rashi (cf. Rashi 1997: 4:271) and affirmed by some scholars (see Sutcliffe 1937: 441–442; Eissfeldt 1939: 226), explaining why Balaam was so well known to Balak – and Balaam had even prophesied that Balak was destined to rule (*Tan.* 4; *Num. Rab.* 20.7; Rashi 1997: 4:271). Such an interpretation, however, calling for a non-Moabite Balak to be a chieftain of Moab, is problematic (see Gross 1974: 113). In Deuteronomy, a more detailed place of origin is given, namely *pĕtôr 'ăram nahărayim*, an Aramean region between the two rivers (Tigris and Euphrates), which fits the location of Pitru in upper Mesopotamia known today as Jezirah (Younger 2016: 17–20; cf. C. S. Ehrlich 2018). In favour of an Aramean locale, Moyer, after performing an analysis of non-standard language in the Balaam narrative (e.g. *'immāhem*, 22:12; *rĕgālîm*, 22:28, 32, 33; *min-'ărām*, 23:7), concluded these linguistic features were intentionally aimed at infusing the story with an Aramean flavour, calling to mind the speech of Balaam's homeland in the upper Euphrates (2009: 77–168). The phrase 'his people' (*'ammô*) is confirmed by the LXX (*huiōn laou autou*) and the Targums. Others suggest it may refer to the place Amau in the Levant (Albright 1950: 15–16), or to the Egyptian *'Āmu*, with reference to Asiatics or Semites associated with North Syria (Yahuda 1945); originally, it might have read 'Ammon', as with some of the versions (SamP, Syr and Vg) (Lust 1978), or may simply designate Balaam as a foreigner (Robker 2019: 311). In favour of reading Ammon, the expression 'sons of Ammon' (*bĕnê-'ammôn*) is used widely in the Pentateuch (see Gen. 19:38; Deut. 2:19, 37; 3:11, 16), including in Numbers (21:24), and the expression is quite similar to 'sons of his people' (*bĕnê-'ammô*) here (cf. Barré 1997: 255). Also, if Balaam were an Ammonite, it may explain why in the last four prophetic utterances, directed against surrounding nations, Ammon is missing (Leson 2007: 237) – however, since his words are given and constrained by YHWH, the enigma remains. If 'Ammon' is preferred, then the river must be the Jabbok (Num. 21:24; Deut. 3:16). As no such site as Pethor is known in the area of Ammon, however, a locale near the Euphrates river is assumed (cf. Kaiser 1996: 96–97). Deuteronomy forbids an 'Ammonite or Moabite' from entering the assembly of YHWH, listing as one of the reasons 'because they hired Balaam the son of Beor of Pethor of Mesopotamia against you to curse you' (23:3–6); so, while Ammonites are grouped with Moabites against Israel, Balaam is separated from them as a Mesopotamian. Some have suggested that 'sons of his people' portrays Balaam as a foreigner, making his blessing of Israel all the more unexpectedly magnificent (cf. Sutcliffe 1937: 441). Foreignness and the distinction of peoples is an underlying theme throughout the narrative, and perhaps the phraseology at the story's conclusion should be given more weight, as Balaam says (24:14), 'Now, look, I am going to *my people* (*'ammî*). Go, I will guide you as to what *this people* (*hā'ām hazzeh*) will do to *your people* (*'ammĕkā*) at the end of days' (similarly, Burnett 2018: 168–169). In any case, while 'Ammon' and 'Edom' require emendations to the MT, 'Aram' does not (23:7; Deut. 23:5), so I will proceed with the widely accepted view that Balaam is a Mesopotamian diviner, with any use of 'prophet' made loosely. As Keil and Delitzsch point out, Scripture nowhere calls Balaam a 'prophet' (*nābî*') or 'seer' (*ḥōzêh*), although assuming he regards himself as a seer is part of the text's lampooning of Balaam – rather, he is dubbed 'the soothsayer' or 'the diviner' (*haqqôsēm*, Josh. 13:22), a designation never used of true prophets (Guyot 1941: 235–237; Keil and Delitzsch 1973: 3:159–160; on possible overlap between prophecy and divination, see Kitz 2003). Philo's description of Balaam in his *Vita Mosis* (1.264), as one who 'obtained a name of wide celebrity', remains reasonable (1993: 484):

> Now there was a man at that time very celebrated for his skill in divination, dwelling in Mesopotamia, who was initiated in every branch of the soothsayer's art. And he was celebrated and renowned above all men for his experience as a diviner and prophet.

More narrowly, Burnett points to a 'common tradition of Balaam as an archetypal doomsayer beholden to no single kingdom, a spokesman for the divine at an international level' (2018: 136), and Coats, similarly, to 'the image of a non-Israelite seer with an international reputation, famous for his ability to bless and curse with power', and whose skills 'were available for hire' (1982b: 53). Balak, then, sends messengers to Balaam, a famous Mesopotamian soothsayer, imploring him to use his magic arts to strike down Israel with curses, weakening them enough for Balak to drive them out of his land.

Balak's message to Balaam includes three major parts: (1) a twofold indication of the situation (namely, Israel's status), presented as a problem; (2) a plea for Balaam to come to curse the Israelites; and (3) a threefold justification of his call for Balaam, explaining (a) Balak's need for the curse ('they are mightier than I'), (b) the desired goal of the curse ('I will be able to strike them down and drive them out of the land') and (c) the basis for the curse ('whom you curse will be cursed'). The opening twofold indication of the situation uses two *hinnê* (Look!) clauses, perhaps already reflecting the theme of seeing and vision:

> Look! A people has come forth from Egypt;
> Look! They cover the eye of the earth, and they are dwelling over
>   against me.

It is significant that Balak offers a naturalistic explanation of the exodus (cf. Num. 20:16; Josh. 2:8–11) – the Balaam narrative instructs its audience about the nature of God through Balak's experience. Through Balaam's mouth, YHWH will twice correct Balak's 'A people has *come* forth from Egypt' with 'El *brought* them forth from Egypt' (23:22; 24:8) (cf. Rashi 1997: 4:296; noted as well by Frisch 2005: 113; Bazak 2014a: 310–311). The expression to 'cover the eye of the land' (*kissā ʾet-ʿên* hā'āreṣ – cf. v. 11) is also used in Exodus (10:5, 15), and may originally have been an idiom related to the Egyptian sun-god Ra (Yahuda 1933: 62–63). Rendsburg (1990), noting that *TgO* translates 'the eye of the sun of the (whole) land' in the Exodus and Numbers passages, suggests the reference to Israel's coming forth out of Egypt in Numbers 22:5 made the idiom appropriate here, likely meaning that, as with the hordes of locusts, the multitude of Israelites has blocked the sun. Locust imagery was employed in the ancient world to convey the devastating swarms and destruction of a militia, the vastness of opposing forces, overwhelming in their invasion (Marcus 1977: 98–99). Taking 'eye' to mean 'view' or 'appearance' by extension (see Lev. 13:55; Num. 11:7), Milgrom suggests Israel's army, like a locust plague (cf. Judg. 6:5; 7:12), has covered the view of the land (1990: 186). As part of a recurring exodus motif, the phraseology parallels Balak and Moab with Pharaoh and Egypt. As Helfgot observes (2012a: 169), 'the entire Balak/Bil'am narrative appears to be a mini-Exodus from Egypt experience for the new generation'. Moreover, the use of 'eye' here and in verse 11 feeds into the motif of 'seeing', especially ironic inasmuch as it is a 'covered' eye (see the uncovering of Balaam's eyes, 22:31; 24:3, 4, 15, 16). As related in verse 4, Moab is threatened by the great numbers of Israel, especially in regard to the land's resources. Israel's status – the nation's large numbers and encampment on the plains of Moab, and its recent military victories over the Amorites – becomes the basis for Balak's proposed resolution, summoning Balaam to curse them. The urgent note of the *hinnê* (Look!) statements is further underlined in his plea for Balaam to come, using 'now' and 'please'. The necessity for Balaam's cursing of Israel is explained and supported by the simple clause 'because (*kî*) they are mightier than I'. In other words, the desired solution is for Moab to strike down and drive Israel out of the land, but to do so will first require help through sorcery: for Balaam to curse Israel, making them vulnerable. Balak's language recalls that of the faithless scouts about the inhabitants of the land: 'they are stronger (*ḥāzāq*) than we' (13:31; Sherwood 2002: 174), and thus marks a triumphant reversal of Numbers 13 – 14. In the Chronicle of Balaam, it is the nations who scout out Israel's encampment, and are filled with dread. Israel's identity and purpose are inseparable from the blessing of God (cf. Gen. 12:1–3; Num. 6:22–27), so that Balak may be seen as attacking the very essence and heart of God's people: in seeking their curse, Moab 'goes to Israel's jugular vein' (Seerveld 2001: 25).

The summons ends with the grounds for Balak's hope, which may also be seen as an encomium of motivating praise for Balaam: 'because (*kî*) I know that whom you bless will be blessed and whom you curse will be cursed'. In the immediate context, his words demonstrate Balaam's international reputation as a sorcerer. Balak's single-minded desire is for Balaam to curse Israel, so the inclusion of blessing at this point ironically foreshadows YHWH's sovereign purpose. More than this, Balak's closing phrase echoes YHWH's promise to Abram in Genesis 12:3: 'I will bless those who bless you, and the one who curses you I will curse,' and thus 'alerts us to the fact that God's covenant purpose is now on trial' (Naylor 1994: 189). Through Balak's lips, Balaam is set up in opposition to YHWH, hired to counter directly YHWH's purposes for his people. With Israel encamped on the cusp of the land of Canaan, allusions to YHWH's promises to Abraham begin to resound triumphantly, especially in Balaam's own oracles, much to Balak's dismay. Balak's plea in verse 6 forms the opening bracket of an inclusio, closed in Numbers 24:9, 10, with the closing words of Balaam's third blessing of Israel, followed by Balak's anger and dismissal of Balaam – his original purpose of cursing his enemies having resulted in their exceeding benediction. Part of the message of the Balaam narrative is found here: what Balak thinks he 'knows' (*yāda'tî*), that Balaam or any pagan sorcerer is able to hex God's people, is wrong – God alone is sovereign over the nations and history, and has determined to bless his people. Given other echoes of the exodus story, Balak's 'I know' resonates with Pharaoh's infamous 'I do not know (*yāda'tî*) YHWH, and so I will not release Israel!' (Exod. 5:2); both rulers, Pharaoh and Balak, are humbled under YHWH's demonstration of faithful love and mighty power for his people.

Balak desires to turn YHWH against his people. The basic scheme of the narrative moves from Balak to Balaam to God to Israel, as Balak seeks to manipulate Balaam with riches and honour to curse Israel by God, and Balaam seeks to manipulate God through repeated approaches, sacrifices and sorcery, so that God will curse Israel. While Balak's role will diminish as Balaam takes centre-stage, the narrative sets Balak in opposition against YHWH (cf. Isbell 2002; on Balak's role, see W. W. Lee 2004; Lipscomb 2012). Three times Balak uses the verb *'arar* for 'curse', recalling its use in the divine promise to Abram (Gen. 12:3), but the term is first used by YHWH God against the serpent (Gen. 3:14) and later against Cain (Gen. 4:11) – in these latter two cases, used with *min*, *'arar* has the sense of 'to ban' (Speiser 1960: 198). In Genesis 1 – 11, *'arar* occurs fives times, while 'bless' (*bārak*) occurs five times in the call of Abram (Gen. 12:1–3), so that the biblical story of humanity, centred on Israel's role in redemption, may be understood along the paradigm of divine curse versus divine blessing. The Akkadian cognate *araru* carries the notion of 'binding' with a curse (Bezold 1926: 69). Speiser accordingly writes that Balaam was hired for the express purpose of 'immobilizing Israel', and translates Balak's summons as 'Come, cast a spell for me against that people' (1960: 198). It should be noted at the outset that, in so doing, Balak called for a curse on himself and the Moabites, since YHWH had promised Abraham that he would 'curse him who curses you' (Gen. 12:3; van Groningen 1990: 241), the prospect of which is given explicitly in Balaam's fourth parable (24:17). Curses were widespread throughout the ANE, used to manage nearly 'every feature of life from simple business affairs to complex international relations', writes Kitz (2007a: 615). Curses were especially sought as a preliminary to military conflict, considered as important as the battle itself (Powell 1982: 99). Among the common properties of curses, Kitz mentions divine judgement and the arousal of divine wrath; curses were petitions, importuning deities to some form of intervention based on the 'eye for eye' talionic principle, and which aimed at separating the god or gods from the offending individual or people (2007a: 618–619). Both in the ANE and in the culture of Israel, blessings and curses were taken with utmost seriousness, as having the power to shape history, determining the character and fate of people and nations (cf. Gressmann 1913: 332; Brichto 1963; Hayes 1968). In pagan cultures, the gods and forces of nature could be manipulated through magic and sorcery, whereas in Israel YHWH steadily taught his people that his hand alone was sovereign, and his prophetic word alone was effectual. The clash of these two disparate world views is at the heart of the narrative's drama. Balaam will learn that YHWH cannot be manipulated, and his purposes – in this case, to bless Abraham's descendants, the nation of Israel – cannot be thwarted. An underlying question of the Balaam narrative, then, is whether or not YHWH's fierce anger can be aroused against his people. The initial response includes that he has not observed 'iniquity in Jacob' (23:21) for any talionic principle to apply.

The Balaam narrative, among other purposes, functions to reaffirm the spiritual realties of the covenant community, especially as encompassed within the theologically rich opening section of Numbers on the structure and purity of the Camp (chs. 1–6). One facet of this link is found in the key term *bārak* (to bless), which occurs three times for the priestly blessing of the Camp (Num. 6:23, 24, 27), and fourteen times in the Balaam story (22:6 [twice], 12; 23:11 [twice], 20 [twice], 25 [twice]; 24:1, 9 [twice], 10 [twice]) – the only two places where *bārak* appears in Numbers.

22:7–14 Scene 1: Balaam's first call to Moab from Balak

7. Having mutual interest against Israel's nearness, Moab and Midian send messengers to Balaam – their joint intrigue that begins as soon as Israel encamps on the plains of Moab (22:4) continues into the enticement of Israel to spiritual harlotry (25:1, 6, 14–18). The embassy is comprised of the 'elders' (*ziqnê*), lending the delegation a sense of dignity and gravity – elders were senior community leaders, aged and presumably wise. In verse 8, they are called 'princes' (*śārîm*), a designation implying high rank, which can also have military connotations. The elders go with 'divinations' (*qĕsāmîm*), the same word used when

Joshua refers to Balaam as a 'soothsayer' or 'diviner' (*qôsēm*, Josh. 13:22). Balak, who knows (of) Balaam, identifies him as a soothsayer, a practice forbidden in Israel (see Deut. 18:10, 14; 1 Sam. 15:23; 2 Kgs 17:17), undermining scholarly speculation as to Balaam's saintly character (see Donner 1977: 129). The root *q-s-m* is used regularly in the HB with a polemical sense, providing a negative appraisal of Balaam from the start so that readers 'expect a problematic story about a strange diviner' (Heckl 2013: 3–4; contra Milgrom 1990: 187). Through Balaam himself, YHWH will declare 'there is no divination (*qesem*) against Israel' (23:23; cf. 24:1). The detail that the elders took 'divinations' in hand with them is often understood as referring to the payment or fees for divination (G. B. Gray 1903: 329), or that diviners ('colleagues') were sent for the purpose of honouring Balaam (Milgrom 1990: 187), or that the elders carried tools of divination in hand. However, each of these options is unsatisfying: fees were commonly withheld until the service was performed (cf. Num. 22:17, 37; 24:11), the men are called 'elders', not diviners, and the latter were typically rivals, not colleagues, in the ancient world, and lastly, as a famous diviner himself, Balaam would have no need for divination equipment, and in any case would have preferred his own tools of the trade. Rather, based on divinatory practice in Mari, Hurowitz (1992) clarifies that *qěsāmîm*, which finds a partial overlap with the Akkadian term *têrētum*, almost certainly refers to the physical results of divination, often in the form of clay models (e.g. of entrails), which in cases of obscure or ominous forecasts would be sent to more authoritative diviners, for reasons such as national security. The *qěsāmîm* 'may well have been baked clay models of the entrails predicting Moab's downfall and Israel's ascendancy', writes Hurowitz (1992: 13), and were brought to Balaam, either because the results foretold disaster or were unclear to Balak's diviners – 'Balak was afraid and sent them to Balaam for a second, more favourable opinion which only he will know how to provide.' If, alternatively, the omens were favourable, indicating that Israel was capable of being hexed, then these divinations were brought to Balaam as an encouragement for him to come to Moab and perform the curse – in other words, as Wiggershaus states, Balak sent the 'results to show Balaam the clear decision of the divine courtroom', since he 'assumed his request to curse Israel was approved, and he sought Balaam to carry it out' (2021: 111–112). This reading would explain why 'Balak's ire burned greater with each of Balaam's attempts,' since Balak had never asked for more signs – rather, given the favourable and to his mind decisive divinations, he had hired Balaam only to curse his enemy (2021: 112–113). Moreover, the divinations were most likely the results of Moabite specialists consulting the god Chemosh, and it may be that, given ANE notions of territorial claims or jurisdiction among gods, YHWH (and/or El) needed to be consulted since he was the God of Israel and perhaps because the plains of Moab were now under his jurisdiction (see Burnett 2018: 177–179; Wiggershaus 2021: 109–111). Finally, in relation to 'divinations', Moyer points out the chiastic interaction between the prosaic and poetic uses of 'divination' and 'enchantment' (2009: 181). (See Table 6.)

Table 6: 'Divination' and 'enchantment' usage

	Numbers 22:7	Numbers 23:23a	Numbers 23:23b	Numbers 24:1
Prose	qĕsāmîm			nĕḥāšîm
Poetry		naḥaš	qesem	

The presence of the elders of Midian, closely linked with the divinations, prepares readers for the role of Midian in the story of Baal Peor in chapter 25 (vv. 15–18; 31:1–11; cf. Kislev 2014).

Balaam's character was apparently well known to the original audience, a context lost to us. However, we may glean insight into Balaam's reputation most deeply through the perception and engagement of Balak, the character who knows and introduces him.

8. In response, Balaam bids the messengers to lodge for the night, avowing to bring them word 'just as YHWH will speak to me'. His words assume a night vision, as described also in the Deir 'Alla inscription. Consistently, throughout scenes 1 and 2, Balaam refers to God by the name 'YHWH' when speaking to the delegation of Moab, but the narrator describes Balaam's encounters with him using the designation 'God', a rhetorical device that calls into question the nature of the relationship with YHWH Balaam claims and tries to portray (cf. Cassuto 2008: 48) – there is a 'flagging of discrepancy' between Balaam's presumption of God and what the narrator knows (Sharp 2009: 136). As Allen writes (1973: 243), 'one suspects that had the oracle been intended against another nation, he would have used the name of the god of that nation'. His use of 'YHWH', then, may be expected since, as a soothsayer with an international reputation, 'it would be Balaam's care to know the gods of each nation' (Guyot 1941: 238). It is reported that the 'princes of Moab' stayed with Balaam, omitting any reference to the elders of Midian, whose absence continues through the rest of the scene – only the Moabite elders are noted (22:13, 14), leaving open the possibility that the Midianite delegation did not stay, or they are simply subsumed under Moab, the story's main concern. Spero reads this verse as Balaam's standard response, understood as 'Let me consider your offer,' so that when the living God actually appears to him, he is both overwhelmed and shaken (2013: 194). Perhaps, like Laban who, after hearing of Jacob's dire straits (Gen. 29:13–14), determined to get full use of him, Balaam on hearing of the desperate straits of Moab and Midian understands he may stall for greater riches. Shenk wisely asks (1993: 39), how righteous is Balaam when he never pauses to consider whether the Israelites *ought* to be cursed?

9. 'And God came to Balaam'. The narrator switches to the more generic use of 'God', withholding the covenant name of YHWH from Balaam's interaction. The phrase is used elsewhere in the Torah only in relation to God's dealings with non-Israelites, and in all of Scripture is never used to depict God's interaction with a prophet: 'And God came to Abimelech in a dream by night' (Gen. 20:3); 'And God came to Laban the Aramean in a dream by night' (Gen. 31:24). In both cases in Genesis, God visits a pagan at night for the sake of safeguarding his own people as well as his promises to them – warning the recipients of his visitation (Abimelech, Laban), so they do not carry out their intentions, precisely at issue in the present narrative. Balaam's own rhetoric aside, the narrator does not portray this Mesopotamian soothsayer as a true prophet of YHWH. God asks him, 'Who are these men with you?' giving Balaam an opportunity for explanation; his questioning recalls the early narratives of Genesis when God questions Adam and Eve (Gen. 3:9–13) and then Cain (4:6–10). Hirsch reads God's question as an unexpected divine intervention, and proof that Balaam had not appealed to God for a decision (2007a: 482).

10–11. Balaam's response focuses on Balak as king of Moab and his words (vv. 5–6), the 'words of Balak' that had been spoken to him by the elders (v. 7). Narrative tension begins, as Balaam finds himself increasingly wedged in by the kingship of YHWH and that of Balak. Whereas God asks who 'these men' are with him, Balaam's response begins with emphasis on 'Balak son of Zippor king of Moab', taken by Rashi as haughtiness, as if to say, 'Although I am not esteemed in your eyes, I am esteemed in the eyes of kings' (1997: 4:275; cf. *Num. Rab.* 20.9). His retelling of Balak's summons includes two stylistic changes: from 'curse' (*'ārāh*) to 'condemn' (*qābāh*), and from 'strike down' (*nakkeh*) to 'battle' (*hillāḥem*). The first change, to 'condemn', is the first of ten instances of the verb *qbb* in the Balaam story (see 22:11, 17; 23:8, 11, 13, 25, 27; 24:10), which, as it occurs nowhere else in the Pentateuch, Sherwood suggests (2002: 175) may prepare for the incident at Baal Peor where the Midianite woman is pierced through the 'belly' (*qŏbātāh*) in a 'tent-shrine' (*qubbâ*, Num. 25:8). God uses 'curse' in verse 12, citing Balak's original words. Two further omissions – 'and they are dwelling over against me' and 'for they are mightier than I' – may be inconsequential, largely assumed in Balaam's summary. A third and final omission, however, is telling: Balaam leaves out 'for I know that whom you bless will be blessed and whom you curse will be cursed'.

12. Notably, God's response to Balaam is unequivocal, with two strong prohibitions, each beginning with *lō'*, and an emphatic statement regarding Israel's status: 'You will not go with them,' 'You will not curse the people,' 'because they are blessed'. The response is key for understanding the rest of the narrative, and deciphering the motivations of Balaam. Balaam's instruction, as J. M. Cohen points out (1988: 113),

is merely negative: he is not to curse Israel; his blessing is not required since Israel is already blessed – even his later 'blessings' are but acknowledgements of Israel's qualities and character as blessed by YHWH. A rabbinical saying brings out the force and finality of God's words by filling in the gaps of Balaam's presumed reply (*Num. Rab.* 20.10; Slotki 1951: 6:796): *You shall not go with them.* 'Well, then,' says Balaam, 'I will curse them from where I am.' *You shall not curse the people.* 'In that case,' says Balaam, 'let me bless them!' They do not need your blessing, *for they are blessed.* Israel's blessedness, however, should not be generalized; the reference is to the nature of Israel's Camp under the light of YHWH's face – the priestly benediction (6:22–27).

13–14. For one who regularly touts his reporting only 'just what' YHWH speaks to him (v. 8), Balaam's report to the princes of Moab is anything but a faithful conveying of YHWH's words and will: 'Go to your land, for YHWH refused to let me go with you.' Indeed, as the recurring drumbeat of the narrative is the obligation of God's spokesman to announce exactly the word of YHWH (see 22:8, 18, 20, 35, 38; 23:12, 26; 24:13; Margaliot 1990: 81), Balaam appears anything but a loyal representative of YHWH. If Balaam had been a true prophet, Hirsch observes (2007a: 483), he would have accurately conveyed God's pronouncement to Balak's emissaries, and the purpose of God's intervention would have been achieved without any need for the rest of the narrative. This withholding of information, writes Sharp (2009: 137), 'is clearly telegraphed to the reader' and 'renders all of what Balaam says suspect'. He reports only the first of God's threefold statement, withholding the crux of the matter (cf. M. Douglas 1993: 419): 'You will not curse the people, for they are blessed.' His omission leaves open – and, perhaps, solicits – Balak's further pursuit of his services. Already the narrative cautions evaluating Balaam's character solely on his own assertions. The princes of Moab, in turn, report to Balak that 'Balaam refused to go with us,' omitting reference to YHWH. Clearly, they understood Balaam's words as 'merely a negotiating ploy' (Sherwood 2002: 175). Symmetry is created between the two incomplete reports, as both begin with the 'rising' (*qûm*) of the messenger(s). Rabbinical interpreters noted how Balaam's reply, not only neglecting to state that he was forbidden to curse Israel, appears to emphasize the point 'with you' (*'immākem*), taken by them (as well as by Balak) as implying that he may go with officers of higher rank (*m. Av.* 5.19; *Tan.* 6; *Num. Rab.* 20.10; Rashi 1997: 4:276).

22:15–20 Scene 2: Balaam's second call to Moab from Balak

15–17. Yet again Balak sends princes to Balaam, this time 'many more' and more 'honourable' (from *kābēd*) than the previous ones – indeed, for he 'knew his man' (Hirsch 2007a: 484). This larger and weightier delegation implies a larger honorarium (Maarsingh 1987: 80; Shenk 1993: 35). Such a practice, of sending weightier men – from regional leaders ('elders') to men of the royal court representing Balak himself – who were authorized to negotiate terms, having mastered the art, reflects accurately the known realities of diplomacy in the ANE (Wiggershaus 2021: 93–95). The formal pattern of increasing magnitude and intensity is hereby set, which will be repeated through the narrative, eventually reinforcing the message of YHWH's sovereign rule over history in the incrementally soaring prophetic oracles (I. Clark 1982: 139). What insight into Balaam's character does this approach by Balak, the one who knows him, provide? Whether by intention or mishap, Balaam's unexplained refusal is received – naturally, within its ANE context of negotiations (see e.g. Gen. 23) – as haggling for a higher offer. The audience is invited to entertain the possibility of construing Balaam's motive as greed (Sherwood 2002: 175), or, more strongly, we are 'likely meant to condemn Balaam', given this 'is the only motivation overtly suggested in the text for Balaam's asking God a second time – clearly God's anger with the seer would have a just basis' (Shenk 1993: 35). Likely, both the story's tension and ironic humour lie in the fact that Balaam is now acting and speaking as Balak has always known him to do – except this time, having dealings with the one true God, Balaam actually means what he says.

'Thus says (*kō 'āmar*) Balak son of Zippor,' the princes say, introducing Balak's message in language that both disregards and mimics God's authority (cf. Exod. 4:22). 'Let nothing, please, hinder you from coming to me . . . so come, please, condemn this people for me': the opening and closing of Balak's plea directly opposes God's own message to Balaam, 'you will not go with them; you will not curse the people', creating tension as Balaam endeavours to serve two masters. Along with the display of a more glorious entourage of noble messengers, the centre of Balak's message assures Balaam of great riches, the key motivation for why he should come and curse Israel: 'for (*kî*) I will surely honour you greatly', using an emphatic doubling of 'glory' (*kabbēd 'ăkabbedkā*) magnified by the adverb 'very' (*mě'ōd*).

18–19. Balaam's response is carefully crafted and curious; he does not report to these new messengers God's previous unambiguously definite message that he may neither go to Balak nor curse the people because they are blessed by YHWH. Rather, he focuses upon Balak's offer: 'If Balak gave me the fullness of his house, silver and gold, I would not be able to pass beyond the mouth of YHWH my God to do small or great,' with 'small or great' being a merism that includes everything in between (i.e. 'I cannot do anything at all'). The phrase 'pass beyond the mouth of YHWH' (*'ăbōr 'et-pî yhwh*, repeated verbatim in 24:13) recalls Moses' questioning the Israelite rebels of the first generation,

'Why do you transgress the mouth of YHWH' (*'ōběrîm 'et-pî yhwh*, 14:41). While Balaam's words may be taken as displaying his faithfulness to YHWH, they may also be interpreted as the rhetoric of negotiation, soliciting – planting the seeds for – greater riches. His 'faux protestation', seeming to demur, actually signals his expectation for enhanced compensation, heightening the session of bargaining, not unlike when Ephron the Hittite, under the guise of graciously demurring, indicated the amount required of Abraham in Genesis 23:15 (Sharp 2009: 137; cf. Lapsley 2006). Jewish tradition suggests that Balaam, seeing Moab's dire prospects, calculated and justified his extravagant payment, for otherwise Balak would have had to hire many armies and even this would be without any guarantee of victory (see *Num. Rab.* 20.10; Rashi 1997: 4:277). Similarly, his emphasis on YHWH as 'my God' may be read in two different ways. Is he a devout adherent of YHWH – and even if so, why underscore this point? Perhaps it is precisely because YHWH is Israel's God, and Balak, who had seen all that Israel had done to the Amorites (v. 2), wants to hire a soothsayer to curse Israel. Few scholars have appreciated the necessity for a people to be cursed specifically by their own deity (a notable exception, Margaliot 1977: 281 n. 10). Burnett, who does observe Balak's acknowledgement that cursing Israel would require YHWH's consent, also includes the issue of geography (at least in the view of Balak and Balaam), with YHWH having jurisdiction over Israelite territory (2018: 178–179; cf. C. W. Mitchell 1987: 91–92). Ashley, who takes a decidedly neutral view of Balaam's character, affirms that Balaam 'cannot be made into a great devotee of Yahweh', and that he is depicted as a Mesopotamian seer and exorcist (1993: 436). Balaam's routine might have been to claim influence and expertise with whatever gods the situation demanded (so, too, von Pakozdy 1958: 169–170) since in the ANE it was standard that soothsayers 'professed expertness in transmitting the supernatural' (Orlinsky 1969: 250). His self-deprecating words of inability were likely aimed to demonstrate why Balak needs him, a form of braggadocio. Some have reasonably read Balaam's character here as 'a paradigm of arrogance and condescension who proclaims for all to hear that by his sorcery and magic he can "walk with God" and ascertain his thoughts' (Hattin 2014: 338; so, too, Heckl 2013: 6). The least that may be said, as Wiggershaus explains (2021: 99), is that 'the sobriquet "my God" in no way connoted exclusivity in the ancient Near East' (see also Burnett 2018: 177, who reads Balaam as touting a rapport with El, Shadday and Elyon, 'the highest level of the pantheon on an international scale'). In the context of a business transaction, moreover, suggesting that he may not be able 'to do anything small or great' may be a way of hedging the stakes in the event Israel defeats Moab in battle after Balaam's sorcery – a soothsayer's fine print (cf. Shenk 1993: 39).

Balaam's words may reveal the tension within himself: riches, a house full of silver and gold, entice him, *yet* he may not pass beyond YHWH's words. Here one finds no righteous servant of YHWH, who *wants* only to honour his God faithfully, but someone with 'an evil thought in his heart' (Ibn Ezra 1999: 184), a soul who covets wealth even as he affirms a divine *prohibition* – that he is *not able* 'to pass beyond' or 'to transgress' (*la'ăbōr*) YHWH's word. Although Balaam has just avowed his inability to pass beyond the mouth of YHWH his God, and although God has already declared his word and intent to him, he bids the messengers to stay the night so that he may know 'what more' YHWH will speak to him. Why? God's previous message was not 'a particular issue of time or circumstance', as Moberly observes (1999: 6), 'but a fundamental principle' that will not change; namely, that Israel is blessed. Moberly continues (1999: 7), consulting God a second time shows that Balaam does not mean what he says; rather, he is 'acceding to Balak's construal of his earlier refusal, that it was not a genuine refusal but a negotiating ploy' – the language of his religious vocation has become 'a tool of self-interested financial negotiation'. He thus dubs Balaam's willingness to approach God a second time 'a pious smokescreen' (Moberly 2006: 141).

The conciliatory use of 'please' (*nā'*) may also indicate Balaam's concern not to miss out on this lucrative prospect. But can God be manipulated to change his purpose? If Balaam knows YHWH's will, and desires only to perform his will, why dither at all – rather than declare that Israel is blessed, and this must be so? Balaam's seeming piety dissolves further when one appreciates more fully the nature of Balak's request. If, for example, one replaces 'curse' with 'destroy' and then replaces 'the people' with 'YHWH's bride' – how devoted to YHWH does Balaam appear when, far from being offended even by the suggestion of harming God's people, he vacillates, hosting rather than chiding the antagonists, and awaiting another word from God just in case he may after all be permitted to go with some suggestion of cursing Israel? Arama expresses the thought well, explaining how Balaam, on hearing of such a wicked notion as cursing YHWH's people, should have refused even under threat of death – he should have said, 'Far be it from me to destroy the herd of the Lord and the flock of his pasture,' and should have upbraided Balak's messengers (quoted in Leibowitz 1982: 311–312). Often missed, Balaam's repeated approach to God, bringing up the matter of the denunciation of Israel a second time, should be seen as greatly affronting to God (Shenk 1993: 36), for he who touches Israel touches the apple of YHWH's eye (Zech. 2:8; cf. *Num. Rab.* 20.6). Balaam's action and words misrepresent YHWH as one who may change his purpose, undermining the divine word – a point that will be addressed in the second oracle (23:19). Nachmanides speaks of Balaam's profanation of God's name later when he went with the princes of Moab, giving them the impression that YHWH had granted permission to curse his people (1975: 255).

20. Again, although Balaam had spoken of 'YHWH', the narrator defers to 'God' for describing their actual interaction, undermining any suggestion of such a relationship (see v. 9). This time God says, 'If the men come to call you, arise, go with them . . .' While many commentators get boggled by the contrast between this verse and verse 22 (scene 3), when God's fierce anger is kindled at Balaam's going, the real puzzle is found within its present context of scenes 1 and 2, which otherwise are consistent with God's anger in scene 3. Why does God allow him to go now? Wiggershaus interprets verses 12 and 20 as paraphrased dialogues by the narrator, indicating only Balaam's (mis)interpretations of divination, not actual prophetic oracles (2021: 191–197), a view challenged by the direct speeches. The ancient rabbis provide a sufficient answer: because Balaam is bent on going. Based on the principle 'In the direction a man is determined to walk, Heaven lets him go' (*Mak.* 10b; *Num. Rab.* 20.12), J. M. Cohen observes that when Balaam displayed his resolute determination and consuming desire to undertake the mission of cursing Israel, God, rather than standing in his way, removed the barrier, allowing 'Balaam's evil impulse to impel him onwards to his ultimate objective – and undoing' (1992: 160; cf. Trapp 1650: 46–47). Having already forbidden him to go, God tells him to do what he is bent on doing already. Micaiah's prophecy in 2 Chronicles 18 serves as an instructive parallel (cf. 1 Kgs 22). Having been directed by a messenger to speak precisely what king Ahab wanted to hear from YHWH; namely, divine encouragement to war against Ramoth Gilead, Micaiah, who avows, 'As YHWH lives, whatever my God speaks, that I will speak,' nevertheless says, 'Go and prosper.' Afterward, he unveils that YHWH, amid his divine council, had determined to persuade Ahab to go to war in order to bring disaster on him. Having already told him not to go, God sends Balaam, who will eventually be slain with the sword for his avarice and duplicity (see 31:8). However, YHWH's ultimate purpose in sending Balaam is, in the wonders of his infinite wisdom and goodness to his people, to bless Israel in a threefold manner even while making a mocking display of Israel's enemies, overturning their hostile schemes on their own heads.

'God's words' in verse 20, as Moberly observes (1999: 9), 'are not just to be taken at face value as straightforward permission to go'. Moyer (2012: 173) points out that while all other divine commands are given as simple, direct commands, here God's word is conditional, marked by the particle *'im* (if), and that part of the condition includes Balaam's doing 'only' (*'ak*) what YHWH speaks:

> What, we may ask, is the 'word' that God speaks to Balaam? It has been detailed precisely only a few verses earlier, in Num. 22:12, 'You shall not go with them; you shall not curse the people, for it is blessed' – and, although this second half of the verse receives the stress, Balaam nevertheless makes the wrong choice and provokes the fierce anger of YHWH.

Kaiser reads the conditional statement quite literally, that Balaam was to wait for the men to come and call him in the morning but, instead of waiting, he, being anxious to go, saddled his donkey and sought them out (Kaiser et al. 1996: 167–168). Levy suggests a similar reading: that God's fierce anger 'is raised because Balak's people have not returned to implore Balaam yet again, as they had done before. Perhaps it is Balaam's own decision this time to rise and go to curse' (2012: 4). A further nuance is possible. Cohen reads the phrase 'If the men come *to call you* to go' (*liqrō' lěkā*) as technical language for being emotionally enslaved: 'If the coming of those men *has so overwhelmed you*, then arise and go with them' (J. M. Cohen 1992: 161–162; cf. Moyer 2009: 486–487). Supporting this usage, he points to the warning of apostasy in Exodus, as the inhabitants of the land 'call to you' (*qārā' lěkā*) to eat their sacrifices, which would end with their whoring after their gods (34:15), so that the notion involved indulging the passions and thereby becoming easy prey to apostasy. This, as Cohen points out, is precisely what happens, through Balaam's ingenuity (31:16), in the Baal Peor episode where the daughters of Moab 'called to the people' (*wattiqre'nā lā'ām*) to the sacrifices of their gods, leading to Israel's apostasy (25:2). It seems possible, then, that *q-r-' l-* may have the nuance of being enticed, and the parallel between 22:20 and 25:2 is noteworthy: as Balaam was enticed by Balak's riches to pursue execrating Israel to his own demise, so the sons of Israel were enticed by the daughters of Moab to pursue sexual indulgence and apostasy to their own destruction.

God's permission contains a strict condition: 'but only (*wě'ak*) the word which I will speak to you, that is what you will do'. The divine response to Balaam accords with a relenting on God's part, as if to say, 'All right, you may go, *but* . . . !' The 'but' not only delimits the previous clause, but sets up a contrast: the men call 'for you' (*lěkā*), but it is only the word I speak that you will do. M. Douglas reads God's response not as an injunction, but as information, announcing what will happen: that the journey will be fruitless (1993: 420). On either scenario, why would Balaam need any such admonition? First, contrary to his own assertions, Balaam has already failed to convey God's speech faithfully, neglecting to report his determined will regarding the whole enterprise (v. 12). Second, God sees Balaam's covetous intent. On this point, God and Balak agree; both see the same rapacious character that has eluded modern interpreters. Rashi glosses this verse by saying that 'But' means that 'against your will you shall do what I command you', adding that Balaam went thinking that maybe he could lead God astray into consenting to curse Israel (1997: 4:278). Here another question surfaces: Given God's proviso, that he might do exactly only as God instructed, why would Balaam bother to go? On the one hand, Balak has drawn him with bands of wealth; on the other, he entertains notions of manipulating God – if YHWH has yielded regarding the first part of his original declaration, forbidding him to go, perhaps he may also be persuaded on the second part, allowing Balaam to curse Israel.

God's instruction that Balaam is to do only what YHWH speaks recalls Balak's message to Balaam in verse 17 with irony (Castello 1994: 36).

22:21–35 Scene 3: Balaam journeys to Moab on his donkey

The donkey episode is formed by threefold repetitions, as the messenger of YHWH takes a stand along Balaam's path three times, the donkey veers off the path three times, Balaam strikes his donkey three times, and the phrase 'these three times' occurs three times (cf. Marcus 1995: 104–107). Balaam is wedged between what Balak wants him to perform against Israel and what YHWH God explicitly forbids him to do. As dominant rival authorities, Balak and God 'do not act in the same scene at the same time' (Sals 2008: 327, referencing Weise 2003: 27; cf. Margaliot 1990: 81–82; Levy 2012: 3). While the offer of riches has begun to tip the scale toward Balak's demands, YHWH's threat of death in this scene serves to balance the scales. Full of humour and irony, the donkey episode most obviously derides Balaam as a charlatan, and has been dubbed a 'burlesque' (Rofé 1979; Moore 1990: 3). With Balaam presented as an expert in the interpretation of omens, especially omens concerning unusual animal behaviour (Way 2005), there is no little irony in his inability to read the abnormal behaviour of his jenny, behaviour she herself must point out to him as being completely contrary to her lifelong habit (22:30). While lampooned, with his own donkey able to see more than he does, Balaam will nevertheless utter true oracles of God, with this scene offering an explanation beforehand: just as YHWH is able to open the mouth of a donkey, so is he able to speak through Balaam, a pagan sorcerer greedily bent on cursing Israel (cf. *Num. Rab.* 20.14), who is 'nothing but a tool in God's hands' (Levy 2012: 5). Embarking on a new life in the land, Israel rests secure among the nations under the protective care of her sovereign God YHWH – no powers operate outside his kingship.

21. The lengthy description of Balaam's departure betrays his eagerness to go (cf. Shamah 2011: 795). Balaam the seer and diviner goes, not realizing he does so 'as an ox to the slaughter' (Prov. 7:22), unable to see that it will end with his own destruction (Num. 31:8; so *Num. Rab.* 20.11). With a slight variation of terms, this verse echoes remarkably that of Genesis 22:3, when Abraham arose to sacrifice Isaac on Mount Moriah:

> And Balaam arose (*wayyāqām*) in the morning, and saddled his donkey (*'ătōnô*). (Num. 22:21)

> And Abraham arose early (*wayyaškēm*) in the morning, and saddled his donkey (*ḥămōrô*). (Gen. 22:3)

In rabbinic tradition, the contrast between Abraham and Balaam was brought out through parallels such as this, duly noting that Abraham arose *earlier* in the morning than Balaam, thwarting the latter's purposes (see *b. Sanh.* 105b; *Gen. Rab.* 55.8; *Num. Rab.* 20.12; *Pirk. Av.* 5.19). Both are quasi-prophetic figures (Gen. 20:7) who appear to come from the same homeland of 'Mesopotamia' (*'ăram nahărayim*; cf. Gen. 24:4, 10; Num. 23:7; Deut. 23:5). Other parallels between these stories include a journey of the main character as the setting for each story, each beginning with God's command to 'go' (*lēk*, Gen. 22:2; Num. 22:20); the presence of the messenger of YHWH (*mal'ak-yhwh*) who reverses the goal of each character's mission, whether to sacrifice Isaac or to curse Israel (Gen. 22:11, 15; Num. 22:22, 23, 24, 25, 26, 27, 31, 32, 34, 35); the presence of two servant lads who accompany the main character on his journey, the expression 'his two servant-lads' occurring only these two times in the Torah (Gen. 22:3; Num. 22:22); use of *rā'āh* (to see) as a key word, used five times in the Akedah story (Gen. 22:4, 8, 13, 14) and five times in the donkey episode (Num. 22:23, 25, 27, 31, 33); Balaam claims to have a 'vision' (*maḥăzêh*) of Shaddai, a term used only once more elsewhere in the Pentateuch, when YHWH comes to Abram in a 'vision' (Gen. 15:1; Num. 24:4, 16); the later language of Balaam's 'lifting up his eyes and seeing' echoes similar language from Abraham's binding-of-Isaac episode, where the phrase is used twice (Gen. 22:4, 13; Num. 24:2); use of the rare word 'anything' (*mě'ûmāh*), occurring nine times in the Pentateuch, whereby Abraham is not to do 'anything' to Isaac (Gen. 22:12), and Balaam has no power to speak 'anything' (Num. 22:38); both journeys lead to the summit of mountains, where whole burnt offerings are offered on altars (Gen. 22:13; Num. 22:41–23:3; 23:14–15; 23:28–30); a similarly phrased return from the journey, with a use of three verbs (*qûm*, *hālak* and *šûb*) that occur together in the Torah in only these two instances (Gen. 22:19; Num. 24:25); and both Abraham and Balaam are used to confirm YHWH's blessing of Israel, using the doubled, emphatic form of the verb 'to bless' (Gen. 22:17; Num 24:10) – such connections serve to underscore the contrast between Abraham and Balaam (see Safren 1988; Marcus 1995: 38–39; Friedman 2001: 504; Frisch 2005: 110; Waxman 2006a; R. Novick 2007). As result of Abraham's obedience, YHWH promised to multiply Abraham's seed as the stars of heaven and as the sand on the seashore, and that his seed would possess the gate of his enemies (Gen. 22:17). Now it is the many thousands of them encamped nearby that causes Balak and Moab to dread Israel, even as Balaam's final utterances will pronounce ultimate defeat for all of Israel's enemies (Num. 24:15–24).

The nature and language of YHWH's blessing of Israel, as promised to Abraham and uttered through Balaam, correspond in three instances (cf. R. Novick 2007: 32). First, Balaam's exclamation at the conclusion of his third utterance, 'Who blesses you is blessed, and who curses you is cursed!' (Num. 23:24), echoes directly YHWH's word at the original call of Abram, 'I will bless the one who blesses you, and curse him who dishonours you' (Gen. 12:3) – indeed, in Balaam's 'call', Balak declares, 'I know whom you bless will be blessed and whom you curse will be cursed' (22:7; cf. Waxman 2006a: 5). Second, when in his first prophetic speech, Balaam asks, 'Who has counted (*mānāh*) the dust (*'ăpar*) of Jacob?' (Num. 23:10), his language parallels YHWH's promise to Abram, 'I will make your descendants as the dust (*'ăpar*) of the earth, so that if a man could count (from *mānāh*) the dust (*'ăpar*) of the earth, then your descendants could also be counted (from *mānāh*)' (Gen. 13:16). In the third instance, more broadly, Balaam prophesies the destruction of Israel's enemies, such as shattering the brow of Moab and that Edom would become a 'possession' (*yĕrēšāh*) (Num. 24:17–18), along with the doom of the other Transjordan nations (24:20–24), which recalls YHWH's confirming oath on Abraham's obedience, that 'your descendant will possess (*yāraš*) the gate of his enemies' (Gen. 22:17). The undercurrent of YHWH's promises to Abraham continues thematically, and Balaam's journey – despite himself – will end in blessing for Israel. Given some Ugaritic parallels, the phrase 'saddled his donkey' may be an ancient idiom for setting out (Avishur 1999: 99–101), although in this case the donkey will play a key role in the rest of the scene. Jewish interpretation, reflecting on the parallel between Abraham and Balaam as men of means who had servants for such menial labour, saw the personal saddling of donkeys as a display of their zeal for the journey (see *b. Sanh.* 105b; *Gen. Rab.* 55.8; *Num. Rab.* 20.12): Abraham was so zealous to obey God, even at the risk of great personal loss, that he saddled his own donkey; Balaam, coveting the riches of Balak's house, is so eager to set out and curse Israel in defiance of God's will, he too saddles his own donkey. One important function of these parallels, theologically, is that Abraham's life with God, from his call out of Ur to his obedient submission to God's will, in the near sacrifice of Isaac, whereby YHWH promised and confirmed by oath his blessing on Israel, is the irrevocable and indestructible foundation of Israel's life and blessing in the land. Abraham's previous journey, in other words, counteracts the journey of Balaam, an import to which the Midrash gestures: 'Let the saddling done by our father Abraham in order to go and fulfil the will of Him at whose word the world came into existence counteract the saddling done by Balaam in order to go and curse Israel' (*Gen. Rab.* 55.8; H. Freedman 1939: 1:489; cf. R. Novick 2007: 30). With Israel encamped on the plains of Moab, on the cusp of realizing the inheritance of the land of Canaan, echoes of Abraham's life underscore that Israel enters the land because of YHWH's divine promise to the patriarchs (cf. Waxman 2006a: 6–7). 'It is not because of your righteousness or the uprightness of your heart that you are going to possess their land,' Moses declares on the plains of Moab, 'but because of the wickedness of these nations, YHWH your God is dispossessing them from before you, and *for the sake of confirming the word that YHWH swore to your fathers, to Abraham, Isaac, and Jacob*' (Deut. 9:5; emphasis added). Moreover, in thwarting Balak's scheme to curse Israel in such a way that Moab itself becomes the subject of a prophetic curse (24:17), there comes a literal fulfilment of YHWH's promise to Abram that he would curse whoever dishonours Abram (Gen. 12:3; cf. Num. 24:9).

There is yet a deeper significance to the parallels, found in the dynamic of cursing versus blessing. In Genesis 1 – 11, before the call of Abram, the word 'curse' (*'ārāh*) occurs five times (Gen. 3:14, 17; 4:11; 5:29; 9:25), while for his call YHWH uses the word 'bless' (*bārak*) five times, confirming that through Abram he will restore blessing to all the families of the earth (Gen. 12:1–3; see Morales 2020: 21). The word 'curse' (*'ārāh*) occurs seven times in the Balaam narrative, beginning with Balak's call to him, knowing that 'whom you curse is cursed' (Num. 22:6 [three times], 12; 23:7; 24:9 [twice]), but the word 'bless' (*bārak*) occurs fourteen times, exactly double, demonstrating that the 'power of Abraham's blessing outweighs the attempt to curse' (Waxman 2006a: 8). Justly, Waxman reads Balaam as a foil for Abraham, bringing the Abraham story into the context of this part of Numbers (2006a: 9): 'While Balak may well have contracted an anti-Abraham, from the same place and supposedly possessing the same powers, to reverse the divine promises and blessedness granted to Abraham, this project is doomed to failure.' While the near-sacrifice of Isaac has been understood widely as a foundation story for the Jerusalem cult (see Morales 2020: 28–32), here an even broader significance is mapped out: Israel enters the land through the billows of smoke ascending from Abraham's whole burnt offering on Moriah's summit – having demonstrated unswerving loyalty to YHWH, he received the promises afresh, confirmed by divine oath (Gen. 22:15–17).

While contrasted against Abraham, Balaam is often compared, and even identified, with Laban in his greedy exploits of Jacob (see *TgJon* on Num. 22:5; *Yalk. Shim., Shem.* 168; *b. Sanh.* 105a; P. Kahn 2007a). Others, such as Rashbam (on Gen. 32:26), have noted parallels with Moses' near-death encounter in Exodus 4:24–26 (cf. Shenk 1993: 37; Hepner 2011: 183–184). Embry points to the following characteristics and features shared by Exodus 4 and Numbers 22 (2010: 180, 185–191): the main character has been allowed/commanded by YHWH to proceed with a journey; both characters, 'arousing his fierce anger' (*wayyiḥar-'ap*), are attacked by YHWH; both characters are sent to deliver a word from YHWH, and both to a foreign ruler (Pharaoh, Balak); both are saved through the intervention of another female character; both have trouble speaking and are accompanied by a figure who speaks; both have their 'foot' (*regel*) directly involved in the process (Exod. 4:25; Num. 22:25); both are equipped with a staff; and he also notes the similarity between 'Zippor' and 'Zipporah'. He understands the parallels to suggest a 'missional journey' type-scene, a rite of passage in which the character must pass through a near-death scenario, and sees, in line with rabbinic interpretation, that the likely function of the correspondences is to present Balaam as something of a counter-hero to Moses (cf. Embry 2010: 178).

22. Balaam's journey immediately kindles the fierce anger of God. The phrase 'fierce anger was kindled' (*wayyiḥar-'ap*) occurs five times in Numbers with 'YHWH' as subject (11:10; 12:9; 32:10, 13; cf. 11:1), and in every case having his own sinful people as the cause for kindling his anger. In this case, the fierce anger of 'God' (*'ĕlōhîm*) is kindled, once more distancing Balaam's knowledge of God from Israel's relationship with YHWH. The phrase also forms a literary link throughout the story's development: Balaam's fierce anger is kindled against the donkey (22:27), and then Balak's fierce anger is kindled against Balaam (24:10). Connecting chapter 25 to the Balaam narrative, YHWH's fierce anger will be kindled against his people for the last time when Israel joins to Baal of Peor (25:3).

The reason for God's fierce anger is explained: 'because (*kî*) he was going', using the pr. (*hû'*) for emphasis. Attempts by some to read the particle *kî* temporally (versus causally), so that God was angered *as he was going* (Cox 1884: 53; Ashley 1993: 454), are not convincing and do not resolve the matter. One must resort to God's previous words to Balaam for deeper understanding: God had first declared, 'You will not go with them,' forbidding Balaam to curse the people because they were blessed (v. 12), and in a second response he instructed Balaam to go, adding the stipulation that he was to do only YHWH's word (v. 20). The natural implication is that Balaam, enticed by the riches of Balak, has undertaken the journey intent on cursing Israel. Rashi discerns Balaam's inner intent based on the change of vocabulary in the previous verses: whereas God permitted Balaam to go 'with them' (*'ittām*, v. 20), Balaam goes 'with them' (*'im*, v. 21), implying the same goal in their hearts was now in his heart (1997: 4:278–279; cf. Anisfeld 2013: 228). Leibowitz refers to the nineteenth-century commentators Mecklenburg and Malbim, who make the same point: that *'im* implies an active going along with, an equality of purpose (1982: 310–311). Previously noted, Balaam's waking early in the morning and saddling his own donkey may be read as a depraved eagerness on Balaam's part to go to curse Israel and, at their expense, gain riches for himself. Just as YHWH's fierce anger was kindled at the voraciousness with which Israel consumed the meat he had provided (11:33), so now God's fierce anger is kindled at how Balaam is going, at the wicked intentions of his heart. Making a similar correlation, Gane writes that both the Israelites (in Num. 11) and Balaam fail to show restraint, incurring divine anger 'by single-mindedly gravitating to self-gratification' (2004: 693). Such a reading explains the function of the previous verse (v. 21). Ultimately, as Keddie recognizes (1992: 207), Balaam's going would serve God's sovereign determination to bless his people, but Balaam was nevertheless intending to do something wicked.

As a result of God's kindled anger, the 'messenger' (*mal'ak*) of YHWH stations himself on the way. Balak had sent 'messengers' (*mal'ākîm*) to Balaam (22:5), and now God sends his own 'messenger' (*mal'ak*) to Balaam (cf. Savran 1994: 35). The angel of YHWH appears repeatedly throughout Genesis, notably in the binding of Isaac story (Gen. 22:11, 15), and was YHWH's agent for the exodus deliverance out of Egypt (Exod. 3:2; 14:19) as well as his promised agent for the conquest of Canaan, called simply 'angel/messenger' (Exod. 23:20, 23; 32:34; 33:2). Most recently, Moses' appeal to Edom had rehearsed how, in response to his people's cry, YHWH had sent an angel to bring Israel forth out of Egypt (Num. 20:16), whereas now he sends his messenger to obstruct Balaam's journey. Historically, the church (beginning with Justin Martyr) has understood appearances of the messenger of YHWH not only as theophanies but as Christophanies, appearances of the pre-incarnate Son, although others, including Augustine, cautioned against such precise identification. Biblical scholars and theologians favouring an association with the second Person of the Godhead point both to the Messenger's identification with YHWH, bearing his Name and authority, as well as his distinction from YHWH, speaking of him in the third person (see e.g. Reymond 2003: 72–77); others, however, observe that in the ANE such a dynamic was typical of royal messengers, the 'angel' functioning as an agent or ambassador of YHWH (see Walton 2001: 462–466; cf. W. G. MacDonald 1975). It is fitting to acknowledge mystery in these appearances of YHWH's messenger, even while affirming they indicate 'a real manifoldness in the inner life of the Deity', the Messenger conveying something of God's 'sacramental' intent to be present among his people even while safeguarding his spiritual nature, that he cannot be seen, a 'fundamental arrangement' that finds its 'supreme expression' in the incarnation of the Messiah (Vos 1975: 73–74).

The messenger of YHWH is 'stationed' (*yāṣab*, hith. stem) on Balaam's way with the purpose of being an 'adversary' or 'accuser' (literally, *śāṭān*) against him, a purpose involving a severe threat to Balaam's life (vv. 32–33). As a functional concept, used without a definite article (i.e. not as a proper noun), *śāṭān* describes one who intervenes on behalf of YHWH (see P. L. Day 1988: 45–145). Intensity heightens the storyteller's art: the audience knows both that God's fierce anger has been kindled against Balaam and that his messenger has been stationed on the way, while Balaam the diviner who boasts an intimate relationship with YHWH is oblivious to the divine threat to his life – 'he was riding his donkey and two of his servants were with him'. As 'his two servant-lads' (*něʻārāyw*) do not appear to play a significant role in the story, their mention here may serve as a contrasting echo of Abraham's previous journey (Gen. 22:3, 5, 19). It may be that Balaam's rage over being mocked by the donkey (v. 29) stems in part from its public nature, that it was in the presence of his servant-lads and the princes from Moab (this appears to be their dramatic function; cf. Levy 2012: 6). Alternatively, Sutcliffe suggested that Balaam's journey here, on his donkey and with his two servant-lads, only presents his travelling to join the Moabite caravan, which had camped outside town – the messenger stood in his way on the journey to his meeting-place with the princes of Moab, a scenario that may explain both his (temporary) use of a donkey and the renewed statement that 'Balaam went with the princes of Balak' in verse 35 (1937: 440–441). This scenario also implies God's condition had not been met (v. 20), explaining his kindled anger. The 'way' or 'road' (*derek*) is a key word in the Balaam narrative, gaining metaphoric value (cf. Levy 2012: 5); *derek* is used eight times in the donkey episode (22:22, 23 [three times], 26, 31, 32, 34) and is the last word in the larger narrative (24:25).

23–27. The donkey, 'a model of obedience' in the story (Savran 1994: 36), makes three attempts at avoiding the angel of YHWH and his sword, her avoidance narrated with escalation, each time by three words – 22 words (v. 23), 25 words (vv. 24, 25), 28 words (vv. 26–27). At the same time, space increasingly narrows upon Balaam, from field (v. 23) to a furrow with barriers on either side (v. 24) to a narrow place with no chance of turning aside (v. 26), so that he must finally confront the angel of YHWH. The ever-decreasing space, narrowing as Balaam progresses, reiterates visually both his stubbornness and his blindness, even while limiting his 'relative freedom to do as he pleases' (Leson 2007: 159). Comically, Balaam, whose profession and international repute make him out as one able to read omens, cannot discern any significance in the extraordinary behaviour of the she-ass, his long-standing mount.

That 'the donkey saw' (*wattēreʼ hāʼātôn*) the angel of YHWH is both ironic and humorous at the expense of Balaam, who will later proclaim to have his eyes opened (24:3); it is near the end of this scene when YHWH opens his eyes so that he can see what the donkey has already seen (22:31). Through the donkey's sight we gain the added detail that the angel's sword is drawn in his hand, intensifying the threat to Balaam. Possibly, the angel of YHWH and his sword recall the cherubim and sword placed at the eastward entrance to the garden of Eden (Gen. 3:24). An angel with sword drawn in hand will also be spotted by Joshua before conquering Jericho (Josh. 5:13–15), and later in Israel's history David will see the nation threatened by the angel of YHWH with his sword drawn and stretched out over Jerusalem (1 Chr. 21:16). Seeing the angel of YHWH stationed on the way with drawn sword, the donkey saves Balaam, 'turned' (*nāṭāh*) from the way and 'went into the field'. The language of the places where Balaam is forced to go by his donkey is strikingly similar to that used by Moses when requesting passage through Edom, explaining where Israel will *not* go (cf. 20:14–21). Balaam's response is to 'strike' (*nākāh*) the donkey in order to 'turn' her (*nāṭāh*) back on to the way. The dissonance between his spared life and his striking the donkey in return is part of the lampoon against Balaam, portraying him as a sorry diviner indeed, unable to perceive the situation. The Midrash brings out some of the scene's mockery (*Num. Rab.* 20.14; Slotki 1951: 6:799): 'This villain was going to curse an entire nation which had not sinned against him, yet he has to smite his ass to prevent it from going into a field!'

In the second instance, the angel of YHWH stood in the 'furrow' through the vineyards (*mišʿôl* referring to 'a road shut in between vineyards', BDB 1043); that is, a narrow path with a 'barrier' (*gādēr*) on either side. Bolger suggests 'vineyards' (*hakkĕrāmîm*) may form a play on 'cherubim' (*hakkĕrubîm*), calling to mind the Eden narrative (Gen. 3:24) – the 'sword'-bearing angel between the vineyards guards the 'way' to Israel as the cherubim and 'sword' guarded the 'way' to the garden's tree of life (1993: 224). For the second time verbatim we read that 'the donkey saw the angel of YHWH' (vv. 23, 25), again underscoring Balaam's lack of vision. Unable to turn aside, the donkey 'presses' or 'squeezes' (*lāḥaṣ*) to the 'wall' (*qîr*), so that Balaam's 'leg' or 'foot' (*regel*) gets crushed (for a possible sexual euphemism here, see Twersky 2022: 154). While 'barrier' (*gādēr*) is used twice in verse 24, 'wall' (*qîr*) is used twice in verse 25; *gādēr* implies a stone wall, while *qîr* more particularly refers to the side (or surface) of the wall (cf. *TWOT*, 798). The term *lāḥaṣ* refers to pressing strongly, including the threat of military force (Judg. 1:34) or holding a person fast against a door (2 Kgs 6:32), and is also used with the connotation of affliction or oppression (Pss 44:24; 106:42; Amos 6:14). The donkey's pressing into the wall then 'presses' (*lāḥaṣ*) Balaam's foot into the 'wall' (*qîr*), leading him to strike her 'again' (*yōsep*) – the next clause will open with *yōsep* (v. 26), repetition that dramatically highlights each unfolding stage of the narrative (Wendland 2012: 176).

On the third occasion, the angel 'again' (*yōsep*) passed over (i.e. went ahead of Balaam's way) and stood, this time in a 'narrow' or 'tight' (*ṣār*) place, one with no possibility of 'turning' to the right or left as happened in the first instance (v. 23). For the third time verbatim 'the donkey saw the angel of YHWH' while Balaam did not; and the tension has escalated since we know the donkey cannot turn away – what will she do? Apparently, the donkey fears YHWH's messenger more than she does Balaam's beatings. Saving Balaam a third time, the donkey 'lies down' (*rābaṣ*) – rather than *yāšab* (to sit down); *rābaṣ* implies an animal's repose. Here, too, as well as in the donkey's response in verse 30, Twersky finds sexual innuendo (2022: 153), and certainly Jewish tradition asserts – *perhaps* derived from taunting hints in the text – that Balaam was committing bestiality with his donkey. Although the detail would have been assumed, we are told the donkey lies down 'under Balaam', since part of the humour lies in appreciating the frustration from his point of view. The 'fierce anger of Balaam was kindled' against the donkey, just as later Balak's fierce anger will be kindled against (the donkey-like) Balaam (24:10). In his anger, Balaam 'strikes' (*nākāh*) the donkey a third time, the text adding 'with his rod' (*maqqēl*). This is the singular occurrence of *maqqēl* in Numbers; the term is used for the poplar rods employed by Jacob (Gen. 30), and for the staff to be kept in hand while Israelites ate the Passover meal (Exod. 12:11) – Balaam beats his donkey with a staff of wood. Likely, on the two previous occasions when Balaam struck the jenny (vv. 23, 25) he had also used his rod (Rendsburg 2019: 57–60). If Balaam's striking the donkey in anger with his rod (*wayyak 'et-hā'ātôn*, 22:27) intentionally recalls an angered Moses striking the rock with his staff (*wayyak 'et-hassela'*, 20:11), there may be a subtle critique of the latter.

28–35. The third scene telescopes in a twofold manner for (1) the donkey's engagement with Balaam (vv. 28–30), and (2) the angel of YHWH's engagement with Balaam (vv. 31–35), both dialogues preceded by an act of YHWH: 'And YHWH opened the mouth of the donkey' (v. 28); 'And YHWH uncovered the eyes of Balaam' (v. 31). (See Table 7.)

Table 7: Act 1, scene 3

The donkey and Balaam, vv. 28–30	The angel of YHWH and Balaam, vv. 31–35
YHWH opened the mouth of the donkey	YHWH uncovered the eyes of Balaam
She (donkey) said to Balaam	The angel of YHWH said to him (Balaam)
Balaam said to the donkey	Balaam said to the angel of YHWH
The donkey said to Balaam	The angel of YHWH said to Balaam
And he (Balaam) said	

God's kindled fierce anger, which leads to opposition of Balaam by the messenger of YHWH, opens the scene (22:22), so that YHWH's three acts three times become the starting point for consequences (Weise 2003: 78–90, noted by Sals 2008: 325). YHWH's sovereign power guides the close of scene 3. As YHWH opens the mouth of the donkey, so he uncovers the eyes of Balaam – in both the third scene of the donkey episode and in the third prophetic utterance, Balaam's eyes are opened (24:4; cf. Milgrom 1990: 192). The donkey and the messenger of YHWH both open their respective dialogue by asking for what cause Balaam has 'struck' (*nākāh*) the donkey 'these three times' (*zeh šālôš rĕgālîm*) (vv. 28, 32). By contrast, Balaam does not answer the angel of YHWH a second time, as he does the donkey. Use of 'feet' (*rĕgālîm*) for 'times' is rare, and may underscore the three occasions as distinct journeys; that is, 'these three journeys' (cf. Gen. 29:1; 30:30; 33:14), a usage which may further highlight the foolishness of Balaam's journey in the crushing of his 'foot' (*regel*, 24:25). Aside from the three instances in the Balaam narrative as 'time', a similar usage of *rĕgālîm* is found only once more, related to the annual feasts Israel is to keep 'three times' (*šālōš rĕgālîm*, 'three journeys') in the year (Exod. 23:14; cf. Rendsburg 2019: 55), a link not lost on Jewish interpreters who explained the adversarial role of the angel of YHWH as due to Balaam's wanting to uproot the nation, so as to keep Israel from celebrating these feasts (see e.g. *Num. Rab.* 20.14; Rashi 1997: 4:282). As the high point of Israel's life in the land (cf. Deut. 12:5–7), the pilgrimage feasts to Zion are an apt way to summarize what is at stake in the cursing or blessing of Israel on the brink of inheriting the land. The she-ass, hoping to reason with Balaam, asks him two questions, while the angel of YHWH asks him one question, explains to him the situation and then gives him instructions about going with the men. The angel of YHWH's dialogue, moreover, is framed by descriptions of Balaam's action (vv. 31, 35).

YHWH opens the mouth of the donkey, an act given a variety of interpretations (for comparisons with the serpent of Gen. 2 – 3, see Savran 1994). Stebbins (1885: 389), seeing Balaam as a mere charlatan, assumed that he made up this story – it is but his report to Balak's princes – in order to make his mission seem more momentous (although the story actually *lessens* Balaam's reputation). Margaliot reads the donkey's speech as a literary device, 'a monologue of Balaam who talks with himself' (1990: 80), while Spero suggests a psychological explanation, the result of Balaam's overheated imagination and sense of guilt (2013: 198 n. 2; cf. Canney 1916), Blumenthal reads the scene allegorically, with the talking donkey as a symbol of Balaam's inner voice (2006: 84) and Maimonides interpreted the scene as a prophetic vision (see *Guide for the Perplexed*, 2.42). The straightforward understanding is that God caused true speech to come forth from the mouth of an unreasoning donkey, although the hearing and understanding of that speech might have been perceived differently. Harrison, for example, explained that the donkey was heard by onlookers to be braying in protest while Balaam comprehended her speech (1990: 300). Enchantment and divination involve seeking to discern divine providence through omens, typically through the behaviour or parts of lesser creatures (reading the flight pattern of a hawk or the liver of a goat); in an ironically fitting act, therefore, God communicates with Balaam, who was made in his image and likeness, through an animal's speech – he stoops to Balaam's level, showing its absurdity. Similarly, Kaufmann observed that the opposition between God and the sorcerer is really between two domains, two forms of wisdom, divine and heathen; Balaam trusts in his enchantments, divinations, and altars in his heathen pride and ambition to be like the gods, but is forced finally to submit to the power of God (1960: 463, 497). Nevertheless, the miracle of the talking donkey is a supernatural wonder, which gets one closest to the fundamental message: in no less a wonder, God will soon utter beatific prophecies through the mouth of Balaam. The narrative's greater marvel, for which the speaking donkey serves only as preparation, is YHWH's transformation of Balaam's attempted curses into ever-increasing blessings, exalting Israel above the nations. The donkey's speech, in other words, enables the audience to read Balaam himself as merely a pawn in YHWH's hand, a mouthpiece to accomplish his sovereign will (Isbell 2002: 90; cf. *Num. Rab.* 20.14). The donkey's use of 'struck' (*nākāh*) may be intended to recall Balaam's original agenda to 'strike down' (*nākāh*) Israel (22:6). Balaam, contrary to his humbled posture before the angel of YHWH, apparently finds his donkey's speech unremarkable, or is perhaps portrayed as too livid to register the astounding oddity. The donkey asks, 'What have I done to you' that you have struck me these three times? The audience knows what she has done; namely, spared his life three times. His declared reason for striking her three times is that she has 'taunted', 'mocked' or 'made sport of' (*ʿālal* in hith.; BDB 759; *HALOT* 2.834) Balaam. Here, we are given further insight into Balaam's character, as well as the likely function of the earlier mention of his two servant-lads (v. 22) and the princes of Moab/Balak (vv. 21, 35): having carefully crafted a dignified image as a diviner and devout follower of YHWH, he is enraged that the donkey's actions have made him look a fool in the presence of his entourage. 'At this point in the story', Spero observes similarly (2013: 195), 'we must see events as they appear to the distinguished princes of Moab who have come to honour the famous sorcerer.' Balaam's language of what the donkey has done to him ('made a mockery of me', *hitʿallalt*), further resonates with the language of what YHWH had done to Egypt in the exodus, when he says that the Israelites will be able to tell their children and grandchildren how 'I made a mockery' (*hitʿallaltî*) in Egypt (Exod. 10:2; 1 Sam. 6:6) (cf. Isbell 2002: 86; Hepner 2011: 182). The angel of YHWH, after asking the same question, will vindicate the donkey's actions, making Balaam blameworthy for smiting the animal three times (vv. 32–33). Adding to the humour, Balaam, in his rage over being taunted, exclaims that 'if only there were a sword (*ḥereb*) in my hand . . . I would slay you now', which reminds the audience that the angel of YHWH even now stands with a 'sword' (*ḥereb*) in hand, ready to slay Balaam – precisely what the she-ass has been attempting to avoid! In due time, Balaam will indeed be slain by a 'sword' (*ḥereb*) (31:8). Rather than explaining the situation to Balaam, which the angel of YHWH will do, the donkey continues to reason with

Balaam, asking him leading questions as if condescending to a child: 'I (*'ānōkî*), have I not been your donkey, which you have ridden for so long until this day – was it ever my habit to do so to you?' Here, 'habit' (*sākan* in hiph.) is underscored by repetition. The she-ass is pointing out Balaam's failure to discern the strangeness of the present situation when compared to his long and consistent history of riding her – can he not deduce she must have had a sound reason for her actions? The point is only magnified by his failure to register the strangeness of her speech. Balaam's brief answer, 'No' (*lō'*), opens the way for a reassessment of the situation given by the messenger, one that begins with a second act of YHWH.

YHWH 'uncovered' (*gālāh* in pi.) the eyes of Balaam. Later, before uttering an oracle, Balaam will describe himself as one having 'his eyes uncovered' (24:16). The expression, however, is not ever used for prophetic vision. As YHWH performed an unusual and presumably temporary act for the donkey's mouth, so he does for Balaam – YHWH is utterly sovereign over both speech and vision, mouth and eyes. As a result, Balaam's sight finally accords with his donkey's original sight, a point brought out through verbatim repetition of the donkey's original view:

> v. 31: Balaam saw the angel of YHWH stationed on the way, and his sword drawn in his hand.
> v. 23: The donkey saw the angel of YHWH stationed on the way, and his sword drawn in his hand.

As the prospect of his near death at the hands of this divine messenger – and having barely escaped three times despite himself – sinks in, Balaam falls to the ground; with two wayyiqtols we read that he 'bowed' (*wayyiqqōd*) and 'prostrated himself' (*wayyištaḥû*) to his brow or 'face' (*'ap*). Bartelmus observes how Balaam progressively sinks lower; whereas he had been sitting on the donkey which eventually lay down under him (v. 27), now, in prostrating himself, Balaam bows lower than his donkey (2005: 37–38). Bolger draws several parallels between the Balaam story and the Eden narratives of Genesis 2 – 3 (1993: 223–225): including imagery of YHWH's 'planting' (*nāṭa'*, Gen. 2:8; Num. 24:5–7), 'opening' of eyes motif (different Hebr. terms, Gen. 3:5, 7; Num. 22:31; 24:3), talking animals, and angels with drawn sword, guarding 'the way' (Gen. 3:24; Num. 22:23).

In verse 32, the angel of YHWH opens the dialogue with the same pointed question as the donkey to Balaam: 'Why have you struck your donkey these three times?' The divine concern over the donkey is like a parable, the lesson of which is captured well by the Midrash: If the angel of YHWH demands satisfaction from Balaam for beating a donkey, which possesses neither merit nor the covenant of the patriarchs, how much more so in the case of Israel (*Num. Rab.* 20.15), an entire nation he has redeemed out of Egypt to make his treasured possession? With some irony the messenger then says 'Look!' (*hinnê*), so that Balaam sees what he had earlier missed; namely, that the messenger of YHWH himself (*'ānōkî*) had set forth as an adversary. The last clause (*kî-yārat hadderek lĕnegdî*) is extremely difficult on a number of counts. Does it read 'because your way was perverse before me?' (see Ibn Ezra 1999: 188). The first challenge to this reading is that the MT reads 'the way' not 'your way'. While the SamP and LXX read 'your way' (as does the Vg), the MT seems more consistent with the rest of the story's use of 'the way' (22:22, 23, 34) – although one may argue this frequency led to a copyist's error. Second, the verb *yārat* is ambiguous, lexicons guessing 'be precipitate' or 'rush headlong'. Recourse to the other possible use of this word in Job 16:11 is of little value since that passage appears to use a different root, *rātāh*. The SamP reads *hāraʿ* (evil) adjectivally for 'your evil way', and 4QNum^b has *rāʿāh* (evil) in a verbless nominal clause, 'the way is evil'. Replacing *yārat* with *rāʿāh* is no less viable than imposing the meaning 'perverse' for *yārat*. Third, how one understands *yārat*, likely signifying to cast down (*HALOT* 1.438 suggests a slippery slope for Num. 22:32), will influence whether one reads *kî*, as 'because', 'that', 'when' or as an intensive ('indeed'). Reading *yārat* as 'perverse' provides a motive for the messenger ('I came forth as an adversary *because* the way was perverse before me'). While this understanding would offer the clearest statement as to Balaam's character in the whole story, it nevertheless involves a few changes to MT, and includes a fourth difficulty. The translation of *lĕnegdî* as 'before me' is problematic since it is typically used with an object, whether physical, such as an angelic being standing before or in front of someone (Josh. 5:13; Dan.8:15) or conceptual such as YHWH's judgements or sacrifices being set before or in front of someone (Pss 18:22; 50:8). The present verse, however, requires an idiomatic use of *lĕnegdî* that basically means 'your way was perverse *in my estimation*'. P. L. Day argues that *lĕnegdî* can mean 'in my evaluation' or 'in my judgement', and translates: 'because the journey was hasty in my judgement' (1988: 65–66, citing BDB 617). Such a usage, however, is questionable since the idiom is otherwise expressed with 'in my eyes' (see v. 34) or 'to me' (using *lî*). Through Balaam's own words in verse 34, one may deduce much of the significance of the typical (mis)translation of verse 32, albeit on a sounder textual basis. Ashley, to take one example, suggests textual corruption only because the transparent MT reading 'makes little sense here' – however, his construal ('because the way in front of me is steep') is hindered by reading *yārat* as a predicate adjective (1993: 453). Rather, the idea of a path steeply descending before the divine messenger fits with the previous narrative portrayal (Hirsch [2007a: 491] refers 'to a road that descends in a steep slope'). Accepting the MT, especially the clear phrase 'the way in front of me', and weighing the semantic ranges of *kî* and *yāraṭ*, leads most naturally to a translation describing the messenger of YHWH's previous action in the narrative: 'I myself came forth as an adversary when (or intensified 'indeed') the way hastened in front of me'; that is, as described in verses 22, 23, 24, 25 and 26, the angel of YHWH is now having Balaam see ('Look!') that on every occasion the way Balaam traversed led to his certain destruction. This, then, becomes the divine accusation against Balaam for beating his donkey three times: 'Why have you struck your donkey these three times – do you not realize she deviated in every case only to spare your life since I had come out as your adversary, stationing myself on the way before you; indeed, the pathway led directly to me so that you were headed straight into my drawn sword?'

On this reading, verse 33 follows most naturally: 'The donkey saw me' – stationed on the way right in front of you – 'and turned aside from my face these three times. Now, had she not I would have slain you and let her live.' Use of 'these three times' demonstrates the angel of YHWH is still reprimanding Balaam for striking the donkey 'these three times'. Balaam's twofold response also supports my reading of verse 32. The first part of his response 'I did not know that you were stationed to encounter me on the way' accords precisely with a reiteration of the messenger's words in my reading. While the second part of his response 'if it is evil in your eyes let me return' would appear to support the translation of verse 32 as 'your way is perverse before me', yet the difference of expressions is telling: Balaam uses 'evil' (*ra'*) and 'in your eyes' (*bě'ênêkā*) – there is no lexical link between the two verses. Use of 'also' (*gam*) and other phraseology ('you *also* I would have slain and her I *would have* left alive') led to the notion that the angel in fact killed the donkey (perhaps in place of Balaam since he witnessed her speech; see *Num. Rab.* 20.14, 15; Ibn Ezra 1999: 189), but the messenger's point is rather, as Nachmanides discerned, that the she-ass's turning away was entirely for Balaam's benefit, not her own, and yet he repaid her evil for good (1975: 261).

Suddenly faced with a threat to his life, Balaam declares, 'I have sinned' (*ḥāṭā'tî*). The explanation he offers defines the limits of his confession: 'because I did not know that you were stationed to encounter me on the way'. He confesses that he had sinned in beating his donkey three times – for he had beaten her only because he had not known the messenger of YHWH was on the path before him. To be sure, his confession responds adequately to the opening questions by both the donkey and the angel, including the angel's ensuing defence of the donkey (vv. 28, 32–33). His 'I did not know' (*lō' yāda'tî*), as the sages put it, testifies against his self-proclaimed knowledge of the Most High (cf. *Tan.*, Balak 10). What remains to be addressed is how Balaam responds to his original fault, the *reason* why the angel of YHWH stationed himself on the way in the first place – and, here, Balaam's words are revealing: 'if it is evil in your sight let me return'. The designation 'evil' is qualified in two ways, with 'if' (leaving the possibility an open question) and 'in your eyes' (a subjective judgement). Balaam does not repent of setting out on the journey, nor of his motives for doing so; his 'if . . . (then) let-me-return (cohort.)' demonstrates he is bargaining for his life. Regardless, Balaam's words are a telling confirmation that his journey, accompanying the princes of Moab, was rebellion against YHWH's will (cf. Hawk 2017: 86). Frisch compares Balaam's display to the fleeting words of Pharaoh, who had similarly said, 'I have sinned' (Exod. 9:27; 10:16–17), an apt comparison (2005: 105), since Balaam's words are likely meant to recall those of Pharaoh. More directly, Balaam's 'if' (*'im*) recalls God's earlier 'if' in verse 20, 'precisely where he [Balaam] had gone wrong' (Moyer 2012: 182).

The angel of YHWH responds, directing Balaam to 'go' (*lēk*) with 'the men' (*hāʾănāšîm*), the consistent divine designation for the princes of Moab (see 22:9, 20, 35), reiterating YHWH's original warning (in v. 20): 'but only' (*wĕʾepes*) the word which I will speak to you – that (alone) you will speak'. While in verse 20 it was 'the word which I will speak to you, that is what you will do (*taʿăśeh*)', here it is 'that is what you will speak (*tĕdabbēr*)'. The difference may point to a deeper significance. Had Balaam set out on the journey presuming some level of liberty with his own speech (versus actions), only to be more narrowly limited now? Or, had Balaam somehow disobeyed God's command on his journey 'because he was going' (v. 22) or perhaps having separated from 'the men' with whom he was commanded to go – note again the curious detail in v. 22, that (only?) Balaam's two servant-lads were with him, whereas now the focus is on his speech before Balak? As noted for verse 22, Sutcliffe suggested that this donkey journey was merely to meet the Moabite caravan, so that only now does Balaam reach the princes of Balak (1937: 440–441). At the least, it now becomes clear that Balaam's speech concerning Israel will not be out of his own resources – he will be forced to speak only what YHWH would have him speak (see 22:38; 24:13). More significantly, the divine demands of obedience form an inclusio around the donkey episode (22:20, 35) and, cast as a resolving of matters in both instances, serves to shade Balaam's character negatively, justifying God's anger at his journey.

The donkey episode, and Balaam's encounter with the angel of YHWH, is what 'brings home to Balaam that he would not succeed in his purpose, and that his journey would be fruitless' (J. M. Cohen 1988: 112), and clarifies that without YHWH's intervention Balaam had no real power as a seer – even his own donkey demonstrated more insight than the famous diviner. Once more, Balaam is bidden to go in an incongruous manner. Whereas earlier, the divine allowance resonated with YHWH's previous refusal (22:12, 20), presenting the instruction as a concession or test, here, after Balaam's life-threatening encounters with the angel of YHWH, the instruction also 'reverberates with divine anger and displeasure' (Hawk 2017: 86). Frisch sees Balaam's adventure en route to Moab as aimed at making him realize that 'his intentions are evil and unacceptable', and just as his evil intentions against his donkey were unveiled as folly and malignity, the question remains: Will he 'ask himself whether there is any justification for the harm he is planning to wreak on Israel?' (2005: 111). Just as he spurned the donkey's message, continuing his journey, so Balaam continues his plan to curse God's people – the donkey episode reveals Balaam's character flaw vividly (Frisch 2005: 111).

The apostle Peter describes the speaking ass episode as a rebuke for Balaam's iniquity, an attempt at hindering the prophet's madness in pursuing the aim of cursing Israel because he loved the wages of unrighteousness (2 Peter 2:15–16). The exegetical clues for such a widely held reading include Balaam's second questioning of God (22:19), God's kindled anger at Balaam's journey (22:22), the divine hindrance to his journey (22:22, 24, 26), Balaam's infuriated impatience and beating of his donkey, refusing – out of his desire for Balak's wages – to submit to YHWH's expressed will and providential hindrances (22:23, 25, 27), and the angel of YHWH's rebuke and admonition (22:32–33, 35).

22:36 – 24:25 Act 2: Balaam constrained by YHWH to bless Israel

Despite YHWH's original forbidding of him to do so, Balaam now finds himself before Balak, who continues to press him with the assurance of wealth and honour in exchange for cursing Israel. But just as Balaam, even with beatings, could not control his donkey, so Balak, either by enticements or threats, is not able to control Balaam, whose words, as with the donkey, are controlled by YHWH. Just as the donkey obeyed a being stronger and more threatening than his master, so now Balaam will obey YHWH who is stronger and more threatening than his master Balak (see Bartelmus 2005: 38). As with the previous act, there are three scenes, the last of which, scene 6, escalates and expands with four more parables. As Licht points out (1986: 72), all three scenes contain similar elements: (1) Balak takes Balaam to a high place; (2) altars are built and sacrifices offered; (3) Balaam seeks and receives inspiration; (4) Balaam returns to Balak and delivers a divine speech; (5) there is a confrontation between Balak and Balaam (see also Allen 1973: 254–255; Olson 1996: 145–147; Cole 2000: 398; Leson 2007: 51). Significantly, the fourth oracle will break the established pattern, forming a rhetorical climax (Wendland 2012: 179).

Correspondences with the exodus have already been noted, Sailhamer observing further parallels between Exodus 1 and 2 and the rest of the Balaam story (1992: 406–407): just as Pharaoh had made three attempts to counteract God's blessing of Israel and hence to decrease their number (Exod. 1:11–14, 15–21, 22), so Balak also makes three attempts to thwart God's blessing on Israel (23:1–12, 13–26; 23:27–24:9), and in both scenarios God intervened on each of the three occasions, blessing his people all the more; both scenarios culminate, after the third attempt, with an announcement of the dawning of God's chosen deliverer – in the first case, Moses (Exod. 2:1–10), and in the second, the Davidic Messiah (24:15–19). Associations with Israel's exodus out of Egypt position YHWH's thwarting of Balak's scheme to curse Israel through Balaam, a Mesopotamian sorcerer, as a mighty act of God for the sake of his people.

22:36–40 Setting: Balak meets with Balaam

36–40. The perspective shifts from Balaam back to Balak, in a setting not unlike the chapter's opening; whereas earlier Balak 'saw' (22:2), now Balak 'heard'. His continuing anxiety over Israel's nearness is evident in the urgency of his actions. First, having heard that Balaam had decided to come, he goes forth to meet him at the Arnon border, 'on the outskirts' (*biqṣêh*) of the border – to the earliest possible place within Moab's border in which to meet him. Doing so also demonstrated 'the maximum respect' to Balaam (Milgrom 1990: 193), underlining Balak's craven desire for his help. Israel's wilderness journey had begun with YHWH's judgement 'on the outskirts' (*biqṣêh*) of the Camp (11:1), language that resurfaces in Balaam's attempts to curse Israel (22:41; 23:13), but which also marks the progress of Israel's journey to the outskirts of the lands of the nations (20:16; cf. 33:6, 37; 34:3). Reference to the 'city of Moab' may imply Ar, the capital of Moab located on its border (Num. 21:15; Deut. 2:18; Isa. 15:1; cf. G. B. Gray 1903: 286; Levine 2000: 160). Second, encountering Balaam the very moment he enters the outskirts of Moab's border, Balak immediately chides him for his delay: 'Did I not surely send for you to call for you – why did you not come to me?' Balak's urgency is underscored by repetition and emphasis (*šālōaḥ šālaḥtî/'ēlêkā liqrō'-lāk*), and by his question 'Why did you not come to me?' after the fact of Balaam's arrival. So, Balaam responds, 'Look! I came to you.' Balak's question – essentially, 'what took you so long?' – contains an undercurrent of humour for the audience, which has just rehearsed the threefold delay with Balaam's she-ass, along with his harrowing brush with death by the sword of YHWH's messenger. Once more, as the character who knows Balaam best (aside from YHWH), Balak assumes Balaam's avaricious character (cf. Sherwood 2002: 178): 'Truly (*'umnām*), am I not able (*'ûkal*) to honour you?' The only reason he can think of for Balaam's delay is that Balaam had somehow doubted his reward. That Balak is indeed willing to offer him extravagant riches further underscores his desperate anxiety over Israel.

Balak's questions also reveal his own damaged pride, according to Wiggershaus (2021: 96–97), since in the ancient world the treatment of envoys was tantamount to such treatment of the envoy's lord himself: 'Based on the way you have treated my representatives, do you assume that I am not able to honour you?' Moreover, the construction of Balak's second question lends itself to a foreshadowing that in Jewish tradition is taken as prophetic – Balaam will indeed leave humiliated and without honours (see *Tan.* 10; Rashi 1997: 4:286). This insight may be supported textually (Wiggershaus 2021: 97): whereas Balaam had refused the first envoys, saying, 'Go back to your land, for YHWH has refused (*mē'ēn*) to grant me to go with you' (22:13), later Balak will say, 'Flee to your place . . . YHWH has withheld (*mē'ēn*) honour from you' (24:11).

Balak receives two responses from Balaam. First, that he is here now, then regarding Balak's 'ability' (*'ûkal*) to honour him with wealth, Balaam prepares him for disappointment over Balaam's own ability: 'Now am I even able (*'ûkal*) to speak (just) anything? The word that God puts in my mouth, that is what I will speak.' While the statement sounds pious, the audience knows the divine threatening and reiteration required for Balaam's compliance (22:12, 20, 33, 35), as well as the humorous parallel with Balaam's donkey, whose mouth YHWH opened.

Having gone forth to the outskirts of Moab, by the Arnon, to meet Balaam, Balak now returns, and Balaam, neglecting to report God's forbidding of any attempt to curse Israel, 'went with Balak'. Mention of Arnon recalls Israel's recent conquests and nearness to Moab (Num. 21:13, 26). They come to Kiriath-Huzoth, meaning something along the lines of 'village of courts', if *ḥuṣôt* is taken to derive from *ḥāṣēr*, or 'village of streets/divisions', if from *ḥûṣ* (cf. LXX, which has *poleis epauleōn*, 'City of Habitations'). In either case, the name feeds into the idea of a peripheral first engagement between Moabites and Israel, and underscores the boundary or separateness of Israel from other peoples (cf. v. 41). Dijkstra, who observes the 'geography' of the text, mapping emphasis on centre and periphery, suggests the pun 'village of half-way', being the 'meeting-place halfway down the road from where both Balaam and Balak enter the central scene of action' (1995a: 86–87). Balak prepares a feast and 'sends' (*wayĕšallaḥ*) again (see 22:5, 10, 15, 37) for Balaam and the princes who were with him. The designation 'sacrifice' (*wayyizbaḥ*) implies the feast was part of a ritual, in this case likely to Chemosh, the god of the Moabites (see Num. 21:29; Jer. 48:46), also associated with the Ammonites and their god Molech or Milcom (Judg. 11:24). 'Chemosh' may mean something like 'Destroyer' or 'Subduer' (cf. Strawn 2000); he is called 'the abomination of Moab' (1 Kgs 11:7).

Wiggershaus believes that 'Chemosh, though not named, looms in the background of the narrative,' arguing that the earlier *qĕsāmîm* ('divinations', 22:7) 'undoubtedly appealed to Chemosh for their inquiries' (2021: 109–110). As with the ensuing offerings preliminary to Balaam's utterances (23:1, 14, 29–30), the sacrifices may be intended to obtain divine favour for Balak's object of cursing Israel. On this scenario, the present feast may have YHWH in its purview, hoping to manipulate him against his people (cf. 23:27).

22:41 – 23:12 Scene 4: Balaam's first parable

41. Each of the scenes of act 2 takes place at a different locale, presumably positioned as a place of favour to God and as providing a unique view of the Camp of Israel from which to curse the people (22:41; 23:13–14, 27–28). In Babylonian practice, which may be an assumed context for Balaam, the place of divination was important and carefully chosen, referred to as places of divination, decision or judgement (Daiches 1909: 63). In the morning Balak 'took' (*lāqaḥ*) Balaam, a reminder that the soothsayer is pulled by two opposing wills: Balak's desire to curse Israel, enticing him with riches, and YHWH's desire to bless Israel, threatening him with sure destruction. They ascend the 'Heights of Baal' (*bāmôt bāʿal*), apparently 'a well-known site for the worship of the Canaanite fertility god, Baal' (Wendland 2012: 182). High places in Scripture often refer to places of pagan idolatry (1 Kgs 12:32; 13:2, 32; 15:14; 2 Kgs 12:3; 14:4; 15:4, 35; 17:29; 18:4; 21:3; 23:9, 13, 15, 19, 20; etc.). The form of *bāmôt* here always occurs within cultic contexts, designating a sanctuary (Vaughan 1974: 13–14). Likely, we are to presume the presence of a staff of priests – at least, 'the seven altars and sacrifices are indicative of such Levantine Baalism' (Wiggershaus 2021: 100). The Heights of Baal is later listed among the territory allotted to the tribe of Reuben (Josh. 13:17); Ibn Ezra identifies the Heights of Baal with the high places of Arnon, *bāmôt ʾarnōn*, noted in Numbers 21:28 (1999: 190). Reference to Baal links the Balaam narrative with the following story, where Israel 'joins Baal of Peor' (25:3), a link that led ancient rabbis to see Balak as a diviner who had divined the places where Israel would fall (see *Num. Rab.* 20.18). Yet even from the Heights of Baal, Balaam saw only the 'outskirts' (*qĕṣêh*) of the people, who under God's blessing have been fruitful, becoming an abundant host. The root *qāṣeh* was used in verse 36, and resurfaces here almost as a motif: Balak of Moab, along with his hired diviner Balaam, will make a first attempt at execrating Israel by focusing on the *outskirts of the Camp* (22:41; 23:13), which recalls the focal place of judgement as soon as Israel had left Sinai for the wilderness journey, when the fire of YHWH had consumed the 'outskirts of the Camp' (*biqṣêh hammaḥăneh*, 11:1). Nachmanides captures well the arrangement of the Camp (Num. 1 – 6) as a subtext in his gloss (1975: 263–264): 'Balaam did not see the whole camp [of Israel] because they were encamped in four standards [positioned in all] four directions of heaven,' and further explains that Balak's changing of locales was in the hope of viewing other parts of the Camp that, due to unrighteousness, might be open to being cursed of God.

23:1–2. As a skilled practitioner of his divining trade, Balaam instructs Balak to build 'for me' (*lî*) seven altars and to prepare 'for me' (*lî*) seven bulls and seven rams. Noth suggests the likelihood that the new altars served to avoid any taint from previous cultic use (1968: 182), demonstrating the care with which Balaam sought to procure divine favour. The phrase 'seven bulls and seven rams' (*šibʻāh pārîm wěšibʻāh ʼêlîm*) occurs also at Numbers 23:29 and elsewhere in Ezekiel 45:23, Job 42:8 and 1 Chronicles 15:26. An astrological explanation, with seven altars for the seven planets, seems the likeliest reason for the number (so, too, Milgrom 1990: 194). There will also be seven oracles (23:7, 18; 24:3, 15, 20, 21, 23). Balak does just as Balaam speaks, as he had said he would (22:17), willing to spare no expense for the sake of Israel's destruction. By this ritual, von Rad understands that 'Balaam still intends to curse the people and makes all the necessary preparations for doing so' (2011: 79). The excessive and lavish sacrifices are acts of intercession, attempts by Balaam – at Balak's expense – to change YHWH's disposition toward Israel and persuade him in favour of Moab (cf. v. 4). Their excessive nature, repeated three times, betrays Balaam's knowledge of YHWH's determination that Israel be blessed and not cursed, his 'great stock of gifts' aimed at persuading YHWH to reconsider (Hawk 2017: 86). It was commonplace in the ANE for patrons of divination to endeavour to procure favourable results by catering to the deities' appetites, and the sacrifices also served as an appeal for the gods to convene in their heavenly courtroom for the purposes of giving a verdict (Wiggershaus 2021: 118, 172). Daiches points out that the building of altars and offering of sacrifices – by both the diviner and the one for whom he divines – was a necessary part of Babylonian divination ceremonies, one of which included seven altars and seven lambs, further portraying Balaam as a sorcerer (1909: 61–62). The prophets of Israel do not chase after prophecy. Rather than seeking it, prophecy is thrust on them, but Balaam by contrast 'hankers after prophecy, and strives, through magical means, to obtain such power, to force it down from Heaven, as it were, through the medium of seven altars, seven bullocks, enchantments and solitude' (Leibowitz 1982: 284). Rhetorically, the scene creates tension for the audience, which observes Israel's enemy sparing no expense in seeking their demise.

3–6. Balaam now instructs Balak to 'station himself' (*hityaṣṣēb*) by his whole burnt offering, use of *yāṣab* possibly recalling the angel of YHWH, who had stationed himself on the way (22:22, 23, 31, 34).

Mention of 'whole burnt offering' might have created tension for an Israelite audience which surely perceived that the whole burnt offering, the basis of Israel's engagement with YHWH God, central to the cult (Exod. 29:38–46), and significant at both a cosmic (Gen. 8) and covenantal (Gen. 22) level, was highly cherished by YHWH, its smoke rising to heaven as a propitiating fragrance (see Morales 2019a): with such lavish whole burnt offerings, will YHWH be persuaded by Balaam to curse Israel? In some Babylonian rituals, the offeror would stay by the sacrifice and pray while the diviner did his work, and even the language of Balaam's going may reflect the practice of magic, whereby the diviner 'goes' in the sense of seeking a divine judgement (Daiches 1909: 63; cf. Weinfeld 1977a: 186–187). Balak, anxious to deal with the problem of Israel's nearness, is like a dog eager to perform obediently for the morsel in his master's hand. Not only does he build the altars and prepare the offerings, but, on Balaam's return, is found waiting unflinchingly where Balaam had directed him, comically pointed out by use of 'Look!' (*hinnê*, v. 6). Waiting by one's sacrifice might have been a ritual in the Levant intended to assure efficacy (Weinfeld 1977a: 186–187). Balaam says he will go (to his own secluded place), described as a 'bare height' (*šepî*, referring to a treeless place of outlook, a higher summit area), on the chance (*'ûlay yiqqārêh*) that YHWH will encounter him. Later, whatever it is Balaam does in seclusion will be dubbed 'divination' or 'enchantments' (*něḥāšîm*, 24:1). Since even for the third utterance, Balaam had instructed Balak to build seven altars, offering up seven bulls and rams, the divination cannot be linked directly to the sacrifices (23:29–30), but to whatever Balaam practised after going off into seclusion. Enchantment or divination was a practice forbidden by YHWH (Lev. 19:26), so perhaps the details were deliberately withheld.

Balaam avows to 'report' (*nāgad*, or 'interpret' if referring to omens) whatever YHWH causes him to 'see' (*yar'ēnî*), presumably expecting a vision. Balaam's ongoing reference to 'YHWH', setting himself as one with influential access to Israel's deity, continues to be undermined by the narrator who reports that 'God' met Balaam. The term translated 'meet' and 'met' (vv. 3, 4) is *qārāh*, which carries the notion of a chance meeting or to 'befall'. Twersky finds in this usage a possible sexual innuendo, as the same root may be used for 'ritually unclean nocturnal emissions' (2022: 153–155; see BDB 899b). Hoping to curse Israel so as to obtain the promised wealth from Balak, Balaam straightaway recounts to God how he has lavishly 'arranged' (*'ārak*) the seven altars and has offered up a bull and a ram on each, endeavouring to change YHWH's mind and procure a favourable word for Moab. Making God out in his own image, easily manipulated by the prospect of riches and honour, Balaam attempts to cajole and bribe God to be unfaithful to his people (to which YHWH responds directly, vv. 7–8). In a suspenseful way, we are told only that YHWH put a word in Balaam's mouth, but, unlike the previous encounters (22:12, 20), we are not allowed to overhear that word. Since the word is 'put' or 'placed' (*śîm*) 'in Balaam's mouth' (*bĕpî bilʿām*), used in cases of biblical prophecy (see Deut. 18:18; Jer. 1:9), there is an assurance that what Balaam speaks *will* (unlike the previous scenarios) be precisely what YHWH desires to express. The suspense, then, is directed at YHWH himself: Was he in any way appeased or persuaded by Balaam's lavish offerings? Could his heart be turned against Israel? Jewish interpretation likens God's putting a word in Balaam's mouth to a hook, forcing a fish against its will (*b. Sanh.* 105b), and to a bit in a horse's mouth or to a nail driven into a board (*Num. Rab.* 20.16). Von Rad dubbed this 'the central lesson of the whole story', that Balaam 'has ceased to be master of himself', behaving as 'an automaton': while serious enough in all he does, he behaves as a caricature, having no control over his own words – 'where, then, is his ancient fame as a diviner?' (2011: 79–80). Balaam returns and sees Balak, along with his cadre of princes, waiting by his smoking whole burnt offering, and eagerly anticipating the sought-after curse on Israel. This view of Balak and the princes of Moab, given as the prelude to Balaam's taking up his parable, functions comically: we hear the divine blessing of Israel through the ears of Balak and the princes of Moab.

7–10. Before Balak and the princes of Moab, Balaam 'took up' (*nāśāʾ*) his parable. The word translated 'parable', *māšal*, may also be translated 'proverb', 'allegory' or 'discourse' and carries the notion of likeness or similarity, using sentences constructed in parallelism or, more generally, a saying or discourse characterized by poetry, typically having an object lesson (*TWOT*, 533; BDB 605). Noordtzij provides a description of poetic discourses that fits the present material and its context well, defining Balaam's prophetic *māšal* as having 'a deep meaning or with more or less cryptic allusions', and which 'creates curiosity and stimulates reflection because of its content' (1983: 216). To 'take up a parable' may be understood as 'to utter solemnly', and the function of a 'parable' includes that 'of quickening an apprehension of the real as distinct from the wished for, or complacently accepted; of compelling the hearer or reader to form a judgement on himself, his situation or conduct' (Herbert 1954: 196). Outside its sevenfold use in Numbers (23:7, 18; 24:3, 15, 20, 21, 23), anticipated once in the previous section (21:27), the phrase 'take up a parable' occurs five other times in the HB (see Job 27:1; 29:1; Isa. 14:4; Mic. 2:4; Hab. 2:6).

Balaam's first parable or poetic discourse recounts his summons by Balak, pronounces the futility of threatening Israel, since their God is sovereign, and proclaims the blessedness of Israel in terms of the nation's consecrated status and vocation, and its divinely induced proliferation and abundance – all with echoes of YHWH's promises of blessing to Abraham. His utterance consists of fourteen lines organized as seven distichs (pair of verse lines) set in synonymous parallelism. One way the parable may be structured is in two loosely parallel stanzas of three distichs (cf. Witte 2002: 201), the stanzas dealing with curse and blessing, respectively, and with the distich of 10b either expanding the second stanza or serving as a cap to the whole parable (Gall 1900: 25–26). (See Table 8.)

Table 8: Curse and blessing in the first parable

Stanza one: curse	Stanza two: blessing
7aFrom Aram Balak has led me, The king of Moab, from the mountains of the east:	9aFor from the summit of rocky-crags I see him, and from the hills I behold him.
7bGo, curse for me Jacob, And go doom Israel!	9bLook! A people dwelling alone, And not reckoned among the nations!
8How shall I condemn whom El has not condemned? Or how shall I doom whom YHWH has not doomed?	10aWho has counted the dust of Jacob? Or numbered a fourth of Israel?
	10bMay my soul die the death of the upright, And may my latter end be like his!

There is debate on approaches to metric analysis, whether by counting stress patterns (e.g. Albright 1944: 211) or by counting syllables (see p. xxxii of D. N. Freedman's 'Prolegomenon' in G. B. Gray 1972), and due caution is necessary to avoid constructing an artificial balance not found in the MT (see Isaacs 1918; D. N. Freedman 1960: 101; Gordon 1967: 131; Powell 1982). The two stanzas sum up the movement of the narrative's two acts, from cursing to blessing, from Balak's scheming against Israel to their state of well-being under YHWH's sovereign care. The first stanza, then, rehearses act 1. Balak 'led' or 'brought' (*nāḥāh* in hiph.) Balak from 'Aram' (*'ărām*), a designation that without a modifier (such as Padan-Aram) is ambiguous enough to suggest various peoples, but is more narrowly defined as 'Mesopotamia' (*'ăram nahărayim*) in Deuteronomy 23:4 (cf. Knauf 2004). One viable option for resolving some of the difficulties of identifying Aram with 'the mountains of the east' would be to take the latter as referring to Balak, creating a scenario whereby Balaam speaks from an Israelite perspective (Robker 2019: 315); otherwise, as referring to Mesopotamia, 'mountains' may be taken in a general manner.

Alternatively, the poem may be divided into strophes (cf. Mowinckel 1930: 262–263; Tournay 1964: 284), with a chiastic arrangement (Tosato 1979: 99–100, his tr.; cf. Kosmala 1964: 430). (See Table 9.)

Among the salient points supporting Tosato's structure 'of 14 stichs, 7 verses (each of two stichs), 3 strophes (each of two verses) placed

Table 9: Balaam's first parable, 23:7–10

Preface	From Aram has brought me Balak,	7a
	the king of Moab from the eastern mountains.	7b
A.	'Come, curse for me Jacob!	7c
	Come, execrate Israel!'	7d
	How can I denounce him who God has not denounced?	8a
	How can I execrate him whom YHWH has not execrated?	8b
B.	For from the top of the rocks I see him,	9a
	from the hills I behold him:	9b
	Lo, a people dwelling alone,	9c
	not reckoning itself among the nations.	9d
A'.	Who can count the dust of Jacob?	10a
	Who can number a fourth of Israel?	10b
	Let me die the death of the righteous!	10c
	Let my end be like his!	10d

in a concentric scheme (A–B–A'), with 1 introductory distich' are the following (1979: 100–101): the first distich (7a–b) is chiastic, setting it apart as introductory; the regular repetition of the first stich in the second; every second stich begins with vav and three times out of six also repeats the first word of the first stich (7d, 8b, 10b); the central strophe (B), on the theme of the vision of Israel, is double-framed by the first and third strophes: rhetorical questions (8ab, 10ab) and hortative exclamations (7cd, 10cd).

The opening verse presents Balak's nefarious designs against Israel: he sends Balaam ('Go!') to curse ('*arar*) Jacob / doom (*zā'am*) Israel. Balak is named 'king of Moab' here, but as the kingship theme spreads across the prophetic utterances it is YHWH's kingship that is magnified (23:21), along with that of a future ruler of Israel (24:7, 17) – in the second proverb, Balak is called merely 'son of Zippor' (23:18). The word pair 'Jacob' and 'Israel' is used seven times throughout Balaam's poems (23:7, 10, 21, 23 [twice]; 24:5, 17). Used in synonymous parallelism, '*arar* is the standard designation for 'curse', and *zā'am* carries the sense of indignation and hostile speech, to denounce. Balaam's response in verse 8 that, for all the parables, addresses 'the assemblage' of Balak and his princes (cf. Seerveld 2001: 8) expresses his inability to do as Balak bids him, apart from God's own determination. His second term 'doom' (*zā'am*) matches Balak's second term in 7b, but Balaam's first term 'condemn' (from *qābab*) is unique, adding variety, and, reading '*eqqōb* (qal impf., first common sg.), may be intended as wordplay on 'Jacob' (*ya'ăqōb*) in Balak's first command, and may stress the point that Jacob will not be cursed (Tosato 1979: 101). The root *q-b-b* (to condemn) is used ten times in this narrative (22:11, 17; 23:8 [twice], 11, 13, 25 [twice], 27; 24:10; cf. Job 3:8; 5:3; Prov. 11:26; 24:24), linking it to the Baal of Peor incident (cf. 'tent', 25:8). The pair 'condemn' (*qābab*) and 'doom' (*zāʿam*) occurs also in Proverbs 24:24. The heaping up of three words of malevolence against Israel also portrays rhetorically the level of Balak's ill-will toward God's people, intensifying the narrative. The basic message is that God has not cursed his people and, therefore, as noted in the second parable, 'there is no enchantment against Jacob, nor divination against Israel' (23:23). YHWH God is King above all gods and powers so that nothing and no one can overturn his determined plans and providence. To be sure, God had already instructed Balaam, 'You will not curse (*'arar*) the people because they are blessed' (22:12). Far from cursing his people, God has blessed them. If one should ask, 'When has YHWH blessed his people?' the answer is found within the section on the theology and spiritual essence of the Camp of Israel, the priestly blessing (6:22–27). Through the upraised palms of the high priest, YHWH's own name is placed on the covenant community, lifting up his countenance upon the Camp – a blessing that includes keeping or guarding them, as the present scenario entails. The name El, which occurs eight times in the oracles (23:8, 19, 22, 23; 24:4, 8, 16, 23), is paralleled with YHWH, and was a general Semitic designation for deity, likely signifying divine power, leadership and sovereignty – the Mighty One (cf. Jacob 1958: 44; Eichrodt 1976b: 1:178–179; BDB 42). The first half of the poetic utterance ends with the key point that YHWH is sovereign: doom cannot be proclaimed, let alone enacted, against any people, and especially not against Israel, unless YHWH himself has determined to do so – but he has positively determined to bless his people abundantly. Because YHWH, sovereign Lord over all creation, is their God, Israel is invulnerable to sorcery.

Double use of the prefixed prep. *min* (from) in verse 9a, mirrors the same in verse 7a, but whereas 7a describes the place from which Balaam came, 9a describes the place from which he sees Israel, a beholding that justifies his inability to condemn Israel (v. 8), as the line begins with 'for' or 'because' (*kî*). Given the encampment's might and numbers, it is evident to Balaam that YHWH, having blessed Israel so abundantly already, can have no intentions whatsoever of cursing them now – indeed, Israel appears so favourably, even triumphantly, blessed that Balaam will want a share in their destiny, in their 'latter end'. From the heights of Baal, now described as 'the summit of rocky-crags' (*rōʾš ṣurîm*) and 'the hills' (*gĕbāʿôt*), Balaam could see the 'outskirts of the people' (22:41). Balaam 'sees' (*rāʾāh*) and 'beholds' (*šûr*) the Camp unbeknown to the Israelites, perhaps an inverse of the scouting expedition in chapter 13. There is a progression of seeing toward the focal point of the proverb: from the twofold 'I see him'/'I behold him' to the call for the audience to see with 'Look!' (*hen*). Through his eyes, we see a people dwelling alone, not reckoned among the nations. The description may be interpreted literally the Camp of Israel in the wilderness dwells 'alone' (*bādād*), not 'accounted' or 'thought of' (*ḥāšab*, a singular instance in the hith.) as among the nations – for the people are like a migratory city abiding in no-man's-land. But there is also a spiritual aspect to what Balaam sees: the people are consecrated, set apart, from the nations to God; they comprise a priestly kingdom created and called by God for the sake of restoring blessing to the nations (Gen. 12:3). The significance of circumcision (Gen. 17) and of the Sinai covenant, whereby Israel becomes YHWH's special treasure above all peoples, a kingdom of priests and a holy nation (Exod. 19:5–6), flows into Balaam's vision of the wilderness encampment. What Balaam sees and points out to his audience is nothing less than *the election of Israel by YHWH*. Moses' inspired blessing in Deuteronomy resonates with Balaam's description of Israel, that 'Israel will dwell in safety, the fountain of Jacob alone' (Deut. 33:28), including the context of YHWH's deliverance from enemy hostility (Deut. 33:27, 29; cf. Waxman 2012: 445–448). Given the progression of Balaam's poetic discourses, Israel as the object of God's eternal choice is the logical starting point since the nation's election 'is the basis of all its further blessings' (Stubbs 2009: 191). YHWH's taking of Israel to himself as a treasured possession explains why the nation cannot be doomed (v. 8), and demonstrates that Balak's designs to have Israel cursed are not peripheral, but form an attack on the very root of their existence, identity and purpose: Israel was created for the sake of blessing (Gen. 12:3; 22:18). The designation 'alone' (*bādād*) also carries the notion of safety and security, that Israel dwells *securely* (cf. Deut. 33:28; Jer. 49:31; Ps. 4:8), underscoring the point that Israel cannot be condemned by sorcery. Israel is 'alone' and 'secure' among the nations, as taken by YHWH for his special inheritance (Deut. 4:20; 9:29) – his 'portion' is Israel (Deut. 32:9, 12), leading to Moses' exclamation 'Israel will dwell safely alone (*bādād*) . . . Happy are you, O Israel! Who is like you, a people saved by YHWH!' (Deut. 33:28–29). The picture is the opposite of the Kenites in the sixth proverb, who appear to have a 'firm' dwelling place, like an eagle's nest set on a high crag, and yet will end up destroyed and its people taken captive. Here, Israel appears defenceless, abiding in the open without fortifications or encircling wall; yet, because of YHWH's central presence, the people rest securely on the Rock. It is this very aloneness, Israel's consecration to YHWH God, that is betrayed in Numbers 25, as the Israelites 'join Baal of Peor' (25:3). Calamity ensues when Israel becomes too intimate with the nations (Sals 2008: 332). Considering the word 'reckoned', *ḥāšab* may also signify 'to devise evil against' (see BDB 363), so that rather than 'among' the nations, the *b*- particle may be read as 'against', with the following implication: 'since Israel does not conspire against the nations, why should they be cursed?' (so Hertz 1933). While such a reading is possible, the immediate context favours Israel's not being 'counted' among the nations. YHWH's incomparability is what makes Israel unique among the nations – just as he is incomparable among the gods, so Israel, bound to him by covenant and having his presence among them, is incomparable among the nations (see Labuschagne 1966: 149–153). At Mount Sinai YHWH had declared that if Israel would heed his voice and keep his covenant, the nation would be his 'treasured possession' (*sĕgullā*) above all peoples, even a priestly kingdom and holy nation (19:5–6) – a status and role of separation to God (cf. J. A. Davies 2004: 54).

What Balaam sees, in sum, is that this people is blessed by YHWH God: they are his treasured possession, evident in the creation blessing Israel has experienced, for 'who has counted the dust of Jacob, or numbered a fourth of Israel?' Clearly, Israel has been fruitful and has multiplied; they are filling the earth and will surely subdue and rule it (see Gen. 1:28) – precisely what has prompted the angst of the nations (Exod. 1:6–14; Num. 22:3–4). Likewise, Stubbs correlates the blessing of fruitfulness, as the first sign of Israel's election, with the first result of God's blessing on humankind: 'Be fruitful and multiply, and fill the earth and subdue it' (Gen. 1:28; 2009: 191), for Israel is a new creation, the new humanity, called out by God for re-establishing his original purposes for creation. Just as being fruitful, multiplying and filling the earth is evident in Balaam's first prophetic utterance, so subduing and ruling will surface among his oracles as well (23:24; 24:7–9, 17–19). The 'outskirts' of the people, described by Balaam as 'a fourth' of Israel, even this cannot be numbered (10a). It may be that 'a fourth' should be translated as 'dust-cloud' (Albright 1944: 213; see Moyer 2009: 105–111), but in either case, especially with the parallelism 'dust of Jacob', the point remains: God's people have miraculously increased (for the notion that dust/dust-cloud refers to a common practice among sorcerers and soothsayers in ancient Mesopotamia, see Powell 1982: 104–105). That a mere fraction of Israel may be dubbed 'the dust (*'ăpar*) of Jacob' that cannot be 'numbered' (*mānāh*) calls to mind YHWH's promises to the patriarchs. To Abram YHWH had said, 'I will make your descendants as the dust (*'ăpar*) of the earth which if a man could number (*mānāh*) the dust (*'ăpar*) of the earth, (only) then also could your descendants be numbered (*mānāh*)' (Gen. 13:16). And to Jacob, YHWH had promised, 'Your descendants will be as the dust (*'ăpar*) of the earth, and you will spread out to the west and to the east and to the north and to the south – and in you and in your descendants all the families of the ground will be blessed' (Gen. 28:14), a description that, mapped along the cardinal points of the compass, resonates with the description of the Camp of Israel (cf. M. Douglas 1993: 420). The phrase 'numbered' a fourth of Israel, using the term *mispār*, surely recalls the census for establishing Israel's camp, with nineteen instances in the opening chapters (1:2, 18, 20, 22, 24, 26,

28, 30, 32, 34, 36, 38, 40, 42; 3:22, 28, 34, 40, 43; cf. 14:29; 25:53), and 'fourth' (*rōbaʿ*) naturally recalls the Camp's four major divisions (cf. *TgO* on this passage: Who can count 'one of the four divisions of Israel') as described in Numbers 2 (cf. Keil 1869: 180; for understanding the reference as 'the seed of Israel', see Twersky 2022: 153). Ibn Ezra thus glosses the phrase with 'One standard' (of the four that comprised the Camp, 1999: 196; cf. Nachmanides 1975: 268; on reading ' encampment' here, see A. Guillaume 1962). Balak's original summons to Balaam involved his trembling revulsion over the hordes of Israel (22:4–5), paralleling Pharaoh's earlier aversion to the abundant growth of the Israelites (Exod. 1:8–12), and now Balaam prophetically praises the vastness of God's people, exalting the source of Balak's fear. Balaam's parable, then, portrays Israel as set apart to God from among the nations, and as fulfilling the patriarchal promises, rooted in the original divine blessing on humans at the time of creation.

Israel's eminence is such that even their end, 'the death of the upright', is enviable, declared by Balaam at the close of his parable with words of personal yearning ('my soul', 'my latter end', v. 10b). Here *yĕšārîm* (upright) may be a wordplay on *yiśrāʾēl* (Israel) (cf. Wendland 2012: 180 n. 31), or perhaps on Jeshurun (Deut. 33:5; Loewenstamm 1965: 185–186; Nachmanides 1975: 268). Albright surmised these lines formed a self-maledictory oath, and were not intended to compare Israel to a just man (1944: 224), but such a reading unnecessarily disconnects the flow of thought. Rather than becoming a cursed people, Israel's community is so blessed the hired sorcerer himself longs to be identified with them, especially with their destined end. The fourth prophetic utterance will focus on the 'latter days' (*'aḥărît hayyāmîm*, 24:14), and will pronounce dominion and glory for Israel. There is strong encouragement for Israel: not only is the nation's beginning enviable, but their destined end – viewed through the power of God – was exclaimed as even more desirable than the beginning. Inasmuch as Balaam will die with the enemy camp (31:8, 16), the lines are full of irony, expressing a futile desire and forlorn hope (Allen 1981: 86). Citing the parallel between 'the upright' (*yĕšārîm*) and 'the mighty' (*gibbôr*) in Psalm 112:2, Levine argues for reading this line as 'the death of the valiant', focusing on Israel's destiny to be victorious over its enemies (2000: 177–178). However, while the theme of Israel's military strength is stressed in the other prophetic utterances, the first proverb appears to focus on Israel's consecrated status. It may be that 'my latter end' (*'aḥărîtî*) refers to Balaam's posterity, with 'like his' (*kāmōhû*) more properly meaning 'like him/it' with reference to the abundant posterity of Jacob, pointing once more to the sheer magnitude of God's people rather than to their militaristic nature (so Moyer 2009: 121–122). LXX appears to favour this understanding, translating *'aḥărîtî* with *to sperma mou* (my seed) (cf. Hulst 1960: 11). Assuming progression, with 'latter end' following 'death', Nachmanides understood 'latter end' as referring to the destiny of the righteous in the world to come, that they are inheritors of the garden of Eden (1975: 268), a fitting notion since the Camp itself will soon be described in terms of an Edenic paradise (24:5–6). In any case, the emphasis is on Israel's supreme blessedness: 'If this encampment is how YHWH has *begun* to bless his people, then imagine their end, when all that YHWH has promised them springs forth abundantly into fruition – would that I might have a share in their end!'

11–12. Balak's response is comically desperate: after the prolonged ordeal of urging Balaam to Moab, his utterance, far from cursing Balak's enemies, blesses them – and at Moab's expense. 'What are you doing to me?' he says to Balaam, and reminds him of the agenda, *why* Balak had 'taken' (*lāqaḥ*) Balaam in the first place, 'to curse my enemies' (fronting the verb for emphasis). Whereas previously he had referred to Israel as 'the/this people' (22:5, 6, 17), here Balak refers to them as 'my enemies' (*'ōyĕbay*). 'Look,' he ironically compels Balaam to see, 'you have surely blessed (*bērakta bārēk*) them' (repeating the root *b-r-k* emphatically). Balaam answers in the form of a helpless question, 'Must I not keep (*šamar*) to speaking (only) what YHWH puts in my mouth?' That YHWH had 'put' (*śîm*) a word in Balaam's mouth (23:5, 12) may be interpreted as a word Balaam is compelled to speak without a choice. Alternatively, Balaam's keeping to YHWH's word may be the result of his fearful, threatening encounter with the angel of YHWH who, with drawn sword, had reiterated God's previous command to speak only what God spoke to him (22:35; cf. 22:20).

23:13–26 Scene 5: Balaam's second parable

13–15. Undaunted, Balak immediately urges ('please', *nā'*) Balaam to go to another place from which to see Israel, but, again, 'only' (*'epes*) to see their 'outskirts' (*qāṣeh*), a term used first in Numbers with reference to the Camp (11:1; cf. 22:36, 41). The phrase *'epes qāṣeh* may also be read as 'the end of its edge', implying that now Balak is showing Balaam 'an even smaller segment of the Israelite camp than before out of fear that the sight of too many Israelites would once again turn his curse into a blessing' (Milgrom 1990: 198). 'All of them (*kullô*) you will not see,' Balak reiterates, and 'you will curse them (*qābĕnô*) for me from there'. Just as Balak had manipulated Balaam by increasing the prospect of riches and honour, so now Balak and Balaam will attempt to persuade YHWH from a different place and with more lavish sacrifices (YHWH responds directly to this, v. 19). As Granot writes (2014a: 325), 'This thinking is characteristic of a culture of magic, divination, and enchantment, where everything depends on technique and on the order of the rituals that act on nature, rather than on the absolute will of God.'

With a threefold use of 'to see' (*rāʾāh*), Balak expresses his desire for Balaam only to see enough of the divine encampment to be able to curse Israel, but not so much so as to be filled with dread and awe (cf. 22:1–3). Another superstitious notion may be that if Balaam can glimpse some corrupt portion of the Camp, then YHWH will be more agreeable to cursing them (note the divine response, v. 21). Presumably, it is Balak who takes Balaam (in verse 14; cf. 22:41) to the field of Zophim ('watchers' or 'lookouts'), likely a guard post to keep watch against attacks, to the summit of Pisgah; or, alternatively, it might have been intended for astronomical observation and the observing of omens (see Milgrom 1990: 198). In Numbers 21:20, Israel journeys from Bamoth (*bāmôt*) in the field of Moab to the summit of Pisgah, which looks toward the wasteland; now Balak takes Balaam from the 'Heights' (*bāmôt*) of Baal to the 'summit of Pisgah' (23:14), and then he will take him to 'the summit of Peor, which looks out to the wasteland' (23:28), tracing, as it were, the steps of Israel. Pisgah is also the summit from which Moses will be granted a vision of the land of Canaan before his death (see Deut. 3:27; 34:1). Ancient rabbis, followed by Rashi, suggest Balak was a greater sorcerer than Balaam, having some premonition that Israel would be weakened through this summit – but he could not discern this would happen by Moses' death, rather than by Balaam's cursing them from there (Rashi 1997: 4:292; cf. *Num. Rab.* 20.7). For a second time, Balak builds seven altars and offers up a bull and a ram on each. Once more Balaam directs Balak in a verse that balances their separation: you (Balak) 'station' (*hityaṣṣēb*) yourself 'here' (*kō*) by your whole burnt offering, and 'I myself' (*ʾānōkî*) will 'chance-to-meet' (*ʾiqqāreh*) God there (*kō*). The twofold use of *kō* may, as suggested by Daiches (1909: 67), have its more usual meaning 'thus', so that Balaam is now, in the hope of a better result, showing Balak just how to stand by his burnt offering and how he will try to obtain a decision from God in his favour, underscoring his use of sorcery.

16–17. Whereas for Balaam's first proverb, we read that 'God met Balaam . . . and YHWH put a word in Balaam's mouth' (23:4–5), here we read that 'YHWH met Balaam and put a word in his mouth', marking some progression. Nachmanides suggested that once the divine attribute of mercy had been displayed in blessing (rather than cursing) the Israelites in Balaam's first proverb, the description could change from Elohim, symbolizing his attribute of justice (1975: 269). Before the third parable, we read that Balaam observed it was good in the eyes of YHWH to bless Israel (24:1), marking further progression. Just as Balaam had directed Balak, so YHWH commands Balaam, 'Return to Balak, and just so (*kō*) you will speak.' Language from scene 4 continues to be repeated, but with a deviation that creates dramatic escalation. Again Balaam goes to Balak and we see through Balaam's eyes (*hinnô*) that Balak has remained obediently by his whole burnt offering, and the princes of

Moab with him. In this case, however, Balak's anticipation manifests itself: rather than waiting for Balaam to take up his parable (as in vv. 6–7), he immediately asks, 'What has YHWH spoken?'

18–24

Balaam's second parable, rebuking Balak for his second attempt at cursing Israel, reinforces the immutability of YHWH's character and purposes, and further adds to the image of Israel's invulnerability that of the people's mightiness under the guidance of YHWH, portending the conquest of the land and the destruction of its enemies. (See Table 10.)

My outline, independently worked, matches precisely that of Tosato, who arranged the poem into '22 stichs, 11 verses (each of two stichs), 5 strophes (each of two verses) placed in a concentric scheme (A–B–C–B'–A'), with 1 introductory stich' (1979: 101–104; cf. Powell 1982: 174). As with the first poem, the preface is chiastically arranged, setting it apart from the main strophes, and the central strophe (C) is

Table 10: Balaam's second parable, 23:18–24

Preface	Arise, Balak, and hear,	18a
	Give ear unto me, O son of Zippor!	18b
A. God's character	No man is El so as to lie,	19a
	Nor a son of a human so as to relent.	19b
	Has he said, and will he not do,	19c
	Or has he spoken, and will he not fulfill?	19d
B. Balaam vs Israel: curse vs blessing	Look! To bless I was taken,	20a
	He has blessed and I cannot revoke it.	20b
	He has not observed iniquity in Jacob,	21a
	Nor has he seen trouble in Israel.	21b
C. YHWH is with Israel	YHWH his God is with him,	21c
	The trumpet blast of a King is among them.	21d
	God brought them forth from Egypt,	22a
	He has the horn-strength of a wild ox.	22b
B'. Balaam vs Israel: curse vs blessing	For there is no enchantment against Jacob,	23a
	Nor divination against Israel.	23b
	At once it must be said to Jacob,	23c
	And to Israel, what El will do!	23d
A'. Israel's character	Look! A people like a king of beasts arises,	24a
	And like a lion lifts himself up.	24b
	He will not lie down until he devours the prey,	24c
	And drinks the blood of the slain!	24d

double-framed by strophes B and B' – note the parallel expressions in 21ab and 23ab, along with their references to both 'Jacob' and 'Israel'.

YHWH's presence with Israel marks the central statement of the parable, along with his mighty deliverance of his people out of Egypt (21b–22). Serving as an inner frame to these lines are references to Balaam's inability to bring a curse upon God's people (20–21a, 23). The outer frame describes, first, the character and nature of God, who will fulfil his intention to bless Israel without relenting, and, second, the character of God's people (19, 24): God is not as a human being, and Israel rises like a mighty lion.

It is instructive to trace the particle of negation (*lō'*) throughout Balaam's second parable: God is *not* a man, to *not* do or *not* fulfil what he has spoken (19); Balaam is thus *not* able to reverse God's blessing (20); for God has *not* observed iniquity, he has *not* seen mischief in his people (21); there is, therefore, *no* enchantment and *no* divination that will be effective against Israel (23); for Israel, like a mighty lion, will *not* lie down until vanquishing all his enemies (24).

18–19. Balaam, for a second time, takes up his parable (cf. 23:7), which begins with a sharp rebuke of Balak – not from Balaam, but from YHWH who had put this word into Balaam's mouth. Given the basic comparison – rather, incomparability – between El and man, it is fitting that here Balak is called 'son of Zippor' rather than 'king of Moab', as in the previous proverb (23:7). Addressed personally ('Balak . . . O son of Zippor!'), Balak is called to attention ('Arise . . . hear, / Give ear to me') and given a lesson on theology: 'God' (*'ēl*) is not like a 'man' (*'îš*) or 'son of man' (*ben-'ādām*), for he neither 'lies' (*kāzab*, also entailing 'to fail, or disappoint'; see BDB 469) nor relents ('to change one's mind, repent', *n-ḥ-m*) – the negation *lō'* (not), heading the line, is emphatic. Scripture elsewhere affirms this aspect of YHWH's glory, that the 'Strength of Israel will neither lie nor relent, for he is not a man that he should relent' (1 Sam. 15:29), for as he says of himself, 'Even I am YHWH, I change not; therefore you, sons of Jacob, are not consumed' (Mal. 3:6), an apt declaration for which the Balaam narrative serves as a fine illustration. Israel's security rests in the faithful character of God, that he is *not* capricious. Not only is it impossible to manipulate YHWH in the first place, but once he has already spoken his will and sovereign determination (in the first parable), it is utterly vain and foolish to hope he will change his mind. What he has (already) said, that is what he will do; and what he has spoken, that is what he will establish. The root of the last term 'establish', *qûm*, was also the opening word of the parable, spoken to Balak ('Arise!'); it will be used once more, to describe Israel's rising like a mighty lion (v. 24). Taking the first six lines together, lines 1and 2 with 5 and 6, Balak is to hear and hearken to what YHWH has already said and spoken, for this is what he will surely do and establish. Lines 3 and 4, at the heart of YHWH's rebuke of Balak, are a declaration of God's nature and character by way of negation: he is not like a sinful human creature, characterized by falsehood and regretful changes of mind. God is true and faithful, all-wise and unchanging in his purposes, which means he will fulfil his promises to the patriarchs of Israel. The rebuke applies to Balaam as well, who, after receiving God's unequivocal response that Israel is blessed (22:12), nevertheless, when enticed with greater honour, approached him a second time (22:19).

20–22. After being commanded to arise and hear, now Balak is called to 'Look!', with Balaam himself as the object: 'I (Balaam) was taken (*lāqaḥ*) to bless.' Whereas we have read about Balak's 'taking' Balaam three times (22:41; 23:11, 14), and he will do so twice more (23:27, 28), this for the purpose of cursing Israel, in reality YHWH has sovereignly 'taken' Balaam so that he can only bless his people. The verb 'to take' is qal perfect, 'I have taken' (*lāqāḥĕtî*), opening the possibility of Balaam's no longer speaking in the first person for himself, but transmitting a divine saying as God's mouthpiece: 'I (= El) have taken (him = Balaam) to bless' (Notarius 2008: 62), or perhaps 'Bless! (is the command) I received,' so that 'Bless!' is the word YHWH had put in his mouth (Powell 1982: 158). Yet, as Wiggershaus points out (2021: 171), there is no indication that the perspective has changed, with the middle of the line continuing Balaam's perspective. He, therefore, proposes treating *bārēk* as the object of *lāqāḥtî*, since inf. absolutes may fill such a role especially in poetry, so that Balaam is reporting on the results of his divination: 'Behold! "*bārēk*" I received!' (Wiggershaus 2021: 171). On this scenario Balaam might have used lots designated 'bless' and 'curse'. Clearly, whatever the case, YHWH has determined blessing and Balaam cannot 'revoke' (or 'turn it back', *šûb*). Marking progression through the poetic discourses, what the first discourse had stated only negatively – namely, that Balaam had been taken to curse Israel, but could not (23:7, 8) – is now stated only positively: YHWH had taken him to bless and Balaam cannot revoke the blessing.

Incredibly, even as a statement regarding the second generation, YHWH declares through Balaam that he has not 'observed' (*hibbît*) iniquity (*'āwen*) in Jacob, nor 'seen' (*rā'āh*) 'trouble' (*'āmāl*) in Israel. There are only two other uses of 'observe' (*nābaṭ*) in Numbers, the first declaring that Moses observes the form of YHWH (12:8), and the second describing how a bitten person, when he observed the brazen serpent, would live (21:9). 'Iniquity' and 'trouble' overlap in meaning, but the first leans more to the range of wickedness while the second toward mischief: God has not studied the wickedness of his people, nor even seen any mischief among them. Since *'āmal* relates to the grievous and wearisome aspects of toil or labour (*TWOT*, 675), the latter statement may include the idea that YHWH has not grown weary with his people throughout the wilderness era. The entire Balaam narrative amounts to a vivid demonstration of YHWH's loyalty to his people. Justly, Hooke focused on this statement, that YHWH had not observed iniquity in Jacob, as what Micah refers to as the supreme example of YHWH's character, his 'righteous acts' (6:5), here 'the goodness of which Yahweh had spoken to Moses shines out against the dark background of Israel's disobedience and unbelief' (1961: 37). Alternatively, the pair of words may be understood to proclaim that YHWH (the true 'seer') has not observed calamity in Israel's future, with *'āwen* signifying 'looming disaster' (*HALOT* 22), complementing *'āmāl*'s basic meaning of 'trouble'. Such a message would be especially pointed against Balak, who is trying to bring calamity against Israel. In the chiastic arrangement, no looming disaster/trouble against Jacob/Israel corresponds well with no enchantment/divination against Jacob/Israel (v. 23). However, a more ethical connotation (as 'no iniquity' in Israel) would correspond with no enchantment *in* (i.e. practised by) Israel, or even as the cause for there being no enchantment against Israel. The immediate context, describing YHWH's royal presence in the Camp (v. 21b) relates both to Israel's purity and protection (see Powell 1982: 160–162; Ward 2009: 193). That it is YHWH who sees and observes would seem to favour the ethical reading. Ibn Ezra surmised that Balak learned from this utterance to send Moabite women into the Camp of Israel, seeing that Israel's divine blessedness was conditional upon the absence of iniquity among them (1999: 199).

The central statement of the parable comes in 21b–22. 'YHWH his God is with him' sets forth the heart of the covenant relationship, often expressed with the threefold covenant formula 'I will be your God, you will be my people, and I will dwell in your midst' (see Morales 2015: 103–106). The source of Israel's uniqueness and blessing is found in that YHWH God, the Creator of the heavens and earth, abides in their midst, as an ever-present source of life, of goodness and protection, and of help and guidance (cf. Deut. 4:7). YHWH's being 'with' his people gestures toward the Incarnation of Immanuel, 'God with us' (Isa. 7:14; Matt. 1:21–23). The former generation in the wilderness had tested YHWH, asking, 'Is YHWH among us or not?' (Exod. 17:7) – now the glory of his presence among Israel is proclaimed by a pagan seer. Whereas Balaam had earlier referred to 'YHWH my God' (22:18), here, constrained to speak only the word YHWH has put in his mouth, it is 'YHWH his (Israel's) God' – Israel alone may boast in such covenant relationship with YHWH. This line is paralleled with a reference to YHWH as king, 'The trumpet blast of a King is among them,' kingship being the underlying theme of Numbers 21 – 25. Incredibly, the first naming of YHWH as 'king' in the Bible is uttered through the lips of Balaam, a pagan sorcerer (although Exod. 15:18 exclaims that YHWH 'will reign' for ever and ever) (cf. Allen 1973: 401). The word *tĕrû'āh* has also been translated as a 'shout'; while it can refer to a shout of joy, especially in public worship, both the subject and the context favour a blast of the trumpet as something of a battle-cry, a depiction of YHWH as King leading forth his hosts, from Egypt with the horn-strength of a wild ox, and onward to the conquest. Psalm 47, proclaiming YHWH as the 'great King over all the earth', says he has 'gone up with a shout, YHWH with the sound of a shofar' (vv. 2, 5). BHS suggests emending with the Hebr. root *yāra'*, for a meaning of 'majesty of', which while an extremely rare use of the term is supported by the versions and favoured by several scholars: *TgO* reads *šĕkīntā* (presence, glory), the Syriac has *tisbōḥtā* (majesty) and LXX translates as *ta endoxa* (glory) (Powell 1982: 139). One might argue that the majesty of a King, with possible reference to YHWH's glory Cloud, parallels the previous stich fittingly ('YHWH his God is with him), but the emendation is not necessary. The 'trumpet blast of a King' speaks of military majesty in particular, which works well with the further imagery of the conquest. The term *tĕrû'āh* recalls its earlier uses after the formation of the Camp, as the King's means for directing his hosts. In Numbers 10, where YHWH had directed Israel to fashion two silver trumpets, the *tĕrû'āh* blasts are used to lead forth each of the four major camps in the wilderness, beginning with Judah's division in the east, and the *tĕrû'āh* blast is also designated for going to war against Israel's oppressive enemies in the land, so that YHWH will remember his people and save them (10:5, 6, 9). Once more, Balaam's vision interprets the Camp of Israel as established in the opening chapters: YHWH resides in the midst of his people (Num. 2) and the trumpet blast of YHWH, the King, is in their midst (Num. 10:5–6). The central Dwelling of YHWH amid the tribal encampments, surrounded by Levites and adorned with the colours of blue, purple and crimson, and marked by a lavish use of pure gold for its furnishings, including the ark as the divine throne and footstool, all of these marking the tabernacle as the palace of the most holy King (cf. Cole 2000: 412).

The exodus out of Egypt, whereby bitterly oppressed Hebrew slaves triumphed over the ancient world's superpower, is a prime illustration that 'YHWH his God is with him' and that YHWH is king. After crossing the sea, Moses had led the Israelites in singing, 'YHWH will reign (*yimlōk*) for ever and ever' (Exod. 15:18; the song also refers to the trembling dread of Moab, v. 15; cf. Num. 22:2–3). Whereas Balak had earlier said 'a people has come forth out of Egypt' (22:5), as if of their own accord, God now corrects him through Balaam: 'El brought them forth from Egypt' (*Num. Rab.* 20.20). God (*'ēl*) brought forth Israel out of Egypt, displaying great strength, the 'horn-strength' of a 'wild ox'. The exodus out of Egypt is the paradigm of salvation, foreshadowing the resurrection of the Messiah from the dead, and all his people with him (see Morales 2020). Use of 'wild ox' (*rĕ'ēm*) forms an image of a fiercely strong animal with potential to wreak great devastation (see also 24:8; cf. Leson 2007: 294). The imagery of a huge wild ox was employed in the ancient world to portray military might in trampling down a foe's land (cf. Marcus 1977: 87). 'Horn-strength' (*tôʻăpōt*, likely derived from *y-ʻ-p*), literally 'eminence' or 'mountain peaks', is a rare word (cf. Num. 23:22; 24:8; Job 22:25; Ps. 95:4). Although using a different Hebr. term, horns are a symbol of royalty (Pss 89:17; 132:17), so the notion of kingship may also be in the foreground (Budd 1984: 268). The rare use of a pl. suff. for Israel (*môṣîʼām*, 'brought them forth') might have been intended to clarify that it is El (rather than Israel) who has the horn-strength of a 'wild ox' (*rěʼēm*), a symbol of divinity and divine power in the ancient world – although, through their God, Israel may be presented as endowed with enormous power (Noth 1968: 187). AV's 'unicorn' for *rěʼēm* is off the mark, as is LXX's *monokerōtos* ('unicorn'; see Godbey 1939: esp. 284; BDB 910). In Deuteronomy 33:17, the glory of the tribe of Joseph is portrayed with 'the horns of a wild ox' (for similarities between Balaam's oracles and Moses' blessings, see Spiegelman 2012: 458–459), one of the references that led early interpreters to assign the image of a wild ox to the standard of Ephraim's westward camp in particular. Psalm 22 refers both to the 'lion' (*ʼaryêh*) and to the horns of 'wild oxen' (*rēmîm*, v. 21), both animals mentioned in Balaam's oracle (23:22, 24). Curiously, Balaam's parables include metaphors that encompass the four images supposed for the four major standards of the Camp: lion (Judah, 23:24; 24:9), ox (Ephraim, 23:22; 24:8), man (Reuben, 24:7–9) and eagle (Dan, 24:21). While the last two metaphors, those of a man and an eagle, cannot be linked with their respective tribes – referring, rather, to Judah's line and the Kenites – the lion and ox may be traced to Judah and Ephraim, respectively, underscoring the leading tribes of the eventual northern and southern kingdoms (on a possible correlation with the figures of the Zodiac, see Burrows 1938: 71–74). M. Douglas, noting the parallels to the blessings of Jacob and Moses, and how the wild ox and lion imagery are repeated in the next oracle (24:5–9), similarly regards these as symbolizing Joseph and Judah, and their respective kingdoms, underscoring the message of Israel's solidarity (2004: 100–101). With the strength by which YHWH had brought Israel out of the land of Egypt, he will also bring them into the land.

23. Once more the parable turns to Balaam's inability against Israel: because 'YHWH his God is with him,' there is no 'enchantment' (*naḥaš*) or 'divination' (*qesem*) that can be effective against Israel. Both terms are used with reference to Balak's use of Balaam to curse Israel: Balak had sent elders of Moab and of Midian with 'divinations' (*qěsāmîm*) in hand (22:7), and, in chapter 24, Balaam's activity is defined clearly as seeking 'enchantments' (*něḥāšîm*, 24:1). It is possible that rather than 'against', the twofold use of *bě-* is to be understood as 'in' Israel/Jacob. The thought would then be contrastive: rather than using enchantment or divination in Israel, God announces to Israel, through Moses and other prophets, what he will do, or that Israel merits blessing since no enchantment or divination is found within – used by – them (cf. Rashi 1997: 4:297–298).

While this latter reading may be aligned with the notion of verse 21 ('He has not observed iniquity in Jacob'), both the immediate (El's strong presence among them, v. 22) and broader context (of Balak's hiring Balaam to curse Israel) resonates rather with there being no augury that can be effective against God's people (cf. Nachmanides 1975: 271). Perhaps, as Levine suggests (2000: 185), a double entendre is intended. Possibly, the 'divinations' and 'enchantments' refer not to the practice but its result, with Balaam reporting that none of the omens he read came up against Israel (cf. Wiggershaus 2021: 169–170).

Use of *naḥaš* links the Balaam cycle with the opening chapter of the subdivision (chs. 21–25), with its sevenfold use of the same root in the story of the fiery serpents (*nāḥāš*; see 21:6, 7, 9). Gane remarks that, given the preceding reference to a creature (the 'wild ox'), *naḥaš* would naturally be read as 'snake' until one reads the parallel expression 'divination' – and further reflects on the irony that snakes were effective against Israel when sent by YHWH (2004: 702). Savran links 'enchantment' here with the 'serpent' of Genesis 2 – 3 as a homophone that reflects contrasting approaches to humanity's relationship with God (1994: 51): as enchantment constitutes an indirect approach to understanding God's will, so the snake's counsel in Genesis 3 betrayed a desire to control the divine by human means. In Deuteronomy, Moses will list both 'enchantment' (*naḥaš*) and 'divination' (*qesem*) as 'abominations' (*tô'ăbat*) – completely abhorrent and detestable – to YHWH, practised by the nations in the land but that should not be found among God's people, for those nations 'listened to fortune-tellers and diviners (*qĕsāmîm*)' (18:10–14; cf. Gen. 30:27; 44:5; Lev. 19:26; 2 Kgs 17:17). YHWH's loathing of enchantment and divination should factor strongly in how the audience is meant to view Balaam's character. Moab is doing what the nations do, and Balaam cannot but be regarded as a pagan diviner, a soothsayer, just as Joshua dubs him (Josh. 13:22). Here, with YHWH's word placed in his mouth, Balaam is made to confess his own inability before the king and princes who have hired him. By contrast to the nations' vain use of augury, Israel is 'at once' ('this time', *kā'ēt*) informed ('it must be said', *'āmar* in niph.) what El will 'do' (*pā'al*). If 'what El has done' is the preferred reading, then perhaps the whole verse summarizes the Balaam narrative as revealed to Israel. As future-oriented ('will do'), the whole prophetic corpus lies within its compass (see Ibn Ezra 1999: 200–201). The term *pā'al* here designates God's deeds of deliverance and judgement in his providence. Through the Torah of Moses, along with God's faithful supply of prophets, Israel is not ignorant of God's intention for human history, and never has need to resort, with the nations stumbling in darkness, to mediums and diviners. Contrasting Balaam's approach, Moses sees the form of YHWH, who speaks to him plainly as with a friend (12:7–8). Verse 22 began with *'ēl* and verse 23 ends with *'ēl* (God).

24. The parable ends with a magnificent view of Israel, calling the audience to 'look' (*hen*). Israel's nature and character are described with a common ancient metaphor for military might: that of a mighty lion, an image especially fitting for the leading tribe of Judah (Gen. 49:9), which encamped on the east and led the hosts of YHWH on the march to Canaan (Num. 2:1–9), and that may have had a lion depicted on its standard. Whether Balaam was able to see relevant images on the tribal banners, his prophetic descriptions nevertheless unfold their presumed theological significance, the character and destinies of each tribe as revealed prophetically by God through Jacob (Gen. 49) and Moses (Deut. 33). M. Douglas notes that both images from this utterance, of a wild ox and a lion, signifying the tribes of Joseph and Judah, respectively, are repeated in the third oracle, demonstrating their intentionality (1993: 421).

As Alter notes (2004: 808), biblical Hebrew has four synonyms for 'lion' (*lābî'* and *'ărî* are used here) but their distinctions are lost to us. Both the terms *lābî'* and *'ărî* refer to an adult male lion (Strawn 2005: 294–304, 311–319). AV's 'great lion' is to be preferred over ESV's 'lioness' for *lābî'* (cf. Notarius 2008: 69 n. 47, who cites Kaplan 1989), since arguments for this term being f. have been judged 'philologically dubious' – when a lioness is intended, the same word may occur with a f. ending in both sg. and pl. (*lĕbîā'*, *lĕbā'ôt*; see Ezek. 2:19 and Nah. 2:13) instead of m. as here (Strawn 2005: 267, 311–319). The first two lines portray the king of beasts as 'getting up' (*qûm, nāśā'*) to attack and devour his prey, and the last two declare that he will not repose until he has satisfied himself on his enemies, devouring the prey and drinking the blood of the slain. Such martial rhetoric was commonly employed by nations to instil their enemies with dread and fear – and is, ironically, uttered by the very soothsayer Moab has hired against Israel. In the ANE, and equally in the HB, the lion's primary symbolism was that of military boldness and magnificence (Marcus 1977: 87), of threat and power – the 'lion captures prey with the purpose of devouring it (Prov. 22:13; cf. Gen. 37:33)', its 'victims are torn, broken (1 Kgs 13:26), and struck (1 Kgs 20:36; Jer. 5:6); their bones are crushed (Dan. 6:25); finally, they are killed (1 Kgs 13:24, 26; 2 Kgs 17:25–26; Dan. 6:25)' (Strawn 2005: 26–27, 36; cf. Bovati 1994: 294).

By analogy with the donkey episode (scene 3), 'Balak has now just been led off the road into the field but feels his leg crushed against the wall' (Alter 2004: 808). In the last couplet 'prey' (*ṭerep*) is sg. and 'slain' (*ḥălālîm*) is pl., understood in Jewish tradition as referring to Balaam and the Midianite kings, respectively, even as Joshua stated that the sons of Israel did slay 'Balaam the son of Beor the soothsayer' with the sword 'among them that were slain (*ḥălĕlêhem*)' (Josh. 13:22; cf. *Tan.* 14; *Num. Rab.* 20.20; Nachmanides 1975: 272; Rashi 1997: 4:299; Ibn Ezra 1999: 201). Such a reading properly understands the events of Numbers 31 as an immediate application or initial fulfilment of what is a broader, more generalized statement regarding the divinely wrought military strength and prowess of Israel. The noun 'prey' is found with 'lion' thirteen times in the HB, and connects Numbers 23:24 with Genesis 49:9 (see also Job 4:11; Ps. 104:21; Isa. 5:29; 31:4; Ezek. 19:3, 6; 22:25; Amos 3:4; Nah. 2:13–14; 38:39; Strawn 2005: 337). The chiastically arranged closing words (he devours the prey / the blood of the slain he drinks) may be a literary device to lend a sense of climax. The movement in imagery from 'he will not lie down until he devours the prey' in this second prophetic utterance (23:24) to 'he crouched, he lay down as a lion' in the third utterance (24:9) most directly applies to Israel's conquest and settlement of the land: Israel will not lie down (i.e. settle in the land) until, like a mighty lion, the nation has conquered all their enemies; then, once lying down (inherited and settled in the land), the surrounding nations will tremble at any attempt to unsettle them ('who will rouse him?', 24:9). With YHWH in their midst, Israel is like a mighty lion: strong, fierce and invincible. Within the context of divination in the ancient world, Balaam's report functioned to discourage Balak from any military engagement with Israel – far from being diminished by a curse, the people of Israel grow in might, shown to be abundantly blessed by the God who resides in their Camp. As Wiggershaus observes (2021: 175), Balaam's divination reports a favourable verdict for Israel in a fourfold manner: first, divine judgement is 'pronounced' (*'āmar, dibber*, v. 19b); second, no misdeeds were found (*'āwen, 'āmāl*, v. 21a); third, God is present with Israel (v. 21b); and fourth, Israel is like a lion militarily and cannot be overcome (v. 24) – there can be no curse that will prevail against YHWH's blessing.

25–26. Balak realizes that his plot to curse Israel is not only failing Moab, but is strengthening Israel. He would rather retreat to having 'neither any curse' (*qōb lō' tiqqŏbennû*) 'nor any blessing' (*bārēk lō' tĕbārăkennû*) – no curse against Israel is better than positively blessing them. This finally answers the question as to why YHWH had told Balaam to go with Balak's men (22:20): so that YHWH might bless his people boldly in the face of Israel's enemies. Balaam answers Balak with a defensive question: 'Did I not tell you already that I must do (*'āśāh*) what YHWH speaks?' The previous report (22:38; 23:12) had likely been received by Balak as mere rhetoric, but it appears that Balaam is unable to utter anything apart from the word YHWH has put in his mouth – he is divinely prevented from speaking forth contempt against Israel, despite Balak's lucrative offer of gain. Such a scenario fits the understanding of later inspired interpreters, who speak of YHWH's turning the curse into blessing. 'YHWH your God was not willing to hearken to Balaam,' Moses declares in Deuteronomy; rather, he 'overturned (*hāpak*) the curse (*qĕlālāh*) into blessing (*brākāh*) for you, because YHWH your God loved you' (23:5).

23:27 – 24:25 Scene 6: Balaam's third and further parables

Balaam's third prophetic utterance marks a plateau before moving on to the culminating and climactic fourth proverb, along with the three short discourses that follow. The text underscores the special significance of his third speech in several ways: Balaam did not use divination as at other times; he was able to view the entire encampment of Israel instead of just a portion; the 'Spirit of God' (*rûaḥ 'ĕlōhîm*) came upon him; and this discourse is described not only as a parable but as an 'oracle' (*nĕ'um*; the fourth speech is also described this way; cf. 24:15–16).

27–30. Balak, whose desperation has mounted with the direness of his situation, pleads for another try, 'Go, please, let me take you to another place,' hoping that 'perhaps' (*'ûlay*) at a different locale it will then seem pleasing, agreeable or 'right' (*yāšar*) in the eyes of God to allow Balaam to curse Israel 'from there' (*miššām*). The cumulative effect of changing locales is triumphant for Israel: YHWH's blessing on Israel knows no boundaries or limitations, and is utterly resistant to outside malicious forces and manipulation, which can only serve to confirm the people's blessedness (cf. Cole 2000: 415). By contrast to his previous 'curse them for me' (v. 13), Balak's helpless dilemma has become evident – he is coming to see that 'he must reckon with the power of Israel's God' (Milgrom 1990: 201). The response to Balak's second attempt at cursing Israel had been a divine rebuke addressed directly to Balak son of Zippor, proclaiming that God is not like man to change his will, but will indeed establish what he has spoken – marking the second attempt as vain and rebellious. Yet Balak ignores YHWH's word. He has not learned that YHWH does not fit the mould of Balak's pagan notion of gods, cast in the image of humans, so that, despite any professed intentions to the contrary, they can be manipulated to do one's will. Just as by a more lucrative offer he had persuaded Balaam to change his original refusal, so he tries again to persuade God, to make cursing Israel seem good 'in the eyes' (*bĕ'ênê*) of God – but YHWH is not like Balaam. While Balak here attempts to persuade 'God' (*hā'ĕlōhîm*), later he will blame 'YHWH' for withholding Balaam's honour (24:11). Balaam is perhaps more blameworthy than Balak, for he has already been told the will of God plainly (22:12), has been warned repeatedly (22:20, 35; 23:5, 16) and spoke the divine reprimand through his own lips (23:19), yet he is willing to cater to another attempt at cursing Israel for Balak.

Balak takes Balaam to the summit of Peor, which overlooks the wasteland. Earlier Israel was said to reach the summit of Pisgah, 'which overlooks the wasteland' (21:20). Israel will soon fall into heinous spiritual harlotry with the daughters of Moab and Midian, joining themselves to 'Baal of Peor' (25:3; see Josh. 22:17), at the instigation of Balaam (31:16); so, this site, as with the 'Heights of Baal' (22:41), was likely a locale for Baal worship (on Peor as a local god, see Mendenhall

1973: 108–109; Spronk 1995) and close to the sanctuary of Baal of Peor, where many Israelites would commit apostasy (25:3, 5). As with his gloss on Pisgah (23:28), Rashi again suggests Balak took Balaam to the summit of Peor because he, Balak, was a great sorcerer, and had discerned that Israel would be made to stumble from this place, although he did not know how this would happen, whether by a curse or something else (1997: 4:300; cf. *Tan.* 4, 11). Far from being reluctant to approach God again with the prospect of cursing Israel, Balaam calls for the same building of seven altars and the preparation of the offerings, a bull and a ram on each altar. Again, Balak complies with Balaam's instruction.

24:1. Amid the repetition involved in the three attempts to curse Israel, a significant deviation now occurs. This time Balaam does not direct Balak to wait by his whole burnt offering while he, Balaam, goes off in seclusion for a chance encounter with YHWH – a point underscored by the narrative: 'he did not go as at other times to encounter by enchantments'. Since Balaam did in fact have the seven altars built, offering up bulls and rams, the 'enchantments' (*nĕḥāšîm*) refers to whatever he was doing when he had gone to secluded places in the first two attempts (23:3, 15), perhaps looking for omens in animal parts from the sacrifices (cf. Noordtzij 1983: 214). In Babylonian divination, the result depended on liver-omina (omens) or oil-omina (Daiches 1909: 65), so it could be that Balaam had assumed his previous encounters with God had been the result of his magic arts. Had he been engaged in sorcery, such as inspecting animal livers of the sacrifices, or was he by some other means seeking to induce an ecstatic state? Whatever his precise practice, Balaam had clearly been resorting to sorceries in his approach of God. The text, perhaps avoiding any description of forbidden practice, is silent on the details. Noted previously, *nĕḥāšîm* in 24:1 and 23:23 (*naḥaš*) links the Balaam narrative (chs. 22–24) with the previous chapter's story on the serpent and its brass image (*nāḥāš*, *nĕḥaš nĕḥōšet*, 21:4–9) – the *Zohar* translates 'toward snakes' in 24:1 (1.126a). Kaiser notes that the connection is often made between divination, augury, omens and the serpent in the biblical and ANE worlds, and that the phrase here implies Balaam's use of 'certain mysterious ceremonies' (1996: 105). Possibly the similarity is more than lexical: in both cases a threatening *n-ḥ-š* is turned by YHWH to Israel's good. Chen suggests use of *naḥaš* not only links Numbers 21 and 22 – 24 together, but also links back to the enmity between the seed of the woman, who will descend from Israel, and the seed of the serpent, whose head will be crushed by the Messiah (Gen. 3:15; 2019: 201). Balaam's lack of movement on this instance signals 'the story's *dénouement* is at hand' (Leson 2007: 175). Again, there is progression with each parable: seeing in the previous utterance that there is no 'enchantment' (*naḥaš*, 23:23) against Jacob, Balaam forsakes use of 'enchantments' (*nĕḥāšîm*) now; and, as we will observe, whereas the second parable portrayed the conquest, the third utterance portrays Israel's tranquil settlement in the land, foretasted by the encampment. His forsaking of enchantments may also be read as an attempt to avoid 'encountering' (*liqra't*) God at all.

Balak had hoped that to 'curse' (*qābab*) Israel would be 'pleasing' (*yāšar*) 'in the eyes' of God (23:27), but Balaam sees that to 'bless' (*bārak*) Israel is 'good' (*ṭôb*) 'in the eyes' of YHWH. The expression echoes Balaam's previous statement to the angelic messenger that his journey to Moab may be 'evil in your eyes' (22:34). Just as the previous word put in his mouth by YHWH had declared there was no 'enchantment' (*naḥaš*) against (or, possibly, in) Jacob, and that God speaks his will directly to Israel (23:23), Balaam leaves off enchantments. Finally, realizing that YHWH is so pleased to bless Israel, inducements to the contrary are futile and, equally, inducements for their blessing are unnecessary, Balaam forsakes attempting to encounter God – he simply sets his 'face to the wilderness' (cf. 23:28). What a message for the people of God! YHWH so loves his people that he is not only determined to do them good, but doing so is 'pleasant in his eyes' – he needs absolutely no cajoling, bribery or manipulation to open freely and abundantly the storehouse of heaven's blessing upon their heads. Balaam, however, has not finally submitted to YHWH's heavy hand; rather, he now seeks to avoid God long enough to spew out a curse against Israel. Gane offers just such a dramatic reading: Balaam, seeing that to bless Israel is pleasant in the eyes of YHWH, seeks to short-circuit his divine word – he leaves off sorcery so as *not* to encounter and be controlled by YHWH, in order 'to satisfy Balak and claim his reward' (2004: 709). The language of Balaam's 'setting his face' (*wayyāšet . . . pānāyw*) to the wilderness supports this reading. While the phraseology widely refers to establishing one's determination (Gen. 31:21; 1 Kgs 2:15; 2 Kgs 12:17; Dan. 11:17; and may also use *nātan*, Lev. 17:10; 20:3, 6; 26:17; Ezek. 14:8; 15:7; Dan. 9:3; 10:15; or *kûn*, Ezek. 4:3, 7), in several instances in Ezekiel the idiom is used particularly for prophesying oracles of doom against nations, including Israel:

> Son of man, set your face to (*'el*) the mountains of Israel, and prophesy against them. (6:2)

> Now, son of man, set your face to (*'el*) the daughters of my people . . . and prophesy against them. (13:17)

> Son of man, set your face toward the southward way (*derek têmānāh*) . . . and prophesy against the forest of the Negev field. (20:46)

> Son of man, set your face to (*'el*) Jerusalem . . . and prophesy against the land of Israel. (21:2)

> Son of man, set your face to (*'el*) the sons of Ammon, and prophesy against them. (25:2)

Son of man, set your face to (*'el*) Sidon, and prophesy against her. (28:21)

Son of man, set your face against (*'al*) Pharaoh king of Egypt, and prophesy against him and against all Egypt. (29:2)

Son of man, set your face against (*'al*) Mount Seir, and prophesy against it. (35:2)

Son of man, set your face against (*'al*) Gog . . . and prophesy against him. (38:2)

Note that while in some cases 'setting the face' is explicitly 'against' a nation by use of *'al*, yet in the majority of cases *'el* is used with the same significance, matching precisely the wording of our present verse: 'Balaam . . . set his face to (*'el*) the wilderness.' In the absence of any other instance in the HB whereby a prophet sets his face toward a place or people for the sake of blessing, it may well be the idiom's connotation here would have been heard originally as presaging doom or at least implying Balaam's ill intent: 'he set his face to the wilderness, and prophesied against Israel' would fit precisely with the idiom's use in Ezekiel. The overall thought would be that Balaam, seeing it pleased YHWH only to bless Israel, did not go as at other times to encounter God by enchantments – not wanting to encounter God at all, but instead, apart from such divine control, to pronounce doom on Israel by setting his face against them in the wilderness. A further point in favour of understanding Balaam's action as seeking to curse Israel, his three sought-out encounters with YHWH grow more distanced, progressively: 'Perhaps YHWH will meet to encounter me' (23:3), 'I will seek to meet there' (23:15) and, finally, 'he did not go as at other times' (24:1). The plain sense of the third attempt is that Balaam did not seek any encounter with YHWH since he, Balaam, was convinced YHWH *only* wanted to bless Israel and would not relent. This time, he endeavoured to *avoid* an encounter with YHWH in the hope that by doing so he would be able to fulfil Balak's commission and earn his reward. On this reading, the coming of God's Spirit on Balaam stands as a mighty act of intervention, only just 'in the nick of time', transforming his malediction into a sublime beatific revelation. Centuries ago, Trapp (1601–69) offered a similar reading, glossing *he did not go as at other times* with 'As being resolved to curse howsoever, and without God's leave; yea in spite of God (*al despito di Dio*), to take his own course whatever came of it,' and explaining *he set his face* with 'As fully bent to do it, and nothing should hinder him' (1650: 52).

Rather than as previously when, under Balak's fearful direction, he only saw a small portion of the outskirts of the Camp, Balaam now boldly 'sets his face' to the wilderness to view the entirety of the encampment (cf. Milgrom 1990: 202). Mention of 'the wilderness' (*hammidbār*) recalls the opening verse of Numbers, the setting for the divine revelation of the Camp of Israel (1:1), the glory of which is about to be unveiled to Balaam. Mention of 'the wilderness' underscores the great contrast with the description of the encampment's spiritual essence as an Edenic garden that follows (v. 5).

2. Dramatically, the lifting up of Balaam's eyes is 'narrated' (*wayyiśśā'*) – finally, he begins 'to see what YHWH sees' (Ward 2009: 52). Two highly significant points are made. First, Balaam 'saw' (*rā'āh*) Israel 'dwelling' (*šōkēn*) by 'his tribes' (*lišbāṭāyw*); that is, according to the arrangement of the Camp as rehearsed in Numbers 1 – 4, 'the sons of Israel, each man encamped by his standard with the emblems of their father's house, at a distance from the Tent of Meeting' (2:2). He sees the outer camp, with the twelve tribes encamped along the four points of the compass; he sees the inner camp of the Levites, with Moses and Aaron encamped at the eastward side; and he sees the central Dwelling of YHWH, the camp of the *Shekhinah*. Ibn Ezra's terse gloss 'He saw all the standards' captures the idea well (1999: 202). Second, upon seeing the sacred encampment, the paradigmatic covenant community, and before he could utter an execration, the 'Spirit of God' (*rûaḥ 'ĕlōhîm*) came upon him (cf. 1 Sam. 10:10; 16:16; 2 Chr. 15:1), both sovereignly controlling his actions and enabling him to see the spiritual significance of the Camp of Israel. Given the exchange of enchantments for the Spirit of God, Levine observes that Balaam now speaks not as a pagan diviner but as a prophet of YHWH (2000: 191; cf. Hildebrandt 1993: 165) – clearly, 'Balaam's message rises to a different level' (Powell 1982: 255). The first major division of Numbers focused entirely on the nature and character of YHWH's Camp, its physical arrangement and spiritual reality (chs. 1–10), and its threefold concentric camps of holiness served as a paradigm to display the failures of the first generation (the outer camp in chs. 13–14; the inner camp in chs. 16–17; the central camp in ch. 20). Now, finally, through the Spirit-empowered eyes of Balaam, we are given to see the heavenly realities of the Camp of Israel, which had been detailed in the opening chapters. Like Balaam on his donkey, Israel had been blind to the divine glories of the wilderness encampment, and observing them now with open eyes is the key for unlocking the book's message and import. Just as Balaam's eyes had been opened to see the messenger of YHWH after beating his donkey three times (22:31), so now on his third attempt his eyes are opened to see the covenant community of YHWH (24:3). In a narrative about vision, which employs the root 'to see' (*rā'āh*) eighteen times (22:2, 23, 25, 27, 31, 33, 41; 23:3, 9, 13 [three times], 21; 24:1, 2, 17, 20, 21), Balaam's vision of Israel's Camp is of central significance. It could be we are meant to hear a distant echo of the priestly blessing here: 'YHWH lift up' (*yiśśā' yhwh*) his face (6:26); 'Balaam lifted up' (*wayyiśśā' bil'ām*) his eyes (24:2). The leaving off of enchantments, the coming of the Spirit of God upon him and the dubbing of his utterance as an 'oracle', along with its being the third poem in a story that plays on cycles of three, all contribute to underscoring this oracle as a mounting crescendo, higher than the previous utterances (although penultimate, with the four proverbs reaching the climactic point of the Balaam chronicle). (See Table 11.)

The twelve parallel units may serve as a poetic reference to the tribes of Israel (Wendland 2012: 183), fittingly so since Balaam views 'Israel encamped tribe by tribe' (Gane 2004: 709). Smick (1974: 246, 251–252) noted the correspondence between the opening and closing bicolons (5a–b, 9c–d), both exclamations using the 2nd m. sg. pr. suff., and how the exaltation of the king (7c–d) serves as the axis and key line of the poem, centred structurally and notionally, and framed by antithetical scenes of the nation at peace and at war, respectively. The Camp, as the

Table 11: Balaam's third parable, 24:3–9

Preface	Oracle of Balaam son of Beor,	3b
	And oracle of the man whose eye is opened.	3c
	Oracle of the one hearing the words of El,	4a
	Who envisioned a vision of Shaddai,	4b
	The one falling and his eyes uncovered:	4c
A. Introduction: The loveliness of Israel	How goodly are your tents, O Jacob,	5a
	Your dwelling places, O Israel!	5b
B. Israel, like a well-watered garden planted by YHWH. (*Peace scene*)	Like palm groves they stretch forth,	6a
	Like gardens by the riverside,	6b
	Like aloes planted by YHWH,	6c
	Like cedars by the waterside.	6d
		7a
	He will pour out waters from his buckets,	7b
	And his seed in many waters.	
C. The king exalted	May his king be exalted above Agag,	7c
	And his kingdom be lifted up!	7d
B'. Israel's king, like a lion will destroy his enemies (*War scene*)	El brought him forth from Egypt,	8a
	He has the horn-strength of a wild ox.	8b
		8c
	He will devour the nations of his hostile-foes,	8d
	And their bones he will crush,	8e
	And his arrows will pierce them!	9a
	He crouched, he lay down as a lion,	9b
	And as a king of beasts, who will rouse him?	
A'. Conclusion: The blessedness of Israel('s king)	Who blesses you is blessed,	9c
	And who curses you is cursed!	9d

paradigmatic covenant community, is observed as a foretaste of Israel's life in the land. Wiggershaus points out a cause and effect dynamic, between the imminent and distant future, given in three cycles (2021: 185–186). (See Table 12.)

Table 12: Balaam's third parable: Israel in the land

Imminent future	Distant future
Israel has sprawled across Canaan (24:5–6)	As a result, resources, population, and power will be increased (24:7)
El, having brought him out of Egypt, continues to be present with Israel (24:8a–b)	As a result, Israel's adversaries will be overcome (24:8c–e)
Israel is an established lion, unchallenged by its neighbours (24:9a–b)	As a result, any challengers will be dominated (24:9c–d)

3–4. Balaam, for the third time, 'takes up his parable'. He further dubs this speech an 'oracle' or 'divine utterance' (*něʾum*) three times, as he will do in the fourth speech (24:15–16). Crucially, as Milgrom points out (1990: 202), the term is never used of divination. These prophetic openings for the third and fourth oracle, noticeably lacking in the first and second, are meant to reflect Balaam's change in practice from divination now to actual prophecy (Margaliot 1990: 77), a change that signals the narrative's dramatic turning point. Wiggershaus conveys this turning point, with its shift from divination to prophecy as shown in Table 13 (2021: 215).

The designation 'oracle' underscores these two utterances, although, as with many aspects concerning Balaam, some ambiguity remains inasmuch as the standard formula is 'Oracle of YHWH' (*něʾum-yhwh*) – some 268 times (see Gen. 22:16; Num. 14:28; etc.); a rare exception occurs in the last words of David, dubbed an 'oracle of David' (*něʾum dāwid*, 2 Sam. 23:1; cf. Ps. 36:1; Prov. 30:1). Balaam refers to himself as the 'man' (*geber*) whose eye is 'opened' (*šětum*) – and who has envisioned a vision of Shaddai – lending greater gravity to this parable than the previous two. The words of verse 3 are repeated verbatim in verse 15, the only two uses of *šātam*, and verse 4 is repeated nearly verbatim in verse 16. The wording 'the eye' in sg. fed the Jewish lore that Balaam was blind in one eye (*b. Sanh.* 105a; Rashi 1997: 4:303; for a connection to *šatama*, 'reviled', possibly implying ' grim-faced', see Allegro 1953). Verses 3 and 4 are in parallel: with 'oracle of the man whose eye is opened' expanded by 'who envisioned a vision of Shaddai, / Falling and having his eyes uncovered.' Having 'the eye (*hāʿayin*) opened (*šětum*)' is paralleled by his having 'the eyes (*ʿênāyim*) uncovered (*gālāh*)'. Since *šětum* can mean 'open' and 'shut', Sharp suggests a double entendre appropriate to Balaam's ambiguous characterization (2009: 146). Citing Genesis 15:12,

Table 13: From divination to prophecy

Conventions of divination (Num. 22 – 23)	Num. 24:1–2	Conventions of prophecy (Num. 24)
1. The qĕsāmîm (22:7)	T U R N I N G P O I N T	1. Divine possession (24:2)
2. 'Three-strike rule' / three queries (22:9–20; 23:3, 15; 24:1)		2. Fourth oracle is initiated by the deity despite Balaam's attempt to leave (24:14)
3. Balak sacrifices only with each enquiry (23:1–3, 14, 29–30)		3. No sacrifice before fourth oracle (24:10–14)
4. Importance of location (22:41; 23:13–14, 27–28)		4. No switching locations before the fourth oracle (24:10–14)
5. Balak stops enquiring after three attempts (24:10–11)		5. No enquiry before the fourth oracle (24:10–14)
6. Balaam offers two divination report oracles (23:7–10, 18–24)		6. Balaam offers two visions as prophetic oracles (24:3–9, 15–19)
7. Balak gets increasingly angry closer to the final attempt (24:10)		
8. 'Previously' sought omens (24:1)		

Hummelauer understood this as Balaam's receiving divine revelation while in a state of ecstatic sleep (1899: 289), but the notion may simply refer to prophetic vision without implying any abnormal psychological state (cf. H. C. Ackerman 1920). Similarly, Wiggershaus explains that Balaam's physical vision is 'shuttered' (nōpēl, v. 4c) 'as it temporarily gives way to the opening of his supernatural vision by God during the possession event' (2021: 179–180). The term gālāh, used also in 24:16, was used earlier when YHWH had 'opened' the eyes of Balaam so that he saw the messenger of YHWH standing in the way (22:31), his eyes being opened in the third scene of the donkey episode, as well as here in the third prophetic utterance, drawing an analogy between the two (cf. Postell 2019: 291).

Shaddai is the divine name used regularly throughout the patriarchal narratives (Gen. 17:1; 28:3; 35:11; 43:14; 48:3; 49:25), often as 'El Shaddai', widely held to mean 'El, the One of the mountain' or 'Mountain-dweller', possibly derived from the Akkadian šadû, 'mountain' (cf. Albright 1935; Jacob 1958: 46; L. R. Bailey 1968; de Moor 1997: 179–180, 246; Knauf 1998; Steins 2004). The word 'vision' (maḥăzêh) is also used for when YHWH came to Abram in a vision (Gen. 15:1). In its verbal form, ḥāzāh (envisioned) was used when the nobles of the sons of Israel viewed God on Mount Sinai (Exod. 24:11) and for the visions of later prophets (Isa. 1:1; Ezek. 12:27; Amos 1:1; Mic. 1:1; Hab. 1:1; and diviners viewing a lie, Zech. 10:2). As prophets are called 'seers' (*ḥōzêh*, 2 Sam. 24:11; 2 Kgs 17:13; 1 Chr. 21:9; 25:5; 29:29; 2 Chr. 9:29; 12:15; 19:2; 29:25, 30; 33:18; 35:15; Isa. 29:10; 30; 10; Amos 7:12; Mic. 3:7), use of *ḥāzāh* and *nĕ'um* depict Balaam's parable as true prophecy – although he is never called a seer or prophet in Scripture. The focus is on this particular vision, which as with the donkey's speech is understood as an isolated occasion, unique, and not a description of his status. Both 'hearing' and 'falling' are rendered as participles, the latter (*nōpēl*) supplied with the phrase 'into a trance' in AV, a common interpretation (LXX reads 'falling asleep', *en hypnō*).

5–6. After the preface related to Balaam's self-description (vv. 3–4), his vision is related, which portrays the Camp of Israel as paradise, both beautiful and bountiful. The oracle, opening with *mah* (How . . . !), bursts forth with an exclamation (on the use of *mah* adverbially followed with a verb, see BDB 553). Not surprisingly, these 'words of wonderful excellence and beauty' were deemed by Simpson (1885: 127) to 'find no parallel outside of the Bible, and are unsurpassed within it'. They were also destined to become famous in Judaism, with Numbers 24:5 being recited as the opening prayer in Shabbat morning services. The opening exclamations are not only about Israel, but are addressed *to* Israel: '*your* tents . . . *your* dwelling places' (cf. Notarius 2008: 64). Not only is this the first time Balaam addresses Israel directly, a 'fundamental and dramatic shift' (Twersky 2022: 151), but the oracle closes with the same feature, framing the oracle (A, A') – the only instances within the prophetic utterances. Rather than addressing Balak directly, as with the first two utterances (23:7, 18), this oracle stands out further as rising beyond the present audience, speaking to the subject of the vision, Israel. The encampment of Israel – Jacob's tents, paralleled with Israel's dwelling places – is described as 'goodly' (*ṭôb*), which, as with the LXX *kaloi*, also refers to beauty, here to such an extent it draws an exclamation from the beholder: 'How beautiful!' With good reason, this verse 'remained among the most cherished passages in Scripture throughout Synagogue history' (Gordon 1962: 41). At the peak of the enemy's malicious intent, the Spirit of God intervenes and, through the enemy's own tongue, utters passionate exclamations to Israel about their splendour and blessedness.

Whereas the first oracle had described Israel's 'dwellings' in reference to being set apart from the nations, the third oracle proclaims the loveliness and paradisal nature of Israel's dwellings, 'compared to an aromatic garden planted by God himself' (Twersky 2022: 152). With four different designations, the beauty of the Camp is described in terms of a lush garden, each simile (note the fourfold use of the *k* prefix, 'like') drawing out a different aspect within the idyllic vision. First, 'like palm groves' (*kinḥālîm*), given the further description of 'stretching out' (*nāṭāh*), appears to describe the magnitude of the Camp. *Naḥal* could refer to a torrent-valley or wady as well as to a palm grove, in which case the stretching out refers to streams; the other three similes, however, being arboreal in nature make (well-watered) 'palm groves' the likelier intention. Palm groves are images of life in the midst of a wilderness, and these 'stretch out' in sumptuous abundance. One is reminded of Israel's early encampment at Elim, with its twelve springs of water and seventy 'palm trees' (*těmārîm*, Exod. 15:27). Second, the Camp is 'like gardens' (*kěgannōt*) by the 'river' (*nāhār*). The first garden mentioned in the Torah is the garden of Eden, noted for its abundant water supply from a fourfold river (*nāhār*; Gen. 2:10–14). Israel's encampment, in community with YHWH God, is described in terms of life *before* the divine curses of Genesis 3:14–19; Balaam portrays Israel in a state of creational blessedness (cf. Savran 1994: 42–43). That being well-watered was apparently one of the garden of Eden's leading features is evident in the following passage: 'And Lot lifted (*nāśā'*) his eyes and he saw all the valley of the Jordan, that it was well-watered everywhere . . . like the garden of YHWH' (Gen. 13:10). There is a marked similarity between the visions of Lot and Balaam: they both 'lift up their eyes and see' verbatim (*wayyiśśā'* [-*lôṭ*/*bilʿām*] *'et-'ênāyw wayyar' 'et-*), and the objects they behold are described as Edenic gardens (Gen:13:10; Num. 24:2, 6). The phrase 'he lifted up his eyes and saw' may be a formula of transition (Avishur 1999: 101). Genesis 22 uses the phrase twice to describe Abraham's vision, first of Mount Moriah and then of a ram caught in the thicket (vv. 4, 13), momentous junctures. The Camp, likened to a well-watered garden, is depicted as abundantly fruitful and life-giving. Third, the Camp is described 'like aloes (*ka'ăhālîm*) planted by YHWH'. Sharing the same root letters ('*-h-l*), 'aloes' may serve as a play on Israel's 'tents', to which the aloes are compared. LXX reads 'like tents God has pitched' (*hōsei skēnai, has epēxen kyrios*). Only of the garden of Eden is it also said that it was 'planted (*nāṭaʿ*) by YHWH' (Gen. 2:8). In the Song of the Sea, Moses had led Israel to sing that 'You (YHWH) . . . will plant them (Israel) on the mountain of your inheritance' (Exod. 15:17), pointing to the Edenic imagery of Canaan (cf. Bolger 1993: 279–280). This simile makes most explicit that YHWH is the source of Israel's abundant life and beauty – Israel's blessedness is absolutely YHWH's doing. Moreover, just as Genesis 2:4–25 marks a shift from Elohim as transcendent Creator, to YHWH as one who personally formed man from the dust of the ground and breathed into his nostrils the breath of life, so the image here of YHWH's planting Israel portrays his intimate covenantal care for and dealings with Israel. Fourth, the encampments of Israel are likened to cedars by the waterside, an image that speaks of strength and fixedness, power and majesty, cedars, the king of trees, being renowned for their great height (see e.g. Ezek. 31:3) – and traditionally believed to have grown in Eden, 'the garden of God' (Ezek. 31:8). G. J. Wenham justly faults interpreters concerned over scientific accuracy (1981b: 199) – the point is not whether cedars are actually found growing beside waters, but the image of abundantly nurtured strength. In the Psalms, the righteous are said to flourish like palm trees, and to grow like cedars of Lebanon (92:12), which are 'full (of sap)', 'planted' by YHWH (104:16). Cedar wood also happens to be one of the ingredients required for cleansing from defilement (Lev. 14:52; Num. 19:6), and cedar trees were used for the palaces of David (2 Sam. 5:11; 7:2) and Solomon (1 Kgs 7:1–12) and for the Temple (1 Kgs 5–6).

Lines 6b, d with their 'by the riverside' and 'by the waterside' reinforce the idea of water as a source of life and fertility. Psalm 1, describing the righteous one who delights in and meditates on YHWH's Torah 'like a tree planted by streams of water' (1:3), uses a similar image to speak of spiritual realities, and even the river of Eden is echoed in Scripture as a symbol of God's life-giving supply, especially through the outpouring of his Spirit (see Ps. 46:4; Isa. 32:15; 44:3; 55:1; Ezek. 47; Joel 3:18; Zech. 12:10; 13:1; 14:8). Such water-supply, according to Psalm 1:3, ensures that the tree brings forth much fruit, and its leaves will not wither under scorching heat, signifying that whatever the righteous one does will prosper. Nachmanides has it that Balaam's vision reached to the eschatological Zion, quoting from Isaiah 58:11, wherein Israel is likened to 'a watered garden, and like a spring of water, whose waters fail not' (1975: 279). These similes vividly portray the blessings *already* being experienced by Israel, even through the wilderness journeys, through YHWH's central Dwelling within the Camp. YHWH is like a fountain of life, an endless supply of life-giving water, in the midst of the Camp that journeys through the arid wilderness. The arboreal images portray the Camp, the covenant community of YHWH, as regal, strong and growing, resplendent with abundance and life, as 'fragrant, exotic and strong trees' (Ashley 1993: 490). In the ANE, one type of curse, dubbed a 'proverb' by scholars, involved the use of similes, such as the Sumerian proverb 'Like a clod thrown into water, (so) may he perish as he slowly dissolves' (Kitz 2007a: 624–625). Balaam, sovereignly overruled by the Spirit, uses similes to extol and bless God's people, to such a degree it 'is as if Israel has returned to the garden of Eden' (Stubbs 2009: 193). (See Figure 3.)

7. The first couplet of this verse is difficult and has been translated in a variety of ways (for emmendations, see G. B. Gray 1903: 363–366); for example, 'Water flows from his buckets, and his seed (*zeraʻ*) is in many waters,' or 'Water flows from his branches, and his root is in many waters.' JPS, Milgrom, Levine and Alter translate *zeraʻ* as 'root', with Alter mistakenly noting that *zeraʻ* 'frequently designates "root" in poetry (repeatedly, in Job)' (2004: 812; cf. Morag 1981: 14–16; Savran 1994: 42), whereas there is not a single other instance where such a rendering is preferable and Job consistently uses *šōreš* for 'root' (see Job 8:17; 14:8; 18:16; 29:19). The phrase 'from his buckets' (*middālĕyāw*)

may use either the dual form of 'bucket' (*dĕlî*), portraying a person with a bucket full of water in each hand or on either end of a pole returning from abundant springs (so e.g. G. B. Gray 1903: 364), or that of 'branch' or 'bough' (*dālît*), although elsewhere, as in Ezekiel (17:6, 7; 19:11; 31:7, 9, 12), the word is f. Given the arboreal language of the previous verse, it would be natural to understand the water as flowing or dripping from 'his branches', which, in turn, makes possible the (albeit unusual) interpretation of *zera‘* as 'root', conveying imagery that resonates with the picture in Ezekiel 17:3–10 of a tree planted by abundant waters (although *šōreš* is used in Ezek. 17:6, 7, 9). 'All the versions, except the Vulgate', as Vermes observes (1961b: 159), 'are messianic in interpretation' (see also M. F. Collins 1978: 16–57). LXX reads, 'There shall come a man out of his seed, and he shall rule over many nations' (*exeleusetai anthrōpos ek tou spermatos autou kai kyrieusei ethnōn pollōn*; Brenton 1986: 209), reflecting the messianic expectations of the intertestamental period (see also Biersdorff 2014: 77–85). As Vermes points out (1961a: 159), the LXX treatment of this verse is similar to the Targumim (*TgO, TgPs-J,* and *Frg. Tg.*), which have 'king' in place of 'man'. The MT's imagery seems intended to portray the virility and fruitfulness of Israel, either under the guise of a well-watered tree or, more likely, the figure of a man carrying irrigation buckets overflowing with water (cf. Smick 1974: 250). Water pours out of Israel's buckets, and Israel's seed – either 'semen' (as euphemism; see Allen 2012: 326, 328) or 'offspring' (cf. Harrison 1990: 316; see BDB 282–283) – will be like flowing waters (see Burrows 1938: 72 n. 2). Rather than 'in' flowing waters, Israel's seed may be likened to – 'as' or 'like' – flowing waters (for the comparative use of the particle *b-*, see BDB 89). Just as a seed planted near water flourishes, so Israel's generations will flourish and prosper (cf. Rashi 1997: 4:305). Proverbs uses the imagery of cisterns, flowing waters, fountains and streams, for sexual intercourse with one's wife (5:15–20), and the imagery here may likewise refer to virility and an abundant posterity, as blessed of YHWH. Hirsch reads the line as (2007a: 510) the water flows from God's buckets, and every human seed that is sown beside these streams is his – God's – seed. 'The dry dust of Jacob', writes J. S. Ackerman (1987: 87), 'becomes his seed in "many waters" – an indication of the coming proliferation of the nation, sustained by YHWH's mastery over the waters of chaos.' There is some irony in that this prophecy is uttered from the summit of Peor (23:28), a place likely given over to pagan rites of sexual immorality to which the sons of Israel would soon succumb (25:1–3) – Israel forsook the divine blessing of fecundity for illicit pleasure, leading to divine judgement and death.

Although some see an abrupt shift to royal imagery (e.g. Wendland 2012: 184), yet either notion, whether that of a tree planted by many waters, a common ANE image of kingship (cf. Ezek. 17; 31; Dan. 4; see Widengren 1951; Wyatt 2014), or that of seed, a key term with

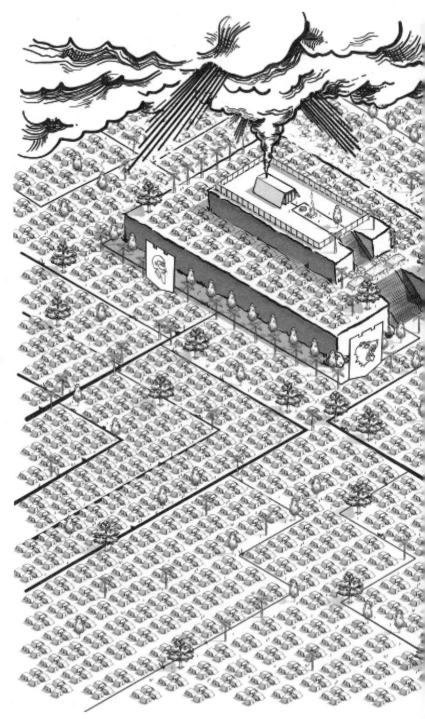

Figure 3: Balaam's vision

Messianic implications (Gen. 3:15; 22:18; Ruth 4:18–20; Matt. 1:1–17; see Alexander 2003), leads naturally to the topic of Israel's king and kingdom in the next couplet. The phrase 'many waters' (*mayim rabbîm*) is used only one other time in Numbers, with reference to the 'many waters' that poured forth from the rock, demonstrating YHWH's abundant provision for his people (20:11), a scene and message not unlike the vision now proclaimed by Balaam.

Three times in Genesis, YHWH had promised that kings would come from the seed of Abraham (17:6, 16; 35:11) (cf. G. J. Wenham 1981b: 200; Milgrom 1990: 204). The main textual issue in the next couplet is the reference to Agag, since other versions have 'Gog'. Agag is the name of the Amalekite king whom Saul failed to execute, leading to the rejection of Saul's dynasty (1 Sam. 15:10–35). Later in Israel's history, the rivalry between Saul's tribe of Benjamin and the descendants of Agag would be renewed (cf. Esth. 2:5; 3:1), and indeed YHWH had sworn to battle Amalek from generation to generation (Exod. 17:16). Reading a historical and chronological progression among the oracles has led interpreters to understand the third utterance as referring to Israel's settlement in the land, along with the dawning of the monarchy under Saul. Rashi, for example, read the first line (Israel's king 'exalted above Agag') as a reference to Saul, while the second line (Israel's kingdom 'lifted up') to the rise of David and Solomon's reigns after Saul (see Rashi 1997: 4:305–306). Nachmanides supports this reading by connecting the language of David's reign to the second line (23:7), 'his kingdom lifted up (*naśśē' malkutô*)': David understood that YHWH had 'exalted his kingdom' (*niśśē' mamlaktô*, 2 Sam. 5:12) (1975: 278–279, 281–282). Agag might also have been a title, like 'Pharaoh', referring to a current prominent ruler of the Amalekites (cf. BDB 8). On any reading, 'Agag' likely represents an archetypal enemy of God's people (H.-C. Schmitt 2001: 244–245), leaving open a definitive fulfilment for Israel's ideal king, a hope that through YHWH's covenant with David flowed into the expectations for the Messiah. More generally, the reference to Agag may signify the founding of Israel's monarchy. As noted, several key witnesses read 'Gog' (*gôg*) instead of 'Agag' (here I am following Postell 2019: 299–300): these include the LXX, the SamP, the DSS (4QNum[b] f24ii), Aq, Sym and Theo. In Ezekiel, Gog stands as a 'last days' (*bĕ'aḥărît hayyāmîm*, 38:16) enemy of God's people, whom YHWH will utterly defeat (chs. 38–39), before establishing his glory in the New Jerusalem, patterned after the wilderness Camp of Israel (chs. 40–48), an eschatological victory reasserted in John's Revelation (cf. 20:8). In Ezekiel, YHWH refers to Og as one 'spoken about in former times' (38:17), making Balaam's oracle an attractive referent (cf. Postell 2019: 299–300). Regardless, both 'Agag' and 'Gog' stand for archetypal enemies of Israel whom YHWH will decisively conquer in the last days. Powell suggests a reference to the Akkadian *Igigi*, the gods of the sky in Babylonian mythology, with Israel's king being 'higher than the gods of the sky' (1982: 278–279), but this notion finds no support within the rest of the HB. Albright suggested the possibility that the imagery of being 'above Agag' may derive from a play on *gag* (roof) (1944: 218). I cautiously retain the reading of 'Agag', taking the reference – at least in the first place – as a prediction that Israel would eventually defeat its earliest arch-enemy, as also foretold in the fifth utterance (24:20; cf. G. J. Wenham 1981b: 178), a view that may readily incorporate the notion that 'Agag' was a dynastic title among the Amalekites (cf. Keil 1869: 189). Ultimately, the blessing for Israel's king to be 'exalted above' (*rûm*) Agag and for his kingdom to be 'lifted up' (*nāśā'*) is brought into YHWH's promises for the royal line of David: 'I will make him my firstborn, higher (*'elyôn*) than all the kings of the earth' (Ps. 89:27), promises that find their culmination in the Messiah, whose victory over 'Og' is itself a token of his triumph over all powers. Using the same two verbs as Numbers 24:7b, Isaiah proclaims the Servant of YHWH will be 'exalted (*rûm*) and lifted up (*nāśā'*) very high' (52:13), glorified after being despised and rejected, a man of sorrows who, taking the iniquity of God's people upon himself, makes atonement for them, offering up his life as a sacrifice for their healing (53:3–12).

8–9. The king of Israel, introduced in the previous couplet, is the focus for the rest of Balaam's oracle. The second discourse (23:18–24), which otherwise consistently refers to Israel or Jacob in the 3rd m. sg., used the pl. in verse 22, 'God brought *them* (*môṣî'ām*) out of Egypt,' to distinguish the people both from the aforementioned king (v. 21) and from God ('He') in the following line (v. 22b). Balaam's second and third discourses use similar language but whereas the second discourse focused on Israel as a people, the third focuses on Israel's king (Postell 2019: 294–296). In the second utterance of Balaam, El brought the people out of Egypt, who are like a lion (23:22, 24), but here El brings *him* (*môṣî'ô*) out of Egypt, and he, the king, is like a lion. Rather than El having the horn-strength of a wild ox (23:22b), here it is the king who possesses such strength that he will devour the nations of his hostile foes (*ṣar*; see also 10:9; 22:26; 24:8; 25:17, 18; 33:55), crushing their bones and smashing them with his arrows. For 'wild ox' (*rĕ'ēm*), see 23:22. In the ANE, blessing was understood as including the defeat of one's enemies, and here the utter defeat of Israel's enemies is pictured vividly, a point made in previous divine promises (e.g. Gen. 22:17). Most directly, 'the nations of his hostile-foes' refers to the Canaanites in the land, or 'the kings of Canaan' as Ibn Ezra glosses (1999: 205). That he 'devours' (*yō'kal*) the nations and crushes or 'gnaws' (*yĕgārēm*) on their bones, already brings in the imagery of a lion devouring its prey, made explicit in the first couplet (v. 9). The last clause of verse 8 would fit the couplet better if the enemies' arrows were being smashed like the bones of the previous clause, as with Fox's translation: 'their bones they will crush; their arrows they will smash!' (1995: 780), and JPS, 'Crush their bones, And smash their arrows'; however, the 3rd m. sg. suff. 'his arrows' makes this reading difficult (for a belomancy, see Powell 1982: 283–284). Friedman suggests the chain of alliteration (*môṣî'ôm mimmiṣrayim . . . ṣārāyw wĕ'aṣmōtêhem . . . ḥiṣṣāyw yimḥāṣ*) may be intended to convey the defeat of Egypt through puns (2001: 510). While verse 8 envisions the conquest of Israel's enemies, led by her king, verse 9 portrays Israel, again through the headship of the nation's king, as resting undisturbed in the land of their inheritance (cf. G. B. Gray 1903: 366). Keenly, Leibowitz links this verse with the covenantal blessing described at the end of Leviticus, where YHWH says, 'And I will give peace in the land, and you will lie down (*šĕkabtem*) and nothing will make you afraid' (26:6) (1982: 295).

Echoing the end of Balaam's second utterance (cf. 23:24), but with *'ărî* (lion) and *lābî'* (king of beasts) chiastically reversed, and with an allusion to Jacob's prophetic blessing of Judah's line (Gen. 49:9), Israel's king is likened to a mighty lion (with different terms for 'lie down': *rābaṣ* and *šākab*, respectively). The term 'crouched' (*kāra'*) is used of a lion in only these two instances (Gen. 49:9; Num. 24:9), and 'rise'/'rouse' (*qûm*) with reference to a lion connects Genesis 49:9, Numbers 23:24 and 24:9 with the phrase 'who will rouse him' occurring only in Genesis 49:9 and Numbers 24:9 (Strawn 2005: 332). Clearly, then, the lion imagery in Balaam's oracles is not simply an example of the use of a widespread metaphor in the ancient world, but functions more particularly as an allusion to and a divine reaffirmation of Jacob's blessing of Judah, whose tribal banner (so tradition holds) had the insignia of a lion. (See Table 14.)

Table 14: The blessing of Judah

Genesis 49:9	Numbers 24:9
He crouched (*kāra'*),	He crouched (*kāra'*),
he lay down as a lion (*kĕ'aryêh*),	he lay down as a lion (*ka'ărî*),
and as the king of beasts (*ûkĕlābî'*)	and as the king of beasts (*ûkĕlābî'*)
who will rouse him (*yĕqîmennû*)?	who will rouse him (*yĕqîmennû*)?

The next verse in Jacob's prophetic blessing declares that 'the scepter will not depart from Judah' and that 'to him will be the obedience of the people' (Gen. 49:10), divine promises that fall upon the head of David and, through his line, to the Messiah (Pss 2; 89; 2 Sam. 7; Isa. 9:6–7; 11). Parallels between Balaam's third and fourth speeches also favour reading verse 9 in relation to Israel's future king rather than the nation. Twersky, observing how the 'narrative climaxes with Balaam reluctantly showering Israel with three blessings, which are topped off by an apocalyptic, end of days oracle', notes both the progressive intensification of the blessings and how their unified message heralds the Israelite monarchy by following the 'template' of Jacob's blessing to Judah in Genesis 49 (2022: 146, 159–168). The Messiah will be a majestic king (Gen. 49:9; Num. 24:9a), conqueror of Israel's enemies (Gen. 49:8; Num. 24:8), and a channel of blessing to the nations (Gen. 49:10; Num. 24:9b) (see Postell 2019: 298).

The second prophetic utterance had ended by declaring that Israel as a mighty lion would not lie down until he devours the prey (23:24), referring to the conquest – that Israel would not rest or settle the land until destroying their enemies within it. The crouching and lying down in the third prophetic utterance therefore describes Israel's settling in the land of Canaan with strength and might and tranquility (cf. *TgO*; Ibn Ezra), so that surrounding nations are unable and too fearful to disturb them or attempt to drive them out, a meaning that holds even with Israel's king and head in focus. Ultimately it is under the Messiah's reign alone that God's people will dwell securely in the land, with no threat either of invading enemies or of exile – that is when Israel 'will no more be prey to the nations . . . and will dwell safely, with none to make them afraid' (Ezek. 34:28; cf. Jer. 30:10; 32:37; Amos 9:15).

The last couplet of Balaam's third utterance alludes to the Abrahamic blessing, when YHWH avowed, 'I will bless (*bārak*) those who bless (*bārak*) you, and he who dishonours you I will curse (*'arar*)' (Gen. 12:3; cf. Gen. 22:18; 27:29). Far from cursing God's people, Balaam's utterance forms a powerful *reaffirmation* of YHWH's original plans of blessing for the 'great nation' he would make of Abraham (Gen. 12:2), and particularly for Abraham's seed as ultimately fulfilled by the king who represents the whole nation – whoever blesses the (singular) seed of Abraham, even the Messiah Lord Jesus, is blessed indeed (see Gal. 3:16). Even referring to the king, the declaration encompasses Israel as his people, paralleling structurally and thematically the declaration in verse 5 about Israel. The proclamation also serves as a divine warning to Balak himself that cursing Israel would lead to his own demise, a warning fulfilled in the fourth parable (24:15–19). The nations will experience either blessing or cursing, depending on their regard for the seed of Abraham. MacKintosh's comment is worth quoting, as he captures the exuberance of the oracle (1869: 386):

> 'Higher and higher yet' is surely the motto here. We may well shout 'Excelsior,' as we mount up to the top of the rocks, and hearken to those brilliant utterances which the false prophet was forced to give out. It was better and better for Israel – worse and worse for Balak. He had to stand by and not only hear Israel 'blessed,' but hear himself 'cursed' for seeking to curse them.

10–13. In response, Balak's 'fierce anger was kindled' (*wayyiḥar-'ap*), the third and final use of this phrase in the Balaam narrative (22:22,

27; 24:10). Just as Balaam had been furious over his donkey's third failure on the journey to Moab, so now Balak is enraged over Balaam's failure to curse Israel. The phrase will be used again in Numbers 25, for YHWH's fierce anger against Israel for their apostasy with Baal of Peor (v. 3; cf. also 11:1, 10; 12:9; 32:10, 13). The description of Balak's anger is underscored, targeting the amusement of listeners: he claps his hands and states the obvious, that he had called Balaam to curse his enemies, but, 'look, you have thoroughly blessed (*bēraktā bārēk*) them these three times!' Clapping one's hands at another might have been a derogatory and even vicious expression against someone in the ancient world (Job 27:23; Lam. 2:15; cf. Budd 1984: 269). The words 'these three times' (*zeh šālōš pĕʿāmîm*), while using slightly different phraseology, can hardly keep from recalling the similar expression of Balaam's striking his donkey 'these three times' (*zeh šālōš rĕgālîm*, 22:28, 32, 33), once more drawing an analogy between the threefold journey of Balaam with his donkey and Balak's threefold attempt at cursing Israel through Balaam. By ANE divination customs, only three chances were permitted for receiving a desired result, a point – that his chances had been exhausted – which may feed Balak's rage (cf. Wiggershaus 2021: 116). In anger, Balak tells Balaam, 'Now, flee for yourself to your place!' Balak's outrage may involve a play on words: Balaam likes to 'bless' (*bārēk*), so now he had better 'flee' (*bĕraḥ*)! To flee 'for yourself to your place' signals that Balaam is no longer welcome in Moab; he is to return to the place from which he had been called (22:5). Whereas twice, in seeking Israel's curse, Balak had led Balaam to 'another place' (*ʾaḥēr māqôm*), now Balak bids him to flee 'to your own place'. Once more Balak sets himself, and the allure of wealth, as a competing and powerful motivation for Balaam, Balak versus YHWH: Balak wanted to honour Balaam greatly, but YHWH has withheld such honour from him. Maligning God's character, Balak emphasizes YHWH's withholding of riches from Balaam by use of 'look!' (*hinnê*), as if he is pointing out a malicious act. Perhaps it was this last word from Balak that led to Balaam's scheme, a renewed attempt against Israel revealed later (see 31:16). Whereas Balaam had refused the first envoys, saying, 'Go back to your land, for YHWH has refused (*mēʾēn*) to grant me to go with you' (22:13), now Balak, perhaps mocking that earlier refusal in spite, says, 'Flee to your place . . . YHWH has withheld (*mēʾēn*) honour from you' (24:11).

Balak's statement, beginning with 'I had said', holds up the impotence, contingent uncertainty and waywardness of human words, serving as a contrast to YHWH's word, upheld and reaffirmed (23:19–20). Both Balak and Balaam come full circle to their own previous words (22:17–18). Balaam responds by resorting to his previous response to Balak's call. Yet, again, the differences in his reporting are curious. Comparing his words in 22:18 with 24:13, they are repeated nearly verbatim. Previously, however, he had referred to YHWH as 'my God', but now omits 'my God' – a rhetorical distancing of himself from YHWH not lost on interpreters (e.g. Rashi 1997: 4:308). He had also previously confessed that he was 'unable to do small or great', whereas as now he is 'unable to do good or evil from my own heart', distancing himself from YHWH's will. Bonchek sees this latter difference as deviousness on Balaam's part (2004: 112–113): whereas previously he had hedged his bet in case his curse did not accomplish anything ('to do a small or a big thing', 22:2), now that he has brought disaster ('evil') on Balak's head by blessing Moab's enemy, he relies on saying, 'I told you so,' but changes his own previous words ('to do good or evil', 24:13). At least in two ways, by leaving out 'my God' and by separating his own desire to do good or evil from what YHWH speaks, Balaam demonstrates that his prophetic utterances have been by compulsion alone and that he, left to himself, would be in good rapport with Balak, whose honours he craves. Surely this is no Moses, whose heart is conformed to the will of YHWH, serving Israel, the apple of his eye, selflessly. On the contrary, that Balaam even stands before Balak now is due only to the hope he had entertained of somehow persuading YHWH to curse his chosen people. The thematic refrain of Balaam's speaking only what YHWH speaks underscores the story's message that 'there is no autonomous realm of word magic and vision that a technician of the holy can manipulate; all blessings and curses are dictated by the LORD' (Alter 2004: 813).

14. Separated from the first three poetic discourses by Balak's summary dismissal, this oracle should be grouped with the final three as a set of four. Uniting these last proverbs thematically, each predicts doom for the enemies of Israel – fittingly beginning with Moab (24:17) – and, as a finale, the set forms a reversal and denouement for the Balaam narrative: the story that began with a desire to curse Israel ends with that curse falling on Israel's hostile foes. It was not enough, then, for Israel to be blessed – divine justice addresses the intentions of the wicked: for YHWH makes himself known when the wicked are ensnared in the work of their own hands (Ps. 9:15–16; cf. Ps. 141:10; Prov. 5:22; 12:13).

'Now, look, I am going to my people' parallels Balak's demand (v. 11). However, he bids Balak to follow for the time being ('Go' or 'Come,' *lĕkāh*) so that he may guide ('advise, counsel', *yāʻaṣ*) him. Although the context has the fourth and following prophetic utterances in its immediate purview, some interpreters have noted that this moment of Balaam's counsel may explain (or at least hint at) the scheme later revealed (31:16; see *Num. Rab.* 20.21). Isbell notes (2002: 96) that the root *y-ʻ-ṣ*

> is used often in Scripture to describe the most trusted confidant to a king, and entire military operations sometimes hinged on the validity of the advice each side received from such persons (see 2 Sam. 15:31–37; 16:23; 17:1–23).

The Targums make this clue explicit: 'Come and I will advise you what to do to this people. Cause them to sin or you will not prevail against them' (*Frg. Tg.*), 'Come, I will advise you. Go and set up taverns and appoint within them seductive women' (*TgPs-J*) (quoted from Vermes 1961b: 162; cf. Blumenthal 2006: 85). Typically, this understanding, assuming an elliptical verse, divides Balaam's brief statement in two: 'I will advise you' (as to how to bring about Israel's downfall by causing them to sin) and, in addition, I will tell you 'what this people will do to your people' (how Israel is destined to harm Moab) (*TgO*; *b. Sanh.* 106a; *Tan.* 18; Rashi 1997: 4:308–309). Milgrom registers the disjunctive Masoretic accentuation (*zaqef qaton*), interpreted as indicating that information was omitted (1990: 206). The focus of the text, however, is narrower: Balaam says he will counsel Balak 'as to what this people will do to your people at the end of days'. These words underscore the fourth prophecy as containing the principle message, the one that most directly responds to the reason for which Balak had summoned Balaam to begin with; namely, Moab's fate at the hands of Israel (Granot 2014a: 327). The nations or peoples is a theme for this whole verse, as with the utterances that follow: 'my people', 'this people', 'your people' (cf. McCarter 1980: 57; Burnett 2018). The divine judgement against the various nations in the last four prophetic utterances may be read under the rubric of against 'your people' (Moab), if the other peoples are considered partners in a coalition led by Balak against Israel (as suggested by Margaliot 1990: 80). 'My people' (*'ammî*) forms an inclusion with 'his people' (*'ammô*) in 22:5, framing the Chronicle of Balaam (cf. Milgrom 1990: 206).

Arguably, the phrase 'end of days' (or 'latter days', *bĕ'aḥărît hayyāmîm*), while it may refer to an indeterminate historical future, is in this context eschatological in nature, a significant concept in the Torah (Gen. 49:1; Num. 24:14; Deut. 4:30; 31:29) and in the rest of the HB, where it tends to be used in a technical sense for the eschatological future especially in the classical prophets (Isa. 2:2; Ezek. 38:16; Dan. 2:28; 10:14; Mic. 4:1; cf. Bateman et al. 2012: 53–54). The word 'latter end' (*'aḥărît*) also occurs in the oracles, in parallel with the 'death of the righteous' (23:10), and in the 'latter end' of Amalek (24:20). The expression 'end of days' refers to the final period of the future from the speaker's perspective (G. B. Gray 1903: 368, quoting S. R. Driver), but a good argument can be made that 'Scriptural usage ordinarily indicates messianic times' (Guyot 1940: 337). At the end of Genesis, Jacob gathered his sons to report what would befall their tribes in the 'end of days' (49:1), and, similarly, Moses tells the gathered tribes what will befall them (Deut. 4:30; 31:29). The phrase 'latter days', then, forms another link particularly, within the context of other allusions throughout Balaam's oracles, to Judah's blessings, portending kingship in Israel. Sailhamer noted the convergence of macrostructure, narrative motifs and terminology among these three poetic discourses (1992: 36–37):

In each of the three segments, the central narrative figure (Jacob, Balaam, Moses) calls an audience together (imperitive: Gen. 49:1; Num. 24:14; Deut. 31:28) and proclaims (cohortative: Gen. 49:1; Num. 24:14; Deut. 31:28) what will happen (Gen. 49:1; Num. 24:14; Deut. 31:29) in 'the last days' (Gen. 49:1; Num. 24:14; Deut. 31:29).

Twersky reads Balaam's fourth prophecy as 'an apocalyptic, end of days oracle' (2022: 146). Following a chronological reading of the oracles, progressing through the history of Israel, Nachmanides discerned that 'this prophecy refers to Messianic times', explaining the scheme as in Table 15 (1975: 281–288).

Table 15: Nachmanides' chronological reading of Balaam's oracles

First prophecy Num. 23:7-10	Israel is YHWH's portion and inheritance (cf. Deut. 32:9; exodus out of Egypt, Sinai covenant and wilderness journeys).
Second prophecy Num. 23:18-24	Israel's conquest of the land and destruction of Canaanite kings.
Third prophecy Num. 24:3-9	Israel's dwelling in the land, increasing and multiplying therein; the appointment of Saul as king, and his defeat of Agag; and the further exaltation of the kingdom under the dynasty of David.
Fourth prophecy Num. 24:15-19	The Messianic era of Israel, when the Messiah gathers the dispersed of Israel from all the corners of the earth, ending the exile of Rome (Edom).
Last prophecies Num. 24:20-24	The fourth beast, Kittim (Rome), destroyed by the hand of the Messiah (cf. Dan. 7).

24:15–19

The climax of the Balaam narrative is found in these verses, as Balaam prophesies further of a coming one, the Ruler out of Israel introduced in the heart of his third discourse, who will establish the kingdom of God against the enemies of YHWH and of his people (cf. van Groningen 1990: 242). The future-orientation of the oracle, within the broader context of the prose story and the first three proverbs, along with the ripple effect of the three minor oracles that follow in the wake of its crescendo (M. F. Collins 1978: 59), all mark this fourth prophetic utterance as the pinnacle of the Balaam chronicle and, perhaps, of Numbers. This oracle, as Milgrom observes (1990: 202, 468), culminates the theme of blessing and cursing, as its resolution: in the first, the message is delivered that only God determines blessing and cursing (23:8); in the second, the point is made that God's blessing cannot be revoked (23:20); the third declares that whoever blesses or curses Israel will in turn be either blessed or cursed themselves (24:9); and, finally, in the fourth oracle, and in 'a stunning reversal' of Moab's desired curse against Israel (Pressler 2017: 199), Balaam, still possessed of the Spirit of God, prophesies that Moab will fall under Israel's domination, fulfilling the measure-for-measure principle invoked in the previous oracle (24:15–19). Set apart from the others by its directly future orientation, the parable may be outlined as in Table 16 (cf. Wendland 2012: 186–187).

Table 16: Balaam's fourth parable, 24:15–19

Preface	Oracle of Balaam son of Beor,		15b
	And oracle of the man whose eye is opened.		15c
	Oracle of the one hearing the words of El,		16a
	And who knows the knowledge of Elyon,		16b
	Who envisioned a vision of Shaddai,		16c
	The one falling and his eyes uncovered:		16d
A. Israel's future ruler	I see him but now,		17a
	I behold him but not nearby.		17b
	A star treks forth from Jacob,		17c
	A scepter rises from Israel		17d
B. Israel's enemies defeated	He will shatter the brow of Moab,		17e
	And the pate of the sons of Sheth.		17f
B'. Israel's enemies defeated	And Edom will be dispossessed,		18a
	And Seir will be dispossessed by his enemies.		18b
A'. Israel's future ruler	But Israel will do valiantly.		18c
	And from Jacob he will exercise dominion,		19a
	And he will destroy survivors from the city.		19b

The central theme of the destruction of Israel's enemies forms a bridge into parables 5, 6 and 7, which focus on the same. Also observed with the previous prophecy, Wiggershaus points out the shift from the immanent future, that Balaam sees a coming Israelite king who does not exist in the historical present (24:17a–b), to the distant future, as a result, when the king will expand his territory, defeating and taking possession of his neighbours (24:17c–20) (2021: 186).

15–16. For the fourth of seven times (23:7, 18; 24:3, 15, 20, 21, 23), Balaam takes up his parable – the fourth parable telescoping into four parables (24:15–19, 20, 21–22, 23–24). This parable, as with the third (cf. 24:3–4), is also dubbed an 'oracle' (*něʼum*) three times. Balaam's opening self-description is the same verbatim as the third parable, except for the addition now of 'who knows the knowledge of Elyon'. The repetition implies that the Spirit of God remained on Balaam for these last utterances, while the additional line referring to Elyon increases further the climactic sense of mounting exuberance. Elyon means 'upper' or, with reference to God, 'Most High' or 'Lofty One', and was used earlier in the Torah in one pericope alone, in Abram's encounter with Melchizedek, who is dubbed a priest of 'God Most High' (*'ēl 'elyôn*, Gen. 14:18, 19, 20, 22; cf. Deut. 32:8), and seems to refer to God's sovereignty over the nations, being higher than their gods. The note of his supremacy as Most High, above the nations, comes out in the following passages (cf. Allen 1973: 400):

> The kingdom and dominion, and the greatness of the kingdom under the whole of heaven, will be given to the people of the saints of Elyon, whose kingdom is an everlasting kingdom, and all dominions will serve and obey him. (Dan. 7:27)

> For YHWH Elyon is feared, a great King over all the earth. He will subdue the peoples under us, and nations under our feet. (Ps. 47:2–3)

> That all may know that you, whose name alone is YHWH, are Elyon over all the earth. (Ps. 83:18)

Not only does Balaam claim to have heard the words of El and to have seen a vision of Shaddai (cf. 24:3–4), but he knows or has learned Elyon's knowledge. From Elyon's lofty position, God has ordained and sees the affairs of the peoples, including what will befall them in the latter days, and Balaam, who has learned this divine knowledge, will tell it forth now to Balak. The word 'knowledge' (*da'at*), in this context, refers to 'prophetic knowledge', insight possessed by God but taught by him to people (BDB 395). Balaam's self-advertisement is profuse in the extreme, especially by contrast with the marked meekness of Moses, and ironic in the light of the donkey episode.

17. J. S. Ackerman (1987: 87) justly considers this speech of Balaam to be 'the most far-reaching and positive vision of Israel's future found in the entire Pentateuch'. In keeping with the 'end of days' context for the oracle, Balaam declares that he sees him 'but not now' and beholds him 'but not nearby' – the ruler he announces is one he sees through the mists of future history. In his first parable, Balaam had said, 'From the summit of rocky-crags I see him (*'er'ennû*), and from the hills I behold him (*'ăšûrennû*),' and went on to describe the consecrated uniqueness of the nation of Israel (23:9). With similar language, Balaam 'sees' (*'er'ennû*) and 'beholds' (*'ăšûrennû*) Israel's future king. A star, a metaphor for kingship, 'treks forth' (*dārak*) from Jacob, and a sceptre 'rises' (*qām*) from Israel. This is the only abs. form of 'star' (*kôkāb*) in the HB (cf. Lewis 1995: 2). As a poetic feature the verbs have been exchanged: one would expect a star to rise, and a sceptre (in a king's host) to march

forth into battle. LXX, Syr and Vg read that the star 'shall arise', perhaps reading *zāraḥ* instead of *dārak*, easily interchanged in Hebr. (cf. Guyot 1940: 333). The stars, along with the greater lights, are said to 'rule' (*memšālāh*) the night (Gen. 1:16; Ps 136:9), and Isaiah uses astral imagery in his portrayal of kingship (Isa. 14:12–13). In Genesis, the imagery of stars is used to portray the innumerable posterity of Abraham under God's blessing (15:5; 22:17) and for the sons of Jacob in Joseph's dream, which augured his own rise to rule (37:9). That this passage was embraced messianically by ancient Jews is evident in the adoption of the name 'star' by Simeon Bar Kochba ('son of a star', changed from 'Ben Kossevah'), as he – hailed as the Messiah by Akiva ben Yosef – led the unsuccessful revolt against Hadrian in AD 132–5 (cf. Avi-Yonah 1969: 162). The Essenes of Qumran refer to Numbers 24:17 in three of their scrolls: the *War Scroll (1QM)*, *Testimonia (4QTest)*, and the *Damascus Document (CD)*, each assuming an eschatological and Messianic interpretation (cf. Grundke 1995: 8; Marek 2020; for other ancient Jewish and early Christian interpretations, see Pick 1885; Vermes 1961b: 127–177; M. F. Collins 1978: 58–161; Lewis 1995; Caulley 2014; Jacobus 2015a). Since the 'scepter' will shatter the brow of Moab, it not only represents dominion (Judg. 5:14; Ps. 45:6; Ezek. 19:11, 14; Amos 1:5, 8; Zech. 10:11), but signifies a war mace (Pss 2:9; 125:3; Isa. 10:15; 14:5; Mic. 5:1), wielded by ANE rulers for shattering the skulls of their enemies in battle (Bateman et al. 2012: 54). In place of 'scepter', LXX reads 'man' (*anthrōpos*), a messianic reading in line with the Syr, which has 'a leader will arise from Israel' (Haymen 1991: 78). The Aramaic translations also evince a messianic understanding (Cathcart 1998: 512–513): *TgO* reads, 'A king will arise from Jacob, and the Messiah will be consecrated from Israel' (Sperber 1959: 266; cf. Grossfeld 1988: 138–139), while *TgNeof* has, 'A king will arise from the house of Jacob and a redeemer and ruler from the house of Israel' (Díez Macho 1974: 239) and the later *TgPs-J* reads, 'When the mighty king from the house of Jacob will reign, and the Messiah, the mighty scepter from Israel will be anointed' (Rieder 1974: 2:231–232). The *Testaments of the Twelve Patriarchs*, which is generally dated 200 BC as a Jewish work, perhaps with Christian interpolations (200 AD), uses the rising star of Balaam's prophecy in its apocalyptic vision of a messianic priestly king: 'And his star shall rise in heaven like a king' (*T. Levi* 18:3; see also 8:14; Kee 1985: 794). While there is no reference to Numbers 24:17 in the New Testament, the church fathers widely regarded the verse as predicting the incarnation, signalled by the star the magi followed in Matthew 2:12, implied in their question 'Where is he who has been born king of the Judeans – for we have seen his star in the East?' (see Cathcart 1998: 517–519; Lienhard 2001: 3:243–249; Hannah 2015; cf. Baskin 1983; Jacobus 2015a). While some exclude this possibility, arguing the absence of any fulfilment formula, it is a common error to reduce Matthew's use of the HB in such a way (see Instone-Brewer 2008). Numbers 24:17 as a prophecy of the Messiah can be found in Justin Martyr ('The First Apology'), Athanasius ('On the Incarnation of the Word'), Theodoret (*Quaest. in Oct.* c. 44 PG 80, 394), Jerome (ep. 77, *ad Oceanum*, PL 22, 695), Origen (*In Numeros*, MPG 12, 619), Irenaeus (*Fragmenta*, MPG 7, 1242) and Augustine (*Mir. S.S.*, MPL 35, 2173) (cf. Guyot 1940: 336; Allen 1973: 41–43). The *Zohar* (Exodus, *Vayera*, v. 478; Numbers, *Balak*, v. 501) associates a star from the east with the Messiah (cf. Maas 1893: 1:240; on Jewish astronomical observations related to the Messiah's advent, see Rosenberg 1972). There may also be a reference to Balaam's star in Zacharias's prophecy of the Messiah as the 'Dayspring' (*anatolē*) in Luke 1:78, possibly playing on the LXX translation for 'rising (*anatelei*) star'.

A ruler will descend from Jacob to conquer the enemies of God's people, establishing the kingdom of God. Focus on a descendant recalls YHWH's original promise regarding the seed of the woman (Gen. 3:15), which was also announced first to the foe of God's purposes, the serpent. The reference to a ruler recalls the divine promise that kings would spring forth from Abraham (Gen. 17:6; cf. 17:16; 35:11), a promise and genealogy that would eventually blossom forth through the line of Judah, as Jacob had proclaimed, 'the scepter will not depart from Judah, nor a ruler's staff from between his feet until he to whom it belongs comes, and to him will be the obedience of the peoples' (Gen. 49:10). Both Numbers 24:17 and Genesis 49:10 refer to a 'scepter' (*šēbeṭ*). Some read 'scepter' as a 'comet', in parallel with 'star' (cf. Gemser 1925; Mowinckel 1930: 246). Historically, both Genesis 49:9–12 and Numbers 24:17–19 have been interpreted as heralding the advent of the Messiah (see e.g. Merrill 2019; Gordley 2005: 113). Perhaps the star of Balaam's oracle inspired the description of Jesus as 'the bright and morning star' in Revelation 22:16 (cf. Vermes 1961b: 165). Many read the fourth oracle as a presentation of David and his mighty conquests (e.g. Seybold 1973), with his dynasty in view (see e.g. Ibn Ezra), and David became a type of the Messiah in the prophetic corpus (e.g. Jer. 30:9; Ezek. 34:23–24; Hos. 3:5; Amos 9:11–12; Mic. 5:2–5; see Vos 2001: 107–116; Morales 2020: 123–127). The announced regal figure is part of, but distinct from, the entire people of Israel, and, within the arc of the scriptural narrative, leads ineluctably to the royal house of David – to a king who will exercise dominion, establishing peace and security for God's people, and bringing definitive judgement on those who oppose YHWH and his purposes (van Groningen 1990: 244, 246). There are, moreover, a variety of lexical and thematic links between Balaam's fourth poetic discourse and Psalm 110, which portrays the divine enthronement and conquest of David, arguably signifying the Messiah's reign. Both texts use the imagery of smashing the enemy's head (cf. Gen. 3:15): Balaam's oracle describes the 'shattering' (*māḥaṣ*) of the brow of Moab and pate of Sheth (Num. 24:17), while the psalm refers to 'smiting' (*māḥaṣ*) the heads of many lands (110:6). Both texts also refer to 'rule' or 'dominion' (*rādāh*, Num. 24:19; Ps. 110:2), and mention 'oracle' (*nĕ'ūm*, Num. 24:15; Ps. 110:1), 'valour' or 'strength' (*ḥayil*, Num. 24:18; Ps. 110:3) and refer to a 'scepter' (Num. 24:17; Ps. 110:2), albeit with different terminology (cf. de Vaulx 1972: 292; G. J. Wenham 1981b: 205).

The third couplet shows that the coming king is a conqueror, who will smash the brow of Moab and the pate of all the sons of Sheth. Again, a foretaste of the Messianic conquest is seen in the life of David, who 'struck down Moab' (2 Sam. 8:2). This oracle, along with the following three, may be regarded as a 'curse oracle', forming a reversal of Balak's original intent – this was precisely the sort of speech he had hired Balaam to speak against Israel (Allen 1973: 322–323). Appropriately, the threatened destruction begins with Moab, who hired Balaam to curse Israel and so incurred the curse on its own head (cf. Gen. 12:3). In the prophets, Moab functions as 'an archetype for all hostile Gentile nations (Isa. 11:14; 15:1–9; 16:2–14; 25:10; Jer. 9:26; 48:1–47; Ezek. 25:8–11; Amos 2:1–3; Zeph. 2:8–11)' (Bateman et al. 2012: 56–57). 'Shattering' (*māḥaṣ*) the brow of Moab, which may signify Moab's border defences (van Groningen 1990: 244), feeds into the developing theme of crushing the head of the serpent (Gen. 3:15), used also for when Jael shattered Sisera's head (Judg. 5:26), and for YHWH's piercing of Rahab, the sea dragon often used to designate Egypt (Job 26:12). While the serpent, as enemy of God's people, may be temporarily linked with human powers and nations, the Scriptures ultimately link the serpent with Satan, whom the Messiah will conquer (Rev. 12:9; 20:2; see Morales 2020: 62–65). The prophet Habakkuk describes YHWH's coming as a warrior with his Messiah for the salvation of his people, 'smashing' (*māḥaṣ*) the head of the wicked (3:13; cf. Ps. 68:21), and in the Psalms, the Davidic servant, widely taken as the Messiah, 'smashes' (*māḥaṣ*) his enemies' heads so they fall at his feet (18:38; 110:5–6).

The 'pate' of the sons of Sheth will also be shattered. Who precisely are meant by the 'sons of Sheth' (*šēt*) is ambiguous. The referent may be to the third son of Adam (Gen. 4:25–26; 5:3); namely, the entire human race as the ruler's dominion (so *TgO*, Rashi 1997: 4:310; Ibn Ezra 1999: 208), or, perhaps more probable, to 'sons of tumult' as a parallel description of Moab – a reading that requires a slight emendation: from *šēt* to *šē't* (see Lam. 3:47 for *šē't* as 'destruction'; cf. BDB 981). Favouring the reading of Seth as Adam's third son is the fact that 'Cain' (for the Kenites) appears only a few verses later (24:21–22; cf. J. Day 2015: 55). Milgrom favours a reference to nomadic groups descended from Abraham and over whom Israel was promised dominance (1990: 208; see Gen. 25:1–18; 27:29). That verses 18–19a refer to one people by two names ('Edom', 'Seir'), followed by two names for God's people ('Israel', 'Jacob'), favours a double description of Moab. Moreover, Jeremiah 48:45 reads 'shall devour the brow of Moab, and the pate of the sons of tumult'; here 'tumult' is *šā'ôn* in the Hebr. – perhaps a folk etymology on *šēt* (cf. Mowinckel 1930: 254). Sayce suggested that 'Sheth' was the Moabite god Baal Peor (1887); on this scenario, the name still stands as a parallel referent to Moab. Albright favoured reading *Šûtu*, an archaic tribal designation for peoples around Moab (1944: 220; cf. Powell 1982: 358), which again correlates the referent with Moab. Although uncertainty remains, Guyot's suggestion is a reasonable possibility, that 'Seth' might have been an ancient name for Moab, as Seir was for Edom, perhaps playing on 'sons of Shaon', which was likely applied to the Moabites for their aggressive, bellicose nature (1940: 334). He sums up the verse with 'Israel is promised a king clothed with splendour (star) and endowed with authority (scepter); this king will destroy the enemies of Israel, Moab and Edom; he will rule over his enemies' (Guyot 1940: 335). As a parable of what Israel will do to Moab (v. 14), these lines have been anticipated ominously and stand as Moab's punishment for attempting to curse Israel.

18–19. From the descendants of Lot, Moab, the focus then turns to the descendants of Esau, Edom, who will be 'dispossessed' (*yĕrēšāh*) (cf. Ps. 60:8, where Moab is God's 'washpot', followed by God's casting his shoe over Edom). While 'Edom' refers to the people, their locale is designated by their prominent mountain, 'Seir' (cf. Judg. 5:4). As with Moab, Edom also serves as an archetype in prophetic literature for all hostile nations (Isa. 34:5–8; 63:1; Jer. 49:7–22; Ezek. 25:12–14; 32:29; 35:15; 36:5; Joel 3:19; Amos 1:6–11; 9:11–12; Obad. 1:8; Mal. 1:4) (Bateman et al. 2012: 57; see Rouillard 1985: 470–471; B. A. Anderson 2012: 44–50). Through the prophet Obadiah, YHWH would renew his proclamation against Edom, especially for their violence against Jacob their brother, rejoicing in Judah's destruction and captivity. Mention of Edom reminds one that the context (chs. 21–25) concerns the journeys east of the Jordan; while Edom and Moab have been bypassed (20:14–21; 21:10–22:1), yet, in the future, these lands will also be conquered by Israel (Granot 2014a: 328). While, as Kaiser points out (1995: 55), David did subjugate Moab and then Edom (1 Sam. 14:47; 2 Sam. 8:1, 14), the prophet Jeremiah would later echo Balaam's prophecy, placing it yet in the future (Jer. 48 – 49). Within its literary context, this oracle of doom pronounced against Edom can hardly be read without taking into account the recent refusal by Edom to allow Israel safe passage through its territory (20:14–21). Having recounted 'all the hardships' that had befallen Israel, Moses and the people of God were threatened harshly with military force and rebuffed by Edom's king, forcing Israel to turn away and continue its journey via a longer route – hardly a model of kinship and hospitality. Here again the measure-for-measure principle first articulated to Abram by YHWH (Gen. 12:3) surfaces – YHWH's eye is on his beloved people, and any ill-treatment of them will be redressed in due course.

By contrast ('But', with the subject fronting the verb: *wĕyiśrā'ēl*), Israel will do 'valiantly', *ḥāyil* often having a military connotation. The phrase *'ōśeh ḥāyil* could be translated 'gain wealth' (see Deut. 8:18), in which case the context would signify the spoils of victory (over Edom/ Seir), this the direction taken by the Syr and in *TgO*, *TgNeof* and *TgPs-J* (cf. M. F. Collins 1978: 117, 156). This line, then, may be taken as a contrastive inclusio with 'And Edom will be dispossessed' (Powell 1982: 301–302), or perhaps better as a couplet with the following line, forming a pair with Jacob (see Israel/Jacob in 23:7, 10, 21, 23 [twice]; 24:5, 17) – in either case, there is one tristich in the poem. Since Jacob occurs before Israel in every other instance, Milgrom prefers reversing the sequence of lines to read 'Jacob shall rule over his enemies and Israel shall be triumphant' (1990: 208). There is, however, no textual support for his otherwise attractive suggestion; perhaps the names are reversed as a chiastic parallel with Jacob and Israel in verse 17. 'From Jacob' (*mîa'ăqōb*) points back to the ruler that treks forth 'from Jacob' (*mîa'ăqōb*) in verse 17, and 'to exercise dominion' (*rādāh*) echoes humanity's original commission to 'exercise dominion' (*rādāh*) over all creation as those who, created in God's image and likeness, were to rule on his behalf (Gen. 1:26–28). That 'he will destroy survivors from the city' is idiomatic for a complete conquest. Some prefer to read 'Ar' (*'ār*), the leading Moabite city, instead of 'city' (*'îr*) (BHS suggests 'from Seir', *miśśē'îr*). Adam, as 'son of God' (cf. Luke 3:38), his firstborn son, was entitled to rule over God's kingdom, which encompassed all the earth. Adam's mantle was later given to the line of David who, as YHWH's 'firstborn', is 'higher than the kings of the earth' (Ps. 89:27), and so promised dominion over all the nations on behalf of God as his due inheritance (Ps. 2; Isa. 9:6–7; Dan. 7:13–14; see Matt. 28:18–20). David's victories over Moab and Edom were an initial fulfilment of these prophecies (1 Sam. 14:47; 2 Sam. 8:2–14), serving as a foretaste of their ultimate fulfilment in the Messiah – 'David in the history, Christ in the mystery' (Trapp 1650: 54).

To summarize the parallels between Balaam's third and fourth discourses (cf. Postell 2019: 302–303), both (1) are dubbed 'oracles' (*nĕ'um*; Num. 24:3–4, 15–16); (2) reference a 'vision of El Shaddai' (24:4, 16); (3) refer to Balaam's 'opened eye' (*šĕtum hā'āyin*; 24:3, 15); (4) refer to his eyes being 'uncovered' (*gālāh*; 24:4, 16); (5) portray Israel's king 'shattering' (*māḥaṣ*) his enemies, the only two uses of this root in Numbers (24:8, 17); (6) allude to Jacob's prophecy of a Judahite ruler: first, to the lion imagery of Gen. 49:9 (Num. 24:9), and then to the 'scepter' (*šēbeṭ*) of Genesis 49:10 (Num. 24:17).

24:20–25

While Balaam's first four prophetic utterances focus on YHWH and the destiny of Israel, and may be said to rise climactically in blessing for Israel, the final three parables attend to the destiny of other nations and more properly constitute 'curse oracles', directed against nations. Curse one (v. 20), Curse two (vv. 21–22) and Curse three (vv. 23–24) (cf. Wendland 2012: 172). Milgrom observes that from the height of the Moabite plateau Balaam would have been able to see into the Negeb, the home of the Amalekites, Asshurim (assuming an early nomadic tribe) and Kenites (1990: 209). There is an 'unto destruction' (*'ădê 'ōbēd*) inclusio in verses 20 and 24, framing all three utterances as oracles of destruction against Israel's enemies. Whereas the first four prophetic utterances portray the conquest of the land by Israel and the establishment of the monarchy and the rise of the Messiah's reign, this last set of discourses, whose central theme is the perishing of Israel's enemies (Cole 2000: 429), describes the expansion of his kingdom and glory. The growth of God's kingdom involves a steady demise of the powers and nations arrayed against his rule, and prophecies concerning the vanquishing of surrounding hostile realms would be received as declarations of glad tidings by Israel. Indeed, the context of Isaiah's 'How beautiful on the mountains are the feet of him who brings good tidings, who proclaims peace, who brings good tidings of gladness, who proclaims salvation – who says to Zion, Your God reigns!' (52:7; cf. Rom. 10:15) is precisely that of a messenger declaring battle victory, for, as Nahum adds, 'the wicked will never again march through you – they will be utterly cut off' (1:15). Such an establishment of peace, in the conquest of the wicked, is the work of YHWH through his Adam-like vice-gerent, the Messiah (Ps. 2; Dan. 7:13–14). Balaam's last parables prophesy the growing dominion of Israel under the Davidic dynasty's Messiah, developing into the leading world-power, not unlike Daniel's prophecies of the kingdom of God, when the One like the son of man is 'given dominion and glory and a kingdom, that all peoples, nations, and languages should serve him – his dominion is an everlasting dominion, the one that will not pass away, and his kingdom the one that will not be destroyed' (Dan. 7:14; cf. Vos 2001: 114). Later biblical prophets would also pronounce oracles against the nations (Isa. 13 – 23; Jer. 46 – 51; Ezek. 25 – 32; Amos 1 – 2; Zeph. 2:4 – 3:7).

20. The fifth and sixth parables begin with 'and-he-saw' (*wayyar'*), implying that Balaam was either looking to the direction of the people's lands or seeing them in a vision. In Genesis, Amalek is said to have been born of Timna, a concubine of Esau's son Eliphaz, and was considered a 'chief' (*'allûp*) of Edom (Gen. 36:12, 16). In Exodus, Amalek attacks Israel along their journey to Mount Sinai; Joshua leads the battle as Moses raises his hands in prayer – and YHWH avows to wipe out the remembrance of Amalek from under heaven, making war with Amalek from generation to generation (Exod. 17:8–16). The only other mention of Amalek in Numbers was in the scouts' original report of the strong people and large, fortified cities in the land, with 'Amalek dwelling in

the land of the Negev' (13:29). Using a pair of antonyms commonly employed in the HB (e.g. Isa. 46:10), Balaam's parable declares that while Amalek is the 'first' (*rēʾšît*) of the nations, his 'latter end' (*'aḥărît*) will be destruction. 'Latter end' echoes the end of the first utterance, when Balaam expressed the desire for his 'latter end' to be like Israel's (23:10), a marked contrast from Amalek's latter end. The phrase also recalls the context for Balaam's final oracles (24:14). As the Amalekites were neither first in origin nor in prominence, 'first' may signify that they were the first to attack Israel, after the people's exodus out of Egypt (Exod. 17:8–16; cf. Rashi 1997: 4:311; Ibn Ezra 1999: 210). There are, moreover, indications that this was an especially vicious attack that had incurred YHWH's ire (Deut. 25:17–19):

> Remember what Amalek did to you on the way as you were going forth out of Egypt, how he encountered you on the way and attacked your rear ranks, all those who were lagging behind at your rear, when you were faint and weary – and he did not fear God. So it will be, when YHWH your God has given you rest from your enemies all around, in the land which YHWH your God is giving to you as an inheritance to possess, you will blot out the remembrance of Amalek from under the heavens. Do not forget.

The context for YHWH's covenant with David was when 'YHWH had given him rest from all his enemies all around' (2 Sam. 7:1) and, under the reign of Hezekiah, the sons of Simeon struck down 'the remnant of Amalek that had escaped' (1 Chr. 4:42–43).

21–22. Next, Balaam saw the Kenites and took up another parable that, like the previous one against Amalek, involves a dramatic reversal: from a lofty and secure dwelling place, likened to an eagle's nest established on a high crag, Cain will be burned up and taken captive by Ashur. In the ancient world, the eagle's innate characteristic of building large nests on mountain cliffs was used metaphorically for an enemy's flight for refuge on a steep mountain, the natural habitat of an eagle (Marcus 1977: 95–96). Although the term 'eagle' is not used, the eagle imagery here supplies the last of the four emblems traditionally supposed for the four main standards of Israel's Camp (along with lion, man and ox). 'Kenites' (*qênî*) are thought to derive from 'Cain' (*qāyin*), and the presence of copper mining and smelting in the southern desert region of Canaan where they lived is in accord with the association of Cain's line with craftsmanship in bronze and iron (Gen. 4:22) (see Halpern 1992; McCrory 2000; J. Day 2015). Moses' brother-in-law, Hobab, was a Kenite (Judg. 1:16), as was Heber, the husband of Jael (Judg. 4:11, 17). The word 'nest' (*qēn*) is a play on 'Cain' (cf. Albright 1944: 222).

'Ashur' (*'aššûr*) is first mentioned as one of the reference points for the third branch of Eden's river, which flowed east of 'Assyria' (Gen. 2:14).

Ashur, listed as the second son of Shem (Gen. 10:22), went on to build the city of Nineveh (Gen. 10:11) – he is the eponymous ancestor of the Assyrians. The city of Ashur was an established city and major religious centre, with a temple dedicated to Ishtar, by the early third millennium BC (Chavalas 2000). However, 'Asshurim' (*'aššûrim*), the great-grandson of Abraham by Keturah, and possibly to be identified with Syrians or a nomadic tribe among the Canaanites, has also been suggested as a probable referent (Gen. 25:3; 2 Sam. 2:9; Ps. 83:8; see de Vaulx 1972: 295; Matthews 1992). Here the focus is on Ashur's razing Cain's city to ashes and carrying away the Kenites into captivity (yet in the next parable Ashur will, in turn, be afflicted by the Kittim, v. 24). That Cain will be 'burned up' (*bāʿēr*) may, as Albright suggested (1944: 222), be a play on the relation of Cain to forgers and smiths, or to folk etymology (see Gen. 4:22; one thinks also of 'Beor', 24:15). Since Kenites are generally viewed as amicable neighbours, Mauchline proposed emending the verse to 'For even if it be burned, Forever blessed will be thy dwelling' (1945: 91). Although I do not follow him, it is worth noting that Albright emends 'Ashur' (*'aššûr*) to *'āšûr*, deriving from the root *šûr*, for 'to behold, watch' (cf. 23:9; 24:17; see BDB 1003), yielding a mournful gaze on the Kenites' demise (1944: 222; cf. Powell 1982: 387). Nachmanides reads these verses as a warning and assurance to the Kenites that, by joining with Israel instead of with Amalek, they will not be destroyed when in captivity (with Israel, 'Eber') (1975: 285–286). Significantly, the only two references to Kenites in the Torah are here (24:21) and in Genesis 15:19, where Kenites head the list of nations whose land is promised to Abram's descendants by YHWH (Leson 2007: 223). Mention of the Kenites, then, joins the many other allusions to YHWH's promises to Abraham.

Uniquely, the Kenites are the only other nation (aside from Israel in the third utterance, 24:5, 9) addressed directly with 2nd m. sg. suffixes. Contrary to Israel's 'dwelling places' (*miškĕnōtêkā*) secured by YHWH's central Dwelling (24:5), the Kenites' seemingly secure 'dwelling place' (*môšābekā*) will be destroyed.

23–24. The seventh and final prophetic utterance is not preceded by a report that Balaam 'saw' any people, reverting to the language of the first four oracles: 'he took up his parable and said', perhaps offering a wider summary perspective for this final speech. LXX has, 'And seeing Og' (*kai idōn ton Ōg*), but there is no other textual support for this reading. Unfortunately, these verses are the least intelligible of all the utterances of Balaam. What is clear is that the empires of the ANE are now overcome by a burgeoning power from the west, the Kittim. 'Alas' translates the Hebr. interjection *'ôy*, sometimes translated 'Woe!' but here carrying more the idea of grief than of warning, an emotional expression of despair (cf. BDB 17). This interjection occurs only twice in Numbers – and these are the only two instances in the Pentateuch – and, given that the other instance was, 'Woe to you, Moab!' (21:29), this *'ôy*, pronounced before the king of Moab, may recall the former warning and taunt. The question 'Who will live (*ḥāyāh*) when El sets (*śîm, miśśumô*) to it?' may be the earliest expression of what later prophets would refer to as the 'Day of YHWH' (see Isa. 2:12; 13:6, 9; Jer. 46:10; Ezek. 13:5; 30:3; Joel 1:15; 2:1, 11, 31; 3:14; Amos 5:18, 20; Obad. 15; Zeph. 1:7, 14; 14:1; Mal. 4:5), the eschatological in-breaking of YHWH God into history to judge the nations and his people, and to establish his kingdom definitively. The line, again, is extremely difficult: *śîm* may refer to a 'determination' or 'to set/place', the suff. may refer to a person, and the SamP reads 'will be' rather than 'will live'. Rhetorically, it may function like 'what God will do!' in the second prophetic utterance (23:23).

'Kittim', descendants of Japheth who settled the coastlands (Gen. 10:2–5; cf. Ezek. 27:6), may refer to Cyprus (for 'ships from the farthest sea', see Albright 1944: 226). The maritime link may have in mind the incursion of the Sea Peoples or Philistines into the Levant, and the designation seems to have become proverbial for a distant place, but was gradually identified by interpreters with Alexander the Great's Macedonia and then with Rome (Baker 1992). The designation is used by Daniel in what many take as a prophecy of Roman naval might over the Seleucids (Dan. 11:30), but the precise historical scenario envisioned here remains enigmatic. Nachmanides read the four beasts of Daniel 7 as Babylon, Persia, Greece and Rome, identifying 'Kittim' here as the fourth beast, Rome (1975: 289). Wifall's (1970) suggestion that the reference is to the clan of 'Ḥeber' (versus Eber, Gen. 46:17) within the tribe of 'Asher' (versus Ashur) requires unwarranted emendations and remains unconvincing. The subject of 'afflict Ashur and afflict Eber', being third person pl., is likely the ships of Kittim. Eber was a descendant of Shem (Gen. 10:21, 24; cf. Gen. 11:14–17), and is apparently the name from which 'Hebrew' derives, although the identification of Eber here is difficult. Levine may be correct that Eber is short for *'ēber hannāhar* ('across the river', Josh. 24:2–3), designating the land west of the Euphrates that designates the Persian satrapy (*'abār naharāh* in Aramaic, *eber nāri* in Akkadian), and with *'arām* (Syria) being one of the 'peoples of Eber' (*benê 'ēber*, Gen. 10:21–22) (2000: 206). 'And he also unto destruction' may possibly read 'it will end in destruction', referring to Kittim or back to Amalek (v. 20). Favouring the latter option, verses 20 and 24 end with the same phrase 'unto destruction!' (*'ădê 'ōbēd*). If referring to Kittim, the idea is that after their ships have punished Ashur and Eber, they themselves will be defeated. The references to Kittim, Ashur and Eber may allude to Noah's prophetic word concerning his sons (Gen. 9:26–27; 10:4, 11, 22–24; and Canaan in Num. 21:1–3). An early scenario for these prophecies would involve the Kenites being subdued by the local neighbouring tribe of Asshur, and then the Asshurites themselves, possibly along with some of the Hebrews or another local tribal group (Eber), are afflicted by the Philistines who will in turn be defeated – this being one of the triumphs of David's rise (cf. G. J. Wenham 1981b: 204). Especially given the incomplete nature of such a historical development, these partially fulfilled prophecies served as a paradigm for a more eschatological scenario (cf. Vos 2001: 114). The same theology of providence is manifested in more detail throughout the prophetic corpus: YHWH sovereignly raises up one nation to judge another but, although a tool in his hands, that nation remains accountable for its wicked actions and will in turn be judged by yet another. The kingdoms of the world rise and fall, destined to perish – and yet all the nations, peoples from every tongue and tribe, are granted the sure hope of life in the kingdom of God. While destruction awaits his enemies, the Messiah's reign is a refuge for all who turn to YHWH (Ps. 2), for all who rejoice to hear that 'he will have dominion from sea to sea, and from the river to the ends of the earth' (Ps. 72:8), and that 'the kingdom of this world has become the kingdom of our Lord and of his Messiah, and he will reign for ever and ever' (Rev. 11:15).

The last four utterances of Balaam focus on the destruction of nations, implying that, rather than blessing God's people, they as enemies of God's kingdom will have cursed Israel (Gen. 12:3; Num. 24:9). In God's sovereign plan, even to bring blessing on the nations, his everlasting kingdom is destined to overcome and subdue all worldly powers. Arranged in the order of appearance, the names of the peoples exhibit a progression from centre to periphery, concentric circles around Israel as the centre: Jacob/Israel (fourth oracle), to Moab and Edom, two of Israel's closest neighbours and oldest enemies (fourth oracle), to Amalek and Kenites, a second circle (fifth and sixth oracles), to Ashur, Kittim and Eber, the most distant nations at the periphery of the known world (sixth and seventh oracles) (Leson 2007: 231–232).

25. With three successive wayiqqtols, Balaam arises, goes and returns 'to his place' (*limqōmô*), following Balak's earlier charge to 'flee to your place' ('*el-měqômekā*, v. 11), albeit after speaking four more parables. This closing verse echoes the closing verse of Abraham's intercession for Sodom: 'And YHWH went, when he had finished speaking to Abraham, and Abraham returned to his place' (Gen. 18:33). Having joined YHWH and the (angelic) men, wherein YHWH disclosed his purposes regarding Sodom, Abraham had repeatedly interceded for the city's deliverance – whereas Balaam had joined Balak with the purpose of destroying God's people. It was perhaps on this setting out 'to his place' that Balaam, still desirous of riches, fell in with the Midianite kings, who had been counselling with the Moabites (22:4), and directed them to allure Israelites into sexual immorality and apostasy (cf. 31:8, 16). As in Judges 9:55 and 1 Samuel 14:46, 'returning to one's place' might have been a conventional way of ending a narrative (Wendland 2012: 191), but the impression left is that Balaam began his journey back to Mesopotamia. It is also just possible that the force of 'also' (*wĕgam* fronting 'Balak')

has in mind that Balak also went his (i.e. Balaam's) 'way' (*derek*), and that this account ends in suspense: Will there be another attempt? Balaam's hand in the events of the next chapter, which involved his conspiring with Midianites, will eventually be revealed (31:8, 16). The term 'way' (*derek*) was a key word in the donkey episode, used eight times, so its final appearance now as the closing word seems to have underlying value, perhaps as reinforcing the analogy with the donkey episode and the fruitless, threatened end for those attempting to curse God's people.

Explanation

The Balaam narrative is set within a subsection of Numbers that deals with Israel's engagement with foreign nations, particularly underscoring the theme of kingship (chs. 21–25). Earlier, in a passage that adumbrates the subsection as a whole, Israel encountered the king of Edom (20:14–21), then had engagements with the king of Arad (21:1–3), the king of the Amorites (21:21–31) and the king of Bashan (21:33–35); now Balak the king of Moab presents another obstacle to their entering the Promised Land: having observed their military strength, he schemes Israel's demise through sorcery (cf. Barré 1997: 254; Sals 2008: 316). From one perspective, the threat of Balaam's wizardry presents 'the severest crisis of the wilderness wandering – severest because here there stands over against Israel no ordinary mortal foe, but the concentrated powers of evil', and yet YHWH sovereignly delivers Israel 'more miraculously than ever, because he has transformed the curse into blessing' (Wharton 1959: 45). Within this context, the plot of Numbers 22 – 24 involves the antagonism of Balak, king of Moab, against Israel, and how YHWH sovereignly used the situation, along with Balak's hired diviner Balaam, not only to preserve and bless his people, but also to prophesy the advent of Israel's king, the Messiah, who would conquer all enemies, establishing his glorious dominion over the earth.

Lending poignancy to the story, the entire narrative occurs, uniquely, outside Israel's wilderness encampment and from the perspective of foreign nations, completely apart from Israel's knowledge (cf. Mann 1988: 138). Such a setting allows the original audience, ancient Israel, both to observe YHWH's continual protection and care for his people, even when unbeknown to them, shielding them from the malevolent schemes of hostile enemies, and to view *themselves*, the covenant community, from an outsider's perspective. Through the Spirit-empowered eyes of a foreigner, Israel are enabled to observe themselves, the spiritual realities, blessings and promises of YHWH's community. Margaliot notes that 'the beautiful blessings of Israel pronounced by Balaam, which actually amount to a magnificent eulogy of Israel and its singular relationship to Y[HWH] their God, the like of which is found nowhere else in the Pentateuch, and all the more appealing because uttered by a non-Israelite' function as 'a counterbalance to those narratives which describe Israel's almost continuous rebellion against the religio-political leadership of Moses as a messenger of Y[HWH]' (1977: 279). Indeed, as Shenk writes, the wondrous visionary promises of the Balaam story are precious precisely because they are uttered by the very mouth of one who opposed Israel (1993: 48; cf. Westermann 1967: 75). 'You prepare a table before me', David fittingly sings, 'in the presence of my enemies' (Ps. 23:5). This reality of YHWH's sovereign governance remains a fortress of encouragement for God's people today. Satan, the vicious dragon, evil deceiver and violent adversary, and the spiritual realm, filled with his conspiring demonic hosts, are ever-threatening to persecute, seduce and to destroy. Thankfully, YHWH, unchangeable in his being and character, is always the keeper of his people (Ps. 121), and surely, just as Israel's encampment was ignorant of the apocalyptic threat posed by Moab, God's protective ways remain largely unknown to us as well although no less sure (cf. Seerveld 2001: 59–61).

As exemplified when YHWH opened the mouth of the donkey, the prophecies of Balaam, although uttered by a pagan diviner, were inspired by YHWH and bear his divine authority – and may be relied upon as his word. Within the context of ANE divination conventions, Balaam emerges as a diviner who was practising divination but then experienced prophecy by the Spirit of God at the crucial and climactic point in the story (24:1–9), not only demonstrating the supremacy of prophecy over divination, but offering an urgently relevant message for Israel on the cusp of Canaan; namely, that YHWH's plans as promised to the patriarchs would not be thwarted – least of all by the mantic practices of the nation's enemies (Wiggershaus 2021: 205–206; cf. Hattin 2014: 333). Rather than displaying a devotion to YHWH's word, the narrative portrays – and other biblical texts, such as Deuteronomy 23:5, interpret – Balaam as *constrained* by the prophetic word, pronouncing blessing rather than his desired curse (cf. Wharton 1959; Lindblom 1973: 90–95; contra Coats 1973), making the drama all the more triumphant. As Balak and Balaam change locales and heights in their attempts to curse Israel, from the Heights of Baal (22:41) to Pisgah (23:14) to the summit of Peor (23:28), every vantage point portrays ever more clearly the blessed election of Israel and YHWH's fierce devotion to them as the sovereign God who in love chose them (cf. I. Clark 1982: 142). Arguably, God's love of Israel is stressed increasingly with every vision of Balaam (Sals 2008: 327). Other passages of Scripture are equally clear that YHWH, far from giving Balaam a sympathetic audience, overturned his intention to curse, and transformed the threat into an opportunity to bless Israel superabundantly – because he loves them (Deut. 23:5–6; Josh. 24:9–10; Neh. 13:1–3).

Von Rad closed his book on the life of Moses with the Balaam narrative, stating, 'In a wonderful way, this story sums up the whole of the revelation of the purpose of God given through Moses' (2011: 76). Justly, the oracles of Balaam may be considered 'the capstone' of Israel's wilderness-era narratives (Wharton 1959: 45). Highlighting Israel's consecrated nature and fruitful multiplication (23:9–10), invincibility and military strength (23:24; 24:8–9), and lush prosperity (24:5–7), the prophetic utterances communicate that in spite of Israel's rebellions and YHWH's judgements in the wilderness, the divine promises to the patriarchs and his original intentions for Israel will yet be fulfilled (Alexander 2003: 37–38). Through these oracles, the Balaam narrative 'incrementally soars into a prophetic vision imbued with the awesome might of God ordering history through his chosen people' (I. Clark 1982: 138). The oracles prophesy the advent of a ruler, called 'king' (24:7), a rising 'star' and conquering 'scepter' (24:17), who would, as set out in the fourth and final three proverbs, vanquish the Transjordan nations, the archetypal enemies of God's people – hopes that, while having token historical fulfilment with the rise of David's kingship, point ultimately to the eschatological triumph of the Messiah over all nations (cf. Bateman et al. 2012: 52–58). Isaiah's prophecies of an ideal Davidic ruler, the Messiah, include the conquest of Moab and Edom as part of his establishing a universal reign (see e.g. v. 14 of Isa. 11:1–16; cf. 16:6). The nations mentioned in Balaam's last four oracles may be understood as 'types and forerunners of all those nations who war against the Israel of God . . . the front line of an innumerable host, advancing in every epoch of history, until the final conflict with Gog and Magog at the end of the world' when 'the royal scepter of David's greater son' establishes the kingdom of God in triumph over all the hostile nations (Briggs 1886: 108–109; cf. Rev. 20:7–10). Taken together, Balaam's oracles sum up Israel's participation in YHWH's redemptive purposes through history, from the promises to their patriarch Abraham, to their covenantal consecration at Sinai by the hand of Moses, their conquest of the land under Joshua's leadership and the initial glories of the kingdom of David, a foretaste of the Messiah's universal reign. Indeed, Balaam's vision of an Israelite king flowers into the universal dominion described in Psalm 72, where the king will 'reign from sea to sea and from the river to the ends of the earth', whose 'enemies will lick the dust' (vv. 8–9), and 'the peoples will be blessed in him, all nations will call him blessed' (v. 17b).

The development of the kingship theme may be traced across the prophetic discourses. In the first, Balak is named 'king of Moab' (23:7), while in the second he is merely dubbed 'son of Zippor' and YHWH himself is declared the 'King' who is among his people. In the third utterance there is mention of an Israelite 'king' being exalted over Agag, and whose 'kingdom' is lifted up (24:7), likely referring to the development of the monarchy in Israel from Saul to David's dynasty, and then, climactically, in the fourth poetic discourse, which speaks of a star and rising sceptre who will conquer all the kingdoms of Israel's enemies (24:17), the Messiah's reign is predicted, along with his triumph over all earthly kingdoms. Beginning with Balak the king of Moab, the prophetic utterances come full circle as the Messiah shatters the brow of Moab. Moyer suggests the following chronological scenario, correlating the oracles with the history of Israel (2009: 466–473; cf. Milgrom 1990: 473):

1. the first proverb represents the Wandering period, with Israel as a numerous people but without an established system of rule;

2. the second proverb represents the Pre-monarchy period, Israel's incursions into the promised land, and the lion imagery indicating the nation's ferocity as a conquering force in their first steps along the path toward monarchy;

3. the third proverb represents the Early Monarchy period, with an implicit reference to the reign of Saul, and the establishment of internal security conveyed by floral imagery;

4. the fourth proverb represents David's Reign, whose firmly established kingdom leads to the conquest of neighboring nations.

5. the fifth proverb: Past (David's reign)

6. the sixth proverb: Present (Assyrian threat)

7. the seventh proverb: Future (unspecified events)

Evidently, Moyer dates the pericope to as early as the tenth century BC, regardless of which, his 'impressionistic' observation on the Judah-centric perspective on Israel's enemies is noteworthy (2009: 474–476): Moab is to the east of Judah; Edom/Seir is to the south; the activities of Assyria (and the Kenites) in the region would have begun in the north; Amalek was a group residing primarily in areas internal to Judah; and the ships represent peoples to the west, across the Mediterranean. Balaam's oracles flow beautifully into the church's confession of the kingship of Jesus the Messiah, that he executes the office of a king 'in ruling and defending us, and in restraining and conquering all his and our enemies' (Westminster Shorter Catechism, 26), for 'he must reign until he has put all enemies under his feet' (1 Cor. 15:25).

A comprehensive theological layer spreads across the oracles, presenting the present and future blessedness of Israel as the sprouting and blossoming forth of the kernel of YHWH's promises to Abraham.

As Naylor observes, each of the four prophetic utterances 'takes up one of the promises of the Abrahamic covenant and confirms it' (1994: 190; see also Stubbs 2009: 193, 196) – the following expands on Naylor's insights:

1. The first oracle confirms the promise that Abraham's descendants would be as the dust of the earth (23:10), and affirms God's covenant separation of Israel to himself (23:9). Emphasis falls on the numerous descendants promised to Abraham, that he would become 'a great nation' (Gen. 12:3), for God would 'multiply you exceedingly' and 'make you exceedingly fruitful' (Gen. 17:2, 6) so that his descendants, if it were possible to 'number' them, would be as 'the dust of the earth' (Gen. 13:16; cf. 15:5; 22:17).
2. The second oracle, declaring 'YHWH their God is in their midst' (23:21), affirms the relationship aspect of God's promises to Abraham, to establish his covenant with Abraham's descendants after him, to be their God (Gen. 17:7).
3. The third oracle, which includes a vision of Shaddai, the name by which God had appeared to Abraham (Gen. 17:1), confirms that Israel will inherit the land (24:4–5), stressing the land promised to Abraham (Gen. 12:1; 13:14–15; 15:18–20). The defeat of Agag, the Amalekite king, along with their devouring hostile nations (24:7–8), confirms God's promise that Abraham's descendants would 'possess the gate of their enemies' (Gen. 22:17). Its concluding lines, 'Who blesses you is blessed, and who curses you is cursed,' make plain the flowering of the Abrahamic promise (Gen. 12:3; 22:18).
4. The fourth oracle, referencing Elyon, invoked by Melchizedek to bless Abraham (Gen. 14:18–20; cf. Ps. 110:4), promises a victorious king in the distant future, anticipating the triumphs of David (2 Sam. 8:2), and looks beyond him to the Messiah's reign. God had promised Abraham that 'kings will come from you' (Gen. 17:6; cf. Gen. 17:16; 35:11), and that all the families and nations of the earth would be blessed through his 'seed' (Gen. 12:3; 22:18), a promise realized ultimately through the seed and son of David, the Messiah (Matt. 1:1; Gal. 3:16).

Even the exodus motif in the oracles (23:22; 24:8), moreover, confirms the redemption out of Egypt first proclaimed in a vision to Abraham (Gen. 15:7–21; see Morales 2020: 23–25).

Most profoundly, the Balaam Chronicle is a narrative about YHWH, unfolding his sovereign power over scheming forces of darkness and his faithful devotion to his people, Israel, in a magnificent display that hearkens back to the exodus deliverance out of Egypt. Indeed, given the maladies, the defeat and destruction that would have befallen Israel had YHWH regarded Balak's desires to curse Israel through Balaam, the narrative reads as a story of deliverance, one of the mighty acts of God – Israel were delivered from their enemies, who had conspired the nation's ruin through spiritual forces. The kingship of YHWH, Lord of creation and history, is supreme and absolute, he alone 'frustrates the signs of liars and makes fools of diviners' (Isa. 44:25), and he alone 'changes the times and the seasons; he removes kings and raises up kings' (Dan. 2:21). Both the plans of Balak, 'the Devastator', and the sorcery of Balaam, 'the Destroyer of the People', are not only powerless before God Almighty but actually promote the sure promises and glorious purposes of YHWH for his people. Even 'the most sinister purposes of the enemy against the people of God', von Rad exclaims (2011: 79), 'are bound to be transformed in such a way as to benefit them; Balaam comes to curse – but he stays to bless'. The message of the Balaam narrative is akin to what YHWH would later declare through the prophet Isaiah: 'No weapon formed against you will prosper, and every tongue that rises against you in judgement you will condemn' (54:17); and to what the apostle Paul would later declare to the church:

> If God is for us who can be against us? . . . No, in all these things we are more than conquerors through him who loved us. For I am persuaded that neither death nor life, nor angels nor rulers nor powers, nor things present nor things to come, nor height nor depth, nor anything else in all creation, will be able to separate us from the love of God in Christ Jesus our Lord. (Romans 8:31–39)

YHWH is superior to all of his foes, so that no enemy, no destroyer – not even death itself – has the last word over his own determined will and plan of salvation for his people, a message of glory and hope indeed (see Sousek 1967: 185; cf. Grundke 1995: 104–105). Balaam's oracles set forth the attributes of YHWH God exuberantly, declaring his incomparability, his sovereignty and never-failing providence, his immutability, the veracity of his word and his love for his people and faithfulness to them (see Allen 1981: 86–96).

Because this great King, YHWH – the High and Lofty One, the Mighty One – is with Israel, dwelling in the midst of the covenant community, all of Balaam's oracles flow into one fundamental and unchangeable fact: *Israel is blessed*. As Mowinckel asserted (1930: 255), the theme and theology of Balaam's prophetic utterances *in nuce* may be found in the declaration 'Who blesses you is blessed, and who curses you is cursed' (24:9). YHWH's greatness and uniqueness lift Israel to rest upon his high clouds. He sovereignly reigns and overrules any effort to hinder his will, transforming the hostility of foes and forces into abundant blessing for Israel, actually accomplishing his prophetic word and furthering Israel's priestly role, and turning the curse back on the heads of those who oppose him by attempting to destroy his people. YHWH's reign is supreme at all times and places, and over all nations – he determines the destinies of Egypt (24:8), Moab (24:17), Edom (24:18), Amalek (24:20), the Kenites (24:21–22), the Kittim, Ashur and Eber (24:22, 24) – and his plan of redemption and covenant promises to Israel, called to be a priestly kingdom and holy nation, stand resolutely and triumphantly (cf. van Groningen 1990: 242). Israel's own uniqueness – their blessedness, security, prosperity and triumph – is bound up with and flows out of their covenant relationship with YHWH, the incomparable, sovereign King.

Ultimately, the miracle of turning cursing into blessing, so that the merciful, gracious and eternal goodness of God pours out abundantly upon his people, has been accomplished through the suffering and exaltation of the Messiah proclaimed by Balaam:

> Messiah has redeemed us from the curse of the law, having become a curse for us – for it is written: Cursed is everyone who is hanged on a tree – so that in Messiah Jesus the blessing of Abraham might come upon the Gentiles, that we might receive the promised Spirit through faith (Gal. 3:13–14; cf. 2 Cor. 5:21; see Wharton 1959: 48).

As a Mesopotamian diviner looked at the encampment of Israel 'from the summit of rocky-crags' (23:9) and 'the Spirit of God came upon him' (24:2), the Balaam narrative triumphantly offers Israel *insight*, a view into the spiritual glories of the covenant community that has YHWH God as her sovereign King, whose reign would be established by a future ruler, the Messiah. Balaam's vision, preserved in Scripture for Israel's hope, reaches into the cloud-filled glories of the Apocalypse as John, being carried away 'in the Spirit to a great and high mountain', was shown 'that great city, Holy Jerusalem, descending out of heaven from God' (21:3, 10), the paradisal kingdom of God established by his Messiah, 'the Lion of the tribe of Judah, the Root of David' (5:5). In the Torah, the two explicit Messianic prophecies, clearly parallel, are pronounced first by Jacob to Judah and his brothers (Gen. 49) and then by Balaam to Balak the king of Moab and his entourage (Num. 24), the two audiences whose people would encompass the lineage of David, ancestor of the Messiah (Ruth 4:13–22; cf. Matt. 1:1–17)!

NUMBERS 25: YHWH'S JEALOUSY OVER THE SECOND GENERATION'S HARLOTRY

Translation

[25:1] And Israel dwelled at Shittim (Acacia Grove), and the people began to whore with the daughters of Moab. [2] And they (the daughters) called to the people to the sacrifices of their gods, and the people ate and prostrated themselves to their gods. ³And Israel was joined to Baal of Peor, and the fierce anger of YHWH was kindled against Israel. ⁴And YHWH said to Moses, 'Take all the heads of the people, and impale them before YHWH, in front of the sun, that the burning fierce anger of YHWH may turn away from Israel.' ⁵And Moses said to the judges of Israel, 'Slay each man his men who were joined to Baal of Peor.'

⁶Now look! A man from the sons of Israel coming, and he brought near to his brothers the Midianitess before the eyes of Moses and before the eyes of all the community of the sons of Israel, as they were weeping at the door of the Tent of Meeting. ⁷Now Phinehas the son of Eleazar the son of Aaron the priest saw and he arose from the midst of the community and he took a spear in his hand. ⁸And he came after the man of Israel to the tent-chamber, and he pierced through the two of them, the man of Israel and the woman to her womb, and the plague was stayed from the sons of Israel. ⁹And those who died in the plague were twenty-four thousand. ¹⁰And YHWH spoke to Moses saying, ¹¹'Phinehas son of Eleazar son of Aaron the priest has turned away my fury from over the sons of Israel, for he acted-jealously with my jealousy in their midst, so I would not finish off the sons of Israel in my jealousy. ¹²Therefore say, "Look at me!" I am giving him my covenant of peace. ¹³It will be for him and for his descendants after him, a covenant of everlasting priesthood, as a recompense since he acted jealously for his God and made atonement for the sons of Israel.'

¹⁴Now the name of the man of Israel who was struck down, struck down with the Midianitess, was Zimri son of Salu, a prince of a father's house belonging to the Simeonites. ¹⁵And the name of the woman who was struck down, the Midianitess, was Cozbi daughter of Zur; he was head of a people, a father's house in Midian. ¹⁶And YHWH spoke to Moses saying, ¹⁷'Be hostile to the Midianites and strike them down, ¹⁸for they are the ones who were hostile to you with their guiles to beguile you with the matter of Peor and with the matter of Cozbi daughter of a prince of Midian, their sister, the one struck down on the day of the plague over the matter of Peor.' ¹⁹And it happened after the plague . . .

Notes on the text

1. 'began': LXX reads *wayyāḥel* as 'profane themselves' (*ebebēlōthē*), but the construction *wayyiqtol* of *ḥ-l-l* followed by an inf. const. typically means 'began' (see Judg. 13:25; 16:19, 22; 20:31; Jon. 3:4; 2 Chr. 3:1, 2; 29:17). The prep. *'el* is used as 'with' following the verb *zānāh*; also in Ezek. 16:26, 28.

4. 'heads': as in 'leaders'; BHS suggests *r-š-'* (wicked). SamP explains that the people commanded to be impaled are those 'who joined themselves to Baal Peor'. Some Gk texts omit 'all' possibly out of concern that not all chieftains were involved in the idolatry (Wevers 1998: 421).

5. 'judges' (*šōpĕṭê*): SamP and LXX read 'tribes' (*šibtê, phylais*).

6. 'brought near to his brothers the Midianitess': LXX reads that a man 'brought his brother to the Midianitess' (*prosēgagen ton adelphon autou pros tēn Madianitin*).

'the Midianitess': the Hebr. has a definite article (*ha*), possibly representing a class of people (Davidson, *Syntax* § 22; R. J. Williams 2007: §92).

12. 'covenant of peace': some minor variants read 'covenant of requital' (see Tov 2001: 58). Rather than as an appositive construction ('my covenant, that is, peace'), we take this as a const.-gen. (cf. D. N. Freedman 1972).

13. 'a recompense since': *taḥat* here introduces a causal clause (R. J. Williams 2007: §§353, 354).

17. 'Be hostile': *ṣārôr* is inf. abs., although translated as imp. (cf. SamP), an irregular but recognized occurrence (R. J. Williams 2007: §211; GKC, § 113bb; Davidson, *Syntax* § 88b).

19. 'And it happened after the plague': this verse, separated from the next chapter by a paragraph marker in MT, will be treated as the opening chapter 26 – it 'refers back to vv. 8b–9 and connects to Num. 26' (Schäfers 2018: 138).

Form and structure

The chapter divides into two main sections, with verses 1–5 offering a broad scenario of Israel's apostasy with the daughters of Moab, and verses 6–18 narrowing on one paradigmatic example involving a Midianite woman and the resolution by Phinehas the priest. Source-critical scholarship usually assigns verses 1–5 to J, E, combined JE or even D, and verses 6–18 to P or as a late addition (see Baentsch 1903: 622–625; Holzinger 1903: 126; J. W. Rudolph 1938: 128–131; Noth 1968: 195–196; Boudreau 1991; Levine 2000: 195–196; Kim 2008: 116; Kislev 2011; Blenkinsopp 2012: 88–89; Albertz 2013: 222), often reading post-exilic xenophobia into the text (e.g. Quesada 2002; Waters 2017: 43). Yet the 'grounds for maintaining this chapter as a conflation of sources', Milgrom observes (1990: 476), 'are patently insufficient', making it more profitable to struggle with the narrative as it stands, especially since verses 1–5 cannot be understood well apart from verses 6–18 and vice versa (see e.g. Smend 1912: 233). Assertions that other scriptural passages preserve alternative traditions (Josh. 22:17; Ps. 106:28–31; Hos. 9:10), simply from the absence of details, are unconvincing not only as arguments from silence but in neglecting the summary nature of the references (e.g. Monroe 2012: 214).

The Baal Peor story employs literary gapping and ambiguity, rhetorical devices used to bring both unity and focus to a message by blurring peripheral elements (see e.g. Burnham 2014; cf. Alter 1981: 13, 133; Sternberg 1987: 235–263). Not only the later revelation of the names of Zimri and Cozbi (25:14, 15), but also YHWH's explanation of the Midianite ruse (25:16–18), signal a 'flashback' rhetorical strategy, developed further when Balaam's role is later revealed (31:8, 16) (Samet 2014a: 343–344). Changes in vocabulary, moreover, often have a stylistic function: as when gathered at the Tent of Meeting to weep corporately, there is every reason to refer to the people as the *'ēdāh*, the cultic community, and the term 'Israel' occurs fourteen times altogether. YHWH has three speeches (vv. 4, 10–13, 16–18), each as a response to previous information or action (vv. 1–3, 6–9, 14–15), the last two being linked as subsets within the second section (vv. 4, 10, 16). The concluding speech connects both sections with two references to 'the matter of Peor', mention of the 'plague' and references to 'Cozbi' and 'the Midianites'. The panel structure of narratorial action (or information) plus divine speech forms three A–B cycles:

I. The matter of Peor, vv. 1–5

    A. Israel was joined to Baal of Peor, vv. 1–3

    B. YHWH's first speech (and Moses' relay of it), vv. 4–5

II. The matter of Cozbi, the Midianite princess, vv. 6–13

    A'. Paradigmatic offenders, and Phinehas's response, vv. 6–9

    B'. YHWH's second speech, vv. 10–13

III. Conclusion, vv. 14–18

    A". Naming the paradigmatic offenders, vv. 14–15

    B". YHWH's third speech, vv. 16–18

In the second section (vv. 6–13), the offenders are generalized and anonymous while Phinehas and his lineage are detailed (vv. 6–9), and YHWH's speech pertains exclusively to Phinehas (vv. 10–13; cf. Seebass 2003: 43); in the third (vv. 14–18), the offenders and their lineage are named while Phinehas's details are absent (vv. 14–15), and YHWH's speech pertains entirely to Cozbi and the Midianites, again with no mention of Phinehas (vv. 16–18). That Phinehas is entirely missing from this third panel, while the names of the offending couple are withheld from the second panel evinces narrative strategy, especially when combined with the first section to form three cycles of panels: the first section centres on Israel's sin and punishment (vv. 1–5), the second on Phinehas's jealous act and reward (vv. 6–13), and the third on the Midianites' culpability and prescribed retribution (vv. 14–18). Clearly, the literary centre is also the thematic focus of the chapter; namely, the atoning work of Phinehas:

Israel's Apostasy at Peor	1–5 (5 verses, 55 words)
Phinehas's jealousy for God	6–13 (8 verses, 112 words)
The Midianite scheme	14–18 (5 verses, 62 words)

Comment

25:1–19

1–3. Israel 'dwelled' (*wayyēšeb*) at Shittim; this stay on the borders of the land will signal the major threat to their relationship with YHWH once in the land: the embrace of false gods, especially through the enticement of foreign women. As such the notice of their 'dwelling', linked closely with 22:1, marks a shift in focus from the military campaigns of Numbers 21 to that of settlement (Fleurant 2011: 287–288). Shittim, short for Abel-shittim, the last stay before the land of Canaan (Num. 33:49), was located in the plains of Moab directly north-east of the Dead Sea (Grohman 1962), among the Transjordan heights that overlook the Jordan river and the lands beyond it (cf. Boudreau 1993: 129–130). Presumably, this area was formerly under Sihon, king of the Amorites, and inhabited by both Moabites and Midianites. It is from Shittim, notably, that Joshua will eventually send out two spies, and from which the Israelites will journey to cross the Jordan (Josh. 2:1; 3:1). The name Shittim means 'acacias' (from the *shittah* or acacia tree) and Abel-shittim 'stream of the acacias', perhaps indicating once-forested hills of Moab (Slayton 1992; or perhaps 'well' or 'meadow of the acacias'). Josephus places Shittim near the Jordan River and full of palm trees (*Ant.* 4.176). Shittim wood was used extensively for the structure and furnishings of YHWH's Dwelling, typically overlaid with gold (see Exod. 25:5; 35:7, 24). Given that the otherwise exclusive use of 'Shittim' in the Torah relates to the construction of YHWH's Dwelling, including the ark (Exod. 25:10, 13; 37:1, 4), the table of the presence (Exod. 25:23, 28; 37:10, 15), its upright boards (26:15, 26; 36:20, 31), its four pillars (Exod. 26:32, 37; 36:36), the altar of whole burnt offering (27:1, 6; 38:1, 6; cf. Deut. 10:3) and the incense altar (Exod. 30:1, 5; 37:25, 28), one may be inclined to read of Israel's dwelling in Shittim as an ideal picture of the tribes encamped in the sanctuary of God. Throughout the Tabernacle instructions in Exodus, LXX translates 'Shittim' with *asēptos*, 'incorruptible', wood, perhaps making an association with the garden of Eden. The Camp had just been described with floral and paradisal imagery (24:5–7; cf. Isa. 41:19, which includes the *shittah* tree), yet here among the acacias Israel will commit apostasy, enticed through sexual relations with the daughters of Moab.

While dwelling at Shittim, the Israelites began 'to whore, play the harlot' (*zānāh*) with the daughters of Moab, making this Baal Peor incident 'a paradigmatic example' of Israel's bent toward apostasy (Mendenhall 1973: 106). Milgrom repoints *yāḥel* to *yeḥel*, reading 'profaned themselves' (in place of 'began'), which agrees with LXX (*ebebēlōthē*, 'profane themselves') – and *ḥ-l-l* (profane) is joined with *zānāh* in Lev. 19:29; 21:9 (1990: 212, 323). Even without retaining the translation 'defiled/profaned themselves', however, the story certainly regards the purity of the Camp, and is, therefore, in association with the purity laws of Numbers 5 – 6. In the light of the Balaam narrative (chs. 22–24), which demonstrated YHWH's tenacious faithfulness to Israel, such waywardness on the part of his people is especially shameful, how 'within a mere three verses' his people join themselves to Baal in idolatry (Leveen 2010: 413). As Milgrom puts it, 'The nation that dwells alone with its God (23:9, 21) pollutes itself with idolatry' (1990: 211). In the light of the nuptial imagery of the story, Seerveld's language is appropriate, that through Balaam, Israel was made into a whore (2001: 57) – a jarringly severe contrast with YHWH's triumphant loyalty.

Again, this failure is but a preview of Israel's future life in the land when they would 'play the whore with the Egyptians' and 'play the whore also with the Assyrians' (Ezek. 16:26, 28), to give but two examples among many. The phrase 'to whore' or 'play the harlot' is similar to the notion of 'following after other gods' or engaging in idolatry (see Isa. 57:3; Jer. 2:20; Ezek. 16:15; Hos. 2:7; cf. Bird 1989), but *zānāh* is also marked by sexual imagery (see Gen. 38:24; Lev. 21:9; Deut. 22:21; Hos. 4:13–14), since the larger controlling motif is marital (Ortlund 2002: 32). The majority of its uses in the Torah refer to sexual harlotry, although it is also used figuratively as the spiritual harlotry of apostasy, the worship of pagan gods, which often also included an element of sexual activity. Possibly, the construction *zānāh* plus *'el*, as found here and in the Ezekiel references, implies idolatry (cf. Keil and Delitzsch 1973: 3:204); the sexual immorality, in other words, has both a physical and a spiritual sense – in the covenantal sphere, idolatry stands as spiritual whoredom (cf. G. J. Wenham 1981b: 185; Balorda 2002: 26–27). Milgrom notes that this is the only instance in the Bible where *zānāh* in its literal sense takes a m. subject (1990: 212), a point underscored by Davidson, who argues that by using a verb elsewhere reserved to describe the sexual activity of women, the narrator 'clearly links the sexual activity to the spiritual harlotry of Israel against Yahweh' (Davidson 2007: 100). The term '*zānāh*, which everywhere else has a feminine subject, can have Israel as its subject here, because Israel plays the female role in relationship to Yahweh' (Erlandsson 1980: 100). As Weinfeld explains, the Sinai covenant between God and Israel was based on the metaphor of marriage in the

ANE, with its contract formula 'I will be to you a husband and you will be to me a wife', so that the 'term *'ēl qannā'* [jealous God] as well as the usage of *zānāh* for deviation in the Torah are rooted in the husband–wife metaphor' (1975: 125 n. 5). This is the understanding of the Sinai covenant assumed by the prophets – note, for example, how YHWH declares through Jeremiah that Israel broke YHWH's covenant 'even though I was a husband to them' (31:32). With 'the Sinaitic covenant as a marriage between YHWH and Israel' (Sohn 1999: 358), Israel is YHWH's bride. In Deuteronomy, YHWH tells Moses that 'this people will rise up and whore (*zānāh*) after the gods of the strangers in the land', forsaking YHWH and breaking his covenant (31:16). Within Numbers, the language of spiritual harlotry throughout chapter 25 contextualizes Israel's apostasy and breaking of the Sinai covenant within the sphere of marital unfaithfulness to YHWH, linking this sin with the purity law concerning the strayed woman, a law signalling the spiritual nature of the Camp (Num. 5:11–31). Like the guilty strayed woman, Israel has committed unfaithfulness against her spiritual Husband (see Gane 2004: 724–725). The wilderness sojourn thus ends 'with the ultimate rebellion', writes Fox (1995: 782), 'the moment of serious unfaithfulness in the "marriage" between God and Israel'. In Leviticus, YHWH had warned that for anyone 'whoring' (*zěnôt*) with the Canaanite god Molech or with any mediums or necromancers, he would set his face against that person and his family, cutting him off (20:1–8). Also sobering, YHWH's judgement on the first generation was for them to 'bear your whoredoms (*zěnûtê*) until your carcasses are made an end in the wilderness' (Num. 14:33).

The designation 'daughters' likely refers to unmarried females (cf. Mendenhall 1973: 111), and their being 'of Moab' connects this occasion with the preceding Balaam narrative, along with the juxtaposition of the two texts and mention of Midianites (25:6, 14, 15, 17, 18; cf. 22:4, 7; 31:3, 7, 8, 9). The daughters of Moab 'called' (*wattiqre'nā*) to the people, an instance of 'call' (*qārā' l-*) implying a summons and, in the present context, seduction (J. M. Cohen 1992: 161–162). The Midrash observes that these daughters are completing the act of their matron, Lot's eldest daughter, who not only seduced Lot with wine, bearing the child 'Moab' (from-father), but then taught her younger sister the same act of whoredom (*Num. Rab.* 20.23). The echo may reach even further back, to the 'daughters of men' (*běnôt hā'ādām*) whom the 'sons of God' took for wives (dubbed an 'unmistakable' connection by Balorda 2002: 28–29), especially on the view whereby this transgression involved the mingling of Seth's descendants of YHWH-followers with Cain's wicked line (Gen. 6:1–7). In being 'called' away from obedience to YHWH, Israel is depicted like Balaam (cf. 22:20). Here, the daughters' enticement is specifically 'to the sacrifices of their gods'. The sense may rather be 'their god', intending Chemosh, the national deity of Moab (cf. Judg. 11:24; Levine 2000: 283). The sacrifices most immediately recall those of Balak and Balaam, in Moab's effort to persuade YHWH to curse Israel (22:40; 23:1, 2, 4, 14, 29, 30), marking a contrast between YHWH's response and that of Israel. As an instance whereby apostasy involves eating, Israel's eating of sacrifices forms a bookend with the start of the wilderness sojourn, when the Camp had rebelled through the people's intense lust for flesh, despising the heavenly manna and longing for the fare of Egypt – then, too, Israel had been influenced by foreigners, the 'gathered-rabble' (11:4–6). The sexual indulgence might have been an aspect of ritual worship, an orgiastic or fertility rite; in either case, the goal was Israel's participation in the sacrifices of their gods, that was the plot, for it will later be revealed to have been a deliberate scheme (25:15–18; 31:8, 16); namely, to entice Israel to offend severely against YHWH. If the Moabite system of sacrifices resembles that of Israel in any way, then partaking of the sacrifices (i.e. 'and the people ate') would involve well-being sacrifices, signalling Israel's table fellowship – their communion and bond – with the gods and people of Moab.

The sacral feasting led to Israel's bowing down to their gods, acknowledging submission and obeisance to their supremacy and sovereignty. 'Falling prostrate before their gods' (wayyištaḥăwû lē'lōhêhen) recalls the second commandment, in Exodus 20:5, prohibiting just such activity (cf. Deut. 5:9): 'You shall not prostrate yourself before them (tištaḥweh lāhem) nor serve them, because I, YHWH your God, am a jealous God ('ēl qannā').' Israel's actions, whoring with the daughters of Moab, partaking of the sacrifices, eating and bowing down before their gods, culminates with a definitive statement, horrific in its terse summary 'Israel was joined to Baal of Peor.' The root for 'was-joined' (ṣāmad in niph.) is also used for yoking oxen together (cf. e.g. 1 Kgs 19:19, 21), and describes a strong attachment or binding (cf. *Num. Rab.* 20.23). It is used again to describe Israel's joining with Baal Peor in verse 5 and in Psalm 106:28. Milgrom notes that the root ṣ-m-d was used in Ugarit for the permanent transfer of property, and also had sexual connotations in some Mesopotamian texts (1990: 212; 323 n. 11; Sturdy [1976: 181] also finds an indication of sexual union). In the present context, being 'yoked' or 'coupled with' carries both cultic and sexual connotations, implying ritual intercourse whereby Israel becomes one with Baal (Mendenhall 1973: 111–112; Ashley 1993: 517; Organ 2001: 206). The Midrash fills in the gap of this brief narration, describing how Moabites set up a market, selling wares in booths staffed with young seductive women. Solicited by the Israelite men, they would respond, 'I will not listen to you until you slaughter this animal to Peor and bow down to the idol,' and thus led them astray (*Num. Rab.* 20.23; Slotki 1951: 6:821–822). The yoke of Baal Peor bound Israel together with Moab and Midian, 'a binding commitment at a cultic place' (Seebass 2003: 42), and constituted a flagrant repudiation of Israel's loyalty to YHWH, the heart of her covenant commitment (G. J. Wenham 1981b: 186). The prophet Hosea summarizes this episode with 'Like grapes in the wilderness I found Israel ... but they went to Baal Peor and separated themselves (*wayyinnāzĕrû*) to shame, and became as detestable as what they loved' (9:10). Rather than deprivation, being with Israel in the wilderness was for YHWH like discovering grapes, choice fruit in an impossible place – but not so for Israel. Significantly, Hosea uses the root *nāzar* (separate), which occurs twenty-four times in Numbers with reference to the Nazirite vow (Num. 6:1–21), reading the idolatrous whoring at Baal Peor in terms of the strayed woman (5:11–31), set forth as the wayward path contrary to the Nazirite's separation to YHWH. Rather than consecrating themselves to YHWH as solicited by the Nazirite vow, gladly and temporarily forsaking earthly pleasures through the wilderness sojourn, the covenant community has betrayed YHWH like a wayward wife. In Numbers 31, this incident of Peor is described as Israel's acting 'treacherously' (*ma'al*) against YHWH (v. 16), precisely the term used to describe the wayward woman's act in Numbers 5 (see vv. 12, 27) – the Baal Peor incident being the book's only use of *ma'al* outside the Camp's purity regulations (5:6, 12, 27; 31:16).

This account presents Israel's *first* encounter with Baal (cf. a person's name 'Baal Chanan' in Gen. 36:38, 39; the locale 'Baal Zephon' in Exod. 14:2, 9; and 'high places of Baal' in Num. 22:41). As Spronk observes (1995), 'Baal of Peor' was apparently a local god associated with the Peor mountain in Moab (23:28), and the place Beth-Peor (Deut. 3:29; 4:46; 34:6; Josh. 13:20). Likely, there were many manifestations of the one Baal, and the fertility rites alluded to in the text are consistent with a Baal cult (Habel 1964: 25). Since 'Peor' is related to the Hebr. *p'r* (open wide), used for the mouth of the netherworld (Isa. 5:14), this Baal probably represents the underworld aspect of the Canaanite god of fertility (Spronk 1995): in Canaanite mythology, Baal, temporarily defeated by Mot the god of death, repeatedly engages with a heifer sexually in the netherworld, so that his Moabite cult may be understood as a cult of the dead involving fertility rites. Israel's licentious feasting, having been seduced by the Moabite women, is therefore preserved in Psalm 106:28 as eating 'the sacrifices of the dead' (see Brichto 1973: 28). Balorda notes that the practice of necrolatry and necromancy (cf. Lev. 19:31; 20:6, 27; coupled with *zānāh* in Lev. 20:26) only intensifies the seriousness of Israel's sin (2002: 30). The incident at Baal Peor marks a battle for the allegiance of Israel – it concerns the kingship of YHWH versus the kingship of Baal. As Habel observes (1964: 24–26), Israel's harlotry was no mere peccadillo, but a yoking of the community to Baal, religious harlotry and treachery likely expressed through cult prostitution, and making necessary the covenant renewal recorded in Deuteronomy, 'in the valley over against Beth Peor' (Deut. 3:29; cf. 4:46; 34:56). Comparing the language of the Sinai covenant with the renewal on the plains of Moab (cf. Exod. 19:4; Deut. 4:3–4), he further describes the redemption experienced by the tribes at Baal Peor as analogous to the release experienced in the exodus out of Egypt (1964: 26). What is crucial for the text's theological message is that the name 'Baal' also signifies 'husband', its verbal form *bāʻal* meaning 'to marry'. Examples of such usage include Isaiah 62:5, 'As a young man marries (*yibʻal*) a maiden / so will your sons marry you (*yibʻālûk*); / as a bridegroom rejoices over his bride / so will your God rejoice over you,' and Jeremiah 3:14, 'Return, O wayward children, utters YHWH, for even I am your Husband (or 'married to you', *bāʻaltî*)'. Justly, then, Sohn points out that *bāʻal* is 'one of the important terms used to describe the YHWH–Israel relationship in terms of the marriage concept' (2002: 12). That 'Israel was yoked to Baal/Husband' therefore brings out the spiritual harlotry involved in the episode, along with other prominent sexual and marriage-related language, portraying Israel's marital treachery that enables the earlier law of the strayed woman (Num. 5:11–31) to serve as a key for interpretation. Verses 1–3 progress symmetrically: Israel, the people, the daughters of Moab, they [the daughters of Moab], the people, Israel; 3rd m., sg. verbs with Israel as a corporate body foreshadow the sg. example that follows with 'a man from the sons of Israel' in verse 6.

The chain of events leads precisely to the wanted outcome on the part of Moab: 'the anger of YHWH was kindled against Israel'. What Moab was powerless to do with Balak's hiring of Balaam, the Israelites have done to themselves – the holy displeasure of YHWH has been turned *against* (*bě*) Israel. The exact phrase 'the anger of YHWH was kindled' (*wayyiḥar-ʼap yhwh*) has appeared twice already in relation to the first generation of Israel, when they had craved meat and the food of Egypt (see 11:10; cf. 11:1) and after Miriam and Aaron had spoken against Moses (12:9), and occurs twice more later when Moses refers to the first generation's failure to trust YHWH in taking the land (32:10, 13). Further, 'kindled anger' occurs three times in the Balaam chronicle (22:22, 27; 24:10), one of several links with the Baal Peor incident. YHWH's fierce anger, as we discover later (vv. 8–9), has been unleashed in the form of a plague. The plague, however, is no surprise; a similar circumstance has already taken place: 'the wrath (*qeṣep*) has gone forth from before YHWH – the plague has begun' (16:46).

4–5. As the God who abounds in loving-kindness and steadfast mercy to his people (Exod. 34:6; Num. 14:17–19; cf. Ps. 103:4, 8), YHWH immediately reveals to Moses the remedy for his fierce anger, for the sake of his wayward people, and this before the 'plague' is even mentioned. While the living God cannot change his holy nature, so that ignoring sin and rebellion is not an option, he is, however, always faithful, all-wise and all-powerful, to provide deliverance out of his own consuming judgements. He instructs Moses to 'take' (*lāqaḥ*) the chiefs, the leaders ('heads', *rōʼš*) of the people, and to impale them to or before

YHWH 'against' (*neged*) the sun, so that 'the burning, fierce anger of YHWH will turn away from Israel'. His declared judgement, then, '*is already thought of as an act of redemption*' (Seebass 2003: 40; emphasis original).

The instructions to 'take the heads' may be understood in several ways, some ambiguity resulting from a perceived disjunction between the chiefs and the actual offenders. The SamP has 'slay the ones who joined themselves to Baal Peor', making the execution of only the offenders explicit. E. W. Davies prefers to leave the MT as it stands 'and to assume that the chiefs are here singled out for punishment as representatives of the people, or because they had neglected their duty of vigilance in permitting the Israelites to act in such a fashion' (1995b: 286). In 'Take all the heads of the people' there may be an echo of YHWH's original command at the book's opening 'Lift up the heads of all the community' (1:2). Although not the intuitive reading, however, it seems likely that the referent of 'and impale them' is 'the people' of the present and previous verses (cf. Keil 1869: 204–205), and that Moses is being instructed by YHWH to 'take the heads of the people' in order to facilitate obedience to YHWH's instruction – and this is precisely what follows in the narrative, with Moses instructing 'the judges of Israel' (cf. Grossman 2007: 57–58; Keil 1869: 204–205). Such is the traditional interpretation, understanding that the leaders were designated to bring judgement on the idolaters (see e.g. Rashi, Ibn Ezra ad loc.). The summary statement in verse 3 that 'Israel was joined to Baal of Peor' implicates the community as a whole, including its chieftains, and in verses 14–15 one of the leading offenders, Zimri, was 'a prince' of his ancestral house, and Cozbi's father was a 'head (*rōʾš*) of a people'. The judges, however, as with Moses and other heads of the people, had not engaged in the harlotry.

The term translated 'impale' (*yāqaʿ*) is unclear, and may refer to hanging, exposing or putting out of joint (BDB 429; *HALOT* 1.431), or to some form of dismemberment after death (Seebass 2003: 42), likely for covenant violation (cf. Cross 1973: 266). Perhaps the most relevant parallels, in hiph. stem, are found in 2 Samuel 21:6, 9 (cf. 1 Sam. 31:10; and hoph. stem in 2 Sam. 21:13), with a similar context implying some form of hanging, perhaps by impaling (see Milgrom 1990: 478; Levine 2000: 300–301). Presumably, Moses' use of 'slay' (*hārag*) in the next verse refers to the same act in more general terms. Contrary to a host of interpreters who accuse Phinehas of vigilantism and murder (e.g. Collins 2003; Claussen 2015; Y. S. Miller 2015; Rees 2015; Waters 2017; Grafius 2018), of acting without divine authority, the terms used for his executing of the man and woman 'pierced through' (*dāqar*, v. 8) and 'struck down' (*nākāh*, vv. 14–15) are in accord with both YHWH's instructions to impale and with Moses' use of slay. Collins, for example, refers to 'the killing of others without benefit of judicial procedure' (2003: 4), whereas Phinehas's act is clearly portrayed as judicial in nature, fulfilling the prescribed judgement – the fact that source critics typically sever the judicial verdict (vv. 4–5) from Phinehas's response (vv. 7–8) has only compounded the misreading. Fleurant, while dubbing Phinehas's act as 'murder', nevertheless concedes that the command in verse 4 'foreshadows the impalement of the Midianite', so that Phinehas's act 'is thus seen as being a lawful execution that meets the divine requirement' – yet this scenario, so Fleurant, is merely the concoction of a later priestly redactor who welded two completely unrelated stories together (2011: 292). Even on wholistic readings, Phinehas's actions have had a mixed reception (see Feldman 2002), nearly always due to an underappreciation for, or complete neglect of, the divine judgement commanded in verses 4 and 5, along with a justified concern that others follow Phinehas's example while *presuming* the same divine sanction (cf. Steinberg 2007). While due caution is justified, such care should not cloud the point that in this instance, clearly sanctioned by YHWH, all scriptural appraisals of Phinehas's deed are lavishly commendatory (vv. 10–13; cf. Ps. 106:28–31). As Kaiser avers (Kaiser et al. 1996: 169), 'Phinehas was no vigilante. He was heir apparent to the priesthood; thus he, no doubt, was one of the appointed judges whom Moses had ordered to slay all known offenders.' Due hesitation and proper nuance should be observed, moreover, in how one understands Phinehas's act as exemplary: the text commends his *jealousy* for YHWH's honour, and the expression of that jealousy inasmuch as YHWH had called for such action and relayed his will through Moses publicly as a judicial authority – an objective scenario not replicated by zealots claiming subjective divine sanction. 'Phinehas can be defended: He did not act on his own initiative but followed God's command' (Milgrom 1990: 477). As such, the universal, transferrable example is that of zeal for YHWH's honour, but Phinehas's execution of the couple was a particular and historical application not intended as a paradigm – indeed, his was a *priestly* act, committed in the authoritative capacity of his office and done in fulfilment of God's judicial command through Moses. YHWH's reward of an everlasting priesthood ensured that such acts would remain only within the priestly charge of guarding sacred space.

Presenting the bodies 'to YHWH' (*layhwh*) signifies not only that the execution is by his bidding, but that it is done to satisfy his justice and appease his righteous anger. Similarly, exposure of the bodies 'in front of the sun' (*neged haššāmeš*), that is, 'publicly' (cf. 2 Sam. 2:11–12; Ibn Ezra 1999: 214), completes the symbolism of the act, with the offenders being exposed to YHWH's 'burning' (*ḥārôn*), fierce anger so that it is 'turned away from Israel' as a whole. More than a sanction of judgement, the order aims at the redemption of the community, propitiation (Seebass 2003). Such execution of criminals proclaims the depth of the sin committed and re-establishes the idea of holiness, so as to maintain YHWH's relationship with Israel (Hirsch 2007a: 523).

Moses relays YHWH's instructions to 'the judges of Israel' (*šōpĕtê yiśrā'ēl*) who, as noted above, are likely to be identified as 'the heads of the people' in the previous verse, designated to help Moses carry out YHWH's instruction. Judges, as an office, were chosen and installed by Moses in Exodus 18 through the counsel of his father-in-law Jethro, and were designated by Moses to be 'heads over the people' (*rā'šîm 'al-hā'ām*), further defined as 'rulers' (*śar*) over divisions of the people (Exod. 18:25) (cf. Weinfeld 1977b). That these heads 'judged' (*šāpaṭ*, Exod. 18:26) the people, demonstrates a synonymous understanding of 'heads' and 'judges'. Moses' command for the judges to 'slay each man (*hirgû 'îš*) his men' recalls his command for Levites to 'slay each man (*hirgû 'îš*) his brother, and each man his friend, and each man his neighbour' after Israel's apostasy with the golden calf (Exod. 32:27), one of many links between the two passages. Here the death penalty is explicitly directed to the offenders, to those 'who were joined to Baal of Peor'. As the narrative progresses, however, it becomes evident that YHWH's instruction, along with Moses' direction, was not carried out comprehensively, in the light of the new situation that arises in verse 6 (cf. G. J. Wenham 1981b; Milgrom 1990: 214; Ashley 1993: 519; Seebass 2003: 40; Monroe 2012: 213) – Phinehas's action, a singular and exemplary case of obedience, will be accepted by YHWH as a comprehensive fulfilment of his original order. There may be, then, an intended progressively narrowing focus: from the 'heads of the people' (v. 4), to 'his men' (the transgressors, v. 5), to 'a man' (a high-ranking prince, v. 6).

6. Within the larger summary of Israel's apostasy and YHWH's response (vv. 1–5), the narrative zooms in on a particularly aggravated and exemplary scenario, drawing the audience's focus through use of 'Now look!' (*wĕhinnê*). The narration, using a participial form, causes the scene to unfold before the audience's eyes: 'Look! A man from the sons of Israel coming (*bā'*).' Then the man's purpose for coming unfolds: he 'brought near' (*wayyaqrēb*) to his brothers the Midianitess. The anonymity employed, with use of 'a man' and 'the Midianitess', functions to lift the event as an exemplary microcosm of the entire situation, and the withholding of details also allows for greater surprise and impact upon the later revelation of their names (vv. 14–15). While use of the definite article for the Midianitess may function to represent a class of people, it appears to stress her high-ranking prominence. Only one other character in the Bible is referred to in the same way as 'the Midianite', namely, 'Hobab son of Reuel the Midianite (*hammidyānî*)' (10:29), so that Israel's dealings with Midianites bracket the wilderness sojourn (cf. Fleurant 2011: 289).

The Israelite man's appalling audacity is exhibited by the text in a sevenfold manner: first, his act takes place within the context of YHWH's fierce anger, in the midst of an ongoing plague (vv. 3–4, 8) – and *after* YHWH's command; that is, knowing 'God's righteous decree that those who practise such things are worthy of death' (Rom.

1:32); second, rather than committing his act discreetly, he brings the Midianite woman 'to his brothers'; third, he does so 'before the eyes of Moses' himself, disregarding his sacred office and authority; fourth, he also does so before the eyes of 'all the community of the sons of Israel' (*kol-'ădat bĕnê-yiśrā'ēl*), affronting the covenant community, the holy assembly belonging to YHWH; fifth, his dissolute behaviour is set against the community's weeping, in marked contrast to their expression of grief and (possibly) contrition – and within the context of a communal lament, some form of abstinence was likely in order (Rees 2015: 81); sixth, the community's weeping took place at the door of the Tent of Meeting, the focal point of Israel's sacrificial rituals of reconciliation with YHWH (cf. Lev. 1:3) – the couple demonstrates no dread or shame as they parade before the sacred Tent of God; and seventh, mention of the door of YHWH's holy Tent, the threshold of Israel's gathering to meet with YHWH, positions the man's flagrant act in the midst of the Camp where YHWH dwells, causing profanation, as it were, before the divine face. To be sure, notions of sacred place underline the narrative (Schäfers 2018: 148; emphasis original): 'the Israelites had turned to foreign women outside the camp and away from JHWH to foreign gods, now, a foreign woman is introduced *into* the camp and near the tent of meeting and into the congregation'. The 'entrance to the Tent of Meeting', as Hundley observes (2011: 24), refers to the area around and between the altar and the literal tent entrance, or anywhere in the court, and marks the closest place for Israelites to come before YHWH, whether to participate in rituals or to observe them. The man's aggravations create a mounting tension and expectation in the face of YHWH's consuming anger, dispelling any notion of injustice over the judgement that must inevitably befall the unabashed couple. While the first function of noting that his act took place before the eyes of Moses is to underscore the man's blameworthiness and flagrancy, it is also likely that Moses' stunned passivity serves as a foil to Phinehas's zealous action (cf. e.g. Cross 1973: 203; Milgrom 1990: 478; Quesada 2002: 34; Monroe 2012: 226), the latter also forming a stark contrast to Aaron's passive disposition throughout his tenure as high priest, especially so during the golden calf episode (see Exod. 32:21–24; cf. Num. 12:1; 16:46). A mitigating factor in critiquing Moses is that he is described as being at the Tent of Meeting, either just having received YHWH's instructions or in the midst of carrying them out. Part of the message is that for the sake of Israel's spiritual well-being, the new generation must be marked by a zealous following after YHWH, and the priesthood especially, charged with maintaining the covenant community's reconciliation with YHWH, must be marked by this quality. With life in the land in view (Num. 26 – 36), Phinehas is the sort of priest especially needed post-Moses.

The narrowing focus of the *hinnê*-clause functions also in a spatial manner, moving the narrative from the larger Camp dwelling at Acacia

Grove near Moabite territory to within the Camp near YHWH's central Tent, the camp of the *Shekhinah* – this as an Israelite brings a foreign woman into the midst of the mourning community to engage in sexual immorality of an idolatrous nature. Sivan similarly explains (2001: 77; cf. G. J. Wenham 1981b: 210), 'The drama unfolds by moving from the edge of the camp, where the worship of Baal takes place, to its very heart, the tent of the Tabernacle.' The term *qārab* (in hiph.), used regularly within the context of the cult to describe offering a sacrifice, adds to other associations (cf. Levine 2000: 286), including 'the door of the Tent of Meeting' (*petaḥ 'ōhel mô'ēd*), at which sacrifices would be brought and offered (*qārab*; cf. Lev. 1:3), that together give the story a cultic aura (cf. e.g. Monroe 2012: 221) and may even imply the background of a fertility rite. Use of *qārab* with sexual connotations elsewhere (Gen. 20:4; Deut. 22:14) led Ibn Ezra to presume a brothel scenario involving 'his brothers' (1999: 215). The Israelite man and the Midianitess might have been consummating an intermarriage or engaging in cultic prostitution; in either case, the scene brims with sexual, political and cultic overtones, and is set forth literarily as the prime example of Israel's spiritual harlotry and apostasy against YHWH (cf. Organ 2001: 208). The Vg refers to the 'harlot' (*scordum*) of Midian. Seebass understands the scenario with the Midianite woman as escalating the already grave situation with an 'extremely dangerous religiopolitical connection under the auspices of Baal Peor': here was 'the threat of a real political bond with the Midianites underlined through family ties of very high-ranking persons', with a prospect of Cozbi becoming 'the mother of high-ranking Israelites under the yoke of Baal Peor' (2003: 40). He also understands their act as demonstrative and with a high hand (cf. 15:30), the worst case of guilt, even while not respecting the weeping of the covenant community at the door of the Tent of Meeting (Seebass 2003: 43). Magonet takes a similar view of the political function of their sexual display (2013: 118): 'This symbolic act would have created a permanent link between the two peoples and their gods.' The Israelite man and Midianite woman represent the broader communal apostasy in microcosm, the nation of Israel's spiritual harlotry against YHWH – and Phinehas, who incarnates YHWH's just jealousy will make atonement for the nation as a whole by bringing divine judgement on this one couple.

The community's weeping echoes the start of the wilderness journey, with a fivefold reference (11:4, 10, 11, 18, 20), so that the wilderness is bookended by Israel's weeping to YHWH. Why, in this instance, was all the community of the sons of Israel weeping? Friedman, noting that the last reference to weeping was for the death of Aaron (*wayyibkû*, 20:29), makes the intriguing deduction that 'this episode occurs during the thirty days that they were mourning Aaron' (2001: 513). Such a connection, however, faces the challenge of making chronological sense of the intervening material (chs. 21–24), although the ensuing emphasis on 'Phinehas . . . son of Aaron' forms another link between chapters 20 and 25. The context of YHWH's kindled anger (vv. 3–4), later reported as an unleashed plague that killed 24,000 people (v. 9), would indicate that the ongoing death-toll among the community had awakened them to their great transgression, and their grief is here expressed as penitent weeping (cf. BDB 113). Community-wide laments are associated elsewhere with disasters (cf. Deut. 1:45; Judg. 20:23, 26; Joel 2:12–16; Waters 2017: 40 n. 4). To be sure, in many other settings in Numbers (11:4, 10, 13, 18, 20; 14:1), 'weeping' constitutes 'murmuring', but this is not always the case (see Num. 20:29; cf. Schäfers 2018: 148). That the locale of their weeping is the entrance to the Tent, their nearest designated meeting-place with YHWH, further indicates they understood the deaths as his righteous judgement and were seeking his face in repentance (see also Baruchi-Unna 2015). Between verses 1–5 and verse 9, the focal episode of verses 6–8 has been inserted by the author, offering archetypal cases of both Israel's apostasy and YHWH's just retribution.

The evident focus on sight in verses 6–7, employing 'look' (*hinnê*), 'before the eyes (*lĕʿênê*) of Moses', 'before the eyes (*lĕʿênê*) of all the community of the sons of Israel' (v. 6) and 'Phinehas saw (*wayyar'*)' (v. 7) may be intended to recall the tassels legislation of Numbers 15:37–41, as the function of the tassels was expressly for this purpose: Israelites were to 'look' (*rĕʾîtem*) upon them and so remember YHWH's commands, rather than seeking after 'your own eyes (*ʿênêkem*), after which you go whoring'. Twice, Israel is called to 'remember' (*zākar*, 15:39, 40), but now, on the verge of inheriting the land, the sons of Israel have forgotten YHWH their God who brought them out of Egypt (cf. Deut. 6:10–15). Listing witnesses, the eyes of Moses and the community of the sons of Israel, may also serve a judicial role, further exonerating Phinehas's act.

7–9. Twice the narrative had reported that the man's act of bringing the Midianitess near was 'before the eyes' – first of Moses, then of all the community. With that background information, the narrative view shifts from the Israelite man and the Midianitess to the eyes of one man, Phinehas: 'he saw' (*wayyar'*). While the brazen act was paraded before the eyes of Moses and of all the community of Israel, one man would not only see, but act, animated by YHWH's spirit of jealousy. By contrast to the offender's anonymity, Phinehas is introduced by name, lineage and office: 'Phinehas the son of Eleazar the son of Aaron the priest.' Here the Torah's genealogies, beginning with Adam, reach their climax: from the archetypal high priest in the garden of Eden to the young Aaronide priest who acts with YHWH's own jealously for the sake of his people, to whom the high priesthood is granted. He is first introduced in the Levitical genealogy of Exodus 6: 'And Eleazar son of Aaron took to himself one of the daughters of Putiel for his wife, and she bore him Phinehas; these are the heads (*rāʾšê*) of the fathers of the Levites according to their families' (v. 25; cf. 1 Chr. 6:4; 6:50; Ezra 7:5; 8:2). He appears again in Numbers 31 as sacral leader of the Israelites in their holy war against Midian, in Joshua 22 to settle a cultic controversy over an altar constructed in Gilead by the tribes on the east side of the Jordan, and in Judges 20 – 21during a tribal war against the tribe of Benjamin, where he is associated with the ark of God; in every case, he appears as an authority when there is a question of cultic purity and national survival (Organ 2001). Phinehas was an ancestor of Ezra, the scribe used of God among the returned exiles in Jerusalem to lead and instruct them in Moses' Torah (Ezra 7:1–6). The Chronicler writes that Phinehas was a 'prince' (*nāgîd*) over the Korahites and that 'YHWH was with him' (1 Chr. 9:20), and the psalmist encapsulates his role at Baal Peor, writing that Phinehas 'stood up and he made intercession (*wayĕpallēl*)', adding that his action 'was accounted to him for righteousness (*wattēḥāšeb lô liṣdāqāh*), from generation to generation for ever' (Ps. 106:28–31), characterizing the young priest in a manner remarkably similar to Israel's patriarch Abraham (*wayyaḥšĕbehā lô ṣĕdāqāh*, Gen. 15:6). Based on this psalm's description of his making intercession, a tradition arose in Judaism that portrayed Phinehas in prayer, as a Moses-figure who interceded on behalf of Israel at a crucial moment (Bernat 2007: 282). Elijah, for his own zeal (1 Kgs 19:10), is traditionally identified with Phinehas (see *Pirkei de-Rabbi Eliezer*, 47; *TgPs-J* Jon on Exod. 6:18 and Num. 25:12; cf. Spiro 1953; Cohen 2013: 16). Although often misapplied, his legacy would include serving as a paradigm of zeal (see Hayward 1978); in 1 Maccabees, for example, Mattathias is described as one who 'burned with zeal for the law, just as Phinehas did against Zimri the son of Salu' (1 Macc. 1.26; cf. Farmer 1952; Klassen 1986). This Phinehas should not be confused with one of the sons of the priest Eli at Shiloh who went by the same name, but was exceedingly wicked (1 Sam. 1:3; 2:34; 4:4, 11, 17, 19; 14:3), nor with another figure in the post-exilic era (Ezra 8:33).

The name 'Phinehas' appears to be an Egyptian loan word along the lines of 'the southern one' signifying 'the dark-skinned one' (Ashley 1993: 520), 'the Nubian' or 'the Cushite' (Hays 2003: 81), or even perhaps 'the second king' (Thon 2006: 2), apparently a common New Kingdom name in Egypt implying either a true African or one with unusually dark skin (Propp 1999: 280; cf. Hays 2003, 82). 'Bronze-coloured one' has also been suggested (*TWOT*, 473), along a more Hebraic reading. Hebr. wordplay may be involved with his name meaning 'mouth of brass' (Easton 1894: 548) or, more likely, 'mouth of a serpent' (cf. Strong 1890: 94; Kolatch 1984: 186–187), derived by reading *pî* (mouth) and *nĕḥāš* (serpent). If intended the wordplay would relate Phinehas's divine role of executing judgement with the episode of the released serpents (21:4–9), the only other occasion of the second generation's rebellion and judgement. Returning to Phinehas's possible association with Cushites, Hays points out the irony in that Moses first marries into a *Midianite* family (Exod. 2:16–22) and later marries a *Cushite* woman (Num. 12:1), and then Phinehas, the great-nephew of Moses, whose name conceivably means 'the Cushite' is used by YHWH to bring judgement on Midianites, including their women (Hays 2003: 83 n. 31; cf. 2000). Midrashic traditions have Zimri chide Moses: 'How can she [the Midianitess] be forbidden to me when you yourself, Moses, married a Midianite?!' (*Num. Rab.* 20.24; *b Sanh.* 82a; quoted in Cohen 2013: 15).

Given Phinehas's Levite heritage and Zimri's Simeonite ancestry, the story of Genesis 34 seems to fade in and out of the present episode mist-like. In that story, Leah's daughter Dinah had gone out to see the daughters of the land, and was subsequently seen, taken and violated by Shechem, a prince, whose father then proposed for Jacob and his house to integrate with the inhabitants of the land through intermarriage, even to become 'one people' (34:22). Simeon and Levi devised a plan of vengeance, making intermarriage conditional upon the people's circumcision, so that on the third and painful day after the procedure, the brothers, taking sword in hand, went and slew all the males in the city. In the Phinehas episode, as Cohen writes (2013: 17):

> There is supreme and bitter irony in the fact that Simeon, who took the moral high ground in defence of his sister's honour, would be the progenitor of Zimri, who leaped from that dizzy height into the moral abyss below; and that Levi, his fellow conspirator, would be the very one whose descendant, Phinehas, ended up punishing the tribe of Simeon for their failure to comply with the moral perfection that supposedly justified massacring the Shechemites.

In Deuteronomy, using language similar to Genesis 34:9, Moses applies the lesson as a sober warning for life in the land (7:3–4):

> You will not intermarry with them; your daughter you will not give to his son, nor will you take his daughter for your son. For they will turn away your son from following after me, so they may serve other gods – so the fierce anger of YHWH will be kindled against you, and destroy you suddenly.

Moses further explains that this must be so since Israel is a holy nation, chosen by YHWH to be his own 'treasured possession' (*sĕgullā*), a people upon whom he has set his love (Deut. 7:6–9).

Not only by YHWH's pronounced judgement, and by Phinehas's position and duty as a 'head' of the people (v. 4), but especially by his priestly office, as chief over the guardians of sanctuary gates (1 Chr. 9:19–20), Phinehas's ensuing act was fully authorized, even divinely compelled. Earlier in Numbers, Eleazar was declared to be the prince of the princes of the Levites, appointed over them who keep the charge of the sanctuary, a charge that includes executing any outsider who 'comes near' (*haqqārēb*, 3:32, 38). With Aaron's death, Eleazar had become high priest (20:22–29), making Phinehas the chief guardian (cf. Gane 2004: 718). As the high priest is not to come into contact with death (Lev. 21:10–12), there is a narrative pattern whereby the next highest-ranking priest performs a duty in his place (see 16:37; 19:3–4), a role performed here by Phinehas, since Eleazar is high priest (cf. Frevel 2013b: 157). The Levitical duty of putting to death the stranger who draws near, guarding YHWH's Tent from profanation, is repeated several times in Numbers (see 1:51; 3:10, 38) and is the special charge of the priesthood, not only as supervisors over the rest of the Levites, but as those who encamp eastward of the Dwelling, guarding its entrance (3:38). This Levitical duty, moreover, is so that 'there will be no plague (*negep*) among the sons of Israel when the sons of Israel approach (*běgešet*) the Sanctuary' (8:19; 18:22–23). The language of the man's 'bringing near' (*wayyagrēb*) the Midianitess, along with reference to the entrance of the Tent of Meeting (v. 6), and in the context of a divine plague, all serve to depict the scenario in the light of the previous warnings concerning the Levitical duty to put such persons to death. Such 'discriminate bloodshed' was a part of the responsibility of the priesthood, taking the life of one who encroaches upon sancta in order to protect the rest of the community (S. D. Mason 2008: 203). Incarnating the character of God by his priestly office (G. J. Wenham 1981b: 211), Phinehas acted within his authority, not only fulfilling God's command, but unveiling the very jealousy of YHWH himself, who had unleashed a plague that was quickly decimating the people. Precisely as a priestly duty, and especially in being motivated to that duty by a heart enflamed after YHWH's glory, Phinehas's line would be confirmed in the priesthood, and granted its highest office.

With its quick and climactic succession of five wayyiqtol verb-form acts by Phinehas – he 'saw' (*wayyar'*), he 'arose' (*wayyāqām*), he 'took' (*wayyiqqaḥ*), he 'went' (*wayyābō'*), he 'pierced through' (*wayyidqōr*) – the narrative impression is of a priest who does not hesitate, who takes initiative, possessing a firm knowledge of YHWH's will in exactly this situation and who is compelled to act by jealousy for the honour of YHWH. As Organ observes, Moses' only active role is to reinterpret YHWH's command; while he fades into the background, Phinehas, the main character, 'is clearly at center stage' (2001: 205). Phinehas's redemptive action parallels that of Aaron as high priest in 16:44–55, even with its context of a divine plague (cf. Thon 2006: 59; Achenbach 2010: 245). Phinehas's decisive action, perhaps impelled by a divine 'spirit of jealousy' (cf. Num. 5:14), forms a sharp contrast to Aaron's passivity in the worship of the golden calf (Exod. 32), the parallel event of the first generation (cf. Olson 1997: 234). Although the couple had walked before the eyes of all, yet when Phinehas saw, he acted (cf. *Num. Rab.* 20.25).

Phinehas's seeing led to his rising, and to that of the nation with him. His rising was from 'the midst of the community' (*mittôk hā'ēdāh*), language that may imply his position as priest near YHWH's Dwelling, in the midst of the Camp, but more narrowly that he had been with the community weeping at the door of the Tent of Meeting – he thus leaves the mourning community in order to defend YHWH's honour. The man's transgression was before the eyes of the 'whole community' (v. 6), from the midst of which Phinehas rises to act. Whether a spear was the given weapon for threatening encroachers to sacred space, or as intending to follow the instruction to 'impale' offenders before YHWH (v. 4), Phinehas takes a 'spear' or 'lance' (*rōmaḥ*) in his hand. As guardian of YHWH's Tent, he would likely have been armed with a short-shafted spear (Steinberg 2007: 125 n. 1). His deliverance of Israel with spear 'in his hand' (*bĕyādô*) echoes Moses' deliverance of Israel out of Egypt with rod 'in his hand' (*bĕyādô*, Exod. 4:20; cf. Exod. 4:17; 7:15; 17:5).

Pursuing the man of Israel, he 'entered after' (*wayyābō' 'aḥar*) him into 'the tent-chamber' (*haqubbāh*). The word *qubbāh* is exceedingly rare, making the discernment of its intended meaning difficult. One function of its use may be as a link with the Balaam narrative where *qābāh*, 'curse', occurs ten times (22:11, 17; 23:8 [twice], 11, 13, 25 [twice], 27; 24:10), offering a subtle hint at Balaam's role in this scheme (Shamah 2011: 808; cf. Garsiel 1991: 217–219). *Qubbāh* appears to signify a large, vaulted tent, and may be related to *qēbāh*, the word for 'stomach' or 'belly', which appears later in the verse (BDB 866, 867) – there is wordplay (cf. Strack 1894: 446). Morgenstern suggested an association between this vaulted tent and the pre-Islamic tent shrine that was served by young women from prominent families and set near the chieftain's tent, used for seeking oracles (1942: 162–163; cf. Organ 2001: 208), but it is perhaps enough to point out that, given other cultic and sexual nuances in the account, the couple's usage of this tent hints at a cultic significance. The question remains: *Which* tent-chamber is indicated? The tent-chamber may refer to the Israelite man's own dwelling, to a tribal cultic shrine, a marriage canopy or even to YHWH's central Tent of Meeting. Cross, who understands *qubbāh* as 'the Tent of Meeting itself', reads the account as the couple entering YHWH's Tent and engaging in rites of ritual prostitution (1973: 202; cf. Sweeney 2017: 90), and M. Douglas underscores the heinousness of the offence – and appropriateness of Phinehas's response – by reading the couple as committing their act 'in the inner room of the Tent of Meeting' (2001: 191; cf. Sturdy 1976: 184–185). De Vaux understood *qubbāh* along the lines of a Bedouin tent shrine housing idols and used for divination, also identifying it within Israel's context as YHWH's Tent (de Vaux 1961: 296–297). Friedman, following Cross, presents the strongest arguments for identifying *qubbāh* as the Tent of Meeting (2001: 513–514; cf. 1981: 112): (1) the episode begins precisely at the Tent of Meeting; (2) as a ritual violation of sacred space no trial was necessary, since the law required execution (1:51; 3:10, 38; 18:4, 7), thus explaining the seeming omission; (3) the Torah's report concerning the plague points to a ritual violation of sacred space as warned in 8:19, 'so there will be no plague . . . when the children of Israel would come near to the Holy' and as had happened in the aftermath of the Korah rebellion (16:46). Allen even proposes emending 'to his brothers' (*'el-'eḥāw*) in verse 6 to 'to the tent [of God]' (*'el-'ōhel*), related to the last words of the verse (2012: 342). In Numbers 18, linked to the present episode by an 'everlasting covenant' granted to the priesthood (18:19; 25:12–13), YHWH had declared that Aaron and his sons would bear the iniquity of the sanctuary and of their priesthood, being warned that the sons of Israel must not 'draw near' (*yiqrĕbû*) the Tent of Meeting, lest they die (vv. 1, 22). Others, however, suggest the Israelite had installed the Midianitess in a *qubbāh* (as a shrine) next to his own tent within the Camp in order to engage her as a diviner or in cultic activity (involving sexual rites) as a means to staying the plague – usurping Israel's priesthood and YHWH's cult (Reif 1971: 205), or that the *qubbāh* served as a nuptial tent (Milgrom 1990: 215), perhaps underscoring the political bonds being forged by their consummation of marriage. LXX has *kaminos*, 'furnace' or 'oven', perhaps a euphemism for the heat of physical engagement, while the Vg goes further, translating *qūbbāh* as *lupanar*, 'brothel' (cf. Waters 2017: 53). Steiner observes that the account appears to contain all the ingredients of the sacred marriage ceremony, as described at length in Papyrus Amherst 63 (2020: 582): sexual union in a sacred bridal chamber erected on a sacred height in a sacred grove. While ambiguity remains, their action in the *qubbāh* takes place at least near or before the Tent of Meeting (cf. Rees 2015: 103), and was committed with a high hand, announced before the eyes of Moses and the eyes of the whole community at the door of the Tent, and YHWH's response itself vindicates Phinehas. Wherever precisely their violation took place, it was indeed a heinous sacrilege that called for their being cut off, and Phinehas's action was well within both YHWH's earlier command and his own priestly duty of safeguarding YHWH's cult. Both idolatry and whoredom pollute God's people and his sacred space, whether the sanctuary, the land or in this case the divine Camp, to such a degree there is no ritual remedy; rather divine judgement must be executed, such pollution being framed within the context of national survival (cf. Frymer-Kensky 1983: 407–408) – and it is the priesthood that is charged with guarding sacred space. Embracing the deliberateness of the text's ambiguity as a literary technique, J. S. Ackerman understands the scene as a 'gross parody' of the priestly office, whereby Phinehas enters the 'inner chamber' and pierces the couple right through her 'inner chamber', making atonement (1987: 88).

In Chronicles, Phinehas is honoured with a twofold description: he was a 'ruler' (*nāgîd*) over Levites, specifically over the sons of Korah, and 'YHWH was with him' (1 Chr. 9:20). Intriguingly, the previous verse portrays the sons of Korah as guardians of the Tent threshold, with their ancestors having had charge of the entrance of 'the camp of YHWH' (*maḥănêh yhwh*, 1 Chr. 9:19), referring either to the whole Camp broadly or to YHWH's central encampment. 'It is no surprise', writes Rees (2015: 80), 'to discover that Phinehas was present at the Tent and on the look-out, fulfilling his role as chief guardian of the sacred precinct, particularly given that the entire house of Israel was gathered at a moment of crisis.' Similarly, Burnham remarks that the 'righteousness and exemplary zeal of the temple guard remitted the plague, intervened for the people, and reestablished the purity of the congregation' (2014: 146). Whether the Midianitess was brought into the Tent of Meeting, she was indeed brought into the Camp, whose eastward entrance was guarded by the priesthood and was therefore under Phinehas's purview and charge. Moreover, the whole theology of the Camp constructed in Numbers 1 – 6 conveys that it is set apart from the wilderness and the world by YHWH's central, holy presence, and must maintain a state of purity. That the Israelite and his consort conducted their liaison within the Camp already justifies Phinehas's action, quite aside from the many aggravations involved in the couple's transgression. More than other priestly figures, whether Aaron or Eleazar, Phinehas is portrayed as the guardian of YHWH's sanctuary (cf. Kim 2008: 114). Accepting the scene's portrayal as a parody of the priestly office, the *qubbāh*, in my view, was a nuptial tent set up brazenly near the sacred precincts of the sanctuary, flaunted before the eyes of all, wherein the couple would consummate their marriage as a sexual rite, ritual intercourse having both political and religious ramifications. This scenario matches closely YHWH's precise warning in Exodus 34:15–16 whereby sexual enticement by foreign women would lead to cultic feasting after their gods and then to intermarriage (cf. Milgrom 1990: 212).

The ambiguity of the *qubbāh* may be intentional, with cultic resonances displaying the transgression of the Israelite and Midianitess as an act of tremendously serious profanation. Since Zimri and Cozbi enter the *qubbāh* while Moses and the community are consulting with YHWH at the Tent of Meeting, it could be that the couple's action forms a challenge or antithesis to YHWH and his sanctuary as central to the Camp and life of the community – there may be two rival tent shrines, with the *qubbāh* set up in sight of YHWH's Tent and 'standing in opposition to the Tent of Meeting' (Organ 2001: 208; cf. Baruchi-Unna 2015: 514). Within the tent, Phinehas 'pierced through' (*wayyidqōr*) the two of them, referring to them as 'the man of Israel and the woman'. The term *dāqar* occurs elsewhere for being run through with a sword (Judg. 9:54; 1 Sam. 31:4; 1 Chr. 10:4; Isa. 13:15; implied in Zech. 13:3) and perhaps by an arrow (cf. Jer. 51:3–4), and occurs in a prophecy where YHWH says, 'They will look on me whom they have pierced (*dāqārû*)'

(Zech. 12:10; cf. John 19:37). The implication of piercing them through together, given the wider context of 'whoring' (v. 1), is that Phinehas executed them while they were engaged in sexual activity, likely part of a fertility rite of Baal worship. It has been suggested, further, that the woman might have been a local prophetess or priestess (Lutzky 1997: 547), but there is not enough narrative detail to yield such a conclusion firmly. The piercing of the man and woman reaches 'to her womb' or 'inner parts' (*'el-qŏbātāh*; cf. BDB 867; HALOT 2.1060), perhaps a euphemism for her private parts (see e.g. *Sif. Num.* 131; *b Sanh.* 87b; cf. Thon 2006: 49), and again forming a wordplay with 'to the tent-chamber' (*'el-haqqubbāh*; LXX reads 'in the womb', *dia tes mētras*, while Vg has 'in the genitals', *in locis genitalibus*). Some scholars understand *qŏbātāh* as the same word as *qubbāh*, with Phinehas running the couple through in 'her tent-shrine' or 'the tent-shrine', doubling the beth to read *qobbātāh* (see Noth 1968: 194; Reif 1971: 206; Cross 1973: 202; Lutzky 1997: 546; Levine 2000: 287–288), a reading suggested by Ibn Ezra (1999: 215). One function of the wordplay is to draw out the poetic justice involved in Phinehas's action: committing an outrage before YHWH in a 'tent-chamber' (*qubbāh*), the seductress is put to death through her 'womb' (*qŏbātāh*). Significantly, there was a similar talionic judgement appointed for the strayed woman in the jealousy law, wherein her thigh would rot and her 'belly' (*beṭen*) would swell, the bitter waters entering through her 'inward parts' (*mēʿeh*) (5:21, 22, 27). However, the symbolism of spearing her womb may involve less the issue of illicit sexual engagement and pertain more to the political notion of her becoming the matriarch of high-ranking sons, patriarchs of the new alliance under the auspices and blessing of Baal Peor. Phinehas's act functioned to protect Israel's separateness and singularity in the ancient world, as consecrated to YHWH alone (Seebass 2003: 44–45). Blenkinsopp similarly suggests the sexual engagement concerns Israel's acceptance of the offer by the host society (Moab, Midian) to be incorporated into their lineages or, perhaps, reinforcing an already existent bond of kinship, a contractual social covenant involving intermarriage, and the sharing of sacrifice and sacrificial meal (2012: 90). The word for her womb probably occurs one other time, in Deuteronomy, where *haqqēbāh* refers to the stomach of a sacrificial animal, assigned as part of the priest's due from the people when they offer a sacrifice (18:3). Possibly, then, *qŏbātāh* adds to the cultic imagery of the episode: the Midianitess who had been 'brought near' like a sacrifice before the Tent of Meeting is slain by an Israelite priest (Gane 2004: 719). *TgPs-J* on Numbers 25:13 understands the term as referring either to the woman's womb or private parts, noting that the priesthood was gifted with the shoulder, jaw and stomach of sacrificial animals because Phinehas took the spear with his arm (meriting the shoulder), prayed on behalf of Israel with his mouth (meriting the jaw) and struck the Midianite woman through her womanhood (meriting the stomach). Given other cultic resonances, the woman's womb – *qŏbātāh* – may symbolize the *qubbāh*-shrine.

Immediately, as a result of Phinehas's decisive action, 'the plague was stayed' (*wattēʿāṣar hammaggēpāh*) from the sons of Israel. The precise phrase *wattēʿāṣar hammaggēpāh* was used after Aaron had offered incense, making atonement as he stood between the living and the dead (16:48) – in both cases, 'atonement' being the key for staying the plague (*wayĕkappēr*, 16:47; 25:13). Phinehas's execution of the couple was an act of intercession (Schäfers 2018: 147). The phrase 'from the sons of Israel' demonstrates that Phinehas's priestly act of impaling the two offenders served to spare the rest of the community from death – this was the declared aim of the Levitical duty to put to death any unauthorized persons who drew near to YHWH's Dwelling (8:19; cf. 1:51; 3:10, 38; 18:22–23). 'The introduction of the plague', Organ writes (2001: 209), 'shifts the reader's understanding of the whole scene: it is not simply about an aberrant act but about the survival of the whole people'. In Numbers, this is precisely the role of the priesthood; namely, the nation's survival in the wilderness through atonement (cf. Frevel 2013b: 154–155) – Phinehas acted out of zeal for YHWH and for the sake of Israel, not only according to YHWH's command (v. 4) but in fulfilment of his office. 'Thus, Phinehas's "impassioned action for his God" (v. 13) was actually the ideal – and appropriate – behaviour of the sanctuary guard,' writes Milgrom (1990: 478). 'His prompt action "ransomed" Israel by terminating God's wrath/plague.'

As with the account in chapter 16, the staying of the plague is followed by a death-toll: 'And those who died in the plague were . . .' (16:49; 25:9), the verbatim repetition highlighting the one drastic difference, this time almost 10,000 more people dying: 24,000, rather than 14,700 – indeed, the Baal Peor plague comprises the deadliest expression of YHWH's fierce anger during the sojourn, aside from the entire generation's demise through the thirty-eight years of 'wandering'. The round number 24,000 cannot fail to imply the symbolism of twelve tribes with a loss of 2,000 for each of them – a dramatically sobering loss on the cusp of the land. The *Gemara* fills the gap, stating that 'Zimri arose and gathered 24,000 men of Israel, and went to Cozbi' (*b. Sanh.* 82a, quoted in Rashi 1997: 4:315–316 n. 11), perhaps drawing a parallel with Korah (cf. Num. 16:1–2). Given a variety of links to the golden calf episode, the death-toll appears even more astonishing, for only 'about 3,000 men from the people fell on that day' (Exod. 32:28; cf. *Num. Rab.* 20.23). In his first letter to the Corinthians, the apostle Paul mentions that '23,000 fell in one day' for committing sexual immorality (1 Cor. 10:8), instigating 'the infamous case of "the missing thousand", for which there is not an entirely satisfying solution' (Fee 1987: 456), whether by resorting to a thousand dying before or after the 'one day', by differentiating those who died of the plague from those who died through Moses' instructions for judicial execution or by surmising some conflation with the golden calf episode (see e.g. Mody 2007; Lincicum 2011). The Midrash remarks that 'on every occasion when Israel fell they were numbered' (see Slotki 1951: 6:826), a reminder that aside from the positive census counts in Numbers 1 and 26, there has been a 'wilderness census' taking place, underscoring the judgement of God's rebellious people.

In the census figures of chapter 26, Simeon's tally comes out to 22,200, having lost about two-thirds of the tribe's population, which was 59,300 in the former census (1:23), demonstrating that YHWH's fierce anger had 'especially impacted the tribe of the evil doer' (Albertz 2013: 223). Such a diminishment further underscores that YHWH's judgement was indeed on the *second* generation, which in committing such apostasy experienced its own 'golden calf episode'. The point stands as a needed correction to the commonly touted notion that the Baal Peor sin was committed by the last remnants of the elderly generation, finally purged from the Camp (e.g. Olson 1997). Rather, the purging was among the second generation, as Joshua later intimates, declaring that God's people had not yet been fully cleansed from 'the guilt of Peor' despite the plague among the community of YHWH (22:17). By contrast to the guilt of the golden calf episode, which fell with the first generation in the wilderness, the Baal Peor incident was a blot on the present generation of Joshua. In Deuteronomy, Moses plainly states that the old generation had already perished before crossing the Zered valley (Deut. 2:14–16; cf. Num. 21:12). Zimri and Phinehas, rather, symbolize the alternative paths of the younger generation, this time for life in the land: either, like the strayed woman, forsaking the nation's loyalty to YHWH by whoring after Canaanite gods, or, like the Nazirite, embodying the nation's calling to be a priestly kingdom. Moreover, while the whole community bound together by covenant was under threat of divine destruction, it seems the plague slew primarily and perhaps only the transgressors who joined themselves to Baal. Moses would later declare that 'every man who followed Baal Peor, YHWH your God destroyed from your midst – but you who held fast to YHWH your God are alive, every one of you today' (Deut. 4:3–4). Also relevant, the term 'held fast' (*dābaq*, 'to cleave') is used to define the archetypal marital relationship within the garden of Eden (Gen. 2:24), which Paul understood as signifying the mystery of the Messiah's union with the church as his bride (Eph. 5:30–32) – such bridal imagery and theology already informing Israel's view of the relationship established with YHWH in the Sinai Covenant. After his people strayed again into Baal worship in the land, YHWH vows to remove from Israel's mouth 'the names of the Baals', promising, 'I will betroth you to me for ever' (Hos. 2:14–20).

10–11. Not only is the plague immediately stayed, but YHWH himself is compelled to explain, commend and reward the young priest's action, all the more significant as this takes place in the wilderness section wherein YHWH's approval is nearly absent. Once more the full appellation of Phinehas is given, perhaps indicating that his action was in his capacity as 'the priest'. Fronting the verb, Phinehas's role in saving the sons of Israel is underscored: 'It is Phinehas the son of Eleazar the son of Aaron the priest who has turned away my fury from over the sons of Israel.' YHWH's 'fury' (*ḥămātî*) had been on his people, but Phinehas's action caused it to 'turn away' (*hēšîb*). Note that YHWH's original purpose for impaling the violators was to 'turn back' (*šûb*) his anger from Israel (v. 4), precisely what was accomplished through Phinehas's action – he 'turned back' (*šûb*) YHWH's fury, a further indication that Phinehas was not acting as a vigilante, but in accord with YHWH's expressed will. Whereas scholarly engagement tends to focus on the brutality of the priest's action, the enigma of the narrative itself is how the prescribed execution of merely one set of offenders could make atonement for the thousands among Israel's community. Phinehas is a hero because he turned away YHWH's fury from the rest of the sons of Israel, whom YHWH would otherwise have 'finished off' (*killîtî*).

Asking further *how* Phinehas's act functioned to turn away YHWH's fury, part of the answer, later dubbed making 'atonement' (v. 13), relates to Phinehas's driving motivation, to how he acted: 'for he acted-jealously' (*qan'ô*) with 'my jealousy' (*qin'ātî*) in their midst, so that YHWH would not make an utter end of the sons of Israel in 'my jealousy' (*qin'ātî*) – in other words, by incarnating YHWH's jealousy in executing the pair of offenders, Phinehas the priest answered or satisfied YHWH's jealousy, which otherwise would have consumed Israel. That he so closely sympathized with the sentiments of YHWH, that his actions so perfectly mirrored YHWH's own character and will, leads inexorably to the reality that Phinehas had been filled with the divine Spirit of the God whose name is Jealous, with the 'spirit of jealousy' (cf. Num. 5:14). 'Phinehas's uncompromising jealousy – or "zeal" – is again mentioned as background to the divine grant of "my covenant of well-being" (v. 12)' (J. A. Davies 2004: 186; see also Kugler 1996: 9–22). As priest, his action was mediatorial in nature, for the sake of the sons of Israel. By allusions to Exodus 32, Phinehas is portrayed as acting the way that Aaron should have done in the golden calf episode (Seebass 2003: 45). In the midst of the onslaught of YHWH's plague, while most of the community could do nothing but weep before YHWH, however penitential, and while others brazenly carried on their rebellious indulgence before his face, Phinehas alone acted in obedience to YHWH's command to slay the leaders of the apostasy.

Given the prominence of the notion of jealousy in YHWH's overwhelming commendation of Phinehas, a biblical understanding of jealousy is key for grasping the significance of Phinehas's action (Balorda 2002: 2–3). First and foremost, 'jealousy' is presented as a divine attribute, the phrase 'jealous God' ('*ēl qannā*') occurring five times in the Torah, linked especially to his demand for exclusive loyalty and worship (Exod. 20:5; 34:14; Deut. 4:24; 5:9; 6:15). As an emotion that springs from the very depths of personality, jealousy, von Rad explains (1962: 1:207–208), is the most personal of all the manifestations of YHWH's being, manifested in his ardent will, expressed both as intense passion in salvation and severe threat of wrath, to be the only God for Israel. YHWH as a jealous God 'determines the whole slant of Mosaic religion' and is found in every period of Israel's history as 'the basic element' in the scriptural notion of God (Eichrodt 1976a: 1:210). By contrast with other divine attributes, such as holiness or glory, YHWH's jealousy is a relational sentiment, conveyed in relation to his people Israel – divine jealousy is the supreme marital emotion expressed within the covenant bond (Balorda 2002: 83–84).

12–13. YHWH is so pleased with the sparing of Israel from his own just anger, so pleased with Phinehas's jealousy over YHWH's honour as covenant husband to Israel, that he rewards him grandly and publicly – 'Therefore' (*lākēn*) makes the correlation between Phinehas's act and divine bestowal explicit, and 'Look at me!' (*hinĕnî*) calls to attention, regarding Phinehas's reward as an object lesson for the entire covenant community. More than this, the *hinĕnî* language may correspond to YHWH's side of the eternal covenant enunciated in Numbers 18, so that Phinehas is being rewarded by YHWH for upholding the priestly duties of Aaron that were introduced by *wĕ'attā* (as for you) in Numbers 18:7 (S. D. Mason 2008: 217). More broadly, the two focal points of the narrative are introduced with 'Look!', the Israelite man's brazen act of bringing the Midianitess before the watching community to commit harlotry against YHWH, and, now, YHWH's bestowal of the office of high priest upon Phinehas and his line ('for him and for his descendants after him', *lô ûlĕzarʿô 'aḥărāyw*). As with the previous *hinnê* clause, a ptc. follows setting the action before the audience as it unfolds: 'I am giving' (*nōtēn*) to him 'my covenant of peace' (*bĕrîtî šālôm*), a 'perpetual' or 'everlasting' ('*ôlām*) priesthood. The covenant of priesthood is hereby narrowed within Aaron's house specifically through the line of Phinehas. While likely having the office of high priest primarily in view, Milgrom observes that, historically, his (Zadokite) line eventually encompassed the priesthood as a whole (cf. Ezek. 44:15–16; 1990: 217) – the covenant need not be understood as excluding Ithamar's line from the priesthood (1 Chr. 24:1–6; cf. Ashley 1993: 523). Moreover, Phinehas does not simply inherit the priestly privilege due to his being a descendant of Aaron, but now in his own right as a reward. As with Numbers 20, the narrative calls for new leadership of the second generation, and Phinehas rises up as a divine demonstration of the sort of leadership, zealous for YHWH's honour, needed for Israel's survival. Perhaps an overstatement, Phinehas like his grandfather Aaron becomes a new fountainhead for the line of high priests. Later priestly sons will trace their ancestry not only to Aaron vaguely, but to Phinehas especially – his jealous action and divine reward become a (re)founding story for Israel's priesthood. Phinehas's line will eventually blossom into the Zadokites, who serve in Solomon's Temple in Jerusalem (cf. 1 Kgs 2:26–27, 35; 1 Chr. 5:30–41; 6:35–38; Ezra 7:1–5; see also Sir. 45.23–24; 50.24; 1 Macc. 2.54). With the promise of divine privilege for his lineage, Phinehas experiences the exact opposite of the *kareth* penalty, presumably being experienced by the transgressors at Baal Peor; namely, the severe excommunication from the covenant community by death and the destruction of one's lineage.

The form 'my covenant (*běrîtî*) of peace', using a broken construct is rare, occurring in Leviticus 26:42 as 'my covenant with Jacob, and also my covenant with Isaac, and also my covenant with Abraham', a point of comparison Milgrom uses to suggest that 'covenant of peace' signifies 'My pact, a pact of friendship' (1990: 216), even as Rashi had already conceived of the covenant as an expression of YHWH's 'feelings of friendship' with Phinehas (1997: 4:321). Ibn Ezra, by contrast, observing that Zimri had come from a powerful family that would surely want to avenge his death, suggested the covenant of peace was a form of divine assurance, that Phinehas should not fear Zimri's brothers (1999: 216). Although these 'brothers' are in fact mentioned in verse 6, this reading does not seem likely. Covenant of 'peace', in parallel with covenant of 'priesthood', may rather describe the priestly work of reconciliation through atonement – especially in the present context whereby Phinehas's action served to heal a covenant breach. Von Rad wrote that 'peace' designates the wholeness and communion shared between two parties of a covenant (1962: 1:130). Moreover, the cessation of divine wrath appears to be a common motif linking other covenants 'of peace' (cf. Isa. 54:10; Ezek. 34:25; 37:26–27; Williamson 2007: 161). Since it was the marriage-like relationship between YHWH and Israel established through the Sinai covenant whose rupture Phinehas acted to repair by way of atonement, his perpetual priesthood should also be understood, as with the Levitical system as a whole, as part and parcel of the Sinai covenant – it is for the sake of the covenant community. Aside from commending Phinehas and establishing his line as the future line of high priests, YHWH's reward of his covenant of peace also functions to renew 'the numinal marriage between God and the people of Israel, legally contracted at Sinai, since the priests also served as representatives of the congregation before God' (Balorda 2002: 93). Returning to the word 'peace', it is intriguing that the following order is observed in the purity laws of the Camp (Num. 5 – 6): strayed woman (5:11–31), Nazirite vow (6:1–21), priestly blessing with its climactic final word 'peace' (*šālôm*, 6:26); arguably, Numbers 25 presents the same sequence: Israel as strayed woman (25:1–4), Phinehas as jealous husband and true Nazirite (25:6–9), followed by the divinely granted covenant of 'peace'

(25:10–13). Strengthening the latter connection, Numbers 6:26 and 25:12 form the only uses of the word 'peace' in Numbers, and both are related to the Camp's reception of YHWH's benevolence as a result of the priesthood's action. The phrase 'covenant of peace' occurs also in Isaiah 54:10 and Ezekiel 34:25 and 37:26; in Malachi 2:4–5, YHWH's covenant with Levi is described further as a covenant 'of life and peace'. References similar to 'perpetual priesthood' are found also in Exodus, where the priesthood is granted to Aaron's house as a 'perpetual statute' (*ḥuqqat 'ôlām*, 29:9), and Aaron and his sons are then anointed into a 'perpetual priesthood' (*khunnat 'ôlām*, 40:15; 'covenant of priesthood', *bĕrît hakkĕhunnā*, occurs again only at Neh. 13:29). The notion of a 'perpetual covenant' appears here for the last time in the Torah (see Gen. 9:16; 17:7, 13, 19; Exod. 31:16; Lev. 24:8; Num. 18:19; 25:13). This 'covenant of priesthood perpetually' (*bĕrît kĕhunnat 'ôlām*) is likely to be connected to the 'covenant of salt perpetually' (*bĕrît melaḥ 'ôlām*) in 18:19. S. D. Mason thereby reads Phinehas's act as fulfilling Aaron's eternal covenant of Numbers 18, marking the theological climax of the Pentateuch's development of *bĕrît 'ôlām*, providing ultimate hope for Israel's future and vocation in the land, and ensuring that the priestly covenant will be promulgated by his line (2008: 207).

More narrowly, YHWH grants the office of high priest to Phinehas's descendants (cf. Noth 1968: 199). As noted for the priestly grant and 'covenant of salt perpetually' in Numbers 18:7, 19, the gift nature of the covenant as a royal grant should not be pitted against the notion of conditionality. J. A. Davies points to Eli as an example of one who, in defaulting on the expected loyalty, forfeited his priestly status (1 Sam. 2:30; 2004: 186). He further writes that the unified picture of a covenant of grant is that 'of an honoured position of service, where faithfulness is expected and disloyalty will be punished, but where the primary emphasis is not on the imposition of terms, but of the high honour bestowed on the favoured recipient of the grant' (2004: 186). The death of Phinehas is not recorded in Scripture, but the last verse of Joshua registers the death of Eleazar the son of Aaron, noting that he was buried 'in a hill of Phinehas his son, which had been given to him in the mountain of Ephraim' (24:33). Later through the prophet Ezekiel, YHWH would commend the priestly line of Zadok, descendants of Phinehas, for staying loyal to him even while the rest of the Levites had gone far from God when Israel strayed after idols (Ezek. 44:10–16; 48:11; cf. 1 Chr. 9:20; Ezra 8:2). The Levitical approach to YHWH was integral to the Mosaic covenant, itself linked to the old creation with its Sabbath sign (Exod. 31:13; cf. Gen. 2:1–3). As such the 'covenant of salt' with the Aaronic priesthood (Num. 18:19), the 'covenant of peace/perpetual priesthood' with Phinehas's line (Num. 25:12–13) and the covenant with Levi (cf. Neh. 13:29; Jer. 33:21–22; Mal. 2:4–5, 8) are encompassed by the broader national covenant with Israel, the Sinai covenant (Williamson 2007: 42).

Turning away YHWH's fury and saving the people from being finished off in verse 12 is paralleled with 'made atonement for the sons of Israel' in verse 13, both ascribing his action to 'jealousy' – 'with my jealousy in their midst', 'jealously for his God'. Phinehas is commended by YHWH for having 'turned away my fury', also described as making 'atonement', two statements associated with Moses' intercession in the golden calf episode (Exod. 32:12, 30), so that Phinehas, Israel's future high priest, is portrayed in a manner as filling Moses' role (Kim 2008: 120–121). His action, in terms of maintaining the community's relationship with YHWH through cultic mediation, is precisely why YHWH had consecrated Aaron's house. It would be nearly impossible to overemphasize the significance of Phinehas's priestly act, which was of Noahic proportions: one man, displaying singular zeal, saved the entire nation of Israel from destruction. Phinehas's reward, the covenant of perpetual priesthood, is ultimately a gift for all Israel, since the priesthood of Aaron's house functions at a fundamental level to ensure the nation's survival, saving Israel from the consuming anger of YHWH. Indeed, within the context of the Balaam oracles, whereby YHWH had pronounced abundant blessing on his people, Phinehas's act ensured that there would even be a nation of Israel at all, including its priesthood, to experience those blessings (cf. S. D. Mason 2008: 218). As Balorda summarizes, Phinehas was rewarded for demonstrating, in his divine jealousy, three covenantal principles (2002: 87). First, he demonstrated extreme hatred for the sin of idolatry as the manifestation of marital harlotry before God. Second, he demonstrated supreme love for YHWH as the only legitimate Husband of Israel. Third, he demonstrated sympathy for the polluted nation as the covenant bride whom he saved and for whom he made atonement. While a tremendous amount of ink has been spilled in either questioning or defaming Phinehas for his action, precious little consideration of YHWH's commendation of Phinehas has been given. Even from a purely literary perspective, however, YHWH's voice has absolute validity, even more so than that pronounced by the narrator (Bar-Efrat 2004: 54).

In the HB, 'atonement' (*kipper*) functions as a means to an end, that of reconciliation with YHWH God, a prerequisite for life in his presence. A formerly presumed Arabic cognate meaning 'to cover' or 'to hide' is now widely rejected in favour of an Akkadian and Aramaic root signifying 'to wipe off', and the Hebr. noun *kōper* means 'to ransom' (see R. L. Harris 1961; Feder 2010). Scriptural usage regularly refers to the outcome or effect of *kipper*, to purify, atone, or expiate, as brought out in the contrived English word 'at-one-ment', rather than to the means ('wipe', 'rub', 'cover'), and, by varying degrees, implies a twofold meaning: ransom from death, and purification from pollution (Sklar 2005). As Milgrom explains, the accomplishment includes cleansing the offenders of impurities and sin so that they are reconciled, made 'at one', with God (1991: 1083). Helpfully, Brodie writes that Numbers is about both division and unity, 'the divisions that can tear a community apart, and the atonement and unity that are nonetheless possible under God', with atonement being central in every sense, for (2008: 455, 467) 'Atonement counters the forces of death; and purity brings vitality, in effect a form of blessedness.' The connection between Phinehas's act of atonement and the reward of a priestly covenant is not incidental, as the 'whole sacrificial system serves to atone and finds its meaning in the atoning function of sacrifice itself' (Gese 1981: 103; cf. Low 2009). Indeed, 'acted-jealously for his God and made atonement for the sons of Israel' is a fine summary of priestly duty. The last uses of *kipper* in Numbers narrated how Aaron the high priest, positioned between the dead and the living, offered up incense and thus 'made atonement for the people' so that 'the plague was stayed' (16:46–48), two phrases connecting with Phinehas's act in Numbers 25 – Phinehas has acted as a priest. YHWH and Israel had been estranged and, worse, set in hostile opposition by the latter's spiritual harlotry with Baal; but Phinehas, the young priest, jealous for his God, made atonement, reconciling the covenant partners and thus re-establishing peace. In this case, given the nature of the sin, atonement was not – and could not be – made merely through sacrifices. Israel's sexual idolatry and spiritual harlotry, joining themselves to Baal, was a spurning of YHWH's kingship, exchanging his life-yielding reign for the yoke of Baal ('Lord', 'Master', 'Husband') – prostrating themselves in allegiance to a pagan husband. At the culmination of the exodus deliverance, Israel had proclaimed the kingship of YHWH (Exod. 15:18), but now, on the verge of life in the land, that kingship has been rejected – a severe breach of the covenant loyalty due him, a treacherous act of 'unfaithfulness', *ma'al*. Certain classes of sin such as murder, sexual abominations and idolatry, each involving defiant rebellion tantamount to apostasy, are said to 'defile the land' and cannot be remedied through the sacrificial system – divine justice calling for exile or execution, being 'cut off' (cf. Frymer-Kensky 1983). These are the very sins for which YHWH had declared he was casting out the nations from the land, threatening Israel with the same punishment – 'lest the land vomit you out also when you defile it, just as it vomited out the nations who were before you' (Lev. 18:28; see vv. 24–30). Later, in Numbers 35:29–34, YHWH declares that for murderers the only atonement possible is through the death penalty, sparing the rest of the community, precisely the dynamic involved in Phinehas's action. On the cusp of the land, Israel commits, before the face of YHWH, the very abominations for which he intends to bring judgement on the Canaanites. The category of sins that merited being 'cut off' include the desecration of sacred (or cultic) objects, time and space, including the divine sanctuary (Num. 19:13, 20), which may also have been involved in the Israelite's sin with the Midianitess (25:6–8). In such instances of heinous, land-defiling crimes, atonement for the rest of the community is not offered through the sacrificial cult, but mercifully and graciously granted often through justice on the particular offenders, by meting out the divinely prescribed punishment, usually death. In Exodus 31, concerning the defiling of the Sabbath, the penalty of being 'cut off' (*nikrĕtāh*) is paralleled by the statement that such a person shall 'surely be put to death' (*môt yûmāt*, v. 14), connecting the two synonymously (cf. Num. 4:18–20). YHWH had already prescribed the judgement necessary for satisfying divine justice; namely, death for at least the leading offenders. This act of atonement is what Milgrom refers to as a 'secondary function of *kippur*', which has 'the immediate goal of preventing the already kindled divine wrath from incinerating innocent and guilty alike' (1990: 370), and so it is aligned with Aaron's 'atonement' for the people through his incense offering amid the plague in Numbers 16 (vv. 46–48) – it is akin to 'when the Levitical guard cuts down the encroacher on God's sancta' and so 'provides a ransom that stays God's wrath from venting itself upon Israel' (1990: 217). While the divine plague had already begun to decimate the community, it does not appear, however, that the edict of execution declared by YHWH and relayed by Moses had begun to be accomplished (vv. 4–5). Such divine communications with Moses and pronouncements to the community would take place at the entrance of the Tent of Meeting (see e.g. Lev. 8:3–4; Num. 7:89; 10:3; 16:18–19; 20:6), precisely where we find Moses and the rest of the community stunned into passivity before the brash Israelite paraded with the Midianitess (v. 6; cf. Organ 2001: 208). In his mercy, YHWH accepted the deaths of Zimri and Cozbi, apparent leaders of the rebellion, as 'atonement' for the sons of Israel, both staying the plague and reckoning as satisfied the as-yet-unfulfilled charge to impale offenders (cf. Nachmanides 1975: 294–295). Sklar includes Israel's apostasy in Numbers 25 with other instances in Israel's history that involve an outright rejection of YHWH (Exod. 32:1–10; Num. 11:1–3; 14; 16:1–40; 16:41–50; 21:4–9); it is met with dire consequences and is not atonable by means of sacrifice, but YHWH's rejection of the people is avoided through the actions of a mediator (2012: 477, 486–489). With the exception of Aaron's role in offering incense (16:47), forgiveness or 'atonement' is pursued outside the sacrificial system (Exod. 32:30; Num. 14:20; 25:13); however, the Levites' role after the golden calf incident (Exod. 32:26–29), Aaron's role after Korah's rebellion (Num. 16:46–50) and Phinehas's role in the Baal Peor incident all underscore the necessity of the cult for the survival of the covenant community, with the stories progressing from Aaron's spiritless passivity and actually supporting the people's apostasy, to Phinehas's zealous activity, initiating divine judgement on the apostate Israelite and his consort. Although 24,000 had been struck down by plague, YHWH mercifully spared the second generation of Israel from total destruction, because of Phinehas's mediation. Atonement, as Sklar writes (2012: 490), guarantees the relationship with YHWH will continue, but not that his discipline for sin will be avoided. After the golden calf incident, Levites were rewarded with cultic service for their display of zeal after being prompted by Moses (Exod. 32:25–29), an episode in Israel's life that required Herculean mediation on the part of Moses (Exod. 32:30–35; 33:12–23; 34:1–9), but which nevertheless called for a plague from YHWH (Exod. 32:35). The present apostasy at Baal Peor also entailed carrying out human execution, aside from the punishment of a divine plague, an efficacious mediation that resulted in YHWH's sparing of the whole community. Phinehas's role encompassed that of the Levites and Moses in Exodus 32, and he is commended by YHWH – itself the highest reward – and then given an everlasting covenant of priesthood. Rather than having his lineage cut off, Phineas's lineage is awarded an everlasting honour, granted the holiest status on earth as high priest, divinely consecrated to enter the holy of holies, the earthly throne room of the divine King – there chiefly to do what he has already demonstrated he is zealous to accomplish: the reconciliation of Israel to YHWH, to make atonement for the community, restoring the covenant marriage and making peace. Use of 'atonement' by YHWH, then, explains how the 'plague was stayed' (v. 8) through Phinehas's act, since *kipper* functions to avert the retribution of YHWH's wrath, terminating it before it can be fully exhausted (Milgrom 1990: 477) – by his act of atonement, Phinehas the priest saved the entire community of Israel.

The priesthood of Aaron was ordained by YHWH God to maintain Israel's relationship with YHWH, and Numbers is an exposition as to the necessity of this priestly work. The covenant goal of having YHWH dwell among his people in blessing, in fellowship and communion, among them as their King, defender and fountain of life, requires, as the Camp's structure so eloquently maps out, mediators encamped between YHWH and the twelve tribes – it requires the priestly cult with its shedding of sacrificial blood for cleansing and atonement, its daily whole burnt offerings, sending up their fragrant, propitiating smoke, and the priestly instruction of God's people in his Torah, the way of life. Early in Numbers, the Levites are instructed to encamp around the Dwelling of Testimony, as a cordon separating YHWH's encampment from the rest of the twelve tribes, so that no wrath would fall upon the community of the sons of Israel (1:53) – all of which leads to the question 'How did the Levites allow this Israelite man and his Midianite consort to enter through their protective encampment so as to flaunt their rebellion before the Tent of Meeting?' Whatever the precise nature of the fault, the solution is clearly a priestly remedy. The cult, in other words, is the linchpin of the Camp, of Israel's life with God. Whereas this point was confirmed in chapters 16–17, with the vindication of Aaron as God's chosen high priest, here the point is demonstrated, as the second generation, rather than facing its utter demise in a plague of God, will – through the atonement of its priest Phinehas – progress to the security of a new beginning on the plains of Moab, with a new census in chapter 26 to signal the end of the wilderness era and to mark out those who will inherit the land. Perhaps a contrast between Balaam and Phinehas is intended: Balaam the pagan diviner with multiple altars of whole burnt offerings sought to curse Israel despite YHWH's desire to bless his people, whereas Phinehas the priest sought to atone for Israel in the midst of YHWH's ensuing plague of destruction.

With YHWH's reward and commendation of Phinehas, granting him the priestly lineage that will eventually serve in the Jerusalem temple, the wilderness sojourn concludes with a significant pinnacle, which had been signalled by Aaron's genealogy in 3:1–4, and anticipated with the listing of Levi's descendants in Exodus 6, which ends on a single descendant: 'and she bore him Phinehas' (v. 25).

14–15. These verses function rhetorically as a punchline, a staged surprise. The incident had been narrated according to its paradigmatic nature, suppressing particulars, but now the previously withheld details are supplied; yet even these are given dramatically only at the end of a lengthy summary description: 'Now the name of the man of Israel who was struck down, struck down with the Midianitess.' His name was Zimri son of Salu, a prince of an ancestral house of the tribe of Simeon, which encamped on the south side of YHWH's Tent, under Reuben's banner – the next place of honour after Judah's in the east. Monroe suggests the name 'Zimri' carries villainous connotations, used symbolically to identify a scoundrel of any name (2012: 217–219), although any negatively freighted nuances in her cited references (1 Kgs 16; 2 Kgs 9:31; 1 Chr. 2:4–7) may derive from the Baal Peor incident itself – showing that Zimri's name lived on in infamy. The Hebr. root *z-m-r* is related to an Arabic root meaning 'thing to be protected, sacred, inviolable' (BDB 275, no. III) and the root for 'Salu' suggests weightiness and the notion of being devoted or consecrated (BDB 698) (cf. Stubbs 2009: 200). The revelation of Zimri, a prince among Israel, demonstrates Phinehas's obedience to YHWH's original command to bring justice upon the leaders of the apostasy (cf. Milgrom 1990: 217).

The greater surprise, however, dawns with the revelation of 'the woman who was struck down, the Midianitess': her name was Cozbi, a princess – the daughter of Zur, who was a 'tribal head' (*rōʾš ʾummôt*) of a Midianite ancestral house. The rare term for 'tribal', *ʾummôt*, occurs again only in Genesis 25:16, for Ishmael's genealogy, both Ishmaelites and Midianites being tribally based and related peoples (Milgrom 1990: 217). Hirsch understood *bêt ʾāb* as one of the tribal branches of Midian, and *rōʾš ʾummôt* as signifying that Zur was 'one who wielded influence over the united tribes' (2007a: 530). The name 'Zur' (*ṣûr*) means 'rock' (cf. 23:9) and appears elsewhere in Numbers within theophoric names among Israel (Eli-zur, Zuri-shaddai, Pedah-zur, Zuri-el; cf. 1:5, 6, 10; 2:10, 12, 20; 3:35; 7:30, 35, 36, 41, 54, 59; 10:18, 19, 23). From Numbers 31:8, it is evident that Zur was one of five kings, a head over one of Midian's five tribal houses, which aligns Cozbi with Zimri since he was a prince over one of the five houses of Simeon (see 26:12–13), although hers was an even higher rank. The presence of this very high-ranking daughter of a chieftain in the midst of Israel's community has all the overtones of a cleverly contrived plot, that she was sent to seduce one of the princely houses of Israel as part of a deliberate scheme. Rashi remarks how the revelation of her name and status serves to underscore Midian's level of hatred for Israel, that they would 'cast loose the daughter of a king to harlotry' (1997: 4:322), a notion strengthened by YHWH's use of 'their sister', and Nachmanides adds that their names stress Phinehas's zeal for God since he displayed no fear in executing an Israelite prince and heathen princess (1975: 297). Samet refers to the unveiling of 'a big surprise', that behind Israel's harlotry with the daughters of Moab, joining themselves to Baal, and behind Zimri's act with Cozbi, 'stands a Midianite scheme! . . . [It] turns out to be a case of Israel falling into a trap set by the Midianite enemy!' (2014a: 341). Likely, Cozbi's name is itself wordplay for the root 'to deceive' (Niditch 1993b: 45). Lutzky points out that the West Semitic name Cozbi is not neutral, having both sexual and religious connotations: the first form of the Semitic root *kzb* means 'to lie, deceive, disappoint, fail' and a second form means 'to be voluptuous, luxuriant, abundant', and 'to be magnificent', with the Akkadian equivalent (*kuzbu*) meaning 'voluptuousness, abundance, attractiveness, charm, sexual rigor' and euphemistically 'sexual parts' (1997: 547; cf. BDB 469; HALOT 1.468; TDOT 105). YHWH's retribution implies just such an interpretation (vv. 16–18). Cozbi's name, moreover, forms one of several significant links between the Balaam narrative and the sin of Baal Peor: Balaam's second oracle had proclaimed: '*El* is no man that he should lie (or 'deceive', *kāzab*)' (23:19), using the same root as for 'Cozbi' (cf. Sherwood 2002: 182). Israel's well-being was guaranteed because YHWH is not like Cozbi – because he remains loyal, his people continue to experience blessing.

The term 'struck down' (*nākāh*), occurring five times here (vv. 14 [twice], 15, 17, 18), often implies a fatal smiting, and was used previously to describe how YHWH had struck down the firstborn in the land of Egypt (Num. 3:13; 8:17), how YHWH struck down with a great plague the lusters after flesh (11:33), what YHWH had proposed to do to the faithless first generation after their rejection of the land (14:12), as well as the fate of those who rebelliously attempted to take the land (14:45), how Moses twice struck the rock (20:11), for the defeats of Sihon and Og (21:24, 35), what Balak had wanted to do to Israel (22:6), for Balaam's repeated striking of his ass (22:23, 25, 27; cf. 22:28, 32) – and it will be what YHWH commands Israel to do to the Midianites (25:17–18). As a general term, it satisfies the semantic range of both YHWH's instruction to 'impale' the offenders, as well as Phinehas's act of piercing the couple through with his spear.

16–18. In verses 6–9, the offenders were generalized while Phinehas was detailed, and YHWH's response in verses 10–13 also focused on Phinehas, on the reward for his action. Similarly, verses 14–15 feature the offenders Zimri and Cozbi, detailing their names while that of Phinehas is completely absent, and YHWH's response in verses 16–18 focuses on retribution for the Cozbi ruse plotted by the Midianites. YHWH's two speeches (vv. 10–13, 16–18), then, respond to the paradigmatic episode separately, first to commend Phinehas, second to wreak judgement on the Midianites – and, tellingly, in that order. The two divine utterances (vv. 10–15, 16–18) present just retribution for two parties, reward for Phinehas, and punishment for the Midianites (cf. Samet 2014a: 340) – both given in relation to the effects of their respective actions toward Israel, and both given in perpetuity, with ongoing consequences.

YHWH calls on Moses to attack or 'be hostile' (*ṣārôr*) to the Midianites. Possibly a play on the name of Cozbi's father 'Zur' (*ṣûr*), *ṣārôr* is variously translated as 'vex' or 'harass', and has the basic meaning of being hostile against another or to treat as an adversary (cf. BDB 865). The order to attack the Midianites forms an instance of 'an eye for an eye', since they were 'the ones who were hostile (*ṣōrĕrîm*) to you'. The inf. form, as Rashi noted, implies ongoing hostility (1997: 4:323). Such an attack is further defined as striking them down (*wĕhikkîtem*). The root *ṣ-r-r* occurs seven times in Numbers, beginning with a twofold use in chapter 10 related to the use of the silver trumpets when going against 'the hostile-foe that is hostile to you' in the land (*haṣṣar haṣṣōrēr*, 10:9), then for a 'narrow' place in the Balaam narrative (22:26) and for the king of Israel's 'enemies' in Balaam's third oracle (24:8); the final use regarding the need for Israel to drive out the inhabitants from the land who will otherwise 'be hostile' ('harass'/'attack') to you (33:55). That *nākāh* was also used for Zimri and Cozbi (vv. 14–15), may be intended to communicate that the judgement for the paradigmatic case will also be applied to those who planned the scheme – they are just as culpable as Cozbi 'their sister, the one struck down (*hammukkā*)'. In the case of Midian, their 'being hostile' was in the form of sending Cozbi to seduce an Israelite chieftain, along with his clan ('his brothers', v. 6), into apostasy. They 'were hostile to you with their guiles (*bĕniklêhem*) to beguile (*nikkĕlû*) you', a clear statement assessing both the broader 'matter of Peor' and the matter of 'Cozbi daughter of a prince of Midian' as a deliberate plot against Israel – she 'was deliberately sent to the Israelites' (Samet 2014a: 341). The word *nākal* carries the notion of craftiness and deceit, wiles and faithlessness (cf. BDB 647); its first and only other use in the Torah is for Joseph's brothers who, having seen him coming from afar off, 'conspired (*yitnakkĕlû*) against him to kill him' (Gen. 37:18; cf. Exod. 1:8–22; Ps. 105:25).

Why is the attack limited to the Midianites, excluding the Moabites? In Deuteronomy, Moses declares that YHWH had already commanded him *not* to 'be hostile' (*tāṣar*) to the Moabites because their land had been granted to the descendants of Lot as a possession (2:9; cf. Nachmanides 1975: 301). Numbers, however, underscores that it was the Midianites who 'deceived the Israelites in the affair of Peor *and* in the matter of Cozbi' (Organ 2001: 205; emphasis original). The ploy, apparently at the behest of Balaam (31:16), was led by the Midianite elders or kings. Aside from seducing Israel into idolatry so as to incur God's anger, it seems the Midianites, already a confederation of peoples, sought to lure Israel into a political alliance, consummated by the joining of Zimri and Cozbi's houses, intended to yield a similar nomadic status for Israel as with the Midianites (versus Israel's inheriting or 'dwelling' in the land). In sum, Israel would lose that very status Balaam had only recently marvelled at, the nation's 'separateness' from other peoples (23:9), their 'dwelling alone', the root of their consecration to YHWH. Sicherman develops the political aspects of the Zimri and Cozbi affair, remarking first on the geography of Israel's Camp, especially its southern flank with Reuben's tribe in the centre, Gad to the west of Reuben and Simeon to the east (2008). Since the Midianites were nomadic sheep and camel herders, caravanners and raiders, ranging over the wide area south and east of Canaan (Parr 1996; cf. Seligsohn 1906), the connection between a prince of Simeon's tribe with his consort, a Midianite princess, fits geographically, writes Sicherman (2008: 22–23), as well as politically, forming a royal liaison that often functioned in the ancient world to consolidate treaties or alliances among peoples. Such a Simeon–Midian union would have had devastating effects (2008: 23): first, it would have made Israel's southern flank vulnerable to attack; second, and as testing Moses' authority, it would have led to disunity among the Camp; and third, it would have further impaired Israel's relationship with YHWH. Such a reading deepens the twofold conclusion to the narrative, as the results of Phinehas's action: Phinehas is granted a covenant of peace since 'he kept Israel at peace, unified and preserved', and his action 'ensured that Midian and Israel would be at odds', a point continued with YHWH's order to take vengeance on the Midianites (2008: 23). Regarding the latter point, Milgrom explains (1990: 214), 'There can hardly be a more heinous crime than the open and deliberate murder of a princess by one of the highest officials of another nation' – so Phinehas's action, in obedience to YHWH's command to impale the leaders of apostasy, had the further effect of ensuring ongoing hostility between Midian and Israel. This point perhaps explains the details that Cozbi was both 'a daughter of a prince of Midian' and 'their sister', thus obligating Midian to retaliation (cf. Milgrom 1990: 218). By comparison with the first census (Num. 1), the following census in Numbers 26 shows the most losses for the southern flank of the Camp, with Simeon's tally dropping by 37,100 (and Reuben's down by 2,770, Gad's by 5,150), surely instructing that the tribe of Simeon justly bore the brunt of divine punishment in the Baal Peor affair (cf. Sicherman 2008: 22). The divinely commanded 'hostility' between Israel and Midian may be likened to the 'enmity' YHWH established between the seed of the woman and the serpent (Gen. 3:14–15).

The follow-through fulfilment of YHWH's order is given in chapter 31 for literary-strategic reasons (discussed in that section), which is linked to the present chapter by a number of thematic and lexical features; for example, the form *hammidyānîm* occurs only in Numbers 25:17 and 31:1 (cf. Monroe 2012: 230). Here we note two points: among the slain kings of Midian is 'Zur', Cozbi's father (31:8), and only in that section is the reader informed that it was the counsel of Balaam, also slain in the battle against the Midianites, that had led to Israel's apostasy (31:16). Balaam's involvement is withheld here to focus on Israel's own culpability: the sons of Israel chose to whore after the daughters of Moab and Midian, they chose to feast on the sacrifices of foreign gods, they chose to prostrate themselves before those gods and to join themselves to Baal of Peor. In divine justice, each party is accountable and dealt with in turn: Israel suffers a terrible, divine plague, and the leading offenders, including Zimri, are to be impaled. The attention then turns to the instigators: Cozbi the Midianitess is slain, then the Midianites who sent her are to be struck down, and finally Balaam, who had counselled the scheme, is himself slain. In the light of YHWH's faithfulness in the face of Balaam's wizardry, Israel's faithlessness is underscored, precisely by withholding the deceit through Balaam's counsel. The chapter thus begins with the people's action: they 'began to whore' – their culpability results from this fact, regardless of Midian's beguiling. The Midianites will be held responsible for their own involvement, but that accountability is reserved for the narrative conclusion, after YHWH deals with his own covenant community and rewards Phinehas for his action that was aimed at restoring YHWH's relationship with Israel.

The third divine speech functions also to reassert YHWH's kingship over his people. Through the guile of the Midianites, along with the daughters of Moab, Israel had been yoked to Baal Peor and separated from YHWH; now, rejoined with YHWH, Israel will, under his leadership, attack those who had driven a wedge into the covenantal bond between YHWH and Israel.

19. The chapter ends abruptly with 'And it happened after the plague,' the Masoretes inserting an athnak under 'the plague', a major disjunctive accent, and then adding a paragraph-break marker, severing the sentence that continues in 26:1. Perhaps this was to parallel 26:1 with 1:1, both beginning with YHWH's revelation to Moses (cf. Cole 2000: 446), or to disassociate more vividly the community that would inherit the land from the apostates who were judged.

Positioning the apostasy with Baal of Peor after the Balaam narrative leads to two observations. First, the great contrast between the covenant partners, YHWH and Israel, is manifest. YHWH could not be compelled to turn his back on his people and, rather than cursing them, faithfully blessed them with almost surreal abundance, and then brought the curse on the heads of their enemies in retribution. By contrast, Israel, on the cusp of inheriting the land, abandons YHWH at the first possible opportunity, bowing to the gods of the Moabites and joining themselves to Baal. As Seerveld expresses it (2001: 54):

> The virginity of Israel was ruined in the plains of Moab despite the protecting faithfulness of her Covenanting God. That damned Balaam, stopped from cursing, still connived to get the sons of Israel to break their married vows to Yahweh.

Israel's apostasy and spiritual whoredom took place, he continues, just after YHWH had reaffirmed his nuptial vows, singing 'the old love songs' to his bride (2001: 56). Second, the nature of Israel's greater threat is made clear: rather than fearing the military threat of the Canaanites and surrounding nations, Israel needed to fear their own flesh – the principle of sin within their own hearts, compelling them to stray from YHWH after the foreign women of the lands who would inevitably lead them into idolatry. Israel's core problem, more deeply, was in failing to fear YHWH. Through his terrible judgements, however, Israel would be taught such reverential dread.

THE BAAL PEOR INCIDENT IN THE TORAH'S LITERARY CONTEXT

The heinousness of Israel's apostasy at Baal Peor is profound, standing as the second generation's fall, comparable only to the first generation's golden calf episode (Exod. 32). There are a number of parallels between the two stories, including their structure (based on Grossman 2007: 59–61; cf. also Olson 1996: 153–154; Helfgot 2014: 418–420). (See Table 17.)

The loathesomeness of these defections is aggravated by their contexts, the golden calf apostasy occurring within the covenant at Sinai, on the verge of constructing YHWH's Dwelling (Exod. 32), and the Baal Peor apostasy juxtaposed with YHWH's turning Moab's attempted curses into abundant blessings, on the verge of inheriting the land (Num. 25). Arguably, the Baal Peor incident was more inciting of divine anger, since it occurred within the context of the Camp, with YHWH's dwelling in the midst of his tribes. Moreover, while both scenarios entail a transgression of the first command to have no other gods before YHWH,

Table 17: Baal Peor and the golden calf

Parallels	Golden Calf	Baal Peor
Idolatry involving ritual feasting and sexual immorality	'And they . . . offered whole burnt offerings, and brought peace offerings; and the people sat down to eat and drink, and rose up to make sport' (Exod. 32:6).	'And the people began to whore with the daughters of Moab. And they called to the people to the sacrifices of their gods, and the people ate and prostrated themselves to their gods' (Num. 25:1).
YHWH responds with kindled fierce anger (ḥārāh 'ap) and plague (nāgap, maggēpāh)	'that my fierce anger may kindle against them' (Exod. 32:10). 'YHWH plagued the people' (Exod. 32:35).	'the fierce anger of YHWH was kindled against Israel' (Num. 25:3) 'those who died in the plague were 24,000' (Num. 25:9).
Human response of slaying (hārag) as judicial execution	Moses called Levites to 'slay each man his brother' (Exod. 32:27).	Moses called judges to: 'slay each man his men' (Num. 25:5).
Atonement (kipper) sought	'perhaps I can make atonement for your sin' (Exod. 32:30).	'he made atonement for the sons of Israel' (Num. 25:13).
A cultic reward	Levites: 'Consecrate yourselves today to YHWH . . . so he may bestow on you a blessing' (Exod. 32:29; see Num. 3:5–13; 8:5–26).	Phinehas: 'It will be for him and for his descendants after him, a covenant of priesthood perpetually' (Num. 25:13).

their differing contexts yield different nuances: the golden calf apostasy formed a denial of YHWH's hand in the exodus out of Egypt (Exod. 32:1, 4), but the apostasy at Baal Peor concerns the seduction of the nations upon entering the land, with Israel enticed to sexual immorality and idolatry. The temptations were particular for the given generations: the first generation's challenge was to die to the life of Egypt, whereas the second generation's challenge was to live out Israel's vocation in the land. Finally, focusing only on the roles of Aaron the high priest in Exodus 32 and Phinehas the future high priest in Numbers 25, it becomes evident that Phinehas's action, which moves the story from idolatry to atonement and reconciliation out of jealousy for YHWH, marks a reversal of Aaron's passivity and timidness, which had led to his own complicity in the golden calf incident (Exod. 32:1–5).

In Exodus 34, within the context of renewing the Sinai covenant through the persistent entreaties of Moses as mediator, YHWH, in the aftermath of the golden calf betrayal, underscores the first commandment, saying, 'for you shall not prostrate yourself before any other god, for YHWH whose name is Jealous is a jealous God' (34:14; cf. Exod. 20:3). The words 'prostrate yourself' (*tištaḥăweh*) and 'Jealous' (*Qannā'*) are found in the Baal Peor episode (Num. 25:2, 11, 13), linking the two texts closely (cf. Seforno: 1997: 782). But the association runs much deeper; Exodus 34:15–16 reads:

> Lest you cut a covenant with the inhabitants of the land when they whore after their gods, and sacrifice to their gods, and one calls to you and you eat of his sacrifice. And you take from their daughters for your sons, and their daughters go whoring after their gods, causing your sons to go whoring after their gods.

Lexical links with Numbers 25, in addition to the above-mentioned 'prostrate yourself' (*ḥāwāh*) and 'jealous' (*qannā'*), include 'whore' (*zānāh*), 'sacrifice' (*zebaḥ*), 'their gods' (*'ĕlōhêhem*), 'calls' (*qārā'*), 'eat' (*'ākal*) and 'daughters' (*bĕnôt*), reinforcing the message that the second generation of Israel has committed precisely the treachery YHWH had warned against in the aftermath of the golden calf episode – they have broken the first and all-encompassing command that forms the basis of Israel's covenant relationship with YHWH. Based, no less, on YHWH's jealousy, 'the Israelites were to reject any future (1) covenant or yoke with other nations, (2) invitation from pagan women to worship their idols, (3) meal sacrificed to idols, (4) and intermarriage with these women', all of which demonstrates that Israel's behaviour at Shittim was a 'wilfull pursuit of the Moabite women' and the ensuing idolatry was 'a deliberate crime against YHWH' (Bechara 2012: 38). Exodus 34, with its use of 'call' (*qārā' l-*), reads as a warning of Israel's seduction in Numbers 25. In Deuteronomy YHWH will warn Israel against intermarrying with the inhabitants of the land 'for they will turn your son away from following me, and they will serve other gods', adding that this would 'kindle the fierce anger of YHWH' (*wĕḥārāh 'ap-yhwh*) against you to destroy you suddenly (7:3–4), precisely the scenario of Baal Peor.

Within the bounds of Numbers, the second generation's apostasy at Baal Peor is akin to the first generation's malicious rejection of the land (Num. 13 – 14): both occur on the brink of entering the land, result in a plague of divine judgement (14:37; 25:9) and showcase a faithful few (Caleb and Joshua, 14:6–10; Phinehas, 25:6–7) (Olson 1985: 160). Significantly, after the judgement on the first generation, YHWH had instituted the wearing of tassels on the borders of the Israelites' garments, specifically intended to safeguard Israel against the sort of sin depicted at Baal Peor:

that you may look upon it and remember all the commands of YHWH to do them, and not scout after your own heart, after your own eyes through which you go whoring (*zōnîm*) after them. So that you remember and do all my commands, and so you will be holy to your God. (Num. 15:39–40)

Framed by reminders to remember YHWH's commands, the central purpose statement underscored not having any other gods before YHWH (Exod. 20:3), with an application remarkably similar to Exodus 34:14. The tassel law closes with the exodus formula 'I am YHWH your God, who brought you out of the land of Egypt to be your God' (v. 41), which also serves as the opening to the Decalogue (Exod. 20:2), again reinforcing how whoring after other gods definitively breaks the first command, and Israel's covenant with YHWH. The fruit of the exodus deliverance was to be borne in the life with YHWH in the land, with Israel's joyful worship of him alone (cf. Deut. 12). Now on the verge of inheriting the land, the second generation of Israelites stray from YHWH, delving into sexual immorality with the daughters of Moab, and idolatry, prostrating themselves before their gods and joining in bonds to Baal of Peor. In Deuteronomy, YHWH commands Moses to teach his people a song, as a witness against them, including the lyrics 'They incited him to jealousy with strange gods' (32:16), precisely what the second generation had just done.

Lexical and thematic features also link Phinehas's action with the actions of Moses and Aaron, by way of contrast, in Numbers 20. Focal references to 'the door of the Tent of Meeting' (*petaḥ 'ōhel mô'ēd*, 20:6; 25:6), to Moses or Phinehas's 'taking' (*wayyiqqaḥ*) the spear or rod in 'his hand' (*yādô*) (20:8, 9, 11; 25:7) and to action 'before the eyes' (*lĕ'ênê*) of the community (20:8, 12; 25:6) set the two stories as mirror images, with Phinehas reversing the action of Moses and Aaron the priest, a point brought out in YHWH's alternative responses: the termination of leadership by way of exclusion from the land and death on the one hand, and the gift of perpetual leadership by way of a grant of priesthood on the other. In arresting the nation's apostasy by slaying offenders who were engaged in a sexual rite near the Tent of Meeting, therefore, Phinehas acted to prevent the sanctuary from being defiled and 'can be viewed as doing what Moses and his grandfather Aaron were punished for failing to do: namely, affirming the sanctity of the Lord in the sight of the Israelite people' (Spero 1993: 112).

Finally, the Baal Peor incident alludes to another text within Numbers, the law for the strayed woman (5:11–31) in the section on the Camp's purity laws, setting forth the spiritual nature of the covenant community (Num. 5 – 6). As observed in that section, the language describing a strayed wife is similar to the later portrayals of Israel's unfaithfulness to YHWH by the prophets, with the Sinai covenant understood as establishing a relationship between YHWH and Israel analogous to that of a husband and wife, a spiritual marriage and union, evident also in the Torah's language of 'whoring' after other gods. As a hermeneutical device, the strayed-woman law characterizes Israel's apostasy at Baal Peor as *māʿal*, a treacherous act of unfaithfulness against YHWH (5:12), and Moses indeed dubs the incident in precisely these terms: 'Look! They [the Midianite women] caused the sons of Israel, through the counsel of Balaam, to commit treachery (*māʿal*) against YHWH in the matter of Peor, so that the plague came against the community of YHWH' (31:16). Use of *zānāh* in 25:1 is, arguably, even more forceful than *māʿal* (Bechara 2012: 36). The parallel with Numbers 5, further, explains the act of Phinehas as taken on behalf of YHWH, Israel's faithful husband possessed of 'the spirit of jealousy'. In this law, called 'the law of jealousies' (*tôrat haqqĕnāʾōt*, 5:29), the husband who brings his wife to YHWH through the priest is animated by a 'spirit of jealousy' (*rûaḥ-qinʾāh*). The root for jealousy occurs no fewer than ten times in the law for the strayed woman, functioning as its key idea (5:14 [four times], 15, 18, 25, 29, 30 [twice]). Now, in YHWH's commendatory explanation of Phinehas's act, 'jealousy' occurs four times (25:11, 13; the only other instance is in 11:29), underscoring that the young priest had acted not only on behalf of YHWH but with YHWH's *own* jealousy; that is, as Israel's divine husband. Given the association with the law for the strayed woman, along with the description of Phinehas as 'jealous', the deduction that YHWH's 'spirit of jealousy' had come upon Phinehas is reasonable. Urging that law (Num. 5) and narrative (Num. 25) were meant to be interpreted together, Bechara points out the literary parallels shown in Table 18, somewhat modified (2012: 27):

This comparison in mind, we may be more attuned to the literary strategy at work in Numbers 25: the shift from the corporate sin of 'Israel'/'the people' whoring with the 'women of Moab' (vv. 1–5) to the paradigmatic couple, the 'man from the sons of Israel' and 'the Midianitess' (vv. 6–9), functions to enable the audience to view the nation of Israel in terms of a single person engaged in sexual offence; that is, through the lens of the strayed woman law, with Israel as YHWH's wife: 'those yoked to Baal are represented in Zimri, who is called "one of the people of Israel" (Num. 25:6) and "a man of Israel" (v. 8); the foreign seductresses are in turn represented in Cozbi' (Bechara 2012: 41). In the strayed-woman section, it was argued that the law itself created a figural representation of 'the relationship between YHWH and Israel in the wilderness, where YHWH is the jealous husband and Israel, the wife suspected of unfaithfulness' (N. MacDonald 2008a: 59). Moreover, in both cases YHWH adjudicates through the priest, and, while using different terminology, it is striking that the strayed woman's judgement reaches to her womb, even as the Midianite woman's judgement reaches to her belly – a connection Bechara determines 'cannot be accidental'

Table 18: Baal Peor and the strayed wife

Numbers 5	Numbers 25
If any *man* (*'îš*) whose wife goes astray (v. 12).	A *man* (*'îš*) from Israel brings a Midianite into the Camp (v. 6).
The sexual offence is hidden from *the eyes of* (*'ênê*) her husband (v. 13).	Couple parade in *the eyes of* (*'ênê*) Moses and in *the eyes of* (*'ênê*) the people (v. 6).
Spirit of *jealousy* (*qin'āh*) comes over him, and he is *jealous* (*qinnē'*) over his wife (v. 14).	Phinehas was *jealous* with my *jealousy* (*qin'āh*) so I did not consume Israel in my jealousy (*qin'āh*) . . . in that he was *jealous* (*qinnē'*) for his God (vv. 11, 13).
Woman taken to *the priest* (*hakkōhēn*) at the Dwelling (*hammiškān*) (vv. 15–17), the priest places the offering of jealousy in her *hands* (*kappêhā*), the water of affliction *in the hand* (*běyad*) of the priest (v. 18).	Phinehas *the priest* (*hakkōhēn*) leaves the Tent of Meeting (*'ōhel mô'ēd*) with spear in *his hand* (*běyādô*) (vv. 6–7).
Water of bitterness *goes into bowels* (*běmē'ayik*), thigh falls and *womb* (*beṭen*) swells (vv. 19–22).	Phinehas goes *into chamber* (*'el-haqqubbā*), spear driven *into her* belly (*'el-qŏbātāh*) (v. 8).
Either free to bear *seed* (*zera'*) (v. 28), or takes unlawful *seed* (*zera'*) of copulation (vv. 13, 20).	Phinehas and his *seed* (*zera'*) receive covenant of perpetual priesthood (v. 13).

(2012: 32). The sexual offence, while hidden from the eyes of the strayed woman's husband, in Zimri's case is flaunted before the eyes of Moses and the eyes of the community, while they are weeping over the divine judgement at the Tent of Meeting. Since, however, Zimri and Cozbi enter a tent-shrine, the public display relates primarily to their entering into seclusion, precisely the scenario for a strayed woman. While Phinehas follows them into the *qubbāh*-tent, so indeed knows of the sexual offence and treachery of Israel, the locale of their brazenness near 'the door of the Tent of Meeting' (along with divine omniscience), however, makes it clear their offence was in no way hidden from the eyes of Israel's Husband. Understanding the couple's actions as exemplary of the earlier statement that 'Israel yoked herself to Baal,' underscores the marital infidelity to YHWH, especially since 'Baal' also signifies 'Husband'. Balorda refers to the 'numinal marriage', that covenantal bond between YHWH in the role of Husband and Israel in the role of bride or wife, as the primary context for understanding the divine jealousy displayed by Phinehas, so that the breaking of the covenant through idolatry may be viewed as marital unfaithfulness, adultery or harlotry, and YHWH's 'jealousy' encapsulates the most sublime affection, the feeling of intense, passionate marital love, with its resilient sentiment of commitment and loyalty (2002: 86). The strongest link between the two passages, as noted, binding them together indissolubly, is their use of the root *q-n-'* (jealous, jealousy) in both cases as a response to the *mā'al* of marital infidelity. Tellingly, of the four uses of *mā'al* in Numbers, two relate specifically to the strayed woman (5:12, 27), and the last use is in relation to Israel's harlotry at Baal Peor (31:16). The strayed woman ritual involved an ordeal instigated by the 'spirit of jealousy' and the role of the priest resolving the matter before YHWH, both of which aspects are embodied by Phinehas. The fact that Phinehas himself penetrated to the spiritual reality that Israel's sexual offence and idolatry constituted spiritual harlotry against YHWH, filling him with the 'spirit of jealousy' on YHWH's behalf, is what in the end leads to his reward of the covenant of perpetual priesthood. Phinehas's jealousy is what YHWH commends: 'for he acted-jealously with my jealousy in their midst' (v. 11). If the community of the sons of Israel is cast as a wayward wife, then Phinehas is cast not only as a stand-in for YHWH, the jealous husband, but also as a devoted Nazirite – the alternative path set before Israel. In the Nazirite section (6:1–21), parallels between a Nazirite and the priesthood were noted. What is profoundly astounding is that the treachery of Israel's being joined to Baal, bringing divine anger and plague on the entire nation, could be counteracted by the jealousy of a single man, the Nazir-like priest, Phinehas, whose act purifies the Camp. What Burnham writes of Phinehas equally describes the role of the Nazir within the Camp (2014: 172): 'Phinehas became a shining example of a member of God's community who, through obedience and motivation, matched a passion for holiness that emanated only from Yahweh.' Part of the story's drama is found in tracing the roles of Phinehas (Bechara 2012: 41–43): he is first seen as a *representative of the remnant assembly*, gathered with Moses at the door of the Tent of Meeting to weep over Israel's apostasy, and who 'arose in the midst of the community' (vv. 6–7); second, he stands as a *representative for YHWH*, identifying with his jealousy over his wayward bride, Israel (vv. 11, 13); and, finally, he becomes the *representative of a new hereditary line of high priests* (vv. 12, 13).

Explanation

By literary juxtaposition, the 'Peor' location of the account (cf. 23:28), the continuation of the 'seeing' motif and other wordplay, through the continuing involvement of the Moabites and Midianites (22:4, 7; 25:1,

6, 17), and by the connection of Balaam (later revealed in 31:8, 16), the Baal Peor incident was evidently intended to be read in conjunction with the Balaam story (cf. Olson 1997: 232–233; Samet 2014a: 345–347). Such a holistic reading magnifies Israel's sin in the face of YHWH's unrestrained display of devotion to them. Whatever the precise nature of Israel's whoring with the daughters of Moab, being joined to Baal Peor, the apostasy of the sons of Israel was an undoing of the very first ascription of praise Balaam had uttered concerning Israel, the people's separateness: 'dwelling alone, not reckoning itself among the nations' (23:9) – and a breaking of the first and second commands, which form the heart of their covenant relationship with YHWH (Exod. 20:1–6). Their separateness, a key for Israel's spiritual strength, had not been challenged through the isolation of the wilderness sojourn – devastatingly, YHWH's people join the gods of the peoples at their earliest opportunity (cf. Wellhausen 1885: 356), a sin all the more egregious since these are 'the victorious Israelites, the new generation' (Levine 2000: 292). Although YHWH had just lavished bountiful blessings on them from the 'heights of Peor' (23:28), Israel plunges headlong into spiritual harlotry in joining 'Baal of Peor' (25:3), an act 'etched in the collective memory as a nadir in Israel's history (Deut. 4:3; Hos. 9:10; Ps. 106:28)' (Milgrom 1990: 480).

As a subunit, Numbers 21 – 25 deals with the second generation's encounters with the nations surrounding the land, auguring the sorts of challenges the nation would continue to face once settled in the land (cf. Samet 2014a: 347–348). Sadly, the apostasy at Baal Peor would indeed be repeated in Israel's later history (see e.g. Judg. 2:11–13; 1 Kgs 11:1–2; 16:30–33). In Numbers 21 a preview is given of the second generation's conquest of the land; in chapters 22–24 the second generation's covenantal status as YHWH's people, blessed of him, is confirmed; in chapter 25, in being seduced into idolatry by foreigners, the second generation yields the dismal trajectory of Israel's life in the land. Even as Balaam's oracles foretell heights of glory for the nation, the Baal Peor incident also forecasts Israel's cyclic downfall into idolatry and apostasy. The leading male characters, Zimri and Phinehas, are both Israelite princes, and represent the two alternative paths set before Israel in prospect of life in the land, just as the strayed woman and Nazirite laws had set two alternative paths before Israel's first generation in prospect of the wilderness journey (Num. 5 – 6).

Sexual nuances in the text – that Israel 'began to whore with the women of Moab', was 'called' by them, and 'joined' to Baal (Husband), along with the Israelite man's 'bringing near' a Midianite woman, into 'the tent-chamber', and their being pierced apparently while engaged sexually so that she is speared through 'her womb' – portray Israel as committing spiritual adultery against YHWH, that the nation chose the path of the strayed woman (5:11–31). While in verses 1–5 Israel is described as one body ('Israel dwelled', 'Israel was joined'), verses 6–9 focus on one paradigmatic couple, 'a man from the sons of Israel' and 'a Midianitess', who symbolize the harlotry and apostasy taking place on the national scale and who, by their high-ranking positions in their respective communities, in all likelihood represent the leading roles in the affair (as contrived by the Midianites at the behest of Balaam, 25:17; 31:16). The two sections of the passage (vv. 1–5 and 6–18) are placed in a reciprocal relationship, lending cultic overtones to sensual activity and vice versa. Israel's sin is grave and heinous, a point underscored by another textual feature, the suppressing of details until later (31:8, 16). As a microcosm of the national harlotry against YHWH as Israel's Husband, Zimri the Israelite represents Israel cast as the strayed woman. The last major division of Numbers (chs. 26–36) will feature women prominently (cf. Sivan 2001: 69), especially the daughters of Zelophehad whose efforts to preserve the name and inheritance of their father form bookends around this section (Num. 27, 36). Perhaps, in a manner not unlike Proverbs, an intentional contrast is being made: between the sexual allure of pagan daughters, which leads to idolatry and death, and the lasting blessing of Israelite daughters who are faithful to YHWH and do good for their households.

The idea that Sinai's covenant established a sort of marriage relationship between YHWH and his people is ancient, informing traditional Jewish readings of Song of Songs, and is brought out in the language and imagery of the prophets. In Hosea, YHWH speaks of alluring Israel in the wilderness so that she will desire to return 'to her first husband' and call him 'My Husband', no longer calling him 'My Baal' (*ba'lî*), for he will take away the names of the Baals from her mouth (2:7, 14–16; cf. Jer. 2:2); and Isaiah proclaims, 'as the bridegroom rejoices over the bride, so will your God rejoice over you' (Isa. 62:5). Through the nuptial motif of Psalm 45, such imagery was applied to the Messiah, reigning as YHWH's vice-gerent, and his bride, Israel. The apostle Paul understood the church's relationship to Jesus Christ in terms of bridal theology, a development of Israel's relationship with YHWH. Concerned over a congregation's unfaithfulness to the gospel, he even wrote, 'I am jealous over you with a godly jealousy, for I espoused you to one husband, to present you as a chaste virgin to Christ' (2 Cor. 11:2; cf. Gibson 2008: 218–221). Elsewhere Paul explains that the mystery of the church's union with Christ is typified by the original nuptial account in the garden of Eden between Adam and the Woman, and how the Son loved the church and gave himself for her, cleansing her so as to present her to himself a glorious and holy bride (Eph. 5:25–32). In divine jealousy, the Son rose up amid the heavenly assembly and descended through the incarnation to deliver the people of God. He entered the tent of a broken creation plagued with spiritual harlotry and uncleanness; he himself was impaled – crucified – and the storm of God's righteous fury broke upon his own head, his shed blood reconciling both Jewish people and the nations to God, and to one another. By the everlasting mercies of God, Jesus himself 'is our peace' (Eph. 2:14). The Messiah endured afflictions and torments for YHWH's sake, because 'jealousy (*qin'at*) for your house has consumed me' (Ps. 69:9; John 2:13–22).

Leibowitz asks why the Torah does not reveal the evil schemes of Balaam before the description of Israel's sin, or even when it talks of Midian's scheming? Her answer is profound: the Torah teaches 'a special lesson', that despite Balaam's initiative and the compliance of Midian and the daughters of Moab, 'the moral responsibility ultimately rested on the Israelites themselves', who were guilty (1982: 377–378). In recounting only the sin of Israel and their punishment, the narrative's focus remains on Israel's own culpability for the nation's harlotry, even though it was the fruit of a deceptive political scheme on the part of the Midianites. Especially as juxtaposed against YHWH's lavish blessing of his people despite Balak's efforts, Israel is left without excuse. The nation cannot attribute its sufferings to any divine curse, but must face the reality of having incurred divine displeasure due to their own disobedience (Leibowitz 1982: 306). Numbers 25 underscores deeply the sinfulness of Israel's apostasy, not allowing Balaam's scheme to mitigate the people's blameworthiness; justly, 24,000 Israelites died. Nevertheless, retribution does come at last to Midian as well as to the original schemer, Balaam, who was found to be the starting point of a long line of treachery (31:8, 16).

In the light of the second generation's dismal failure, the central figure of the story is Phinehas the priest, commended and rewarded by YHWH with a covenant of perpetual priesthood because he had acted with jealousy for the honour and worship of YHWH. Within the context of Israel's apostasy, the action of an Israelite man and his Midianite consort had 'threatened the purity of the community and its cult', compelling the priest Phinehas as 'the guardian of purity' to deliver God's people through 'his zeal for the purity of God's sanctuary' (Kugler 1996: 14–15). God's people had given themselves over to their carnal passions, engaging in fertility rites, even to the point of bowing before idols. Phinehas's act of passion – out of YHWH's own jealousy – counters Israel's apostasy, applying divine judgement in a manner that mirrored the sin: Zimri and Cozbi's sexual engagement is countered by their mutual impalement, with Phinehas's spear, the instrument of judgement, reaching to her womb. The genealogy of Aaron's house in 3:1–4 had already suggested that the movement of Numbers would on some level concern the story of Israel's priesthood, and, indeed, major focal points throughout the wilderness journey highlight with urgency Israel's need for Aaron's divinely consecrated priesthood: the priestly benediction, safeguarding the community throughout the sojourn (6:22–27), Aaron's atoning, plague-defying incense offering (16:46–48), his sprouting, almond-bearing staff (17:8), YHWH's reinstitution of the priesthood, along with Levites (18:1–32), the role of Eleazar in the red heifer ritual, marking the second generation's cleansing from the sin and death pollution of the first (19:1–22), the transfer of the high priesthood from Aaron to his son Eleazar (20:22–29), and now the role of Phinehas, grandson of Aaron, in delivering Israel from the consuming anger of YHWH, and his divine reward of a covenant of perpetual priesthood (25:6–13) – and, once in the land, the death of the high priest will release the one guilty of manslaughter from his city of refuge (35:9–34). The wilderness sojourn has tracked Aaron's genealogy to Phinehas, ancestor of the Zadokites who will serve in Solomon's Temple. More than this, by turning immediately to a new census in prospect of inheriting the land (ch. 26), Numbers communicates that Phinehas's jealous act of atonement has enabled the wilderness era, with all of its testing and death-tolls, to conclude. There will be no more journeys, rebellions or deaths for the remainder of the book. The final major section (chs. 26–36) will be taken up entirely with Israel's life in the land.

Just as Israel's priesthood ensured the nation's survival in the wilderness, so what Israel needs for assurance of life in the land, is a faithful, zealous priesthood that will strive for the purity of the people, maintaining the community's life with YHWH in their midst, precisely what Phinehas represents. Not only so, but as demonstrated in Numbers 16 – 17, an active, faithful priesthood is the *sine qua non* for the Camp – for the community – to function as a fruition of the covenant relationship, for YHWH to be able to dwell in the midst of his people without consuming them. In parading his consort *within* the Camp, even through the Levitical cordon and before the Tent of Meeting, the Israelite Zimri and his sexual activity with the Midianite princess fell within the sphere of Phinehas's guardianship (aside from v. 4). Whereas Numbers 21 underscored the military role of the twelve tribes and their needed faithfulness, Numbers 25 underscores the vital role of the priesthood for the sake of the covenant community – these two aspects of the Camp bracket the Balaam narrative, which offers a glimpse into YHWH's intent to bless Israel for the sake of his sovereign purposes in the world (chs. 22–24). Granted a covenant of 'peace', Phinehas's movement, like the priestly benediction that ends with 'peace' (Num. 6:26), goes out from the Tent of Meeting in the centre of the Camp, and, although he pursues for the sake of execution, the result of his mediation is the staying of the plague – peace within the Camp. The Son's atoning death has brought a fulfilment of the Mosaic covenant and an end to the old creation, transforming both by his resurrection from the dead, and opening a new and living way to God's heavenly presence. Jesus has become the everlasting high priest of the new creation and covenant for the people of God, fully able to save since he ever lives to intercede for them (Heb. 7:11 – 10:25; for the theology of this transition, see Morales 2020: 166–172).

The theme of kingship pervades the present subsection (chs. 21–25). Phinehas's priestly act was a means, but the end and goal relates deeply to the *kingship* of YHWH. In being joined to another 'Husband' or 'Master' (Baal), Israel had committed apostasy against YHWH, whose sovereign kingship was so gloriously exhibited in the Balaam Chronicle. By atoning for Israel through the execution of a flagrant couple, one of whom was a Midianite princess, Phinehas also severed political bonds with Midian and reasserted Israel's loyalty to YHWH God, the only King over Israel. This is precisely how the covenant community, structured as the Camp of Israel, works: the outer camp of twelve tribes is atoned for by the inner camp of Levites and priests, for the sake of the nation's relation to the central camp of the *Shekhinah* – so that blessing rather than destruction may flow from YHWH's central throne to the outermost reaches of his people.

NUMBERS 26: THE SECOND GENERATION TALLIED TO INHERIT THE LAND

Translation

$^{25:19}$And it happened after the plague . . . $^{26:1}$Now YHWH said to Moses and to Eleazar the son of Aaron the priest, saying: ^{2}'Lift up the head of the whole community of the sons of Israel from twenty years old and upward, by their fathers' house, all who go out in the host in Israel.' ^{3}And Moses, along with Eleazar the priest, spoke with them in the plains of Moab by Jordan near Jericho, saying, ^{4}'From a son of twenty years and upward, just as YHWH had commanded Moses, with the sons of Israel who went forth from the land of Egypt.'

^{5}Reuben the firstborn of Israel, the sons of Reuben: Hanoch, the clan of Hanochites; for Pallu, the clan of Palluites; ^{6}for Hezron, the clan of Hezronites; for Carmi, the clan of Carmites; ^{7}these are the clans of the Reubenites. And those who were appointed were forty-three thousand, seven hundred and thirty. ^{8}And the sons of Pallu, Eliab; ^{9}and the sons of Eliab, Nemuel and Dathan and Abiram – these are the Dathan and Abiram who were called forth of the community, who strove against Moses and against Aaron in the community of Korah, when they strove against YHWH. ^{10}And the earth opened her mouth and swallowed them and Korah when that community died, when the fire consumed the two hundred and fifty men – and they became a sign. ^{11}But the sons of Korah did not die.

^{12}The sons of Simeon by their clans: for Nemuel, the clan of the Nemuelites; for Jamin, the clan of the Jaminites; for Jachin, the clan of the Jachinites; ^{13}for Zerah, the clan of the Zerahites; for Shaul, the clan of the Shaulites. ^{14}These are the clans of the Simeonites, twenty-two thousand and two hundred.

¹⁵The sons of Gad by their clans: for Zephon, the clan of the Zephonites; for Haggi, the clan of the Haggites; for Shuni, the clan of the Shunites; ¹⁶for Ozni, the clan of the Oznites; for Eri, the clan of the Erites; ¹⁷for Arod, the clan of the Arodites; for Areli, the clan of the Arelites. ¹⁸These are the clans of the sons of Gad according to those who were appointed, forty thousand and five hundred.

¹⁹The sons of Judah were Er and Onan, and Er and Onan died in the land of Canaan. ²⁰And the sons of Judah by their clans were: for Shelah, the clan of Shelahites; for Perez, the clan of Perezites; for Zerah, the clan of the Zerahites. ²¹And the sons of Perez were: for Hezron, the clan of the Hezronites; for Hamul, the clan of the Hamulites. ²²These are the clans of Judah according to those who were appointed, seventy-six thousand and five hundred.

²³The sons of Issachar by their clans: Tola, the clan of the Tolaites; for Puvah, the clan of the Puvahites; ²⁴for Jashub, the clan of the Jashubites; for Shimron, the clan of the Shimronites. ²⁵These are the clans of Issachar according to those who were appointed, sixty-four thousand and three hundred.

²⁶The sons of Zebulun by their clans: for Sered, the clans of the Seredites; for Elon, the clan of the Elonites; for Jahleel, the clan of the Jahleelites. ²⁷These are the clans of Zebulunites according to those who were appointed, sixty thousand and five hundred.

²⁸The sons of Joseph by their clans were Manasseh and Ephraim. ²⁹The sons of Manasseh: for Machir, the clan of the Machirites. And Machir begot Gilead: for Gilead, the clan of the Gileadites. ³⁰These are the sons of Gilead: for Jiezer, the clan of the Jiezerites; for Helek, the clan of the Helekites; ³¹and of Asriel, the clan of the Asrielites; and of Shechem, the clan of the Shechemites; ³²and of Shemida, the clan of the Shemidaites; and of Hepher, the clan of the Hepherites. ³³Now Zelophehad the son of Hepher had no sons, only daughters; the name of the daughters of Zelophehad were Mahlah and Noah, Hoglah, Milcah, and Tirzah. ³⁴These are the clans of Manasseh and those who were appointed, fifty-two thousand and seven hundred. ³⁵And these are the sons of Ephraim by their clans: for Shuthelah, the clan of the Shuthelahites; for Becher, the clan of the Becherites; for Tahan, the clan of the Tahanites. ³⁶These are the sons of Shuthelah: for Eran, the clan of the Eranites. ³⁷These are the clans of the sons of Ephraim according to those who were appointed, thirty-two thousand and five hundred. These are the sons of Joseph by their clans.

³⁸The sons of Benjamin by their clans: for Bela, the clan of the Belaites; for Ashbel, the clan of the Ashbelites; for Ahiram, the clan of the Ahiramites; ³⁹for Shephupham, the clan of the Shuphamites; for Hupham, the clan of the Huphamites. ⁴⁰And the sons of Bela were Ard and Naaman. The clan of the Ardites; for Naaman, the clan of the Naamanites. ⁴¹These are the sons of Benjamin by their clans, and they were appointed, forty-five thousand and six hundred.

⁴²These are the sons of Dan by their clans: for Shuham, the clan of the Shuhamites. These are the clans of Dan by their clans. ⁴³All the clans of the Shuhamites according to those who were appointed, sixty-four thousand and four hundred.

⁴⁴The sons of Asher by their clans: for Imnah, the clan of the Imnahites; for Ishvi, the clan of the Ishvites; for Beriah, the clan of the Beriahites. ⁴⁵For the sons of Beriah: for Heber, the clan of the Heberites; for Malchiel, the clan of the Malchielites. ⁴⁶And the name of the daughter of Asher was Sarah. ⁴⁷These are the clans of the sons of Asher according to those who were appointed, fifty-three thousand and four hundred.
⁴⁸The sons of Naphtali by their clans: for Jahzeel, the clan of the Jahzeelites; for Guni, the clan of the Gunites; ⁴⁹for Jezer, the clan of the Jezerites; for Shillem, the clan of the Shillemites. ⁵⁰These are the clans of Naphtali according to their clans, and they were appointed, forty-five thousand and four hundred. ⁵¹These were the appointed of the sons of Israel, six hundred and one thousand, seven hundred and thirty.
⁵²Now YHWH spoke to Moses, saying, ⁵³'For these the land will be divided as an inheritance by the number of names. ⁵⁴For the large you will cause his inheritance to be large, and for the small you will cause his inheritance to be small, each according to the word of his appointment will his inheritance be given. ⁵⁵Nevertheless, by lot the land will be divided, according to the names of the tribes of their fathers they will inherit. ⁵⁶According to the word of the lot his inheritance will be divided, between the large and the small.'
⁵⁷These were appointed of the Levites by their clans: for Gershon, the clan of the Gershonites; for Kohath, the clan of the Kohathites; for Merari, the clan of the Merarites. ⁵⁸These are the clans of Levi: the clan of the Libnites, the clan of the Hebronites, the clan of the Mahlites, the clan of the Mushites, the clan of the Korahites. And Kohath begot Amram. ⁵⁹And the name of the wife of Amram was Jochebed the daughter of Levi who was born to Levi in Egypt; and she bore to Amram Aaron and Moses and Miriam their sister. ⁶⁰And to Aaron was born Nadab and Abihu, Eleazar and Ithamar. ⁶¹And Nadab and Abihu died when they offered unauthorized fire before YHWH. ⁶²And those who were appointed were twenty-three thousand, all males from a month old and upward, for they were not appointed among the sons of Israel, for no inheritance was given to them among the sons of Israel.
⁶³These are the ones appointed of Moses and Eleazar the priest, who appointed the sons of Israel in the plains of Moab by Jordan near Jericho. ⁶⁴But among these there was not a man appointed of Moses and Aaron the priest, who appointed the sons of Israel in the wilderness of Sinai. ⁶⁵For YHWH had said to them, They will surely die in the wilderness, and not a man of them was left except for Caleb the son of Jephunneh, and Joshua the son of Nun.

Notes on the text

25:19. This fragment is taken as transitioning to chapter 26.
  26:1. 'said': SamP reads 'spoke'.
  'son of Aaron': missing from LXX.

4. A clause directing Israel to 'lift up the head' must be assumed (cf. Paterson 1900: 60).

5. 'sons of Reuben': *BHS* suggests inserting 'by their clans' in conformity with vv. 12, 15 (so too Paterson 1900: 60).

8. 'sons of': perhaps should read as sg., with *Sebir*.

9, 12. 'Nemuel': Syr has Jemuel in v. 12; *BHS* proposes removing Nemuel from v. 9. Gen. 46:10 and Exod. 6:15 list six names: Jemuel, Jamin, Ohad, Jachin, Zohar and Shaul. If Zerah accounts for Zohar, the absence of Ohad is not readily explicable – Ashley surmises the Ohadites, headed by Zimri, died out (1993: 526).

13. 'Zerah': likely the same as Zohar.

15. LXX places this material on Gad, vv. 15–18, after Zebulun (v. 27), followed by Asher (vv. 44–47), perhaps to conform with Gen. 46.

'Zephon': reads as Ziphion in Gen. 46:16.

16. 'Ozni': reads 'Ezbon' in Gen. 46:16.

'Eri': although SamP, LXX and Syr read Adi, Gen. 46:16 has Eri.

17. 'Arod': SamP, LXX and Syr read Arodi, as does Gen. 46:16.

'Areli': SamP has Aroli, LXX and Vg have Ariel, and Syr has Adil.

18. 'forty thousand and five hundred': some Gk witnesses have 'forty-four thousand five hundred'.

21. 'Hamul': reads Hamuel in SamP and LXX.

23. 'Puvah': reads Puah in SamP, LXX, Syr, Vg and 1 Chr. 7:1.

'Puvahites': actually Punites in MT.

24. 'for Jashub': Gen. 46:13 has 'Job'.

27. See note on v. 15.

30. 'for Jiezer': following *BHS* addition of 'for' (*lĕ*). Perhaps an alternative form of Abiezer (cf. Josh. 17:2); SamP and LXX read 'Ahiezer'.

32. 'of Hepher . . . Hepherites': LXX reads 'Opher . . . Opherites'.

34. 'fifty-two thousand and seven hundred': Some Gk witnesses have 'sixty-two thousand and five hundred'.

35. 'Becher . . . Becherites': lacking from LXX.

'Tahan': reads Taham in SamP, and Tanak in LXX.

36. 'Eran': reads Edan in SamP, LXX and Syr.

38. 'Ashbel': reads Ashbeel in SamP, and Ashuber in LXX.

39. 'Shephupham': reads 'Zophan' in LXX. *BHS* suggests 'Shupham', with a few Hebr. MSS, some Gk MSS, Syr, Tg and Vg.

40. 'Naaman': missing from SamP.

41. 'forty-five thousand and six hundred': reads 35,500 'thirty-five thousand and five hundred' in some Gk witnesses.

42–43. Considering the large number for this tribe, it may be other clans of Dan have been lost (see Paterson 1900: 60).

'Shuham': perhaps alternative form of 'Hushim' (cf. Gen. 46:23; 1 Chr. 7:12).

44. See note on v. 15.

'Ishvi': SamP and LXX read Ishvah, while Gen. 46:17 lists both.

45. 'Beriah': lacking in SamP and LXX, but found in Gen. 46:17.

50. 'forty-five thousand and four hundred': reads 'thirty thousand and three hundred' in some Gk witnesses.

57. 'Levites': reads 'sons of Levi' in SamP, Syr and Tg.

58. 'clans of Levi': reads 'sons of Levi' in SamP and LXX. The MT order, Mushites and Korahites, is inverted in LXX.

59. 'who was born to Levi': MT reads obscurely 'who begat her to Levi'.

61. LXX closes the verse adding *en tē erēmō Sina*, paralleling Num. 3:4.

Form and structure

Although a variety of scholars see chapters 26–36 as a 'series of appendixes' or a 'miscellaneous collection of legislation and narrative' (Sakenfeld 1995: 8, 11), there is a clear structure to the material and thematic unity centred on possessing the land of Canaan. The census of the second generation in chapter 26, signalling the end of the wilderness sojourn and the renewed prospect of life in the land, may be outlined as follows:

1. Introduction: YHWH commands the census of the whole community of Israel by Moses and Eleazar (vv. 1–4)
2. The tribal tallies (vv. 5–51)
    As Kislev observes (2013: 237), this principle section gives the census results in twelve paragraphs related to each of the tribes and is composed of the following four elements:
    (1) a heading, normally formulated by the expression 'sons . . . by their clans';
    (2) an elaboration of the clans constituting the tribe, usually through the formula 'for . . . the clan of . . .';
    (3) a summary statement, such as 'these are the clans of . . .';
    (4) the sum total for the tribe.
3. YHWH explains to Moses the division of land by lot (vv. 52–56)
4. The Levite tally (vv. 57–62)
5. Conclusion: Summary statement noting that none who were tallied in the original census were included in this one, except Caleb and Joshua (vv. 63–65)

Comment

25:19

The tally of the second generation takes place 'after the plague', a distinction of significance since it had been the second generation of

Israelites who had been decimated under YHWH's kindled wrath in the matter of Baal Peor (cf. 25:18). It is only now, upon a second census, that the wilderness journey, along with its trials, can be said to have ended – from Numbers 26:1 onward, life in the land is assumed. The second generation also had their own period of testing in the wilderness (chs. 20–25), and at least some 24,000 who died in the plague would be excluded from life in the land (25:9). Adding the Israelites who had died in the plague to the present tally would bring the count to 625,730, demonstrating how, under YHWH's faithfulness, they had flourished in the wilderness beyond the census figures of the first generation. Nevertheless, it is the actual census figure of 601,730 that defines Israel. Given the destruction wreaked by the plague on the second generation, as well as Israel's new, forward-looking, beginning on the plains of Moab, the census may be said to *reconstitute* the covenant community (so, too, Budd 1984: 294). In a sense, the Israel that will inherit Canaan could not be defined by way of census until those of the second generation who would not possess it were excluded – 'after the plague' (cf. Y. Kahn 2014b: 354). Soberingly, only now, through this census that will determine the inheritance within the land of Canaan, are we able to perceive all that was at stake when the sons of Israel succumbed to sexual licence and apostasy in the Midian plot – on the cusp of the land, many sons failed to enter the rest of YHWH's land. This reality, in turn, explains the ensuing judgement on Midian (ch. 31).

26:1–4. YHWH's command to Moses and Eleazar, concerning the census on the plains of Moab, is the singular occasion where YHWH includes Eleazar in direct speech, underscoring the importance of the tally. That Eleazar is 'the son of Aaron the priest' reminds us that this is the second generation of Israel, and recalls the original census in the opening chapter, a comparison made explicit at the close of verse 4. Eleazar was installed as high priest on the death of his father, Aaron, in a transitional chapter (20:22–29), signalling the death of the old generation's leadership and the full emergence of Israel's second generation. Although arranged in different order, the phrases 'Lift up the head of the whole community of the sons of Israel,' 'from twenty years old and upward', 'by their fathers' house', 'all who go out in the host in Israel' occur verbatim in the original census, which had further specified 'according to their clans', 'by the number of names' and 'all males by their skulls' (1:2–3). By contrast, this census mentions the 'host', with its military connotations, only once, whereas the designation occurs some sixty-one times in Numbers 1 – 10, with reference to the Camp (forty-two times directly related to the census in chapters 1–4). Such a feature strikes one as counterintuitive as Israel is now on the cusp of the land, poised to embark on the conquest – why not underscore the people's military nature here? While Israel's martial strength, under YHWH's leadership, is literarily central with Israel's absolute victory over Midian (ch. 31), this last major section of Numbers anticipates life in the land, and is given less to the conquest, which is almost assumed (the exception, chs. 31–32, function as a foretaste of the conquest). Rather than seeing the differences as military (chs. 1–4) versus land (ch. 26), the deeper analogy is between wilderness life with God in the Camp (Num. 1 – 10) and settled life with God in the land (chs. 26–36). Israel's Camp served as the model and the wilderness sojourn as the training period for Israel's life in the land. While the Camp had been arranged by the tallied tribes (chs. 1–2), the land allotment will be by family clans; hence this tally by clans.

YHWH had charged Moses alone, apart from Aaron, with the first census (Num. 1:1, 19; cf. 1:17, 44), a detail seemingly conveyed now in the omission of Eleazar in verse 4, a verse with several difficulties (cf. Paterson 1900: 60). Has some part of the command to *number* the Israelites been omitted? Whatever the case, the gist of 'From a son of twenty years and upward' is clear. More difficult, how does the clause about the sons of Israel fit? YHWH had charged Moses alone, and only 'Moses' is preceded by the definite direct object marker (*'et*), although the 'sons of Israel' may still be included in the charge generally (assumed by Masoretic pointing). Some commentators (e.g. G. B. Gray 1903: 387; Ashley 1993: 534) and translations (e.g. JPS, NRSV, ESV) split the verse after 'Moses', and take 'the sons of Israel' as a heading for verses 5–51. This, however, identifies the tallied clans as 'those who went forth from the land of Egypt', leading some to render 'sons' as 'descendants' of Israelites, a rare connotation for the stock phrase *běnê yiśrā'ēl* (e.g. Levine 2000: 313–314; JPS). Rather, the end of verse 4 fits better with the backward look to the original census, leading us to translate the vav of *ûběnê yiśrā'ēl* as 'with' the sons of Israel (a 'vav of association'; cf. BDB 253). As such, the whole verse was spoken to the second generation of Israelites, communicating that this census puts them in place of the previous generation, which had also been tallied. Mention of 'Moses' and 'the sons of Israel' further underscores the similarity between these two censuses, between those who were delivered out of Egypt and Israel now in the plains of Moab. While there had been a severe and just punishment of his people in the wilderness, YHWH the God of the exodus was faithful to fulfil his purposes for their deliverance out of Egypt; namely, to bring them into the land of Canaan (Gen. 15:7–20). The 'plains of Moab by Jordan near Jericho' recurs as a unifying locale throughout the last major section of the book (Num. 26:3, 63; 33:48, 50; 35:1; 36:13).

26:5–51

The order of the tribes is similar to that of the first census, with one exception related to the tribes of Joseph: whereas Ephraim had been numbered before Manasseh earlier (Num. 1:32–36), here Manasseh comes first. The listing is not by birth order alone but according to the tribal encampments, by their banners (cf. Ibn Ezra 1999: 222 n. 33), beginning with Reuben's southern encampment. While the tallies are given according to tribal divisions, the focus is on the clans or 'families' (*mišpaḥat*) within each tribe, whose lines and names derive from the sons of Jacob as listed in Genesis 46:8–28 (cf. Josh. 12 – 19; 1 Chr. 2 – 9), and the terms for 'tribe' (*šēbeṭ, maṭṭeh*) do not occur in the tally itself, vv. 5–51 (cf. v. 55). The sons of the twelve patriarchs appear to have constituted patriarchal houses ('father's house', *bêt 'āb*), a concept that always implies ownership of land, but the 'clans' (*mišpāḥôt*) originated with the grandsons of the tribal eponym, this term expressing a relation of kinship (Levine 2000: 331).

Comparing the tallies between the two censuses, seven tribes increased while five decreased in number. There is not enough evidence to demonstrate the impression clearly, yet, given the variety of punishments recounted throughout the wilderness sojourn, it appears that, generally, a decrease in number represents that tribe's diminishment under YHWH's discipline in the wilderness. Reuben's tribe, for example, was noted as involved in the rebellion of Korah's band (16:1), which is recalled explicitly (vv. 9–10), and his tribe decreased by 2,770. More convincing, one of the leaders singled out in the second generation's recent apostasy at Baal Peor was Zimri a prince of the tribe of Simeon (25:14). Given his leadership, Zimri's tribe probably took the highest death toll under God's wrath. That judgement occurred *after* the second generation's emergence, rendering the Simeonites the smallest tribe by far at only 22,200, a sum even smaller than the 24,000 who had died in the plague. Simeon's tally positions the tribe remarkably close to the tribe of Levi – the two patriarchal brothers often linked together (see Gen. 34:25, 30; 49:5–7; N. Price 2020: 41–76). A tribe's loyalty or disloyalty to YHWH through the wilderness period had a bearing on the size of that tribe's inheritance in the land – God knows how to reward the righteous, remaining faithful to their descendants. It is harder to explain deductions for the remaining three tribes: Ephraim and Naphtali both incur a loss of 8,000, and Gad's figure drops by just over 5,000. Tally differences according to the four major camps show that only the southward camp, led by Reuben, suffered a great deduction, while the eastward, westward and northward camps gained in number. At 201,300, the eastward camp is the largest by far, with Judah remaining the leading tribe by over 10,000 at 76,500. As with its honoured encampment across from the entrance to the Tent of Meeting in the east, Judah's numerical prominence seems to reflect YHWH's sovereign design and promise concerning Israel's future ruler (Gen. 49:8–12), recalled in Balaam's oracles (Num. 24:7–9, 17). Curiously, the tallies are all rounded at 100, with the single exception of Reuben's, rounded at 10 (43,730), as was the case with Gad in the original census (45,650), and each tribe of the northward camp ends with 400. (See Table 19.)

Table 19: Census tallies: a comparison

Tribal census totals of Numbers 26		First census	Tally changes by tribes	Tally totals, changes by camps
1. Reuben	43,730	46,500	−2,770	
2. Simeon	22,200	59,300	−37,100	SOUTH: 106,430 Loss: 45,020
3. Gad	40,500	45,650	−5,150	
4. Judah	76,500	74,600	+1,900	
5. Issachar	64,300	54,400	+9,900	EAST: 201,300 Gain: 14,900
6. Zebulun	60,500	57,400	+3,100	
7. Manasseh	52,700	32,200	+20,500	
8. Ephraim	32,500	40,500	−8,000	WEST: 130,800 Gain: 22,700
9. Benjamin	45,600	35,400	+10,200	
10. Dan	64,400	62,700	+1,700	
11. Asher	53,400	41,500	+11,900	NORTH: 163,200 Gain: 5,600
12. Naphtali	45,400	53,400	−8,000	
Totals	601,730	603,550	−1,820	

Beyond the tally figures themselves, there are two further differences, of greater import, between the original census and the present one in the plains of Moab. First, in Numbers 1 only the tribal patriarch is mentioned, while in Numbers 26 the tribal clan lines are listed to the third generation. In other words, the major families of each tribe are noted, and this primarily for the sake of their land inheritance, the census determining the size of their allotted lands. Second, and underscoring the same motif of land inheritance, glosses are interspersed throughout the tribal listings, arguably under the three leading tribes, Reuben, Judah and Manasseh: the deaths of Dathan and Abiram, along with the survival of Korah's sons in Reuben's section (26:9–11); the deaths in the land of Canaan of Er and Onan in Judah's section (v. 19); and mention of Zelophehad's daughters in Manasseh's section (v. 33). Nadab and Abihu's death will also be noted in the Levite section (v. 61). In each case, the notice relates in some way to their family line *not* inheriting the land, that they were 'cut off', with the survival of Korah's sons being an exception that proves the rule (along with the later resolution for Zelophehad's daughters, 27:1–11). 'Thus,' writes Rimon (2014a: 377), the narratives that appear in the midst of the census are directly related to it: they describe different situations in which a person loses his inheritance in the land – whether in the wake of a serious transgression, or because he had no heirs.

Only the reference to Sarah, the daughter of Asher (v. 46), appears somewhat out of place, perhaps simply carried over from the traditional list found in Genesis 46, which also includes Judah's sons Er and Onan (see Gen. 46:12, 17). For the probable significance of the clan eponyms, see Levine 2000: 315–324.

Including the daughters of Zelophehad (v. 33) and the Levites (vv. 57–62), as Milgrom points out (1990: 219; following Jacob 1909: 92–98, 113), the community of Israel comprises seventy clans, so that Israel, having descended into Egypt numbering seventy individuals (Gen. 46:27; Exod. 1:5), is now poised to enter the land of Canaan as seventy clans. Shamah, similarly, refers to the seventy clans as a 'macrocosm of the seventy individuals who descended to Egypt' (2011: 816).

5–11. The clans of Reuben, designated 'the firstborn (*běkôr*) of Israel', head the census (cf. Gen. 46:9). Reuben's own firstborn is named 'Hanoch' (or 'Enoch'), which signifies 'dedication'. Two other firstborn sons are called 'Enoch' (Gen. 4:17; 5:18). The first Enoch, born to Cain, may signify the dedication of a city (cf. Levine 2000: 315–316; he also presumes that all Enochs were firstborn sons), and the second Enoch, who walked with God and was divinely 'taken' (Gen. 5:24), likely illustrates the name as 'dedicated to El/YHWH', illumining the theology of firstborns as belonging to God.

Fully half of this section is dedicated to recalling the demise of Dathan and Abiram, when they, with Korah's band, strove against Moses and Aaron (Num. 16). Again, the logic for these glosses appears to be as an explanation for why some clan lines were not entitled to inherit the land, having been cut off in divine judgement. Ironically, Dathan and Abiram had faulted Moses, saying, 'You have not brought us into a land that flows with milk and honey, nor given us an inheritance of fields and vineyards' (16:14) – and now they are mentioned as excluded from the inheritance of land. Those who participated in Korah's rebellion are deemed as cut off, disqualified from the land promise (cf. *b. Bav. Bat.* 117b), precisely the understanding communicated by the daughters of Zelophehad (see 27:3–4). When Dathan and Abiram and the community of Korah 'strove' (*nāṣāh* in hiph.) against Moses and Aaron, they actually 'strove' against YHWH himself, struggling against his will and order, and consequently endured his judgement when the earth opened to swallow them and their houses, and when fire came forth to consume the 250 princes who offered incense. Samet (2017c) suggests the notice of Dathan and Abiram's sin accounts for Reuben's tribal figure not being rounded to the nearest hundred (i.e. ending in 30), since the lack (of '70' no less) gives a sense that Reuben's tribe was missing some of its numbers.

Verse 10 ends with 'And they became a sign (*nēs*).' The 3rd m. pl. verb *hāyāh* presumably refers to the 250 princes who were consumed in fire, although in the original story it is the censers that became a sign (16:38). The hammered-out censers used for plate coverings for the altar, serve to remind Israel of the men's judgement, that 'no stranger who is not of Aaron's seed' should draw near to offer incense to YHWH (16:40), so it may be said the men themselves became a sign. Moreover, in the original story the term for 'sign' is *'ôt*, and also 'memorial' (*zikkārôn*, 16:38, 40), whereas here it is *nēs*. The word *nēs* normally designates a standard or banner to which people or armies gather (Isa. 11:10; Jer. 50:2), and was used earlier in the Torah when, after Israel's victory over the Amalekites at Rephidim, Moses built an altar and called it 'YHWH is my banner' (Exod. 17:15–16), and more recently for the standard on which the brazen serpent had been set (Num. 21:8, 9). The fiery destruction of these men – their divine judgement – stands as a warning sign.

The survival of Korah's sons comes as a surprise (cf. Kislev 2019: 499–500), likely a narrative technique. The wording in 16:32 is vague: 'every man (*hā'ādām*) who belonged to Korah'. While the immediate context favours identifying 'every man' with Korah's followers, the members of his community, the impression left open the possibility that his entire household had also been destroyed. Given the probable function for the glosses interspersed throughout this census, to explain why some clan lines failed to inherit the land by being cut off, the notice that the sons of Korah did not actually die is a needed clarification – as Levites they will not inherit land, but were not cut off. Earlier, YHWH had warned Moses and Aaron to ensure that the clans of the Kohathites would not be 'cut off' (*'al-takrîtû*, 4:17), and this notice reassures their survival. Evidently, Korah's descendants would become temple musicians and singers (see Pss 42 – 49, 84, 85, 87 – 88; 1 Chr. 26:1–19). Ibn Ezra points out that the sin of Dathan and Abiram, whose lines were cut off, was worse than Korah's since they refused Moses' summons and insulted him (Num. 16:12–14; 1999: 221). Since the place for Levites is in verses 57–62, mention of the sons of Korah here and as an exception that proves the rule, underscores the exclusion of Dathan and Abiram from the clan scheme of land allotment. 'Thus,' writes Rimon (2014a: 377), 'the narratives that appear in the midst of the census are directly related to it: they describe different situations in which a person loses his inheritance in the land – whether in the wake of a serious transgression, or because he had no heirs.'

12–14. Comparing this section with Genesis 46:10 and Exodus 6:15, it becomes apparent that the clan of Ohad is missing. Ashley suggests the possibility that Zimri was specifically a prince of the Ohadite clan, and that the plague destroyed this clan entirely (1993: 535). A gloss to this effect, however, would have been in keeping with their use elsewhere in the chapter. In any case, the omission occurs again in 1 Chronicles 4:24, so it does appear the line of Ohad did not continue. Simeon's massive population decrease, by 37,100, is commonly accounted for by attributing the majority of the 24,000 who perished at Baal Peor to this tribe, having been led by Zimri. Perhaps Zimri's disgraced name was intentionally withheld, just as 'Moses refrained from blessing Simeon explicitly prior to his death' in Deuteronomy 33 (Y. Kahn 2014b: 356; cf. *Pesikta de-Rav Kahana*, Addenda 1). As a diminished tribe, Simeon's territory would fall within the land of Judah (Josh. 19:9).

15–18. Gad's tally drops by just over 5,000 from the previous census. While no explanation is given for this decline, it is likely significant that Gad is linked with Reuben and Simeon, comprising the southward camp, the only one of the four major camps that did not grow larger by at least 5,000 – instead declining by over 45,000. Divine blessing often spills over to those associated with a person being blessed (e.g. Gen. 30:27), and the same principle holds for those associated with ones who fall under God's judgement.

19–27. The eastward camp remains the largest, now by almost 40,000, reflecting YHWH's blessings and promises especially as focused on the tribe of Judah (Gen. 49:8–12), and reaffirmed in Balaam's oracles (Num. 24:7–9, 17). For the original list of the sons/clans of Judah, Issachar and Zebulun, see Genesis 46:12–14. The gloss concerning the deaths of Er and Onan, recounted in Genesis 38, explains why no land inheritance is assigned to their (cut off) lines.

28–37. Joseph's line again includes two tallies, counting the clans of Manasseh and Ephraim separately, keeping the tribal listing at twelve, given the omission of Levi's tribe. Although Manasseh was Joseph's firstborn son (Gen. 41:50–52), the earlier census had begun with Ephraim (1:32–33), the priority established by Jacob (Gen. 48:12–20). While their varying order in lists, as G. B. Gray noted (1902: 240), appears 'to have been used indifferently by all writers', the change here, with Manasseh's tally listed before that of Ephraim, may mirror their changes in size (cf. Chinitz 1996: 40). Earlier, Ephraim had been the larger tribe by over 8,000, but now Manasseh exceeds Ephraim by over 20,000 – even as Ephraim decreased by 8,000. Alternatively, it may be the two censuses are to be taken together, as complimentary. The Netziv (Naftali Zvi Yehuda Berlin, 1816–93) contrasted the two censuses, with the first for the sake of forming the Camp, the earthly Chariot of the *Shekhinah*, in an era of miracles, whereas the second was for the sake of inheriting the land, transitioning to practical, non-supernatural life: Ephraim, being more spiritual, preceded Manasseh in the first census, and Manasseh, being more practical, took priority in the second, so that their diverse order reflected the transition between these two distinct eras, marked by the change in God's dealings with his people (cf. Berlin 1840). Sasson suggests the switch was intended to give Manasseh the prominent seventh place, with the daughters of Zelophehad comprising the seventh generation, since Zelophehad will be given special focus in chapters 27 and 36 (1978: 181–182; cf. Dozeman 1998: 212; Rimon 2014a: 374). The theme of reversal related to these sons of Joseph may be traced back to Jacob's blessing when he reversed his hands, designating the younger Ephraim as the firstborn (Gen. 48). The priority of the tribe of Manasseh in the census may be the result of Manasseh's 'central role in the conquest of Sihon and Og' (Hattin 2012: 294), although their role is indicated only later in 32:41 and then in Deuteronomy 3:14–15 (cf. Craigie 1976: 122–123; Tigay 1996: 36). Their priority in the census, along with the tribe's significant population increase, are only a few of the ways the last section of Numbers emphasizes the tribe of Manasseh (chs. 26–36): the Manassite daughters of Zelophehad are listed in the census, and then their story is given in chapter 27 and continued in chapter 36, closing the book with a notice of their marriages, and the half-tribe of Manasseh receives land in Transjordan in chapter 32.

The census gloss about Zelophehad the son of Hepher notes that 'he had no sons' (*lō'-hāyû lô bānîm*), but daughters – five will be named. Presumably, then, his line has been cut off, so as not to inherit land. Further stories concerning the daughters of Zelophehad, however, will overturn this conclusion, and form an inclusio around the third major section of the book (chs. 27, 36). As the crisis of Zelophehad's name and inheritance will be resolved in the next chapter (27:1–11), this gloss serves as an introduction. Manasseh shows up again when part of its tribe joins Reuben and Gad in settling on the east side of the Jordan (see 32:33–42). Every clan of Manasseh, except the clan of Hepher, will settle with Reuben and Gad in Transjordan: on the one hand, the settlement east of Jordan serves as a foretaste and seal of the later conquest; on the other hand, Zelophehad's daughters, within the clan of Hepher, stand as banners to the undaunted hope and resolute aspiration for life in the land promised by God. Their inheritance of land is recorded in Joshua 17:3–6. The name 'Zelophehad' likely derives from the combination of *ṣēl* (shadow, divine protection) and *paḥad* ('fear, awe', perhaps theophoric as with 'fear of Isaac'), referring to divine power – thus, 'one protected by divine power' (Levine 2000: 322), and akin to 'Bezalel' for 'sheltering in God's shadow', with 'Zelophehad' being a shortened form of 'sheltering in the shadow of God whom he fears' (Ben-Barak 2006: 55). One is reminded of Joshua and Caleb's impassioned declaration that the Canaanites' shade (from *ṣēl*) had been removed (Num. 14:9). Machir will appear again in Numbers 32, given Gilead by Moses (32:39; cf. Josh. 17:1–3). Several of the names here are associated with cities (see Ashley 1993: 536–537), a phenomenon observed in the earliest biblical reference to a city (Gen. 4:17).

38–41. The clans of Benjamin, along with those of Joseph, had formed the westward camp, which grew by nearly 23,000 overall (in spite of Ephraim's decline). Benjamin's tribe grew by over 10,000. For differences in Benjamin's line, see Genesis 46:21; 1 Chronicles 7:6–12; 8:1–40. Five sons of Benjamin have been omitted from the list in Genesis 46:21, their lines, so the Midrash says (*Num. Rab.* 21.8), having perished through the whoredom that resulted from Balaam's counsel (Num. 25). Rashi, however, assigning the 24,000 who died in the plague completely to Simeon's tribe, relates the legend that after Aaron's death, when the glory Cloud disappeared, the Israelites were resolved to return to Egypt, but the Levites pursued them, killing several families in the confrontation (see Rashi 1997: 4:328–329; cf. *y. Yom.* 1.1; *m. Sot.* 1.10). Interestingly, the name of Benjamin's firstborn, Bela, is cognate with Balaam (Levine 2000: 323); several of the names in this chapter recall events of the wilderness sojourn.

42–50. The clans of Dan, Asher and Naphtali had comprised the northward camp, the second largest major camp with 163,200. At 64,400, the sons of Dan made up the second largest tribe, after Judah, and this, remarkably, with only a single clan, the Shuhamites. The listing in Genesis affirms this quandary (46:23), while the Chronicler is silent on Dan's genealogy (2 Chr. 2 – 8). For Asher and Naphtali, see the listings in Genesis 46:17; 24; 1 Chronicles 7:13, 30–31. Asher's daughter Sarah is named, perhaps merely in keeping with Genesis 46:17 (cf. 1 Chr. 7:30). Rashi, following *Seder 'Olam*, says Sarah is mentioned 'because she was still alive' (cf. 1997: 4:334; see Bronner 1994). Nachmanides links her reference to the principle for mentioning the daughters of Zelophehad (v. 33); namely, that Sarah was able to inherit land – following the *TgO* translation 'daughter of Asher's wife' by a previous husband who died with no sons (see 1975: 311–312). Demsky notes three alternative reasons for the inclusion of a woman in patriarchal genealogies (2021b): importance (as with Miriam, in 26:59), relationship (whereby she 'constitutes an inter-tribal/clan alliance') or blemish (socially or ethnically, 'like being a concubine or a foreigner, which will impinge on the inheritance rights of her children'). Perhaps, as she shares the name of the first matriarch (Gen. 17:15–16), Sarah's importance would be the implied reason she is listed (even in Gen. 46:17).

51. The total count for the sons of Israel is 601,730. While the tally is just under that of the original census, yet, incorporating the 24,000 who died in the recent plague, the total would have exceeded the first census. In Numbers 2, the tallied tribes are organized into the four major camps, yielding four new tallies. The present census numbers are not reorganized into four camps, although I have done so in the comments for purposes of comparison. Whereas the first census was preliminary for Israel's life with YHWH in the Camp, the paradigm for the covenant community, the present census anticipates Israel's life with YHWH in the land.

26:52–56

As a speech by YHWH 'to Moses', the text makes clear that even the inheritance of land is Mosaic in origin. The tribal allotments are under Moses' authority, under YHWH's foundational revelation, the Torah. The purpose for the tally of the tribes by clans, central to this chapter (cf. Auld 1980: 73), is given clearly as the division of land inheritance according to the number of names. The whole chapter is 'oriented towards the entry into Canaan and the distribution of the allotments' (Kislev 2013: 251). The land distribution will also involve casting lots, a widespread custom in the ANE (see Westbrook 1991: 17–18), but which has led to some consternation among scholars who pit the census figures against the lots as two competing ways for dividing the land (as with Baentsch 1903: 627–635). Likely, casting lots is for determining precise locations (see Num. 33:54; 34:13), while the apportioned sizes of land inherited will be in proportion to the size of the tribe, by clans, as determined in the census (cf. Abarbanel 2015: 295–298; so, among others, Dillmann 1886: 175; Snaith 1967: 185). The enumeration of clans in the census is, therefore, meant for establishing the principle of equality in land distribution, not only among the tribes, but among the clans within the tribes (cf. Weinfeld 1988: 279–280; Aḥituv 1992). A possible variation may be the inclusion of more lots for larger tribes (cf. Josh. 17:14–18). Every judgement or decision (*mišpāṭ*) of the 'lot' (*gôrāl*) is sovereignly determined by YHWH (Prov. 16:33; cf. Acts 1:23–26; Derby 1997: 171; Shapira 2012: 277–280), and so guards against disputes and rivalries regarding the allotted regions (cf. Prov. 18:18) – YHWH is the true Landowner who gives the tribes their allotments as his tenants (cf. Habel 1995: 98–101). This passage is the Torah's first use of 'lot' in relation to land, whereas previously lots were cast as part of the Day of Atonement ritual (Lev. 16:8–10; cf. Hausoul 2018: 83–84). A *gôrāl* originally referred to a stone or pebble, marked in some fashion, which would be cast or thrown (Lindblom 1962: 166–168). The procedure has been understood as involving Eleazar's use of the Urim and Thummim (cf. Exod. 28:30), guided by the Spirit, and Jewish tradition adds the drawing of two sets of twelve tickets, the one set inscribed with the tribal names and the other with the territories of the land (see e.g. Rashi 1997: 4:335).

I take it that the larger inheritances for the larger tallies refers to the larger tribes receiving more land, whereas Nachmanides understood that each of the twelve tribes received equal allotments and only the clans within them received varied territory sizes, according to their clan's population (see 1975: 321–322). Seforno compromised by suggesting the tribes received territories equal in value but not in size, with a larger plot of inferior land being comparable to a smaller plot of rich soil (see 1997: 788–790; cf. *b. Bav. Bat.* 122a). Through Jacob's deathbed blessing, YHWH had already indicated the land apportionment to some extent;

for example, that Zebulun would dwell by the shore of the sea, and Issachar between the sheepfolds (Gen. 49:13, 14). Caleb and Joshua, not part of the second generation, are exceptions to the rule of division by lot – their land was given according to the word of YHWH (Judg. 1:20; Josh. 19:49–50).

Regarding the division of land according to the names of the tribes 'of their fathers', Hirsch observes that the Israelites take possession of the land in the name of their ancestors as something akin to delegates, only as heirs (2007a: 544–545; cf. *b. Bav. Bat.* 117b), a notion that unfolds more fully with the pursuit of land by the daughters of Zelophehad for their deceased father's sake (27:1–11). In relation to the land division, verse 55 is the chapter's only use of 'tribe', whereas the primary focus is on level of clans (*mišpaḥat*). Nevertheless, these verses also emphasize the land divisions per tribe, so that 'number of names' (v. 53) may refer to the names of the twelve tribal patriarchs, and 'each' (*'îš*, v. 54) may denote 'each tribe', even while 'they will inherit' refers to the clan families (see Jeyaraj 1989: 129–131). The land is received as an inheritance of the land-grant made originally to the patriarchs, beginning with Abraham (see Weinfeld 1970). As Westbrook observes (1991: 23), that the 'sons of Israel', as direct descendants of the patriarchs, 'do take possession of their father's estate, and divide it between them like heirs . . . For the purposes of allocation the head of each *mšpḥh* within the tribe is treated as an heir *per stirpes* of the eponymous tribal ancestor.' In Numbers 33, which rehearses the wilderness journeys in prospect of possessing the land, the land's division is described in similar terms, perhaps forming an inclusion (compare 26:52–56 with 33:54).

26:57–62

Levites had been excluded from the nation's tally in Numbers 1:47–53, since they were designated over the Dwelling of the Testimony in the Camp (see 1:50, 53). In the present census, Levites are excluded from the nation's tally because 'no inheritance was given to them among the sons of Israel' (26:62), demonstrating once more the focus on Israel's life in the land, along with the analogy between sojourning life with God in the wilderness Camp (first census) and settled life with God in the land of Canaan (second census). The phrase in verse 62 that Levites 'were not appointed among the sons of Israel' is repeated verbatim from the earlier census (Num. 2:33; cf. 1:47, 49), and 'no inheritance was given to them among the sons of Israel' echoes earlier statements as well (see 18:23, 24) (cf. Kislev 2013: 253). Previously, YHWH had spoken to Aaron directly, saying, 'You will have no inheritance in their land' (18:20), a statement similar to the end of verse 62. Later, Levites will be granted forty-eight cities (35:1–8), perhaps in view of which they are tallied here. Of Simeon and Levi, Jacob had prophesied, 'I will divide them in Jacob, and scatter them in Israel' (Gen. 49:7), a word fulfilled positively for Levites as they are scattered throughout the land in order to teach the tribes divine *torah*, but negatively for Simeon's decreased people, who will be allotted a small portion of territory within the land of Judah (Josh. 19:9). In Numbers 18, YHWH had twice said of the Levites, 'Among the sons of Israel they will have no inheritance,' an inclusio around the central statement that he would give the tithes of the sons of Israel, lifted up to YHWH as a contribution, to them as their inheritance (vv. 23–24). So, while not having their own land, Levites will nevertheless receive the best of the fruits of the land as their inheritance. Reminding the house of Aaron that they will have no inheritance in the land, YHWH said, 'I myself am your portion and inheritance' (18:20) – priests would get a tithe of the tithes received by Levites (18:25–32).

Levi's line had been delineated in Numbers 3:14–39 (cf. Gen. 46:11), in view of each clan's responsibility in the transport and set up of YHWH's Dwelling. Numbers 26:57–62 now presents only a summary of that fuller record (cf. Levine 2000: 307). Based on the genealogical details in Exodus 6:16–19 and in Numbers 3:17–20, the 'clans of Levi' as delineated here (v. 58) refer to the clans that derive from Levi's three sons, Gershon, Kohath and Merari, as follows: the Libnites derive from the first son of Gershon (his second son, Shimei, not noted); the Hebronites derive from the third son of Kohath (his first two sons, Amram and Izhar, and his fourth, Uzziel, not noted); the Mahlites and the Mushites derive from the two sons of Merari; and the Korahites derive from the first son of Izhar, who was the second son of Kohath, and seems to stand in his place here. These clans are followed by a reference to the birth of Kohath's first son, Amram, and the ensuing births of the leaders of the exodus: Aaron, Moses and Miriam their sister. The exodus motif is appropriate within the present context of inheriting the land, but their names also recall chapter 20, the last occasion where all three siblings were mentioned, beginning with the death of Miriam and ending with the death of Aaron. Amram and Jochebed are also mentioned in Exodus 6:20, along with the births of Aaron and Moses, and in the account of Moses' birth in Exodus 2:1–10 the couple is designated generically as 'a man of the house of Levi' and a 'daughter of Levi', Miriam is called the babe's 'sister', and the infant is named, climactically, 'Moses'. Ashley deems it unlikely that the Amram of verse 58 is the same one as in verse 59, even though it appears the two are fused here and elsewhere (1993: 539–540; see the lists of Exod. 6; 1 Chr. 6:3). Nachmanides refers to Jochebed as a 'joyful mother of children' (cf. Ps. 113:9), as she gave birth to the redeemers of Israel (see 1975: 326), a worthy honour bestowed even more wondrously upon Mary (Luke 1:26–38).

Kohath's line focuses on the priesthood, continuing through Aaron to his four sons Nadab and Abihu, Eleazar and Ithamar, and recounting the deaths of the first two brothers when they offered 'unauthorized fire before YHWH'. The notice is nearly verbatim that of 3:4, except the latter passage states their death, in addition to their offering, was 'before YHWH' and 'in the wilderness of Sinai'. The genealogy of Numbers 3:1–4 also records that Nadab and Abihu 'had no sons' (or 'children'), which is likely the point here: their specific lines have been cut off. The genealogy in Number 3 had also signalled that to some extent the ensuing narrative would trace the Levitical line, and indeed the story transitions from Aaron to Eleazar (20:22–29) and then to Phinehas, Eleazar's son, who is granted the priesthood in perpetuity for his atoning deliverance of Israel (25:10–13).

In Numbers 3, tallies were given for each of the major clans, Gershon, Kohath and Merari, but this was because the purpose of their census was to assign their specific camps – westward (3:23), southward (3:29) and northward (3:35), respectively – and to assign their specific duties related to the Dwelling. Here only the combined total of 'all males from a month old and upward' is given, 23,000, marking an ideal increase from their previous total of 22,000 (3:39).

26:63–65

63. 'These are the ones appointed' (v. 63) forms an inclusion with the chapter's opening verses, and serves as a secondary concluding statement (following v. 51), this time incorporating the separately tallied Levites (vv. 57–62). Again, Moses and Eleazar are mentioned, as well as the census locale 'in the plains of Moab by Jordan near Jericho', a phrase that unifies the third major section of Numbers (26:3, 63; 33:48, 50; 35:1; 36:13).

64–65. This census with 'Moses and Eleazar the priest' is contrasted with the original census with 'Moses and Aaron the priest', the transition from Aaron to Eleazar encapsulating that of the first generation to the second, whom they represent, respectively. That 'there was not a man' left from the tally of the wilderness of Sinai demonstrates soberly both the faithfulness of YHWH to fulfil his word of judgement (14:20–35) and the perfection of the judgement itself. Both attributes are underscored further by the two exceptions, Caleb and Joshua. Of the nine references to Caleb in Numbers, he is always designated 'the son of Jephunneh' except twice (13:30; 14:24; cf. 13:6; 14:6, 30, 38, 65; 32:12; 34:19). Of eleven references, Joshua is always 'the son of Nun' except once (27:22; cf. 11:28; 13:16; 14:6, 30, 38; 26:65; 27:18, 22; 32:12, 28; 34:17). Caleb and Joshua are listed as a pair five times (14:6, 30, 38; 26:65; 32:12). The context of Numbers 13 – 14 singles them out as the two faithful scouts who gave a good report of the land and of YHWH's ability to bring them in. Eleazar the priest and Phinehas, who might have been born in Egypt (Exod. 6:23, 25), do not count as exceptions to 'not a man' since Levites had not been appointed with the rest of the tribes in the original census, and the decree of death in the wilderness pertained only to the outer camp of tribes (cf. Nachmanides 1975: 326; *b. Bav. Bat.* 121a). Twelve princes, one per tribe, along with Eleazar the priest and Joshua son of Nun, will be chosen to oversee the division of the land inheritance (see Num. 34:16–29).

The census closes with a contrast between those who 'die in the wilderness' and those who will inherit life in the land, underscoring the theme of death versus life, with the former associated with the old generation and the wilderness, and the latter associated with the second generation and the land. The land, as a place of divine abundance and lushness, is like a new Eden (cf. Ottosson 1988; Stager 1999). As Bick states, the summary statement in verses 63–65 signifies that 'the world of the desert is over' (2014c: 428). Psalm 37 proclaims that those blessed by YHWH 'will inherit the earth', while those cursed by him 'will be cut off' (v. 22) – the census of Numbers 26 functions as an exclamation point to this reality.

Explanation

YHWH charges Moses and Eleazar the priest to conduct a census of the Israelite community on the plains of Moab 'after the plague'. The census on the plains of Moab signals the end of the sojourn in the wilderness, a return to divine order and cosmos, in view of inheriting the land of Canaan.

Failing to appreciate the emergence of the second generation in Numbers 20, Olson regards chapter 26 as signalling questions such as (1996: 157): 'Will the second generation find a way to be faithful and enter the promised land, or will they rebel and fail as the first generation had done?' Such questions, however, were already asked and answered in chapters 21–25, and the census now forms a new stage, not of sojourn or trial and testing, but of anticipation and expectation: chapters 26–36 find their parallel, rather, in chapters 1–10, sections where the need for obedience remains but is almost assumed. The census after the plague is a result of the atoning act of Phinehas the priest, and ushers in a period of rest whereby the journey has finally ended and there is no more question over whether Israel will be brought into the land. The purpose of the census was not to signal the emergence of the second generation; rather, its purpose *explicitly* was to mark out the Israelite families that would inherit the land: 'to these the land will be divided for an inheritance' (26:53). To be sure, the analogy between a census for life in the Camp (Num. 1 – 4) and a census for life in the land (ch. 26) falls out according to the old and new generations, respectively

– but the second generation did experience its own wilderness sojourn (chs. 20–25) and at least 24,000 among them did not inherit the land (25:9). The questions that do remain all pertain to matters concerning the inheritance of the land; for example, whether Zelophehad will be divided his portion despite having no sons (27:1–11), and who will lead Israel into the land (27:12–23), what offerings will be brought once in the land (chs. 28–29), and whether tribes may settle on the east side of the Jordan (ch. 32). Although it does not signal the *emergence* of the second generation (which takes place in chs. 19–20), nevertheless the census, coming full circle in its recall of the original census (Num. 1 – 4), does officially confirm the replacement of the first generation, now that their children have completed the sojourn and are poised to inherit the land of Canaan – the census *defines* Israel's second generation as those who will inherit the land. The theme of succession pervades the final third of Numbers, seen, for example, in the daughters' preservation of Zelophehad's name and inheritance (27:1–11) and in Joshua's succession of Moses (27:12–23) (Hattin 2012: 295–298), although the transition stretches back to chapters 19 and 20, and to Eleazar's succession of Aaron as high priest (20:22–29).

While 'after the plague' looks back to the people's unfaithfulness and destruction, 'by Jordan near Jericho' looks forward to life in the land (cf. Hirsch 2007a: 533). Levine explains the threefold purpose of a census in the ancient world (2000: 307): (1) backward looking, to recapitulate recent history, summarizing changes since the last accounting; (2) forward looking, to take account of resources before embarking on a pursuit, such as a military or migratory campaign – in this case, the conquest and settlement of Canaan; (3) to serve as a basis for apportioning the land. Numbers 26 focuses primarily on the latter, the tribal inheritance of the land. The census also registers the fulfilment of YHWH's decree that the exodus generation would not survive the wilderness period, but also accounts for the more recent change within the second generation: 'after the plague'.

The entire old generation that died in the wilderness, along with the rebels mentioned in the glosses – Dathan and Abiram, Korah and his community – serve as warnings to the ensuing generations of God's people, not to imitate such rebellion. The apostle Paul accordingly warned the church that the wilderness stories function as examples, written for our admonition and humility – that we should take heed, lest we too fall (see 1 Cor. 10:1–12). That the inheritance of land was according to the size of each tribe after the wilderness sojourn, with its decimating judgements, is a reminder that this present life in the wilderness counts for ever, one's loyalty to YHWH now is worthwhile and has eternal significance for life in the renewed land later – the journey and its end are deeply related. The high-tally numbers, delineated by families related to the twelve sons of Jacob, recall God's promise to the patriarchs, that he would multiply their seed into a great nation (Gen. 12:2; 26:24; 46:3) – an agenda despised by the noted rebels Dathan and Abiram, with Korah's community (vv. 9–11; see ch. 16), Er and Onan (v. 19; see Gen. 38:2–9), Nadab and Abihu (v. 61; see Lev. 10:1–3) and the old generation who came out of Egypt (vv. 64–65; see chs. 13–14) (G. J. Wenham 1981b: 212–213). The exceptions to divine judgement in the wilderness, Caleb and Joshua, formed living banners to YHWH's faithfulness and the sure rewards of following closely after him.

The Midrash relates the census on the plains of Moab to a shepherd who numbers the entrusted flock upon his return, Israel having been entrusted to Moses for the journey out of Egypt to the Promised Land (*Num. Rab.* 21.7). David understood that YHWH is our shepherd, a reality that ensures all his people will arrive safely at his banquet house (Ps. 23). Jesus the Good Shepherd who laid down his life for the sheep avowed that no one can snatch any of his sheep out of his hand (John 10). The presence of Israel on the plains of Moab, these 'little ones' whom their faithless fathers had presumed would become spoils of the enemy (14:3), are a testimony to the character of God as entreated by Moses, 'YHWH is slow to anger and of abundant loving-kindness, forgiving guilt and transgression, but by no means clearing wholly' (14:18).

The real focus and purpose of the tally is the gift of land. YHWH had directed Abram to lift his eyes northward, southward, eastward and westward, promising, 'All the land which you see I will give to you and your descendants for ever (Gen. 13:14–15; cf. 12:1). The chief sin of the ten chieftains who had scouted the land was in slandering the land (13:32), leading to its loss by their entire generation. The second generation, journeying to possess the land, were blocked along the way, denied travel through the lands of other nations protective of their own territory: Edom (20:14–21), Arad (21:1–3), Amorites (21:21–30) and Bashan (21:33–35) – but now they encamp on the plains of Moab by Jordan, near the city that will become their first conquest within the land, Jericho. Hausoul makes three significant points about the Torah's theology of the land (2018): (1) As the creator of the whole earth, YHWH owns the land. As owner, he may freely grant land to the patriarchs and their descendants, and even the nations' possession of their lands derives from him (e.g. Deut. 2:2–5, 8–9). The tribes are tenants of YHWH, acknowledging him as Landowner through the offering of first-fruits and tithes, which belong to YHWH (Exod. 13:11–14; 23:19; 34:26; Lev. 19:23–25; 23:10; 27:28–33). (2) YHWH sovereignly gives the land to Israel, bringing them in and causing them to inherit Canaan. Not only is the land divided by lot (26:52–56), but other divine regulations ensure that the land remains the property of the family clans he has designated in the census (27:1–11; 36:1–12). The land never ceases to be his property, enjoyed as a favour from God. (3) YHWH's presence is in the land. By his sovereign determination, YHWH planned to live with his people in the land (cf. Exod. 15:17; Lev. 26:10–12), his special presence among them marking the good land as something of a return to Eden.

NUMBERS 27: SECURING THE INHERITANCE OF LAND

Translation

27:1Now the daughters of Zelophehad, the son of Hepher, the son of Gilead, the son of Machir, the son of Manasseh, of the clans of Manasseh, the son of Joseph, drew near; and these were the names of his daughters: Mahlah, Noah and Hoglah and Milcah and Tirzah. ²And they stood before Moses and before Eleazar the priest, and before the chieftains and the whole community, at the door of the tent of meeting, saying, ³'Our father died in the wilderness, but he was not in the midst of the community that gathered themselves against YHWH in the community of Korah; for he died through his own sin, and he had no sons. ⁴Why should the name of our father be removed from the midst of his clan because he has no son? Give us a holding in the midst of the brothers of our father.' ⁵So Moses brought-near their case before YHWH.

⁶And YHWH said to Moses, saying, ⁷'Rightly the daughters of Zelophehad have spoken. You will surely give them a holding of inheritance in the midst of their father's brothers, and cause the inheritance of their father to pass over to them. ⁸And to the sons of Israel you will speak, saying, "If a man dies and he has no son, then you will pass over his inheritance to his daughter. ⁹And if he has no daughter, then you will give his inheritance to his brothers. ¹⁰And if he has no brothers, then you will give his inheritance to the brothers of his father. ¹¹And if his father has no brothers, then you will give his inheritance to his nearest kin from his clan, and he will possess it. And it will be for the sons of Israel for a statute of judgement, just as YHWH commanded Moses."'

¹²And YHWH said to Moses, 'Ascend to this Mount Abarim (Mount of the Crossings), and see the land that I have given to the sons of Israel. ¹³And when you have seen it, then you also will be gathered to your people, just as Aaron your brother was gathered. ¹⁴For you (both) rebelled against my word (mouth) in the Wilderness of Zin in the contention of the community, to sanctify me through the waters before their eyes – those are the waters of Meribah (Contention) of Kadesh in the Wilderness of Zin.'

¹⁵Now Moses spoke to YHWH, saying, ¹⁶'Let YHWH, the God of the spirits of all flesh, appoint a man over the community, ¹⁷who will go forth before them and come in before them, who will lead them forth and bring them in, so the community of YHWH will not be as a flock that has no shepherd.' ¹⁸And YHWH said to Moses, 'Take for yourself Joshua son of Nun, a man in whom is the Spirit, and lean your hand upon him. ¹⁹And you will stand him

before Eleazar the priest and before the whole community, and you will charge (command) him before their eyes (as with water from rock). ²⁰And you will put some of your majesty upon him, so the whole community of Israel will heed. ²¹And before Eleazar the priest he will stand, and he will enquire for him with the judgement of Urim before YHWH. Upon his word (mouth) they will go forth and upon his word they will come back, he and all the sons of Israel with him, even the whole community.' ²²And Moses did just as YHWH had commanded him: he took Joshua and stood him before Eleazar the priest and before the whole community, ²³and he leaned his hands upon him and charged him, just as YHWH had spoken by the hand of Moses.

Notes on the text

1. 'the son of Manasseh': lacking in LXX, and Vg lacks 'the clans of Manasseh'.

4. 'a holding': SamP reads 'holding of inheritance' (cf. v. 7).

6. 'YHWH said . . . saying': two Hebr. MSS, SamP and LXX read 'YHWH spoke . . . saying'.

7. 'them', 'their': the first two occurrences are m. (*hem*) in MT but must be read as f., which is not unusual (cf. GKC §135*o*; Davidson, *Syntax* §1 Rem. 3); but some MT MSS and SamP use f., as with the final 'them' (*hen*) in the verse (cf. Paterson 1900: 61).

12–13. LXX appears to harmonize this verse with Deut. 32:48–50, reading Nebo instead of 'Abarim', adding 'of Canaan' to 'land' (as does Syr) and adding 'as an inheritance', and identifying 'Mount Hor' as the place where Aaron died.

17. 'go forth before them': *TgPs-J* glosses this phrase as pertaining to war.

20. 'majesty': from *hôd*; LXX, Syr and Vg read 'glory'.

23. 'hands': SamP and Syr read sg., and Vg lacks 'by the hand of Moses'; whereas LXX and *TgPs-J* read 'as YHWH/the Lord commanded Moses' in place of this latter phrase. SamP adds Deut. 3:21b–22 here.

Form and structure

Numbers 27 is comprised of two sections (vv. 1–11, 12–23), involving human-initiated requests, which uncover a problem (the loss of a father's name, and the loss of Israel's leader), and their resolution by divine response. Both problems look back to a sin in the wilderness sojourn (vv. 3, 14) that calls into question some aspect of the second generation's inheritance of land – a father's name and holding in the event he has no sons in the first instance, and how Israel will be led into the land in the second. Although the second scenario begins with a speech of YHWH

(vv. 12–14), it serves as the backdrop to Moses' request (vv. 15–17). The backdrop for the first scenario is in Numbers 26:33, an indication that chapters 26–27 form a unified unit. The motif of transition unifies the two major sections, as Zelophehad's inheritance 'passes' to his daughters (*'ābar*, 27:7, 8) and Moses is divinely called to ascend the 'Mount of Crossings' (*'ābar*, 27:12).

I. Daughters allotted land in place of their father Zelophehad (vv. 1–11)

A. The daughters of Zelophehad request a holding in the midst of their father's brothers (vv. 1–5)

1. The daughters of Zelophehad draw near before Moses, Eleazar, the chieftains, and the whole community at the door of the Tent of Meeting (vv. 1–2)
2. The daughters request a holding of land to keep their father's name from being removed from his clan (vv. 3–4)
3. Moses brings their case before YHWH (v. 5)

B. YHWH responds favourably, granting the daughters a holding of inheritance and establishing a statute for Israel (vv. 6–11)

1. YHWH concedes the justness of, and grants, the daughters' request (v. 6–7)
2. YHWH establishes a statute for Israel (vv. 8–11)

II. Joshua installed to lead Israel into the land in place of Moses (vv. 12–23)

A. YHWH tells Moses to see the land before he dies for rebelling against his word (vv. 12–14)

1. YHWH tells Moses to ascend Mount Abarim to see the land he is giving to the sons of Israel (v. 12)
2. YHWH tells Moses that after seeing the land he will die, just as Aaron had died (v. 13)
3. YHWH explains the cause for Moses' and Aaron's death as their rebellion against his word (v. 14)

B. Moses requests YHWH to appoint a man to take his place leading the community (v. 15–17)

C. YHWH appoints Joshua in place of Moses to lead Israel into the land (vv. 18–23)

1. YHWH tells Moses to install Joshua as Israel's next leader (vv. 18–20)
2. YHWH subordinates Joshua under Eleazar the priest (v. 21)
3. Moses installs Joshua just as YHWH had commanded (vv. 22–23)

The second section (vv. 12–23) forms a panel outline (Mattingly 2001: 193, with some rephrasing). (See Table 20.)

There is no reason the events of chapter 36 could not have taken place immediately after this episode with Zelophehad's daughters since the two stories are separated only to serve a compositional function. Indeed, as Frevel points out (2013a: 24 n. 91; cf. Tov 1998: 353–354), in the 4Q365 fragment 36, the framing function is suspended with Numbers 36:1 following immediately after 27:11. Taking the two daughters of Zelophehad passages (27:1–11 and 36:1–13) as one cycle, the case law may be structured as follows (Ben-Barak 2006: 14; cf. M. Douglas 2001: 102–126; Kislev 2010):

Segment 1: Story of Zelophehad's daughters (27:1–7)
Segment 2: Law of inheritance in Israel (27:8–11)
Segment 3: Story of the chief fathers of Manasseh and their claim (36:1–4)
Segment 4: Law of marital limitation for daughters who inherit property (36:5–9)
Segment 5: Story of Zelophehad daughters' compliance (36:10–12)

Table 20: Moses' prayer for a new shepherd

	I. YHWH solicits Moses' prayer, 12–17		II. YHWH satisfies Moses' prayer, 18–23
A	YHWH announces Moses' death, 12–14 1. Introductory identifier, 12a 2. Request, 12b 3. Leader issues, 13 4. Congregation issues, 14	A'	YHWH instructs Moses to install Joshua, 18–21 1. Introductory identifier, 18a 2. Request, 18b 3. Leader issues, 18c–20a 4. Congregation issues, 20b–21
B	Moses' prays for a new shepherd, 15–17 1. Introductory identifier, 15 2. Request, 16 3. Leader issues, 17a, b 4. Congregation issues, 17c	B'	Moses installs Joshua, 22–23 1. Introductory identifier, 22a 2. Response to request, 22b 3. Leader issues, 22c–23a 4. Congregation issues, 23b

Together with the account in Joshua, when they obtain their allotments of land, a complete story of the daughters of Zelophehad unfolds in three acts (Hunt 2010: 181–201): act 1, where the quest is introduced (Num. 27:1–11), act 2, where a complication arises and is resolved (36:1–13), and act 3, where the quest is finally realized (Josh. 17:3–6).

Comment

27:1–11

Women pervade the third major section of Numbers (chs. 26–36), which addresses issues related to women's vows (ch. 30) and to female captives of war (ch. 31). Most prominently, scenes related to the daughters of Zelophehad form a frame for the entire section (27:1–11; 36:1–13) (cf. Olson 1996: 165). Zelophehad's daughters, as with Ruth the Moabitess who became an ancestress of King David and eventually of the Messiah (cf. Ruth 4:13–22; Matt. 1:1–17), stand as exemplary women of virtue. Ruth, even as Tamar before her (Gen. 38), sacrificed herself for the sake of preserving the line of promise, conveyed in terms of preserving a deceased man's name (cf. Ruth 4:5). Similarly, the daughters' main concern is to keep their father's name from being removed (27:4). There is, perhaps, a contrast intended between the two sets of daughters noted in Numbers 25 and 27. The 'daughters' (*běnôt*) of Moab had committed harlotry with Israelite men, calling them away from YHWH to join Baal – one man shamelessly 'bringing near' (*qārab*) a Midianite princess before Moses and the whole community – leading to the swift destruction of many, who thus forfeited life in the land of Canaan (25:1–9). By contrast, the 'daughters' (*běnôt*) of Zelophehad courageously 'draw near' (*qārab*) Moses, Eleazar the priest, the chieftains and the whole community in order to preserve the name and inheritance of land on behalf of their dead father. One set of daughters brought death and destruction, while the other brings life and preservation – these are the forking paths of the immoral woman and the wise virtuous woman described in Proverbs (see Prov. 1:20–33; 5:1–23; 6:20–35; 7:1–27; 8:1–11; 9:1–18; 14:1; 31:10–31). More than this, and contrary to the faithless scouts alluded to in the preceding verse (26:65; cf. 13:31–33), these women stand as exemplary Israelites who demonstrate a robust confidence in YHWH's promise to grant the land of Canaan to the tribes of Israel. The Midrash, pointing out the language of 'not a man' (26:65), contrasts the men of the old generation, who were unwilling to enter the land, with the daughters of Zelophehad, who 'drew near to ask for an inheritance in the land' (*Num. Rab.* 21.10; see Slotki 1951: 6:836).

Given the bridal theology implicit in Israel's harlotry in Numbers 25, along with its connections to the strayed-woman ritual (5:11–31), whereby Israel is viewed from the vantage point of the nation's marriage-like covenant with YHWH, it is especially fitting that the first narrative glimpse of the second generation after its spiritual harlotry is of these five daughters of Zelophehad, who will close Israel's story with marriage in the land (36:10–12). The rabbis, writes Claassens (2013: 324), celebrated the daughters' love for the land. With their claim on the land, fully assured of YHWH's promise, and their zealous desire to preserve the name of their father, these women symbolize Israel as the faithful bride of YHWH.

1–2. Although the information had already been conveyed related to the census (26:28–34), the daughters of Zelophehad are honoured once more in being introduced according to their full sevenfold genealogy and by the formal notice of their names. They are introduced first as 'the daughters' of Zelophehad and then again 'his daughters' is noted before their names are listed, solidifying the link that will become the basis of their preservation of his name – they stand as a testimony to his presence in the narrative. Zelophehad's daughters are referenced in a variety of passages: Numbers 26:28–34; 27:1–11; 36:1–13; Joshua 17:1–6; 1 Chronicles 7:14–19, a feature taken by the Midrash as honourable recognition for their faithfulness and courage (cf. *Sif. Num.*, Pinḥas, v. 2) (see Shemesh 2007; cf. Ilan 1994). The fact that Zelophehad had no sons (26:33) is omitted here, to be mentioned in the daughters' speech (v. 3). Their drawing near (from *qārab*) recalls the recent occasion where an Israelite man 'brought near' a Midianite woman for spiritual harlotry (25:6). Within a juridical sphere, the act of drawing near indicates coming forward to present one's case, a formal appeal to leaders for an authoritative decision (Gane and Milgrom 2004: 138).

That they 'stood' (from *ʿāmad*) designates an official and formal occasion, as does the audience – 'before' (*lipnê*) Moses, 'before' Eleazar the priest, 'before' the chieftains and the whole community – and the locale, at the entrance of the Tent of Meeting, signifying 'before YHWH' inasmuch as this entrance 'directly evoked the presence of YHWH, supreme judge and lawgiver of the people in whose presence the most important juridical questions were presented and settled' (Cocco 2020: 134). The locale, beyond the appropriate space for legal proceedings, the 'locus of all legislation' after Sinai (Chavel 2009b: 12), implies the daughters are appealing to YHWH himself. This is the book's last of twelve uses of *petaḥ 'ōhel môʿēd* (door/opening of the Tent of Meeting), the last instance was in relation to Zimri's rebellion with the Midianitess (25:6), another link between the two texts (cf. Grossman 2007: 65). The echo to Zimri's flagrant display, 'bringing near' the Midianite woman before the eyes of Moses and all the community who were weeping at the 'entrance to the Tent of Meeting', may be intended to exhibit Zelophehad's daughters, in their petition of YHWH's goodness to keep their father's name among Israel in the land, as a reversal of Zimri's rebellion. The list of leaders before whom the daughters' appeal acknowledges the structure of the Camp, whereby Moses is linked to the central camp of the *Shekhinah*, Eleazar to the priests and Levites, which form the inner camp, and the chieftains, leaders of 'the whole community', represent the outer encampments of the twelve tribes. Their appeal, by contrast with Korah's rebellion, respects divine order. Aside from their commendable kinship loyalty, the daughters display deep conviction, courage and a strong desire for justice, by their coming before such an august gathering of Israel's highest leadership. The setting for the daughters' approach (as well as in 36:1–13 and Josh. 17:3–6) is that of the law court (cf. Hunt 2010: 188–190).

3–4. The daughters' speech begins with a statement of their father's death in the wilderness. The catalyst for their claim, and the logic of the episode's placement immediately following the census, derives from YHWH's recent words to Moses: 'To these the land will be divided as an inheritance, by the number of names' (26:52–53; Samet 2003). Fronting 'our father' before the verb, followed in the next clause by 'but he' (*wĕhû'*, again fronting the verb) emphasizes the contrast between Zelophehad and those who were in 'the community of Korah' who had gathered 'against YHWH'. The daughters quote nearly verbatim Moses' own assessment of Korah during the rebellion, that his 'community' (*'ēdāh*) had 'gathered themselves together against YHWH' (*hannō'ādîm 'al-yhwh*, 16:11), perhaps deliberately demonstrating that their own loyalties remained with YHWH and his community. As an apostate 'community' (*hā'ēdāh*), Korah and his followers were cut off from YHWH and his established covenant community, the Camp, and so had no claims on his promises of land. As Shemesh observes, the members of Korah's insurgency 'were punished by losing their rights of inheritance (and bequest) in the land' (2007: 85). Zelophehad's death is then explained (*kî*, 'for/because of') as 'through his own sin' (*bĕḥeṭ'ô*), presumably the comprehensive judgement of God on the first generation for embracing the land-slander of the ten faithless scouts (Num. 14:26–35; cf. Noth 1968: 211), some strands of Jewish tradition identifying the failed attempt at conquest in 14:39–45 as the occasion of his demise, while others identify him as the stick-gatherer in 15:32–36 (see *b. Shab.* 96b–97a) – noting the use of 'in the wilderness' (*bammidbār*) in both texts (15:32; 27:3). The latter is unlikely since, as a high-handed sin (see 15:30–31), Zelophehad would have merited being 'cut off', precisely the penalty his daughters are disputing in relation to the Korah incident. Cited by many (see e.g. Malamat 1988: 175–176; Blenkinsopp 1997: 54), the story of Naboth's vineyard is instructive (1 Kgs 21; cf. 2 Kgs 9:25–26): proclaiming, 'YHWH forbid!' Naboth was fully able to refuse even King Ahab of the inalienable patrimony estate of his fathers, yet by the (false) charge of blasphemy against YHWH and the king, meriting the punishment of being cut off (Lev. 24:10–16), his patrimony became forfeit, acquired by Ahab. Similarly, had Zelophehad been guilty of any treasonable activity, his inheritance-estate would have been forfeit, apart from any divine judgement leading to his physical demise – so the daughters' statement served to assure the court that there 'was no legal impediment to the transfer of Zelophehad's property to his lawful heirs' (Weingreen 1966a: 518, 521). Their plea implies the reverse: 'the fate pending over their father's inheritance risks causing an injustice within the midst of the people of Israel who are waiting to take possession of the promised land' (Cocco 2020: 139). Their declaration that their father 'died in the wilderness' parallels the closing verse of the previous chapter (26:65), supporting further the notion that Zelophehad died under this general judgement of God, not for a further particular deed of rebellion (cf. Nachmanides 1975: 328; Kislev 2013: 256). Especially in the light of the reference to Baal Peor (26:1; see Deut. 4:3–4), it is significant that the daughters assume no need to separate their father from Israel's harlotry with Moabite and Midianite daughters. The reason is simple: Baal Peor was the second generation's failure, not that of the first (see also Deut. 2:13–19).

Positively, the original judgement (14:29–30) included hope for that generation's children to inherit the land: 'But your little ones, which you said would be for prey, I will bring them in, so they will know the land which you have despised' (14:31) – *it is this divine promise the daughters are tenaciously claiming*. The daughters, in clarifying the nature of their father's demise, remove any obstacle to entitlement of Zelophehad's patrimony by his heirs (Ben-Barak 2006: 17), and perhaps also imply that their own irregular appeal was not meant to be understood as defying authority or God's established order as was the case with Korah's rebellious challenge (Shemesh 2007: 85; cf. Hunt 2010: 207). Fishbane understands their statement as alluding 'to the support their father Zelophehad gave Moses' contested leadership during the Korah affair', which 'helped allay any timidity' in their request (1986: 98–99). The phrase 'in the wilderness' also rhetorically distances the present moment from that (previous) context, further signalling that the 'wilderness era' has come to a close.

The account in Numbers 27 is one of four similarly structured legal stories in the Pentateuch, including Leviticus 24:10–23; Numbers 9:6–14; 15:32–36; and 27:1–11 (see Fishbane 1986: 98–105; Chavel 2009b). The episode parallels the Passover story in 9:1–14 in an especially similar way. Both accounts include the following:

1. A problem that threatens to *exclude* members from the community of Israel (9:6; 27:3).
2. A request for adjudication, similarly phrased (9:7; 27:4): *lāmmā* (Why?) + *gāraʿ* (remove).
3. Moses seeks YHWH's will on the matter (9:8; 27:5).
4. YHWH responds favourably, the particular case leads to new legislation (9:9–14; 27:6–11).

One may also add the final step of carrying out YHWH's solution, although this element occurs only in Numbers 15:36 and 36:10–12 (cf. de Vaulx 1972: 319). Both the Passover sacrifice and the inheritance of land form pillars of Israelite identity in Numbers: to be excluded from Passover, symbolizing the nation's redemption out of Egypt, was to have one's identification with Israel lessened, and, similarly, to have one's name removed from the list of inheritance in the land, the goal of the exodus out of Egypt and fulfilment of the divine promises to the patriarchs, was to be excluded from the membership and life of Israel (cf. B. P. Y. Lee 2003: 82; Rimon 2014a: 380). At just this point in the narrative, brimming over with the expectation of inheriting the land, the matter of who belongs to 'all Israel' surfaces, just as it did with the creation of the Camp in Numbers 9 – for, as Habel expressed (1995: xi), 'Land claims and communal identity are often inextricably interrelated.' The land, moreover, is defined as a place of divine justice through YHWH's ruling on behalf of the daughters of Zelophehad.

Having distinguished their father's death from the judgement that fell on Korah and his community, the daughters come to the situation from which the problem arises: 'he had no sons'. The critical issue is that 'the name of our father' will be 'removed' (from *gāra'*, 'diminished', 'withdrawn'), a crisis emerging from the fact that 'he has no sons' (stated three times, 26:33; 27:3, 4). In Israel, writes Davies (1981: 140), 'it was regarded as a great misfortune for a man to die without male issue' since such a fate 'would have meant the extinction of his family and his own annihilation'. One's '*šēm* (name) constitutes a reality that guarantees the bearer an existence, however hard to define, that endures beyond death' (A. P. Ross 1997). Samet (1997) observes that a man's name represented the metaphoric continuation of his existence on earth after his death, with the loss of his name and memory constituting a negation of his previous life, a grievous loss. Having one's children live in the same ancestral portion of land, he further explains, was a means of continuing a living connection from generation to generation. If Zelophehad's estate had transferred to his brothers (i.e. who are not direct descendants), rather than passing to his descendants, then his name would no longer have existed – because his land would not have passed to his own descendants. While the patronymic ('son of') ensured the continued memory of a father no longer living, the ongoing possession of his patrimony from generation to generation by his descendants also perpetuated his name (Cocco 2020: 140). The survival of one's 'name' thus depended on the family's continued maintaining of the ancestral estate (Westbrook 1991: 64).

The verb *gāra'*, which in a juridical context refers basically to 'depriving someone of something' (Ringgren 1978), further 'indicates the greatest calamity that could befall a man and his house, expressing one of society's greatest fears' (Ben-Barak 2006: 17–18), and may imply 'theft or erasure by another party' in contrast to 'being cut off' through one's own sin (Litke 2002: 214). The root *g-r-'* occurs in three stories in Numbers: once for the second Passover legislation (9:7), once for this daughters of Zelophehad legislation (27:4) and three times in the addendum to the daughters of Zelophehad legislation (36:3–4). Gevaryahu observed that the root carries the notion of hewing a chunk from the whole or 'to diminish, subtract, cut off', with the ancient legal principle 'that a group has the right to be kept intact' underlying all three stories: the daughters endeavour to keep the family name intact, while their uncles seek to keep the tribal lands intact, and the Passover claimants had wanted to keep the nation of Israel intact (2013: 109–110). Actually, although from different angles, each of the stories concerns membership in Israel (cf. Fishbane 1986: 99; Chavel 2009b: 15), along with the rights and privileges – anchored in the promises of YHWH – that such membership entails. Cocco rephrases the daughters' question, bringing out the dire implications (2020: 141): 'Why should the heritage which goes back to Manasseh, whose last proprietor in the line of descent was our father, be taken away from his family because he did not have any male heirs?' The allotment of land for his family has ultimately to do with whether Zelophehad's name will count in the census of Israel, by way of his female progeny (in seeking to preserve their father's name, the daughters were not 'the first feminists'; cf. Sakenfeld 1988: 41; Samet 1997; contra Ron 1998). In this way, the reference to the daughters in 26:33 is a result of the ruling in 27:6–7, added 'secondarily to indicate that the daughters ultimately inherited and became clans of their own' (Milgrom 1990: 230). The daughters' pursuit brings the essence of the census into focus; namely, 'landholding and the continuity of a namesake' (B. P. Y. Lee 2003: 85).

The dire situation is caused not by Zelophehad's death, but by his lack of sons to inherit, so that his name and house are not included in the census for inheriting a patrimonial estate, being wiped out from among the Israelites. As Levine discerned (2000: 346), 'their father's name would be deleted from the register of his *mišpāḥāh* [family, clan]'. Moreover, if his name is omitted from the list of family heads it may well be that the tribe of Manasseh itself will consequently receive a diminished share of land (cf. Jeyaraj 1989: 136). Noth observes that a person's name 'could be preserved only in association with the inheritance of land by his descendants' (1968: 211). Since the permanent allocation of land relates to those alive *on the occasion of the census*, at that point in time, moreover, the levirate process, is irrelevant (Litke 2002: 213). Whereas the *levir* (a woman's brother-in-law) is to propagate a son who will raise up the name of a deceased brother (Deut. 25:6; cf. Ruth 4:5), in Numbers 27 the perpetuation of Zelophehad's name is through the allocation and ongoing inheritance of land (cf. Sakenfeld 1988; Embry 2016: 35–37). Whether the tribe of Manasseh would have received a reduced portion of land, with Zelophehad's name not counting at all since he had no sons (cf. Stubbs 2009: 208), or even in the unlikely scenario that his portion of land would have gone to his brothers straightaway, the problem remains for Zelophehad's name (Samet 1997): his brothers, not being his direct descendants, would not continue his name – but, and this is their main point, the daughters of Zelophehad, as his daughters, his direct descendants, may continue Zelophehad's name by receiving his allotment of land and passing it on to their children. The main issue is Zelophehad's name, while the allocation of land is the application, becoming a means for preserving his name. As Meinhold observes, in the ancient world a 'name' includes 'everything that belongs to a person physically (one's own existence and family), materially (one's health and possessions), and spiritually (one's fame and honour)' (1985: 245; he cites van der Woude 1997). The land allotment, then, serves as something of a 'memorial' to the father's name (Rimon 2014a: 378). As Zelophehad was not in 'the midst of' Korah's community, his name should not be removed from 'the midst of' his family clan in the land allotment. Zelophehad's name is in danger of being cut off, not as due punishment, but simply because he begot no sons. The dilemma is phrased rhetorically as a question: *Why* should his name be removed . . . (just) because he had no sons? As he had sired five daughters, Zelophehad was clearly virile, but the dilemma arises simply because none of his children were sons (Russaw 2013: 187). As the entire old generation of fathers had died in the wilderness (excepting Joshua and Caleb), and the second generation will be given land as promised to the patriarchs, an underlying principle is clearly at work, that the sins of the fathers have not negated YHWH's promise and plan to give the land of Canaan to Israel – the episode serves to underscore this theological message.

Another principle at work is that families and the allocation of land to them are accounted by males, those with more sons receiving more land (Litke 2002: 213): 'The census had been done, and the lack of such males has meant that the house of Zelophehad does not count.' Since the tally had already taken place, having catalogued the current males who would inherit, levirate marriage was irrelevant – only allowing the daughters themselves to stand in as a 'just surrogate for a family' could resolve the matter (Litke 2002: 213). In any case, that levirate marriage, established so a deceased husband's 'name not be blotted out from Israel' (Deut. 25:6), is not mentioned implies that Zelophehad's wife had also died (cf. Noth 1968: 212; Budd 1984: 301; Sakenfeld 1988: 41; Levine 2000: 358). Having one's name removed from the list, not having a possession among his people, is a 'metaphoric death' – the issue is not merely about the family's inheriting but the family's *counting* among Israel and so being given land by YHWH (Litke 2002: 210, 214). A deep and abiding association between names and particular tracts of land is assumed. The daughters' plea flows directly out of the divine pronouncement on the purpose of the census (cf. Levine 2000: 341): 'For these the land will be divided as an inheritance *by the number of names (šēmôt)*' (26:53) – what will happen to the 'name' (*šēm*) of Zelophehad? Bergsma also brings up a possible implicit motivation, that the daughters are unmarried and their father has died without leaving them a dowry. To be destitute (i.e. dowry-less) might have meant being unmarriable, precluding any further descendants at all, so the ruling they proposed would provide 'both land and descendants for the "name" of Zelophehad' (2007: 120–121; for land as dowry, see Westbrook 1991: 163–164).

Zelophehad's daughters not only bring up the problem and its apparent injustice, but propose the remedy as well, using the imp. form 'Give to us' (*tĕnāh-lānû*) a holding in the midst of the brothers of our father. Since 'holding' (*'ăḥuzzā*) indicates not just any property but the portion of land received by inheritance upon a father's death, the daughters are asking to be 'included in the line of succession of the family of Manasseh' (Cocco 2020: 142). With loyal boldness, they claim the right to be named full heirs of their father's patrimonial estate, keeping it in their father's house (cf. Ben-Barak 2006: 18). In effect, they claim to 'be accorded the legal status of heirs and thus be entitled to inherit their deceased father's property' (Weingreen 1966a: 518). Rather than merely counting as Zelophehad's sons, they claim to be counted among Zelophehad's brothers – each one, as with Zelophehad himself, standing for a clan of Manasseh, a scenario that recalls Jacob's claiming of Joseph's sons as his own (Gen. 48:5). The term 'holding' (*'ăḥuzzā*) refers to an estate of property held solely by the *paterfamilias* of a house as an inalienable right, a patrimony, whereas 'inheritance' (*naḥălāh*) includes the notion of Israel's original possession of the land of Canaan, divided and granted out of YHWH's own inheritance (Ben-Barak 2006: 18–19; cf. Lev. 25:23–24, 41; *TWOT*, 32, 569).

5. As the situation had not previously been addressed, Moses seeks YHWH's will, 'bringing-near' (from *qārab*) the case or cause, possibly even the daughters' own 'resolution/judgement' (*mišpāṭ*), before YHWH. Their 'cause' (*mišpāṭān*) may form a wordplay with 'clan' (*mišpāḥāh*). Use of *mišpāṭ* means the daughters did not bring a mere request or plea to YHWH, but a judgement or argued right, 'a strong demand for justice' (Litke 2002: 214). Rather than indicating any weakness or deficiency on Moses' part, his bringing the case before YHWH serves to legitimize the ruling with divine authority, especially given its probable controversial nature (Cocco 2020: 152–153).

6–7. YHWH's response, literarily and thematically central (cf. Hunt 2010: 198), is definite in its favour, opening with 'Right' (*kēn*), assessing their cause as just, which goes beyond acquiescing to a request for land. The formula *kēn* + *d-b-r* (right + to speak) is exceedingly rare, occurring only three times in the Bible, twice related to Zelophehad's holding (27:7; 36:5) and once in Exodus (10:29), in each case representing 'a solemn ratification of something that has previously been affirmed by others' (Cocco 2020: 153). YHWH thus grants their remedy with emphasis: Moses will 'surely give' (*nātōn tittēn*) to them a 'holding of inheritance' (*'ăḥuzzat naḥălāh*), a 'hereditary holding' (Elitzur 2020: 503) in the midst of the brothers of their father, causing their father's inheritance to 'pass over' (*'ābar* in hiph. stem) to them. The const., which heaps patrimony nouns together, underscores their right. That YHWH begins by assessing their speech as just is significant, especially so within a book that recounts much evil speech – murmuring (11:1, 4–6; 20:3–5; 21:5) and slandering (12:1, 8; 13:31–33; 16:3, 12–14) – and even Moses' failed speech (20:8) (cf. Zornberg 2015: 263). In this context, as Orlinsky points out (1986: 31–32), *n-t-n* (give) carries the legal force of 'assign, deed, transfer, convey'. Use of *'ābar* may be restricted to the case of daughters (cf. Rashi 1997: 4:344), and represents YHWH's direct intervention in changing established practice (cf. Cocco 2020: 156). Calvin well observes that such a divine confirmation, given openly before the assembly, would have encouraged all of God's people to imitate the example of these five daughters, especially in their faith that God would soon fulfil his promise of the land (2003b: 4:256). How it pleases God when his people boldly claim his own promises, esteeming the very gifts he fervently desires to give them.

Litke outlines YHWH's three imp. statements as (2002: 215–216) (1) vindicating the daughters' claim, (2) granting the daughters' request, and (3) giving the daughters an honourable standing in the community (as heads of houses), understanding the phrase 'cause to pass' as 'a statement of transference of standing' in place of sons, who were normally thought of as extensions of the father. He is likely correct to distinguish the second and third imp. as a progression in YHWH's dealing with the daughters: not only are they made to take part in the land grant, but are also 'given the right of inheritance for their family' (2002: 216). Both m. and f. suffixes are used with reference to the daughters in verse 7, which may reflect the situation where 'female characters are thrust into roles typically occupied by males' (Embry 2016: 38; cf. Hirsch 2007a: 555). Particularly, the second statement, 'give *them* a holding of inheritance in the midst of *their* father's brothers', uses m. suffixes, while the third statement, 'cause the inheritance of *their* father to pass over to *them*', uses f. suffixes. If progression is intended, the idea may involve the movement from their status as daughters to that of wives/mothers: the land is received by the daughters in place of sons (m. suffixes), but the land will, from the wives/mothers (f. suffixes), eventually transfer to their sons.

Not simply the eldest daughter, but each of the five daughters will be treated as being in the place of Zelophehad, as one of the brothers of Zelophehad, so that in the ten shares that fell to Manasseh in the division of land, the five brothers of Zelophehad and the five daughters each receive one share (Josh. 17:3–6; cf. Hiers 1993: 128; cf. Elitzur 2020: 504–507; contra Snaith 1962: 310; 1966: 127; and Hunt 2010: 222, who, ignoring the five brothers, read the text as assigning each daughter the double-portion of a firstborn son). In this way, each daughter is treated as a son of Hepher, considered as 'heads of families regarding inheritance of the land', and, in sum, will hold about half of Manasseh's western territory, perhaps explaining the prominence of both the tribe and the daughters in Numbers (Bin-Nun 2011).

Through the daughters' case and YHWH's confirmatory ruling, Zelophehad's name is preserved – since his daughters have inherited 'from' him, Zelophehad has indeed received a portion, which remains with his descendants. The underlying sense seems to rest on the understanding that the generation of Israelites who had been delivered out of Egypt, including Zelophehad, had been granted the land by YHWH, formulating the possession of land now by the second generation as an 'inheritance' from the former generation's allotment. By 'inheriting' the land, the second generation upholds and continues the name of their fathers. Had the daughters not inherited land, their father's name would have been cut off. By inheriting land, they preserve Zelophehad's name. Perhaps all the fathers' names of the first generation are to be thought of as redeemed by their children (cf. Gane 2004: 742). While the previous generation had been faithless, this 'general sin' by which they themselves forfeited inhabiting the land, was not punished by YHWH with the penalty of being 'cut off'.

YHWH's speech is characterized by the term 'say' (*'āmar*) in verse 6, intensifies to the stronger 'speak' (*dābar*) in verse 8, and finally concludes with the even stronger term 'command' (*ṣāwāh*) in verse 11 (Litke 2002: 215).

8–11. The case settled, YHWH now directs Moses to convey to the sons of Israel a new statute of judgement, addressing similar situations in four tiers (cf. Lev. 25:48–49). Again, the daughters were not merely making a request to be granted, but making a case that an aspect of the land allotment system was unjust. YHWH, in commending the justness of their cause, therefore, adjusts and applies the legislation as a statute of judgement for all Israel. The collocation 'there is no son to him' (*bēn 'ên lô*) occurs only here and with reference to the Levirate law (Num. 27:8; Deut. 25:5).

The foundational command, expressed by *kî* ('if/when', v. 8), relates to the inheritance of daughters, whereas the secondary situations utilize the conditional *'im* (if) conjunction (vv. 9–11) (see B. P. Y. Lee 2003: 89–90). First, the scenario for a situation like that of Zelophehad, having no sons, is for the inheritance to 'pass over' to any daughters. Language for the 'passing' of property, used consistently in both narrative (v. 7) and legislation (v. 8), versus 'giving' as the standard language for inheritance along the male line, is apparently reserved for unusual situations of transfer, and may imply that the property will transfer through the daughter to her husband or son as an inheritance (*Sif. Num.*, Pinḥas, v. 134). Significantly, albeit in the absence of sons, Israelite daughters are divinely and legally established as legitimate heirs of patrimonial estates. Hiers is likely right to assume the inheritance of land includes only unmarried daughters (1993: 129), for whom the ensuing constriction in chapter 36 would be able still to apply. Second, if there is no daughter, then the inheritance is given to the brothers of the deceased father. Third, if the father has no brother, then the inheritance is given to the brothers of the deceased man's father, to his uncles. Fourth, if there is no uncle, then the inheritance is given to the nearest 'kin' (šĕ'ēr) of his family clan. Daughters, then, are granted priority above their uncles, grand-uncles and other nearest kin. Inheritance moves in a direct line of descent, applying to a parallel line, to a brother or uncle of the deceased, only as descendants of the deceased's father or grandfather, respectively (Hirsch 2007a: 558). The instructions, initiated by the daughters of Zelophehad, become a 'statute of judgement' (ḥuqqat mišpāṭ), bearing the weight of torah, 'as YHWH commanded Moses'. The designation 'statute of judgement' occurs again only in Numbers 35:29, related to God's provision of cities of refuge and the instructions related to the land's defilement through bloodshed.

In honouring their father's memory and name, the daughters of Zelophehad are themselves honoured and rewarded. The goal of their petition, and of the legislation that flowed from it, should not be lost: to preserve an Israelite's name – and through his name, his membership – among the community of God's people, and so retain the land given by God within his family as a legacy. By their appeal, the daughters of Zelophehad were demonstrating the preciousness of the covenant community, of the divine promise of land, and even of the goodness of the land, in a sense reversing the previous generation's rejection of the land (Num. 14:1–4). Their story is about inclusion in Israel and bears further significance in the ensuing drama (ch. 32), as half their tribe chooses to settle outside the boundaries of Canaan (Litke 2002: 210; cf. Lerner 2014: 57). While here Manasseh's claim to land west of the Jordan is central (Snaith 1966; Levine 2000: 360–361), the real focus is on YHWH's sovereign gift for all his people, including orphaned, husbandless daughters, who reveal a tenacious hold on his promises and demonstrate their confidence in his good and just character.

KINSHIP, LAND AND INHERITANCE IN ANCIENT ISRAEL: THE DAUGHTERS OF ZELOPHEHAD

Kinship in ancient Israel

With Ben-Barak we may define Israelite society as 'a three-tiered traditional structure united by ties of blood and kinship' (2006: 1; cf.

Bendor 1996: 45–47): (1) the *bēt 'āb*, the 'father's house', (2) the *mišpāḥāh*, the (extended) family or clan, and (3) the *šēbeṭ* or *maṭṭeh*, the 'tribe'. A fourth and largest social group, of course, was the nation itself, the whole community of the sons of Israel (cf. Stager 1985: 22; Matthews and Benjamin 1993: 7–9). The *bēt 'āb* consisted of three generations, possibly four, including wives and concubines, sons (natural and adopted), the wives of sons, daughters, grandchildren and servants, including temporary sojourners, the *gēr*, who came under the *bēt 'āb*'s protection while rendering labour. Many of Israel's customs, laws and world view were shaped by this smallest social unit, the *bēt 'āb*, which was patriarchal, led and ruled solely by the *paterfamilias*, typically the grandfather, and focused on the firstborn son as the legitimate agnate heir (descending through the male line) (Stager 1985: 20; Westbrook 1991: 12–14; Borowski 2003: 22; Ben-Barak 2006: 1–3). Jacob's household serves as a classic three-generation house (cf. Gen. 45:10; 46:6–7). Likely, tribal chiefs and elders, the *nāśī'* and *zāqēn*, including judges and military leaders, were drawn from among the heads of 'father's houses' (*bātēy 'āb*) (cf. Andersen 1969: 37). The father's house, moreover, was deeply connected to the land, with its economy, including the daily duties of each member, revolving around the land – for 'the Israelites were farmers' with a central 'agrarian identity' (Meyers 1997: 3, 18–21; cf. Bendor 1996: 134–140). A 'father's house', writes Westbrook (1991: 17), 'survives as long as the family property remains intact; it is the decision to divide the property rather than the father's death which changes the structure of the family, breaking it up into a series of new, independent houses, each with its own head'.

The *mišpāḥāh* was comprised of several father's houses, each including three or four generations, with kinship circles broadening to the brothers of the *paterfamilias*, the brothers of his father and the next of kin, forming a clan (cf. King and Stager 2001: 36–38). The largest subdivision of a tribe, the clan, formed a 'protective association of families', with families here referring to fathers' houses (Gottwald 1999: 257), and 'often corresponded to a whole town or village community' (Bimson 1988: 119; cf. Meyers 1997: 13). Similarly, Wright describes the *mišpāḥāh* as 'a grouping of several family units into a largely self-sufficient and self-protective organism' (1990: 48–49). This 'kin group', he further adds, was the most important social unit to which an Israelite belonged, and comprised a territorial unit with a key role in Israel's system of land tenure, with the kin group name even serving as something of a person's geographical address (1990: 49–50; following Andersen 1969). In essence, 'the *mišpāḥāh* is the kinship unit intermediate between the "tribe" (*šēbeṭ*, *maṭṭeh*) and the ancestral "household" (*bayit*, *bēt 'āb*)' (Blenkinsopp 1997: 50). Naturally enough, however, these terms are relative, so that a 'tribe' (*šēbeṭ*, *maṭṭeh*), comprised of several *mišpĕḥôt*, may be referred to by its originating patriarchal house, and *mišpāḥāh* may even be used as a synonym for 'tribe' (cf. Andersen 1969: 35; Bendor 1996: 67–86). The 'tribe' of Levi, for example, may be referred to as the *bēt 'āb* of Levi, and the head of Levi's tribe may be called the head of the house of their fathers (cf. Num. 17:3), while the chieftains over clans may also each be called a 'chief of the house of the father of the Gershonites' (Num. 3:24) – and the twelve patriarchal sons, whose houses eventually formed tribes, originally belonged to the great 'father's house' of Jacob. Levine's attempts to distinguish between 'house' (beneath the clan level) and 'father's house' (above the clan level) are, therefore, unnecessary, and scriptural usage does not support his distinction (cf. Bendor 1996: 54–56) – when Joshua, for example, spares Rahab's 'father's house' (*bêt 'ābîhā*), it is clearly defined as a house beneath the clan level, with father, mother, brothers and possessions (cf. Josh. 6:23, 25). Broadly conceived, the four-tiered structure – from nation or whole community, to tribe, to clan, to father's house – presents the basic form of Israelite society, and is especially clear in certain passages, such as when Achan was singled out by lot, through concentrically decreasing social units (Josh. 7:14): first, one 'tribe' (*šēbeṭ*) was taken out of the twelve (out of the nation of Israel), then one 'clan' (*mišpāḥāh*) was taken out of the many within the tribe, and then one 'house' (*bayit*) was taken out of the several within the clan, and, finally, the 'man' himself (*geber*) was taken (see also 1 Sam. 10:20–22). In Numbers, the first census moves from the whole 'community' to the 'clans' to the 'father's house' to every 'male' (*zākār*), and while the tribe level is not noted, chieftains from each of the twelve tribes are chosen to help conduct the count, clearly inserting tribes between the whole community and its clans (1:1–5). The term *'elep* is sometimes used with a meaning closely related to *mišpāḥāh*, as a subdivision of a tribe (Judg. 6:15; 1 Sam. 10:19, 21; 23:23; Mic. 5:2), likely with military connotations (Andersen 1969: 36; Dybdahl 1981: 41–42; Bendor 1996: 94–97; Meyers 1997: 13; cf. HALOT 59–60).

Land in ancient Israel

The terminology related to land used in Numbers includes *naḥălāh* and *'ăḥuzzā*. The root *n-ḥ-l* occurs 46 times in noun forms and 13 more times in verbal forms. The first use occurs in 16:14, followed by 9 uses in chapter 18 (vv. 20–26); aside from those 10 instances, the rest – 49 occurrences – appear in chapters 26–36, culminating the book with the sure hope of life with YHWH in the land of inheritance (7 times in ch. 26; 6 times in ch. 27; 5 times in ch. 32; 4 times in Num. 33:54; 7 times in ch. 34; 3 times in ch. 35). The noun *naḥălāh* is regularly defined as 'inheritance, hereditary possession, inalienable property' (*HALOT* 1.687; BDB 635), with the emphasis falling more 'upon possession generally than upon the process of succession, though this idea is not altogether absent' (Nixon

1962: 562). The verb *n-ḥ-l* is used for obtaining a patriarchal estate, while *y-r-š* signifies acquiring or taking possession of alien property (Lipiński 1998: 320–321). Forshey critiqued the typical 'inheritance' translation of *naḥălāh*, which he linked to a nomadic understanding of Israel, and proposed 'possession' instead, suggesting a feudal model whereby the apportionment of land is seen as land grants from YHWH to his devoted servants, primarily for military service rendered (1972: 233–235; cf. Dybdahl 1981: 55–58). While not offering a precise definition, Horst (1961) noted the connection between *naḥălāh* and the social sphere (even if his view of communal land tenure is rejected), implying a relationship to the clan. Dybdahl, noting parallels with *ḥ-l-q* (divide, share), observes that *naḥălāh* often has the connotation of referring to a part, share or portion of land in relation to the whole, and offers 'share, portion' as a definition (1981: 59–60). He further draws out that in Numbers (and Joshua) Levites receive no *naḥălāh* (18:20, 23, 24; 26:62), or *ḥeleq* (18:20), yet they do receive cities and pasturelands for their use, leading to an understanding of *naḥălāh* as *a portion or share of agricultural land*; that is, *farmland* specifically. He cites Dathan and Abiram's complaint that Moses had not given them a *naḥălat* of field and vineyard; that is, agricultural land. In Joshua 21:11–12, moreover, he also points out how the city of Hebron and its pastureland was given to Levites, while Caleb retained Hebron's 'field' (*śādeh*) and its villages – agricultural villages and farmlands (and not cities) being the basis of *naḥălāh*. With these observations, Dybdahl narrows the definition of *naḥălāh* to the right to a portion or share of something that is a means to a livelihood, having primary reference to agricultural land: the 'right to a share of land for living and farming' – a 'right' since YHWH God is the land's owner, giving a portion of it to Israel for their livelihood (1981: 60–62). YHWH's sovereign ownership of the land served 'to justify and explain the inalienability of patrimonial domain' (Blenkinsopp 1997: 54). The Levites, as a non-agrarian, priestly tribe, have a right to 'cities' (*'ārîm*) and 'pasturelands' (*migrashîm*), but not to *naḥălāh* farming land – not to 'fields' (*śadōt*). However, the tithes (as the produce of Israel's *śadōt*, the fruit of the *naḥălāh* of the other tribes) and sacrifices of Israel become the *naḥălāh* of Levites: as a means of their own livelihood and reward for their service, they receive of the fruits of the *naḥălāh* of the other tribes. In this sense, YHWH and the lay-priestly service may be called the *naḥălāh* of Levites (Num. 18:20; Deut. 10:9; 18:2), just as Israel may be considered YHWH's own share, his livelihood in terms of revealing himself to the nations (Dybdahl 1981: 62–63, 81). The translation 'inheritance' is thus misleading since the term at a basic level refers to 'apportioned land', with each of its part called a 'portion', *ḥeleq* (Kennett 1933: 73–74; cf. Malamat 1988: 172). However, given the inalienability of the ancestral patrimony, the land was normally transferred only through inheritance. Habel sums up the matter helpfully (1995: 35):

A *naḥalah* is a rightful share or allotment, an approved entitlement to land, property, or people . . . A *naḥalah*, in its primary meaning, is not something simply handed down from generation to generation, but the entitlement or rightful property of a party that is legitimated by a recognized social custom, legal process, or divine charter. Only in familial contexts, where the head of the ancestral household gives the *naḥalah* to children, does a derived meaning of 'inheritance' fit this term (Ruth 4:5–6; Judg. 11:2; Num. 27:7).

Within Numbers, *naḥălāh* has 'patrimony' or 'ancestral estate' in view.

All twelve occurrences of the root '-ḥ-z (holding, possession) fall within the final division of Numbers (chs. 26–36), in four groupings: (1) daughters of Zelophehad, 27:4, 7; (2) spoils given to the Levites, 31:30, 47 (designating a 'portion'); (3) Gad and Reuben's land east of the Jordan, 32:5, 22, 29, 32; (4) cities of refuge legislation, 35:2, 8, 28, and is usually translated as 'possession, holding, landed property' (*HALOT* 1.32; BDB 28). Differentiating '*ăḥuzzā* from *naḥălāh* is not a simple matter, as the terms are closely associated. Gerleman (1977) concluded that '*ăḥuzzā* refers not simply to property or possession, but specifically to a tillable area, land able to be cultivated, given for Israel's use. His distinction between *naḥălāh* as *Wohnrecht* (right of residence) and '*ăḥuzzā* as *Nutzrecht* (right of use), however, appears too sharply demarcated; whereas Dybdahl found the usage of these terms – at least in Numbers and Joshua – to be nearly synonymous (1981: 65). Lipiński regards '*ăḥuzzā* as a 'possession' that usually refers to land, implying a legal right of ownership. Noting that the tribe of Levi has an '*ăḥuzzā*, but without receiving a *naḥălāh*, he writes (1998: 321):

> Strictly speaking, *nḥl* refers only to an allotted portion to which one has a claim by right of inheritance, while '*ḥz* refers to all the property that one has actually acquired, whether by purchase or by some other bilateral transaction, gift, inheritance, prescription, usucapion, or the like.

Habel makes the following distinction (1995: 105):

> The term '*aḥuzzah* normally designates acquired property used for cultivation. This term is to be distinguished from *naḥalah*, which is a wider concept covering any land or portion of land to which a person or group is entitled by charter, decree, allotment, or inheritance.

It may be that while the daughters of Zelophehad had asked for a 'holding' ('*ăḥuzzā*), YHWH in fact grants them more by referring to the land as *naḥălāh*, denoting a lasting heritage preserved through inheritance. Milgrom's distinction is helpful (1990: 232): '*ăḥuzzā* denotes 'inalienable property received from a sovereign', while *naḥălāh* refers to 'inalienable property transmitted by inheritance', so that 'the land seized by the Israelites (*'ăḥuzzā*) will become their inheritance (*naḥălāh*)'.

Canaan as YHWH's land

Regarding Israel's possession of land, the starting point is YHWH's ownership and sovereign authority: 'The land must not be sold in perpetuity, because the land is mine – so you are but guests and my tenants' (Lev. 25:23). YHWH's possession of the land was the theological rationale for Israel's system of land tenure and the principle of inalienability (Wright 1990: 58). He granted Israelites tenancy in his land, and they gratefully returned to him of its bounty and firstfruits, and rendered homage and worship to him solely. In terms of distribution and ownership among Israel, Dybdahl makes a case for land control in the hands of the *mišpāḥāh* leaders (1981: 53–54; cf. Henrey 1954): The *mišpāḥāh* was the basic land holding entity during the settlement period, rather than the *bēt 'āb* or individual Israelite. An individual's apportionment of land was temporary, depending on his membership within the *mišpāḥāh*, which required military service and the working of the land, presumably as part of his 'father's house', since the *bēt 'āb* was the key farming or land-working unit. As such, the *bēt 'āb* would receive a portion of the land under the supervision of the *mišpāḥāh*, which could redistribute apportionments on the Jubilee year, adjusting land allocation according to the proportional growth or decline of its various fathers' houses, changing the actual size and shape of their lots. The Jubilee, Dybdahl proposes (1981: 73, 74), was the time 'when clan land was "released" from its present users and redistributed by lot to the "fathers houses" of legitimate *mišpāḥāh* members', and served to keep individual *bātēy 'āb* 'from getting a permanent hold on more than their fair share of *mišpāḥāh* land'. Dybdahl further suggests this land holding structure manifests the concern of the chiefs of the *mišpaḥat* of Gilead in Numbers 36 (1981: 68–70). If Zelophehad's daughters married outside the tribe of Manasseh, transferring their holdings to their husbands, then at the time of Jubilee, when the land was redistributed, land would be lost to the *mišpāḥāh* since the aggregate amount of land would have been diminished. Even though the regulation is to keep land from transferring among tribes (36:9), he supports his argument with Moses' three statements that the daughters must marry within their *mišpāḥāh* (not simply within their tribe), thus keeping the land within the ownership and supervision of the clan (see vv. 6, 8, 12). The *mišpāḥāh*'s common land would be parcelled out to its various *bātēy 'āb* for communal reaping, not only a practical custom but a social event as well (cf. Ruth 2:3; Dybdahl 1981: 88). Along similar lines, Lipiński avers that in some cases *'ăḥuzzā* signifies 'collective property' (Gen. 17:8; 36:43; 48:4; Lev. 14:34; etc.), which belonged to the *mišpāḥāh*, the clan (1998: 327). In this construct, a sonless marriage becomes a crisis for the *mišpāḥāh*, which kept a tenacious hold on its land, preserving its boundaries. Dybdahl's proposal is helpfully mitigated by his conceding that vineyards, orchards and vegetable gardens were likely privately held and not redistributed, able to be passed on as an inheritance to future generations, while woodlands and pasture lands were probably held as commons for use as the need arose – the grain-producing fields being the primary holdings of the *mišpāḥāh*, apportioned to the *bātēy 'āb* as a form of communal tenure (Dybdahl 1981: 96; cf. Kennett 1933: 77).

It may well be that *some* grain-producing fields were held in common by the *mišpāḥāh*, which allowed for communal efficiency in their sowing and harvesting, while village homes, vineyards and other property (including family burial plots) remained within the inalienable estates of each *bēt 'āb*'s possession. The legislation of Numbers 36 concerns especially the lands as divided among the tribes – the tribe, as von Rad observed (1966: 86), 'was the trustee of the *naḥălāh*, and held the ultimate title to the land over and above the family'. Narrowly, however, Wright is probably correct that YHWH's ownership of the land (Lev. 25) ensured the security of individual families; that is, each *bēt 'āb* – by preventing permanent alienation of their land, so that each family head regarded his land holding as derived from the hand of YHWH, given to him from God (1990: 63; cf. Perdue 1997: 234–237). Wright observes how, as YHWH's *gērîm* ('sojourner, temporary resident', Lev. 25:23), Israelites had the right to dwell in the land, residing as it were in his house, enjoying his security and protection (1990: 64). It is within this context that Scripture repeats the divine injunction 'You must not move your neighbour's boundary stone, set up in ancient times, in the inheritance you will inherit in the land that YHWH your God is giving you to possess' (Deut. 19:14; cf. 27:17; Job 24:2; Prov. 22:28; 23:10), for the 'boundaries of a family's estate were marked by cairns of stones' and the 'loss of the landmarks amounted to loss of a family's claim to its land' (Bimson 1988: 127). Against formerly widespread notions of communal lands controlled by the *mišpāḥāh*, and periodically redistributed to different families, Wright points out that institutions such as inheritance, levirate marriage and the Jubilee functioned emphatically to protect family (*bēt 'āb*) land, with families forming a strong attachment to their land, especially in connection to the ancestral burial place (1990: 69; cf. Lipiński 1998: 326–327; King and Stager 2001: 39–40). 'The family was attached to the soil,' writes Brichto (1973: 5), 'as the notion of the burial place as the ancestral home was extended to the surrounding fields'. Moreover, maximizing the limited potential of particular farmlands required 'family-specific ecological knowledge', a familiarity that comes only from the generational experience of tending patrimonial lands (Meyers 1997: 30). As already noted, it is probable that outside family patrimonies there was some land that was communal and even occasionally redivided, land – *migraš* (open land, pasture) and *śādeh* (field) – that was cultivated or used for pasturage (conceded by Wright 1990: 70; cf. Ps. 16:5–6; Mic. 2:5). Nevertheless, the *bēt 'āb* 'was the basic unit of the land-tenure system, each family and lineage having its own inheritance (*naḥălāh*; Num. 27:8–11)' (King and Stager 2001: 48). The emerging portrait, as Jeyaraj explains, is that there was 'ownership of land by families and a common use of the territory by all the members of the tribe' (1989: 132; on land redistribution, see Bendor 1996: 141–160).

Name and patrimony

The inheritance process was designed to preserve the two main components of the *bēt 'āb*'s integrity (Ben-Barak 2006: 3–5, for the rest of the paragraph): (1) the father's name and memory, and (2) the patrimony estate, which was the *bēt 'āb*'s 'economic, social, and legal basis, from generation to generation'. During the life of the *paterfamilias*, grown sons who married and begot children remained within their father's house, contributing to the main *bēt 'āb*. Upon the death of the father, the estate lands would pass to his natural sons, with the firstborn, who as chief heir would carry on the ancestral traditions, likely inheriting a double-portion (cf. Deut. 21:15–17; 2 Kgs 2:9; Blenkinsopp 1997: 72; King and Stager 2001: 47–48). Daughters would, conventionally, leave their father's house upon marriage, helping their husbands to establish houses for themselves. The great crisis facing any *bēt 'āb* would be the lack of an heir, typically the absence of sons to inherit, threatening the 'name' and patrimony of the father with extinction – this is the traumatic predicament addressed by the daughters of Zelophehad (27:4). A father's name and estate were linked in a profound way – indeed, 'name' may even refer to the inheritance itself (Neufeld 1944: 47). Meyers writes (1997: 21): 'The identity of any family unit was . . . inseparable from its land, which was the material basis of its survival.' A man's 'name', writes Ben-Barak (2006: 18), 'exists only in connection with his patrimony, the two principles inseparably intertwined in the foundation of the *bēt 'āb*'. Indeed, there was 'a sacrosanct link between a man's name and his land' (Hunt 2010: 194). In 2 Samuel 14, the prospect of losing her last son leads a widow to exclaim that the destruction of the heir would leave her husband with neither 'name' (*šēm*) nor 'remnant' (*šě'ērît*) on the ground (v. 7). With 'remnant' (from *šā'ar*) likely referring to descendants, 'name' here probably refers to her husband's estate, although, again, the two concepts are so intertwined that both may be in view.

Keeping the household and its land together was the aim of many of Israel's laws and institutions, whether Jubilee requirements (Lev. 25:10,

28), levirate marriage (Deut. 25:5–6; Ruth 4:10) or laws of redemption (Lev. 25:23–34), and many biblical stories centre on 'the preservation of the family on its ancestral land (e.g. Gen. 38; Ruth 2; 2 Kgs 4:1–7; 8:1–6; Neh. 5)' (Bimson 1988: 127; Meyers 1997: 20). A widow's children would support her, but if they were still young, she likely 'administered their *naḥălāh* as guardian (Prov. 15:25; 23:10)' (Lipiński 1998: 326). Presumably, a widow had legal charge or usufruct rights over the estate in the absence of sons but did not inherit it (see 2 Kgs 8:1–6; Ruth 4:3; cf. Bimson 1988: 130; Lipiński 1998: 325) – although the possibility that a widow without an adult son could inherit her deceased husband's property should not be excluded (so King and Stager 2001: 53; cf. Westbrook 1991: 65; Hiers 1993: 130–134). Through the levirate process, whereby the deceased man's brother sired a son with the widow, an heir could be raised to inherit the estate and continue the 'name' of the *paterfamilias* (her previous husband) who had died – one of the major functions of the levirate law being 'to assure retention of ancestral property within the family or clan' (Hiers 1993: 135; cf. Westbrook 1991: 74), preserving the close connection between patrimony and the *bēt 'āb* (or 'name'). That the possibility of levirate marriage, which is also concerned that the deceased husband's 'name not be blotted out from Israel' (Deut. 25:6), is not brought up in the case of Zelophehad leads to the presumption that his wife had also died (cf. Noth 1968: 212; Budd 1984: 301; Sakenfeld 1988: 41; Levine 2000: 358).

The concept of continuing a name apparently did *not* involve taking on the deceased father's actual name, perhaps because his name was so deeply linked with the land itself, rendering such a literal application unnecessary. Ancients understood 'name' in ways that went beyond an appellation, but include one's estate, the permanent place of lineage. The word 'name' may even have the metonymic force of 'family line', as observed by Brichto (1973: 22), so that 'raising up a name' stood for 'raising up a seed' (cf. Gen. 38:8 with Ruth 4:5, 14). When Saul, for example, confessed his knowledge that David would be established as king over Israel, he asked David to swear an oath before YHWH neither to 'cut off my seed' nor to 'destroy my name from my father's house' (1 Sam. 24:22; cf. Ps. 109:13–15), bringing the two ideas into parallel. The profound connection of patrimony and 'name' underlies the request by Zelophehad's daughters. As Noordtzij explains (1983: 253), 'Since Zelophehad had only daughters, and thus no heir, his family could not receive any land when Canaan was divided, and consequently his name would no longer exist in the Israelite community.' The continued existence of a man's 'name', as Noth perceived (1968: 211), 'could be preserved only in association with the inheritance of land by his descendants'. Neufeld suggested that 'name' in the speech of the daughters of Zelophehad may refer to 'property' (1944: 47), an observation that has exegetical merit, given the parallel statements in verse 4:

Why should the *name* of our father be removed from the midst of his clan . . . ?

Give us a *holding* in the midst of our father's brothers.

Westbrook similarly understands name and place to be deeply connected here, likely referring to 'landed estate', and further posits that 'name' was used as a legal term for 'title' (1991: 75; cf. Levine 2000: 346).

Land and covenant community

Obtaining a portion in the land of Canaan can be appreciated as supremely significant especially within the context of the covenant community. YHWH's goal of dwelling among his people, the chief reality of Israel's covenant relationship with him, was entering a new era, life in the land. A place in the land, therefore, was tantamount to membership in the covenant community no less so than one's place in the wilderness Camp among the tribes surrounding YHWH's central Dwelling – this is the significance of both census accounts (chs. 1–4, 26). 'Thus,' as Litke states (2002: 208; emphasis original),

> having a land possession within Israel became tightly related to keeping the name of a family within the lists of the people of God. Conversely, *to have one's name cut off* means variously to be . . . removed from membership in the covenant people, or killed.

Likely, the tower builders have something of this idea of place and the permanence of one's name in mind when they exclaim, 'Come, let us build a city and a tower, whose summit will reach into the heavens – let us make a name for ourselves, lest we be scattered upon the face of all the land' (Gen. 11:4). The loss of one's memory from the land, the loss of one's 'name', means to be 'cut off' in biblical terms – the *bêt'āb*, including not only lineage but patrimony, is destroyed and irrevocably lost. To be sure, in the regular process of inheritance natural sons were rarely given their father's name, and the same applies with the levirate process (Davies 1981: 141), but they still continued his 'name' nevertheless – perhaps because having belonged to his father's *bēt 'āb*, and still belonging to the patrimony connected to that *bēt 'āb*, remains a permanent aspect of the son's identity, his lineage and geographical address even after the father's death. The inheritance itself preserves the father's name, continuing the patrimony within the family's *bēt 'āb* (Ben-Barak 2006: 18). The 'name of the deceased is preserved as long as his descendants remain associated with his property' (Davies 1981: 142). In Genesis, Jacob blessed Manasseh and Ephraim, saying: 'in them let my name be perpetuated, and the name of my ancestors Abraham and Isaac; and let them grow into a multitude on the earth' (48:16; tr. King and Stager 2001: 42). As the Thompsons express it (1968: 87):

> In Israel a man's 'name' comes to mean his property to such an extent that his name achieves thereby an existence separate from his own person. On the other hand, his person is continued through his progeny. The effort, therefore, to maintain one's name becomes precisely the effort to keep progeny and property (name and person) together; i.e., to keep one's property within his immediate family.

Having explained that the death of their father, who had no sons, should not result in the cutting off of his name, the Zelophehad daughters claim a 'holding' among their father's brothers (Num. 27:3–4). Similarly, in Psalm 37 the wicked will be 'cut off', while the righteous will 'inherit the land' (v. 9), the latter's 'inheritance' or 'estate' (*naḥălāh*, v. 18) being assured – being 'cut off' forming the polar opposite fate of obtaining and retaining one's land of inheritance (see Brichto 1973: 26–27).

Land and daughters

On the rare scenario that property was given to a woman while in her father's house, such property would remain with her and eventually pass on to her husband's patrimony through her sons (Ben-Barak 2006: 6), precisely the concern raised by Zelophehad's brothers (Num. 36:3–4). For the sake of her security and future well-being, and reflecting concern for daughters in Israel, it was customary for a daughter to be given upon marriage a dowry (such as money, clothing and furniture), all or part of the bride price paid to her father by the groom or groom's father, and other gifts, which remained rightfully hers even within marriage and served as some provision in case of divorce or widowhood (Ben-Barak 2006: 5–9). A *paterfamilias* having daughters but no sons might have had the opportunity to adopt a son-in-law so that the first of his grandsons, and perhaps all of them, would count as his own heir, preserving his name and patrimony. Such a scenario may explain why the son of Hezron of the tribe of Judah, born through Hezron's marriage to the daughter of Machir, appears to continue his mother's line, with his own son Jair remaining in Gilead – assuming Hezron's marriage occurred *before* Machir begot sons (cf. Ben-Barak 2006: 83, and 71–77, perhaps the situation with Laban's daughters in Gen. 29 – 31). Whether such a development occurred with Zelophehad's daughters when they married their cousins, namely, that their sons and patrimony remained within the household of the deceased father (Zelophehad), as Ben-Barak appears to assume (cf. 2006: 102, 106–107; so also Dybdahl 1981: 69), is hard to discern. It may well be, as Andersen suggests (1969: 36), the patrimony estate was so closely (and 'indissolubly') connected to the family name that, on the scenario where a man married into a patrimony held by daughters, the husband necessarily forfeited his own patronymic. The tribal chiefs of Manasseh, however, certainly do not appear to assume such a scenario as they bring their concern to Moses (Num. 36).

It was not uncommon in the ANE for daughters, in the absence of sons, to inherit the patrimony (see Ben-Barak 2006; cf. Milgrom 1990: 482; Russaw 2013: 24–25). By assuming a late date of composition for Numbers 27:1–11, various scholars question the purpose of the Zelophehad story, asserting that inheritance laws related to daughters were already established in Israel, as well as in the wider ANE (e.g. see Aaron 2009: 5–7) – a presumption that neglects the narrative's context. Before Israel possessed the land of Canaan, inheritance laws were irrelevant, and the narrative of Zelophehad's daughters is presented as the precedent for the statute that follows, a claim supported by the verbal links between the story and law, as well as by the prominence given to the Zelophehad daughters by the repeated listing of their names and by their literary placement, shaping the book's structure (the inclusio of chs. 27, 36). Without the daughters' divinely justified case, allowing them to 'count' as sons, moreover, *there would be no land to inherit*, for Zelophehad's house would not have counted in the census – that is the main point at issue, obtaining the land grant in the first place, with the ensuing legislation providing for later (related but different) scenarios regarding inheritance alone.

Historical evidence by way of archaeological and geographical findings suggest the daughters' prominence, as cities in central Israel, within the mountainous regions of Manasseh's tribe, can be linked by name to each of the daughters of Zelophehad. In 1910 in the storehouse of the fortress city of Samaria, some sixty-three ostraca from the eighth century BC were found. Likely bills of lading used for taxes, the ostraca's Hebr. inscriptions recorded dates, place names, individuals and families, as well as quantities of oil and wine – including the names of Jeezer, Shemida, Helek, Hoglah, Noah and Asriel. 'Noah' is listed on Ostracon 50 'as the name of a settlement or administrative district in the Manasseh area west of the Jordan', possibly located between Shechem and Hepher, and 'Hoglah' is a geographical term on Ostraca 45 and 47 designating a locale in north-eastern Samaria, Hoglah possibly having 'married a cousin from the Peresh-Sheresh branch of the family' (Ben-Barak 2006: 56). The city of Tirzah, previously a Canaanite city, is presented as a royal capital in Scripture, renowned for its beauty, compared to the loveliness of Jerusalem (Songs 6:4; cf. Josh. 12:24; 1 Kgs 14:17; 15:21, 33; 16:6, 8, 9, 15, 17, 23; 2 Kgs 15:14, 16) (Ben-Barak 2006: 57; on the locations of Mahlah and Milcah, see Lemaire 1972). Among the sixty-three inscriptions on the Samaria ostraca, seven districts correspond to the *mišpāḥāh* clan names of the tribe of Manasseh, underscoring once more the territorial importance of the *mišpāḥāh* (Wright 1990: 49–50), as well as indicating that 'at least some of the old clan and lineage divisions retained their integrity until much later' (Stager 1985: 24). The finding confirms the general view of Joshua 17, writes Elitzur (2020: 507), with the districts 'given permanent names for the major households of Manasseh, as well as for Zelophehad's five daughters!' The daughters of Zelophehad episode thus looks forward to the apportionment of land in chapters 34–35. Demsky (2021a) argues that the Zelophehad story 'reflects the historical reality of five localities that were associated with the sisters in proximity to each other from the period of the settlement until the Assyrian conquest of the Northern Kingdom of Israel in the 8th century'. Using archaeological, topographical and documentary evidence, along with Arabic toponyms, he suggests the following locations for the daughters' territories, as mapped below (Demsky 2021a; cf. Z. H. Ehrlich 1983; Zertal 1991; 2004: 54–56, 74–77, 116–120, 507–509): Tirzah is identified with Tel el Far'ah, and Mahlah with the biblical Abel Meholah (cf. Judg. 7:22; 1 Kgs 4:12; 19:16); the Samaria Ostraca mention both Hoglah (nos. 45, 47) and Noah (no. 50) without geographical reference, but since Hoglah is named together with Yeset, the present-day Arab village of Yasid, a reasonable suggestion is that the village of Yeset fell within the territory of Hoglah; Milkah is placed contiguous with Hoglah and Tirzah on the stepped eastern side of the Samarian hills in the same order as typically listed in the Bible.

Just as the census of Numbers 26 focused on 'clans'('kin groups', *mišpĕḥōt*), the word 'tribes' (*maṭṭôt*) occurring only once, in relation to the land division (v. 55), so the statute concerning the daughters of Zelophehad focuses on the plight of the clan – 'Why should the name of our father be removed from the midst of his clan?' (27:4). In Numbers 36, however, the focus of concern broadens to the tribal level.

27:12–23: Moses' final intercessory prayer

12–14. YHWH commands Moses to 'ascend' (*'ălêh*) this Mount Abarim, literally, mountain of 'crossing' or 'transferring', using the same root *'-b-r* that was used earlier for the 'transfer' of a father's inheritance to his daughters (vv. 7–8), connecting the two passages by the motif of transition. Both episodes also concern the land/inheritance, making use of 'give' (*n-t-n*; vv. 4, 7 [twice], 9, 10, 11, 12, 20), and involve 'standing' (*'āmad*) 'before Eleazar the priest and the whole community' (vv. 2, 19, 22). Use of the adjective 'this' (cf. Deut. 32:49) lends the name 'Abarim' a descriptive quality: the mountain range, allowing a view of the land, not only reflects the crossing of Moses' vision into the land, but his crossing from life to death, perhaps even from earthly to heavenly existence, and

Israel's transition both into the land and into life without Moses. In Deuteronomy, the notion of crossing is made more explicit: 'Ascend to this Mount Abarim (*'ăbārîm*)' (32:39), 'but to there (the land) you will not cross over (*ta'ăbōr*)' (34:4). The mountain range is associated with Mount Nebo and Pisgah (Num. 21:11; 33:44, 47–48; Deut. 3:27; 32:49; 34:1).

From Mount Abarim, he is to 'see the land' (*rĕ'êh 'et-hā'āreṣ*) YHWH has given to the sons of Israel. The phrase recalls Moses' original charge to the scouts to 'see the land' (13:18; cf. 32:9), and perhaps resonates with their consequent failure. While he will not enter or possess the land himself, Moses is granted to see the land. As Balaam was given a picture of the glory of Israel's encampment (24:2), Moses' vision would enable him to experience the glories of Israel's life in the land. By sight of the landscape, Moses will taste from afar the fulfilment of YHWH's promise to the patriarchs – through a compassionate concession from God, he is able to see the land YHWH 'has given' (*nātattî*) to the sons of Israel. Note the contrast from YHWH's earlier words in 13:2: 'the land of Canaan which I am giving (*nōtēn*) to the sons of Israel', whereas here it is 'the land I have given (*nātattî*) to the sons of Israel'. Similarly, Caleb had said, 'If YHWH delights in us then he will bring us into this land and will give it (*nĕtānāh*) to us' (14:8), and, after the first generation's failure, YHWH had reaffirmed 'the land . . . which I am giving (*nōtēn*) to you' (15:2); Dathan and Abiram, moreover, had complained that Moses had not given them an inheritance in the land (16:14). As of chapter 20, with the arrival of Israel's second generation, YHWH's language changes to 'I have given' the land (20:12, 24) – and especially within this last major section (chs. 26–36), YHWH's promise is so sure it is almost as if the conquest, division and possession of land have already taken place. In the fulfilment of this episode, Deuteronomy explains that 'YHWH showed' (*wayyar'êhû*) Moses the land, expansively describing the tribal territories, with YHWH himself saying, 'This is the land which I swore to Abraham, to Isaac and to Jacob, saying, "To your seed I will give it. I have caused you to see it (*her'îtîkā*) with your eyes, but to there you will not cross over"' (34:1–4). That YHWH is the giver of the land is pointed out several times in Numbers' last section (27:12; 32:7, 9; 33:53; cf. Hausoul 2018: 85).

After Moses has 'seen the land' (*rā'îtāh 'ōtāh*), YHWH explains, he will 'be gathered to his people', perhaps an idiom for death that may relate to the ancient practice of burial in family tombs. Milgrom, observing that the phrase occurs in the Torah only for the ancestors of Israel Abraham (Gen. 25:8), Ishmael (25:17), Isaac (35:29), Jacob (49:29, 33), Aaron (Num. 20:44; Deut. 32:50) and Moses (Num. 27:13; 31:2; Deut. 32:50), deduces that it means 'be reunited with one's ancestors . . . in *Sheol*' (1990: 169–170), but other meanings are possible (cf. Levine 1993: 494). Being 'gathered' reminds one of the opening chapter of the wilderness sojourn where *'āsap* was a key word used seven times (11:4, 16, 22, 24, 30, 32 [twice]). YHWH's 'you also' is made explicit with 'just as Aaron your brother was gathered', forming a link between Moses' impending death (27:12–14) and that of Aaron (20:22–29), as well as with their momentous sin (20:1–13). Both Aaron and Moses ascend mountains, are each told 'you will be gathered to your people', are kept from entering 'the land I have given to the sons of Israel', are reminded that 'you rebelled (*měrîtem*) against my word (*pî*)' at 'Meribah'. A final parallel is the result of Moses' intercession (27:15–17); namely, a successor is installed on both occasions (Eleazar and Joshua, respectively) – perhaps Moses' intercession deliberately addressed this omitted parallel with Aaron's scenario (20:25–28). The differences between the two scenarios are also significant: Aaron dies soon after his rebellion, does not see the land and is fully replaced by Eleazar; whereas Moses' death-sentence is delayed, he does see the land and Joshua will receive only Moses' political role of leadership, some of his 'majesty'. Not only with Aaron's death, but the parallels connect with the account of Moses and Aaron's sin earlier in chapter 20 – most of the connections found within YHWH's response (20:1, 12–13): 'Wilderness of Zin', 'sanctify me in the eyes' of Israel, 'waters of Meribah' and 'land that I have given' Israel. Reminding Moses that he 'rebelled' forms poetic justice for his having called God's people 'rebels' (20:10; cf. 20:24). Through these connections, a window of narrative is framed between Numbers 20, including Aaron's death, and the prospect of Moses' death in Numbers 27, underscoring the role of Moses in between: he led the second generation, supplying them water, leading them in victories over Sihon and Og and conducting the census that sealed their inheritance of the land.

The links with chapter 20 established, YHWH's previous pronouncement explains the placement of this section precisely here: 'therefore you will not bring this assembly into the land' (20:12). The census of Numbers 26 seals the gift of the land to the current, second generation of Israel. The episode with Zelophehad's daughters was a needed addendum to the census, including them as full recipients of land allotments within Israel's inheritance of Canaan (27:1–11). Even though Moses' ascent, viewing of the land and death will not yet occur (see Deut. 34:1–8), now – when Israel has been fully assured of possessing the land – is the first opportunity to reaffirm YHWH's judgement on Moses and the need of a leader for the conquest. The Midrash observes that YHWH's command to Moses concerning the daughters of Zelophehad '*you* will surely give them a holding' (v. 7) might have led to the false impression that Moses would, after all, lead the people into Canaan and distribute the land, a notion YHWH immediately corrects (*Num. Rab.* 21.13). More deeply, with this section's enthusiastic emphasis on inheriting the land, here is the logical point at which to answer the question 'Who will bring Israel into the land?' Ever since YHWH's sober pronouncement 'you will not bring this assembly into the land which I have given them' (20:12), the shadow of Moses' death has been cast – before any further material related to possessing the land and the jubilant assurance of YHWH's promise follows, it is necessary to address this great question, so as to keep its uncertainty from tarnishing the second generation's triumph. Within the sweep and movement of the material in chapters 26–36, this episode is really about YHWH's provision of Joshua for Israel *through Moses*, allaying any concerns about land entry in the light of the prohibition on Moses. As will become clear, even the provision of Joshua is rendered as a gift granted Israel through the mediation of Moses – one of Moses' last acts for the people of God. The provision of Joshua nevertheless does not eliminate the pathos of the moment, as the death of Moses, Israel's profoundly Godlike leader, draws near. From Moses' perspective, the reminder of his approaching death adds urgency to the following material: before he dies, Moses must be used of God to conclude a variety of matters related to Israel's life in the land (cf. Abarbanel 2015: 311).

Aaron is still in view in verse 14, evident by YHWH's use of the pl.: 'For you (both) rebelled (*mĕrîtem*)', characterizing the events of chapter 20 as a joint sin. The words 'rebelled' (*mĕrîtem*), 'in the contention' (*bimrîbat*), 'Meribah' (*mĕrîbat*), and even the two uses of 'wilderness' (*midbar* – note *bĕmidbar* with *bimrîbat*), seem to form wordplay, as with 'sanctify' and 'Kadesh' (cf. Budd 1984: 306). Just as Zelophehad's death was distinguished from Korah's rebellion, as having died under the general judgement on the first generation, so Moses' death is distinguished from the first generation's sin of unbelief – rather, Moses is denied entry into Canaan for having failed to sanctify YHWH before the eyes of Israel (see Rashi, ad loc.; cf. Štrba 2006: 344). In being invited to 'see the land', Moses is granted a grace expressly forbidden the first generation: 'Surely they will not see the land which I swore to their fathers – none who despised me will see it' (14:22).

15–17. When YHWH reminds him of his impending death, Moses' first concern is for the community of Israel, interceding for them immediately with passion and urgency – and with selflessness and humility. The momentous nature and boldness of his intercession is brought out in the construction *wayĕdabbēr mōšeh 'el-yhwh lē'mōr*. Typically, *wayĕdabbēr . . . lē'mōr* (And he spoke . . . saying) describes YHWH's speaking to Moses. This verse, reversing (as it were) the roles of YHWH and Moses, is unique (cf. Exod. 6:12). The parallel passage for Aaron, whereby it is YHWH who initiates the installation of Eleazar as high priest to replace his father (20:22–29), also underscores the role reversal here. Adding even greater emphasis, this is *the last time* the Torah narrates Moses' speaking to God. Friedman compares this last engagement between YHWH and Moses with the first time (Exod. 3), observing that both occasions concern the well-being of Israel and have shepherding as a context (2001: 521).

Addressing YHWH, Moses calls him 'the God of the spirits of all flesh', a designation used only once elsewhere in the entire HB, in a telling reference, also in Numbers: 'Then they (Moses and Aaron) fell on their faces and said, "O El, God of the spirits of all flesh, will the one man sin, but you be angry against the whole community?"' (16:22). Within the context of Korah's rebellion, YHWH had announced he would consume the community within a moment, moving both Moses and Aaron to pray urgently. Now, Moses in effect pleads that the punishment for his own sin will not penalize the whole community, berefting them of a leader to bring them into the land. Levine, noting similarities with Genesis 6:17, 'all flesh (*kol bā'sār*) in which there is breath (*rûaḥ*)', understands the phraseology as signifying YHWH's sovereignty over life and death, that Moses is alluding to his own death with resignation but without complaint (2000: 349). As 'spirit' may be used of an inward bent and disposition (Gen. 41:8; 45:27; Exod. 6:9; 35:21), even supplied by God (Exod. 28:3; 31:3; 35:31; Num. 5:14, 30; 11:17, 25), especially as the spirit that gives life to flesh (Gen. 7:15), Moses perhaps beseeches God not merely as the one who gives life to all flesh, but who sovereignly knows the heart of people and so may appoint the right leader for Israel, the shepherd who will be faithful to YHWH, serving them selflessly. This notion comes out through YHWH's previous description of Caleb as one 'who has another spirit within him' (14:24) and here in YHWH's response, regarding Joshua as 'a man in whom is the Spirit' (27:18). The same theology will be foundational for the secondary fulfilment of Moses' prayer, when David is anointed king over Israel, shepherd of God's flock, chosen by YHWH, who does not observe the outward appearance, but 'looks to the heart' (2 Sam. 16:7). Moses, then, does not simply pray for a leader, but for the sort of leader only YHWH, who looks to the heart, can supply. Moses pleads for a faithful man of God, who will not stray from the word of YHWH, nor abandon his flock. His own compassion for YHWH's people makes the community's plight and need his highest concern – 'appoint (*yipqōd*) a man over the community'.

Moses defines the role of the 'man' whose appointment he seeks, according to his understanding of the community's direst need upon his own death. There is a double use of the verbs *yāṣā'* (go forth) and *bô'* (come in) related first to the leader's own going forth (*yēṣē'*) and coming in (*yābō'*), then, using the hiph. causative, of his leading the people themselves to go forth (*yôṣî'ēm*) and bringing them in (*yĕbî'ēm*) – this is the biblical paradigm of leadership, captured most genuinely by the image of a shepherd, as the last line makes explicit. The language of 'going forth' relates to *military* leadership, used of YHWH in battle (Judg. 4:14; 2 Sam. 5:24), and used especially of kings, as when the Israelites declared their desire to be like all the nations, having a king who will 'go out before us and fight our battles' (1 Sam. 8:20; cf. Josh. 14:11; 2 Chr. 20:17) – fitting language for Joshua's role in the conquest. The full expression is used of David: 'But all Israel and Judah loved David, because he is the one who would go forth and come in before them' (1 Sam. 18:16; cf. 1 Sam. 8:13; 29:6; 2 Sam. 5:2; 1 Chr. 14:8). While both the language, 'leading forth' and 'bringing in', and the imagery of a shepherd, have royal connotations, the primary focus restricts the application, 'employed here not to denote the leader as political, but rather as a military chief' (Frevel 2018: 103). Given the military context, the first set of verbs relate to a leader's courage, while the second set pertains to wisdom in the sense of military strategy (cf. Abarbanel 2015: 313–314).

But Moses has more than the military aspects of the conquest of Canaan in mind. Just before his death in Deuteronomy, Moses says, 'I am one hundred and twenty years old this day, and no longer able to go forth (*lāṣēʾt*) and to come in (*lābôʾ*)' (31:2). The main purpose of his plea for YHWH to appoint a man is because the flock of YHWH needs a man who will incarnate the shepherding of YHWH himself (cf. 2 Sam. 5:2). Although Israel is the community *of YHWH*, and he himself is their Shepherd (Ps. 23:1; 80:1; 100:3; Isa. 40:11; Jer. 31:10; 50:19), nevertheless, they need an appointed man. There is a strong and urgent note of compassion in his plea that the *ʿēdāh* of YHWH be not 'as sheep without a shepherd'. Without a human shepherd after YHWH's heart, his flock would be scattered and a prey for their enemies: 'I saw all Israel scattered along the mountains as sheep without a shepherd' (1 Kgs 22:17; cf. Isa. 13:14; Ezek. 34:5). Moses had experience shepherding flocks before YHWH set him over his own flock, the community of Israel (Exod. 3:1–3; Ps. 77:20; Isa. 63:11), just as David also would be taken from shepherding his father's sheep and be set over the people of God (1 Sam. 16:11; 2 Sam. 7:8). 'Thus the image of David', writes Milgrom (1990: 235), 'is forged along the Mosaic model' (see Morales 2020: 148–153). A shepherd lives to care for the sheep, providing guidance and protection (cf. Stubbs 2009: 212–213). Israel's need, and so, too, Moses' concern, is more deeply rooted than the supply of Joshua for the present generation can satisfy – the prayer's answer moves to the kingship of David, looking ultimately to his seed, the Messiah. Moses' compassion would be taken up by the Messiah who 'was moved with compassion' over God's people 'because they were as sheep without a shepherd' (Matt. 9:36; Mark 6:34). Jesus is the Good Shepherd who tends and feeds the flock of YHWH, who seeks and saves the lost – who lays down his life for the sheep (John 10).

18–21. YHWH's response begins with 'Take', reminiscent of his provision of Eleazar for Aaron as high priest before the latter's death (20:25), in this case 'Take for yourself (*qaḥ-lĕkā*) Joshua son of Nun.' Moses had prayed for YHWH to appoint a man, but YHWH gives him the honour and consolation of having Moses do so – that is how

Abarbanel explains *lĕkā*, 'for yourself' (2015: 314). It is significant that YHWH describes Joshua as 'a man in whom is the Spirit' (*'îš 'ăšer-rûaḥ bô*), since 'Spirit', specifically as short for 'the *rûaḥ* of YHWH/Elohim' (cf. Levine 2000: 350), is the *sine qua non* of biblical leadership, granting the person both wisdom and empowerment to lead God's people. Lack of a definite article does not preclude a reference to the Holy Spirit (cf. Wood 1998: 49–50). While all flesh has 'spirit' (v. 16), as in 'life' (cf. Ps. 31:6), Joshua possesses the 'Spirit of YHWH' (Vogels 1982: 5–6), and this before the laying on of Moses' hands (cf. Hymes 2010: 270–271). A similar statement was made of Joseph, noting the Spirit 'of God', *'îš 'ăšer rûaḥ 'ĕlōhîm bô* (Gen. 41:38), enabling him to rule over Egypt with wisdom (cf. Exod. 31:3). In Judges, the Spirit of YHWH would rush upon his chosen leaders, empowering them to overcome Israel's enemies (Judg. 3:10; 6:34; 13:25; 14:6, 19; 15:14). In this case, spirit, likely referring to the 'Spirit of God', signifies Joshua's loyalty to YHWH, his own zealous commitment to Israel's faithfulness, just as Caleb, the other faithful scout, had been described as having 'another spirit with him' (Num. 14:24), opposite to that of the faithless scouts who led the community astray in disobedience. One also recalls the endowment of the seventy elders with YHWH's Spirit (who was upon Moses), enabling them to supplement Moses' leadership (11:16–17, 23–29). Based on his loyalty to YHWH, Joshua will receive a separate endowment of the Spirit through the laying on of Moses' hands, conferring upon him greater authority, power and wisdom (cf. Gispen 1964: 2:190). The account in Deuteronomy reads that Joshua was 'full (*mālē'*) of the Spirit of wisdom, *because* (*kî*) Moses had leaned his hands upon him' (34:9). A lifelong apprentice of Moses, and as a faithful scout who had explored the land of Canaan, Joshua was a fitting choice to succeed Moses (cf. G. J. Wenham 1981b: 217).

After taking Joshua, Moses is to lean his hand upon him, an act that has influenced ordination rites in both Jewish and Christian traditions (cf. Mattingly 2001: 191; see Acts 8:17–19; 19:6). The act of leaning hands, *sāmak*, in this case involves a conferring of authority that also includes a divine transfer of spiritual enablement. Verse 18's 'take and lean your hand upon' summarizes the more detailed delineation in verses 19–20, which instructs Moses to stand Joshua before Eleazar the priest and the whole community, to charge him before their eyes and to put some of Moses' majesty on him – the latter act referring to the hand-leaning rite. Perhaps not unrelated to the hand-leaning rite within the sacrificial system, using one hand, which conveyed a ritual transfer or establishing of identity (cf. Lev. 8:10; Morales 2015: 127–129; for hand-leaning and status in the ANE, see Mattingly 1997: 24–82), Moses is conferring some of his own identity and role, his authority and power as Israel's leader, to Joshua.

'Eleazar the priest and the whole community' defines the two main entities of YHWH's covenant people: the spiritual leader (especially post-Moses) and the people themselves – separate, given the double use of 'before' (*lipnê*), but inseparable. Moses is to 'stand' Joshua before them, a ritual procedure involving their presence and for their benefit, acknowledging him as their chosen leader by YHWH through Moses – but also for Joshua's benefit, that he would acknowledge himself as their servant under YHWH's guidance. For the same purpose, Moses is to 'charge' ('command', *ṣiwwîtāh*) Joshua specifically 'before their eyes' (*leʿênêhem*, vv. 14, 19), an expression used elsewhere in Numbers only with reference to YHWH's instructions for watering his flock through the rock (Num. 20:8). The substance of the charge was probably similar to YHWH's own charge described in Joshua 1:1–9, to lead the people across the Jordan in conquest, being strong and courageous in YHWH, and by carefully and wholeheartedly following Moses' teaching, the 'Book of Torah'. Moses, as narrated in Deuteronomy, is specifically to charge Joshua with the goal of encouraging and strengthening him on his divine mission: he will go before the people and cause them to inherit the land (3:28). The encouragement and strength derive from YHWH's own presence and commitment ('YHWH your God himself fights for you'), and from his past faithfulness, that YHWH would do to the Canaanites just as he had done to the two kings Sihon and Og (Deut. 3:21–22).

YHWH also instructs Moses to put some of his 'majesty' upon Joshua, descriptive of the hand-leaning rite and as a summary of the entire installation ceremony. The term *hôd* refers to splendour, majesty and even vigour (see BDB 217), and, especially with royal overtones in ascription of praise to YHWH (Pss 45:3; 96:6; 104:1; 145:5; 148:13), may serve to express the greatness or magnificence of a person or beast. YHWH would later magnify Solomon in the eyes of all Israel and put upon him 'majesty of kingship' (*hôd malkût*), such as no king before him had in Israel (1 Chr. 29:25). Levine explains *hôd* as 'an aura that commands awe and respect' (2000: 351). Since the rabbinical sages described Moses' radiant face as 'rays of splendour (*hôd*)' (see Exod. 34:35), Rashi surmises Moses transferred some of the radiance of his face on to Joshua, depicting Moses' face like the sun and Joshua's like the moon (cf. 1997: 4:350). Central to Moses' greatness was his superabundant possession of YHWH's Spirit, the reception of which is never narrated but everywhere assumed, displayed in Numbers 11, where merely some of the Spirit on him is distributed among seventy elders. Again, this point – that Moses passed a portion of YHWH's Spirit on to Joshua – is explicit in Deuteronomy 34:9. The purpose for putting some of Moses' majesty on Joshua is clear: so (*lěmaʿan*, 'in order that') the whole community of Israel 'will heed' (*yišměʿû*). YHWH will guide his people through Joshua, so that in heeding Joshua, who will not depart from Moses' divine instruction, they will be heeding YHWH. Although he will not be 'another Moses' (cf. Deut. 34:10–12), Joshua, who was ever by Moses' side as his personal aide – the 'minister of Moses' (*měšārēt mōšeh*) – was nevertheless the most Moses-like figure in his era (Num. 11:28; 13:16; cf. Exod. 24:13; 33:11). Both Moses' prayer and YHWH's answer contain purpose clauses: Moses prays for an appointed man so that the community of YHWH will not be as sheep without a shepherd (v. 17), and here YHWH instructs Moses to put some of his majesty on the appointed man, Joshua, so that the community of Israel will heed that man (v. 20) – the first focuses on the needs of the people; the second, that of the leader, also for the people's sake.

The limits on Joshua's authority are seen not only in his receiving merely some of Moses' majesty, but also in his manifest subordination to the high priest. YHWH establishes a clear channel of authority: Joshua will stand before Eleazar the priest and enquire of him for leadership guidance. As Albertz observes (2013: 225), 'In all places within Num. 26–36, where Joshua is mentioned after his installment, he is preceded by Eleazar (32:12, 28; 34:17).' The phrase 'before Eleazar the priest' (*lipnê el'āzār hakkōhēn*) fronts the verb, adding emphasis to the hierarchy. He – the priest – will enquire of YHWH through the Urim, on behalf of Joshua, with the result that it is at his – the priest's – word (lit. 'mouth', *pî*) that Joshua and Israel will go forth, and at his – the priest's – word they will come back. In the absence of Moses, with whom YHWH spoke 'mouth to mouth' (12:8), the new channel of divine guidance will be from YHWH to the priest via the Urim and Thummim, and from the priest to Joshua, who would then lead forth God's people according to the divine will. As Shamah points out (2011: 820–821), using the identical verbs Moses employed, YHWH 'radically modified the meaning . . . placing the word of God derived through the Urim and Thummim as the guideline for leader and nation'. The foundational revelation given through Moses, the Torah, would be the life-giving guide for Israel's life in the land, but in seeking God for immediate, *ad hoc* counsel, such as whether Israel should go forth into battle against a particular enemy, YHWH would reveal his will through the priest's use of the Urim, which might have yielded a simple yes or no answer. What is true of Joshua's role as political leader will also hold for the future office of kingship (and later governors) in Israel (see 1 Sam. 23:9–12; 28:6; 30:7–8; Ezra 2:63; Neh. 7:65; cf. LXX of 1 Sam. 14:41).

Urim may be shorthand for 'Urim and Thummim' (cf. 1 Sam. 28:6). The name 'Urim' likely signifies 'light' (*'ôr*), and together with the Thummim (perhaps 'faultless'), was worn by the high priest in his breastpiece connected to the ephod (cf. Exod. 28:15–30; Lev. 8:8; Deut. 33:8), serving as an oracle by sacred lot (see BDB 22; IDB 739–740; Milgrom 1990: 484–486). Harrison points out that Urim begins with the letter aleph and Thummim with tau, the first and last letters of the Hebr. alphabet, perhaps a merismus motif implying the totality of their revelation (1990: 359). The 'judgement' (*mišpaṭ*) of the Urim refers to the divine answer to the query – having solicited YHWH's decision on a matter, his response through the Urim and Thummim is a ruling, a judgement, which Joshua would be bound to observe. In answer to Moses' intercession, YHWH does provide a leader who will go forth and come in, but he and all the sons of Israel will do so only by the priest's word. In retrospect, it may be that Moses had selflessly asked God for a successor equal to himself, a leader endowed with the same measure of authority and power, so as to be able to lead Israel as Moses himself had done, through YHWH's direct revelation; if that was the case, then such was clearly denied by God (Milgrom's view, 1990: 234–236). Such a channel limits only the self-willed leader, who has no interest in God's guidance for his people; otherwise, the process serves to safeguard the flock of YHWH, since it is the priest who has the means for obtaining an oracle from God.

Recalling the language of going forth and bringing in used of kings in Scripture, and with particular reference to leadership in battle, the conquest of the land under Joshua is within the immediate purview of Moses' prayer, especially so in the context of Numbers 26 – 36, which has Israel's inheritance of the land as a major emphasis. Fittingly, then, the Torah first introduces Joshua as Moses' choice leader in the battle against Amalek, the archetypal enemies of Israel (Exod. 17:8–16; cf. Num. 24:20; Deut. 25:17–19). Indeed, the present scene brings together three elements that were encountered in Joshua's first appearance. Numbers 27:12–23 relates (1) Moses' failure in drawing water from the rock in Numbers 20, (2) Moses' call to ascend a mountain, while (3) Joshua continues his earthly role of leading Israel in the conquest. In Exodus 17, (1) Moses had drawn water from the rock (vv. 1–7), and then (2) ascended to the summit of a hill, while (3) Joshua led Israel in battle against Amalek (vv. 8–16). In Deuteronomy, YHWH himself encourages Joshua, saying, YHWH his God will be fighting for him, and then reminds Moses that Joshua will 'go before' the people, causing them to possess the land (3:21–22, 28).

22–23. Moses faithfully obeys YHWH's command, the compliance formula ensuring that what was done was indeed according to the divine will, vouchsafed by God himself, with Moses' 'charge' (*wayĕṣawwêhû*, v. 23) to Joshua, derived from YHWH's 'command' (*ṣiwwā*, v. 22) to Moses (Mattingly 2001: 200). The delineation of his follow-through uses the same verbs from YHWH's previous instructions: he 'took' Joshua, 'stood' him before Eleazar the priest and before the whole community, 'leaned' his hands and 'charged' him. The last statement – 'just as YHWH had spoken by the hand of Moses' – may refer to the substance of the charge given to Joshua. Based on passages from Deuteronomy (3:21–28; 31:1–8, 14, 23) and Joshua (1:1–9), Mattingly summarizes a four-part commission (2001: 200). First, Joshua was encouraged to be strong and courageous based on his experience with YHWH. Second, Joshua was reminded that he was commissioned to accomplish the twofold goal of crossing the Jordan into the land in conquest, and of dividing the land among the tribes. Third, Joshua was reminded that YHWH would be with him, go before him and fight for him. Fourth, Moses exhorted Joshua to read and keep the Torah, meditating on it day and night.

The exact or similar expression of YHWH's speaking 'by the hand of Moses' occurs some thirty-one times throughout the HB, and its use here appears 'to be no accident', since Moses' laying on of hands becomes 'a visible enactment of the "word" of YHWH' (Mattingly 2001: 207). One wonders, more deeply, if the 'hand' of Moses here may serve to call further attention to the discrepancy of verses 17 and 23. The Jewish sages picked up on a detail in Moses' follow-through that differs from YHWH's precise instruction: while YHWH had directed Moses to 'lean your *hand* (sg.) upon Joshua' (v. 18), Moses, the narrative reports, actually 'leaned his *hands* (pl.) upon him' (v. 23), explaining his action, motivated by his ardent concern for Israel, as his endeavour to convey as much of the Spirit of YHWH upon Joshua as possible (cf. *Num. Rab.* 21.15; Rashi 1997: 4:351). Noted already, Deuteronomy reads that Joshua was 'full (*mālē'*) of the Spirit of wisdom, *because* (*kî*) Moses had leaned his *hands* (*yādāyw*, pl.) on him' (34:9). Since this episode began with YHWH's reference to Moses' failure at the waters of Meribah in chapter 20, one may also hear a distant echo from that account, how Moses had 'raised his hand' in defiance (20:11), for which he was forbidden entry into the land, requiring the leadership of Joshua. Tracing the arc of Moses' hand thus highlights the grace of God and the growth of his faithful servant Moses – the hand that had once sinned grievously now passes on spiritual gifts and graces to his protégé, and the revelation of God to his people. At the least, Moses' use of two hands 'preempts anyone from criticizing Joshua later as not having been Moses' choice' (Friedman 2001: 522; cf. Calabro 2017). In a book that centres on YHWH's shepherding of his flock through the wilderness, bringing Israel to the cusp of the land of Canaan, designating a successor to Moses who will be used of God to bring them to their inheritance is of utmost moment, and underscores the honoured stature of Joshua. As a public ceremony 'before the eyes' of the community, the appointment of Joshua served to reassure Israel of YHWH's commitment to bring them into the land.

In Deuteronomy, YHWH himself will confirm Joshua's appointment, charging him, 'Be strong and courageous because you are the one who will bring in the sons of Israel to the land which I have sworn to them – and I myself will be with you' (31:14–15, 23). And in Joshua, the community of Israel pledges to 'heed' (*š-m-'*) him just as they 'heeded' (*š-m-'*) Moses in all things, vowing to put to death any who rebel against his command – 'only let YHWH your God be with you . . . only be strong and courageous' (1:17–18). Closer to the actual narration of Moses' death (Deut. 34:4–8), YHWH's call for Moses to ascend Mount Abarim will be rehearsed (Deut. 32:48–52), followed by YHWH's announcement to Joshua 'Moses my servant is dead' (Josh. 1:2).

ENDING WITH JOSEPH

The last major section of Numbers (chs. 26–36), relating to Israel's inheritance of land, highlights Joseph's tribes in an uncanny way. In chapter 26, the tribe of Manasseh increases significantly in the census, is listed before Ephraim and includes a lengthy genealogy for the daughters of Zelophehad (26:28–34). Chapter 27 highlights the tribes of Joseph's two sons, Manasseh and Ephraim, recounting the successful allotment of land to Zelophehad's daughters, of the tribe of Manasseh (27:1–11), and narrating the transition of leadership from Moses to Joshua bin Nun, of the tribe of Ephraim (27:12–23). In chapter 32, part of the tribe of 'Manasseh the son of Joseph' is portrayed conquering lands east of the Jordan (32:33, 39–42), and Numbers closes with the preservation of Manasseh's lands through the marriage of Zelophehad's daughters (ch. 36), their inheritance story forming an inclusio around the book's last major section (chs. 27; 36). Arguably, Joseph's tribes are structurally and theologically central in the book's opening census (1:10), with five tribes preceding (vv. 5–9) and following (11–15), perhaps reflecting Joseph's right of primogeniture from Jacob (Gen. 48; cf. 49:26). The name Joseph occurs twelve times in Numbers, eight in the last section (26:28, 37; 27:1; 32:33; 34:23; 36:1, 5, 12; and 1:10, 32; 13:7, 11). Why does Numbers end with Joseph?

As a prelude to understanding the function of the Joseph motif in relation to Israel's land inheritance, an earlier use of this motif needs to be explored, when Israel's first generation failed to take possession of the land (Num. 13 – 14). In the scouts narrative, Moses 'sent' (*šālaḥ*, 13:1, 16) the sons of Israel 'to see' (*rā'ah*, 13:18) and 'bring back word' (*šûb dābor*, 13:26), which led to a 'bad report' (*dibâ*, 13:32; 14:36, 37) that the land 'devours' (*'ākal*, 13:32) its inhabitants, followed by the 'tearing of clothes' (*qāra' bāgad*, 14:6) and much 'weeping' and 'mourning' (*bākâ*, 14:1; *'ābal mĕ'ōd*, 14:39). Taken together, these terms echo the sale of Joseph in Genesis 37, where Jacob 'sends' Joseph, who had given a 'bad report' of his brothers, to go and 'see' and 'bring back word' (Gen. 37:2, 13–14). The brothers conspire against Joseph, selling him and claiming an animal has 'devoured' him (37:18, 33); Reuben and Jacob each 'tears his clothes' (*qāra' bāgad*, 37:29; *qāra' śimlâ*, 37:34), and Jacob 'weeps' and 'mourns' greatly (*bākâ, 'ābal*, 37:34–35). Broader conceptual parallels include a decision to return to Egypt (Gen. 42:2; 43:1–15; Num. 14:4), the accusation that the sons of Jacob were 'spies' come to view the land (Gen. 42:9, 14), and a ten versus two brothers scenario. Some links are especially firm: the Torah's only uses of 'bad report' occur in these stories (Gen. 37:2; Num. 13:32; 14:36, 37), and the first two uses of the collocation 'bring back word' are for these stories as well (Gen. 37:14; Num. 13:26). Joseph, moreover, was sent from 'Hebron' (Gen. 37:14) and ends up 'in the wilderness' (37:22), precisely the geography reversed in the scouts story (Num. 13:22). These parallels underscore an underappreciated point about the Joseph story, that it narrates the occasion whereby the sons of Israel lost the land of Canaan – it is a story of departure, beginning with the betrayal and exile of Joseph. Fittingly, echoes of Israel's departure from Canaan into Egypt resurface as Israel anticipates the reversal of that exile, with the re-entry into Canaan.

The story of Joseph, who was separated from his family as the first to experience Egyptian exile out of the land of Canaan, is integrated deeply into the last major section of Numbers. Considering Numbers 27 as a whole, with its first section centring on the tribe of Manasseh (27:1–11) and the second on the transition to Joshua of the tribe of Ephraim (27:12–23; cf. 13:8, 16), Joseph's story – especially Genesis 41 and 48 – serves as a subtext. Joseph named his firstborn 'Manasseh', derived from *nāšâ* in pi., 'to make one forget', since God had caused him to forget his 'misery' (*'āmal*) and his 'father's house' (*bêt 'āb*) (41:50–52). He named his second son 'Ephraim', from *pārâ* (fruitful), acknowledging: 'God has caused me to be fruitful in the land of my affliction' (41:52). Emphasis on Manasseh at the end of Numbers appears to hold a similar message: on the other side of a devastating forty-year judgement and in the light of anticipating life in the land of Canaan as YHWH's good gift, Israel can also declare, 'God has caused me to forget my misery' and 'has made me fruitful.' The daughters of Zelophehad reverse their tribal name's significance, causing their 'father's house' to be remembered, and, curiously, while Ephraim's census figures decline, the tribe of Manasseh increases significantly from 32,200 to 52,700, exhibiting 'fruitfulness' indeed. With Israel on the verge of re-entering the land of Canaan, ending a four-centuries-long exile, how fitting to shine a spotlight on Manasseh's descendants in particular. The first of the twelve patriarchal brothers to experience exile in Egypt, Joseph is honoured in having his descendants showcased on the verge of Israel's entry to the land of Canaan – and the nation will be brought into the land under the leadership of Joshua of the tribe of Ephraim, Joseph's second son whom Jacob chose to receive the firstborn's blessing (Gen. 48; Num. 27:12–23). The Midrash interprets Jacob's reference to the younger brother being greater than the older, as referring to 'Joshua, who will come from the tribe of Ephraim and will conquer the land' (Etshalom 2015: 243). Moses' hand-leaning rite on the head of Joshua, conferring on him military leadership over Israel's tribes, forms but a long echo and fulfilment of Jacob's own placing of his right hand on the head of Ephraim.

On his deathbed, Jacob had declared that Israel would invoke Joseph's sons in blessing, saying, 'May God place you as Ephraim and as Manasseh!', after which he offered the prophetic reassurance that 'God will be with you and will bring you back to the land of your fathers' (Gen. 48:20–21), a divine promise about to be realized at the end of Numbers. Joseph's life thus represents the ideal of longing for the land. Although he has risen to prominence and lived long enough to see Ephraim's children to the third generation in Egypt, Genesis closes with Joseph's deathbed demand for an oath from his brothers: 'God will surely visit you to bring you into the land he swore to Abraham, Isaac, and Jacob, and you must carry up my bones from here' (50:22–26) – and his bones did experience the exodus (Exod. 13:19) and were brought into the land (Josh. 24:32). The daughters of Zelophehad, as Rashi pointed out (1997: 4:340), in their ardent desire for the land prove true daughters of Joseph. Although Joseph died outside the land, he was looking for the promised deliverance and inheritance of the land, and YHWH proved faithful, bringing not only his bones but his descendants into the land of Canaan. Numbers ends with a threefold reference to 'Joseph', as his descendants are granted a divine provision to ensure their tribe retains its land inheritance (36:1, 5, 12).

More profoundly, another key to the emphasis on Joseph in Numbers may be found in relation to the book's use of the pattern of the Nazirite, given as an exemplary path for Israel's wilderness sojourn (6:1–21). The last section of Numbers anticipates the completion of the 'Israel as Nazirite' pattern, whereby, after a period of privation (chs. 11–25), including cleansing from corpse pollution and a new start (ch. 19), the nation's worship with tribute and drink offerings (chs. 28–29) and the fulfilment of vows (ch. 30) is portrayed, completing the paradigm with abundance and blessing. The Torah's first use of the root *n-z-r* is in a description of Joseph as being a *nězîr* (usually translated 'separate' or 'a prince') among his brothers, given in Jacob's climactic blessing at the end of Genesis. More, this verbatim blessing on Joseph bookends the Torah, as Jacob and then Moses pronounce heaven's outpoured gifts on 'the crown of the head of Joseph', who was 'a Nazirite (*nězîr*) among his brothers' (Gen. 49:26; Deut. 33:16), even as the priestly benediction follows the Nazirite-vow legislation (Num. 6:22–27). Joseph's life thus seems to form the paradigm for the Nazirite vow: he not only rejects the path of the strayed woman (Gen. 39; cf. Num. 5:11–31), but waits on YHWH to fulfil his promises, even beyond his own death. The final section of Numbers offers a sustained contemplation of the tribes of Joseph, whose life conformed to the spirit of the Nazirite vow and whose head was thus crowned with divine blessing. Indeed, Jacob had prophesied, 'In you Israel will bless, saying: God make you as Ephraim and Manasseh!' (Gen. 48:20).

Explanation

Thematically, Numbers 27 should be considered together with chapter 26, both chapters confirming the second generation's hope of inheriting the land by taking a backward glance at the wilderness era and resolving issues of transition. *Life* in the land is contrasted with *death* in the wilderness. The phrase 'in the wilderness' occurs in three significant sections within these chapters, looking back on the first generation's death in the wilderness (twice in 26:64–65), looking back on Zelophehad's death in the wilderness (27:3), and looking back on Moses' rebellion in the wilderness for which he will die (27:14). Enabling a forward hope, resolution comes, respectively, with the second generation's land allotment (26:52–56), the allotment of land for Zelophehad's daughters (27:6–11) and the installation of Joshua as Israel's military leader to bring Israel into the land (27:18–23), each of these resolutions comprised of divine speeches (26:52; 27:6,18) whereby YHWH confirms in each case that he is giving the land to Israel (*nātan*, 26:54; 27:7, 12). The latter two divine resolutions were prompted by human initiative (27:1, 15), structurally uniting the chapter. In both scenarios of chapter 27, a problem arises through the death of an old generation Israelite (Zelophehad, then Moses), which leads to a request for resolution, assuring the second generation's inheritance of land and favourably granted by YHWH. Moreover, the census in Numbers 26 focused on two issues that are continued in chapter 27: first, there was the extended genealogy of Manasseh, including the five daughters of Zelophehad (26:33), addressed in Numbers 27:1–11 with a resolution to the daughters' plight, granting them to share in the land allotments; and, second, the goal of the census was stated explicitly in relation to the distribution of the land (26:52–56), addressed in Numbers 27:12–23 with the appointment of Joshua, who will distribute the land among the tribes (Mattingly 1997: 183–184).

Zelophehad of the tribe of Manasseh died as part of the general judgement on the first generation, but he had no sons, which meant his line would not receive a portion of land, and his name would be removed from his clan list – a dreadful tragedy. Selflessly and boldly, Zelophehad's five daughters approach Moses, Eleazar the priest, the chieftains and whole community of Israel and claim an allotment of land in his stead, ultimately entreating YHWH himself who, acknowledging the justness of their plea, fully grants them an inheritance, their case becoming the basis for an established ruling on inheritance in the absence of sons. In a sense, these daughters, who are the opposite of the strayed woman (5:11–31), are bidding YHWH to fulfil the principle of the restitution law (5:5–10), to give them what would otherwise have gone to Zelophehad's sons. The daughters' proposed solution did not, in the first place, have marriage in view (cf. ch. 36). On the one hand, if thinking only of themselves, their own well-being would have been secured by marriage to any Israelites among the tribes; on the other hand, in thinking of preserving their father's name, he would have no land to redeem through levirate marriage since his name would not have counted in the allocation census. Broadly, and as part of the inclusio formed around the last major section of Numbers (chs. 27, 36), the episode of the daughters of Zelophehad sets the tone of longing for the land, the tenacious hope of claiming YHWH's promises that will pervade the rest of the material. In many ways, their bold plea forms a reversal of the previous generation's sin, providing 'an example of the duty to cleave to the land and believe in the divine promise', a point brought out in *Sifre* to Numbers (Shemesh 2007: 98): 'The power of women is greater than the power of men. Men say, "Let us appoint a head and return to Egypt" (Num. 14:4), but women say, "Give us a portion among our father's brothers."' The daughters of Zelophehad, as Rashi pointed out (1997: 4:340), prove true daughters of Joseph, who so longed for the land that he made his brothers take an oath to carry up his bones out of Egypt and into the land of Canaan (Gen. 50:25; cf. Exod. 13:19; Josh. 24:32). Framing the last major section of the book, the daughters of Zelophehad episodes infuse all the material with a sense of excitement for obtaining (27:1–11) and retaining (36:1–12) the land as God's good gift, creating an appropriately zealous expectation on the part of the people and conveying YHWH's own divine affirmation of that desire – he reassures his people, reaffirming his promised intention to give them the land.

Emphasis on land in the last third of Numbers is no peripheral matter, but rather the culminating goal of the exodus out of Egypt, which remains an incomplete redemption outside life with God in Canaan. In Psalm 2, the Messiah, as YHWH's Adam-like vice-gerent, is promised the nations as his 'inheritance' (*naḥălāh*) and the ends of the earth as his 'possession' (*'aḥuzzah*) (v. 2; see Habel 1995: 25), and his people, the meek, will inherit the earth (Matt. 5:5) – membership in the covenant community remains inseparable from the hope of enjoying life in the land with God. This goal, to be consummated in the new heavens and earth as all of God's people – renewed Israel and the remnant of all the nations – are raised up and brought into the new Jerusalem (Rev. 21 – 22), is the culmination of the Messiah's redemption, the new exodus (cf. Morales 2020).

The census and ensuing episode with Zelophehad's daughters has affirmed YHWH's will to bring Israel into possession of the land of Canaan, renewing Israel's expectant hope. Just here, the major question surfaces as to *who* will lead Israel into the land. While YHWH had declared that Moses and Aaron would not lead Israel into the land due to their rebellion (20:12), he had never announced who would do so. Naturally, given that the office of high priest was hereditary, Aaron was replaced by his eldest living son, Eleazar (20:22–29), and even the subsequent high priest, Phinehas, was revealed as well (25:10–13), underscoring the omission all the more in relation to Moses' replacement. Here, for the first time, Joshua is revealed to be Moses' successor. YHWH bids Moses to ascend Mount Abarim to see the land, after which he will be gathered to his fathers, an event that will be fulfilled later in Deuteronomy 32:48–52, but noted here since it led to the appointing of Joshua. In response to the sobering news of his own impending death, Moses immediately intercedes for the sake of Israel, selflessly, urgently and compassionately pleading that YHWH will appoint a man to lead them so the community will not be as sheep without a shepherd. While situations of corrupt, false or no shepherds inevitably cause the scattering of the flock, a good shepherd after YHWH's heart will ensure the tribes are led and established in the land. That is the critical issue: without a shepherd to guide and protect the second generation of Israelites, there can be no inheritance of land. In response to Moses' prayer, YHWH provides Joshua, a man in whom resides God's Spirit and who will follow God's judgements through the high priest Eleazar's mediation. Through the hand-leaning rite by Moses, Joshua will receive more of the divine Spirit's enablement, including authority and wisdom – even some of the majesty of Moses. This majesty, along with the public ceremony of inauguration before the eyes of the community, will ensure that the people heed Joshua.

NUMBERS 28 – 29: WORSHIPPING YHWH IN THE LAND

Translation

$^{28:1}$And YHWH spoke to Moses, saying, ^{2}"Command the sons of Israel and say to them, "My near-offering, my bread, for my fire offerings, my restful aroma, you will guard to bring near to me at its appointed time." ^{3}And say to them, "This is the fire offering that you will bring near to YHWH: two lambs, a yearling without blemish, per day as a continual whole burnt offering. ^{4}The one lamb you will do in the morning, and the second lamb you will do at twilight (between the evenings). ^{5}And a tenth of an ephah of flour for a tribute offering, mixed with a fourth of a hin of beaten oil. ^{6}A whole burnt offering as ordained at Mount Sinai for a restful aroma, a fire offering to YHWH. ^{7}And its drink offering will be a fourth of a hin for the one lamb, you will pour out in the sanctuary the drink offering of strong drink to YHWH. ^{8}And the second lamb you will do at twilight, as the tribute offering of the morning, and as its drink offering you will do, a fire offering of restful aroma to YHWH.

^{9}"And on the Sabbath day, two lambs, yearlings without blemish, and two-tenths of flour for a tribute offering, mixed with the oil, and its drink offering. ^{10}The whole burnt offering of the Sabbath in its Sabbath, beside the continual whole burnt offering and its drink offering.

[11]"'And in the beginnings of your months you will bring near a whole burnt offering to YHWH, two bulls, sons of the herd, and one ram, seven lambs, yearlings without blemish, [12]and three-tenths of flour for a tribute offering, mixed with the oil, for one bull, and two-tenths of flour for a tribute offering, mixed with the oil, for each one ram, [13]and one-tenth (tenth-tenth?) of flour for a tribute offering, mixed with the oil, for each one lamb, a whole burnt offering of restful aroma, a fire offering to YHWH. [14]And their drink offerings will be half a hin for the bull, and a third hin for the ram, and a fourth hin for the lamb – of wine. This is the whole burnt offering of the month in its month, throughout the months of the year. [15]And one kid of the goats for a purification offering to YHWH, beside the continual whole burnt offering, will be done, and its drink offering.

[16]"'And on the first month, the fourteenth day of the month, is Passover to YHWH. [17]And on the fifteenth day of the month, this is a festival: seven days unleavened bread will be eaten. [18]In the first day there will be a holy convocation, any work of labour you will not do. [19]You will bring near a fire offering, a whole burnt offering to YHWH: two bulls of the herd, and one ram, and seven yearling lambs; they will be without blemish for you. [20]And their tribute offerings will be flour mixed with the oil, three-tenths for the bull, and two-tenths for the ram you will do. [21]One-tenth you will do for each lamb, for the seven lambs. [22]And one goat for a purification offering to make atonement for you. [23]Beside the whole burnt offering of the morning, which is for the continual whole burnt offering, you will do these. [24]As these you will do for every day, seven days, the bread of the fire offering of restful aroma to YHWH, aside from the continual whole burnt offering it will be done, and its drink offering. [25]And on the seventh day there will be a holy convocation for you, any work of labour you will not do.

[26]"'And in the day of firstfruits when you bring near the new tribute offering to YHWH, on your (Feast of) Weeks, there will be a holy convocation for you; any work of labour you will not do. [27]But you will bring near a whole burnt offering for a restful aroma to YHWH: two bulls of the herd, one ram, seven yearling lambs. [28]And their tribute offerings of fine flour, mixed with the oil, three-tenths for each one bull, two-tenths for each one ram, [29]a tenth for each one lamb, for the seven lambs. [30]One kid of the goats to make atonement for you. [31]Beside the whole burnt offering and its tribute offering you will do, they will be without blemish for you, and their drink offerings.

[29:1]"'And in the seventh month, on the first of the month, there will be a holy convocation for you; any work of labour you will not do – it is a Day of (Shofar) Blast for you. [2]You will do the whole burnt offering, for a restful aroma to YHWH: one bull of the herd, one ram, seven yearling lambs without blemish. [3]And their tribute offering of flour, mixed with the oil, three-tenths for the bull, two-tenths for the ram, [4]and one-tenth for each lamb, for the seven lambs. [5]And one kid of the goats for a purification offering, to make atonement for you. [6]Beside the whole burnt offering of the month, and its tribute offering, and the continual whole burnt offering and its tribute offering, and their drink offerings, according to their rule (*mishpat*) for a restful aroma, a fire offering to YHWH.

⁷"And on the tenth of this seventh month, there will be a holy convocation for you, and you will afflict your souls, any work you will not do. ⁸You will bring near a whole burnt offering to YHWH, a restful aroma, one bull of the herd, one ram, seven yearling lambs; they will be without blemish for you. ⁹And their tribute offering, flour mixed with the oil, three-tenths for the bull, two-tenths for each one ram, ¹⁰and a tenth for each one lamb, for the seven lambs. ¹¹One kid of the goats for a purification offering beside the purification offering of the atonements and the continual whole burnt offering and its tribute offering, and their drink offerings.

¹²"And on the fifteenth day of the seventh month, there will be a holy convocation for you; any work of labour you will not do; you will celebrate a festival to YHWH seven days. ¹³And you will bring near a whole burnt offering, a fire offering, a restful aroma, to YHWH, thirteen bulls of the herd, two rams, fourteen yearling lambs; they will be without blemish. ¹⁴And their tribute offering, flour mixed with the oil, three-tenths for each one bull, for thirteen bulls, two-tenths for each one ram, for the two rams, ¹⁵and a tenth for each one lamb, for fourteen lambs. ¹⁶And one kid of the goats for a purification offering, beside the continual whole burnt offering, its tribute offering and its drink offering.

¹⁷"And on the second day: twelve bulls of the herd, two rams, fourteen yearling lambs without blemish. ¹⁸And their tribute offerings and their drink offerings for the bulls, for the rams, and for the lambs, by their number, according to the rule. ¹⁹And one kid of the goats for a purification offering, beside the continual whole burnt offering, and its tribute offering, and their drink offerings.

²⁰"And on the third day: eleven bulls of the herd, two rams, fourteen yearling lambs without blemish. ²¹And their tribute offerings and their drink offerings for the bulls, for the rams, for the lamb, by their number, according to the rule. ²²And one goat for a purification offering, beside the continual whole burnt offering, and its tribute offering, and its drink offering.

²³"And on the fourth day: ten bulls, two rams, fourteen yearling lambs without blemish. ²⁴Their tribute offerings and their drink offerings for the bulls, for the rams, and for the lambs, by their number, according to the rule. ²⁵And one kid of the goats for a purification offering, beside the continual whole burnt offering, its tribute offering, and its drink offering.

²⁶"And on the fifth day: nine bulls, two rams, fourteen yearling lambs without blemish. ²⁷And their tribute offerings and their drink offerings for the bulls, for the rams, for the lambs, by their number, according to the rule. ²⁸And one goat for a purification offering, beside the continual whole burnt offering, and its tribute offering and its drink offering.

²⁹"And on the sixth day: eight bulls, two rams, fourteen yearling lambs without blemish. ³⁰And their tribute offerings and their drink offerings for the bulls, for the rams, for the lambs, by their number, according to the rule. ³¹And one goat for a purification offering, beside the continual whole burnt offering, its tribute offering, and its drink offering.

³²"And on the seventh day: seven bulls, two rams, fourteen yearling lambs without blemish. ³³And their tribute offerings and their drink offerings for the

bulls, for the rams, for the lambs, by their number, according to the rule. ³⁴And one goat for a purification offering, beside the continual whole burnt offering, its tribute offering, and its drink offering.

³⁵"'And on the eighth day there will be an assembly for you, any work of labour you will not do. ³⁶You will bring near a whole burnt offering, a fire offering, a restful aroma to YHWH, one bull, one ram, seven yearling lambs without blemish. ³⁷And their tribute offerings and their drink offerings for the bull, for the ram, for the lambs, by their number, according to the rule. ³⁸And one goat for a purification offering, beside the continual whole burnt offering, its tribute offering, and its drink offering. ³⁹These you will do to YHWH on your appointed times, beside your vow offerings and your freewill offerings, for your whole burnt offerings and your tribute offerings and your drink offerings and your peace offerings."' ⁴⁰And Moses said to the sons of Israel according to all that YHWH had commanded Moses.

Notes on the text

2. 'near-offering': BHS proposes pl., as with LXX, but the MT sing. matches the sing. suff. at the end of the verse.

'my bread': BHS proposes repointing as 'bread of', referencing 28:24 (which, however, does not include a final yod).

'appointed time': MT is sg.; SamP and LXX read pl.

5. 'beaten': missing from SamP and LXX.

7. 'you will pour out . . . to YHWH': Paterson sees this as a late gloss (1900: 61; cf. G. B. Gray 1903: 409; Noth 1968: 221).

9. 'two lambs': LXX, Vg and *TgNeof* supply 'you will offer' before listing the offerings.

10. 'beside': MT *'al*, 'over and above' (cf. R. J. Williams 2007: §292).

14. 'of wine': should perhaps be moved to before 'for the bull' with SamP, Syr, Vg and *TgO*.

'the bull . . . the ram . . . the lamb': SamP and LXX read 'for each one'.

17. 'will be eaten': SamP and LXX have 'you will eat', perhaps harmonizing with v. 18 (cf. Ezek. 45:21).

27. SamP adds 'a fire offering' after 'whole burnt offering' and 'they will be without blemish for you' at the end of the verse (cf. 28:19; 29:8) – LXX also adds, and BHS suggests, the latter phrase.

30. 'One kid of the goats': SamP and LXX add 'for a purification offering', supported by BHS.

29:6. 'fire offering': lacking in LXX.

7. 'any work': LXX, Syr and Vg have 'work of labour' (cf. 29:12, 35).

8. 'they will be . . . for you': lacking in Syr.

12. 'the seventh month': reads 'this seventh month' in SamP, LXX and Syr.

13. LXX includes 'on the first day'.

'without blemish': SamP adds 'for you' (cf. 28:19; 29:8).

14. Possibly, 'drink offering' has been omitted (see vv. 18, 21, 24, etc.); included by SamP at the end of v. 15.
16. 'its . . . its': LXX has plurals.
36. LXX reads 'for a restful aroma, a fire offering to YHWH' as in 29:6.
40. This is 30:1 in MT, but a paragraph break separates it from the rest of ch. 30 – it functions as a summary bridge between chs. 28 and 29 and 30.

Form and structure

The structure of chapters 28 and 29 is straightforward, covering the fire offerings the sons of Israel are to bring to YHWH on the sacred appointed times, and moves logically and chronologically from the daily, weekly and monthly offerings to those required for the annual holidays:

Introduction	28:1–2
1. Daily offerings	28:3–8
2. Weekly offerings	28:9–10
3. Monthly offerings	28:11–15
4. Annual offerings	28:16 – 29:38
Spring	
a. Passover/ Unleavened Bread	28:16–25
b. Weeks	28:26–31
Autumn	
c. Trumpets	29:1–6
d. Day of Atonement	29:7–11
e. Booths	29:12–38
Conclusion	29:39–40

While source-critical scholars tend to date this calendar late, in the post-exilic era (e.g. G. B. Gray 1903: 403; Kraus 1965: 35–36; Noth 1968: 219–220; Budd 1984: 314–315), its similarity to a Ugarit calendar (fourteenth century BC) positions this one well within its literarily presumed historical context (see Fisher 1970).

Comment

28:1–2: Introduction

YHWH instructs Moses to 'command' (*ṣaw*) the sons of Israel to 'guard' (*tišměrû*, 'keep', 'carefully observe') to offer YHWH's fire offerings at their appointed times. As Nachmanides points out, the command is appropriately placed here since YHWH had recently confirmed that 'to these the land will be divided' (26:53), and Israel previously had no need to bring any additional offerings for the Sabbaths and festivals, nor drink offerings, while in the wilderness (1975: 332). Given the structural delineation of the appointed times, it is easy to lose the actual focus of the text; namely, *the required fire offerings*. While Leviticus 23 has sacred time as its focus, Numbers 28 – 29 underscores the fire offerings divinely mandated for each occasion – the legislation creates recurring 'ritual moments' by synchronizing ritual activities with particular times (Morgan 1974: 215–219). As a result, form and function, liturgical order and cosmos are established for Israel's life in the land (cf. Gorman 1990: 216–217), anticipating the nation's vocation as a priestly kingdom and holy nation, which exhibits a society – a *living* in the land – that shows forth God's original purposes for creation. Leviticus 23, further, underscores the sacredness of time and consequent prohibitions of work, while Numbers 28 – 29, through the legislation of additional offerings, emphasizes the public, celebratory role of the nation of Israel (Bin-Nun 2011).

The fourfold 'my' (yod suff.) – 'my near-offerings', 'my bread', 'my fire offerings', 'my restful aroma' – establishes a sovereign claim to the offerings, adding gravity to the command, and justifying Israel's need to 'keep' the charge carefully – withholding such offerings in their appointed times is to rob God of his due. These offerings are also meant to ensure that once in the land Israel will be drawn continually to YHWH, deepening the nation's relationship with God and remembering the vocation it has received from him, which flows from Israel's fellowship and communion with him. Tellingly, previous calendric and sacrificial concerns were prefaced by the phrase 'when you enter the land' (Lev. 23:9; Num. 15:2), which is absent here because, to a degree, the inheritance is already assumed.

The burning on the altar of the whole or a part of an offering, sending it up to heaven in billows of aromatic smoke, is fundamentally what defines an offering as an 'approach' (*qorbān*) to YHWH, a 'gift by fire' (*'iššeh*) and a propitiating or 'restful' aroma (*reaḥ nîḥôaḥ*) (Eberhart 2004; cf. Morales 2019a: 33–36). Israel's basic sacrifices are legislated in Leviticus 1:1 – 6:7, where the whole burnt, tribute and communion offerings are each dubbed an *'iššeh* and restful aroma to YHWH, although the whole burnt offering's role dominates. Focus on the required fire offerings is related to the increasing anticipation of Israel's life in the land, for they serve to acknowledge both that the land and everything in and derived from it belong to YHWH, and that Israel's place in the land wherein YHWH dwells requires a continual cultic service: the manipulation of atoning blood and the ascent of propitiating smoke to heaven as a pleasing aroma are continually needed to enable the continual presence of YHWH's Dwelling among his people in the land. The phrase 'restful aroma' occurs first in Genesis when Noah, having emerged from the ark after the deluge, offers up whole burnt offerings, and 'YHWH smelled the restful aroma' (8:21), a propitiating incense that pacifies his wrath and the 'unrest' of his heart, yielding a divine resolve to uphold creation in spite of humanity's bent toward evil.

Strikingly, the priesthood of Aaron's house is nowhere mentioned, although its cultic service is assumed. Rather, the emphasis is placed on the obligation and participation of the 'sons of Israel' as a priestly kingdom and holy nation (Exod. 19:6) once in the land. The focus is on the people's contribution: note the uses of 'you' in the m. pl. (28:2, 3; 29:1, 2) – even the exceptional case, related to the daily *tāmîd*, which uses 'you will do' in m. sg. (28:4, 8) is addressed 'to them' (v. 3). Comparing this text with the offerings of the tribal princes in Numbers 7, a twofold movement is detected: from life in the Camp to life in the land, and from a focus on leaders (the chieftains) to a focus on the people.

The appropriate offerings are to be brought-near to YHWH at the 'appointed time' (*môʿăd*). In the creation account of Genesis, where the cosmos is presented as God's sanctuary, the central fourth day narrates the creation of the night sky, with its greater and lesser lamps and its hosts of stars, for the purpose (*lĕ-*) of 'appointed times' (*môʿădîm*, Gen. 1:14). While many translations render the term 'seasons', the Hebr. root for *môʿădîm* refers some 135 times (out of 160 occurrences) in the Torah to the Tent of 'Meeting' (*môʿēd*), with the majority of the other uses referring to the 'appointed time' of a festival or even as a synonym for the festival itself, and never to the seasons of the year, so that Genesis 1:14 refers to the fixed times of the annual festivals whereby humanity was to 'meet' with the Creator (Vogels 1997: 164–165; cf. Snaith 1963: 175; D. J. Rudolph 2003; Morales 2015: 43–45). Consequently, 'the appointed times of the liturgical order have been built into the very structure of the created order' (Gorman 1990: 218). As fire offerings centred on the whole burnt offering, the goal of the sacrifices and focus of the text is on the 'restful aroma' created by the offerings, the clouds of smoke that *continually* rise as propitiating plumes heavenward. The whole burnt offerings, moreover, solicited a Godward life of consecration from Israel. The Midrash, similarly, teaches that the sacrifices are not required because God needs to eat or drink, but for the sake of the pleasing aroma, reminding Israel to please him like the pleasing aroma (*Num. Rab.* 21.19). Aside from the daily and Sabbath cultic requirements, as Milgrom points out (1990: 237–238), there are 30 days per year of public sacrifices, including seven feasts (including Passover and the eighth day of Sukkot, *ʿăṣeret*). Ashley also counts 7 feasts but, perhaps more in line with the text's aims, reckons the sum as follows (1993: 562): Sabbath, New Moon, Unleavened Bread, Weeks, Day of Trumpet Blowing, Day of Atonement and Tabernacles. There are, moreover, 7 days of sacred assembly throughout these feasts, with 6 uses of 'holy convocation' (*miqrā'-qōdeš*, 28:18, 25, 26; 29:1, 7, 12) and a final use of 'assembly' (*'ăṣeret*, 29:35): for the first and seventh days of Unleavened Bread, on the day of firstfruits in the feast of Weeks, the Day of (Shofar) Blasts, the Day of Atonement, the first day of Booths, and for the eighth day after the week of Booths. Finally, offerings are prescribed in multiples of 7, with for example 70 bulls (7 × 10) as whole burnt offerings along with 7 male goats as purification offerings required for the feast of Booths.

28:3–8: Daily whole burnt offering

This section relates the requirements for the daily *tāmîd* ('continual', simply called *tāmîd*; cf. Dan. 8:11) whole burnt offerings, originally legislated in Exodus 29:38–46. While it is Leviticus 23 that designates sacred times, nevertheless Numbers 28 – 29, because it focuses on the appropriate offerings for those times, also highlights the sacred calendar. The whole burnt offering functioned as a marker of sacred time on a cosmic level, coordinated with the creation account's movement: day 1 (Gen. 1:3–5), as the period of each day, morning and evening, is marked by the daily *tāmîd* whole burnt offering; day 4 with its 'lamps' (*mĕ'ōrōt*) establishes the annual cultic festivals, the *mô'ădîm* (Gen. 1:14–19), which are marked by numerous whole burnt offerings; and day 7, the weekly, blessed and holy Sabbath (Gen. 2:1–3), is marked by adding two lambs to the *tāmîd* whole burnt offerings (see Gorman 1993: 52–53; Greenstein 2001: 4; Morales 2012: 85–86; 2015: 44–45, 198–200). The creation account presents not only a sacred place, the earth as a sanctuary and theatre for humanity's relationship with God, but its movement from day 1 to 4 to 7 is a musing on time as the atmosphere within which humans engage with God: the meaning and purpose of creation, and especially of humanity, are found not in creation itself but in time. Accordingly, beginning with the period of day, YHWH explains through Moses, 'This is the fire (offering) which you (pl., the sons of Israel) will bring-near (offer) to YHWH,' delineating the *tāmîd* whole burnt offering requirements: two yearling lambs without blemish per day. The expectation of Israel's life in the land of Canaan is hereby infused with cosmic significance well beyond a migratory people's territorial conquest. Sanctifying every transitional cycle of creation – from day to week to month, along with the annual seasons – Israel's cultic life in the land becomes a theatre for a divine calendar, acknowledging and proclaiming the Creator's sovereignty, holiness and redeeming power. The twofold daily offerings will be paralleled by the twofold annual offerings (for spring and autumn).

The Hebr. term for 'without blemish', *tamîm*, refers to blamelessness or 'wholeheartedness in devotion to YHWH' (see Trevaskis 2011:

202–207), and is first used of Noah (Gen. 6:9) and then of Abram, whom YHWH charges, 'be blameless' (Gen. 17:1). Such references are not irrelevant for the sacrificial system's symbolism: the animal, a vicarious substitute for the worshipper, represents a blameless proxy through its physical wholeness, being without spot or blemish. YHWH's heavenly abode may only be approached through a blameless substitute, through a life of wholehearted submission to the will of God (cf. Morales 2015: 127; 2019a: 33). The sacrifice of a blameless animal was to solicit such a life – 'You will be blameless with YHWH your God' (Deut. 18:13).

Central to Israel's worship, the whole burnt offering was its 'paradigmatic offering' holding 'pride of place' (Watts 2006: 125), the very 'basis and foundation of all the offerings' (Hirsch 2007a: 570). The whole burnt offering was not only the centre of the sacrificial system, but a summation of Israel's cult (see Morales 2019a; cf. Snaith 1957: 312; McCarthy 1969: 175), and given a prominent role in the Torah and the rest of the HB. Noah offered whole burnt offerings immediately after the deluge, propitiating YHWH's heart (Gen. 8:20–21); God tested Abraham, calling him to sacrifice Isaac 'as a whole burnt offering' (Gen. 22:2); and whole burnt offerings formed Israel's central means of engagement with YHWH at Mount Sinai (Exod. 24:5–8), the dominant focus of worship at the Tent of Meeting, through the 'altar of the whole burnt offering' (Exod. 29:38–46). Indeed, legislation for the whole burnt offering comprised YHWH's opening speech from the newly consecrated Tent of Meeting (Lev. 1:1–17), and is listed as the fundamental offering at the place where YHWH would choose to cause his name to dwell, for the worship envisioned in Deuteronomy (12:6, 11–14); and the list could go on – David offered up whole burnt offerings to halt a divine plague, dramatically unveiling the future site of the temple (2 Sam. 24).

Perhaps the main text, however, that demonstrates the cherished role of the whole burnt offering in the divine estimation is the present one; even a peripheral reading of Numbers 28 – 29 is striking in relation to the whole burnt offering's significance, not only for marking and consecrating every single day of Israel's life but also for being the principal event of virtually every sacred occasion, regardless of seasonal cycle or theological stress. These chapters portray, as Watts observes (2006: 133), 'regular priestly services as consisting mostly of *'ōlôt* offerings'. Incredibly, the first day of Booths required no fewer than thirty-one whole burnt offerings. The significance may be traced to the original majestic summary statement by YHWH concerning the continual whole burnt offering, linked to the altar, in Exodus 29:42, 45:

> This will be a continual whole burnt offering throughout your generations at the door of the Tent of Meeting before YHWH, where I will meet with you and speak with you there . . . And I will dwell among the sons of Israel and I will be their God.

These daily whole burnt offerings are concerned primarily with YHWH's continual presence among his people (cf. Gorman 1990: 220). Bick (1997) explains that just as the altar fulfils the purpose of the Dwelling, so the continual whole burnt offering fulfils the purpose of the altar: since YHWH's presence among Israel in the land is intended to be permanent, the altar, as the basis for his presence, must be in a state of continual offering, that of the whole burnt offering. *The tāmîd whole burnt offering, then, signals YHWH's presence in the land among Israel.* The altar is justly called 'the altar of the whole burnt offering' (*mizbaḥ hāʿōlāh*) – so designated seven times in Exodus (30:28; 31:9; 35:16; 38:1; 40:6, 10, 29), seven times in Leviticus 4 (vv. 7, 10, 18, 25 [twice], 30, 34) and five times in Chronicles (1 Chr. 6:34; 16:40; 21:26, 29; 2 Chr. 29:18). All other sacrifices were added to flames and smoke of the morning's whole burnt offering, incorporated into the *tāmîd* (J. W. Kleinig 2003: 40). Every day, in the morning and at twilight ('between the evenings', *bên hāʿarbāyim*), Aaron's priestly house was to offer up a yearling lamb as a whole burnt offering, this 'continual' offering to God bookending, and therefore subsuming, all of the day's other sacrifices – along with all Israel – within the ascending smoke of their soothing aroma. In this way, Israel's daily life was lived out within the context of the flames of these whole burnt offerings: whether plowing a field or weaving a basket, all of the Israelite's life was offered up to God, by the priesthood on behalf of Israel, through the soothing aroma that, morning and evening, ascended continually to YHWH's heavenly abode from the altar (Morales 2019a: 29). The Midrash offers a similar understanding: answering the question of how it could be that there 'was never a man in Jerusalem to whom iniquity adhered', *Numbers Rabbah* explains, 'The continual offering of the morning atoned for the transgressions of the night, while that of the dusk atoned for transgressions committed during the day' (21.21; Slotki 1951: 6:848). According to the Mishnah, the evening sacrifice took place at the ninth hour or around 3 p.m. (*m. Pes.* 5.1; cf. *m. Pes.* 58a).

Grasping the theological significance of the whole burnt offering begins with its name, '*ōlāh*, the 'ascending one' (or 'ascending offering'), focusing on the column of smoke that ascends from the altar heavenward, where YHWH God breathes in, as it were, the 'soothing aroma' (*rēaḥ nîḥōaḥ*) and is propitiated. The burning rite, the process of burning a part or the whole of an animal or other offering (such as grain), uses the Hebr. verb *hiqṭîr*, a technical term for cultic burning, signifying the transformation of the sacrifice into smoke. Whereas, for example, *śārap* is the general word used for burning for the sake of elimination in the common spheres of life, *hiqṭîr* is used specifically for the burning that takes place on the altar and focuses on the idea of transformation into smoke – the root *q-ṭ-r* is used for 'incense', which basically refers to 'that which goes up in smoke (to the Deity)' (Snaith 1957: 314–315). As Eberhart has shown (2004: 489–493; cf. G. A. Anderson 1992b: 873), the *hiqṭîr* rite of burning sacrificial material on the altar – whether for a whole burnt, tribute, communion, purification or reparation offering – is the *defining and climactic rite* of a sacrifice: the burning of sacrificial material on the altar makes it an *'iššeh*, a 'fire offering', transforms that material into smoke, a 'pleasing aroma', which rises to heaven and so constitutes an 'offering', a *qorbān* – literally, an 'approach' to God. The whole burnt offering, as the only sacrifice wherein all the parts of the whole animal (apart from its skin) are burned on the altar, presents the *hiqṭîr* rite par excellence and is thus fittingly dubbed 'ascending offering'.

Two aspects of the *hiqṭîr* rite flow into the theology of the whole burnt offering. First, that the *whole* animal is offered up, rather than merely the animal's fat as with the communion, purification and reparation offerings, leads more deeply to the essential meaning of the whole burnt offering as an utter consecration of one's whole life. Its aroma was pleasing to YHWH because it represented the life of self-denial and wholehearted submission to divine will, an absolute surrender to him, a yielding entirely to YHWH in total obedience to his law. Such consecration, again, unfolds the logic of why this offering so pleased and appeased YHWH: the whole burnt offering, offered daily, morning and evening, signified a complete dedication of oneself – of the people of Israel – to YHWH that can be summed up as 'loving YHWH God with all one's heart, soul and strength' (Deut. 6:5) (see Morales 2019a: 34–35).

The second aspect of the *hiqṭîr* rite brings us back to the Hebr. name for the whole burnt offering, the *'ōlāh* or 'ascending one'. As the fire transformed the sacrificial animal into an aroma pleasing to God, the offering as a vicarious substitute for the worshipper – and through its transformation into smoke – was made to ascend to the heavenly abode of YHWH. In the *hiqṭîr* rite, therefore, 'the offering is not destroyed but transformed, sublimated, etherealized, so that it can ascend in smoke to the heaven above, the dwelling-place of God' (F. C. N. Hicks 1953: 13; cf. Kurtz 1863: 154–155; Gayford 1953: 79; Blenkin 1964: 29; Low 2009: 27–29). As Lyonnet and Sabourin write, through this rite the ascending smoke becomes a visible presentation of humanity's restoration to God (1970: 169):

> The holocaust, therefore, was considered as 'the most perfect sacrifice,' because it expressed perfectly that oblation inasmuch as the whole victim, apparently transformed into the vapor of smoke (but not destroyed or reduced to nothing), could ascend unto God 'in fragrant odor' (see Eph. 5:2) and thus represent in a visible manner, as it were, the return of man to God.

The burning rite, stated differently, was for the sake of transferring the animal, as a vicarious substitute, from the ordinary earthly plane to the divine heavenly realm, to God's ownership. R. D. Nelson explains (1993: 60), 'the altar fire was a pipeline into the other world, vaporizing a burnt offering, the fat of a communion sacrifice, some grain, or even wine (Num. 15:7), up to Yahweh's domain'. So, too, Leach states the 'fire of the altar is the gateway to the other world, the channel through which offerings can be transmitted to God' (1985: 144). The idea of ascending to heaven through the sacrificial fire of a whole burnt offering is realized in a profound way in Judges: after Manoah offered up a whole burnt offering, we read that 'as the flame ascended heavenward from the altar, the messenger of YHWH ascended in the flame of the altar!' (Judg. 13:20). Through the daily *tāmîd*, the morning and evening whole burnt offerings, Israel ascends, as it were, ushered into YHWH's presence with the clouds (Morales 2019a: 35–36). With good reason the morning and evening *tāmîd* offerings were marked as times of prayer throughout the history of Israel, as God's people offered up praises and supplication with the high priest's offering of incense. The psalmist proclaims, 'From the rising of the sun to its setting' – the very times marked by the whole burnt offerings – 'the name of YHWH is to be praised' (Ps. 113:3), and 'May my prayer be affirmed as incense before your face, and the lifting of my palms (in prayer) as the evening tribute offering' (141:2; cf. Dan. 9:21; Mal. 1:11; Acts 3:1; Rev. 5:8; 8:3–4).

The vicarious entrance into God's heavenly abode, moreover, explains the logic of the tribute offering that normally accompanied the whole burnt offering, for one brings tribute when visiting a king. Here, the tribute offering is delineated as a tenth of an ephah of flour, mixed with a fourth of a hin of beaten oil – the grain or cereal is made into a cake of bread. The 'beaten' (*kātît*) oil was especially pure, having been pressed in a mortar (Milgrom 1990: 239; cf. BDB 510), and was the pure oil used to light the menorah (Exod. 27:20; Lev. 24:2). This section assumes the fuller treatment on accompanying tribute offerings and libations in Numbers 15:1–21, which had also served to encourage Israelites as a reaffirmation of God's intention to bring his people into the land even after the scouts' rebellion. Given the reference to a 'tenth of an ephah' in Exodus 16:36 in the story where YHWH first gave Israel bread from heaven in the wilderness, Hirsch suggests the tribute offerings also reminded Israel of how God had provided manna, and that he providentially supplies the needs of all his creatures (2007a: 577). A drink offering is then added, a fourth of a hin per lamb, poured out as a 'drink offering of strong drink' to YHWH. Pre-Sinai, the only recorded drink offering was offered by Jacob at the 'House of God', Bethel (Gen. 35:14). The Hebr. root for *šēkār* denotes intoxication, thus indicating a strong or 'fermented drink'; beer, widely used in the ANE, is unlikely since it was otherwise forbidden in the cult – rather, some sort of distinctly strong wine is probably meant (Alter 2004: 832; SamP and some MSS of LXX supply 'of wine'), wine that is undiluted with water.

Normally wine would be poured out, according to tradition, in a cavity at the side of the altar (cf. Sir. 50.15; *m. Meil.* 87b; *Sif. Num.*, Pinḥas 143; Nachmanides 1975: 335), although here *šēkār* is prescribed to be poured out 'in the sanctuary' (*baqqōdeš*) – possibly a general designation for the court area which included the altar (cf. Ashley 1993: 565). Israel approaches YHWH, the heavenly King, with a tribute of bread and with strong drink.

Verse 6 stands between the tribute and drink offerings, keeping the latter from being subsumed into the former – and they are clearly distinguished in verse 8 as well. More fundamentally, this verse anchors the legislation to Mount Sinai. While whole burnt offerings were performed pre-Sinai, by Noah and Abraham, and also at Sinai on the day of convocation (see Exod. 24:5), the reference here – taking *hāʿăśuyāh* as 'ordained' – is to the legislation for the *tāmîd*, the daily morning and evening sacrifices of lambs, revealed by YHWH to Moses at Sinai, thereby carrying its full weight of authority, as recorded in Exodus 29:38–46 (cf. Rashi's comments: 1997: 4:354). Reading *hāʿăśuyāh* as 'performed', Ibn Ezra takes this verse as proof that whole burnt offerings were not offered during the wilderness sojourn (see 1999: 231) – at the least, his understanding of 'sojourn' must exclude the stay at Sinai since the inaugural ceremony of the Tent of Meeting included the morning *tāmîd* (Lev. 9:17). The point here seems to be that the altar of whole burnt offering, as well as the entire Tent of Meeting cult, functioned to perpetuate the Mount Sinai experience, even through the wilderness sojourn. At Sinai, moreover, an altar had been constructed, surrounded by twelve pillars, a ritual scene parallel to Mount Sinai and the twelve tribes, with the altar and its fire consuming whole burnt offerings (Exod. 24:4–6) and representing Mount Sinai, whose summit was ablaze with YHWH's fiery presence – 'like a consuming fire on the summit of the mountain' (Exod. 24:17) – so that the altar of whole burnt offering itself recalls the Sinai experience (see Morales 2012: 232–243; cf. Hirsch 2007a: 578).

The Sinai institution of the *tāmîd* had the goal of a 'restful aroma' to YHWH, noted three times in verses 1–7, and this section on the daily whole offering also ends on this phrase. The *tāmîd*, morning and evening, functions as perpetual incense, causing propitiating billows of smoke to rise heavenward continually, ensuring YHWH's continual presence, through his Dwelling, in the land. The lamb, moreover, forms a theological link connecting the lamb to be provided by YHWH in Abraham's binding of Isaac (Gen. 22:7–8, 14), the divine provision of lambs in place of Israel's firstborn sons on Passover (Exod. 12:4–5), the daily *tāmîd* lambs (Exod. 29:38–46) and the suffering Servant of Isaiah (see Morales 2020: 30–32, 101–103, 143–145, 162). Hirsch even refers to the *tāmîd* offered by priests on the heights of Mount Moriah in Jerusalem as 'basically a continuation of the Pesach offering' (2007a: 571). For another connection, the time of the evening *tāmîd* sacrifice (28:8) is also the time delineated for the slaying of Passover lambs (Lev. 23:5; Num. 9:3; cf. G. J. Wenham 1981b: 221). The Lamb of God was crucified at the third hour, the time of the morning *tāmîd* (Mark 15:25), and died at the ninth hour, the time of the evening *tāmîd* (Mark 15:33–34, 37).

28:9–10: Weekly (Sabbath) whole burnt offering

From the daily *tāmîd*, the legislation moves to the weekly whole burnt offerings: on the Sabbath day two lambs are offered, along with two-tenths of fine flour mixed with oil ('beaten' oil is understood, v. 5), and its drink offering. While the regular daily whole burnt offerings mark the period of a day, the seventh – Sabbath – day is marked out by two extra whole burnt offerings, the *'ōlat šabbat bĕšabbattô*. The principle assumed throughout these chapters on calendric offerings is that the more frequent offerings take precedence, and are offered before the less frequent offerings: the morning *tāmîd* is offered before the Sabbath offerings, which are in turn offered before the monthly offerings, which in turn precede the offerings for the Day of (Shofar) Blasts (cf. *m. Zeb.* 10.1) – note the language of 'beside' (i.e. 'in addition to') the *tāmîd* (28:10, 15, 23, etc.).

The Sabbath day, rooted in creation as the first and only object of sanctification in Genesis (Gen. 2:1–3), is the designated sign of the Sinai covenant (Exod. 31:12–13), with Israel required to 'keep' the Sabbath, both in imitation of God's own rest from creative work (see Exod. 20:8–11; 31:14–17; 35:1–3), and because Israel was redeemed from Egyptian bondage in order to enter into this divine rest (Deut. 5:15). 'The common starting point for the entire legislation with regard to the feasts', wrote Kurtz (1863: 342), 'was the seventh day . . . and as such infolded prototypically within itself the fundamental idea of every festal celebration.' As a sign of the covenant, the Sabbath links the Mosaic covenant deeply to God's purposes for creation, and the divine redemption that brings creation to its glorious end and renovation – the Messiah ushers in a new creation through his own bodily resurrection on the 'eighth' or (new) 'first day' (cf. John 20:1, 19, 26; see Morales 2020: 166–168). In Isaiah, YHWH says 'from Sabbath to Sabbath (*šabbāt bĕšabbattô*) all flesh will come to worship before me' (66:23). The Sabbath, moreover, was sanctified for the sake of sanctifying Israel: 'You will surely keep my Sabbaths, because it is a sign between me and you throughout your generations, for you to know that even I, YHWH, am the one who sanctifies you' (Exod. 31:13). As the daily whole burnt offerings mark times of daily prayer, and each of the public fire offerings throughout the year – especially for the three pilgrimage feasts – mark occasions for Israel to enter YHWH's presence, the

Sabbath principle applies by degree to the entire liturgical calendar, for meeting with God is the basis and goal of sanctification (see Morales 2015: 185–220).

Previous legislation on keeping the Sabbath is assumed, the point here being to prescribe the required public offerings. Verse 10 clarifies that the Sabbath whole burnt offerings are aside from the daily *tāmîd* with its drink offering. The tribute offering is omitted only as subsumed with the whole burnt offering, which it always follows (cf. Lev. 9:16–17, 22). Finally, while Leviticus 23 noted only that the Sabbath calls for a holy convocation, in keeping with that chapter's focus on sacred time, Numbers fills the information gap on what offerings are required for the sacred gathering.

28:11–15: Monthly whole burnt offering

The rhythm continues from daily to weekly, and now to monthly, whole burnt offerings. The 'beginnings of your months' refers to the first day of the month, or the 'new moon' (*ḥōdeš*), marked in the cult by lavish sacrifices: two bulls, each with three-tenths of flour, mixed with oil, for a tribute offering, along with half a hin of wine as a drink offering; seven lambs, each with two-tenths of flour, mixed with oil, for a tribute offering, along with a third hin of wine as a drink offering; and seven lambs, each with one-tenth of flour, mixed with oil, for a tribute offering, along with a fourth hin of wine as a drink offering. As with the Sabbath ordinance (v. 10), there is a clear statement for the monthly ordinance: 'This is the whole burnt offering of the month in its month, throughout the months of the year'; in other words, to be performed twelves times annually. The new moon set of offerings, moreover, becomes the basis or archetype for all the *môʿădîm*, the annual feasts (Hirsch 2007a: 584). Just as marking the period of a day finds its epitome in the Sabbath, so the marking of months finds its epitome and purpose with the seventh month.

A new offering is added for the monthly ritual, which will also recur for the annual festivals: 'a kid of the goats for a purification offering'. The purification offering, legislated in Leviticus 4 – 5, focused on the manipulation of blood, thus emphasizing atonement and cleansing, since 'the life (*nepeš*) of the flesh is in the blood, and I have given it to you on the altar to make atonement for your lives (*nepeš*) – for it is the blood that makes atonement for the life (*nepeš*)' (Lev. 17:11; see Morales 2015: 130–132). The *ḥaṭṭāʾt* offering (Lev. 4) is regularly prefixed to the standard triad of offerings, whole burnt, tribute and peace offerings (Lev. 1 – 3), where it then functions to expand the atonement (blood) aspect of the whole burnt offering (cf. Levine 1965; Rainey 1970; Morales 2019a: 32–33). In isolation the focus and significance of the purification offering is on cleansing sancta and eliminating impurities, while as part of a set of sacrifices the purification offering signifies atonement for moral offences, or collective cleansing (Nihan 2007: 183–184). Nevertheless, in accord with rabbinic interpretation (*m. Shev.* 1.4–5), Milgrom understands the purification offering here as providing cleansing for the sanctuary and its sancta (1990: 242; followed by Frevel 2013c: 372–373). As Sklar demonstrated, the purification offering always includes both notions by degree of atonement and cleansing (2005: 186–187). The phrase 'to YHWH' is unusual for the purification offering (see Maimonides' discussion in *Guide for the Perplexed*, 3.46). Again, when not prefixed to the whole burnt offering, purification offerings serve to cleanse the individual offeror and YHWH's Dwelling from the defilement of particular sins, the priest thereby making atonement so the worshipper may be forgiven by YHWH (Lev. 4), and on the Day of Atonement, which revolves around an expanded purification offering ceremony, Israel as a nation, the priesthood and the Tent of Meeting, with its altar and cultic furnishings, were atoned for and cleansed (Lev. 16). The phrase 'one kid of goats' is used, employed seven times in this legislation (28:15, 30; 29:5, 11, 16, 19, 25), while 'one goat' is used six times (28:22; 29:22, 28, 31, 34, 38), probably a stylistic change. A variation is also found with the phrase 'to make atonement for you' added to the purification offering (28:22, 30; 29:5, 11) or its absence (28:15; 29:16, 19, 22, 25, 28, 31, 34, 38). Hirsch connects the purification offering with the new moon, implying the divine lesson that, like the moon, humanity may be renewed, attaining light after any darkness (2007a: 587).

Although the *tāmîd* is referenced in relation to the purification offering in verse 15, the reckoning of the new moon whole burnt offerings is also 'beside' the daily whole burnt offering. Note that 'its drink offering' relates to the *tāmîd*, as the purification offering is never accompanied by a drink offering (cf. Rashi 1997: 4:357). In Isaiah, 'new moon' festivals are mentioned alongside Sabbaths, convocations and assemblies, as well as with 'your appointed feasts' (1:13–14).

28:16 – 29:38: Annual whole burnt offerings

Now from daily, weekly and monthly whole burnt offerings, the legislation progresses to the annual appointed times, marked by special whole burnt offerings. The daily, weekly and monthly times are *cyclical* and relate to creation. The annual times, while cyclical to the extent that they coincide with annual seasons and their harvests, moving from spring (Passover, Unleavened Bread, Weeks) to autumn (Trumpets, Day of Atonement, Booths), are also *linear* or covenantal, commemorating the history of redemption (cf. Sacks 2017: 5). Creation and redemption, while distinct, are inseparable theologically. For these appointed times the language differs from that of the daily, weekly and monthly offerings: the annual holidays are designated 'holy convocations' (*miqrā'-qōdeš*) in which no 'work of labour' (*mĕle'ket 'ăbōdāh*) is permitted – even though, as per Leviticus 23:3, the Sabbath, too, is a holy convocation in which no work (*mĕlā'kāh*) is to be done.

28:16–25: Passover and Feast of Unleavened Bread whole burnt offering

The fourteenth day of the first month is Passover (*pesaḥ*) to YHWH (see Exod. 12:1–20; Lev. 23:4–8; Deut. 16:1–8). The term *pesaḥ* may refer to 'protection' rather than 'hopping' or 'passing over' (Levine 2000: 380). In Exodus 12, when YHWH had instituted Passover as the ritual to experience and later commemorate the exodus deliverance, he had reformulated Israel's calendar: 'This month will be for you the beginning (*rō'š*) of the months, it is the first (*ri'šôn*) of the months of the year for you' (v. 2), formerly called Abib (cf. Exod. 13:4; 23:15; Deut. 16:1), but after the return from Babylonian exile called Nisan. 'Abib' refers to green or unripe corn, specifically, ears of barley grain (cf. BDB 1), reflecting the period of early spring, and correlating to the present month of April. The text, aside from acknowledging Pesach, focuses attention on the feast of Unleavened Bread – a feature explained by the fact that these chapters are dealing with the prescribed public and communal sacrifices, whereas the Passover sacrifice was still at this point in history conceived as a household celebration (cf. Exod. 12:1–14).

Although practically Judaism begins the year with Rosh HaShanah, and treatments on the festivals correspondingly begin with the seventh month, which begins the agricultural year, yet the Torah consistently delineates the months and their feasts beginning with Passover (Lev. 23:4–8; Num. 28:16–25), this logical ordering also being manifest in their respective historical-redemptive dimensions, with the exodus (Passover) preceding life in the wilderness (Booths). The Gospel of John presents Jesus' life and death in terms of the Passover 'Lamb of God', so that even in death his bones were not broken, fulfilling the ceremonial regulation of the Passover lamb (cf. Exod. 12:46; John 1:29, 36; 19:31–37; Morales 2020: 159–166).

After one verse on Passover, the rest of the paragraph relates to the feast of Unleavened Bread, the fifteenth day designated a 'festival' (*ḥāg*). Considering parallels between Leviticus 23:14 and Joshua 5:11, LeFebvre argues this festival, the convocation on the first day of Unleavened Bread, is 'best understood as the Feast of Firstfruits, which is here dated to the fifteenth . . . just as the convocation on the Feast of Weeks was also called "the day of [wheat] firstfruits" (Num. 28:26)' (2019: 42–43). The requirements for observing Passover are detailed in Exodus 12, while those for Unleavened Bread are given in Exodus 12:18–20 and 13:3–10. In keeping with their differing agendas, Leviticus 23 states in passing that 'an offering made by fire' must be offered to YHWH for the seven days of Unleavened Bread (23:8), but the revelation of the nature and details of those offerings is given only now in Numbers.

The first and seven days are set apart for holy convocations (*miqrā'-qōdeš*, the first two of the year), prohibiting any 'work of labour' (*mĕle'ket 'ăbōdāh*), widely understood to refer to any form of industry that requires labour; that is, occupational work. By contrast, the Day of Atonement (and the Sabbath) is more strict, forbidding 'any work' (29:7), whereas the other festivals allow for non-laborious work. In Leviticus 23, both the Sabbath and the Day of Atonement forbid any work (vv. 3, 28), requiring complete rest (*šabbat šabbātôn*, see Exod. 16:23; Lev. 16:31). For the seven-day period unleavened bread (*maṣṣôt*) is eaten, and each of the seven days requires the same three sets of sacrifices, and their tribute offerings, as required for the monthly offerings above (vv. 11–15). Two bulls of the herd, one ram and seven yearling lambs, along with their tribute offerings, and one goat for a purification offering, are required. Doing these same sets of sacrifices 'every day, seven days' is by way of contrast to the feast of Booths, which will involve a progressively decreasing number of bulls throughout the seven days (see 29:12–34; cf. Rashi 1997: 4:359). The principle of telescoping, which will continue into the seventh month, is thus employed: on the first month, the new moon offerings are expanded for seven days. Rashi employs interesting symbolism here, taken from HaDarshan, whereby (1997: 4:358) the bulls represent Abraham (see Gen. 18:7), the rams, Isaac (see Gen. 22:13) and the lambs, Jacob (see Gen. 30:40).

28:26–31: Firstfruits, Feast of Weeks whole burnt offering

On the day after the Passover Sabbath, Israel was to bring a firstfruits 'sheaf' (*'ōmer*) of the spring barley harvest, and then to count seven Sabbaths, bringing a 'new tribute offering' (*minḥāh ḥădāšāh*), now of the wheat harvest, to YHWH on the fiftieth day (see Lev. 23:9–14, 15–22), hence the name 'Weeks' (*šābu'ōt*) or 'Pentecost'. The 'day of firstfruits' called for a 'holy convocation', the third of the year. Occurring at the beginning of the wheat harvest, again, which comes seven weeks after the beginning of the barley harvest, the feast of Weeks is also defined as the 'Firstfruits of the wheat harvest' (Exod. 34:22; Lev. 23:15–16; cf. Exod. 23:16). Two wheat loaves comprised the main firstfruits offering (Lev. 23:17), and a liturgy of rejoicing for the offering is supplied in Deuteronomy, which recounts the exodus out of Egypt, confessing that YHWH 'brought us into this place and gave to us this land, a land flowing with milk and honey. And now, look, I have brought the firstfruits of the land, which you, O YHWH, have given me' (26:9–10).

The whole burnt offering requirements are the same three sets of sacrifices, and their tribute offerings, as required for the monthly offerings above (vv. 11–15). Also as with the new moon and other feasts, a kid of the goats for a purification offering is done, in this instance including the phrase 'to make atonement for you' (cf. v. 15). As with all the weekly, monthly and annual offerings, these are aside from and in addition to the daily *tāmîd*. The feast of Weeks is the only festival in Leviticus 23 for which fire offerings are delineated, but the number of bulls and rams is reversed (cf. 23:18), a discrepancy for which there is no satisfactory answer (cf. Ashley 1993: 567–568).

Traditionally, the story of Ruth, with its literary and theological background of a wheat harvest, has been connected with the feast, which also drew in Messianic hopes, since it culminates with David's genealogy (Ruth 4:18–22; cf. Cole 2000: 476–477). Given the chronology of redemptive history, that Israel entered into covenant with YHWH at Sinai in the third month after their Passover deliverance out of Egypt (Exod. 19:1), the feast of Shavuot naturally became closely linked with the giving of the Decalogue at Sinai, likely before the writing of the New Testament. Already in the second century BC, Jubilees associates Shavuot not only with the Sinai covenant, but with the covenants with Noah and Abraham as well (1:1–2; 6:17; 15:2). In Acts, the outpouring of the Spirit by the heavenly enthroned Messiah takes place on Pentecost, a divine gift that inscribes the Decalogue on the hearts of God's people (Acts 2:1–4, 32–39; cf. Jer. 31:31–34; Ezek. 36:25–27).

29:1–6: Day of (Shofar) Blast whole burnt offering

Even as the creation week progressed to the blessed, holy Sabbath, the seventh day, so the year culminates with the awe-inspiring holiness of the seventh month. The first day of the seventh month called for a 'holy convocation', the fourth of the year. Earlier in Numbers, YHWH had commanded Israel to fashion two silver trumpets, saying that

> in the day of your gladness and at your appointed times (*mô'ădîm*) and on the first of your months, you will sound (*tāqa'*) the trumpets over your whole burnt offerings and over your sacrifices of peace offerings, and they will be to you for a memorial before the presence of your God. (Num. 10:10)

But this day in particular is a 'Day of Blast' (*yôm těrû'āh*), which sounded in a way that was distinct from the regular sounding of trumpets for the first day of the months (*těrû'āh* rather than *tāqa'*;

see also Lev. 23:24). Probably, as traditionally understood, this 'Day of Blast' entailed the sounding of a ram's horn, a shofar – Psalm 81:3: 'Sound the shofar on the new moon, on the full moon, for the day of our festival.' The blast is an alarm, calling for attention, a summons to return to God and prepare oneself for the Day of Atonement as if for the Day of Judgement. The shofar 'is about the future', writes Sacks (2017: 19); it 'is always a signal of something about to come: the imminent arrival of the king, a warning of impending danger, or the sound of a trial about to begin'. Similarly, Steinsaltz observed that the sound of the shofar is that 'of a cry, of sobbing and moaning', that the shofar's sound 'is not meant to be pleasant to the ear', but meant 'to shock, to awaken those who slumber in the endless routine of life and guide them towards *teshuva* [repentance]' (2011: 4; cf. Rambam, *Hilkhot Teshuva* 3.4).

Insightfully, Milgrom observes (1990: 246):

> Perhaps Psalms 47 and 95–100, in which shofar blowing is prominent, were sung; and their theme of cosmic judgement – 'he is coming to rule the earth' (Pss 96:13; 98:9) – was incorporated as a permanent theme in the liturgy of this day.

Hirsch remarks on the confluence of the morning *tāmîd*, the new moon offering and the sound of the Rosh HaShanah shofar blast (2007a: 598):

> For on this day the thoughts that lead joyfully to God spring from three sources: from the light of the morning, which proclaims God's glory; from the new moon, which calls for renewal; and the sound of the *tĕrû'āh*, which stirs us to repentance.

Historically in Judaism this day came to be celebrated as New Year's Day (Rosh HaShanah), with the seventh month considered the beginning of the agricultural year. Balaam had gazed at Israel from the summit of Pisgah and declared, 'the shout (*tĕrû'āh*) of a King is among them' (23:21), and likely this annual shofar blast served to remind Israel of the same.

The number seven continues to feature prominently for YHWH's appointed times: the daily *tāmîd* repeats seven times, ascending into the seventh day, the Sabbath day, and after Passover seven Sabbaths are counted until the feast of Weeks, and now the initial first month moves to the seventh month, climactically underscored in a threefold manner with three feasts, (Shofar) Blast, Day of Atonement and Booths, with the third feast lasting seven days, capped by a holy convocation on the eighth.

On the first day of the seventh month, and in addition to the daily *tāmîd* and new month whole burnt offerings, with their tribute and drink offerings (v. 6), a whole burnt offering of restful aroma is offered to YHWH, similar to the monthly triad of offerings and their tribute offerings (see 28:11–15), except that the number of bulls is one instead of two – as will be the case also for the Day of Atonement.

29:7–11: Day of Atonement whole burnt offering

The tenth day of the seventh month is also a holy convocation (the fifth of the year), the Day of Atonement, literally, 'atonements', *kippurîm* (cf. Lev. 16; 23:27; see Morales 2015: 167–180). For both the Sabbath (cf. Lev. 23:3) and the Day of Atonement (Num. 29:7), there is a prohibition of 'any work', which is more restrictive than for the other festivals where only 'any labour of work' is prohibited. On the Day of Atonement, Israelites are also called to 'afflict your souls' (*wĕ'innîtem 'et-napšōtêkem*), understood traditionally as – but not reduced or limited to – fasting. The word *'ānāh* refers to being 'bowed down', 'humbled' or 'afflicted', and there are examples in the Bible where afflicting or humbling oneself – also 'denying yourselves' (Lev. 16:29) – is accomplished through fasting. In Psalm 35, the psalmist says 'I afflicted my soul (*'innêtî . . . napšî*) with fasting (*baṣṣôm*)' (v. 13). In Isaiah 58, YHWH recounts how the people ask, 'Why have we fasted (*ṣamnû*)? . . . Why have we afflicted (*'innînû*) our souls?' (v. 3). And Ezra proclaimed 'a fast' (*ṣôm*) in order that 'we might afflict (or 'humble', *hit'annôt*) ourselves' before God (8:21). As with the Day of (Shofar) Blasts, the requirement for the Day of Atonement whole burnt and tribute offerings is the same as for the new month (see 28:11–15), except that the number of bulls is one instead of two. One kid of the goats is also required for a purification offering; this aside from the purification offering of 'the atonements' (*hakkippuîm*), having reference to the atonement ceremony detailed in Leviticus 16 – there the two identical goats, one sacrificed to YHWH and the other sent away into the wilderness loaded down with Israel's sins, are referred to as one purification offering (cf. Lev. 16:5). Again there is a statement that the Day of Atonement whole burnt and purification offerings are aside from the *tāmîd* and its tribute and drink offerings. By contrast with Leviticus, where Aaron the high priest is addressed and the Day of Atonement rituals are given in detail (Lev. 16:2), this section, addressed to the sons of Israel (28:2), focuses only on the public offerings to be supplied by Israel.

Although the Day of Atonement is most clearly anchored within the context of the newly established cult in Leviticus, where it was placed as the book's literary and theological centre (ch. 16), Jewish tradition also connects the ceremony to the renewal of the Sinai covenant after the golden calf incident (cf. Exod. 32:30; see e.g. Hirsch 2007a: 600). On this reading the annual feasts obtain relative redemptive-historical chronology: Passover (exodus out of Egypt), Weeks (receiving the Decalogue at Sinai), Day of Atonement (renewal of covenant after golden calf apostasy), Booths (journey through the wilderness to the land). Hebrews offers a sustained reflection on how God's Son has accomplished a Day of Atonement to cleanse not merely the Tent of Meeting, a microcosm of creation, but the cosmos, having entered heaven itself, of which the Tent's holy of holies was merely a copy (Heb. 9).

29:12–38: Feast of Booths whole burnt offerings

The third appointed time of the seventh month occurs on the fifteenth day and is then expanded for seven days. Not only is the feast a 'holy convocation', the sixth sacred assembly of the year, wherein no 'work of labour' must be done, but Israel is called to 'celebrate a festival' (*wĕḥaggōtem ḥag*) to YHWH for seven days, each day requiring its own set of sacrifices, and is capped by an eighth day of assembly. Although the name of the feast is not given, in Leviticus 23 it is called 'The Feast of the Booths' (*ḥag hassukkôt*, v. 34; cf. Deut. 16:13), since its celebration included the Israelites' building and dwelling in booths, temporary shelters (see Lev. 23:39–43; cf. Neh. 8:13–18), and in Exodus, the 'Feast of Ingathering' (*ḥag hā'āsîp*, 23:16; 34:22). Just as the Day of Atonement came to be known simply as 'The Day' (see *m. Yom.*), the Feast of Booths came to be called 'The Feast' (1 Kgs 8:22; 12:32). As with the spring feast of Unleavened Bread, which begins on the fifteenth day of the first month and telescopes into seven days, so the autumn feast of Booths begins on the fifteenth day of the seventh month and telescopes into seven days. On this day, Israel's life 'which was planted on the fifteenth of the first month, blossoms and bears fruit' (Hirsch 2007a: 601). Each of the seven days requires two rams and fourteen yearling lambs, but for the bulls thirteen are required on the first day, counting down to seven bulls on the seventh day (for a total of seventy). The standard tribute offerings are listed for the first day, with mention made also of the drink offering, but for each subsequent day a summary statement is supplied instead: the tribute and drink offerings are required 'by their number, according to their rule'. Each day also requires one goat for a purification offering. The eighth day marks a distinct occasion, a separate day of 'assembly' (*'ăṣeret*; cf. also Lev. 23:36) – the final, seventh sacred assembly (although 'holy convocation' is used for the other six) – wherein no work of labour is done, and that requires its own set of sacrifices: one bull, one ram, seven yearling lambs, along with their tribute and drink offerings – the same requirements as for the first and tenth of the same month (29:2, 8). The root of *'ăṣeret* includes the notion of being confined or restrained (see BDB 783b–784a), perhaps connected here to being restrained from doing work, or, alternatively, from departing immediately after the seven days so as to remain for the eighth-day ceremonies (Rashi 1997: 4:365). The eighth day stands as the day of renewal or recreation, coming after the seventh-day consummation of creation, evident in the significance of circumcision on the eighth day (Gen. 2:1–3; 17:9–14) and the role of the eighth day in cleansing rituals (Lev. 14:10; Num. 6:10), and here likely signifies the new beginning on the other side of divine judgement and the consummation of history. This eighth day gathering, Shemini Atzeret, has been likened to the more intimate gathering of close friends and relatives after the major festivities among the broader circle of people have ended – the smaller 'private reception' between God and his people (see Sacks 2017: 155–158).

Occurring in the autumn, coalescing with the last harvest ingathering of the year, especially that of grapes, the feast of Booths eventually took an eschatological meaning, with the prophet Zechariah proclaiming the ingathering of the nations to Jerusalem 'to worship the King, YHWH of hosts, and to celebrate the feast of Sukkot' (14:16), again underscoring the kingship-of-God motif. Aptly Hirsch observes (2007a: 604):

> World history begins with the building of the Tower and ends with the building of the *sukkah*. The builders of the Tower worshipped human power and sought to conquer heaven; the builders of the *sukkah* will render homage to God and rejoice in their lives on earth.

The last ingathering, moreover, which took place after typically parched summers, also carried concerns of prayer that God would grant the necessary rains for the ensuing year (see *Sif. Num.* 150), imagery that became linked theologically with the people's need for the outpouring of the Holy Spirit (see e.g. Isa. 32:15; 44:3; 51:3), and which led to the incorporation of a water-pouring ritual during the feast (see Morales 2020: 173–179). John's Gospel records that on the great day of this feast Jesus cried out, 'If anyone thirsts let him come to me and drink. The one who believes in me, as the Scripture says, out of his heart rivers of living water will flow,' speaking of his gift of the Spirit (7:37–38).

The required whole burnt offerings data, including all the appointed times, may be charted as in Table 21, with numbers in parentheses indicating the inclusion of the *tāmîd* and/or new moon whole burnt offerings (cf. G. J. Wenham 1981b: 21; Ashley 1993: 563):

The precise tally of sacrifices is tentative due to an array of variables. On the seventh day of Booths, for example, I have included four more lambs, since the required offerings are aside from the two *tāmîd* lambs and the two additional lambs for the Sabbath – whether such adjustments mar any intended numeric ideal, symbolism or numerology is difficult to determine. The Midrash observes that the seventy bullocks, as the sum total for the feast of Booths, were offered as atonement for the seventy

Table 21: Whole burnt offerings in Numbers 28 – 29

Appointed times		Bulls	Rams	Lambs	Total
Daily *tāmîd*		–	–	2	2
Weekly Sabbaths		–	–	2 (4)	4
Monthly new moons		2	1	7 (9)	12
Annual feasts					
Unleavened bread		2	1	7 (9)	12
Sum for seven days		14	7	49 (65)	86
Firstfruits/Weeks		2	1	7 (9)	12
Trumpets		1 (3)	1 (2)	7 (16)	21
Day of Atonement		1	1	7 (9)	11
Booths	Day 1	13	2	14 (16)	29 (31)
	Day 2	12	2	14 (16)	28 (30)
	Day 3	11	2	14 (16)	27 (29)
	Day 4	10	2	14 (16)	26 (28)
	Day 5	9	2	14 (16)	25 (27)
	Day 6	8	2	14 (16)	24 (26)
	Day 7	7	2	14 (18)	23 (27)
Sum for seven days		70	14	98 (114)	182 (198)
	Day 8	1	1	7 (9)	11

nations, while the eighth-day assembly was more intimately about Israel's own special relationship with YHWH (cf. *Num. Rab.* 21.24) – and the decrease in bulls relates to the decreased contrast between Israel and the nations, in terms of acknowledging and serving the one true God, as Israel fulfils their mission among them (cf. Hirsch 2007a: 603). Given that seventy nations are listed in the 'table of nations' (Gen. 10), such symbolism makes sense (cf. Sacks 2017: 106; contra Ayali-Darshan 2015). Jewish tradition also suggests the ninety-eight sum total of lambs, which represent Israel, were intended to guard Israel against the ninety-eight curses mentioned in Deuteronomy 28:15–68 (see Rashi 1997: 4:363). At the least, the large number of sacrifices, built on the number 7 (cf. Nihan 2008: 185–186), demonstrates the importance of this culminating autumn festival (cf. Rubenstein 1996; Ulfgard 1998: 90). The table includes only the whole burnt offerings, but it is noteworthy that seven goats as purification offerings, the total for the seven days of Booths, are also required. As Leibtag (2017) observes, there are three groups of sacrifices: (1) the first New Moon, Unleavened Bread and Weeks each included a 2–1–7 scheme (for bulls, rams and lambs, respectively), and all take place in the spring and relate to the exodus out of Egypt (if the New Moon is regarded as the 'first month'); while (2) (Shofar) Blast, Day of Atonement and the Eighth-Day Gathering (Shemini Atzeret) follow a

1–1–7 scheme, all taking place in the seventh month and perhaps dealing with the theme of judgement; (3) Booths doubles daily the second and third figures in the set to 2–4 (rams–lambs), in effect doubling the number of the first two groups.

In a profound sense, the Feast of Booths celebrates the inheritance of the land, and, as a celebration of all Israel, including the participation of Levites and priests, in a festival to YHWH, it becomes a culminating expression of the inheritance theme that pervades the last section of Numbers (chs. 26–36; cf. Naylor 1994: 193).

29:39–40

A summary statement reiterates that 'these (fire offerings) you (pl.) will do unto YHWH on your appointed times' or 'on your feasts' (*bĕmô'ădêkem*), a reminder that the speech is directed, through Moses, from YHWH to the sons of Israel (28:1). Remarkably, no priests are mentioned at all in these chapters, nor is 'the place which YHWH your God will choose out of all your tribes to put his Name there' ever noted, the refrain that recurs throughout Deuteronomy 12 (vv. 5, 11, 14, 18, 21, 26) – yet neither is the Tent of Meeting or its altar ever mentioned. The speeches of Leviticus 23 are also for the sons of Israel (vv. 2, 10, 24, 34, 44), and while 'priest' occurs three times in Leviticus 23 (vv. 10, 11, 20), there are no references to the Tent of Meeting (or future 'place') or its altar, since these, as with Numbers 28 – 29, are assumed in the language of 'fire offering to YHWH' – as detailed already in Leviticus 1 – 5. Since the material in Numbers assumes that of Leviticus, the feasts are not explained in detail, nor is their theological rationale explained. The feast of Booths, for example, is described in detail in Leviticus 23:33–43, whereas even its name does not occur in Numbers 29:12–38. The present chapters are supplemental in a precise manner, listing the required fire offerings, repeating the phrase *rêaḥ nîḥōaḥ* (soothing aroma) eleven times (28:2, 6, 8, 13, 24, 27; 29:2, 6, 8, 13, 36), the last occurrences of the Torah – whereas the phrase appears only twice in Leviticus 23 (vv. 13, 18).

Although not mentioned until verse 39, the 'peace offering' (*šĕlāmîm*) was nevertheless a required staple for some of the appointed times, for example, the feast of Weeks (see Lev. 23:17–21), demonstrating that these present chapters do indeed assume the previous legislation. The peace offering, part of the standard triad of offerings (whole burnt offering, tribute offering and peace offering; see Lev. 1 – 3), enabled the worshipper to dine on the sacrificial meat as a joyful communion meal in God's presence, and, as with the tribute offering, may be explained in relation to the whole burnt offering's ascent: having entered the heavenly abode of God and offered him tribute, one then enjoys his unsurpassed hospitality. With YHWH as host in the custom of the ANE, Israel is amply sated by the abundance of God's house (Ps. 36:8–9) as he prepares a table before them and anoints their head with oil (Ps. 23:5) (see Morales 2015: 137–140).

These designated offerings are aside from 'your vow offerings and your freewill offerings' (cf. also Lev. 23:38), the latter detailed in Leviticus 1 – 5. Both vow and freewill offerings are grouped together in Leviticus 22:18–23 (cf. Lev. 28) and in Numbers 15:1–21 (see v. 3). In Numbers, vows are referenced in relation to the Nazirite (6:2, 5, 21), for the second generation's victory over the Canaanites at Hormah (21:2) and finally in chapter 30, where the binding nature of vows is underscored, along with exceptional cases related to women. The admonition that 'these' required fire offerings were to be offered aside from 'your vows and freewill offerings' assumes that vows and freewill offerings pledged throughout the year would normally be fulfilled during the pilgrimage festivals, so Israelites would not need extra journeys to Jerusalem (Rashi 1997: 4:367). The chapters have presented public, communal offerings, which are distinct from the private, individual ones. The reference to 'vow offerings' in 29:39 serves as a key word link for chapter 30's discussion of vows.

A summary statement concludes the fire offerings legislation, reporting that Moses indeed conveyed to the sons of Israel all that YHWH had commanded him (29:40). Nachmanides aptly notes how this concluding statement, in excluding the priesthood, as with 28:2, underscores the nature of the laws, that they call Israelites to observe these days, the bringing of offerings and refraining from labour, and so on, when they enter the land (cf. 1975: 338–340).

Explanation

Once the census has designated those who will inherit the land (Num. 26; 27:1–11) and Joshua has been inaugurated to lead the people into their possession of the land (27:12–23), the first consideration, the priority and goal for Israel's life in the land must be established; namely, *the worship of YHWH God*. By analogy to other parts of the Torah, the position of these chapters on sacrifices will be manifest. As the foundation for the Sinai covenant, the Decalogue opens with the object, means, place and day of Israel's worship, instructing Israel to have no other gods before YHWH, not to make any graven images, not to bear his Name vainly and to keep his Sabbath day holy – the worship of YHWH God was the primary end for their deliverance out of Egypt, as the preamble implies (Exod. 20:1–11). Moreover, as the so-called 'law of the altar' shows, manufacturing idols is countered by offering whole burnt offerings on an earthen altar wherever YHWH causes his Name to be remembered (Exod. 20:22–24), establishing the close relationship between the second and third command – YHWH's Name is to be invoked in worship, not through idols, but through whole burnt offerings (cf. Gen. 4:26; 12:8; 26:25). The altar law, however, also indicates that the third command has much to do with place: *wherever* YHWH causes his Name to be remembered, just as Deuteronomy anticipates the 'place where YHWH will cause his Name to dwell' (12:5–7; again in contrast to idols, vv. 2–4) – the Name designates the place where Israelites are to journey annually to offer up whole burnt offerings in worship. After the Decalogue is rehearsed in Deuteronomy 5, the next two sections of the book, chapters 6–11 and 12–26, both begin with a similar emphasis on the opening instructions of the Decalogue: Deuteronomy 6 – 11 pertains completely to the first two commands, and the second section, opening with chapter 12, begins with a sustained application of the second and third commands – Israel is not to worship YHWH as the Canaanite nations worshipped their gods, through idols, but rather to seek the place where he will cause his Name to dwell, and there to worship him with whole burnt offerings. Structurally and theologically, then, Moses' farewell exhortations to Israel in Deuteronomy, which form the nation's constitution and guiding instruction for life in the land, underscore, thoroughly and at every level, the priority of the right worship of YHWH God in the land. Israel's relationship with YHWH, lived out in the land within the context of regular worship, was to be the spring and fountainhead of the nation's vocation among the nations. This foray into Deuteronomy unfolds the similar structural and theological logic for the last major section of Numbers, which is also given with anticipation of life in the land. As soon as Israel's possession of the land has been divinely assured (Num. 26 – 27), the priority of worshipping YHWH in the land is conveyed (chs. 28–30). The rationale is abundantly clear: the land is the arena and historical context for Israel's relationship with YHWH.

From one perspective, these chapters may be said to rest entirely on the daily whole burnt offering, with every ensuing sacred time delineating those sacrifices and offerings that are 'beside' or 'in addition' to the daily whole burnt offering, the details for these accompaniments (*mussaf* offerings) being a central contribution of this section. The laws for whole burnt offerings underscore the sacred calendar rooted in the creation account of Genesis 1, with its marked emphasis on the periods of time that unfold on days one (daily service), four (annual feasts) and seven (Sabbath service), and anticipate a life of abundance, fertility and prosperity in the land – the fruit of God's own life-yielding presence in the land, giving his blessing on wombs, pasture lands, agricultural fields, crops, vines and trees. As G. J. Wenham notes, the annual offerings included 113 bulls, 32 rams, 1,086 lambs, more than a ton of flour, and a thousand bottles of oil and wine (1981b: 220). Surely, for the hosts of Israelites who had endured the long wilderness sojourn, such an accounting would have stirred pangs of longing and hopeful anticipation. In rhythm with the cyclical time of nature, the annual festivals also celebrate 'linear time', God's saving acts for and covenant relationship with Israel – they mark redemptive history. The sacrificial laws are a reminder that life in the land is part of Israel's vocation before the nations, that God's people were meant to shine as a light in darkness, drawing scattered humanity to the life, wisdom and power of God (cf. Deut. 4:5–8). More than a reminder, the liturgical calendar, based on the holy Sabbath, established times for Israel to meet with YHWH God, marking daily times of prayer along with the three annual pilgrimage feasts, which served to sanctify Israel – the meeting times were part of God's programme of sanctification for his people (see Morales 2015: 185–220).

Israel's calendar acknowledges the Creator at every transitional moment of time, the people's whole burnt offerings, with their tribute and drink offerings, and supplemental purification offerings, making atonement and sending up billows of propitiating incense to YHWH God's heavenly abode, so that Israel's cultic service functioned, as it were, to uphold creation itself through the microcosm of Israel's own life in the land. The significance of the whole burnt offerings solicited a life of utter consecration to YHWH, lived with complete devotion to his will. Even the tribute offerings and libations underscore the same idea since, as G. J. Wenham observes (1981b: 229), loaves, too, may represent the twelve tribes of Israel (Lev. 24:5–8), and a vineyard is used as a symbol for Israel (Isa. 5:7). The transitional periods of each day, week and month are acknowledged and sanctified through whole burnt offerings, the shorter periods serving as foundations for the longer, and the offerings likewise being cumulative. In the clockwork of Israel's liturgical calendar, the daily periods of morning and evening form the smallest and leading cogs, animated by the fires of the *tāmîd*. The morning and evening *tāmîd* sacrifices function as a merism, so the whole day is rendered a *continual* act of consecration and worship – a complete, wholehearted living to God. The annual cycles are acknowledged in a twofold manner, dividing the year into two halves and underscoring the first month of the first half, and the first month of the second half (i.e. the seventh month), just as the day is divided into morning and evening (each with a *tāmîd*), and the week is divided in two (with the Sabbath set apart from the other six days). The following chart summarizes the annual calendar (based on Olson 1996: 172):

Spring festivals: first half of the year
   First month
      1st day: monthly offerings (28:11–15)
      14th day: Passover offerings (28:16)

15th–21st days (7 days): Feast of Unleavened Bread offerings (28:17–25)

Seven weeks (a Sabbath day plus 7 × 7 days): Feast of Weeks (28:26–31)

Autumn festivals: second half of the year
  First (seventh) month
    1st day: Day of Trumpets (29:1–6)
    10th day: Day of Atonement (29:7–11?)
    15th–21st days (7 days): Feast of Booths (29:12–34)
    22nd day (eighth day): Assembly (29:35–38)

The calendar, while founded on cycles of creation, also underscores redemptive history, this linear understanding of time, which progresses under YHWH's sovereign activity, overlaying rhythms of cyclical time and deepening their meaning. The spring feasts of Passover, with Unleavened Bread, and Weeks integrated the spring harvests of barley and wheat, with the historical exodus out of Egypt and, at least eventually, with the giving of the Decalogue at Sinai. The autumn feasts of Trumpets (Rosh HaShanah), Day of Atonement and Booths integrated the autumn harvest of vineyards, olives, dates, figs, pomegranates and other fruits (and vegetables), with God's provision of cleansing and atonement, along with his providential care of Israel throughout the wilderness sojourn. God's goodness and faithfulness in creation and providence thus form the foundation for his mercy and grace in the history of redemption, just as the Noahic covenant, establishing that 'While the earth remains, seed and harvest, cold and heat, summer and winter, day and night will not cease (*šābat*)' (Gen. 8:22), undergirds the history of redemption, upholding all creation as the arena and stage for God's redeeming drama to unfold.

The concern of Numbers 28 – 29 is on the responsibility of the people of Israel themselves (Budd 1984: 314), on their own obligation of public sacrifices once in the land, and thus forms an analogy with the offerings of the tribal princes delineated in chapter 7. There, within the context of the newly established and consecrated Tent of Meeting cult, which would form the centre of the wilderness encampment, one prince representing each of the twelve tribes gave offerings for the 'dedication of the altar' (*ḥănukkat hammizbēaḥ*), and here, within the context of life in the land, the people of Israel regularly offer up fire offerings on that altar as a pleasing aroma to YHWH, throughout the cycles of creation and redemption. The whole burnt offering, emphatically the heart of Israel's cult, solicits the complete dedication of God's people, their lives yielded wholeheartedly to him (cf. Deut. 6:4–5). Long before, God had called Abraham to offer up his beloved seed of promise, Isaac, as a whole burnt offering on one of the mountains he would show him – and

Isaac had been spared through a divinely provided substitute ram, a foreshadowing basis for the Passover provision of lambs (Gen. 22), and the provision and story that would serve as the foundation of Israel's worship on that same mountain in the land. The whole burnt offering, within the cult's system of substitution, solicits utter consecration from the people of Israel, a life in the land lived to God's glory that would fulfil the nation's vocation of bringing divine blessing to the nations (cf. Gen. 22:18). As the first major division of Numbers, chapters 1–10, focused on life within the Camp as a covenant community, with twelve tribal princes bringing offerings for the altar, which would form the centre of the Camp, so now in the last major section of Numbers, chapters 26–36, focused on life in the land as a covenant community, all Israel is called to supply the public offerings – founded on the daily whole burnt offerings – demonstrating that, once in the land, the altar would remain the centre of the nation's life. The liturgical calendar underscores the goal of Israel's redemption and covenantal vocation: the nation is called not merely to live in the land, but to serve YHWH God in the land. More than this, the annual liturgy forms Israel's life according to the pattern of God's created order (cf. Gorman 1990: 219). The anticipation created by the cultic legislation of Numbers 28 – 29 is profound: finally, with Israel's life in the land, there will be a confluence of creation, time and ritual – as Israelites live according to the rhythms of this cosmic liturgy, the nations may catch a glimpse of God's original purposes for humanity.

Following the paradigm of the Nazirite vow, whereby a period of abstention (wilderness sojourn, chs. 11–25) is followed by an act of worship (sacrifices in the land, chs. 28–29), it is likely not fortuitous that these two chapters on sacrifices in the land end with a notice about fulfilling vows during the appointed feasts of YHWH, nor that this section is followed by an entire chapter whose main object is to affirm that vows made to YHWH must be fulfilled (ch. 30). Indeed, Moses' two missions he must accomplish before 'being gathered' in death (27:12–23 and 31:1–2) form a frame around chapters 28–30, calling for a unified reading of the 'additional sacrifices' with the 'oaths and vows' sections (Albertz 2013: 225). The pattern of the Nazirite vow includes (1) a period of abstention, (2) cleansing from corpse pollution and, at the fulfilment of the vow period, (3) worship in the land, marked by purification, whole burnt and peace offerings, along with tribute and drink offerings. This is precisely the experience of Israel: the wilderness sojourn was a period of meagre provision (in a place without grapes), wherein the second generation of Israelites were eventually cleansed from the corpse pollution of the first (ch. 19), and now, in the first anticipation of life in the land, the chapters are marked by sacrifices with accompaniments rendered to YHWH (chs. 28–29) and the fulfilment of vows (ch. 30). The centrality of the whole burnt offering, soliciting the consecration of Israel, melds deeply with the path of the Nazirite set before Israel, calling the nation to live a life fully devoted to God. The death of Jesus Christ, the culminating fulfilment of the sacrificial system and to which the near sacrifice of Isaac had gestured, is fittingly called 'an offering and sacrifice to God for a fragrant aroma' (Eph. 5:2) because it was the offering up of his life lived entirely consecrated to God. Similarly, his people are urged to present their bodies – their lives and conduct on earth – as living sacrifices, pleasing to God (Rom. 12:1).

NUMBERS 30: FULFILLING VOWS TO YHWH IN THE LAND

Translation

[30:1]Now Moses spoke to the heads of the tribes, for the sons of Israel, saying, 'This is the word that YHWH has commanded: [2]"If a man vows a vow to YHWH or swears an oath to bind a bond on his soul, he will not profane his word – according to all that went forth from his mouth he will do. [3]And if a woman vow a vow to YHWH and bind a bond in the house of her father's house in her youth, [4]and her father hears her vow and her bond which she bound on her soul, and her father keeps silent to her, then all her vows will stand, and every bond which she bound on her soul will stand. [5]But if her father forbids her on the day he hears it, all her vows and her bond which she bound on her soul will not stand, and YHWH will forgive her, because her father forbid her. [6]Now if she has become married to a husband and her vows are upon her or the rash utterance of her lips which she bound on her soul, [7]and her husband hears but on the day he hears he keeps silent to her, her vows will stand, and her bonds which she bound on her soul will stand. [8]But if on the day her husband hears he forbids her, he annuls her vow which was on her, and the utterance of her lips which she bound on her soul, and YHWH will forgive her. [9]Now a vow of a widow and of a divorced-woman, all which she binds on her soul will stand against her. [10]But if in her husband's house she vowed or bound a bond on her soul by an oath, [11]and her husband heard but kept silent to her, did not forbid her, all her vows will stand, and every bond which she bound on her soul will stand. [12]But if her husband surely annuls them on the day he hears, all that went forth from her lips concerning her vows and concerning the binding of her soul will not stand – her husband has annulled them, and YHWH will forgive her. [13]Every vow and every binding oath to afflict a soul, her husband may cause it to stand or her husband may annul it. [14]If her husband surely keeps silent to her from day to day, then he causes to stand all her vows or all her bonds which are on her, he causes them to stand because he kept silent to her on the day he heard. [15]But if he surely annuls them after he has heard it, then he will bear her guilt.'" [16]These are the statutes which YHWH had commanded Moses, between a man and his wife, between a father and his daughter in her youth, in her father's house.

Notes on the text

MT 30:1 is 29:40 in English translations, so its versification for chapter 30 is one ahead of the English (e.g. MT 30:3 = English 30:2).

2. 'his word': SamP reads pl. ('words').
4. 'vow', 'bond . . . bond': these are pl. in SamP, LXX (except for second 'bond') and Syr.
8. 'her vow': SamP, LXX and Syr have pl. 'vows' (cf. v. 7). LXX adds explanatory gloss.
9. 'divorced-woman': from root g-r-$š$, 'to drive out (of the house)'.
11. 'bond': pl. in LXX, SamP, Syr and Tg.
15. 'her guilt': LXX, SamP and Syr have a m. suff.

Form and structure

After the inclusio of verses 1 and 16, verses 2 and 13–15 form a general frame related to the binding nature of vows and oaths on a man, and verses 3–12 describe three scenarios of vows and oaths of women, particularly within a woman's relationship to her father and then her husband. (See Table 22.)

The common factor in these cases appears to be marriage, with the scenarios progressing from a woman's situation before (Scenario A), during (Scenario B) and after (Scenario C) marriage (cf. Cocco 2020: 190), with the summary (vv. 13–15) offering the general principle of vows

Table 22: Numbers 30: structure

Introduction: 'This is the word YHWH has commanded'	v. 1
Summary of principle: a man must perform his vow or oath to YHWH	v. 2
Contingencies for women	vv. 3–12
Scenario A: vow/oath of a woman while in her father's house	v. 3
1. Her father keeps silent	v. 4
2. Her father forbids: 'YHWH will forgive her'	v. 5
Scenario B: vow/oath of a woman who has a husband	v. 6
1. Her husband keeps silent	v. 7
2. Her husband forbids/annuls: 'YHWH will forgive her'	v. 8
Scenario C: vow/oath of a widow or divorced woman	v. 9
1. Late or previous husband had kept silent	vv. 10–11
2. Late or previous husband had annulled: 'YHWH will forgive her'	v. 12
Summary of contingency principle: A man accountable for his wife's vows and oaths	vv. 13–15
Conclusion: 'These are the statutes which YHWH had commanded'	v. 16

and oaths within marriage (for a valid alternative, see G. J. Wenham 1981b: 230–233).

VOWS AND OATHS IN ANCIENT ISRAEL

The word 'vow' occurs over ninety times in the HB, attesting to the popularity of this practice in ancient times. Although vows will be our focus, vows and oaths were similar, as reflected by the parallelism in Psalm 132: 'He swore (*nišbaʻ*) to YHWH, vowed (*nādar*) to the Mighty One of Jacob' (v. 2). Vows, which were open to a variety of applications, were always made to YHWH, and it was common practice in Israel to vow in relation to the offering of sacrifices. The previous chapter closed with the reminder that YHWH's required whole burnt offerings, with their tribute and drink offerings, designated on Israel's appointed times, were to be performed 'beside your vow offerings and freewill offerings' (29:39), and earlier, in Numbers 15, 'vow and freewill offerings' were also grouped with whole burnt and peace offerings (vv. 3, 8). Leviticus provides legislation related to these offerings (see Lev. 7:16–17; 22:17–33; 23:38; 27:1–34), while Deuteronomy assumes Israel's worship at the place where YHWH will cause his Name to dwell will include vow offerings (see Deut. 12:6, 11, 17, 26; 23:18, 21–23). Of Elkanah we read, for example, that it was his custom to go up and sacrifice to YHWH the yearly sacrifice 'and his vow' (1 Sam. 1:21). The earliest example of a vow in the Bible is by Jacob who vowed that if YHWH would be with him, provide for his needs and return him to his father's house in wellness, then YHWH would be his God, the stone he set up would be for God's house and Jacob would give a tenth back to him of all that YHWH would give him (Gen. 28:20–22) – a vow Jacob fulfilled after YHWH had answered overwhelmingly abundantly (see Gen. 33:18–20; 35:1–15).

In ancient Israel vows to YHWH were often used in order to intensify prayers of petition. When one's plight became severe or desperate – for example, when a man became seriously ill or was besieged by enemies so as to fear death, or when a woman's womb remained barren – a vow was joined to the petition, exhibiting the person's urgency and resolve. The vow was typically in the form of promising an offering to God, which then became an expression of thanksgiving for answered prayer, and might have involved a public testimony, declaring YHWH's goodness and faithfulness. A reference in Job outlines the practice succinctly: 'You will make your entreaty to him [God], and he will hear you, and you will fulfil your vow' (22:27). Alternatively, out of gratitude for some deliverance, a person may spontaneously vow to offer a thanksgiving sacrifice to God. In Jonah, not only do the mariners offer sacrifices and make vows to YHWH when delivered from the raging storm at sea (1:16), but Jonah in the midst of the sea, with his life waning, had offered up a 'prayer' to YHWH, which apparently included a vow, for on his deliverance through the great fish, he proclaimed, 'I myself, with the voice of thanksgiving, will sacrifice to you, I will fulfil what I had vowed – salvation belongs to YHWH!' (2:7, 9). Psalm 40, although not using the term 'vow', appears to assume such a scenario: YHWH heard the petitioner's cry and delivered him out of the horrible pit (some threat of death), with the result that (when the petitioner pays his vow publicly at the temple) many will hear his praise of God and similarly put their trust in him. This idea is explicit in other psalms, as the psalmist declares, 'My praise will be of you in the great assembly – I will fulfil my vows before those who fear him' (22:25), and 'Your vows are with me, O God – I will fulfil the thanksgivings to you' (56:12). The Psalter, as part of the liturgy of the Temple where such vow offerings would be brought and offered, contains many references to vow offerings: 'For you, O God, have heard my vows, you have given me the possession of those who fear your Name . . . So I will sing praises to your Name for ever, to fulfil my vows from day to day' (61:5, 8); 'Praises await you, O God, in Zion, and to you the vow will be fulfilled' (65:1). Again, fulfilling a vow often involved a public testimony, an ascription of praise to God that fulfilled a divine purpose for answered prayer, not only that of God's own glory but for the encouragement of others to trust in him as well: 'I will fulfil my vow to YHWH in the presence of all his people' (Ps. 116:14, 18).

Such a fulfilment of one's vow was costly, involving the sacrifice of offerings: 'I will enter your house with whole burnt offerings, I will fulfil my vows to you' (Ps. 66:13); 'My peace offerings are with me, today I will fulfil my vows' (Prov. 7:14). Because of the costliness of sacrifices, ignoring the fulfilment of one's vows became a strong temptation, especially when the immediate danger, or 'moment of crisis' (Milgrom 1990: 251), had already passed, having been resolved favourably by God's good and faithful hand. Scripture, therefore, contains a variety of admonitions to fulfil one's vows. In Deuteronomy, Moses teaches (23:21–23):

> When you vow a vow to YHWH your God, you will not delay to fulfil it, for YHWH your God will surely require it of you – and it would be sin with you. If you refrain to vow, it will not be sin with you. What proceeds from your lips you will observe and do, just as you vowed to YHWH your God, your freewill offering which you spoke with your mouth.

Elsewhere we read, 'Sacrifice to God thanksgiving – fulfil your vows to the Most High' (Ps. 50:14); 'Vow and fulfil to YHWH your God: let all who surround him bring gifts to the Feared One' (Ps. 76:11). Ecclesiastes admonishes, 'When you vow a vow to God do not delay to fulfil it, for he takes no pleasure in fools – fulfil what you have vowed. Better that you did not vow than to vow but not fulfil' (5:4–5; see also Prov. 20:25; Isa. 19:21; Jer. 44:25; Nah. 1:15). The prophet Malachi similarly warns, 'Cursed is the deceiver, who has a male in his flock, but vows and sacrifices a corrupt offering to the Lord' (1:14).

Although vows did not necessarily require sacrifices, their performance was nevertheless within the cultic sphere, involving some sort of dedication to the sanctuary (see Milgrom 1990: 488). There are instances in Scripture where one's life or possessions are vowed to YHWH, yielded to the priesthood in service of him. Leviticus 27 deals with some of these scenarios. A famous case is the vow vowed to YHWH by Hannah whereby she, distraught over her barrenness, prayed that if God would give her a son, she would apply the Nazirite vow to him all the days of his life, surrendering him to serve at God's house in Shiloh – this the divinely orchestrated setting for raising up the prophet and king-maker Samuel (1 Sam. 1:8–18). The most infamous case of a 'foolish' vow in Scripture is that of Jephthah who, in a prayer for victory over the Ammonites, vowed to YHWH that he would offer up as a whole burnt offering whatever would come out of the doorway of his house to meet him upon his return in peace after battle – only to have his daughter do so (Judges 11:29–40). In terms of oaths at least, the accidental breaking of an oath required a reparation offering (Lev. 5:4–13), while the regular punishment for breaking oaths is understood as being beaten with many stripes, but not to exceed forty (Deut. 25:1–3; Nachmanides 1975: 351 n. 29).

Comment

30:1–2. Moses conveys to 'the heads of the tribes' (*rā'šê hammaṭṭôt*) the matter YHWH has commanded 'for the sons of Israel' (*libnê yiśrā'ēl*). It is not immediately apparent why this legislation is conveyed to Israelites through tribal leaders. Rashi (ad loc.) points out this was likely the common practice for Moses' instruction, offering Exodus 34:31–32 as exemplary, and suggests the tribal leaders are noted here since they, as judges, would have the authority – and so needed the expertise of these laws – to annul vows. Ibn Ezra (ad loc.) connects these 'heads of the tribes' with the 'chieftains of the community' in Numbers 32:2, and one may add 'the heads of the fathers of the tribes' (32:28), since they will be accountable for ensuring that the tribes of Reuben and Gad 'do according to what has proceeded from your mouth' (32:24), referring to their agreement before Moses to take part in the conquest as a vanguard.

The opening 'This is the matter that YHWH has commanded' (*zeh haddābār 'ăšer ṣiwwā yhwh*), occurring eight times in the Pentateuch (see Exod. 16:16, 32; 35:4; Lev. 8:5; 9:6; 17:2; Num. 30:2; 36:6), emphasizes Moses' mediatorial role in relation to the people (Cocco 2020: 187).

Broadly, the subject matter relates to Israel's *speech* in the land: vows to YHWH or oaths sworn must be performed – not to do according to what has proceeded from one's mouth is to 'profane' (*yaḥēl*) one's word, a legal principle affirmed in Deuteronomy 23:22–24 (cf. Lev. 27:1–13). The wilderness section of Numbers (ch. 11–25) is filled with evil speech in nearly every episode: the people 'complained' (11:1); the sons of Israel wept, saying, 'Who will give us flesh to eat?', and complained about the manna (11:4–6); Miriam and Aaron spoke against Moses (12:1–2, 8); ten scouts slandered the land, causing the people to complain (13:32–33; 14:36–36); Korah and his band spoke against Moses and Aaron (16:3, 12–14); and after YHWH's judgement the people complained against them as well (16:41); Moses spoke harshly to the people, calling them 'rebels' (20:10); and the second generation of Israel spoke against God and Moses (21:5, 7). In Numbers 21, however, we see how the second generation makes use of a standard vow formula, deepening their relationship with YHWH: 'Israel vowed a vow to YHWH, and said, *If* you will surely give this people into my hand, *then* I will utterly devote their cities to destruction' (21:2). And with the daughters of Zelophehad, such righteous or 'just' speech continues on the part of the people (27:6–7), and is solicited in chapter 30 by the admonition for Israelites not to profane their word, but to do that which goes forth from their mouths, fulfilling their vows to YHWH and their oaths. Moreover, in chapter 32 the sons of Reuben and Gad agree to serve as the advance guard in the conquest until the land is subdued, while their women, children and livestock remain to possess lands east of the Jordan, and Moses, in language similar to 30:2, charges them to 'do what went forth from your mouth' so as to be innocent of sin (32:20–24).

The designation *'îš* (a man) here does not exclude women (cf. Cocco 2020: 188): as a general principle the rule applies to all. Even if certain contingencies will apply to women, whereby they may be forgiven for not fulfilling certain pledges, these are exceptions. If particularly a man's own obligation is within the immediate scope of concern, then the rest of the legislation derives from this solemn statement, since the diverse rules related to a woman's vows or oaths entail scenarios whereby fathers and husbands may or may not be accountable for pledges made by women (cf. Olson 1996: 174). Nevertheless, there is also a focus on women, and a concern to protect them within their various spheres of life, including widowhood and divorce, which are not subject to a man's authority – so the legal status of women in the realm of vows and oaths may justly be called the text's 'truce concern' (Levine 2000: 425). The daughters of Zelophehad episodes also concern daughters' relation to both fathers and husbands (26:33; 27:1–11; 36:1–13), and the topic of women occurs again after the battle with the Midianites (31:9–20).

The narrative frame concerning Moses' being 'gathered to your people' (Num. 27:12–23 and 31:1–2), unifies the material within chs.

28–29 and 30. The subject of vows and oaths is indeed more connected to the previous chapters on offerings (Num. 28 – 29) than is usually appreciated, since vows commonly involved the self-imposed obligation to offer sacrifices (cf. de Vaulx 1972: 346). Numerous passages in the Torah connect sacrifices with vows (see Lev. 7:16; 22:18, 21, 23; 23:38; Num. 15:3, 8; 29:39; Deut. 12:6, 11, 17, 26). Numbers 29 closed with the reminder that the holiday fire offerings were 'beside your vow offerings and your freewill offerings' (v. 39), and it could be, as Rashbam suggested (ad loc.), vow offerings were intended to be fulfilled during the three pilgrimage holidays, so that not to fulfil them at these times was to be 'late' in fulfilling one's word – relying on Genesis 8:10 and Judges 3:25 for understanding *yaḥēl* as derived from *yāḥal*, 'late, delay, tarry' (versus 'profane'). The parallel legislation in Deuteronomy 23:21–23 does focus on not delaying fulfilment of vows, but it uses the term *'āḥar*, while the focus in Numbers 30 appears to be on the validity of vows and the need to fulfil them. Certainly, pilgrimage feasts provided the main opportunity and context for fulfilling one's vows at the temple. A person must be careful to do '*his* word', which proceeded from his mouth – although there will be instances where other people or circumstances (such as death, or, for a woman, the resistance of a father or husband) cut short the fruit of one's word, the focus here is on the resolve of the one who utters a vow or oath.

Vows are directed 'to YHWH', but oaths, even when not sworn to YHWH, would be sworn by the name 'YHWH', lending them similar gravity (on vows, see Berlinerblau 1996; on oaths, see Ziegler 2008; on vows and oaths in the ANE, see Cocco 2020: 168–172). In Leviticus, YHWH thus says, 'You will not swear (*tiššābĕ'û*) in my Name falsely, nor profane (*ḥillaltā*) the Name of your God – I am YHWH' (19:12). Both vows and oaths, although – or *because* – they are taken upon oneself freely and voluntarily are of utmost seriousness, involving the sacredness of YHWH's own Name. Breaking either a vow or an oath was 'to take the Name of YHWH in vain' (Exod. 20:7). Vows, however, were usually contingent, as the first biblical instance, Jacob's vow at Bethel (Gen. 28), indicates: 'Jacob vowed a vow, saying: *If ('im)* God . . . *then* YHWH will be my God' (28:20–22). It is also possible that in response to a blessed providence, such as deliverance from death, one would make a vow (*Since* . . . *then* . . .) – in other words, a 'condition' was met even without a preliminary vow, so that out of gratitude the worshipper brings an offering of thanksgiving, expressing the weight of thankfulness and indebtedness to God for his mercies by vowing to bring an offering (cf. Jon. 1:16). Vows, moreover, were always directed to YHWH: they were pledges directly between a person (or people) and YHWH God himself, involving the dedication of oneself or some object to him. As such, vows were expressions of one's devotion to God (cf. Ashley 1993: 574). Oaths, by contrast, were given in YHWH's Name in order to confirm one's word or intention – Milgrom dubs these 'assertory' and 'promissory' oaths, respectively (1990: 488). Confirming one's word was a necessary part of daily civil, cultic and judicial life (see Lev. 6:1–7; Josh. 9:19–20). In Exodus 22:11, for example, an 'oath of YHWH' between neighbours is sworn to ensure amicable relations, diffusing suspicions of property theft. Beyond a confirmation of one's word, oaths sworn to bind oneself, confirming one's intention, such as the sort dealt with in Numbers 30, created an obligation for a person either to do something or to refrain from doing something. When such oaths were also sworn to YHWH, they were akin to vows. Swearing an oath is to 'bind' oneself – literally to 'bind a bond' (*le'sōr 'issār*), with *'āsar* being used for fastening one's horse or donkey securely (cf. Gen. 49:11; 2 Kgs 7:10), binding an animal with cords to the altar (Ps. 118:27) and for binding a prisoner with cords or fetters (Gen. 42:24; 2 Kgs 25:7), with a *bêt hāsûrîm* being a 'prison house' (cf. Judg. 16:21, 25; Eccl. 4:14; see BDB 63). An oath metaphorically fastened one as if by cords to his or her word. G. J. Wenham points out that the *neder* (vow) stands for a positive pledge, while *'issār* for a negative one, a pledge of abstinence (1981b: 231; cf. Cartledge 1992: 25). Although rare, oaths could include conditions, clearing the one bound to an obligation (cf. Gen. 24:8). To give his people added assurance of his promises, YHWH who cannot lie nevertheless swore by his own Name (Gen. 22:16–18; 26:3; cf. Heb. 6:13–18). Traditionally, if overly simplistic, vows entail a dedication of certain *objects* (including oneself), while oaths bind oneself to do or not do certain *actions* (cf. *Ned.* 2b; Nachmanides 1975: 346–351). Even seeming exceptions may be pressed into this template: a vow to offer a sacrifice, for example, sets apart one's animal from common use, and even Jacob's vow may be understood as casting aside idols.

Within the context of Numbers, where the root for 'vow' (*n-d-r*) occurs 27 times (16 times in ch. 30), vows appear first in the purity regulations for the Camp related to the Nazirite vow (4 times, 6:2 [twice], 5, 21), while the strayed woman is charged with an 'oath' (*šĕbu'at*) of cursing (5:21). Each of the major purity cases involves an oath or vow (5:5–10; 5:11–31; 6:1–21). Given that chapter 30 entails familial relationships in the land, especially between a wife and her husband, there may be an intended parallel with Numbers 5 – 6 on the analogy between life in the Camp and life in the land. Another link occurs in the aftermath of the battle with the Midianites, where the princes conduct a census (31:49; cf. 26:2), and on discovering that not a single fighter has lost his life, they give an offering for YHWH from their plunder (31:50), an offering that resonates with the fulfilment of thanksgiving vows. Numbers 21:1–3, moreover, as an exemplary foretaste of the land's conquest, demonstrates how the topic of vows and oaths is relevant for Israel on the plains of Moab, on the verge of engaging in the conquest under Joshua.

30:3–16: Contingencies for women in relation to fathers and husbands

This section presents three cases of scenarios whereby a woman's vow or oaths are either binding or annulled in relation to her father (vv. 3–6), her husband (vv. 7–8) or, as a widow or divorcee, in relation to a late or previous husband (vv. 9–12), each of which concludes with the statement that 'YHWH will forgive her' for failing to fulfil her word in the event her vow or oath has been cancelled by her father, husband or a deceased or previous husband. The cases move through three ever-narrowing spheres: within her father's house as a youth, within her marital relationship as a wife and, finally, alone as a widow or divorcee. Recalling that a 'father's house' was the basis for the census of the tribal encampments (20 times in Num. 1 – 2), including the Levitical camps (13 times in Num. 3 – 4), detailed in narratives where tribal affiliations are concerned (e.g. Num. 7:2; 17:2, 3, 6; 18:1; 25:14–15), it may be the three life-scenarios for vows and oaths mirror the three purity cases (Num. 5:5–10, 11–31; 6:1–21) in being aligned with the Camp structure: (1) tribal encampment: vows/oaths within her father's house, paralleled with restitution for false oaths in the neighbourly sphere; (2) Levitical encampment: vows/oaths within marriage, paralleled by the strayed-woman ritual, which assumes a marital vow and involves an oath of malediction; (3) *Shekhinah* encampment: vows/oaths of the woman isolated, as a widow or divorcee. In every sphere of relationship, as with the Camp's purity laws, vows and oaths involve YHWH – but the narrower the sphere, the more focused is the individual's relationship with God. Since the purity laws for the Camp had pertained to 'a male or a female', with the Sotah ritual focusing on a wife, the parallels are apt, and reinforce the analogy between life in the Camp and life in the land.

The section ends with a concluding summary of a husband's accountability (and, presumably, a father's as well). The authority structure, of a father over his daughter and of a husband over his wife, may factor in the cultural reality that vowed commodities, whether of livestock or land, typically belonged to the father's house, requiring his permission. Even – or especially – vows and oaths concerning oneself alone (a daughter or wife) would also necessarily affect a father's house (conceivably in terms of daily management and chores, or in relation to a planned betrothal), as well as a husband's marital relations. Providing good and wise pathways in the relationship between a daughter and her father, and between a wife and her husband, these regulations protect both a father or husband's interests and a woman's well-being in the various stages of her life. Although the head of a father's house enjoyed a high level of autonomy, there was no individualism within the household – major decisions, such as vows and oaths, affected many and needed careful consideration. From the legislation's perspective, the annulment of one's vow or binding oath is not viewed as a loss of one's rights, but rather as a serviceable loophole releasing a person from a weighty obligation, which might have been taken on unadvisedly ('in her youth', v. 3; 'rash utterance', v. 6; 'to afflict a soul', v. 13) – in other words, the father and husband function in a protective role, and are accountable to YHWH to be faithful in this duty ('he will bear her guilt', v. 15), for which reason the man's passivity, perhaps culpably so, is underscored (he 'keeps silent', vv. 4, 7, 11). The guidelines may even have Israel as bride and YHWH as faithful husband within their theological purview. Presumably, too, within a healthy and pious house, there would be a variety of scenarios whereby the vow or oath of a daughter or wife was happily affirmed and upheld with encouragement. Moreover, and again within the context of a pious house, there is no reason to think that a woman's own desire and intention would not be factored in. Rather, the case scenarios all presume situations whereby the woman had pledged naively or rashly and even to her soul's affliction, so that the provision of a father or husband's nullifying authority comes as a welcomed deliverance. For a male, by contrast, there was no such deliverance, naively spoken or not, rashly uttered or not – even to the severe affliction of his soul, he must perform 'all that went forth from his mouth' and 'not profane his word'. It may be, however, that the 'restitution offering' (*'āšām*) made atonement for failing to keep his oath, providing forgiveness – at least in the case where the man was 'unaware' of his pronouncing an oath (see Lev. 5:4–6). Finally, given the detailed limitations of how and precisely when a husband (or father) may nullify the pledge of his wife (or daughter), these case laws may be read as serving to *limit* a man's right to void her vows and oaths, or, put differently, they may function to create greater liberty for women in the realm of their devotion to God, expressed through vows and oaths, than was common in ancient times. Another principle underlying these cases is that a person's self-imposed religious obligations may not undermine God-given duties, whether a child's duty to obey parents or a wife's duty to submit to her husband – a principle Jesus upheld, reproaching those who used vows to escape their responsibility to parents (G. J. Wenham 1981b: 232; Matt. 15:3–9).

A level of imprecision or vagueness remains in the legislation: What age defines 'in her youth'? What period actually encompasses 'on the day he hears' it? What happens in the event a father or husband has not heard the vow or oath that nevertheless affects him? In the Mishnah a whole tractate is devoted to a variety of scenarios of vow-taking, which fills in some of these gaps, and addresses the possibility of nullifying vows through a court or Beis Din (see *Ned.*).

3–5. These verses concern the contingency of a woman's vow or oath in relation to her father. The woman is an *'iššā*, but the context is 'in the house of her father' and 'in her youth' (*bin'urêhā*), so the scenario envisioned may be the contingency for a *later* fulfilment, as an adult, of a vow or oath that was made while still a youth. Jewish tradition defines 'in her youth' as around 11 years of age (i.e. having begun her twelfth year), within the narrow timeframe between being a minor, who is not authorized to make any vows, and being mature, which basically begins at the age of 12, when signs of puberty have developed (see e.g. *Sif. Num.* 153; Rashi 1997: 4:372–373). The time envisioned may refer to the whole period of time before marriage, while the young woman resided in her father's house – a period that would normally close in any event around the age of 12 when she was betrothed. The underlying assumption is that an adult woman, while under his provision, within his house, is no longer subject to his authority as regarding her vows and oaths. Within the limited period of 'her youth', a father may 'forbid' her, the text using the hiph. form of *nw'* (restrain, forbid, hinder), which appears to have a technical legal sense within the present context (as in Num. 32:7, 9; Budd 1984: 322). Even within this period of youth, more narrowly, a father's window of opportunity for annulling his daughter's vow is restricted to the timeframe of 'the day he hears it'. When her father hears her vow or oath ('bind a bond'), his positive and deliberate affirmation is not necessary for vows or oaths to 'stand' (*yāqûm*) – his silence or passive inaction is enough for 'all' her vows and 'every' oath to stand, which evinces a sphere of autonomy for young girls. The word *qûm* has technical meaning in a juridical context, expressing validity. His remaining silent is expressed by the Hebr. word *ḥārēš* (to be speechless, dumb, silent), which may imply criticism of his inaction. More positively, within the ideal of a father's godly, protective role, any silence on his part assumes that the burden of his daughter's vow or oath is inconsequential in terms of potentially harming her or her future. Silence, in any case, is considered assent (cf. *b. Yev.* 87b).

If, however, her father forbids her on the day he hears it, then 'all' her vows and oaths will not stand. The suff. for 'he-hears-it' (*šāmĕ'ô*), refers to his hearing of the vow or oath, not necessarily hearing 'her' (i.e. at the moment of her making the pledge). Not all vows and oaths were public or formal affairs, but especially if her vow or oath would affect him substantially, the father must eventually hear of 'it', and when he does so – presumably, even if his hearing of it takes place long after her actual words – he has an opportunity at that moment to nullify the commitment. The term translated 'forbid' is *hēnî'*, from the root *nw'* (frustrate, hinder, dissuade, discourage), a rare term that occurs only five times in the Torah, all within Numbers: three times in this chapter (30:5, 8, 11) and twice in chapter 32 (vv. 7, 9), connecting the two texts (cf. Pss 33:10; 141:5).

Even if the commitment does not affect him directly, the father still has the authority to nullify the vow or oath upon hearing about it, which would be a favourable scenario if she had made it rashly to her own hurt. If the father nullifies her vow or oath, it cannot be upheld or enforced, it will not stand or be fulfilled, a reality that would likely have caused some trepidation for the original audience, given the weightiness of YHWH's Name – to whom the vow was made, or by whom the oath was taken. For this reason, a divine word of comfort and assurance is provided: 'YHWH will forgive her' (*sālaḥ*). Even within a legal context yielding the sense of 'release', that these words are given apart from atonement is striking. In the Pentateuch, statements of YHWH's forgiveness – and *sālaḥ* has only God as subject in the HB – are otherwise always preceded by a priest's making atonement (see Lev. 4:20, 26, 31, 35; 5:10, 13, 16, 18; 6:7; 19:22; Num. 15:25, 26, 28; aside from Moses' direct intercession; cf. Exod. 34:9; Num. 14:19–20), even for cases of a man's oaths (Lev. 5:4–10). The omission is all the more significant since, as Milgrom points out (1990: 252), the expression is always in the (niph.) passive within cultic contexts, demonstrating that sacrifices 'were not inherently efficacious but dependent on the divine will', so that here, in relation to vows, the point is that 'God will automatically forgive her'. The rationale for YHWH's forgiveness is, 'because her father forbade her'. It is not her fault if the pledge goes unfulfilled in the event that her father (or husband) has himself kept her from fulfilling it – and yet that she must still be 'forgiven' or 'released' by YHWH demonstrates the seriousness of the circumstance. In Genesis 24, Abraham, who had bidden his servant to swear an oath by YHWH that he would obtain a bride for Isaac only from Abraham's own country and family, also added a proviso: 'If (*'im*) the woman is not willing' to come, then 'you will be clear (*wĕniqqîtā*) of this my oath' (v. 8). Although Abraham's servant, like the woman, would not be able to fulfil his oath due to the unwillingness of another, the term used is not *sālaḥ*, but *nāqāh* (niph.), 'to be free from guilt, clean, innocent' (cf. BDB 667), the word used for the case of the strayed woman (Num. 5:19, 28, 31) and for the result when Gad and Reuben fulfil their pledge to serve as the vanguard of tribes in conquering the land (Num. 32:22), which usages also do not imply that anyone is being forgiven, but rather that one is being cleared of any charges of guilt or iniquity. In other words, *nāqāh* establishes that there is nothing to forgive, for there is no true guilt – otherwise, YHWH declares he 'surely will not clear the guilty' (*yĕnaqqeh lō' wĕnaqqê*, Num. 14:18). Perhaps use of *sālaḥ* in Numbers 30 may be explained in that the present cases deal not simply with oaths sworn in YHWH's Name, but, as with all vows, the oaths envisioned here are sworn *to* YHWH himself, thus requiring his forgiveness. Also noteworthy, that 'her father forbade her' is the *only* circumstance allowed for not fulfilling her vow or oath – the provision in no way leaves room for complacency in performing one's word, nor for taking YHWH's Name lightly. But, through a father's protection, YHWH himself – the One to whom she had vowed or in whose Name she had sworn an oath – forgives her.

6–8. From the sphere of a father's house, the legislation now addresses the woman within the sphere of marriage: 'she has become (married) to a husband' (wĕ'im-hāyô tihyeh lĕ'îš). As with the daughter–father relationship, whereby the daughter might have spoken a vow or oath while yet a youth, unable properly to weigh the consequences, so it seems the scenario here involves a vow or oath – 'rashly uttered' – while yet unmarried, which she brings into the marriage. In both scenarios, the male protective figure, whether father or husband, is able to deliver her from the burden by nullifying the vow or oath later, 'on the day he hears'. It may be that specific stages of a young woman's life are in mind. If, in the first stage of life, a young girl ('in her youth') makes a vow or oath within her father's house, she is protected by her father. However, what happens if, in the next stage of life, when, no longer in her youth, she makes a vow or oath within her father's house? In this case, a future husband may protect her from its consequences, even for pledges made during betrothal (according to *Ned.* 67a). Alternatively, it may be assumed rather that a father or husband always has a preliminary right to cancel the vows and oaths of a daughter or wife, and these scenarios may be addressing only the vague situations whereby there has been a transition of time (from 'in her youth' to young adult, and from young adult to marriage) before a father or husband has discovered the pledge. In any case, the husband 'takes over the previously held responsibilities of the father' (Levine 2000: 432).

The woman enters a marriage having a vow upon her or having bound her soul by the 'rash utterance' (*mibṭā'*) of her lips (vv. 6, 8). The word *mibṭā'* derives from *bāṭā'*, which refers to speaking thoughtlessly, unadvisedly, rashly or even babbling (BDB 104–105; cf. Lev. 5:4; Ps. 106:33). Vows and oaths made to or in the Name of YHWH are serious matters, and must be fulfilled even if spoken in one's youth or rashly. As Gane observes (2004: 762), however, here the woman's situation rather than character appears to be in view: when she made her pledge she had not foreseen 'the potential effects of a change in circumstance', entering a marriage wherein her 'husband may feel adversely affected by an obligation she incurred while single'. On such a scenario the possibility of having the pledge annulled through this protective (escape) clause would have been liberating for the young woman (cf. Allen 2012: 394). A father or husband is a divine provision of security and protection, functioning somewhat akin to a kinsman redeemer, able to deliver the woman from her looming obligation. As with a father in the previous case, so with a husband here: if he remains silent on the day he hears of the vow or oath, then it will stand. He does not need positively to affirm the vow or oath: it already stands by the woman's own speech. However, he cannot remain passively silent and deliver her – he must positively 'forbid her' (*yānî'*) so as to 'annul' (*hēpēr*) the vow or utterance. Whereas the previous case used *nw'* (v. 5), here in addition to *nw'*, *pārar*, which signifies 'to frustrate, make ineffectual, invalidate, annul', is also used. Whether this means that a husband in this situation requires an additional juridical act (*pārar*), over and above that of a father (*nw'*), as suggested by Cocco (2020: 196–200), is questionable. 'To annul', *hēpēr*, is the legal antonym of *hēqîm*, 'to cause to stand' (vv. 13–14; G. B. Gray 1903: 416), and the same dynamic appears to apply for *nw'* (vv. 4–5, 11). Within the context of a burdensome pledge, spoken rashly, the focus of blameworthiness shifts to the husband – he at least shares the fault for having remained silent. But if he annuls the pledge by forbidding her, then 'YHWH will forgive her.' Possibly, the designation 'rash utterance' limits a new husband's authority over a young woman's previous vows.

9–12. From the spheres of a father's house, and that of marriage, the third case deals with the scenario of a woman alone, either as a widow or through divorce. Both scenarios were especially tragic for a woman in ancient times. A 'widow' (*'almaānāh*) was bereft of both the compassion and support of her husband, and likely grieving the loss (whatever the circumstances of his death), and a divorced woman was by definition one who was 'driven out' (*gāraš*) from her husband's home. She might have been able to secure support in her father's house, or among her brothers or sons, but none could relieve her of the burden of a vow or oath. By contrast with the previous two cases, this one begins with the statement that 'all which she binds on her soul will stand against her', before moving on to contingent circumstances. As a single, adult woman she is obligated to fulfil her word, and is accountable to YHWH for doing so even though, as the language of its standing 'against her' (or 'over, upon', *'ālêhā*) seems to imply, fulfilling her word entails severe consequences. The scenario of a destitute widow or divorced woman making a vow to YHWH or an oath in his Name that would further her own affliction, compounding her burden, would presumably have been exceedingly rare – and there are no instances of such in the Bible, although Anna, a widow of 84 years, who served God at the temple with fasting and prayers night and day, makes for an endearing candidate (cf. Luke 2:36–38). Furthermore, no *future* contingencies – whether returning to her father's house or entering a new husband's house – are provided for the nullification of vows or oaths made while in the state of widowhood or as a divorcee. Release from the burden of a pledge was possible, however, under certain *past* conditions. This legislation deals with the vows or oaths she might have made when circumstances were presumably brighter, while she was still married.

The rest of the legislation (vv. 10–12), as with the first two cases, addresses the circumstance that arises through the transition from one sphere to another, from the context of her husband's house to that of singleness, either as a widow or through divorce: Do her previous vows or oaths stand now that she is in a new and different sphere? A wide survey of commentaries will show that many exegetes take verses 10–12 as unrelated to widows or divorced women (v. 9). Yet the form of the previous two cases argues in favour of understanding these verses in relation to widows and divorced women. The awkwardness of isolating a single verse on widows and divorced women before moving – *returning* – to basic legislation within marriage, in effect separating the legislation related to a married woman (vv. 6–8 and 10–12), is evident in Cocco's otherwise fine study, which leaves verse 9 aside to deal with lastly, considering it 'secondary and additional in nature' and 'inserted right in the middle of our law', interrupting its natural progression – he sees the verse as a 'bizarre thematic intrusion' because he assumes the verses that follow relate the scenario of a married woman, which should most naturally follow the second case of verses 6–8 (2020: 198, 202–204). Without textual evidence, other scholars have similarly determined that verse 9 is an interpolation (see e.g. Holzinger 1903: 147; Heinisch 1936: 117). My understanding of the text accords with that of Ibn Ezra (1999: 240):

> If the widow vowed in an earlier time and her husband disallowed it, then she does not have to keep the vow in her widowhood. This speaks about a vow which she vowed regarding the future, and the husband died before the vow was to take effect.

Abarbanel also agrees (2015: 323–234) that

> the Torah now refers back to the previous category, that of a widow or divorcee . . . She cannot now say: 'Since I am not married now therefore the revocation was not total, and it should now become resurrected.' 'It is not so!' the Torah says.

The Mishnah seems to take the same reading, teaching that if a husband abrogated a vow, then 'even though she was widowed or divorced', even within thirty days, the vow remains annulled (see *Ned.* 11.9E–H in Neusner 1988: 429). Milgrom counters these arguments, but his own observation about the caustic legal form of the material, with the primary case introduced by *kî* (when) and the subsections with *'im* (if), argues against his view, a point only partially alleviated by his taking verse 9 as an interruption, an 'editorial parenthesis' – since he still regards verses 10–12 as a separate case, requiring *kî* rather than *'im* (1990: 250, 253). Taking the text as we have it, the two possibilities introduced by *'im* in verses 10 and 12 must flow from the main statement regarding widows and divorcees in verse 9, even without its use of *kî*. Levine agrees that verses 10–12 relate to vows or binding agreements of a woman presently widowed or divorced, but that had been undertaken previously while that woman had still been married (2000: 433). The previous paradigms, then, apply to the widow or divorced woman. If, while still married, her husband had remained silent and did not forbid her when he had heard of her pledge, then 'all her vows' and 'every bond' will stand even now as a widow or divorcee. But if, on the day he had heard, he 'surely annulled' (*hāpēr yāpēr*) them, then all that went forth from her lips will not stand – 'YHWH will forgive her.' The basic point remains: a husband has limited authority over his wife's vows and oaths, and his voiding or affirming of her pledge stands even if he later dies or divorces her.

13–16. A summary of a husband's protective role and accountability for his wife's every vow and oath 'to afflict her soul', is provided; namely, he may either confirm or annul it. Although some take this section as introducing a new special category of pledges, those of 'self-affliction' (e.g. Levine 2000: 433), I take this section as a comprehensive summary akin to verse 2 (as does Milgrom 1990: 254). That the Temple Scroll (11Q19–20) concludes the topic of women's vows and oaths with verse 13 likely indicates the Qumran sect also understood this section 'as a recapitulatory conclusion' (cf. Cocco 2020: 200). While the language qualifies the right of a husband (and presumably father) over his wife's vows and oaths to those that 'afflict her soul' through some consequential abstention, this limit has traditionally been interpreted to include any vow that has an impact on her marital relationship, given the further language of verse 16, which explains that the statutes address concerns 'between a man and his wife' (cf. *Ned.* 79b). Once more, confirming a vow or oath, causing it 'to stand' is accomplished merely by his keeping silent 'from day to day', understood as a period of the day when 'he heard' of the pledge; that is, until sunset that day (cf. *Ned.* 76), although some prefer a twenty-four-hour period (see Abarbanel, ad loc.). Milgrom points out that a different biblical idiom is used for a twenty-four-hour period (cf. Ezek. 4:10–11), so that here annulment must be made on the same day the father or husband hears of the pledge (1990: 254). Elkanah's response to Hannah provides a remarkable example of affirming a wife's vow, moving beyond mere silence to encouragement, even though the cost to him was in the highest extreme, his own firstborn son by her: 'Do (*'ăśî*) what is good in your eyes; wait until you have weaned him – only let YHWH confirm (*yāqēm*) his word' (1 Sam. 1:23).

'But if he surely annuls them after he has heard it, then he will bear her guilt' presumes that 'after' means 'after the day when he heard has passed'; that is, this statement follows the previous verse's scenario chronologically. Consequently, when he annuls the vow or oath after the period of a day, he himself must bear 'her guilt' for not fulfilling it, which in a manner also provides her with a layer of protection from God, for, as Ibn Ezra writes, 'she is under his care' (1999: 241). The same result holds for a father, related to the first case (cf. *Sif. Num.* 155; Nachmanides 1975: 353; Milgrom 1990: 254). The 'guilt' here is completely aside from the husband's possible guilt of negligence in handling the vow or oath, but relates to the wife's guilt for not having fulfilled her vow. Whereas in the previous instances, she was forgiven by YHWH, here her guilt remains but is transferred for her husband to bear. As with the case of the strayed woman, the phrase here 'he will bear her guilt' (*wĕnāśā' 'et-'ăwōnāh*) implies some sort of divine punishment (cf. Zimmerli 1954: 8–11) – although, at least under certain conditions, there was a possibility of making atonement with a reparation offering (Lev. 5:4). This is not the same consequence as the judgement recorded for a high-handed sinner, whose 'guilt' is prefaced by the *kārēt* penalty of being cut off, in Numbers 15:31 (contra Stubbs 2009: 226–227). He, through his authority over her, has prevented her from fulfilling her vow or oath, and she, in submitting to her husband, will not be held accountable. Given their one-flesh union (Gen. 2:24) and the husband's protective role, it is as if he himself had taken the vow or oath upon himself and not fulfilled it. Assuming a scenario whereby the husband regrets not having nullified the vow in time, this possibly becomes a last-ditch scenario whereby he can rescue her through a late, and therefore invalid, nullification, which transfers the guilt to himself. Alternatively, Eichler (2021), pointing out that 3rd sg. verbs may be indefinite in Hebr. and that *nāśā'* may have a 'good' sense, proposes the translation 'her sin will be lifted' as a variation on the phraseology 'she will be forgiven'. While the variation in terminology is not an insurmountable objection, the parallel phrasing in 5:31, whereby the woman 'will bear her guilt' (*tiśśā' 'et-'ăwōnāh*), is a strong challenge against his alternative reading.

The concluding statement reiterates two points. First 'these statutes' spoken by Moses were expressly commanded by YHWH, bearing his authority. Second, the statutes address relationships, that 'between a man and his wife', and that 'between a father and his daughter in her youth, in her father's house'. They may be seen justly as divine protective measures for women at different stages of their lives, and as such serve to complement the inheritance law derived through the daughters of Zelophehad (27:1–11; so, too, Hirsch 2007a: 628).

Explanation

The laws concerning women's vows should be understood within the context of a daughter's social status in the ancient world. Ben-Barak helpfully summarizes as follows (2006: 5):

> Two main principles determined the daughter's legal, social and economic status. The first was that as her father's direct offspring . . . he was obliged to provide for her and assure her future. The second was her marriage. A daughter in her father's house was destined for marriage. With it, she left her father's house and joined that of her husband's father. From then on the husband was obliged to provide for her and her offspring as an integral part of his house. Objectively,

therefore, the daughter was never an independent being: her life was divided between two periods of dependency. In the first, until her marriage, she belonged to her father's house and depended on him and on her brothers legally, economically and as regards her security. In the second, after marriage, she belonged to her husband's *bēt 'āb* and was dependent on her husband, his father and her sons legally, economically and as regards her security.

In the purity law regarding the strayed woman (Num. 5:11–31), we noted the application to the covenantal relationship of YHWH and Israel, as husband and wife, a nuptial theology observed in Numbers 25 as well. So, too, vows 'are like a covenant in miniature', writes Stubbs (2009: 227), 'and the consequence of breaking a vow is similar to Israel's breaking covenant with God'. Of utmost weight is the seriousness and crucial nature of the obligations the people took upon themselves at Sinai, which was like a marriage covenant: 'All that YHWH has spoken we will do' (Exod. 19:8; cf. 24:7). As Milgrom observes (1990: 488; cf. Williamson 2007), 'A covenant, by definition, is a promissory oath (e.g. see Gen. 21:22–32; 31:44–53),' so that, in a sense, each Israelite's keeping of vows and oaths becomes a reflection of the nation's covenant relationship with YHWH. Asking whether it is 'possible to see the women in this passage as veiled figures of Israel in relationship to God', as is apparently the case with the strayed woman, Stubbs reflects on how these laws may gesture toward the profound notion of how God as the husband of Israel will himself bear the guilt rather than enforcing the entire fulfilment of punishments due Israel for breaking her vows in unfaithfulness (2009: 229). M. Douglas interprets the laws on women's vows and oaths likewise, arguing that their literary placement is fitting when one reads the unnamed woman as Israel, referring to Israel's commitment to God and expressing the comfort of the Lord's dealing with his people as husband or father (2001: 170–171). She draws on Hosea's description of Israel in the wilderness era as 'the days of her youth' (2:15; cf. Ezek. 23:1–4), observing how the law of the strayed woman (Num. 5:11–31) portrays Israel as an erring wife, but whose vows to false gods at Baal Peor (Num. 25) may be nullified by YHWH her husband, if she repents – 'she has made vows to new husbands and defiled herself, but the Lord, her first husband, has heard her vows and made them void at once, she will not have to bear the consequences, and he is mercifully willing to take her back' (M. Douglas 2001: 171). Perhaps the narrative logic of the material unfolds as follows: Israel had 'joined' with Baal (master, husband), committing harlotry – a pledge YHWH abrogated through Phinehas (Num. 25); Moses here explains the divine law, whereby a husband has the authority to abrogate his wife's vows and oaths – she is forgiven and not expected to follow through on the previous commitment she voiced (Num. 30); under YHWH's leadership, and free from any bonds with Midian created through Zimri and Cozbi, Israel then exacts vengeance on the Midianites (Num. 31; see *mā'al* in 5:12, 27 and 31:16).

Ideally, the legislation of Numbers 30 has in view the relieving of a woman's burden. Even more than for a man, observes Hirsch (2007a: 621), the 'moral greatness of a woman's calling' requires her to 'avoid the constraint of extraordinary guidelines in her life, for they are likely to be an impediment to her in the fulfilment of her calling', so the legislation 'seeks to insure the vowing woman against the consequences of her own words' through the limited rights granted fathers and husbands that offer a form of protection for women throughout the various stages of their lives (cf. Cocco 2020: 204). Aside from protecting the women themselves, there was also the practical concern of protecting a father's house in the scenario where a woman, whether as daughter or wife, had pledged to give either herself or possessions (of estates, flock, cattle or even children), which would harm the family.

An overriding concern of the legislation is that one's word, especially as pledged to YHWH or in his Name, be fulfilled. In canto 5 of Dante's *Paradiso*, within the realm of the moon, with its ever-shifting phases, the pilgrim meets those saints who reneged on their vows. He learns that vows are especially sacred because the self – the will's liberty, which derives from humanity's being made in the image of God – is the greatest gift one can offer to God. Once this pact is sealed, to take back one's pledge in exchange for whatever works of kindness is like trying to pay for charitable works with stolen money (cf. lines 13–33). The concern for fulfilling vows and oaths in particular relates, more deeply, to faithfulness in fulfilling one's expressed *intentions*, which is especially relevant within Israel's historical context, on the verge of receiving the gift of the land. Within the literary context of Numbers, the pledge of the tribes of Reuben and Gad in Numbers 32 forms a significant example of how life on the cusp of the land is filled with noble intentions – for all the tribes of Israel so much depended on Reuben and Gad's keeping their word (cf. Sacks 2017: 369). Although the world has learned by experience to put little value on words, God, whose Son, the *Logos*, is truth, takes human words – especially when uttered to him or in his Name – with utmost seriousness. Made in his image and likeness, people should speak sincerely and truthfully (Matt. 5:37), fulfilling oaths even when sworn to one's own hurt (Ps. 15:4; see also Lev. 5:4; Ps. 106:33; Prov. 20:25; Eccl. 5:2; James 5:12).

The land of Canaan was to be a foretaste of the new earth, or paradise, where devotion to YHWH God is the priority, manifest not only in the offering of whole burnt offerings throughout the liturgical calendar (chs. 28–29), but even in the details of daily speech within the average Israelite home (ch. 30). Such commitments to keep one's word reflects YHWH's own character and word, for he cannot lie and always fulfils his word. But beyond truth-telling, vows and oaths speak to each Israelite's relationship with YHWH, and the need to fulfil one's original intention when the soul, out of gratitude for life and blessing or even out of humility over one's desperate plight, had originally turned to YHWH for praise, thanksgiving or deliverance. Fulfilling one's intention, perhaps long after the heart has turned to rest or grown fat with complacency, becomes the very means of returning to YHWH, of persevering in following him closely. Fulfilling vows and oaths to YHWH, from this perspective, is the remedy and antidote to the sort of straying into apostasy described by Moses in his farewell speeches to the nation. Shortly after warning Israel that, after YHWH fulfils his oath of bringing them into the land, giving them houses they did not build, filled with good things, wells they did not dig, vineyards and olive trees they did not plant, and they eat and are full, so that they should beware of forgetting YHWH, he immediately says, 'You will fear YHWH your God and serve him, and will take oaths in his Name' (Deut. 6:10–13). Within the context of Numbers as well, following the legislation on Israel's liturgical calendar, the legislation on vows and oaths functions to underscore their relationship with YHWH and the sort of life demanded of those who live before his face. Just as in Numbers 27:1–11, room was made for women to possess lands, so now in chapter 30, room is made for women to fulfil a main purpose for life in the land, to express devotion to YHWH through vows and oaths, even while mitigating their burden. Within the broad theological structure of Numbers, these women stand for Israel in the nation's covenant marriage with YHWH. Following the paradigm of the Nazirite vow, Israel, having endured a period of deprivation (chs. 11–25), with cleansing from corpse pollution (ch. 19), now anticipates offering sacrifices and accompaniments in the land (chs. 28–29), fulfilling her vow of separation (ch. 30).

NUMBERS 31: ISRAEL'S VENGEANCE ON THE MIDIANITES

Translation

$^{31:1}$And YHWH spoke to Moses, saying, ^{2}'Avenge, the vengeance of the sons of Israel against the Midianites, after which you will be gathered to your people.' ^{3}And Moses spoke to the people, saying, 'Arm men from among you for the host, and let them be against Midian, to set the vengeance of YHWH against Midian. ^{4}A thousand per tribe: a thousand per tribe for all the tribes of Israel you will send to the host.' ^{5}And they were mustered from the thousands of Israel, a thousand per tribe, twelve thousand armed for the host. ^{6}And Moses sent them, a thousand per tribe to the host, them and Phinehas the son of

Eleazar the priest to the host, with the holy vessels and the trumpets for the trilling blast in his hand. ⁷And they battled against Midian, just as YHWH had commanded Moses, and they struck down all the males. ⁸And all the kings of Midian they struck down, beside the others of the slain: Evi and Rekem and Zur and Hur and Reba, the five kings of Midian – and Balaam the son of Beor they struck down with a sword. ⁹And the sons of Israel took-captive the women of Midian, and their little ones, and all their beasts, and all their livestock, and all their wealth they despoiled. ¹⁰And all their cities, their dwellings, and all their encampments, they burned with fire. ¹¹And they took all the booty and all the plunder (the takings), both human and beast. ¹²And they brought to Moses and to Eleazar the priest, and to the community of the sons of Israel, the captives and the plunder and the booty, to the Camp, to the plains of Moab, which was by Jordan near Jericho.

¹³And Moses and Eleazar the priest and all the chieftains of the community went forth to encounter them, to outside the Camp. ¹⁴And Moses was enraged (wrath) against the appointed ones of the force, the chiefs over thousands and the chiefs over hundreds, who came from the hosts of the war. ¹⁵And to them Moses said, 'Have you left alive every female? ¹⁶Look, these caused the sons of Israel, through the word of Balaam, to muster in unfaithfulness against YHWH concerning the matter of Peor, and so the plague happened among the community of YHWH. ¹⁷Now, strike down every male among the little ones, and every woman who has known a man by lying with a male you will strike down. ¹⁸But the young among the women who have not known lying with a male keep alive for yourselves. ¹⁹You yourselves encamp outside the Camp seven days, all who have struck down a soul and all who have touched any slain purify yourselves on the third day and on the seventh day, you and your captives. ²⁰And every garment and every vessel of leather and everything made of goat (hair) and all vessels of wood you will purify.'

²¹And Eleazar the priest said to the men of the host who went to the war, 'This is the statute of the law which YHWH had commanded Moses: ²²Only the gold and the silver, the bronze, the iron, the tin, and the lead, ²³everything that may go through the fire, you will pass through the fire; then it will be clean; nevertheless, by the waters of separation it will be purified, and everything that cannot go through fire you will cause to pass through the waters. ²⁴You will wash your garments on the seventh day, and you will be clean, and afterward you may come into the Camp.'

²⁵And YHWH said to Moses, saying, ²⁶'Lift up the head of the plunder that was taken, both human and beast, you and Eleazar the priest, and the heads of the fathers of the community. ²⁷And divide the plunder between those who wielded (sword) in the war, who went forth to the host, and the whole community. ²⁸And raise a levy to YHWH from the men of the war who went forth to the host: one soul out of five hundred, from human and from cattle and from donkeys and from flock. ²⁹From their half you will take and give to Eleazar the priest, a contribution to YHWH. ³⁰And from the sons of Israel's half you will take one held from every fifty, from humans, from cattle, from donkeys,

and from flock, from all the beasts, and you give them to the Levites who keep the charge of the Dwelling of YHWH.' ³¹And Moses, along with Eleazar the priest, did just as YHWH had commanded Moses. ³²Now the plunder, the spoil left over beyond what the people of the host despoiled, were sheep, six hundred and seventy-five thousand, ³³and cattle, seventy-two thousand, ³⁴and donkeys, sixty-one thousand, ³⁵and human souls, from the women who had not known lying with a male, every soul, thirty-two thousand. ³⁶And the half, the portion of those went forth to the host, the number of sheep was three hundred and thirty-seven thousand and five hundred. ³⁷And the levy for YHWH from the sheep, six hundred and seventy-five. ³⁸And the cattle, thirty-six thousand, and their levy to YHWH, seventy-two. ³⁹And donkeys, thirty thousand five hundred, and their levy to YHWH, sixty-one. ⁴⁰And human souls, sixteen thousand, and their levy to YHWH, thirty-two souls. ⁴¹And Moses gave the levy contribution of YHWH to Eleazar the priest, just as YHWH had commanded Moses. ⁴²And from the sons of Israel's half, which Moses had divided from the men of the host – ⁴³the community's half from the sheep was three hundred and thirty-seven thousand and five hundred, ⁴⁴and cattle, thirty-six thousand, ⁴⁵and donkeys, thirty thousand and five hundred, ⁴⁶and human souls, sixteen thousand – ⁴⁷and from the sons of Israel's half Moses took one held from every fifty, from human and from beast, and gave them to the Levites who keep the charge of the Dwelling of YHWH, just as YHWH had commanded Moses.

⁴⁸And the appointed ones, who were over thousands of the host, the chiefs of the thousands and the chiefs of the hundreds, came near to Moses, ⁴⁹and they said to Moses, 'Your servants have lifted the head of the men of the war who were in our hand, and there is not a man unaccounted (appointed) from us! ⁵⁰So we have brought near a near-offering for YHWH, for every man who found a vessel of gold, armlet and bracelet, ring, earring and pendant, to make atonement for our souls before YHWH.' ⁵¹And Moses, with Eleazar the priest, took the gold from them, every vessel of workmanship. ⁵²And all the gold of the contribution which they levied to YHWH was sixteen thousand seven hundred and fifty shekels, from the chiefs of the thousands and from the chiefs of the hundreds. ⁵³The men of the host had despoiled, each man for himself. ⁵⁴And Moses, with Eleazar the priest, took the gold from the chiefs of the thousands and the hundreds, and brought it into the Tent of Meeting, a memorial for the sons of Israel before YHWH.

Notes on the text

3. 'let them be': *BHS* suggests reading 'YHWH' instead, an unnecessary emendation.

5. 'mustered': a rare word, likely intended as 'provided', with Syr and Tg; LXX reads *exērithmēsan*, 'were numbered'.

6. 'per tribe': LXX adds *syn dynamei autōn* here, 'son of Aaron' after Eleazar and omits the second reference to 'the host'. *TgJon* refers to 'Urim and Thummin' after 'holy vessels' (cf. Num. 27:21).

10. 'encampments': Vg implies towns here, while Tg understands cultic sites.

13. 'went forth': reads sg. in SamP, LXX and one MT MS.

15. 'Have you left alive?': SamP, LXX, Syr and Vg read 'Why have you left alive?'

16. 'muster': as with v. 5. LXX explains the children of Israel despised the word of the Lord, and Syr notes they revolted against YHWH; plausibly, *BHS* suggests changing *limsor* to *limʻōl* for 'committed a transgression against YHWH'.

21. SamP prefaces Eleazar's speech with Moses' direction for him to declare that statute.

23. 'you will pass through the fire': lacking in LXX; likely, as *BHS* suggests, through homeoteleuton.

28. SamP adds 'and cattle' to the end of the list of animals (cf. v. 30); whereas LXX adds 'cattle' to the front of the list.

29. 'you will take': pl. in MT, but sg. in SamP and Syr.

30, 47. 'held': same root as 'holding'; lacking in LXX, Syr and Vg.

37. 'six hundred and seventy-five': reads 'six thousand seven hundred and fifty' in Syr, which also multiplies by ten the other numbers in vv. 36–40.

Form and structure

G. B. Gray dubbed this 'not history, but *Midrash*' (1903: 418), a common position, including Snaith who defined midrash as 'a story invented to illustrate a theme, a law or a regulation' (1962: 324; cf. Sturdy 1976: 214–215). While some of Gray's reasoning, such as the later presence of Midianites in history, has since been overturned by scholarship (see e.g. Dumbrell 1975), yet his instinctive assessment gestured toward a fundamental insight about this text, which presents a historical account in a stylized manner. In various ways, Israel's divinely ordained battle against Midian is depicted as paradigmatic for the conquest, and symbolic, employing imagery of the Camp's structure and embracing its purity laws. While a historic military victory, regarded as 'holy war', the account can also be read 'in a more spiritual manner' as Stubbs observes (2009: 230). Cole, who considers the passage historically reliable, nevertheless agrees that it may be understood as midrashic, defined as 'a literary tool for teaching certain lessons or principles', inasmuch as provides 'case law precedents for future holy war endeavours', apt for the impending conquest (2000: 490). Seebass regards 'midrash' as an imprecise term for Numbers 31, even while underlining the chapter's obvious use of other texts (2007: 3:316–317), and K. Brown also recognizes the chapter 'does not simply recount a historical event; it reapplies and reformulates a wide range of earlier biblical legislation in novel and surprising ways'

(2015: 66). This narrative is certainly more than case law, even more than a foretaste of the conquest; there is a note of triumph and idealism that lifts up the battle and its plunder into ethereal realms – here, the Torah presents the Camp of Israel, the paradigmatic covenant community, functioning as the earthly hosts of YHWH, the flowering of all the latent potential accumulated in the first ten chapters of Numbers.

Milgrom posits a chiastic structure (1990: 491–492), which appears forced; although followed by a few scholars (e.g. Staubli 1996: 331), it was rightly critiqued by Seebass (2007: 3:289–290). Numbers 31 comprises two halves, marked by a major paragraph break in the MT (vv. 1–24, 25–54), each beginning with YHWH's charge to Moses (vv. 1, 25). These two halves may be subdivided further into four units. The first, 1–12, begins with YHWH's charge to Moses for the sons of Israel to bring vengeance against the Midianites in battle (vv. 1–2) and resolves with the return of the Israelites with their hoard of victory plunder (v. 12). The second unit, 13–24, involving the matter of Midianite women and purification from corpse pollution, begins 'outside the Camp' (v. 13) and ends with entrance 'into the Camp' (v. 24). The third unit, 25–47, begins with YHWH's charge to inventory and divide the plunder (vv. 25–27) and concludes with a threefold obedience (vv. 31, 41, 47). The fourth unit, 48–54, recounting the gold offering by the chiefs, a ransom for their souls, begins with the chiefs' approach to Moses (v. 48) and ends with Moses and Eleazar bringing the gold to the Tent of Meeting as a memorial (v. 54). The two halves form a panel construction (see also Seebass 2007: 3:290; K. Brown 2015: 68–69). (See Table 23.)

Table 23: Numbers 31: structure

I. Vengeance on the Midianites, vv. 1–24	II. Victory spoils for the Camp, vv. 25–54
A. War against Midian, vv. 1–12	**A. Spoils for tribes, priests and Levites, vv. 25–47**
'YHWH spoke to Moses, saying', v. 1 'just as YHWH had commanded Moses', v. 7 'human and beast', v. 11	'YHWH said to Moses, saying', v. 25 'just as YHWH had commanded Moses', vv. 31, 41, 47 'human and beast', v. 26
B. Re-entering the Camp, vv. 13–24	**B. Spoils for Tent of Meeting, vv. 48–54**
'chiefs over thousands/ hundreds', v. 14	'chiefs over thousands/hundreds', v. 48

The first column (vv. 1–24) pertains to making 'reparation' or *tikkun* for the Baal Peor incident (ch. 25), even verses 13–24 being shaped by the need to conclude the matter by dealing with the women of Midian who had seduced the Israelites. Cleansing the fighters, captives and plunder from death pollution, for reintegration into the Camp concludes the mission of YHWH's retribution against the Midianites. The 'Midianites' or 'Midian' occurs seven times in the first unit (I.A., vv. 2, 3 [twice], 7, 8, 9), although clearly the 'females' and 'women' of the second unit (I.B.) are 'the women of Midian' from the first unit (v. 9). The second column of the panel (vv. 25–54) pertains entirely to the distribution of the spoils throughout the threefold Camp. Even the last episode resolves with gold being brought to the Tent of Meeting, the heart of the Camp (v. 54).

In discerning a rationale for the chapter's placement, the inclusion created with Numbers 25 must be factored in, as well as the chapter's central placement, structurally and theologically, within the book's last major movement (chs. 26–36). By narrating the vengeance on Midian in this section, which focuses on the conquest and division of land, the battle and division of plunder becomes a foretaste of the conquest, even though no land was taken from the Midianites – marking the battles against Sihon and Og more strongly as tokens of conquest, although these occurred during the 'wilderness sojourn' section (cf. Bick 2014c: 429). The Midianite inclusio (chs. 25, 31), more deeply, demonstrates that military victory follows on fulfilment of the Nazirite path, as Israel's second generation (chs. 26–27) brings offerings and accompaniments to YHWH in the land (chs. 28–29), fulfilling their vows (ch. 30). Finally, as Ashley, among others (e.g. Budd 1984: 329; Olson 1996: 179–180), well-observes, chapter 31 weaves together many of the other passages in the book, as something of 'a summary and conclusion' of what has gone before, as shown in Table 24 (1993: 587).

The wide-ranging interlacing of previous passages, expanded below, exhibits an intention to set this account as the exemplary epitome of its subsection (chs. 28–32), and perhaps the entire book. Chapter 31 serves

Table 24: Battle with Midian as culmination

Numbers 31	Previous passages
Vengeance on Midian, vv. 2–3	25:16–18
Moses' coming death, v. 2	27:13
The trumpets, v. 6	10:2–10
Zur the Midianite, v. 8	25:15
Balaam, vv. 8, 16	chs. 22–24
The incident of Baal Peor, v. 16	25:6–9
Purification from corpse defilement, vv. 19–24	6:9–12; 19:11–19
Care for priests and Levites, vv. 28–47	18:8–32
Costly offerings, vv. 48–54	chs. 7; 28–29
Counting or mustering, vv. 3–5, 26, 32–47	chs. 1–4; 26

as the culmination of the second generation's journey with YHWH, the consummate view of the second generation's Camp of Israel.

Comment

31:1–12: The Camp of Israel's symbolic holy war against Midian

Following preliminaries that anticipate the gift of the land – the census (ch. 26), the inheritance concern of the daughters of Zelophehad (27:1–11), the appointment of Joshua (27:12–23) and the laws concerning the calendric whole burnt offerings (chs. 28–29) and vows and oaths (ch. 30) – the text continues where the narrative ended: the war against the Midianites justly resolving their role in both the Balaam (chs. 22–24) and Baal Peor (ch. 25) stories, and reaches back even to the divine sentence against Moses at the waters of Meribah (ch. 20).

1–2. YHWH 'commands' (*wayĕdabbēr*) Moses to 'avenge' (*nĕqōm*) the 'vengeance (*niqmat*) of the sons of Israel' against the Midianites, forming an inclusion with the previous, similar command in Numbers 25:16–18 for Israelites to 'be hostile' to the Midianites, striking them down for having beguiled the Israelites. The precise form 'the Midianites' (*hammidyānîm*) is rare, occurring only twice (25:17; 31:2), with YHWH's charge here forming a resumption of the earlier command. As with 25:17, YHWH's ire focuses on the Midianites, rather than the Moabites. Rashi offers two reasons: first, Moab justly feared Israel, whereas Midian was meddling in a business not their own, and second, God wanted to preserve Ruth, ancestress of David (see Rashi 1997: 4:378, incl. n. 4).

As Milgrom notes (1990: 255), when *nāqam* (vengeance) takes a *min*-prep., the associated meaning is to redress past wrongs, whereas when it takes a *be*-prep., as it does in verse 3, it signifies the exacting of retribution. Akin to the notion of *tikkun* in Judaism, Israel's battle against the Midianites functions to restore or repair the Baal Peor incident, making amends for it inasmuch as the sons of Israel reverse the previous failure by responding rightly this time, including with regard to the women who had seduced them (vv. 15–18). G. J. Wenham describes the campaign 'as punishment for the Midianites' seduction of Israel from their true husband, the LORD (cf. 25:1–13)' (1981b: 234). Stubbs, similarly and without negating a 'historical' reading, suggests an 'allegorical or spiritual reading' underlining the 'battle for Israel's soul . . . against the spiritual forces or temptations that confront Israel and keep it from fulfilling its role to be a holy nation' (2009: 233). More than retribution, which is relevant (v. 3), the battle against Midian functions pedagogically for Israel, giving opportunity for the sons of Israel to demonstrate loyalty to YHWH, reversing the failure at Baal

Peor. The purpose, adds Hirsch (2007a: 629), 'is to raise Israel up *from* the Midianites, to effect Israel's spiritual and moral liberation from the power of Midian's wiles' (emphasis original). The battle is imbued with spiritual significance; a campaign against a foe who had plotted Israel's spiritual destruction, to sever the people's relationship with YHWH God. YHWH calls for the battle as the 'vengeance of the sons of Israel', aiming to guide them in redressing their own previous wrong, while Moses instructs the people to battle for the 'vengeance of YHWH' (v. 3); that is, to accomplish the divine retribution against Midian.

Through use of the m. sg. for the command, along with YHWH's explanation that afterward Moses would be gathered to his people, the war against Midian is portrayed as a final act of Moses. The war is an action that must be accomplished by Moses before he dies, not left for Joshua. At the least, YHWH ensures that the grievance which occurred under Moses' watch is not left for Joshua to resolve, whose role is forward-looking to the land. Yet the emphasis on Moses' impending death leads to the conclusion that there is 'something personal in Moses' life which is the reason for the war and Moses' involvement in it', as Bick explains (2014c: 430–433), adding that the phrase 'after which you will be gathered to your people' encourages Moses to understand the impending war in terms of fulfilling his life mission, a final act of educating Israel, and repairing his previous passivity at Baal Peor. The war expresses a *changed attitude* toward the culture of licentiousness and idolatry awaiting Israel in the land (cf. 33:51–56). As with his speeches in Deuteronomy, Moses' task is to prepare the people *spiritually* to enter the land. This was not Joshua's role. Nor was it Phinehas's role, who accompanies the hosts of Israel to battle as Moses' template – his exemplary model – for the spirit of jealousy that should characterize the life of Israel in the land. The battle is linked to the tassels legislation (15:37–41) via Numbers 25 where, instead of remembering YHWH and his commands, the Israelites followed 'your own eyes, after which you go whoring'.

The phrase 'after which you will be gathered to your people' echoes the similar and fuller divine remark in Numbers 27:12–14, about both Aaron's death and the reason for their judgement, having rebelled against YHWH's command to hallow him. Both Numbers 31:1–2 and 27:12–14 look back further to Moses' failure to sanctify YHWH at the waters of Meribah (Num. 20). The context of Numbers 20 thus forms an interpretative layer that undergirds Moses' call to enact vengeance on Midianites with the ultimate purpose of sanctifying YHWH before the Israelites. Comparing 31:1–2 with 27:12–14 places Moses' seeing the land in parallel with Moses' avenging Israel against Midian, perhaps marking the battle as a foretaste of the land's conquest. Thus, YHWH's notice to Moses regarding his approaching death adds urgency to the command to avenge against the Midianites, and lends the act meaningful gravity as Moses' final accomplishment.

3–6. Moses relays the message to 'the people' (*hāʿām*), a signal of the national importance of the battle against Midian. While 12,000 men will be appointed for battle (cf. 2 Sam. 17:1; 1 Kgs 10:26), they represent all the tribes of Israel, so that the war itself becomes a profound gesture of all the people, their *tikkun* for and rejection of the Baal Peor incident. The figure 12,000 also represents half of the Israelites who died in the plague of YHWH's wrath, 24,000 (cf. 25:9). Twelve signifies Israel, explicitly since one thousand is taken from each tribe, an ideal or stylized representation of *the outer camp*, recalling the unity displayed in Numbers 7, as does the later offering by the chiefs (vv. 48–54). Phinehas's presence completes the representation of the Camp structure, as George explains, although he has in mind the threefold tabernacle complex, whereby the outer court represents the outer camp of twelve tribes (2013: 41):

> The fact that they (the twelve tribes) join together as a fighting force and are accompanied by a priest – Phinehas, who brings with him sacred vessels from the tabernacle – symbolically reproduces tabernacle socio-spatial logic in battle, since items and persons from all three spaces of the tabernacle complex are involved in it.

Moses instructs them to 'arm' (*ḥālaṣ*, 'to equip') men 'for the host' (*laṣṣābā'*), for battle. The construction *l* + *ṣābā'* occurs twenty times in chapters 1–10, with reference to the newly constructed Camp; Numbers 31 marks the first occurrence since then, appearing six times, demonstrating that the newly reorganized second generation is fulfilling what it means to be YHWH's earthly hosts. The link by use of *ṣābā'* is significant, as the term does not appear even once in the wars against Sihon and Og (cf. Bick 2014c: 431). These men, the vanguard of Israel, the Camp in microcosm, are to be 'against Midian', to 'set' (*nātan*) the 'vengeance of YHWH against Midian' (cf. Jer. 50:15, 28; 51:11). As noted above, the form of *nāqam* with a *be*-prep., refers to vengeance as retribution, or 'punitive vindication' (so Mendenhall 1973: 99). Their battle is not merely for the sake of YHWH's honour, but a retribution delivered *by* YHWH against Midian through his people. As such, the battle is paradigmatic for the conquest (cf. Gen. 15:16), and the fight 'against Midian' becomes a tangible way for Israelites to realign themselves – consciously and deliberately – with YHWH over against Midian, precisely repairing the failure at Baal Peor. As YHWH once did in the garden of Eden, when he reasserted the fitting enmity between the seed of the woman and the seed of the serpent (Gen. 3:15), so now, aside from bringing judgement upon Midian for their deceitful enticing of his sons, he instils the proper militant posture against idolatry and sexual immorality within the nation's soul.

From the general statement in verse 3, Moses' instructions are detailed in verse 4: a thousand men must be appointed 'per tribe' and this 'for all the tribes of Israel', underscoring the point that the whole nation must partake in the battle – its significance far surpasses any ordinary military endeavour whereby pragmatic concerns may play a role. Each of the twelve tribes will 'send to the host' its representative thousand. The paradigmatic role of this war becomes immediately evident in the next chapter, where the sons of Reuben and Gad, who desire for their tribes to settle east of the Jordan, are pressed to commit their fighting men to join the other tribes in the conquest of the land: all tribes must be represented, not only in bringing divine judgement on the Canaanites, but in possessing the land. The 'thousands of Israel' (*'alpê yiśrā'ēl*, v. 5) is used only four times in Numbers, 3 within chapters 1–10, including the epic and climactic final verse 'Return, O YHWH, to the many thousands of Israel' (10:36; cf. 1:16; 10:4), and here in 31:5, another indicator of the central significance of the battle. Once more verse 5 spells out 'a thousand per tribe', adding 'twelve thousand', emphasizing how the warriors represent Israel's twelve tribes – in other words, the outer camp of the Camp of Israel. The 12,000 are 'armed for the host/battle', a phrase that picks up the language of verse 3, demonstrating the people's compliance.

In verse 6 the spotlight returns to Moses: he sent them – again, 'a thousand per tribe' – to the host, to war. He also sends Phinehas the son of Eleazar the priest, creating another substantial link to Numbers 25: the priestly figure who made atonement for Israel, turning back the wrathful plague of YHWH God by slaying a Midianite princess (along with Zimri the Simeonite), will represent the sacral nature of the battle, embodying once more, as he had done at Baal Peor, the divine jealousy of the One whose Name is Jealous (cf. Exod. 34:14; see *Num. Rab.* 22.4). A Jewish tradition that has Phinehas personally slaying Balaam (see *TgPs-J* on v. 8; *b. Sanh*. 106b) perceives the essence of the battle as Phinehas versus Balaam who, as a *bārû* – a Mesopotamian diviner – accompanied the Midianite armies, so Milgrom aptly describes Phinehas's 'acting as the antidote to Balaam' (1990: 256–257). As with Balaam, Phinehas's role is as spiritual advisor, not military commander, also evidenced by 'the fact that Moses does not scold him but only the officers (v. 14)' (Milgrom 1990: 257, following Shadal). On a more pragmatic level, Phinehas is sent since Eleazar, as high priest, must avoid death-defilement, even as earlier Eleazar had been sent to collect censers from among the dead in place of his father Aaron (16:37). According to Deuteronomy, part of Phinehas's role would be to encourage the Israelite fighters against fear, reminding them that 'YHWH your God goes with you, to fight for you against your enemies, to save you' (20:1–4).

'While Phinehas is not the major character in Numbers 31,' writes Barbara Organ (2001: 210), 'he holds the key to the narrative nonetheless', since his 'presence marks this war as a war of YHWH, a holy war'. Although the Midianite war is not dubbed *ḥerem* in the story, she suggests it functions as a 'narrative justification' for what is articulated as the law of *ḥerem* in Deuteronomy (Organ 2001: 211): 'Why must all the inhabitants of an enemy town be destroyed? Only look back to the incident of Peor and the Midianite war for the rationale.' In terms of *ḥerem* within Canaan, however, the notion of YHWH's due judgement for the inhabitants' guilt is also relevant (cf. Gen. 15:16). Phinehas, representing *the inner camp*, is accompanied by the 'holy vessels' and the 'trumpets for the trilling blast' in hand, representing the camp of the *Shekhinah*. There is some precedent for suggesting the 'vessels' refer to the Urim and Thummim, by which military stratagems may be decided (see Num. 27:21), and the ark of the covenant (see Num. 10:35; 14:44; cf. *Num. Rab.* 12.4). Mention of the trumpets and trilling blast recalls YHWH's original command to Moses to make the trumpets, along with his explanation of their use and purpose in chapter 10, another link between the Midian war and the first major section of the book. One purpose for the trumpets is given as follows:

> And when you enter war in your land against the hostile-foe who is being hostile (*haṣṣar haṣṣōrēr*) against you, make a trilling blast with the trumpets and you will be remembered before YHWH your God and you will be saved from your enemies. (Num. 10:9; cf. 2 Chr. 13:2)

The root *ṣārar* occurs only seven times in Numbers, twice in the verse just quoted (10:9) and twice more in the Baal Peor narrative, directly related to Midianites (25:17, 18), making the presence of the trumpets now obvious in relation to their function: the trilling alarm-blast will be sounded by Phinehas so that Israel will be remembered before YHWH God, who will deliver them from their enemy, Midian. The threefold link among chapters 10, 25 and 31 also flows into the significance of the Midianite battle as fulfilling the original divine intent for the covenant community established as YHWH's Camp. Since, moreover, the military use of trumpets was intended for 'in your land' (10:9), their use now may portray further the battle against Midianites as a foretaste of the conquest.

7–8. They 'battled' (*wayyiṣbĕ'û*) against the Midianites 'just as YHWH had commanded Moses' (*ka'ăšer ṣiwwā yhwh 'et-mōšeh*). Recalling the opening of Numbers, where it appears five times (1:19; 2:33; 3:51; 8:3, 22), the fulfilment formula occurs four times in chapter 31 (vv. 7, 31, 41, 47) – not only was the organization of the Camp according to YHWH's direction, but its life, movement and action are as well. The term for 'struck down' (*hārag*) refers not to killing within the context of battle (where *nākāh*, 'to smite', is used), but to 'wholesale slaughter after battle' (BDB 246–247, 645–646). Note, however, the kings who here are 'struck down' were, in Joshua, 'smitten' (*nākāh*) by Moses (13:21). Here the Israelite fighters 'struck down all the males', opening the way for verse 9 and the controversy in verses 14–18, where Moses heatedly points out the role of Midianite women at Baal Peor. First, however, the significant males struck down are delineated; namely, the five kings of Midian: Evi, Rekem, Zur, Hur and Reba (see Josh. 13:21–22), who might have been those designated 'elders' earlier in Numbers 22:4 (so Ashley 1993: 592). Encouraging a spiritual reading of the battle, Stubbs offers possible meanings for each of the kings, along with their BDB reference (2009: 233). (See Table 25.)

Table 25: The five kings of Midian

Name	Root	
Evi	'wn – 'trouble, sorrow, wickedness'	BDB 19
Rekem	rqm – 'variegated'; hence, 'impure'	BDB 955
Zur	ṣr – 'adversary, foe'	BDB 865
Hur	ḥrr – 'to bore or pierce', 'be parched, a parched place'	BDB 359
Reba	rbʻ – 'to lie down, copulate'	BDB 918

Origen of Alexandria also used his understanding of the kings' names to apply the Midianite battle in spiritual terms, to 'destroy beastly and savage morals' (for 'Evi'), against the 'worthlessness' of the nations (for 'Rekem'), and so on – in short, to battle against 'fleshly lusts that wage war against the soul' (Origen 2009: 155–156). Whether or not the kings' names function in such a manner, the battle against Midian truly is conceived thus, as Israel's fight against the sexual seduction to idolatry that had led to the destruction of thousands among their hosts at Baal Peor, and which they would encounter regularly among the nations. Zur forms a link to the Baal Peor incident since he was the father of Cozbi the princess (25:15).

Most notably, 'Balaam the son of Beor' was also struck down. For his death, the phrase 'with a sword (ḥereb)' is tacked on, which forms a deeper connection with the Balaam narrative where the sword of YHWH's messenger had threatened him repeatedly (see 22:23, 29, 31) – for his schemes against YHWH's people, the divine sword finally smote him. The natural question that arises – namely, what was Balaam doing with these Midianite kings? – is answered in verse 16 . Rather than inept editing, the later filling-in of gaps is part of the Torah's literary strategy, which 'often omits in one part of the narrative important details, only to allude to them, at a later stage' (Leibowitz 1982: 376). Rhetorical suspense aside, Balaam's presence and demise in Israel's battle against Midian not only unifies the Balaam (chs. 22–24) and Baal Peor (ch. 25) narratives, but resolves the latter apostasy more completely since it was he who had instigated the Midianites to the ruse of sending Cozbi among the Israelites. One may even wonder about a wordplay between *Bilʿām* son of *bĕʿôr* and *Baʿal* of *pĕʿôr* (cf. Ingalls 1991: 168). Reading between the lines, the Midrash postulates that when Balaam heard that 24,000 Israelites had fallen as a result of his counsel, he returned to get his reward from the five kings (*Num. Rab.* 20.20; cf. *b. Sanh.* 106a). Numbers 25 presented the final challenge for the second generation, in which they failed. After YHWH's judgement and Phinehas's atoning act, the community was reconstituted via the census (ch. 26) and assured of inheriting the land (chs. 27–29). After such divine grace, it is fitting for the second generation to return to their colossal failure and make reparation under YHWH's guidance by the hand of Moses. Scripture warns of the judgement due to those who cause others – especially among God's people – to sin (cf. Mark 9:42), and here Israel forms the means by which YHWH brings swift judgement on the Midianites, their kings and on Balaam, who had devised the original scheme against Israel.

9–12. The sons of Israel 'took-captive' (*šābāh*) the women of Midian, their little ones, all their cattle and all their livestock, and 'despoiled' (*bāzaz*) all their 'wealth' (*ḥayil*). The term 'livestock' (*miqneh*) will be a key word in the next chapter, used four times in the opening verses, with Gad and Reuben's 'much livestock' becoming a major impetus for their wanting to settle in Transjordan (32:1–4). Their action accords with rules for warfare in Deuteronomy (20:13–14; cf. 21:10–14). Aside from the captives and spoils, the overthrow is complete: not only were all males struck down, but 'all their cities and dwellings and all their encampments' were burned with fire. Milgrom makes a good case for *bĕhēmāh* signifying donkeys here (1990: 258), although the usage in verses 11 and 26 is typical of the generic label for domesticated animals. While older scholarship dismissed the utter destruction of the Midianites here, since Midianites appear again in later history (see Judges 6 – 8), it is now better understood that 'Midianites formed a large confederation of tribes, associated with various smaller groups such as the Ishmaelites (Gen. 37:28; Judg. 8:22, 23), the Moabites (Num. 22:4, 7), the Amalekites (Judg. 6:3, 33), and Ephah (Gen. 25:4; Isa. 60:6),' so that only those Midianites linked with Moab are referenced in the present account (G. J. Wenham 1981b: 233; cf. Dumbrell 1975).

The return from battle is then described, fronting with emphasis the recipients before the plunder: 'to Moses and to Eleazar the priest and to the community of the sons of Israel', a threefold list reflecting the hierarchical structure of the Camp. Next, the enormous horde of captives, cattle and flocks, along with the mass of plundered objects, is listed before designating the location 'to the Camp, to the plains of Moab', with the prep. *ʾel* before 'Camp' not implying that they actually entered, as verses 13, 21–24 make clear. The location 'plains of Moab, which was by Jordan near Jericho' recurs in Numbers, beginning with Israel's encampment there (22:1), and frames the census (26:3, 63) as well as YHWH's concluding commandments (35:1; 36:13), being noted also in the travelogue (33:48–50). Since the first reference to the plains of Moab occurs as the setting for the Balaam narrative, the nearly identical phrase used here functions as one of several unifying links (cf. Monroe 2012: 223).

31:13–24: Reintegrating into the Camp

A major tension arises as Moses castigates the military leaders over their sparing of the Midianite women. This matter, however, may be subsumed under the broader idea of reintegration into the Camp, requiring resolution. The repair for Baal Peor must be completed, along with the purification of the army and their plunder, before re-entering the Camp.

13–16. Moses, Eleazar the priest, and all the chieftains of the community 'go forth' to meet them – alternatively, 'to outside the camp' (*'el-miḥûṣ lammaḥăneh*), underscoring the Camp's purity and the militia's need for cleansing, along with their plunder, before being reintegrated into the *life* of the Camp. The precise expression 'to outside the camp' occurs five times in Numbers, twice with reference to the purity regulations (5:3, 4) and once in the red heifer ritual (19:3), both of which serve as contextual backdrops for the present account. The locale 'outside the camp' (without *'el*) occurs a further five times, related to Miriam's being shut out of the camp (12:14, 15), and then again in relation to the red heifer ritual (19:9) as well as in the present story (31:19). Both forms of the phrase occur, finally, in relation to the Sabbath violator (15:35, 36). The battle against Midian exhibits the second generation of Israel as fulfilling the form, function and nature of the Camp set out in chapters 1–10.

Moses is 'enraged' (*qāṣap*; cf. 1:53; 16:22; 16:46; 18:5), not against the entire 12,000 but with their chiefs ('princes, captains', *śar*), the 'appointed ones of the force' (*pĕqûdê heḥāyil*), who came from the hosts of war. The designation *pĕqûdê* recalls the tallies of chapters 1–4 and 26, where the same form appears over sixty times (cf. Ashley 1993: 594). Verse 9 had already intimated the problem being addressed by Moses: 'the sons of Israel took-captive the women of Midian', although the wrathful encounter is still jarring in view of the outstanding victory and the enormous hoard of plunder. Incredulously, he asks, 'Have you left alive *every female* (*kol-nĕqēbāh*)?' Moses' further instructions in verse 18 make it clear that the emphasis is on 'every' – including the very women who were the most culpable for seducing Israel. Use of both 'Look' and 'these' (note the alliteration, *hēn henna hāyû*) portray Moses as if he is pointing to particular women, the very ones who caused the sons of Israel to 'muster' against YHWH. Rashi similarly understands *hēn henna* as 'they are the very ones' (see Rashi 1997: 4:384). The term 'muster' (*māsar*) occurs only twice in Numbers, both in chapter 31: first in verse 5 for the 12,000 who were gathered to battle against Midian, and now in verse 16 to describe how Israelites had been gathered against YHWH through the Midianite women in the matter of Peor, demonstrating once more the intention for this battle to reverse and repair Israel's failure in chapter 25. Moses also rehearses the result of Israel's being lured to their women, YHWH's destructive plague whereby 24,000 had died – the losses were twice as many as those who battled Midian. Lest they draw divine ire again, Israelite men must not be blindly allured by their attraction for the women, but should act foremost out of loyalty to YHWH, and so repair the previous 'unfaithfulness' (*ma'al*). The only other uses of the term *ma'al* were in relation to the purity of the Camp (5:6, 12, 27), portraying Israel's treachery against YHWH at Peor as the unfaithfulness of a strayed wife.

Mention of Balaam's role in verse 16 is as surprising as his presence in verse 8, yet the words 'through the word (i.e. 'counsel') of Balaam' form something of a capstone, simultaneously unifying the Balaam narrative (chs. 22–24) with the apostasy at Baal Peor (ch. 25), and explaining both Balaam's presence with the Midianite kings and the justice of his being struck down. Perhaps, in his wrath Moses is being presented in a parallel fashion to Phinehas in chapter 25, filled with divine jealousy, calling for execution of those guilty of seducing Israel. At the least, the passive portrayal of Moses in Numbers 25 is here reversed. Moses' wrath underscores the nature of the war as repair for the Baal Peor incident, supporting the original mandate (25:16–18), whereas the soldiers had acted according to 'normal' holy war regulations (see Deut. 20:13–15).

17–20. Having presented the grave error of the Israelite fighters, which threatened repetition of Peor, Moses now instructs them on how to amend the fault: every 'male' (*zākār*) among the little ones must be struck down, along with every 'woman' (*'iššā*) who has 'known a man by lying (*miškab*) with a male'. Although commonly touted, the Midianite battle does *not* employ the 'ban' (*ḥ-r-m*) – indeed, that not all of the enemy is slain is part of the distinctive war ideology of Numbers 31 (Niditch 1993a: 81). Given Moses' heated explanation in verse 16, slaying all the women who were not virgins is intended to ensure that none of the guilty among them, who had enticed the Israelites into sexual immorality and idolatry, would escape due punishment. The carnal use of 'lying down' (*šĕkābāh*), occurring three times here (31:17, 18, 35), is only used elsewhere in Numbers for the strayed woman (four times: 5:13 [twice], 19, 20), positioning the issue at hand under the scheme of Israel's purity and spiritual integrity. The young women, who have not known 'lying down' with a man may be 'kept alive', echoing Moses' earlier question in verse 15, so that the real emphasis in the previous verse had not been on either 'kept alive' or 'female' but on 'every' (*kol*).

The common interpretation of these verses is that, while the young virgins would be incorporated into Israelite households by marriage, the young males were put to death based on the potential threat of their revenge in the future. We must also consider the binding nature of vows and oaths established in the previous chapter. Given the probability that Midian had endeavoured to seduce Israel into being joined together as a people, it is only the bond of these virgin girls that may be overturned, by an Israelite husband. Perhaps the same dynamic is at work regarding the fundamental identity of Midianites: only a virgin girl may, through marriage to an Israelite, transform her identity. That vows and oath requirements function within the narrative in chapter 32 as an instance of 'God providing the cure before the disease' (*Meg.* 13b; *Midrash Lekaḥ Tov*, *Parashat Shemot*, 3.1), whereby the tribes of Reuben and Gad must keep their word to lead the armies in the conquest (Sacks 2017: 369), makes their also playing a role in chapter 31 possible.

In retrospect, the scene of Moses' appropriate anger functions to underscore two points. First the nature of the mission to wreak vengeance on Midian – repairing the apostasy at Beth Peor – was in danger of being diffused if no form of judgement was meted out to the women themselves, who had personally enticed the Israelites into sexual immorality and idolatry. Second, the correction shapes the narrative's ongoing portrait of the second generation as teachable, able to be guided along in their covenant relationship with YHWH.

Moses further instructs the Israelite warriors to encamp 'outside the Camp seven days', in accord with the corpse-pollution regulations delineated in the red heifer ritual: any who have 'struck down a soul' or touched a 'slain' person must purify themselves, along with their captives, with the ashes of a red heifer on the third and seventh days (19:12, 19). The juxtaposition between Moses' call to strike down the enemy and his explanation of the required purification from corpse defilement underscores a fundamental dynamic: the retributive slaying of Israel's enemies notwithstanding, the community of YHWH's people, the Camp of Israel's having YHWH's own Tent in its midst, was characterized by abundant life and blessing. Outside a single reference in one of Balaam's oracles (23:24), 'slain' (*ḥālāl*) occurs only in the red heifer ritual (19:16, 18) and here for the Midianite battle and the reintegration into the Camp (31:8, 19), exhibiting the summative quality and symbolic nature of this account. Directions are also given to purify garments and vessels, detailed as a 'statute of law' in verses 21–24. The epitome of concern and logic of purification, as enunciated in Numbers 19, and orchestrating Moses' instructions here, is that whoever fails to purify himself 'defiles the Dwelling of YHWH – and that soul will be cut off from Israel . . . that soul will be cut off from the midst of the assembly because he has defiled the Sanctuary of YHWH' (19:13, 20). Reintegration into the Camp, then, mimics membership within the covenant community, where

YHWH dwells. The need to forbid entry into the Camp for those defiled by death functions like the expulsions in Numbers 5:1–4, underscoring the Camp's purity, defined as its 'essence-of-life'.

21–24. Eleazar the priest, who had featured in the red heifer ritual even though Aaron his father and high priest was still alive (see 19:1–4), now assumes leadership in communicating to the men of the host who had gone to battle the 'statute of the law' (*ḥuqqat hattôrāh*). Since the terminology 'statute of law' occurs only here and in 19:2, one may infer the following details were revealed earlier in relation to the red heifer ritual even though they have been apportioned for the present context. In 19:2, it had been YHWH himself speaking to Moses and Aaron, while here Eleazar refers to YHWH's command specifically to Moses. It is fitting, as Gane observes (2004: 770), for Eleazar to speak on God's behalf, especially since, with Moses' impending death, the people need to learn to listen to the high priest, precisely the role asserted earlier in 27:21–22. The instructions pertain to the additional purification of objects: precious and other metals – and 'everything that may go through fire' – are to be purified by passing them through fire, so they will be 'clean' or pure (*ṭāhēr*). The following 'nevertheless' or 'only' in verse 23 (cf. v. 22) has the force of making the 'waters of purification' a requisite part of the cleansing process for metals in addition to their passing through fire. Whatever cannot be passed through fire must be passed through water, and then also be sprinkled with 'waters of purification' containing the ashes of a red heifer as regulated in Numbers 19 (cf. Wright 1985: 218–219). The 'waters of purification' (*mê niddā*) in verse 23 is the only use of the designation in Numbers outside chapter 19, where it occurs five times.

After washing their garments on the seventh day, the men (and their captives) will be considered clean, after which they are able to enter the Camp (*wĕ'aḥar tābō'û 'el-hammaḥăneh*), reintegration being the focus. Rashi (ad loc.), employing a three-camp hermeneutic, understands this 'camp' as the camp of the *Shekhinah* only, arguing that those defiled by a corpse were not excluded from the camp of the Levites or the camp of the twelve tribes.

31:25–54: Distributing the plunder throughout the Camp

While the first half of the chapter represents something of a military microcosm of the Camp (vv. 1–24), the second half focuses on how distributing the plunder serves as an affirmation of both the hierarchical structure and the spiritual nature of the Camp (vv. 25–54). Both begin with YHWH's communication to Moses: *wayĕdabbēr* in verse 1, and *wayyō'mer* in verse 25. The detailed description here of the plunder is in stark contrast to almost all other battles described in the Torah

(Helfgot 2012c: 141), a feature that points to its theological significance, both exhibiting and undergirding the covenant community's threefold hierarchy, structured by the Camp.

25–31. YHWH instructs Moses as to the distribution of the plunder, beginning with a tally of the human and animal captives only, since the other spoils belonged to the fighters who were able to seize objects 'each man for himself' (v. 53). The term 'levy' (*mekes*) refers to a computed portion of payment, a tax. The wording of the tally, literally 'lift up the head' (*śā' 'ēt rō'š*, 31:26; cf. 31:49), was used for the censuses at the opening of the first (1:2; 4:2, 22) and third (26:2) major sections of the book. The tally, then, echoes the construction and reconstruction of the Camp and reaffirms its hierarchical and theological structure. The threefold nature of the Camp is evident already in the list of leaders accountable for carrying out the distribution: 'Moses, Eleazar the priest and the heads of the fathers of the community.' Divine revelation regarding the distribution of the plunder, as with the detailed organization of the Camp in Numbers 1 – 4, suggests a theological message. Practically, the distribution reinforces hierarchies and roles, ultimately designated via spheres of holiness, vividly portrayed in the structure of the Camp. Eleazar will oversee the distribution for the Levites (and priests), and the heads of the fathers will oversee distribution to the community of Israel.

The plunder is to be divided in half, shared between the fighters – those who 'wielded' (*tāpaś*) a sword in war, who went forth to the host – and the 'whole community' (*kol-hā'ēdāh*), confirming the battle as an act of the entire *'ēdāh*, represented and symbolized by the 12,000 men (cf. 1 Sam. 30:23–25). From the militia's half, 1 out of every 500 captives, cattle, donkeys and flocks is to be taken and given to Eleazar the priest as 'a contribution (*těrûmāh*) to YHWH'. In Numbers 18:8 YHWH had given charge of his contribution offerings to Aaron's priestly house as a perpetual due, a *ḥaq-'ôlām*, and this occasion becomes the first realization of that divine designation. The *těrûmāh* occurs in four clusters in Numbers: twice for the purity regulations of the Camp (5:9; 6:20); seven times for the laws on grain and drink offerings *in the land*, as part of YHWH's reassurance after the outer camp's failure (15:19, 20, 21); sixteen times throughout the laws on dues for priests and Levites, reaffirming the priestly role of Aaron's house after it had been challenged by Korah's band (18:8–32); and now four times for the distribution of plunder (31:29, 41, 52; cf. 31:28). The contribution that flows out of the victory over Midian, therefore, reinforces the inner dynamic of the Camp as YHWH's divinely organized covenant community, and becomes a foretaste of Israel's life in the land.

From the other half, divided to 'the whole community', which had not gone to war, 1 out of every 50, of captives, cattle, donkeys and flocks, is to be given for the Levites, for their service of keeping the charge of

YHWH's Dwelling – a giving on the part of the twelve tribes that both prioritizes YHWH's central Dwelling, whose presence in their midst is the source of every blessing (cf. 6:22–27), and reaffirms their own acceptance of and support for the divinely established hierarchy as mapped out in the Camp's structure. Nevertheless, as Milgrom also points out (1990: 263), this giving is not labelled either a *mekes* or a *tĕrûmāh* (both of which are in const. with 'YHWH'), but an *'āḥuz*, a withholding, the root of which occurs only in the last section of Numbers, twelve times, related to a 'holding' or possession of the land (27:4, 7; 32:5, 22, 29, 30, 32; 35:2, 8, 28; cf. 31:30, 47). What is given 'to Eleazar the priest' is 'a contribution to YHWH', since the priests represent God, but Levites receive their share as those who 'keep the charge' of YHWH's Dwelling. The function of 'keeping the charge' (*šōmĕre mišmeret*) defined the Levites' office since the construction of the Camp (3:28, 32, 38; 8:26), and had been reasserted after Korah's rebellion (18:3), and now reappears twice (31:30, 47), as part of the battle's culminating significance, reaffirming YHWH's intent for the structure and life of his earthly hosts, the covenant community. The portion for Levites, ten times as much as what the priests receive, recalls the tithing regulation in Numbers 18:25–32 (cf. G. B. Gray 1903: 424), exhibiting the second generation as living in accord with their divine calling.

The fulfilment formula echoes the steady obedience of the first major section of Numbers where it occurs 6 times (1:19; 2:33; 3:42, 51; 8:3, 22), and which becomes a regular feature of the third section, occurring 8 times (26:4; 27:11, 22; 31:7, 31, 41, 47; 36:10) – it appears only 3 times during the wilderness sojourn (15:36; 17:11; 20:27). That the formula appears 4 times in chapter 31 alone adds to the overall sense that the battle against Midian and its aftermath function as an ideal portrayal of Israel.

32–47. The tally figures for the plunder are given, first the total amount (vv. 32–35), then the distributions from the fighters for Eleazar's priestly house (vv. 36–41) and from the sons of Israel for the Levites (vv. 42–47). The numbers are aside from 'what the people of the host despoiled', that is, from the personal spoil-taking that was exempt from the levy. The large totals for the plunder, which included 675,000 sheep, 72,000 cattle, 61,000 donkeys and 32,000 virgin women, underscore the blessings of victory Israel may anticipate experiencing during the conquest if the people remain loyal to YHWH. The division, precisely half, divvied out to the fighters and to the sons of Israel, then, are 337,500 sheep, 36,000 cattle, 30,500 donkeys and 16,000 virgin women. The contribution of the fighters, who were to give 1 out of every 500 is as follows: 675 sheep, 72 cattle, 61 donkeys and 32 virgin women. This levy, defined as a contribution belonging to YHWH, is given by Moses to Eleazar for his priestly house. The gift of the sons of Israel, amounting to 1 out of 50, is not enumerated; Moses gives them to the Levites, who are again characterized as those who keep the charge of YHWH's Dwelling. The fantastical nature of the figures may be informed by a symbolism or accounting code as yet undiscerned, likely applicable to the census figures for Israel as well.

48–54. An already triumphant account now expands in its spiritual depths, as the military leaders, 'the appointed ones' who were chiefs over thousands and hundreds – representing the whole 12,000 – approach Moses, expressing their desire to offer yet more of the plunder to YHWH in gratitude, and as a ransom for their souls, for the divine preservation of every Israelite in the battle against Midian. The language of 'drawing near' (*qārab*) to Moses recurs in Numbers (9:6; 27:1, 5; 36:1; cf. also 25:6). In a sense this narrative forms the counterpart to the spontaneous gifts of the chieftains in Numbers 7 (cf. G. B. Gray 1903: 419; Olson 1996: 179–180; Helfgot 2012c: 149–150). The designation 'appointed ones' (*happĕqudîm*) appears eight times in chapters 1–10 (1:44, 46; 2:9, 16, 24, 31; 4:46; 7:2) and here (31:38) alone, forging a link to the establishment of the Camp.

The military leaders, who refer to themselves as 'your servants', report to Moses that they conducted their own census – 'lifted the head of the men of war' – and not a single man was 'unaccounted' (*lō'-nipqad*). Although using different terminology, this statement may recall that 'not a man' was left of the previous generation (26:64, 65), and possibly also the question of Zelophehad's daughters, 'Why should our father's name be diminished?', since the question was about inclusion within the community, and there are other parallels between the daughters and the chiefs, such as the distribution of property, and 'drawing near' to Moses (cf. Grossman 2007: 76). As the Israelites spared in battle were 'in our hand', under their charge, the leaders demonstrate care and grateful sensitivity. They bring-near (or 'offer', *q-r-b*) an 'offering' (*qorban*) for YHWH comprised entirely of plundered gold objects ('found', *māṣā'*) by every man: vessels, armlets, bracelets, rings, earrings and pendants. The term translated 'bracelet' (*ṣāmîd*) may echo when Israel 'joined' (*yiṣṣāmed*) themselves to Baal Peor (25:3).

The motivating logic of their offering is 'to make atonement for our souls' before YHWH, meaning 'to ransom our souls'. Atonement evokes the Baal Peor incident (cf. 25:13), both accounts resolving with atonement. Why, however, do their souls need ransoming? The idea may be that since the men *should have* died in battle, a ransom must be paid even if after the fact. More deeply, the Midianite war was an event of YHWH's judgement. After Noah and his household through God's mercy survived the universal judgement of the deluge, he offered up atoning sacrifices (Gen. 8:20–21). A similar understanding may be at work with Passover: the firstborn Israelites had been spared the death of the firstborn when God visited Egypt in judgement, and consequently belonged to YHWH, needing to be ransomed (cf. Exod. 13:1–2, 11–16;

Num. 8:16–18). Seforno explains the atonement as an expiation 'for the episode of Peor, because we did not protest against the sinners' (1997: 808). Whether he was correct, his observation does capture well the link to Numbers 25, along with the function of the Midianite battle as a reaffirmation and strengthening of Israel's loyalty to YHWH: after the battle, the fighters sensed their previous failure at Peor more deeply. However one understands the precise dynamic at work, the note of thanksgiving is underscored (see Philo, *Moses*, 1.317). Nachmanides explains their thanksgiving over God's 'great salvation', that he 'redeemed' the men from death in war (see 1975: 369; cf. Sturdy 1976: 217). Alternatively, the wording is close to Exodus 30:12, where YHWH commands that whenever a census is taken ('lift the head', *tiśśā' 'et-rō'š*) of the sons of Israel, 'according to their appointment' (*lipqudêhem*), then 'a ransom for his soul to YHWH' must be given, repeating 'when you count them' (*bipqōd 'ōtām*) twice – so that 'there will be no plague among them'. The memorial function of the offering forms another link to the Exodus passage, where the atonement silver also becomes a '*zikkārôn* before YHWH' (30:16). Census-taking, apparently, demonstrated sovereign ownership so that any counting of his people would incite his jealousy, resulting in plague (see 2 Sam. 24). Following this approach does not require any suppression of thanksgiving on the part of the chiefs. Their gratitude is only magnified since their contribution was of gold rather than the prescribed silver, and the weight far surpassed – more than double – the required half shekel per person that was mandated (Exod. 30:13). Moreover, the contribution derived from the personal plunder, which had not been subject to the original levy (v. 53). The golden vessels, a 'contribution' (*tĕrûmāh*) levied to YHWH, amounted to 16,750 shekels (over 600 pounds), when only 6,000 shekels of silver had been required. The contribution appears to have been given solely from the plunder of the chiefs of thousands and hundreds, contributed on behalf of the men under their charge.

The account closes with Moses and Eleazar taking 'the gold' from the chiefs of thousands and hundreds and bringing it to the Tent of Meeting, perhaps used for crafting vessels for the sanctuary. The centrifugal movement with which the chapter began, sending forth 12,000 fighting Israelites from the Camp, is now fully reversed: as the Israelite warriors return to outside the Camp (31:12–20), they and their plunder are brought into the Camp (vv. 21–24), then the levied plunder is distributed to the priests and Levites (vv. 25–47), then the chiefs of thousands and hundreds 'draw near' to Moses, with the result that the gold is brought into the Tent of Meeting at the heart of the Camp (vv. 48–54). The gold stands as a 'memorial for the sons of Israel before YHWH'. A 'memorial' (*zikkārôn*) first appeared in Numbers within the purity law for the strayed woman (5:15, 18), then related to the silver trumpets sounded on sacred occasions (10:10), and again for the bronze censers that were hammered out as a covering for the altar (16:39–40). In each case the object serves to bring something, an event or person(s), to mind, whether to bring to YHWH's mind the strayed woman's sin, to bring Israel to YHWH's mind for deliverance and blessing, or to bring to Israel's mind the divine judgement that had fallen upon Korah's would-be priests, so serving as a warning. In the present case, Israel's devotion, expressed through the contribution of gold, and the reality that their lives had indeed been ransomed, is set before YHWH's remembrance. This remembrance of Israel's vengeance on Midian reverses remembrance of their harlotry at Baal Peor, negating the strayed woman's 'memorial' (z-k-r occurs four times: 5:15 [twice], 18, 26). *TgNeof*, perceiving the function of the battle against Midian as *tikkun* for the Baal Peor incident, describes the merit of the Israelite fighters who, upon seeing and desiring the Midianite daughters, were able to remove their gold crowns, earrings, necklaces, clasps and rings *without* engaging with them sexually, a sharp contrast to the debacle at Shittim (see also *Shab.* 64a–b). The tassels legislation had twice used the language of Israel's remembering YHWH and his commands so as not to go whoring 'after your own eyes', the precise sin at Baal Peor. Possibly 'memorial' (*zikkārôn*) here creates a link to 'remember' (*zākar*) in 15:39–40.

THE DIVISION OF PLUNDER IN THE TORAH'S LITERARY CONTEXT

Numbers 31, beginning with YHWH's charge to 'Avenge the vengeance of the sons of Israel against the Midianites' (vv. 1–2), clearly resumes the story of Israel's apostasy at Baal Peor from chapter 25. Under 'The Baal Peor incident in the Torah's literary context', I showed that the Baal Peor apostasy was the second generation's version of the golden calf episode in Exodus 32, a parallel long-observed in the history of interpretation. After listing various parallels between Exodus 32 and Numbers 25, as perceived by the Jewish sages, Helfgot continues by comparing the division of plunder after the battle against Midian in Numbers 31 with the offerings collected for YHWH's Dwelling in Exodus 35 (2012c: 146):

> The only other place in the Torah where we find a similarly detailed qualitative and quantitative description of gold, silver, and materials brought to the Priests and Levites is, of course, the story that immediately follows the Golden Calf episode – the building of the Tabernacle by the Jewish people.

I add that through Moses' mediation (Exod. 32 – 34), YHWH granted his gracious mercy to the first generation, after which and out of thanksgiving and gratitude the people gave so abundantly an offering to YHWH – gold, silver, bronze, and blue, purple and scarlet thread, fine linen, earrings, nose rings, rings and necklaces – that Moses had to restrain them from giving further. By parallel, Israel's military victory over Midian, perhaps as an extension of action by Phinehas (25:7–13), becomes YHWH's display of gracious mercy, demonstrating his favour to Israel – a point underlined by the astonishment of the chiefs over not having lost a single man in battle (31:49). Moreover, the offerings in Exodus further demonstrated the people's repair for the golden calf idolatry, inasmuch as all the gifts contributed to building the Dwelling of YHWH, renewing the people's commitment to worship him only, through the tabernacle cultus (Exod. 35 – 40). Similarly, the division of plunder represents Israel's renewed commitment to YHWH, the covenant relationship as expressed in the threefold structure of the Camp, with the final section narrating the chiefs' gold offerings being brought into the Tent of Meeting (31:48–54), which not only strikes the note of thanksgiving but directly alludes to a tabernacle text (Exod. 30:11–16).

Table 26: Numbers 31 and the Tabernacle offerings

Division of Plunder, Numbers 31	Offerings for Tabernacle, Exodus 35 – 40
'vessels of gold' (kĕlî-zāhāb), 'rings' (ṭabbaʿat), 'pendant' (kûmāz) (v. 50)	'rings' (ṭabbaʿat), 'pendant' (kûmāz), 'vessels of gold' (kĕlî-zāhāb) (35:22)
'contribution to YHWH' (tĕrûmat yhwh); occurs twice (v. 29, 41)	'contribution to YHWH' (tĕrûmat yhwh), occurs three times (35:5, 21, 24; cf. 25:2; 30:15)
'just as YHWH had commanded Moses' (ka'ăšer ṣiwwā yhwh 'et-mōšeh), occurs four times (vv. 7, 31, 41, 47)	'just as YHWH had commanded Moses' (ka'ăšer ṣiwwā yhwh 'et-mōšeh), occurs fourteen times (39:1, 5, 7, 21, 26, 29, 31; 40:19, 21, 23, 25, 27, 29, 32; cf. 39:32, 42, 43; 40:16, 22)
'lifted the head' (nāśĕ'û 'et-rōʾš); 'ransom for our souls before YHWH' (lĕkappēr ʿal-napšōtênû lipnê yhwh); 'memorial for the sons of Israel before YHWH' (zikkārôn libnê-yiśrā'ēl lipnê yhwh); 'into the Tent of Meeting' ('el-'ōhel môʿēd) (vv. 48–54)	'when you lift the head' (tiśśā' 'et-rōʾš); 'ransom for his soul to YHWH' (kōper napšô layhwh); 'for the sons of Israel for a memorial before YHWH' (libnê yiśrā'ēl lĕzikkārôn lipnê yhwh); 'for the service of the Tent of Meeting' ('ăbōdat 'ōhel môʿēd) (30:12–16)

The significance of the allusion to the ransom payment of Exodus 30:11–16 in Numbers 31:48–54 should not be lost simply because it occurred before the golden calf incident – on the contrary, when the context is factored in the reference serves to underscore the parallels. The half-shekel ransom due for every Israelite counted in a census is set near the end of the section of instructions for building the Dwelling (chs. 25–31) for a reason, as an 'offering to YHWH' appointed for the 'service of the Tent of Meeting' (Exod. 30:14, 16). As Alexander observes (2017: 603), 'The atonement payment mentioned here [Exod. 30:11–16] is a once-only prescription related to the initial construction of the sanctuary.' After God's forgiveness of the golden calf incident, however, the people respond by giving in abundance, daily, 'more than enough for the service of work' (Exod. 36:5). In the unfolding of the narrative, the prescription in Exodus 30 functions to underscore the people's magnificent gesture of gratitude. Similarly, the allusion to Exodus 30 in Numbers 31 accomplishes the same, bringing the division of plunder in line with the people's original giving for the Tent of Meeting's construction and operation.

Helfgot draws several parallels between the people's offering in Exodus (chs. 35–39) and the distribution of plunder in Numbers 31 (2012c: 146–150), which are presented in Table 26, expanded with further correspondences.

Within the context of Numbers, as noted by several scholars (cf. G. B. Gray 1903: 419; Olson 1996: 179–180; Helfgot 2012c: 149–150), the division of the plunder, especially as the offering of the chiefs, recalls the gifts of the chieftains in Numbers 7, demonstrating their tribes' support for the priests and Levites, and their affirmation of the central place, both spatially and theologically, of YHWH's Tent of Meeting within the life of the covenant community. The point for the account of the Midianite battle and plunder is that the second generation has 'returned' to the original plan for the Camp of Israel, affirming God's own design and intention for the covenant community and displaying his wisdom in action.

Explanation

Forming an inclusion with Numbers 25, YHWH charges Moses to wreak the vengeance of the sons of Israel on the Midianites, a final accomplishment of Moses before his death. In dealing with both the Midianites and Balaam, the battle brings closure to previous events for Israel's second generation (chs. 22–24, 25; 31:8). Moses sends a militia comprised of 12,000 Israelite fighters, 1,000 per tribe, along with Phinehas, who brings 'the holy vessels' and trumpets. After a complete victory, in which all the males are struck down, including five kings of Midian and Balaam the diviner, and all the Midianite cities and encampments are destroyed with fire, Moses, Eleazar the priest and the tribal chieftains meet the warriors outside the Camp. Moses rebukes them for sparing 'every female' since many of the women had seduced the Israelites into sexual immorality and idolatry, marking the battle as a repair for Israel's failure at Baal

Peor. Male infants, representing the seeds of future Midianite revenge, and the women who have known a man, representing those who seduced Israel, are executed. The virgin girls, presumably, were assimilated into Israel through marriage, helping to build the nation's households. Moses and then Eleazar provide instructions for purification from corpse pollution, after which the Israelite fighters, along with their captives and plunder, are brought into the Camp. YHWH then charges Moses to take a tally of the plunder, equally divided between the fighters and the rest of the community, and raising a levy from the soldiers' half, 1 out of every 500, as a 'contribution to YHWH' for the priests, and from the community's half taking 1 out of every 50 for the Levites. Finally, after the chiefs who led the battle count the soldiers under their charge and discover that not a single one had died, they freely offer gold vessels from their personal plunder to make atonement for their souls before YHWH. Moses and Eleazar the priest take the 'contribution' of gold and bring it into the Tent of Meeting as a memorial for the sons of Israel before YHWH.

The battle against Midian, the central narrative of the last section of Numbers (chs. 26–36), is presented as an idealized and symbolic portrait of the second generation of Israel, a theological well fed by many undercurrents sourced in earlier chapters of the book. Midianites had a vested interest in barring Israel from the land, demonstrated by their continual plotting against God's people both in the hiring of Balaam (22:4, 7) and in the seduction of Israelites at Baal Peor (25:6, 15) – a hostile craftiness underscored by YHWH (25:16–18), and that demanded a conclusive reprisal. Midian's hostility would only have been stoked further with the slaying of Cozbi, a princess of one of Midian's royal houses, leading some to understand Israel's battle as a 'pre-emptive strike' (see Bin-Nun 2019a). The military victory and distribution of the plunder throughout the Camp, including to the central Tent of Meeting, allude to earlier sections of the book by way of fulfilment: the ideal of the Camp of Israel as YHWH's covenant community and earthly hosts in Numbers 1 – 10, including its threefold structure (chs. 1–4), purity (chs. 5–6), gifts by the tribal princes for YHWH's Dwelling (ch. 7) and the use of silver trumpets (ch. 10); recalling the altar-coverings that served as a 'memorial' (chs. 16–17); fulfilling the instructions on offerings and tithes for supporting priests and Levites (ch. 18); undergoing the red heifer ritual of purification from corpse-defilement (ch. 19); destroying cities and taking captives in victory (ch. 21); bringing divine retribution on Balaam (chs. 22–24), and repairing Israel's seduction and apostasy by Midianite women (ch. 25); and the reference to Moses' impending death recalls the earlier statement (27:12–23), as well as the original occasion when Moses had struck the rock twice (ch. 20). Philip Budd also discerned that the battle, which he reads as 'a midrashic construction', presented an opportunity to show aspects of priestly legislation in operation, referring to Numbers 10, 18, 19, and even to the opening chapter's depiction of Israel as an army, here shown 'fighting Yahweh's sacred war' (1984: 333). As the apostasy at Baal Peor in Numbers 25 was also a failure of applying the tassels legislation of 15:37–41, the *tikkun* of the war on Midian also reinforces that legislation's admonition to remember YHWH and his commands instead of whoring 'after your own eyes'.

Every aspect of the chapter reinforces the threefold hierarchical structure of the Camp, which embodies the ideal covenant community and its theological dynamic: the battle hosts are comprised of 12,000 fighters representing the twelve tribes of the outer camp, along with Phinehas and the sacred vessels representing the Levitical inner camp and the camp of the *Shekhinah*, respectively (vv. 1–12). Indeed, Susan Niditch rightly points out (1993a: 82) that chapter 31 presents a 'strongly hierarchical vision of war', which has more in common with the priestly apocalyptic Qumran War Scroll than with the descriptions of Joshua's battles. The next section begins 'outside the Camp' and ends with 'into the Camp', tracing the reintegration of hosts, along with their captives and spoils, into the Camp (vv. 13–24). The second half of the chapter, narrating the distribution of spoils, features Moses, Eleazar the priest, the heads of the fathers of the community, representing the three divisions that comprise the Camp from the centre outward: the camps of YHWH, the priests and Levites, and the twelve tribes, respectively. The plunder is then delineated for the whole community (vv. 32–35), the priests and Levites (vv. 36–41, 42–47), and the final story narrates the offering of gold by the chiefs, which is brought to the centre of the Camp, 'into the Tent of Meeting' (vv. 48–54). *Chapter 31 marks the second generation's realization of the Camp of YHWH's earthly hosts, the outer camp's fulfilment of the vision laid out in Numbers 1 – 2.* It can be no surprise the scene is a military one: the first generation's outer camp, the twelve tribes, had feared the Canaanites and failed to take the land, rebelling against YHWH's word via Moses' prophetic office. Now, the second generation's outer camp, heeding YHWH's word through Moses, strikes down the Midianites absolutely and without a single life lost. Israel's victory is elevated further by its literary placement: Why was the battle separated from YHWH's original command (25:17–18), with five intervening chapters? After reconstituting the second generation to inherit the land (chs. 26–27), the laws on offerings and accompaniments in the land (chs. 28–29) and the fulfilment of vows (ch. 30) present Israel's victory over the Midianites as a culmination, a divine gift, that follows upon Israel's fulfilment of the Nazirite vow paradigm. Israel's story in Numbers is the Nazarite vow writ large: a period of deprivation in the wilderness (chs. 11–25), including a setback requiring cleansing from corpse pollution and a new start (ch. 19), followed by offerings with accompaniments in the land (chs. 28–29), fulfilling the vow (ch. 30).

Moses' death notices further frame chapters 28–30 as a unit (cf. 27:12–13; 31:1–2) within the Midianite inclusio. While no lands were taken in the victory over Midian, it is not by chance that in the following chapter land is distributed (ch. 32). Delaying the distribution of land from the conquests of Sihon and Og (ch. 21) to this point allows the theme of land inheritance to govern the close of the book, but it also coordinates with the Midianite war as a basic paradigm: battle victory leads to a division of spoils (ch. 31) and to the distribution of land (ch. 32; Josh. 13:21 links the five Midianite kings with Sihon of the Amorites). The overall message for Israel is that consecration to YHWH as a priestly kingdom, fulfilling the nation's covenant vow in joyful worship, will lead to a victorious realization of Israel's vocation in the land.

Beyond wreaking divine vengeance on Midian for the matter of Baal Peor, the war is as much a demonstration of Israel's renewed loyalty to YHWH, and a foretaste of the entire conquest. The sexual immorality and idolatry at Baal Peor, whereby Israel abandoned YHWH and joined themselves to Baal, was the second generation's 'fall', their repeat of the first generation's apostasy and sexual licence via the golden calf (Exod. 32), but, more than this heinous offence, it represented a foretaste of the spiritual threat Israel would face among the nations in the land (cf. Exod. 34:15–16), and even among the Israelites themselves, who should also be put to death (see Deut. 13). The destruction of the Midianites symbolizes Israel's final repudiation of the spiritual and sensual enticements of the nations before entering the land. As such, it is conspicuous that Joshua is nowhere mentioned – this battle, divinely mandated by YHWH, is rather one of the last acts of Moses before his death, his divinely wrought glimpse into the magnificent potential of the covenant relationship between YHWH and Israel. Although not permitted to cross the Jordan, Moses fulfils all that is necessary for Israel on the east side of the Jordan, not only conquering Sihon and Og, and dividing their lands to Reuben, Gad and Manasseh, but also bringing God's retribution on the Midianites (cf. Nachmanides 1975: 357).

While the atrocities of war, bitterly experienced by many, inevitably mar the reception of this chapter, when read on its own terms within an ANE context (see Craigie 1978), it narrates one of the high joys of ancient life: victory over one's hostile enemies. The prophet Isaiah, for example, describes the joy of the gospel as the rejoicing that occurs when victors 'divide the spoil' after their oppressor has been vanquished 'as in the day of Midian', so that all hostility is finally brought to an end (9:4–5). Indeed, 'the righteous rejoice in seeing vengeance (*nāqām*)' on the wicked (Ps. 58:10). The drama of the Bible revolves around the unfolding warfare between the seed of the woman and the serpent (Gen. 3:15), glimpsed in David's victory over Goliath (1 Sam. 17), and fulfilled in the Messiah's slaying of the dragon through his own crucifixion and resurrection (see Morales 2020: 62–65), with the gospel herald being likened to 'the feet of him who bears good news', referring to the proclamation of lasting peace through a definitive victory over enemies (Isa. 52:7; Nah. 1:15; Rom. 10:14–15). Upon his exaltation to the Father's right hand, the Son poured out the Spirit, whose distribution of gifts is likened to the distribution of spoils of war after a resounding victory (Eph. 4:7–10), having conquered the Adversary and his hosts. The church's warfare is spiritual in nature, requiring the full armour of God (Eph. 6:10–20), with every 'soldier' needing to put to death the deeds of the flesh (Rom. 8:12–17). In union with the Messiah in his death, burial and resurrection, God's people will finally be raised from the dead, experiencing their Saviour's consummate victory, as the last enemy, Death, is destroyed for ever (1 Cor. 15:26).

NUMBERS 32: POSSESSING THE TRANSJORDAN LANDS

Translation

32:1Now much livestock there was for the sons of Reuben and for the sons of Gad, exceedingly numerous; and they saw the land of Jazer and the land of Gilead, and look: the place was a place for livestock. 2And the sons of Gad and the sons of Reuben came and said to Moses and to Eleazar the priest, and to the chieftains of the community, saying, 3'Ataroth and Dibon and Jazer and Nimrah and Heshbon and Elealeh and Sebam and Nebo and Beon – 4the land YHWH struck before the community of Israel – it is a land for livestock, and your servants have livestock. 5And they said, If we have found favour in your eyes, let this land be given to your servants for a holding and do not have us pass over the Jordan.'

6And Moses said to the sons of Gad and to the sons of Reuben, 'Will your brothers go to war, but you, you dwell here? 7Why would you discourage the heart of the sons of Israel from passing over to the land which YHWH has given them? 8Just so did your fathers do when I sent them from Kadesh Barnea to see the land! 9They ascended to the Valley of Eshcol, and they saw the land, and discouraged the heart of the sons of Israel so as not to go to the land which YHWH had given to them. 10YHWH's anger was kindled on that day, and he swore, saying, 11"The men who ascended out from Egypt, from twenty years old and upward, will not see the ground which I have sworn to Abraham, to Isaac and to Jacob, because they did not follow wholly after me. 12Except Caleb the son of Jephunneh the Kenizzite and Joshua the son of Nun, because they followed wholly after YHWH." 13And YHWH's anger was kindled against Israel, and he caused them to wander in the wilderness forty years, until they came to an end – the whole generation that had done evil in the eyes of YHWH. 14And look! You have arisen in place of your fathers, a brood of sinful men, to add still more to the burning anger of YHWH against Israel! 15For if you turn away from following after him, he will add still more to their stay (rest) in the wilderness, so you will destroy this whole people!'

¹⁶And they approached him, and they said, 'We will build sheepfolds for our flocks here and cities for our little ones. ¹⁷But we ourselves will hasten armed before the sons of Israel, until we have brought them to their place, and our little ones (sing.) will dwell in cities of fortification on account of the inhabitants of the land. ¹⁸We will not return to our houses until the sons of Israel have inherited each man his inheritance. ¹⁹For we will not inherit with them across the Jordan and beyond, for our inheritance has come to us on the eastward side of the Jordan.'

²⁰And to them Moses said, 'If you will do this thing, if you go armed before YHWH to war, ²¹you will all, armed, pass over the Jordan for yourselves before YHWH, until he has dispossessed his enemies from before him, ²²and the land is subdued before YHWH, and afterward you return, then you will be free (innocent) of YHWH and of Israel, and this land will be for you for a holding before YHWH. ²³But if you do not do just so – look! – you will sin against YHWH, and you will know your sin, which will find you. ²⁴Build for yourselves cities for your little ones, and sheepfolds for your sheep, and do what went forth from your mouth.' ²⁵And the sons of Gad and the sons of Reuben said (sg.) to Moses, saying, 'Your servants will do just as my lord commands. ²⁶Our little ones, our wives, our livestock and all our cattle will be there in the cities of Gilead. ²⁷But your servants will pass over, everyone armed for the host before YHWH to war, just as my lord speaks.' ²⁸So, concerning them, Moses commanded Eleazar the priest and Joshua the son of Nun and the heads of the fathers of the tribes of the sons of Israel. ²⁹Moses said to them, 'If the sons of Gad and the sons of Reuben pass with you over the Jordan, everyone armed for war before YHWH, and subdue the land before you, then you will give for them the land of Gilead for a holding. ³⁰But if they do not pass over armed with you, then they will have holdings among you in the land of Canaan.' ³¹And the sons of Gad and the sons of Reuben answered, saying, 'What YHWH has spoken to your servants, just so we will do. ³²We ourselves will pass over armed before YHWH into the land of Canaan – ours, the holding of our inheritance, will be on this side of the Jordan.'

³³So, Moses gave to them, to the sons of Gad and to the sons of Reuben and to half of the tribe of Manasseh the son of Joseph, the kingdom of Sihon king of the Amorites, and the kingdom of Og king of Bashan, the land according to her cities, within the borders of the cities of the land all around. ³⁴And the sons of Gad built Dibon, and Ataroth, and Aroer, ³⁵and Atroth-Shophan, and Jazer, and Jogbehah, ³⁶and Beth-Nimrah, and Beth-Haran, fortified cities and sheepfolds. ³⁷And the sons of Reuben they built Heshbon, and Elealeh, and Kiriathaim, ³⁸and Nebo, and Baal-Meon (their name changed around), and Sibmah, and they called by (other) names the names of the cities that they built. ³⁹And the sons of Machir the son of Manasseh went to Gilead, and seized her, and dispossessed the Amorite who was in her. ⁴⁰And Moses gave Gilead to Machir son of Manasseh, and he dwelled in her. ⁴¹And Jair son of Manasseh he went and seized

their villages, and called them Villages of Jair. [42]And Nobah he went and seized Kenath and her daughters, and called her Nobah, by his name.

Notes on the text

1. 'the sons of Reuben and . . . the sons of Gad': SamP adds 'and the half-tribe of Manasseh' here and in vv. 2, 6, 25, 29, 31.

2. 'the sons of Gad and the sons of Reuben': MT switches the order after v. 1. LXX maintains 'sons of Reuben' first here and in vv. 25, 29, 31, and Syr reads 'sons of Reuben' first here and, with SamP, at vv. 6, 25, 29, 31, 33.

3. 'Sebam': apparently the same as Sibmah (v. 38). SamP and LXX read Sibmah, Syr has Sebah, and TgO reads Simah.

'Beon': apparently the same as Baal-Meon (v. 38) – see BHS.

4. 'struck': LXX has *paredōken*.

'community of Israel': reads 'people of Israel' in LXX, Syr and Vg.

11. 'twenty years old and upward': LXX adds 'those knowing between evil and good'.

12. 'the Kenizzite': LXX reads *ho diakechōrismenos*.

13. 'wander': see 1 Sam. 15:20; Ps. 59:11; cf. Gen. 4:12, 14.

14. 'against Israel': reading *'al* with SamP, instead of MT's *'el*.

15. 'their stay': Syr reads in the second person.

17. 'hasten': BHS proposes emending *ḥušîm* to *ḥămušîm*, as in Josh. 1:14; 4:12; Judg. 7:11 (see Paterson 1900: 64; GKC §72p).

22. 'you will be free' of guilt, innocent (BDB 579; G. B. Gray 1903: 431; cf. Job 4:17).

23. 'look!': lacking in LXX and Syr.

'sin': pl. in SamP and Syr.

25. 'said': MT has sg., but SamP, LXX, Syr, Vg and some MT MSS have the required pl.

26. 'there': lacking in LXX, Syr and Vg.

30. LXX adds details such as going armed 'before the Lord' and listing 'wives and their cattle' with their possessions.

32. 'the holding . . . this side of the Jordan': LXX reads 'you will give us our inheritance on this side of the Jordan'.

33. 'son of Joseph': pl. 'sons' in LXX.

35. 'Atroth-Shophan': LXX has 'Shophar', SamP 'Shaphim', Syr 'Shopham' and Vg 'Etroth and Shophan'.

'Jogbehah': SamP reads 'Jogbohah'.

36. 'Beth-Nimrah': LXX reads 'Nimrah'.

38. 'Nebo': lacking in LXX; TgJon glosses Nebo as the place of Moses' death.

'Baal-Meon': reads 'Baalmon' in SamP and Syr.

39. 'dispossessed': MT has sg., but pl. required, as with SamP, Syr and TgJon.

41. 'Villages of Jair': Syr includes 'to this day'.
42. 'Nobah . . . Nobah': LXX reads 'Nabau . . . Naboth'.

Form and structure

Chapter 32 concludes the first half of the last major section of Numbers (chs. 26–32), and resolves the narrative of the Transjordan lands begun in Numbers 21 (cf. Levine 2000: 477–478). There is no agreement among scholars regarding the chapter's compositional history (Marquis 2013: 408; see Loewenstamm 1972; Budd 1984: 337–342). Although forming a complete unit, Numbers 32 is linked with chapters 30 and 31 by a variety of terms and motifs. The binding nature of Gad and Reuben's pledge to lead Israel's armies as vanguard in the conquest is underscored by allusion to the previous section on oaths and vows (compare 30:2 with 32:24). Formally, the structure of chapter 32 resembles that of 31, whereby Moses heatedly responds to a situation, which then displays the second generation's readiness to comply with Moses' instruction, not only avoiding a negative scenario but also rounding out the story in a positive manner. Read together with chapter 31, the distribution of land follows naturally after a military victory as one pattern of conquest, spoils and possession of land, which, along with Gad and Reuben's pledge to lead the armies into Canaan, functions to foreshadow the conquest. To be sure, the land distributed here was not from the battle of Midian, but from the earlier victories over Sihon and Og, which makes its placement here the more significant. Just as it was Moses who directed the battle against Midian (31:1–6), so it is Moses now who 'gives' the land to the tribes of Reuben and Gad, and to the half-tribe of Manasseh (32:33, 40), completing the conquest pattern with tribal settlement.

Intrinsic to the final acts of Moses is the fact that the giving of land occurs on the east side of the Jordan: chapters 31 and 32 conclude matters related to the east side of the Jordan, including the pending retribution on Midian (chs. 22–25), and the question of the lands gained from the kingdoms of Sihon and Og (ch. 21). Not only is Moses allowed to experience a foretaste of the conquest within the bounds of the east side of the Jordan, but having settled such matters, the narrative is free to turn fully to those topics that remain within the borders of Canaan, *on the west side of the Jordan* (chs. 33–36) – a point that explains the restart nature of chapter 33, summarizing Israel's journeys and narrating YHWH's renewed charge to conquer the land (33:50–56).

Milgrom has pointed out the sevenfold recurrence of five key terms, lending unity to the narrative (1990: 492–493): (1) Gad and Reuben, in this order (vv. 2, 6, 25, 29, 31, 33, 34/37); (2) 'possession' (vv. 5, 22, 29, 30, 32) and 'inheritance' (vv. 19, 32), taken together; (3) 'pass over' the

Jordan (vv. 5, 7, 21, 27, 29, 30, 32); (4) 'armed' (vv. 17, 20, 21, 26, 29, 30, 32); and (5) 'before YHWH' (vv. 20, 21, 22 [twice], 27, 29, 32). He has also discerned a palistrophic structure, which builds on the three dialogue exchanges, centring on the acceptance of Moses' reformulated proposal by Gad and Reuben (Milgrom 1990: 493–494). (See Table 27.)

Table 27: Numbers 32: tribal lands east of the Jordan River

A. Gad and Reuben request land in Transjordan 1. They specify nine towns (vv. 1–5) 2. Moses rejects request, with a heated warning (vv. 6–15)	vv. 1–15
B. Their compromise proposal is revised by Moses 1. The two tribes' compromise (vv. 16–19) 2. Moses accepts, requiring a double condition/oath (vv. 20–24)	vv. 16–24
X. Gad and Reuben accept Moses' revisions	vv. 25–27
B'. Moses' revised proposal is offered the leaders 1. Consequences if double condition/oath is rejected (vv. 28–30) 2. Gad and Reuben repeat their acceptance (vv. 31–32)	vv. 28–32
A'. Moses provisionally grants land in Transjordan 1. The grant, including the half-tribe of Manasseh (v. 33) 2. Gad and Reuben rebuild fourteen towns (vv. 34–38) 3. Manassite clans conquer and settle in towns (vv. 39–42)	vv. 33–42

As highlighted in the centre, the narrative drama revolves around Moses' role in averting another disaster along the lines of the scouts episode: Gad and Reuben's acceptance of Moses' revisions (vv. 25–27). Moses, understanding that Gad and Reuben were irreversibly bent on the lands east of the Jordan, aimed for a compromise that would entail the best scenario for the rest of the tribes – this instead of trying to convince Gad and Reuben to set their hearts on settling across the Jordan. Moses' achievement on behalf of the tribes is triumphant, even if tension remains over the self-chosen plight of the sons of Gad and Reuben, along with the half-tribe of Manasseh.

Comment

32:1–5. The opening verse begins awkwardly, fronting 'much livestock' (*ûmiqneh rab*) for emphasis. Indeed, *miqneh* occurs four times within these verses – six times in the chapter (32:1 [twice], four [twice], 16, 26), only twice more in the book (20:19; 31:9), underscoring that to a large degree the issue of livestock is one of the keys for understanding the story. The double uses of *miqneh* in both verse 1, where it appears as the first and last word, and in verse 4, where it also comes as the last word, form an inclusio. The term *miqneh*, which is general in scope, used for cattle, sheep, goats and other domesticated animals, had also occurred in chapter 31 for 'all their livestock', which the Israelites had taken as spoil from the Midianites (v. 9), providing continuity for the present story. The root of *miqneh* is *qānāh*, 'to acquire or create', referring to livestock as the principal possession of herdsmen, first associated with Jabal in Genesis 4:20 (Levine 2000: 483), so one may wonder if there is a hint of association of Reuben and Gad with the line of Cain. The Chronicler notes how the Reubenites settled eastward 'because their livestock multiplied' (*miqnêhem rābû*) in the land of Gilead (1 Chr. 5:9). Gilead's lush southern region was renowned for its livestock (1 Chr. 5:9; Song 4:1; Mic. 7:14; cf. Milgrom 1990: 266–267). That the sons of Reuben and of Gad had 'much livestock', even 'exceedingly numerous' (*'āṣûm mě'ōd*), is a narratorial detail that functions to explain their request, even as it resonates with past stories that, together with other elements, including Moses' own rebuke, appear to critique their decision. Leibowitz observes how the opening verses summarize the spiritual outlook of the children of Reuben and Gad (1982: 380): instead of focusing on fulfilling Israel's mission in the land, they 'desire to settle down comfortably in the first stretch of fertile, cultivated country that they encountered'.

The sons of Reuben and Gad 'saw' (*wayyir'û*) the land of Jazer and of Gilead and 'look!' (*hinnê*) – prompting readers to see sympathetically through their eyes – the place was 'a place for livestock'. The language recalls the story where Lot parts ways from Abram (cf. A. D. Kahn 2013: 266), they having too much 'livestock' to stay together, with Lot lifting his eyes so that he 'saw' the plain of the Jordan and journeyed east (Gen. 13:1–11). Similarly, Esau would later depart from his brother Jacob, taking his 'livestock' (*miqneh*) and all his 'possessions' (*qinyānô*), for they could not dwell together because of their 'livestock' (*miqneh*). Just as Lot separated from Abram, heading eastward to Sodom, and Esau separated from Jacob, departing eastward to Seir, so the sons of Reuben and Gad will separate from their brothers, remaining in the lands east of the Jordan. Such comparisons seem to signal subtle disapproval of the tribes who chose to remain in the lands east of the Jordan. The Midrash reads their motives quite negatively, explaining that since the sons of Gad and Reuben were willing to separate from their brethren and settle outside Canaan because of their possessions, they were, consequently, the first tribes to go into exile, quoting 1 Chronicles 5:26: *And he carried them away, even the Reubenites, and the Gadites, and the half-tribe of Manasseh* (*Num. Rab.* 32.8; Slotki 1951: 6:859). Within its literary context, preceded by the laws on oaths and vows (ch. 30) and the Midianite war (ch. 31), in both of which material possessions are dedicated to YHWH, so that spiritual matters are prioritized before physical and material considerations, Gad and Reuben's concern over their livestock, including their plea to be released from crossing the Jordan, reads as a contrast. Waxman detects the resonance of another 'livestock rationale' story; namely, when Joseph tells his brothers to say they are in the 'livestock' (*miqneh*) trade, which would result in the Israelites being allowed to live in the land of Goshen, separately from the Egyptians, since shepherding was an abomination to the Egyptians (Gen. 46:34; 2014c: 438–439): 'In making their request, the tribes of Gad and Reuben subtly equate the Land of Israel with the land of Egypt,' and, distrusting God's goodness, they 'reject the land of the forefathers, the divine promise, and the divine plan for history'.

Some, however, point out that the text does not necessarily or explicitly impugn their decision, and that Moses' later blessing of the tribe of Gad contains no hint of censure (see Deut.33:20–21). The perspective taken will normally follow one's view of the status of the lands east of the Jordan. Helfgot, for example, notes that *in contrast* to Lot and Esau, the sons of Reuben and Gad remain united to their Israelite brethren, arguing that the territory east of the Jordan was destined to be inhabited by Abraham's descendants since his defeat of the five kings entitled him to their lands (Gen. 14), a point divinely reaffirmed when, in the Covenant of the Pieces (Gen. 15) – the first scriptural defining of the Promised Land – YHWH grants him the lands of all ten nations, rather than the familiar seven within Canaan (2012b: 164). He further observes that while the children of Lot and Esau were given the southern areas of Transjordan as an inheritance, the northern area remained open for the children of Jacob to capture, which they do in Numbers 21 (2012b: 164). Tension remains since Moses, on YHWH's behalf, will make the concession, validating the inclusion of Transjordan, and Deuteronomy 3:18 reads as an, albeit isolated, instance where Moses assigns the Transjordan as YHWH's gift: 'YHWH your God has given you this land to possess' (cf. Helfgot 2012b: 165).

In addition to the allusions to the stories of Lot and Jacob, which are strong exegetical features, along with the possible allusion to the Joseph narrative, one may also compare the present account of the sons of Gad and Reuben with similarly structured stories in Numbers, whereby a legal transmission originates through an instigating request on the part of the people. Such a scenario takes place in relation to the celebration of Passover (9:1–14), the daughters of Zelophehad (27:1–11) and the chieftains of Manasseh (36:1–12). Although the present account resolves with the lands east of the Jordan being permitted for settling by Israelites, based on their pledge to lead the conquest within Canaan, yet that no actual legislation springs out of the sons of Gad and Reuben episode may prove a significant exception, marking the story in contrast to the other three. YHWH had vindicated the daughters of Zelophehad's request (27:6), whereas there is no divine approbation given regarding the sons of Gad and Reuben, only a concession by Moses after a harsh rebuke. More deeply, each of the other stories entails a desire to maintain the integrity of Israel (9:7; 27:4; 36:3–4), a motif brought out by the use of *gāra'*, but which is absent in the language of the sons of Gad and Reuben, who want to be kept back in the east rather than joining their brethren on the other side of the Jordan. The other three scenarios involve a desire to maintain the unity and integrity of God's people, in the light of which Gad and Reuben's desire to remain in the east, separated from the other tribes, takes on particular force, especially given the allusions to the similar decision by Lot. Etshalom explores precisely these comparisons with stories of unity, with their sense of common destiny and mutual responsibility, to portray the opening request by Gad and Reuben as 'abandonment . . . a dire threat indeed' (although they redeem themselves in vv. 16–19; 2010).

The tribes of Reuben and Gad encamped together, along with the tribe of Simeon, under Reuben's banner in the southern quadrant of the Camp of Israel (see 2:10–16). Given the devastating role of Simeon's tribe at Baal Peor and its consequently diminished numbers (25:14; 26:12–14), it may be that Reuben and Gad are perceived as tainted from the start of this account. Helfgot points out that both Reuben and Gad were firstborn sons of Leah and her handmaid Zilpa, respectively, just as Manasseh was the firstborn of Joseph, but all three firstborn sons were displaced by younger brothers (2012b: 155–156). Jobling also observes that 'lost precedence' forges a link among Reuben, Gad and Manasseh, and suggests that 'Reuben and Gad grasp for precedence in the gift of the land,' which in one sense they get even while in another sense 'they go to the bottom of the list' since they will receive land first only if they are willing to enjoy it last (1986: 2:109). The other sense in which grasping for precedence may place them last among the tribes is in relation to the ambiguous status of the lands east of Jordan.

After the first verse, the order of names places 'Gad' in the initial position consistently, indicating that Gad's tribe led the effort, with Reuben named first in the opening verse simply out of deference for his firstborn status (cf. Deut. 3:16). They came to 'Moses and to Eleazar the priest and to the chieftains of the community', reinforcing the threefold hierarchy of the Camp. These addressees were the same leaders who went to meet the victorious fighters outside the Camp after the battle against Midian (31:13; cf. 4:34), connecting these chapters, and they, along with Joshua, will also be charged with dividing the land (34:16–29). Although using different terms, the scene is similar to when the daughters of Zelophehad 'drew near' (*q-r-b*) before the same three levels of the Camp's hierarchy (27:1–2). They point out the 'land YHWH struck (*nākāh*) before the community of Israel', *nākāh* having been used for the victories over Sihon and Og (cf. 21:24, 35), except that in these previous uses Israelites are the subject. While YHWH was surely responsible for the victories, Gad and Reuben distort the narrative in an attempt to justify their settling in these lands (cf. Milgrom 1990: 268). They also list the variety of villages and towns, three of which were named explicitly in chapter 21, linking the two accounts: 'Dibon' (21:30 and 32:3, 34, 35, 46), 'Jazer' (21:32 and 32:1, 3, 35) and 'Heshbon' (21:25, 26, 27, 28, 30, 34; 32:3, 37). The Mesha Inscription (or 'Moabite Stone', 830 BC) records how the men of Gad lived in Ataroth 'from of old' (see Sergi 2020). They respectfully speak what the narrator had already explained to readers: 'the land . . . is a land for livestock, and your servants have livestock'.

Since their previous speech (vv. 2–4) had not been interrupted, there is some question as to why verse 4 ends with a minor (*samek*) paragraph break and verse 5 opens a new speech (*wayyō'mrû*). They were perhaps sounding out Moses, presenting the facts before him in the hope he would make the deduction and offer them the Transjordan lands himself (Leibowitz 1982: 381), but nothing could have been further from Moses' mind. Abarbanel thus reads the sons of Gad and Reuben's wavering in hesitation, hoping fruitlessly for Moses to fill the silence (referenced in Hattin 2012: 300). Having presented a basis, they now make their request, again respectfully, 'If we have found favour in your eyes let this land be given to your servants for a holding.' Although the expression of finding favour in one's eyes is used some 21 times in the Torah (Gen. 6:8; 18:3; 30:27; 32:6; 33:8, 10, 15; 34:11; 47:25, 29; 50:4; Deut. 24:1), 6 times for Moses' mediation after the golden calf incident (Exod. 33:12, 13 [twice], 16, 17; 34:9), it occurs only 3 times in Numbers (11:11, 15; 32:5). The referent of *'your* servants' is Moses, the one who will *give* (*nātan*) this land (32:5, 33, 40). They ask for the land to be given for a 'holding' (*'ăḥuzzā*, 32:5, 22, 29, 32), a designation that occurs 9 times, only in the third section of Numbers (cf. 35:2, 8, 28), and which makes the scene somewhat similar to the story of Zelophehad's daughters (27:4, 7), since both stories involve a request for holdings under unusual circumstances, perhaps forming an inclusio for the first half (chs. 27–32) of the last section. The punchline, saved for the end, brings one to the heart of the matter and justifies Moses' concern: 'do not (*'al*) have us pass over (*taʿăbirēnû*) the Jordan'. Given the scriptural boundaries of Canaan, limited to the lands west of the Jordan, their 'proposal meant, therefore, nothing short of a divided Israel' (Ashley 1993: 606–607).

6–15. By their initial request, as Jobling discerns (1986: 2:103), the sons of Gad and Reuben 'break the integrity of Israel', since the one people 'about to enter one land becomes two groups with different territorial intentions'. Moses drives the conversation to its concrete implication, not about livestock, but about the unity of Israel's commitment to go to war: 'Will your brothers go to war, but you (emphatic, *wĕ'attem*) – you just sit (*tēšĕbû*) here?' Especially in the light of the war against Midian, which had included 1,000 fighters from each of the twelve tribes, demonstrating a united, concerted effort, the thought of two tribes abandoning 'your brothers' – note the rhetorical effect of this term, highlighting familial obligation – so that only ten tribes 'go to war' (*yābō'û lammilḥāmāh*) is exceedingly offensive and, more deeply, will 'discourage the heart' of the 'sons of Israel' (rather than 'the other tribes', again reinforcing the people's unity). The word 'war' (*milḥāmāh*) connects chapters 31 and 32 (31:14, 21, 27, 28, 49; 32:6, 20, 27, 29; cf. also 10:9; 21:14, 33). While the sons of Israel need to be fortified to conquer the land, Moses phrases the matter as 'passing over (*'ăbōr*) to the land which YHWH has given them', picking up on Gad and Reuben's own language in verse 5, and implying that in discouraging Israel they will also be acting against the intention of YHWH, who 'has given' the land to them. That YHWH 'has given' the land to the sons of Israel not only alludes to the patriarchal promises that undergird the conquest but also speaks to military victory, sovereignly given by YHWH, just as he had 'surely given' the Canaanites and then Og king of Bashan earlier (see 21:3–4, 34). Moses' reference to 'the land which YHWH has given them' reprioritizes the divine will, correcting the implication of Gad and Reuben's opening speech regarding the Transjordan lands as 'the land YHWH struck before the community of Israel' (v. 4). Moses' first speech employs a sevenfold use of 'YHWH', demonstrating that he presents YHWH's interests and will in the dialogue (fourteen of the eighteen uses of 'YHWH' in this chapter come from Moses' lips).

Such a possibility, of discouraging Israel from possessing the land, naturally leads Moses to draw a parallel spanning thirty-eight years, when the first generation had been on the cusp of realizing the promises of the land only to turn away and experience bitter judgement. The rebellion at Kadesh 'functions as a paradigmatic narrative, aimed at preventing the disobedience of the next generations' of Israel (Artus 2013: 375). While in Deuteronomy Moses focuses on the accountability of the people themselves (1:19–46), the emphasis in Numbers is on leaders and their influence, both in chapters 13–14 and here: 'Just so did your fathers' clearly has reference to the ten faithless scouts who had 'discouraged (*wayyānî'û*) the heart of the sons of Israel so as not to go to the land which YHWH had given them' – a statement that parallels Moses' previous accusatory question in verse 7, making his point rhetorically explicit:

v. 7: *tĕnî'ûn   'et-lēb bĕnê yiśrā'ēl mē'ăbōr 'el-hā'āreṣ 'ăšer-nātan lāhem yhwh*
v. 9: *wayyānî'û 'et-lēb bĕnê yiśrā'ēl lĕbiltî-bō' 'el-hā'āreṣ 'ăšer-nātan lāhem yhwh*

The verb for 'discourage' (*n-w-'*), more literally 'restraining' their hearts from conquering the land, occurs only six times in the Torah, all in Numbers, twice here in 32:7, 9 and four times in chapter 30 (vv. 5 [twice], 8, 11), another lexical feature connecting chapters 30, 31 and 32. Moses twice defines the land as the land YHWH has given 'to them' (*lāhem*), rather than 'to you (all)' (see also 13:1–2; 14:8, 16, 30). It may be that from Moses' perspective, the tribes of Gad and Reuben have separated themselves from Israel (cf. Waxman 2014c: 441). If this detail was not intended to exclude Gad and Reuben from the land prematurely, then it probably functions to underscore the priority of the people and the possibly negative influence on them by these leaders as had occurred in the debacle with the scouts – a point that fits with Moses' warning 'So *you* will destroy this whole people!' Beyond underscoring their accountability, Moses appeals to them to have concern for the other tribes, whereas the sons of Gad and Reuben seem focused only on their own possessions. In verse 17, Gad and Reuben will speak of bringing *them* (the other tribes) into *their* place (Canaan), their own hearts having already settled for the Transjordan lands.

Moses continues the historical review, reminding them that the action of 'your fathers' had kindled YHWH's anger so that he 'swore' (*wayyiššābaʻ*) the men of the first census who had experienced the exodus out of Egypt would not 'see' (*yirʼû*) the 'ground' (*hāʼăd̄āmāh*) he had 'sworn' (*nišbaʻtî*) to the patriarchs, listing each one – to Abraham, to Isaac and to Jacob – so as to emphasize the definite nature of the divine intention and the sure gift that had been rejected. YHWH's 'oath' to give the land to the patriarchs occurs also at 11:12, 14:16, 23, and forms a backdrop to the entire narrative of Numbers. A new oath sworn by YHWH, of judgement, will prolong the realization of the previous oath he had sworn to the patriarchs concerning the land. The oath-swearing vocabulary (32:10, 11) forms a relevant link to chapter 30 and the topic of vows and oaths (30:3 [twice], 14). Choice of 'ground' likely functions with 'see' for the sake of rhetorical emphasis: they will not even glimpse a spot of the land, much less live there. The scouts' discouragement of the people, influenced them not to 'follow wholly after' YHWH – the exceptions being Caleb son of Jephunneh the Kenizzite (cf. Josh. 14:6, 14; Judg. 1:13; on the ancestor Kenaz, see Gen. 36:11, 15, 42; 1 Chr. 1:36) and Joshua son of Nun because they 'followed wholly after YHWH'. The language of verses 11–12 echoes Numbers 14:23–24, so that the story of Gad and Reuben becomes another potential Kadesh Barnea episode, except being resolved pleasantly, with disaster avoided and a renewed commitment to conquer the land. The paradigm for life that pleases YHWH, inheriting his promises, is one of following him wholly, resonating with the zeal solicited in the Nazirite vow, and as displayed by Caleb and Joshua, and later by Phinehas (cf. Stubbs 2009: 235–236).

For the second time, Moses says 'YHWH's anger was kindled,' here as a preface to the forty-year judgement on the 'whole generation' that had done evil in the eyes of YHWH, so that 'they wandered' (*wayĕniʻēm*) in the wilderness 'until they came to an end (*tōm*)'. The term 'wandered' (*nûaʿ*) echoes Cain's judgement to be a 'wanderer', settling in the 'City of Wandering' (Gen. 4:12, 14). The complete end of a generation, which had almost been the end of Israel as a people (see 14:11–12) and *as instigated by the tribal leaders*, is what causes the intensity of Moses' response: 'For if you turn away from following after him . . . so you will destroy this whole people!' Moses' assumed connection between their request 'do not have us pass over the Jordan' and a desire 'not to follow after YHWH' is logical since following closely after YHWH means, concretely, to follow him across the Jordan into the land. Such an assumption regarding these tribes who settle in Transjordan would come up again in Joshua 22 (see Jobling 1986: 2:98–100). In this latter context, the language of Phinehas the priest, along with ten princes of the other tribes, leaves the status of the lands east of the Jordan as questionable: 'However, if the land of your holding is unclean, then pass over for yourselves to the land of YHWH's holding, there where the Dwelling of YHWH dwells, and take a holding among us' (Josh. 22:19).

Earlier, the sight of a place for livestock by the sons of Reuben and Gad was introduced by 'look!' (*wěhinnê*, v. 1); now Moses bids them to 'look!' (*wěhinnê*) at themselves, as a brood (*tarbût*) of sinful men who have arisen in place of their fathers. The root of 'brood' is 'many' or 'increase' (*rābāh*), perhaps an ironic play on the 'much' (*rab*) livestock of the opening verse. Moses refers to YHWH's 'burning anger' against Israel for a third time as he warns them about adding still more to Israel's stay in the wilderness. The threefold reference to YHWH's anger uncovers a reality that was largely hidden from the masses of Israel, experienced by Moses alone in his role as mediator, standing in the gap before the ignited wrath of YHWH: Moses alone had heard the thunderous intention to strike Israel with pestilence and disinherit them (14:11–25) – he who knows YHWH more intimately than any other and perceived most fully that Israel had been on the brink of utter destruction is now the one most concerned about any challenges to the divine plan. The phrase 'to their stay (*lěhannîḥô*) in the wilderness, so you will destroy (*wěšiḥattem*) this whole people', in addition to the conceptual parallel to the Deluge story, where a whole generation had been destroyed, uses two words that recall the world's destruction: *nûaḥ* ('Noah', Gen. 6–9; cf. 8:4) and *šāḥat* (Gen. 6:11, 12, 13, 17; 9:11, 15) – a similar literary strategy was employed for the golden calf incident (cf. Exod. 32:7, 10).

As made explicit in Moses' speech, the request of Gad and Reuben has brought the second generation to a potentially parallel situation as faced by the first generation in Kadesh Barnea when the ten scouts had brought a bad report about the land. A variety of words and phrases in Moses' speech find a direct parallel in Numbers 13 – 14 (cf. Cole 2000: 509; Helfgot 2012a: 170–171): 'the land YHWH has given them' (13:1–2; 14:8, 16, 30; 32:7, 9), Moses sends men to scout/see the land (13:2;

32:8), 'Valley of Eshcol' (13:23, 24; 32:9), 'not one of the men 20 years old and upward' (14:29; 32:11), 'be shepherds/wander in the wilderness forty years' (14:33; 32:13), death/destruction 'in the wilderness' (14:33, 35; 32:15). Given these parallels, Ulrich writes (1998: 532), 'The spy story (Numbers 13–14) and the request of the Gadites and Reubenites (Numbers 32) are the two pivotal events – one for each generation. Each concerns Israel's hesitation to enter the promised land.' Clearly, Moses' rhetoric is aimed squarely at preventing a recurrence of the divine judgement that fell on Israel some thirty-eight years before, a challenge and threat to the second generation that was indeed averted through his engagement and exhortation, as well as by the teachableness displayed by the sons of Gad and Reuben. The recall of the scouts incident is not limited to Moses' speech, but pervades the narrative itself, G. J. Wenham noting several more connections (1981b: 238 n. 19): 'place' (14:40; 32:1), 'smite' (14:45; 32:4), 'pass over' (13:32; 14:7, 41; 32:21, 27, 29, 30), 'little ones' (14:3, 31; 32:16, 17, 24, 26), 'inhabitants of the land' (14:14; 32:17), 'fortified cities' (13:19; 32:17, 36), 'return' (13:25; 14:36; 32:18, 22), 'drive out' (14:12, 24; 32:21, 39), along with more common terms such as 'land' and 'community'. The narrator, not merely the character of Moses in the story, intends the scenario in chapter 32 to be interpreted as an averting of what was potentially another scouts incident (chs. 13–14). Whereas in the scouts episode there were ten false and two faithful scouts, here there are two (whole) tribes that are negative and ten that remain faithful (cf. Milgrom 1990: 268).

Moses' refusal of their proposal is complete and presumes that any desire to settle east of the Jordan is 'to turn away from following after' YHWH across the Jordan. Because, however, he focused on the negative influence their proposal would have on the other tribes, paralleling the negative influence of the ten scouts, the window has been opened for the compromise Gad and Reuben will suggest.

16–19. Verse 2 had narrated how the sons of Gad and Reuben 'came' (*wayyābō'û*) to Moses, to Eleazar the priest, and to the chieftains of the community, whereas now they 'approach' (*wayyiggĕšû*) Moses specifically. Their response functions as a counterproposal: they now commit to serving in the frontline, in hopes of gaining approval for their request. Boldly, they begin their speech with 'Sheepfolds we will build for our livestock here (*pō*),' their second reference to 'here' (32:6, 16), 'and cities for our little ones (*lĕṭappēnû*)' (likely, *ṭappēnû* in this instance includes other dependents, such as wives). The word 'little ones' unifies chapters 31–32 (31:9, 17, 18; 32:16, 17, 24, 26; cf. 14:3, 31; 16:27). Does their placement of livestock before little ones betray misplaced priorities? The Midrash indeed accuses them of cherishing their possessions more than human lives, and points out how Moses' response corrects their disordered love by reversing the order in verse 24 (*Num. Rab.* 32.9). Possibly mitigating their language, it is the issue of livestock that validates their settling east of the Jordan, forming the gist of their request (vv. 1, 4), not the fact that they like every other tribe have little ones. In their next line (v. 17), moreover, they mention their little ones dwelling in fortifications, without any reference to livestock. Nevertheless, they mention their own concerns first (v. 16), ahead of the needs of the other tribes (v. 17), an order Moses will reverse in his response (vv. 20–24).

Addressing Moses' major concern, they state emphatically, 'But we ourselves (wa'ănaḥnû) will hasten armed before the sons of Israel,' forming a vanguard for the conquest until each of the other tribes receives its place. They employ the verb 'hasten' (ḥušîm) to show that taking the lead in the conquest will not be done reluctantly, requiring compulsion, and that their original request did not intend to imply fear of battle on their part – they are only too eager to realize YHWH's victories in Canaan. In verse 18 they reiterate their pledge in detail: 'We will not return to our houses until the sons of Israel have inherited (hitnaḥēl) each man his inheritance (naḥălātô).' Whereas the previous generation used 'our wives and our little ones' as an excuse for refusing the land of Canaan, the second generation, while wanting to provide for their wives and little ones in Transjordan, are willing to go forth in conquest (cf. Olson 1996: 182–183). Etshalom, who characterizes Gad and Reuben's earlier proposal as an abandonment of Israel (vv. 3–5), nevertheless observes that this story was not placed in chapter 21, after the conquests of Sihon and Og, or within the 'troubles' section (chs. 11–25) – the story is, rather, included in an optimistic section of Numbers due to this counterproposal wherein they now, in parallel with other favourable accounts (9:1–14; 27:1–11; 36:1–12), request inclusion with Israel by serving in the frontline of the conquest, demonstrating 'their willingness and desire to maintain a common destiny with the rest of the sons of Israel' (2010). While the ambiguous status of the lands east of the Jordan tinges their request, the counterproposal, the fruit of Moses' engagement, releases tension in averting another catastrophe like the scouts episode.

They go on to explain that their request is a matter of the place of inheritance, not about whether they will discourage the hearts of their brothers by refusing to join the militia – no, they will even serve as the lead army, fighting in the forefront of the battle. The issue is that 'we will not inherit with them across the Jordan and beyond, because our inheritance has come to us on the eastward side of the Jordan'. The rhetoric, that the 'inheritance has come to us', rather than 'we would choose an inheritance on the eastward side', is probably intended to support their understanding that the lands of the Transjordan were given by YHWH, as the battles against Sihon and Og demonstrate (ch. 21). In verse 5 they had requested a 'holding' ('ăḥuzzā), whereas now they dub the lands east of the Jordan an 'inheritance' (naḥălāh), typically reserved for Canaan. It is difficult to know whether there is significance to the alternation of these terms. Moses' response, for example, consistently refers to their requested lands as a 'holding' (vv. 22, 30), while the sons of Gad and Reuben will go on to refer to 'the holding of our inheritance' (v. 32), the same designation used for the lands within Canaan given to the daughters of Zelophehad (27:7). The latter case, moreover, was a speech by YHWH, which had begun with his declaration as to the rightness of their request, and then proceeded to transform the daughters' own wording of 'holding' to his grant of a 'holding of an inheritance'. In the present instance, the sons of Gad and Reuben speak of 'inheritance', while Moses speaks (only?) of a 'holding'. While a 'holding before YHWH', the lands east of the Jordan, writes Waxman (2014c: 444–445), will never constitute a covenantal *naḥălāh* like the land of Israel, and living there cannot be a fulfilment of the divine promises or realization of covenantal life. Notably, their speech nowhere mentions YHWH, whereas Moses' reply will refer to him seven times (vv. 20–24: 'YHWH' six times, 'him' once).

20–24. The tone of Moses' response, after their explanation, is palpably different, since the primary source of contention for Moses was whether the sons of Gad and Reuben would cross the Jordan to join in the conquest and so keep from discouraging the heart of the other Israelites – this remained the chief dilemma he endeavoured to resolve, albeit by compromise. Nevertheless, he neither placates nor praises them for this commitment, but launches into further negotiations, demonstrating that he had not misunderstood their earlier request (i.e. originally, they had *not* intended to help with the conquest). The sons of Gad and Reuben had been justly accused, and Moses' response has achieved its intended effect (cf. Samet 2017b). The major theological point is that all the tribes remain united in their commitment to YHWH and to realizing his gift of the land, as well as his purposes for his people in the land. Moses is satisfied with the resolution, which also clarifies that inheriting land on the east side of the Jordan, outside Canaan proper, was not of itself necessarily a choice to be stigmatized. Moses reiterates the conditions clearly, as an if–then statement, repeating 'if' (*'im*) as if to say 'if and *only* if'. Gad and Reuben, Moses says, must go armed 'before YHWH', rather than their statement 'before the sons of Israel' (v. 17). The phrase 'before YHWH' (*lipnê yhwh*) is repeated by Moses four times (vv. 20, 21, 22 [twice]), plus 'before him', 'of YHWH' and 'sin against YHWH (*layhwh*)', weighing his charge, and transforming their proposal as an oath before YHWH. The sevenfold reference to YHWH could not contrast more with Gad and Reuben's language, as Leibowitz brings out (1982: 383):

> The abyss separating their two outlooks stands revealed here. The two and a half tribes saw it in the light of a *quid pro quo* between themselves and the rest of Israel; they would contribute their share

in helping to conquer the land and, in return, would be allotted the region they desired. Not so Moses. He stated everything in terms of responsibility to and dependence on God who alone drives out the enemy and apportions the land.

Moses' language underscores that every element of the conquest, from mustering the militia to crossing the Jordan, is an act of YHWH: 'until he (YHWH) has dispossessed his enemies from before him' – the militia is not merely about camaraderie with the 'sons of Israel' but solidarity with the person and purposes of YHWH himself, a battle against his enemies. As an instance of holy war, the Israelites are a tool in the hand of YHWH, who has chosen, as part of Israel's own education, to bring judgement through military means rather than plague, pestilence or other 'natural' forces. Moreover, although the sons of Gad and Reuben must participate in the conquest, its success will not be due to them but because of YHWH himself (Boorer 1992: 407). Clearly, YHWH is able to subdue the land even through a diminished militia, but, as with the 1,000 from each of the twelve tribes established as a paradigmatic ideal in chapter 31, and even as twelve scouts representing the twelve tribes had been sent to scout the land in chapters 13–14, so the conquest requires 'all Israel'.

Moses also repeats 'you go armed (*tēḥālĕṣû*) . . . you will all, armed (*ḥālûṣ*)'. This term, *ḥ-l-ṣ*, occurs nine times in Numbers, only within chapters 31–32 (cf. 31:3, 5) – a significant observation, since the root was not used at all in Israel's three battles narrated in chapter 21. The extended phrase 'armed for the host' (*ḥălûṣ ṣābā'*) occurs only twice, once in each chapter (31:5; 32:27). The seven uses of *ḥ-l-ṣ* in the present chapter serve as an entry to the fuller anticipation of the conquest in chapters 33–36 (32:17, 20, 21, 27, 29, 30, 32). The conquest will lead to the land being 'subdued' (*nikbĕšāh*) before YHWH, stated twice (32:22, 29). Intriguingly, the only other instance of *kābaš* in the Torah is in Genesis 1:28, where God blessed humankind, male and female, charging them to 'subdue her' (*wĕkibšuhā*), 'the land' (*hā'āreṣ*). The opening of the exodus out of Egypt had narrated Israel's experience of humanity's original blessing to 'be fruitful and multiply and fill the earth' (Gen. 1:28; Exod. 1:6), and now, in the conquest of Canaan, Israel will begin to fulfil God's primordial charge. If only 'afterward' (*'aḥar*), after leading the armies before YHWH until he has dispossessed his enemies and subdued the land, they return to the Transjordan, *then* that land 'will be for you for a holding', and this, again, 'before YHWH'. Defining the results of fulfilling the conditions (*protasis*) for their request, Moses begins his 'then' (*apodosis*) clause with a higher priority than merely receiving the land as a holding – the real and weighty issue is that then 'you will be free (*nĕqîîm*) of YHWH and of Israel'. The term *nāqî* relates to be being free from guilt, innocent of blame, so as to be exempt from punishment (BDB 667). Elsewhere in Numbers, the term was used three times in the strayed-woman ritual (5:19, 28, 31), also in the context of an oath (cf. Gen. 24:8, 41; Josh. 2:17, 20; Zech. 5:3), and twice in YHWH's judgement of the first generation (14:18). The sons of Gad and Reuben, if they fulfil their obligation, will be free not only of guilt but of reprisal – punishment – from YHWH and from their fellow tribes.

Moses, however, is not content to leave the contrary prospect merely implied, but states explicitly that if they do not do 'just so (kēn), you will have sinned (ḥāṭā'tem layhwh) against YHWH', underscoring the consequence with another 'look!' (hinnê) – a grave warning that understands the arrangement as an oath before YHWH. Defining the nature and severity of failing to follow through on their word, that it would be sin and, particularly, sin against YHWH, Moses proceeds to warn them about its sure penalty. Whatever else the idiom 'you will know (ûdĕ'û) your sin, which will find you' means, Moses assures the sons of Gad and Reuben that any betrayal of their word will not simply be forgotten just because they have settled on the east side of the Jordan out of sight; rather, their sin will 'find' (timṣā') them such that they will know, that is, experience – the judgement upon – their sin, be made to know the depths of its heinousness by the severity of its punishment. Marquis notes the literary play (2013: 414–415): whereas in verse 5 the sons of Gad and Reuben speak of 'finding (māṣā') favour' in his sight, Moses reminds them that just because they found favour does not mean that their sin will not 'find' (māṣā') them if they fail to fulfil their pledge. Only after this threat does Moses grant permission to the sons of Gad and Reuben to build, reversing the order (and priority) of their speech in verse 16: first 'cities for your little ones' and then 'sheepfolds for your sheep' – and they follow that reversal in their later language (v. 26). The Hebr. term 'your sheep' is unusual, lĕṣōna'ăkem, and Hirsch suggests the possibility that Moses drew the word out, lingering on it, as if to imply, 'your sheep, about which you care too much' (2007a: 650). Moses' admonition closes with 'do what went forth from your mouth' (hayyōṣē' mippîkem ta'ăśû), a phrase that evokes the text on vows and oaths, and their severity before YHWH: 'If a man vows a vow to YHWH or swears an oath to bind a bond on his soul, he will not profane his word – according to all that went forth from his mouth he will do' (hayyāṣē' mippîw ya'ăśeh, 30:2). This strong link to chapter 30 not only binds the chapters together as a unit, but serves to unfold their interpretation: chapter 32 exemplifies why the binding nature of one's pledge is crucial, and chapter 30 adds serenity to the conclusion of the Gad and Reuben affair – there is no lingering suspicion or anxiety over the tribes' total and united commitment to the conquest. While Noordtzij goes as far as dubbing this account as 'nothing more or less than the making of a covenant' (1983: 281; cf. Ashley 1993: 612), a binding pledge or oath is sufficient and more fitting.

25–27. As Moses' words had underscored the obligations of the tribes to YHWH and to Israel (the other tribes), the compliance of the sons of Gad and Reuben, therefore, expresses a reaffirmation of this dual loyalty. Perhaps to demonstrate that they speak with one voice, 'said' (*wayyō'mer*) is in the 3rd m. sg. form (cf. Rashi, ad loc.). Their speech, pledging to fulfil ('to do', *ya'ăśû*) Moses' stipulations, employs a twofold use of 'your servants' as well as a twofold use of 'just as my lord commands/speaks'. Between these declarations, they state, this time using Moses' order, that their little ones, wives, livestock and cattle will be 'there' (*šām*), in the cities of Gilead (cf. v. 1). In Joshua, the 'cities of Gilead' are granted to the tribe of Gad (13:25), the use here perhaps reflecting their initiative in the speech. The collocation of 'little ones' and 'wives' occurs only in chapters 31 and 32 (31:18; 32:26).

In the Decalogue, YHWH states that he will not hold a person 'blameless' (*yĕnaqqeh*) who takes up his Name in vain (Exod. 20:7), a penalty that would apply to the sons of Gad and Reuben since their pledge was before YHWH. Considering again the unequivocal statement in 30:2, the matter is resolved in a definite way: the sons of Gad and Reuben *will* cross the Jordan armed for the host before YHWH to war. Nevertheless, as Jobling points out (1986: 2:95–96), they still put their own interests (v. 26) ahead of the interests of the other tribes (v. 27). Their original request included only their interests (vv. 3–5), and here, although the interests of others is noted, those come after their own. Moses, however, places the interests of the tribes first, followed by those of the sons of Gad and Reuben (vv. 20–24), an order the sons of Gad and Reuben will finally embrace (v. 32).

28–32. The sons of Gad and Reuben had approached Moses for an exchange (vv. 16–27), and now Moses relays the results as a command, not only to the previous audience, Eleazar the priest and the heads of the fathers of the tribes of Israel, but also to Joshua the son of Nun, centrally placed as the one who, recalling 27:12–23, will lead Israel in the conquest of the land. In something of an official and judicial ceremony, Moses details the stipulations of the pledge, its conditions and result, before designated leaders of the covenant community, Eleazar the high priest, Joshua the political and military leader and the tribal heads. If the sons of Gad and Reuben fulfil the conditions, then the land of Gilead will be their holding; if not, such land is forfeit despite their building of fortifications and the settling of their families and livestock – they must instead have holdings in the land of Canaan with the other tribes. That the land will be 'subdued' (*kābaš*), recalling Genesis 1:28 (cf. Hausoul 2018: 85), may serve to portray Canaan as another Eden or renewed creation.

Moses' statement is followed by the pledge of the sons of Gad and Reuben, declared before the community leaders and acknowledging Moses' divine authority: 'What YHWH has spoken to your servants, just so we will do,' succinctly phrasing the condition and the reward, both opening with an emphatic reference to themselves: 'We ourselves (*naḥnû*) will pass over armed before YHWH into the land of Canaan,' and 'but ours' (*wě'ittānû*), the 'holding of our inheritance' (*'ăḥuzzat naḥălātēnû*) will be on this side of the Jordan. Alluding to this text, Joshua records that indeed 'the sons of Reuben and the sons of Gad and the half-tribe of Manasseh passed over armed before the sons of Israel, just as Moses had spoken to them', having sent 40,000 men to serve in the militia's frontline (4:12–13; cf. Josh. 22).

33–38. In Joshua 13, the authority of Moses for granting the lands assigned east of the Jordan is emphasized, with the phrase 'Moses had given' recurring repeatedly (see 13:8 [twice], 15, 24, 29; cf. 13:32, 33). Moses, who directed the battle against Midian, continues to resolve all unfinished business pertaining to matters east of the Jordan. As a further final act connected to the battle of Midian in the previous chapter, he now officially gives the lands of Transjordan. Given the conditions of the pledge set forth already (vv. 20–24), the lands are now given only provisionally, and will not become a 'holding' until the sons of Gad, Reuben and half the tribe of Manasseh have returned from subduing the land of Canaan in conquest (see v. 29). A comparison with 34:13 demonstrates that *ḥăṣî* refers to 'half' or 'part' of Manasseh's tribe, whereas the other half will settle west of the Jordan – and not to its being a half of Joseph's tribe, alongside Ephraim.

Curiously, half the tribe of Manasseh son of Joseph is suddenly added to the sons of Gad and the sons of Reuben as those to whom Moses gave lands, without any apparent explanation. The order, however, follows the explanation delineated afterward, beginning with 'the sons of Gad' (vv. 34–36), 'the sons of Reuben' (vv. 37–38) and 'the sons of Machir the son of Manasseh' (vv. 39–42), the latter section explaining the addition of Manasseh in verse 33, which stands as a summary statement of all the lands Moses gave – not merely summarizing the preceding account (vv. 1–32). The backstory for Manasseh's involvement is not supplied, but is in accord with the spotlight on this tribe in the last major section of Numbers (27:1–11; 32:33, 39–42; 36:1–12). In the entire Pentateuch, the precise phrase 'Manasseh the son of Joseph' occurs only at Numbers 27:1, 32:33 and 36:12, and all three stories deal with land-allotment issues. It may well be that these Manassite conquests occurred alongside those of Sihon and Og, which had included possession of their lands (cf. 21:24, 35), and even Israel's 'dwelling' (*yāšab*) in the land of the Amorites (21:31; cf. Marquis 2013: 410), or, with greater uncertainty, that the Manassite captures took place much earlier. Milgrom explains that this upper Gilead territory, unlike that of Reuben and Gad, was considered part of the Promised Land (1990: 276, 501–502), so perhaps the account of the giving of these lands to part of Manasseh was placed here for topical reasons, concluding the subunit with land-grants east of the Jordan (cf. Levine 2000: 478). Since the rest of Manasseh's tribe will inherit within the land of Canaan (Num. 27:1–11; see Josh. 17:1–13), there is no question of whether they will go armed across the Jordan for battle, enabling them to encourage the participation of Gad and Reuben as well. The part-tribe of Manasseh is listed in Joshua 4:12 as joining the vanguard with the sons of Reuben and Gad, which may presume that these clans of Manasseh were also brought under the same agreement and pact as Reuben and Gad.

Including Manasseh only at the end of the story serves, among other factors, to separate the part-tribe from the stigma of Gad and Reuben's initial request. Although commentators loosely include the half-tribe of Manasseh as being motivated by much livestock, common cause with the sons of Gad and Reuben should *not* be assumed – the scenario for Manasseh's half-tribe is utterly distinct. That the tribe of Manasseh will obtain lands on both sides of the Jordan functions to unify the tribes, one of the leading motifs of the narrative, and was perhaps an impulse in Moses' willingness to include them. Reference to 'the kingdom of Sihon king of the Amorites and the kingdom of Og king of Bashan', including their lands and cities, recalls the complete victories narrated triumphantly in chapter 21, with a fourfold use of the root *m-l-k*. Again, *ḥăṣî* signifies merely 'a part of' the tribe, designating here the Machirites and Gileadites, two of the eight Manasseh families, as Nachmanides explains (1975: 373–374; see Josh. 17:1–6).

The sons of Gad (re)built eight 'fortified cities and their sheepfolds': Dibon, Ataroth, Aroer, Atroth-Shophan, Jazer, Jogbehah, Beth-Nimrah and Beth-Haran. Only four of these had been noted in verse 3, in different order: Ataroth, Dibon, Jazer and Nimrah. In Joshua, Jazer is listed as a Levitical city (21:39). That cities belonging to Gad were the first four listed in verse 3 supports understanding the priority of the sons of Gad throughout (cf. v. 2) as communicating their leadership and initiative in the story. That 'fortified cities and sheepfolds' is omitted from the cities of the sons of Reuben may function likewise. These are the towns built by the Gadites for their dependents even though, as Ashley observes (1993: 615), some would later be reassigned to Reuben. There are six cities listed for the sons of Reuben: Heshbon, Elealeh, Kiriathaim, Nebo, Baal-Meon and Sibmah, five of which were mentioned in verse 3, assuming that Sibmah (*śibmāh*) is the same as Sebam (*śĕbām*), and Baal-Meon (*ba'al mĕ'ôn*) is a longer form of Beon (*bĕ'ōn*). The phrase 'their name changed around' is understood by Rashi as referring to the sons of Reuben who altered the names of Nebo and Baal-Meon since those cities had the names of pagan deities (cf. 1997: 4:400), but Nachmanides, questioning why, if Rashi were correct, the text should use the pagan names here (as well as in Isa. 15 and Jer. 48) instead of the new ones, explains that these city names had been changed by the Amorites when they were captured from Moab – but Israel now used the previous names, both to shame Moab and because the Amorites called their cities by the names of their idols (see 1975: 375–378). The fact remains, however, that the names listed, Nebo and Baal-Meon, reflect pagan idols. G. J. Wenham's suggestion, similar to Rashi's, justifies their use here instead of the new names given by the sons of Reuben, since the old names were revived when the Moabites reconquered these cities (1981b: 241; cf. Isa. 15:2; Ezek. 25:9). Alternatively, the phrase may instruct Israelites to read the names differently, such as 'Beon' (v. 3) in place of 'Baal-Meon' (Ashley 1993: 616). Nebo is likely the mountain where Moses was buried (see Deut. 32:49; 34:1; cf. Ibn Ezra ad loc.).

39–42. Completing the record of Israel's lands east of the Jordan, accounts of the lands conquered by sons of Manasseh and given by Moses are now noted, related to the territory in northern Transjordan. The capture of Gilead from 'the Amorite' by Manasseh is summarized (v. 39), along with Moses' subsequent giving of that land to them (v. 40), followed by two detailed accounts of how Jair went and seized their villages, and Nobah went and seized Kenath and her villages. Whereas Gad and Reuben request lands already conquered, the Manassites conquer lands for themselves (cf. Milgrom 1990: 496), campaigns that might have taken place in the aftermath of Israel's victories over Sihon and Og (cf. 21:21–32). The sons of Machir are referenced also in chapters 27 and 36 in relation to the daughters of Zelophehad (cf. Artus 2013: 367).

The names of both Jair and Nobah are emphasized by fronting the verb (*hālak*), delineating their respective possession, underscored also by their naming the cities/villages after themselves, an ancient practice displayed in Cain's naming his city after his son Enoch, and the city-builders, who sought to 'make a name for ourselves' (Gen. 4:17; 11:4). Naming a captured city likely served to demonstrate the victor's conquest (cf. Scolnic 1995: 127–128). Without any clear antecedent for 'their' villages, some interpret 'villages of Ham' (cf. Gen. 14:5), which may be preferable (Snaith 1962: 334; cf. Noordtzij 1983: 285; Levine 2000: 497). If verse 40 is taken as parenthetical, then 'their villages' in verse 41 refers to Gilead (v. 39). Jair was also of the tribe of Judah (see 1 Chr. 2:18–24), but is called by his mother's tribe, Manasseh, since he chose to inherit with her tribe (cf. Nachmanides 1975: 378–379; Ibn Ezra 1999: 254). Machir appears to have been a prominent family line, generating leaders (cf. Judg. 5:14; L. Hicks 1962), and 'the most warlike members of Manasseh' (Segal 1918: 126). Having conquered territories for themselves, without the help of the rest of the tribes, the Manassites needed ratification of their conquests by Moses for the sake of national recognition (Segal 1918: 127). For the sons of Machir, Jair and Nobah, the text says each 'captured' (*lākad*), which is used only one other time in Numbers, related to the capture of the villages of Jazer (21:32), whereas for the sons of Gad and Reuben the text simply states, 'they built', since their lands had already been taken in the victories over Sihon and Og. Land assignments are given more precisely in Joshua 13:8–32.

When in Numbers 34 the boundaries of the land of Canaan are delineated, it will clearly mark the Jordan River as an eastern limit. While expanding Israel's territory, 'effectively enlarging the borders of the promised land (v. 33)' (so Marquis 2013: 421), may be seen as a resulting benefit of the present story (cf. Calvin 2003b: 4:286), the Transjordan lands do not appear to achieve the same status as Canaan, where the land is seen as YHWH's gift. While the status of the lands east of the Jordan remains ambiguous, Jobling sees a distinction whereby the land north of the Jabbok River, settled by the half-tribe of Manasseh, is less problematic than the lands south of the river, which were settled by Gad and Reuben (1986: 2:110–117). He further suggests that the tribe of Manasseh, in its bipartition, 'recapitulates and *mediates* the bipartition of Israel', ensuring 'Israel's singleness by straddling the border' – while south of the Jabbok Israel is divided, in the north it is joined (Jobling 1986: 2:116, 119; emphasis original). This nuanced understanding finds support in Moster's thesis (2017), which demonstrates that it was indeed possible for the tribe of Manasseh to inhabit both sides of the Jordan River while maintaining social cohesion and tribal unity, since it was easy to cross the Jordan in the region of Manasseh.

History would demonstrate that being separated from the other tribes made the Transjordan especially susceptible to enemy attacks, as Noordtzij points out (1983: 277):

> As Deuteronomy 33:6 clearly shows, Reuben was unable to stand up to the pressure of the Moabites, who would soon push forward again (Judg. 3:12ff.), followed later by the Midianites (Judg. 6). Reuben would soon fall into decline, so that the Moabite king Mesha, a contemporary of Ahab (ca. 850 B.C.) makes no mention of it at all.

And, although Gad achieved much more prominence, yet the 'overwhelming superiority of Damascus finally overpowers Gad (2 Kings 10:32f.)' (see Milgrom's challenge to this view, 1990: 494–496). In the Bible's historical record, Gad's tribe is prominent, whereas the tribe of Reuben is often conspicuously absent (see 1 Sam. 13:7; 2 Sam. 24:5; cf. 1 Kgs 4:19 in LXX), perhaps because, as Milgrom suggests (1990: 267), Reuben's territory was restricted to the Heshbon area, surrounded and eventually absorbed by the towns assigned to Gad. At the same time, as Noordtzij notes (1983: 278–279), being separated from the rest of the tribes would also make the tribes of Reuben and Gad, after the conquest, reluctant to join in later battles of the confederacy within the land – as memorialized in Deborah's song, which, aside from naming both Reuben and Gad, individually, as complacent tribes, states, 'Gilead stayed beyond the Jordan' (see Judges 5:15–17). Moses had rightly perceived, then, that Gad and Reuben, so overly focused on their wealth of livestock, were not factoring the well-being of the other tribes in their decision. Within the context of Moses' imminent death (cf. 31:2), his priority was on maintaining the unity of the tribes of Israel, and their commitment to the mission of YHWH *in the land*. His negotiation of a compromise with the tribes of Gad and Reuben was a victory inasmuch as he had avoided another disaster along the lines of the scouts incident. The story may even be read as Moses' 'leadership skills in action' (Waxman 2014c: 442).

Within the flow of Numbers, the distribution of lands follows naturally from the victory and plunder of the war on Midian, and becomes a foretaste of the conquest. If YHWH granted such victory, spoils and lands outside the Promised Land, how much more confidence should Israel have to conquer the land of Canaan, which YHWH has repeatedly defined as his gift to Israel? The allusions to the scouts episode, moreover, demonstrate a positive contrast for the second generation, and likely explains the Manassite addendum (vv. 39–42). Just as the scouts incident was followed by a failed attack of the sons of Israel (14:39–45), a resounding defeat continually linked to the scouts story (see Deut. 1:41–45), so here not only does the second generation pass the challenge of a potential scouts incident, through Moses' mediation and through the willingness of the tribes of Gad and Reuben to compromise for the sake of the rest of Israel, but, as an inversion of Israel's failed attempt at conquest, the story is followed immediately by an account of successful attacks by Manassite leaders. Helfgot, observing how chapter 32 parallels and inverts the pattern of the scout episode, including its failed-attack addendum, enriches the point with the Talmudic tradition that Zelophehad had died as one of the *ma'apilim* (presumptuous ones) who were killed in the failed attack of 14:39–45 (2012a: 172–173): when the daughters of Zelophehad marry their cousins from the clan of Machir son of Manasseh, who captured and settled Gilead, we have an instance of *tikkun* since the 'children of Manasseh fight for the land and are rewarded by God, thus reversing the sin of their ancestors, who attempted to battle against His wishes'. While there is no explicit scriptural witness to Zelophehad's demise, Helfgot's overarching assessment is on point (2012a: 173):

> The second generation re-experienced many of the seminal events of the first generation. Since the mission of the first generation had gone awry, the second generation now had to relive their history, overcome it, and continue ... [T]hey confronted the major crisis-mistakes of the first generation ... and were able to emerge victorious.

Tellingly, while Jobling underscores how the story of the sons of Gad and Reuben (1986: 2:96–97) 'is put into a hermeneutical relationship' with that of the scouts story so that 'paradigmatic analysis becomes imperative', he also states that the final episode of the scouts story, 'the abortive attempt, appears to have no relevance to the new situation', because he restricted his analysis to verses 8–13 of Numbers 32 rather than taking the chapter as it stands.

A BACKSTORY TO THE MANASSITES?

Several questions surface as to the presence of the tribe of Manasseh in Numbers 32: Why were the sons of Manasseh not mentioned at all until verse 33? Why are they mentioned only at the point of Moses' allotment of lands east of the Jordan? Why, moreover, is the tribe of Manasseh so prevalent in the last major section of Numbers (chs. 26–36), showcased with the daughters of Zelophehad (27:1–11), with capture of lands east of the Jordan (32:33, 39–42), and finally concluding the book with the chieftains of Manasseh (ch. 36)? Why, furthermore, does the half-tribe of Manasseh gain more eastern lands than the territories of Gad and Reuben combined – essentially all the area that had been ruled by Og king of Bashan (see Deut. 3:13–15; 4:43)? Additionally, a comparison of the census figures in Numbers 1 and 26 shows that the tribe of Manasseh increased disproportionately in relation to the other tribes, from 32,200 to 52,700 – and, for this second census, Manasseh is listed *prior* to Ephraim, reversing the established order (26:28–34; cf. Gen. 48:20). What happened to cause Manasseh's census figures to surge dramatically, over 63%?

One possible explanation for the presence of the tribe of Manasseh in Numbers 32, which factors in the other curious elements noted and which goes back at least to a tenth-century commentary on 1 Chronicles by a disciple of Sa'adia Gaon (cf. 1873: 12), suggests the presence of Manassite clans in the Gilead and Bashan regions since the time of Joseph's reign in Egypt. The proposal, perhaps most fully articulated by Elitzur, is as follows (2020: 525–530; see also Hayman 1898; Etshalom 2015: 100–105; Medan 2016). As a preliminary observation, some of Jacob's grandsons were named for places related to the land of Israel while still living in Egypt, an occurrence especially prevalent among Manassites, who used names such as Gilead, Hepher, Shechem and Tirzah – names that may hint at a former connection to those regions on the part of Jacob's sons. The Chronicler's accounts of the early generations of the tribe of Judah relate the conquests in Gilead and Bashan by Jair son of Manasseh, whose paternal grandfather descended from Judah while his paternal grandmother descended from Manasseh (1 Chr. 2:21). The commentary by the disciple of Sa'adia Gaon intimates that Machir and his sons had taken these lands during the rule of Joseph in Egypt. In Genesis, we read that 'Joseph saw the sons of Ephraim to the third generation – the sons of Machir son of Manasseh were raised on the knees of Joseph' (50:23), and the second census in Numbers reports that 'Machir bore Gilead' (26:29). Joseph, then, had lived to see Gilead the firstborn of Machir, and, given Joseph's clout, his descendants might have traversed to the lands of Gilead under the auspices of Egypt. As Hayman expressed it (1898: 38):

> But suppose Machir, Joseph's heir by adoption, to have led a victorious settlement north-eastward from the Egyptian frontier, with all his grandfather's Egyptian influence to second him, we see at once why his eldest son should share the name of the region which he first won by conquest.

It appears there were Egyptian provinces on both sides of the Jordan, confirmed with the discovery of the Tell el-Armarna tablets (cf. Hayman 1898: 41), and some trace those provinces to Joseph's purchase of lands during the famine (Gen. 47:13–26). From the angle of the Chronicler's genealogy of Manasseh's tribe, it appears that Manasseh or his son had a concubine from Aram, the western-most regions that included Gilead and Bashan (1 Chr. 7:14). Aram being far from Egypt, Medan (2016) postulates the concubine might have been a woman of some distinction, even the daughter of an Aramean nobleman, surmising whether Machir might have inherited Gilead from his mother (or grandmother), thus naming his son after his inheritance. Interestingly, Gilead's sister is called 'Queen regnant' (*hammōleket*) (1 Chr. 7:18; Hayman 1898: 41, 47). Otherwise it would be quite prescient of him to name his son after territories that his descendants would later conquer. According to one version of the theory, then, the remark that 'Machir the firstborn of Manasseh was a valiant warrior, and was assigned the lands of Gilead and Bashan' (Josh. 17:1) and the land-capture accounts in Numbers 32:39–42, refer to the time of Joseph, explaining why years later those territories were granted to Machir's descendants. After Joseph's death, the lands he had acquired were possessed by the people of Ammon and Moab, until Machir, who was something of an Egyptian general, conquered them (see Munk 1995: 30–31). Nuancing this view is the suggestion that Machir's lands had in the meantime been taken by the Amorites, so that the descendants of Machir needed to capture them so as to reclaim their ancestral homestead (E. Fischer 2016). In 1 Chronicles, moreover, it even appears that Ephraim had built and settled in cities some six generations before Joshua (7:20–27), making the idea of engagement with the lands of their heritage plausible in some of the stages of Israel's stay in Egypt. In Numbers 32:39–42, Moses confirms the right of Machir's descendants to lands originally acquired by Joseph, and confirms their right to Jair's towns (cf. 1 Chr. 2:21–23), which had been named 'Jair' to preserve his memory since he had no children of his own (Munk 1995: 30–31).

Regarding the dramatic increase in Manasseh's census figures, Elitzur points out that some of the thousands added to Manasseh's tribe might have derived from the descendants of Machir, Jair and Nobah, who had never returned to Egypt after establishing settlements in Transjordan, but who were recently liberated from Og king of Bashan by the Israelites (2020: 526–529; cf. Medan 2016). The situation is compared by way of analogy with the families of Jewish people who had already been living in Palestine for centuries but are often overlooked in the narrative of the modern state of Israel, which usually focuses on the arrival of post-Holocaust Jewish immigrants from Europe and Arab countries. This theory is thus used to explain the increased size of Manasseh's tribe (as well as the after-the-fact statement in Deut. 2:12). The book of *Jubilees* takes for granted the presence of some Israelites in Canaan while the majority resided in Egypt (ch. 46; Medan 2016). Along with answering most of the questions raised at the start, assuming a pre-Mosaic conquest by Manassite warriors may explain other obscure references as well. Hayman, for example, points out the words of 'Jepthah the Gileadite' in Judges (11:1), who confronted the Ammonites, arguing that Israel had lived in the territory beyond the Jordan for 'three hundred years', possibly referring to his tribe's ancestral settlements (1898: 48). He further points to the otherwise awkward statement by Moses in Deuteronomy that 'Jair called Bashan after his own name, Villages of Jair, *to this day*' (3:14; Hayman 1898: 49). Finally, he also reflects on the definiteness of the inheritance claimed by the daughters of Zelophehad as embodying the title of descent from Machir, Gilead and Hepher (1898: 51): 'a heritage which had come down through some two centuries of user, and had only been *de facto* interrupted through an intrusive hostile possession'. Perhaps, the Manassite desire to reclaim these lands of Gilead and Bashan led to the decision for Israel to turn and go northward (Num. 21:33) after the conquest of Sihon's land rather than remaining in the area between the Arnon and the Jabbok, from which Israel could eventually have crossed the Jordan into Canaan (cf. Medan 2016).

In sum, it is feasible that Manasseh's tribe already had lands east of the Jordan, which had been captured and settled generations earlier, *possibly* retaining some vestige of a Manassite population, but which had fallen under Amorite control. The settlement language used in Numbers, between the (re)building of cities by the sons of Gad and Reuben (32:34–38) and the taking of cities and villages by sons of Machir (32:39–42), is starkly different, calling for some explanation. As the chapter stands, the Manassite conquests form a victorious inversion of the failed attempt at conquest that closes the scouts episode (14:39–45). Moreover, given the desire for maintaining the integrity of God's people and their land displayed in the other Manasseh stories (27:1–11; 36:1–12), the conquests by the sons of Machir seem to function as an attempt at maintaining the connection between the sons of Gad and Reuben in the east with the other ten tribes in the west, inasmuch as the tribe of Manasseh straddles both sides of the Jordan River.

Explanation

Having much livestock, the tribes of Gad and Reuben approach Moses, Eleazar the priest and the chieftains of the community, and ask to be given territory east of the Jordan River for their holding, since this land was a place for livestock, specifically requesting that they not pass over the Jordan. Moses, concerned over the unity of the tribes in conquering the land, rebukes them strongly, warning them about how their behaviour would discourage the other tribes and possibly turn them from following YHWH closely, inciting YHWH's judgement just as the scouts of the former generation had done. The narration is layered richly with allusions to previous 'livestock' events in Genesis, such as Lot's parting of ways with Abram (Gen. 13), Esau's separation from Jacob (Gen. 36:6–8), and possibly also Israel's separation from the Egyptians in Goshen (Gen. 46:31–34), which, combined with Moses' own linking of their request with the scouts debacle of the first generation (Num. 13 – 14), shades the sons of Gad and Reuben negatively. Their language betrays a fixation on their possessions, with the key term 'livestock' used repeatedly, even listed before their 'little ones' and before their obligation to the other tribes of Israel, and there is scant reference to YHWH himself – all of which Moses discerns and overturns.

The sons of Gad and Reuben draw near to Moses and propose a compromise whereby they build sheepfolds for their flocks and cities for the little ones, but commit their fighting men to cross the Jordan and serve in the frontline before the sons of Israel in the conquest, not returning to their houses until the other tribes had each gained their inheritance. Moses accepts their proposal, rephrasing it in a way that prioritizes the other tribes before themselves (and their own little ones before their livestock), and that emphasizes their obligations not only to the rest of Israel but to YHWH himself, repeating the phrase 'before YHWH' numerous times. The sons of Gad and Reuben pledge to fulfil this plan, which recollects the severity of men's oaths before YHWH (Num. 30), and Moses accordingly instructs Eleazar, Joshua and the other tribal heads about the agreement. There is some tension in the Bible regarding the status of Transjordan: whereas the 'covenant of pieces' includes the east bank of the Jordan (Gen. 15:18–21), later passages clearly define the land as on the other side of the Jordan (Num. 34:10–12; 35:10–14), and it may be that the eastern lands were only appropriate as an eventual outgrowth of the land of Canaan, sanctified 'before YHWH' *only as annexed to Canaan* after the conquest (cf. Bin-Nun 2019b). The larger boundaries promised to Abraham in the covenant of pieces in Genesis 15 had already been partially distributed to his relations, the lands of three of the ten nations (given to Edom, Moab, Ammon). Possibly, these lands were restricted only for a time, intended eventually to be inherited by Israelites – a scenario that made the lands of Sihon and Og, by contrast, subject to immediate conquest since they were not connected to Abraham's descendants already (cf. Deut. 2). Moses' negotiations did, in a sense, secure the possession of the land of Canaan before that of Transjordan, and he also unified both sides of the Jordan through the tribe of Manasseh, which would claim lands on either side of the Jordan River.

The account closes with an official record that 'Moses gave' the Transjordan lands to the sons of Gad, Reuben and to the half-tribe of Manasseh, delineating the cities rebuilt by Gad and Reuben, and describing the capture of places in the Gilead area by Manassite warriors Machir, Jair and Nobah. Following the victorious note of Israel's defeat of the Midianites, and the distribution of spoils, the division of lands now – albeit from the earlier victories of Sihon and Og (21:21–35) – completes the pattern of conquest. While the status of the lands east of the Jordan remains ambiguous, the overall atmosphere of the chapter is optimistic. On the brink of the conquest, with the shadow of Moses' imminent death looming, another potential scouts incident had emerged, but was transformed both by Moses' engagement and by the reverent compliance of the sons of Gad and Reuben. The story, therefore, ends with a note of triumph, not only with the division of lands, but with a reversal of the failed attack that had closed the scouts episode as the Manassites go and seize villages, a foretaste of the conquest in the land (cf. 14:39–45).

NUMBERS 33 – 35: ISRAEL'S JOURNEYS TO YHWH'S LAND

Translation

[33:1]These are the journeys of the sons of Israel who went forth from the land of Egypt, according to their hosts, by the hand of Moses and Aaron. [2]And Moses wrote their going-forths, according to their journeys by the word (mouth) of YHWH. Now these are their journeys, according to their goings-forth:

[3]And they journeyed out from Ramesses on the first month, on the fifteenth day of the first month, on the morrow of the Passover, the sons of Israel went forth with a high hand before the eyes of all the Egyptians. [4]The Egyptians they buried all their firstborn whom YHWH had struck down among them, and against their gods YHWH executed judgements.

⁵And the sons of Israel journeyed out from Ramesses, and encamped at Succoth.

⁶And they journeyed out from Succoth, and encamped at Etham, which is on the outskirts of the wilderness.

⁷And they journeyed out from Etham, and turned by Pi-Hahiroth, which is before Baal-Zephon, and they encamped before Migdol.

⁸And they journeyed out from before Hahiroth, and passed over through the midst of the sea to the wilderness, and went a three-days' way in the Wilderness of Etham, and encamped in Marah.

⁹And they journeyed out from Marah, and came to Elim. Now in Elim there were twelve springs of water and seventy palm trees, and they encamped there.

¹⁰And they journeyed out from Elim, and encamped by the Sea of Suph.

¹¹And they journeyed out from the Sea of Suph, and encamped in the Wilderness of Sin.

¹²And they journeyed out from the Wilderness of Sin, and encamped in Dophkah.

¹³And they journeyed out from Dophkah, and encamped in Alush.

¹⁴And they journeyed out from Alush, and encamped in Rephidim – and there was no water there for the people to drink.

¹⁵And they journeyed out from Rephidim, and encamped in the Wilderness of Sinai.

¹⁶And they journeyed out from the Wilderness of Sinai, and encamped in Kibroth-Hattaavah.

¹⁷And they journeyed out from Kibroth-Hattaavah, and encamped at Hazeroth.

¹⁸And they journeyed out from Hazeroth, and encamped in Rithmah.

¹⁹And they journeyed out from Rithmah, and encamped in Rimmon-Perez.

²⁰And they journeyed from Rimmon-Perez, and encamped in Libnah.

²¹And they journeyed out from Libnah, and encamped in Rissah.

²²And they journeyed out from Rissah, and encamped in Kehelathah.

²³And they journeyed out from Kehelathah, and encamped at Mount Shepher.

²⁴And they journeyed out from Mount Shepher, and encamped in Haradah.

²⁵And they journeyed out from Haradah, and encamped in Makheloth.

²⁶And they journeyed out from Makheloth, and encamped in Tahath.

²⁷And they journeyed out from Tahath, and encamped in Terah.

²⁸And they journeyed out from Terah, and encamped in Mithkah.

²⁹And they journeyed out from Mithkah, and encamped in Hashmonah.

³⁰And they journeyed out from Hashmonah, and encamped in Moseroth.

³¹And they journeyed out from Moseroth, and encamped in Bene-Jaakan.

³²And they journeyed out from Bene-Jaakan, and encamped at Mount Gidgad.

³³And they journeyed from Mount Gidgad, and encamped in Jotbathah.

³⁴And they journeyed out from Jotbathah, and encamped in Abronah.

³⁵And they journeyed out from Abronah, and encamped in Ezion-Geber.

³⁶And they journeyed out from Ezion-Geber, and encamped in the Wilderness of Zin – this is Kadesh.

³⁷And they journeyed out from Kadesh, and encamped at Mount Hor on the outskirts of the land of Edom. ³⁸And Aaron the priest ascended into Mount

Hor, by the word of YHWH, and died there, in the fortieth year after the sons of Israel went forth from the land of Egypt, in the fifth month, on the first of the month. ³⁹Now Aaron was one hundred and twenty-three years old when he died in Mount Hor.

⁴⁰And the Canaanite, king of Arad – he was dwelling in the Negev in the land of Canaan – heard when the sons of Israel came.

⁴¹And they journeyed out from Mount Hor, and encamped in Zalmonah.

⁴²And they journeyed out from Zalmonah, and encamped in Punon.

⁴³And they journeyed out from Punon, and encamped in Oboth.

⁴⁴And they journeyed out from Oboth, and encamped in Iye-Abarim, on the border of Moab.

⁴⁵And they journeyed out from Iye-Abarim, and encamped in Dibon-Gad.

⁴⁶And they journeyed out from Dibon-Gad, and encamped in Almon-Diblathaim.

⁴⁷And they journeyed from Almon-Diblathaim, and encamped in the mountains of Abarim, before Nebo.

⁴⁸And they journeyed from the mountains of Abarim, and encamped in the plains of Moab, by the Jordan near Jericho. ⁴⁹And they encamped by the Jordan, from Beth-Jeshimoth up to Abel-Shittim (mourning of acacia grove) in the plains of Moab.

YHWH's first speech

⁵⁰And YHWH spoke to Moses in the plains of Moab, by the Jordan near Jericho, saying, ⁵¹"Speak to the sons of Israel and say to them, "When you yourselves pass over the Jordan to the land of Canaan, ⁵²you will dispossess all the inhabitants of the land from before you, and you will destroy all their carved figures and all their molten images you will destroy, and all their high places you will demolish. ⁵³And you will possess the land and dwell in her, for to you I have given the land to possess her. ⁵⁴And you will inherit the land by lot according to your clans, for the large you will cause his inheritance to be large, and for the small you will cause his inheritance to be small – wherever the lot falls forth to him, there it will be to him, according to the tribes of your fathers you will inherit. ⁵⁵But if you will not dispossess the inhabitants of the land from before you, then it will be that whoever you have left from among them will be as barbs in your eyes and as thorns in your sides, and they will be hostile to you on the land wherein you are dwelling. ⁵⁶And it will be that just as I had thought to do to them, I will do to you."

YHWH's second speech

³⁴:¹And YHWH spoke to Moses, saying, ²"Command the sons of Israel and say to them, "When you come into the land, Canaan, this is the land which will

fall to you as an inheritance, the land of Canaan by her borders: ³And your southern side will be from the Wilderness of Zin alongside (by the hands of) Edom, and your southern border will be from the outskirts of the Salt Sea eastward. ⁴And your border will go around from the Negev to the Scorpions' Ascent, and pass on to Zin, and its outreaches will be from the Negev to Kadesh Barnea, and go forth to Hazar-Addar, and pass on to Azmon. ⁵And the border will go around from Azmon toward the Wadi of Egypt, and its outreaches will be seaward. ⁶Now the border of the sea (western), the Great Sea will be your border – this will be for the border of the sea (western). ⁷And this will be your northern border: from the Great Sea mark out (the line) for yourselves to Mount Hor. ⁸From Mount Hor mark out (the line) to Lebo (entrance of)-Hamath, and the goings forth of the border will be toward Zedad. ⁹And the border will go forth toward Ziphron, and its goings forth will be Hazar-Enan – this will be your northern border. ¹⁰And you will draw out (the line) for your eastward border from Hazar-Enan toward Shepham. ¹¹And the border will descend from Shepham to Riblah, on the east of Ayin (the spring), and the border will descend and reach the side of the Sea of Chinnereth eastward. ¹²And the border will descend toward the Jordan, and its goings forth will be the Salt Sea – this will be your land, according to her borders all around."'

¹³And Moses commanded the sons of Israel, saying, 'This is the land which you will inherit by lot, which YHWH commanded to give to the nine tribes and the half-tribe. ¹⁴For the tribe of the sons of Reuben, according to their fathers' house, and the tribe of the sons of Gad, according to their fathers' house, have taken, and the half-tribe of Manasseh have taken their inheritance.' ¹⁵The two tribes and the half-tribe have taken their inheritance from across the Jordan near Jericho eastward, from the sunrise.

YHWH's third speech

¹⁶And YHWH spoke to Moses, saying, ¹⁷'These are the names of the men who will divide the inheritance of the land for you: Eleazar the priest, and Joshua the son of Nun. ¹⁸And one chieftain, one chieftain per tribe, you will take to divide the inheritance of the land. ¹⁹These are the names of the men: for the tribe of Judah, Caleb the son of Jephunneh; ²⁰and for the tribe of the sons of Simeon, Samuel the son of Ammihud; ²¹for the tribe of Benjamin, Elidad son of Chislon; ²²And for the tribe of the sons of Dan, chieftain Bukki the son of Jogli; ²³for the sons of Joseph, for the tribe of the sons of Manasseh, chieftain Hanniel the son of Ephod; ²⁴and for the tribe of the sons of Ephraim, chieftain Kemuel the son of Shiphtan; ²⁵and for the sons of Zebulun, chieftain Elizaphan the son of Parnach; ²⁶and for the tribe of the sons of Issachar, chieftain Paltiel the son of Azzan; ²⁷and for the tribe of the sons of Asher, chieftain Ahihud the son of Shelomi; ²⁸and for the sons of Naphtali, chieftain Pedahel the son of Ammihud.' ²⁹These are the ones whom YHWH had commanded to cause the sons of Israel to inherit in the land of Canaan.

YHWH's fourth speech

35:1And YHWH spoke to Moses on the plains of Moab by Jordan near Jericho, saying, 2"Command the sons of Israel, and they will give to the Levites from the inheritance of their holding cities to dwell in, and pastureland for the cities surrounding them you will give to the Levites. 3And the cities will be for them to dwell in, and their pasturelands will be for their cattle and for their livestock, and for all their beasts. 4And the pasturelands of the cities which you will give to the Levites are to be, from the wall of the city and outward, a thousand cubits all around. 5And you will measure from outside the city on the eastward side two thousand cubits, and on the Negev side two thousand cubits, and the sea side two thousand cubits, and on the north side two thousand cubits; and the city will be in the midst – this will be for them the pasturelands of the city. 6And the cities that you will give to the Levites, six cities of asylum you will give, for the murderer to flee there, and along with them you will give forty-two cities. 7All the cities that you will give to the Levites will be forty-eight cities, they with their pasturelands. 8And the cities that you will give from the holding of the sons of Israel, from the large you will give a large portion and from the small you will give a small portion – each one according to the portion of his inheritance which he inherits will give of his cities to the Levites.'

YHWH's fifth speech

9And YHWH spoke to Moses, saying, 10"Speak to the sons of Israel and say to them, "When you pass over the Jordan toward the land of Canaan, 11You will select cities for you; they will be cities of asylum for you, and there the murderer who strikes down a life unintentionally will flee. 12And the cities will be for an asylum for you from the avenger, so the murderer will not die, until he stands before the community for the judgement. 13And the cities that you will give, six will be cities of asylum for you. 14And three cities you will give from this side of the Jordan, and three cities you will give in the land of Canaan; they will be cities of asylum. 15For the sons of Israel, and for the sojourner, and for the resident aliens in their midst, these six cities will be for asylum to flee there, for everyone who strikes down a life unintentionally. 16Now if with a vessel of iron he strikes him and he dies, he is a murderer – the murderer will surely be put to death. 17And if with a stone in hand, by which one may die, he strikes him and he dies, he is a murderer – the murderer will surely be put to death. 18Or if with a vessel of wood in hand, by which one may die, he strikes him and he dies, he is a murderer – the murderer will surely be put to death. 19The avenger of blood, he will put the murderer to death: when he encounters him, he will put him to death. 20And if in hatred he thrusts him or hurls upon him by lying in wait and he dies, 21or in enmity he strikes him with his hand and he dies, then the one who struck will surely be put to death: he is a murderer – the avenger of blood will put the murderer to death when he encounters him. 22But if suddenly, without enmity, he thrusts him or hurls upon him any vessel without lying in wait, ²³or with any stone, by which one may die, without seeing him, and causes it to fall upon him and he dies, but he was not an enemy to him and he did not seek him evil, ²⁴then the community will judge between the one who struck and the avenger of blood, according to these judgements. ²⁵And the community will deliver the murderer from the hand of the avenger of blood, and the community will return him to the city of asylum, there where he had fled, and he will dwell there until the death of the high priest who was anointed with the holy oil. ²⁶But if the murderer surely goes forth from the boundary of the city of his asylum, there where he had fled, ²⁷and if the avenger of blood finds him outside the border of the city of his asylum, and the avenger of blood murders the murderer, he has no bloodguilt. ²⁸For in the city of his asylum he should have dwelled until the death of the high priest, but after the death of the high priest the murderer will return to the land of his holding. ²⁹And these will be for you for a statute of judgement throughout your generations in all your dwellings. ³⁰Everyone who strikes down a life, by the mouth of witnesses the murderer will be killed, but one witness will not answer against a life to die. ³¹And you will not take a ransom for the life of a murderer, he who is guilty (wicked) to die, for he will surely be put to death. ³²And you will not take a ransom for the one who has fled to the city of his asylum so that he returns to dwell in the land, until the death of the priest. ³³So you will not pollute the land wherein you are, for the blood it will pollute the land, and for the land there is no ransoming for the blood that was shed in her except by the blood of him who shed it. ³⁴So do not defile the land wherein you dwell, where I myself dwell in her midst – for I am YHWH dwelling in the midst of the sons of Israel.'"

Notes on the text

33:7. 'turned': MT is sg.; but pl. is required, as with SamP and *TgJon*. LXX and Syr read 'encamped' (cf. Exod. 14:2).

8. 'from before Hahiroth': should probably be emended to 'from Pi-Hahiroth', as with SamP, Syr, Vg.

9. 'encamped there': LXX includes 'by the waters' (cf. Exod. 15:27).

12. 'Dophkah': LXX reads 'Raphaka' (also in v. 13).

13. 'Alush': SamP reads 'Alish' (also in v. 14).

16. 'Kibroth-Hattaavah': LXX translates 'Graves of Lust'.

20. 'Libnah': SamP has 'Lebonah' (also in v. 21).

21. 'Rissah': LXX has 'Dessa' (also in v. 22); *TgJon* reads 'Beth-Rissah'.

22. 'Kehelathah': LXX has 'Makelath' (also in v. 23), similar to 'Makeloth' in vv. 25–26.

23. 'Mount Shepher': LXX reads only 'Shepher' (also in v. 24).

24. 'Haradah': LXX reads 'Charadath' (also in v. 25).

26. 'Tahath': LXX has 'Kataath' (also in v. 27).

27. 'Terah': LXX has 'Taphath' (also in v. 28).

28. 'Mithkah': LXX has 'Matekka' (also in v. 29); SamP has 'Mithikah.
29. 'Hashmonah': LXX has 'Zelmonah' (also in v. 30).
30. BHS suggests inserting vv. 36b–41 after Hashmonah.
31. 'Bene-Jaakan': LXX has 'Banaia' (also in v. 32).
32. 'Mount Gidgad': MT reads 'Hor-Haggidgad'; possibly the 'hollow of Gidgad'; Mount Gidgad follows LXX, some MT MSS and Vg.
33. 'Jotbathah': LXX has 'Etebatha' (also in v. 34).
36. 'Wilderness of Zin': LXX inserts 'and they journeyed out from the Wilderness of Zin and encamped in the wilderness of Paran' (cf. Num. 10:12).
38. 'Mount Hor': lacking in LXX.
42. 'Punon': LXX has 'Phino', SamP and Syr 'Phinon' (also in v. 43).
44. 'Iye-Abarim': LXX has 'Gai' (also in v. 45).
46. 'Almon-Diblathaim': LXX has 'Gelmon Deblathaim' (also in v. 47).
49. 'Beth-Jeshimoth': LXX reads 'in the middle of Asimoth'.
'Abel-Shittim': LXX has 'Belsattim'.
53. 'possess': LXX references destroying (*apoleite*) the inhabitants of the land; Vg refers to purifying the land.
54. 'there it will be to him': LXX includes a reference to 'his name'.
34:2. 'Canaan': BHS suggests deleting its first occurrence (cf. Paterson 1900: 65), as 'the land' and 'Canaan' are both absolutes in apposition; a few SamP MSS have them in regular const.-gen. (see *Sebir* note in BHS). Perhaps Canaan is underscored in contrast with Transjordan (Num. 32; 34:14–15).
4. 'Hazar-Addar': LXX has 'Arad' (see Josh. 15:3).
'will be': reading pl. with Q.
5. 'seaward': or 'the sea' with SamP and LXX as suggested by BHS.
9. 'Ziphron . . . Hazar-Enan': LXX has 'Dephrona . . . Asernain'.
10. 'draw out': MT reads 'desire for yourselves'.
11. 'Riblah': SamP and LXX have 'Arbela'.
20. 'the sons of': lacking in LXX, Syr and Vg.
21. 'Elidad': SamP, LXX and Syr have 'Eldad', perhaps two forms of the same name (cf. 11:26).
22. 'chieftain': lacking in Syr, Vg and one MT MS.
'Bukki': LXX has 'Bakchir'.
23. 'chieftain': lacking in Syr, Vg and two MT MSS.
'Ephod': LXX has 'Ouphi'.
24. 'chieftain': lacking in Syr and Vg.
25. 'chieftain': lacking in Syr and Vg.
26. 'chieftain': lacking in Syr.
'Azzan': LXX has 'Oza', Syr has 'Azor'.
27. 'chieftain': lacking in Syr and Vg.
'Ahihud': reads 'Achior' in LXX.
28. 'chieftain': lacking in Syr, Vg and two MT MSS.
'Ammihud': reads 'Benamioud' in LXX (likely repeating 'son of').

35:2. 'you will give': LXX and Syr have third person pl.
3. 'their pasturelands': MT's suff. is m., referring to Levites; SamP has f., referring to cities.
4. 'thousand': LXX has 'two thousand', harmonizing (cf. v. 5).
5. 'for them': SamP, LXX, Syr, *TgJon* have 'for you'.
6. 'to flee': Syr includes that the murderer killed unintentionally.
8. 'he inherits': MT is pl.; SamP, Syr and one MT MS have sg.
10. 'When you pass over': LXX has 'you will pass over'.
12. 'avenger': LXX, Syr and Tg include 'of blood'.
17. 'put to death': SamP has 'will die'.
18. 'Or if': SamP, LXX, Syr, Vg read 'And if'.
20. 'thrusts': Syr reads 'struck'.
'hurls upon him': LXX infers throwing an object (cf. v. 22).
25. 'the murderer': SamP reads 'the one who struck'.
30. 'killed': uses same root *r-ṣ-ḥ* for 'murderer' in talionic justice.
32. 'the priest': SamP, LXX and Syr read 'high priest' (cf. vv. 25, 28).
33. 'wherein you are': SamP, LXX, Syr, Vg and *TgNeof* read 'you live'.
34. 'do not defile': MT is sg., but SamP, LXX, Syr, Tg and some MT MSS have pl.

Form and structure

Within the unit of chapters 33–35, the itinerary forms a summation of the wilderness sojourn from Egypt to the plains of Moab (33:1–49) that functions as an introduction to YHWH's last five speeches to Moses, related to Israel's life in the land: 33:50–56; 34:1–15; 34:16–29; 35:1–8; and 35:9–34. The MT further subdivides the itinerary, into verses 1–39 and 40–49, distinguishing the journeys of the first and second generations, respectively.

Numbers 33:1–49 possesses the traits of a genuine ANE itinerary (Cole 2003: 341), making it preferable to take the list of journeys and stations as a whole (for source-critical approaches, see G. B. Gray 1903: 442–452; Coats 1972; de Vaulx 1972: 372–381; J. T. Walsh 1977; G. I. Davies 1983; Budd 1984: 350–353; cf. Ashley 1993: 624–625). Following Dillmann (1886), Milgrom soundly argues that chapter 33 comprises a master list recorded by Moses, akin to other ancient itineraries which also included expansions (rather than editorial glosses; 1990: 497–499; contra Roskop 2011: 223–232). Since there is no consensus as to the wilderness route itself, geographical and archaeological approaches are hindered (cf. e.g. Davies 1979: 67–69; 1990; Kitchen 1992; Fritz 2016; see Elitzur 2020: 758–767 for stations to the Sinai wilderness, 439–449 for stations from the Sinai wilderness to Rithmah, 481–493 for the final stations). Part of the itinerary, through the Transjordan (33:44–49), receives historical confirmation among maps of ancient Egypt preserved in list form, recording an important fixed and official route utilized and maintained during Egypt's 300-year jurisdiction in the Late Bronze Age (1560–1200 BC) over Palestine (Krahmalkov 1994). (See Table 28.)

Formally, Davies points out (1974), repeated use of a stereotyped formula, continuity of references to movement, and short sections with historical or geographical material are all markers of the sorts of itineraries found among the annals of Hittite and Assyrian kings, especially those recording royal military campaigns. Given the triumphant start of Israel's journeys in chapter 33, the sons of Israel going forth with 'a high hand' after YHWH's victory over the gods of Egypt, the itinerary is likely meant to be a record of the triumphant marches of YHWH's earthly hosts – 'Arise, O YHWH! Your enemies be scattered, and those who hate you flee from your face!' (10:35).

Expansions can be grouped into three sorts:

1. *Location or route clarification*: 'which is on the outskirts of the wilderness' (v. 6), 'which is before Baal-Zephon' (v. 7), 'a three-days way in the wilderness of Etham' (v. 8), 'this is Kadesh' (v. 36), 'on the outskirts of the land of Edom' (v. 37), 'on the border of Moab' (v. 44), 'before Nebo' (v. 47), 'by the Jordan near Jericho . . . by the Jordan' (vv. 48–49).

2. *Location feature*: 'Now in Elim there were twelve springs of water and seventy palm trees' (v. 9), 'there was no water there for the people' (v. 14).

3. *Notable event at location*, sometimes including notice of date: 'on the fifteenth day of the first month, on the morrow of the Passover' (vv. 3–4), 'Aaron the priest ascended Mount Hor . . . in the fifth month, on the first of the month' (vv. 38–39), 'the Canaanite king Arad heard' (v. 40).

The expansion 'passed over through the midst of the sea to the wilderness' (v. 8) may be categorized under either 'route clarification' or 'notable event', depending on the degree to which one identifies the language with the miracle at the sea. There are several expansions within verses 3–14, which then begin again at Kadesh through the rest of the second generation's journeys (vv. 36–49), with none occurring in the middle section. The itinerary list, then, highlights the departure and arrival eras as one overarching journey that began with the departure out of Egypt, culminating with the arrival in the plains of Moab by the Jordan on the cusp of the land of Canaan. These two eras are related to the two generations of Israel: the first generation is the generation that departed out of Egypt; the second is the generation that inherited the land. The generations, however, form the one people of God who were

Table 28: Arabah – Plains of Moab road

Late Bronze Age Egyptian name	Biblical name
(Yamm) ha-Melach	Melah (Salt)
Iyyin	Iyyim
Heres/Hareseth	Heres/Hareseth
Aqrabat	
Dibon/Qarho	Dibon
Iktanu	
Abel	Abel-shittim
Jordan	Jordan

led like sheep by their divine Shepherd through the wilderness on one purposeful journey.

Another feature that stands out when considering the expansions is so obvious as to be missed easily; namely, that each has to do with *a place* – its location or special feature, or an event that took place there. Given that several notable events, such as the supply of manna and the giving of the Decalogue, were omitted, how can one discern a rationale for the few that are included? The purpose of the 'notable event' expansions appears to be the distinction between the two generations: the first generation, which departed out of Egypt on the morrow of Passover, had its end signalled by the death of Aaron the high priest, marking the transition to the second generation that takes place in chapter 20 of the narrative – these are the two events chosen as expansions (vv. 3–4 and 38–39), while the other notable events were bypassed. Along this line, the only other expansion, referencing the 'Canaanite king Arad' (v. 40), may serve to mark the official start of the second generation's marches to the land, the new progress that begins after the death of Aaron, which marked the end of the first generation. More than this, the Canaanite-king expansion includes a reference to his 'dwelling in the Negev in the land of Canaan' and that 'he heard when the sons of Israel came', which makes it likely this gloss functions to explain why Israel had to change its route. Even given Israel's utter defeat of Arad's Canaanites, YHWH had chosen to bring the Camp around for eastern entry into the land, across the Jordan, from the plains of Moab, perhaps because the plains of Moab were more suitable as a locale for Moses' final preparation of Israel (i.e. Deuteronomy), whereas the southern entry would have involved continual battles – the conquest would necessarily have begun, but Moses was forbidden from taking part in Israel's entry (20:12), perhaps explaining his absence in 21:1–4. Other expansions, 'route clarification' and 'location features' all focus on *place*, marking the entrance into and emergence out of the wilderness, with the two features being exemplary of the highs and lows of the journeys: some places in the wilderness abundantly supplied with water provided comfort, while others, lacking water, challenged the people to depend on YHWH, trusting his good intentions for them. The emphasis on places accords with the major theme of the book's final subsection, given completely to a focus on the land. As an introduction to the focus on land, the wilderness stations may be read as something of a divine tutelage on place, instructing and disciplining Israel so the nation would not only appreciate the land more fully but remain dependent on YHWH once in the land.

The number of stations, forty-two, has long solicited a search for symbolic meaning. Several patristic exegetes pointed to a parallel with the forty-two generations in Jesus' genealogy (de Vaulx 1972: 381; cf. Matt. 1:1–17), while in Jewish tradition forty-two lines are prescribed for the Torah's columns, reflecting the Torah's guidance through life's journeys (Tur, *Yoreh Deah* 275; cf. Bernstein 2021). The number 42 occurs in Numbers, with reference to the cities of refuge (see 35:6), which perhaps encourages a similar perspective on the forty-two stations of the journey, whereby all Israel lived as Levites in the wilderness, trusting in YHWH as their inheritance, and vice versa: each Levitical city is like a replica of the wilderness Camp of Israel. Differently angled, Israel under YHWH's forty-year judgement may be likened to their residing in a city of refuge. Strengthening this notion, the death of Aaron appears to signal the second generation's release to the land, even if this idea relates more to the six cities of refuge. Subtracting the places of departure (Ramesses) and final arrival (the plains of Moab), leaves forty stations, perhaps recalling the forty years spent in the wilderness (cf. Knierim 1995a: 383; Scolnic 1995: 96, 128), a notion that does not require correlating one station per year in a trite, literalistic manner. Most surely, the forty-two stations and their overview form a triumphant demonstration of YHWH's faithful guidance of Israel through the wilderness, from the deliverance out of Egypt to the plains of Moab.

Israel's journeys (33:1–49) function as the introduction for the final five speeches of YHWH, each of which focuses on the land: (1) possessing the land (33:50–56), (2) the boundaries of the land (34:1–12), (3) the leadership for dividing the land (34:16–28), (4) the Levitical cities in the land (35:1–8), and (5) the cities of refuge in the land (35:9–34). There is a clear logical progression to YHWH's speeches, moving from (1) dispossessing the land's inhabitants, along with destroying all remnants of idolatry so as to clear the land of offence, to (2) delineating the land's borders, a prerequisite for (3) dividing the land. Once the land is allotted, then, within those allotments (4) Levitical cities need to be designated, and, finally, among those Levitical cities, (5) several must be chosen to function as cities of refuge. In the final climactic statement of the fifth speech YHWH declares, 'for I am YHWH dwelling in the midst of the sons of Israel' (35:34), a statement demonstrating the land of Canaan is the intended fulfilment not only of the Camp structure as the ideal covenant community (see 5:3), but of the original purpose statements given in connection with YHWH's Dwelling (see Exod. 25:8; 29:45–46). Although Moses would not cross the Jordan to achieve these five acts himself, reserving the five messages for this point, before his death, ensures that Israel's eventual accomplishment of them will be done under his authority (cf. Milgrom 1990: 282; Abarbanel 2015: 338–339).

The five speeches are also arranged chiastically, creating a central focus on the ten princes who will divide the land for their respective tribes, under the leadership of Eleazar the priest and Joshua son of Nun (34:16–29). YHWH's opening instructions to Moses in each case make the arrangement clear: 'speak' – 'command' – x – 'command' – 'speak', with the central speech not including any reference whatsoever as to the need or even manner in which Moses is to relay its substance to the sons of Israel. Numbers 36 does not contain direct divine speech (see Frevel 2009: 115), and should be separated as forming a narrative inclusio with 27:1–11.

> 1. Speak to the sons of Israel and say to them, 'When you pass over the Jordan to the land of Canaan, you will dispossess all the inhabitants of the land'
>
> 2. Command the sons of Israel and say to them, 'When you come into the land of Canaan, this is the land which will fall to you as an inheritance, the land of Canaan by her borders' (Moses' fulfilment, 34:13–15)
>
>> 3. These are the names of the men who will divide the inheritance of the land for you . . .
>
> 4. Command the sons of Israel, and they will give to the Levites from the inheritance of their holding . . .
>
> 5. Speak to the sons of Israel and say to them, 'When you pass over the Jordan into the land of Canaan, you will select for yourselves cities'

With this aerial view, other connections surface. YHWH's first speech clears the land of idolatry, and his fifth speech is concerned with avoiding the land's defilement by the shedding of innocent blood since he will be dwelling in the land. The latter concern enables one to understand more deeply that Canaanite idolatry also defiles the land and must be cleared out so that YHWH may dwell in the land with his people. Three transgressions defile the land: idolatry, murder and sexual abominations (cf. Frymer-Kensky 1983: 407–408). Through the prophet Ezekiel, YHWH addresses both bloodshed and idolatry as defiling the land: 'I poured my fury upon them (Israel) for the blood which they shed on the land, and for their idols by which they defiled her (the land)' (36:18). The second and fourth speeches, by contrast, pertain to inheritance, the boundaries of the inheritance for the tribes, and the cities 'from their inheritance' which will be given to the Levites – corresponding precisely to the outer and inner camps, respectively, and demonstrating how the community's life in the land is patterned after that of Israel's Camp. The central speech, 'These are the names', is secluded as the culminating speech, wherein Israelite princes, under the leadership of Eleazar the priest and Joshua son of Nun, will divide the land to their respective tribes. Part of the significance relates to the speech's function as a foretaste of the giving of the land. More than this, these princes of the second generation recall the previous list of princes (Num. 13:1–16), which had concluded with 'These are the names of the men whom Moses sent to scout the land' (13:16) and which had ended in disastrous failure. Brilliantly, while ten princes had failed, slandering the land, here ten princes – since those of Gad and Reuben are not included – now divide the land on behalf of YHWH for their tribes. Once more, the notion of *tikkun*, repair, is prominent, as the second set of ten princes will reverse the catastrophic faithlessness of the first generation's ten scouts. 'These (*'ēlleh*) are the names' (34:17), moreover, turns out to be central within the broader structure of the section as well, the centre of an inclusion: 'These are the journeys' (33:1) and 'These are the commandments and judgements' (36:13). More than mere legal requirements, these divine speeches, as G. J. Wenham points out (1981b: 257), are implicit promises from YHWH God, that he will, along with the gift of land, give his people victory over their enemies and pursue their holiness, even as he abides in their midst.

One curiosity remains related to this literary outline; namely, the fact that only speeches 1 and 4 include an introductory formula verbatim: 'And YHWH spoke to Moses in the plains of Moab by Jordan near Jericho, saying' (33:50; 35:1). This feature yields a twofold movement within the five speeches, the first comprised of speeches 1–3, and the second of speeches 4–5. Observing the subject matter of each speech, including the parallel between speeches 2 and 4, and between 1 and 5, the puzzle is resolved so as to reinforce the entire composition. The first formula (33:50) introduces speeches that concern the 'outer camp', the twelve tribes of Israel, while the second (35:1) introduces speeches that concern the 'inner camp', the Levites. The formulae function, then, as division markers, designating the division between the tribes and the Levites, within the unified composition whereby the land assumes the Camp structure as the new locale for the covenant community with YHWH in its midst (see Table 29).

Table 29: YHWH's final speeches

Focus on the tribes' place		
A	Speech 1	YHWH spoke to Moses in the plains of Moab by the Jordan near Jericho saying Speak to the sons of Israel: *dispossessing Canaanites* / *(land's defilement by idolatry)* (33:50–56)
B	Speech 2	YHWH spoke to Moses saying Command the sons of Israel: *delineating tribal lands* (34:1–15)
Focus on the Levites' place		
B'	Speech 4	YHWH spoke to Moses in the plains of Moab by the Jordan near Jericho saying Command the sons of Israel: *delineating Levitical cities* (35:1–8)
A'	Speech 5	YHWH spoke to Moses saying Speak to the sons of Israel: *banishment of accidental killer* / *land's defilement by blood-guilt* (35:9–34)

Turning to Numbers 34:1–15, some scholars take the boundaries as ideal (cf. G. B. Gray 1903: 452–453), while others, noting the detailed nature of the account, look for historical reference points (e.g. Mazar 1986; Kallai 1997; Levin 2006), including comparison with other boundary lists (see Aharoni 1979: 61–93), such as Ezekiel 47 and Joshua 15 (see Hutchens 1993; Levin 2006). Levin points out that the 'sites mentioned are not precise points along a boundary-line in the modern sense, but rather towns, whose hinterlands or surrounding villages and fields were within the delineated territory' (2006: 71; for the relation to purity concerns, see Hutchens 1993). Lack of any reference to Transjordan in verses 1–12 has tended to discourage attempts at understanding the land of Canaan's boundaries as either idealistic or reflecting a geopolitical reality, but this is to miss the literary context whereby Moses immediately addresses the lands east of the Jordan (vv. 13–15). Within the narrative flow, as Stubbs observes (2009: 244), the 'description of the physical boundaries of the land provides some sense of completion to the story of the journey of Israel' – details are thus no barrier to the presentation of Israel's boundaries as an ideal (cf. Davies 1995b: 350).

Numbers 35:1–8 comprises the fourth of YHWH's final five speeches, all related to the land. The structure is straightforward, beginning with the basic command for Israel to give the Levites cities and pasturelands (vv. 1–3), followed by details related to the pasturelands (vv. 4–5) and then to the cities (vv. 6–8).

Numbers 35:9–34 relates the instructions for the cities of asylum, beginning with their function (vv. 9–15), the qualifications for obtaining asylum (vv. 16–28) and the logic of the cities of asylum; namely, to prevent defilement of the land wherein YHWH dwells in the midst of his people (vv. 29–34). The cities of asylum are intimated in Exodus 21:13–14, explained in Numbers 35:9–34, in Deuteronomy 4:41–43 and 19:1–13, realized in Joshua 20, referenced in 1 Chronicles 6:54–81 and are related at least somewhat to narratives in 1 Kings 1:50–53 and 2:28–34. Source-critical scholars, according to their varied dating of purported strands, come with 'radically different' presentations in their historical reconstructions of the cities of refuge (Rofé 1986: 207). The different emphases on the legislation, however, are readily explained by the distinct concerns of each book, our focus being on the agenda of Numbers 35 within its literary context.

Comment

33:1–49: Israel's journey from Egypt to the plains of Moab

With the lengthy and eventful stay at Mount Sinai, taking up the second half of Exodus, the entirety of Leviticus and the first ten chapters of Numbers, it is easy to forget that the central books of the Torah narrate a *journey*: Israel's journey from Egypt, which began after the first Passover celebration, to the plains of Moab, from which Moses will deliver the speeches of Deuteronomy before his death and Israel's conquest of the land of Canaan under the leadership of Joshua. Numbers 33 summarizes Israel's journeys (vv. 1–49) as a prelude to YHWH's charge through Moses for Israel to dispossess the Canaanites (vv. 50–56). The importance of the present chapter relates not only to Numbers but structurally and thematically to the Pentateuch. Having completed the journeys that began at Exodus 13:17–22 after the Passover sacrifice and which continued through Numbers 21, and having resolved circumstances related to the Transjordan (Num. 22 – 32), the list of journeys provides the hinge by which to focus entirely on the immediate concerns of life in the land of Canaan (cf. Milgrom 1990: 277). The list of journeys, moreover, is Janus-faced, looking back to the distribution of Transjordan and forward to the distribution of the land of Canaan in the remaining chapters (cf. Frevel 2009: 116). The summary nature of the chapter serves as a momentum-gaining restart, for the last subsection's focus on Israel's inheritance of the land of Canaan (chs. 33–36).

While forty-two stations (with forty-one journeys) are narrated, the effect of the list is to unify them into one continuous journey from Egypt to the lands of Moab. Although the journeys may be divided into two paragraphs, related to the first and second generations of Israel (vv. 1–39, 40–49), the solidarity of the two generations is established by the continuum of this one journey from exile to the land. Generally, the sites of verses 6–15, from Succoth to the wilderness of Sinai, correspond with Exodus 13:17 – 19:1, and those of verses 16–49, from the wilderness of Sinai to the plains of Moab, with Numbers 10:11 – 22:1 (Olson 1996: 184). The suggested meanings for some of the place-names add colour to Israel's journeys with YHWH through the wilderness, *TgPs-J* containing many such explanatory glosses (see McNamara and Clarke 1995: 284–286; names also taken from Levine 2000: 519–522; Allen 2012: 427–429, 432): Succoth (booths, the place that seven clouds of Glory covered), Pi Hahiroth (mouth of burning), Migdol (tower), Baal Zephon (Baal of the north), Marah (bitter spring), Elim (place of trees, terebinths), Yam Suph ('sea of end' or, more commonly, 'sea of reeds'), Dophka (beaten), Rephidim ('spreading', 'because their hands were neglectful of the words of the Law'), Kibroth Hattaavah (graves of lust), Hazeroth ('settlements' or 'courtyards'), Rithmah (binding, place of Broam trees), Rimmon Perez (pomegranate gorge, whose fruit is firm), Libnah (white, a place built of brick), Kehelathah (assembly, a place where Korah and his company gathered against Moses and Aaron), Mount Shepher (mount of beauty, mountain whose fruits were beautiful), Haradah ('frightening' or 'trembling', 'a place where they were anxious about the evilness of the plague'), Makheloth (place of assembly), Tahath (foot of the mountain), Mithcah (sweetness, a place of sweet waters), Moseroth (bands, place of chastisement), Bene Jaakan (sons of Ya'aqan, wells of distress), Hor Haggidgad (hollow or cave of Gidgad, cliffs), Jotbathah (pleasantness, good and restful place), Abronah (regions beyond, the ford), Ezion Geber (mighty trees), Kadesh (sanctuary), Mount Hor (Hor the mountain), Zalmonah ('resemblance' or 'darkness', 'a place of briars and thorns'), Oboth (water skins), Iyye-Abarim (ruins of the passes), Dibon Gad (built up by Gad, Dibon the chance), Almon Diblathaim (perhaps 'hidden figs', 'there the well was hidden from them because they had abandoned the words of the Law which are sweet as figs'), mountains of Abarim (the mountains beyond, ... before the place of Moses' grave). Israel's final encampment stretches from Beth-Jeshimoth to Abel-Shittim, that is from 'wasteland' to 'acacia trees' (Levine 2000: 522) or from 'place of desolation' to 'brook of the acacias' (Allen 2012: 432), perhaps symbolically summing up their journeys. Such an approach resonates with Scolnic's proposal that 'if Num. 33 is a map at all, it is a map of symbolic geography, based on theological rather than topographical considerations' (1995: 100). Shamah, who takes 8 as signifying the covenant relationship, points out that from Sinai the eighth station is *qĕhēlātâ*, related to the 'day of assembly' at Sinai (Deut. 9:10; 10:4; 18:16), which is followed by *har-šāper*, 'the mountain where the shofar was blown' and *ḥărādâ* (trembling), where the nation trembled, noting that 'the words *har*, *shofar*, and *vayeḥerad* are all attested in the same Exodus 19:16 verse describing the lawgiving' (2011: 848).

1–2. The opening word 'These' (*'ēlleh*) is typical for an archival document, including genealogies and land allotments (Davies 1974: 48–49; Scolnic 1995; Roskop 2011: 230–231). This verse serves as a heading, identifying the list of journeys as those of the sons of Israel, adding three significant descriptions: 'who went forth from the land of Egypt' (cf. 26:4) 'according to their hosts' (cf. Exod. 12:41, 51), and 'by the hand of Moses and Aaron', summarizing the exodus out of Egypt and ensuing march in a triumphant manner. Aaron's death will be noted in verse 38, forming an inclusio with verse 1, marking out the 'generation of the exodus'. All of the journeys, including those within the 'lost years', the thirty-eight years of judgement in the wilderness, are nevertheless part of purposeful and spiritual movement *from* Egypt and *toward* the land of Canaan, for the people of God as a whole, so that every individual journey within the wilderness becomes part of the original departure from Egypt. Intriguingly, the focus of the heading's language is not so much on the places as encampments, but on the places as 'going-forths', places of departure, and on the journeys themselves to the land. There is a forward thrust, leading naturally into YHWH's charge in verses 50–56. Noting the militaristic connotations of 'journeys' (as 'marches'), 'hosts' and 'by the hand of Moses and Aaron', with *bĕyad* possibly signifying 'under the (military) command of' (c. 2 Sam. 18:2), Scolnic reads verse 1 as describing Israel in terms of an army's ordered and triumphant marches under the command of its generals (1995: 72–76). The language here echoes the triumphant chord of Israel's departure from Sinai verbatim, lending the whole account an aura of exultant victory:

10:28: *'ēlleh masʿê bĕnê-yiśrā'ēl* . . .

33:1: *'ēlleh masʿê bĕnê-yiśrā'ēl* . . .

The second verse is chiastically arranged: 'their going-forths, according to their journeys' – 'their journeys, according to their going-forths', yielding a fitting introduction to the list of journeys (cf. Cole 2003: 344). Hirsch makes an interesting homiletical point, aligning the first part with God's perspective, so that the departures were for the educative sake of the journeys, progressively attaining new goals, while the second part reveals Israel's perspective, being dissatisfied with every station, and simply wanting to depart (2007a: 657). Although there is every reason to presume he did write at YHWH's bidding, the clause 'by the word of YHWH' (*'al-pî yhwh*) is not linked to Moses' writing but to Israel's journeys, which are everywhere described in this manner (see Exod.

17:1), especially in Numbers 9, where the description occurs seven times (vv. 18 [twice], 20 [twice], 23 three times), and climactically in chapter 10 as Israel's Camp first sets out (10:13; cf. 13:3). The theology of the present chapter is founded on the iconic portrayal of Israel following after YHWH's Cloud in the wilderness (9:15–23; Exod. 40:36–38). The same ideal is expressed through the prophet Jeremiah, as YHWH declares: 'I remember you, the loving-kindness of your youth, the love of your espousals, how you followed after me in the wilderness, in a land not sown' (2:2). At a more basic level, to declare that the journeys were 'at YHWH's command' is to communicate that they were, each and every one, *necessary*, an integral part of God's wise purposes for his people.

Adding to the positive portrayal of Israel's long journey through the wilderness is the omission of any reference to murmuring and rebellion. Through YHWH's own faithfulness, and in spite of Israel's own rebellions, the marriage-like covenant relationship established at Sinai held and he securely brought Israel to the land of Canaan. Obtaining the aerial view of Israel's precise forty-two stations, enables one to reflect more deeply on the reality that through the seeming trials, chaos and digressions of history, our sovereign God is indeed carrying out his purposes and working out all things for the good of his people (cf. Rom. 8:28). This point brings out the significance of the report that Moses recorded the journeys with their stations, which goes well beyond its being an explicit instance of his writing activity (cf. Exod. 17:14; 24:4; 34:28; Deut. 31:9, 22, 24). *Why* does Moses write these journeys down? What use would the record serve? Moses understood the significance of the journey itself. What is the Torah if not a book of journeys through the wilderness, a testimony of God's relationship with his people in the wilderness, a guide for all who realize that life is a pilgrimage? There is no pause in narration between Egypt and Canaan; on the contrary, most of the text is about the era of transition, the passage through the wilderness – and Israel's call to follow her divine Husband closely and devotedly. No arrival along the way is final, no station is lasting; each station is temporary, a stage along the way of a greater pilgrimage. The stages are treasured, however, because each one is a step closer to the fulfilment of YHWH's promises, and a testimony to his faithfulness – this is the record of Israel's divinely guided journey *home*, to the land where they would dwell with YHWH God.

3–5. Describing the original place of departure (Ramesses/Egypt), these verses include an unusual amount of descriptive narrative, a feature recurring only once more (in vv. 37–39). Many of the turns of phrases mirror or recall the account in Exodus 11 – 14, defining Israel's departure out of Egypt through the lens of Passover: YHWH had declared the month of Abib would be the beginning of months, with the Passover sacrifice performed on the fourteenth day (Exod. 12:1–6); he would 'strike all the firstborn in the land of Egypt . . . and against all the gods of Egypt I will execute judgement' (Exod. 12:12; cf. 12:29–30), quoted now with the language of fulfilment; Israel departed 'with a high hand' (Exod. 14:8). The first journey, from Ramesses to Succoth, 'with a high hand' in the sense of boldly and triumphantly, likely with military connotations, sets the tone for receiving the whole list as a victorious march (cf. Scolnic 1995: 80).

The patriarchs' journeys had also begun with a kind of exodus experience (see Gen.15:7; Deut. 26:4–10), just as the spiritual journey of every one of God's people begins with an exodus (Morales 2020: 19–36).

6–15. The journeys from Succoth to Etham, including the latter's description as 'on the outskirts of the wilderness', and from Etham to Pi-Hahiroth, including references to 'before Baal-Zephon' and 'Migdol', are narrated in Exodus (13:20; 14:1–2, 9), as is the journey through the midst of the sea to the wilderness (14:21–31), which implies but does not actually describe the miracle of parting the sea, and the 'three days' journey to Marah (15:22–23), then on to Elim (15:27) (see Fritz 2016: 235–252). 'Etham' is the Egyptian name, whereas the Hebr. 'Shur' is used in Exodus 15:22 – both meaning 'wall, fortification' (Milgrom 1990: 279). In Exodus 13:20–22, the journey from Succoth to the encampment at 'Etham on the outskirts of the wilderness' is first given, along with an extremely significant point:

> YHWH went (*hōlēk*) before them by day in a pillar of cloud, to lead them on the way, and by night in a pillar of fire, to shine light upon them, to go by day and by night. The pillar of cloud did not depart by day, nor the pillar of fire by night, from before the people.

As soon as Israel entered 'the outskirts of the wilderness' YHWH had appeared in the pillar of cloud and pillar of fire to guide and protect his people, recalling once more the statements of Israel's following after the Cloud in the wilderness (Exod. 40:36–38; Num. 9:15–23), which underlies the theology of the present list: it was only when the Cloud lifted that Israel would break camp to set out on the journey – 'At the word of YHWH they encamped, and at the word of YHWH they journeyed forth; the charge of YHWH they kept, at the word of YHWH by the hand of Moses' (Num. 9:23). *TgPs-J* identifies Succoth as 'the place which seven clouds of Glory covered' (McNamara and Clarke 1995: 284; cf. *MekhSh* 20.4). The itinerary displays YHWH as divine Shepherd and King, and Israel, his flock, marching forth as his earthly hosts.

Why is there no mention of the bitter waters in Marah, while Elim's details, its having twelve springs and seventy palm trees, are given? Miracles such as turning bitter (undrinkable) waters into sweet (drinkable) are by-passed, while the geographical features of Elim, that it was a place for respite, are noted, perhaps because those features factored into the choice or length of encampment. Both Exodus 15:27 and Numbers 33:9 describe Elim *before* Israel's encampment: the Israelites first 'came' (*wayyābō'û*) to Elim, then the description of 'twelve springs of water and seventy palm trees' is given, followed by the statement that they 'encamped there' (*wayyaḥănû-šām*). Ascribing symbolic significance to this ideal scene is nearly inescapable: with the number twelve signifying the twelve tribes of Israel and seventy representing the nations, the scene may portray Israel's vocation as a source of life-giving blessing to the nations (*TPs-J*, ad loc., compares the twelve springs to the twelve tribes and the seventy palm trees to the seventy sages granted a share of the Spirit in Num. 11).

Exodus 16:1 gives the journey from Elim to the Wilderness of Sin, omitting reference to the Sea of Suph, and Exodus 17:1 gives the journey from the Wilderness of Sin to Rephidim, omitting reference to Dophkah and Alush, but includes, as with 33:14, the fact that 'there was no water there for the people to drink'. Bypassing comments regarding the Shur wilderness, Mara and Kadesh, the itinerary offers two comments: the natural abundance of water and shade in Elim, and the lack of water at Rephidim, perhaps serving as singular examples of the highs and lows, comforts and hardships, of the journey (cf. Rimon 2014c: 460–461). Since, within the literary context of the Torah, readers know of YHWH's wondrous supply of water from the rock at Rephidim (Exod. 17), perhaps the two examples relate to YHWH's providential (Elim) and supernatural (Rephidim) supplies of water in the wilderness. Y. Kahn, observing how these expansions occur in the opening stages of the wilderness journeys (vv. 3–14), with none in the verses of the wilderness 'wanderings' that follow (vv. 15–35), suggests the opening stages of the list form something of a narrative, relating how the people of Israel 'leave a civilized and irrigated land and follow the clouds of glory into the wilderness, armed only with a promise that they will eventually be taken to the Land of Israel' (2014b: 452).

Exodus 19:1–2 gives the journey from Rephidim to the Wilderness of Sinai, adding that it was the third month after the exodus out of Egypt and that Israel specifically camped 'before the mountain'. Almost incredibly there is not a single hint that 'Wilderness of Sinai' includes all the thunderous drama of YHWH's advent on the mountain, the covenant inauguration, the golden calf apostasy and subsequent judgement, the building of the divine Dwelling, along with the consecration and installation of Aaron's priesthood and inaugural worship service, nor of the establishment of the sacred Camp of Israel, the substance of Exodus 19 – 40, the whole of Leviticus, and the first ten chapters of Numbers are by-passed, yet the heading to this list had indeed made clear that only the journeys themselves are recounted (33:1–2).

16–17. Events along these journeys are narrated earlier, in chapters 11–12 (cf. 11:35). While the broad journey from the Wilderness of Sinai to the Wilderness of Paran is summarized in 10:12, with the Wilderness of Paran given as the general location for the episode of the scouts (cf. 12:16; 13:3), the Wilderness of Paran, which encompasses a wide, general region, is here perhaps subsumed under Hazeroth or exchanged for a more precise encampment, such as 'Rithmah' in verse 18 (Ashley, e.g. suggests the journey from Sinai to Kadesh has been mixed with the wilderness wandering stations, 1993: 630; cf. Aharoni 1979: 199). Assuming the former, then, these verses encompass Numbers 11 – 14. There is another possibility, however, which is strengthened by the fact that, generally, in comparison with the narratives of Exodus and Numbers, the list in Numbers 33 *adds* to our knowledge of places – the Wilderness of Paran, in other words, is an instance where the list detracts from what readers already know from Numbers itself, omitting a locale that is mentioned in previous narrative sections. From a source-critical perspective, Budd observes that all of P's stations are included except for the Wilderness of Paran, and speaks of 'the failure' to include a station that is 'important to the priestly story' (1984: 350, 357). Cross assumes 'Wilderness of Paran' got omitted through haplography, a scribe continuing at '*encamped* at Rithmah', having accidentally passed over '*encamped* at Wilderness of Paran' (1973: 315 n. 74; followed by Milgrom 1990: 330 n. 19). With Kadesh Barnea set within the Wilderness of Paran as the precise locale from which the scouts were sent, mentioned explicitly by Moses in the previous chapter (32:8; cf. 12:16; 13:26), Gane, too, 'raises a question that remains unresolved' (2004: 786): 'Why doesn't Numbers 33 mention the long stay at Kadesh?' Scolnic also asks, 'Why is there no mention of the wilderness of Pa'ran, as in Num. 10:12 and 12:16?', and remarks that 'Qadesh seems to be only an afterthought,' suggesting the possibility that the itinerary pre-dates traditions of Israel's failure to inherit the land (1995: 71, 86, 97–99). Bin-Nun similarly points out (2019b), 'There is no reference to the story of the scouts, to the crisis in its wake, or to the decree of forty more years in the wilderness. "Kadesh Barnea" in "the wilderness of Paran" is not even mentioned as a station!' The same astonishment is expressed by Rimon over 'this riddle' (2014c: 464):

> This is most surprising; after all, Kadesh-Paran is not a minor, insignificant station in *Benei Yisrael's* travels! This is where the spies give their report and the people cry, as a result of which they wander for another thirty-eight years in the wilderness. Surely this station is of great significance!

Rashi discerned and overcame the problem by having the Wilderness of Paran renamed 'Rithmah' after the scouts incident, a name he ingeniously connects to the 'Juniper plant' (*rōtem*), linked to the 'false tongue' in Psalm 120:3–4 (cf. 1997: 4:406; see Rimon 2014c: 464). In what the translator refers to as a 'slight disagreement' with Rashi, Abarbanel has the scouts being sent from the Kadesh of verse 36, stating that the nineteen stops since Hazeroth all occurred in fewer than two months, which, he explains, is why they were omitted from the main narrative – due to their swift and insignificant nature (2015: 330–331). Rimon suggests the likelihood that the route of Rithmah through to Ezion Geber (vv. 18b–35) is to be correlated with Israel's wanderings 'by way of the Reed Sea' (cf. 14:25), again, underscoring that Kadesh-Paran remains unaccounted for (2014c: 465). The omission is all the more odd by the inclusion of Kadesh Barnea in the next chapter, delineating the southern boundary of the land of Canaan (34:4). The inclusion of Kadesh Barnea, the place of the scouts' mission (13:1–26) and the failed attempt to enter the land (14:40–45), 'as a central site' of the southern border is considered by Levin to be 'one of the most peculiar aspects' of Numbers 34:1–12 (2006: 63). A deliberate omission of the Wilderness of Paran, which, as an argument from silence, must remain conjecture, would resolve these difficulties, and is an appealing idea given the other references to 'Wilderness of Paran' and 'Kadesh Barnea' within Numbers (12:16; 13:3, 26; 32:8). The book's audience would be expecting the now infamous Kadesh Barnea / Wilderness of Paran to appear and certainly note its obvious absence. As Schart states, Kadesh Barnea 'played the central role on the route from Sinai to Moab' (2013: 177). Shamah writes (2011: 847), 'It is as if mention of the station from where the scouts were sent is eliminated from the list at the point of transgression,' comparing the edit to Job's diatribe against the day of his birth, that it 'should not be counted among the days of the year, and should not be included in the count of the months' (Job 3:6). On the scenario of a purposeful omission, the rhetorical function would be to by-pass the failed inheritance of the land of Canaan by the first generation, which in turn serves to portray the whole list as one purposeful journey of Israel from Egypt to Canaan. In the sovereign purposes of YHWH God, and without mitigating human responsibility and accountability, this was the intended journey all along. Bin-Nun offers a similar explanation (2019b): 'Kadesh Barnea represents a crisis and failure on the way to the land of Israel. The book of journeys, in contrast, describes the journey that succeeded despite the crisis and the failure.' The omission of Kadesh-Paran conveys that the wandering in the wilderness was not meaningless, writes Rimon (2014c: 466–467), but part of the process of preparing Israel to enter the land – the wilderness years were not *only* punishment for sin but a necessary time of preparation. The march continues, its triumphant note unsullied by even the most disastrous of Israel's failures, proving the divine promises sure.

18–35. None of the eighteen stations listed here, after Hazeroth and until Kadesh in the Wilderness of Zin, have been mentioned thus far in the Torah, most not appearing in the rest of the HB. With the naming of 'Taberah' (11:3) and 'Kibroth Hattaavah' (11:34) as examples, it would not be surprising if names given by Moses to these wilderness encampments, which were not linked to events in the narrative, were lost to history save for the list itself – these were not established cities or villages, but stopping-places amid a wilderness region. The cluster of places in verses 31–33, however, are also noted in Deuteronomy. A journey from Bene-Jaakan to Moserah (= 'Moseroth'), reversing the order of Numbers 33:31, and, more challenging, placing Aaron's death and burial in Moserah, is given in Deuteronomy 10:6 (but see Deut. 32:50), while the journey from 'Gudgodah' (= 'Mount Gidgad') to Jotbathah, adding that Jotbathah was 'a land of rivers of waters', is recorded in Deuteronomy 10:7. Ezion-Geber (vv. 35, 36) is mentioned in Deuteronomy 2:8 (cf. 1 Kgs 9:26; 22:49; 2 Chr. 8:17; 20:36). The name 'Libnah' occurs outside the Torah (likely unconnected to this one; cf. Josh. 10:29 [twice], 31, 32, 39; 12:15; 15:42; 21:3; 2 Kgs 8:22; 19:8; 22:31; 24:18; 1 Chr. 6:57; 2 Chr. 21:10; Isa. 37:8; Jer. 52:1).

The narrative of Numbers, bypassing this era of divine judgement, resumes only at the dawn of the second generation (ch. 20). Listing the journeys and places here functions in a variety of ways, beyond reminding readers that a long period of Israel's life in the wilderness was omitted from the story. Recording the journeys amid the thirty-eight intervening years underscores not only God's continued providential care and guidance of his people throughout this time, but redeems those journeys as the early history of the second generation, who were born and/or grew into maturity throughout those years. That Moses continued to record the journeys throughout the punishment era is evidence of his own understanding that God had not abandoned his people, that these journeys, while spotted with the deaths of the first generation, were nevertheless stations of progress for the rising generation. Borrowing words from the apostle Paul, the second generation was not to lose heart, even amid the perishing of the older generation, for their light and momentary afflictions were working for them a far more exceedingly good life in the land (cf. 2 Cor. 4:16–17). While the wilderness of Paran station, where Israel had rejected the land, might have been omitted, these journeys were not for they comprised a significant part of the second generation's journey to the land, preparing them to grow into the role of YHWH's community which becomes official in Kadesh in the Wilderness of Zin (v. 36; cf. 20:1, 12). As such, the journeys link the original departure with the final arrival: though spanning two generations, their solidarity as 'Israel' enables a reading of Numbers 33:1–49 as one continuous journey from Egypt to the plains of Moab. The beautiful portrayal of Israel's Camp following YHWH's Cloud of Glory through the wilderness (Num. 9:15–23) is no less true for these journeys, and, indeed, the text gives no indication whatsoever that these journeys and stations should be thought of any differently from the rest. Even for the first generation, the daily mercies of God in this listing of journeys and encampments are evident, inasmuch as the average journey-encampment cycle would appear to have taken place only once every two years (see Rashi 1997: 4:404).

36–39. The journey from Kadesh to Mount Hor corresponds with the events of Numbers 20:22–29. As with the opening journey out of Ramesses, this section includes a mini-narrative. The story relates to the death of Aaron the priest, but includes thematic parallels with the opening narrative related to the exodus out of Egypt (vv. 3–4). Both texts include the following:

1. Narrative interpolations into the journey-station record.
2. The death of firstborn sons (Aaron).
3. Chronological references: 'fifteenth day of the first month' of the first year (v. 3), and 'first day of the fifth month' in the 'fortieth year' (v. 38).
4. References to the exodus out of Egypt.
5. The only references to the name 'YHWH' within the travelogue.

Given these similarities, the two passages may be understood to form headings for the first and second generations' journeys, respectively. The first generation was released to journey through the Passover death of firstborn sons, even as the second generation was released to make progress to the land of Canaan once Aaron, who represented the first generation as their priestly mediator, died in the fortieth year, marking the end to YHWH's judgement. The thought relates to the manslayer's need to remain in a city of refuge until the death of the high priest, whose death apparently yielded a general atonement for the generation he served (see 35:25–34). 'Aaron's death symbolizes the passing of the entire generation and the end of wandering in the wilderness,' writes Rimon (2014c: 467; cf. Twersky 2022: 39); 'After his death, the nation can enter the land.' Aaron dies on 'the first day', a new moon of the fifth month, as Miriam had apparently died on New Year's Day, a new moon of the first month (20:1), and Moses on the new moon of the eleventh month (Deut. 1:3; 32:48–50) (see LeFebvre 2019: 72–73).

Taking these verses on their own, a feature that stands out is the lack of any reference to the circumstances that led to Aaron's death, maintaining the optimistic note of the recorded journeys. The note functions, as Scolnic observes (1995: 90), to provide chronological bearings. More, Aaron's ascent of Mount Hor is validated as being 'by the word of YHWH' (*'al-pî yhwh*), the only such attribution within the list, even though the introduction had already conveyed that all the journeys were 'by the word of YHWH' (v. 2). As with Israel's journeys through the wilderness, the last journey of the nation's high priest, Aaron's ascent to the summit of Mount Hor to die, was no less by God's command, part of his divine purposes – which also included the death of the first generation and even that of Moses himself – for Israel's spiritual journey to the land. Aaron's age of 123 years is given, his longevity conveying a further mark of honour.

40–49. These journeys encompass the second generation's experience as narrated in Numbers 21 – 25. Oddly verse 40 includes a parallel reference to Numbers 21:1, narrating how the Canaanite king of Arad had heard of Israel's arrival, omitting his ensuing response and Israel's ultimate victory. The likely function of this mention of 'the Canaanite' is to mark Israel's arrival near 'the land of Canaan', where he was dwelling. As soon as Aaron the priest dies (vv. 37–39), the second generation enters a new stage in the wilderness journeys – Israel's triumphant marches anticipate the conquest of the land. The strength of the second generation may be seen in that their journeys, as the assembly of YHWH, began with mourning the death of Aaron and progressed under the shadow of the nations' threats (Edom, Arad, Sihon, Og, Moab, Midian).

The stations of Zalmonah, Punon and Almon-Diblathaim occur nowhere else in the Torah or the rest of the HB. Ibn Ezra suggested the possibility that Almon-Diblathaim may be a general name encompassing the journeys related to Beer, Mattanah and Nahaliel (cf. Num. 21:18; 1999: 172, 257). Other stations, such as Oboth and Iye-Abarim, overlap with previous narratives (21:10, 11), with Abel-Shittim being the infamous locale of Israel's apostasy (25:1) – although as with other sites of notorious sin, the negative associations are completely suppressed. In the previous chapter, we read that 'Gad built Dibon' (32:34), so that here the place is called 'Dibon-Gad' (33:45), whereas in Joshua we find that Dibon was eventually given to the tribe of Reuben (Josh. 13:17). If given full appellative force, Iye-Abarim would be translated 'the ruins on the other side', and the same may be done with 'mountains of Abarim' (J. M. Miller 1989: 581), clearly a general locale, but that also occurs in the sg. 'mount Abarim' elsewhere (Num. 27:12; Deut. 32:49). Beth-Jesimoth occurs three times, outside the Pentateuch (Josh. 12:3; 13:20; Ezek. 25:9). The precise station 'in the plains of Moab by the Jordan near Jericho' recurs as a unifying clause for the last major section of Numbers (26:3, 63; 33:48, 50; 35:1; 36:13) – it is from here that YHWH will give the charge to the sons of Israel to destroy all elements of idolatry when possessing the land (v. 50). With 'the land of Canaan' (v. 40) and 'encamped by the Jordan . . . in the plains of Moab' (49) bookending the second generation's final stations, the Jordan River being the place of crossing into the land of Canaan, the record of Israel's journeys come to a place of culmination and triumphant expectation. YHWH's next speech to Moses for the sons of Israel begins, 'When you pass over the Jordan to the land of Canaan' (v. 51). In this way, Frevel observes (2009: 115), Israel's current encampment on the plains of Moab is configured as a conclusion to the exodus out of Egypt. The journey, writes Cole (2003: 345), traces the steady historical fulfilment of YHWH's ancient promise to Abraham, 'To your offspring I will give this land' (Gen. 12:7; 13:14–17; 15:7, 18–21; 17:8; 24:7; etc.)

33:50–56 YHWH's first speech: possessing the land by clearing it of idolatry

50–52. This first of YHWH's last five speeches continues logically from the previous twofold mention that Israel had encamped 'by the Jordan near Jericho . . . they encamped by the Jordan' (vv. 48–49), opening not only with the locale 'in the plains of Moab by the Jordan near Jericho', but instructing the sons of Israel, 'When you yourselves pass over the Jordan . . .' The journeys of 33:3–49 brought Israel to the Jordan, and now they are instructed as to their first act and priority after crossing the Jordan, to dispossess the land of her Canaanite inhabitants, wiping out all traces of idolatry from the land. The military flavour of the itinerary, as YHWH leads forth his earthly hosts on a royal campaign, makes for a natural transition to the present charge from YHWH for the sons of Israel to dispossess the Canaanites, and destroy their idolatrous practices. Before the land can be repurposed as the arena for Israel's relationship with YHWH God, who will dwell among them in the land, it must be cleared of defiling idols. By participating in the destruction of idols and high places, Israelites, much like their participation in the war against Midian (ch. 31), not only demonstrate loyalty to YHWH but will be reaffirmed in their commitment to him and his purposes.

There is emphasis on the reality that Moses' audience, the sons of Israel, will finally and actually enter the land of Canaan: When 'you yourselves' (*'attem*) pass over the Jordan to the land of Canaan. Structurally, verses 52–53 and 55–56, both relating Israel's dispossession of the inhabitants of Canaan, enclose the central verse 54, which focuses on Israel's dwelling in the land (cf. Knoppers 2004: 140). The opening of the inclusion, verse 52, gives the positive guideline to dispossess the inhabitants and destroy all vestiges of their idolatry, while the closing verses, 55–56, warn of a negative scenario whereby Israel does not dispossess all the inhabitants. The instructions are twofold. First, Israel is to dispossess the land's inhabitants 'from before you', language that implies military campaigns whereby YHWH, fighting for his people, drives out the Canaanites before them (cf. Exod. 23:29–31; 34:24; Lev. 18:24; 20:23; Num. 10:35; 32:21; Deut. 2:21–22; 4:38; 6:19; 7:1, 20–22; 9:4–5; 12:29–30; 18:12; 33:27). Second, after dispossessing the inhabitants, Israelites are to destroy all remnants of their idolatrous culture – the latter, defiling the land with idolatry, is what leads to the former, to

Canaanites losing the land. Indeed, if Israel also goes the way of idolatry, then just as YHWH 'had thought to do' to the Canaanites, he 'will do' to Israel (v. 56), a point made abundantly clear in the Torah (see Exod. 23:24; 34:13–14; Lev. 18:24–30; Deut. 8:19–20; 9:4–6; 12:1–4, 29–31; 18:9–14). Ridding the land of idolatry begins with ridding it of idolaters, then moves to a threefold dealing with the remnants of their culture: 'destroy' or 'cause to perish' (*'ābad*) all their 'carved images' (*maśkît*; cf. also Lev. 26:1; Tg interprets as 'places of worship'), 'destroy' (*'ābad*) all their 'molten images' (*ṣalmê massēkōtām*; cf. also Exod. 34:17; Lev. 19:4) and 'demolish' (*šāmad*) all their 'high places' (*bāmôt*; cf. also Lev. 26:30; Num. 21:28; Deut. 32:13; 33:29). Note the comprehensiveness in YHWH's instructions to rid the land of idolators and idols, employing a fourfold use of 'all'(*kol*): *all* the inhabitants, *all* their carved images, *all* their molten images, *all* their high places – he brooks absolutely no compromise in his call for Israel to heed the first and second commands (Exod. 20:1–6; Deut. 5:6–10), summarized in Deuteronomy as a threefold loving YHWH your God with *all* your heart, *all* your soul, and *all* your strength (6:5). The term 'images' (*ṣelem*) here is the last of six uses in the Torah, the other five references found in Genesis, mostly related to human beings as the 'image' of God (Gen. 1:26, 27 [twice]; 9:6; cf. 5:3). While the Canaanites filled the land with idols, the images of beasts and birds and humans, the Israelites will themselves fill the land with images of God. The structural and thematic parallel between YHWH's first (33:50–56) and last (35:9–34) speeches is manifest: just as shedding the blood of human beings, because they are made in God's image (Gen. 1:26–27; 9:6), would defile the land (35:32–34), so here the worship of idols – images – defiles the land (Jer. 3:2, 9). Both prohibitions have in view God's dwelling in the land (stated explicitly in 35:34).

53–54. Only after dispossessing the Canaanites *and* clearing the land of the vestiges of their idolatrous culture does the statement come 'And (or *then*) you will possess the land and dwell in her,' almost as if Israel, like YHWH, could not dwell in a defiled land. The first speech emphasizes Israel's dwelling in the land (33:53), the last YHWH's dwelling in the land (35:34), mutually reinforcing the covenant relationship. The basis for Israel's life in the land is clear: for ('because', *kî*) to you I *have given* (*nātattî*) the land to possess her. Observed previously, the land will be inherited by lot. Aside from their cultic use (Lev. 16:8–10), lots occur in the Pentateuch only in Numbers and only with reference to the division of the land, seven times (26:55–56; 33:54 [twice]; 34:13; 36:2–3). It is no accident that after the reference to the census, which had dividing the land by lot as its purpose (26:52–56), the remaining five instances all occur within the last subsection (chs. 33–36), beginning with the present text, which essentially repeats the information given at the census (26:52–56), using similar expressions, such as 'by lot', 'the lot', 'inheritance', 'the land', 'according to the . . . tribes of their fathers they will inherit' and 'for the large you will cause his inheritance to be large, and for the small you will cause his inheritance to be small'. The inheritance of the land, given by YHWH, does not occur merely by passing over the Jordan nor by the conquest of the Canaanites – that is all preliminary. The land, again as in the census instruction (26:52-56), is given from YHWH (1) by lot, which falls by his sovereign determination since 'its every judgement is from YHWH' (Prov. 16:33), and (2) according to their 'clans'/'tribes of your fathers' in terms of the size of the inheritance, whether large or small. The momentous occasion, then, is focused on the lot.

55-56. Forming an inclusion with the opening of YHWH's speech (vv. 51-52), these verses present a threat in the event Israel does not follow the instructions of dispossessing the Canaanites, which necessarily entails not ridding the land of their idolatry – 'But if' (*wĕ'im*). On the scenario that Canaanites 'are left (*yātar*) from among them', there will be a twofold result. First, those Canaanites who remain will be as 'barbs'(*ś-k-k*) in your eyes and as 'thorns' (*ṣānîn*) in your sides. The idea seems to be that even a small remnant of Canaanites – even the smallest deviation from YHWH's instructions, or the slightest level of incompleteness in Israel's obedience – will prove a torment, even as a little barb in the eye may cause excruciating pain, or a thorn in one's side. Alternatively, there may be two different ideas at play if 'barbs' is understood rather as blinding Israel – that is, misleading them away from YHWH (see Exod. 23:33; cf. Nachmanides 1975: 387; Milgrom 1990: 284). Tolerating even a small remnant of idolaters would eventually blind Israel to the heinous offence of idolatry in the eyes of God, while 'thorns in your sides' would still refer to the aspect of hostility. Milgrom aligns 'barbs in your eyes' (v. 55aß) with Israel's call to 'destroy cult objects' (v. 52aßb), with the idea that Canaanites will 'sting Israel with their cult' and 'harass Israel militarily' as two separate problematic issues (1990: 500-501). The next statement explains that these inhabitants 'will be hostile to you' on the land wherein you are dwelling. The choice of 'hostile' (*ṣārar*) recalls the three other times this language is used in Numbers: in the scenario of war in your land against 'the hostile (enemy) who is hostile' (*haṣṣar haṣṣōrēr*) against you (10:9), and twice related to Midianites (25:17, 18). Given these previous uses, Israel could anticipate both military hostility and cultural seduction into sexual immorality and idolatry (cf. Josh. 23:11-13). Although in failing to drive out the Canaanites, Israel would face such a dire reality (see Judges 3:5-6), the tenor of the closing section of Numbers is full of hope.

The latter potential of apostasy explains the second result of Israel's incomplete obedience in dispossessing the inhabitants. Second, YHWH will do to Israel as he had intended to do to the Canaanites. 'This verse', writes Allen (2012: 434), 'encapsulates the theology of the land *in nuce*. It is God's land. He will give and will take it back as he wills.' When Israel becomes like the original inhabitants of the land whom YHWH intended to destroy and remove from the land, then Israel too will be judged and exiled. Inasmuch as this threatened path would be taken by Israel, eventually incurring divine judgement and exile, Ashley observes how these verses (33:50 – 36:13) anticipate and introduce the literature of Deuteronomy and Joshua through Kings (1993: 634). These warnings apply within the context of sanctification and spiritual warfare: wilfully failing to put to death the deeds of the flesh, complacency in mortifying the old nature, and flirtations with sin often result in tragic spiritual disasters that, even when healed, leave behind their scars – corruption spreads like cancer, and God will not be mocked (cf. Luke 9:23; Rom. 8:13; 1 Cor. 9:26–27; Gal. 6:7–8, 14; Col. 3:5–6).

34:1–15 YHWH's second speech: defining the land of Canaan

1–12: The land of Canaan

1–2. The borders of the land of Israel are, much as the structure of the Camp had been (chs. 1–4), divinely revealed, the subject of YHWH's speaking to Moses, which is then conveyed to Israel as a divine 'injunction' (*ṣāwāh*). In its immediate context, the text is structurally and thematically complemented by YHWH's fourth speech concerning Levitical cities (35:1–8), and, as with all five speeches, carries the weight of YHWH's final instructions for Israel through Moses. While it is true that defining the land's boundaries is necessary since a host of commands apply only to life 'in the land' (cf. Hirsch 2007a: 668), yet the tenor of this passage, as with the last third of Numbers in general, is on the realization of possessing the land as YHWH's gift.

'When you come into the land, Canaan, this is the land' almost reads as if Canaan is waiting in pristine purity, verdant and vacant, for Israel simply to claim and enjoy. This portrayal, however, is in view of the previous speech by YHWH (33:50–56), and the order is instructive: only after the Canaanites have been dispossessed and the land cleansed of idolatry are the borders of Israel's inheritance described. Just as the gift of fashioned gold is given only after the dross has been melted away by fire, so YHWH's gift of the land is contemplated only after his fiery judgement has first removed its idolatrous defilement.

The adjective in 'This (*zō't*) is the land' is emphatic as it serves to introduce the details of verses 3–12. Although it may be argued that YHWH is concerned only with defining the lands to be inherited by the nine-and-a-half tribes, the adjective *zō't* does appear to function as excluding the lands east of the Jordan (cf. Seforno 1997: 818–819), and the following section also contains hints of a less than completely positive view of the Transjordan 'inheritance' (vv. 13–15). That the land 'will fall' (*tippōl*) to Israel as an inheritance has the method of casting lots in view (cf. Rashi, ad loc.), as with the complementary statement in verse 13.

The description of the land's boundaries begins with the south, the south-east outskirts of the Salt Sea (vv. 3–5, later known as the 'Dead Sea'), and then moves, clockwise and continuously, to the west (v. 6), the north (vv. 7–9) and ending with the east (vv. 10–12), completing the 'circle' – note the use of *sābîb* that closes verse 12.

3–5. The 'southern side' (or 'edge of Negev', *pĕ'at-negeb*) is located from the Wilderness of Zin beside Edom, bounded on the east by the Salt Sea and the west by the Great Sea, stretching through Kadesh Barnea to the Wadi of Egypt, which formed a natural boundary between Egypt and the land of Canaan. The locations of Scorpions' Ascent and Zin (unless conflated with 'Wilderness of Zin') are unknown (cf. Aharoni 1979: 63). The absence of Kadesh in the previous chapter's journey log is all the more notable given the place's surprising appearance here (cf. Levin 2006: 63–66). Levin makes the crucial observation that the scouts episode, especially Numbers 13:21–26, appears to be 'interwoven' with the present text, since they had scouted the land 'from the wilderness of Zin to Rehob, at Lebo-Hamath', and return to Moses 'at Kadesh in the wilderness of Paran' (2006: 56). One rhetorical feature of this repetition, as Olson points out (1996: 187), is to reassure 'the new generation that the original promise of the land to the old wilderness generation has been extended in its entirety to the new generation'. Especially evident in the next passage, where ten princes from the second generation are chosen by God to divide the land among the tribes (34:16–29), YHWH's speeches conclude Numbers by presenting a victorious reversal to the first generation's disastrous failure.

As Judah's tribe will inherit the majority of the southern region, Judah's pre-eminence here parallels that of the tribal encampment, which had begun with its place of prominence in the east (see 2:3), and continues as Caleb is named first in the list of those who will divide the inheritance among the tribes (34:19).

6. Just as the southern westward boundary was 'seaward' (*hayyāmmā*), the Great Sea, the Mediterranean, naturally serves as the western border for the rest of the land. With the brief exception of David and Solomon's reigns, this western boundary was occupied by Philistines, along with other Sea Peoples and Phoenicians (cf. e.g. Josh. 13:2–6; Judg. 1; 3; 2 Sam. 5:17–25; 8:1–14).

7–9. The clockwise movement continues, again picking up where the previous section ended, with the northern border demarcated from the Great Sea to Mount Hor, presumably one of the sacred peaks of the Lebanese range (not to be confused with the site of Aaron's death, in the south), toward Lebo (*lĕbō'*, 'entrance of')-Hamath, which may possibly be identified as Libweh, 'north of the watershed between the Orontes and Liṭani' (Aharoni 1979: 65–67). The language then changes to the border's 'going-forths' (*tôṣā'āh*)/'go forth' (*yāṣā'*) – or 'concluding stretches' where the boundary 'comes out' (Levine 2000: 533) – toward Zedad, then Ziphron and Hazar-Enan. Lebo-Hamath recalls the scouts episode, being the northernmost area of land they had surveyed (13:21).

10–12. Starting once more at the place where the last section had ended, the northern boundary moves from Hazar-Enan toward Shepham, down to Riblah, east of Ayin (spring), descending down to the Sea of Chinnereth (harp-shaped) on the eastward 'side' (or 'shoulder', *ketep*), downward along the Jordan and to the Salt Sea, completing the circle (cf. 'Salt Sea', v. 3). Shepham's location is unknown, and there is some controversy concerning Riblah. A Riblah north of Lebo-Hamath would become notorious as a place of tragedy for God's people – indeed, every other scriptural reference to Riblah records calamity (2 Kgs 23:33; 25:6, 20–21; Jer. 39:5–6; 52:9–10, 26–27; cf. Levin 2006: 68–71). This site in the north makes little sense for discussing the eastern boundary, so is rejected by some as the referent here (e.g. Aharoni 1979: 67), although Levin makes the identification, maintaining that such precision asks too much from the text (2006: 71).

While many of the places cannot be identified with certainty, the general portrayal is readily recognized. The description moves in a continuous line, clockwise, from south to west to north to east, with each quadrant beginning with the last locale of the previous one. Three features of this description, that it was given by divine revelation, detailed according to the four points of the compass, and begins with Judah's location, recall the wilderness encampment in relation to the twelve tribes, the outer camp (chs. 1–2). It is key, then, to incorporate the parallel text within the structural palistrophe that comprises YHWH's five speeches, namely Numbers 35:1–8, focusing on Levitical cities, for this is the counterpart to the inner, Levitical camp (chs. 3–4). The tribal boundaries of the land (34:1–12), dotted with Levitical cities (35:1–8) forms the counterpart of the Camp, the covenant community in the land, within which YHWH will dwell among his people – precisely the final and climactic statement of chapter 35: 'I myself dwell in her midst – I am YHWH dwelling in the midst of the sons of Israel' (v. 34; similarly, see George 2013: 42). (See Figure 4.)

34:13–15: The lands east of the Jordan

This section reports Moses' fulfilment of YHWH's instruction (vv. 1–2) to command the sons of Israel concerning the land's boundaries – 'This is the land' (v. 13) – and further explains why this command applies only to the nine-and-a-half tribes since the tribes of Reuben and Gad, along with half of Manasseh's tribe, have already 'taken' their inheritance on the other side of the Jordan near Jericho 'eastward, from the sunrise'

(vv. 14–15). Answering the question of whether the Transjordan lands are excluded from the boundaries of the divine gift remains difficult. As an idealistic portrait of the land, verses 1–12 certainly make no mention of the Transjordan. Moses' explanation here, however, may be read as speaking directly to the point, that YHWH was describing only the land that still remained to be inherited, rather than intending to *delimit* once and for all the borders of his land. Moreover, that three cities of asylum will be set east of the Jordan encourages an embrace of the Transjordan lands as part of Israel's divinely granted territory. Nevertheless, a more negative reading is also possible, given the threefold use of 'take' (*lāqaḥ*) – the two-and-a-half tribes have 'taken' their inheritance, rather than receiving them as God's gift by lot (a negative parallel with 16:1 *may* be unwarranted). Noordtzij detects a reproach in the use of *lāqaḥ* (1983: 294), although the language in Numbers 21, when Transjordan was conquered, may serve as a counterbalance, since YHWH had said 'I have given him into your hand, with all his people, and all his land' (v. 34; cf. Olson 1996: 188).

This section, as Ashley recognized (1993: 642), connects to previous portions of the book's last major section: verse 13 alludes to 26:52–56, where the division of the land by lot is addressed, and verses 14–15 recall chapter 32, where the tribes of Reuben and Gad, along with the half-tribe of Manasseh gained lands east of the Jordan. Whereas in chapter 26 the land was to be divided as an inheritance 'to these' (26:53), referring to the number of names from the census, now two-and-a-half tribes have been excluded from the previous general statement, a fact explained by Numbers 32 and 34:14–15.

34:16–29 YHWH's third speech: tribal princes to divide the land inheritance

16–18. YHWH's third and central speech, moving from the last speech's 'This is the land' (vv. 2b, 13) now to 'These are the names of the men', designates by divine revelation the tribal chieftains who, under the authority and oversight of Eleazar the priest and Joshua son of Nun, will divide the inheritance of the land. Underscoring this speech further, this listing of princes is the seventh and final climactic listing of the patriarchal descendants in Numbers (1:1–44; 2; 7:12–84; 10:14–28; 13:1–16; 26:1–62; 34:16–29), a feature of significant emphasis (M. Douglas 2004: 20). The inf. const. of verse 18 ('to divide the inheritance of the land') designates the chieftains in particular as the referent of 'the men', while the 'you will take' of the same verse, which reads pl. (*tiqḥû*), encompasses Eleazar and Joshua as the overseers along with Moses. Eleazar and Joshua replace the original duo, Moses and Aaron (see 1:17) – and the difference is noteworthy: now Eleazar the priest takes priority, as

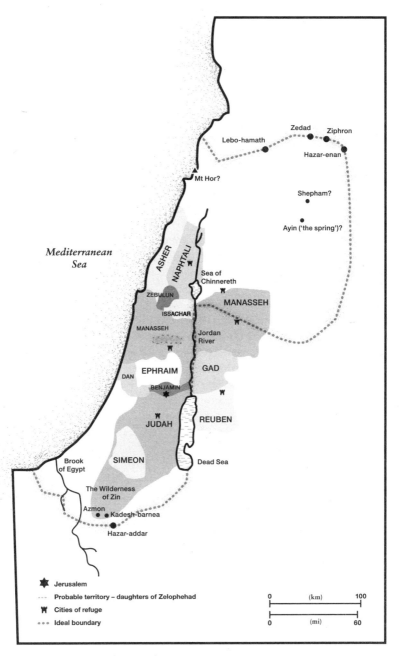

Figure 4: Promised Land, Numbers 34

Joshua is not fully Moses' replacement. Significantly, the phrase 'These are the names of the men' occurs four times in Numbers. Outside its twofold use here (vv. 17, 19), it opened Numbers with the twelve chieftains who were appointed to help conduct the census of their respective tribes for the sake of establishing the Camp (1:5), and then it was used again to designate the twelve chieftains who were sent to scout out the land (13:16), a mission that ended in disaster. Both earlier uses are exceptionally crucial for understanding the weight and function of the present text. On the one hand, there is an analogous relationship between the tribal placements in the Camp and in the land, the former being paradigmatic and preparatory for the latter. Recalling further that Numbers is primarily focused on leadership, the ten princes designated by YHWH to 'divide the inheritance of the land' form the reversal of the original ten princes who, after their scouting mission, had brought back a negative report of the land. Whether inclusion of the two leaders, Eleazar and Joshua, for a sum of twelve, symbolic of Israel, is intended seems unlikely in this instance. Structurally, the threefold use of 'These (*'ēlleh*) are the names/those' (34:17, 19, 29) is central, not only within the last five divine speeches, but for the last section as well – between 'These are the journeys' (33:1) and the closing 'These are the commands and judgements' (36:13). The chieftains are chosen to represent their tribes in the division of the land, which will establish the tribal territories, so their roles would involve 'providing the details of the size of their tribe, and witnessing the casting of the lots, and helping in the future apportioning and distribution of land to families' (Jeyaraj 1989: 134).

19–28. Discerning the logic of the order of listed names, especially as it differs from the order of the actual conquest in Joshua 14 – 19, is a challenge but is not insurmountable. Other lists in Numbers had begun with the triad of Reuben, Gad and Simeon, so, given the removal of Reuben and Gad, whose tribes had taken possession of lands east of the Jordan (ch. 32), it makes sense that Simeon remains near the opening of the list. Levi's tribe is also omitted since Levites have no inheritance in the land, but will receive of its bounty through the people's tithes (18:23–24). Judah's pre-eminence, attested also in having the largest population at 76,500, explains why this tribe is listed first. Both delineations in chapter 34, of the land's boundaries (vv. 3–5) and of the tribal leaders (v. 19), begin with Judah. As Table 30 demonstrates (significance of names taken from Levine 2000: 537–538; and Allen 2012: 442), the order of tribes follows their settlements in the land.

With their eventual land allotments according to Joshua in view, the progression of tribes appears to move along a vertical axis, beginning with the southern tribes (Judah, Simeon, Benjamin), moving to the central tribes (Dan, Manasseh, Ephraim) and then to the tribes in the northern section (Zebulun, Issachar, Asher, Naphtali). Given that Joshua the son of Nun has already been mentioned as the tribes' military and

Table 30: Ten tribal leaders

Tribes	Camp	Land	Significance of Names
Judah	East	South	Caleb ('Dog') son of Jephunneh ('he makes clear'?)
Simeon	South	South	Samuel ('his name is El') son of Ammihud ('the Majestic one is my kinsman')
Benjamin	West	South	Elidad ('my El is the friend' or 'my El loves') son of Chislon ('one of hope')
Dan	North	Central	Bukki ('proven'?) son of Jogli ('led away')
Manasseh	West	Central	Hanniel ('El has been gracious to me') son of Ephod ('costly, embroidered garment', priestly garment)
Ephraim	West	Central	Kemuel ('El establishes') son of Shiphtan ('judgement')
Zebulun	East	North	Elizaphan ('my El has protected') son of Parnach ('splendorous one')
Issachar	East	North	Paltiel ('El is my deliverance') son of Azzan ('mighty')
Asher	North	North	Ahihud ('my brother is majesty') son of Shelomi ('[Yah] is my covenant' or 'my peace')
Naphtali	North	North	Pedahel ('El redeems') son of Ammihud ('the Majestic one is my kinsman')

political leader in place of Moses, moreover, it is fitting for the list of tribal princes to begin with Caleb the son of Jephunneh, who was the first scout to urge possessing the land (13:30) and was marked out by YHWH as 'My servant Caleb' who had followed YHWH closely and would inherit the land he had scouted (14:24). Caleb, a remnant of the first generation, would have been much older than the rest, warranting their respect and his place of honour. Judah's tribe aside, the central tribe of the remaining nine, which is bracketed by 'the son of Ammihud' (vv. 20, 28), is Ephraim (v. 24), which is perhaps not incidental. The tribes of Judah and Benjamin alone are not described as 'the sons of the tribe of', all the more odd since Simeon's tribe, listed between them, does conform to the list of other tribes: 'the tribe of the sons of Simeon'. Also notable, after Judah, Simeon and Benjamin, the last seven names beginning with the tribe of Dan include the label 'chieftain'. Hirsch explained these features by the future site of the Temple (2007a: 673): since the sanctuary would reside in their territories, the tribes of Judah and Benjamin are not defined according to their collective individuals ('tribes of the sons of') but only 'as parts of the national community', and, in the light of

YHWH's sovereignty represented by his sanctuary, the term 'chieftain' would also have been inappropriate. Likely, given the twofold nature of the final six tribes, according to their encampment locales (W–W, E–E, N–N), the list is to be read by twos, which brings out yet another feature, that the twofold groups of tribes will be adjacent to each other in the land: Simeon's territory will be within Judah, Benjamin and Dan will lie next to each other, as will Manasseh and Ephraim, Zebulun and Issachar, and Asher and Naphtali.

Aside from Caleb, these tribal leaders, whose names are ceremoniously recited, never appear again in Scripture. Nevertheless, their names are preserved here in monumental fashion, as those who led in the historic realization of the patriarchal promises of land. Although the precise meaning of the names is debatable, many include the designation El (God), which accords with the antiquity of its historical context.

29. Forming an inclusion with the double-use of 'These are the names' (vv. 17, 19), verse 29 confirms that 'These are the ones' YHWH had 'commanded' (*ṣiwwā*). As with the census and construction of the Camp, the leaders who will direct Israel's inheritance in the land are designated by God directly, by divine command. In contrast to verses 17 and 18, where the definite direct object particle (*'et*) is prefixed to 'the land' (*hā'āreṣ*), here, likely as a prep. of advantage ('for', see R. J. Williams 2007: §341), it is prefixed to 'the sons of Israel', underscoring how the ten princes will benefit *the sons of Israel*, causing the tribes to inherit (*nāḥal* in pi.) 'in the land of Canaan'. Focus is placed on the tribes' *geographical arrangement* in the land, as Levine's translation brings out (2000: 531, 538): 'These are the ones whom YHWH commanded to install the Israelite people in their estates in the Land of Canaan,' a focus we discerned in the order of the chieftains.

As the central speech, in which their names are ceremoniously listed, and with the benefit of the sons of Israel in view, these chieftains form the celebratory reversal of the previous generation's ten princes who had caused the sons of Israel to lose the land, falling under YHWH's forty-year death sentence in the wilderness.

35:1–8 YHWH's fourth speech: designating forty-eight Levitical cities

YHWH's fourth speech, concerning the cities in which Levites will reside in the land, parallels YHWH's second speech, delineating the boundaries of the land in which the tribes will reside. Recalling the analogy between Israel's life in the Camp and in the land, the second speech is comparable to the arrangement of the twelve tribes in the Camp (Num. 1 – 2), while the fourth speech is comparable to the place and function of Levites in the Camp (Num. 3 – 4). The distribution of land hereby continues from the allotment of the tribes to the place for the Levites. Language of inheritance is avoided, as Levites receive no inheritance (Num. 18:24; 26:62) – even the cities and pasturelands are merely used – rather than owned – by Levites.

1–3. The form of YHWH's fourth speech parallels the second speech: 'Command the sons of Israel' (*ṣaw 'et-běnê yiśrā'ēl*, 34:2; 35:2). The second and fourth speeches are also in parallel structurally and thematically. The second speech, which delineates the boundaries of the land of Canaan, defines the land that will fall to the sons of Israel as an inheritance (34:1–15), and the fourth speech determines that cities and pasturelands from the inheritance of the sons of Israel will be given as dwellings for the Levites and their animals. Only when the speeches are combined is the picture of Israel – both the twelve tribes and the Levites – dwelling in the land complete.

Verse 2 begins and ends with the phrase 'you will give to the Levites', surrounding and creating a parallel between the two gifts for the Levites: the cities from Israel's inheritance and the pasturelands surrounding the cities. Verse 3 then provides the purpose for each gift: the cities are for the Levites to dwell in (repeated from v. 2), and the pasturelands will be for the Levites' cattle, livestock and other beasts (i.e. donkeys, mules). Both occurrences of *lāšābet* ('to dwell', vv. 2, 3) are marked as emphatic by the athnak. Although Levites do not inherit the land, there are nevertheless sure, divinely ordained places for them to reside in the land. YHWH God is their inheritance (see Num. 18:20, 24; Deut. 10:9), and he, through his people – as a divine command (v. 2) – will provide for their needs abundantly. The prohibition on land for Levites, moreover, relates to farmland or agricultural fields rather than pastureland for raising animals (cf. Dybdahl 1981: 81; Milgrom 1990: 289). 'Pasturelands' (*migrāš*) apparently derives from the notion of 'driving' (*gāraš*) or corralling animals. That Levites can live together as Levites, within distinct, walled cities among the tribes, also serves 'to preserve their identity in Israel' (Naylor 1994: 196).

4–5. The detailed explanation now begins with the pasturelands (vv. 4–5), before moving to further details about the cities (vv. 6–8). In Numbers 18:20–24, YHWH informed Aaron concerning the role of Levites, that they would serve at the Tent of Meeting in place of the sons of Israel, bearing their guilt, and receive their tithes from the land's produce since Levites would not inherit an allotment of land with its produce. Numbers 18:22, 24, as Dybdahl points out (1981: 82), had denied Levites any *ḥēleq* (portion, share) of *naḥălāh* (inheritance), terms that are not used here to describe the cities and lands for them. While Levites are denied agricultural land, they are given pastureland, grassy acreage for their cattle, livestock and other animals, which are necessary for their sanctuary service. Most ancient cities were surrounded by common or public lands, freely used by its residents for pasturing animals. As a legal part of the city, Milgrom includes the pastureland as part of the safe zone of asylum cities (1990: 289).

The biggest challenge to understanding the pasturelands is in relation to coordinating the measurement of a thousand cubits around the city's wall in verse 4, with the two thousand cubits measured 'from outside the city' along the four points of the compass in verse 5 (*m. Sot.* 5.3), whereby it appears that the writer, in the words of G. B. Gray (1903: 468), 'forgot to allow for the dimensions of the city'. Given, moreover, that their rectangular dimensions, as Wellhausen noted (1885: 159), would have been impractical in the mountainous regions of Canaan, the idealistic nature of Levitical cities and pasturelands has also been appreciated. The simplest interpretation first traces a square around the city and then measures 1,000 cubits outward from each side in the four cardinal directions, and assumes that the 2,000 cubits measurement, which must presume a mere point for the city, is exemplary and, therefore, flexible. M. Greenberg (1968) pointed out that offering dimensions for the city, beyond the economical size of zero, would have unnecessarily complicated matters. The 2,000 cubits measurement on four sides, he explained (1968: 63), 'is paradigmatic and given only to bring home the square shape; without it, the direction to extend the pasture "a thousand cubits outside the town wall all around" could have been misconstrued to mean a circular area.' Levine reads the 2,000 cubits as projecting each side of the walled town itself, which would be 2,000 cubits square, yielding an entire jurisdiction, including the 1,000 cubits of pastureland all around, of 4,000 cubits square (2000: 552, 571). Another possible scenario, noted by Naylor (1994: 196), entails measuring 1,000 cubits from the corners of the square boundary traced around the city – although the language of the text, describing one measurement per the points of the compass (rather than two each), accords more firmly with M. Greenberg's simpler solution. One may further ask, especially given the idealistic – and even utopian – character of the passage, what is intended by these square-shaped dimensions so perfectly symmetrical? Given the parallel between the second speech, delineating the idealistic boundaries of the tribal land of inheritance, and this fourth speech, it may be the city dimensions are intended to recall the dimensions of the Camp (Num. 1 – 4) for, as Nachmanides glossed, 'Thus the city given to the Levites was in the form of a square' (1975: 390). The portrayal of these cities with their pasturelands, measured from the eastward side and progressing clockwise to the south, west and then north, may convey that Levites in the land would function analogously to their role in the Camp.

6–8. The number of cities is designated, focusing first on the six cities of 'the asylum' (*hammiqlāṭ*) which have the stated purpose of being 'for the murderer (*hā-rōṣēaḥ*) to flee (*nûs*) there'. Twelve uses of 'give' (*nātan*) in the chapter, all referring to the Israelites' giving of cities and pasturelands to Levites, means the people – each of the twelve tribes (matching the twelve uses of *nātan*) – are called to imitate YHWH: as he gave them an inheritance of land for their good and well-being, they in turn, out of his abundant gift, are to give to the Levites for their good and well-being, precisely the same dynamic found in chapter 18 related to the offerings and tithes.

Aside from the six cities of asylum, forty-two more cities will be given for a total of forty-eight cities, with their pasturelands (cf. Josh. 21). Various Jewish interpreters understand that every Levitical city could serve or, at least historically, eventually came to serve, as an asylum – it was a secondary purpose for the forty-two cities, but the primary purpose of the six (consult Elitzur 2020: 531–552). The numbers appear idealistic, and possibly symbolic: 6 is half the number of tribes, while 42 is 6 multiplied by 7, the number of completion; and 48 is 12, the number of tribes, multiplied by 4 (like foursquare cities in verse 5). Rofé noted that all the figures appear to be based on the number 12, its multiple (48) and divisors (2, 3, 4, 6) (1986: 226), a number related to the tribes of Israel. Keil, taking the number 4 as 'the seal of the kingdom of God', suggested that 4 times 12 towns represented 'the idea of the kingdom of God' (Keil and Delitzsch 1973: 3:261). Plaut cites a Chasidic interpretation whereby the 6 cities of refuge are compared to the 6 Hebr. words of the Shema (Deut. 6:4), and the 48 cities to the 48 words of that paragraph in Deuteronomy 6:4–9 (Plaut 1979: 342). Intriguingly, inasmuch as the cities of asylum might have formed expansions of the altar (cf. Exod. 21:12–14), scholars have noted that beyond some similar functions, Levitical cities, 'bounded by an exact square of pastureland', have 'the very shape of an altar' (Burnside 2010a: 260–261 n. 24; cf. Jacob 1992: 635). As Levites, ironically fulfilling both the derivation of the name 'Levi' ('to join, attach' Gen. 29:34) and YHWH's judgement through Jacob ('I will divide them in Jacob, and scatter them in Israel,' Gen. 49:7), they will be scattered throughout the land in a manner intended to raise up the tribes spiritually, spreading the instruction of Torah among them. And just as the split tribe of Manasseh joins together the lands east and west of the Jordan, so the spread-out Levitical cities unify the tribal lands spiritually. HaCohen (1997), noting how the altar may serve as a 'city of refuge', suggests an analogy between the role of the Dwelling in the wilderness and the cities of asylum in the land, as the centre(s) from which both Torah and holiness radiate to the nation as sources of spiritual development.

Giving will be proportionate to the size of tribal holdings, more cities from the larger tribal territories. The language of Levitical cities, 'from the large a large portion (*hārab tarbû*) and from the small a small portion (*ûmē'ēt ham'aṭ tam'îṭû)*', relates closely to the language of tribal inheritance (*lārab tarbû . . . wĕlam'aṭ tam'îṭ*, 33:54), language that further recalls the tribal census where the size of each tribe was determined: *lārab tarbeh . . . wĕlam'aṭ tam'îṭ* (26:54). As the twelve tribes receive land in proportion to their size, so they will give cities to Levites in proportion to their size. Once more, YHWH's fourth and fifth speeches concerning the place of Levites in the land (34:1–8, 9–34), parallel Numbers 3 – 4 concerning the place of Levites in the Camp.

35:9–34 YHWH's fifth speech: establishing cities of asylum

35:9–15: Selecting cities of asylum

9–10. YHWH's charge to Moses, 'Speak (*dabbēr*) to the sons of Israel', matches the form of the first speech (cf. 33:51), as does the initial occasion clause – nearly verbatim:

> 35:10: *dabbēr 'el-bĕnê yiśrā'ēl wĕ'āmartā 'ălêhem kî 'attem 'ōbĕrîm 'et-hayyardēn 'arṣāh kĕnā'an*
> Speak to the sons of Israel and say to them, 'When you pass over the Jordan toward the land of Canaan'

> 33:51: *dabbēr 'el-bĕnê yiśrā'ēl wĕ'āmartā 'ălêhem kî 'attem 'ōbĕrîm 'et-hayyardēn 'el-'ereṣ kĕnā'an*
> Speak to the sons of Israel and say to them, 'When you pass over the Jordan to the land of Canaan'

Both speeches, moreover, are structurally set in parallel, a clue that each will be understood more deeply when interpreted with the others. In the first speech the sons of Israel are called to dispossess the inhabitants of the land and to destroy all the appurtenances of idolatry, while in the last speech the sons of Israel are called to select cities of asylum, with the goal of preventing the land's defilement with bloodguilt. Although not mentioned explicitly in the first speech, idolatry, like bloodguilt, defiles the land. The urgency of the first speech lends urgency to the last – among the first duties to which Israel must attend after crossing the Jordan, they must clear the land of idolatry *and* set aside cities of asylum, both in the light of YHWH's presence in the land. The need for the latter is so urgent that, before he dies, Moses will set aside three cities of refuge in the Transjordan (Deut. 4:41–43).

11–15. While in the previous speech YHWH had clearly noted that asylum cities were from those given to Levites (35:6), the Levites are not actually mentioned at all in this final speech, as the focus shifts to the asylum these cities will offer for 'the sons of Israel, and for the sojourner, and for the temporary alien in their midst' (v. 16), and to the legislation regarding various scenarios of murder and qualifications for one's stay in a city of asylum. The Levitical character of these cities, however, is everywhere assumed, and Milgrom observes the appropriateness of a manslayer to be put in the custody of Levites since they should not be influenced by the clan or tribe of either the victim or the one who killed (1990: 290). The sons of Israel are to 'select' (hiph. of *qārāh*) cities that are four times designated 'for you' (*lākem*) – their gift to the Levites will benefit the tribes and the nation as a whole. Levine brings out the nuance of *hiqrîtem* as 'make accessible' for yourselves (2000: 554). One of the cities of asylum ('*ārê miqlāṭ*) becomes the destination – 'there' (*šāmmā*) – for the murderer who strikes down (*nākāh*) a life (*nepeš*) unintentionally (*bišgāgāh*) to flee (*nûs*). To 'flee', as Levine points out (2000: 553), is a key term that appears in nearly all biblical references regarding asylum (Num. 35:11, 15, 25–26, 32; cf. Exod. 21:13; Deut. 4:42; 19:3–5, 11; Josh. 20; 1 Kgs 2:28–29). The term *miqlāṭ* denotes asylum or refuge and, in later Judaism, connotes 'reception', with some linking that idea here as well: 'cities of reception', which receive the unintentional murderer (cf. Feinberg 1946: 412; Auld 1978: 38; Levine 2000: 552–553; Hirsch 2007a: 679). Hebr. does not use different labels to distinguish between 'murder' and 'manslaughter', adding instead 'unintentionally' to the designation 'murderer' (*rōṣēaḥ*), taken from *rāṣaḥ*, 'to murder, slay' (cf. BDB 953). This approach appreciates the common denominator, the victim – both murder and manslaughter kill a person, unjustly or undeservedly cutting short a life. M. Greenberg explains (1959: 127), 'Shedding an innocent man's blood, even unintentionally, involved bloodguilt, and no manslayer was considered clear of this guilt . . . Yet the avenger is not regarded as a murderer. Why? Because the manslayer was not guiltless.' Those who deny an expiatory death of the high priest typically fail to appreciate the bloodguilt incurred by inadvertent murder (e.g. Vasholz 1993). The other commonality between murder and manslaughter is that the victim's avenger, likely the nearest male kin, is obligated to exact retribution by killing the one responsible. The term 'avenger' is *gō'ēl*, from the root *gā'al* (to redeem or act as kinsman), and designates a kinsman within a clan who is designated with a variety of duties, including raising up children for a kinsman's widow, redeeming family members from bondage, redeeming a kinsman's field, and avenging a kinsman's murder (BDB 145). Each of these duties involves 'redemption' in the sense of restoring order or equilibrium, stability – as Milgrom explains, he delivers 'a descendant to the deceased, the slave to freedom, the land to its rightful owner', even 'restoring the ecological balance' from bloodguilt so that the 'earth again yields its fruit' (1990: 291–292). Because the avenger may exact retribution against a kinsman's murderer with impunity (and, more, was duty-bound to do so), the cities of asylum are established 'so the murderer will not die, until he stands before the community for judgement'. Rather than undoing the kinsman-gō'ēl's role, YHWH establishes a means for ensuring justice: the community will render judgement (*mišpāṭ*), determining whether the murder was unintentional, in which case the murderer may continue to receive asylum in the Levitical city. The 'community' (*hā'ēdāh*) occurs well over fifty times in Numbers (the last four uses here, 35:12, 24, 25 [twice]), broadly signifying the twelve tribes unified as the covenant people of Israel, while its authoritative and representative assembly was likely comprised of male members above the age of 12. Here the delegation envisioned would be smaller, such as the local elders of the village where the person was murdered (see Deut. 19:12; 21:6). Feinberg helpfully explains (1947: 38) that here 'the community' refers 'to those leaders in each community, representing all the congregation, who were entrusted with the administration of justice among the people of Israel'. Even as a smaller, representative delegation, the *'ēdāh* further signifies that the pollution of the land in the midst of which YHWH dwells is a crisis that concerns all the tribes of Israel.

Of the six (initial) cities of asylum to be given by the tribes, three must be given on the east side of the Jordan, and three within the land of Canaan. Including the tribes of Reuben and Gad, who will reside outside 'the land of Canaan', beyond expressing the intention of justice throughout these lands, creates a unifying conception of Israel. More deeply, given the main purpose for the cities of asylum legislation in Numbers as defined in the chapter's closing verses, namely, YHWH's dwelling in the midst of his people in the land (vv. 33–34), it may be that the Transjordan lands are hereby embraced as contiguous to and encompassed within 'YHWH's land', which must also avoid defilement. In Deuteronomy, Moses designates the three Transjordan cities to serve as asylums: Bezer, in the wilderness, the plateau, for the Reubenites; Ramoth in Gilead, for the Gadites; and Golan in Bashan for the Manassites (4:43). Joshua names the three within Canaan: Kedesh in the north in Naphtali, Shechem in the centre in Ephraim, and Hebron (Kiriath-arba) in the south in Judah (Josh. 20:7). These asylum cities will be for 'everyone' (*kol*) who strikes down a life unintentionally, including not only Israelites but also the 'sojourner' (*gēr*) and 'temporary resident' (*tôšāb*). The sojourner is well defined by Zehnder (2021: 21):

> The noun *ger* likely refers to a person of foreign origin who immigrates into Israel because of war, famine, poverty, or impending debt slavery or the like. He is typically a person who has come to stay in Israel for an extended period of time; it seems that in many cases it is implied that he intends to become part of the Israelite society. This implies a willingness to assimilate on all levels.

Given the sojourner's willingness to be incorporated into Israel, including undergoing the rite of circumcision, so that the *gēr* was basically regarded as a proselyte (Stigers 1980), this potentially permanent status is recognized by the inclusion of sojourners in a variety of statutes and judgements, such as Passover and the Feast of Unleavened Bread (cf. Exod. 12:19, 48–49; Num. 9:14), whereas others, such as temporary residents, are excluded. At a broader level, YHWH had declared in Leviticus that 'the land is mine', defining Israelites themselves as 'sojourners and temporary residents' residing there 'with me' (Lev. 25:23), so that Israel in the land was, in a manner, likened to refugees seeking asylum in the land, under YHWH's protection (see Joosten 1996: 181–192). When it comes to a just society, and to preventing the defilement of the land with bloodguilt – resulting from the unjust execution of one who killed unintentionally – then all, even the temporary resident, whose circumstances in Israel are more tenuous, are included. As the cities of refuge legislation is founded upon the sanctity of human life, created in the image of God, so the law of asylum applies naturally to all human beings.

35:16–28: Prescribing refuge in the cities of asylum

This section divides broadly into two halves: the first dealing with scenarios pertaining to a guilty murderer who must be put to death (vv. 16–21), and the second dealing with scenarios whereby the murderer is innocent, having killed without intention (vv. 22–28). The first division may be further subdivided, relating to the guilty murderer's weapon (vv. 16–19) and malicious intent (vv. 20–21). The second division may also be subdivided, related to determining the innocence of the one who killed without intention (vv. 22–24), and the non-guilty murderer's stay in the city of asylum (vv. 25–28).

16–19. Three scenarios, related to three vessels used as weapons of murder – 'he strikes' (*hikkāhû*) with a vessel of iron, a stone or a vessel of wood, are given that end with the same refrain: 'he is a murderer – the murderer will surely be put to death' (vv. 16, 17, 18). The phrase 'surely die / be put to death' (*môt yûmat*) as a divine verdict for transgression begins within the garden of Eden (Gen. 2:17) and is often applied for especially heinous sins in YHWH's sight (see Gen. 20:7; Exod. 19:12; 31:14–15; Lev. 20:2, 9, 10, 11; etc.), including murder (Exod. 21:12–15; Lev. 24:17). As Kislev explains (2020: 254), *môt yûmat* refers to 'an execution that is sanctioned by a sovereign authority and performed by its agents'. There are two conditional 'if' (*'im*) clauses, beginning verses 16 and 17, while 'or' (*'ô*) connects verse 18 to the previous scenario in verse 17, so that two main conditions are set forth: striking with an iron (or presumably any metal) vessel (v. 16), which may 'reflect the beginnings of the Iron Age, when it was used exclusively for weapons' (Milgrom 1990: 292), and striking with a vessel in 'hand' (*yad*), whether of stone or wood (vv. 17–18). Perhaps the distinction is that a heavy metal object may be thrown from a distance with the intent of killing a person, while other objects, such as a regular stone or piece of wood, small enough to be carried in hand, will normally involve the force of striking while in hand (excluding, of course, a catapult stone or an arrow, both of which are weapons of battle used with the clear intention to kill). The iron vessel scenario omits both 'in hand' and 'by which one may die', while all three portray the murder with 'he strikes him and he dies', along with the same conclusion that the murderer must be put to death. In verse 31, the necessity of the murderer's execution and the impossibility of accepting a ransom in place of the guilty murderer's death is stated definitely. After the threefold declaration that the murderer will surely be put to death, verse 19 identifies the avenger of blood, literally '(kinsman) redeemer of blood' (gō'ēl haddām), as the executioner. Surprisingly, the execution is not described as an official or public affair, but reads as a typical vendetta situation: 'the avenger of blood will put the murderer to death when he encounters (pāga‘) him'. The function of the cities of asylum, as a restraining control – but not abolishment – of vendetta killing, is evident.

20–21. The second subdivision of the guilty murderer relates to the malicious intent involved when killing a person: 'If in hatred (śin'āh) . . . or in enmity ('ēbāh).' The first scenario describes the aggressor who 'thrusts' – he 'shoves, pushes' (hādap) – a person whom he hates, or, by lying in wait, he then 'hurls' (or 'flings', šālak in hiph.) either himself or an object upon him (see 'any vessel' in v. 22), with the result that 'he dies'. A second scenario, linked to the first, is when an aggressor 'strikes' (nākāh in hiph.) a person – one with whom he is at 'enmity' – with his hand so that 'he dies'. This one 'who struck' is also dubbed '(guilty) murderer' and must surely be put to death (cf. Exod. 21:12–15). The same phraseology as verse 19, in slightly different order, is used as a summary conclusion at the end of verse 21: the avenger of blood will put the murderer to death when he encounters him. As a near-kinsman of the victim there is poetic justice involved in the avenger's sanction to slay the murderer since the kinsman represents the victim.

22–24. The scenarios for the (innocent) murderer, who killed unintentionally, are listed comprehensively and in chiastic reversal of those for the (guilty) murderer: verse 22 forms a contrast to verses 20–21, and verse 23 is contrasted against verses 16–19 (so, too, Milgrom 1990: 292).

Verse 22 sets forth three contrasting qualifications to describe the otherwise same acts of verses 20–21 ('he thrusts' or 'hurls upon him any vessel'), but which demonstrate a lack of intention to murder: 'suddenly' (peta‘), 'without enmity' (lō'-'ēbāh) and 'without lying in wait' (lō' ṣĕdîâ). Verse 23 continues with three contrasting qualifications to the act of using any 'stone by which one may die' (cf. v. 17): 'without seeing him' (lō' rĕ'ôt), 'he was not an enemy to him' (lō'-'ôyēb) and 'he did not seek him evil' (lō' mĕbaqqēš rā'ātô). Use of a vessel such as an axe head, which may kill certainly, is not proof of guilt when the person using it had not seen, lain in wait or held any grudge against the victim; that is, if there had been no malicious intent in the use of that item.

The community, rather than the 'bereaved kinsman' (Milgrom 1990: 291), will then 'judge' (šāpaṭ) between two parties, 'the one who struck' (hammakkeh) and the avenger of blood. In verse 21, it was declared that 'the one who struck' (hammakkeh) with the intention of killing must be put to death, whereas here, in verse 24, where there was no malicious intent, the community arbitrates according to 'these judgements' (hammišpāṭîm hā'ēlleh), which are prescribed in the verses that follow (vv. 25–28). The cities were designated as an asylum particularly 'from the avenger' (miggō'ēl), so the murderer would not die 'until he stands before the community for the judgement' (v. 12). 'Avenger' is not a just translation, since the gō'ēl sought equity, a restoration or balance, rather than mere vengeance (cf. W. Driver 1960: 7). The verb gā'al essentially means 'to act as kinsman', and it was the duty of a gō'ēl, whether brother, uncle, cousin or other blood relative, to vindicate a family member within the mišpāḥāh, write King and Stager (2001: 38–39), adding that the blood avenger's role was 'intimately involved with kinship and genealogy', a point that makes the topic especially relevant for this section. Andersen underscores that the duties of the gō'ēl, including the execution of blood vengeance, was one of the measures, along with the institution of Jubilee, 'for keeping the land of a mišpāḥāh intact' (1969: 36). The inclusio established between verses 12 and 24, as a preface to the judgements listed in verses 25–28, removes judicial authority from the kinsman avenger. The provision of the cities of asylum serves, in the first place, as a haven from the avenger for the sake of the community's mediation, its investigation and judgement concerning the nature of the killing that has taken place. While divine *torah* must guide a person's behaviour, even beyond kinship ties and tribal affiliations (cf. Cocco 2016), it is nevertheless a marvel, however, to what degree the legislation refrains from restricting the kinsman's right to avenge a death in the family: rather than prohibiting the avenger's right to kill with impunity even before the community has met to render judgement, the legislation rather provides cities to 'help' the murderer escape the avenger's lawful threat. The ANE context needs to be appreciated: in the absence of any police force, the immediate – and lawful – threat of a kinsman's vengeance served as a necessary deterrent to violence.

25–28. With direct reference to the scenario of an innocent murderer (vv. 22–24), the community is called to 'deliver (wĕhiṣṣîlû) the murderer (hārōṣēaḥ) from the hand (mîad) of the avenger of blood', and to 'return (wĕhēšîbû) him to the city of asylum', both actions presuming a context whereby the adjudications have taken place outside the city of asylum. The second half of verse 25 states, 'he will dwell there until ('*ad*) the death of the high priest who was anointed with the holy oil', a scheme restated in verse 28: 'For in the city of his asylum he should have dwelled until the death of the high priest.' In between these statements, the scenario whereby the innocent murderer leaves the refuge of the city of asylum before the death of the high priest is addressed, instructing that the avenger of blood, if 'he murders (*rāṣaḥ*) the murderer (*hārōṣēaḥ*)' outside the bounds of the city of asylum, incurs 'no bloodguilt', literally, 'there is not to him blood' ('*ên lô dām*), a reality that once more assumes the underlying right of the kinsman avenger to exact retribution. In Deuteronomy's asylum-city regulations, the cities are granted lest 'innocent blood' be shed in the land with the result that 'bloodguilt will be upon you' (*wĕhāyāh 'ālêkā dāmîm*, 19:10), precisely what the avenger does not incur here if the unintentional murderer leaves the asylum city prematurely. Although 'bloodguilt' is typically rendered with a dual ending as in the Deuteronomy passage, the sg. *dām* occurs as well. Likely, the city's 'boundary' included the pastureland. The basic notion conveyed is that if the innocent murderer leaves the city of asylum prematurely (before the death of the high priest), then he is in part to blame for his own death: 'because (*kî*) in the city of his asylum', fronted before the verb for emphasis, 'he should have dwelled until the death of the high priest' – and note '*his* asylum' (*miqlāṭô*), underscoring that he in some way spurned his protection. The point underscores the complex nature of the cities of asylum, serving as both protection and punishment (cf. Peters 2000; Clarke 2003: 126; Lévinas 2007: 39). Rather than absolutely prohibiting the role of a kinsman avenger, the legislation provides a protective shelter for the innocent murderer. This point is also evident in Deuteronomy, where Israel is further instructed to 'establish roads' leading to the cities of refuge and to spread out the cities in three areas lest the avenger pursue and overtake the murderer 'because the way is long' (19:3, 6).

After the death of the high priest, the innocent murderer will return to the land of his holding. Given that the 'high priest was one of the most important figures in ancient Jewish life, cult, and tradition', it is, as Morgenstern wrote (1938: 1), 'surprising, therefore, even a bit startling, to find how extremely infrequently this title [*hakkōhēn haggādôl*] does occur'. In the Torah, the designation 'the high priest' (or 'the great priest', *hakkōhēn haggādôl*) occurs only four times, three of which occur in the present passage (35:25, 28 [twice]) and once earlier in Leviticus in a reference that is relevant, as it also includes 'the oil of anointing' upon his head (21:10–12):

> The great priest (*hakkōhēn haggādôl*) among his brethren, upon whose head the oil of anointing had been poured, and whose hand had been filled (i.e. 'who was consecrated') to wear the garments, must not uncover his head nor rend his garments. And he will not come by any

dead person, nor defile himself for his father or for his mother. And from the Sanctuary he will not go forth, nor defile the Sanctuary of his God, for the crown (*nēzer*) of the oil of anointing is upon him – I am YHWH.

Within context, the Leviticus reference relates the high priest's holy status and anointing to his place within the sanctuary, the place symbolizing utmost life where YHWH the fountain of life abides, and the need, therefore, for the high priest to avoid corpse pollution, even for the death of his father or mother – death and defilement being other points of contact with the cities of asylum. By intertextual links to Leviticus 21, the high priest's role and function in relation to the holiness and life of YHWH are recalled. The death of the great priest who was so defined by YHWH's realm of life that he could neither attend a parent's funeral nor even display the signs of mourning a loved one, surely, the death of such a one may count in place of the death of an accidental murderer. As representing his generation, the high priest's death indeed stands for the passing of an era, along with the putting away of the generation's sins, just as Aaron's death in Numbers 20 represented the death of the first generation and the end of YHWH's forty-year judgement. While some views on the function of the high priest's death focus only on his representative role (cf. Bissell 1884: 67; Feinberg 1947: 38; for the administrative view, see W. Driver 1960: 19–20; cf. Kislev 2020: 252), his representation was primarily for the sake of his work of atonement, since, as Gane states (2004: 799): 'only a priest was authorized to bear the culpability of others (cf. Exod. 28:38; Lev. 10:17)'. Emphasis on the high priest as the one 'who was anointed with holy oil' (*'ăšer-māšaḥ 'ōtô běšemen haqqōdeš*) underscores *both* his representative function (cf. Gorman 1990: 71, 91–102) and his annual entrance into the holiest to make atonement for all Israel. The Babylonian Talmud, engaging the significance of the innocent murderer's exile, whether the exile itself atones (*b. Sanh.* 37a), concludes, 'It is not exile that expiates, but the death of the high priest' (*Mak.* 11b; see Lévinas 2007: 34–52). Elsewhere, the Babylonian Talmud states, 'Just as the clothing of the high priest expiates, so the death of the righteous man expiates' (*MQ* 28a; cf. *Zeb.* 88b). The Mishnah also explains that in the scenario whereby the high priest dies just after the sentencing of an inadvertent murderer, then the latter need not go into exile at all (*Mak.* 2.6).

The long-standing explanation, then, for why the high priest's death enables the innocent murderer to leave the city of refuge and return to the land of his holding is that the death of the high priest, anointed to represent and mediate on behalf of Israel, procures a general atonement that covers an innocent murderer's act of murder – by dying in his place. As Morgenstern expressed it, 'the death of the high priest was regarded as the fitting, expiatory substitute for the death of the manslayer himself'

(1932: 87). Nicolsky, noting the high priest's role as representing the people, argued that his death was 'death for death' in place of the innocent murderer (1930; referenced in Feinberg 1946: 416–417). M. Greenberg, similarly, wrote (1959: 130):

> The sole personage whose religious-cultic importance might endow his death with expiatory value for the people at large is the high priest. During his life the priest expiates one type of religious guilt incurred by the people at large through the gold plate that he wears on his forehead . . . By his death he expiates that guilt which can be expiated only through death, but which could not be so expiated before.

The high priest had been anointed especially for the sake of his annual access to the holy of holies on the Day of Atonement, to make atonement for Israel, providing cleansing from all their sins (Lev. 16:30). As he lived, so he dies, to make atonement for God's people. In Deuteronomy, YHWH provides a ritual of purification in the event a slain human body is found without any clue as to the identity of the murderer (21:1–9). The procedure involved breaking the neck of a heifer over flowing water in a valley, and praying for YHWH to grant atonement, not imputing to Israel the guilt of innocent blood. The heifer stands in for the death of the murderer, only because the killer's identity is hopelessly unknown – but the principle of substitution is upheld, supporting a similar view of the high priest's death, with the phrase 'the death of the (high) priest', *môt (hakkōhēn) haggādōl*, occurring four times (vv. 25, 28 [twice], 32). Release from a city of refuge, upon the death of the high priest, appears as another expression of substitution on which the entire sacrificial system was founded. Such lines, like rivulets, flow together and cascade into Isaiah's theology of a suffering servant (Isa. 52:13 – 53:12; cf. M. Greenberg 1959: 130 n. 12, citing *Yefeh To'ar*).

Since the book's last subdivision (chs. 33–36) focuses almost exclusively on the land, moreover, the innocent murderer's exile from his land also appears to be a form of *lex talionis*, whereby the punishment matches the crime, since he did deprive an Israelite from enjoyment of the land (even if accidentally). Whitekettle explains (2018: 333) that an

> inadvertent killer was confined to a city of refuge in order to equalize the circumstances of the killer and his family/kin group with the circumstances of the victim and his family/kin group: specifically, the confinement of the killer in a city of refuge removed his presence and labour from his family/kin group just as the death of the victim had removed his presence and labour from his family/kin group.

That poetic justice is at play in the innocent murderer's exile appears evident in the description of his release upon the high priest's death: the murderer will return to 'the land of his holding' (*'ereṣ 'ăḥuzzātô*). The words are remarkably similar to the Jubilee legislation of Leviticus:

Num. 35:28: *yāšûb hārōṣēaḥ 'el-'ereṣ 'ăḥuzzātô*
the murderer will return to the land of his holding

Lev. 25:10: *wĕšabtem 'îš 'el-'ăḥuzzātô*
each man will return to his holding

The correspondence is not incidental, since Jubilee is proclaimed on that year's Day of Atonement, while the murderer goes free after the death of the high priest: 'As with Jubilee, return to one's land [from a city of refuge] coincides with a purificatory event' (Kawashima 2003: 382). There is a deep correspondence, therefore, between this section and the next (ch. 36), which refers to the Jubilee (36:4). The Jubilee, as Kawashima explains (2003: 372), would begin with 'the proclamation of "liberty" on the Day of Atonement, at which point each man returns to "his family" and/or "his land" (Lev. 25:10, 13, 27, 28, 41). It signifies the return of cosmic order to Israel.' The Day of Atonement, in the year of Jubilee, was accompanied by themes of redemption and liberation, including a person's return to the land of his or her inheritance, a pattern that may be discerned in the release of the accidental murderer to the land of his holding, through the death of the anointed high priest. Moreover, differences – that Numbers 35:28 includes 'the land', and Leviticus 25:10 includes a return to 'his family' (*mišpaḥtô*) – emphasize the primary concern of this last section of Numbers on the tribal inheritance of land (chs. 26–36). For a period of time, the innocent murderer had been removed, separated, from the land of his holding, dwelling – fittingly enough – in a Levitical city, the place provided by YHWH for Levites who had no land-holdings. Since Levitical cities formed liminal space, reflecting the Levite's liminal status, between the holiness of the priesthood and profane character of the tribes (cf. Olson 1996: 189–190), the accidental killer's experience via a city of asylum may be interpreted through the rubric of a rite of passage (cf. Whitekettle 2018: 351 n. 30).

35:29–34: The logic of the cities of asylum

29–32. Additional, clarifying laws are given, summing up the whole as a 'statute of judgement' (*ḥuqqat mišpāṭ*), a phrase used elsewhere only in Numbers 27:11, and that relates to civil, versus ritual, law (cf. Milgrom 1990: 294). The first stipulation requires that a murderer, who must be convicted by witnesses, cannot be convicted by only one witness. The second stipulation is twofold: a 'ransom' (*kōper*) cannot be taken for murder, neither for the guilty murderer nor for the innocent murderer who receives asylum. The guilty murderer must surely be put to death, and the innocent murderer must not 'return to dwell in the land, until the death of the priest'. The parallel between verses 31 and 32 argue forcefully for interpreting the high priest's death as in place of the innocent murderer: just as the guilty murderer cannot ransom himself but must be put to death to atone for his incurred bloodguilt, so the innocent murderer cannot ransom himself but must await the death of the priest before returning to dwell in the land. While the verse specifies only 'the priest', it has three times been established already that the high priest is intended (vv. 25, 28; cf. Lev. 16:32). In the covenant established with Noah and his descendants (all humanity), YHWH had declared he would require ('demand an accounting for', *dāraš*) 'the life of man' (*nepeš hā'ādām*), Genesis 9:5–6:

> Surely for your blood of your lives I will demand an accounting . . .
> Whoever sheds the blood of man (*dam hā'ādām*),
> by man his blood will be shed,
> for in the image of God he made man.

Genesis 9, in turn, points back to Genesis 1, the Torah's prologue, which teaches that humans were created in God's own image and likeness (1:26–27), endowing their lives with special dignity and sanctity 'unparalleled in ANE law' (M. Greenberg 1959: 129). A period of years spent in a city of asylum cannot atone for shedding the blood of another human being, even by accident. It is this principle, that only the life (blood) of a human being can atone for the life, the shed blood, of another human being, which makes the death of a representative mediator, that of the high priest, utterly necessary. The case of an innocent or accidental murderer is complex: only a death can atone for the shedding of blood, and yet, being an accidental crime, the murderer in this case does not deserve capital punishment. What is justice in such a scenario? Nagen captures the dilemma well, writing (2019: 271):

> Exile in a city of refuge cannot atone for the killing, as only blood can atone for blood. In order to remove the stain of such a horrific act, there is need for something equally powerful and symbolically equivalent to balance it out, a type of measure for measure . . . But if only blood can atone for blood, how is the accidental killer to atone for his actions?

The riddle is resolved by the death of the high priest, whose death as a representative of his generation may count as in the place of the innocent murderer's death. Especially on the Day of Atonement, the high priest's anointing above that of other priests is realized as he, representing the entire Israelite community, enters the holiest to sprinkle blood before the throne of YHWH; this to secure atonement and cleansing for God's people (cf. Nagen 2019: 272–273). When the 'whole community' (*kol-hā'ēdāh*) saw that Aaron, Israel's first high priest, had died, they – even the 'whole house of Israel' (*kōl bêt yiśrā'ēl*) – mourned for him thirty days (Num. 20:29). Such a momentous occasion, wherein all Israel mourned the death of the nation's highest spiritual leader and mediator, becomes a fitting context for the release of an accidental killer (cf. W. Driver 1960: 17–18), whose own 'death' has been tasted by the high priest, clearing him of bloodguilt. Ben Asher similarly notes (cf. 2003: 6:2342): 'the death of the high priest serves as a measure of consolation and comfort for the relatives of the slain person who will no longer bear a grudge concerning that killing'. While the sacrificial blood of animals was given by YHWH to atone for his people's sins (Lev. 17:11), the guilt of murder was not included – such is the sanctified nature of God's image, and the profound sacrilege that shedding the blood of a human being constitutes. Exceptions for bloodguilt include (Milgrom 1990: 510) homicide in self-defence (Exod. 22:1), judicial execution (Lev. 20:9–16), already suggested with 'by man his blood will be shed' (Gen. 9:6) and war (1 Kgs 2:5–6).

33–34. The last verses unravel the logic of the chapter: the cities of asylum legislation is placed precisely here within the book's flow to make a theological statement about the land itself; namely, that it is the place, analogous to the Camp in the wilderness, where YHWH will be dwelling in the midst of his people. This final speech of YHWH uses the term 'land' 8 times (35:10, 14, 28, 32, 33 [3 times], 34), 5 times in these final two verses, plus 2 more references ('in her', 'in her midst'). Both verses begin similarly, with a reference to not polluting/defiling the land, yielding a twofold emphasis:

v. 33: *wĕlō'-taḥănîpû 'et-hā'āreṣ 'ăšer 'attem bāh*
you will not pollute the land wherein you are

v. 34: *wĕlō' tĕṭammē' 'et-hā'āreṣ 'ăšer 'attem yōšĕbîm*
you will not defile the land wherein you dwell

As van Wolde states (2009: 234), the point of reference throughout these verses is the same: 'the land'. The focus, as Grossman observes (2014a: 481; emphasis original), is 'not on the murderer himself, but rather on the ramifications of murder to the *land*'. Allowing either a guilty murderer to ransom himself from the death penalty or an innocent murderer to ransom himself apart from the death of the high priest would be to pollute the land. Just as the city of asylum is an allowance for the innocent murderer's sake, even while the avenger would be innocent of bloodguilt for striking down the innocent murderer either before the latter reached the city of asylum or afterward if he left the city of asylum prematurely, so the death of the innocent murderer at the hands of the avenger would not defile the land – only the scenarios of verses 31 and 32 are in view. The term 'pollute' (*ḥānēp*) nearly always refers to the defilement of the land (Num. 35:33; Ps. 106:38; Isa. 24:5; Jer. 3:1, 2, 9; for exceptions, see Jer. 23:11; Dan. 11:32; Mic. 4:11). In her study of defilement terms, van Wolde determined that *ḥānēp* and *ṭimmē'* are so similar that they function as synonyms (2009: 236); although, as Levine suggests (2000: 560), *ḥānēp* also carries the notion of especially reprehensible behaviour, characteristic of evildoers. Even the innocent murderer must be removed from the land, from 'the land of his holding' (v. 28), and not be allowed 'to dwell in the land' (v. 32), because his doing so would defile the land. More than his own life is at stake in his residing in asylum – he must be separated from the land upon which he has shed blood.

The principle is clearly stated: 'for the blood it (*hû'*) will pollute the land, and for the land there is no purification (or 'atonement', 'ransoming', *yĕkuppar*) for the blood that was shed in her except by the blood of him who shed it.' The Torah is clear that even accidental or 'unintentional' (*bišgāgāh*) sins require atonement (see Lev. 4:27–31). Moreover, while other transgressions classified as 'unintentional' may be atoned through the cult by purification or reparation offerings (see Lev. 4:2, 22, 27; 5:15), murder – even accidental manslaughter – cannot be atoned in this manner. The pollution occurs when the bloodguilt for shedding the blood of the victim, a human made in the image of God, is not atoned for by the just death of another – either the death of the murderer (intentional or unintentional) or that of the high priest in the stead of the unintentional murderer. Once more the legislation here is given, not as a general consideration of the sixth command (Exod. 20:13; Deut. 5:17), nor to highlight the sanctity of life and the need for justice in the land as elsewhere (cf. Deut. 19:1–13), but *as a statement about the land*, that it will not be cleansed of murder except by the blood of another, whether murderer or high priest, and that the land's purity is an urgent concern because YHWH dwells there in the midst of his people. The high priest's death is necessary, not as a psychological resolution for the victim's family, but for the land itself. YHWH's presence in the land, as was the case of his presence in the Camp, is central to the life of Israel's community (cf. Budd 1984: 384). The Levites' role in the land is similar to their role in the Camp, guarding against pollution (cf. Olson 1996: 190; Stubbs 2009: 246).

Turning to the original case of murder in human history, Cain's murder of his brother Abel (Gen. 4:1–17), a number of links to the cities of asylum may be discerned. First, shed (human) blood is related in some way to the ground, an association perhaps traced to the creation of Adam of dust 'from the ground' (*min-hā'ădāmāh*, Gen. 2:7) – for the voice of Abel's blood cried 'from the ground' (*min-hā'ădāmāh*, Gen.

4:10). The relationship between Cain and the land was clearly affected by murder: Cain is 'cursed' from the ground, which has opened her mouth to receive Abel's blood (4:11), the ground will no longer yield her strength at his tilling, he will be a fugitive and wanderer on the earth (4:12) and is 'driven' from the face of the ground (4:14). Second, Cain fears that 'anyone who finds me will slay me' (4:14), even as the innocent murderer would fear being slain if found by the avenger. Lamech, Cain's descendant, will boast that if Cain is 'avenged' (*nāqam*) sevenfold, Lamech will be seventy-sevenfold (Gen. 4:24). Third, that Cain built a city under the motivation of self-protection is evident by the context of his expressed fear; somewhat similarly, the city of asylum provides for the innocent murderer's protection. While the unintentional murderer is not guilty of malicious, calculated murder, the land/ground nevertheless will be defiled apart from his own death (at least via the death of the high priest), and until this happens, it appears that his exile away from the land, as with Cain's banishment farther east of Eden 'from before the face of YHWH' (*millipnê yhwh*, Gen. 4:16), facilitates a sort of mitigation of the bloodguilt, until it has been cleansed (see also Lev. 18:25–28). The exiled person is not 'dwelling on his land', as Grossman writes (2019: 168), 'and only thus can land that was tainted with innocent blood come to rest'. In the primordial era, the earth would be cleansed through the waters of the flood (Gen. 7 – 8), the cosmic counterpart to the Day of Atonement in Israel's cult (cf. e.g. Kawashima 2003: 374–379). Other stories in the Bible, as Rofé points out, follow a pattern of banishment or escape after a murder, whether intentional or innocent: Cain after slaying Abel (Gen. 4), Moses after killing an Egyptian (Exod. 2:11–19), Absalom after killing Amnon (2 Sam. 13:37; 14:13, 32), with the possible implication that banishment from the land might have been perceived as a mitigating alternative to putting the murderer to death (1986: 237; cf. M. Greenberg 1959: 128–129; see Burnside 2010a). One may also add Israel's exile from the land, due to bloodshed among other heinous acts (cf. Isa. 1:15, 21). Shedding innocent blood, whether intentionally or inadvertently, defiles the land, and since the land cannot suffer the presence of a person who shed the blood of another, as Grossman states (2014a: 487), 'the accidental murderer is exiled to the city of refuge, symbolizing a temporary migration from the land' where YHWH God dwells. Since the land's defilement calls for the death of the one who shed blood, he further explains, but 'legal ethics' cannot allow execution for an accidental murder, the legislation provides a twofold compromise (Grossman 2014a: 487): 'the murderer's symbolic detachment from the land, and atonement through the death of the high priest'. Whereas the guilty murderer is removed from the land by death, the innocent murderer is removed by exile to the city of asylum until the high priest's death (cf. van Wolde 2009: 235). Exile did indeed constitute 'a form of social death', as Plaut explains (1979: 340–341), and even the accidental manslayer needed to be confined to keep 'the body social from further contamination' until the process of full expiation was completed by the high priest's death. The Midrash, expounding on the compassions and mercies of God, compares the city of refuge legislation, whereby an accidental murderer is spared a death-sentence, to the banishment of Adam from the garden of Eden, since Adam had deserved to die immediately (*Num. Rab.* 23.13), a reading that connects Israel's land with Eden.

The focus on the land in Numbers 35 is especially evident when compared to the cities of asylum legislation in Deuteronomy, which makes no reference to the Levitical character of the cities of refuge nor to the role of the high priest's death (cf. M. Greenberg 1959: 125), and where the ultimate reason given for not shedding innocent blood in the land is to avoid 'bloodguilt upon you' (*'ālêkā dāmîm*, Deut. 19:10). The point of urgency in Numbers is for Israel not to 'defile (*tĕṭammē'*) the land', here using *ṭāmē'* instead of *ḥānēp*, which more clearly manifests the analogy between the Camp and the land in relation to YHWH's presence in the midst of Israel (cf. Leder 2010: 161):

Num. 5:3: *wĕlō' yĕṭammĕ'û 'et-maḥănêhem 'ăšer 'ănî šōkēn bĕrôkām*
And do not defile your camps where even I am dwelling in the midst of them.

Num. 35:34: *wĕlō' tĕṭammē' 'et-hā'āreṣ . . .'ăšer 'ănî šōkēn bĕtôkāh kî 'ănî yhwh šōkēn bĕtôk bĕnê yiśrā'ēl*
And do not defile the land . . . where even I am dwelling in the midst of her, for I, YHWH, am dwelling in the midst of the sons of Israel.

The statement in 5:3 was climactic as the first realization of the divine purpose-statements in Exodus:

Let them make for me a Sanctuary so that I may dwell in their midst. (Exod. 25:8)

I will dwell in the midst of the sons of Israel, and will be their God. And they will know that I am YHWH their God, who brought them forth from the land of Egypt in order to dwell in their midst – I, YHWH, am their God. (Exod. 29:45–46)

The ultimate goal, however, was for YHWH God to dwell in the midst of his people *in the land*, marking the last verse of Numbers (35:34), before the concluding inclusio related to the Zelophehad daughters (ch. 36), as both climactic and emphatic, with its *'ănî yhwh*: 'for I, YHWH, am dwelling in the midst of the sons of Israel' (recalling Exod. 29:46). Also remarkable, the ptc. form *šōkēn* is used: 'I *am dwelling* in the midst of her (the land) . . . for I, YHWH, *am dwelling* in the midst of the sons of Israel (in the land).' Aptly, Frevel observes that on a conceptual level, Israel's wilderness Camp represents both the ideal walled city with a sanctuary in its centre (i.e. Jerusalem) and the ideal land (Israel, the Promised Land) (2013c: 378–379), an analogy assumed and cultivated in Numbers. The cities-of-asylum legislation functions to highlight the wondrous reality that YHWH God will dwell in the midst of Israel in the land – what was once experienced in the land of Eden will be tasted in some measure by the redeemed people of God. His presence, his dwelling in the land, raises the urgency over the land's defilement, since the goal of the covenant is for YHWH to dwell among his people in the land. This reality, YHWH's presence in the land, with all goings-on occurring before 'his face' (cf. Gen. 4:16), must determine the conduct of Israel, just as his presence had called for purity of life in the Camp. As the purity laws in Numbers 5 – 6 designated periods of expulsion from the Camp and highlighted the role of the priesthood for restoration, the same may be said of the cities of asylum. Just as Numbers 3 – 4 delineated the Levites' place and role within the Camp after it was established with the tribes (chs. 1–2), so YHWH's last two speeches (ch. 35) delineate the place and role of Levites in the land of the tribes (chs. 33–34).

Verse 34, therefore, forms an appropriate conclusion not only 'for the regulations involving conquest, occupation, and distribution of the land' (Grossman 2014a: 482), but in terms of its climactic statement regarding YHWH's presence in the land among his people: 'The Lord's demand in the wilderness that the camp be kept pure (see 5:3) is, in Canaan, extended to all of God's land' (Milgrom 1990: 296) – since Israel's Camp was the 'prototype' for the entire land (Milgrom 1997: 242). (See Figure 5.)

Explanation

The second half (chs. 33–36) of the third major section of Numbers (chs. 26–36) begins with Moses' written record of Israel's journeys through the wilderness by the word of YHWH, out of Egypt to the plains of Moab. The journeys are divided into two major sections, each headed by short narrative descriptions (vv. 3–5 and 38–39), related to the first (vv. 3–36) and second generations (vv. 37–49), respectively. Factoring in the overlap between stations of encampment and departure, the first section offers the first generation's journey toward the land as fourteen stations (vv. 3–17), and the journeys through the thirty-eight years of judgement as twenty stations (vv. 18–36), while the second section details the journeys of the second generation with ten stations (vv. 37–49). The style of the list is similar to the military marches of ANE kings (as found e.g. in ninth-century BC Assyrian annals), portraying Israel's journeys

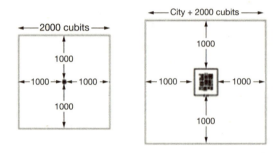

Figure 5: Levitical cities and cities of refuge

as the marches of the earthly hosts of YHWH, the divine King (Davies 1974; cf. G. J. Wenham 1981b: 245). Scolnic refers to the list of marches as 'uplifting and victorious . . . a paean of triumph' (1995: 129). The itinerary map recalls the movements of YHWH's glory Cloud for Israel's setting out and encampments (Exod. 40:36–38; Num. 9:15–23), and the 'Song of the Ark' voiced by Moses: 'Arise, O YHWH! Your enemies be scattered, and those who hate you flee from before your face!' when Israel journeyed forth, and 'Return, O YHWH! To the myriad thousands of Israel' upon encampment (10:35–36).

The Midrash offers a number of expositions of the stages of Israel's journeys, each capturing something of how the list forms a record of God's faithful compassion to his people, miraculously shielding them from fiery serpents and scorpions in the wilderness (cf. Deut. 8:15), and how he 'led his people like a flock by the hand of Moses and Aaron' (Ps. 77:20; *Num. Rab.* 23.1). The mere recollection of forty-two stations brings to mind the miraculous wonder of Israel's survival in the wilderness for forty years (cf. Maimonides, *Guide for the Perplexed*, 3.50). One midrashic story captures YHWH's solidarity with and care for Israel, likening the list of wilderness journeys to the case of a king whose son was ill (*Num. Rab.* 23.3; Slotki 1951: 6:865): 'He took him to a certain place to cure him. On their return journey his father began to recount all the stages, saying: Here we slept; here we cooled ourselves; here you had a headache.' Israel's illness was spiritual in nature, and their wilderness journeys, full of provocations against YHWH, were nevertheless, by his sovereign wisdom, ordained for their spiritual growth so that, in retrospect, the stations might be appreciated for their healing purpose. The Midrash exclaims further that for having welcomed God's people, these stopping places will be the first to experience the fulfilment of prophetic promises for the wilderness to be transformed into the garden of Eden (*Num. Rab.* 23.4; cf. Isa. 35:1–2; 41:18; 43:19). Similarly, Abarbanel refers to each station as a 'signpost' for the prophesied second exodus of the Messiah (citing Mic. 7:15 and Ezek. 20:35; 2015: 329–330; cf. ben Asher 2003: 6:2332–2333).

That the journeys involved both blessings and hardships is evident by the two isolated references, one to much water, 'twelve springs of water' (v. 9), and the other to none, 'there was no water there for the people' (v. 14). Aside from these geographical observations, however, there are no mentions of the spiritual struggles and failures that occurred throughout the journeys. By suppressing the negative elements of the previous narrative accounts, such as Israel's grumblings, disobedience and rebellions, but also equally suppressing the positive elements, such as YHWH's miraculous provisions of water, bread and meat, along with bypassing his supernatural judgements of fire and plague, the travelogue lays bare a single, underlying thread, exposing it as a wonder worthy of contemplation in and of itself; namely, the ongoing relationship of YHWH and his people Israel throughout the wilderness era. The rhythm of repeated departure and encampment, the underlying steady obedience under YHWH's guidance, would eventually overcome the dramatic valleys of rebellion and intense peaks of divine judgement. The spiritual success of life's journey is much more dependent on the monotony of persevering commitment, on the slow and steady growth that comes through the ordinary means of grace, than on the manufactured highs of immature spirituality. The journeys themselves, with Israel following after YHWH through a barren wilderness, is testimony to the enduring covenant relationship, rooted in the love of YHWH, that otherwise may be lost in the drama of the events that transpired along the way. As an elderly couple, celebrating their golden anniversary, may relish with tranquil satisfaction and comfort the marvel that they have remained together faithfully throughout the current of years, this without denying times of strain, perplexity and hardship, but quietly focusing on the thread of togetherness throughout their journeys in the world, so Moses' record of Israel's journeys with YHWH, from the beginning to the end of the wilderness years, functions as an enduring testimony to a love and faithfulness that would serve as a foundation for Israel's life in the land – and a wellspring of hope in the face of exile. 'I remember you,' YHWH cries out through Jeremiah, 'the loving-kindness of your youth, the love of your espousals, how you followed after me in the wilderness, in a land not sown' (2:2). 'Therefore, look!' he says through Hosea, 'I myself will allure her and bring her into the wilderness, and will speak soothingly to her . . . as in the days of her youth when she came up out of the land of Egypt' (2:14–15).

As with the journey of our lives, every stage is a further departure and reliving of the original exodus, and a step forward toward the final destination – even delays and reversions in geography were divinely intended for spiritual progress. While each of the stations might not have been required to get to Canaan, every one was necessary for departing Egypt and for living well in the land: 'each travel was a new exodus from the land of *Mitzrayim*, another step away from the immorality and idolatry of Egypt' (Malbim 2013: 469–470). The journeys, each departure and encampment, as a comprehensive whole completed the one process of leaving the land and life of Egypt – every month of the wilderness years was necessary, not only for leaving Egypt more fully but for learning to cleave to YHWH God, Israel's Redeemer and Shepherd. Deuteronomy looks back to the wilderness years as a time for YHWH to teach Israel special lessons that would serve as the foundation for life in the land, a notion captured well in *Mekhilta de-Rabbi Shimon ben Yoḥai* (W. D. Nelson 2006: 80):

> The Holy One, blessed be He, said, 'If I bring them now into [the Land of Israel] by the straight route, they will [immediately begin] seizing the fields and vineyards, and they will neglect the Torah. Rather, I will make them go around in the wilderness for 40 years, and they will eat the manna and drink the water of the well, and the Torah will [have time to] take root in their bodies.'

The itinerary creates continuity not only across geography but across time, unifying the stories of two separate generations as the one that went forth out of Egypt eventually merges and transforms into the generation that enters the land (cf. Y. Kahn 2014b: 456). The long list of stages has one beginning and one end, which creates not only continuity as a single itinerary, but demonstrates divine purpose and intention by the One who promises that 'all things work together for good for those who love God and have been called according to his purpose' (Rom.

8:28). Given the rich significance of Israel's list of journeys, it is no surprise that in some Jewish traditions the itinerary is treated as a song, the journeys read in a special melody (cf. Bin-Nun 2019b). The itinerary stands, in the words of Scolnic (1995: 122), as 'perhaps the best example in the entire Bible of God's guidance in the wilderness', underscoring Israel's experience of divine mercy faithfully supplied by YHWH. Contemplating the nation of Israel in the present day, along its arduous road of suffering and survival, one cannot doubt the divine assurance that 'all Israel will be saved' (Rom. 11:26) – for YHWH, their merciful Father, is faithful.

Israel's lyric of journeys, culminating in 'the plains of Moab' (33:49), forms the introduction to YHWH's final five speeches, chiastically arranged as a unit, which functions as a vision of life in the land beyond the Jordan. Life in the land with YHWH is portrayed in a manner analogous to life with him in the Camp, including separate places and roles for the twelve tribes and Levites. YHWH's first speech (33:50–56) calls on Israelites to dispossess the land's inhabitants, destroying all vestiges of idolatry. Being paralleled with the fifth speech (35:9–34), and related to the Levitical cities of asylum, allows one to discern an underlying concern related to idolatry's defilement of the land (in which YHWH will dwell). Pertinently, the first speech relates to *conquest*, precisely the military failure of the outer camp of twelve tribes, when the first generation rebelled against YHWH's word through Moses (Num. 13 – 14). YHWH's call for Israelites to drive out the Canaanites, destroying all vestiges of their idolatrous culture, resonates with the theology of the Midianite war (ch. 31). Rather than decimating Canaanites with a divine plague for their offensive wickedness, YHWH uses Israelites as instruments of warfare in order to teach Israel the appropriate response to idolatry (33:50–53), to safeguard his people from the sort of judgement they endured at Baal Peor (33:55–56; cf. 25:9).

YHWH's second speech (34:1–12, with Moses' obedience, vv. 13–15), delineating the boundaries of the land, sets before Israel a portrait, both historical and ideal, that functions as a tangible reality and spiritual paradigm. Aptly, Allen refers to the boundary list as 'a liturgy of geography' (2012: 436), a triumphant and celebratory view of YHWH's gift to his people. Such a vision of the land would fill Moses' own eyes before he entered the glory of heaven (Deut. 32:48–52). YHWH's third and central speech (34:16–29), announces the ten princes who will divide the inheritance of land to Israel. Recalling not only the book's opening ('These are the names of the men', 1:5), but also the disastrous scouts mission ('These were their names', 13:4), the second generation's ten chieftains, chosen to divide the land to their respective tribes, stand as those who will finally repair the failure of the ten scouts who had, a generation earlier, given a bad report of the land.

After the division of the land by Eleazar the priest, Joshua the son of Nun and the ten princes – via divine speech – completing the focus on the twelve tribes, YHWH's fourth speech (35:1–8) turns topically to the place of Levites in the land. Through the other tribes, YHWH grants Levites holding cities, with their surrounding pasturelands, to dwell in. The envisioned forty-two cities plus six cities of refuge are analogous to the Levites' place in the Camp (chs. 3–4). In his fifth and final speech (35:9–34), which continues the Levitical focus, YHWH establishes cities of refuge to keep the land from defilement, concerns analogous to the purity regulations for the Camp (chs. 5–6). Just as with the motif of atonement made by the high priest that pervades the section on the inner camp (chs. 16–18), so the death of the high priest is underscored here as the sole means for an unintentional murderer to be released from his city of asylum. The priesthood is just as necessary for Israel's survival in the land, as it was for Israel's survival in the wilderness. Feinberg, noting that biblical references to God as the believer's refuge are too numerous to mention (cf. Psalms), applied the teaching of the cities of refuge to the Messiah provided by God as the refuge for all humanity (1947: 45–48): Israel's dire need of God's provision of the cities, their accessibility and the manslayer's peril apart from them underscore the preciousness of the salvation found only in the Lord Jesus Christ. The atoning death of the high priest gestured toward a hope and way realized by the Messiah, the 'anointed one', whose blood speaks a better word than Abel's (Heb. 12:24; cf. Allen 2012: 451).

As with the extraordinary statement of YHWH's dwelling in the Camp (5:3), proclaiming the new reality of the covenant relationship (cf. Exod. 25:8; 29:45–46), the last view of life in the land – indeed, the concluding statement of YHWH's speeches – announces that *YHWH will be dwelling in the midst of his people in the land* (35:34). YHWH's presence among his people in the land, the fruition of the Sinai covenant, mapped out after the pattern of Israel's Camp (cf. Leder 2010: 161), is the impetus for not defiling the land; that is, for pursuing purity and holiness. In a similar way, union with Christ is a deterrent to defiling behaviour in the life of God's people (see e.g. 1 Cor. 6:15–20; 10:14–22). Wondrously, the last words of YHWH's last speech proclaim the realization not only of the Sinai covenant, but of the ancestral promises: 'where I myself dwell in her (the land's) midst – for I am YHWH dwelling in the midst of the sons of Israel'. The resplendent rays of effulgent glory pale only under the greater luminescence of the consummation in a new heaven and earth (Rev. 21:3): 'And I heard a great voice out of heaven, saying: Behold! The Dwelling of God is with people, and he will dwell with them, and they will be his peoples, and God himself will be with them and be their God!'

NUMBERS 36: PRESERVING THE INHERITANCE OF LAND IN MARRIAGE

Translation

³⁶:¹And the heads of the fathers according to the clan of the sons of Gilead, the son of Machir, the son of Manasseh, from the clans of the sons of Joseph, drew near and spoke before Moses and before the chieftains of the heads of the fathers of the sons of Israel. ²And said, 'YHWH commanded my lord to give the land as an inheritance by lot to the sons of Israel, and my lord was commanded by YHWH to give the inheritance of Zelophehad our brother to his daughters. ³But should they become wives to one of the sons of the (other) tribes of the sons of Israel, their inheritance will be removed from the inheritance of our fathers, and will be added upon the inheritance of the tribe to which they would belong, and from the lot of our inheritance it will be removed. ⁴And when there is a Jubilee for the sons of Israel, then their inheritance will be added upon the inheritance of the tribe to which they would belong, and from the inheritance of the tribe of our fathers their inheritance will be removed.' ⁵And Moses commanded the sons of Israel by the word of YHWH, saying, 'Rightly the tribe of the sons of Joseph have spoken. ⁶This is the matter which YHWH has commanded for the daughters of Zelophehad, saying, 'To whoever is good in their eyes, let them be wives; only, within the clan of the tribe of their father let them be wives. ⁷So the inheritance of the sons of Israel will not go around from tribe to tribe, for the sons of Israel will cling each man to the inheritance of the tribe of his fathers. ⁸And every daughter who possesses an inheritance from the tribes of the sons of Israel may become wife to anyone from the clan of the tribe of her father, in order that the sons of Israel may possess each man the inheritance of his fathers. ⁹So the inheritance will not go around from tribe to another tribe, for the tribes of the sons of Israel will cling each man to his inheritance.' ¹⁰Just as YHWH had commanded Moses, just so the daughters of Zelophehad did. ¹¹And Mahlah, Tirzah, and Hoglah, and Milcah, and Noah, the daughters of Zelophehad, became wives to the sons of their uncles. ¹²Within the clans of the sons of Manasseh, the son of Joseph, they became wives, and their inheritance was (still) with the tribe of the clan of their father. ¹³These are the commands and judgements that YHWH had commanded by the hand of Moses to the sons of Israel, on the plains of Moab by the Jordan near Jericho.

Notes on the text

1. 'the clans': LXX, Syr and Vg have sg.

'before Moses': LXX and Syr include 'and before Eleazar the priest' (cf. 27:2).

2. 'my lord was commanded by YHWH': *BHS* suggests emending to 'and YHWH commanded us' (see Paterson 1900: 66 for 'YHWH commanded my lord').

3. 'sons of the (other) tribes': LXX and Syr lack 'sons of' here.
'our fathers': Syr has 'their' (also in v. 4).

6. 'their father': MT has m. suff., but f. is required here, with many MT MSS and SamP (see GKC §135o).

7. 1Q3:9 commands men as well to marry only within their tribe (implied in Vg).

11. The order is changed from what appears to be the standard listing (26:33; 27:1; cf. Josh. 17:3), but SamP and some Gk MSS retain the previous order.

12. 'the clans': LXX, Syr, Vg and one MT MS have sg.

Form and structure

Chapter 36 is typically dubbed an appendix (cf. Budd 1984: xvii, 388–389) or 'editorial afterthought' (Milgrom 1990: 512), composed by a different author than that of Numbers 27 (e.g. Baentsch 1903: 697; G. B. Gray 1903: 477; E. W. Davies 1995b: 368). Yet, beyond presupposing and supplementing the ruling in chapter 27 (cf. Fishbane 1986: 104), Numbers 36 forms an inclusio with Numbers 27:1–11, both dealing with land inheritance concerns related to the daughters of Zelophehad (cf. Olson 1985: 175; Ulrich 1998). Since, moreover, the same feature, a census plus inclusio, has shaped the parallel opening chapters (chs. 1–10), the nature and function of the episode's placement should, rather than being dismissed, be studied for its exegetical and theological value. In this regard, Kawashima's observation is on point (2003: 380; cf. Joosten 1996: 137–148): 'the camp prefigures the nation [in the land] as a spatial distribution of kinship'. The chapter may be outlined as follows:

1. The potential problem of losing tribal lands (vv. 1–4)
2. The divine ruling for heiresses (vv. 5–9)
3. The daughters of Zelophehad comply (vv. 10–12)
4. Postscript (v. 13)

Comment

1–4. The introductory narration and speech of the heads of Gilead is strikingly similar to the earlier daughters of Zelophehad episode that it continues (27:1–11), beginning with a drawn-out genealogical introduction to a son(s) of Gilead, use of the verb 'to draw near' (*q-r-b*), designating a formal (and perhaps judicial) approach, and turning on a concern over 'diminishment' (*gāra'*) of Zelophehad's name and land, respectively (cf. Samet 2003; Shemesh 2007: 92; Kislev 2010: 249–250). Inclusion of 'son of Machir' makes the allotment concern inclusive of the Transjordan and Cisjordan areas (21:21–35; 32:33–42). Form, context and key terms (including *q-r-b* and *g-r-'*) relate this episode not only to the prior daughters of Zelophehad account (27:1–11), but also to the second Passover episode (9:1–14). Whereas the daughters of Zelophehad had drawn near specifically to speak to Moses, Eleazar the priest, the princes and all the congregation, the heads of the sons of Gilead speak before Moses and the highest chieftains of Israel. The daughters' concern had related to the preservation of their father's name, separating his sin from that of Korah's rebellion, perhaps explaining the presence of Eleazar the priest. Now, however, the focus has shifted to the retention of YHWH's gift of land, a tribal concern addressed only to Moses and the princes of the tribes of Israel. The movement from chapter 27 to 36 includes a broadening of the concern from family to tribe. Chapter 36 safeguards lands at the clan level, but, ultimately, the resolution will serve to avoid intertribal conflict (Uffenheimer 1979: 8; cf. Gottwald 1999: 265–266). The former concern of the daughters of Zelophehad related to the integrity of the family within the tribe, and the later concern of their uncles relates to the integrity of the tribes within the nation (Etshalom 2010; cf. Weingreen 1966a: 519; Ben-Barak 2006: 36). Chapters 33–36 all pertain to the inheritance of the land, 'carried out in a tribal framework' (Samet 2003). Within this tribal system, nevertheless, Numbers 36 is deeply concerned about the *mišpāḥāh* as well (cf. Bendor 1996: 145, 162–163).

Their preliminary twofold statement (v. 2a, b) serves as background to their concern and begins each time with 'my lord', even as a direct object in the first case (*'et-'ădōnî*), underscoring their respectful address of Moses: 'my lord YHWH commanded . . . my lord was commanded by YHWH'. The first part relates the general divine command to give the land as an inheritance by lot to the sons of Israel (26:52–56), while the second relates the divine command to give Zelophehad's inheritance to his daughters (27:1–11). Along with their identification with the 'sons of Gilead' (v. 1), their use of 'our brother' as a descriptor of Zelophehad justifies their vested interest in the previous ruling. The word 'inheritance' (*naḥălāh*) occurs *seventeen times* in this thirteen-verse story (cf. Ziegler 2014: 10), bringing the book to a climactic close: Israel will receive the inheritance of land divinely promised to the patriarchs.

The twofold preliminary statement is then reversed in verse 3, demonstrating how the second command may undo the first: if the daughters of Zelophehad marry someone from another tribe, the result will be the 'removal' (*g-r-'*) of lands 'from the lot of our inheritance', echoing the original command to give the land 'as an inheritance by lot'. Since the original division of land was by lot, understood as determined by God's will (Prov. 16:33), then the recent ruling (27:6–11), could potentially work against God's determination of tribal boundaries (cf. Hirsch 2007a: 704). Use of 'lot', then, strengthens their claim, since the divisions fixed by God were to be immutable (Kislev 2010: 258). The divinely ordained tribal distribution of land formed a sacred bond between the tribe and its land (Derby 1997: 171). Since the daughters' sons would inherit their lands, and because sons trace their lineage through their father's tribe, the lands would be 'added' to the tribe of the husbands whom the daughters of Zelophehad marry (cf. Rashi 1997: 4:432). Use of *yāsap* in verses 3 and 4 may be a pun on Joseph's name, as mentioned in verses 1, 5 and 12 (*yôsēp*). Not only does their concern involve a removal or diminishment, as with the daughters' original concern, but they also, as with the daughters' plea, seek to preserve a father's possession: the daughters sought to preserve the name (and land) of their father (cf. 27:4), and these heads of Gilead seek to preserve 'the inheritance of our fathers'. While in both cases, their appeals include personal benefit as well, this does not lessen their familial concern. Use of 'sons of Israel', 'our brother', 'his daughters', 'wives' and 'our fathers', all contribute to the focus on maintaining family ties and harmony via the barring of further land-division after its distribution by lot – in other words, maintaining the unity of the land is related to the unity of each tribe. From this perspective, inasmuch as losing land is linked to losing an ancestor's name, the requests on the part of the daughters of Zelophehad, on the one hand, and by the chieftains of Gilead, on the other, are nearly the same if from different perspectives. In both scenarios God rules in favour of those 'who stood to lose their land' (Ulrich 1998: 529). Q. Day (2023: 18) points out the 'series of losses' emphasized in verse 3: the daughters' inheritance, the inheritance of the uncles' fathers and, finally, the inheritance of the uncles themselves. The concern of the Gileadite chieftains highlights the sacred nature of marriage, the one-flesh union (Gen. 2:24), which supersedes other ties of kinship, especially in the patriarchal cultures of the ancient world. As Ben-Barak writes (2006: 24), 'Ancient Israelite and Near Eastern custom decreed that with her marriage a daughter and all her possessions went over to her husband's father's house.'

The third part of their speech (v. 4) includes 'a brief and tantalizing reference' to Jubilee (Bergsma 2007: 114), and serves not only as an illustration but to demonstrate the irreversible nature – and therefore urgent gravity – of their concern: the Jubilee would confirm the transfer of land from the inheritance of only one tribe to another, ensuring that the 'inheritance of the tribe of our fathers . . . will be removed'. The logic of the Jubilee reference has been debated, with some scholars asserting its complete lack of relevance (e.g. Noth 1968: 257–258; E. W. Davies 1995b: 369). The simplest understanding, offered by Rashi (cf. 1997: 4:432), is that, since the Jubilee returns only lands exchanged in sale (Lev. 25:13–55) versus property gained by inheritance or marriage, then *even the Jubilee*, ordained by God specifically to restore and safeguard the tribal inheritance of land, would fail to preserve the tribal inheritance of

lands (see Gane 1990: 8–10). Ibn Ezra also interpreted 'Even if the Jubilee
. . .' (see 1999: 266; cf. Fishbane 1986: 105; Levine 2000: 577), understanding the reference as precluding a false remedy, since the Jubilee
legislation was given as 'the great remedy' for problems concerning loss
of land in Canaan (Ashley 1993: 659; cf. Gane 2004: 796). To experience
loss on Jubilee – the occasion of redemption and restoration, even of
Messianic anticipation (see Isa. 61) – would be, therefore, harshly incongruous with and inimical to YHWH's purpose not only for the Year
of Jubilee, but for his gift of the land as well. G. Robinson describes
(1988: 345–346, 357) the sabbath, including the Jubilee year, 'the seventh
sabbath of years', as 'a symbol of salvation and freedom for Israel. It is
the symbol of *měnûḥâ* ['rest'], the ideal living condition in the *naḥălāh*,
in the promised land,' with the Jubilee legislation 'aimed at restoring
the condition of *měnûḥâ* to every Israelite . . . in recovering his ancestral
rights to the *naḥălāh*'. Far from being an irrelevant intrusion, the Jubilee
reference reinforces the uncles' argument 'that Jubilee, as intended by
Yahweh, cannot occur, at least for the tribe of Manasseh, unless the law
changes' – this tribe will experience loss (Q. Day 2023: 21; see also Aaron
2009: 16–18; Gevaryahu 2013: 109).

The name 'Jubilee' (*yōbēl*) derives from 'ram's horn', *yôbēl*, which
was blown to announce the dawn of liberty, triumphantly and with
all of its celebratory associations. Leviticus 25 offers the foundational
legislation for Jubilees, which establishes the following features, relevant
to our passage: the shofar blast is sounded on the tenth day of the
seventh month, the Day of Atonement (v. 9); the fiftieth year is to be
consecrated (v. 10); liberty is to be proclaimed throughout the land (v.
10); each 'man' (*'îš*) will return to 'his holding' (*'ăḥuzzātô*), each man
will return to 'his family' (*mišpaḥtô*) – note the parallelism between
'holding' and 'family' (v. 10; cf. v. 13); on the Jubilee year sold lands
must return to their original owner (vv. 13–17, 23–34). In all, Leviticus
25 uses the word 'return' (*šûb*) some eleven times, with five uses referring
to people's return to their land holding (vv. 10, 13, 27, 28, 41) and two
referring to people's return to their family. The rule of return holds
priority over the other legislative features of Jubilee (Q. Day 2023: 18; see
Westbrook 1991: 52–57). The word 'liberty' (*děrôr*) contains the idea of
flowing freely (BDB 204; *HALOT* 233), and the use here includes one's
unencumbered restoration to family lands. With the focus on YHWH's
gift of land to the tribes in the final section of Numbers (chs. 26–36),
the possibility of losing the fathers' inheritance is addressed. The laws
of inheritance, as Breland observes (2019: 204), serve a similar objective
to the Jubilee, in preserving Israel's system of land tenure at the clan
level – 'land and family belong together'. Sakenfeld is, therefore, correct
in taking the Jubilees reference as forming 'an appropriate climax' to
the uncles' speech (1988: 45–46), for if *even* the time of Jubilee will not
restore the land to Zelophehad's clan but, worse, confirm its loss, then

additional legislation is needed to safeguard the intent of Jubilee. The dilemma occurs *because* the daughters are the rightful owners, a right that would transfer to the family (and clan and tribe) into which each daughter adhered in marriage – so while Zelophehad's name has been secured, his inheritance would eventually be transferred to another tribe (Embry 2016: 41).

The unity and narrative logic of chapters 35 and 36 surfaces through the underlying text of Leviticus 25, which address both Levitical cities (vv. 32–34) and the restoration of tribal holdings (vv. 13–17, 23–31) (cf. Bergsma 2007: 119). Both chapters, moreover, indirectly rest on the Day of Atonement: in the innocent murderer's release from the city of refuge through the death of the anointed high priest (35:25, 32), recalling his work on the Day of Atonement, and in the reference to Jubilee (36:4), which is inaugurated on the Day of Atonement.

5–9. The new ruling, as with the previous ones (cf. v. 2), comes as a command (v. 5: *wayĕṣaw*; v. 6: *ṣiwwā*; cf. vv. 10, 13) from the word ('mouth') of YHWH (*'al-pî yhwh*) – no serious significance, then, should be derived from the fact that the narration omits Moses' consultation of YHWH, as recounted earlier (27:5), especially since YHWH might have even revealed this addendum during Moses' original consultation (similarly, Milgrom 1990: 297). The separation and form of the two Zelophehad episodes were determined by structural and thematic concerns.

Mirroring YHWH's previous response to the daughters of Zelophehad (27:7), it is now said of the tribe of the sons of Joseph, 'Rightly' (*kēn*) they have 'spoken' (*dōbĕrîm*). The broader emphasis on 'Joseph' accords with the similar note on which Genesis ends (Gen. 48; 49:22–26; 50:22–26), and functions to position the dilemma at the *tribal* level with the chieftains of Gilead speaking on behalf of the tribe (cf. Ibn Ezra 1999: 266), since the current situation would allow for lands to 'go around from tribe to tribe' (vv. 7, 9). Although Joseph had died outside the land, he was looking for the promised deliverance, to which YHWH had proven faithful: his bones and, more, his descendants were brought in to inherit the land (Gen. 50:24–25; Exod. 13:19; cf. Josh. 24:32).

Moses' speech moves from YHWH's command particularly 'for the daughters of Zelophehad' (v. 6), to its rationale (v. 7), and the command and its rationale are given as a general, binding judgement for all Israel in verses 8 and 9, respectively, so that verses 8–9 parallel verses 6–7 as a panel construction. The command of verse 6 is expressed in a liberal manner, beginning with the daughters' complete liberty to choose whoever is 'good (*ṭôb*) in their eyes', a phrase that fronts the command, and then adding one restriction by use of *'ak* (only), that their choice must fall within the 'clan' (*mišpāḥāh*) of their father's tribe – affirming land distribution and retention at the clan level. That a m. suff. is used in 'their eyes' (*bĕʿênêhem*) does not suggest the uncles chose husbands for the daughters (contra Ginsberg 1972) – in the same verse 'their father', clearly referring to the daughters, also uses a m. suff. (cf. 27:7). The purpose of this one restriction is clearly stated from the onset of verse 7: 'No going-around' (*lōʾ-tissōb*) of the inheritance from tribe to tribe – here, the verb means 'to transfer' (Levine 2000: 578). This negative scenario is then replaced beautifully with 'for' (*kî*) each 'man' (*ʾîš*) will cling to the inheritance of the tribe of his fathers, repeated twice to emphasize its significance (vv. 7, 9; cf. G. J. Wenham 1981b: 266). The term for 'cling' (*dābaq*) is intimate, meaning 'to cleave, keep close' (see BDB 179–80), its first use in Scripture referring to a man's cleaving to his wife so as to become one flesh (Gen. 2:24). It is also used of close relationships, whether with God (cf. Deut. 10:20; 11:22) or with family members (cf. Ruth 1:14). The rhetoric is startling enough that some have mistakenly understood Moses' speech as creating a new 'primary relationship' between a man and his land, shifting even the marriage relationship to his wife as secondary (cf. Hunt 2010: 236). The portrait of YHWH's gift of land thus develops through this episode into a personal inheritance safeguarded by God for every family. The case of the Zelophehad daughters within the tribe of Manasseh is then generalized in verses 8–9 to 'every daughter' (*kol-bat*), 'for the tribes of the sons of Israel'. Traditional Jewish interpretation (Tobit 6.13 excepted) understands this ruling as applying only to the second generation of Israel; that is, to those who would first inherit the land. The ancient rabbinical sources do not explain why the law should only apply to the generation that entered and conquered Canaan, but Malbim noted that otherwise the tribes might have been discouraged from conquering the lands allotted to them (ref. in Derby 1997: 170). Samet (2003) suggests the pertinent timing of the concern relates *only* to the scenario of the heiresses getting married sometime before the conquest and subsequent division of the land. Presumably, once the inheritance divisions were determined, as continuing to the ensuing generation within the tribe, then the threat of losing tribal inheritances was mitigated (see Nachmanides 1975: 401–403; cf. *b. Taʿan.* 30b; *b. Bav. Bat.* 117a, 120a; *Sif. Deut.* 233; *TgJon*, ad loc.). Far from detracting from or negating the original ruling in favour of Zelophehad's daughters (as per Kislev 2010: 250), the law of chapter 36 'guarantees the possibility of its implementation' (Cocco 2020: 165). The ruling resolves the essence of the problem, as Ben-Barak accurately describes (2006: 25; contra Fishbane 1986: 104–105):

> On the one hand it protects the daughter's right to inherit and preserves the *bēt ʾāb*'s name and patrimony when it has no son, and on the other hand it dispels the danger to the tribal inheritance from the daughter's marriage, by commanding the inheriting daughter to marry within her tribe.

While some critics emphasize the limitation set on the daughters' liberty in marriage (cf. Sakenfeld 1988: 43), Shemesh observes that there is nothing in the text that leads one to surmise the daughters were troubled by the new ruling (2007: 94). Building on this observation, Ortiz-Roberts writes (2020: 154; emphasis original):

> Given that most people across the ancient world remained close to home and the fact that travel could be dangerous (cf. Gen. 34:1–2), it is unlikely the daughters would start 'shopping' for husbands throughout all Israel. It is more likely that most of the marriageable men in the daughters' acquaintance are of their own clan, probably cousins. Most importantly, Num. 27 says *nothing* regarding the daughters' marriages. Prior to this so-called 'restriction' their marriages would be negotiated by older relatives as was the custom for both daughters *and sons*. Any assumption the marriage restriction is somehow 'painful' imprints a modern marriage custom (marry whomever you want) onto an ancient culture.

10–12. The book closes on an encouraging note, commending the faithful obedience of the daughters of Zelophehad 'just as YHWH had commanded Moses', a hopeful prospect inasmuch as they may represent all Israel. The daughters' submission in verse 10 to the new ruling highlights magnificently their own sacrificial desire to maintain family harmony and clan unity – having heard God's will for the tribes, they maintain its spirit even at the clan level (cf. Seforno 1997: 825). As with the story of Ruth, the daughters of Zelophehad model the sort of horizontal *ḥesed* necessary to foster the life of the covenant community. The daughters are not tainted by individualistic aspirations: they do not seek their own, but submit for the good of the whole tribe. Numbers 'presents these daughters as examples of true Israelites', writes Ulrich (1998: 536), 'who persist in their commitment', and to whom 'God delights to give an inheritance'. Zelophehad's daughters are indeed so remarkable in terms of character and strength, some scholars simply dismiss them as a fictional contrivance (e.g. Aaron 2009: 23). The Jewish Sages' disagreement with such a sentiment could not be more complete, lavishing limitless praise on the daughters, who 'were wise women, skilled in interpreting Scripture, and virtuous' (*b. Bav. Bat.* 119b, quoted in Shemesh 2007: 95–102; see *b. Sanh.* 8a; *Sif. Num.* 133; *Tan.*, Gen. 42:1). Within the structure and theology of Numbers, these daughters are set forth as *the* portrait of Israel, both representatives and models for the people of God of every age, tokens of that obedient faith that inherits the land. Stubbs points out that the episode's 'two main pressing issues' are, first, the inheritance of land and, second, 'the character of the daughters as representatives of the new generation', the latter needing further contemplation 'desperately' (2009: 248–249).

Verses 11–12 follow the same panel-structured content as verses 6–7 and 8–9. Once more honouring the five daughters by listing each of their names, verse 11 narrates their obedience, that they married their uncles' sons, while verse 12 follows through with the implication for the clans of the sons of Manasseh, son of Joseph, that the inheritance remained within the clan of their father. The daughters not only married within their tribe, as per the ruling, but within their clan as well, which, as Westbrook observes (1991: 148; cf. 22), was especially useful since 'their husbands' landed inheritance would have been contiguous to their own shares'. Milgrom points out the practical wisdom of their decision inasmuch as keeping the heiress's land close to her husband's (i.e. within the clan division) would enable the husband to work both lands jointly (1990: 512). Deciding to marry within their own extended family, a common custom in ancient societies, the daughters kept their offspring and their patrimony within the framework of both clan and tribe (Ben-Barak 2006: 38). Most people married 'inside their clan', writes van der Toorn (1996: 200–201):

> Custom encouraged a man to marry a woman from among the girls of his clan. One of the considerations in favour of endogamy was economic: the marriage money would thus remain within the clan, so would the paternal inheritance of orphaned women.

Under normal circumstances, as Bergsma further observes (2007: 122–123), the daughters would marry inside the clan and their inheritance would remain clan property – so the Gileadite chieftains were addressing the possible exception to custom, and the daughters would not have perceived a burdensome restriction by the new ruling.

The listing of their names here follows a different order than the original list in 26:33 and 27:1, reversing the position of the second and fifth names (Noah and Tirzah). The original list (26:33; 27:1), also used in Joshua 17:3, likely represents the order of birth, while the alternative order may represent their social standing or prominence, perhaps derived from their eventual respective marriages (so, too, Ibn Ezra 1999: 267; ben Asher 2003: 6:2346; but *b. Bav. Bat.* 102a and Rashi, ad loc., reverse this approach). The suff. for 'their father' is f., demonstrating that this second episode served the same cause as the original request to preserve their father's name – in the former case by granting him land (via his daughters), and in this case by ensuring his land would not be diminished (via the marriage of his daughters). It is not necessary to assume the daughters married immediately upon YHWH's ruling through Moses. The verses simply tell us 'the end of the story', whenever they happened to marry, as a fitting conclusion. Intriguingly, narration of the land division in Joshua lists the daughters only as approaching Joshua and Eleazar the priest, once more of their own accord (Josh. 17:3–6), and states clearly that each received an inheritance among her father's brothers; that is, the land allotments were divided as if each daughter counted in place of Zelophehad, rather than as one of his sons, precisely the language of their request and of YHWH's affirmation (27:4, 7).

The possibility of losing part of their fathers' inheritance of land functions rhetorically in a manner that underscores the secure nature of the gift, so the book closes with an even more triumphant note than with the mere giving of the land, for the land given by YHWH to the tribes of Israel will be *preserved* as their sure inheritance for generations to come. YHWH's gift – not simply 'the land', but life in the land – is a lasting one. The daughters of Zelophehad who frame the last major section of Numbers portray the second generation of Israel as the faithful bride of YHWH, following his word and will closely, its spirit as well as its letter. In terms of closure, Douglas noted how chapter 36 uses language reminiscent of the opening chapter, particularly in the use of 'father's houses', recalling the original census, counted tribe by tribe, with every family given its proper place in the Camp – precisely the analogical concern in the land (M. Douglas 2001: 111, 246–247; cf. J. S. Ackerman 1987: 89–90; Ashlock 2002: 174–177). Israel's life with God in the land is seen as the fuller realization of the wilderness Camp experience (cf. Joosten 1996: 137–148). Bernat (2021) also speaks of chapter 36 as a 'nuanced yet fully coherent exemplar of literary closure', which underscores the covenantal link between God and the land, ending Numbers 'with the notion that every family, and every individual, through each generation, is to be the beneficiary of the self-same *berit*-promises first granted to Abraham and his family.

13. The statement echoes the close of the first daughters of Zelophehad episode concerning the statute of judgement that was 'just as YHWH had commanded Moses' (27:11), likely intended not only to close chapter 36 but, together with 27:11 as bookends enclosing the whole section after the census, chapters 27–36, pertaining to what YHWH had commanded Moses for the sons of Israel while 'on the plains of Moab by the Jordan near Jericho'. The whole final section of chapters 26–36 relates to the inheritance of the land, foretasted nearly to the point of actual experience, making the closing words 'by the Jordan near Jericho' especially poignant.

Explanation

The daughters of Zelophehad frame closes the book in a way that underscores 'the intense connection between the nation of Israel and the land' God's people are about to inherit (Rimon 2014a: 381–382). Sakenfeld goes further, calling the question of land addressed in chapter 36 'the climax of the tetrateuch', linked as it is 'to maintaining *tribal* holdings intact' (1988: 38, 43; emphasis original). Plaut, observing 'the Torah's pervasive genealogical interest', underscores that there are ten generations apiece, from Adam to Noah, from Noah to Terah (Abraham's father) and now from Abraham to the daughters of Zelophehad, making the point that the 'end of the wanderings is thus related to creation' (1979: 330). Given the exuberant focus of Numbers 26 – 36 on inheriting the land of Canaan, Plaut's observation may be adjusted to reflect YHWH's gift of the land as an all-encompassing theme: the ten generations from Abraham to the daughters of Zelophehad relate Israel's inheritance of the land of Canaan to humanity's inheritance of Eden. The daughters represent that generation which will mark the fulfilment of YHWH's ancient promise to Abraham. It is also fitting that Numbers ends with a reference to the Jubilee. In the Sabbath-breaker story (Num. 15:32–36), which caps the section on the failure of the first generation (i.e. the outer camp, chs. 11–15), it was noted how rejecting the Sabbath was an image for disinheriting the land (cf. Noonan 2020), since Sabbath fellowship with YHWH God was to culminate within the land of Canaan. Purposefully, Numbers ends with the prospect of the second generation's inheritance of the land, conveyed in terms of the grand, fiftieth-year Sabbath, the Jubilee – the entire last section of Numbers is framed by this anticipation (chs. 27, 36).

After the last verse of chapter 35 had climactically unveiled that YHWH dwells in the land among the sons of Israel, Numbers 36 closes the book by underlining the everlasting nature of YHWH's gift, that 'the sons of Israel will cling each man to the inheritance of the tribe of his fathers' (vv. 7, 9) – beams of radiant light flowing from YHWH's original promise to Abraham: 'I will give to you and to your descendants after you . . . all the land of Canaan for an everlasting possession, and I will be their God' (Gen. 17:8; following G. J. Wenham 1981b: 267). The land is linked to the covenant formula 'I will be your God, you will be my people, and I will dwell in your midst' (see Morales 2015: 103–106), demonstrating that YHWH's gift of the land is but a means for the gift of himself. 'The ultimate goal of life in the land is salvation,' writes Stubbs (2009: 249), 'a new life for Israel in which God will dwell among them and bless them (cf. 6:22–27; 24:2–9) so that all nations will see their life, glorify God, and receive the blessing of God as well (cf. Gen. 12:1–3).' Within the bridal theology of the Sinai covenant, Israel is on the verge of experiencing life in the land with her Lord and divine Husband, YHWH. This context in mind, it is surely significant that Numbers concludes with reference to the daughters' marriages and the prospect of new life in the land. The Zelophehad women are amazing, displaying zest and verve in their willingness to contravene traditional inheritance rights (27:1–11), as well as dutiful compliance for the sake of their tribe's well-being (ch. 36). The faithful daughters of Zelophehad close Israel's story as wives devoted to the will of YHWH through Moses, countering the portrayal of Israel as engaging in spiritual harlotry (chs. 5, 25), even as their previous pursuit of the land in chapter 27 for the sake of their father's name formed a counter to the scouts who had rejected the land (chs. 13–14). Numbers closes with a vivid eschatological picture of life with YHWH in the land with the *marriage* of Zelophehad's daughters, who, in representing Israel, symbolize the bride of YHWH.

Aptly, Leveen writes (2002: 263), 'This concluding vision of a successful and blessed future in a land not yet conquered remains the ultimate aim and message conveyed by Numbers.' Closing Numbers with the vision of Israel in the land, with each tribe's inheritance divinely bounded and secured for all generations, recalls the splendorous third vision of Balaam, who, when he saw 'Israel dwelling according to his tribes', was overwhelmed by the Spirit of God to erupt with praise – the paradisal dwelling places of Israel, with their palm groves and riverside gardens, were a foretaste of Israel's life in the land (24:1–6). The vision points God's people to life in a new creation, lived before the face of God and the Lamb, where a pure river of life flows, feeding a tree of life that bears twelve kinds of fruits, twelve months of the year, and whose leaves are for the healing of the nations – when God's people, adorned as a Bride for her Husband, will feast at the Wedding Supper of the Lamb (Rev. 21 – 22).

> Uncover my eyes, that I may observe wonders out of your Torah,
> And we will praise you, YHWH God of hosts,
> To Whom be glory and eternal dominion!

BIBLIOGRAPHY

COMMENTARIES ON NUMBERS

Abarbanel, R. Y. (2015), *Abarbanel – Selected Commentaries on the Torah: Bamidbar*, tr. Rav I. Lazar, Brooklyn, N.Y.: CreateSpace.

Ackerman, J. S. (1987), 'Numbers', in R. Alter and F. Kermode (eds.), *The Literary Guide to the Bible*, Cambridge: Belknap, 78–91.

Ainsworth, H. (1619), *Annotations upon the Fourth Book of Moses, Called Numbers: Wherein, by Conference of the Scriptures, by Comparing the Greek and Chaldee Versions, and Testimonies of Hebrew Writers; the Lawes and Ordinances given of Old unto Israel in This Book, Are Explained*, Amsterdam: G. Thorp.

Alexander, T. D. (2017), *Exodus*, AOTC, Nottingham: Apollos; Downers Grove: InterVarsity Press.

Allen, R. B. (2012), 'Numbers', in T. Longman III and D. E. Garland (eds.), revised, *Numbers–Ruth*, EBC, Grand Rapids: Zondervan, 2:23–455.

Alter, R. (2004), *The Five Books of Moses: A Translation with Commentary*, New York: W. W. Norton.

Asher, B. ben, Rabbi (2003), *Torah Commentary: Midrash Rabbeinu Bachya*, 2 ed., vol. 6, Jerusalem: Urim.

Ashley, T. R. (1993), *The Book of Numbers*, NICOT, Grand Rapids: Eerdmans.

Baentsch, B. (1903), *Exodus, Leviticus, Numeri*, HAT, Göttingen: Vandenhoeck & Ruprecht.

Barnes, A. (1973), *The Bible Commentary: Exodus–Ruth*, ed. F. C. Cook and F. M. Fuller, Grand Rapids: Baker Book House.

Bekhor Shor, J. (1983), *Commentary on the Torah*, ed. H. Gad, Jerusalem: Mosad ha-Rav Kook.

Bellinger, W. H. (2001), *Leviticus and Numbers*, Peabody: Hendrickson.

Berlin, N. Z. Y. 'Netziv' (1840–80), *Haamek Davar on Numbers*, from Sefaria: www.sefaria.org.

——— (1879), *Sefer Torat Elohim: Chumash Ha'amek Davar: Sefer Bamidbar*, vol. 4, Vilna: Bi-defus ha-almanah ve-ha-aḥim Rom.

Binns, L. E. (1927), *The Book of Numbers*, London: Methuen.

Boyce, R. N. (2008), *Leviticus and Numbers*, WBC, Louisville, Ky.: Westminster John Knox.

Brown, R. (2002), *The Message of Numbers: Journey to the Promised Land*, BST, Downers Grove: InterVarsity Press.

Brueggemann, D. A. (2005), 'Numbers', in P. W. Comfort (ed.), *Cornerstone Biblical Commentary*. Carol Stream, Ill: Tyndale House, 2:215–443.

Budd, P. J. (1984), *Numbers*, WBC 5, Waco, Tex.: Thomas Nelson.
Burns, R. J. (1989), *Exodus, Leviticus, Numbers: With Excurses on Feasts, Ritual and Typology*, Old Testament Message 3, Wilmington: Glazier.
Bush, G. (1858), *Notes, Critical and Practical, on the Book of Numbers*, New York: John F. Trow.
Butzer, A. G. (1953), *Numbers*, Nashville: Abingdon-Cokesbury.
Caine, I., and N. S. Fox (2007), 'Numbers, Book Of', in *Encyclopaedia Judaica*, 2nd ed., 15:330–333, New York: Macmillan.
Calmet, A. (1709), *Commentaire littéral sur tous les livres de l'ancien et du nouveau testament: Les Nombres et le Deuteronome*, Paris: Pierre Emery.
Calvin, J. (2003b), *Commentaries on the Four Last Books of Moses: Arranged in the Form of a Harmony*, tr. C. W. Bingham, vol. 4, Grand Rapids: Baker.
Cole, R. D. (2000), *Numbers*, NAC, v. 3B, Nashville: Broadman & Holman.
——— (2009), 'Numbers', in J. Walton (ed.), *Zondervan Illustrated Bible Backgrounds Commentary: Genesis, Exodus, Leviticus, Numbers, Deuteronomy*, Grand Rapids: Zondervan, 1:338–417.
Currid, J. D. (2009), *Numbers*, Darlington: Evangelical.
Davies, E. W. (1995b), *Numbers*, NCBC, Grand Rapids: Eerdmans.
——— (2015), *Numbers: The Road to Freedom*, Sheffield: Sheffield Phoenix.
Dentan, R. C. (1962a), 'Numbers, Book Of', *IDB* 3:567–571.
Dillmann, A. (1886), *Die Bucher Numeri, Deuteronomium und Josua*, Leipzig: S. Hirzel.
Dorival, G. (1976), *La Bible d'Alexandrie LXX, tome 4: Les Nombres*, Paris: Le Cerf.
Dozeman, T. B. (1998), 'The Book of Numbers', in *The New Interpreter's Bible, 2: Numbers–Samuel*, Nashville: Abingdon, 1–268.
Fox, E. (1995), *The Five Books of Moses*, New York: Schocken.
Friedman, R. E. (2001), *Commentary on the Torah: With a New English Translation*, San Francisco, Calif.: HarperSanFrancisco.
Gane, R. E. (2004), *Leviticus, Numbers*, NAC, Grand Rapids: Zondervan.
Gispen, W. H. (1959), *Het Boek Numeri*, vol. 1, COT, Kampen: Kok.
——— (1964), *Het Boek Numeri*, vol. 2, COT, Kampen: Kok.
Goldberg, A. (1970), *Das Buch Numeri*, Düsseldorf: Patmos-Verlag.
Gray, G. B. (1903), *A Critical and Exegetical Commentary on Numbers*, The International Critical Commentary on the Holy Scriptures of the Old and New Testaments, Edinburgh: T. & T. Clark.
Greenstone, J. H. (1948), *Numbers: With Commentary*, Philadelphia: Jewish Publication Society.
Harrison, R. K. (1990), *Numbers: An Exegetical Commentary*, Grand Rapids: Baker.
Heinisch, P. (1936), *Das Buch Numeri, Übersetzt und Erklärt*, Bonn: Hanstein.
Held, S. (2017), *The Heart of Torah, Volume 2: Essays on the Weekly Torah Portion: Leviticus, Numbers, and Deuteronomy*, Philadelphia: Jewish Publication Society.

Hertz, J. H. (1988), *The Pentateuch and the Haftorahs*, London: Soncino.
Hirsch, S. R. (2007a), *The Hirsch Chumash: Bemidbar*, tr. D. Haberman, Jerusalem: Feldheim.
—— (2007b), *The Hirsch Chumash: Bereshis*, tr. D. Haberman, Jerusalem: Feldheim.
Holzinger, H. (1903), *Numeri: Erklart*, Tübingen: Mohr Siebeck.
Hummelauer, F. de (1899), *Commentarius Numeros*, Cursus Scripturae Sacrae, Paris: P. Lethielleux.
Ibn Ezra, A. (1999), *Ibn Ezra's Commentary on the Pentateuch, Vol. 4: Numbers (Ba-Midbar)*, tr. H. N. Strickman and A. M. Silver, New York: Menorah.
Jacob, B. (1909), *Die Abzählungen in den Gesetzen der Bücher Leviticus und Numeri*, Frankfurt am Main: J. Kaufmann.
Jamieson, R., A. R. Fausset and D. Brown (1973), *A Commentary, Critical, Experimental, and Practical, on the Old and New Testaments*, vol. 3, Grand Rapids: Eerdmans.
Jensen, I. L. (1964), *Numbers: Journey to God's Rest-Land*, Chicago: Moody.
Jeyaraj, B. (1989), 'Land Ownership in the Pentateuch: A Thematic Study of Genesis 12 to Deuteronomy 34', PhD diss., Sheffield: University of Sheffield.
Keddie, G. J. (1992), *Numbers: According to Promise*, Welwyn, UK: EP.
Keil, C. F. (1869), *Numbers*, Edinburgh: T. & T. Clark.
Keil, C. F., and F. Delitzsch (1973), *Commentary on the Old Testament: Pentateuch*, tr. J. Martin, vol. 3, Commentary on the Old Testament, Grand Rapids: Eerdmans.
Knierim, R. P. (1995a), 'The Book of Numbers', in *The Task of Old Testament Theology: Substance, Method, and Cases*, Grand Rapids: Eerdmans, 380–388.
Knoppers, G. N. (2004), 'Establishing the Rule of Law? The Composition Num 33,50–56 and the Relationships Among the Pentateuch, the Hexateuch, and the Deuteronomistic History', in E. Otto and R. Achenbach (eds.), *Das Deuteronomium zwischen Pentateuch und Deuteronomistischem Geschichtswerk*, Göttingen: Vandenhoek & Ruprecht, 135–152.
Leibowitz, N. (1982), *Studies in Bamidbar (Numbers)*, tr. A. Newman, Jerusalem: World Zionist Organization, Department for Torah Education and Culture in the Diaspora.
Levine, B. A. (1976b), 'Numbers, Book Of', in K. Crim (ed.), *IDB Supplement*, 631–635.
—— (1993), *Numbers 1–20: A New Translation with Introduction and Commentary*, in AB 4A, New York: Doubleday.
—— (2000), *Numbers 21–36: A New Translation with Introduction and Commentary*, in (eds.), AB 4A, New York: Doubleday.
Licht, J. (1985), *A Commentary on the Book of Numbers*, vol. 1, Jerusalem: Magnes.

―――― (1991), *A Commentary on the Book of Numbers*, vol. 2, Jerusalem: Magnes.
Lienhard, J. T. (ed.) (2001), *Exodus, Leviticus, Numbers, Deuteronomy*, 3rd ed., vol. 3, ACCS: OT, Downers Grove: InterVarsity Press.
Luzzato, M. C. (2016), *Ramchal on the Parsha: Bamidbar*, tr. H. Berkin, Jerusalem: Targum.
Luzzatto, S. D. (2012), *Torah Commentary*, tr. E. Munk, vol. 3, Brooklyn, N.Y.: Lambda.
Maarsingh, B. (1987), *Numbers. A Practical Commentary*, tr. J. Vriend, Grand Rapids: Eerdmans.
MacDonald, N. (2012a), 'The Book of Numbers', in R. S. Briggs and J. N. Lohr (eds.), *A Theological Introduction to the Pentateuch: Interpreting the Torah as Christian Scripture*, Grand Rapids: Baker, 113–144.
MacKintosh, C. H. (1869), *Notes on the Book of Numbers*, London: G. Morrish.
McNeile, A. H. (1911), *The Book of Numbers*, Cambridge: Cambridge University Press.
Manoach, C. ben (2013), *Chizkuni: Torah Commentary*, tr. E. Munk, vol. 4, Brooklyn, N.Y.: KTAV.
Meir, S. ben (2001), *Rashbam's Commentary on Leviticus and Numbers: An Annotated Translation*, tr. M. I. Lockshin, BJS 330, Providence: Brown University.
Milgrom, J. (1990), *The JPS Torah Commentary: Numbers = [Ba-Midbar]: The Traditional Hebrew Text with the New JPS Translation*, Philadelphia: Jewish Publication Society.
―――― (1992), 'Numbers, Book Of', *ABD* 4:1146–1155.
Moriarty, F. L. (1968), 'Numbers', in R. E. Brown, J. A. Fitzmyer and R. E. Murphy (eds.), *Jerome Bible Commentary*, Englewood Cliffs, N.J.: Prentice-Hall, 86–100.
Nachmanides, M. (1975), *Ramban Commentary on the Torah: Vol. 4 Numbers*, tr. C. B. Chavel, New York: Shilo Publishing House.
Naylor, P. J. (1994), 'Numbers', in G. J. Wenham, J. A. Motyer, D. A. Carson and R. T. France (eds.), *New Bible Commentary, 21st Century Edition*, Downers Grove: InterVarsity Press, 158–197.
Noordtzij, A. (1983), *Numbers*, Bible Student's Commentary, Grand Rapids: Zondervan.
Noth, M. (1968), *Numbers: A Commentary*, Philadelphia: Westminster.
Nowell, I. (2011), *Numbers*, New Collegeville Bible Commentary, Collegeville, Minn.: Liturgical.
Olson, D. T. (1996), *Numbers*, IBC, Louisville, Ky.: John Knox.
Paterson, J. A. (1900), *The Book of Numbers: Critical Edition of the Hebrew Text*, Leipzig: J. C. Hinrichs.
Philip, J. (1987), *The Communicator's Commentary, Numbers*, Waco, Tex.: Word.
Pressler, C. (2017), *Numbers*, AOTC, Nashville: Abingdon.

Rashi (1997), *The Torah: With Rashi's Commentary: Numbers*, ed. Y. Herczeg, vol. 4, Brooklyn, N.Y.: Mesorah.
Riggans, W. (1983), *Numbers*, DSB, Philadelphia: Westminster; Edinburgh: Saint Andrew.
Riskin, S. (2009), *Torah Lights: Bemidbar: Trials and Tribulations in Times of Transition*, 2nd ed., New Milford, Conn.: Maggid.
Sacks, J. (2017), *Covenant & Conversation, a Weekly Reading of the Jewish Bible: Numbers, the Wilderness Years*, New Milford, Conn.: Maggid & The Orthodox Union.
Sakenfeld, K. D. (1995), *Journeying with God: A Commentary on the Book of Numbers*, Grand Rapids: Eerdmans; Edinburgh: Handsel.
Schneerson, M. M., and M. Y. Wisnefsky (eds.) (2009), *The Torah: Chumash Bemidbar: With an Interpolated English Translation and Commentary Based on the Works of Lubavitcher Rebbe*, Brooklyn, N.Y.: Kehot Publication Society.
Seebass, H. (1993), *Numeri: Kapitel 10,11–22,1*, vol. 2, BKAT 4, Neukirchen-Vluyn: Neukirchener Verlag.
—— (2007), *Numeri: Kapitel 22,2–36,13*, vol. 3, BKAT 4, Neukirchen-Vluyn: Neukirchener Verlag.
Seforno, O. ben Jacob (1997), *Commentary on the Torah*, tr. R. Pelcovitz, Brooklyn: Mesorah.
Shamah, M. (2011), *Recalling the Covenant: A Contemporary Commentary on the Five Books of the Torah*, Jersey City: KTAV.
Sherwood, S. K. (2002), *Leviticus, Numbers, Deuteronomy*, Berit Olam, Collegeville, Minn: Liturgical.
Slotki, J. J. (tr.) (1951), *The Midrash Rabbah: Numbers II*, vol. 6, London: Soncino.
Snaith, N. H. (1962), 'Numbers', in M. Black and H. H. Rowley (eds.), *Peake's Commentary on the Bible*, London: Thomas Nelson, 179–348.
—— (1967), *Leviticus and Numbers*, London: Thomas Nelson.
Sprinkle, J. M. (2015), *Leviticus and Numbers*, Teach the Text Commentary, Grand Rapids: Baker.
Staubli, T. (1996), *Die Bücher Levitikus, Numeri*, NSKAT 3, Stuttgart: Katholisches Bibelwerk.
Steele, D. (1891), *Commentary on the Old Testament: Leviticus and Numbers*, vol. 2, New York: Hunt & Eaton.
Stubbs, D. L. (2009), *Numbers*, Brazos Theological Commentary on the Bible, Grand Rapids: Brazos.
Sturdy, J. (1976), *Numbers*, Cambridge: Cambridge University Press.
Sweeney, M. A. (2012), *Tanak: A Theological and Critical Introduction to the Jewish Bible*, Minneapolis: Fortress.
Trapp, J. (1650), *A Clavis to the Bible. Or a New Comment upon the Pentateuch: Or Five Books of Moses*, London: Timothy Garthwait.
Twersky, Y. (2007b), *Amittah Shel Torah II: Vayikra, Bemidbar, Devarim*, vol. 2, Southfield, Mich.: Targum.

Vaulx, J. de (1972), *Les Nombres*, Paris: Gabalda.
Wenham, G. J. (1981b), *Numbers: An Introduction and Commentary*, TOTC, Leicester: Inter-Varsity Press; Downers Grove: InterVarsity Press.
——— (1997), *Numbers*, OTG, Sheffield: Sheffield Academic Press.
Wevers, J. W. (1998), *Notes on the Greek Text of Numbers*, Atlanta: Society of Biblical Literature.
Woods, C. M., and J. Rogers (2006), *Leviticus–Numbers*, The College Press NIV Commentary, Joplin, Mo.: College Press.
Zornberg, A. G. (2015), *Bewilderments: Reflections on the Book of Numbers*, New York: Schocken.

OTHER WORKS

Aalders, G. C. (1949), *A Short Introduction to the Pentateuch*, London: Tyndale.
Aaron, D. H. (2009), 'The Ruse of Zelophehad's Daughters,', *HUCA* 80:1–38.
Abba, R. (1978), 'Priests and Levites in Ezekiel', *VT* 28 (1):1–9.
Abbott, A. (1933), 'Was Moses the Meekest of Men?', *ExpTim* 45:524–525.
Abela, A. (2008), 'Shaming Miriam, Moses' Sister, in Num 12,1–16', in T. Römer (ed.), *The Books of Leviticus and Numbers*, 521–534, Leuven: Peeters.
Abrams, J. Z. (1993), 'Metzora(at) Kashaleg: Leprosy, Challenges to Authority in the Bible', *JBQ* 21:41–45.
Achenbach, R. (2003a), 'Die Erzählung von der Gescheiterten Landnahme von Kadesch Barnea (Numeri 13–14) als Schlüsseltext der Redaktionsgeschichte des Pentateuchs', *Zeitschrift für Altorientalische und Biblische Rechtsgeschichte* 9:56–123.
——— (2003b), *Die Vollendung der Tora: Studien zur Redaktionsgeschichte des Numeribuches im Kontext von Hexateuch und Pentateuch*, Wiesbaden: Harrassowitz.
——— (2010), 'Zippora und Kosbi: Zwei exemplarische Fallbeispiele zur Problematisierung exogamer Verbindungen im Pentateuch', *ZABR* 16:225–248.
——— (2013), 'Complementary Reading of the Torah in the Priestly Texts of Numbers 15', in C. Frevel, T. Pola and A. Schart (eds.), *Torah and the Book of Numbers*, Tübingen: Mohr Siebeck, 201–232.
——— (2016), 'The Empty Throne and the Empty Sanctuary: From Aniconism to the Invisibility of God in Second Temple Theology', in N. MacDonald (ed.), *Ritual Innovation in the Hebrew Bible and Early Judaism*, BZAW 468, Berlin: de Gruyter, 35–53.
Ackerman, H. C. (1920), 'Critical Notes Concerning the Nature of Balaam's Vision (Num. 24:3–4)', *AThR* 2:233–234.
Ackerman, S. (2014), 'Moses' Death', in D. E. Callender Jr (ed.), *Myth and Scripture: Contemporary Perspectives on Religion, Language, and Imagination*, Atlanta: Society of Biblical Literature, 103–117.

Ackroyd, P. (1968), *Exile and Restoration: A Study of Hebrew Thought of the Sixth Century B.C.*, Philadelphia: Westminster.

Adamo, D. T. (1989), 'The African Wife of Moses: An Examination of Numbers 12:1–9', *African Theology Journal* 18:230–237.

Aharoni, Y. (1979), *The Land of the Bible: A Historical Geography*, tr. A. F. Rainey, Philadelphia: Westminster.

Aḥituv, S. (1992), 'Land and Justice', in H. G. Reventlow and Y. Hoffman (eds.), *Justice and Righteousness: Biblical Themes and Their Influence*, Sheffield: Sheffield Academic Press, 11–28.

Albertz, R. (2013), 'A Pentateuchal Redaction in the Book of Numbers?', *ZAW* 125 (2): 220–233.

Albright, W. F. (1915), 'The Home of Balaam', *JAOS* 35:386–390.

——— (1925), 'The Administrative Districts of Israel and Judah', *Journal of the Palestine Oriental Society* 5:17–54.

——— (1935), 'The Names Shaddai and Abram', *JBL* 54 (4):173–204.

——— (1938), 'What Were the Cherubim?', *BA* 1:1–3.

——— (1944), 'The Oracles of Balaam', *JBL* 63 (3):207–233.

——— (1950), 'Some Important Recent Discoveries: Alphabetic Origins and the Idrimi Statue', *BASOR* 118:11–20.

——— (1953), *Archaeology and the Religion of Israel*, Baltimore: Johns Hopkins University Press.

——— (1963), 'Jethro, Hobab and Reuel in the Early Hebrew Tradition', *CBQ* 25:1–11.

——— (1968), *Yahweh and the Gods of Canaan*, Garden City, N.Y.: Doubleday.

Alden, R. L. (1966), 'Ecstasy and the Prophets', *Bulletin of the Evangelical Theological Society* 9 (3):149–156.

Alexander, T. D. (1995), 'The Passover Sacrifice', in R. T. Beckwith and M. J. Selman (eds.), *Sacrifice in the Bible*, Carlisle: Paternoster; Grand Rapids: Baker, 1–24.

——— (2003), *The Servant King: The Bible's Portrait of the Messiah*, Vancouver: Regent College Publishing.

——— (2009), *From Eden to the New Jerusalem: An Introduction to Biblical Theology*, Grand Rapids: Kregel.

Allegro, J. M. (1953), 'The Meaning of the Phrase Šetūm Hā'ayin in Num. XXIV 3, 15', *VT* 3:78–79.

Allen, R. B. (1973), 'The Theology of the Balaam Oracles: A Pagan Diviner and the Word of God', PhD diss., Dallas: Dallas Theological Seminary.

——— (1981), 'The Theology of the Balaam Oracles (Numbers 22–24)', in J. S. Feinberg (ed.), *Tradition and Testament: Essays in Honor of Charles Lee Feinberg*, Chicago: Moody, 79–119.

Allis, O. T. (1943), *The Five Books of Moses*, Philadelphia: Presbyterian & Reformed.

——— (1972), *The Old Testament: Its Claims and Its Critics*, Philadelphia: Presbyterian & Reformed.

Alter, R. (1981), *The Art of Biblical Narrative*, New York: Basic.
Altmann, P. (2011), *Festive Meals in Ancient Israel: Deuteronomy's Identity Politics in Their Ancient Near Eastern Context*, Berlin: de Gruyter.
Amy-Dressler, J. A. (1986), 'Moses and the Rod', *Proceedings, Eastern Great Lakes and Midwest Biblical Society* 6:18–31.
Andersen, F. I. (1969), 'Israelite Kinship Terminology and Social Structure', *BT* 20:29–39.
Anderson, B. A. (2012), 'Edom in the Book of Numbers: Some Literary Reflections', *ZAW* 124:38–51.
Anderson, B. W. (1986), *Understanding the Old Testament*, 4th ed., Englewood Cliffs, N.J.: Prentice-Hall.
Anderson, G. A. (1987), *Sacrifices and Offerings in Ancient Israel: Studies in Their Social and Political Importance*, Atlanta: Scholars.
——— (1992a), 'The Interpretation of the Purification Offering in the Temple Scroll (11QTemple) and Rabbinic Literature', *JBL* 111 (1):17–35.
——— (1992b), 'Sacrifice and Sacrificial Offerings, Old Testament', *ABD* 5:870–886.
——— (2008), 'To See Where God Dwells: The Tabernacle, the Temple, and the Origins of the Christian Mystical Tradition', *Letter & Spirit* 4:13–45.
——— (2022), 'The Date of the Tabernacle's Completion and Consecration', *TheTorah.Com* (blog), https://www.thetorah.com/article/the-date-of-the-tabernacles-completion-and-consecration.
Anisfeld, M. (2011), 'Why Was Moses Barred from Leading the People into the Promised Land? A Psychotheological Answer', *JBQ* 39 (4):211–220.
——— (2013), 'The Psychology of Balaam', *JBQ* 41 (4):227–235.
Anthonioz, S. (2014), 'Water(s) of Abundance in the Ancient Near East and in Hebrew Bible Texts: A Sign of Kingship', in E. Ben Zvi and C. Levin (eds.), *Thinking of Water in the Early Second Temple Period*, Berlin: de Gruyter, 49–75.
Archer, G. L. (1994), *A Survey of Old Testament Introduction*, Chicago: Moody.
Arden, E. (1957), 'How Moses Failed God', *JBL* 76:50–52.
Armgardt, M., B. Kilchör and M. P. Zehnder (eds.) (2019), *Paradigm Change in Pentateuchal Research*, BZAR 22, Wiesbaden: Harrassowitz.
Artus, O. (1997), *Etudes sur le livre des Nombres: Récit, histoire et Loi en Nb 13, 1–20, 13*, Göttingen: Vandenhoeck & Ruprecht.
——— (2008), 'Le Problème de l'unité Littéraire et de La Spécificité Théologique du Livre des Nombres', in T. Römer (ed.), *The Books of Leviticus and Numbers*, BETL 215, Leuven: Peeters, 121–144.
——— (2013), 'Numbers 32: The Problem of the Two and a Half Transjordanian Tribes and the Final Composition of the Book of Numbers', in C. Frevel, T. Pola and A. Schart (eds.), *Torah and the Book of Numbers*, Tübingen: Mohr Siebeck, 367–382.
——— (2017), 'Gouverner et Parler au Nom de Dieu: La Question du Pouvoir en Nb 11–12', *RB* 124 (1):26–37.

Asher, N. (1984), 'Moses and the Spies', *Dor le Dor* 12 (3):196–199.
——— (1989), 'Why Was Aaron Punished?', *JBQ* 18:44–45.
Ashlock, R. O. (2002), 'As the Lord Commands: Narrative Endings and Closure Strategy in Exodus, Leviticus and Numbers', PhD diss., Waco, Tex.: Baylor University.
Attridge, H. W. (1989), *Hebrews: A Commentary on the Epistle to the Hebrews*, Philadelphia: Fortress.
Auld, A. G. (1978), 'Cities of Refuge in Israelite Tradition', *JSOT* 10:26–40.
——— (1980), *Joshua, Moses and the Land*, Edinburgh: T. & T. Clark.
Aune, D. E. (1998), *Revelation 6–16*, WBC 52b, Nashville: Thomas Nelson.
Aurelius, E. (1988), *Der Fürbitter Israels: eine Studie zum Mosebild im alten Testament*, Stockholm: Almqvist & Wiksell.
Averbeck, R. E. (1997), 'Offering by Fire, "iššeh"', *NIDOTTE* 1:540–549.
Avishur, Y. (1999), *Studies in Biblical Narrative: Style, Structure, and the Ancient Near Eastern Literary Background*, Tel Aviv-Jaffa: Archaeological Center Publication.
Avi-Yonah, M. (ed.) (1969), *A History of the Holy Land*, Jerusalem: The Jerusalem Publishing House.
Awabdy, M. A. (2018), 'The Holiness Composition of the Priestly Blessing', *Bib* 99 (1):29–49.
Ayali-Darshan, N. (2015), 'The Seventy Bulls Sacrificed at Sukkot (Num 29:12–34) in Light of a Ritual Text from Emar (Emar 6, 373)', *VT* 65:9–19.
Bach, A. (1999), 'Good to the Last Drop: Viewing the Sotah (Numbers 5:11–31) as the Glass Half Empty and Wondering How to View It Half Full', in A. Bach (ed.), *Women in the Hebrew Bible*, New York: Routledge, 503–522.
Baden, J. S. (2009), *J, E and the Redaction of the Pentateuch*, FAT 68, Tübingen: Mohr Siebeck.
——— (2013a), 'Source Stratification, Secondary Additions, and the Documentary Hypothesis in the Book of Numbers: The Case of Numbers 17', in C. Frevel, T. Pola and A. Schart (eds.), *Torah and the Book of Numbers*, Tübingen: Mohr Siebeck, 233–247.
——— (2013b), 'The Structure and Substance of Numbers 15', *VT* 63 (3):351–367.
——— (2014), 'The Narratives of Numbers 20–21', *CBQ* 76:634–652.
Baigent, M. (1994), *Astrology in Ancient Mesopotamia: The Science of Omens and the Knowledge of the Heavens*, Rochester: Bear.
Bailey, L. R. (1968), 'Israelite 'El Sadday and Amorite Bel Sade', *JBL* 87 (4):434–438.
Bailey, R. (1991), 'Beyond Identification: The Use of Africans in Old Testament Poetry and Narratives', in C. H. Felder (ed.), *Stoney the Road We Trod: African American Biblical Interpretations*, 165–186, Minneapolis: Fortress.
Baker, D. W. (1992), 'Kittim', *ABD* 4:93.

Baker, L. S., K. Bergland, F. A. Masotti and A. R. Wells (eds.) (2020), *Exploring the Composition of the Pentateuch*, Bulletin for Biblical Research Supplement Series, University Park: Eisenbrauns.

Baldensperger, L., and G. M. Crowfoot (1931), 'Hyssop', *PEQ* 63:89–98.

Balentine, S. E. (1985), 'Prayer in the Wilderness Traditions: In Pursuit of Divine Justice', *Hebrew Annual Review* 9:53–74.

Balorda, A. (2002), 'The Covenant of Phinehas as a Reward for the Jealousy of Numinal Marriage', M.A. thesis, Berrien Springs, Mich.: Andrews University Seminary.

Baltzer, K. (1975), *Die Biographie der Propheten*, Neukirchen-Vluyn: Neukirchener.

Bar-Efrat, S. (2004), *Narrative Art in the Bible*, London: T. & T. Clark.

Bar-Ilan, M. (1989), '"They Shall Put My Name upon the People of Israel" (Num. 6:27)', *HUCA* 60:19–31.

Barker, D. (2005), 'Voices for the Pilgrimage: A Study of the Psalms of Ascent', *ExpTim* 116:109–116.

Barker, P. A. (2004), *The Triumph of Grace in Deuteronomy: Faithless Israel, Faithful Yahweh in Deuteronomy*, PBM, Milton Keynes: Paternoster.

Barnouin, M. (1977), 'Recensements du Livre des Nombres et l'astronomie Babylonienne', *VT* 27 (3):280–303.

Baron, S. W. (1972), 'Population', in C. Roth (ed.), *Encyclopaedia Judaica*, New York: Macmillan, 13:866–903.

Barré, M. L. (1997), 'The Portrait of Balaam in Numbers 22–24', *Int* 51 (3):254–266.

Bartelmus, R. (2005), 'Von Eselinnen mit Durchblick und Blinden Sehern. Numeri 22:20–35 als Musterbeispiel Narrativer Theologie im alten Testament', *TZ* 61:27–43.

Barth, L. (1984), 'Oxen, Calves and the Heavenly Source of Idolatry', Annual Meeting of the Society of Biblical Literature conference paper, Chicago, 1–26.

Bartlett, J. R. (1969), 'The Use of the Word ראש as a Title in the Old Testament', *Vetus Testamentum* 19 (1):1–10.

——— (1989), *Edom and the Edomites*, JSOTSup 77, Sheffield: Sheffield Academic Press.

Baruchi-Unna, A. (2015), 'The Story of the Zeal of Phinehas and Congregational Weeping at Bethel', *VT* 65:505–515.

Baskin, J. R. (1983), *Pharaoh's Counselors: Job, Jethro, and Balaam in Rabbinic and Patristic Tradition*, BJS 47, Chico, Calif.: Scholars.

Bateman, H. W., D. L. Bock and G. H. Johnston (2012), *Jesus the Messiah: Tracing the Promises, Expectations, and Coming of Israel's King*, Grand Rapids: Kregel.

Bauckham, R. (2013), 'Eldad and Medad: A New Translation and Introduction', in R. Bauckham, J. R. Davila and A. Panayotov (eds.), *Old Testament Pseudepigrapha: More Noncanonical Scriptures*, Grand Rapids: Eerdmans, 1:244–254.

Baumgarten, A. I. (1993), 'The Paradox of the Red Heifer', *VT* 43 (4):442–451.
Bazak, A. (1997), 'The Ideological Foundations of the Sin of the Golden Calf', Yeshivat Har Etzion – Virtual Beit Midrash, https://www.etzion.org.il/en.
——— (2012), 'The Episode of the Cushite Woman', Yeshivat Har Etzion – Virtual Beit Midrash, https://www.etzion.org.il/en.
——— (2014a), 'Balak and Balaam', in E. Bick (ed.), *Torah MiEtzion: New Readings in Tanakh: Bemidbar*, Jerusalem: Yeshivat Har Etzion; Maggid, 307–315.
——— (2014b), 'Benei Yisrael – The New Generation', in E. Bick (ed.), *Torah MiEtzion: New Readings in Tanakh: Bemidbar*, Jerusalem: Yeshivat Har Etzion; Maggid, 275–283.
——— (2014c), 'Why Are the Laws of the Nazir and the Sota Juxtaposed?', in E. Bick (ed.), *Torah MiEtzion: New Readings in Tanakh: Bemidbar*, Jerusalem: Yeshivat Har Etzion; Maggid, 55–62.
Beale, G. K. (1999), *The Book of Revelation*, Grand Rapids: Eerdmans.
Beattie, D. R. G., and J. S. McIvor (eds.) (1994), *The Targums of Ruth and Chronicles*, ArBib 19, Collegeville, Minn.: Liturgical.
Bechara, C. A. (2012), 'A Case for Law and Narrative in Numbers', in W. Kuhn (ed.), *The Book and the Student: Theological Education as Mission: A Festschrift Honoring José Carlos Ramos*, Berrien Springs: Andrews University, 25–43.
Beck, J. A. (2000), 'Geography and the Narrative Shape of Numbers 13', *BSac* 157:271–280.
——— (2003), 'Why Did Moses Strike Out? The Narrative-Geographical Shaping of Moses' Disqualification in Numbers 20:1–13', *WTJ* 65:135–141.
Beegle, D. (1972), *Moses, The Servant of Yahweh*, Grand Rapids: Eerdmans.
Begrich, J. (1936), 'Die Priesterliche Tora', in *Werden und Wesen des Alten Testaments*, BZAW 66, Berlin: A. Töpelmann, 63–88.
Beirne, D. (1963), 'A Note on Numbers 11,4', *Bib* 44 (2):201–203.
Ben-Barak, Z. (2006), *Inheritance by Daughters in Israel and the Ancient Near East: A Social, Legal and Ideological Revolution*, Jaffa, Israel: Archaeological Center.
Bendor, S. (1996), *The Social Structure of Ancient Israel*, Jerusalem Biblical Studies 7, Jerusalem: Simor.
Ben-Yosef, E., and A. Greener (2018), 'Edom's Copper Mines in Timna: Their Significance in the 10th Century', *TheTorah.Com* (blog), https://www.thetorah.com/article/edoms-copper-mines-in-timna-their-significance-in-the-10th-century.
Bergsma, J. S. (2007), *The Jubilee from Leviticus to Qumran: A History of Interpretation*, VTSup 115, Leiden: Brill.
Berlin, A. (1983), *Poetics and Interpretation of Biblical Narrative*, Sheffield: Sheffield Academic Press.
Berlinerblau, J. (1996), *The Vow and the 'Popular Religious Groups' of Ancient Israel: A Philological and Sociological Inquiry*, JSOTSup 210, Sheffield: Sheffield Academic Press.

Berman, J. (1995), *The Temple: Its Symbolism and Meaning Then and Now*, Northvale, N.J.: J. Aronson.
—— (2006), 'Constitution, Class, and the Book of Deuteronomy', *Hebraic Political Studies* 1 (5):523–548.
—— (2016), 'The Kadesh Inscriptions of Ramses II and the Exodus Sea Account (Exodus 13:17–15:19)', in J. K. Hoffmeier, A. R. Millard and G. A. Rendsburg (eds.), *'Did I Not Bring Israel Out of Egypt?', Biblical, Archaeological, and Egyptological Perspectives on the Exodus Narratives*, Bulletin for Biblical Research Supplements 13, Winona Lake: Eisenbrauns, 93–112.
—— (2017), *Inconsistency in the Torah: Ancient Literary Convention and the Limits of Source Criticism*, New York: Oxford University Press.
Bernat, D. A. (2007), 'Phinehas' Intercessory Prayer: A Rabbinic and Targumic Reading of the Baal Peor Narrative', *JJS* 58.2:263–282.
—— (2021), 'Why Conclude with the Daughters of Zelophehad?' TheTorah.com, https://www.thetorah.com/article/why-conclude-with-the-daughters-of-zelophehad.
Bernstein, I. (2021), 'The Journeys of the Children of Israel', Journeys in Torah, https://www.journeysintorah.com/wp-content/uploads/dimensions_masei_2021.pdf.
Bertman, S. (1961), 'Tasseled Garments in the Ancient East Mediterranean', *BA* 24 (4):119–128.
Bewer, J. A. (1905a), 'The Literary Problems of the Balaam Story in Numbers Chapters 22–24', *AJT* 9:238–262.
—— (1905b), 'The Original Significance of the Rite of the Red Cow in Numbers Xix', *JBL* 24:41–44.
Beyerlin, W. (1965), *Origins and History of the Oldest Sinaitic Traditions*, tr. S. Rudman, Oxford: Blackwell.
Bezold, C. (1926), *Babylonisch–Assyrisches Glossar*, ed. A. Bezold and Albrecht Gotze, Heidelberg: Carl Winter's Universitätsbuchhandlung.
Biale, D. (2016), 'Korah in the Midrash: The Hairless Heretic as Hero', *Jewish History* 30:15–28.
Bibb, B. D. (2001), 'Nadab and Abihu Attempt to Fill a Gap: Law and Narrative in Leviticus 10.1–7', *JSOT* 26 (2):83–99.
Bick, E. (1997), 'Tamid', Yeshivat Har Etzion – Virtual Beit Midrash, https://etzion.org.il/en/tanakh/torah/sefer-shemot/parashat-tetzaveh/tetzaveh-tamid-0.
—— (2014a), 'Aliya', in E. Bick (ed.), *Torah MiEtzion: New Readings in Tanakh: Bemidbar*, Jerusalem: Yeshivat Har Etzion; Maggid, 193–200.
—— (2014b), 'The Election of the Tribe of Levi', in E. Bick (ed.), *Torah MiEtzion: New Readings in Tanakh: Bemidbar*, Jerusalem: Yeshivat Har Etzion; Maggid, 233–240.
—— (2014c), 'Moses and Midian', in E. Bick (ed.), *Torah MiEtzion: New Readings in Tanakh: Bemidbar*, Jerusalem: Yeshivat Har Etzion, Maggid, 427–435.

—— (2014d), 'That Day – Again', in E. Bick (ed.), *Torah MiEtzion: New Readings in Tanakh: Bemidbar*, Jerusalem: Yeshivat Har Etzion; Maggid, 81–93.

—— (2017), 'Completing the Machane', Yeshivat Har Etzion – Virtual Beit Midrash, https://www.etzion.org.il/en.

Biderman, A. (2011), *The Mishkan: The Tabernacle: Its Structure and Its Sacred Vessels*, Brooklyn, N.Y.: Mesorah.

Biersdorff, K. A. (2014), 'Translation and Interpretation in the Septuagint Version of the Balaam Account', M.A. thesis, Langley, B.C.: Trinity Western University.

Bimson, J. J. (1978), *Redating the Exodus and Conquest*, Sheffield: University of Sheffield.

—— (1988), *The Compact Handbook of Old Testament Life*, Minneapolis: Bethany House.

Bin-Nun, Y. (2011), 'The Census Taken for the Purpose of Inheritance and the Additional Offerings', Yeshivat Har Etzion – Virtual Beit Midrash, https://www.etzion.org.il/en/tanakh/torah/sefer-bamidbar/parashat-pinchas/pinchas-census-taken-purpose-inheritance-and

—— (2019a), 'Masei: A Song of Biblical Geography', Studies in Parashat HaShavua, https://www.etzion.org.il/en/tanakh/torah/sefer-bamidbar/parashat-masei/masei-song-biblical-geography.

—— (2019b), 'Matot: War and the Morality of War', Yeshivat Har Etzion – Virtual Beit Midrash, https://etzion.org.il/en/tanakh/torah/sefer-bamidbar/parashat-matot/matot-war-and-morality-war.

Bird, P. (1989), '"To Play the Harlot": An Inquiry into an Old Testament Metaphor', in P. L. Day (ed.), *Gender and Difference in Ancient Israel*, Minneapolis: Fortress, 75–94.

Birkan, A. (2005), 'The Bronze Serpent, A Perplexing Remedy: An Analysis of Num. 21:4–9 in the Light of Near Eastern Serpent Emblems, Archaeology and Inner Biblical Exegesis', Master of Arts, Montreal: McGill University.

Bissell, A. P. (1884), *The Law of Asylum in Israel Historically and Critically Examined*, Leipzig: Th. Stauffer.

Black, J. (1930), *Rogues of the Bible*, New York: Harper & Brothers.

Blau, J. L. (1967), 'The Red Heifer: A Biblical Rite in Rabbinic Literature', *Numen* 14:70–78.

Blenkin, H. (1964), *Immortal Sacrifice*, London: Darton, Longman & Todd.

Blenkinsopp, J. (1997), 'The Family in First Temple Israel', in L. G. Perdue, J. Blenkinsopp, J. J. Collins and C. L. Meyers (eds.), *Families in Ancient Israel*, Louisville, Ky.: Westminster John Knox, 48–103.

—— (2012), 'The Baal Peor Episode Revisited (Num 25,1–18)', *Bib* 93 (1):86–97.

Bloch-Smith, E. (1994), '"Who Is the King of Glory?" Solomon's Temple and Its Symbolism', in M. D. Coogan, J. C. Exum and L. E. Stager (eds.), *Scripture and Other Artifacts*, Louisville, Ky.: Westminster John Knox, 18–31.

Block, D. I. (1997), *The Book of Ezekiel: Chapters 1–24*, vol. 1, NICOT, Grand Rapids: Eerdmans.
—— (2012), *Deuteronomy*, The NIV Application Commentary, Grand Rapids: Zondervan.
Blum, E. (1990), *Studien zur Komposition des Pentateuch*, BZAW 189, Berlin, New York: de Gruyter.
—— (2009), 'Issues and Problems in the Contemporary Debate Regarding the Priestly Writings', in S. Shectman and J. S. Baden (eds.), *The Strata of the Priestly Writings: Contemporary Debate and Future Directions*, ATANT 95, Zürich: Theologischer Verlag, 31–44.
Blumenthal, F. (2006), 'Balaam and His Talking Donkey', *JBQ* 34 (2):83–85.
Bobrick, B. (2005), *The Fated Sky: Astrology in History*, New York: Simon & Schuster.
Bodenheimer, F. S. (1947), 'The Manna of Sinai', *BA* 10:1–6.
Bodenheimer, F. S., and O. Theodor (1929), *Ergebnisse der Sinai-Expedition 1927*, Leipzig: Hinrich'sche Buchhandlung.
Boer, P. A. H. de (1982), 'Numbers VI 27', *VT* 32:3–13.
Boer, R. (2006), 'The Law of the Jealous Man', in W. J. Bergen and A. Siedlecki (eds.), *Voyages in Unchartered Waters: Essays on the Theory and Practice of Biblical Interpretation in Honor of David Jobling*, Sheffield: Sheffield Phoenix, 87–95.
Bolger, E. W. (1993), 'The Compositional Role of the Eden Narrative in the Pentateuch', PhD diss. Deerfield, Ill.: Trinity Evangelical Divinity School.
Bonchek, A. (2004), *Studying the Torah: A Guide to in-Depth Interpretation*, Lanham, Md.: Rowman & Littlefield.
Boorer, S. (1992), *The Promise of the Land as Oath: A Key to the Formation of the Pentateuch*, BZAW 205, Berlin; New York: de Gruyter.
—— (2012), 'The Place of Numbers 13–14 and Numbers 20:2–12 in the Priestly Narrative (Pg)', *JBL*, 131 (1):45–63.
—— (2015), 'Miriam, Moses, and Aaron in Numbers 12 and 20: A Feminist Biblical Theology Concerning Exclusion', in P. K. Tull and J. E. Lapsley (eds.), *After Exegesis: Feminist Biblical Theology. Essays in Honour of Carol A. Newsom*, Baylor University Press, 123–139.
Boraas, R. S. (1978), 'Of Serpents and Gods', *Dialog* 17 (4):273–279.
Borger, R. (1956), *Die Inschriften Asarhaddons Königs von Assyrien*, Graz: E. Weidner.
Borowski, O. (2003), *Daily Life in Biblical Times*, Archaeology and Biblical Studies 5, Atlanta: Society of Biblical Literature.
Boudreau, G. R. (1991), *A Study of the Traditio-Historical Development of the Baal of Peor Tradition*, Atlanta: Emory University Press.
—— (1993), 'Hosea and Pentateuchal Traditions: The Case of the Baal of Peor', in M. P. Graham, W. P. Brown and J. K. Kuan (eds.), *History and Interpretation: Essays in Honour of John H. Hayes*, JSOTSup 173, Sheffield: Sheffield Academic Press, 121–132.

Bourke, J. (1959), 'The Spirit of God in the Old Testament', *Life of the Spirit* 13 (156):538–550.
Bovati, Pietro (1994), *Re-Establishing Justice: Legal Terms, Concepts and Procedures in the Hebrew Bible*, tr. M. J. Smith, JSOTSup 105, Sheffield: Sheffield Academic Press.
Boys, T. (1825), *A Key to the Book of Psalms*, London: Seeley.
Breland, C. R. (2019), 'The Year of the Lord's Favor: An Old Testament Theology of the Jubilee', PhD diss., Louisville, Ky.: Southern Baptist Theological Seminary.
Brenner, A. (1982), *Colour Terms in the Old Testament*, JSOTSup 21, Sheffield: JSOT.
Brenton, L. C. L. (1986), *The Septuagint with Apocrypha: Greek and English*, Peabody: Hendrickson.
Brichto, H. C. (1963), *The Problem of 'Curse' in the Hebrew Bible*, Philadelphia: Society of Biblical Literature.
——— (1973), 'Kin, Cult, Land and Afterlife – A Biblical Complex', *HUCA* 44:1–54.
——— (1975), 'The Case of the Sotah and a Reconsideration of Biblical Law', *HUCA* 46:55–70.
Briend, J. (1992), *Dieu dans l'Écriture*, Paris: Cerf.
Briggs, C. A. (1886), *Messianic Prophecy: The Prediction of the Fulfillment of Redemption Through the Messiah*, New York: Scribner.
Briggs, R. S. (2009), 'Reading the Sotah Text (Numbers 5:11–31): Holiness and a Hermeneutic Fit for Suspicion', *BibInt* 17:288–319.
——— (2018), *Theological Hermeneutics and the Book of Numbers as Christian Scripture*, Notre Dame: University of Notre Dame Press.
Brin, G. (1980), 'Numbers XV 22–23 and the Question of the Composition of the Pentateuch', *VT* 30 (3):351–354.
——— (1994), *Studies in Biblical Law: From the Hebrew Bible to the Dead Sea Scrolls*, JSOT 176, Sheffield: JSOT.
Briscoe, T. V. (1995), 'Paran', in G. W. Bromiley (ed.), rev., *International Standard Bible Encyclopedia*, Grand Rapids: Eerdmans, 3:662.
Brodie, T. L. (2008), 'The Literary Unity of Numbers: Nineteen Atonement-Centered Diptychs as One Key Element', in T. Römer (ed.), *The Books of Leviticus and Numbers*, Leuven: Peeters, 455–472.
Bronner, L. (1994), 'Seraḥ and the Exodus: A Midrashic Miracle', in *A Feminist Companion to Exodus to Deuteronomy*, Sheffield: Sheffield Academic Press: 187–198.
Broshi, M. (1975), 'La Population de l'ancienne Jerusalem', *RB* 82:5–14.
Broshi, M., and I. Finkelstein (1992), 'The Population of Palestine in Iron Age II', *BASOR* 287:47–60.
Broshi, M., and R. Gophna (1986), 'Middle Bronze Age II Palestine: Its Settlements and Population', *BASOR* 261:73–90.
Brown, E. (2011), 'The Well Dried Up: Miriam's Death in Bible and Midrash',

in R. Schwartz (ed.), *All the Women Followed Her: A Collection of Writings on Miriam the Prophet and the Women of Exodus*, Mountain View, Calif.: Rikudei Miriam, 42–51.

Brown, F., S. Driver and C. Briggs (2003), *The Brown, Driver, Briggs Hebrew and English Lexicon*, Peabody: Hendrickson.

Brown, K. (2015), 'Vengeance and Vindication in Numbers 31', *JBL* 134.1:65–84.

——— (2020), 'Between Our Ancestors and the Other: Negotiating Identity in the Early Reception of the Water from the Rock', in K. Brown, B. Breed and A. Joseph (eds.), *Reading Other People's Texts: Identity Formation and the Reception of Authoritative Traditions*, LHBOTS 692, London: Bloomsbury T. & T. Clark; Grand Rapids: Eerdmans, 102–123.

Brueggemann, W. (1977), *The Land*, OBT, Philadelphia: Fortress.

Brumberg-Kraus, J. (1999), 'Meat-Eating and Jewish Identity: Ritualization of the Priestly "Torah of Beast and Fowl" (Lev. 11:46) in Rabbinic Judaism and Medieval Kabbalah', *Association for Jewish Studies Review* 24 (2):227–262.

Brütsch, C. (1970), *Die Offenbarung Jesu Christi: Kapitel 1–10*, ZBK, Zürich: Zwingli-Verlag.

Buber, M. (1946), *Moses: The Revelation and the Covenant*, London: East and West Library.

——— (1968), 'The Tree of Knowledge', in N. M. Glatzer (ed.), *On the Bible*, New York: Schocken, 14–21.

Büchler, A. (1967), *Studies in Sin and Atonement in the Rabbinic Literature of the First Century*, New York: Ktav.

Budge, E. A. W. (1969), *The Gods of the Egyptians: Studies in Egyptian Mythology*, vol. 2, New York: Dover.

Buell, S. D. (2012), 'The Characterization of Aaron: Threshold Encounters in Exodus, Leviticus, and Numbers', PhD diss., Waco, Tex.: Baylor University.

Buis, P. (1974), 'Qadesh, un Lieu Maudit?', *VT* 24:268–285.

Bullinger, E. W. (1893), *The Witness of the Stars*, London: Eyre & Spottiswoode.

Burnett, J. S. (2018), 'Prophecy in Transjordan: Balaam Son of Beor', in C. A. Rollston (ed.), *Enemies and Friends of the State: Ancient Prophecy in Context*, University Park: Eisenbrauns, 135–204.

Burnham, J. N. (2014), 'Clarity Through the Blur: An Equivocal Reading of Numbers 25:1–18', PhD diss., New Orleans: New Orleans Baptist Theological Seminary.

Burns, R. J. (1980), '"Has the Lord Indeed Only Spoken through Moses?" A Study of the Biblical Portrait of Miriam', PhD diss., Milwaukee: Marquette University.

——— (1987), *Has the Lord Indeed Spoken Only Through Moses? A Study of the Biblical Portrait of Miriam*, SBLDS 84, Atlanta: Scholars.

Burnside, J. P. (2010a), 'Exodus and Asylum: Uncovering the Relationship between Biblical Law and Narrative', *JSOT* 34 (3): 243–266.

——— (2010b), '"What Shall We Do with the Sabbath-Gatherer?" A Narrative

Approach to a "Hard Case" in Biblical Law (Numbers 15:32–36)', *VT* 60:45–62.

——— (2016), 'Why Was Moses Banned from the Promised Land? A Radical Retelling of the Rebellions of Moses (Num. 20:2–13 and Exod. 2:11–15)', *ZABR* 22:111–159.

Burrows, E. (1938), *The Oracles of Jacob and Balaam*, ed. E. Sutcliffe, The Bellarmine Series 3, London: Burns, Oates and Washbourne.

Calabro, D. (2017), 'A Reexamination of the Ancient Israelite Gesture of Hand Placement', in H. L. Wiley and C. A. Eberhart (eds.), *Sacrifice, Cult, and Atonement in Early Judaism and Christianity*, Atlanta: SBL Press, 99–124.

Callan, T. (1980), 'Pauline Midrash: The Exegetical Background of Gal 3:19b', *JBL* 99 (4):549–567.

Calvin, J. (2003a), *Commentary on a Harmony of the Evangelists, Matthew, Mark, and Luke*, tr. W. Pringle, vol. 1, Grand Rapids: Baker.

Camp, C. V. (2009), *Wise, Strange and Holy: The Strange Woman and the Making of the Bible*, Sheffield: Sheffield Academic Press.

Canney, M. A. (1916), 'Numbers Xxii.21–31', *ExpTim* :568.

Carmichael, C. M. (2012), *The Book of Numbers: A Critique of Genesis*, New Haven: Yale University Press.

Carr, D. M. (2011), *Formation of the Hebrew Bible: A New Reconstruction*, Oxford: Oxford University Press.

Cartledge, T. W. (1992), *Vows in the Hebrew Bible and the Ancient Near East*, JSOTSup 147, Sheffield: Sheffield Academic Press.

Carvalho, C. L. (2014), 'A Serpent in the Nile: Egypt in the Book of Ezekiel', in A. Mein, E. K. Holt and H. C. P. Kim (eds.), *Concerning the Nations: Essays on the Oracles Against the Nations in Isaiah, Jeremiah, and Ezekiel*, London: Bloomsbury, 195–220.

Cassuto, U. (2008), *The Documentary Hypothesis and the Composition of the Pentateuch: Eight Lectures*, tr. I. Abrahams, Jerusalem: Shalem.

Castello, G. (1994), 'Balaam e Balak: Approccio Narrativo a Nm 22–24', in C. Marcheselli-Casale (ed.), *Oltre Il Racconto: Esegesi Ed Ermeneutica: All Ricerca Del Senso*, Naples: M. D'Auria, 29–48.

Cathcart, K. J. (1998), 'Numbers 24:17 in Ancient Translations and Interpretations', in J. Krasovec (ed.), *The Interpretation of the Bible: The International Symposium in Slovenia*, JSOTSup 289, Sheffield: Sheffield Academic Press, 511–520.

Caulley, T. S. (2014), 'Balaam's "Star" Oracle in Jewish and Christian Prophetic Tradition', *ResQ* 56:28–40.

Cavasola, A. G. P. (2020), 'Two Mysterious Numbers of Numbers: Why Exactly Were 603,550 Israelites Invited to Enter the Promised Land?', Academia.edu, https://www.academia.edu/44496050/Two_Mysterious_Numbers_of_Numbers_Why_exactly_603_550_Israelites_were_invited_to_enter_the_Promised_Land.

Chavalas, M. W. (2000), 'Assur', in D. N. Freedman (ed.), *Eerdman's Dictionary of the Bible*, Grand Rapids: Eerdmans, 119.

——— (2003), 'Balaam', in T. D. Alexander and D. W. Baker (eds.), *Dictionary of the Old Testament: Pentateuch*, Downers Grove: InterVarsity Press, 75–78.
Chavel, S. (2009a), 'Numbers 15,32–36 – A Microcosm of the Living Priesthood and Its Literary Production', in S. Shectman and J. S. Baden (eds.), *The Strata of the Priestly Writings: Contemporary Debate and Future Directions*, AThANT 95, Zürich: Theologischer Verlag Zürich, 45–55.
——— (2009b), '"Oracular Novellae" and Biblical Historiography: Through the Lens of Law and Narrative', *Clio* 39 (1):1–27.
——— (2009c), 'The Second Passover, Pilgrimage, and the Centralized Cult', *HTR* 102 (1):1–24.
——— (2012), 'The Face of God and the Etiquette of Eye-Contact: Visitation, Pilgrimage, and Prophetic Vision in Ancient Israelite and Early Jewish Imagination', *JSQ* 19:1–55.
Chen, K. (2019), *The Messianic Vision of the Pentateuch*, Westmont: InterVarsity Press.
Childs, B. S. (1989), *Old Testament Theology in a Canonical Context*, Philadelphia: Fortress.
——— (2004), *The Book of Exodus: A Critical, Theological Commentary*, Louisville, Ky.: Westminster.
Chinitz, J. (1996), 'The Listing of the Twelve Tribes', *JBQ* 24 (1):36–42.
Chou, A. (2013), *I Saw the Lord: A Biblical Theology of Vision*, Eugene: Wipf & Stock.
Christensen, D. L. (1974), 'Num 21:14–15 and the Book of the Wars of Yahweh', *CBQ* 36:359–360.
Claassens, J. (2013), '"Give Us a Portion Among Our Father's Brothers": The Daughters of Zelophehad, Land, and the Quest for Human Dignity', *JSOT* 37.7:319–337.
Clark, I. (1982), 'Balaam's Ass: Suture or Structure?', in K. R. R. Gros Louis and J. S. Ackerman (eds.), *Literary Interpretations of Biblical Narratives*, Nashville: Abingdon, 2:137–144.
Clark, M. (1999), *Etymological Dictionary of Biblical Hebrew: Based on the Commentaries of Rabbi Samson Raphael Hirsch*, New York: Feldheim.
Clark, R. E. D. (1955), 'The Large Numbers of the Old Testament', *Journal of the Transactions of the Victoria Institute* 87:82–92.
Clark, T. S. (2014), 'Firstfruits and Tithe Offerings in the Construction and Narratives of the Hebrew Bible', PhD diss., Atlanta: Emory University.
Clarke, T. A. (2003), 'Cities of Refuge', *DOTP*, 125–128.
Claussen, G. (2015), 'Pinḥas, the Quest for Purity, and the Dangers of Tikkun Olam', in D. Birnbaum and M. S. Cohen (eds.), *Tikkun Olam: Judaism, Humanism and Transcendence*, New York: New Paradigm Matrix, 475–501.
Clines, D. J. A. (1997), *The Theme of the Pentateuch*, 2nd ed., Sheffield, England: JSOT.
——— (2007), 'What Do We Really Want to Know about the Pentateuch?',

Sources of the Pentateuch: Ancient Writings, Modern Constructs, conference paper delivered at SBL International meeting in Vienna.
Coats, G. W. (1968), *Rebellion in the Wilderness: The Murmuring Motif in the Wilderness Traditions of the Old Testament*, Nashville: Abingdon.
—— (1972), 'The Wilderness Itinerary', *CBQ* 34:135–152.
—— (1973), 'Balaam: Sinner or Saint?', *BR* 18:21–29.
—— (1982a), 'Humility and Honor: A Moses Legend in Numbers 12', in D. J. A. Clines, D. M. Gunn and A. J. Hauser (eds.), *Art and Meaning: Rhetoric in Biblical Literature*, JSOTSup 19, Sheffield: JSOT, 97–107.
—— (1982b), 'The Way of Obedience: Traditio-Historical and Hermeneutical Reflections on the Balaam Story', *Semeia* 24:53–79.
—— (1987), *Moses: Heroic Man, Man of God*, Sheffield: Sheffield Academic Press.
—— (1993), 'The King's Loyal Opposition: Obedience and Authority in Exodus 32–34', in *The Moses Tradition*, JSOTSup 61, Sheffield: Sheffield Academic Press, 57–75.
Cocco, F. (2016), *The Torah as a Place of Refuge: Biblical Criminal Law and the Book of Numbers*, FAT 2.84, Tübingen: Mohr Siebeck.
—— (2020), *Women in the Wilderness: The 'Female Legislation' of the Book of Numbers (Num 5,11–31; 27,1–11; 30,2–17)*, FAT 138, Tübingen: Mohr Siebeck.
Cohen, J. M. (1984), 'The Striking of the Rock', *Dor le Dor* 12 (3):152–165.
—— (1988), 'Balaam's Mission – Failure or Success?', *Dor le Dor* 17 (2):112–116.
—— (1992), 'Balaam: Did God Change His Mind?', *JBQ* 20 (3):159–163.
—— (2000), 'Leadership in the Book of Numbers', *JBQ* 28 (2):125–129.
—— (2013), 'Phinehas, Elijah and Circumcision', *JBQ* 41.1:14–18.
Cohen, N. (2016), 'And a Fire Came Down from Before the Lord: Examining the Relationship Between Leviticus 10 and Numbers 16–18', Senior Thesis, Waltham, Mass.: Brandeis University.
Cohn, R. L. (1981), *The Shape of Sacred Space: Four Biblical Studies*, Chico, Calif.: Scholars.
Cole, R. D. (1998), 'Structure, Outline, and Theology of the Book of Numbers', Presented at the Annual Meeting of the Evangelical Theological Society, Orlando, Florida, 1–11.
—— (2003), 'The Challenge of Faith's Final Step', in D. M. Howard and M. A. Grisanti (eds.), *Giving the Sense: Understanding and Using Old Testament Historical Texts*, Grand Rapids: Kregel, 340–359.
—— (2009), 'Numbers', in J. H. Walton (ed.), *Zondervan Illustrated Bible Backgrounds Commentary: Genesis, Exodus, Leviticus, Numbers, Deuteronomy*, Grand Rapids: Zondervan, 1:338–417.
Colenso, J. W. (1862), *The Pentateuch and Book of Joshua Critically Examined*, London: Longman.
Collins, J. J. (1985), 'Artapanus', in J. H. Charlesworth (eds.), *The Old Testament Pseudepigrapha*, Garden City, N.Y.: Doubleday, 2:889–903.

––––––– (2003), 'The Zeal of Phinehas: The Bible and the Legitimation of Violence', *JBL* 122.1:3–21.
Collins, M. F. (1978), 'Messianic Interpretation of the Balaam Oracles', PhD diss., New Haven: Yale University.
Condie, K. (2001), 'Narrative Features of Numbers 13–14 and Their Significance for the Meaning of the Book of Numbers', *RTR* 60 (3):123–137.
Condren, J. C. (2005), 'Yahweh in Their Midst: Analysis of Numbers 1:1–10:10 and Its Relationship to the Theme of Divine Presence in the Pentateuch', PhD diss., Deerfield, Ill.: Trinity Evangelical Divinity School.
––––––– (2013), 'Is the Account of the Organization of the Camp Devoid of Organization? A Proposal for the Literary Structure of Numbers 1.1–10.10', *JSOT* 37 (4):423–452.
Conrad, J. (1980), '*Zāqēn*', *TDOT* 4:122–431.
Cook, S. L. (1999), 'The Tradition of Mosaic Judges: Past Approaches and New Direction', in S. L. Cook and S. C. Winters (eds.), *On the Way to Nineveh: Studies in Honor of George M. Landes*, Atlanta: Scholars, 286–315.
Cooper, A. M., and B. R. Goldstein (1997), 'At the Entrance to the Tent: More Cultic Resonances in Biblical Narrative', *JBL* 116 (2):201–215.
Cornelius, F. (1966), 'Moses Urkundlich', *ZAW* 78 (1):75–78.
Cornhill, C. H. (1891), 'Beiträge Zur Pentateuchkritik', *ZAW* 11:20–33.
Cotton, R. D. (2001), 'The Pentecostal Significance of Numbers 11', *JPT* 10:3–10.
Cox, S. (1884), *Balaam: An Exposition and a Study*, London: Kegan Paul, Trench.
Craigie, P. C. (1976), *The Book of Deuteronomy*, NICOT, Grand Rapids: Eerdmans.
––––––– (1978), *The Problem of War in the Old Testament*, Grand Rapids: Eerdmans.
––––––– (1983), *Psalms 1–50*, WBC 19, Waco, Tex.: Word.
Creach, J. F. D. (2008), *The Destiny of the Righteous in the Psalms*, St. Louis: Chalice.
Croatto, J. S. (1998), 'The Function of the Non-Fulfilled Promises: Reading the Pentateuch from the Perspective of the Latin-American Oppressed People', in I. R. Kitzberger (eds.), *The Personal Voice in Biblical Interpretation*, London: Routledge, 38–52.
Cross, F. M. (1973), *Canaanite Myth and Hebrew Epic: Essays in the History of the Religion of Israel*, Cambridge, Mass.: Harvard University Press.
Cruzer, H. J. (2010), 'Spies and Lies: Faithful, Courageous Israelites and Truthful Spies', *Journal for The Study of The Old Testament* 35 (2):187–195.
Cumming, J. E. (1880), 'Christ in the Tabernacle: No. IV The Most Holy Place (Concluded)', *Life & Work: A Parish Magazine with Gaelic Supplement*, 188–190.

Currid, J. D. (1997), *Ancient Egypt and the Old Testament*, Grand Rapids: Baker.
Curwin, D. (2023), *Kohelet: A Map to Eden*, Jerusalem: Maggid.
Daiches, S. (1909), 'Balaam – a Babylonian Bārū. The Episode of Nu 22,2–24,24 and Some Babylonian Parallels', in *Hilprecht Anniversary Volume: Studies in Assyriology and Archeology*, Leipzig: Hinrichs, 60–70.
Darnov, A. M. (2007), 'Equivocal Narrative in the Hebrew Bible', PhD diss., New York: The Jewish Theological Seminary.
Daube, D. (1973), *Ancient Hebrew Fables: The Inaugural Lecture of the Oxford Centre for Postgraduate Studies*, Oxford: Oxford University Press.
Davidson, A. B. (1896), *Hebrew Syntax*, Edinburgh: T. & T. Clark.
Davidson, R. M. (2007), *Flame of Yahweh: A Theology of Sexuality in the Old Testament*, Peabody: Hendrickson.
Davies, E. W. (1981), 'Inheritance Rights and the Hebrew Levirate Marriage, Part 1', *VT* 31.2:138–144.
——— (1995a), 'A Mathematical Conundrum: The Problem of the Large Numbers in Numbers i and Xxvi', *VT* 45:449–469.
Davies, G. I. (1974), 'The Wilderness Itineraries: A Comparative Study', *TynB* 25:46–81.
——— (1979), *The Way of the Wilderness: A Geographical Study of the Wilderness Itineraries in the Old Testament*, SOTSMS 5, Cambridge: Cambridge University Press.
——— (1983), 'The Wilderness Itineraries and the Composition of the Pentateuch', *VT* 33:1–13.
——— (1990), 'The Wilderness Itineraries and Recent Archaeological Research', in Emerton, J. A. (ed.), *Studies in the Pentateuch*, VTSup 41, Leiden: Brill, 161–175.
Davies, J. A. (1998), 'The Temple Scroll from Qumran and the Ultimate Temple', *RTR* 57:1–21.
——— (2004), *A Royal Priesthood: Literary and Intertextual Perspectives on an Image of Israel in Exodus 19.6*, London: T. & T. Clark International.
Davis, J. J. (1968), *Biblical Numerology: A Basic Study of the Use of Numbers in the Bible*, Grand Rapids: Baker Academic.
Day, J. (2015), 'Cain and the Kenites', in *From Creation to Babel: Studies in Genesis 1–11*, London: Bloomsbury T. & T. Clark, 51–60.
Day, P. L. (1988), *An Adversary in Heaven: Śāṭān in the Hebrew Bible*, Harvard Semitic Museum Publications 43, Atlanta: Scholars.
Day, Q. (2023), 'Shall the Daughters of Zelophehad Inherit? Allusions to Jubilee in Numbers 36:1–13', *Africanus Journal* 15 (1):16–22.
De Regt, L. J. (2008), 'Partial Repetition in Sections of Numbers 4 and the Translator', in T. C. Römer (ed.), *Books of Leviticus and Numbers*, Leuven: Peeters, 417–422.

De Vries, S. J. (1975), 'The Time Word Māḥār as a Key to Tradition Development', *ZAW* 87:65–79.

Dearman, J. A. (1984), 'The Location of Jahaz', *Zeitschrift des Deutschen Palästina-Vereins* 100:122–126.

Delcor, M. (1982), 'Bala'am Patorah, Intrete des Songes au Pays d'Ammon d'apres Nombres 22:5. Les Temoignages Épigraphiques Paralleles', *Sem* 32:89–91.

Démare-Lafont, S. (1987), 'L'interprétation de Nombres 5,31 à La Lumière des Droits Cunéiformes', in J.-M. Durand (ed.), *La Femme Dans Le Proche-Orient Antique: Compte Rendu de La 33e Recontre Assyriologique Internationale (Paris, 7–10 July 1986)*, Paris: ERC, 49–52.

Demsky, A. (2021a), 'The Daughters of Zelophehad: A Historical-Geographical Approach', *TheTorah.Com* (blog), https://www.thetorah.com/article/the-daughters-of-zelophehad-a-historical-geographical-approach.

——— (2021b), 'Manasseh's Genealogies: Why They Change Between Numbers, Joshua, and Chronicles', *TheTorah.Com* (blog), https://www.thetorah.com/article/manassehs-genealogies-why-they-change-between-numbers-joshua-and-chronicles.

Dentan, R. C. (1962b), 'Wars of the Lord, Book of The', *IDB* 4:805.

Derby, J. (1997), 'The Daughters of Zelophehad Revisited', *JBQ* 25.3:169–171.

DeRouchie, J. S. (2013), 'The Blessing-Commission, the Promised Offspring, and the Toledot Structure of Genesis', *JETS* 56 (2):219–247.

——— (2020), 'How Does Isaiah 12:2 Use Exodus 15:2?', in B. L. Merkle (ed.), *40 Questions About Biblical Theology*, Grand Rapids: Kregel, 303–312.

Derrett, J. D. M. (1993), 'The Case of Korah Versus Moses Reviewed', *Journal for the Study of Judaism in the Persian, Hellenistic and Roman Period* 24 (1):59–78.

Destro, A. (1989), *The Law of Jealousy: Anthropology of Sotah*, Atlanta: Scholars.

Diamond, E. (1997), 'An Israelite Self-Offering in the Priestly Code: A New Perspective on the Nazirite', *JQR* 88:1–18.

Díez Macho, A. (1974), *Neophyti 1: 4 Numeros*, Madrid: Consejo Superior de Investigaciones Científicas.

Dijk, H. J. van (1968), 'A Neglected Connotation of Three Hebrew Verbs', *VT* 18:16–30.

Dijkstra, M. (1995a), 'The Geography of the Story of Balaam: Reading as a Help to Date a Biblical Text', in J. C. de Moor (ed.), *Synchronic or Diachronic: A Debate on Method in Old Testament Exegesis*, OtSt 34, Leiden: Brill, 72–97.

——— (1995b), 'Is Balaam Also Among the Prophets?', *JBL* 114 (1):43–64.

Dobin, J. C. (1983), *The Astrological Secrets of the Hebrew Sages: To Rule Both Day and Night*, New York: Inner Traditions International.

——— (1999), *Kabbalistic Astrology: The Sacred Tradition of the Hebrew Sages*, new edition of *The Astrological Secrets of the Hebrew Sages*, Rochester, Vt.: Inner Traditions.

Donner, H. (1977), 'Balaam Pseudopropheta', in H. Donner, R. Hanhart and

R. Smend (eds.), *Beiträge zur Alttestamentlichen Theologie: Festschrift für Walther Zimmerli zum 70. Geburtstag*, Göttingen: Vandenhoeck & Ruprecht, 112–123.

Douglas, C. E. (1936), 'The Twelve Houses of Israel', *Journal of Theological Studies* 37 (145):49–56.

Douglas, J. D., M. C. Tenney and M. Silva (eds.) (2011), *Zondervan Illustrated Bible Dictionary*, rev. ed., Grand Rapids: Zondervan.

Douglas, M. (1993), 'Balaam's Place in the Book of Numbers', *Man, New Series* 28 (3):411–430.

—— (2001), *In the Wilderness: The Doctrine of Defilement in the Book of Numbers*, rev. ed., JSOT 158, Oxford: Oxford University Press.

—— (2004), *Jacob's Tears: The Priestly Work of Reconciliation*, Oxford: Oxford University Press.

—— (2007), *Thinking in Circles: An Essay on Ring Composition*, New Haven: Yale University Press.

Dozeman, T. B. (2000), 'Masking Moses and Mosaic Authority in Torah', *JBL* 119 (1):21–45.

—— (2008), 'The Midianites in the Formation of the Book of Numbers', in T. B. Dozeman (ed.), *The Books of Leviticus and Numbers*, Leuven: Peeters, 261–284.

—— (2009), *Commentary on Exodus*, ECC, Grand Rapids: Eerdmans.

—— (2017), *The Pentateuch: Introducing the Torah*, Grand Rapids: Fortress.

Driver, G. R. (1956a), 'Three Technical Terms in the Pentateuch', *Journal of Semitic Studies* 1 (2):97–105.

—— (1956b), 'Two Problems in the Old Testament Examined in the Light of Assyriology', *Syria* 33:70–78.

—— (1960), 'Abbreviations in the Massoretic Text', *Textus* 1:112–131.

Driver, S. R. (1902), *Deuteronomy*, ICC, Edinburgh: T. & T. Clark.

—— (1906), *An Introduction to the Literature of the Old Testament*, 12th ed., Oxford:Clarendon.

Driver, W. (1960), 'The Release of Homicides from the Cities of Refuge', *Grace Journal* 1 (2):7–22.

Dumbrell, W. J. (1975), 'Midian – A Land or a League?', *VT* 25.3:323–337.

Durham, J. I. (1970), 'Shalom and the Presence of God', in J. I. Durham and J. R. Porter (eds.), *Proclamation and Presence: Old Testament Essays in Honour of Gwynne Henton Davies*, Richmond, Va.: John Knox, 272–293.

Dybdahl, J. L. (1981), 'Israelite Village Land Tenure: Settlement to Exile', PhD diss., Pasadena, Calif.: Fuller Theological Seminary.

Easton, M. G. (1894), *Illustrated Bible Dictionary*, London: Thomas Nelson.

Eberhart, C. (2002), *Studien zur Bedeutung der Opfer im alten Testament: Die Signifikanz von Blut- und Verbrennungsriten im kultischen Rahmen*, Neukirchen-Vluyn: Neukirchener Verlag.

—— (2004), 'A Neglected Feature of Sacrifice in the Hebrew Bible: Remarks on the Burning Rite on the Altar', *HTR* 97.4: 485–493.

Edwards, J. R. (1989), 'Markan Sandwiches: The Significance of Interpolations in Markan Narratives', *NovT* 31 (3):193–216.
Ehrlich, A. (1899), *Scripture in Its Plain Sense*, vol. 1, Berlin: M. Poppelauer.
——— (1908), *Randglossen zur Hebräischen Bibel*, vol. 2, Leipzig: Hinrichs.
Ehrlich, C. S. (2018), 'Balaam the Seer: From the Bible to the Deir 'Alla Inscription', *TheTorah.Com* (blog), https://www.thetorah.com/article/balaam-the-seer-from-the-bible-to-the-deir-alla-inscription.
Ehrlich, Z. H. (1983), 'The Inheritance of Hoglah, Daughter of Zelophehad (Num. 27)', *Beit Mikra* 28.3:232–235.
Eichler, R. (2014), 'The Meaning of יֹשֵׁב הַכְּרֻבִים', *ZAW* 126 (3):358–371.
——— (2015), 'Cherub: A History of Interpretation', *Bib* 96 (1):26–38.
——— (2016), 'The Poles of the Ark: On the Ins and Outs of a Textual Contradiction', *JBL* 135 (4):733–741.
——— (2021), 'A Sin Is Borne: Clearing up the Law of Women's Vows (Numbers 30)', *VT* 71.3:317–328.
Eichrodt, W. (1976a), *Theology of the Old Testament*, tr. J. A. Baker, vol. 1, Philadelphia: Westminster.
——— (1976b), *Theology of the Old Testament*, tr. J. A. Baker, vol. 2, Philadelphia: Westminster.
Eidelberg, S. (1980), 'Trial by Ordeal in Medieval Jewish History: Laws, Customs and Attitudes', *Proceedings of the American Academy for Jewish Research* 46/47:105–120.
Eisenstein, J. D. (1906), 'Zodiac', in I. Singer (ed.), *The Jewish Encyclopedia*, New York: Funk and Wagnalls, 12:688–89.
Eissfeldt, O. (1939), 'Die Komposition der Bileam-Erzählung. Eine Nachprüfung von Rudolphs Beitrag zur Hexateuchkritik', *ZAW* 57:212–241.
——— (1965), *The Old Testament: An Introduction*, tr. P. Ackroyd, New York: Harper & Row.
Elior, R. (1993), 'Mysticism, Magic, and Angelology: The Perception of Angels in Hekhalot Literature', *JSQ* 1 (1):3–53.
——— (1997), 'From Earthly Temples to Heavenly Shrines: Prayer and Sacred Song in Hekhalot Literature and Its Relation to Temple Traditions', *JSQ* (3):217–267.
——— (1999), 'The "Merkavah" Tradition and the Emergence of Jewish Mysticism', in A. Oppenheimer (ed.), *Sino-Judaica, Jews and Chinese in Historical Dialogue*, Tel Aviv: Tel Aviv University Press, 101–158.
Elitzur, Y. (2020), *Places in the Parasha: Biblical Geography and Its Meaning*, Jerusalem: Maggid.
Ellingworth, P. (1993), *The Epistle to the Hebrews: A Commentary on the Greek Text*, NIGTC, Grand Rapids: Eerdmans; Carlisle: Paternoster.
Ellul, J. (1973), *The Meaning of the City*, Grand Rapids: Eerdmans.
Embry, B. (2010), 'The Endangerment of Moses: Towards a New Reading of Exodus 4:24–26', *VT* 60 (2):177–196.
——— (2016), 'Legalities in the Book of Ruth: A Renewed Look', *JSOT* 41:31–44.

Emmrich, M. (2003), 'The Case Against Moses Reopened', *JETS* 46:53–62.
Enns, P. (2000), *Exodus*, NAC, Grand Rapids: Zondervan.
Erlandsson, S. (1980), '*Zānāh*', *TDOT* 4:99–104.
Erlanger, G. (2000), *Signs of the Times: The Zodiac in Jewish Tradition.* Jerasalem: Feldheim Publishers.
Etheridge, J. W. (trans.) (1862), *The Targums of Onkelos and Jonathan Ben Uzziel on the Pentateuch [Includes Fragmentary Targum]*, vol. 2, London: Longman, Green and Roberts.
Etshalom, Y. (2010), 'Siyyum on Sefer Bamidbar: Parshas Matos Masei', Torah.org, https://torah.org/torah-portion/mikra-5770-matos.
—— (2015), *Between the Lines of the Bible: Genesis*, Jerusalem: Urim.
Ewald, H. (1891), *Syntax of the Hebrew Language of the Old Testament*, tr. J. Kennedy, Edinburgh: T. & T. Clark.
Fabry, H.-J. (1998), '*Něḥōšet*', *TDOT* 9:370–380.
Fairholm, D. D. (2002), 'Moses the Transgressor: Identifying the Sin of Moses in Numbers 20:1–13', Master of Christian Studies, Vancouver, B.C.: Regent College.
Farber, Z. (2016), 'The Cherubim: Their Role on the Ark in the Holy of Holies', *TheTorah.Com* (blog), http://thetorah.com/the-cherubim.
—— (2021), 'The Song of the Well, Psalm 136, Was Removed from the Torah', *TheTorah.Com* (blog), https://www.thetorah.com/article/the-song-of-the-well-psalm-136-was-removed-from-the-torah.
Farmer, W. R. (1952), 'The Patriarch Phinehas', *AThR* 34:26–30.
Faulkner, R. O. (tr.) (1969), *The Ancient Egyptian Pyramid Texts*, Oxford: Clarendon.
Fauna and Flora of the Bible (1980), 2nd ed., Helps for Translators, London: United Bible Societies.
Feder, Y. (2010), 'On kuppuru, kippēr and Etymological Sins that Cannot be Wiped Away', *VT* 60.4:535–545.
—— (2014), 'The Semantics of Purity in the Ancient Near East: Lexical Meaning as a Projection of Embodied Experience', *Journal of Ancient Near Eastern Religions* 14:87–113.
Fee, G. D. (1987), *The First Epistle to the Corinthians*, NICNT, Grand Rapids: Eerdmans.
Feilchenfeldt, W. (1952), 'Die Entpersönlichung Moses in der Bibel und Ihre Bedeutung', *ZAW* 64 (1):156–178.
Feinberg, C. L. (1946), 'The Cities of Refuge', *BSac* 103:411–417.
—— (1947), 'The Cities of Refuge', *BSac* 104:35–48.
Feinstein, E. L. (2012), 'The "Bitter Waters" of Numbers 5:11–31', *VT* 62 (3):300–306.
Felder, C. H. (1989), *Troubling Biblical Waters: Race, Class, and Family*, Maryknoll, N.Y.: Orbis.
Feldman, E. (1977), *Biblical and Post-Biblical Defilement and Mourning: Law as Theology*, The Library of Jewish Law and Ethics, New York: Yeshiva University Press.

Feldman, L. H. (1993), 'Josephus' Portrait of Moses, Part Three', *JQR* 83:301–330.

―――― (2002), 'The Portrayal of Phinehas by Philo, Pseudo-Philo, and Josephus', *JQR* 92 (3–4):315–45.

Ferguson, S. B. (1996), *The Holy Spirit*, Downers Grove: InterVarsity Press.

Findlay, J. (2006), 'The Priestly Ideology of the Septuagint Translator of Numbers 16–17', *Journal for The Study of The Old Testament* 30 (4):421–429.

Finkelstein, I. (1988), *Archaeology of the Israelite Settlement*, Jerusalem: Israel Exploration Society.

Finkelstein, I., and R. Gophna (1993), 'Settlement, Demographic, and Economic Patterns in the Highlands of Palestine in the Chalcolithic and Early Bronze Periods and the Beginnings of Urbanism', *BASOR* 289:1–22.

Fisch, H. (1986), '"Eldad and Medad are Prophesying in the Camp" – Structuralist Analysis of Numbers XI', in U. Simon (ed.), *Studies in Bible and Exegesis*, Ramat Gan: Bar Ilan University Press, 2:45–55.

Fischer, E. (2016), 'The Manassite Conquests', On the Contrary, https://adderabbi.blogspot.com/2006/07/manassite-conquests.html.

Fischer, I. (2000), 'The Authority of Miriam: A Feminist Rereading of Numbers 12 Prompted by Jewish Interpretation', in A. Brenner (ed.), *A Feminist Companion to Exodus to Deuteronomy*, Sheffield: Sheffield Academic Press, 159–173.

Fishbane, M. A. (1974), 'Accusations of Adultery: A Study of Law and Scribal Practice in Numbers 5:11–31', *HUCA* 45:25–45.

―――― (1983), 'Form and Formulation of the Biblical Priestly Blessing', *JAOS* 103:115–121.

―――― (1986), *Biblical Interpretation in Ancient Israel*, 2nd ed., Oxford: Oxford University Press.

Fisher, L. R. (1970), 'A New Ritual Calendar from Ugarit', *HTR* 63:485–501.

Fisk, B. N. (2008), 'Pseudo-Philo, Paul and Israel's Rolling Stone: Early Points Along an Exegetical Trajectory', in K. Pomykala (ed.), *Israel in the Wilderness*, Themes in Biblical Narrative 10, Leiden: Brill, 117–136.

Fleurant, J. (2011), 'Phinehas Murdered Moses' Wife: An Analysis of Numbers 25', *Journal for The Study of The Old Testament* 35 (3):285–294.

Fokkelman, J. P. (1999), *Reading Biblical Narrative: An Introductory Guide*, Louisville, Ky.: Westminster John Knox.

Forshey, R. O. (1972), 'The Hebrew Root NḤL and its Semitic Cognates', PhD diss., Cambridge, Mass: Harvard University.

Fouts, D. M. (1992), 'The Use of Large Numbers in the Old Testament', ThD diss., Dallas: Dallas Theological Seminary.

―――― (1997), 'A Defense of the Hyperbolic Interpretation of Large Numbers in the Old Testament', *JETS* 40:377–387.

―――― (2005), 'Numbers, Large Numbers', in B. T. Arnold and H. G. M.

Williamson (eds.), *Dictionary of the Old Testament: Historical Books*, Downers Grove: InterVarsity Press, 750–754.
—— (2007), 'The Demographics of Ancient Israel', *Biblical Research Bulletin* 7 (2):1–10.
Fowler, S. W. (1978), 'The Visual Anthropomorphic Revelation of God', ThD diss., Dallas: Dallas Theological Seminary.
Frankel, D. (1998), 'Two Priestly Conceptions of Guidance in the Wilderness', *JSOT* 81:31–37.
—— (2014), *The Murmuring Stories of the Priestly School: A Retrieval of Ancient Sacerdotal Lore*, Leiden: Brill.
Franken, H. J. (1967), 'Texts from the Persian Period from Tell Deir 'Alla', *VT* 17:480–481.
Freedman, D. N. (1960), 'Archaic Forms in Early Hebrew Poetry', *ZAW* 72 (2):101–107.
—— (1972), 'The Broken Construct Chain', *Bib* 53:534–536.
—— (1975), 'The Aaronic Benediction (Numbers 6:24–26)', in J. L. McKenzie, J. W. Flanagan and A. W. Robinson (eds.), *No Famine in the Land: Studies in Honor of John L. McKenzie*, Missoula, Mont.: Scholars, 35–48.
Freedman, H. (tr.) (1939), *The Midrash Rabbah: Genesis*, vol. 1, London: Soncino.
Frendo, A. J. (2004), 'Back to Basics: A Holistic Approach to the Problem of the Emergence of Ancient Israel', in J. Day (ed.), *In Search of Pre-Exilic Israel: Proceedings of the Oxford Old Testament Seminar*, JSOTSup 406, London: T. & T. Clark, 41–64.
Fretheim, T. E. (1978), 'Life in the Wilderness', *Dialog* 17 (4):266–272.
—— (1996), *The Pentateuch*, Nashville: Abingdon.
Frevel, C. (2009), 'Understanding the Pentateuch by Structuring the Desert: Numbers 21 as a Compositional Joint', in J. van Ruiten and J. Cornelius de Vos (eds.), *The Land of Israel in Bible, History, and Theology. Studies in Honour of Ed Noort*, VtSup 124, Leiden: Brill, 111–135.
—— (2012), 'Struggling with the Vitality of Corpses: Understanding the Rationale of the Ritual in Numbers 19', in J.-M. Durand, T. Römer and J. Hutzli (eds.), *Les Vivants et Leurs Morts*, OBO 257, Göttingen: Vandenhoeck & Ruprecht, 199–226.
—— (2013a), 'The Book of Numbers – Formation, Composition, and Interpretation of a Late Part of the Torah. Some Introductory Remarks', in C. Frevel, T. Pola and A. Schart (eds.), *Torah and the Book of Numbers*, Tübingen: Mohr Siebeck, 1–38.
—— (2013b), 'Ending with the High Priest: The Hierarchy of Priests and Levites in the Book of Numbers', in C. Frevel, T. Pola and A. Schart (eds.), *Torah and the Book of Numbers*, Tübingen: Mohr Siebeck, 138–163.
—— (2013c), 'Purity Conceptions in the Book of Numbers in Context',

in C. Frevel and C. Nihan (eds.), *Purity and the Forming of Religious Traditions in the Ancient Mediterranean World and Ancient Judaism*, Leiden: Brill, 369–411.

——— (2016), 'Practicing Rituals in a Textual World: Ritual and Innovation in the Book of Numbers', in N. MacDonald (ed.), *Ritual Innovation in the Hebrew Bible and Early Judaism*, BZAW 468, Berlin: de Gruyter, 129–150.

——— (2018), 'Leadership and Conflict: Modelling the Charisma of Numbers', in K. Pyschny and S. Schulz (eds.), *Debating Authority: Concepts of Leadership in the Pentateuch and Former Prophets*, BZAW, Berlin, New York: de Gruyter, 89–114.

Frick, F. S. (1989), 'Ecology, Agriculture and Patterns of Settlement', in R. E. Clements (ed.), *World of Ancient Israel*, Cambridge: Cambridge University Press, 67–93.

——— (2002), 'Ritual and Social Regulation in Ancient Israel: The Importance of the Social Context for Ritual Studies and a Case Study – The Ritual of the Red Heifer', in D. M. Gunn and P. McNutt (eds.), *"Imagining" Biblical Worlds: Studies in Spatial, Social and Historical Constructs in Honour of James W. Flanagan*, JSOTSup 359, London: Sheffield Academic Press, 219–232.

Friedman, R. E. (1981), *The Exile and Biblical Narrative: The Formation of the Deuteronomistic and Priestly Works*, Chico, Calif.: Scholars.

——— (2003), *The Bible with Sources Revealed*, San Francisco: HarperCollins.

——— (2012), 'The Sotah: Why Is This Case Different from All Other Cases?', in I. W. Provan and M. Boda (eds.), *Let Us Go Up To Zion: Essays in Honor of H.G.M. Williamson on the Occasion of His Sixty-Fifth Birthday*, VTSup, Leiden: Brill, 371–382.

Frisch, A. (2005), 'The Story of Balaam's She-Ass (Numbers 22:21–35): A New Literary Insight', *HS* 56:103–113.

Fritz, G. A. (2016), *The Lost Sea of the Exodus: A Modern Geographical Analysis*, San Antonio: Geo Tech.

Fritz, V. (1970), *Israel in der Wüste*, Marburg: Elwert.

Frymer-Kensky, T. (1976), 'Judicial Ordeal', In IDBSup, 638–640.

——— (1983), 'Pollution, Purification, and Purgation in Biblical Israel', in C. L. Meyers (ed.), *And the Word of the Lord Shall Go Forth*, Winona Lake: Eisenbrauns, 399–414.

——— (1984), 'The Strange Case of the Suspected Sotah (Numbers 5:11–31)', *VT* 34:11–26.

Fuller, M. E. (2006), *The Restoration of Israel: Israel's Re-Gathering and the Fate of the Nations in Early Jewish Literature and Luke–Acts*, Berlin: de Gruyter.

Gaffin, R. B. (1987), *Resurrection and Redemption: A Study in Paul's Soteriology*, 2nd ed., Phillipsburg, N.J.: Presbyterian & Reformed.

Galbraith, D. (2014), 'Interpellation, Not Interpolation: Reconsidering Textual Disunity in Numbers 13–14 as Variant Articulations of a Single Ideology', *The Bible & Critical Theory* 10 (1):29–48.

Galil, G. (1985), 'The Sons of Judah and the Sons of Aaron in Biblical Historiography', *VT* 35 (4):488–495.
Gall, A. F. von (1900), 'Zusammensetzung und Herkunft der Bileam-Perikope in Num. 22–24', in W. Diehl, R. Drescher, K. Eger, A. F. von Gall, E. Preuschen and H. Weinel (eds.), *Festgruss Bernhard Stade zur Feier Seiner 25 Jährigen Wirksamkeit als Professor*, Giessen: Ricker, 1–47.
Gane, R. E. (1990), 'The Laws of the Seventh and Fiftieth Years', *JAGNES* 1:1–16.
——— (2005), *Cult and Character: Purification Offerings, Day of Atonement, and Theodicy*, Winona Lake: Eisenbrauns.
——— (2008), 'The Function of the Nazirite's Concluding Purification Offering', in B. J. Schwartz, D. P. Wright, J. Stackert and N. S. Meshel (eds.), *Perspectives on Purity and Purification in the Bible*, New York: T. & T. Clark, 9–17.
——— (2009), *In the Shadow of the Shekinah: God's Journey with Us*, Hagerstown, Md.: Review and Herald.
——— (2010), 'Loyalty and Scope of Expiation in Numbers 15', *Journal for Ancient Near Eastern and Biblical Law* 16:249–262.
——— (2016), 'Innovation in the Suspected Adulteress Ritual (Num 5:11-31)', in N. MacDonald (ed.), *Ritual Innovation in the Hebrew Bible and Early Judaism*, BZAW 468, Berlin: de Gruyter, 113–127.
Gane, R. E., and J. Milgrom (2004), '*Qārab*', *TDOT* 13:135–148.
Ganzel, T. (2020), *Ezekiel: From Destruction to Restoration*, Maggid Studies in Tanakh, Jerusalem: Koren.
Gaon, S. (1873), *Divrei Ha-Yamim*, Frankfurt: R. Kirchheim.
García López, F. (2008), 'La Place Du Lévitique et des Nombres Dans La Formation Du Pentateuque', in T. C. Römer (ed.), *The Books of Leviticus and Numbers*, BETL 215, Leuven: Peeters, 75–98.
Garsiel, M. (1991), *Biblical Names: A Literary Study of Midrashic Derivations and Puns*, Ramat Gan: Bar-Ilan University Press.
Garton, R. E. (2017), *Mirages in the Desert: The Tradition-Historical Developments of the Story of Massah-Meribah*, BZAW 492, Berlin: de Gruyter.
Gaster, M. (1925), *The Samaritans: Their History, Doctrines and Literature*, London: British Academy.
Gaster, T. H. (1981), *Myth, Legend, and Custom in the Old Testament*, Gloucester, Mass.: Smith.
Geikie, C. (1897), *Old Testament Characters*, New York: James Pott.
Geller, S. A. (1992), 'Blood Cult: Toward a Literary Theology of the Priestly Work of the Pentateuch', *Prooftexts* 12 (2):97–124.
Gellis, J., ed. (1993), *Sefer Tosafot Hashalem*, vol. 1, Jerusalem: Mifal Tosafot Hashalem.
Gemser, B. (1925), 'Der Stern aus Jakob (Num 24 17)', *ZAW* 43:301–302.
George, M. K. (2009), *Israel's Tabernacle as Social Space*, Atlanta: Society of Biblical Literature.
——— (2013), 'Socio-Spatial Logic and the Structure of the Book of

Numbers', in M. K. George (ed.), *Constructions of Space IV: Further Developments in Examining Ancient Israel's Social Space*, London: T. & T. Clark, 23–43.

Gerleman, G. (1977), 'Nutzrecht und Wohnrecht – zur bedeutung von 'ăḥuzzah und naḥălah', *ZAW* 89: 313–325.

Gertel, E. B. (2002), 'Moses, Elisha, and Transferred Spirit: The Height of Biblical Prophecy? Part 1', *JBQ* 30 (2):73–79.

Gertz, J. C., B. M. Levinson, D. Rom-Shiloni and K. Schmid (eds.) (2016), *The Formation of the Pentateuch Bridging the Academic Cultures of Europe, Israel, and North America*, Tübingen: Mohr Siebeck.

Gese, H. (1981), 'The Atonement', in K. Crim (tr.), *Essays on Biblical Theology*, Minneapolis: Augsburg, 93–116.

Gevaryahu, G. J. (2013), 'The Root G-R-A in the Bible: The Case of the Daughters of Zelophehad and Beyond', *JBQ* 41.2:107–112.

Gibson, R. (2008), 'Name Above All Names: Preaching Exodus', in B. S. Rosner and P. R. Williamson (eds.), *Exploring Exodus*, London: IVP Academic, 196–223.

Gilbert, R. A. (ed.) (1983), *The Sorcerer and His Apprentice*, Wellingborough: Aquarian.

Gilders, W. K. (2006), 'Why Does Eleazar Sprinkle the Red Cow Blood? Making Sense of a Biblical Ritual', *Journal of Hebrew Scriptures* 6:2–16.

Ginsberg, H. L. (1972), 'Zelophehad', *Encyclopaedia Judaica* 16:979–980.

Ginsburg, C. D. (1966), *Introduction to the Massoretico-Critical Edition of the Hebrew Bible*, New York: KTAV.

Ginzberg, L. (1967), *Legends of the Jews*, vol. 3, Philadelphia: Jewish Publication Society.

Godbey, A. H. (1939), 'The Unicorn in the Old Testament', *American Journal of Semitic Languages and Literatures* 56 (3):256–296.

Goldstein, A. (2012), 'Large Census Numbers in Numbers: An Evaluation of Current Proposals', *Presb* 38 (2):99–108.

Goldwasser, O. (2010), 'How the Alphabet Was Born from Hieroglyphs', *BAR* 36 (2):40–53.

Gophna, R., and J. Portugali (1988), 'Settlement and Demographic Processes in Israel's Coastal Plain from the Chalcolithic to the Middle Bronze Age', *BASOR* 269:11–28.

Gordley, M. E. (2005), 'Seeing Stars at Qumran: The Interpretation of Balaam and His Oracle in the Damascus Document and Other Qumran Texts', *Proceedings – Eastern Great Lakes and Midwest Biblical Societies* 25:107–119.

Gordon, C. H. (1959), 'Higher Criticism and Forbidden Fruit', *Christianity Today*, 131–136.

——— (1962), *Before the Bible: The Common Background of Greek and Hebrew Civilizations*, London: Collins.

——— (1967), *Ugaritic Textbook: Grammar, Texts in Translation, Cuneiform Selections, Glossary, Indices*, AnOr 38, Rome: Pontifical Biblical Institute.

Gordon, R. P. (1991), 'Compositeness, Conflation and the Pentateuch', *Journal for The Study of The Old Testament* 51:57–69.

Görg, M. (1976), 'Die "Heimat" Bileams', *BN* 1:24–28.

Gorman, F. H. (1990), *Ideology of Ritual: Space, Time, and Status in the Priestly Theology*, JSOTSup 91, Sheffield: JSOT.

——— (1993), 'Priestly Rituals of Founding: Time, Space, and Status', in M. P. Graham, W. P. Brown and J. K. Kuan (eds.), *History and Interpretation: Essays in Honour of John H. Hayes*, Sheffield: JSOT Press, 47–64.

Gottwald, N. K. (1999), *The Tribes of Yahweh: A Sociology of the Religion of Liberated Israel, 1250–1050 BCE*, Sheffield: Sheffield Academic Press.

Gradwohl, R. (1963), 'Das "Fremde Feuer" von Nadab und Abihu', *ZAW* 34 (3):288–296.

Graetz, N. (1991), 'Miriam: Guilty or Not Guilty?', *Judaism* 2:184–192.

Grafius, B. R. (2018), *Reading Phinehas, Watching Slashers: Horror Theory and Numbers 25*, Lanham, Md.: Lexington.

Granot, T. (2012), 'Remembering the Revelation in Moses' Speech', in E. Bick and Y. Beasley (eds.), *Torah MiEtzion: New Readings in Tanach: Devarim*, Jerusalem: Maggid, 63–71.

——— (2014a), 'A Commentary on Balaam's Prophecies', in E. Bick (ed.), *Torah MiEtzion: New Readings in Tanakh: Bemidbar*, Jerusalem: Yeshivat Har Etzion; Maggid, 317–329.

——— (2014b), 'The Differences Between Kalev and Joshua', in E. Bick (ed.), *Torah MiEtzion: New Readings in Tanakh: Bemidbar*, Jerusalem: Yeshivat Har Etzion; Maggid, 173–182.

——— (2014c), 'Through the Plains of Moab', in E. Bick (ed.), *Torah MiEtzion: New Readings in Tanakh: Bemidbar*, Jerusalem: Yeshivat Har Etzion; Maggid, 293–304.

Gray, G. B. (1900), 'The Nazirite', *Journal of Theological Studies* 1:201–211.

——— (1902), 'The Lists of the Twelve Tribes', *The Expositor* 6 (5):225–240.

——— (1972), *The Forms of Hebrew Poetry*, New York: KTAV.

Gray, J. (1963), *I & II Kings*, Philadelphia: Westminster.

Green, W. H. (1893), '"The Story of the Spies" Once More', *The Biblical World* 1 (5):328–344.

——— (1895), *The Higher Criticism of the Pentateuch*, New York: Scribner's Sons, repr. 1978.

Green, Y. (1985), 'The Rebellion of the Bechorim', *Dor le Dor* 14 (2):77–81.

Green, Y., and P. Kahn (2011), 'The Mystery, Meaning and Disappearance of the Tekhelet', *JBQ* 39 (2):108–114.

Greenberg, M. (1959), 'The Biblical Conception of Asylum', *JBL* 78.2:125–132.

——— (1968), 'Idealism and Practicality in Numbers 35:4–5 and Ezekiel 48', *JAOS* 88.1:59–66.

——— (1971), 'Ḥerem', in F. Skolnik (ed.), *Encyclopaedia Judaica*, 2nd ed., Detroit: Thomson Gale, 9:10–13.

——— (1983), *Ezekiel 1–20: A New Translation with Introduction and Commentary*, New York: Doubleday.

——— (1995), 'The Etymology of נִדָּה "(Menstrual) Impurity"', in Z. Zevit, S. Gitin and M. Sokoloff (eds.), *Solving Riddles and Untying Knots: Biblical, Epigraphic and Semitic Studies in Honor of Jonas C. Greenfield*, Winona Lake: Eisenbrauns, 69–77.
Greenberg, M. A. (1997), 'The Red Heifer Ritual: A Rational Explanation', *JBQ* 25:44–46.
Greenstein, E. L. (2001), 'Presenting Genesis 1, Constructively and Deconstructively', *Prooftexts* 21.1:1–22.
——— (2017), 'What Was the Book of the Wars of the Lord?', *Torah.Com* (blog), https://www.thetorah.com/article/what-was-the-book-of-the-wars-of-the-lord.
——— (2018), 'Signs of Poetry Past: Literariness in Pre-Biblical Hebrew Literature', in M. L. Satlow (ed.), *Strength to Strength: Essays in Appreciation of Shaye J.D. Cohen*, Providence: BJS, 5–25.
Gregor, Z. (2000), 'Edrei', in D. N. Freedman (ed.), *Eerdman's Dictionary of the Bible*, Grand Rapids: Eerdmans, 373.
Greifenhagen, F. V. (2002), *Egypt on the Pentateuch's Ideological Map: Constructing Biblical Israel's Identity*, JSOTSup 361, New York: Sheffield Academic Press.
Gressmann, H. (1913), *Mose und seine Zeit: ein Kommentar zu den Mose-Sagen*, Göttingen: Vandenhoeck & Ruprecht.
——— (1922), *Die Anfänge Israels: (von 2. Mose bis Richter und Ruth)*, Göttingen: Vandenhoeck & Ruprecht.
Grohman, E. D. (1962), 'Shittim', *IDB* 4:339.
Groningen, G. van (1990), *Messianic Revelation in the Old Testament*, Grand Rapids: Baker Book House.
Gros Louis, K. R. R. (1982), *Literary Interpretations of Biblical Narratives*, vol. 2, Nashville: Abingdon.
Gross, W. (1974), *Bileam: Literar- und Formkritische Untersuchung der Prosa in Num 22–24*, SANT 38, Munich: Kösel-Verlag.
Grossfeld, B. (1988), *The Targum Onqelos to Leviticus and Numbers*, ArBib 8, Wilmington: Michael Glazier.
Grossman, J. (1998), 'Two Complaints of the Nation, and the Re-Appointment of Aharon', Yeshivat Har Etzion – Virtual Beit Midrash, https://www.etzion.org.il/en.
——— (2002), 'How Good Are Your Tents, Yaakov: The Organization of God's Dwelling Place', Yeshivat Har Etzion – Virtual Beit Midrash, https://www.etzion.org.il/en.
——— (2007), 'Divine Command and Human Initiative: A Literary View of Numbers 25–31', *BibInt* 15:54–79.
——— (2012), 'Changes in Deuteronomy', in E. Bick and Y. Beasley (eds.), *Torah MiEtzion: New Readings in Tanach: Devarim*, Jerusalem: Maggid, 41–51.
——— (2014a), 'The Inadvertent Murderer and the Cities of Refuge', in E. Bick (ed.), *Torah MiEtzion: New Readings in Tanakh: Bemidbar*, Jerusalem: Yeshivat Har Etzion, Maggid, 481–487.

―――― (2014b), 'Military and Political Espionage', in E. Bick (ed.), *Torah MiEtzion: New Readings in Tanakh: Bemidbar*, Jerusalem: Yeshivat Har Etzion; Maggid, 167–171.

―――― (2014c), 'The Mishkan and the Nazir', in E. Bick (ed.), *Torah MiEtzion: New Readings in Tanakh: Bemidbar*, Jerusalem: Yeshivat Har Etzion; Maggid, 63–70.

―――― (2014d), 'Moses and Ḥovav', in E. Bick (ed.), *Torah MiEtzion: New Readings in Tanakh: Bemidbar*, Jerusalem: Yeshivat Har Etzion; Maggid, 109–117.

―――― (2014e), 'The Symbolic Significance of the Earth "Opening Her Mouth"', in E. Bick (ed.), *Torah MiEtzion: New Readings in Tanakh: Bemidbar*, Jerusalem: Yeshivat Har Etzion; Maggid, 223–231.

―――― (2017), 'The Message of the Non-Chronological Opening of Numbers', *TheTorah.Com* (blog), https://www.thetorah.com/article/the-message-of-the-non-chronological-opening-of-numbers.

―――― (2019), *Creation: The Story of Beginnings*, tr. S. Daniel, Jerusalem: Maggid.

Gruber, M. I. (2009), 'The Many Faces of Hebrew Nāśā' Pānîm "Lift up the Face"', *ZAW* 95 (2):252–260.

Grundke, C. L. K. (1995), 'A Literary Examination of the Masoretic Balaam Cycle (Numbers 22–24)', Master of Arts, Wolfville, Nova Scotia: Acadia University.

Grushcow, L. (2006), *Writing the Wayward Wife: Rabbinic Interpretations of Sotah*, Leiden: Brill.

Gudme, A. K. de Hemmer (2009), 'How Should We Read Hebrew Bible Ritual Texts? A Ritualistic Reading of the Law of the Nazirite (Num 6,1–21)', *SJOT* 23 (1):64–84.

Guillaume, A. (1962), 'A Note on Numbers XXIII 10', *VT* 12 (3):335–337.

Guillaume, P. (2004), 'Metamorphosis of a Ferocious Pharaoh', *Bib* 85:232–236.

―――― (2009), *Land and Calendar: The Priestly Document from Genesis 1 to Joshua 18*, New York: T. & T. Clark.

Gunneweg, A. H. J. (1965), *Leviten und Priester: Hauptlinien der Traditionsbildung und Geschichte des israelitisch-jüdischen Kultpersonals*, Göttingen: Vandenhoeck & Ruprecht.

―――― (1990), 'Das Gesetz und die Propheten. Eine Auslegung von Ex 33,7–11; Num 11,4–12,8; Dtn 31,14 f.; 34,10', *ZAW* 102 (2):169–180.

Guyot, G. H. (1940), 'The Prophecy of Balaam', *CBQ* 2 (4):330–340.

―――― (1941), 'Balaam', *CBQ* 3 (3):235–242.

Habel, N. C. (1964), *Yahweh Versus Baal: A Conflict of Religious Culture*, New York: Bookman Associates.

―――― (1985), *The Book of Job: A Commentary*, OTL, Philadelphia: Westminster.

―――― (1995), *The Land Is Mine: Six Biblical Land Ideologies*, OBT, Minneapolis: Fortress.

Haberman, B. D. (2000), 'The Suspected Adulteress: A Study of Textual Embodiment', *Prooftexts* 20 (1, 2):12–42.
Hackett, J. A. (1980), *The Balaam Text from Deir 'Allā*, HSM 31, Chico, Calif.: Scholars.
HaCohen, A. (1997), 'The Order and Contents of Sefer Bemidbar, Part 1', Yeshivat Har Etzion – Virtual Beit Midrash, https://www.etzion.org.il/en.
Halperin, D. J. (1982), 'Merkabah Midrash in the Septuagint', *JBL* 101 (3):351–363.
—— (1988), *The Faces of the Chariot: Early Jewish Responses to Ezekiel's Vision*, Tübingen: Mohr Siebeck.
Halpern, B. (1992), 'Kenites', *ABD* 4:17–22.
Hannah, D. D. (2015), 'The Star of the Magi and the Prophecy of Balaam in Earliest Christianity, with Special Attention to the Lost Books of Balaam', in P. Barthel and G. van Kooten (eds.), *The Star of Bethlehem and the Magi: Interdisciplinary Perspectives from Experts on the Ancient Near East, the Greco-Roman World, and Modern Astronomy*, Leiden; Boston: Brill, 433–462.
Hanson, J. (1985), 'Demetrius the Chronographer', in J. H. Charlesworth (ed.), *The Old Testament Pseudepigrapha*, Garden City, N.Y.: Doubleday, 2:843–854.
Hanson, P. D. (1968), 'The Song of Heshbon and David's Nir', *HTR* 61:297–320.
Haran, M. (1985), *Temples and Temple Service in Ancient Israel: An Inquiry into Biblical Cult Phenomena and the Historical Setting of the Priestly School*, Winona Lake: Eisenbrauns.
—— (1990), 'Book-Size and Thematic Cycles in the Pentateuch', in E. Blum, C. Macholz and E. Stegemann (eds.), *Die Hebräische Bibel und Ihre Zweifache Nachgeschichte*, Neukirchen-Vluyn: Neukirchener Verlag, 165–176.
Harrelson, W. (1959), 'Guidance in the Wilderness', *Int* 13:24–36.
—— (1962), 'Testimony', *IDB* 4:579.
Harrington, H. K. (1993), *The Impurity Systems of Qumran and the Rabbis: Biblical Foundations*, SBLDS, Atlanta: Scholars.
Harris, R. L. (1961), 'Exegetical Notes: Meaning of Kipper', *JETS* 4.1:3
Harris, R. T. (1998), 'The Ritual of the Red Heifer', *JBQ* 26 (3):198–200.
Harrison, R. K. (1954), 'The Biblical Problem of Hyssop', *EvQ* 26:218–224.
—— (2004), *Introduction to the Old Testament: Including a Comprehensive Review of Old Testament Studies and a Special Supplement on the Apocrypha*, Peabody: Hendrickson.
Harvey, W. Z. (1986), 'The Pupil, the Harlot and the Fringe Benefits', *Prooftexts* 6 (3):259.
Hattin, M. (2012), *Passages: Text and Transformation in the Parasha*, Jerusalem: Urim.
—— (2014), 'Requiem for Balaam', in E. Bick (eds.), *Torah MiEtzion: New Readings in Tanakh: Bemidbar*, Jerusalem: Yeshivat Har Etzion; Maggid, 331–338.

Hauge, M. R. (2001), *The Descent from the Mountain: Narrative Patterns in Exodus 19–40*, Sheffield: Sheffield Academic Press.

Hausoul, R. R. (2018), 'The Land in the Books of Exodus, Leviticus, and Numbers', in H. J. Koorevaar and M.-J. Paul (eds.), *The Earth and the Land: Studies about the Value of the Land of Israel in the Old Testament and Afterwards*, Edition Israelogie 11, Bern, Switzerland: Peter Lang, 65–95.

Havrelock, R. (2014), 'The Scout Story: A Guided Reading', TheTorah.com: A Historical and Contextual Approach. http://thetorah.com/the-scout-story.

Hawk, L. D. (2017), 'A Prophet Unlike Moses: Balaam as Prophetic Intercessor', *Asbury Journal* 72 (2):80–90.

Hayes, J. H. (1968), 'The Usage of Oracles Against Foreign Nations in Ancient Israel', *JBL* 87:81–92.

––––––– (1999), 'Prophecy and Prophets, Hebrew Bible', in J. H. Hayes (eds.), *Dictionary of Biblical Interpretation*, Nashville: Abingdon, 2:310–17.

Hayman, H. (1898), 'Gilead and Bashan; Or, the Pre-Mosaic Manassite Conquest', *BSac* 55.217:29–52.

Haymen, A. P. (ed.) (1991), *The Old Testament in Syriac According to the Peshiṭta Version*, Leiden: Brill.

Hays, J. D. (1996), 'The Cushites: A Black Nation in the Bible', *BSac* 153 (612):396–409.

––––––– (2000), 'Moses: The Private Man Behind the Public Leader', *BRev* 16.4:16–26, 60–62.

––––––– (2003), *From Every People and Nation: A Biblical Theology of Race*, NSBT 14, Leicester: Apollos; Downers Grove: InterVarsity Press.

Hayward, R. (1978), 'Phinehas – The Same is Elijah: The Origins of a Rabbinic Tradition', *JJS* 29:22–34.

––––––– (1992), 'Red Heifer and Golden Calf: Dating Targum Pseudo-Jonathan', in P. V. M. Flesher (ed.), *Targum Studies*, Atlanta: Scholars, 1:9–32.

Healy, M. (2001), *Qadesh 1300 BC: Clash of the Warrior Kings*, Campaign 22, London: Osprey Military.

Hebrew Union College (2015), 'Comprehensive Aramaic Lexicon', https://www.cal1.cn.huc.edu.

Heckl, R. (2013), 'Balaam. Numbers 22–24 as a Parody of the Tradition about the Strange Divinator', paper given at SBL International meeting, St. Andrews, UK, 1–9.

Heifetz, R. (1994), *Leadership Without Easy Answers*, Cambridge, Mass.: Harvard University Press.

Heinzerling, R. (1999), 'Bileams Rätsel. Die Zählung der Wehrfähigen in Numeri 1 und 26', *ZAW* 111 (3):404–415.

––––––– (2000), 'On the Interpretation of the Census Lists by C. J. Humphreys and G. E. Mendenhall', *VT* 50 (2):250–252.

––––––– (2008), 'Akzent 8: Levi's Secret – Sidereal Moon Astronomy',

Homepage of Rüdiger Heinzerling (blog), 30 August 2008, www.ruediger-heinzerling.de.
Heiser, M. S. (2012), 'Divine Council', in J. D. Barry and L. Wentz (eds.), *The Lexham Bible Dictionary*, Bellingham, Wash.: Lexham.
Helfgot, N. (1993), '"And Moses Struck the Rock": Numbers 20 and the Leadership of Moses', *Tradition* 27 (3):51–58.
——— (2012a), 'The Conclusion of the Book of Numbers', in *Mikra & Meaning: Studies in Bible and Its Interpretation*, Jerusalem: Maggid, 167–173.
——— (2012b), '"Shall Your Brothers Go into Battle While You Remain Here?" An Analysis of Numbers 32', in *Mikra & Meaning: Studies in Bible and Its Interpretation*, Jerusalem: Maggid, 151–166.
——— (2012c), 'Unraveling the Message of Numbers 31', in *Mikra & Meaning: Studies in Bible and Its Interpretation*, Jerusalem: Yeshivat Har Etzion; Maggid, 141–150.
——— (2014), 'The War with Midian and Its Meaning', in E. Bick (ed.), *Torah MiEtzion: New Readings in Tanakh: Bemidbar*, Jerusalem: Maggid, 417–425.
Helfmeyer, F. J. (1986), 'Ḥānâ; Maḥaneh', *TDOT* 5:4–19.
Hendel, R. S. (2001), 'The Exodus in Biblical Memory', *JBL* 120:601–622.
Hendriksen, W. (1998), *More Than Conquerors: An Interpretation of the Book of Revelation*, Grand Rapids: Baker.
Hengel, M. (2002), *Septuagint As Christian Scripture*, tr. M. Biddle, Grand Rapids: Baker Academic.
Hengstenberg, E. W. (1848), *A Dissertation on the History and Prophecies of Balaam*, tr. J. E. Ryland, Edinburgh: T. & T. Clark.
Henrey, K. H. (1954), 'Land Tenure in the Old Testament', *PEQ* 86: 5–15.
Hepner, G. (2011), 'The Mockery of Kings and Prophets: The Balaam Narrative Contains an Implied Critique of Moses', *RB* 118 (2):180–185.
Herbert, A. S. (1954), 'The "Parable" (māšāl) in the Old Testament', *SJT* 7 (2):180–196.
Hertz, J. H. (1933), 'Numbers XXIII, 9b, 10', *ExpTim* 45 (11):524.
Hicks, F. C. N. (1953), *The Fullness of Sacrifice: An Essay in Reconciliation*, London: SPCK.
Hicks, L. (1962), 'Machir', *IDB* 3:218.
Hieke, T. (2009), 'Die Unreinheit der Leiche Nach der Tora', in T. Nicklas, F. V. Reiterer and J. Verheyden (eds.), *The Human Body in Death and Resurrection*, Berlin: de Gruyter, 43–65.
Hiers, R. H. (1993), 'Transfer of Property by Inheritance and Bequest in Biblical Law and Tradition', *Journal of Law and Religion* 10:121–155.
Hildebrandt, W. (1993), *An Old Testament Theology of the Spirit of God*, Grand Rapids: Baker Academic.
Hill, C. A. (2003), 'Making Sense of the Numbers of Genesis', *Perspectives on Science and Christian Faith* 55 (4):239–251.
Hillers, D. R. (1969), *Covenant: The History of a Biblical Idea*, Baltimore: Johns Hopkins University Press.

Hobbes, T. (1997), *Leviathan: Authoritative Text, Backgrounds, Interpretations*, ed. R. E. Flathman and D. Johnston, New York: W. W. Norton.

Hobson, G. T. (2010), 'Cut Off From (One's) People: Punitive Expulsion in the Torah', PhD diss., St. Louis, Mo.: Concordia Seminary.

Hoegger, M. (1984), 'L'interprétation des Grands Nombres Dans l'Ancien Testament', *Hokhma* 25:2–12.

Höflmayer, F., H. Misgav, L. Webster and K. Streit (2021), 'Early Alphabetic Writing in the Ancient Near East: The "Missing Link" from Tel Lachish', *Antiquity* 95 (381):705–719.

Hoftijzer, J. (1973), 'De Ontcijfering van de Deir 'Alla-Teksten', *Mededelingen van Het Oosters Genootschap in Nederland* 5:111–134.

Hölscher, G. (1927), 'Zu Num 20:1–13', *ZAW* 45:239–240.

Hooke, S. H. (1952), 'The Theory and Practice of Substitution', *VT* 2 (1):2–17.

––––––– (1961), *Alpha and Omega*, London: Nisbet.

Horbury, W. (1985), 'Extirpation and Excommunication', *VT* 35:13–38.

Horn, B. (1993), 'Spies, Sacrifices, and Fringes', *Essays in Literature* 20 (1):31–53.

Horst, F. (1961), 'Zwei Begriffe für Eigentum (Besitz): naḥăla und 'ăḥuzza,' in A. Fuschke (ed.), *Verbannung und Heimkehr*, Tübingen: J. C. B. Mohr: 135–156.

Hort, G. (1959), 'The Death of Qorah', *ABR* 7:2–26.

Hulse, E. V. (1975), 'The Nature of Biblical Leprosy', *PEQ* 107:87–105.

Hulst, A. R. (1960), *Old Testament Translation Problems*, Leiden: Brill.

Humann, J. (2011), 'The Ceremony of the Red Heifer: Its Purpose and Function in Narrative Context', PhD diss., Durham, UK: Durham University.

Humphreys, C. J. (1998), 'The Number of People in the Exodus from Egypt: Decoding Mathematically the Very Large Numbers in Numbers i and Xxvi', *VT* 48:196–213.

––––––– (2000), 'The Numbers in the Exodus from Egypt: A Further Appraisal', *VT* 50:323–328.

Hundley, M. B. (2011), 'Before YHWH at the Entrance of the Tent of Meeting: A Study of Spatial and Conceptual Geography in the Priestly Texts', *ZAW* 123:15–26.

Hunt, M. C. (2010), 'Dutiful Daughters and the Fathers Who Fail Them: The Application of Feminist Insights and the Retrieval of Resistance Strands of Women's Traditions Via a Narrative Analysis of Four Unmarried Daughter Texts in the Hebrew Bible', PhD diss., Adelaide, South Australia: Flinders University.

Hurowitz, V. A. (1992), 'The Expressions Ûqsāmîm Bĕyādām (Numbers 22:7) in Light of Divinatory Practices from Mari', *HS* 33:5–15.

––––––– (2004), 'Healing and Hissing Snakes: Listening to Numbers 24:4–9', *Scriptura* 87:278–287.

––––––– (2007), 'YHWH's Exalted House – Aspects of the Design and Symbolism of Solomon's Temple', in J. Day (ed.), *Temple and Worship in Biblical Israel*, London: Bloomsbury T. & T. Clark, 63–110.

Hutchens, K. D. (1993), 'Defining Boundaries – A Cultic Interpretation of Numbers 34:1–12 and Ezekiel 47.13–48.1, 28', in M. P. Graham, W. P. Brown and J. K. Kuan (eds.), *History and Interpretation: Essays in Honour of John H. Hayes*, Sheffield: JSOT Press, 215–230.

Hutton, R. R. (1992), 'Korah', *ABD* 4:100–101.

——— (1994), *Charisma and Authority in Israelite Society*, Minneapolis: Fortress.

Hymes, D. (1998), 'Numbers 12: Of Priests, Prophets, or "None of the Above"', *Annual of the Japanese Biblical Institute* 24:3–32.

——— (2006), 'Heroic Leadership in the Wilderness, Part 1', *Asian Journal of Pentecostal Studies* 9 (2):295–318.

——— (2007), 'Heroic Leadership in the Wilderness, Part 2', *Asian Journal of Pentecostal Studies* 10 (1):3–21.

——— (2010), 'Numbers 11:A Pentecostal Perspective', *Asian Journal of Pentecostal Studies* 13 (2):257–281.

Ibn Ezra, A. (1995), *The Secret of the Torah: A Translation of Abraham Ibn Ezra's Sefer Yesod Mora Ve-Sod Ha-Torah*, tr. and annotations H. N. Strickman, Northvale, N.J.: Aronson.

——— (2004), *Ibn Ezra's Commentary on the Pentateuch: Leviticus (Va'yikra)*, tr. H. N. Strickman, vol. 3, New York: Menorah.

Ilan, T. (1994), 'The Daughters of Zelophehad and Women's Inheritance: The Biblical Injunction and Its Outcome', in A. Brenner (ed.), *A Feminist Companion to Exodus to Deuteronomy*, Sheffield: Sheffield Academic Press, 176–186.

Imes, C. J. (2018), *Bearing Yhwh's Name at Sinai: A Reexamination of the Name Command of the Decalogue*, BBRS 19, University Park: Eisenbrauns.

——— (2019), 'Between Two Worlds: The Functional and Symbolic Significance of the High Priestly Regalia', in A. Finitsis (ed.), *Dress and Clothing in the Hebrew Bible: 'For All Her Household Are Clothed in Crimson'*, New York: T. & T. Clark, 29–62.

Ingalls, A. D. (1991), 'The Literary Unity of the Book of Numbers', PhD diss., Dallas: Dallas Theological Seminary.

Instone-Brewer, D. (2008), 'Balaam–Laban as the Key to the Old Testament Quotations in Matthew 2', in D. M. Gurtner and J. Nolland (eds.), *Built Upon the Rock: Studies in the Gospel of Matthew*, Grand Rapids: Eerdmans, 207–227.

Isaacs, E. (1918), 'The Metrical Basis of Hebrew Poetry', *American Journal of Semitic Languages and Literatures* 35:20–54.

Isbell, C. D. (2002), *The Function of Exodus Motifs in Biblical Narratives: Theological Didactic Drama*, Studies in the Bible and Early Christianity 52, Lewiston, N.Y.: Mellen Press.

Israel, A. (2013), *I Kings: Torn in Two*, Maggid Studies in Tanakh, New Milford, Conn.: Maggid; Yeshivat Har Etzion.

Jacob, B. (1992), *Exodus*, tr. W. Jacob, New York: KTAV.

Jacob, E. (1958), *Theology of the Old Testament*, New York: Harper & Row.
Jacobus, H. R. (2015a), 'Balaam's "Star Oracle" (Num 24:15–19) in the Dead Sea Scrolls and Bar Kokhba', in P. Barthel and G. van Kooten (eds.), *The Star of Bethlehem and the Magi: Interdisciplinary Perspectives from Experts on the Ancient Near East, Greco-Roman World, and Modern Astronomy*, TBL 19, Leiden: Brill, 339–429.
——— (2015b), *Zodiac Calendars in the Dead Sea Scrolls and Their Reception: Ancient Astronomy and Astrology in Early Judaism*, IJS Studies in Judaica 14, Leiden: Brill.
——— (2021), 'Zodiacs of Heaven and Earth', in A. Paluch (ed.), *Representing Jewish Thought: Proceedings of the 2015 Institute of Jewish Studies Conference Held in Honour of Ada Rapoport-Albert*, Leiden: Brill, 186–217.
Jart, U. (1970), 'The Precious Stones in the Revelation of St. John XXI. 18–21', *ST* 24:150–181.
Jastrow, M. (1926), *Dictionary of the Targumim, the Talmud Babli and Yerushalmi, and the Midrashic Literature*, Peabody: Hendrickson.
Jenson, P. P. (1992), *Graded Holiness: A Key to the Priestly Conception of the World*, Sheffield: JSOT.
Jeon, J. (2007), 'Two Laws in the Sotah Passage (Num. v 11–31)', *VT* 57:181–207.
——— (2015), 'The Zadokites in the Wilderness: The Rebellion of Korach (Num 16) and the Zadokite Redaction', *ZAW* 127 (3):381–411.
——— (2020), 'The Scout Narrative (Numbers 13) as a Territorial Claim in the Persian Period', *JBL Literature* 139 (2):255–274.
Jeremias, J. (1997), 'נָבִיא' (*nābi'*), *TLOT* 2:704.
Jobling, D. (1978), *The Sense of Biblical Narrative: Structural Analyses in the Hebrew Bible*, vol. 1, JSOTSup 7, Sheffield: JSOT Press.
——— (1986), *The Sense of Biblical Narrative: Structural Analyses in the Hebrew Bible*, vol. 2, JSOTSup 39, Sheffield: JSOT Press.
Johnsgard, P. A. (1988), *The Quails, Partridges, and Francolins of the World*, Oxford: Oxford University Press.
Johnson, P. J. (1996), 'The Murmuring Tradition: A Paradigm for Every Age', *Indian Journal of Theology* 38 (1):16–41.
Joines, K. R. (1968), 'The Bronze Serpent in the Israelite Cult', *JBL* 87 (3):245–256.
——— (1974), *Serpent Symbolism in the Old Testament: A Linguistic, Archaeological, and Literary Study*, Haddonfield, N.J.: Haddonfield House.
Joosten, J. (1996), *People and Land in the Holiness Code: An Exegetical Study of the Ideational Framework of the Law in Leviticus 17–26*, VTSup 67, Leiden: Brill.
Jørstad, M. (2016), 'The Ground That Opened Its Mouth: The Ground's Response to Human Violence in Genesis 4', *JBL* 135 (4):705–715.
Josephus, Flavius (1987), *The Works of Josephus: Complete and Unabridged*, tr. W. Whiston, Peabody: Hendrickson.

Kahn, A. D. (2013), *Echoes of Eden: Sefer B'midbar: Spies, Subversives and Other Scoundrels*, Jerusalem: Gefen.

Kahn, P. (2007a), 'Balaam Is Laban', *JBQ* 35 (4):222–230.

——— (2007b), 'Moses at the Waters of Meribah: A Case of Transference', *JBQ* 35 (2):85–93.

Kahn, Y. (2012), 'Moses' Interpretation of the Torah', in E. Bick and Y. Beasley (eds.), *Torah MiEtzion: New Readings in Tanach: Devarim*, Jerusalem: Maggid, 15–22.

——— (2014a), 'Three Books of Numbers', in E. Bick (ed.), *Torah MiEtzion: New Readings in Tanakh: Bemidbar*, Jerusalem: Yeshivat Har Etzion; Maggid, 119–127.

——— (2014b), 'The Second Census', in E. Bick (ed.), *Torah MiEtzion: New Readings in Tanakh: Bemidbar*, Jerusalem: Yeshivat Har Etzion; Maggid, 351–359.

——— (n.d.), 'Parashat Shelach: Lack of Confidence, Lack of Faith', The Israel Koschitzky Virtual Beit Midrash, https://www.etzion.org.il.

Kaiser Jr., W. C. (1995), *The Messiah in the Old Testament*, Grand Rapids: Zondervan.

——— (1996), 'Balaam Son of Beor in Light of Deir 'Allā and Scripture: Saint or Soothsayer?', in J. Coleson and V. Matthews (eds.), *Go To The Land I Will Show You: Studies in Honor of Dwight W. Young*, Winona Lake: Eisenbrauns, 95–106.

Kaiser Jr., W. C., P. H. Davids, F. F. Bruce and M. T. Baruch (1996), *Hard Sayings of the Bible*, Downers Grove: InterVarsity Press.

Kalisch, M. M. (1877), *Bible Studies Part 1: The Prophecies of Balaam (Numbers XXII to XXIV), or the Hebrew and the Heathen*, London: Longmans, Green.

Kallai, Z. (1997), 'The Patriarchal Boundaries, Canaan and the Land of Israel: Patterns and Applications in Biblical Historiography', *IEJ* 47:69–82.

Kamin, S. (1991), *Jews and Christians Interpret the Bible*, Jerusalem: Magnes.

Kapelrud, A. S. (1957), 'How Tradition Failed Moses', *JBL* 76 (3):242.

Kaplan, M. (1989), *The Lion in the Hebrew Bible: A Study of a Biblical Metaphor*, Ann Arbor: UMI Dissertation Service.

Kaufman, S. (1991), 'An Emphatic Plea for Please', *Journal for the Study of the Northwest Semitic Languages and Literatures* 7:195–198.

Kaufmann, Y. (1960), *The Religion of Israel: From Its Beginnings to the Babylonian Exile*, tr. M. Greenberg, Chicago: University of Chicago Press.

——— (1970), *The Babylonian Captivity and Deutero-Isaiah*, tr. C. W. Efroymson, New York: Union of American Hebrew Congregations.

Kautzsch, E. (ed.) (1910), *Gesenius' Hebrew Grammar*, tr. A. E. Cowley, Oxford: Clarendon.

Kawashima, R. S. (2003), 'The Jubilee Year and the Return of Cosmic Purity', *CBQ* 65:370–389.

Kee, H. C. (1977), *Community of the New Age: Studies in Mark's Gospel*, Philadelphia: Westminster.

―――― (1985), 'The Testaments of the Twelve Patriarchs', in J. H. Charlesworth (ed.), *The Old Testament Pseudepigrapha*, Garden City, N.Y.: Doubleday, 1:775–828.
Keel, O. (1974), *Wirkmächtige Siegeszeichen im alten Testament*, Freiburg, Schweiz: Universitätsverlag.
Keel, O., and M. Küchler (eds.) (1982), *Orte und Landschaften der Bibel: Ein Handbuch und Studeien-Reiseführer zum Heiligen Land*, vol. 2: Der Süden, Göttingen: Vandenhoeck & Ruprecht.
Keel, O., and E. Uehlinger (1998), *Gods, Goddesses, and Images of God in Ancient Israel*, Minneapolis: Fortress.
Kellermann, D. (1970), *Die Priesterschrift von Numeri 1,1 bis 10,10: Literarkritisch und traditionsgeschichtlich untersucht*, BZAW 10, Berlin: de Gruyter.
Kelly, P. H. (1970), 'Israel's Tabernacling God', *RevExp* 67:485–494.
Kennett, R. H. (1933), *Ancient Hebrew Social Life and Custom as Indicated in Law, Narrative, and Metaphor*, London: Oxford University Press.
Kidner, D. (1982), 'Sacrifice: Metaphors and Meaning', *TynB* 33:119–136.
Kim, Y. (2008), 'The Levitical Heptateuch and Phinehas the High Priest', PhD diss., Berkeley, Calif.: Graduate Theological Union.
King, P. J., and L. E. Stager (2001), *Life in Biblical Israel*, Louisville, Ky.: Westminster John Knox.
Kislev, I. (2010), 'Numbers 36,1–12: Innovation and Interpretation', *ZAW* 122:249–259.
―――― (2011), 'P, Source or Redaction: The Evidence of Numbers 25', in T. B. Dozeman, K. Schmid and B. Schwartz (eds.), *The Pentateuch. International Perspectives on Current Research*, Tübingen: Mohr Siebeck, 387–399.
―――― (2013), 'The Census of the Israelites on the Plains of Moab (Numbers 26): Sources and Redaction', *VT* 63.2:236–260.
―――― (2014), 'How Ancient Scribes Tried to Make Sense of the Composite Story of Baal Peor', *TheTorah.Com* (blog), https://www.thetorah.com/article/how-ancient-scribes-tried-to-make-sense-of-the-composite-story-of-baal-peor.
―――― (2017), 'Joshua (and Caleb) in the Priestly Spies Story and Joshua's Initial Appearance in the Priestly Source: A Contribution to an Assessment of the Pentateuchal Priestly Material', *JBL* 136 (1):39–55.
―――― (2019), 'What Happened to the Sons of Korah? The Ongoing Debate Regarding the Status of the Korahites', *JBL* 138.3:497–511.
―――― (2020), 'The Cities of Refuge Law in Numbers 35:9–34: A Study of Its Sources, Textual Unity and Relationship to Deuteronomy 19:1–13', *JANEBL* 26:249–264.
Kitchen, K. A. (1992), 'Exodus, The', *ABD* 2:700–708.
―――― (2006), *On the Reliability of the Old Testament*, Grand Rapids: Eerdmans.
Kitz, A. M. (2003), 'Prophecy as Divination', *CBQ Quarterly* 65:22–42.

——— (2007a), 'Curses and Cursing in the Ancient Near East', *Religion Compass* 1 (6):615–627.

——— (2007b), 'Effective Simile and Effective Act: Psalm 109, Numbers 5, and KUB 26', *CBQ* 69:440–456.

Kiuchi, N. (1987), *The Purification Offering in the Priestly Literature: Its Meaning and Function*, vol. 56, JSOTSup, Sheffield: Sheffield Academic Press.

Klassen, W. (1986), 'Jesus and Phinehas: A Rejected Role Model', SBL Seminar Paper Series 25, Atlanta: Scholars, 490–500.

Klein, N. (2017), 'The Chronicler's Code: The Rise and Fall of Judah's Army in the Book of Chronicles', *Journal of Hebrew Scriptures* 17 (3):1–20.

Klein, S. (2014), 'But to the Sons of Kehat He Gave None', https://www.etzion.org.il/en/sons-kehat-he-gave-none.

——— (2015a), 'For the Cloud Rested Upon It', https://www.etzion.org.il/en/tanakh/torah/sefer-shemot/parashat-pekudei/cloud-rested-upon-it.

——— (2015b), 'Introduction to the Book of Bamidbar', https://www.etzion.org.il/en/tanakh/torah/sefer-bamidbar/parashat-bamidbar/introduction-book-bamidbar.

Kleinig, J. W. (2003), *Leviticus*, Concordia Commentary, Saint Louis, Mo.: Concordia.

Kleinig, V. (1985), 'Providence and Worship: The Aaronic Blessing: Numbers 6:22–27', *Lutheran Theological Journal* 19:120–124.

Kline, M. G. (1999), *Images of the Spirit*, Eugene: Wipf & Stock.

Knauf, E. A. (1998), 'Shadday', in K. van der Toorn, B. Becking and P. W. van der Horst (eds.), *Dictionary of Deities and Demons in the Bible*, 2nd ed., Leiden: Brill, 749–753.

——— (2004), 'Welches "Israel" Bileam Sah', in F. Ninow (ed.), *Wort und Stein*, Studien zur Theologie und Archäologie, Frankfurt: Peter Lang, 179–186.

Knierim, R. P. (1995b), 'The Composition of the Pentateuch', in *The Task of Old Testament Theology: Substance, Method, and Cases*, Grand Rapids: Eerdman, 355–379.

Knierim, R. P., and G. W. Coats (2005), *Numbers*, The Forms of the Old Testament Literature, vol. 4, Grand Rapids: Eerdmans.

Knohl, I. (1991), 'The Sin Offering Law in the "Holiness School" (Numbers 15:22–31)', in G. A. Anderson and S. M. Olyan (eds.), *Priesthood and Cult in Ancient Israel*, JSOTSup 125, Sheffield: Sheffield Academic Press, 192–203.

——— (2004), 'The Guilt Offering Law of the Holiness School (Num. V 5–8)', *VT* 54 (4):516–526.

——— (2007), *The Sanctuary of Silence: The Priestly Torah and the Holiness School*, Winona Lake: Eisenbrauns.

Koch-Westenholz, U. (1995), *Mesopotamian Astrology: An Introduction to Babylonian and Assyrian Celestial Divination*, CNI Publications 19, Copenhagen: Museum Tusculanum.

Koehler, L., W. Baumgartner, J. J. Stamm, B. Hartmann, Z. Ben-Hayyim, E. Y. Kutscher, P. Reymond and M. E. J. Richardson (1999), *The Hebrew and Aramaic Lexicon of the Old Testament*, vol. 4, Leiden: Brill.

Koenig, J. (1963), 'Sourciers, Thaumaturges, et Scribes', *Revue de l'histoire des Religions* 164:17–38, 165–180.

Kohata, F. (1977), 'Die Priesterschriftliche Überlieferungsgeschichte von Numeri XX 1–13', *Annual of the Japanese Biblical Institute* 3:3–34.

Kohler, K. (1919), 'SHEMA YISROEL: Origin and Purpose of Its Daily Recital', *Journal of Jewish Lore and Philosophy* 1 (3):255–264.

Kolatch, A. J. (1984), *Complete Dictionary of English and Hebrew First Names*, Middle Village, N.Y.: Jonathan David.

Konkel, A. H. (1997), 'Gwr I', *New International Dictionary of Old Testament Theology & Exegesis*, 1:836–839, Grand Rapids: Zondervan.

Kooten, G. H. van, and J. van Ruiten (eds.) (2008), *The Prestige of the Pagan Prophet Balaam in Judaism, Early Christianity and Islam*, Themes in Biblical Narrative 11, Leiden; Boston: Brill.

Korpel, M. C. A. (1989), 'The Poetic Structure of the Priestly Blessing', *Journal for The Study of The Old Testament* 45:3–13.

Kosmala, H. (1964), 'Form and Structure in Ancient Hebrew Poetry', *VT* 14 (4):423–445.

Kosman, A. (2002), 'The Story of a Giant Story: The Winding Way of Og King of Bashan in the Jewish Haggadic Tradition', *HUCA* 73:157–190.

Krahmalkov, C. R. (1994), 'Exodus Itinerary Confirmed by Egyptian Evidence', *BAR* 20 (5):55–62, 79.

Kraus, H.-J. (1965), *Worship in Ancient Israel: A Cultic History of the Old Testament*, tr. G. Buswell, Richmond: John Knox.

Kselman, J. S. (1976), 'A Note on Numbers XII 6–8', *VT* 26 (4):500–505.

Kuenen, A. (1878), 'Bijdragen tot de critiek van Pentateuch en Jozua. IV. De Opstand van Korach, Dathan En Abiram', *Theologische Tijdschrift* 12, 139–162.

Kugler, R. A. (1996), *From Patriarch to Priest: The Levi-Priestly Tradition from Aramaic Levi to Testament of Levi*, Atlanta: Scholars.

Kurtz, J. H. (1863), *Offerings, Sacrifices and Worship in the Old Testament*, tr. J. Martin, Peabody: Hendrickson.

Labuschagne, C. J. (1966), *The Incomparability of Yahweh in the Old Testament*, Leiden: Brill.

——— (1982), 'The Meaning of bĕyād rāmā in the Old Testament', in *Von Kanaan bis Kerala: Festschrift für Prof. Mag. Dr. J.P.M. van der Ploeg O.P. zur Vollendung des siebzigsten Lebensjahres am 4. Juli 1979*, AOAT 211, Kevelaer/Neukirchen-Vluyn: Neukirchener Verlag, 143–148.

Lambdin, T. O. (1971), *Introduction to Biblical Hebrew*, Saddle River, N.J.: Prentice-Hall.

Landy, F. (2015), 'For Whom God's Name Is Blotted Out', in F. Landy, L. M. Trevaskis and B. D. Bibb (eds.), *Text, Time, and Temple: Literary,*

Historical and Ritual Studies in Leviticus, Sheffield: Sheffield Phoenix, 170–195.

Lapsley, J. E. (2006), '"Am I Able to Say Just Anything?" Learning Faithful Exegesis from Balaam', *Int* 60:22–31.

Largement, R. (1964), 'Les Oracles de Bile'am et la Mantique Sumero-Accadienne', in *Ecole des Langues Orientales Anciennes de L'Institute Catholique de Paris: Memorial du Cinqyantenaire 1914–1964*, Paris: Bloud & Gray, Travaux de L'Institute Catholique de Paris, 37–50.

Launderville, D. (2004), 'Ezekiel's Throne-Chariot Vision: Spiritualizing the Model of Divine Royal Rule', *CBQ* 66 (3):361–377.

Lawlor, J. I. (2011), 'The "At-Sinai Narrative": Exodus 18–Numbers 10', *BBR* 21 (1):23–42.

Lawrence, P. (2011), *The Books of Moses Revisited*, Eugene: Wipf & Stock.

Lawrence, T. E. (1927), *Revolt in the Desert*, New York: G. H. Doran.

Layton, S. C. (1992), 'Whence Comes Balaam? Num 22,5 Revisited', *Bib* 73:32–61.

Leach, E. (1985), 'The Logic of Sacrifice', in B. Lang (ed.), *Anthropological Approaches to the Old Testament*, Philadelphia: Fortress, 136–150.

Leder, A. C. (2010), *Waiting for the Land: The Story Line of the Pentateuch*, Phillipsburg, N.J.: Presbyterian & Reformed.

——— (2016), 'From the Mountain of Yhwh to Israel's מנוחה: The Desert Itinerary of Numbers 10:11–36', *OTE* 29 (3):513–534.

Lederman, R. (2015), 'What Is the Biblical Flying Serpent?', *TheTorah.Com* (blog), https://thetorah.com/article/what-is-the-biblical-flying-serpent.

Lee, B. P. Y. (2003), 'Reading Law and Narrative: The Method and Function of Abstraction', PhD diss., Toronto: Wycliffe College and University of Toronto.

Lee, W. W. (2003a), 'The Exclusion of Moses from the Promised Land: A Conceptual Approach', in M. A. Sweeney and E. Ben Zvi (eds.), *The Changing Face of Form Criticism for the Twenty-First Century*, Grand Rapids: Eerdmans, 217–239.

——— (2003b), *Punishment and Forgiveness in Israel's Migratory Campaign*, Grand Rapids: Eerdmans.

——— (2004), 'Balak: The Forgotten Character in Numbers 22–24', in J. H. Ellens, D. L. Ellens, R. P. Knierim and I. Kalimi (eds.), *God's Word for Our World: Studies in Honor of Simon John De Vries*, New York: T. & T. Clark International, 247–261.

——— (2008), 'The Conceptual Coherence of Num 5,1–10,10', in T. Römer (ed.), *The Books of Leviticus and Numbers*, Leuven: Peeters, 473–489.

LeFebvre, M. (2019), *The Liturgy of Creation: Understanding Calendars in Old Testament Context*, Downers Grove: IVP Academic.

Lehrman, S. M. (trans.) (1983), *The Midrash Rabbah: Exodus*, vol. 3, London: Soncino.

Leibtag, M. (2012), 'Can Man Return to Gan Eden?', in E. Bick and Y. Beasley

(eds.), *Torah MiEtzion: New Readings in Tanach: Devarim*, Jerusalem: Maggid, 361–369.
—— (2017), 'The Chagim in Parshat Pinchas: The Internal Structure of the Holiday Torah Reading', Tanach Study, https://tanach.org/bamidbar/pin/pins2.htm.
—— (2023), 'An Almost Perfect Finale', *HaMizrachi Parsha Weekly*, 17–18.
Leiman, S. Z. (1974), 'The Inverted Nuns at Numbers 10:35–36 and the Book of Eldad and Medad', *JBL* 93:348–355.
Lemaire, A. (1972), 'Le "pays de Hepher" et les "filles de Zelophehad" á la lumiere des ostraca de Samarie', *Sem* 22:13–20.
Leonard Jr., A. (1989), 'Archaeological Sources for the History of Palestine: The Late Bronze Age', *BA* 52 (1):4–39.
Lerner, E. R. (2014), 'Manasseh: Reflections on Tribe, Territory and Text', PhD diss., Nashville: Graduate School of Vanderbilt University.
Lesko, L. H. (1991), 'Ancient Egyptian Cosmogonies and Cosmology', in B. E. Shafer (ed.), *Religion in Ancient Egypt: Gods, Myths, and Personal Practice*, Ithaca: Cornell University Press, 88–122.
Leson, M. S. (2007), 'The Balaam Texts: A Theme and Motif Approach', PhD diss., Washington, D.C.: The Catholic University of America.
Leveen, A. (2002), 'Falling in the Wilderness: Death Reports in the Book of Numbers', *Prooftexts* 22 (3):245–272.
—— (2008), *Memory and Tradition in the Book of Numbers*, New York: Cambridge University Press.
—— (2010), 'Inside Out: Jethro, the Midianites and a Biblical Construction of the Outsider', *Journal for The Study of The Old Testament* 34 (4):395–417.
—— (2013), '"Lo We Perish": A Reading of Numbers 17:27–20:29', in C. Frevel, T. Pola and A. Schart (eds.), *Torah and the Book of Numbers*, Tübingen: Mohr Siebeck, 248–272.
Levin, Y. (2006), 'Numbers 34:1–12, the Boundaries of the Land of Canaan, and the Empire of Necho', *JANES* 30:55–76.
Lévinas, E. (2007), *Beyond the Verse: Talmudic Readings and Lectures*, tr. G. D. Mole, London: Athlone.
Levine, B. A. (1965), 'The Descriptive Tabernacle Texts of the Pentateuch', *JAOS* 85.3:307–318.
—— (1974), *In the Presence of the Lord: A Study of Cult and Some Cultic Terms in Ancient Israel*, Leiden: Brill.
—— (1976a), 'More on the Inverted Nuns of Num. 10:35–36', *JBL* 95:122–124.
—— (1989), *[Va-Yikra] = Leviticus*, New York: Jewish Publication Society.
Levison, J. R. (2003), 'Prophecy in Ancient Israel: The Case of the Ecstatic Elders', *CBQ* 65:503–521.
Lévi-Strauss, C. (1973), *From Honey to Ashes: Introduction to a Science of Mythology*, vol. 2, New York: Harper & Row.
Levy, S. (2012), 'Angel, She-Ass, Prophet: The Play and Its Set-Design', in *Jews*

and Theater in an Intercultural Context, Jewish Studies 46, Leiden: Brill, 1–21.
Lewis, J. P. (1995), 'Balaam's Star: A Study of an Early Apologetic Motif', Presented at the 47th Annual Meeting of the Evangelical Theological Society, Philadelphia, Pa.
Licht, J. (1986), *Storytelling in the Bible*, Jerasalem: Magnes.
Lichtenstein, M. (2014a), 'The Crisis of Leadership – A Generation Gap', in E. Bick (ed.), *Torah Mietzion: New Readings in Tanakh: Bemidbar*, Jerusalem: Yeshivat Har Etzion; Maggid, 141–150.
—— (2014b), 'Moses' Leadership and the Transition of Generations', in E. Bick (ed.), *Torah Mietzion: New Readings in Tanakh: Bemidbar*, Jerusalem: Yeshivat Har Etzion; Maggid, 285–291.
Liddell, H. G., R. Scott and H. S. Jones (eds.) (1996), *A Greek–English Lexicon*, 9th ed., Oxford: Clarendon.
Liebreich, L. (1995), 'The Songs of Ascent and the Priestly Blessing', *JBL* 74:33–36.
Lim, J. T. K. (1997), *The Sin of Moses and the Staff of God: A Narrative Approach*, SSN 35, Assen: Van Gorcum.
—— (2001), 'A Puzzle in the Pentateuch?', *JBQ* 29 (2):127–130.
Lincicum, D. (2011), 'Philo on Phinehas and the Levites: Observing an Exegetical Connection', *BBR* 21.1:43–49.
Lindblom, J. (1962), 'Lot-Casting in the Old Testament', *VT* 12:164–178.
—— (1973), *Prophecy in Ancient Israel*, Minneapolis: Fortress.
Lipiński, E. (1998), 'Nāḥal; naḥălâ', in *TDOT* 9:319–335.
Lipscomb, A. I. (2012), 'Identifying Balak's Role and Significance in Numbers 22–24: A Study in Participant Reference', Master of Arts in Biblical Interpretation, Virginia Beach, Va.: Regent University.
Liss, H. (2000), '"It Is Not Permitted to Ponder the Deeper Meaning of the Verse": An Interpretation of the Merkava-Vision in Ezekiel According to the Commentaries of Rabbi Shelomoh Jitzchaqi (Rashi) and Rabbi Eli'ezer of Beaugency', *JSQ* 7:42–64.
Litke, J. (2002), 'The Daughters of Zelophehad', *CurTM* 29.3:207–218.
—— (2011), 'Moses at the Waters of Meribah', *JBQ* 39:31–34.
Liver, J. (1961), 'Korah, Dathan and Abiram', in C. Rabin (ed.), *Scripta Hierosolymitana*, Jerusalem: Magnes, 8:180–217.
Lobel, A. D. (2013), 'From Babylon to Jerusalem: The Root of Jewish Astrological Symbolism', in N. Campion and L. Greene (eds.), *Sky and Symbol*, Lampeter: Sophia Centre, 85–101.
Loewenstamm, S. E. (1965), 'The Death of the Upright and the World to Come', *JJS* 16:183–186.
—— (1972), 'The Relation of the Settlement of Gad and Reuben in Nu. 32:1–38. Its Background and Its Composition', *Tarbiz* 42:12–26.
Lohfink, N. (1969), 'Die Ürsunde in der Priesterlichen Geschichtserzählung', in G. Bornkamm and K. Rahner (eds.), *Die Zeit Jesu*, Freiburg, Schweiz: Herder, 38–57.

—— (1994), *Theology of the Pentateuch: Themes of the Priestly Narrative and Deuteronomy*, Minneapolis: Fortress.
Lohr, M. (1927), 'Bileam, Num 22, 2–24, 25', *Archiv für Orient-Forschung* 4:85–89.
Low, B. (2009), 'The Logic of the Atonement in Israel's Cult', *Scripture and Interpretation* 3.1:5–32.
Lucas, A. (1944), 'The Number of Israelites at the Exodus', *PEQ* 76:164–168.
Lund, N. W. (1930), 'The Presence of Chiasmus in the Old Testament', *American Journal of Semitic Languages and Literatures* 46 (2):104–126.
Lunn, N. P. (2010), 'Numbering Israel: A Rhetorico-Structural Analysis of Numbers 1–4', *Journal for The Study of The Old Testament* 35 (2):167–185.
Lust, J. (1978), 'Balaam, an Ammonite', *ETL* 54:60–61.
Luther, B. (1938), '"Kahal" und "Edah" als Hilfsmittel der Quellenscheidung im Priesterkodex und in der Chronik', *ZAW* 56:44–63.
Luther, B. P. (2011), 'Creating a Creation: Ancient Interpretation of Korah's Rebellion', PhD diss., Glenside: Westminster Theological Seminary.
Lutzky, H. (1997), 'The Name "Cozbi" (Numbers XXV 15, 18)', *VT* 47.7:546–548.
—— (1999), 'Ambivalence Toward Balaam', *VT* 49 (3):421–425.
Luzarraga, J. (1973), *Las Tradiciones de la Nube en la Biblia y en el Judaismo Primitivo*, AnBib 54, Rome: Biblical Institute.
Lyonnet, S., and L. Sabourin (1970), *Sin, Redemption, and Sacrifice: A Biblical and Patristic Study*, Rome: Pontifical Biblical Institute.
Maas, A. J. (1893), *Christ in Type and Prophecy*, vol. 1, New York: Benziger Brothers.
McBride Jr., S. D. (1987), 'Polity of the Covenant People: The Book of Deuteronomy', *Int* 41 (3):229–244.
—— (1990), 'Transcendent Authority: The Role of Moses in Old Testament Traditions', *Int* 44:229–239.
McCarter, P. K. (1980), 'The Balaam Texts from Deir 'Allā: The First Combination', *BASOR* 239:49–60.
McCarthy, D. J. (1969), 'The Symbolism of Blood and Sacrifice', *JBL* 88 (2):166–176.
Maccoby, H. (1997), 'The Corpse in the Tent', *Journal for the Study of Judaism* 28 (2):195–209.
McConville, J. G. (1983), 'Priests and Levites in Ezekiel: A Crux in the Interpretation of Israel's History', *TynB* 34:3–31.
McCrory Jr., J. H. (2000), 'Kenites', in D. N. Freedman (ed.), *Eerdman's Dictionary of the Bible*, Grand Rapids: Eerdmans, 763.
MacDonald, N. (2008a), '"Gone Astray" Dealing with the Sotah (Num. 5:11–31)', in S. D. Walters (ed.), *Go Figure!: Figuration in Biblical Interpretation*, Eugene: Wipf & Stock, 48–64.
—— (2008b), *Not Bread Alone: The Uses of Food in the Old Testament*, Oxford: Oxford University Press.

——— (2012b), 'The Hermeneutics and Genesis of the Red Cow Ritual', *HTR* 105 (3):351–371.
MacDonald, W. G. (1975), 'Christology and "The Angel of the Lord"', in G. Hawthorne (ed.), *Current Issues in Biblical and Patristic Interpretation: Studies in Honor of Merrill C. Tenney Presented by His Former Students*, Grand Rapids: Eerdmans, 324–335.
McEvenue, S. E. (1969), 'A Source Critical Problem in Num. 14,26–38', *Bib* 50:454–456.
——— (1971), *The Narrative Style of the Priestly Writer*, AnBib 50, Rome: Biblical Institute.
McKane, W. (1980), 'Poison, Trial by Ordeal and the Cup of Wrath', *VT* 30 (4):474–492.
McKenzie, J. L. (1959), 'The Elders in the Old Testament', *Bib* 40 (2):522–540.
McNamara, M. (1966), 'Some Early Rabbinic Citations and the Palestinian Targum to the Pentateuch', *Rivista Degli Studi Orientali* 41 (1):1–15.
McNamara, M., and E. G. Clarke (eds.) (1995), *Targum Neofiti 1; Targum Pseudo-Jonathan*, ArBib 4, Collegeville: Liturgical.
Madge, S., and P. McGowan (2002), *Pheasants, Partridges & Grouse: Including Buttonquails, Sandgrouse and Allies*, London: Helm.
Magness, J. (2005), 'Heaven on Earth: Helios and the Zodiac Cycle in Ancient Palestinian Synagogues', *DOP* 59:1–52.
Magonet, J. (1982), 'The Korah Rebellion', *Journal for The Study of The Old Testament* 24:3–25.
——— (2013), *A Rabbi Reads the Torah*, London: SCM.
Maier III, W. A. (2015), 'The Divine Presence Within the Cloud', *CTQ* 79:79–102.
Malamat, A. (1970), 'The Danite Migration and the Pan-Israelite Exodus-Conquest: A Biblical Narrative Pattern', *Bib* 51:1–16.
——— (1988), 'Pre-Monarchic Social Institutions in Israel in the Light of Mari', *Congress Volume Jerusalem 1986*, ed. J. A. Emerton, Leiden: Brill, 165–176.
Malbim (M. L. ben Jacob) (2013), *The Essential Malbim: Flashes of Insight on Vayikra, Bamidbar, Devarim*, Brooklyn: Mesorah.
Mann, T. W. (1977), *Divine Presence and Guidance in Israelite Traditions: The Typology of Exaltation*, Baltimore: Johns Hopkins University Press.
——— (1979), 'Theological Reflections on the Denial of Moses', *JBL* 98 (4):481–494.
——— (1987), 'Holiness and Death in the Redaction of Numbers 16:1–20:13', in J. H. Marks and R. M. Good (eds.), *Love & Death in the Ancient Near East: Essays in Honor of Marvin H. Pope*, Guilford: Four Quarters, 181–190.
——— (1988), *The Book of the Torah: The Narrative Integrity of the Pentateuch*, Atlanta: John Knox.
Marcus, D. (1977), 'Animal Similes in Assyrian Royal Inscriptions', *Or* 46 (1):86–106.

———— (1995), *From Balaam to Jonah: Anti-Prophetic Satire in the Hebrew Bible*, Atlanta: Scholars.
Marek, L. (2020), *A Star from Jacob, a Sceptre from Israel: Balaam's Oracle as Rewritten Scripture in the Dead Sea Scrolls*, Hebrew Bible Monographs 88, Sheffield: Sheffield Phoenix.
Margaliot, M. (1977), 'The Connection of the Balaam Narrative with the Pentateuch', in A. Shinan (ed.), *Proceedings of the Sixth World Congress of Jewish Studies*, Jerusalem: World Union of Jewish Studies, 1:279–290.
———— (1983), 'The Transgression of Moses and Aaron, Num 20:1–13', *JQR* 74 (2):196–228.
———— (1990), 'Literary, Historical and Religious Aspects of the Balaam Narrative, Numbers 22–24', in D. Assaf (ed.), *Proceedings of the Tenth World Congress of Jewish Studies*, Jerusalem: World Union of Jewish Studies, 75–82.
Marguerat, D., and Y. Bourquin (1999), *How to Read Bible Stories: An Introduction to Narrative Criticism*, tr. J. Bowden, London: SCM.
Markose, H. M. (2015), 'Metaphor in the Book of Numbers', PhD diss., Ramat Gan, Israel: Bar-Ilan University.
Marquis, L. M. (2013), 'The Composition of Numbers 32: A New Proposal', *VT* 63:408–432.
Martínez, F. G. (1996), *The Dead Sea Scrolls Translated: The Qumran Texts in English*, tr. W. G. E Watson, Leiden: Brill.
Mason, H. J. M. (1818), 'Essay on the Nature and Symbolical Character of the Cherubim of the Jewish Tabernacle', *Transactions of the Royal Irish Academy* 13:81–122.
Mason, S. D. (2008), *'Eternal Covenant' in the Pentateuch: The Contours of an Elusive Phrase*, LHBOTS 494, New York: T. & T. Clark.
Mathews, K. A. (1996), *Genesis 1–11:26*, vol. 1A, NAC, Nashville: Broadman & Holman.
Matthews, V. H. (1992), 'Asshurim', *ABD* 1:200.
Matthews, V. H., and D. C. Benjamin (1993), *Social World of Ancient Israel, 1250–587 BCE*, Peabody: Hendrickson.
Mattingly, K. (1997), 'The Laying on of Hands on Joshua: An Exegetical Study of Numbers 27:12–23 and Deuteronomy 34:9', PhD diss., Berrien Springs, Mich.: Andrews University Seminary.
———— (2001), 'The Significance of Joshua's Reception of the Laying on of Hands in Numbers 27:12–23', *AUSS* 39.2:191–208.
Mauchline, J. (1945), 'The Balaam–Balak Songs and Saga', in C. J. Mullo Weir (ed.), *Presentation Volume to William Barron Stevenson*, Studia Semitica et Orientalia 2, Glasgow: Glasgow University, 73–94.
Maunder, E. W. (1909), *The Astronomy of the Bible*, 3rd ed., London: Hodder & Stoughton.
May, H. G. (1955), 'Some Cosmic Connotations of Mayim Rabbîm, "Many Waters"', *JBL* 74:9–21.

―――― (2014), 'Some Cosmic Connotations of Mayim Rabbim, "Many Waters"', in L. M. Morales (ed.), *Cult and Cosmos: Tilting Toward a Temple-Centered Theology*, Biblical Tools and Studies 18, Leuven: Peeters, 259–271.

Mazar, B. (1986), 'Lebo-Hamath and the Northern Border of the Land of Canaan', in S. Aḥituv and B. A. Levine (eds.), *The Early Biblical Period: Historical Studies*, Jerusalem: Israel Exploration Society.

Mazor, L. (2002), 'The Correlation Between the Garden of Eden and the Temple', *Shnaton* 13:5–42.

Medan, Y. (2014), 'The Mission of the Spies', in E. Bick (ed.), *Torah MiEtzion: New Readings in Tanakh: Bemidbar*, Jerusalem: Yeshivat Har Etzion; Maggid, 153–166.

―――― (2016), 'Matot-Masei: The Tribes Who Remained in Israel', Torat Har Etzion, https://www.etzion.org.il/en/tanakh/torah/sefer-bamidbar/parashat-matot/matot-masei-tribes-who-remained-israel.

Meek, T. J. (1929), 'Some Emendations in the Old Testament', *JBL* 48 (3):162–168.

Meer, M. N. van der (2008), 'The Next Generation: Textual Moves in Numbers 14, 23 and Related Passages', in T. C. Römer (eds.), *Books of Leviticus and Numbers*, Leuven: Peeters, 399–416.

Meinhold, A. (1985), 'Zur Beziehung Gott, Volk, Land im Jobel-Zusammenhang', *BZ* 29.2:245–261.

Mendenhall, G. E. (1958), 'The Census Lists of Numbers 1 and 26', *JBL* 77 (1):52–66.

―――― (1973), *The Tenth Generation: The Origins of the Biblical Tradition*, Baltimore: Johns Hopkins University Press.

Merrill, E. H. (2019), 'Genesis 49:8–12 the Lion of Judah', in M. Rydelnik and E. Blum (eds.), *The Moody Handbook of Messianic Prophecy: Studies and Expositions of the Messiah in the Old Testament*, Chicago: Moody, 271–284.

Mettinger, T. N. D. (1982a), *The Dethronement of Sabaoth: Studies in the Shem and Kabod Theologies*. Lund: CWK Gleerup.

―――― (1982b), 'YHWH SABAOTH – The Heavenly King on the Cherubim Throne', in T. Ishida (eds.), *Studies in the Period of David and Solomon and Other Essays*, Winona Lake: Eisenbrauns, 109–138.

Meyers, C. L. (1976), *The Tabernacle Menorah: A Synthetic Study of a Symbol from the Biblical Cult*, Missoula, Mont.: Scholars.

―――― (1997), 'The Family in Early Israel', in L. G. Perdue, J. Blenkinsopp, J. J. Collins and C. L. Meyers (eds.), *Families in Ancient Israel*, Louisville, Ky.: Westminster John Knox, 1–47.

Michalowski, P. (2000), 'Amorites', in D. N. Freedman (ed.), *Eerdman's Dictionary of the Bible*, Grand Rapids: Eerdmans, 55–56.

Michel, D. (1994), 'Nœpœš als Leichnam?', *ZAH* 7:81–84.

Miles, J. A. (1981), 'Radical Editing: Redaktionsgeschichte and the Aesthetic of Willed Confusion', in B. Halpern and J. D. Levenson (eds.), *Traditions in Transformation: Turning Points in Biblical Faith, Festschrift F.M. Cross*, Winona Lake: Eisenbrauns, 9–31.

Milgrom, J. (1970a), 'The Levitical 'Abodā', *JQR* 61 (2):132–154.
―― (1970b), *Studies in Levitical Terminology*, vol. 1, Berkeley: University of California Press.
―― (1981a), 'The Case of the Suspected Adulteress', in R. E. Friedman (eds.), *The Creation of Sacred Literature*, Berkeley: University of California Press, 69–75.
―― (1981b), 'The Paradox of the Red Cow (Num. XIX)', *VT* 31:62–72.
―― (1983a), 'Magic, Monotheism, and the Sin of Moses', in H. B. Huffmon, F. A. Spina and A. R. W. Green (eds.), *The Quest for the Kingdom of God: Studies in Honor of George E. Mendenhall*, Winona Lake: Eisenbrauns, 251–265.
―― (1983b), *Studies in Cultic Theology and Terminology*, SJLA 36, Leiden: Brill.
―― (1987a), 'The Literary Structure of Numbers 8:5–22 and the Levitical Kippur', in E. W. Conrad and E. G. Newing (eds.), *Perspectives on Language and Text: Essays and Poems in Honor of Francis I. Andersen's Sixtieth Birthday*, Winona Lake: Eisenbrauns, 205–209.
―― (1987b), 'The Structures of Numbers: Chapters 11–12 and 13–14 and Their Redaction. Preliminary Groupings in Honor of Robert Gordis', in J. Neusner, B. A. Levine and E. S. Frerichs (eds.), *Judaic Perspectives on Ancient Israel*, Philadelphia: Fortress, 49–61.
―― (1991), *Leviticus 1–16: A New Translation with Introduction and Commentary*, New York: Doubleday.
―― (1997), 'Encroaching the Sacred: Purity and Polity in Numbers 1–10', *Int* 51 (3):241–253.
Milgrom, J., and D. P. Wright (1998), 'Niddâ', *TDOT* 9:232–234.
Miller, D. (2010), 'Another Look at the Magical Ritual for a Suspected Adulteress in Numbers 5:11–31', *Magic, Ritual, and Witchcraft* 5 (1):1–16.
Miller, J. M. (1989), 'The Israelite Journey Through (Around) Moab and Moabite Toponymy', *JBL* (4):577–595.
Miller, P. D. (1975), 'The Blessing of God: An Interpretation of Numbers 6:22–27', *Int* 29 (3):240–251.
―― (1994), *They Cried to the Lord: The Form and Theology of Biblical Prayer*, Minneapolis: Fortress.
―― (2004), 'Constitution or Instruction? The Purpose of Deuteronomy', in *Way of the Lord: Essays in Old Testament Theology*, 125–141, FAT 39, Tübingen: Mohr.
Miller, R. D. (2018), *The Dragon, the Mountain, and the Nations: An Old Testament Myth, Its Origins, and Its Afterlives*, University Park: Eisenbrauns.
Miller, Y. S. (2015) 'Sacred Slaughter: The Discourse of Priestly Violence as Refracted Through the Zeal of Phinehas in the Hebrew Bible and in Jewish Literature', PhD diss., Cambridge, Mass.: Harvard University.
Mills, W. E. (1997), 'Early Ecstatic Utterances and Glossolalia', *Perspectives in Religious Studies* 24 (1):29–40.

Mirguet, F. (2008), 'Numbers 16: The Significance of Place – an Analysis of Spatial Markers', *Journal for The Study of The Old Testament* 32 (3):311–330.

Mitchell, C. W. (1987), *The Meaning of BRK 'To Bless' in the Old Testament*, SBLDS 95, Atlanta: Scholars.

Mitchell, D. C. (2006), '"God Will Redeem My Soul from Sheol": The Psalms of the Sons of Korah', *Journal for The Study of The Old Testament* 30 (3):243–262.

——— (2015), *The Songs of Ascents: Psalms 120 to 134 in the Worship of Jerusalem's Temples*, Newton Mearns, Scotland: Campbell.

Mitchell, T. C. (1969), 'The Meaning of the Noun Ḥtn in the Old Testament', *VT* 19:93–112.

Moberly, R. W. L. (1999), 'On Learning to Be a True Prophet: The Story of Balaam and His Ass', in P. J. Harland and C. T. R. Hayward (eds.), *New Heaven and New Earth. Prophecy and the Millennium: Essays in Honour of Anthony Gelston*, VTSup 77, Leiden: Brill, 1–17.

——— (2006), *Prophecy and Discernment*, Cambridge: Cambridge University Press.

Mody, R. (2007), '"The Case of the Missing Thousand": Paul's Use of the Old Testament in 1 Corinthians 10:8 – A New Proposal', *Churchman* 121.1:61–79.

Monroe, L. A. S. (2012), 'Phinehas' Zeal and the Death of Cozbi: Unearthing a Human Scapegoat Tradition in Numbers 25:1–18', *VT* 62:211–231.

Moor, J. C. de (1997), *The Rise of Yahwism: Roots of Israelite Monotheism*. 2nd ed., Leuven: Peeters.

Moore, M. S. (1990), *The Balaam Traditions: Their Character and Development*, SBLDS 113, Atlanta: Scholars.

Morag, S. (1981), 'Layers of Antiquity – Some Linguistic Observations on the Oracles of Balaam', *Tarbiz* 50:1–24.

Morales, L. M. (2012), *The Tabernacle Pre-Figured: Cosmic Mountain Ideology in Genesis and Exodus*. Biblical Tools and Studies 15, Leuven: Peeters.

———, ed. (2014), *Cult and Cosmos: Tilting Toward a Temple-Centered Theology*. Biblical Tools and Studies 18, Leuven: Peeters.

——— (2015), *Who Shall Ascend the Mountain of the Lord?: A Theology of the Book of Leviticus*, Downers Grove: IVP Academic.

——— (2019a), 'Atonement in Ancient Israel: The Whole Burnt Offering as Central Israel's Cult', in J. C. Laansma, G. H. Guthrie and C. L. Westfall (eds.), *So Great a Salvation: A Dialogue on the Atonement in Hebrews*, London: T. & T. Clark, 27–39.

——— (2019b), 'The Levitical Priesthood', *SBJT* 23 (1):7–22.

——— (2020), *Exodus Old and New: A Biblical Theology of Redemption*, Downers Grove: InterVarsity Press.

Morenz, S. (1992), *Egyptian Religion*, Ithaca: Cornell University Press.

Morgan, D. F. (1974), 'The So-Called Cultic Calendars in the Pentateuch: A

Morphological and Typological Study', PhD diss., Claremont, Calif.: Claremont Graduate School.

Morgenstern, J. (1911), 'Biblical Theophanies', *Zeitschrift für Assyriologie und Vorderasiatische Archäologie* 25 (1–2):139–193.

—— (1927), 'The Oldest Document of the Hexateuch', *HUCA* 4:1–138.

—— (1932), 'The Book of the Covenant III – The Ḥuqqim', *HUCA* 8–9:1–150.

—— (1938), 'A Chapter in the History of the High-Priesthood', *AJSLL* 55:1–24.

—— (1942), 'The Ark, the Ephod and the Tent of Meeting', *HUCA* 17:153–266.

Morris, L. (1965), *The Apostolic Preaching of the Cross*, Grand Rapids: Eerdmans.

Mortensen, B. P. (2006), *The Priesthood in Targum Pseudo-Jonathan: Renewing the Profession*, Leiden: Brill Academic.

Mosser, C. (2004), 'No Lasting City: Rome, Jerusalem and the Place of Hebrews in the History of Earliest "Christianity"', PhD diss., St Andrews, Scotland: University of St Andrews.

—— (2009), 'Rahab Outside the Camp', in R. Bauckham, D. Driver, T. Hart and N. MacDonald (eds.), *The Epistle to the Hebrews and Christian Theology*, Grand Rapids: Eerdmans, 383–404.

Moster, D. (2013), 'Eshcol (Place)', in C. M. Furey, P. Gemeinhardt, J. LeMon, T. Römer, J. Schröter, B. D. Walfish and E. J. Ziolkowski (eds.), *The Encyclopedia of the Bible and Its Reception*, Berlin: de Gruyter, 7:1208–1209.

—— (2017), 'The Tribe of Manasseh and the Jordan River: Geography, Society, and Biblical Memory', PhD diss., Ramat Gan, Israel: Bar-Ilan University.

Motyer, J. A. (1974), *The Pentateuch and Criticism*, Cambridge: Cambridge University Theological Students Fellowship.

Mounce, R. H. (1998), *The Book of Revelation*, rev. ed., NICNT, Grand Rapids: Eerdmans.

Mowinckel, S. (1930), 'Der Ursprung der Bil'āmsage', *ZAW* 48:233–271.

—— (1953), *Religion und Kultus*, Göttingen: Vandenhoeck & Ruprecht.

—— (2004), *The Psalms in Israel's Worship*, tr. D. R. Ap-Thomas, Grand Rapids: Eerdmans.

Moyer, C. J. (2009), 'Literary and Linguistic Studies in Sefer Bil'am', PhD diss., Ithaca: Cornell University.

—— (2012), 'Who Is the Prophet, and Who the Ass? Role-Reversing Interludes and the Unity of the Balaam Narrative (Numbers 22–24)', *Journal for The Study of The Old Testament* 37 (2):167–183.

Müller, H. P. (1985), 'Das Motiv für die Sintflut. Die Hermeneutische Funktion des Mythos und Seine Analyse', *ZAW* 97 (3):295–316.

Munk, E. (1995), *The Call of the Torah: Devarim*, tr. E. S. Mazer, Brooklyn: Mesorah.

Myśliwiec, K. (2000), *The Twilight of Ancient Egypt: First Millennium B.C.E*, tr. D. Lorton. Ithaca: Cornell University Press.

Na'aman, N. (1981), '"Hebron Was Built Seven Years Before Zoan in Egypt" (Numbers XIII 22)', *VT* 31 (4):488–492.

Nachmanides, M. (1973), *Ramban Commentary on the Torah: Vol. 2 Exodus*, tr. C. B. Chavel, New York: Shilo.

Nagen, Y. (2019), *Be, Become, Bless: Jewish Spirituality Between East and West*, tr. E. Leshem, Jerusalem: Maggid.

Nahmani, H. (1964), *Human Rights in the Old Testament*, Tel Aviv: Joshua Chachik.

Nahshoni, Y. (1989), *Studies in the Weekly Parasha*, vol. 4, New York: ArtScroll Mesorah.

Najman, H. (2000), 'Angels at Sinai: Exegesis, Theology and Interpretive Authority', *DSD* 7 (3):313–33.

Navon, M. (2013), 'On Concealing Tekhelet and Revealing the Shekhinah', *JBQ* 41 (1):44–46.

Nelson, R. D. (1993), *Raising up a Faithful Priest: Community and Priesthood in Biblical Theology*, Louisville, Ky.: Westminster John Knox.

Nelson, W. D. (tr.) (2006), *Mekhilta de-Rabbi Shimon bar Yoḥai*, Philadelphia: Jewish Publication Society.

Neufeld, E. (1944), *Ancient Hebrew Marriage Laws, with Special References to General Semitic Laws and Customs*, London: Longmans, Green.

Neusner, J. (1985), 'Religious Authority in Judaism: Modern and Classical Modes', *Int* 39:373–387.

——— (ed.) (1988), *The Mishnah: A New Translation*, New Haven: Yale University Press.

Newing, E. G. (1987), 'The Rhetoric of Altercation in Numbers 14', in E. W. Conrad and E. G. Newing (eds.), *Perspectives on Languages and Text: Essays and Poems in Honor of Francis I. Andersen's Sixtieth Birthday July 28, 1985*, Winona Lake: Eisenbrauns, 211–228.

Newman, M. L. (1965), *The People of the Covenant*, London: Carey Kingsgate.

Newton, I. (1733), *Observations upon the Prophecies of Daniel, and the Apocalypse of St. John*, London: J. Darby and T. Browne.

Nicholson, E. (1998), *The Pentateuch in the Twentieth Century: The Legacy of Julius Wellhausen*, Oxford: Oxford University Press.

Nicolsky, N. M. (1932), 'Das Asylrecht in Israel', *ZAW* 48:146–175.

Niditch, S. (1993a), *War in the Hebrew Bible: A Study in the Ethics of Violence*, Oxford: Oxford University Press.

——— (1993b), 'War, Women, and Defilement in Numbers 31', *Semeia* 61:39–57.

Nielsen, K. (1986), *Incense in Ancient Israel*, VTSup 38, Leiden: Brill.

Nihan, C. (2007), *From Priestly Torah to Pentateuch: A Study in the Composition of the Book of Leviticus*, Tübingen: Mohr Siebeck.

——— (2008), 'Israel's Festival Calendars in Leviticus 23, Numbers 28–29 and

the Formation of "Priestly" Literature', in T. Römer (ed.), *The Books of Leviticus and Numbers*, Leuven: Peters, 177–231.
Nixon, R. E. (1962), 'Inheritance', in J. D. Douglas (ed.), *New Bible Dictionary*, Grand Rapids: Eerdmans: 562–563.
Noam, V. (2009), 'Corpse-Blood Impurity: A Lost Biblical Reading?', *JBL* 128 (2):243–251.
Noonan, B. J. (2020), 'High-Handed Sin and the Promised Land: The Rhetorical Relationship Between Law and Narrative in Numbers 15', *JSOT* 45:79–92.
North, F. S. (1961), 'Four-Month Seasons of the Hebrew Bible', *VT* 11 (4):446–448.
Notarius, T. (2008), 'Poetic Discourse and the Problem of Verbal Tenses in the Oracles of Balaam', *HS* 49:55–86.
Noth, M. (1930), *Das System der Zwölf Stämme Israels*, Stuttgart: W. Kohlhammer.
――― (1940), 'Num. 21 als Glied der "Hexateuch"-Erzählung', *ZAW* 58 (3):161–189.
――― (1981), *A History of Pentateuchal Traditions*, tr. B. W. Anderson. Chico, Calif.: Scholars.
Novick, R. (2007), 'Abraham and Balaam: A Biblical Contrast', *JBQ* 35:28–33.
Novick, T. (2008), 'Law and Loss: Response to Catastrophe in Numbers 15', *HTR*:1–14.
Oehler, G. F. (1950), *Theology of the Old Testament*, Grand Rapids: Zondervan.
Ogden, G. S. (1996), 'The Design of Numbers', *BT* 47 (4):420–428.
Olson, D. T. (1985), *The Death of the Old and the Birth of the New: The Framework of the Book of Numbers and the Pentateuch*, BJS 71, Chico, Calif.: Scholars.
――― (1997), 'Negotiating Boundaries: The Old and New Generations and the Theology of Numbers', *Int* 51 (3):229–240.
Olyan, S. M. (1998), 'What Do Shaving Rites Accomplish and What Do They Signal in Biblical Ritual Contexts?', *JBL* 117 (4):611–622.
Organ, B. E. (2001), 'Pursuing Phinehas: A Synchronic Reading', *CBQ* 63:203–218.
Origen (2009), *Homilies on Numbers*, tr. T. P. Scheck, ed. C. A. Hall, Downers Grove: IVP Academic.
Orlinsky, H. M. (1969), *Understanding the Bible Through History and Archaeology*, New York: KTAV.
――― (1986), 'The Biblical Concept of the Land of Israel: Cornerstone of the Covenant Between God and Israel', in L. A. Hoffman (ed.), *The Land of Israel: Jewish Perspectives*, Notre Dame: University of Notre Dame Press, 27–64.
Ortiz-Roberts, C. A. (2020), 'The Agency of Daughters in the Hebrew Bible', PhD diss., Berkley, Calif.: Graduate Theological Union.

Ortlund Jr., R. C. (2002), *God's Unfaithful Wife: A Biblical Theology of Spiritual Adultery*, Downers Grove: InterVarsity Press.
Osburn, C. D. (1981), 'The Text of 1 Corinthians 10:9', in E. J. Epp and G. D. Fee (eds.), *New Testament Textual Criticism: Its Significance for Exegesis. Essays in Honor of Bruce M. Metzger*, Oxford: Oxford University Press, 201–212.
Ottosson, M. (1988), 'Eden and the Land of Promise', in J. A. Emerton (ed.), *Congress Volume Jerusalem 1986*, Leiden: Brill, 177–188.
Pakozdy, L. M. von (1958), 'Theological Redactionsarbeit in der Bileam-Perikope (Num 22–24)', in O. Eissfeldt (eds.), *Von Ugarit nach Qumran*, Berlin: A. Töpelmann, 161–176.
Palmer, M. J. (2012), 'Expressions of Sacred Space: Temple Architecture in the Ancient Near East', PhD diss., Pretoria: University of South Africa.
Pardes, I. (2000), *The Biography of Ancient Israel: National Narratives in the Bible*, Berkeley: University of California Press.
Parker, J. D. (2012), 'A Good Meal Gone Bad: Numbers 11 as Meat-Meal Theophany', presented at Annual Meeting of the Society of Biblical Literature, Chicago, 1–12.
—— (2015), 'Moses and the Seventy Elders: Mosaic Authority in Numbers 11 and the Legend of the Septuagint', PhD diss., Durham, UK: University of Durham.
Parr, P. J. (1996), 'Midian (NW Arabia)', in E. Meyers (ed.), *Oxford Encyclopedia of Archaeology in the Near East*, Oxford: Oxford University Press, 4:25.
Paynter, H. (2022), 'Who Is the Wife in Numbers 5? A Reconsideration of the Sotah Text', in P. Hatton and H. Paynter (eds.), *Attending to the Margins: Essays in Honour of Stephen Finamore*, Oxford: Regent's Park, 137–162.
Pearce, L. E. (1995), 'The Scribes and Scholars of Ancient Mesopotamia', in J. M. Sasson (ed.), *Civilizations of the Ancient Near East*, New York: Simon & Schuster, 4:2265–2278.
Perdue, L. G. (1997), 'The Household, Old Testament Theology, and Contemporary Hermeneutics', in L. G. Perdue, J. Blenkinsopp, J. J. Collins and C. L. Meyers (eds.), *Families in Ancient Israel*, Louisville, Ky.: Westminster John Knox: 223–257.
Perrin, N. (2014), *The Exodus Revealed: Israel's Journey from Slavery to the Promised Land*, New York: Faith Words.
Peter, R. (1977), 'L'imposition des Mains Dans l'Ancient Testament', *VT* 27:48–55.
Peters, M. (2000), 'Numbers 35:9–34', *Int* 54.1:60–66.
Petersen, D. L. (1981), *Roles of Israel's Prophets*, JSOTSup 17, Sheffield: JSOT.
Petrie, W. M. F. (1906), *Researches in Sinai*, London: Hazell, Watson and Viney.
Phelps, M. A. (2000), 'Midian', in D. N. Freedman (ed.), *Eerdman's Dictionary of the Bible*, Grand Rapids: Eerdmans, 896–897.
Phillips, A. (1969), 'The Case of the Woodgatherer Reconsidered', *VT* 19:125–128.

Philo (1993), *The Works of Philo: Complete and Unabridged*, tr. C. D. Yonge, Peabody: Hendrickson.
Pick, B. (1885), 'Old Testament Passages Messianically Applied by the Synagogue', *Hebraica* 2 (1):24–32.
Pimpinella, D. (2005), 'Miriam in Numbers 12', *Concept* 29:1–15.
Plaut, W. G. (ed.) (1979), *The Torah: Numbers*, New York: Union of American Hebrew Congregations.
Porten, B. (1993), 'Elephantine Aramaic Contracts and the Priestly Literature', in M. Z. Brettler and M. A. Fishbane (eds.), *Minhah le-Nahum: Biblical and Other Studies Presented to Nahum M. Sarna in Honour of His 70th Birthday*, Sheffield: Sheffield Academic Press, 257–271.
Postell, S. D. (2019), 'Numbers 24:5–9, 15–19: The Distant Star', in M. Rydelnik and E. Blum (eds.), *The Moody Handbook of Messianic Prophecy: Studies and Expositions of the Messiah in the Old Testament*, Chicago: Moody, 285–308.
Powell, T. M. (1982), 'The Oracles of Balaam: A Metrical Analysis and Exegesis', PhD diss., Pasadena, Calif.: Fuller Theological Seminary.
Press, R. (1933), 'Das Ordal Im alten Israel', *ZAW* 51:121–140, 227–255.
Preuss, H. D. (1995), *Old Testament Theology*, vol. 1, Louisville, Ky.: Westminster John Knox.
——— (1999), 'עוֹלָם' '*Ôlām*', *TDOT* 10:530–545.
Price, I. M. (1906), 'Free-Will Offering', in I. Singer (ed.), *The Jewish Encyclopedia*, New York; London: Funk and Wagnalls, 5:506–507.
Price, N. (2020), *Tribal Blueprints: Twelve Brothers and the Destiny of Israel*, Jerusalem: Maggid.
Pritchard, J. B. (ed.) (1969), *Ancient Near Eastern Texts: Relating to the Old Testament*, 3rd ed. with supplement, Princeton: Princeton University Press.
Propp, W. H. (1987), *Water in the Wilderness: A Biblical Motif and Its Mythological Background*, Atlanta: Scholars.
——— (1988), 'The Rod of Aaron and the Sin of Moses', *JBL* 107 (1):19–26.
——— (1999) *Exodus 1–18: A New Translation with Introduction and Commentary*, AB, New York: Doubleday.
Pyschny, K. (2018), 'Debated Leadership: Conflicts of Authority and Leadership in Num 16–17', in K. Pyschny and S. Schulz (eds.), *Debating Authority: Concepts of Leadership in the Pentateuch and Former Prophets*, BZAW, Berlin: de Gruyter, 115–131.
——— (2019), 'From Core to Centre: Issues of Centralization in Numbers and Deuteronomy', *Hebrew Bible and Ancient Israel* 8 (3):287–312.
Quesada, J. J. (2002), 'Body Piercing: The Issue of Priestly Control Over Acceptable Family Structure in the Book of Numbers', *BibInt* 10:24–35.
Rabinowitz, I. (1993), *A Witness Forever: Ancient Israel's Perception of Literature and the Resultant Hebrew Bible*, Bethesda, Md.: CDL.
Rad, G. von (1959), 'The Origin of the Concept of the Day of Yahweh', *Journal of Semitic Studies* 4 (2):97–108.

―――― (1962), *Old Testament Theology*, vol. 1, New York: Harper & Row.
―――― (1966), 'There Remains Still a Rest for the People of God: An Investigation of a Biblical Concept', in *The Problem of the Hexteuch and Other Essays*, tr. E. W. T. Dicken London: SCM, 94–102.
―――― (2011), *Moses*, ed. K. C. Hanson, 2nd ed., Eugene: Cascade.
Rainey, A. F. (1970), 'The Order of Sacrifices in Old Testament Ritual Texts', *Bib* 51 (4):485–498.
Rapp, U. (2002), *Mirjam: Eine Feministisch-Rhetorische Lektüre der Mirjamtexte in der Hebraischen Bibel*, BZAW 317, Berlin: de Gruyter.
Rashi (1994), *The Torah: With Rashi's Commentary: Exodus*, ed. Y. Herczeg, vol. 2, Brooklyn, N.Y.: Mesorah.
Reader, W. W. (1981), 'The Twelve Jewels of Revelation 21:19–20: Tradition History and Modern Interpretations', *JBL* 100 (3):433–457.
Rees, A. (2015) *[Re]reading Again: A Mosaic Reading of Numbers 25*, LHBOTS 589; London: Bloomsbury.
Reif, S. C. (1970), 'A Note on a Neglected Connotation of NTN', *VT* 20:114–116.
―――― (1971), 'What Enraged Phinehas? – A Study of Numbers 25:8', *JBL* 90:2:200–206.
Reis, P. T. (2005), 'Numbers XI: Seeing Moses Plain', *VT* 55 (2):207–231.
Reiss, M. (2010), 'Miriam Rediscovered', *JBQ* (3):183–190.
Rendsburg, G. (1990), 'Targum Onqelos to Exod 10:5, 10:15, Numb 22:5, 22:11', *Henoch* 12:15–17.
―――― (2019), *How the Bible Is Written*, Peabody: Hendrickson.
―――― (2001a), 'An Additional Note to Two Recent Articles on the Number of People in the Exodus from Egypt and the Large Numbers in Numbers I and XXVI', *VT* 51 (3):392–396.
―――― (2001b), 'Reading David in Genesis', *BRev* 17:20–33, 46.
Rendtorff, R. (1998), *The Covenant Formula: An Exegetical and Theological Investigation*, Edinburgh: Continuum.
Reviv, H. (1982), 'The Traditions Concerning the Inception of the Legal System in Israel: Significance and Dating', *ZAW* 94 (4):566–575.
―――― (2014), *The Elders in Ancient Israel: A Study of a Biblical Institution*, Winona Lake: Eisenbrauns.
Reymond, R. L. (2003), *Jesus Divine Messiah: The New and Old Testament Witness*, Fearn, Scotland: Mentor.
Richter, G. (1921), 'Die Einheitlichkeit der Geschichte von der Rotte Korah', *ZAW* 39:123–137.
Ridderbos, J. (1985), *Isaiah*, tr. J. Vriend, Bible Student's Commentary, Grand Rapids: Zondervan.
Rieder, D. (1974), *Pseudo-Jonathan: Targum Jonathan Ben Uziel on the Pentateuch Copied from the London MS (British Museum Add. 27031)*, vol. 2, Jerusalem: Salomon's.
Rimon, S. (2008), 'The Nation and the Shekhina in the Wilderness', Yeshivat Har Etzion – Virtual Beit Midrash, https://etzion.org.il/en.

—— (2014a), 'The Daughters of Tzlofhad', in E. Bick (ed.), *Torah MiEtzion: New Readings in Tanakh: Bemidbar*, Jerusalem: Yeshivat Har Etzion; Maggid, 371–386.

—— (2014b), 'The Incense and Korah's Dispute', in E. Bick (ed.), *Torah MiEtzion: New Readings in Tanakh: Bemidbar*, Jerusalem: Yeshivat Har Etzion; Maggid, 241–249.

—— (2014c), 'And These Are the Journeys of Benei Yisrael', in E. Bick (ed.), *Torah MiEtzion: New Readings in Tanakh: Bemidbar*, Jerusalem: Yeshivat Har Etzion; Maggid, 457–469.

Ringgren, H. (1978), '*Gāra*", *TDOT* 3:66–67.

—— (1986), '*Ḥāqaq*', *TDOT* 5:139–147.

Roberts, B. J. (1951), *The Old Testament Text and Versions*, Cardiff: University of Wales Press.

Robertson, O. P. (2004), *The Christ of the Prophets*. Phillipsburg, N.J.: Presbyterian & Reformed.

Robertson, R. G. (1985), 'Ezekiel the Tragedian', in J. H. Charlesworth (ed.), *The Old Testament Pseudepigrapha*, Garden City, N.Y.: Doubleday, 2:803–820.

Robertson Smith, W. (1927), *Lectures on the Religion of the Semites: The Fundamental Institutions*, New York: Macmillan.

Robinson, B. P. (1985), 'Israel and Amalek: The Context of Exodus 17:8–16', *JSOT* 32:15–22.

—— (1989), 'The Jealousy of Miriam: A Note on Num 12', *ZAW* 101 (3):428–432.

Robinson, E. (1856), *Biblical Researches on Palestine, and in the Adjacent Regions: A Journal of Travels in the Year 1838*, Boston: Crocker and Brewster.

Robinson, G. (1988), *The Origin and Development of the Old Testament Sabbath: A Comprehensive Exegetical Approach*, Beiträge zur Geschichte der Biblischen Exegese 21, Frankfurt am Main: Peter Lang.

Robinson, R. B. (1986), 'Literary Functions of the Genealogies of Genesis', *CBQ* 48:595–608.

Robker, J. M. (2013), 'The Balaam Narrative in the Pentateuch/Hexateuch/Enneateuch', in C. Frevel, T. Pola and A. Schart (eds.), *Torah and the Book of Numbers*, Tübingen: Mohr Siebeck, 334–366.

—— (2019), *Balaam in Text and Tradition*, FAT 131, Tübingen: Mohr Siebeck.

Rock, Y. (2014), 'The Trumpets', in E. Bick (ed.), *Torah Mietzion: New Readings in Tanakh: New Readings in Tanakh: Bemidbar*, Jerusalem: Yeshivat Har Etzion; Maggid, 97–108.

Rofé, A. (1979), *The Book of Balaam: Numbers 22:2–24:25*, JBS 1, Jerusalem: Simor.

—— (1986), 'The History of the Cities of Refuge in Biblical Law', *Scripta Hierosolymitana: Studies in the Bible*, ed. S. Japhet, Jerusalem: Magnes, 31:205–259.

――― (1994), 'The Devotion to Torah-Study at the End of the Biblical Period: Joshua 1:8; Psalms 1:2; Isaiah 59:21', in S. Japhet (ed.), *The Bible in the Light of Its Interpreters: Sarah Kamin Memorial Volume*, Jerusalem: Magnes, 622–628.

――― (2019), 'The Account of Balaam's Donkey: A Late Polemical Burlesque', *TheTorah.Com* (blog), https://www.thetorah.com/article/the-account-of-balaams-donkey-a-late-polemical-burlesque.

Rogers, C. (1986), 'Moses: Meek or Miserable?', *JETS* 29 (3):257–263.

Rogers, J. H. (1998a), 'Origins of the Ancient Constellations: I. The Mesopotamian Traditions', *Journal of the British Astronomical Association* 108 (1):9–28.

――― (1998b), 'Origins of the Ancient Constellations: II. The Mesopotamian Traditions', *Journal of the British Astronomical Association* 108 (2):79–89.

Rolleston, F. (1862), *Mazzaroth: Or, The Constellations*, London: Gilbert and Rivington.

Römer, T. (1997), 'Nombres 11–12 et la Question d'une Rédaction Deutéronomique Dans le Pentateteuque', in M. Vervenne and J. Lust (eds.), *Deuteronomy and Deuteronomic Literature: Festschrift C.H.W. Brekelmans*, BETL 133, Leuven: Peeters, 481–498.

――― (2007), 'Israel's Sojourn in the Wilderness and the Construction of the Book of Numbers', in W. B. Aucker, R. Rezetko and T. H. Lim (eds.), *Reflection and Refraction: Studies in Biblical Historiography in Honour of A. Graeme Auld*, Leiden: Brill, 419–445.

――― (2013), 'Egypt Nostalgia in Exodus 14–Numbers 21', in C. Frevel, T. Pola and A. Schart (eds.), *Torah and the Book of Numbers*, Tübingen: Mohr Siebeck, 66–86.

Ron, Z. (1998), 'The Daughters of Zelophehad', *JBQ* 26.4:260–262.

――― (2003), 'The Genealogy of Moses and Aaron', *JBQ* 31 (3):190–194.

Rosenberg, R. A. (1972), 'The "Star of the Messiah" Reconsidered', *Bib* 53:105–109.

Rosenblum, J. D. (2010), *Food and Identity in Early Rabbinic Judaism*, Cambridge: Cambridge University Press.

Rosen-Zvi, I. (2012), *The Mishnaic Sotah Ritual: Temple, Gender and Midrash*, Leiden: Brill.

Roskop, A. R. (2011), *The Wilderness Itineraries: Genre, Geography, and the Growth of Torah*, Winona Lake: Eisenbrauns.

Ross, A. P. (1997), 'Šēm', *NIDOTTE* 4:147–150.

Ross, J. F. (1962), 'Balak', *IDB* 1:342.

Rothenberg, B. (1972), *Timna: Valley of the Biblical Copper Mines*, London: Thames and Hudson.

Rothkoff, A. (2007), 'Sacrifice, Second Temple Period', in F. Skolnik (ed.), *Encyclopaedia Judaica*, 2nd ed., Detroit: Keter, 17:644–649.

Rouillard, H. (1980), 'L'ânesse de Balaam: Anaylyse Littéraire de Nomb., XXII, 21–35', *RB* 87 (2):211–241.

―――― (1985), *La Péricope de Balaam (Nombres 22–24): La Prose et les Oracles*, Leuven: Peeters.
Routledge, B. (2004), *Moab in the Iron Age: Hegemony, Polity, Archaeology*, Philadelphia: University of Pennsylvania Press.
Rubenstein, J. L. (1996), 'Sukkot, Eschatology and Zechariah 14', *RB* 103.2:161–195.
Rudman, D. (2001), 'The Use of Water Imagery in Descriptions of Sheol', *ZAW* 113:240–244.
―――― (2003), 'Water for Impurity or Water of Impurity?', *OTE* 16:73–78.
Rudolph, D. J. (2003), 'Festivals in Genesis 1:14', *TynB* 54 (2):23–40.
Rudolph, J. W. (1938), *Der 'Elohist' von Exodus bis Josua*, BZAW 68, Berlin: A. Töpelmann.
Runnalls, D. (1983), 'Moses' Ethiopian Campaign', *Journal for the Study of Judaism in the Persian, Hellenistic, and Roman Period* 14:135–156.
Ruppert, L. (1978), '*Nāʾaṣ*', *TDOT* 9:118–125.
Russaw, K. D. (2013), 'Daddy's Little Girls?: An Examination of Daughters in the Hebrew Bible', PhD diss., Nashville: Vanderbilt University.
Rüttersworden, U. (2004), '*Śārap*', *TDOT* 14:218–228, Grand Rapids: Eerdmans.
Sabato, M. (2012), 'Birth of a Nation: The Framing Statements of Moses' Blessing', in E. Bick and Y. Beasley (eds.), *Torah MiEtzion: New Readings in Tanach: Devarim*, Jerusalem: Maggid, 431–441.
Sabo, P. (2014), 'Drawing out Moses: Water as a Personal Motif in the Biblical Character', in E. Ben Zvi and C. Levin (eds.), *Thinking of Water in the Early Second Temple Period*, Berlin: de Gruyter, 409–436.
Sabourin, L. (1974), 'The Biblical Cloud: Terminology and Traditions', *BTB* 4 (3):290–311.
Sadler Jr., R. S. (2009), *Can a Cushite Change His Skin?: An Examination of Race, Ethnicity, and Othering in the Hebrew Bible*, New York; London: Bloomsbury T. & T. Clark.
Safren, J. D. (1988), 'Balaam and Abraham', *VT* 38 (1):105–113.
Sailhamer, J. H. (1992), *The Pentateuch as Narrative: A Biblical-Theological Commentary*, Grand Rapids: Zondervan.
St. Clair, G. (1907), 'Israel in Camp: A Study', *Journal of Theological Studies* 8 (30):185–217.
Sakenfeld, K. D. (1975), 'The Problem of Divine Forgiveness in Numbers 14', *CBQ* 37 (3):317–330.
―――― (1985), 'Theological and Redactional Problems in Numbers 20.2–13', in J. T. Butler, E. W. Conrad and B. W. Anderson (eds.), *Understanding the Word: Essays in Honor of Bernhard W. Anderson*, JSOTSup 37, Sheffield: JSOT, 133–154.
―――― (1988), 'Zelophehad's Daughters', *Perspectives in Religious Studies* 15:37–47.
Salomon, J. (1972), 'When the Ark Set Forward', *Beit Mikra* 51:439–441.
Sals, U. (2008), 'The Hybrid Story of Balaam (Numbers 22–24): Theology for the Diaspora in the Torah', *BibInt* 16:315–335.

Samet, E. (1997), 'Parashat Chukat: A Watershed in Sefer Bamidbar', the Israel Koschitzky Virtual Beit Midrash, https://www.etzion.org.il/en/parashat-chukat-watershed-sefer-bamidbar.

――― (2003), 'Inheritance of the Land by Individual and Tribe', the Israel Koschitzky Virtual Beit Midrash, https://www.etzion.org.il/en/inheritance-land-individual-and-tribe-361-12.

――― (2014a), 'Balaam and the Sin of Baal Peor', in E. Bick (ed.), *Torah MiEtzion: New Readings in Tanakh: Bemidbar*, Jerusalem: Yeshivat Har Etzion; Maggid, 339–348.

――― (2014b), 'The Maapilim', in E. Bick (ed.), *Torah MiEtzion: New Readings in Tanakh: Bemidbar*, Jerusalem: Yeshivat Har Etzion; Maggid, 183–192.

――― (2014c), 'Moses vs. "the Lustful"', in E. Bick (ed.), *Torah MiEtzion: New Readings in Tanakh: Bemidbar*, Jerusalem: Yeshivat Har Etzion; Maggid, 129–140.

――― (2014d), 'Moses vs. the Rebels: A Challenge on Two Fronts', in E. Bick (ed.), *Torah MiEtzion: New Readings in Tanakh: Bemidbar*, Jerusalem: Yeshivat Har Etzion; Maggid, 213–221.

――― (2014e), 'The Waters of Contention', in E. Bick (ed.), *Torah MiEtzion: New Readings in Tanakh: Bemidbar*, Jerusalem: Yeshivat Har Etzion; Maggid, 253–262.

――― (2017a), 'Datan and Aviram', Yeshivat Har Etzion – Virtual Beit Midrash, https://etzion.org.il/en.

――― (2017b), 'Moshe's Speech to Gad and Reuven', the Israel Koschitzky Virtual Beit Midrash, https://www.etzion.org.il/en/tanakh/torah/sefer-bamidbar/parashat-matot/matot-moshes-speech-gad-and-reuven.

――― (2017c), 'Rounding of the Numbers of the Censuses of Bnei Yisrael', the Israel Koschitzky Virtual Beit Midrash, https://www.etzion.org.il/en/tanakh/torah/sefer-bamidbar/parashat-bamidbar/bamidbar-rounding-numbers-censuses-bnei-yisrael.

――― (2020), 'Who Needs This Census?', Studies in Parashat HaShavua, https://torah.etzion.org.il/en/who-needs-census.

Sanchez, S. H. (2000), 'A Literary-Theological Analysis of Numbers 20:1–13', ThM diss., Dallas: Dallas Theological Seminary.

Sandys-Wunsch, J. (1961), 'The Purpose of the Book of Numbers in Relation to the Rest of the Pentateuch and Post-Exilic Judaism', D.Phil., Oxford: University of Oxford.

Sargent, A. D. (2001), 'Why Hassel with a Tassel?: An Exegesis of Numbers 15:37–41', MA, South Hamilton, Mass.: Gordon-Conwell Theological Seminary.

Sasson, J. M. (1972), 'Numbers 5 and the Waters of Judgement', *BZ* 16 (2):249–251.

――― (1978), 'A Genealogical "Convention" in Biblical Chronology?', *ZAW* 90:171–185.

―――― (2011), 'The Lord of Hosts, Seated over the Cherubs', in S. L. McKenzie and T. Römer (eds.), *Rethinking the Foundations: Historiography in the Ancient World and in the Bible. Essays in Honor of John Van Seters*, Berlin: de Gruyter, 227–234.

Savran, G. (1994), 'Beastly Speech: Intertextuality, Balaam's Ass and the Garden of Eden', *Journal for The Study of The Old Testament* 64:33–55.

Sayce, A. H. (1887), 'Balaam's Prophecy (Numbers XXIV, 17–24) and the God Sheth', *Hebraica* 4:1–6.

―――― (1904), 'Recent Biblical and Oriental Archaeology: Who Was Balaam?', *ExpTim* 15:405–446.

Saydon, P. P. (1946), 'Sin-Offering and Trespass-Offering', *CBQ* 8 (4):393–398.

Schäfers, K. M. (2018), '"[. . .] And the LORD's Anger Was Kindled against Israel" (Num 25:3) – Who's in Charge and Who's to Blame?: Punishment, Intercession, and Leadership-Related Competences in Num 25', in K. Pyschny and S. Schulz (eds.), *Debating Authority: Concepts of Leadership in the Pentateuch and Former Prophets*, BZAW, Berlin: de Gruyter, 132–158.

Schart, A. (1990), *Mose und Israel im Konflikt: Eine redaktionsgeschichtliche Studie zu den Wustenerzahlungen*, OBO 98, Freiburg, Schweiz: Göttingen: Vandenhoeck & Ruprecht.

―――― (2013), 'The Spy Story and the Final Redaction of the Hexateuch', in C. Frevel, T. Pola and A. Schart (eds.), *Torah and the Book of Numbers*, Tübingen: Mohr Siebeck, 164–200.

Schechter, S., and C. Levias (1906), 'Gematria', in I. Singer (ed.), *The Jewish Encyclopedia*, New York: Funk and Wagnalls, 5:589–592.

Scheftelowitz, J. (1921), 'Das Opfer der roten Kuh (Num 19)', *ZAW* 39:113–123.

Schenker, A. (1983), 'Das Zeichen des Blutes und die Gewißheit der Vergebung im alten Testament: die sühnende Funktion des Blutes auf dem Altar nach Lev 17.10–12', *MTZ* 34 (3):195–213.

Schiffman, L. H. (1989), 'Architecture and Law: The Temple and Its Courtyards in the Temple Scroll', in J. Neusner, E. S. Frerichs and N. M. Sarna (eds.), *From Ancient Israel to Modern Judaism: Intellect in Quest of Understanding: Essays in Honor of Marvin Fox*, Atlanta: Scholars, 1:267–284.

―――― (2011), 'The Temple Scroll: A Utopian Plan from Second Temple Times', in S. Fine (ed.), *The Temple of Jerusalem: From Moses to the Messiah: In Honor of Professor Louis H. Feldman*, Leiden: Brill, 45–56.

Schmidt, L. (1979), 'Die Alttestamentliche Bileamüberlieferung', *BZ* 23:234–261.

―――― (2004), *Das Vierte Buch Mose, Numeri Kapitel 10,11–36,13*, DATD 7.2, Göttingen: Vandenhoeck & Ruprecht.

Schmidt, P. (2020), 'The Meaning of "Father's House" (Bêt 'āb) and a Chiastic Structure in Numbers 18:1–7', *BT* 71 (1):57–78.

Schmitt, H.-C. (2001), 'Der Heidnische Mantiker als Eschatologischer Jahweprophet. Zum Verständnis Bileams in der Endgestalt von Num 22–24', in *Theologie in Prophetie und Pentateuch: Gesammelte Schriften*, BZAW 310, Berlin: de Gruyter, 238–254.
Schmitt, R. (2004), *Magie im alten Testament*, Münster: Ugarit-Verlag.
Schnittjer, G. E. (2006), *The Torah Story: An Apprenticeship on the Pentateuch*, Grand Rapids: Zondervan.
Schwartz, B. (1995), 'The Bearing of Sin in the Priestly Literature', in D. P. Wright, D. N. Freedman and A. Hurvitz (eds.), *Pomegranates and Golden Bells: Studies in Biblical, Jewish, and Near Eastern Ritual, Law, and Literature in Honor of Jacob Milgrom*, Winona Lake: Eisenbrauns, 3–21.
Schwartz, E. (2020), 'E. Schwartz Reviews Balaam in Text and Tradition (J. Robker)', *Enoch Seminar* (blog), 1 February, http://enochseminar.org/review/16895.
Schwartz, S. (2020), 'From Rhetoric to Demagoguery: A New Reading of the Spies' Report (Num 13,26–33)', *ETL* 96 (4):583–602.
Scolnic, B. E. (1995), *Theme and Context in Biblical Lists*, SFSHJ 119, Atlanta: Scholars.
Scurlock, J. (2006), 'The Techniques of the Sacrifice of Animals in Ancient Israel and Ancient Mesopotamia: New Insights Through Comparison, Part 2', *AUSS* 44 (2):241–264.
Seebass, H. (1978), 'Num. XI, XII und die Hypothese des Yahwisten', *VT* 28:214–223.
——— (1997), 'Edom und Seine Umgehung Nach Numeri XX–XXI: Zu Numeri XXI 10–13', *VT* 47:255–262.
——— (2003), 'The Case of Phinehas at Baal Peor in Num 25', *BN* 117:40–46.
——— (2006), 'YHWH's Name in the Aaronic Blessing (Num 6:22–27)', in G. H. van Kooten (ed.), *The Revelation of the Name YHWH to Moses: Perspectives from Judaism, the Pagan Graeco-Roman World, and Early Christianity*, Leiden: Brill Academic, 37–54.
——— (2009), 'Moses' Preparation of the March to the Holy Land: A Dialogue with R. P. Knierim on Numbers 1:1–10:10', in J. van Ruiten and J. Cornelius de Vos (eds.), *The Land of Israel in Bible, History, and Theology: Studies in Honour of Ed Noort*, Leiden: Brill, 99–110.
——— (2010), 'Old and New, Memory Failure and Outlook for Renewal in the Book of Numbers', in W. Thiel, P. Mommer and A. Scherer (eds.), *Geschichte Israels und deuteronomistisches Geschichtsdenken: Festschrift zum 70. Geburtstag von Winfried Thiel*, AOAT 380, Münster: Ugarit, 265–279.
Seerveld, C. G. (2001), *Balaam's Apocalyptic Prophecies: A Study in Reading Scripture*. Eugene: Wipf & Stock.
Seevers, B. (2013), *Warfare in the Old Testament: The Organization, Weapons, and Tactics of Ancient Near Eastern Armies*, Grand Rapids: Kregel Academic.

Segal, M. H. (1918), 'The Settlement of Manasseh East of the Jordan', *PEQ* 50.3:124–131.

Seiss, J. A. (1882), *The Gospel in the Stars: Or, Primeval Astronomy*, Philadelphia: E. Claxton.

Seligsohn, M. (1906), 'Wars of the Lord, Book of The', in I. Singer (ed.), *The Jewish Encyclopedia*, New York: Funk and Wagnalls, 12:468.

Seligson, M. (1951), *The Meaning of Nephesh Met in the Old Testament*, StOr 16, Helsinki: Societas Orientalis Fennica.

Seraphim, The Very Revd (1900), *The Soothsayer Balaam or The Transformation of a Sorcerer into a Prophet Numbers XXII–XXV*, London: Rivingtons.

Sergi, O. (2020), 'Mesha Inscription', *Encyclopedia of the Bible and Its Reception: Mass – Midnight*, vol. 18, ed. C. M. Furey, J. M. LeMon, B. Matz and T. C. Römer, Berlin: De Gruyter, https://doi.org/10.1515/ebr.meshainscription.

Seybold, K. (1973), 'Das Herrscherbild des Bileamorakels Num 24:15–19', *TZ* 29:1–19.

—— (1977), *Der aaronitische Segen: Studien zu Numeri 6, 22–27*, Neukirchen: Neukirchener Verlag.

Shanks, H. (2007), 'The Mystery of Nechushtan', *BAR Review* 33 (2):58–63.

Shapira, H. (2012), '"For Judgment Is God's": Human Judgment and Divine Justice in the Hebrew Bible and in Jewish Tradition', *Journal of Law and Religion* 27.2:273–328.

Sharp, C. J. (2009), *Irony and Meaning in the Hebrew Bible*, Bloomington: Indiana University Press.

Shectman, S. (2010), 'Bearing Guilt in Numbers 5:12–31', in J. Stackert, B. N. Porter and D. P. Wright (eds.), *Gazing on the Deep: Ancient Near Eastern, Biblical, and Jewish Studies in Honor of Zvi Abusch*, Bethesda, Md.: CDL, 473–493.

Shemesh, Y. (2007), 'A Gender Perspective on the Daughters of Zelophehad: Bible, Talmudic Midrash, and Modern Feminist Midrash', *BibInt* 15:80–109.

Shenk, R. (1993), 'The Coherence of the Biblical Story of Balaam', *Literature and Belief* 13:31–51.

Shiloh, Y. (1980), 'The Population of Iron Age Palestine in the Light of a Sample Analysis of Urban Plans, Areas, and Population Density', *BASOR* 239:25–35.

Shumate, D. R. (2001), 'The Vindication of God's Leadership: The Divine Probation of the Theocratic Order in Numbers 10:11–25:18 and Its Contribution to the Structure and Message of the Book as a Whole', PhD diss., Greenville, S.C.: Bob Jones University.

Sicherman, M. (2008), 'The Political Side of the Zimri–Cozbi Affair', *JBQ* 36.1:22–24.

Simpson, B. F. (1885), 'The Story of Balaam Reconsidered', *Old Testament Student* 5 (3):125–128.

Sivan, H. Z. (2001), 'The Rape of Cozbi (Numbers XXV)', *VT* 51.1:69–80.
Ska, J. L. (2006), *Introduction to Reading the Pentateuch*, Winona Lake: Eisenbrauns.
—— (2014), 'Old and New in the Book of Numbers', *Bib* 95 (1):102–116.
—— (2016), 'Some Empirical Evidence in Favor of Redaction Criticism', in J. C. Gertz, B. M Levinson, D. Rom-Shiloni and K. Schmid (eds.), *The Formation of the Pentateuch Bridging the Academic Cultures of Europe, Israel, and North America*, Tübingen: Mohr Siebeck, 567–577.
Sklar, J. (2005), *Sin, Impurity, Sacrifice, Atonement: The Priestly Conceptions*, Sheffield: Sheffield Phoenix.
—— (2008), 'Num. 15:30–31 as Backdrop to Heb. 10:26', conference paper delivered at annual SBL meeting in Boston, Mass., 1–10.
—— (2012), 'Sin and Atonement: Lessons from the Pentateuch', *BBR* 22 (4):467–491.
Slayton, J. C. (1992), 'Shittim', *ABD* 5:1222–1223.
Smend, R. (1912), *Die Erzählung des Hexateuch: Auf Ihre Quellen Untersucht*, Berlin: Georg Reimer.
Smick, E. B. (1974), 'A Study of the Structure of the Third Balaam Oracle (Num. 24:5–9)', in J. H. Skilton (ed.), *The Law and the Prophets: Old Testament Studies in Honor of Oswald T. Allis*, Nutley, N.J.: Presbyterian & Reformed, 242–252.
Smith, H. P. (1908), 'Notes on the Red Heifer', *JBL* 27 (2):153–156.
—— (1909), 'The Red Heifer', *AJT* 13:207–228.
Smith, J. Z. (2004), 'Manna, Manna Everywhere', in *Religion: Essays in the Study of Religion*, Chicago: University of Chicago Press, 117–144.
Smith, M. (1988), '"Seeing God" in the Psalms: The Background to the Beatific Vision in the Hebrew Bible', *CBQ* 50 (2):171–183.
—— (1999), 'Matters of Space and Time in Exodus and Numbers', in C. Seitz and K. Greene-McCreight (eds.), *Theological Exegesis: Essays in Conversation with Brevard S. Childs*, Grand Rapids: Eerdmans, 182–207.
—— (2010), *The Priestly Vision of Genesis 1*, Minneapolis: Fortress.
Smith, P. A. (1994), 'An Investigation of the Relationship of Theophanies to God's Concealment by Clouds in the Old Testament', PhD diss., New Orleans: New Orleans Baptist Theological Seminary.
Smoak, J. D. (2012), 'May YHWH Bless You and Keep You from Evil: The Rhetorical Argument of Ketef Hinnom Amulet I and the Form of Prayers for Deliverance in the Psalms', *Journal of Ancient Near Eastern Religions* 12:202–236.
—— (2016), *The Priestly Blessing in Inscription and Scripture: The Early History of Numbers 6:24–26*, Oxford: Oxford University Press.
Snaith, N. H. (1957), 'Sacrifices in the Old Testament', *VT* 7.3:308–317.
—— (1963), 'Time in the Old Testament', in F. F. Bruce (ed.), *Promise and Fulfilment*, Edinburgh: T. & T. Clark, 175–186.
—— (1966), 'The Daughters of Zelophehad', *VT* 16:124–127.
—— (1973), 'Note on Numbers 18:9', *VT* 23 (3):373–375.

Snowden Jr, F. M. (1970), *Blacks in Antiquity: Ethiopians in the Greco-Roman Experience*. Cambridge, Mass.: Harvard University Press.
Soden, W. von (1970), 'Mirjām-Maria (Gottes-) Geschenk', *UF* 2: 269–272.
Sohn, S.-T. (1999), '"I Will Be Your God and You Will Be My People": The Origin and Background of the Covenant Formula', in B. A. Levine, R. Chazan, W. W. Hallo and L. H. Schiffman (eds.), *Ki Baruch Hu: Ancient Near Eastern, Biblical, and Judaic Studies in Honor of Baruch A. Levine*, Winona Lake: Eisenbrauns, 355–372.
—— (2002), *YHWH, the Husband of Israel: The Metaphor of Marriage Between YHWH and Israel*, Eugene: Wipf & Stock.
Soloveitchik, J. B. (1974), 'Leadership – Parshas Behaaloscha', tr. Y. Etshalom, https://torah.org.
Sommer, B. D. (1999), 'Reflecting on Moses: The Redaction of Numbers 11', *JBL* 118 (4):601–624.
—— (2011), 'Dating Pentateuchal Texts and the Perils of Pseudo-Historicism', in T. B. Dozeman, K. Schmid and B. J. Schwartz (eds.), *The Pentateuch: International Perspectives on Current Research*, FAT 78, Tübingen: Mohr Siebeck, 85–108.
Sonnet, J.-P. (1997), *The Book Within the Book: Writing in Deuteronomy*, Biblical Interpretation Series 14, Leiden: Brill.
Sousek, Z. (1967), 'Bileam und Seine Eselin: Exegetische-Theologische Bemerkungun Zu Num. 22', *CV* 10:183–186.
Specht, H. (2013), 'Die Verfehlung Moses und Aarons in Num. 20:1–13*P', in C. Frevel, T. Pola and A. Schart (eds.), *Torah and the Book of Numbers*, Tübingen: Mohr Siebeck, 273–313.
Speier, S. (1946), 'The Jerusalem Targum to Num 18:12 and Deut 34:3', *JBL* 65 (3):315–318.
Speiser, E. A. (1960), 'An Angelic "Curse": Exodus 14:20', *JAOS* 80 (3):198–200.
—— (1963), 'Background and Function of the Biblical Nasi'', *CBQ* 25:111–117.
Spencer, J. (1685), *De Legibus Hebraeorum Ritualibus et Earum Rationibus, Libri Tres*, Cambridge: Ex. Officina Joan. Hayes.
Spencer, J. R. (1992), 'Sojourner', *ABD* 6:103–104.
—— (1998), 'PQD, the Levites, and Numbers 1–4', *ZAW* 110:535–546.
Sperber, A. (1959), *The Pentateuch According to Targum Onkelos*, The Bible in Aramaic 1, Leiden: Brill.
Sperling, S. D. (1999), 'Miriam, Aaron, and Moses: Sibling Rivalry', *HUCA* 70–71:39–55.
Spero, S. (1993), 'Two Concepts of the Covenant', *JBQ* 21.2:109–115.
—— (2013), '"Moses Wrote His Book and the Portion of Balaam" (TB Bava Batra 14b)', *JBQ* 41 (3):193–200.
Spiegelman, M. (2012), 'Conclusion', in E. Bick and Y. Beasley (eds.), *Torah MiEtzion: New Readings in Tanach: Devarim*, Jerusalem: Maggid, 455–459.

Spiro, A. (1953), 'The Ascension of Phinehas', *PAAJR* 22:91–114.
Spoelstra, J. J. (2019), 'Apotropaic Accessories: The People's Tassels and the High Priest's Rosette', in A. Finitsis (ed.), *Dress and Clothing in the Hebrew Bible: 'For All Her Household Are Clothed in Crimson'*, New York: T. & T. Clark, 63–86.
Sprinkle, J. M. (1989), 'Literary Approaches to the Old Testament: A Survey of Recent Scholarship', *JETS* 32:299–310.
Spronk, K. (1995), 'Baal of Peor', in K. van der Toorn, B. Becking and P. W. van der Horst (eds.), *Dictionary of Deities and Demons in the Bible*, Leiden: Brill, 147–148.
Stager, L. E. (1985), 'The Archaeology of the Family in Ancient Israel', *BASOR* 260:1–35.
—— (1999), 'Jerusalem and the Garden of Eden', *Eretz-Israel* 26:183–194.
Stallman, R. C. (1999), 'Divine Hospitality in the Pentateuch: A Metaphorical Perspective on God as Host', PhD diss., Philadelphia: Westminster Theological Seminary.
Staubli, T. (2012), 'Cherubim: I. Ancient Near East and the Hebrew Bible/Old Testament', in C. M. Furey, P. Gemeinhardt, J. LeMon, T. Römer, J. Schröter, B. D. Walfish and E. J. Ziolkowski (eds.), *Encyclopedia of the Bible and Its Reception*, 5:55–58, Berlin: de Gruyter.
Stebbins, R. P. (1885), 'The Story of Balaam', *Old Testament Student* 4 (9):385–395.
Steinberg, P. (2007), 'Phinehas: Hero or Vigilante?', *JBQ* 35.2:119–126.
Steiner, R. C. (2020), 'The Book of the Wars of the Lord (Num. 21:14–20): Philology and Hydrology, Geography and Ethnography', *JAOS* 140 (3):565–591.
Steins, G. (2004), 'Šadday', *TDOT* 14:418–446.
Steinsaltz, A. (2011), *Change and Renewal: The Essence of the Jewish Holidays and Days of Remembrance*, Jerusalem: Maggid.
Stephens, F. J. (1931), 'The Ancient Significance of Ṣîṣîth', *JBL* 50 (2):59–70.
Sternberg, M. (1987), *The Poetics of Biblical Narrative: Ideological Literature and the Drama of Reading*, Bloomington: Indiana University Press.
Stigers, H. G. (1980), 'Gēr', *TWOT*, 155–156.
Strack, H. L. (1894), *Die Bücher Genesis Exodus Leviticus und Numeri*, München: C. H. Beck.
Strauss, G. (1979), 'Chronological and Substantial Order in Sefer Bemidbar', *Alon Shvut* 75:13–21.
Strawn, B. A. (2000), 'Chemosh', in D. N. Freedman (ed.), *Eerdman's Dictionary of the Bible*, Grand Rapids: Eerdmans.
—— (2005), *What Is Stronger Than a Lion? Leonine Image and Metaphor in the Hebrew Bible and the Ancient Near East*, Orbis Biblicus et Orientalis 212, Fribourg: Academic; Göttingen: Vandenhoeck & Ruprecht.
Štrba, B. (2006), 'Did the Israelites Realise Why Moses Had to Die?' *RB* 113.3:336–365.

Strong, J. (1890), *A Concise Dictionary of the Words in the Hebrew Bible*, Nashville: Abingdon.
Stronstad, R. (1999), 'The Prophethood of All Believers: A Study in Luke's Charismatic Theology', in W. Ma and R. P. Menzies (eds.), *Pentecostalism in Context: Essays in Honor of William W. Menzies*, JPTSup 11, Sheffield: Sheffield Academic Press, 60–77.
Sutcliffe, E. (1937), 'A Note on Numbers XXII', *Bib* 18 (4):439–442.
Swanson, K. (2002), 'A Reassessment of Hezekiah's Reform in Light of Jar Handles and Iconographic Evidence', *CBQ* 64:460–469.
Sweeney, M. A. (2015), 'The Literary-Historical Dimensions of Intertextuality in Exodus–Numbers', paper presented at SBL International meeting, Atlanta, 1–14.
—— (2017), *The Pentateuch*, Core Biblical Studies, Nashville: Abingdon.
—— (2019), 'Why Moses Was Barred from the Land of Israel: A Reassessment of Numbers 20 in Literary Context', Western Jewish Studies Association conference, Claremont, Calif., 1–14
Taggar-Cohen, A. (1998), 'Law and Family in the Book of Numbers: The Levites and the Tidennūtu Documents from Nuzi', *VT* 48 (1):74–94.
Talmon, S. (1958), 'Divergences in Calendar-Reckoning in Ephraim and Judah', *VT* 8:48–74.
Taylor, D. J. (2010), 'A Narrative Critical Analysis of Korah's Rebellion in Numbers 16 and 17', PhD diss., Pretoria: University of South Africa.
Tedford, J. S. (2013), 'The Agony of Indeterminacy: Sotah Tradition and the Surplus Meaning of the "Cup" Metaphor in Matthew's Gethsemane Narrative', PhD diss., Pasadena, Calif.: Fuller Theological Seminary.
Tengström, S. (1981), *Die Toledotformel und die literarische Struktur der priesterlichen Erweiterungsschicht im Pentateuch*, Lund: CWK Gleerup.
Tervanotko, H. K. (2016), *Denying Her Voice: The Figure of Miriam in Ancient Jewish Literature*, Göttingen: Vandenhoeck & Ruprecht.
Thiessen, M. (2013), '"The Rock Was Christ": The Fluidity of Christ's Body in 1 Corinthians 10.4', *Journal for the Study of the New Testament* 36 (2):103–126.
Thomas, M. A. (2011), *These Are the Generations: Identity, Promise and the 'Toledot' Formula*, New York: Bloomsbury T. & T. Clark.
Thompson, T. (1968), 'Some Legal Problems in the Book of Ruth', *VT* 18:79–99.
Thon, J. (2006), *Pinhas ben Eleasar – der levitische Priester am Ende der Tora. Traditions und literargeschichtliche Untersuchung unter Einbeziehung historisch-geographischer Fragen*, ABG 20, Leipzig: Evangelische Verlagsanstalt.
Tigay, J. H. (1996), *The JPS Torah Commentary: Deuteronomy [Devarim]*, Philadelphia: Jewish Publication Society.
Török, L. (1998), *The Kingdom of Kush: Handbook of the Napatan-Meroitic Civilization*, Leiden: Brill.

Tosato, A. (1979), 'The Literary Structure of the First Two Poems of Balaam (Num. Xxii 7–10, 18–24)', *VT* 29:98–106.
Tournay, R. (1964), 'Bulletin', *RB* 71:283–286.
Tov, E. (1998), 'Rewritten Bible Compositions and Biblical Manuscripts, with Special Attention to the Samaritan Pentateuch', *DSD* 5.3:334–354.
——— (2001), *Textual Criticism of the Hebrew Bible*, 2nd rev. ed., Minneapolis: Fortress.
——— (2018), 'The Septuagint as a Harmonizing Text', in M. Meiser, M. Geiger, S. Kreuzer and M. Sigismund (eds.), *Die Septuaginta – Geschichte, Wirkung, Relevanz*, WUNT 405, Tübingen: Mohr Siebeck, 181–201.
Trevaskis, L. M. (2011), *Holiness, Ethics and Ritual in Leviticus*, Hebrew Bible Monographs 29, Sheffield: Sheffield Phoenix.
Trevett, C. (2005), 'Wilderness Woman: The Taming of Miriam', in R. S. Sugirtharajah (ed.), *Wilderness: Essays in Honour of Frances Young*, Library of New Testament Studies 295, London: T. & T. Clark International, 26–44.
Trible, P. (1994), 'Bringing Miriam out of the Shadows', in A. Brenner (ed.), *A Feminist Companion to Exodus to Deuteronomy*, Sheffield: Sheffield Academic Press, 166–186.
Tunyogi, A. C. (1962), 'The Rebellions of Israel', *JBL* 81:385–390.
——— (1969), *The Rebellions of Israel*, Richmond, Va.: John Knox.
Turnage, M. (2008), 'Is It the Serpent That Heals? An Ancient Jewish Theologoumenon and the Developing Faith in Jesus', in K. Pomykala (ed.), *Israel in the Wilderness: Interpretations of the Biblical Narratives in Jewish and Christian Traditions*, Leiden: Brill, 71–88.
Twersky, G. (2022), *Torah Song: The Theological Role of Torah Poetry*, New York: Kodesh.
Twersky, Y. (2007a), *Amittah Shel Torah I: Bereishit, Shemot*, vol. 1, Southfield, Mich.: Targum.
Uffenheimer, B. (1979), 'Utopia and Reality in Biblical Thought', *Immanuel* 9:5–15.
——— (1988), 'Prophecy, Ecstasy, and Sympathy', in J. A. Emerton (ed.), *Congress Volume: Jerusalem 1986*, VTSup 40, Leiden: Brill, 257–269.
Ulfgard, H. (1998), *The Story of Sukkot: The Setting, Shaping, and Sequel of the Biblical Feast of Tabernacles*, BZGBE 34, Tübingen: Mohr Siebeck.
Ullmann, D. W. (1995), 'Moses' Bronze Serpent (Numbers 21:4–9) in Early Jewish and Christian Exegesis', PhD diss., Dallas: Dallas Theological Seminary.
Ulrich, D. R. (1998), 'The Framing Function of the Narratives About Zelophehad's Daughters', *JETS* 41.4:529–538.
Van Dam, C. (1991), 'The Incense Offering in Its Biblical Context', *Mid-America Journal of Theology* 7 (2):179–194.
Van der Toorn, K. (1996), *Family Religion in Babylonia, Syria, and Israel*, Leiden: Brill.
Van der Woude, A. S. (1997), 'Šem', *THAT* 2:948.

Van Gemeren, W. A. (1981), 'The Sons of God in Genesis 6:1–4 (An Example of Evangelical Demythologization?)', *WTJ* 43:320–348.
Van Seters, J. (1972), 'The Conquest of Sihon's Kingdom: A Literary Examination', *JBL* 91:182–197.
——— (1994), *The Life of Moses: The Yahwist as Historian in Exodus–Numbers*, Louisville, Ky.: Westminster John Knox.
——— (1997), 'From Faithful Prophet to Villain: Observations on the Tradition History of the Balaam Story', in E. Carpenter (ed.), *A Biblical Itinerary: In Search of Method, Form and Content: Essays in Honor of George W. Coats*, JSOTSup 240, Sheffield: Sheffield Academic Press, 126–132.
Vasholz, R. I. (1992), 'Military Censuses in Numbers', *Presby* 18 (2):122–125.
——— (1993), 'Israel's Cities of Refuge', *Presb* 19.2:116–118.
Vaughan, P. H. (1974), *The Meaning of 'bāmâ' in the Old Testament: A Study of Etymological, Textual and Archaeological Evidence*, SOTSMS 3, Cambridge: Cambridge University Press.
Vaux, R. de (1961), *Ancient Israel: Its Life and Institutions*, Grand Rapids: Eerdmans.
——— (1978), *The Early History of Israel*, vol. 2, London: Darton, Longman & Todd.
Vermes, G. (1961a), *Scripture and Tradition in Judaism: Haggadic Studies*, Leiden: Brill.
——— (1961b), 'The Story of Balaam', in *Scripture and Tradition in Judaism: Haggadic Studies*, Leiden: Brill, 127–177.
——— (1997), *The Complete Dead Sea Scrolls in English*, London: Allen Lane; Panguin.
Viberg, Å. (1992), *Symbols of Law: A Contextual Analysis of Legal Symbolic Acts in the Old Testament*, Stockholm: Almqvist & Wiksell International.
Victor, P. (1966), 'A Note on קח in the Old Testament', *VT* 16 (3):358–361.
Viezel, E. (2015), 'R. Judah He-Hasid or R. M. Zaltman: Who Proposed That Torah Verses Were Written After the Time of Moses?', *JJS* 66 (1):97–115.
Vilensky, Z. (1978), *Legends of Galilee, Jordan and Sinai*, vol. 3, Philadelphia: Jewish Publication Society.
Vogels, W. (1982), 'The Spirit in Joshua and the Laying on of Hands by Moses', *Laval théologique et philosophique* 38.1:3–7.
——— (1997), 'The Cultic and Civil Calendars of the Fourth Day of Creation (Gen. 1:14b)', *SJOT* 11 (2):163–180.
——— (2000), 'D'Égypte à Canaan: Un Rite de Passage', *Science et Esprit* 52:21–35.
Vos, G. (1886), *On the Mosaic Origin of the Pentateuchal Codes*, New York: Armstrong.
——— (1975), *Biblical Theology: Old and New Testaments*, Edinburgh: Banner of Truth Trust.

—— (2001), *The Eschatology of the Old Testament*. Phillipsburg, N.J: Presbyterian & Reformed.

Vriezen, T. C. (1950), 'The Term Hizza: Lustration and Consecration', *OtSt* 7:201–235.

Vuilleumier, R. (1996), 'Bileam Zwischen Bibel und Dier Alla', *TZ* 52:150–163.

Wacholder, B. Z. (2004), 'Creation in Ezekiel's Merkabah: Ezekiel 1 and Genesis 1', in C. A. Evans (ed.), *Of Scribes and Sages 1: Ancient Versions and Traditions*, London: T. & T. Clark International, 14–32.

Waite, J. (2010), 'The Census of Israelite Men After Their Exodus from Egypt', *VT* 60:487–491.

Wall, L. (2005), 'Finding Identity in the Wilderness', in R. S. Sugirtharajah (ed.), *Wilderness: Essays in Honour of Frances Young*, Library of New Testament Studies 295, London: T. & T. Clark International, 66–77.

Walsh, C. (2013), 'Where Did God Go? Theophanic Shift in Exodus', *BTB* 42 (3):115–123.

Walsh, J. T. (1977), 'From Egypt to Moab: A Source Critical Analysis of the Wilderness Itinerary', *CBQ* 39:20–33.

—— (2001), *Style and Structure in Biblical Hebrew Narrative*, Collegeville, Minn.: Liturgical.

Waltke, B. K., and C. J. Fredricks (2001), *Genesis: A Commentary*, Grand Rapids: Zondervan.

Waltke, B. K., and M. P. O'Connor (1990), *An Introduction to Biblical Hebrew Syntax*, Winona Lake: Eisenbrauns.

Walton, J. H. (2001), *Genesis: From Biblical Text . . . to Contemporary Life*. NIVAC, Grand Rapids: Zondervan.

Ward Jr., H. D. (2009), 'On Defining a Prophet: A Theological-Ethical Study of the Balaam Narratives of Numbers 22–24', ThD diss., Stellenbosch, South Africa: University of Stellenbosch.

Waters, J. L. (2017), 'The Belly: Phinehas' Target in Numbers 25:8', *Conversations with the Biblical World* 37:38–55.

Watts, J. W. (1998), 'The Legal Characterization of Moses in the Rhetoric of the Pentateuch', *JBL* 117:415–426.

—— (2006), "*Ōlāh*: The Rhetoric of Burnt Offerings', *VT* 56.1:125–137.

—— (2007), *Ritual and Rhetoric in Leviticus: From Sacrifice to Scripture*, Cambridge: Cambridge University Press.

Waxman, C. (2006a), 'For God Is Not a Man . . . (23:19): On Blessing and Betrayal at the Plains of Moab', Yeshivat Har Etzion – Virtual Beit Midrash, www.etzion.or.il/en.

—— (2006b), 'Of Lusts and Laments', Yeshivat Har Etzion – Virtual Beit Midrash, www.etzion.org.il/en.

—— (2012), 'The Blessing, the King and the Torah of Moses', in E. Bick and Y. Beasley (eds.), *Torah MiEtzion: New Readings in Tanach: Devarim*, Jerusalem: Maggid, 443–454.

—— (2014a), 'The Camp and the Chariot', in E. Bick (ed.), *Torah*

MiEtzion: New Readings in Tanakh: New Readings in Tanakh: Bemidbar, Jerusalem: Yeshivat Har Etzion; Maggid, 71–80.

——— (2014b), 'Of Sticks and Stones', in E. Bick (ed.), *Torah MiEtzion: New Readings in Tanakh: Bemidbar*, Jerusalem: Yeshivat Har Etzion; Maggid, 263–273.

——— (2014c), '"A Possession Before God"', in E. Bick (ed.), *Torah MiEtzion: New Readings in Tanakh: Bemidbar*, Jerusalem: Yeshivat Har Etzion, Maggid, 437–445.

——— (2017), 'Of Spy Stories and Heroic Measures', Yeshivat Har Etzion – Virtual Beit Midrash, www.etzion.org.il/en.

Way, K. C. (2005), 'Balaam's Hobby-Horse: The Animal Motif in the Balaam Traditions', *Ugarit Forschungen* 37:679–693.

Webb, B. G. (2008), *The Book of Judges: An Integrated Reading*, Eugene: Wipf & Stock.

Wefing, S. (1981), 'Beobachtungen zum Ritual Mit der roten Kuh (Num 19,1–10a)', *ZAW* 93:342–359.

Weinfeld, M. (1970), 'The Covenant of Grant in the Old Testament and in the Ancient Near East', *JAOS* 90:184–203.

——— (1975), 'Běrît – Covenant vs. Obligation', *Bib* 56 (1):120–128.

——— (1977a), 'Ancient Near Eastern Parallels in Prophetic Literature', *VT* 27:178–195.

——— (1977b), 'Judge and Officer in Ancient Israel and in the Ancient Near East', *Israel Oriental Studies* 7:65–88.

——— (1988), 'The Pattern of Israelite Settlement in Canaan', in J. A. Emerton (ed.), *Congress Volume Jerusalem 1986*, Leiden: Brill, 270–283.

——— (1991), *Deuteronomy 1–11*, Anchor Bible 5, New York: Doubleday.

——— (1992), *Deuteronomy and the Deuteronomic School*, Winona Lake: Eisenbrauns.

Weingreen, J. (1966a), 'The Case of the Daughters of Zelophehad', *VT* 16 (4): 518–522.

——— (1966b), 'The Case of the Woodgatherer (Numbers Xv 32–36)', *VT* 16:361–364.

Weippert, M. (1991), 'The Balaam Text from Deir 'Allā and the Study of the Old Testament', in J. Hoftijzer and G. van der Kooij (eds.), *The Balaam Text from Deir 'Allā Re-Evaluated: Proceedings of the International Symposium Held in Leiden 21–24 August 1989*, Leiden: Brill, 151–184.

Weise, U. (2003), 'Vom Segnen Israels. Eine texpragmatische Untersuchung der Bileam-Erzählung von Num 22–24', diss., Greifswald: University of Greifswald.

Weisman, Z. (1981), 'The Personal Spirit as Imparting Authority', *ZAW* 93 (2):225–234.

Wellhausen, J. (1885), *Prolegomena to the History of Israel*, tr. R. W. Smith, Atlanta: Scholars, repr. 1994.

——— (1889), *Die Composition des Hexateuchs und der Historischen Bücher des alten Testaments*, Berlin: Georg Reimer.

Wells, B. (2009), 'Exodus', in J. H. Walton (ed), *Zondervan Illustrated Bible Backgrounds Commentary: Genesis, Exodus, Leviticus, Numbers, Deuteronomy*, Grand Rapids: Zondervan, 1:160–283.

Wendland, Ernst (2012), 'Two Dumb Donkeys Declare the Word of the Lord: A Literary-Structural Analysis of Numbers 22–24', *Journal for Semitics* 21 (2):167–199.

——— (2016), 'Where Was Korah Killed and What Difference Does It Make? A Brief Structural-Thematic Analysis of Numbers 16:1–40', https://www.academia.edu/26280743/Where_Was_Korah_Killed_And_What_Difference_Does_It_Make_A_Brief_Structural-Thematic_Analysis_Of_Numbers_16_1_40.

Wenham, G. J. (1979), *The Book of Leviticus*, NICOT, Grand Rapids: Eerdmans.

——— (1981a), 'Aaron's Rod (Numbers 17:16–28)', ZAW 93 (2):280–281.

——— (2012), *Psalms as Torah: Reading Biblical Song Ethically*, Grand Rapids: Baker Academic.

——— (2014), 'Sanctuary Symbolism in the Garden of Eden Story', in *Cult and Cosmos: Tilting Toward a Temple-Centered Theology*, Leuven: Peeters, 161–166.

Wenham, J. W. (1967), 'Large Numbers in the Old Testament', *TynB* 18:19–53.

Wénin, A. (2008), 'Le Serpent De Nb 21,4–9 Et De Gn 3,1', in T. Römer (ed.), *The Books of Leviticus and Numbers*, BETL 215, Leuven: Peeters, 545–554.

Wenkel, D. H. (2013), 'A New Reading of Anointing Oil in James 5:14: Finding First-Century Common Ground in Moses' Glorious Face', *HBT* 35:166–180.

Westbrook, R. (1991), *Property and the Family in Biblical Law*, JSOTSup 113, Sheffield: JSOT Press.

Westermann, C. (1967), *Handbook on the Old Testament*, tr. R. H. Boyd, Minneapolis: Augsburg.

——— (1970), 'Die Herrlichkeit Gottes in der Priesterschrift', in H. J. Stoebe (ed.), *Wort, Gebot, Glaube: Beiträge zur Theologie des alten Testaments*, Zürich: Zwingli-Verlag, 227–249.

——— (1984), *Genesis 1–11: A Commentary*, Minneapolis: Augsburg.

——— (1997), 'נֶפֶשׁ' (*nepeš*), TLOT 2:743–759.

Wharton, J. A. (1959), 'The Command to Bless: An Exposition of Numbers 22:41–23:25', I 13:37–48.

Whitekettle, R. (1996), 'Levitical Thought and the Female Reproductive Cycle: Wombs, Wellsprings, and the Primeval World', *VT* 46.3: 376–391.

——— (2018), 'Life's Labors Lost: Priestly Death and Returning Home from a City of Refuge in Ancient Israel', *HTR* 111.3:333–356.

Whybray, R. N. (1987), *The Making of the Pentateuch: A Methodological Study*, London: Bloomsbury T. & T. Clark.

Widengren, G. (1951), *The King and the Tree of Life in Ancient Near Eastern Religion (King and Saviour IV)*, Uppsala: Almqvist and Wiksell.

Widmer, M. (2004), *Moses, God, and the Dynamics of Intercessory Prayer: A Study of Exodus 32–34 and Numbers 13–14*, FAT 8, Tübingen: Mohr Siebeck.
Wiesel, E. (1999), 'Supporting Roles: Eldad and Medad', *BRev* 15 (2):18–19.
Wifall Jr., W. (1970), 'Asshur and Eber, or Asher and Ḥeber?', *ZAW* 82:110–114.
Wiggershaus, B. (2021), 'The Man of Opened Eye: Ancient Near Eastern Revelatory Convention and the Balaam Cycle (Numbers 22–24)', PhD diss., Wilmore, Ky.: Asbury Theological Seminary.
Wijngaards, J. (1965), 'And a Twofold Approach to the Exodus', *VT* 15 (1):91–102.
Wilch, J. R. (1969), *Time and Event: An Exegetical Study of the Use of 'ēth in the Old Testament in Comparison to Other Temporal Expressions in Clarification of the Concept of Time*, Leiden: Brill.
Wilkinson, J. (1974), 'Ancient Jerusalem: Its Water Supply and Population', *PEQ* 106:33–51.
——— (1999), 'The Quail Epidemic of Numbers 11.31–34', *EvQ* 71 (3):195–208.
Williams, J. (2002), 'And She Became "Snow White": Numbers 12:1–16', *OTE* 15 (1):259–268.
Williams, R. J. (2007), *Hebrew Syntax*, Toronto: University of Toronto Press.
Williamson, P. R. (2007), *Sealed with an Oath: Covenant in God's Unfolding Promise*, NSBT 23, Nottingham: Inter-Varsity Press; Downers Grove: InterVarsity Press.
Wilson, R. R. (1979), 'Prophecy and Ecstasy: A Reexamination', *JBL* 98 (3):321–337.
Windsor, G. (1972), 'Theophany: Traditions of the Old Testament', *Theology* 75 (626):411–416.
Winslow, K. S. (2005), *Early Jewish and Christian Memories of Moses' Wives: Exogamist Marriage and Ethnic Identity*, Studies in the Bible and Early Christianity 66, Lewiston, N.Y.: Edwin Mellen.
——— (2011), '"For Moses Had Indeed Married a Cushite Woman": The LORD's Prophet Married Well', *Lectio Difficilior* 1:1–18.
Wiseman, D. J. (1972), 'Flying Serpents?', *TynB* 23:108–110.
Witte, M. (2002), 'Der Segen Bileams – Eine Redaktionsgeschichtliche Problemanzeige zum "Jahwisten" in Num 22–24', in J. C. Gertz, K. Schmid and M. Witte (eds.), *Abschied vom Jahwisten. Die Komposition des Hexateuch in der Jüngsten Diskussion*, BZAW 315, Berlin: de Gruyter, 191–213.
Wold, D. (1978), 'The Meaning of the Biblical Penalty Kareth', PhD diss., Berkeley, Calif.: University of California, Berkeley.
——— (1979), 'The Kareth Penalty in P: Rationale and Cases', *SBL Seminar Papers*, 1–45.
Wolde, E. J. van (2009), *Reframing Biblical Studies: When Language and Text Meet Culture, Cognition, and Context*, Winona Lake: Eisenbrauns.
Wolf, H. (1980), 'Ḥāpap', *TWOT* 310.

Wolf, U. (1946), 'Terminology of Israel's Tribal Organization', *JBL* 65:45–49.
Wolff, H. W. (1974), *Anthropology of the Old Testament*, tr. M. Kohl, London: SCM.
Wong, K. L. (2008), '"And Moses Raised His Hand" in Numbers 20,11', *Bib* 89 (3):397–400.
Wood, A. (2008), *Of Wings and Wheels: A Synthetic Study of the Biblical Cherubim*, Berlin: de Gruyter.
Wood, L. (1966), 'Ecstasy and Israel's Early Prophets', *Bulletin of the Evangelical Theological Society* 9:125–137.
―――― (1998), *The Holy Spirit in the Old Testament*, Eugene: Wipf & Stock.
Wood, W. P. (1974), 'The Congregation of Yahweh: A Study of the Theology and Purpose of the Priestly Document', ThD diss., Richmond, Va.: Union Theological Seminary.
Woudstra, M. H. (1965), *The Ark of the Covenant from Conquest to Kingship*, Philadelphia: Presbyterian & Reformed.
Wright, D. P. (1985), 'Purification from Corpse-Contamination in Numbers XXXI 19–24', *VT* 35 (2):213–223.
―――― (1990), *God's People in God's Land: Family, Land and Property in the Old Testament*, Grand Rapids: Eerdmans.
―――― (1992a), 'Heifer, Red', *ABD* 3:115–116.
―――― (1992b), 'Unclean and Clean', *ABD* 6:729–741.
―――― (2020), 'Atonement Beyond Israel', in M. Botner, J. H. Duff and S. Dürr (eds.), *Atonement: Jewish and Christian Origins*, Grand Rapids: Eerdmans, 40–63.
Würthwein, E. (1979), *The Text of the Old Testament: An Introduction to the Biblia Hebraica*, tr. E. Rhodes, Grand Rapids: Eerdmans.
Wyatt, N. (2014), 'A Royal Garden: The Ideology of Eden', *SJOT* 28:1–35.
Yadin, Y. (1963a), *The Art of Warfare in Biblical Lands: In the Light of Archaeological Study*, vol. 1, New York: McGraw-Hill.
―――― (1963b), *The Art of Warfare in Biblical Lands: In the Light of Archaeological Study*, vol. 2, New York: McGraw-Hill.
―――― (1985), *The Temple Scroll: The Hidden Law of the Dead Sea Sect*, New York: Random House.
Yahuda, A. S. (1933), *The Language of the Pentateuch in Its Relation to Egyptian*, Oxford: Oxford University Press.
―――― (1945), 'The Name of Balaam's Homeland', *JBL* 64 (4):547–551.
Yasur-Landau, A. (2010), *The Philistines and Aegean Migration at the End of the Late Bronze Age*, New York: Cambridge University Press.
Yeung, S. Y. C. (2018), 'Salvation on the Table – Exploring the Role of Sacrificial Meals in the Old Testament', paper presented at St Andrews Symposium for Biblical and Early Christian Studies, St Andrews, Scotland, 1–7.
Yoo, P. Y. (2019), '"He Married a Cushite Woman!": On the Text of Numbers 12:1', in L. Quick, E. E. Kozlova, S. Noll and P. Y. Yoo (eds.), *To Gaul,*

to *Greece and into Noah's Ark: Essays in Honour of Kevin J. Cathcart on the Occasion of His Eightieth Birthday*, Oxford: Oxford University Press, 37–48.

Young, I. M. (1998a), 'Israelite Literacy: Interpreting the Evidence: Part I', *VT* 48 (2):239–253.

——— (1998b), 'Israelite Literacy: Interpreting the Evidence: Part II', *VT* 48 (3):408–422.

——— (2016), 'Trying to Discover When the Good Book Was Written Is a Bad Idea', *Huffington Post*, Australia, http://www.huffingtonpost.com.au/ianyoungau/trying-to-discover-when-the-good-book-was-written-is-a-bad-idea_b_9733926.html

Younger Jr., K. L. (2016), *A Political History of Arameans: From Their Origins to the End of Their Polities*, Archaeology and Biblical Studies 13, Atlanta: Society of Biblical Literature.

Zakovitch, Y. (1985), *Every High Official Has a Higher One Set over Him*, Tel Aviv: Am Oved.

——— (2012), *Jacob: Unexpected Patriarch*, New Haven: Yale University Press.

Zeelander, S. (2015), 'The End of Korah and Others: Closural Conventions in Priestly Narratives', in R. Gane and A. Taggar-Cohen (eds.), *Current Issues in Priestly and Related Literature*, Atlanta: Society of Biblical Literature, 325–346.

Zehnder, M. (2021), *The Bible and Immigration: A Critical and Empirical Reassessment*, Eugene: Pickwick.

Zenger, E. (1996), *A God of Vengeance? Understanding the Psalms of Divine Wrath*, Louisville, Ky.: Westminster John Knox.

Zertal, A. (1991), 'Israel Enters Canaan – Following the Pottery Trail', *BAR* 17.5:28–38, 42–47.

——— (2004), *The Manasseh Hill Country Survey, Volume 1: The Shechem Syncline*, Leiden: Brill.

Ziegert, C. (2009), 'Die Großen Zahlen in Num 1 und 26: Forschungsüberblick und Neuer Lösungsvorschlag', *Bib* 90:237–256.

Ziegler, Y. (2008), *Promises to Keep: The Oath in Biblical Narrative*, VTSup 120, Leiden: Brill.

——— (2014), 'From Generation to Generation', in E. Bick (ed.), *Torah MiEtzion: New Readings in Tanakh: Bemidbar*, Jerusalem: Yeshivat Har Etzion; Maggid, 3–11.

Zimmerli, W. (1954), 'Die Eigenart der Prophetischen Rede des Ezechiel. Ein Beitrag zum Problem an Hand von Ez. 14 1–11', *ZAW* 66 (1):1–26.

——— (1983), *Ezekiel: A Commentary on the Book of the Prophet Ezekiel*, vol. 1, Fortress.

Zobel, H.-J. (2006), '*Tāqa*', *TDOT* 15:765–769.

Zweig, Y.n (1989), 'The Dedication of the Tabernacle', *Tradition* 25 (1):11–16.

Zyl, A. H. van (1960), *The Moabites*, Pretoria Oriental Series 3, Leiden: Brill.

INDEX OF SCRIPTURE REFERENCES AND ANCIENT SOURCES

Note: entries in **bold** indicate the main focus of a section.

OLD TESTAMENT

Genesis
1 *1:32, 1:98, 1:255, 2:348*
1 – 10 *2:351*
1 – 11 *2:120, 2:134*
1:1 – 2:3 *1:172, 1:193*
1:2 *1:149, 1:150, 1:284, 1:286*
1:3 *1:85, 1:170*
1:3–5 *2:329*
1:4 *1:131*
1:4, 6, 7, 14, 18 *1:198, 1:421*
1:4, 10, 12 *1:362*
1:4, 10, 12, 18, 21, 25 *1:331*
1:6, 7, 8, 14, 15, 17, 20 *1:434*
1:11–13 *1:489*
1:14 *1:24, 2:328*
1:14–16 *1:193*
1:14–19 *2:329*
1:16 *2:194*
1:22, 28 *1:353*
1:26 *1:32*
1:26–27 *2:474*
1:26, 27 *2:451*
1:26–28 *1:198*
1:27–28 *1:362*
1:28 *1:88, 1:99, 1:149, 2:157, 2:413, 2:415*
1:29–30 *1:255*
1:31 *1:331, 1:343*
2 *1:291*
2 – 3 *1:141, 1:330, 1:331, 1:432, 1:433, 1:482,*
1:496, 2:140, 2:142, 2:167
2:1 *1:85, 1:104*
2:1–3 *1:234, 1:383, 1.392, 1:489, 2:238, 2:329, 2:335, 2:344*
2:2–3 *1:385*
2:4 *1:120*
2:4–25 *2:179*
2:6–7 *1:362*
2:6, 10 *2:22*
2:7 *1:149, 1:155, 1:481, 1:488, 1:489, 1:493, 1:494, 2:476*
2:7–8, 15 *1:482*
2:8 *2:142, 2:179*
2:8–14 *2:21*
2:9, 17 *1:290, 1:319, 1:363*
2:10–14 *1:53, 1:59, 1:99, 1:174, 1:291, 2:6, 2:45, 2:48, 2:179*
2:12 *1:22, 1:254, 1:255, 1:330, 1:361*
2:13 *1:361*
2:14 *2:200–201*
2:15 *1:90, 1:234, 1:468*
2:16–17 *1:362*
2:17 *2:467*
2:21 *1:309*
2:24 *2:234, 2:368, 2:488, 2:491*
2.9 *1:330*
3 *1:361–364, 2:45, 2:70*
3:1–15 *2:70*
3:4–5 *1:341*
3:4–6 *1:362*
3:5–6 *1:319*
3:5, 6 *1:290*
3:5, 7 *2:142*
3:5, 22 *1:330, 1:363*
3:6 *1:254, 1:290, 1:361, 1:362, 1:363, 1:392, 1:409*
3:8 *1:191*
3:8, 10 *1:362*
3:9, 11, 13 *2:97*
3:9–13 *2:124*
3:10 *2:70*
3:14 *1:149, 2:120*
3:14–15 *2:247*
3:14, 17 *1:149, 2:134*
3:14–19 *2:179*
3:14, 19 *1:155*
3:15 *2:171, 2:184, 2:195, 2:196, 2:379, 2:397*
3:17 *1:363*
3:19 *1:481, 1:493*
3:19, 24 *1:482*
3:21 *1:363, 1:390, 2:43*
3:24 *1:34, 1:35, 1:90, 1:99, 1:147, 1:191, 1:239, 1:362, 1:363, 2:137, 2:138, 2:142*
4 *1:432–433, 2:45, 2:477*
4:1–17 *2:476*
4:2, 8, 9, 10, 11 *1:432*
4:4 *1:440*
4:5 *1:401, 1:426, 1:432*
4:5–6 *1:419*
4:6, 9, 10 *2:97*
4:6–10 *2:124*
4:7 *1:481*
4:8 *1:432*
4:9 *1:432*
4:10 *2:476–477*
4:10–11 *1:426, 1:481*

Genesis (*cont.*)
4:11 *1:149, 1:432, 2:120,*
    2:134, 2:477
4:12 *2:477*
4:12, 14 *2:400, 2:409*
4:12, 14, 16 *1:481*
4:14 *2:477*
4:15 *1:24*
4:16 *1:147, 1:481, 2:477,*
    2:479
4:17 *2:268, 2:271, 2:418*
4:20 *2:403*
4:22 *2:200, 2:201*
4:24 *2:477*
4:25–26 *2:196*
4:26 *1:173, 1:355, 2:348*
5:3 *1:440, 2:196, 2:451*
5:18 *2:268*
5:24 *2:268*
5:29 *1:149, 2:134*
5:32 *1:310*
6 – 8 *1:346*
6 – 9 *1:310, 2:409*
6:1–4 *1:339*
6:1–7 *2:216*
6:3, 17 *1:149*
6:4 *1:339, 1:408*
6:7 *1:149*
6:8 *2:406*
6:9 *1:103, 1:120, 1:481,*
    2:330
6:11 *1:353*
6:11, 12, 13, 17 *2:409*
6:17 *1:149, 1:269, 2:44,*
    2:310
7 – 8 *2:477*
7:4, 23 *1:149*
7:15 *2:310*
7:15, 22 *1:149*
7:16 *1:309*
7:23 *1:279*
8 *2:151*
8:1 *1:149, 1:150, 1:284*
8:4 *1:234, 2:409*
8:7, 8, 10 *2:63*
8:10 *2:358*
8:20–21 *2:330, 2:390*
8:20–22 *1:169*
8:21 *1:375, 2:328*
8:22 *2:350*
9:1 *1:149, 1:353*
9:3–4 *1:255*
9:5 *1:488, 1:489*
9:5–6 *2:474*
9:6 *1:481, 2:451, 2:475*
9:11, 15 *2:409*
9:12–17 *1:24*
9:14 *1:377*
9:16 *2:238*
9:18, 22, 25 *2:80*
9:20–24 *1:362*
9:25 *2:134*
9:26–27 *2:202*
10 *1:291, 2:345*
10:1 *1:120, 1:310*
10:2–5 *2:202*
10:4, 11, 22–24 *2:202*
10:6–9 *1:291*
10:6, 15–18 *2:80*
10:11 *2:201*
10:21–22 *2:202*
10:21, 24 *2:202*
10:22 *2:201*
10:29 *1:331*
11:4 *2:303, 2:418*
11:10, 27 *1:120*
11:14–17 *2:202*
11:31 *2:80*
12:1 *1:231, 1:322, 1:352,*
    2:208, 2:279
12:1–3 *1:167, 1:238,*
    2:119, 2:120, 2:134,
    2:495
12:2 *2:279*
12:2–3 *1:173*
12:3 *1:197, 1:239, 1:351,*
    1:377, 2:57, 2:96, 2:97,
    2:120, 2:133, 2:134,
    2:156, 2:196, 2:203,
    2:208
12:4 *2:80*
12:7 *2:449*
12:8 *1:173, 1:355, 2:348*
12:10 *1:377*
12:10–20 *1:151*
12:12 *2:187*
13 *2:114, 2:424*
13:1–11 *2:403*
13:4 *1:173*
13:10 *2:48, 2:179*
13:14–15 *1:353, 2:208,*
    2:279
13:14–17 *1:325, 1:364,*
    2:449
13:14–18 *1:332*
13:16 *2:133, 2:157, 2:208*
14 *2:404*
14:5 *2:418*
14:11–12 *2:409*
14:13, 24 *1:332*
14:14 *2:57*
14:18, 19, 20, 22 *2:193*
14:18–20 *1:476, 2:208*
15 *1:95, 2:404, 2:425*
15:1 *2:132, 2:177*
15:1–6 *1:99*
15:1–6, 7–21 *1:42*
15:5 *1:24, 1:25, 1:88,*
    2:194, 2:208
15:6 *2:29, 2:226*
15:7 *1:364, 2:443*
15:7, 18–21 *2:449*
15:7–20 *2:265*
15:7–21 *1:99, 2:208*
15:13 *1:215, 1:377*
15:14–16 *2:59*
15:16 *1:335, 2:80, 2:379,*
    2:381
15:18–20 *2:208*
15:18–21 *1:322, 2:424*
15:19 *1:326, 1:378, 2:201*
16:7 *2:36*
16:41 *1:408*
17 *1:95, 2:156*
17:1 *1:86, 2:177, 2:208,*
    2:330
17:1–8 *1:42*
17:2, 6 *2:208*
17:6 *2:195, 2:208*
17:6, 16 *2:184*
17:7 *2:208*
17:7, 13, 19 *2:238*
17:8 *1:377, 2:300, 2:449,*
    2:495
17:9–14 *2:344*
17:11 *1:24*
17:15–16 *2:272*

17:16 *2:195*
17:17–18 *1:474*
18:3 *2:406*
18:7 *2:339*
18:16 *2:63*
18:16–33 *1:421, 1:422*
18:17, 23–32 *1:345*
18:27 *1:493*
18:33 *2:203*
19 *1:421*
19:26 *1:231*
19:30–38 *2:80*
19:38 *2:117*
20:1–17 *1:151*
20:3 *2:124*
20:4 *2:224*
20:7 *1:305, 2:132*
20:17 *2:467*
21:1–3 *2:202*
21:16 *1:341*
21:19 *1:353*
21:22–32 *2:369*
21:33 *1:173*
22 *1:199, 2:151, 2:351*
22:1 *1:352*
22:2 *1:322, 2:132, 2:330*
22:3 *2:131, 2:132*
22:3, 5, 19 *2:137*
22:4, 8, 13, 14 *2:132*
22:4, 13 *2:132, 2:179*
22:7–8, 14 *2:334*
22:11, 15 *2:36, 2:132, 2:136*
22:12 *1:122, 2:132*
22:13 *2:132, 2:339*
22:15–17 *2:134*
22:16 *1:356, 2:176*
22:16–18 *2:359*
22:17 *1:24, 1:88, 2:132, 2:133, 2:185, 2:194, 2:208*
22:18 *1:167, 1:351, 1:377, 2:96, 2:156, 2:184, 2:187, 2:208, 2:351*
22:19 *2:132*
23 *1:332, 2:126*
23:4 *1:215, 1:377*
23:15 *2:127*
24 *2:272*

24:2 *1:156*
24:4, 10 *2:132*
24:7 *2:449*
24:7, 40 *2:36*
24:8 *2:359, 2:363*
24:8, 41 *2:414*
24:16 *1:353*
24:50 *1:330*
24:54 *2:63*
25:1–6 *2:113*
25:1–18 *2:196*
25:3 *2:201*
25:4 *2:383*
25:8 *2:41, 2:307*
25:8, 17 *2:10*
25:9 *1:332*
25:12, 19 *1:120*
25:16 *2:243*
25:17 *2:41, 2:307*
25:24 *1:353*
25:29–34 *2:40*
26:3 *1:322, 1:364, 2:359*
26:4 *1:88*
26:15 *1:353*
26:24 *2:279*
26:25 *2:348*
27:1–42 *2:40*
27:29 *2:187, 2:196*
27:36, 41–45 *2:36*
27:38 *1:341*
27:40 *2:38*
28:3 *2:177*
28:4 *1:364*
28:13 *1:322*
28:14 *1:88, 2:157*
28:14–15 *1:169*
28:15 *1:194*
28:20–21 *1:171*
28:20–22 *2:354, 2:358*
29 – 30 *1:42, 1:95, 1:96*
29 – 31 *2:304*
29:1 *2:140*
29:13–14 *2:123*
29:28 *1:353*
29:31 – 30:24 *1:86*
29:34 *1:464, 2:463*
30 *2:139*
30:14 *1:28*
30:27 *2:167, 2:270, 2:406*

30:30 *2:140*
30:40 *2:339*
31:8 *2:113*
31:11 *2:36*
31:21 *2:116, 2:172*
31:24 *2:124*
31:24, 29 *1:330*
31:44–53 *2:369*
32 – 33 *2:40*
32:3 *2:35*
32:4 *2:63*
32:6 *2:406*
32:26 *2:134*
32:31 *2:74*
33:4 *2:36*
33:8, 10, 15 *2:406*
33:14 *2:140*
33:18–20 *2:354*
34 *1:93*
34:1–2 *2:492*
34:11 *2:406*
34:22 *2:227*
34:25, 30 *2:266*
35:1–15 *2:354*
35:11 *2:177, 2:184, 2:195, 2:208*
35:14 *2:333*
35:22 *1:93, 1:440*
35:23 *1:87*
35:27–29 *1:332*
35:29 *2:10, 2:41, 2:307*
36:1, 9 *1:120*
36:6–8 *2:424*
36:10–11 *1:326*
36:11, 15, 42 *2:408*
36:12, 16 *2:199*
36:32 *2:116*
36:35 *2:113, 2:114*
36:38, 39 *2:218*
36:43 *2:300*
37 – 50 *1:87, 2:36*
37:2 *1:120, 1:338, 2:318*
37:2, 13–14 *2:317*
37:9 *1:24, 2:194*
37:14 *2:318*
37:18 *2:245*
37:18, 33 *2:317*
37:22 *2:318*
37:28 *1:129, 2:383*

Genesis (*cont.*)
37:29 *2:317*
37:31 *1:348*
37:33 *2:168*
37:34–35 *2:317*
38 *2:270, 2:284, 2:302*
38:2–9 *2:279*
38:4 *1:407*
38:8 *1:454, 2:302*
38:18, 25 *1:445*
38:24 *2:215*
39 *2:319*
39:1 *1:254*
40:4 *1:386*
41, 48 *2:318*
41:8 *2:310*
41:10 *1:386*
41:38 *1:150, 1:283, 2:312*
41:45–52 *1:293*
41:50 *1:407*
41:50–52 *2:270, 2:318*
41:52 *2:318*
42 *1:323*
42:2 *2:317*
42:9, 14 *2:318*
42:17 *1:386*
42:24 *2:359*
42:25 *1:353*
43:1–15 *2:317*
43:11 *1:447*
43:14 *2:177*
43:20 *1:306*
44:4 *1:330*
44:5 *2:167*
44:18 *1:306*
44:18–34 *1:87*
45:2 *1:341*
45:10 *2:295*
45:26 *2:29*
45:27 *2:310*
46 *2:262, 2:268*
46:3 *2:279*
46:6–7 *2:295*
46:8 *1:87*
46:8–28 *2:266*
46:9 *2:268*
46:10 *2:262, 2:269*
46:11 *2:275*
46:12–14 *2:270*

46:12, 17 *2:268*
46:13 *2:262*
46:17 *2:202, 2:262, 2:272*
46:21 *2:272*
46:23 *2:262, 2:272*
46:26 *1:156*
46:27 *2:268*
46:31–34 *2:424*
46:34 *2:404*
47:13–26 *2:422*
47:25, 29 *2:406*
48 *1:96, 2:271, 2:317, 2:490*
48 – 49 *1:95*
48:1 – 49:4 *1:440*
48:3 *2:177*
48:4 *2:300*
48:5 *1:96, 1:406, 2:291*
48:5–9 *1:96*
48:10 *1:96*
48:11–15 *1:96*
48:12–20 *2:270*
48:16 *2:36, 2:303–304*
48:20 *2:319, 2:421*
48:20–21 *2:319*
49 *1:23, 1:24, 1:28, 1:86, 1:87, 1:98, 1:103, 2:168, 2:187, 2:210*
49:1 *2:190, 2:191*
49:1–28 *1:91*
49:3 *1:378, 1:478*
49:3–4 *1:406*
49:4 *1:93*
49:5–6 *1:93*
49:5–7 *2:266*
49:6 *1:32*
49:7 *2:275, 2:463*
49:8 *2:187*
49:8–12 *1:87, 1:95, 2:266, 2:270*
49:9 *1:28, 1:29, 1:32, 1:198, 2:168, 2:169, 2:186–187*
49:9–10 *1:24*
49:9–12 *2:195*
49:10 *1:88, 1:98, 1:198, 2:186, 2:187, 2:195*
49:11 *1:332, 2:359*
49:13, 14 *2:274*

49:14 *1:28*
49:22–26 *2:490*
49:25 *2:177*
49:26 *1:96, 1:159, 2:317, 2:319*
49:29 *2:41*
49:29–33 *1:332*
49:29, 33 *2:10, 2:307*
50:4 *2:406*
50:10 *1:309, 2:43*
50:13 *1:332*
50:20 *1:330*
50:22–26 *2:319, 2:490*
50:23 *2:421–422*
50:24–25 *2:490*
50:25 *2:321*
50:30 *1:353*

Exodus
1 *1:51*
1 – 7 *2:4*
1 – 15 *2:36*
1 – 18 *1:16*
1:2, 5, 17, 18, 20, 22 *1:22*
1:5 *2:268*
1:6 *2:413*
1:6–14 *2:157*
1:7 *1:88, 1:99, 1:353*
1:8–12 *2:158*
1:8–22 *2:245*
1:9 *2:112*
1:12 *2:112*
1:13–14 *1:253*
1:14 *1:214, 1:255*
1:22 – 2:10 *1:43*
2 *1:341*
2:1–10 *2:12, 2:275*
2:3, 5 *1:401*
2:4, 7 *1:291*
2:10 *2:25*
2:11–19 *2:477*
2:12, 13 *2:22*
2:14 *1:407*
2:16 *1:353*
2:16–18 *1:229*
2:16–22 *2:227*
2:17 *2:22, 2:28*
2:21 *2:112*
2:22 *1:124, 1:215*

3 2:109, 2:309–310
3:1 1:229, 1:232
3:1–3 2:311
3:2 1:434, 2:36, 2:136
3:5 1:155
3:7–8, 16–17 1:384
3:8 1:330, 1:338
3:8, 17 1:334, 1:337, 1:343
3:12 1:24, 1:425
3:16 1:85
3:17 1:322, 1:330, 1:338
3:18 1:233, 1:263, 1:374
3:19 2:39
3:19–20 2:70
4 2:134
4:1–5 2:70
4:1–9 1:425
4:1, 10, 13 1:304
4:2–3 2:70
4:2–4, 17, 20 1:444
4:6 1:51, 1:304
4:6–7 1:307
4:8 2:29
4:10, 13 1:305
4:14–16 1:304, 2:19
4:15–16 2:17
4:17 2:229
4:18 1:229
4:20 2:229
4:22 1:443, 2:126
4:22–23 1:43
4:24–26 2:134
4:25 2:112, 2:135
4:27 1:232, 1:462
4:29 1:85, 1:263
5 1:265, 1:385
5 – 10 1:341
5:1 2:63
5:2 2:120
5:3 1:233, 1:346, 1:374
5:6–17 1:265
5:14–17 1:265
6 2:243, 2:275
6:1 2:39
6:3 1:86
6:6 1:128
6:6–8 1:384
6:8 1:338, 1:357
6:9 2:310

6:12 2:309
6:14 1:85, 1:87
6:14–19 1:85
6:14–25 1:406, 1:443
6:15 2:262, 2:269
6:16–19 1:124, 2:275
6:16–27 1:43
6:18 1:332
6:20 1:121, 2:275
6:23 1:86, 1:187
6:23, 25 2:277
6:24 1:427
6:25 1:442, 2:225, 2:243
7:1–2 2:19
7:8–12 1:444
7:8–13 2:70
7:15 2:229
7:15–20 1:444
7:25 1:353
7:89 1:445
8:4, 25, 26, 27, 28, 29 1:374
8:8, 28 2:67
8:21 1:353
8:27 1:233
9:3 1:346
9:14 1:358, 1:438
9:15 1:346
9:15–16 2:70
9:17–23 1:220
9:23 1:444
9:27 2:145
9:27–28 2:67
10:2 2:141
10:5, 15 2:119
10:6 1:353
10:12 1:338
10:13, 19 1:285
10:16–17 2:67, 2:145
10:19 1:401
10:25 1:374
10:29 2:291
11 1:277
11 – 13 1:43, 1:199, 1:238, 1:341
11 – 14 2:442
11:22 1:253
12 1:214, 1:237, 1:287, 2:338–339

12:1–6 2:442–443
12:1–14 2:338
12:1–20 2:338
12:1–28 1:212
12:2 2:9, 2:338
12:3 1:85
12:3–13 1:199
12:4–5 2:334
12:5 1:273
12:6 1:348
12:6, 14 1:212
12:8 1:214
12:11 2:139
12:12 2:443
12:13 1:199, 1:346, 1:438
12:18–20 2:339
12:19 1:213
12:19, 48–49 1:215, 2:467
12:21–27 1:214
12:22 1:486, 1:494
12:27 1:374
12:29 2:57
12:29–30 2:443
12:37 1:103, 1:107
12:38 1:252, 1:291, 1:295
12:41, 51 2:441
12:43–45 1:215
12:46 2:338
13 – 14 1:374
13:1–2, 11–16 1:198, 1:199, 2:390
13:1–16 1:441
13:2 1:198, 1:408, 1:440, 1:443
13:3–10 2:339
13:4 2:9, 2:338
13:5 1:330, 1:334, 1:343
13:8 1:355
13:9 2:39
13:11–12 1:128
13:11–14 2:279
13:12–13 1:124
13:13, 15 1:128
13:14–15 1:128
13:17 1:340, 2:63
13:17 – 19:1 2:440
13:17–22 2:439
13:18 1:401, 2:61
13:19 2:319, 2:321, 2:490

Genesis (*cont.*)
13:20 *1:374, 2:443*
13:20–21 *1:219*
13:20–22 *2:443*
13:21–22 *1:233, 1:237*
13:22 *1:220*
13:23–24 *1:34*
13:26–27 *1:374*
13:29 *2:199–200*
14 *1:101*
14 – 15 *1:341, 1:428, 1:429*
14:1–2, 9 *2:443*
14:2 *2:430*
14:2, 9 *2:218*
14:4, 18, 31 *1:429*
14:7 *1:103*
14:8 *2:443*
14:11 *1:352*
14:11–12 *1:341, 1:416, 1:429, 2:14*
14:12 *1:331*
14:14 *1:366*
14:16 *1:444*
14:16, 21 *1:429*
14:19 *2:36, 2:136*
14:19–20 *1:220*
14:19–20, 24–25 *1:233*
14:21 *1:150, 1:285*
14:21–22, 26–28 *1:285*
14:21–31 *2:443*
14:25 *1:429*
14:28 *1:429*
14:30–31 *1:285*
14:31 *2:62*
15 – 30 *1:22*
15 – 35 *2:444*
15:1 *2:76*
15:1–21 *2:73*
15:3 *1:366, 2:76*
15:4, 22 *1:355, 1:401, 2:61*
15:5 *1:429*
15:5, 10 *1:429*
15:5, 12 *1:386*
15:12 *1:426, 1:429*
15:13 *1:128*
15:13, 15, 16 *1:261*
15:14–18 *2:112*
15:15 *2:165*
15:15–16 *2:87*
15:16–18 *2:76*
15:17 *1:232, 2:179, 2:280*
15:18 *2:83, 2:164, 2:165, 2:240*
15:20 *1:295, 1:296*
15:20–21 *1:291, 2:12*
15:22 *1:233, 2:443*
15:22–23 *2:443*
15:22, 23 *2:8*
15:22, 25 *2:63*
15:22–26 *1:249, 2:12*
15:22–27 *1:2, 2:13, 2:49*
15:23 *1:158, 1:352*
15:23–25 *1:149*
15:24 *1:341, 2:8*
15:25 *1:352, 2:8*
15:26 *2:88*
15:27 *2:179, 2:430, 2:443, 2:444*
16 *1:11, 1:244, 1:249, 1:252, 1:256, 1:286–287, 1:370, 1:385, 2:4*
16:1 *2:444*
16:1–36 *2:13*
16:2, 7, 8, 9, 12 *1:341*
16:3 *1:287, 1:340, 1:352, 1:416, 2:14, 2:15*
16:4 *1:256, 1:286, 1:352*
16:4, 28 *1:361*
16:7, 9 *1:271*
16:10 *1:233, 1:344*
16:12 *1:271*
16:13 *1:287*
16:14 *1:307*
16:16, 32 *2:356*
16:18 *1:287*
16:18, 22, 32, 36 *1:287*
16:19–20 *1:352*
16:20 *1:287, 1:407*
16:20, 27–29 *1:284*
16:23–30 *1:383*
16:27 *1:352*
16:33 *1:287*
16:35 *1:232, 1:385*
16:36 *2:333*
17 *1:327, 2:8, 2:12, 2:13, 2:14, 2:16, 2:17, 2:18–22, 2:20, 2:25–26, 2:68*
17:1 *2:4, 2:8, 2:13, 2:441–442, 2:444*
17:1, 5–6 *2:63*
17:1–6 *1:444*
17:1–7 *2:13, 2:315*
17:2 *1:352, 2:8*
17:2, 5 *2:13*
17:2, 7 *1:352, 2:13*
17:2a *2:4*
17:3 *1:416, 2:14, 2:22*
17:3, 6 *1:341*
17:3, 13 *2:13*
17:3–14 *2:444*
17:3b, 4, 5b *2:13*
17:3c *2:4*
17:4 *1:71, 2:8, 2:23*
17:5 *2:18, 2:229*
17:5–6 *2:16, 2:31*
17:5, 6 *2:20*
17:5, 8, 11 *2:13*
17:5c *2:4*
17:6 *2:4, 2:17, 2:19, 2:22, 2:26, 2:48*
17:6f *2:8*
17:7 *1:344, 2:6, 2:164*
17:7b *2:4*
17:8–16 *1:335, 2:199, 2:200, 2:315*
17:8–17 *2:71*
17:9 *1:327, 1:444*
17:10 *2:20*
17:14 *1:335, 2:74, 2:442*
17:15 *2:68*
17:15–16 *2:269*
17:16 *2:184*
18 *1:209, 1:229, 1:233, 1:244*
18 – Num. 10 *1:63*
18:1–2, 5–6, 12 *1:229*
18:2 *2:112*
18:5 *1:232*
18:13–27 *1:263*
18:27 *1:230*
18.25 *1:282, 2:222*
18.26 *2:222*
19 *1:5, 1:199, 1:203, 1:211*
19 – 20 *1:38*
19 – 24 *1:14, 1:16, 1:38, 1:269, 1:341, 2:48*

19 – 40 *1:46, 2:444*
19 – Num. 6 *1:83, 1:175*
19 – Num. 10 *1:85, 1:232, 1:234, 1:239*
19, 24, 33 *1:278*
19:1 *1:97, 1:227, 2:340*
19:1–2 *2:444*
19:1, 2 *1:83*
19:4 *1:32, 2:218*
19:5 *1:175, 1.392*
19:5–6 *1:15, 1:18, 1:55, 1:57, 1:95, 1:159, 1:165, 1:365, 2:156*
19:5, 16, 19 *1:190*
19:6 *1:39, 1:41, 1:48, 1:60, 1:146, 1:225, 1:374, 1:390, 1:391, 1:396, 1:410, 2:328*
19:8 *2:369*
19:9 *1:220, 1:267*
19:9–20 *1:221*
19:10 *1:271*
19:11 *1:269*
19:12 *2:467*
19:13 *1:223*
19:14–15 *1:295*
19:15 *1:233*
19:16 *2:441*
19:16, 19 *1:223*
19:19 *1:274*
19:20 *1:273*
19:22 *1:408*
20:1–6 *2:255, 2:451*
20:1–11 *2:347*
20:2 *1:99, 1:129, 1:393*
20:3 *1:394, 2:250, 2:251*
20:4 *1:91*
20:5 *1:91, 1:150, 2:37, 2:217, 2:236*
20:5–6 *1:347, 1:348*
20:7 *1:173, 2:30, 2:47, 2:358, 2:415*
20:7, 24 *1:355*
20:8–11 *1:383, 1:384, 2:335*
20:11 *1:234, 1:386*
20:13 *2:476*
20:14 *1:47, 1:152*
20:18 *1:190, 1:223*

20:19 *1:302*
20:20 *1:352*
20:22–24 *2:348*
20:24 *1:172, 1:173*
21:8 *1:128*
21:12–14 *2:463*
21:12–15 *2:467, 2:468*
21:13 *2:465*
21:13–14 *2:439*
21:14 *2:85*
21:30 *1:128*
22:1 *2:475*
22:4 *1:416*
22:10 *2:57*
22:11 *2:359*
22:22–25 *2:37*
22:28–29 *1:441*
22:29 *1:440*
22:29–30 *1:199*
23:2 *2:136*
23:10–11 *1:384*
23:14 *2:140*
23:14–19 *1:441*
23:15 *2:9, 2:338*
23:16 *1:199, 2:339, 2:343*
23:17 *1:166*
23:19 *1:378, 2:279*
23:20 *2:37*
23:20, 23 *2:136*
23:20–23, 29–31 *1:337*
23:21–22 *1:190*
23:24 *2:451*
23:28 *2:255*
23:29–30 *1:101*
23:29–31 *2:450*
23:31 *2:116*
23:33 *2:452*
24 *1:244, 1:277*
24:4 *1:21, 2:442*
24:4–6 *2:334*
24:4, 7 *1:71, 1:72*
24:5 *1:373, 1:440, 2:334*
24:5–8 *2:330*
24:6, 8 *1:188*
24:7 *2:369*
24:8–11 *1:287*
24:9–18 *1:269*
24:10 *1:38, 1:39, 1:221*
24:11 *1:277, 2:177*

24:13 *1:232, 2:314*
24:15 *1:220*
24:15–18 *1:220, 1:221*
24:16 *1:218*
24:17 *1:189, 1:190, 1:344, 2:334*
25 – 31 *1:342*
25 – 40 *1:15, 1:16*
25 – 31, 35 – 40 *1:5*
25:2 *2:393*
25:4 *1:39, 1:486*
25:5 *2:214*
25:6 *1:193*
25:8 *1:15, 1:46, 1:83, 1:97, 1:98, 1:146, 1:147, 1:174, 2:436, 2:478, 2:484*
25:9 *1:25, 1:193*
25:10, 13 *2:214*
25:10–40 *1:126*
25:11, 17, 24 *1:170*
25:15 *1:132*
25:16–22 *1:89*
25:17–20 *1:36*
25:17–22 *1:34, 1:191*
25:20 *1:39, 1:388*
25:21 *1:190*
25:21–22 *1:34*
25:22 *1:83, 1:185, 1:190, 1:401, 1:445*
25:23, 28 *2:214*
25:31, 33, 34 *1:447*
25:31–40 *1:192, 1:193*
25:33 *1:447*
25:33–34 *1:192*
25:33, 34 *1:447*
25:40 *1:193*
26 *1:20*
26:1 *1:34, 1:35, 1:221*
26:1, 4 *1:390*
26:1, 4, 31, 36 *1:39*
26:1–14 *1:126*
26:14 *1:221*
26:15, 26 *2:214*
26:15–37 *1:127*
26:30 *1:377*
26:31 *1:34, 1:221, 1:390*
26:31–35 *1:126*
26:32, 37 *2:214*

Genesis (*cont.*)
26:33 1:114, 1:198, 1:421
26:33–34 1:89
26:36-37 1:468
27:1, 6 2:214
27:1–7 1:132
27:1–8 1:187
27:2 1:434
27:9–19 1:127
27:16 1:39, 1:390
27:20 2:333
27:20–21 1:193
28 1:20, 1:155, 2:43
28 – 29 1:451
28:1 1:465
28:3 2:310
28:5, 6, 8 15 1:390
28:5–14 1:22
28:8, 15, 28, 31, 33 1:39
28:12, 29 1:22
28:15–30 1:28, 2:314
28:17 1:23
28:17–20 1:21
28:21 1:91
28:21, 29 1:21–22
28:28, 37 1:390
28:29, 35 1:114
28:30 2:273
28:31 1:390
28:36 1:389, 1:393, 1:447
28:36–37 1:392
28:36–38 1:389
28:37 1:393
28:37–38 1:419
28:38 2:471
28:41 1:122
28:43 1:464
29 1:449
29:4 1:420
29:6 1:159
29:6–7 1:55
29:7, 21 1:200
29:8 2:43
29:9 2:238
29:11 1:348
29:14 1:164
29:20 1:200
29:21 1:122
29:27–28 1:473

29:28 1:373
29:36–46 1:189
29:38–42 1:194
29:38–46 2:151, 2:329, 2:330, 2:334
29:40–41 1:375
29:42 1:190, 1:401
29:42–43 1:185, 1:307
29:42, 45 2:330
29:44 1:411
29:44–46 1:449–450
29:45 1:46, 1:98, 1:147, 1:174, 1:411, 1:445
29:45–46 1:15, 1:19, 1:97, 1:98, 1:146, 1:490, 2:436, 2:478, 2:484
29:46 1:83, 1:84, 2:478
30 2:394
30:1, 5 2:214
30:6, 36 1:401, 1:445
30:7–8 1:194
30:11–16 2:393, 2:394
30:12 2:391
30:12–16 2:393
30:13 1:129, 2:391
30:14, 16 2:394
30:15 2:393
30:17–21 1:132
30:17–21, 29 1:155
30:18 1:132
30:18–21 1:155
30:20 1:132, 1:464
30:28 1:189, 2:331
30:30 1:170
31 1:34, 2:241
31:1–6 1:283
31:3 1:150, 1:353, 2:310, 2:312
31:9 1:189, 2:331
31:12–13 2:335
31:12–17 1:384, 1.392
31:12–18 1:172
31:13 1:396, 2:238, 2:335
31:13–17 1:383
31:13, 17 1:386, 1:435
31:14 1:133, 1:384, 2:241
31:14–15 2:467
31:14–17 2:335

31:16 2:238
31:18 1:89
31:49 2:83
32 1:55, 1:56, 1:121, 1:150, 1:277, 1:352, 2:42, 2:228, 2:235, 2:242, 2:248, 2:397
32 – 33 1:244, 1:277
32 – 34 1:342, 1:346, 1:348–349, 2:392
32:1, 4 2:249
32:1–5 2:249
32:1–10 2:241
32:6 2:249
32:7, 10 2:409
32:9–10 1:261
32:9–14 1:421
32:10 1:346, 2:249
32:10–14 1:346
32:11 1:385, 2:39
32:11–13 1:348
32:12 1:348
32:12, 30 2:239
32:13 1:261
32:15 1:89
32:19 1:418
32:20 2:49
32:21–24 2:223
32:21–35 1:290
32:22 1:305
32:25–29 1:90, 1:124, 1:204, 1:440, 1:465, 2:59, 2:242
32:25–35 1:107
32:26–29 1:441, 1:442, 2:241
32:27 2:222, 2:249
32:28 2:233
32:29 2:249
32:30 1:260, 2:23, 2:241, 2:249, 2:342
32:30–35 2:242
32:32 1:260, 1:278, 1:348
32:34 2:37, 2:136
32:35 2:242, 2:249
33 1:8–9
33:1 1:323
33:1–6 1:9
33:2 2:37

33:3 *1:8, 1:302, 1:330,*
  1:334, 1:337, 1:343
33:5 *2:23*
33:7–11 *1:9, 1:192, 1:233,*
  1:277, 1:298
33:8 *1:278*
33:8, 10 *1:278*
33:9 *1:278*
33:9a *1:278*
33:9b *1:278*
33:11 *1:278, 1:301, 1:354,*
  2:314
33:12 *1:230*
33:12, 13, 16, 17 *2:406*
33:12–23 *1:9, 1:167, 2:242*
33:13 *1:261*
33:14, 17 *1:9*
33:15 *1:8, 1:167*
33:16 *1:8, 1:18*
33:18 *1:347, 2:31*
33:18–23 *1:301, 1:366*
33:19 *1:167*
33:19–23 *1:348*
33:20 *1:220*
33:20–23 *1:277*
34 *1:6, 2:250*
34 – 35 *1:7*
34:1–9 *2:242*
34:5 *1:273, 1:274*
34:5–7 *1:276*
34:5–8 *1:348*
34:6 *1:276, 1:349, 2:28,*
  2:110, 2:219
34:6–7 *1:320, 1:347, 1:348*
34:6–8 *1:274*
34:9 *2:363, 2:406*
34:10–27 *1:441*
34:10–29 *1:441*
34:11, 16 *1:314*
34:13–14 *2:451*
34:14 *1:54–55, 1:150,*
  2:236, 2:250, 2:251,
  2:380
34:15 *1:220, 2:130*
34:15–16 *1.391, 2:231,*
  2:250, 2:397
34:16 *1:150*
34:17 *2:451*
34:18 *2:9*
34:20 *1:128*
34:22 *2:339, 2:343*
34:24 *2:450*
34:26 *1:378, 2:279*
34:27 *1:71*
34:27–28 *1:72, 1:89*
34:27–35 *1:167*
34:28 *2:442*
34:29–35 *1:170*
34:31–32 *2:356*
34:35 *2:313*
35 *1:6, 2:392*
35 – 36 *1:375*
35 – 39 *2:394*
35 – 40 *1:26, 1:27, 1:342,*
  2:393
35:1–3 *1:384, 2:335*
35:2 *1:384*
35:2–3 *1:383*
35:3 *1:373, 1:384*
35:4 *2:356*
35:5–9 *1:366*
35:5, 21, 24 *2:393*
35:7, 24 *2:214*
35:16 *1:189, 2:331*
35:21 *2:310*
35:22 *2:393*
35:31 *1:150, 1:353, 2:310*
36 – 38 *1:6*
36:2–7 *1:375*
36:5 *2:394*
36:8, 11 *1:390*
36:8, 36 *1:34*
36:20, 31 *2:214*
36:35 *1:34*
36:36 *2:214*
36:37 *1:390*
37:1, 4 *2:214*
37:7–9 *1:34, 1:36*
37:9 *1:39, 1:388*
37:10, 15 *2:214*
37:17, 19, 20 *1:447*
37:19–20 *1:192*
37:19, 20 *1:447*
37:25, 28 *2:214*
38:1 *1:189, 2:331*
38:1, 6 *2:214*
38:2 *1:434*
38:8 *1:30, 1:132*
38:18 *1:468*
38:22 *1:434*
39 *1:20*
39:1 *1:486*
39:1, 5, 7, 21, 26, 29, 31
  2:393
39:1, 5, 22, 24, 29, 31
  1:39
39:2, 3, 5, 8 *1:390*
39:8–14 *1:21, 1:28*
39:14 *1:91*
39:21, 31 *1:390*
39:22 *1:390*
39:30 *1:55, 1:159, 1:305,*
  1:389, 1:393
39:30–31 *1:389*
39:31 *1:393*
39:32 *1:401*
39:32, 42, 43 *2:393*
39:40 *1:447*
39:42 *1:72*
40 *1:4, 1:7, 1:181, 1:370*
40:1 *1:227*
40:2 *1:182*
40:2, 17 *1:83*
40:3, 20 *1:89*
40:6, 10, 29 *1:189, 2:331*
40:12–15 *1:4*
40:15 *2:238*
40:16, 22 *2:393*
40:17 *1:5*
40:17, 34–38 *1:216*
40:19, 21, 23, 25, 27, 29,
  31 *2:393*
40:33–34 *1:8*
40:34 *1:6, 1:8, 1:186,*
  1:218, 1:220
40:34–35 *1:7, 1:186,*
  1:202, 1:210, 1:353
40:34–38 *1:6–7, 1:7,*
  1:209, 1:210, 1:216
40:35 *1:6, 1:18*
40:36 *1:8, 1:220*
40:36–37 *1:218*
40:36–38 *1:7, 1:33, 1:122,*
  1:210, 1:216, 1:217,
  1:227, 1:237, 2:442,
  2:443, 2:480
40:38 *1:216, 1:234*

Leviticus

1–3 1:370, 2:336, 2:346
1–5 1:370, 2:346, 2:347
1–10 1:5, 1:7
1–16 1:369
1–26 1:7
1:1 1:182
1:1–3:17 1:376
1:1–6:7 2:327
1:1–17 2:330
1:2 1:90
1:3 2:223, 2:224
1:5 1:483
1:6 1:485
1:53 1:452
2 1:164
2:1–2 1:373
2:2 1:187
2:12 1:378
2:13 1:474
3 1:287
3:1, 6 1:373
3:2 1:483
3:4 1:452
4 1:380, 2:336–337
4–5 1:370, 2:336
4:1–12 1:481
4:1–35 1:379
4:2 1:380
4:2, 22, 27 2:476
4:3, 5, 16 1:455
4:4–5 1:483
4:4, 15, 24 1:483
4:6, 17, 25 1:483
4:7, 10, 18, 25, 30, 34 1:189, 2:331
4:11–12, 21 1:485
4:12, 21 1:164, 1:485
4:13–21 1:481
4:14 1:380
4:15–20 1:452
4:20, 26, 31, 35 1:162, 2:363
4:22 1:198
4:22–35 1:481
4:27–31 2:476
4:31 1:375
5:1 1:379, 1:381
5:1, 17 1:156
5:2 1:146
5:4 2:364, 2:368, 2:370
5:4–10 2:363
5:4–13 2:356
5:6 1:162
5:7 1:162
5:10, 13, 16, 18 1:162, 2:363
5:11 1:153
5:11–31 1:146
5:15 2:476
6–7 1:469
6:1–7 1:147, 1:148, 1:379, 1:381, 2:359
6:2–3 1:148
6:6–7 1:148
6:7 2:363
6:8–23 1:376
6:9, 19 1:471
6:15 1:373
6:18 1:470
6:22 1:455
6:30 1:485
7:6 1:471
7:11–27 1:376
7:16 1:374, 2:358
7:16–17 2:354
7:18 1:156
7:18, 29, 32, 34 1:373
7:20–21 1:155, 1:213
7:30–36 1:469
7:34 1:148, 1:199, 1:476
7:38 1:83
8 1:121, 1:200, 1:449
8–9 1:4, 1:188
8–10 1:451
8:1 1:182
8:2, 14 1:164
8:3 1:421
8:3–4 2:241
8:4, 9, 13, 17, 21, 29, 36 1:122
8:5 2:356
8:6 1:200
8:7–9 2:43
8:8 2:314
8:9 1:159, 1:389, 1:447
8:10 2:312
8:13 1:200
8:17 1:485
8:19 1:452
8:22, 28, 29, 31, 33 1:353
8:23 1:200
8:27 1:200
8:30 1:122, 1:200
8:33–35 1:5
8:79 2:43
9 1:202, 1:370
9–10 1:413
9:4–8, 22–24 1:187
9:4, 22–24 1:189
9:6 2:356
9:7, 10 1:122
9:11 1:485
9:16–17, 22 2:336
9:16–18, 22 1:376
9:17 2:334
9:22 1:90, 1:171
9:22–23 1:46, 1:166, 1:170
9:23 1:413
9:24 1:190, 1:216, 1:413
10:1 1:122, 1:409, 1:413
10:1–3 1:122, 1:127, 1:250, 1:413, 1:428, 1:446, 2:279
10:1–5 1:462
10:2 1:113, 1:216, 1:413
10:3 1:413, 1:430, 2:31
10:4–5 1:413
10:6 1:55, 1:153
10:6, 16 1:413
10:8 1:413
10:8–9 1:160
10:8–11 1:122, 1:462, 1:497
10:9 1:55, 1:57, 1:464
10:10 1:150, 1:198, 1:421, 1:439
10:14 1:373, 1:413
10:14–15 1:473
10:16 1:485
10:17 2:471
11 1:255, 1:489
11–15 1:52, 1:146, 1:150, 1:213, 1:490
11–16 1:7, 1:115, 1:462
11:22 1:338
11:24–40 1:146

11:44 *1:396*
11:47 *1:198*
12:2, 5 *1:488*
12:8 *1:162*
13 *1:294*
13 – 14 *1:303*
13:2 *1:51*
13:4, 5, 21, 26, 31, 33, 50, 54 *1:308*
13:4, 26 *1:308*
13:5 *1:486, 1:489*
13:9–17 *1:308*
13:40, 42, 43, 55 *1:406*
13:45 *1:153*
13:46 *1:49, 1:306, 1:486*
13:55 *2:119*
14:3 *1:486*
14:4 *1:486*
14:4, 6, 49, 51, 52 *1:486, 1:494*
14:5 *1:486*
14:7 *1:486*
14:8 *1:200, 1:486*
14:9 *1:308, 1:489*
14:10 *2:344*
14:12 *1:52*
14:12–14, 24–25 *1:52*
14:14, 17, 25, 28 *1:200*
14:30–31 *1:162*
14:33 *1:488*
14:34 *2:300*
14:38 *1:308*
14:52 *2:180*
15 *1:49, 1:52, 1:146*
15:5, 6, 7, 8, 10, 16, 17, 18 *1:487*
15:13 *1:489*
15:16, 17, 18, 32 *1:52*
15:19–33 *1:488*
15:31 *1:52, 1:159*
15:39 *1:488*
16 *1:5, 1:121, 1:191, 1:307, 1:437, 1:438, 1:446, 2:337, 2:342*
16:1–2 *1:446*
16:2 *1:36, 1:445, 2:342*
16:2, 13 *1:220*
16:2, 14 *1:191*
16:5 *2:342*

16:8–10 *2:273, 2:451*
16:11 *1:481*
16:12 *1:437*
16:27 *1:485*
16:28 *1:485*
16:29 *2:342*
16:30 *1:485, 2:472*
16:31 *2:339*
16:32 *2:474*
17 *1:272*
17 – 25 *1:462*
17 – 27 *1:7, 1:369*
17:2 *2:356*
17:3 *1:348*
17:6, 11–14 *1:188*
17:7 *1.391*
17:10 *1:171, 2:172*
17:11 *1:484, 2:336, 2:475*
17:16 *1:156*
18:20 *1:152*
18:21–23 *1:472*
18:24 *2:450*
18:24–30 *2:240, 2:451*
18:25 *1:339*
18:25–28 *2:477*
18:28 *2:240*
19 *1:148*
19:2 *1:396, 1:410*
19:4 *2:451*
19:12 *2:358*
19:18 *1:148*
19:19 *1:393*
19:20 *1:128*
19:22 *2:363*
19:23–25 *2:279*
19:26 *2:151, 2:167*
19:28 *1:141*
19:29 *1:353, 2:215*
19:31 *2:218*
19:34 *1:216*
20:1–6 *1:472*
20:1–8 *2:216*
20:2, 9, 10, 11 *2:467*
20:3–5 *1:171*
20:3, 6 *2:172*
20:5–6 *1.391*
20:6, 27 *2:218*
20:9–16 *2:475*
20:10 *1:47, 1:152*

20:17 *1:215*
20:23 *2:450*
20:24 *1:330, 1:334, 1:337, 1:343*
20:24, 26 *1:421*
20:25 *1:198, 1:421*
20:26 *1:396, 2:218*
21 *2:471*
21:1 *1:141*
21:1–2 *1:161*
21:1–4, 10 *1:498*
21:1–4, 10–12 *1:213*
21:1–4, 11 *1:498*
21:1, 11 *1:146*
21:5 *1:406*
21:5, 10 *1:55*
21:6 *1:55*
21:9 *2:215*
21:10 *1:153*
21:10–12 *2:228, 2:470–471*
21:11 *1:55, 1:161, 1:488*
21:12 *1:55, 1:159*
21:23 *1:464*
22:1–2 *2:30*
22:2 *1:159*
22:4–7 *1:498*
22:17–33 *2:354*
22:18 *1:374*
22:18, 21, 23 *2:358*
22:18–23 *2:347*
22:20–25 *1:482*
22:21 *1:141, 1:374*
22:28 *1:348*
22:31–32 *2:30*
22:47 *1:146*
23 *1:193, 1:370, 1:375, 2:327, 2:329, 2:336*
23:2, 10, 24, 34, 44 *2:346*
23:3 *2:338, 2:342*
23:3, 21, 31 *1:373*
23:3, 28 *2:339*
23:4–8 *1:213, 2:338*
23:5 *1:212, 2:335*
23:8 *2:339*
23:9 *2:327*
23:9–14 *1:199*
23:9–14, 15–22 *2:339*
23:10 *1:378, 2:279*

Leviticus (*cont.*)
23:10, 11, 20 *2:346*
23:12–14, 18 *1:376*
23:13, 18 *2:346*
23:14 *2:338*
23:15 *2:9*
23:15–16 *2:339*
23:17 *2:339*
23:17–21 *2:346*
23:18 *2:340*
23:20 *1:58*
23:24 *1:224, 2:341*
23:27 *2:342*
23:33–43 *2:346*
23:34 *2:343*
23:36 *2:343*
23:38 *2:347, 2:354, 2:358*
23:39–43 *2:343*
24 *1:473*
24:1–4 *1:193*
24:1–9 *1:193*
24:2 *1:193, 2:333*
24:2–4 *1:194*
24:5–8 *2:349*
24:5–9 *1:373*
24:8 *2:238*
24:10 *1:252*
24:10–16 *2:286*
24:10–23 *1:173, 1:215,
  1:355, 1:370, 1:385,
  2:287*
24:11 *1:386*
24:14 *1:197*
24:15–16 *1:385*
24:17 *2:467*
25 *1:193, 2:300*
25:1–7, 18–22 *1:384*
25:5, 11 *1:160*
25:9 *2:489*
25:10 *2:301–302, 2:473,
  2:489*
25:10, 13, 27, 28, 41
  2:473, 2:489
25:13 *2:489*
25:13–17, 23–31 *2:490*
25:13–17, 23–34 *2:489*
25:13–55 *2:488*
25:23 *2:299, 2:300, 2:467*
25:23–24, 41 *2:291*

25:23–34 *2:302*
25:25, 47–52 *1:141*
25:29 *1:208*
25:32–34 *2:490*
25:48–49 *2:293*
26 *1:158*
26:1 *2:451*
26:6 *2:186*
26:10–12 *2:280*
26:12 *1:191, 1:349*
26:14–39 *2:97*
26:17 *2:172*
26:30 *2:451*
26:34–35, 43 *1:383*
26:40 *1:151*
26:42 *2:237*
27 *2:356*
27:1–8 *1:129*
27:1–13 *2:357*
27:1–34 *2:354*
27:2 *1:141*
27:6 *1:473*
27:10, 13 *1:361*
27:21, 28 *1:469*
27:25 *1:129*
27:27 *1:473*
27:28 *1:472*
27:28–29 *2:58*
27:28–33 *2:279*
27:29 *1:128*
27:30–33 *1:479*
27:34 *1:72*

Numbers
1 *1:25, 1:42, 1:62, 1:92,
  1:95, 1:100–108, 1:182*
1–2 *1:27, 1:42, 1:49,
  1:75–108, 1:97, 1:98,
  1:99, 1:115, 1:122,
  1:124, 1:126, 1:133,
  1:134, 1:173, 1:181,
  1:182, 1:201, 1:218,
  1:224, 1:356, 1:365,
  1:452, 2:265, 2:360,
  2:396, 2:455, 2:460,
  2:479*
1–2, 4 *1:310*
1–3 *1:40*
1–4 *1:42, 1:44, 1:46,*

  *1:87, 1:90, 1:137, 1:228,
  1:444, 1:445, 1:452,
  2:174, 2:264, 2:265,
  2:277, 2:278, 2:384,
  2:388, 2:395, 2:453,
  2:462*
1–4, 26 *2:303, 2:376*
1–6 *1:7, 1:14, 1:18, 1:26,
  1:27, 1:40, 1:46, 1:59,
  1:65, 1:66, 1:84, 1:98,
  1:136, 1:158, 1:166,
  1:168, 1:172, 1:175,
  1:183, 1:185, 1:194,
  1:216, 1:232, 1:235,
  1:411, 1:422, 1:425,
  2:121, 2:150, 2:231*
1–8 *1:7, 1:67, 1:209*
1–9 *1:5*
1–10 *1:9, 1:13, 1:14,
  1:15, 1:17, 1:34, 1:40,
  1:41, 1:61, 1:63, 1:85,
  1:91, 1:201, 1:234,
  1:235, 1:238, 1:239,
  1:250, 1:303, 1:342,
  1:462, 1:496, 2:174,
  2:264, 2:277, 2:379,
  2:380, 2:384, 2:390,
  2:395*
1–10:34 *1:234*
1–16 *1:370*
1–18 *1:499*
1–19 *1:68, 1:80*
1–25 *1:61*
1, 26 *1:96, 1:326, 2:234,
  2:246, 2:421*
1:1 *1:18, 1:62, 1:64, 1:80,
  1:98, 1:124, 1:182,
  1:237, 1:297, 2:174,
  2:247*
1:1–2:34 *1:65*
1:1–10:34 *1:63*
1:1–10:36 *1:64*
1:1–2 *1:82, 1:227*
1:1–4 *1:80, 1:81*
1:1–5 *2:296*
1:1, 10, 20 *1:363*
1:1–16 *1:81*
1:1–19 *1:80, 1:444*
1:1, 19 *1:83, 2:265*

Index of Scripture references and ancient sources

1:1–44 *1:10, 2:456*
1:1–46 *1:80, 1:81*
1:1–54 *1:83–91*
1:2 *1:22, 1:106, 1:114, 2:220, 2:388*
1:2–3 *1:80, 1:82, 2:264*
1:2–4 *1:30*
1:2, 18, 20, 22, 24, 26, 28, 30, 32, 34, 36, 38, 40, 42 *2:157–158*
1:3 *1:124*
1:3–9 *1:82*
1:3, 10, 18, 25 *1:82*
1:3, 20 *1:106*
1:3, 20, 22 *1:26*
1:3, 45 *1:43*
1:4 *1:80*
1:4, 11, 19, 26 *1:82*
1:4, 16 *1:10*
1:5 *1:406, 2:174, 2:458, 2:483*
1:5, 6, 10 *2:244*
1:5, 12, 20, 27 *1:82*
1:5–15 *1:10, 1:29, 1:62, 1:81, 1:96, 1:326*
1:5–16 *1:80, 1:81, 1:83, 1:86–87, 1:229, 1:324, 1:326*
1:5b–9 *1:80*
1:6, 13, 21, 28 *1:82*
1:7, 14, 22, 29 *1:82*
1:8, 15, 23, 30 *1:82*
1:9, 16, 24, 31 *1:82*
1:10 *1:64, 1:65, 1:66, 1:67, 1:80, 2:317*
1:10–16 *1:82*
1:10, 32 *2:317*
1:11 *2:411*
1:11–15 *1:80*
1:12 *1:63*
1:14 *1:80, 1:181, 1:208*
1:15–16 *1:87*
1:16 *1:235, 1:408, 2:380*
1:17 *1:81, 1:82, 1:83, 1:266, 2:456*
1:17–19 *1:81*
1:17, 44 *2:265*
1:18 *1:64, 1:81, 1:82, 1:106*
1:18–24 *1:82*
1:19 *1:81, 1:91, 2:22, 2:381, 2:389*
1:19, 54 *1:91*
1:20 *1:28, 1:81, 1:87*
1:20, 22, 24 *1:87*
1:20–42 *1:81*
1:20–43 *1:62, 1:81, 1:95*
1:20–46 *1:80, 1:81*
1:20–54 *1:83*
1:21 *1:444*
1:21, 23, 25, 27 *1:104*
1:23 *2:234*
1:25–31 *1:82*
1:26–27 *2:451*
1:32–33 *1:82, 2:270*
1:32–36 *2:266*
1:34 *1:82*
1:36, 37 *1:79*
1:44–46 *1:81*
1:44, 46 *2:390*
1:46 *1:100*
1:47 *1:115*
1:47–48 *1:81*
1:47, 49 *2:274*
1:47–50 *1:135*
1:47–51, 53 *1:97*
1:47–53 *1:80, 1:81, 1:356, 2:274*
1:47–54 *1:115, 1:198*
1:48–53 *1:123*
1:50 *1:85, 1:150, 1:217*
1:50–53 *1:134, 1:496*
1:50, 53 *1:273, 1:424, 2:274*
1:51 *1:84, 1:123, 1:208, 1:434, 1:463, 2:228, 2:230, 2:233*
1:51–53 *1:277, 2:73*
1:52 *1:62, 1:79*
1:53 *1:82, 1:94, 1:218, 1:437, 1:443, 1:463, 1:466, 2:242, 2:384*
1:54 *1:81*
2 *1:10, 1:20, 1:42, 1:62, 1:65, 1:84–85, 1:91–2, 1:181, 1:182, 1:228, 1:229, 1:250, 2:158, 2:165, 2:456*
2–3 *1:443*
2–31 *1:92–94*
2, 3 *1:92*
2, 7 *1:96*
2, 7, 10 *1:326*
2:1 *1:91*
2:1–34 *1:91–99*
2:1–2, 17, 34 *2:73*
2:1–3 *2:84*
2:1–9 *2:168*
2:1–31 *1:62, 1:83*
2:1–34 *1:80, 1:83*
2:1–31 *1:62*
2:2 *1:134, 1:228, 1:273, 1:424, 2:69, 2:174*
2:2, 10, 17, 18, 25, 31, 34 *1:62*
2:3 *1:10, 1:127, 1:170, 1:180, 1:354, 1:407, 2:73, 2:454*
2:3–9 *1:95*
2:3, 9 *1:94*
2:3, 12, 27 *1:93*
2:3–29 *1:86*
2:3–31 *1:91, 1:95*
2:5, 12, 20, 27 *1:29*
2:9 *1:84*
2:9, 16, 24, 31 *2:390*
2:10 *1:407*
2:10, 12, 20 *2:244*
2:10–16 *2:405*
2:14 *1:208*
2:14, 22, 29 *1:80*
2:16 *1:84*
2:17 *1:31, 1:83, 1:134, 1:228, 1:233*
2:17, 33 *1:97*
2:21–25 *2:167*
2:33 *1:115, 2:22, 2:274, 2:381, 2:389*
2:34 *1:91*
3 *1:43, 1:44, 1:84, 1:94, 1:136, 1:194, 1:406, 1:440, 2:276, 2:380, 2:418*
3–4 *1:49, 1:66, 1:89, 1:97, **1:109–137**, 1:122, 1:124, 1:125, 1:134, 1:173, 1:181, 1:201, 1:228,*

Numbers (*cont.*)
  1:406, 1:452, 1:467,
  2:360, 2:455, 2:461,
  2:464, 2:479, 2:484
3–4, 8 1:449
3–7 1:224–225
3, 4 1:135
3:1 1:120–122
3:1–4:49 1:65
3:1–4 1:31, 1:43, 1:86,
  1:116, 1:117, 1:120, 1:121,
  1:122, 1:136, 1:429, 2:6,
  2:243, 2:257, 2:276
3:1–4, 6 1:43
3:1–13 1:117
3:1–51 1:120–130
3:2 1:85
3:2–4 1:116, 1:117, 1:121,
  1:122–123
3:3 1:85, 1:353
3:4 1:121, 1:155, 1:413,
  1:428, 1:435, 2:263,
  2:276
3:4, 14 1:83
3:5–6 1:117
3:5–9 1:135, 1:465
3:5, 9 1:117
3:5–10 1:116, 1:117,
  1:123, 1:435, 1:451
3:5–10, 11–13, 14–39,
  40–51 1:115
3:5–13 1:121, 1:123–124,
  1:441
3:5–16 1:43
3:5–51 1:198
3:6, 9 1:129
3:7 1:117, 1:123
3:7–8 1:90
3:7, 8, 25, 28, 31, 32, 38
  1:218
3:8 1:117, 1:123
3:8, 31, 36 1:154
3:9 1:117
3:9, 12 1:467
3:9–13 1:198
3:10 1:117, 1:123
3:10–15, 38 1:496
3:10, 38 1:434, 1:464,
  2:228, 2:230, 2:233
3:11–13 1:113, 1:116,
  1:117, 1:124, 1:467
3:11–13, 40–51 1:50, 1:84,
  1:135
3:11–15 1:127
3:12 1:114, 1:124, 1:467
3:12–13 1:440
3:12, 41, 45 1:266
3:12ab 1:118
3:12c 1:118
3:13 1:288, 1:346, 2:244
3:13–15 1:327
3:13abc 1:118
3:13d 1:118
3:14–16 1:124
3:14–39 1:19, 1:116,
  1:117, 2:275
3:14–51 1:117, 1:121
3:16 1:114, 1:116
3:16–17 1:122
3:16–18 1:127
3:16, 39, 51 1:228
3:17 1:30, 1:113, 1:125
3:17–20 1:116, 1:117,
  1:118, 2:275
3:17–30 1:124–125
3:19 1:332
3:19, 27 1:30
3:21–26 1:116,
  1:125–126
3:21–37 1:116, 1:117,
  1:118, 1:123
3:22 1:114
3:22, 28, 34, 40, 43 2:158
3:23 2:276
3:23, 29, 35, 38 1:134
3:25 1:127
3:25, 31, 36 1:123
3:26, 27 1:290
3:26, 31, 36 1:123
3:27–32 1:116,
  1:126–127
3:28 1:114, 1:126
3:28, 31, 32, 47, 50 1:114
3:28, 32, 38 2:389
3:29 1:125, 1:407, 2:276
3:29–30 1:10
3:30 1:125, 1:406, 1:443
3:32 1:30, 1:119, 1:122,
  1:126, 1:127, 1:434,
  1:466
3:32, 38 2:228
3:33–37 1:127
3:35 2:244, 2:276
3:38 1:116, 1:135, 1:277,
  1:483, 2:73, 2:228
3:38–39 1:135
3:39 1:104, 1:114, 1:116,
  2:276
3:40 1:118, 1:128
3:40–43 1:116
3:40–43, 44–51 1:441
3:40–51 1:117
3:41 1:118, 1:124, 1:128
3:42–43 1:116, 1:118
3:42, 51 2:22, 2:389
3:43 1:100
3:44–45 1:118, 1:128
3:44–51 1:113, 1:128–130,
  1:135
3:46–47a 1:118
3:47 1:129, 1:473
3:47, 49, 50 1:266
3:47b 1:118
3:48 1:118
3:48, 51 1:129
3:49 1:118
3:49–51 1:116
3:50 1:118
3:51 1:117, 1:118, 2:381
4 1:43, 1:58, 1:85–86,
  1:92, 1:126, 1:136,
  1:182, 1:186, 1:229
4:1 1:114, 1:304
4:1–3 1:130–131, 1:201
4:1–16 1:118, 1:119
4:1–20 1:233, 1:464, 1:496
4:1–29 1:130–134
4:1–33 1:118–119
4:1–49 1:115, 1:198
4:2, 22 1:84, 2:388
4:3 1:124, 1:201
4:3, 23, 30 1:200
4:3, 23, 30, 35, 39, 43
  1:26
4:3, 23, 30, 35, 39, 43, 47
  1:30
4:4 1:31, 1:486

Index of Scripture references and ancient sources

4:4–15 *1:229*
4:4, 24, 28, 31, 33 *1:31*
4:5 *1:30, 1:126, 1:208*
4:5–6 *1:39*
4:5–14 *1:30*
4:5–15 *1:31, 1:127, 1:131–133, 1:467*
4:6, 7, 9, 11, 12 *1:390*
4:8 *1:433*
4:8, 10, 11, 12, 14, 25 *1:114*
4:8, 11, 14 *1:114*
4:9 *1:433*
4:9, 10, 12, 14 *1:154*
4:9, 16 *1:193*
4:10 *1:332*
4:12 *1:332*
4:12–13 *2:416*
4:15 *1:133, 1:186*
4:15, 19, 20 *1:133, 1:136*
4:15, 20 *1:114*
4:15, 25 *1:84*
4:16 *1:30, 1:119, 1:127, 1:133, 1:187, 1:439*
4:16–17 *1:31, 1:133*
4:16–20 *1:466*
4:16, 27–28, 33 *1:43*
4:17 *2:269*
4:17–20 *1:31, 1:43, 1:90, 1:119, 1:133*
4:18 *1:133*
4:18, 19 *1:133*
4:18–20 *1:427, 2:241*
4:21–28 *1:119, 1:186*
4:21–28, 29–33 *1:133–134*
4:23 *1:133*
4:23, 30 *1:30*
4:23, 30, 35, 39, 43 *1:30*
4:26, 32 *1:290*
4:27 *1:133, 1:134*
4:27, 28, 31, 32 *1:218*
4:28, 33 *1:187*
4:29–33 *1:119, 1:187*
4:32 *1:114, 1:134*
4:34 *1:134, 2:405*
4:34–37 *1:119*
4:34–45 *1:119*
4:34–48 *1:134*

4:37, 41, 45, 49 *1:228*
4:37, 41, 49 *2:22*
4:37, 45, 49 *1:219, 1:228*
4:38–41 *1:119*
4:42–45 *1:119*
4:46 *1:119, 1:120, 1:134, 2:390*
4:46–48 *1:119*
4:46–49 *1:119*
4:47 *1:119*
4:48 *1:119, 1:120*
4:49 *1:120, 1:134*
4:49a *1:119*
4:49b *1:120*
4:49c *1:120*
5 *1:54, 1:59–60, 1:92, 2:252–253*
5 – 6 *1:13, 1:44, 1:45, 1:46–60, 1:48, 1:49, 1:53–58, 1:60, 1:65,* **1:137–174,** *1:145, 1:146, 1:149, 1:158, 1:168, 1:173, 1:201, 1:203, 1:224, 1:355, 1:387, 1:479, 1:480, 2:215, 2:237, 2:251, 2:255, 2:359, 2:395, 2:479, 2:484*
5 – 8 *1:185*
5, 12, 27 *1:80*
5, 25 *2:496*
5:1 *1:214, 1:304*
5:1 – 6:21 *1:170*
5:1 – 6:27 *1:65*
5:1–3 *1:482*
5:1–4 *1:46, 1:46–7, 1:48, 1:49, 1:52, 1:53, 1:142, 1:143, 1:145–147, 1:147, 1:174, 1:185, 1:214, 1:218, 1:236, 1:303, 1:315, 1:498, 2:387*
5:1, 5, 11 *1:143, 1:168*
5:2 *1:46, 1:48, 1:51, 1:52, 1:58, 1:60, 1:498*
5:2, 3, 13, 14, 19, 20, 27, 28, 29 *1:143*
5:3 *1:46, 1:49, 1:64, 1:67, 1:143, 1:174, 2:436, 2:478, 2:479, 2:484*

5:3, 4 *1:46, 2:384*
5:4–6 *2:361*
5:5 *2:210*
5:5 – 6:21 *1:47, 1:53, 1:142*
5:5–10 *1:46, 1:47, 1:48, 1:49, 1:59, 1:142, 1:143, 1:147–148, 1:174, 2:320, 2:359*
5:5–10, 11–31 *1:50, 1:52, 1:147, 1:172, 2:360*
5:6 *1:142, 1:143, 1:151*
5:6–7 *2:67*
5:6, 12, 27 *1:143, 2:46, 2:218, 2:385*
5:7–8 *1:470*
5:8 *1:58, 1:148*
5:9 *1:141, 1:378, 2:388*
5:10 *1:148*
5:11 *1:155*
5:11–31 *1:32, 1:46, 1:47, 1:48, 1:49, 1:54, 1:60, 1:142, 1:143, 1:148–158, 1:156, 1:174, 1:276, 1:309, 1:312, 1:357, 2:11, 2:216, 2:218, 2:219, 2:237, 2:251, 2:255, 2:284, 2:319, 2:320, 2:359, 2:369*
5:12 *1:148, 1:151, 2:252, 2:253*
5:12–14 *1:144*
5:12–15 *1:386*
5:12, 27 *2:218, 2:254, 2:370*
5:13 *1:52, 1:151, 1:153, 2:253*
5:13, 14 *1:54*
5:13, 14, 19, 20, 27, 28, 29 *1:144*
5:13, 14, 20, 27, 28, 29 *1:151*
5:13, 19, 20 *1:52, 2:385*
5:13, 20 *2:253*
5:14 *2:228, 2:235, 2:253*
5:14, 15, 18, 25, 29, 30 *2:252*
5:14, 30 *1:149, 2:310*
5:14:29, 32 *1:158*

Numbers (*cont.*)
5:14b, 19, 28 *1:152*
5:15 *1:54*
5:15, 16 *1:196*
5:15–17 *2:253*
5:15–18 *1:144*
5:15, 18 *2:391*
5:15, 18, 26 *1:149, 2:392*
5:15, 31 *1:157*
5:15b *1:154*
5:16, 18, 25, 30 *1:155*
5:16, 18, 30 *1:155*
5:17 *1:144, 1:149, 1:154, 1:156, 1:493*
5:18 *1:54, 1:144, 1:153, 1:161, 2:12, 2:253*
5:18, 19, 22, 24, 27 *1:149*
5:18, 19, 23, 24, 27 *1:214*
5:18, 22, 23, 24 *1:154*
5:18b *1:154*
5:19–22 *1:54, 2:253*
5:19–24 *1:144*
5:19, 28, 31 *2:363, 2:414*
5:21 *1:155, 2:359*
5:21–22 *1:156*
5:21, 22 *1:144*
5:21–22, 27 *1:54*
5:21, 22, 27 *1:60, 1:163, 1:356, 2:232*
5:22 *1:156*
5:23 *2:33*
5:24, 26, 27 *1:60, 2:22*
5:25 *1:54, 1:157*
5:25 – 26a *1:144*
5:25–28 *1:144*
5:27 *1:153, 1:156*
5:27–28 *1:144*
5:28 *1:149, 1:152*
5:29 *1:54, 2:252*
5:29–30, 31 *1:144*
5:29–31 *1:156–158*
5:30 *1:156, 1:157*
5:31 *1:157, 1:215*
6 *1:46, 1:54, 1:65, 1:92, 1:203*
6 – 9 *1:344*
6:1 – 2 *1:145*
6:1–2 *1:159–160*
6:1–7 *1:47*
6:1–8 *1:144, 1:161*
6:1–21 *1:46, 1:47–48, 1:49, 1:50, 1:52, 1:54, 1:60, 1:142, 1:143, 1:147, 1:159, 1:159–166, 1:160, 1:172, 1:174, 1:203, 1:210, 1:252, 1:253, 1:312, 1:376, 1:396, 2:58, 2:218, 2:237, 2:254, 2:319, 2:359, 2:360*
6:1, 22 *1:143, 1:168*
6:2 *1:54, 1:143, 1:149, 1:374, 1:396*
6:2–3 *1:327*
6:2, 5, 21 *2:347, 2:359*
6:3 *1:55, 1:57*
6:3–4 *1:145, 1:160*
6:3–4, 20 *1:332*
6:3–8 *1:160–162*
6:4 *2:44*
6:4, 5, 6 *1:160*
6:4, 6, 8 *1:142*
6:5 *1:55, 1:144, 1:153, 1:160, 1:161, 1:162*
6:5–12 *1:52*
6:5, 18 *1:54*
6:5a *1:161*
6:6 *1:162, 1:488*
6:6–7 *1:55, 1:161*
6:6–12 *1:146*
6:6–13 *1:498*
6:7 *1:55, 1:161*
6:7, 9, 12 *1:143, 1:144*
6:8 *1:55, 1:159, 1:160, 1:161*
6:9 *1:57, 1:58, 1:194, 1:487, 1:489*
6:9–12 *1:144, 1:161, 1:162–163, 1:212, 1:237, 1:397, 1:499, 1:500, 2:9*
6:9, 12 *1:54*
6:9, 18 *1:200*
6:10 *2:344*
6:11 *1:161, 1:162, 1:164*
6:12 *1:54, 1:144, 1:163, 1:356, 2:9*
6:13–18 *1:397*
6:13–21 *1:144, 1:161, 1:163–166*
6:13, 21 *1:163*
6:13:23–24 *1:164*
6:14–17 *1:376*
6:15 *1:164*
6:16 *1:54*
6:18 *1:160, 1:165*
6:20 *1:54, 2:388*
6:21 *1:54*
6:22 *1:168, 1:169*
6:22–23 *1:145, 1:168–169*
6:22–27 *1:14, 1:18, 1:46, 1:47, 1:48, 1:49, 1:57, 1:59, 1:65, 1:99, 1:121, 1:142, 1:143, 1:159, 1:166–173, 1:174, 1:202, 1:203, 1:235, 1:250, 1:454, 1:498, 2:50, 2:97, 2:119, 2:125, 2:155, 2:257, 2:319, 2:389, 2:495*
6:23 *1:142, 1:144*
6:23, 24 *1:145*
6:23, 24, 27 *1:59, 2:97, 2:121*
6:24 *1:145, 1:169–170*
6:24, 25, 26 *1:144*
6:24–26 *1:145, 1:168*
6:25 *1:121, 1:169, 1:170–171*
6:25–26 *1:145, 1:418*
6:26 *1:84, 1:169, 1:171–172, 2:174, 2:237, 2:238, 2:258*
6:26, 27 *1:145*
6:27 *1:142, 1:144, 1:168, 1:169*
7 *1:4, 1:13, 1:32, 1:44, 1:65, 1:86, 1:96, 1:185, 1:370, 2:350, 2:390, 2:394, 2:395*
7 – 8 *1:4, 1:7, 1:175–185,* **1:175–204,** *1:185, 1:192, 1:201, 1:203, 1:204, 1:216*
7 – 9 *1:183*

7 – 10 *1:14, 1:65, 1:66,*
    1:185, 1:201, 1:235
7, 28 – 29 *2:376*
7:1 *1:64, 1:124, 1:182,*
    1:183
7:1 – 8:4 *1:185–186,*
    1:192, 1:194
7:1 – 9:14 *1:181, 1:182,*
    1:238
7:1 – 9:23 *1:227*
7:1 – 10:10 *1:65*
7:1–9 *1:184, 1:186–187,*
    1:204
7:1–88 *1:183, 1:184,*
    1:185, 1:186, 1:191,
    1:192, 1:203, 1:227,
    1:229
7:1–89 *1:65*
7:2 *1:10, 2:360, 2:390*
7:2–9 *1:182, 1:183, 1:186,*
    1:189
7:2–88 *1:183*
7:3 *1:36, 1:186*
7:3–9 *1:195*
7:3, 10–11, 12, 18 *1:477*
7:4 *1:193–194*
7:4–9 *1:182*
7:5 *1:186*
7:5–6 *1:186*
7:8 *1:187*
7:9 *1:186*
7:9, 13, 19, 25, 31, 37, 43,
    49, 55, 61, 67, 73, 79,
    85, 86 *1:114*
7:10 *1:186*
7:10–11 *1:180, 1:183,*
    1:187
7:10–88 *1:182, 1:183,*
    1:184, 1:186, 1:187–190,
    1:189, 1:202, 1:204
7:11 *1:182, 1:189*
7:11–88 *1:199*
7:12–17 *1:183*
7:12–83 *1:86, 1:96, 1:99*
7:12–84 *1:10, 2:456*
7:14, 20, 26, 32, 38, 44,
    50, 56, 62, 68, 74, 78
    1:439
7:17 *1:86*

7:18–23 *1:183*
7:21, 27, 33 *1:180*
7:22 *1:190*
7:24–29 *1:183*
7:30–35 *1:183*
7:30, 35, 36, 41, 54, 59
    2:244
7:36–41 *1:183*
7:42–47 *1:183*
7:42, 47 *1:80, 1:208*
7:48–53 *1:183*
7:48–54 *2:379*
7:54–59 *1:183*
7:60–65 *1:183*
7:66–71 *1:183*
7:72–77 *1:183*
7:78 *1:182*
7:78–83 *1:183*
7:84–88 *1:183, 1:188*
7:84, 88 *1:187*
7:86 *1:439*
7:89 *1:18, 1:34, 1:36,*
    1:83, 1:85, 1:183, 1:184,
    1:185, 1:186, 1:188,
    1:189, 1:190–192, 1:191,
    1:192, 1:202, 1:203,
    1:233, 1:235, 1:266,
    1:267, 1:273, 1:278,
    1:297, 1:298, 1:362,
    2:241
7cd, 10cd *2:154*
7d, 8b, 10b *2:154*
8 *1:185, 1:195, 1:236,*
    1:379, 1:451, 1:467,
    1:496
8:1 *1:184*
8:1–3 *1:192–193*
8:1–4 *1:43, 1:117, 1:184,*
    1:185, 1:186, 1:189,
    1:190, 1:191, 1:192,
    1:193, 1:194, 1:202,
    1:203
8:1–7 *1:470*
8:1–26 *1:65*
8:2 *1:184, 1:193*
8:3 *1:184*
8:3, 22 *2:381, 2:389*
8:4 *1:184, 1:193, 1:222,*
    1:447, 2:22

8:5 *1:182, 1:437*
8:5–7 *1:194–195*
8:5–7a *1:184*
8:5–14, 15–26 *1:115*
8:5–14, 16–19 *1:465*
8:5–22 *1:117, 1:184,*
    1:199
8:5–26 *1:129, 1:184,*
    1:185, 1:186, 1:192,
    1:194, 1:198, 1:203,
    1:496, 2:249
8:5–51 *1:194*
8:6 *1:194*
8:7 *1:184, 1:194, 1:200,*
    1:237, 1:487
8:7b–13 *1:184*
8:8 *1:195*
8:8–12 *1:184*
8:8, 12 *1:164*
8:8–13 *1:195–197, 1:470,*
    1:471
8:10 *1:197, 1:378*
8:10, 11 *1:196*
8:10, 19 *1:197*
8:11 *1:197, 1:470*
8:11, 13, 15 *1:196*
8:11, 15, 19, 22, 24 *1:195*
8:12 *1:195, 1:196, 1:197*
8:13 *1:181, 1:184, 1:194,*
    1:197
8:13–19 *1:84, 1:441*
8:14 *1:184, 1:194, 1:197,*
    1:421
8:14–18 *1:441*
8:14–19 *1:184, 1:197–200*
8:15 *1:184, 1:197*
8:16 *1:197, 1:467*
8:16–18 *1:184, 2:391*
8:17 *1:195, 1:197, 1:203,*
    1:288, 1:346, 2:244
8:18 *1:197*
8:19 *1:114, 1:184, 1:197,*
    1:199, 1:203, 1:437,
    1:441, 1:443, 1:467,
    2:228, 2:230, 2:233
8:19, 21 *1:188, 1:470*
8:20–22 *1:200*
8:20–22a *1:184*
8:21 *1:194, 1:200*

Numbers (*cont.*)
8:22b *1:184*
8:23–26 *1:184, 1:195, 1:200–201*
8:23–35 *1:30*
8:24 *1:201*
8:24–25 *1:30*
8:26 *1:90, 1:218, 2:389*
9 *1:238, 1:279, 1:479, 2:9, 2:288*
9 – 10 *1:201,* **1:204–240,** *1:224*
9 – 11 *1:393*
9:1 *1:64, 1:212, 1:213, 2:9*
9:1 – 10:10 *1:65*
9:1 – 10:36 *1:65*
9:1–2, 11 *1:182*
9:1–4 *1:344*
9:1–5 *1:209*
9:1, 5 *1:83*
9:1–14 *1:7, 1:84, 1:185, 1:195, 1:199, 1:203, 1:209, 1:212–216, 1:227, 1:236, 1:237, 1:239, 1:254, 1:385, 1:499, 2:287, 2:404, 2:411, 2:487*
9:2 *1:182, 1:211, 1:212*
9:2–3 *1:212*
9:2–4 *1:210*
9:2–5 *1:212–213*
9:3 *1:212, 2:335*
9:3–4 *1:211*
9:3, 12, 14 *1:209, 1:212*
9:4 *1:213*
9:5 *1:213*
9:5–6 *1:211*
9:5–10 *1:211*
9:6 *1:488, 1:498, 2:287, 2:390, 2:451*
9:6–7 *1:212, 1:213–214*
9:6, 7 *1:213*
9:6, 7, 10 *1:141, 1:214*
9:6–8 *1:209*
9:6–14 *1:209, 2:287*
9:7 *1:211, 1:212, 2:287, 2:288, 2:405*
9:8 *1:211, 2:287*

9:8–12 *1:214*
9:9 *1:211, 1:480*
9:9–14 *1:209, 2:287*
9:10 *1:211, 1:236*
9:10–14 *1:214, 1:385*
9:11 *1:182, 1:254, 2:10*
9:11–13 *1:212*
9:13 *1:133, 1:213, 1:214–215*
9:13, 20 *1:484*
9:14 *1:49, 1:382, 2:467*
9:15 *1:64, 1:186, 1:217*
9:15–16 *1:7, 1:209, 1:210, 1:216–217, 1:220*
9:15–23 *1:7, 1:8, 1:32, 1:33, 1:48, 1:55, 1:84, 1:94, 1:122, 1:202, 1:209, 1:210, 1:211, 1:216–220, 1:218, 1:219, 1:221, 1:223, 1:224, 1:225, 1:227, 1:230, 1:237, 1:238, 1:239, 1:303, 2:73, 2:74, 2:442, 2:443, 2:447, 2:480*
9:15a *1:210, 1:217*
9:15b–23a *1:210, 1:217*
9:16 *1:216, 1:217*
9:17 *1:216, 1:218, 1:236, 1:303*
9:17–18 *1:217*
9:17, 18, 22 *1:218*
9:17, 19, 20, 21, 22 *1:210*
9:17, 21, 22 *1:218*
9:17–23 *1:209, 1:210, 1:216, 1:217–219*
9:18 *1:218, 1:236*
9:18, 20, 23 *1:228, 1:237, 2:442*
9:18, 20, 23a, 23b *1:218*
9:18a *1:210*
9:18bα *1:210*
9:18bβ–19 *1:210*
9:19–20 *1:218*
9:19–22 *1:217, 1:218*
9:19, 22 *1:218*
9:19, 23 *1:218*
9:20, 21 *1:218*
9:20a *1:210*
9:20b *1:210*

9:21–22 *1:210, 1:218*
9:23 *1:214, 1:217, 1:219, 1:223, 1:228, 2:443*
9:23aα *1:210*
9:23aβ *1:210*
9:23b *1:210*
10 *1:62, 1:63, 1:183, 1:229, 1:233, 1:238, 2:165, 2:395*
10 – 11 *1:290*
10 – 15 *1:290*
10, 18, 19 *2:396*
10, 25, 31 *2:381*
10:1–2 *1:222–224*
10:1–10 *1:94, 1:185, 1:209, 1:210, 1:219, 1:225, 1:229, 1:230, 1:238, 1:239*
10:2 *1:236*
10:2, 5, 6 *1:224*
10:2–10 *2:376*
10:3 *1:209, 2:241*
10:3–4 *1:223, 1:224*
10:3, 4, 5, 6, 7, 9, 10 *1:224*
10:3, 7 *1:225*
10:4 *1:104, 2:380*
10:5 *1:224*
10:5–6 *1:223, 1:228, 2:165*
10:5, 6, 9 *2:165*
10:8 *1:209, 1:223, 1:225–226, 1:488*
10:9 *2:185, 2:245, 2:381, 2:407, 2:452*
10:9–10 *1:223, 1:226–227*
10:9, 35 *1:337*
10:10 *1:61, 1:63, 1:209, 2:340, 2:391*
10:11 *1:63, 1:64, 1:182, 1:210, 1:225, 1:227, 1:238*
10:11 – 22:1 *2:440*
10:11–12 *1:62, 1:218, 1:227*
10:11–12, 34 *1:303*
10:11–13 *1:7, 1:84, 1:219*
10:11–28 *1:63, 1:64,*

Index of Scripture references and ancient sources   593

1:209, 1:211, 1:225, 1:229, 1:238, 1:239
10:11, 34   1:227
10:11, 35   1:227
10:11–36   1:7, 1:62, 1:63, 1:64, 1:65, 1:92, 1:209, 1:219, 1:224, 1:227, 1:229
10:12   1:64, 1:83, 1:227–228, 1:229, 1:232, 1:236, 1:238, 1:325, 2:11, 2:431, 2:445
10:12, 28   1:227
10:13   1:219, 1:230, 2:442
10:13–28   1:63
10:14, 18, 22, 25   1:62
10:14–21   1:224
10:14–27   1:62
10:14–28   1:10, 1:96, 2:456
10:17, 21   1:228
10:18, 19, 23   2:244
10:20   1:80
10:21   1:229, 1:233
10:28   1:229, 2:441
10:29   1:216, 1:229, 1:230, 1:231, 1:236, 1:339, 1:361, 1:373, 2:222
10:29–32   1:209, 1:229, 1:229–232, 1:239, 1:254, 1:272, 1:290, 1:295, 1:314, 2:57
10:29, 32   1:246, 1:249, 1:259, 1:330, 1:338, 1:361
10:29–32, 33–36   1:229
10:29–36   1:211
10:31   1:230
10:31–32   1:231
10:32   1:230–231, 1:232–234
10:33   1:217, 1:221, 1:223, 1:231–232, 1:234, 1:236, 1:323, 1:329, 1:360
10:33, 35   1:132
10:33–36   1:35, 1:92, 1:209, 1:229, 1:230, 1:235, 1:238, 1:239
10:34   1:222, 1:233
10:34–36   1:14, 1:65, 1:89
10:35   1:226, 1:236, 1:239, 1:360, 2:16, 2:68, 2:381, 2:433, 2:450
10:35–36   1:63, 1:234, 1:234–235, 2:480
10:36   1:61, 1:62, 1:63, 1:64, 1:234, 2:380
11   1:34, 1:42, 1:46, 1:58, 1:277, 1:297, 1:301, 1:312, 1:340, 1:353, 1:358, 2:62, 2:135–136, 2:313, 2:444
11 – 12   1:63, 1:238, 1:240–315, 1:272, 1:277, 1:290, 1:295, 1:296, 1:298, 1:305, 1:306, 1:308, 1:311, 1:314, 2:60, 2:444–445
11 – 14   1:97, 1:150–153, 1:254, 1:266, 1:283, 1:296, 1:360, 1:363, 1:364, 1:370, 1:373, 1:377, 1:391, 1:392, 1:394, 1:498, 2:445
11 – 15   1:8, 1:42, 1:60, 1:97, 1:122, 1:135, 1:190, 1:192, 1:203, 1:267, 1:302, 1:310, 1:356, 1:361, 1:365–366, 1:389, 1:394, 1:395, 1:401, 1:432, 1:433, 1:447, 1:463, 2:5, 2:6, 2:7, 2:11, 2:26, 2:35, 2:50, 2:84, 2:495
11 – 15, 16–18   1:315
11 – 17   1:499
11 – 18   1:67
11 – 20   2:4, 2:49, 2:55
11 – 25   1:14, 1:17, 1:42–46, 1:45, 1:56, 1:60, 1:61, 1:64, 1:65, 1:66, 1:91, 1:158, 1:227, 1:232, 1:249, 1:251, 1:387, 1:396, 2:319, 2:351, 2:357, 2:371, 2:396, 2:411
11 – 26   1:234
11, 12   2:76
11:1   1:62, 1:63, 1:97, 1:229, 1:234, 1:246, 1:249–250, 1:250, 1:306, 1:314, 2:8, 2:37, 2:44, 2:63, 2:64, 2:135, 2:147, 2:149, 2:159, 2:219, 2:357
11:1 – 14:45   1:66
11:1, 2, 6, 8   1:247
11:1–3   1:245, 1:249–251, 1:250, 1:251, 1:256, 1:257, 1:277, 1:322, 1:355, 1:366, 1:422, 1:423, 1:428, 2:17, 2:60, 2:241
11:1, 3   1:315
11:1–4   1:310
11:1, 4   1:377, 1:378
11:1, 4–6   2:292
11:1, 10   1:244, 2:17, 2:63, 2:188
11:1, 10, 11, 15   1:249, 1:290, 1:330, 1:361
11:1, 10, 33   1:302, 1:418
11:1, 18   1:246, 1:361
11:1a   1:245
11:1b   1:245
11:2   1:251, 1:258, 1:259, 2:8, 2:50, 2:61
11:2, 8, 10, 11, 12, 13, 14, 16, 17, 18, 21, 24, 32, 35   1:289
11:2a   1:245
11:2bα   1:245
11:2bβ   1:245
11:3   1:227, 1:244, 1:251, 2:55, 2:447
11:4   1:243, 1:246, 1:249, 1:251, 1:251–253, 1:269, 1:289, 1:292, 1:293, 1:295, 1:314, 1:340, 1:352
11:4, 5, 13, 18, 19, 21   1:246
11:4–6   1:245, 1.391, 2:217, 2:357
11:4–9   1:56
11:4–10   1:245
11:4, 10, 11, 18, 20   2:224

Numbers (*cont.*)
11:4, 10, 13, 18, 20 *2:225*
11:4, 16, 22, 24, 30, 32
  2:308
11:4, 16, 24, 30, 32 *1:244*
11:4, 20 *1:256*
11:4, 29 *1:283*
11:4–34 *1:245*
11:4, 34 *1:361, 1:364*
11:4–35 *1:244, 1:249,*
  1:250, 1:251, 1:251–290,
  1:295, 1:306, 1:355,
  1:366, 1:423
11:5 *1:214, 1:231, 1:248,*
  1:253, 1:288, 2:15
11:5–6 *1:253–255*
11:5, 18, 20 *1:416*
11:5, 20 *1:331*
11:5b–6 *1:252*
11:6 *1:270, 1:361, 1:427*
11:6, 20 *2:61*
11:7 *1:361, 2:119*
11:7, 8a, 8b, 9 *1:255*
11:7–9 *1:252, 1:254,*
  1:255–256, 1:298, 1:307
11:9 *1:248, 1:273, 1:284*
11:10 *1:246, 1:251, 1:256–*
  258, 1:278, 1:288, 1:418,
  2:135, 2:219
11:10, 11, 15 *1:246*
11:10b *1:256*
11:10b–15 *1:245*
11:11 *1:259, 1:262, 1:266*
11:11–12, 14–15 *1:245*
11:11, 12, 14, 17 *1:263*
11:11–15 *1:239, 1:244,*
  1:245, 1:251, 1:423,
  2:23
11:11, 15 *1:246, 2:406*
11:11–15, 21–22 *1:347*
11:11–17, 25–29 *1:209*
11:12 *1:256, 1:259, 1:306,*
  1:307, 1:323, 1:339,
  2:408
11:12–13 *1:251*
11:12, 14, 21 *1:260*
11:12b *1:270*
11:13 *1:245, 1:259*
11:13–14 *1:251, 1:261*
11:14 *1:259, 1:262*
11:14–15 *1:262*
11:15 *1:66, 1:257, 1:258–*
  262, 1:259, 1:262, 1:278,
  1:281
11:15, 18–20 *1:491*
11:16 *1:10, 1:246, 1:248,*
  1:262–266, 1:269, 1:272,
  1:273
11:16–17 *1:71, 1:262,*
  1:278
11:16–17, 23–29 *2:312*
11:16–17, 24–30 *1:361*
11:16, 24 *1:423*
11:16, 24–25 *1:248*
11:16–24a *1:245*
11:16, 30 *1:242*
11:17 *1:266, 1:266–269,*
  1:267
11:17, 25 *1:247, 1:248,*
  1:276, 1:277, 1:297,
  1:298, 1:299, 2:310
11:17, 25, 26 *1:286*
11:17, 25, 26, 29 *1:150,*
  1:247
11:18 *1:246, 1:249, 1:250,*
  1:270, 1:272, 1:273,
  1:276, 1:287, 1:340,
  1:361, 1:412
11:18–20 *1:245, 1:262,*
  1:269–271
11:18, 20 *1:270*
11:19–20 *1:315*
11:19–20, 24 *1:286*
11:20 *1:246, 1:247, 1:252,*
  1:253, 1:254, 1:264,
  1:340, 2:60
11:21 *1:107, 1:108, 1:246*
11:21–22 *1:245, 1:262,*
  1:272
11:22 *2:431*
11:23 *1:245, 1:246, 1:272–*
  273, 2:60, 2:431
11:23, 24 *1:247*
11:24 *1:272, 1:273, 1:278,*
  1:284, 2:431
11:24–25 *1:279*
11:24–34 *1:32*
11:24a *1:245*
11:24b–25, 30 *1:278*
11:24b–30 *1:245*
11:25 *1:43, 1:62, 1:245,*
  1:246, 1:267, 1:273–278,
  1:277, 1:279, 1:303,
  2:431
11:25, 26 *1:285*
11:25, 26, 27, 29 *1:247*
11:25–27 *1:267*
11:25, 31 *1:150*
11:25a *1:278*
11:26 *1:248, 1:279, 1:281,*
  2:431
11:26–27 *1:245*
11:26–29 *1:261*
11:26–30 *1:278–284*
11:27 *1:281, 1:296, 2:431*
11:27, 28 *1:282*
11:28 *1:245, 1:261, 1:278,*
  1:281, 1:327, 1:342,
  1:354, 1:404, 2:276,
  2:314, 2:431
11:28–29 *1:296*
11:29 *1:245, 1:269, 1:276,*
  1:279, 1:280, 1:281,
  1:283, 1:288, 1:312,
  1:313, 2:252
11:29–30 *1:259*
11:30 *1:245, 1:246, 1:248,*
  1:282, 1:298, 1:310,
  1:424
11:31 *1:247, 1:248, 1:284,*
  1:286, 1:288, 1:290,
  1:306
11:31–32 *1:248*
11:31–33 *1:245, 1:246*
11:31–34 *1:245*
11:31–35 *1:284–290*
11:32 *1:246, 1:248, 1:251,*
  1:253, 1:271, 1:284,
  1:288
11:32–34 *1:315*
11:33 *1:133, 1:246, 1:270,*
  1:271, 1:286, 1:288,
  1:298, 2:135, 2:244
11:34 *1:244, 1:245, 1:254,*
  1:289–290, 2:447
11:34–35 *1:310*
11:35 *1:227, 1:244, 1:290,*

INDEX OF SCRIPTURE REFERENCES AND ANCIENT SOURCES   595

1:309, 1:310, 1:315,
   2:444
12 1:42, 1:46, 1:58, 1:59,
   1:266, 1:277, 1:304–305,
   2:4, 2:10, 2:11–12, 2:23,
   2:42, 2:44, 2:109
12 – 20 2:47
12, 14 1:261, 2:67
12, 17 2:26
12, 19, 20, 29 1:149
12:1 1:266, 1:272, 1:290,
   1:290–296, 1:292, 1:297,
   1:306, 1:314, 1:361,
   1:377, 2:223, 2:227
12:1–2 1:302
12:1–2, 8 2:4, 2:357
12:1–2a 1:245
12:1–3 1:43
12:1, 3 1:362
12:1, 8 2:60, 2:292
12:1–15 1:290, 1:310
12:1–16 1:245, 1:251,
   1:256, 1:291, 1:295,
   1:310, 1:355, 1:366,
   1:423
12:2 1:246, 1:256, 1:294,
   1:295, 1:296–297, 1:363,
   2:63
12:2–3 1:412
12:2, 6 1:247
12:2, 9 1:302
12:2b, 4–5, 9–10 1:245
12:3 1:255, 1:297–298
12:3, 13 1:259
12:4 1:297, 1:298
12:4–5 1:248, 1:423
12:4–9 1:45
12:4–13 1:361
12:4–16 1:43
12:5 1:246, 1:248, 1:273,
   1:299, 1:423
12:5–8 1:192, 1:203, 1:362
12:5, 10 1:303
12:6 1:247, 1:277
12:6a, 8de 1:300
12:6–7 2:23
12:6–8 1:73, 1:277, 1:294,
   1:297, 1:299–302, 2:26
12:6–9 1:267, 1:298

12:7 1:308, 2:4
12:7–8 1:302, 1:313,
   1:353, 1:418, 2:47, 2:167
12:8 1:167, 1:246, 1:277,
   1:294, 1:301, 1:304, 2:4,
   2:163, 2:314
12:9 1:244, 1:246, 1:302–
   303, 1:418, 2:63, 2:135,
   2:188, 2:219
12:9–10 1:294
12:10 1:46, 1:51, 1:52,
   1:60, 1:293, 1:304
12:10, 11–12, 13, 14
   1:305
12:10–12 1:307
12:10–14 1:303–308
12:10, 14–15 1:49
12:10–15 1:249, 1:289,
   2:11
12:11 1:302, 1:304, 2:61,
   2:66
12:11–12 1:245
12:12 1:246, 1:251, 1:306,
   1:307, 2:10
12:12–15 1:248
12:13 1:245, 1:258, 1:307,
   1:423
12:14 1:245, 1:296, 1:306,
   1:362
12:14–15 1:244, 1:246,
   1:247, 1:314, 2:384
12:14–16 1:315
12:15 1:58, 1:242, 1:283,
   1:284, 1:290, 1:298,
   1:308–309, 1:315, 2:4
12:15–16 1:245, 1:248
12:16 1:64, 1:227, 1:228,
   1:238, 1:244, 1:290,
   1:309–310, 1:325, 2:11,
   2:445, 2:446
12:19 1:319
12:20, 22, 23, 24 2:5
12:33 1:331
13 1:96–97, 1:228, 2:82,
   2:155, 2:367, 2:494
13 – 14 1:9, 1:42, 1:43,
   1:56, 1:58, 1:66, 1:90,
   1:233, 1:258, 1:297,
   1:307, 1:310, 1:311,

1:315–366, 1:323–324,
   1:326, 1:328, 1:346,
   1:351, 1:355, 1:364,
   1:369, 1:372, 1:382,
   1:383, 1:384, 1:386,
   1:388, 1:388–391, 1.391,
   1:394, 1:395, 1:416,
   1:452, 2:4, 2:31, 2:32,
   2:44, 2:119, 2:174,
   2:250, 2:276, 2:279,
   2:317, 2:407, 2:410,
   2:413, 2:424, 2:483,
   2:496
13, 14 1:101
13 – 16 1:377–378
13:1 1:10, 1:501
13:1 – 14:45 1:366
13:1–2 1:321, 1:358,
   1:360, 2:408, 2:409
13:1–3 1:322–326
13:1–15 1:356
13:1–16 1:9, 1:10, 1:324,
   1:364, 2:437, 2:456
13:1, 16 2:317
13:1–24 1:321
13:1–26 2:446
13:2 1:85, 1:86, 1:322,
   1:334, 1:335, 1:339,
   1:353, 1:355, 1:373,
   1:388, 2:33, 2:307, 2:409
13:2, 3, 16 1:324
13:2, 3, 16, 17, 27 1:325
13:2, 3, 31 1:415
13:2, 4–16 1:329
13:2, 16, 17, 21, 25, 32
   1:233, 1.391
13:3 1:322, 1:334, 1:341,
   2:22, 2:445
13:3–16 1:67
13:3–20 1:321
13:3, 21 1:325
13:3, 26 1:228, 1:325,
   2:11, 2:446
13:4 2:483
13:4–6 1:326–328
13:4–14 1:11
13:4–15 1:96, 1:325
13:4–16 1:86
13:4–16, 31–33 1:99

Numbers (*cont.*)
13:6 2:276
13:7 1:319
13:7, 11 2:317
13:8 1:352
13:8, 16 1:326, 2:318
13:12 1:348
13:13 1:347
13:13–14 1:347
13:14–15 1:352
13:15 1:347
13:16 1:86, 1:327, 1:348, 1:366, 2:276, 2:314, 2:437, 2:458
13:17 1:328
13:17, 18–20, 21 1:329
13:17, 18, 21, 22, 30, 31 1:328, 1:416
13:17, 29 1:353
13:18 1:329, 1:351, 1:391, 2:307, 2:317
13:18–20 1:328–331
13:19 1:330, 1:334, 2:410
13:19–20 1:362
13:20 1:57, 1:332, 1:334, 1:337, 1:362, 1:372
13:20, 23–24 1:362
13:20, 23–27 1:56
13:20, 23, 31 1:330
13:21 1:331, 2:455
13:21–24 1:321
13:21–26 2:454
13:22 1:333, 1:334, 1:335, 1:353, 2:34, 2:56, 2:318
13:22–25 1:331–333
13:23 1:57, 1:372, 2:15
13:23–24 1:56, 1:133, 1:334, 2:410
13:23–25 1:57
13:23–27 1:376
13:24 2:32
13:25 1:356, 2:410
13:25–29 1:321
13:25–33 1:321
13:26 1:244, 1:324, 1:351, 1:381, 1:386, 2:317, 2:318, 2:445
13:26, 27 1:336
13:26–29 1:333–235, 1:337
13:26–33 1:322
13:26b–27 1:334
13:27 1:330, 1:333, 1:343, 1:373, 1:416
13:27–29 1:329
13:27, 32 1:337
13:27–31 1:9
13:28 1:334–335, 1:351
13:28–29 1:334
13:28, 31 1:336, 1:337
13:29 1:335, 1:355
13:30 1:321, 1:334, 1:335–337, 1:337, 1:343, 1:353, 1:354, 2:276, 2:459
13:30–31 1:320, 1:328
13:31 1:336, 1:338, 1:347
13:31 – 14:4 2:82
13:31–33 1:321, 1:337–340, 1:364, 2:284, 2:292
13:32 1:9, 1:43, 1:331, 1:333, 1:336, 1:338, 1:351, 1:362, 1:364, 1:365, 1:426, 2:279, 2:318, 2:410
13:32–33 1:311, 1:335, 1:337, 1:338, 1:344, 1.391, 2:357
13:33 1:337, 1:339, 1:351, 1:356, 1:388
14 1:152, 1:198, 1:258, 1:369, 1:384, 1:385, 2:9, 2:10, 2:32, 2:241
14 – 12 1:366
14 – 15 1:46
14 – 19 1:198
14 – 27 1–228–229
14, 16 1:382
14:1 1:359, 2:225, 2:317
14:1, 2 1:340
14:1, 2, 5, 7, 10, 27, 35, 36 1:381
14:1–4 1:11, 1:231, 1:270, 1:340–341, 2:294
14:1–5 1:321
14:1–10a 1:321
14:1–38 1:423
14:2 1:355
14:2–3 1:341, 1:356
14:2–4 1:336, 1:386, 1:416
14:2–5 1:321
14:2, 27, 29, 36 1:341
14:3 1:334, 1:340, 1:355, 1:359, 2:279
14:3–4 1:255, 1:340, 1:365, 1:491
14:3, 8, 16, 24, 30, 31 1:373
14:3, 31 1:14, 2:410
14:4 1:342, 1:407, 2:317–318, 2:321
14:4–5 1:344
14:4, 39–45 1:312
14:5–10 1:341–344
14:6 1:354, 2:52, 2:56, 2:317
14:6, 7, 34, 36, 38 1:233
14:6–9 1:9, 1:321
14:6–10 2:250
14:6, 30, 38 2:276
14:6, 30, 38, 65 2:276
14:7 1:331, 1:338, 1:362
14:7–9 1:343
14:7, 41 2:410
14:8 1:343, 1:416, 2:307
14:8, 16, 30 2:408, 2:409
14:9 1:343, 1:355, 1:360, 1:366, 2:32, 2:82, 2:271
14:9, 13, 40, 42, 44 1:416
14:10 1:274, 1:388, 1:423, 2:16
14:10a 1:321
14:10b–12 1:321
14:10b–38 1:321
14:11 1:345, 1:347, 1:350, 1:365, 2:32, 2:46
14:11–12 1:345–346, 1:354, 2:16, 2:17
14:11–12, 20–23 1:350
14:11–20 1:421
14:11, 22 2:69
14:11, 23 1:382, 1:426, 2:32
14:11–25 1:344–345, 2:409
14:12 2:244
14:12, 24 2:410

Index of Scripture references and ancient sources 597

14:13 *1:349*
14:13–14 *1:363*
14:13, 14, 15, 16, 19 *1:347*
14:13–16 *1:347*
14:13–19 *1:258, 1:321, 1:345, 1:346–350, 1:347, 1:350, 1:351, 1:394, 1:423*
14:13–20 *1:382*
14:13, 40, 42, 44 *1:328*
14:14 *1:221, 1:347, 1:349, 1:351, 2:410*
14:15–16 *1:337*
14:15a *1:347*
14:15b–16 *1:347*
14:16 *1:323, 1:348*
14:16, 23 *2:408*
14:16, 23, 30, 40 *1:334*
14:17 *1:347*
14:17–18 *1:347*
14:17–18, 19 *1:349*
14:17–19 *1:347, 1:363, 1:366, 2:219*
14:17–20 *1:375*
14:17c–20 *2:192*
14:18 *2:279, 2:363, 2:414*
14:18, 19 *1:358*
14:19 *1:348, 1:349*
14:19–20 *1:381, 2:363*
14:19b *1:347*
14:20 *1:347, 1:350–351, 2:241*
14:20–23 *1:32*
14:20–25 *1:345, 1:354*
14:20–35 *1:321, 2:276*
14:21 *1:167, 1:351, 1:353, 1:358*
14:21–23, 26–35 *1:373*
14:21–23, 41 *1:43*
14:21, 28 *1:351*
14:22 *1:351, 1:352, 1:362, 1:365, 2:309*
14:22–23 *1:351–352*
14:22, 24 *1:42*
14:23 *1:345, 1:351, 1:352, 1:359, 1:365*
14:23–24 *2:408*
14:24 *1:319, 1:333, 1:352–324, 1:353, 1:354, 2:276, 2:310, 2:312, 2:459*
14:24, 25 *1:360*
14:24, 30 *1:364*
14:25 *1:355, 1:359, 1:412, 2:61, 2:446*
14:25, 45 *2:14*
14:26–27 *2:23*
14:26–28 *1:355–356*
14:26–35 *1:345, 1:354, 1:359, 2:286*
14:27 *1:338, 1:356, 1:358, 1:365*
14:27, 29, 36 *1:355*
14:27–38 *1:258*
14:28 *1:250, 1:346, 1:363, 2:176*
14:28–31 *1:321, 1:341*
14:29 *1:43, 1:58, 1:356, 1:365, 1:453, 2:48, 2:158, 2:410*
14:29–30 *2:287*
14:29, 32 *1:56, 1:59, 2:9, 2:41*
14:29, 32, 33, 35 *1:356*
14:29, 32, 35 *1:356*
14:29–35 *1:356–368*
14:30 *1:351, 1:357, 1:358, 1:359*
14:30–36 *1:43*
14:30, 38 *1:353*
14:31 *1:253, 1:340, 1:356, 1:357, 2:287*
14:32 *1:58, 1:331, 1:365*
14:32–33 *1:356*
14:33 *1:56, 1:58, 1:158, 1:357, 1:372, 1:388, 1.391, 2:216*
14:33–34 *1:359*
14:33, 34, 35 *1:358*
14:33, 35 *2:410*
14:34 *1:32, 1:56, 1:157, 1:158, 1:315, 1:356, 1:357, 1:394*
14:35 *1:315, 1:356, 1:365, 2:50*
14:36 *1:325, 1:362, 1:365, 2:357, 2:410*
14:36–37 *1:9, 1:99, 1:422*
14:36, 37 *1:43, 1:329, 1:338, 1:364, 2:318*
14:36–38 *1:9, 1:358–359, 1:364*
14:37 *1:331, 1:334, 1:362, 1:365, 1:382, 2:250*
14:37, 42 *1:199*
14:38 *1:354*
14:39 *1:359, 2:317*
14:39–40 *1:321*
14:39–45 *1:219, 1:321, 1:328, 1:344, 2:286, 2:420, 2:423, 2:425*
14:40 *2:61, 2:67, 2:410*
14:40, 44, 45 *1:353*
14:40–45 *1:328, 1:345, 1:355, 1:359–361, 2:446*
14:41 *1:326, 2:127*
14:41–43 *1:321*
14:43 *1:353, 1:363*
14:43–44 *2:59*
14:44 *1:235, 1:303, 1:359, 2:381*
14:44–45 *1:321, 1:366*
14:45 *1:43, 1:346, 2:59, 2:244, 2:410*
15 *1:43, 1:57, 1:97, **1:366–397**, 1:498*
15 – 17 *2:125–126, 2:309–311*
15 – 18 *2:9*
15 – 23 *1:8–9*
15 – 28 *1:153–156*
15, 32, 33 *1:386*
15:1–2 *1:372–373*
15:1–3 *1:314, 1:372*
15:1–5 *1:371*
15:1–16 *1:369, 1:372, 1:374, 1:394, 1:396*
15:1, 17, 22, 23, 35, 36, 37 *1:372*
15:1–21 *1:43, 2:333, 2:347*
15:1–29 *1:382*
15:1–31 *1:371, 1:394*
15:2 *1:56, 1:334, 1:372, 1:373, 1:378, 2:33, 2:307, 2:327*
15:2, 18 *1:373, 1:385*

Numbers (*cont.*)
15:3 *1:43, 1:57, 1:373–375*
15:3, 7, 10, 13, 14, 24 *1:375*
15:3, 8 *1:141, 1:396, 2:354, 2:358*
15:3–21 *1:56*
15:4 *1:368*
15:4–5 *1:372*
15:4, 6, 9, 24 *1:418*
15:4–12 *1:375–377*
15:5 *2:16*
15:6–7 *1:371, 1:372*
15:7 *2:333*
15:8–9 *1:376*
15:8–10 *1:372, 1:381*
15:8–16 *1:371*
15:11 *1:371, 1:376*
15:11–12 *1:372*
15:11–31 *1:395*
15:13 *1:377*
15:13–16 *1:372*
15:14 *1:369, 1:377*
15:14, 15 *1:371*
15:14, 15, 21, 23, 38 *1:378*
15:15 *1:377*
15:16 *1:377*
15:17–18 *1:378*
15:17–21 *1:369, 1:370, 1:371, 1:381, 1:394*
15:17–41 *1:370*
15:19, 20, 21 *2:388*
15:20 *1:378*
15:21 *1:371*
15:22 *1:380*
15:22–23 *1:379, 1:395*
15:22–26 *1:369, 1:371, 1:379, 1:381*
15:22–29 *1:379–380, 1:394*
15:22–31 *1:369, 1:370, 1:380, 1:383, 1:395*
15:23 *1:219, 1:371*
15:24 *1:370, 1:371, 1:380, 1:380–381*
15:24, 25, 26, 33, 35, 36 *1:381*
15:25, 26, 28 *1:381, 2:363*
15:25–26, 28–29 *1:381*
15:26 *1:371*
15:27–29 *1:371, 1:379, 1:381, 1:382, 1:481*
15:29 *1:371*
15:30 *1:370, 1:371, 2:25, 2:224*
15:30–31 *1:371, 1:378, 1:381–383, 1:383, 1:385, 1:394, 2:286*
15:30, 31 *1:133*
15:30–36 *1:422*
15:31 *1:386, 1:387, 1:395, 1:490, 2:368*
15:32 *2:286*
15:32–34 *1:385–387*
15:32–36 *1:215, 1:369, 1:370, 1:371, 1:372, 1:373, 1:383–385, 1:392, 1:394, 1:395, 1:396, 2:286, 2:287, 2:495*
15:33 *1:386*
15:33, 34, 36 *1:386*
15:34 *1:375, 1:384*
15:35–36 *1:387–389*
15:35, 36 *1:388, 2:384*
15:36 *1:395, 2:287, 2:389*
15:37–31 *1:369*
15:37–38 *1:388–391*
15:37–41 *1:39, 1:57, 1:173, 1:363, 1:369, 1:370, 1:371, 1:372, 1:393, 1:394, 1:395, 1:396, 1:410, 2:225, 2:378, 2:396*
15:38 *1:39, 1:371, 1:390, 1:393*
15:38, 39 *1:447*
15:39 *1:233, 1:323, 1:363, 1:390, 1:391, 1:396, 1:418*
15:39–40 *1:391–393, 2:225, 2:251, 2:392*
15:40 *1:43, 1:393, 1:395*
15:41 *1:161, 1:393–394, 2:251*
16 *1:135, 1:187, 1:274, 1:302, 1:482, 2:13, 2:241, 2:268, 2:279*
16 – 17 *1:32, 1:44, 1:90, 1:135, 1:136, 1:199, 1:370, 1:389,* **1:397–430**, *1:439, 1:449, 1:462, 1:463, 1:464, 1:468, 1:496, 1:498, 2:5, 2:30, 2:43, 2:44, 2:174, 2:242, 2:258, 2:395*
16 – 17, 25 *1:501*
16 – 18 *1:66, 1:90, 1:116, 1:122, 1:125, 1:190, 1:192, 1:198, 1:203, 1:311, 1:365, 1:389, 1:401, 1:406, 1:410, 1:413, 1:432, 1:433, 1:447, 1:463, 1:499, 2:6, 2:11, 2:26, 2:42, 2:50, 2:484*
16 – 19 *1:45, 1:60, 1:404, 2:5, 2:7, 2:11*
16 – 20 *1:42, 1:43, 1:66, 1:67, 1:403, 1:404, 1:450, 1:453, 1:454, 1:470, 2:3, 2:5, 2:35, 2:43, 2:84, 2:110*
16:1 *1:43, 1:125, 1:135, 1:400–401, 1:420, 1:438, 1:443, 1:467, 2:266, 2:456*
16:1 – 20:13 *1:66*
16:1–2 *1:405, 1:406–408, 2:233*
16:1, 6, 17, 18, 39, 46, 47 *1:401, 1:409, 2:18*
16:1, 6, 17, 18, 39, 46, 47 *1:403*
16:1–35 *1:403, 1:405, 1:406–430, 1:423*
16:1–40 *1:450, 2:241*
16:1, 47 *1:444*
16:2 *1:11, 1:85, 1:410, 1:412, 1:420, 1:432, 1:443*
16:2, 3, 5, 6, 9, 11, 16, 19, 21, 22, 24, 26 *1:409*
16:3 *1:43, 1:225, 1:401, 1:405, 1:408, 1:409, 1:409–412, 1:410, 1:412,*

1:415, 1:421, 1:427,
   1:435, 1:436, 2:13, 2:44
16:3, 5, 7, 37, 38 1:403
16:3, 7 1:414
16:3, 12–14 2:292, 2:357
16:3, 13–14 1:263
16:3–30 1:405
16:4 1:401, 1:417, 1:435,
   2:16
16:4–5 1:412
16:4–11 1:412–415
16:4, 45 1:413
16:5 1:412, 1:413
16:5, 6 1:412
16:5, 6, 11, 16 1:408
16:5–7 1:412, 1:419
16:5, 7 1:403
16:5, 7, 9–10, 16–17 1:417
16:5, 9, 10, 17, 35, 38, 39,
   40 1:403
16:5b 1:414
16:6, 17 1:413
16:7 1:409, 1:410
16:7, 8, 10 1:400
16:7, 16 1:420
16:7b 1:414
16:8 1:401, 2:5, 2:23
16:8–10 1:126
16:8–11 1:43, 1:412,
   1:414
16:9 1:405, 1:421
16:9–10 1:411
16:9, 13 1:414
16:9, 21 1:198
16:10 1:405, 1:443
16:11 1:358, 1:405, 1:417,
   2:286
16:11, 41 1:341
16:12–13 2:13
16:12–14 2:269
16:12–15 1:415–419
16:13 1:426, 1:429
16:13–14 1:417
16:13, 29, 41, 48, 49 1:403
16:14 1:405, 1:416, 1:498,
   2:38, 2:268, 2:296, 2:307
16:15 1:401, 1:410, 1:417,
   1:424, 1:426, 1:432,
   1:433, 2:23, 2:110
16:16 1:415
16:16–22 1:419–422
16:18–19 2:241
16:19 1:420, 1:423, 1:435
16:19, 42 1:413, 2:16
16:20 1:412, 1:477, 1:497
16:20–21 1:435, 1:436
16:20–34 1:421
16:20–35 1:107
16:20–40 1:421
16:20, 44–45 2:16
16:21 1:421, 1:422, 1:426
16:21, 31, 45 1:421
16:22 1:405, 1:423, 1:436,
   1:437, 1:452, 1:466,
   2:310, 2:384
16:22, 45 2:16
16:22, 46 1:403, 1:413,
   1:443, 1:452
16:23, 26 1:401
16:23–27 1:422–425
16:24 1:401, 1:423, 1:430
16:24–25 1:417
16:24, 27 1:417
16:25 1:262, 1:264, 1:416
16:26 1:401, 1:423
16:27 1:14, 1:401, 1:407,
   1:423, 1:430, 2:410
16:28 1:442
16:28–29 1:325
16:28–30 1:44, 1:420
16:28, 30 1:429
16:28–35 1:425–430
16:30 1:401, 1:426, 2:53
16:30, 32 1:432
16:30, 32, 34 1:426,
   1:429
16:30, 33 1:429
16:30–34 1:339
16:31 1:429
16:31–33 1:298
16:31–35 1:405, 2:50
16:31, 35 2:17
16:32 1:401, 1:423, 1:427,
   2:269
16:33 1:409, 1:416, 1:429
16:34 1:429, 1:435, 1:449,
   2:68
16:34, 41 1:435
16:35 1:405, 1:413, 1:414,
   1:426, 1:430, 1:436,
   1:451, 2:64
16:36–38 1:405, 1:433
16:36–40 1:405, 1:413,
   1:433–5
16:36–50 1:403, 1:405,
   1:433–440, 1:450–451
16:36–40 1:435
16:37 1:401, 2:228, 2:380
16:37–38 1:448
16:37, 40 1:413
16:38 1:44, 1:434, 1:435,
   2:269
16:39 1:401, 2:71
16:39–40 1:405, 1:433,
   2:391
16:40 1:411, 1:434, 1:435,
   2:269
16:41 1:405, 1:420, 1:433,
   2:8, 2:357
16:41–42 1:435, 1:449
16:41–50 1:423, 1:435–
   439, 1:477, 2:241
16:42 1:303, 1:404, 1:423,
   1:435
16:42–46 1:405
16:44 1:401
16:44–45 1:435
16:44–55 2:228
16:45 1:401, 1:423, 1:426,
   2:8
16:46 1:435, 1:439, 1:443,
   1:452, 2:42, 2:219,
   2:223, 2:230, 2:384
16:46–47 1:189
16:46, 47, 48, 49, 50 1:199
16:46–48 2:240, 2:257
16:46–49 1:436
16:46–50 2:241
16:47 1:404, 1:405, 1:409,
   1:438, 2:233, 2:241
16:47–48 1:451
16:48 1:405, 1:414, 1:439,
   2:233
16:49 2:233
16:49–50 1:405
16:50 1:439, 2:8
17 1:5, 1:79, 1:85, 1:92,

Numbers (*cont.*)
    1:94, 1:135, 1:192,
    1:446, 1:476–477, 2:18
17 – 19 1:87
17 – 23 1:7
17, 23 2:316
17:1 1:405
17:1–5 1:86, 1:405,
    1:433–435
17:1–5, 10 1:443
17:1–7 1:444–446
17:1–12 1:203
17:1–13 1:193, 1:403,
    1:405, 1:435, 1:443–450,
    1:451
17:2 1:84, 1:401
17:2, 3, 6 2:360
17:2, 4 2:64
17:2, 9 1:403, 2:18
17:3 1:445, 2:296
17:3, 8 1:445, 1:465
17:3, 25 2:69
17:4 1:401
17:5 1:219, 1:401, 1:403,
    1:414, 1:446
17:5, 10 1:341
17:6 1:401, 1:445
17:6–7 1:405, 1:446
17:6–9, 11 1:443
17:6–15 1:435–439
17:7 1:344
17:7, 9 2:22
17:8 1:194, 1:389, 1:404,
    1:447, 2:26, 2:28,
    2:258
17:8–9 1:405
17:8–13 1:446–450
17:10 1:401, 1:421, 1:426,
    1:435, 1:449, 2:5, 2:13,
    2:18, 2:23, 2:24
17:10–11 1:405, 2:27
17:10, 13 1:403
17:11 1:439, 2:389
17:11, 12 1:438
17:11–15 1:466
17:12 1:68, 1:404
17:12–13 1:91, 1:405,
    1:435, 1:444, 1:448–449,
    1:449, 1:455, 2:5

17:13 1:401, 1:403, 1:405,
    1:428, 1:466, 1:484
17:13, 14, 15 1:438
17:27–28 1:474, 1:495,
    2:44
17.6 2:18
18 1:19, 1:58, 1:68, 1:135,
    1:405, 1:420, 1:428,
    1:460, 1:495–496,
    1:497–498, 2:6, 2:236,
    2:238, 2:395, 2:463
18 – 19 1:68, 1:456–502,
    1:479
18, 23 2:316
18:1 1:464, 1:492, 2:360
18:1, 3, 5 1:463
18:1, 3, 5, 8, 9, 10, 16, 17,
    19, 29, 32 1:403
18:1–7 1:435, 1:462,
    1:463–468
18:1, 7 1:463
18:1–7, 8–19, 20–24 1:460
18:1, 8 1:475, 1:476
18:1, 8, 20 1:413, 1:475
18:1–10, 11–13, 14–22
    1:461
18:1–13 1:461
18:1–31 1:115
18:1–32 2:258
18:1a 1:466
18:1b, 5a, 7a 1:466
18:2 1:459, 1:463,
    1:464–465
18:2, 3, 4, 7, 9, 15, 22
    1:403
18:2, 6 1:432, 1:433,
    1:463
18:3 1:123, 1:199, 1:459,
    1:463, 1:466, 2:389
18:3–4 1:460, 1:463
18:3, 4, 5, 7 1:463
18:3–5 1:465–466
18:3, 5, 7 1:463
18:3, 5, 16 1:114
18:3, 7 1:464
18:3, 7, 22, 32 1:403
18:4 1:465
18:4, 6 1:463
18:4, 7 2:230

18:5 1:403, 1:413, 1:443,
    1:449, 1:452, 1:459,
    1:460, 1:463, 1:465,
    1:466, 2:384
18:5–6 1:90, 1:468
18:6 1:404, 1:409, 1:465,
    1:467, 1:470
18:6–7 1:466–468
18:6, 26, 28 1:403
18:7 1:113, 1:445, 1:463,
    1:464, 1:468
18:7, 19 2:238
18:8 1:404, 1:467, 1:469,
    1:470, 1:471, 1:474,
    2:388
18:8, 11, 19, 23 1:460
18:8–19 1:462, 1:467,
    1:469–474, 1:474
18:8, 19 1:469
18:8–32 1:379, 1:432,
    2:376, 2:388
18:9 1:471
18:9–10 1:469, 1:470–471,
    1:473
18:10 1:471
18:11 1:469, 1:471
18:11–13 1:471–472,
    1:472
18:11–18 1:469
18:11–19 1:469, 1:471
18:11, 19 1:471
18:11–25 1:470
18:12 1:377, 1:471
18:12–13 1:469, 1:471
18:12–18 1:469
18:13 1:471
18:13, 20 1:461
18:14 1:459, 1:469
18:14–18 1:472–473
18:14–22 1:461
18:15–17 1:128
18:15–18 1:469, 1:472
18:16 1:129, 1:469
18:18 1:413, 1:459, 2:230
18:19 1:467, 1:469, 1:470,
    1:473–474, 1:475, 1:496,
    2:238
18:20 1:475–476, 2:274,
    2:275, 2:297

Index of Scripture references and ancient sources   601

18:20, 23, 24 *2:297*
18:20, 23d, 24c *1:475*
18:20–24 *1:462, 1:463, 1:475–477, 1:477, 2:461*
18:20, 24 *2:461*
18:20–26 *2:296*
18:20–32 *1:474*
18:21 *1:404, 1:475*
18:21–24 *1:475*
18:21, 24 *1:476*
18:21–24, 31 *1:466*
18:22–23 *1:443, 1:466, 1:475, 1:476–477, 2:228, 2:233*
18:22, 23 *1:466*
18:22, 24 *2:461*
18:23 *1:476, 1:477*
18:23–24 *2:275, 2:458*
18:23, 24 *2:274*
18:24 *1:476, 1:477, 2:461*
18:24b *1:475*
18:25 *1:478*
18:25–29 *1:478*
18:25–32 *1:460, 1:462, 1:469, 2:275, 2:389, 2:477–479*
18:26 *1:475*
18:26–28 *1:478*
18:26–30, 53, 55, 56 *1:475*
18:27 *1:478*
18:29 *1:478*
18:30 *1:478*
18:30–32 *1:478, 1:478–479*
19 *1:32, 1:44, 1:45, 1:49, 1:56, 1:57, 1:58, 1:59, 1:60, 1:67–68, 1:146, 1:198, 1:210, 1:212, 1:237, 1:366, 1:397, 1:421, 1:461, 1:498–502, 2:6, 2:10, 2:48, 2:319, 2:351, 2:387, 2:395, 2:396*
19 – 20 *1:307, 2:278*
19 – 21 *1:378–379*
19, 13, 20 *2:386*
19, 20 *1:153*
19, 24 *2:162*
19, 28, 31 *1:151*

19:1–2 *1:480–482*
19:1–4 *2:387*
19:1–10 *1:491*
19:1–13 *1:480–491, 1:492, 1:500*
19:1–22 *1:237, 1:460, 1:462, 1:479–495, 2:258*
19:2 *1:480, 2:387*
19:2, 4, 6, 17, 18 *1:403, 1:461*
19:2a *1:462*
19:2b–10 *1:462*
19:3 *1:482, 1:483, 2:384*
19:3–4 *2:228*
19:3–4, 6, 7, 9 *1:479*
19:3–6 *1:482–487*
19:3, 9 *1:479*
19:5 *1:482–483, 1:485*
19:5–6 *2:157*
19:5, 6, 8, 17 *2:64*
19:6 *2:180*
19:7 *1:479, 1:483, 1:487*
19:7–8 *1:459*
19:7, 8, 10, 11, 13, 14, 15, 16, 17, 19, 20, 21, 22 *1:479*
19:7–10 *1:487–488*
19:8 *1:483, 1:487*
19:9 *1:460, 1:481, 1:487, 2:384*
19:9, 10 *1:493*
19:9, 12, 13, 17, 19, 20 *1:479*
19:9, 12, 18, 19 *1:479*
19:9, 13, 20, 21 *1:479, 1:487*
19:9, 17 *1:481*
19:9, 20, 21 *1:195*
19:10, 21 *1:460*
19:11 *1:213, 1:489, 2:10*
19:11–12 *1:462*
19:11–13 *1:488–493, 1:492*
19:11, 13, 14, 16, 18 *1:403*
19:11–16 *1:162*
19:11–19 *2:376*
19:12, 13, 20 *1:490*
19:12, 19 *2:386*

19:13 *1:133, 1:462, 1:489, 1:491*
19:13, 18, 19, 20 *1:490*
19:13, 18, 20, 22 *1:488*
19:13, 20 *1:485, 1:490, 1:499, 2:240*
19:14–15 *1:492*
19:14–16 *1:462, 1:492–493*
19:14–22 *1:492–495, 1:500*
19:14a *1:462*
19:16 *1:492*
19:16, 18 *2:386*
19:17–19 *1:462, 1:491, 1:493–494*
19:18, 19 *1:479, 1:490, 1:494*
19:19, 20–21 *1:494*
19:20 *1:133, 1:403, 1:462, 1:491*
19:20–22 *1:494–495*
19:21 *1:487*
19:21a *1:462*
19:21b–22 *1:462*
20 *1:44–45, 1:58, 1:59, 1:60, 1:93, 1:274, 1:306, 1:313, 1:365, 1:404, 1:499, **2:1–50**, 2:53, 2:58, 2:105, 2:174, 2:236, 2:251, 2:275, 2:277, 2:307, 2:315, 2:377, 2:378, 2:395, 2:434, 2:447, 2:471*
20 – 25 *1:45, 1:60, 1:67, 2:264, 2:278*
20 – 36 *1:67, 1:68*
20, 21 *2:39*
20, 24 *2:202*
20, 25 *2:225*
20, 27 *2:308*
20–36 *1:499*
20–43 *1:87–88*
20:1 *1:212, 1:291, 1:296, 1:307, 1:309, 2:10, 2:12, 2:32, 2:34, 2:36, 2:448*
20:1–2 *2:6–13*
20:1, 2, 12, 28–29 *2:3*
20:1–2a *2:4*

Numbers (*cont.*)
20:1–4 *2:380*
20:1, 4, 26, 28 *1:403*
20:1–6 *2:3*
20:1–12 *2:4*
20:1, 12 *2:447*
20:1, 12–13 *2:308–309*
20:1, 12, 13, 14, 16, 22 *1:403*
20:1, 12, 13, 19, 22, 24 *2:3*
20:1–13 *1:423, 2:3, 2:4, 2:5–34, 2:8, 2:34, 2:40, 2:42, 2:75, 2:105, 2:110, 2:308*
20:1, 14 *2:36*
20:1, 14, 16, 22 *2:3, 2:6, 2:10*
20:2 *1:59, 2:8*
20:2, 4, 5 *2:14*
20:2, 4, 6, 8, 10, 12 *2:3*
20:2–5 *2:15, 2:19, 2:76*
20:2, 7–8 *2:63*
20:2–13 *1:308*
20:3 *2:2, 2:3, 2:8, 2:33, 2:34, 2:44, 2:55*
20:3–5 *2:13–16, 2:292*
20:3, 14 *2:36*
20:3, 29 *2:5, 2:44*
20:3a *2:4*
20:4 *2:2, 2:14*
20:5 *1:340, 1:416, 2:2, 2:10, 2:14, 2:38*
20:5a *2:4*
20:6 *1:344, 2:3, 2:8, 2:16, 2:241, 2:251*
20:6–7 *2:28*
20:7–8 *2:16–22*
20:7–8, 10 *2:47*
20:7–8, 11 *1:59*
20:7–11 *2:3*
20:8 *1:60, 1:444, 2:3, 2:4, 2:17, 2:18, 2:19, 2:20, 2:21, 2:22, 2:23, 2:24, 2:27, 2:31, 2:42, 2:76, 2:313*
20:8–9 *1:448, 2:26*
20:8, 9, 11 *2:251*
20:8, 9, 25 *1:403*
20:8, 12 *2:251*
20:8a *2:4*
20:9 *2:3, 2:18, 2:22*
20:10 *1:225, 2:3, 2:5, 2:19, 2:22, 2:24, 2:40, 2:42, 2:308, 2:357*
20:10–11 *2:22–29*
20:11 *2:3, 2:4, 2:8, 2:17, 2:20, 2:21, 2:22, 2:27, 2:28, 2:36, 2:62, 2:139, 2:184, 2:244, 2:316*
20:12 *2:3, 2:4, 2:9, 2:14, 2:18, 2:23, 2:31, 2:32, 2:34, 2:42, 2:46, 2:308, 2:309, 2:321, 2:434*
20:12–13 *2:3, 2:29–34, 2:34*
20:12, 13 *2:6, 2:20*
20:12, 23–24 *2:35*
20:12, 24 *2:42*
20:13 *2:3, 2:10, 2:34, 2:44, 2:48*
20:13b *2:4*
20:14 *2:35, 2:35–36, 2:38, 2:63, 2:79, 2:309*
20:14, 16 *2:5, 2:63*
20:14, 17 *1:45, 2:56*
20:14–21 *1:45, 1:197, 2:3, 2:5, 2:14, 2:34–41, 2:49, 2:54, 2:57, 2:61, 2:79, 2:80, 2:105, 2:114, 2:138, 2:204, 2:279*
20:14b–16 *2:79*
20:15–16 *2:36–37*
20:16 *1:404, 2:15, 2:37, 2:59, 2:103, 2:118, 2:136, 2:147*
20:17 *1:416, 2:5, 2:37–38, 2:38, 2:79*
20:17–18 *2:79*
20:17, 19 *2:40, 2:114*
20:17, 21 *2:5, 2:38*
20:18 *2:38, 2:39, 2:76, 2:79*
20:18, 20 *2:38, 2:112*
20:19 *2:5, 2:38–39, 2:402*
20:19–20 *2:77–78*
20:20 *2:38, 2:82*
20:20–21 *2:39–40, 2:79*
20:21 *2:57, 2:80*
20:22–23 *2:41*
20:22–29 *1:11, 1:123, 1:127, 1:135, 2:3, 2:41–44, 2:55, 2:56, 2:105, 2:228, 2:258, 2:264, 2:276, 2:278, 2:308, 2:309, 2:321, 2:448*
20:23–29 *2:18*
20:24 *2:3, 2:4, 2:24, 2:30, 2:32, 2:33, 2:34, 2:46, 2:308*
20:24–26 *2:41–43*
20:24, 26 *2:10*
20:25 *2:311*
20:25, 26, 28 *2:42*
20:25–28 *2:308*
20:26, 28 *2:43*
20:27 *2:22, 2:389*
20:27–29 *2:43–44*
20:29 *2:13, 2:224, 2:225, 2:475*
20:35 *2:55*
20:44 *2:307*
21 *1:59, 2:16, 2:50–88, 2:111, 2:113, 2:214, 2:258, 2:357, 2:395, 2:397, 2:401, 2:404, 2:411, 2:413, 2:417, 2:439, 2:456*
21 – 24 *2:56, 2:225*
21 – 25 *1:42, 1:44, 1:60, 1:66, 1:197, 2:5, 2:34, 2:35, 2:49, 2:55, 2:63, 2:66, 2:86, 2:164, 2:204, 2:255, 2:259, 2:277, 2:449*
21–22 *2:210*
21, 22 – 24 *2:171*
21 – 24 *2:387*
21 – 25 *1:315, 2:38*
21:1 *2:34, 2:35, 2:52, 2:56–57, 2:57, 2:85, 2:449*
21:1, 2, 17, 24, 25, 31 *2:57*
21:1–3 *2:14, 2:53, 2:55–60, 2:61, 2:62, 2:85, 2:86, 2:88, 2:112, 2:204, 2:279, 2:359*

21:1–3, 4–9, 10–20, 21–35 2:85
21:1–4 2:434
21:1, 21, 22, 26, 29, 33, 34 2:56, 2:84–85
21:1, 21, 33 1:45
21:2 2:55, 2:58–59, 2:59, 2:76, 2:83, 2:347, 2:357
21:2–3 2:57
21:2, 3 1:472
21:3 1:360, 2:57, 2:59–60, 2:63, 2:80
21:3–4, 34 2:407
21:3, 10 2:210
21:4 2:40, 2:55, 2:60, 2:61, 2:62
21:4–5 2:49
21:4–9 2:54, 2:57, 2:60–72, 2:85, 2:86, 2:171, 2:226, 2:241
21:5 1:340, 2:8, 2:52, 2:60–61, 2:62–63, 2:68, 2:76, 2:292
21:5, 7 2:60, 2:357
21:5–16 1:99
21:6 1:434, 2:8, 2:57, 2:62, 2:63, 2:63–66, 2:67
21:6, 7, 8 2:60
21:6, 7, 9 2:60, 2:167
21:6, 21, 32 2:63
21:7 1:59, 1:306, 2:8, 2:61, 2:63, 2:66–67, 2:70, 2:76
21:8 2:67–71
21:8–9 1:92, 2:68, 2:269
21:9 2:8, 2:69, 2:71–72, 2:163
21:10 – 22:1 1:197
21:10, 11 2:449
21:10, 11, 12, 13 2:10
21:10–11, 18–20 2:73
21:10–13 2:74
21:10, 13, 18b 2:77
21:10–15 2:73–75
21:10–20 2:48, 2:54, 2:72–78, 2:84, 2:85, 2:86
21:10–35 2:80
21:11 2:52, 2:307

21:11, 13, 15, 20, 26, 28, 29 2:55, 2:87
21:11, 29 2:87
21:12 2:52, 2:234
21:12–19 2:62
21:13 2:76
21:13–15 2:80, 2:113
21:13–15, 24–26 2:114
21:13, 26 2:148
21:13b, 15b 2:74
21:14 2:53, 2:78
21:14–15 2:55, 2:73, 2:78
21:14–15, 17–18 2:81
21:14–20 2:78
21:14, 33 2:407
21:15 2:147
21:15, 22 2:5, 2:38
21:16 2:62, 2:76, 2:78, 2:84
21:16–18 2:75–77
21:17 2:76
21:17–18 2:55, 2:73
21:18 2:53, 2:77, 2:78, 2:449
21:19 2:77, 2:78
21:19, 20 2:77
21:20 2:53, 2:160, 2:170
21:21 2:5, 2:35, 2:53, 2:54, 2:79, 2:114
21:21–24 2:79–80
21:21–25 2:34
21:21, 25, 31, 34 2:54
21:21–26 2:54
21:21–30 2:279
21:21–31 2:204
21:21–32 2:54, 2:57, 2:74, 2:79, 2:418
21:21–35 2:35, 2:54, 2:78–83, 2:85, 2:86, 2:425, 2:487
21:22 1:416, 2:38, 2:53, 2:79
21:23 2:38, 2:53, 2:57, 2:78, 2:79, 2:82
21:24 2:5, 2:38, 2:117
21:24–25, 34–35 2:84
21:24, 35 2:244, 2:405, 2:416
21:24b–25 2:54, 2:80

21:25 2:80, 2:81
21:25, 26, 27, 28, 30, 34 2:406
21:25–32 2:80–82
21:26 2:53, 2:113
21:26–30 2:113
21:27 2:81, 2:152
21:27–30 2:55, 2:73, 2:75
21:28 2:53, 2:149
21:29 2:81, 2:113, 2:148, 2:201–202
21:30 2:53, 2:81, 2:406
21:31 2:53, 2:81, 2:416
21:31–32 2:54, 2:80
21:32 1:324, 2:5, 2:53, 2:54, 2:406, 2:418
21:33 2:38, 2:423
21:33–35 2:54, 2:57, 2:82–83, 2:85, 2:204, 2:279
21:33, 35 2:83
21:34 2:83
21:35 2:53
22 2:87, 2:105
22 – 23 2:177
22 – 24 1:59, 1:174, 1:277, 2:34, 2:56, 2:57, 2:79, 2:83, **2:88–209**, 2:103, 2:104, 2:106, 2:111, 2:115–116, 2:171, 2:204, 2:215, 2:255, 2:258, 2:376, 2:377, 2:382, 2:395
22 – 24, 25 2:385
22 – 25 2:60, 2:81, 2:401
22, 24 2:55
22 – 24, 25 2:394
22, 25 2:113
22 – 32 2:439
22:1 1:65, 2:10, 2:54, 2:73, 2:78, 2:111, 2:214, 2:384
22:1–3 2:87, 2:160
22:1–6 2:98, 2:111–121
22:1–21 2:105
22:1–35 2:98, 2:111–146
22:2 2:97, 2:111, 2:114, 2:127, 2:147, 2:189
22:2–3 2:81, 2:165

Numbers (*cont.*)
22:2, 23, 25, 27, 31, 33, 41 *2:174*
22:3 *2:62, 2:112–113*
22:3–4 *2:157*
22:3, 33 *2:16*
22:4 *1:45, 2:94, 2:113–114, 2:114, 2:121, 2:203, 2:382*
22:4–5 *2:158*
22:4, 7 *2:216, 2:254, 2:383, 2:395*
22:4, 10 *2:56, 2:85*
22:5 *2:35, 2:94, 2:101, 2:136, 2:165, 2:188*
22:5–6 *2:115–121, 2:124*
22:5, 6, 17 *2:159*
22:5, 10, 15, 37 *2:148*
22:5, 10, 15, 37, 40 *2:63*
22:5, 11, 31, 34 *2:97*
22:5, 20, 34, 36, 37 *2:38*
22:5, 22, 23, 24, 25, 26, 27, 31, 32, 34, 35 *2:5*
22:6 *1:59, 2:57, 2:94, 2:96, 2:107, 2:112, 2:116, 2:120, 2:141, 2:244*
22:6, 12 *2:97, 2:121, 2:134*
22:7 *2:105, 2:113, 2:115, 2:121–123, 2:123, 2:124, 2:133, 2:149, 2:166, 2:177*
22:7–14 *2:98, 2:121–125*
22:8 *2:121, 2:123*
22:8, 18, 20, 35, 38 *2:125*
22:8, 19 *2:99*
22:9 *2:97, 2:124, 2:129*
22:9–12, 20 *2:98*
22:9–20 *2:177*
22:9, 20, 35 *2:145*
22:9, 28, 30, 32, 37, 38 *2:97*
22:10 *2:94, 2:114*
22:10–11 *2:124*
22:11 *2:57, 2:94, 2:118–119*
22:11, 17 *2:97, 2:124, 2:155, 2:229*
22:12 *1:59, 2:97, 2:107,*
2:117, 2:124–125, 2:129, 2:130, 2:135, 2:155, 2:170
22:12, 20 *2:145, 2:152*
22:12, 20, 33, 35 *2:148*
22:12, 20, 35 *2:99*
22:13 *2:94, 2:147, 2:148, 2:188*
22:13–14 *2:125*
22:13, 14 *2:123*
22:15–20 *2:98, 2:125–130*
22:16 *2:382*
22:17 *2:131, 2:150, 2:234*
22:17–18 *2:188*
22:17, 37 *2:122*
22:18 *2:94, 2:104, 2:164, 2:188*
22:18–19 *2:126–128*
22:18, 20, 35, 38 *2:105*
22:18, 38 *2:101*
22:19 *2:146, 2:162*
22:20 *2:94, 2:103, 2:128–131, 2:132, 2:135, 2:137, 2:145, 2:159, 2:169, 2:216*
22:20, 35 *2:102, 2:145, 2:170*
22:21 *2:131, 2:131–135, 2:135, 2:136*
22:21–23, 24–25, 26–27 *2:99*
22:21–35 *2:98*
22:21, 35 *2:141*
22:22 *2:94, 2:99, 2:103, 2:129, 2:132, 2:135–137, 2:139, 2:141, 2:145, 2:146*
22:22, 23, 24, 25, 26 *2:144*
22:22, 23, 24, 25, 26, 27, 31, 32, 34, 35 *2:35, 2:132*
22:22, 23, 26, 31, 32, 34 *2:137*
22:22, 23, 31, 34 *2:150*
22:22, 23, 34 *2:143*
22:22, 24, 26 *2:146*
22:22, 27 *2:187–188, 2:219*
22:22–35 *2:103*
22:23 *2:29, 2:38, 2:60, 2:138, 2:142, 2:166*
22:23, 24, 25, 26–27 *2:137*
22:23, 24, 26 *2:137*
22:23, 25 *2:138, 2:139*
22:23, 25, 27 *2:97, 2:98, 2:146, 2:244*
22:23, 25, 27, 31, 33 *2:132*
22:23, 26, 33 *2:5, 2:38*
22:23–27 *2:137–139*
22:23, 29, 31 *2:5, 2:382*
22:23, 31 *2:38*
22:24 *1:332, 2:38*
22:24, 25 *2:138*
22:25 *2:135*
22:25, 28, 32, 33 *2:5*
22:26 *2:5, 2:38, 2:138, 2:185, 2:245*
22:27 *2:29, 2:135, 2:139, 2:142, 2:354*
22:28 *2:139*
22:28–30 *2:139*
22:28, 30 *2:98*
22:28, 32 *2:29, 2:140, 2:244*
22:28, 32–33 *2:144*
22:28, 32, 33 *2:98, 2:99, 2:117, 2:188*
22:28–35 *2:139–146*
22:29 *2:38, 2:137*
22:30 *2:131, 2:138*
22:31 *2:97, 2:119, 2:137, 2:139, 2:142, 2:174, 2:177*
22:31–35 *2:139*
22:31, 35 *2:140*
22:32 *2:94, 2:98, 2:143, 2:144*
22:32–33 *2:136, 2:141*
22:32–33, 35 *2:146*
22:33 *2:97, 2:144*
22:34 *2:143, 2:172*
22:35 *2:103, 2:137, 2:159*
22:36 *2:37, 2:74, 2:149*
22:36 – 24:25 *2:98*
22:36–40 *2:98, 2:140, 2:147–149*
22:36, 41 *2:60, 2:159*

22:37 2:98
22:38 2:98, 2:132, 2:145, 2:169
22:39 2:94
22:40 2:217
22:41 2:37, 2:73, 2:78, 2:97, 2:99, 2:147, 2:148, 2:149–150, 2:155, 2:160, 2:163, 2:170, 2:177, 2:205, 2:218
22:41 – 23:3 2:132
22:41 – 23:12 2:98, 2:149–159
22.5 2:119
23 1:149, 2:109
23 – 24 2:105
23, 24 2:108
23:1–2 2:150
23:1, 2, 4, 14, 29, 30 2:217/
23:1–2, 14, 29 2:99
23:1–3, 14, 29–30 2:177
23:1–4, 13–15 2:108
23:1, 14, 29 2:98
23:1, 14, 29–30 2:149
23:2 2:94
23:2, 5 2:165
23:3 2:5, 2:38, 2:94, 2:173
23:3, 4 2:151
23:3–6 2:117, 2:150–152
23:3, 9, 13, 21 2:174
23:3, 12, 17, 26 2:99
23:3, 12, 26 2:101
23:3, 15 2:99, 2:171, 2:177
23:4 2:94, 2:150
23:4–5 2:160
23:4, 14, 30 2:94
23:4, 16 2:98
23:5 2:94, 2:169
23:5, 12 2:159
23:5, 16 2:102, 2:170
23:6 2:95
23:6–7 2:161
23:7 2:97, 2:101, 2:108, 2:117, 2:132, 2:134, 2:162, 2:206
23:7–8 2:151, 2:163
23:7–10 2:152, 2:154, 2:191

23:7–10, 18–24 2:73, 2:107, 2:177
23:7, 10, 21, 23 1:198, 2:154
23:7, 18 2:81, 2:99, 2:150, 2:178, 2:192
23:7, 21 2:56, 2:85
23:7, 28 2:152
23:7a, 7b, 8 2:153
23:7a, 9a 2:155
23:7a–b 2:154
23:8 2:97, 2:108, 2:155, 2:156, 2:191
23:8, 11, 13, 25, 27 2:97, 2:124, 2:155, 2:229
23:8, 19, 22, 23 2:155
23:9 2:97, 2:99, 2:193, 2:201, 2:208, 2:243, 2:246, 2:255
23:9–10 2:206
23:9, 13, 21 2:99
23:9, 21 2:215
23:9a, 9b, 10a 2:153
23:10 1:88, 1:101, 2:95, 2:98, 2:133, 2:190, 2:200, 2:208
23:10, 11, 12, 17, 19, 26 2:97
23:10b 2:158
23:11 1:59, 2:98
23:11–12 2:159
23:11, 14 2:163
23:11, 20, 25 2:97, 2:121
23:11, 25 2:106
23:12 2:95, 2:169
23:12, 26 2:105, 2:125
23:13 2:37, 2:60, 2:97, 2:149
23:13–14, 27–28 2:149, 2:177
23:13–15 2:159
23:13–26 2:98, 2:159–169
23:14 2:73, 2:78, 2:99, 2:101, 2:160, 2:205
23:14–15 2:132
23:14, 28 2:99
23:15 2:95, 2:173
23:16 2:95
23:16–17 2:160–161

23:17 2:95
23:18 2:108, 2:154
23:18–19 2:162
23:18–24 2:161, 2:161–169, 2:185, 2:191
23:19 2:98, 2:159, 2:170, 2:244
23:19–20 2:188
23:19, 20, 21, 23, 24 2:162
23:20 1:59, 2:95, 2:108, 2:191
23:20–21a, 23 2:162
23:20–22 2:163–166
23:21 2:97, 2:99, 2:121, 2:154, 2:160, 2:167, 2:208, 2:341
23:21a 2:169
23:21ab, 23ab 2:162
23:21b 2:164, 2:169
23:21b–22 2:162, 2:164
23:22 2:118, 2:166, 2:167, 2:185, 2:208
23:22, 24 2:166, 2:185
23:23 2:60, 2:70, 2:122, 2:155, 2:164, 2:171, 2:172, 2:202
23:23, 24 2:167
23:23a 2:123
23:23b 2:123
23:24 2:133, 2:157, 2:166, 2:168–169, 2:169, 2:186, 2:187, 2:206, 2:386
23:25 2:98
23:25–26 2:169
23:26 2:95
23:27 2:97, 2:149, 2:172
23:27 – 24:9 2:99
23:27 – 24:14 1:42
23:27 – 24:25 2:170–189
23:27, 28 2:163
23:28 2:73, 2:78, 2:99, 2:160, 2:171, 2:172, 2:181, 2:205
23:28–30 2:132
23:29 2:150
23:29–30 2:151
24 1:53, 1:232, 2:102, 2:109, 2:177, 2:210
24:1 1:59, 2:5, 2:38, 2:60,

Numbers (*cont.*)
  2:97, 2:105, 2:122, 2:123,
  2:151, 2:160, 2:166,
  2:171–174, 2:173, 2:177
24:1–2 2:99, 2:112
24:1, 2, 3, 4, 15, 16 2:97
24:1–2, 5–7 1:174
24:1, 2, 17, 20 2:99
24:1, 2, 17, 20, 21 2:174
24:1–6 1:59, 2:496
24:1–9 1:277, 2:97, 2:205
24:1, 9–10 2:97, 2:121
24:2 1:23–24, 1:42, 1:59,
  1:150, 1:277, 2:97, 2:98,
  2:107, 2:132, 2:174,
  2:174–176, 2:177, 2:210,
  2:307
24:2, 5–7 1:92, 1:99
24:2, 6 2:179
24:2–9 2:495
24:2, 13 2:99
24:3 2:95, 2:99, 2:137,
  2:142, 2:174
24:3–4 2:176, 2:176–178,
  2:192
24:3–4, 15–16 1:198
24:3, 4, 15, 16 2:119
24:3–9 2:175, 2:191
24:3–9, 15–19 2:177
24:3–9, 15–19, 20, 21–22,
  23–24 2:73
24:3–9, 15–24 2:107
24:3, 15 2:81, 2:99, 2:109,
  2:176
24:3, 15, 20, 21, 23 2:81,
  2:150, 2:152, 2:192
24:4 2:95, 2:139
24:4–5 2:208
24:4, 7–13 1:422
24:4, 8, 16, 23 2:155
24:4, 16 1:198, 2:132,
  2:176
24:5 1:37, 2:109, 2:201
24:5–6 1:42, 2:70, 2:73,
  2:159, 2:176, 2:178–180
24:5–7 1:90, 1:174, 2:21,
  2:142, 2:206, 2:214
24:5–9 2:166, 2:201
24:5, 13 1:362

24:5, 17 1:198, 2:154
24:5a–b, 9c–d 2:175
24:6 2:5, 2:38
24:6b, d 2:180
24:7 1:42, 2:27, 2:56,
  2:85, 2:95, 2:109, 2:176,
  2:180–183, 2:206
24:7–8 2:208
24:7–9 2:166
24:7–9, 17 2:266, 2:270
24:7–9, 17–19 2:157
24:7, 17 1:45, 2:154
24:7b 2:185
24:7c–d 2:175
24:8 1:42, 2:95, 2:118,
  2:165, 2:166, 2:185,
  2:208, 2:210, 2:245
24:8–9 2:185–187, 2:206
24:8, 17 1:198
24:8a–b 2:176
24:9 1:24, 1:42, 1:59, 1:95,
  1:332, 2:57, 2:97, 2:134,
  2:166, 2:169, 2:185,
  2:192, 2:203, 2:209
24:9–10 2:96, 2:120
24:9, 13, 22, 23 2:97
24:9, 21 2:98
24:9a 2:187
24:9a–b 2:176
24:9b 2:187
24:9c–d 2:176
24:10 2:97, 2:106, 2:124,
  2:132, 2:135, 2:139,
  2:155, 2:177, 2:188,
  2:198, 2:219, 2:229
24:10–11 2:177
24:10–13 2:187–189
24:10–14 2:177
24:10–19 2:99
24:11 2:96, 2:122, 2:148,
  2:170, 2:188, 2:189
24:12 2:5, 2:35, 2:63
24:13 1:330, 2:95, 2:98,
  2:101, 2:104, 2:105,
  2:125, 2:126, 2:145,
  2:170, 2:188, 2:189
24:14 1:197, 2:95, 2:117,
  2:158, 2:177, 2:189–191,
  2:190, 2:200

24:15 2:201
24:15–16 2:170, 2:176,
  2:192–193
24:15–19 2:140, 2:191–
  192, 2:192
24:15–19, 20, 21–22,
  23–24 2:192
24:15–24 2:132
24:16 2:142, 2:177
24:17 1:88, 1:198, 1:404,
  2:95, 2:120, 2:134,
  2:189, 2:193, 2:194,
  2:195, 2:196, 2:201,
  2:206, 2:207, 2:210
24:17–18 2:133
24:17–19 2:195
24:17a–b 2:192
24:18 2:196, 2:210
24:18–19 1:197–198, 2:34
24:18–19a 2:196
24:19 2:95, 2:196
24:20 2:184, 2:190,
  2:199–200, 2:202,
  2:210, 2:315
24:20, 21 2:97
24:20–24 2:99, 2:133,
  2:191
24:20–25 2:198–204
24:21 2:166, 2:185, 2:201
24:21–22 2:196, 2:199,
  2:200–201, 2:210
24:22 2:81, 2:95, 2:185
24:22, 24 2:210
24:22b 2:185
24:23 2:95, 2:98
24:23–24 2:199,
  2:201–203
24:24 2:95, 2:99, 2:199,
  2:201
24:25 2:99, 2:132, 2:137,
  2:140, 2:203–204
24:33 2:238
25 1:53, 1:59, 1:60, 1:150,
  1:151, 1:171, 1:357,
  1:386, 1:438, 1:468,
  1:477, 1:497, 1:499,
  2:42, 2:55, 2:57, 2:80,
  2:102, 2:103, 2:111,
  2:135, **2:210–257**, 2:272,

2:284, 2:369, 2:376,
2:377, 2:378, 2:380,
2:382, 2:383, 2:385,
2:391, 2:392, 2:394,
2:395, 2:396, 2:439
25 – 31 2:394
25, 27 2:284
25, 31 2:376
25:1 1.391, 2:211, 2:232,
2:249, 2:252, 2:449
25:1–3 1:45, 2:181, 2:213,
2:214–219, 2:219
25:1–3, 6–9, 14–15 2:213
25:1–4 1:56, 2:237
25:1–4, 5–9 2:16
25:1–5 2:212, 2:213,
2:214, 2:252, 2:255,
2:256
25:1, 6, 14–18 2:121
25:1, 6, 17 2:254–255
25:1–9 1:199, 2:284
25:1–12 2:396
25:1–13 2:377
25:1–15 2:8
25:1–19 2:214–248
25:1, 22 2:230
25:2 2:130
25:2, 11, 13 2:250
25:3 2:135, 2:149, 2:156,
2:170, 2:188, 2:220,
2:249, 2:255, 2:390
25:3–4 2:225
25:3–4, 8 2:222
25:3, 5 2:171
25:4 1:11, 2:73, 2:211,
2:227, 2:229, 2:233,
2:235, 2:258
25:4–5 2:213, 2:219–222,
2:241
25:4, 8, 11–13 1:382
25:4, 10–13, 16–18 2:213
25:4, 10, 16 2:213
25:5 2:211, 2:217, 2:249
25:6 2:211–212, 2:219,
2:222–225, 2:228, 2:229,
2:251, 2:252, 2:253,
2:285
25:6–7 2:225, 2:250,
2:253, 2:254

25:6–8 2:225, 2:240
25:6–9 2:213, 2:237, 2:245,
2:252, 2:256, 2:376
25:6–13 2:213, 2:214,
2:258
25:6, 14, 15 2:113
25:6, 14, 15, 17, 18 2:216
25:6–15 1:231, 2:395
25:6–18 1:229, 2:212,
2:256
25:7 2:251
25:7–8 2:221
25:7–9 1:438, 2:225–234
25:7–13 1:123, 2:393
25:7–15 1:90
25:7–18 1:56
25:8 1:60, 2:124, 2:155,
2:242, 2:252, 2:253
25:8–9 2:219
25:8, 9, 18, 19 1:199
25:8, 14–15 2:220
25:8b–9 2:212
25:9 2:57, 2:225, 2:233,
2:249, 2:250, 2:264,
2:278, 2:379, 2:483
25:9, 14 1:88
25:10–11 2:234–236
25:10–13 1:11, 1:90,
1:135, 2:213, 2:221,
2:238, 2:245, 2:276,
2:321–322
25:10–18 1:120
25:11 1:151, 2:203, 2:254
25:11, 13 2:252, 2:253,
2:254
25:12 2:212, 2:235, 2:238
25:12–13 1:474, 2:230,
2:236–245, 2:238
25:12, 13 2:239, 2:254
25:13 1:135, 1:151, 2:212,
2:233, 2:235, 2:238,
2:241, 2:249, 2:253,
2:390
25:14 2:266, 2:405
25:14–15 1:11, 2:212,
2:220, 2:222, 2:243–245,
2:245, 2:360
25:14, 15, 17, 18 2:244
25:14–18 2:213, 2:214

25:15 2:376, 2:382
25:15–18 2:123, 2:217
25:15–19 2:187
25:16–18 2:213, 2:244,
2:245, 2:245–247, 2:376,
2:377, 2:385, 2:395
25:17 2:212, 2:247, 2:256,
2:377
25:17–18 2:244, 2:396
25:17, 18 1:226, 2:185,
2:381, 2:452
25:18 2:264
25:19 2:212, 2:247–248,
2:261, 2:263–264
25:53 2:158
26 1:53, 1:61, 1:65, 1:66,
1:96, 1:100–108, 1:133,
1:195, 1:358, 2:82, 2:212,
2:243, 2:259–278, 2:308,
2:347, 2:377, 2:383
26 – 27 2:282, 2:320–322,
2:348, 2:376, 2:396
26 – 32 2:401
26 – 34 2:263
26 – 36 1:14, 1:21, 1:34,
1:40, 1:42, 1:61, 1:64,
1:65, 1:66, 1:67, 1:416,
1:463, 1:475, 1:497,
2:111, 2:223, 2:256,
2:258, 2:265, 2:271,
2:277, 2:284, 2:296,
2:298, 2:307, 2:309,
2:314, 2:315, 2:317,
2:346, 2:351, 2:376,
2:395, 2:421, 2:473,
2:479, 2:489, 2:494–495
26:1 2:247, 2:261, 2:264,
2:287
26:1–4 2:263, 2:264–268
26:1–62 1:10, 2:456
26:2 1:79, 2:359, 2:388
26:3, 63 2:111, 2:265,
2:276, 2:384, 2:449
26:4 2:262, 2:264, 2:265,
2:389, 2:441
26:5 1:87, 2:262
26:5–11 2:268–269
26:5–51 2:263, 2:265,
2:265–272

Numbers (*cont.*)
26:6 *2:186*
26:7, 18, 34 *1:108*
26:8 *2:262*
26:9 *1:408, 2:384*
26:9–10 *2:266*
26:9–11 *2:267, 2:279*
26:9, 12 *2:262*
26:10 *1:426, 1:429, 1:430, 2:68, 2:71, 2:269*
26:11 *1:427, 1:430*
26:12–13 *2:244*
26:12–14 *2:269, 2:405*
26:13 *2:262*
26:14 *1:88*
26:15 *2:262*
26:15–18 *2:270*
26:16 *2:262*
26:17 *2:262*
26:18 *2:262*
26:19 *2:267, 2:279*
26:19–27 *2:270*
26:21 *2:262*
26:23 *2:262*
26:24 *2:262*
26:27 *2:262*
26:28–34 *2:285, 2:421*
26:28–37 *2:270–271*
26:28, 37 *2:317*
26:29 *2:422*
26:30 *2:262*
26:32 *2:262*
26:33 *2:267, 2:268, 2:272, 2:282, 2:285, 2:288, 2:289, 2:320, 2:357, 2:486, 2:493*
26:33, 45 *1:45, 2:85*
26:34 *2:262*
26:35 *2:262*
26:36 *2:262*
26:38 *2:262*
26:38–41 *2:272*
26:39 *2:262*
26:40 *1:430, 2:262*
26:41 *2:262*
26:42–43 *1:101, 2:262*
26:42–50 *2:272*
26:45 *2:263*
26:46 *2:268*

26:50 *2:263*
26:51 *1:100, 2:272, 2:276*
26:52 *2:320*
26:52–53 *2:286*
26:52–56 *2:263, 2:273–274, 2:279, 2:320, 2:451, 2:451–452, 2:456, 2:487*
26:53 *2:274, 2:277, 2:290, 2:327, 2:456*
26:54 *2:320, 2:464*
26:55 *2:266, 2:274, 2:306*
26:55–56 *2:451*
26:57 *2:263*
26:57–62 *2:263, 2:268, 2:269, 2:274–276, 2:276*
26:58 *2:263*
26:58, 59 *2:275*
26:59 *1:121, 1:291, 2:263, 2:272*
26:60–61 *1:122*
26:61 *1:413, 1:428, 2:263, 2:267, 2:279*
26:62 *2:274, 2:297, 2:461*
26:63 *2:276*
26:63–65 *2:263, 2:276–277, 2:277*
26:64 *1:83*
26:64–65 *2:276–277, 2:279, 2:320, 2:390*
26:65 *2:276, 2:284, 2:287*
27 *1:62, 1:66, 1:67, 1:172–173, **2:280–321**, 2:296, 2:492, 2:496*
27 – 29 *2:383*
27 – 32 *2:406*
27 – 36 *2:487, 2:494*
27, 36 *2:256, 2:271, 2:305, 2:418*
27:1 *1:45, 2:85, 2:281, 2:317, 2:416, 2:486, 2:487, 2:493*
27:1–2 *2:282, 2:285–286, 2:405*
27:1–5 *2:282*
27:1, 5 *2:390*
27:1–7 *2:283*
27:1–11 *1:66, 1:96, 1:213, 1:215, 1:358, 1:385,*

2:267, 2:271, 2:274, 2:278, 2:279, 2:282, 2:283, 2:284–294, 2:285, 2:287, 2:305, 2:308, 2:317, 2:318, 2:320, 2:321, 2:347, 2:357, 2:368, 2:371, 2:377, 2:404, 2:416, 2:417, 2:421, 2:423, 2:436, 2:486, 2:487, 2:495
27:1–11, 12–23 *2:281*
27:1, 15 *2:320*
27:2 *2:485*
27:2, 19, 22 *2:306*
27:3 *1:358, 1:402, 1:426, 2:286, 2:287, 2:320*
27:3–4 *2:268, 2:282, 2:286–291, 2:288, 2:304*
27:3, 14 *2:281*
27:4 *2:281, 2:287, 2:288, 2:298, 2:301, 2:302–303, 2:306, 2:405, 2:488*
27:4, 7 *2:389, 2:406, 2:494*
27:4, 7, 9, 10, 11, 12, 20 *2:306*
27:5 *2:282, 2:287, 2:291, 2:490*
27:5–9 *2:317*
27:6 *2:281, 2:404*
27:6–7 *2:282, 2:289, 2:291–293, 2:357*
27:6, 8, 12 *2:299*
27:6–11 *2:282, 2:287, 2:320, 2:487*
27:6, 18 *2:320*
27:7 *2:281, 2:291, 2:298, 2:308, 2:412, 2:490, 2:491*
27:7–8 *2:282, 2:306*
27:7, 12 *2:320*
27:8 *2:293*
27:8–11 *1:385, 2:282, 2:283, 2:293–294, 2:301*
27:9–11 *2:293*
27:11 *1:459, 2:283, 2:473, 2:494*
27:11–15 *2:317*
27:11, 22 *2:389*

27:12 *2:33, 2:34, 2:282,*
   2:307, 2:449
27:12–13 *1:67, 1:352,*
   2:281, 2:397
27:12–14 *2:32, 2:46,*
   2:282, 2:306–309, 2:308,
   2:378
27:12–17 *2:283*
27:12–23 *1:11, 1:66, 1:86,*
   1:96, 1:327, 1:343,
   1:354, 2:10, 2:33, 2:48,
   2:278, 2:282, 2:283,
   2:306–317, 2:315, 2:317,
   2:318, 2:320, 2:347,
   2:351, 2:357, 2:377,
   2:395, 2:415
27:13 *1:57, 2:10, 2:41,*
   2:282, 2:307, 2:376
27:14 *1:404, 2:24, 2:32,*
   2:33, 2:46, 2:282, 2:320
27:14, 19 *2:313*
27:15–17 *2:282, 2:283,*
   2:308
27:16 *1:422, 2:312*
27:17 *1:353, 2:281, 2:314*
27:18 *1:197, 1:353, 2:310,*
   2:312
27:18–20 *1:268, 2:283*
27:18–21 *2:311–315*
27:18, 22 *2:276*
27:18–23 *2:282, 2:283,*
   2:320
27:19–20 *2:312*
27:20 *2:281, 2:314*
27:21 *2:283, 2:374, 2:381*
27:21–22 *2:387*
27:22 *2:22, 2:276*
27:22–23 *2:283,*
   2:315–317
27:23 *1:219, 2:281, 2:387*
28 *1:44*
28 – 29 *1:57, 1:226, 1:375,*
   1:380, 2:278, 2:319,
   2:322–352, *2:370, 2:371,*
   2:376, 2:377, 2:396
28 – 30 *1:56, 1:66, 1:397,*
   2:348, 2:351, 2:397
28 – 32 *1:67, 2:376*
28, 29, 30 *2:357–358*

28:1 *2:346*
28:1–2 *2:326, 2:326–329*
28:1–7 *2:334*
28:2 *2:325, 2:342, 2:347*
28:2, 3 *2:328*
28:2, 6, 8, 13, 24, 27
   2:346
28:3 *2:328*
28:3–8 *2:326, 2:329–235*
28:4, 8 *2:328*
28:5 *2:325, 2:335*
28:5, 8 *1:400*
28:6 *2:334*
28:7 *2:325, 2:328*
28:8 *2:334, 2:335*
28:9 *2:325*
28:9–10 *2:326, 2:335–336*
28:10 *2:325, 2:336*
28:10, 15, 23 *2:335*
28:11–15 *2:326, 2:336–*
   237, 2:339, 2:340, 2:342,
   2:349
28:14 *2:325*
28:15 *2:337, 2:340*
28:15, 30 *2:337*
28:16 *1:212, 2:9, 2:349*
28:16 – 29:38 *2:326,*
   2:337–338
28:16–25 *2:326, 2:338,*
   2:338–339
28:17 *2:325*
28:17–25 *2:350*
28:18, 25, 26 *2:329*
28:19 *1:373, 2:325*
28:22 *2:337*
28:22, 30 *2:337*
28:24 *2:325*
28:26 *2:338*
28:26–31 *2:326, 2:339–*
   340, 2:350
28:27 *2:325*
28:30 *2:325*
28:39 *2:346*
29:1, 2 *2:328*
29:1–6 *2:326, 2:340–342,*
   2:350
29:1, 7, 12 *2:329*
29:2, 6, 8, 13, 36 *2:346*
29:2, 8 *2:343*

29:5, 11 *2:337*
29:5, 11, 16, 19, 25 *2:337*
29:6 *2:325, 2:342*
29:7 *2:325, 2:339, 2:342*
29:7–11 *2:326, 2:342–343,*
   2:350
29:8 *2:325*
29:12 *2:325*
29:12–34 *2:339, 2:350*
29:12, 35 *2:325*
29:12–38 *2:326, 2:343–*
   346, 2:346
29:13 *2:325*
29:14 *2:326*
29:15 *2:326*
29:16 *2:326*
29:16, 19, 22, 25, 28, 31,
   34, 38 *2:337*
29:18, 21, 24 *2:326*
29:22, 28, 31, 34, 38 *2:337*
29:35 *2:329*
29:35–38 *2:350*
29:39 *1:57, 1:66, 2:347,*
   2:354, 2:358
29:39–40 *2:326,*
   2:346–347
29:40 *2:347*
30 *1:57, 2:11, 2:284,*
   2:319, 2:347, **2:350–370**,
   2:351, 2:376, 2:377,
   2:396, 2:403, 2:414,
   2:424
30, 31 *2:401*
30, 31, 32 *2:407*
30, 32 *1:432*
30:1 *2:326, 2:353*
30:1–2 *2:356–359*
30:1, 16 *2:353*
30:2 *2:353, 2:356, 2:357,*
   2:367, 2:401, 2:414,
   2:415
30:2, 13–15 *2:353*
30:3 *2:353, 2:408*
30:3–5 *2:361–363*
30:3–6 *2:360*
30:3, 6, 13, 15 *2:360*
30:3–12 *2:353*
30:3–16 *2:360–367*
30:4 *2:353*

Numbers (*cont.*)
30:4–5, 11 *2:365*
30:4, 7, 11 *2:360*
30:5 *2:353, 2:364*
30:5, 8, 11 *2:362, 2:407*
30:6 *2:353*
30:6–8 *2:363–365, 2:366*
30:6, 8 *2:364*
30:6, 9, 12 *1:357*
30:7 *2:353*
30:7–8 *2:360*
30:8 *2:353*
30:9 *2:353, 2:365–366*
30:9–12 *2:360, 2:365–367*
30:10–11 *2:353*
30:10–12 *2:365–366*
30:11 *2:353*
30:13 *1:157*
30:13–14 *2:365*
30:13–16 *2:367–368*
30:15 *1:157, 2:353*
30:16 *2:367, 2:391*
30:31 *2:368*
31 *1:49, 1:67, 1:229, 1:386, 1:493, 2:104, 2:105, 2:226, 2:247, 2:264, 2:284, 2:370,* **2:371–398,** *2:379, 2:403, 2:413, 2:450, 2:483*
31 – 32 *1:67, 2:265, 2:410, 2:413*
31 – 35 *2:98*
31, 32 *2:415*
31:1 *1:57, 2:247, 2:375*
31:1–2 *1:67, 2:351, 2:357, 2:375, 2:377–378, 2:378, 2:392, 2:397*
31:1–6 *2:401*
31:1–9 *2:113*
31:1–11 *2:123*
31:1–12 *2:375, 2:377–384*
31:1–24 *2:375, 2:387*
31:1–24, 25–54 *2:375*
31:1, 25 *2:375*
31:2 *1:231, 2:10, 2:41, 2:307, 2:376, 2:377, 2:420*
31:2–3 *2:376*
31:2, 3, 7, 8, 9 *2:376*
31:3 *1:244, 2:373, 2:377–378, 2:379*
31:3, 5 *2:413*
31:3–5, 26, 32–47 *2:376*
31:3–6 *2:379–281*
31:3, 7, 8, 9 *2:216*
31:4 *2:379*
31:5 *1:104, 2:373, 2:374, 2:380, 2:385, 2:413*
31:6 *1:123, 1:226, 2:373, 2:376*
31:7 *2:375*
31:7–8 *2:381–383*
31:7, 31, 41, 47 *2:381, 2:393*
31:7, 41, 47 *2:389*
31:8 *1:44, 2:5, 2:38, 2:56, 2:85, 2:100, 2:103, 2:115, 2:129, 2:131, 2:141, 2:244, 2:247, 2:376, 2:394*
31:8–16 *2:103*
31:8, 16 *2:104, 2:158, 2:203, 2:204, 2:217, 2:255, 2:256, 2:257, 2:376*
31:8, 19 *2:386*
31:9 *2:382, 2:402, 2:403*
31:9–12 *2:383–384*
31:9, 17 *1:14*
31:9, 17, 18 *2:410*
31:9–20 *2:357*
31:10 *2:64, 2:374*
31:11 *2:375*
31:11, 26 *2:383*
31:12 *2:111*
31:12–20 *2:391*
31:12–24 *1:499*
31:13 *2:374, 2:405*
31:13–16 *2:384–385*
31:13–24 *2:375, 2:384–387, 2:396*
31:13, 24 *1:49*
31:14 *2:375, 2:380*
31:14–18 *2:382*
31:14, 21, 27, 28, 49 *2:407*
31:15 *2:374, 2:385*
31:15–18 *2:377*
31:16 *1:151, 1:199, 2:46, 2:103, 2:130, 2:170, 2:188, 2:189, 2:218, 2:246, 2:247, 2:252, 2:254, 2:256, 2:370, 2:374, 2:376, 2:385*
31:16–19 *2:405*
31:17, 18, 35 *2:385*
31:17–20 *2:385–386*
31:18 *2:384*
31:19 *1:480, 2:384*
31:19–24 *1:492, 2:376*
31:19–34 *1:492*
31:21 *1:459, 1:480, 2:374*
31:21–24 *1:480, 2:386, 2:391*
31:23 *1:487, 2:374*
31:24 *2:375*
31:24–54 *2:387–392*
31:25 *2:375*
31:25–27 *2:375, 2:391*
31:25–31 *2:388–389*
31:25–47 *2:375*
31:25–54 *1:472, 2:375, 2:376*
31:26 *2:375, 2:388*
31:28 *2:374, 2:388*
31:28–47 *2:376*
31:29 *2:374*
31:29, 41 *2:393*
31:29, 41, 52 *2:388*
31:30, 47 *2:298, 2:374, 2:389*
31:31, 41, 47 *2:375*
31:32–35 *2:389, 2:396*
31:32–47 *2:389*
31:35–40 *2:374*
31:35, 40, 46 *1:213*
31:36–41, 42–47 *2:396*
31:37 *2:374*
31:38 *2:390*
31:42–47 *2:389*
31:48 *2:375*
31:48–54 *1:86, 2:375, 2:376, 2:390–392, 2:391, 2:393, 2:396*
31:49 *2:57, 2:359, 2:388, 2:393*
31:50 *2:359, 2:393*
31:53 *2:388, 2:391*

Index of Scripture references and ancient sources   611

31:54 *2:376*
32 *1:67, 1:204, 2:74, 2:79, 2:83, 2:85, 2:114, 2:142, 2:271, 2:278, 2:296, 2:357, 2:370, 2:386–387, 2:397,* **2:398–425**, *2:456, 2:458*
32 – 34 *1:94*
32:1 *2:400, 2:409, 2:410, 2:415*
32:1–2 *1:94*
32:1, 3, 35 *2:406*
32:1–4 *2:383*
32:1, 4 *2:411*
32:1–5 *2:402,* **2:402–406**
32:1–15 *2:402*
32:1, 16, 26 *2:402*
32:1–32 *2:416*
32:2 *2:356, 2:400, 2:417*
32:2–4 *2:406*
32:2, 6, 25, 29, 31, 33 *2:400*
32:2, 6, 25, 29, 31, 33, 34, 37 *2:401*
32:3 *2:400, 2:417*
32:3–5 *2:411, 2:415*
32:3, 34, 35, 46 *2:406*
32:3, 37 *2:406*
32:4 *2:400, 2:407, 2:410*
32:5 *2:406, 2:407, 2:411, 2:414*
32:5, 7, 21, 27, 29, 30, 32 *2:402*
32:5, 22, 29, 30, 32 *2:389, 2:401*
32:5, 22, 29, 32 *2:298, 2:406*
32:5, 33, 40 *2:406*
32:6–15 *2:402,* **2:406–410**
32:6, 16 *2:410*
32:6, 20, 27, 29 *2:407*
32:7, 9 *1:11, 1:357, 2:34, 2:307, 2:362, 2:407, 2:409*
32:8 *2:410, 2:445, 2:446*
32:8–13 *2:421*
32:9 *1:57, 1:332, 2:307, 2:410*
32:10, 11 *2:408*

32:10, 13 *2:135, 2:188, 2:219*
32:11 *2:400, 2:410*
32:11–12 *1:353, 2:408*
32:12 *1:326, 1:378, 2:276, 2:400*
32:12, 28 *2:276, 2:314*
32:13 *2:400, 2:410, 2:416*
32:14 *2:400*
32:15 *1:11, 1:244, 2:400, 2:410*
32:16 *2:411, 2:414*
32:16, 17, 24, 26 *1:14, 2:410*
32:16–19 *2:402, 2:410–412*
32:16–24 *2:402*
32:16–27 *2:415*
32:17 *2:400, 2:408, 2:410, 2:411, 2:412*
32:17, 20, 21, 26, 29, 30, 32 *2:401, 2:402*
32:17, 20, 21, 27, 29, 30, 32 *2:413*
32:17, 21 *2:16*
32:17, 36 *2:410*
32:18 *2:411*
32:18, 22 *2:410*
32:19, 32 *2:401*
32:20, 21, 22 *2:412*
32:20, 21, 22, 27, 29, 32 *2:402*
32:20–24 *2:357, 2:402, 2:411, 2:412–414, 2:415, 2:416*
32:21 *2:450*
32:21, 27, 29, 30 *2:410*
32:21, 39 *2:410*
32:22 *2:363, 2:400*
32:22, 29 *2:413*
32:22, 30 *2:412*
32:23 *2:400*
32:24 *2:356, 2:401, 2:410*
32:25 *2:400*
32:25–27 *2:402, 2:415*
32:25, 29, 31 *2:400*
32:26 *2:400, 2:414*
32:26, 27 *2:415*
32:27 *2:413*
32:27 – 24:25 *2:98*

32:27–29 *1:121*
32:27, 29 *1:108*
32:28 *2:356*
32:28–30 *2:402*
32:28–32 *2:402, 2:415*
32:29 *2:416*
32:30 *2:400*
32:31–32 *2:402*
32:32 *2:400, 2:412, 2:415*
32:33 *2:54, 2:56, 2:85, 2:317, 2:400, 2:402, 2:416, 2:421*
32:33, 34 *1:44*
32:33–38 *2:416–418*
32:33, 39–42 *2:317, 2:416, 2:421*
32:33, 40 *2:401*
32:33–42 *2:271, 2:402, 2:487*
32:34–35 *2:82*
32:34–36 *2:416*
32:34–38 *2:402, 2:423*
32:35 *2:400*
32:36 *2:400*
32:37–38 *2:416*
32:38 *2:400*
32:39 *2:271, 2:400, 2:418*
32:39–42 *2:402, 2:416, 2:418–421, 2:420, 2:422, 2:423*
32:40 *2:418*
32:41 *2:271, 2:401*
32:42 *2:401*
32:50 *2:41*
33 *2:274,* **2:425–427, 2:439–450**
33 – 34 *2:479*
33 – 35 *1:66, 1:67, 1:364, 2:425–484*
33 – 36 *1:67, 2:401, 2:413, 2:439, 2:451, 2:472, 2:479, 2:487*
33 – 37 *1:116*
33:1 *2:437, 2:441, 2:458*
33:1–2 *2:441–442, 2:444*
33:1–39, 40–49 *2:440*
33:1–49 *2:37, 2:73, 2:432, 2:435, 2:439–450, 2:447*

Numbers (*cont.*)
33:2 *1:71, 2:448*
33:3 *1:212, 1:424, 2:9*
33:3–4 *2:434, 2:448*
33:3–4, 38–39, 40 *2:433*
33:3–5 *2:442–443*
33:3–14 *2:433*
33:3–49 *2:450*
33:4 *2:403*
33:6 *2:37*
33:6, 7, 8, 36, 37, 44, 47, 48–49 *2:433*
33:6–15 *2:440, 2:443–444*
33:6, 37 *2:147*
33:7 *2:430*
33:8 *1:425, 2:430, 2:433*
33:8, 52, 55 *2:16*
33:9 *2:430, 2:444*
33:9, 14 *2:433*
33:10 *2:464*
33:12 *2:430*
33:13 *2:430*
33:14 *2:430, 2:444*
33:15, 16 *1:83*
33:16 *2:430*
33:16–17 *2:444–446*
33:16–49 *2:440*
33:18 *2:445*
33:18b–35 *2:446*
33:20 *2:430*
33:21 *2:430*
33:22 *2:430*
33:24 *2:430*
33:25–26 *2:430*
33:26 *2:430*
33:27 *2:430*
33:28 *2:431*
33:30 *2:431*
33:31 *2:431*
33:31–33 *2:447*
33:32 *2:431*
33:33 *2:431*
33:34 *2:431, 2:449*
33:35, 36 *2:447*
33:36 *2:431, 2:446, 2:447*
33:36–39 *2:9, 2:448–449*
33:36b–41 *2:431*
33:37 *2:37*
33:37–39 *2:442, 2:449*
33:38 *2:431, 2:441, 2:448*
33:38–39 *2:43, 2:434*
33:39 *2:43*
33:40 *2:56, 2:85, 2:434, 2:449*
33:40–49 *2:449–450*
33:42 *2:431*
33:42–43 *2:72*
33:43 *2:431*
33:44 *2:431*
33:44, 47–48 *2:307*
33:44–49 *2:432*
33:45 *2:431, 2:449*
33:46 *2:431*
33:47 *2:431*
33:48 *2:265*
33:48–49 *2:450*
33:48, 49, 50 *2:111*
33:48–50 *2:384*
33:48, 50 *2:276, 2:449*
33:49 *2:214, 2:431, 2:449, 2:483*
33:49–50 *2:111*
33:50 *2:437, 2:449*
33:50 – 36:13 *2:453*
33:50–52 *2:450–451*
33:50–53 *2:483*
33:50–56 *2:401, 2:432, 2:435, 2:438, 2:441, 2:450–453, 2:453, 2:483*
33:50–60 *2:439*
33:51 *2:449, 2:464*
33:51–52 *2:452*
33:51–56 *2:378*
33:52 *2:450*
33:52–53 *2:450*
33:52aßb *2:452*
33:53 *2:34, 2:307, 2:431, 2:451*
33:53–54 *2:451–452*
33:54 *2:273, 2:274, 2:296, 2:431, 2:450, 2:451, 2:464*
33:55 *2:185, 2:245*
33:55–56 *2:450, 2:452, 2:483*
33:55aß *2:452*
33:56 *2:451*

34 *1:63, 2:294, 2:296,* **2:453–460**
34 – 36 *1:63*
34:1–2 *1:94, 2:446, 2:453–454, 2:455*
34:1–8, 9–34 *2:464*
34:1–12 *2:435, 2:438, 2:453–455, 2:455, 2:456, 2:483*
34:1–15 *2:432, 2:438, 2:453–456, 2:461*
34:2 *2:431*
34:2b, 13 *2:456*
34:3 *2:37, 2:147, 2:455*
34:3–5 *2:454, 2:458*
34:3–5, 6, 7–9, 10–12 *2:454*
34:3–12 *2:453*
34:4 *2:431, 2:446*
34:5 *2:431*
34:6 *2:454*
34:7–9 *2:454–455*
34:8 *1:331*
34:9 *2:431*
34:10 *2:431*
34:10–12 *2:424, 2:455*
34:11 *2:431*
34:13 *2:273, 2:416, 2:451, 2:454, 2:455*
34:13–15 *2:436, 2:438, 2:453, 2:455–456, 2:483*
34:14–15 *2:431, 2:455–456, 2:456*
34:15 *2:111*
34:16–18 *2:456–458*
34:16–28 *2:435*
34:16–29 *1:10, 1:11, 1:67, 1:86, 1:96, 1:99, 1:325, 1:364, 2:277, 2:405, 2:432, 2:436, 2:454, 2:456, 2:456–460, 2:483*
34:17 *2:276, 2:314, 2:437*
34:17, 18 *2:460*
34:17, 19 *2:458, 2:460*
34:17, 19, 29 *2:458*
34:18 *1:85, 2:456*
34:19 *2:276, 2:454, 2:458*
34:19–28 *2:458–460*

INDEX OF SCRIPTURE REFERENCES AND ANCIENT SOURCES   613

34:20 *2:431*
34:20, 28 *2:459*
34:21 *1:279, 2:431*
34:23 *2:317*
34:24 *1:279, 2:459*
34:29 *2:460*
34:33 *2:419*
34:34 *2:456*
35 *1:384, 1:421, 2:296,*
   2:460–484, *2:478*
35, 36 *2:490*
35:1 *2:111, 2:265, 2:276,*
   2:384, 2:437, 2:449
35:1–3 *2:438, 2:461*
35:1–8 *2:274, 2:432,*
   2:435, 2:438, 2:453,
   2:455, 2:460–464, 2:484
35:1–39 *2:432*
35:2 *2:432, 2:461*
35:2, 8, 28 *2:298, 2:389,*
   2:406
35:3 *2:432, 2:461*
35:3–5 *2:479*
35:3–17 *2:479*
35:3–36 *2:479*
35:4 *2:432*
35:4–5 *2:438, 2:461*
35:5 *2:432, 2:462*
35:6 *2:390, 2:432, 2:435,*
   2:464
35:6–8 *2:438, 2:461,*
   2:462–464
35:6, 11, 15, 25, 26, 32
   2:68
35:7, 9 *2:495*
35:8 *2:432*
35:9 *2:481*
35:9–10 *2:464*
35:9–15 *2:439, 2:464–467*
35:9–34 *1:141, 1:482,*
   2:258, 2:432, 2:435,
   2:438, 2:439, 2:451,
   2:464–479, 2:483, 2:484
35:10 *2:432*
35:10–14 *2:424*
35:10, 14, 28, 32, 33, 34
   2:475
35:11–15 *2:464–467*
35:11, 15, 22–23 *1:379*

35:11, 15, 25–26, 32 *2:465*
35:12 *2:432, 2:469*
35:12, 19, 21, 24, 25, 27
   1:147
35:12, 24, 25 *2:466*
35:14 *2:481*
35:16 *2:465*
35:16–17 *2:467*
35:16, 17, 18 *2:467*
35:16–19 *2:467*
35:16–28 *2:439,*
   2:467–473
35:17 *2:432, 2:468*
35:17–18 *2:468*
35:18 *2:432*
35:18–36 *2:479*
35:19 *2:468*
35:20 *2:432*
35:20–21 *2:467, 2:468*
35:21 *2:468, 4:69*
35:22 *2:432, 2:468*
35:22–24 *2:467, 2:468–*
   469, 2:469
35:22–28 *2:467*
35:24 *2:469*
35:25 *2:432, 2:469–470*
35:25–28 *2:467, 2:469,*
   2:469–473
35:25, 28 *2:432, 2:470,*
   2:474
35:25, 28, 32 *2:472*
35:25–32 *2:49*
35:25, 32 *2:490*
35:25–34 *2:448*
35:28 *2:470, 2:473, 2:476*
35:29 *1:373, 1:459, 2:294*
35:29–32 *2:473–475*
35:29–34 *2:240, 2:439,*
   2:473–478
35:30 *2:432*
35:31 *1:479, 2:468*
35:31–32 *1:128*
35:31, 32 *2:474, 2:476*
35:32 *2:432, 2:476*
35:32–34 *2:451*
35:33 *2:432, 2:475, 2:476*
35:33–34 *2:466,*
   2:475–479
35:34 *1:64, 1:67, 2:432,*

   2:436, 2:451, 2:455,
   2:475, 2:478, 2:479,
   2:484
35:37–49 *2:479*
35:38–39 *2:479*
35:40–49 *2:432*
36 *1:62, 1:63, 1:65,*
   1:66, 1:67, 1:234–235,
   2:283, 2:294, 2:299,
   2:305, 2:317, 2:320,
   2:421, 2:436, 2:478,
   2:485–496
36 – 37 *1:19*
36 – 49 *2:433*
36, 38, 40 *1:79*
36:1 *2:283, 2:390, 2:485*
36:1–4 *2:283, 2:486,*
   2:486–490
36:1, 5, 12 *2:317, 2:319,*
   2:488
36:1–12 *1:213, 2:279,*
   2:321, 2:404, 2:411,
   2:416, 2:423
36:1–13 *1:96, 2:283, 2:284,*
   2:285, 2:286, 2:357
36:2 *2:485*
36:2–3 *2:451*
36:2, 5, 6, 10, 13 *2:490*
36:2a, b *2:487*
36:3 *2:486, 2:487, 2:488*
36:3–4 *2:289, 2:304,*
   2:405, 2:488
36:4 *2:473, 2:486, 2:488,*
   2:490
36:5 *2:291*
36:5–9 *2:283, 2:486,*
   2:490–492
36:6 *2:356, 2:486*
36:6–7, 8–9 *2:490, 2:493*
36:7 *2:486*
36:7, 9 *2:490, 2:491*
36:8–9 *2:491*
36:9 *2:299*
36:10 *2:389, 2:492*
36:10–12 *2:283, 2:284,*
   2:287, 2:486, 2:492
36:11 *1:45, 2:85, 2:486,*
   2:493
36:11–12 *2:493*

Numbers (*cont.*)
36:12 2:416, 2:486, 2:493
36:13 1:72, 1:219, 2:111,
   2:265, 2:276, 2:384,
   2:437, 2:449, 2:458,
   2:486
36:13, 21–24 2:383
36:18 2:437
37 – 41 1:383
37:26–28 1:19
40 – 51 1:43
44 – 51 1:116
44 – 53 1:88–90
47, 49 1:89
48 – 53 1:88–9
50, 53 1:89
51 1:89, 1:90
52 – 53 1:89–90, 1:90–91
53 1:90

Deuteronomy
1:1, 5 2:111
1:2 1:55, 1:232, 1:253,
   1:309
1:3 2:448
1:4 2:54
1:6 1:410
1:6–8 1:208
1:9–11 1:88
1:10 1:24, 1:25
1:11 2:48
1:19 1:379
1:19–45 1:9
1:19–46 2:407
1:20–23 1:319, 1:322
1:22 1:10
1:23–33 1:10
1:24 1:323, 1:332
1:25, 35 1:343
1:26, 43 1:363, 2:46
1:27–33 1:320
1:32–33 1:323
1:33 1:239
1:35 1:363
1:35–36 1:354
1:36 1:353
1:36, 37, 38 1:354
1:37 2:31
1:37–38 1:354

1:39 1:363
1:41–45 1:360, 2:420
1:42–43 1:359
1:44 1:320
1:45 1:320, 2:225
1:46 – 3:17 2:7
2 2:73, 2:425
2:1–7 2:39
2:2–5 2:37
2:2–5, 8–9 2:279
2:3 1:410
2:6 2:39
2:7 1:1
2:8 2:447
2:8–9 2:114
2:9 2:52, 2:74, 2:87,
   2:246
2:12 2:423
2:13–14, 24 2:73
2:13–19 2:287
2:14 1:356
2:14–16 2:234
2:17–19 2:52
2:18 2:147
2:19 2:80
2:19, 37 2:117
2:21–22 2:450
2:24 2:76
2:24–25 2:53
2:24–35 2:79
2:27 2:53
2:28–29 2:53
2:31 2:53
2:32 2:79
2:37 2:80
3:8 2:74
3:8–10 2:54
3:11 2:59, 2:82
3:11, 16 2:117
3:12–20 2:85
3:13 2:83
3:13–15 2:421
3:14–15 2:271
3:16 2:117, 2:405
3:18 2:404
3:19, 26 1:410
3:20 1:234
3:21–22 2:313
3:21–22, 28 2:315

3:21–28 2:315
3:21b–22 2:281
3:23–29 2:31
3:25 1:343
3:27 2:78, 2:160, 2:307
3:28 2:313
3:29 2:218
4:2 1:275
4:3 2:255
4:3–4 2:218, 2:234, 2:287
4:5–8 2:349
4:7 2:164
4:10–11 1:278
4:12–20 1:202
4:19 1:25
4:20 2:156
4:21–22 1:343, 2:31
4:24 1:250, 1:344, 2:236
4:27 1:279
4:27–28 1:270
4:30 2:190
4:34 2:39
4:38 2:450
4:41–43 2:439, 2:464
4:42 2:465
4:43 2:421, 2:466
4:46 2:218
4:46–47 2:54
4:47 2:82
5 2:348
5:6–10 2:451
5:9 2:217, 2:236
5:11 1:173
5:12–15 1:384, 1:386
5:14 1:234
5:15 1:385, 2:39, 2:335
5:17 2:476
5:22 1:275
5:22–26 1:190
5:23–31 1:232
5:27 1:243
5:31 1:312
6 – 11, 12 – 26 2:348
6:4 – 9 2:463
6:4–5 2:350
6:4–9 1:393
6:5 2:332, 2:451
6:6–9 1:313, 1:391
6:10–13 2:371

INDEX OF SCRIPTURE REFERENCES AND ANCIENT SOURCES   615

6:10–15 2:225
6:15 2:236
6:18 1:343
6:19 2:450
6:21 2:39
7 1:314
7:1 1:101, 1:102
7:1, 20–22 2:450
7:3–4 2:227, 2:250
7:6–7 2:227
7:6–12 1:129
7:7 1:101
7:8 1:128, 2:39
7:13 1:471
7:17 1:101
7:22 1:101
8:1–5, 16 1:361
8:3 1:313
8:7 1:330
8:7–8 2:15
8:7–10 1:364
8:7, 10 1:343
8:15 2:20, 2:33, 2:63, 2:68, 2:480
8:18 1:198
8:19–20 2:451
9:1, 14 1:346
9:3 1:344
9:4–5 2:80, 2:450
9:4–6 2:451
9:5 2:59
9:6 1:343
9:7 2:18
9:10 1:225, 2:440
9:23 1:344, 1:363, 2:29, 2:46
9:26 2:39
9:29 2:156
9.5 2:134
10:3 2:214
10:4 1:225, 2:440
10:6 2:447
10:7 2:447
10:8 1:168
10:8–9 1:476
10:9 2:297, 2:461
10:20 2:491
11:1, 21 1:231
11:6 1:402

11:13–21 1:393
11:14 1:471
11:17 1:343
11:22 2:491
11:24–25 1:325
12 1:272, 2:251
12:1–4, 29–31 2:451
12:1–12 1:232
12:2–4 2:348
12:5–7 2:140, 2:348
12:5, 11 1:172
12:5, 11, 14, 18, 21, 26 2:346
12:6, 11–14 2:330
12:6, 11, 17, 26 2:354, 2:358
12:9 1:234
12:9–10 1:234
12:10 1:234
12:13–14 1:287
12:17 1:471
12:17–19 1:478
12:20–21 1:253
12:29–30 2:450
12:30–32 1:472
12:32 1:275
13 2:397
13, 18 2:109
13:2–4 2:102
14:1 1:141, 1:406
14:22–29 1:478
14:23 1:471
15:1–6, 12–18 1:384
15:12 2:63
15:19 1:160
16:1 2:9, 2:338
16:1–8 2:338
16:6 1:172
16:13 2:343
17:3 1:104
17:4 1:369
17:6 1:152
17:14–20 1:87, 2:35, 2:45
18 1:302
18:1–2 1:476
18:2 2:297
18:3 2:232
18:4 1:471

18:6 1:225
18:9 1:369
18:9–12 1:472
18:9–14 2:451
18:10–14 2:167
18:10, 14 2:122
18:12 2:450
18:13 2:330
18:16 2:440
18:18 2:152
18:18–20 2:102
18:22 1:425
19:1–13 2:439, 2:476
19:3–5, 11 2:465
19:3, 6 2:470
19:10 2:470, 2:478
19:12 2:466
19:14 2:300
19:15 1:152
20:1 1:366
20:1, 3–4 1:366
20:2–4 1:226
20:5–9 1:266
20:13–14 2:383
20:13–15 2:385
21:1–9 2:472
21:3 1:482
21:6 2:466
21:10–14 2:383
21:15–17 2:301
22:7 2:63
22:12 1:393
22:14 2:224
22:21 2:215
22:22–27 1:152
22:23, 25 1:152
23:4 2:153
23:4–5 2:103
23:5 2:60, 2:117, 2:132, 2:205
23:5–6 2:205
23:10–14 1:13, 1:145
23:14 1:366
23:15 1:191
23:18, 21–23 2:354
23:21 1:162
23:21–23 2:355, 2:358
23:22–24 2:357
24:1 2:406

Deuteronomy (*cont.*)
24:8–9 *1:291*, *1:310*
24:9 *1:308*
25:1–3 *2:356*
25:5–6 *2:302*
25:6 *2:289*, *2:290*, *2:302*
25:9 *1:307*
25:17–19 *1:335*, *2:200*, *2:315*
25:19 *1:234*
26 *1:333–334*
26:1 *1:369*
26:1–3 *1:379*
26:4–10 *2:443*
26:5 *2:101*
26:5–10 *1:379*
26:8 *2:39*
26:9–10 *2:339–340*
26:12–14 *1:478*
27:11–26 *1:154*
27:17 *1:287*, *2:300*
28:3–14 *1:169*
28:15–68 *2:97*, *2:345*
28:37 *1:157*
28:38 *1:338*
28:50 *1:171*
28:51 *1:471*
28:62 *1:279*
28:68 *1:365*
29:5–6 *1:57*
29:7 *2:54*
29:10 *1:266*
29:11, 18–19 *1:154*
29:14–29 *1:158*
29:19 *1:154*
30:1–10 *2:28*
30:6 *1:313*
30:11–20 *1:158*
30:14–17 *2:29*
31:1–6 *1:11*
31:1–8 *1:11*
31:1–8, 14, 23 *2:315*
31:2 *2:311*
31:4 *2:54*, *2:82*
31:7 *1:11*
31:9 *1:72*
31:9, 22, 24 *2:442*
31:9, 24 *1:71*
31:14–15, 23 *2:316*
31:16 *1.391*, *2:216*
31:17–18 *1:171*
31:20 *1:345*
31:28 *1:266*, *2:191*
31:29 *2:190*
32 *2:50*
32:4, 15, 18, 30, 31 *2:19*
32:8 *2:193*
32:9 *2:191*
32:9, 12 *2:156*
32:11 *1:32*
32:13 *2:19*, *2:451*
32:14 *2:114*
32:16 *2:251*
32:20 *1:171*, *1:361*
32:21 *1:150*
32:37–38 *1:270*
32:39 *2:307*
32:40 *1:351*
32:44–47 *2:21*
32:48–50 *2:281*, *2:448*
32:48–52 *2:32*, *2:317*, *2:322*, *2:483*
32:49 *2:31*, *2:307*, *2:418*, *2:449*
32:50 *2:10*, *2:41*, *2:307*, *2:447*
32:51 *2:33*, *2:42*, *2:46*
33 *1:23*, *1:28*, *1:38*, *1:39*, *2:168*, *2:270*
33:2 *1:26*, *1:220*, *1:235*, *2:75*
33:5 *2:158*
33:6 *1:28*, *2:419*
33:8 *2:314*
33:8–9 *1:441*
33:8b *2:42*
33:10 *1:413*
33:16 *1:159*, *2:319*
33:17 *1:28*, *1:32*, *2:166*
33:20–21 *2:404*
33:26 *1:27*, *1:221*
33:27 *2:450*
33:27, 29 *2:156*
33:28 *2:156*
33:28–29 *2:156*
33:29 *2:451*
34:1 *2:78*, *2:101*, *2:160*, *2:307*, *2:418*
34:1–4 *2:307*
34:1–8 *2:10*, *2:308*
34:4 *2:307*
34:4–8 *2:317*
34:5–12 *1:70*
34:6 *2:218*
34:7 *1:103*
34:8 *2:43*, *2:111*
34:9 *1:268*, *1:353*, *2:312*, *2:313*, *2:316*
34:9–12 *1:72*
34:10–11 *2:313*
34:56 *2:218*

Joshua
1:1–9 *2:313*, *2:315*
1:2 *2:317*
1:5 *1:194*
1:6, 7, 9 *2:83*
1:7–8 *1:87*
1:7–9 *2:45*
1:10 *1:71*, *1:266*
1:12–16 *2:85*
1:13 *1:234*
1:14 *2:400*
1:17–18 *2:316–317*
2:1 *2:214*
2:1–2 *1:324*
2:8–11 *2:118*
2:8–13 *2:36*, *2:101*
2:9–10 *2:112–113*
2:9–14 *1:314*
2:10 *2:54*, *2:79*, *2:82*
2:12–13 *1:239*
2:17, 20 *2:414*
2:23 *1:324*
3 *1:93*
3:1 *2:214*
3:2 *1:266*
4:12 *2:400*, *2:417*
4:12–13 *1:101*
4:13–14 *1:108*
5:10–12 *1:379*
5:11 *2:338*
5:11–12 *1:385*
5:13 *2:143*
5:13–15 *2:137*
6 – 8 *2:59*
6:5, 10, 16, 20 *1:224*

6:6 *1:235*
6:17 *2:59*
6:17, 18, 21 *1:472*
6:18–19 *1:424*
6:20 *1:328*
6:22, 23, 25 *1:324*
6:23, 25 *2:296*
7:1–11 *2:59*
7:1, 20–26 *1:424*
7:2 *1:324*
7:14 *1:84, 2:296*
9 *2:59*
9:10 *2:54, 2:82*
9:19–20 *2:359*
10:13 *2:74*
10:29, 31, 32, 39 *2:447*
11:4 *1:105*
11:16 – 12:23 *2:88*
12 – 19 *2:266*
12:1–6 *2:88*
12:3 *2:449*
12:4 *2:82*
12:6 *2:85*
12:15 *2:447*
12:24 *2:305*
13 *1:72*
13:2–6 *2:454*
13:8, 15, 24, 29 *2:416*
13:8–32 *2:419*
13:8–33 *2:88*
13:12, 30–31 *2:82*
13:16 *2:74*
13:17 *2:149, 2:449*
13:20 *2:218, 2:449*
13:21 *2:113, 2:114, 2:381, 2:397*
13:21–22 *2:382*
13:22 *2:104, 2:107, 2:116, 2:118, 2:122, 2:167, 2:168*
13:25 *2:82, 2:415*
13:31 *2:82*
13:32, 33 *2:416*
14 – 19 *2:458*
14:6, 14 *1:326, 2:408*
14:6–15 *1:319, 1:333, 1:353*
14:7 *1:324*
14:8, 9, 14 *1:353*

14:11 *2:311*
14:15 *1:331*
15 *2:438*
15:3 *2:431*
15:13–14 *1:331*
15:14–15 *1:328*
15:42 *2:447*
17 *2:306*
17:1 *2:422*
17:1–3 *2:271*
17:1–6 *2:285, 2:417*
17:1–13 *2:417*
17:3 *2:486, 2:493*
17:3–6 *2:271, 2:283, 2:286, 2:292, 2:493–494*
17:14–18 *2:273*
18:3–4 *1:325*
19:9 *2:270, 2:275*
19:40–50 *2:274*
20 *2:439, 2:465*
20:7 *2:466*
21 *2:463*
21:3 *2:447*
21:11–12 *2:297*
21:39 *2:417*
22 *2:226, 2:416*
22:2, 5 *1:72*
22:9 *1:72*
22:17 *2:170, 2:212*
22:19 *2:409*
22:20 *2:44*
23:6 *1:72*
23:11–13 *2:452*
24:2 *2:101, 2:116*
24:2–3 *2:202*
24:9–10 *2:104, 2:205*
24:32 *2:319, 2:321, 2:490*

Judges
1 *2:454*
1:1–2 *1:354*
1:1–4 *1:328*
1:10 *1:331*
1:13 *2:408*
1:16 *1:230, 2:200*
1:20 *2:274*
1:34 *2:138*
2:4 *1:341*
2:10 *1:283*

2:11–13 *2:255*
3 *2:454*
3:4 *1:72*
3:5–6 *2:452*
3:10 *1:150, 2:312*
3:12 *2:419*
3:19 *1:336*
3:25 *2:358*
3:31 *1:103*
4:11 *1:229, 1:230, 1:232*
4:11, 17 *2:200*
4:14 *2:310*
5:4 *1:197*
5:8 *1:101*
5:14 *2:194, 2:418*
5:15–17 *2:420*
5:26 *2:196*
6 *2:419*
6 – 8 *2:383*
6:3, 33 *2:383*
6:5 *1:338, 2:119*
6:7 *1:105*
6:15 *1:104, 2:296*
6:24 *1:171*
6:34 *1:150, 2:312*
7:11 *2:400*
7:12 *1:105, 2:119*
7:22 *2:306*
8:22, 23 *2:383*
8:26 *1:132*
9:53 *1:79*
9:54 *2:231*
9:55 *2:203*
11 *2:103*
11:1 *2:423*
11:2 *2:298*
11:9–22 *2:79*
11:12–28 *2:74, 2:80*
11:17 *2:38, 2:114*
11:20 *2:79*
11:24 *2:81, 2:148, 2:217*
11:25 *2:112*
11:29 *1:150*
11:29–40 *2:356*
13:5 *1:159*
13:20 *2:333*
13:25 *1:150, 2:211, 2:312*
14:6, 19 *1:150, 1:275, 2:312*

Judges (*cont.*)
15:14 *1:150, 2:312*
16:19, 22 *2:211*
16:21 *1:417*
16:21, 25 *2:359*
17:5, 12 *1:122*
18:11, 16, 17 *1:103*
18:11–17 *1:101*
18:30 *1:124*
20 – 21 *2:226*
20:23, 26 *2:225*
20:31 *2:211*
20:47 *1:103*
21:2 *1:341*

Ruth
1:9, 14 *1:341*
1:14 *2:491*
1:16–17 *1:231*
2 *2:302*
2:3 *2:299*
4:3 *2:302*
4:5 *2:284, 2:289*
4:5–6 *2:298*
4:5, 14 *2:302*
4:10 *1:133, 2:302*
4:13–22 *2:210, 2:284*
4:18–20 *2:184*
4:18–22 *2:340*
4:20–22 *1:86*

1 Samuel
1 – 2 *1:440*
1:3 *2:226*
1:3, 11 *1:26*
1:8–18 *2:356*
1:11 *1:159*
1:21 *2:354*
1:23 *2:367*
2:2 *2:19*
2:22 *1:30*
2:28 *1:413*
2:30 *1:356, 2:238*
2:30–33 *1:381*
2:34 *2:226*
4:4 *1:26, 1:34, 1:37*
4:4, 11, 17, 19 *2:226*
6:6 *2:141*
8:13 *2:311*

8:16 *2:311*
8:20 *2:311*
10:6, 10 *1:275*
10:10 *2:174*
10:19 *1:104*
10:19, 21 *2:296*
10:20–22 *2:296*
10:27 *1:375*
11:2 *1:417*
11:4 *1:341*
11:6 *1:275*
12:3 *1:419*
13:7 *2:419*
13:15 *1:103*
14:2 *1:103*
14:3 *2:226*
14:41 *2:314*
14:46 *2:203*
14:47 *1:197, 1:198*
15:6 *1:230*
15:10–35 *2:184*
15:20 *2:400*
15:23 *2:122*
15:29 *2:162*
16:11 *2:311*
16:13 *1:275*
16:16 *2:174*
17 *2:397*
17:4, 16 *1:424*
17:7 *1:103*
17:16 *1:407*
18:10 *1:275*
22:7 *1:416*
22:14 *1:301*
23:9–12 *2:314*
23:13 *1:103*
23:19, 24 *2:78*
23:23 *2:296*
24:16 *1:341*
24:21 *1:133*
24:22 *2:302*
26:1, 3 *2:78*
26:10 *1:351*
27:2 *1:103*
28:6 *2:314*
29:6 *2:311*
30:4 *1:341*
30:7–8 *2:314*
30:9 *1:103*

30:23–25 *2:388*
30:29 *1:230*
31:4 *2:231*
31:10 *2:220*
31:13 *1:309, 2:43*
34 *1:381*

2 Samuel
1:10 *1:159*
1:18 *2:74*
2:1–3 *1:333*
2:9 *2:201*
2:11–12 *2:221*
3:32 *1:341*
5:1–5 *1:333*
5:2 *2:311*
5:11 *2:180*
5:12 *2:184*
5:17–25 *2:454*
5:24 *2:310*
6:1–11 *1:187*
7 *1:88, 1:232, 1:301, 2:186*
7:1 *2:200*
7:1–17 *1:22*
7:2 *2:180*
7:6 *1:349*
7:6–7 *1:191*
7:8 *2:311*
7:23 *1:129*
8:1–14 *2:454*
8:1, 14 *1:197*
8:2 *2:196, 2:208*
8:2, 6 *1:375*
8:2–14 *1:198*
10:18 *1:100, 1:105*
13:36 *1:341*
13:37 *2:477*
14:7 *2:301*
14:13, 32 *2:477*
15:18 *1:103*
15:31–37 *2:189*
16:7 *2:310*
16:23 *2:189*
17:1 *2:379*
17:1–23 *2:189*
18:2 *2:441*
21:6, 9 *2:220*
21:13 *2:220*
22:3, 32, 47 *2:19*

22:11 1:27, 1:37
22:11–12 1:221
23:1 2:176
23:2 1:274
23:3 2:19
24 1:95, 2:330, 2:391
24:5 2:419
24:9 1:102
24:11 2:178

1 Kings
1:5 1:401
1:50–53 2:439
2:1–4 2:45
2:3 1:72
2:5–6 2:475
2:15 2:172
2:24 1:351
2:26–27, 35 2:237
2:28–29 2:465
2:28–34 2:439
4:12 2:306
4:19 2:54, 2:82, 2:419
4:21 1:375
4:26 1:100, 1:105
5 – 6 2:180
6:18–29 1:389
6:20 1:20
7:1–12 2:180
7:25 1:36
8 1:232
8:7–8 1:132
8:9, 16, 21, 51, 53 1:84
8:20 1:172
8:22 2:343
8:53, 56 1:72
8:63 1:188
8:65 1:331
8.30–53 1:25
9:26 2:447
10:14, 16, 29 1:103
10:15 1:323
10:25 1:375
10:26 2:379
11:1–2 2:255
11:6 1:353
11:7 2:148
11:7, 33 2:81
11:26, 27 2:25

12:32 2:149, 2:343
13:2, 32 2:149
13:24, 26 2:168
13:26 2:168
13:33 1:122
14:17 2:305
15:14 2:149
15:21, 33 2:305
16 2:243
16:6, 8, 9, 15, 17, 23 2:305
16:30–33 2:255
18:24 1:173
19:10 2:226
19:16 2:306
19:19, 21 2:217
20:36 2:168
21 2:286
22 1:277, 2:129
22:1–28 2:102
22:8, 18 1:275
22:17 2:311
22:19–23 1:221
22:49 2:447

2 Kings
1:9–17 1:435
2 1:268–269
2:9 2:301
2:15 1:277
4:1–7 2:302
5 1:305
5:7 1:305
5:27 1:52, 1:304
6:32 2:138
7:10 2:359
8:1–6 2:302
8:9 1:375
8:22 2:447
9:25–26 2:286
9:26 1:356
9:31 2:243
9:35 1:79
10:32 2:419
11:12 1:159
12:3 2:149
12:17 2:172
14:4 2:149
15:4, 35 2:149

15:14, 16 2:305
17:3, 4 1:375
17:13 2:178
17:17 2:122, 2:167
17:25–26 2:168
17:29 2:149
18:4 2:66, 2:72, 2:149
18:12 1:72
19:8 2:447
19:15 1:37
21:3 2:149
22:31 2:447
23:9, 13, 15, 19, 20 2:149
23:13 2:81
23:33 2:455
24:18 2:447
25:6, 20–21 2:455
25:7 1:417, 2:359

1 Chronicles
1:32 2:113
1:36 2:408
2 – 9 2:266
2:1–5, 18 1:326
2:4–7 2:243
2:10–17 1:86
2:18–24 2:418
2:21 2:421
2:21–23 2:422
4:24 2:270
4:42–43 2:200
5:1 1:406, 1:440
5:1–2 1:96, 1:440
5:1–3 1:442
5:1, 3 1:87
5:9 2:403
5:26 2:403
5:27–41 1:121
5:30–41 2:237
6:3 1:121, 2:275
6:4 2:225
6:34 1:189, 2:331
6:35–38 2:237
6:39, 43 1:125
6:49 1:72
6:54–81 2:439
6:57 2:447
6:78 2:79
7:1 2:262

1 Chronicles (*cont.*)
7:6–12 *2:272*
7:12 *2:262*
7:13, 30–31 *2:272*
7:14 *2:422*
7:14–19 *2:285*
7:18 *2:422*
7:20–27 *2:422*
7:26–27 *1:86*
7:30 *2:272*
8:1–40 *2:272*
9:19 *1:427, 2:231*
9:19–20 *2:227*
9:20 *2:226, 2:230–231, 2:238*
9:32 *1:125*
10:4 *2:231*
10:10 *1:79*
10:12 *1:309, 2:43*
13:5 *1:331*
13:6 *1:37*
14:8 *2:311*
15:26 *2:150*
16:40 *1:189, 2:331*
18:2, 6 *1:375*
19:18 *1:100, 1:105*
21:5 *1:102*
21:9 *2:178*
21:16 *2:137*
21:26, 29 *1:189, 2:331*
23 *1:116*
23:7–9 *1:125*
23:13 *1:121*
23:24–27 *1:31, 1:201*
24:1–6 *2:236*
25:5 *2:178*
26:1–19 *2:269*
26:1, 19 *1:427*
26:21 *1:125*
28:18 *1:35*
29:25 *2:313*
29:29 *2:178*

2 Chronicles
2 – 8 *2:272*
3:1, 2 *2:211*
5:8–9 *1:132*
6:41 *1:234*
8:17 *2:447*

9:24 *1:375*
9:25 *1:100, 1:105*
9:29 *2:178*
12:15 *2:178*
13:2 *2:381*
13:5 *1:474*
13:12–16 *1:226*
15:1 *2:174*
17:3 *1:103*
17:5, 11 *1:375*
17:14–18 *1:103*
18 *2:129*
19:2 *2:178*
19:3–4 *1:103*
20:17 *2:311*
20:19 *1:427*
20:36 *2:447*
21:10 *2:447*
23:3 *1:31*
23:11 *1:159*
26 *1:305*
26:8 *1:375*
26:11 *1:265*
26:18–21 *1:52*
26:19–21 *1:299*
29:17 *2:211*
29:18 *1:189, 2:331*
29:25, 30 *2:178*
29:27–28 *1:226*
30 *1:210*
31:17 *1:31*
32:23 *1:375*
33:8 *1:72*
33:12–13 *1:383*
33:18 *2:178*
35:6 *1:72*
35:15 *2:178*
36:15–16 *1:381*
36:17 *2:59*
36:21 *1:383*

Ezra
2:63 *2:314*
3:2 *1:72*
3:8 *1:131*
7:1–5 *2:237*
7:1–6 *2:226*
7:5 *2:225*
7:6 *1:72*

8:2 *2:225, 2:238*
8:18–19 *1:125*
8:21 *2:342*
8:33 *2:226*
9:11 *1:301*

Nehemiah
1:4 *1:253*
1:7–8 *1:72*
4:12 *1:352*
5 *2:302*
7:65 *2:314*
8:1 *1:72*
8:11 *1:336*
8:13–18 *2:343*
8:14 *1:72*
9:14 *1:72*
9:15 *1:256, 2:20*
9:19 *1:219, 1:222*
9:22 *2:54, 2:79, 2:82, 2:85*
10:29 *1:72*
10:37 *1:378*
10:38 *1:377*
13:1–3 *2:205*
13:2 *2:104*
13:29 *2:238*

Esther
1:6 *1:389*
2:5 *2:184*
3:1 *2:184*

Job
2:12 *1:341*
2:12–13 *1:253*
3:6 *2:446*
3:8 *2:155*
4:11 *2:169*
4:17 *2:400*
5:3 *2:155*
7:20 *1:258*
8:17 *2:180*
12:10 *1:269*
14:8 *2:180*
15:12 *1:400*
16:11 *2:94, 2:143*
18:16 *2:180*
19:3 *1:352*

22:25 *2:166*
24:2 *2:300*
26:12 *2:196*
27:1 *2:152*
27:23 *2:188*
28:9–10 *2:33*
28:19 *1:291*
29:1 *2:152*
29:19 *2:180*
30:19 *1:493*
33:10 *1:357*
39:5 *2:56*
42:8 *2:150*

Psalms
1 *2:45*
1:2 *1:391*
1:3 *2:180*
1:6 *1:428*
2 *1:88, 1:198, 1:455, 2:186, 2:199, 2:203*
2:2 *2:321*
2:7 *1:455*
2:9 *2:194*
4:6 *1:167*
4:8 *2:156*
7 *1:291*
9:15–16 *2:189*
10:1 *1:258*
11:6–7 *1:174*
13 *1:345*
15:2 *1:481*
15:4 *2:370*
16:1 *1:169*
16:5–6 *2:301*
16:20 *1:256*
18:2 *2:19*
18:2, 31, 46 *2:19*
18:10 *1:37*
18:10–11 *1:221*
18:22 *2:143*
18:38 *2:196*
18.11 *1:27*
19:6, 11 *1:256*
22 *2:166*
22:1 *2:166*
22:2 *1:258*
22:12 *2:114*
22:25 *2:355*

22:26 *1:297*
23 *2:279*
23:1 *2:311*
23:5 *2:205, 2:347*
23:6 *1:1, 1:271*
24:3 *1:233*
24:3–4 *2:193*
24:6 *1:167*
27:8 *1:167*
27:8–10 *1:171*
28 *1:53*
28:1 *2:19*
29:11b *1:171*
31:2 *2:19*
31:3 *2:19*
31:6 *2:312*
31:16 *1:167, 1:170*
33:10 *1:357, 2:362*
34:8 *1:364*
35:13 *2:342*
36:1 *2:176*
36:8–9 *1:271, 2:347*
36:9 *1:174*
37:9, 18 *2:304*
37:22 *2:277*
38:11 *1:92*
40 *2:355*
42 – 49, 84 – 85, 87 – 88 *1:427*
42 – 49, 84, 85, 87 – 88 *2:269*
42:9 *2:19*
44:3 *1:167*
44:24 *1:258, 2:138*
45 *2:256*
45:3 *2:313*
45:6 *2:194*
45:12 *1:375*
46:4 *1:174, 2:48, 2:180*
46:8 *2:78*
47 *2:165*
47, 95–100 *2:341*
47:2–3 *2:193*
48 *1:232*
50:8 *2:143*
50:9, 13 *1:181*
50:10 *1:164*
50:14 *2:355*
51:7 *1:486*

55:15 *1:428*
56:12 *2:355*
58:10 *2:397*
59:11 *2:400*
60:8 *1:197*
61:5, 8 *2:355*
62:2, 6, 7 *2:19*
65:4 *1:414*
66:5 *2:78*
66:13 *2:355*
66:15 *1:181*
67:1 *1:167*
67:1–2 *1:167*
68:1 *1:235*
68:5, 34 *1:27*
68:16–18 *1:232*
68:17 *1:26, 1:39, 1:92, 1:221*
68:18 *1:235*
68:21 *2:196*
68:32 *2:75*
68:33–34 *1:221*
69:9 *2:257*
69:31 *1:376*
71:3 *2:19*
72:8 *2:203*
72:8–9 *2:206*
72:10 *1:375*
72:17b *2:206*
73 *1:53*
75:8 *1:154*
76:11 *2:355*
77:20 *1:228, 2:311, 2:481*
78 *1:1, 1:87, 1:289*
78:9–12 *1:87*
78:60–61 *1:87*
78:67–72 *1:87*
78, 95 *2:50*
78:15 *2:27*
78:15–16 *2:19, 2:19–20, 2:33*
78:17–30 *1:244*
78:19–29 *1:271*
78:20 *2:20*
78:24–25 *1:256*
78:25 *1:254*
78:35 *2:19*
80:1 *1:37, 2:311*
80:3, 7, 14, 19 *1:235*

Psalms (*cont.*)
80:3, 7, 19 *1:167*
80:8–9 *1:161*
81:3 *1:223, 2:341*
81:7 *2:33*
81:16 *2:20*
83:6 *2:36*
83:8 *2:201*
83:18 *2:193*
84:1 *1:37*
87 *1:99*
87:3 *1:99*
88:3–7 *1:425*
89 *1:88, 2:186*
89:6 *1:221*
89:15 *1:167*
89:17 *2:166*
89:26 *2:19*
89:27 *1:198, 2:185*
89:39 *1:159*
90 *1:286, 2:45*
90:4 *2:14*
90:42 *1:346*
91 *1:169*
92:12 *2:180*
92:15 *2:19*
94:22 *2:19*
95:1 *2:19*
95:4 *2:166*
95:8–10 *1:384*
96:6 *2:313*
96:13 *2:341*
98:9 *2:341*
99:1 *1:37*
100:3 *2:311*
103:3, 12 *1:170*
103:4 *1:164*
103:4, 8 *2:219*
103:6–10 *1:348*
103:7 *1:72*
104:1 *2:313*
104:3 *1:27, 1:221*
104:15 *1:160, 1:170, 1:376*
104:16 *2:180*
104:21 *2:169*
105 *2:27*
105:4 *1:167*
105:25 *2:245*
105:39 *1:222*
105:39–41 *1:1*
105:40 *1:256*
105:41 *2:20, 2:33*
106 *1:262, 1:415*
106:7 *1:352*
106:14–15 *1:244*
106:24 *2:32*
106:24–27 *1:344*
106:28 *2:217, 2:218, 2:255*
106:28–31 *2:212, 2:221, 2:226*
106:32–33 *2:14, 2:30*
106:33 *2:4, 2:47, 2:364, 2:370*
106:38 *2:476*
106:42 *2:138*
107:20, 21, 22, 23, 24, 25, 39 *1:234*
109:13–15 *2:302*
110 *2:195*
110:2 *1:454, 2:196*
110:3 *2:196*
110:4 *2:208*
110:5–6 *2:196*
110:6 *2:196*
112:2 *2:158*
113:3 *2:333*
113:9 *2:275*
114:7–8 *2:33*
114:8 *2:20*
116:14, 18 *2:355*
118:22 *1:22*
118:27 *2:359*
119:135 *1:167*
120 – 134 *1:166*
120:3–4 *2:445*
121 *1:169, 2:205*
125:3 *2:194*
132:2 *2:354*
132:8 *1:235*
132:13–14 *1:232*
132:14 *1:234*
132:17 *2:166*
132:18 *1:159*
135:11 *2:54, 2:79, 2:85*
135:11–12 *2:82*
136 *2:77*
136:9 *2:194*
136:19–20 *2:54, 2:79, 2:85*
136:20 *2:82*
137:1 *1:253*
138:6 *1:298*
141:2 *1:437, 2:333*
141:5 *1:357, 2:362*
141:10 *2:189*
144:1 *2:19*
145:5 *2:313*
145:7–9 *1:348*
147:12–14 *1:167*
148:13 *2:313*

Proverbs
1:20–33 *2:284*
3:18 *1:191*
3:34 *1:298*
4:13 *1:191*
4:15 *1:149*
5:1–23 *2:284*
5:15–20 *2:181*
5:22 *2:189*
6:20–35 *2:284*
7 – 8 *1:149*
7:1–27 *2:284*
7:14 *2:355*
7:22 *2:131*
7:25 *1:149*
8:1–11 *2:284*
9:1–18 *2:284*
11:26 *2:155*
12:13 *2:189*
14:1 *2:284*
14:12 *1.392*
15:25 *2:302*
16:25 *1.392*
16:33 *2:83, 2:273, 2:452, 2:487*
18:18 *2:273*
20:25 *2:356, 2:370*
22:13 *2:168*
22:28 *2:300*
23:10 *2:300, 2:302*
23:31 *1:481*
24:24 *2:155*
27:24 *1:159*
29:23 *1:298*
30:1 *2:176*
31:10–31 *2:284*

INDEX OF SCRIPTURE REFERENCES AND ANCIENT SOURCES 623

Ecclesiastes
1:13 *1:323*
4:14 *2:359*
5:2 *2:370*
5:4–5 *2:355–356*
7:25 *1:323*

Song of Songs
4:1 *2:403*
6:4 *2:305*

Isaiah
1:1 *2:177*
1:11 *1:181*
1:13–14 *2:337*
1:15, 21 *2:477*
1:18 *1:481*
2:1–4 *1:339*
2:2 *2:190*
2:3 *1:233*
2:12 *2:202*
2:21 *2:19*
4:5 *1:434*
4:5–6 *1:222*
5:1–2 *1:161*
5:7 *2:349*
5:14 *1:425–426, 2:218*
5:26 *2:87*
5:29 *2:169*
6 *1:221*
6:2, 6 *2:64*
7:11 *1:425*
7:13 *1:345*
7:14 *2:164*
9:4–5 *2:397*
9:6–7 *1:198, 2:186*
10 *2:178*
10:15 *1:196, 2:194*
11 *2:186*
11:1 *1:159*
11:1–16 *2:206*
11:2 *1:277, 1:454*
11:10 *2:87, 2:269*
11:12 *2:87*
11:14 *2:196*
11:15 *1:196*
13 – 23 *2:199*
13:2 *1:196, 2:87*
13:6, 9 *2:202*

13:14 *2:311*
13:15 *2:231*
14:4 *2:152*
14:5 *2:194*
14:12–13 *2:194*
14:12–17 *1:412*
14:29 *2:64*
15 *2:417*
15:1 *2:74, 2:147*
15:1–9 *2:196*
15:2 *2:418*
15:4 *2:79*
16:2–14 *2:196*
16:6 *2:206*
17:10 *2:19*
18:3 *1:224, 2:87*
19:1 *1:27, 1:221*
19:16 *1:197*
19:21 *2:356*
21:1 *1:262*
21:12 *2:75*
22:8 *2:71*
24:5 *2:476*
25:10 *2:196*
27:13 *1:224*
29:10 *2:178*
30 *2:178*
30:1–7 *1:341*
30:6 *2:64*
30:17 *2:87*
30:29 *1:233, 2:19*
31:1–3 *1:341*
31:4 *2:169*
32:15 *1:314, 2:48, 2:180, 2:344*
33:14 *1:344*
34:5–8 *1:197*
34:6 *1:181*
35:1–2 *2:481*
37:8 *2:447*
37:16 *1:37*
39:1 *1:375*
40:11 *2:311*
40:22 *1:339*
41:17–20 *2:48*
41:18 *2:481*
41:19 *2:214*
43:7 *1:172*
43:19 *2:481*

44:3 *1:314, 2:180, 2:344*
44:8 *2:19*
44:25 *2:209*
46:10 *2:200*
48:20–21 *2:48*
48:21 *2:20, 2:33*
49:6 *1:159*
49:22 *2:87*
51:3 *2:48, 2:344*
51:17–23 *1:154*
52:7 *2:199, 2:398*
52:13 *2:87, 2:185*
52:13 – 53:12 *2:472*
53:3–12 *2:185*
53:7 *1:298*
54:10 *2:237, 2:238*
54:17 *2:209*
55:1 *2:180*
57:3 *2:215*
58:11 *2:180*
60:6 *2:383*
61 *2:489*
62:5 *2:219, 2:256*
62:10 *2:87*
63:1 *1:197*
63:2 *1:481*
63:11 *2:25, 2:311*
64:6–7 *1:171*
66:23 *2:335*

Jeremiah
1:9 *2:152*
2 – 3 *1:54*
2 – 4 *1:151*
2:1–2 *1:3*
2:2 *1:55, 1:56, 2:256, 2:442, 2:482*
2:10 *2:78*
2:13 *1:494*
2:14–15 *2:482*
2:18 *1:341*
2:20 *2:215*
3:2, 9 *2:451*
3:8–15 *1:157*
3:14 *2:219*
4:2 *1:351*
4:5 *1:224*
5:2 *1:351*
5:6 *2:168*

Jeremiah (*cont.*)
6:1 *1:224*
7:12 *2:78*
7:16 *1:345*
7:31 *1:472*
8:14 *1:154*
9:16 *2:63*
9:26 *2:196*
11:14 *1:345*
12:7 *1:301*
13:23 *1:293*
14:14 *1:275, 2:110*
15:18 *1:258*
17:13 *1:494*
18:17 *1:285*
20:18 *1:258*
23:5 *1:159*
23:9–40 *2:102*
23:11 *2:476*
23:21 *1:325*
23:33–34, 36, 38 *1:262*
29:27 *1:275*
30 – 31 *1:87*
30:9 *2:195*
30:10 *2:187*
31:10 *2:311*
31:31–34 *2:340*
31:32 *2:216*
32:37 *2:187*
33:15 *1:159*
33:21–22 *2:238*
39:5–6 *2:455*
42:18 *1:157*
44:25 *2:356*
46:10 *2:202*
46:51 *2:199*
48 *2:417*
48 – 49 *1:197*
48:1–47 *2:196*
48:7, 13, 46 *2:81*
48:45 *2:95, 2:196*
48:45–46 *2:81*
48:46 *2:148*
49:7–22 *1:197*
49:31 *2:156*
50:2 *2:269*
50:15, 28 *2:379*
50:19 *2:311*
51:3–4 *2:231*
51:11 *2:379*
51:27 *1:224*
52:1 *2:447*
52:9–10, 26–27 *2:455*

Lamentations
2:10 *1:253*
2:15 *2:188*
3:47 *2:196*

Ezekiel
1 *1:32, 1:33, 1:40, 1:239*
1, 8–10 *1:34*
1:4–5 *1:30*
1:4–28 *1:233*
1:4, 28 *1:220*
1:5 *1:28*
1:5–28 *1:220*
1:6 *1:388*
1:10 *1:30, 1:32, 1:36, 1:92, 1:202*
1:12 *1:31*
1:14 *1:33*
1:15–21 *1:137*
1:24 *1:31*
1:26 *1:31, 1:38, 1:39*
2:2 *1:32, 1:33, 1:181, 1:191*
2:19 *2:168*
3:25–27 *1:32*
4:3, 7 *2:172*
4:4–6 *1:32*
4:10–11 *2:367*
6:2 *2:172*
8:5–6 *1:32*
10 *1:32*
10:4 *1:220*
10:6–17 *1:137*
10:14 *1:36, 1:92*
10:20 *1:38*
11:16 *1:32*
12:27 *2:177*
13 *2:102*
13:5 *2:202*
13:6–9, 23 *2:110*
13:17 *2:172*
14:8 *2:172*
15:7 *2:172*
16, 23 *1:54, 1:151*
16:10 *1:114*
16:15 *2:215*
16:15–59 *1:32*
16:26, 28 *2:211, 2:215*
16:41–42 *1:150*
17 *2:19, 2:181*
17:3–10 *2:181*
17:6, 7 *2:181*
17:6, 7, 9 *2:181*
17:10 *1:285*
17:15 *1:341*
18:6 *1:488*
19:3, 6 *2:169*
19:11 *2:181*
19:11, 14 *2:194*
19:12 *1:285*
20:27–28 *1:381*
20:35 *2:481*
20:46 *2:172*
21:2 *2:172*
22:10 *1:488*
22:25 *2:169*
22:28 *2:110*
22:29–31 *1:259*
23:1–4 *2:369*
23:6 *1:389*
23:32–34 *1:157*
23:37 *1:157*
25 – 32 *2:199*
25:2 *2:172*
25:8–11 *2:196*
25:9 *2:418, 2:449*
25:12–14 *1:197*
27:6 *2:202*
28 *1:412*
28:13 *1:22*
28:14 *1:243*
28:21 *2:173*
29:2 *2:173*
29:10 *1:291*
30:3 *2:202*
31 *2:181*
31:3 *2:179*
31:7, 9, 12 *2:181*
31:8 *2:179*
32:29 *1:197*
34:5 *2:311*
34:23–24 *2:195*
34:25 *2:237, 2:238*
34:28 *2:187*

35:2 2:173
35:15 1:197
36:5 1:197
36:13–14 1:338
36:17 1:488
36:25 1:48
36:25–27 2:340
36:25–29 1:501
36:25, 33–36 1:32
36:26–27 1:32, 1:314
37 1:501
37:4 2:19
37:9–10 1:32, 1:33
37:13–14 1:501
37:15–28 1:87
37:26 2:238
37:26–27 2:237
37:27 1:98
38 – 39 2:184
38:2 2:173
38:16 2:184, 2:190
38:17 2:184
39:18 2:114
39:23–24 1:171
39:29 1:314
40 1:99
40 – 48 1:19, 1:33, 1:171, 1:174, 2:184
41:4 1:20
43:1–5 1:32
43:6 1:181, 1:191
43:7 1:33
44:6 1:410
44:10–16 2:238
44:15–16 2:236
44:28–30 1:377
44:30 1:378
45:9 1:410
45:11 1:376
45:12 1:129
45:17 1:188
45:21 2:325
45:23 2:150
47 2:6, 2:20, 2:45, 2:48, 2:50, 2:180, 2:438
47:1–12 1:174
48:11 2:238
48:30–35 1:19
48:31–34 1:33

58:3 2:342

Daniel
2:21 2:209
2:28 2:190
4 2:181
5:21 2:56
6.25 2:168
7 2:191, 2:202
7:3 1:286
7:13–14 1:198, 2:199
7:27 2:193
8:11 2:329
8:15 2:143
9:3 2:172
9:11 1:72
9:17, 19 1:167
9:21 2:333
10:14 2:190
11:17 2:172
11:30 2:202
11:32 2:476

Hosea
1 – 4 1:54, 1:151
2:7 2:215
2:7, 14–16 2:256
2:7, 14–17 1:56
2:14 1:3, 1:55
2:14–20 2:234
2:16–17 1:219
3:5 1:87, 2:195
4:4–22 1:157
4:13–14 2:215
5:3 1:157
5:8 1:224
6:10 1:157
8:1 1:301
9:10 1:56, 2:212, 2:218, 2:255
10:6 1:375
13:5 1:55

Joel
1:15 2:202
2:1, 11, 31 2:202
2:12–16 2:225
2:15–16, 17 1:223
2:28 – 32 1:312

2:28–29 1:313–314
3:14 2:202
3:18 2:48, 2:180
3:19 1:197

Amos
1 – 2 2:199
1:1 2:115, 2:177
1:5, 8 2:194
1:6–11 1:197
1:11 2:36, 2:40
2:1–3 2:196
2:9 2:54, 2:82
2:10 2:80
2:11 1:243
2:11–12 1:159
3:4 2:169
3:6 1:224
4:1 2:83, 2:114
4:4 2:78
4:10 2:63
5:18, 20 2:202
6:2 2:78
6:8 1:356
6:10 1:336
6:14 2:138
7:1–6, 7–9 1:346
7:12 2:178
8:3 1:336
9:2 1:425
9:11 1:87
9:11–12 1:197, 2:195
9:12 2:36

Obadiah
1:8 1:197
1:21 2:36
15 2:202

Jonah
1:16 2:354–355
2:6 1:425
2:7, 9 2:355
3:4 2:211

Micah
1:1 2:177
2:4 2:152
2:5 2:301

Micah (cont.)
3:7 2:178
3:11 2:110
4:1 2:190
4:2 1:233
4:11 2:476
5:1 2:194
5:2 2:296
5:2–5 2:195
5:9 2:25
6:4 1:129
6:5 2:103, 2:104, 2:164
7:14 2:403
7:15 2:481

Nahum
1:1 1:262
1:15 2:199, 2:356, 2:398
2:13 2:168
2:13–14 2:169
38:39 2:169

Habakkuk
1:1 2:177
1:3, 13 1:258
1:12 2:19
2:6 2:152
2:20 1:336
3:7 1:292
3:13 2:196

Zephaniah
1:7 1:336
1:7, 14 2:202
2:3 1:297
2:4 – 3:7 2:199
2:8–11 2:196
2:9 1:356

Zechariah
2:5 1:222, 1:434
2:8 2:128
2:13 1:336
2:15 1:235
3:8 1:159
5:3 2:414
6:12 1:159
8:2 1:150
8:23 1:396

9:14 1:224
9:16 1:159
10:2 2:178
10:11 2:194
12:1 1:262
12:10 2:48, 2:180, 2:232
13:1 2:48, 2:180
13:3 2:231
14:8 2:48, 2:180
14:8–9 2:50
14:16 2:344

Malachi
1:1 1:262
1:4 1:197
1:11 2:333
1:14 2:356
2:4–5 2:238
2:4–5, 8 2:238
3:6 2:162
4:2 1:396
4:4 1:72
4:5 2:202
23:24 2:162

APOCRYPHA

1 Maccabees
1:26 2:226
2:54 2:237

2 Maccabees
3:49 1:160

Sirach
45:2–5 1:70
45:23–24 2:237
50:15 2:334
50:24 2:237

Tobit
6:13 2:491

Wisdom of Solomon
16:5–7 2:69
16:20 1:256
19:6, 11 1:256

NEW TESTAMENT

Matthew
1:1 2:208
1:1–7 2:184
1:1–17 2:210, 2:284, 2:435
1:4–16 1:86
1:5 1:314
1:21 1:328
1:21–23 2:164
1:21, 23 1:366
2:12 2:194
2:23 1:159
3:7–12 1:314
3:16 1:286
5:5 2:321
5:8 1:171
5:29–30 1:136
5:37 2:370
6:9 2:48
6:9–13 1:169
7:16–17 1:332
9:20 1:396
9:36 2:311
10:2–4 1:99
10:9–10 1:478
11:28 1:234
14:13–21 1:108
15:3–9 2:361
23:12 1:298
24:30–31 1:26
25:31 1:26
26:36–46 1:154
26:64 1:26
27:51–53 1:455
28:2 1:455
28:16–20 1:88
28:18–20 1:198
28:19 1:175
28:20 1:194

Mark
3:13–19 1:99
6:30–44 1:108
6:34 2:311
6:56 1:396
9:38–40 1:282
9:42 2:383
15:25 2:335

15:33–34, 37 *2:335*

Luke
1:26–38 *2:275*
1:52 *1:298*
1:78 *2:195*
2:11 *1:328*
2:36–38 *2:365*
3:23–33 *1:86*
3:38 *1:198*
6:12–16 *1:87, 1:99*
8:44 *1:396*
9:10–17 *1:108*
9:23 *2:453*
10:20 *1:99*
16:29, 31 *1:71*
17:32 *1:231*
24:27 *1:71*
24:44 *1:301*

John
1:9 *1:170*
1:16 *2:358*
1:17–18 *1:73*
1:17, 45 *1:73*
1:18 *1:301*
1:29, 36 *2:338*
1:32–33 *2:48*
1:32–34 *1:501*
2:13–22 *2:257*
3:3–5 *2:48*
3:14–16 *2:87*
3:16 *1:383*
4:10–14 *2:48*
4:13–14 *1:501, 2:50*
5:36 *1:269*
5:46 *1:301*
6:1–14 *1:108*
6:63 *2:48*
7:37–38 *2:344*
7:37–39 *1:501, 2:48, 2:50*
8:12 *1:170*
8:37–47 *1:314*
10 *2:279, 2:311*
10:4, 16, 27 *1:2*
12:32 *2:87*
13:1–17 *1:494*
13:20 *2:36*
14:6 *1:455*

15:1, 5 *1:161*
15:1–8 *1:445*
17:11 *1:175*
19:9–10 *1:298*
19:31–37 *2:338*
19:33–35 *1:501*
19:34 *1:204*
19:37 *2:232*
20:1, 19, 26 *2:335*
20:22 *1:501*

Acts
1 – 2 *1:501*
1:8 *1:314*
1:15–26 *1:87, 1:99*
1:23–26 *2:273*
2 *1:314*
2:1–4, 32–39 *2:340*
2:1–33 *1:313*
2:33 *2:50*
3:1 *2:333*
4:12 *1:455*
7:22 *1:73*
7:38 *1:39*
7:53 *1:26, 1:39*
8:17–19 *2:312*
17:11 *1:269, 1:301*
17:31 *1:455*
18:18 *1:160*
19:6 *2:312*
21:23–24 *1:160*

Romans
1:3 *1:86*
1:21–26 *1:270*
1:32 *2:222–223*
8:3 *2:87*
8:12–17 *2:398*
8:13 *2:453*
8:28 *2:442, 2:482*
8:29 *1:159*
8:31–39 *2:209*
9:6–13 *1:314*
10:5 *1:71*
10:14–15 *2:398*
10:15 *2:199*
11:16 *1:478*
11:22 *1:350*
11:26 *2:483*

12:1 *2:352*
12:1–2 *1:204*
14:4, 12–13 *1:301*
15:27 *1:478*

1 Corinthians
3:12–17 *1:434*
3:16–17 *1:22*
5:5 *2:64*
6:15–20 *2:484*
6:19 *1:22*
9:2–18 *1:478*
9:26–27 *1:136, 2:453*
10:1–12 *2:278*
10:4 *2:50*
10:8 *2:233*
10:9 *2:63*
10:11 *1:1*
10:14–22 *2:484*
10:18 *1:108*
12:12–31 *1:95*
15:20 *1:478*
15:25 *2:207*
15:26 *2:398*
16:1–2 *1:478*

2 Corinthians
3:7–18 *1:167*
4:6 *1:170*
4:16–17 *2:447*
5:21 *2:87, 2:210*
6:11–18 *1:314*
6:16 *1:494*
11:2 *2:256*

Galatians
3:13–14 *2:210*
3:16 *2:187, 2:208*
3:19 *1:26, 1:39*
4:4–5 *2:87*
5:16, 24 *1:314*
6:7 *1:348*
6:7–8, 14 *2:453*

Ephesians
2:14 *2:257*
2:14–22 *1:95*
2:19–22 *1:22, 1:494*
4:7–10 *2:398*

Ephesians (*cont.*)
5:2 *1:455, 2:332, 2:352*
5:25–32 *2:256*
5:30–32 *2:234*
6:10–20 *2:398*

Philippians
2:1–11 *1:494*
2:5–11 *1:455*
3:12–21 *1:136*

Colossians
3:5–6 *2:453*

2 Thessalonians
3:16 *1:172*

1 Timothy
5:17–18 *1:478*

2 Timothy
3:16 *1:73*

Titus
3:5–6 *1:313*

Hebrews
1:1–2 *1:301*
2:2 *1:26, 1:39*
3:1–6 *1:301*
3:2 *1:313*
3:5 *1:301*
3:7 – 4:2 *1:312*
3:7 – 4:11 *1:384*
3:12, 14 *1:365*
3:19 – 4:2 *1:326*
4:9–11 *1:239*
5:4–5 *1:455*
6:13–18 *2:359*
7:11 – 10:25 *2:259*
7:23–25 *2:49*
9 *2:343*
9:13–14 *1:501*
10:19–22 *1:455*
10:26 *1:381*
11:8–10, 14–16 *1:231*
11:26–27 *1:419*
12:1–2 *1:315*
12:14, 28–29 *1:136*
12:24 *2:484*
12:28–29 *1:468*
12:29 *1:250, 1:344*
13:10–13 *1:501*

James
2:20–24 *1:122*
4:6 *1:298*
5:12 *2:370*

1 Peter
1:14–16 *1:136*
2:4–10 *1:22, 1:494*
5:5 *1:298*

2 Peter
1:21 *1:274*
2:15 *2:102, 2:104*
2:15–16 *2:103, 2:104, 2:146*
2:21 *1:73*
3:8 *1:346*

1 John
3:16–23 *1:494*

Jude
11 *2:104*
22 – 23 *1:494*

Revelation
1:5 *1:502*
1:7 *1:26*
2:14 *2:102, 2:104*
4 *1:40, 1:89*
4:6–8 *1:40*
4:7 *1:92*
5:5 *1:28*
5:8 *2:333*
7:9 *1:99*
8:3–4 *2:333*
11:15 *2:203*
12 *2:113*
12:1 *1:24*
12:9 *2:71, 2:196*
20:2 *2:71, 2:196*
20:7–10 *2:206*
20:8 *2:184*
20:9 *1:20, 1:40*
21 *1:40*
21 – 22 *1:20, 1:40, 1:171, 1:174, 1:203, 2:321, 2:496*
21:3 *1:20, 1:40, 1:98, 2:484*
21:9–27 *1:99*
21:11, 23–24 *1:175*
21:12–21 *1:21*
21:13 *1:20*
21:14, 19–21 *1:21*
21:15–16 *1:20*
21:22–24 *1:174*
21:27 *1:174, 1:502*
22:1 *2:48, 2:50*
22:1–2 *1:175, 2:6, 2:20, 2:45*
22:1–3 *1:22*
22:1–5 *1:174*
22:3 *1:175*
22:4 *1:175*
22:5 *1:175*
22:16 *2:195*
40 – 48 *1:40*

ANCIENT SOURCES

Pseudepigrapha
2 Enoch
21:6 *1:24*
Jubilees
1:1–2 *2:340*
1:4, 26 *1:70*
1:27 *1:39*
2:1 *1:39, 1:70*
6:17 *2:340*
12:16–19 *1:24*
15:2 *2:340*
46 *2:423*
Sibylline Oracles
5.512–513 *1:24*
Testament of Abraham
B 7.4–16 *1:24*
Testament of Naphtali
5.1–8 *1:24*
Testaments of the Twelve Patriarchs *2:194*

Dead Sea Scrolls and related texts
1QM *2:194*
    9.7–9 *1:459*

4Q365
  fragment 36 *2:283*
4QMMT *Halakhic Letter*
  1:20
  B 29–33, 58–62 *1:49*
4QNum *2:94, 2:143*
11Q19 Temple Scroll
  1:19–20
  50.4–7 *1:459*
11QT
  46.9 *1:114*
Damascus Document
  (CD) *2:194*
  5.18 *1:39*
Testimonia (4QTest)
  2:194
War Scroll 2:396

Philo
Creation
1.1 *1:70*
On Dreams
2.112–113 *1:24*
Gig
6.24 *1:268*
Leg. Alleg
2.20.79–81 *2:70*
Moses
1.317 *2:391*
2.8 *1:70*
2.24.124 *1:22–23*
2.217 *1:384*
Moses II
25.124 *1:104*
Spec. Laws
1.16.84 *1:22–23*
1.248 *1:165*
1.267–269 *1:461*
Vita Mosis
1:264 *2:118*

Josephus
Ag. Ap. 1.37–40 *1:70*
Ant.
2.10 *1:292*
3.7.5 *1:21*
3.7.7 *1:24*
3.12.5 *1:21*
3.12.6 *1:223*
3.178 *1:389*
3.241–270 *1:20*
4.4.7 *2:41*
4.55–56 *1:430*
4.78–79 *2:12*
4.78–84 *1:499*
4.176 *2:214*
11.331 *1:389*
15.136 *1:39*
Jewish Wars
1.33.2–3 *1:91–92*
5.5.7 *1:21*

Rabbinic literature and other Jewish sources
Mishnah
  17, 19, 23–24 *1:153*
  Avot
    5.19 *2:102, 2:125*
  Berakhot
    1.3 *1:471*
  Hullin 1:378
    24a *1:31, 1:201*
  Kelim
    1.1–4 *1:490*
    10.1–8 *1:492*
  Makkot
    2.6 *2:471*
    10b *2:129*
    11b *2:471*
  Meilah
    87b *2:334*
  Menahot
    5.6 *1:196*
    30a *1:70*
    43b *1.391*
  Middot
    2.5 *1:166*
  Mo'ed Qatan
    17b *1:295*
    28a *2:471*
  Nedarim
    2b *2:359*
    11.9E–H *2:366*
    67a *2:364*
    76 *2:367*
    79b *2:367*
  Parah
    1.1 *1:480*
  2.1 *1:480*
  2.3 *1:482*
  2.5 *1:481*
  4.4 *1:460*
  Pesahot
    5.1 *2:331*
    58a *2:331*
  Pirkei Avot
    5.2 *1:352*
    5.19 *2:132*
  Rosh HaShanah
    3a *1:56*
    3.5 *2:69*
    3.8 *2:71*
  Shevu'ot
    1.4–5 *2:337*
  Sotah
    1.2d *1:151*
    1.10 *2:272*
    5.3 *2:462*
    9.9 *1:148–149*
    34b *1:333*
  Yoma
    1.38b *2:56*
  Zebachim
    10.1 *2:335*
    14.4 *1:440*
    88b *2:471*
Babylonian Talmud
  Arachim
    15a–b *1:352*
    15b *1:51*
  Bava Batra
    14b *1:70, 2:100*
    15a *1:70*
    78b *2:56*
    102a *2:493*
    117a, 120a *2:491*
    117b *2:268, 2:274*
    119b *2:492*
    121a *2:277*
    122a *2:273*
  Bekhorot
    4a *1:114*
    5a *1:28*
  Berakhot
    32b *1:23*
  Ketubot
    111b *1:334*

Rabbinic literature (cont.)
Megilla
　13b 2:386
Menahot
　4.3 1:2
　44a 1.392
Nazir
　45a 1:49
Pesahim
　5.14b, 17a 1:490
　67a 1:49
Sanhedrin
　8a 2:492
　37a 2:471
　42b 1:49
　78b 1:384
　82a 2:227, 2:233
　87b 2:232
　105a 2:134, 2:176
　105b 2:132, 2:133,
　　2:152
　106a 2:190, 2:383
　106b 2:380
　110a 1:407, 1:429
Shabbat
　11a–116a 1:234
　64a–b 2:392
　87b 1:4
　96b–97a 2:286
Sotah
　1.2d 1:47
　36b 1:2
Sukkah
　5.4 1:166
Ta'anit
　30b 2:491
Tamid
　5.1 1:46, 1:166
　7.2 1:46, 1:166
Yevamot
　87b 2:362
Yoma 7.1 1:2
Zebachim
　115b 1:440
　116b 1:20, 1:49
　Gemara 2:56
Jerusalem Talmud
Sotah 5 2:100
Yoma 1.1 2:272

Mekhilta deRabbi
　Ishmael
　4.5 2:12
　16.35 2:12
　20.4 2:443
Sifra
　Emor 14.5 1:384
Sifre
　Numbers
　1 1:48
　39 1:46, 1:166
　84 1:234
　91 1:261
　93 1:268, 1:275
　114 1:384
　115 1.391, 1.392
　117 1:460
　124 1:486
　131 2:232
　133 2:492
　150 2:344
　153 2:362
　155 2:367
　Pinhas
　143 2:334
　v. 2 2:285
　v 134 2:293
　Deuteronomy
　99 1:295
　233 2:491
Sifre Zuta on Numbers
　19.11
　　Genzia fragment
　　1:459
Midrash Rabbah
Genesis Rabbah
　19.2 1:416
　55.8 2:132, 2:133
Exodus Rabbah
　1.30 1:407
　2.5 1:2
　3.12 2:65
　23.13 1:32
Leviticus Rabbah
　2.4 1:198
　16.2 1:51
Numbers Rabbah
　2.3 1:38–39, 1:92
　2.5, 10 1:92

2.6 1:39
2.6–7 1:28
2.7 1:23, 1:91
2.10 1:28
2.13 1:24
3.14 1:128
4.13 1:391
7.4, 5 1:51
7.8 1:48, 1:52
7.10 1:48
8.5 1:147
10.10 2:127
12.4 2:381
14, 15 2:144
15.19 1:268, 1:275,
　1:276, 1:279, 1:282
15.20 1:265
15.24 1:277
15.25 1:269, 1:313
16.5 1:324
16.7 1:323
16.7–8 1:322
16.12 1:328, 1:329
16.21 1:344
17.5 1:39–40
18.2 1:406, 1:410
18.5 1:407
18.19 1:429
18.20 1:407
18.23 1:454
19.1, 5 1:460
19.2 1:461
19.3–5 1:460
19.7 2:36
19.16 2:41
19.20 2:56
19.22 2:70
19.26 2:73
19.30 2:81
20.1 2:109
20.2 2:112
20.4 2:109, 2:114
20.6 2:128
20.7 2:116, 2:117,
　2:160
20.9 2:124
20.10 2:125
20.11 2:131
20.12 2:129, 2:132, 2:133

Index of Scripture references and ancient sources 631

20.14 *2:131, 2:138,*
       2:140, 2:141
20.15 *2:143*
20.16 *2:152*
20.18 *2:149*
20.20 *2:165, 2:168,*
       2:383
20.21 *2:189*
20.23 *2:216, 2:217,*
       2:233
20.24 *2:227*
20.25 *2:228*
21.7   *2:279*
21.8   *2:272*
21.10 *2:284*
21.13 *2:308*
21.15 *2:316*
21.19 *2:328*
21.21 *2:331*
21.24 *2:345*
21.30 *2:81*
22.4   *2:380*
23.1   *2:481*
23.3   *2:481*
23.4   *2:481*
23.13 *2:478*
32.8   *2:403*
32.9   *2:410*
Pesiqta de-Rav Kahana
4.2   *1:461*
4.3–7 *1:460*
4.6   *1:460*
Addenda 1 *2:270*
Pesiqta Rabbati
4   *1:24*
12–13 *1:460*
14.6 *1:461*
Pirke de Rabbi Eliezer
47   *2:226*
53   *1:292, 1:307*
Midrash Tanḥuma
3   *2:109*
4   *2:117*
6   *2:125*
10   *2:148*
14   *2:168*
18   *2:190*
24   *2:81*

Balak
10   *2:144*
Beha'alotcha
12   *1:268, 1:279,*
     1:281
16   *1:268*
Gen. 42:1 *2:492*
Hukat
18   *2:56*
37   *2:7*
Korah
2   *1:410*
23   *1:430*
Metzora 7
24a and 22b *1:51*
Shelach
5   *1:364*
T'tzaveh 11 *1:407*
Midrash Leqaḥ Ṭov
     1:261, 2:386
Parashat Shemot
3.1 *2:386*
Midrash Tehillim
14.6 *1:313*
Mekhilta de-Rabbi Shion
ben Yoḥai *2:482*
Targums
Fragment Targums *2:181,*
     2:190
Jon *2:491*
Ezekiel 1:14 *1:33*
Num. 22:5 *2:134*
Neofiti *1:198, 1:275,*
     1:301, 2:70, 2:194,
     2:392
21:1 *2:12*
Num. 12:6 *2:12*
Onqelos *1:198, 1:275,*
     1:293, 1:301, 2:181,
     2:190, 2:194
Pseudo-Jonathan *1:79,*
     1:198, 1:275, 1:301,
     1:319, 1:320, 1:440,
     1:459, 1:460, 1:480,
     2:56, 2:70, 2:181,
     2:190, 2:194, 2:281,
     2:380, 2:440, 2:443,
     2:444
2.7 *1:92*

11.33 *1:287*
19.6   *1:486*
Exodus 6:18 *2:226*
Numbers
12:12, 16 *2:12*
20:1–2 *2:12*
25:12 *2:226*
25:13 *2:232*
Tosefta
Kel. B Qam 1.12 *1:20,*
     1:49
Levi
8.14 *2:194*
18.3 *2:194*
Megillah 31b *1:38*
Parah 4.10 *1:486*
Shevu'ot 13a *1:383*
Sukkah 3.11–13 *2:12,*
     2:27
Sefer Yetzira
5–6 *1:23*
Zohar
Bemidbar
1.126a *2:171*
1.173 *1:23*
118 *1:104*
Shelah 175 *2:88*
Exodus, Vaycra
v. 478 *1:195*
I:173 *1:24*

Papyri, ostraca etc.
Ostraca
45, 47 *2:305, 2:306*
50 *2:306*
Papyrus Amherst 63
2:230

Other Jewish literature
Akiba ben Joseph *1:208*
Bachya ben Asher *1:255*
Bemidbar
2.2 *1:29, 1:222,*
     1:388
Bekhor Shor *1:446*
Chizkuni *2:33, 2:64*
Elazar ben Levi
Sefer ha–Zikhronot
     1:23, 1:104

Rabbinic literature *(cont.)*
Eliezer ben Jose *1:103*
Kli Yakar (Shlomo
  Ephraim ben Aaron
  Luntschitz)
  Lev. 13:2 *1:51*
  Lev. 14:6 *1:51*
Moses Maimonides
  (Rambam) *1:164,
  1:250, 2:47, 2:140*
  *Guide for the
    Perplexed*
    3:46 *2:337*
    3:50 *2:481*
  Hilkhot Teshuva
    3.4 *2:341*
  Hilkot Sotah
    3 *1:156*
  *MishT, Beit
    Hebechirah*
    7.11–23 *1:20*
  Shemoneh Perakim 4
    2:30
R. Eliezer b. R. Jose *1:103*
Rabbi Joseph
  Targum on 1
    Chronicles *1:440*
Seder Olam
  9–10 *2:12*
Tur
  Yoreh Deah
    275 *2:435*
Yalkult Reuveni
  Num. 16:31 *1:428*
Yalkult Shim'oni
  Deuteronomy 738 *1:295*
    Va'era 181 *2:65*
  Exodus 167 *1:407*

  Shemot 168 *2:134*
  Numbers
    11, 732 *1:250*
    418 *1:23*
    Korah 752 *1:427*

**Classical and ancient
Christian writings**
Aristotle
  Poetics 18 *1:405*
Artapanus of Alexandria
  1:292
Athanasius
  'On the Incarnation of
    the Word' *2:195*
Augustine
  *De diversis
    quaestionbus ad
    Simplicianum*
    2 [PL 40, cols.
    129–130] *2:106*
  De Trinitate
    6.1.1 *1:268*
  *On the Forgiveness of
    Sins and Baptism*
    1.61 *2:87*
  Mir S.S.
    MPL 35, 2173
    2:195
  Quaest. in Num., No
    33 *1:461*
  Sermon
    26.4 *2:87*
  *Sermons on the Old
    Testament*
    6.7 *2:87*
  On the Trinity
    3.9 *2:87*

Barnabas
  8 *1:461*
  8.1–2 *1:501*
Demetrius the
  Chronographer *1:292*
Ezekiel the Tragedian
  1:292
Herodotus
  Histories 3.107
    2:64–5
Irenaeus
  Fragmenta
    MPG 7, 1242 *2:195*
Jerome
  ep. 77, ad *Oceanum*
    PL 22, 695 *2:195*
Justin Martyr
  'The First Apology'
    2:195
Origen *2:382*
  Homilies on Numbers
    6, 7 *1:296*
    6.2.1 *1:268*
    MPG 12, 619 *2:195*
Prado, Jerome de *1:29*
Pseudo-Philo
  11.15 *2:12*
  LAB
    10.7 *2:12*
    20.8 *2:12*
Shepherd of Hermas
  2.3.4 *1:276*
Theodoret
  Quaest. in Oct. c. 44
    PG 80, 394 *2:195*
Trapp, John *1:89, 1:94*
  1650.3 *1:94*

INDEX OF MODERN AUTHORS

Aalders, G. C., 2:100
Aaron, D. H., 2:489, 2:492
Abarbanel, R. Y., 1:67, 2:312
   dragon insignia, 1:28
   Gad and Reuben's sons, 2:406
   Israel and the land, 2:309
   Israel's Camp, 1:41
   land distribution, 2:273
   military strategy, 2:311
   Moses' authority, 2:436
   signpost for Messiah, 2:481
   spies, 1:325
   Wilderness of Paran, 2:446
   women, 2:366
Abba, R., 1:19
Abbott, A., 1:297
Abela, A.
   Hazeroth, 1:290
   Miriam, 1:290, 1:308
Abrams, J. Z., 1:51, 1:304
Achenbach, R., 1:46, 1:243, 1:320, 1:402, 1:408
   congregations, 1:172
   the elders, 1:264
   first generation, 2:59
   Hobab, 1:232
   judgement of YHWH, 1:418, 1:419
   on Num 5-6, 1:142
   Phinehas, 2:228
   red heifer ritual, 1:489
   rich land, 1:372
   the Sabbath, 1:385
   strayed woman, 1:153
Ackerman, H. C., 2:177
Ackerman, J. S.
   Balaam narrative, 2:104, 2:193
   Balak, 2:112
   dry dust of Jacob, 2:181
   Hobab, 1:230
   Phineas episode, 2:230
   red heifer law, 1:460
   tribe and family, 2:494
Ackerman, S., 2:48
Ackroyd, P., 1:30
Adamo, D. T., 1:293
Aharoni, Y.
   land boundaries, 2:438, 2:454
   Mount Hor, 2:41
   Riblah, 2:455
   Sihon's campaign, 2:81
   Sinai location, 1:228
   the wilderness, 2:7
   wilderness journeys, 2:445
Aḥituv, S., 2:273
Ainsworth, H., 1:40
   Camp of Israel, 1:49
   strayed woman, 1:153
Albertz, R., 2:212
   annual sacrifices, 2:351
   Joshua's authority, 2:314
   plagues and executions, 2:234
Albright, William F., 2:75, 2:95
   'Agag', 2:185
   the Ark, 1:31
   Balaam narrative, 2:100, 2:102, 2:107, 2:116, 2:117, 2:153, 2:157, 2:158
   Cain burned up, 2:201
   census figures, 1:102
   chieftain names, 1:86
   the Cushite woman, 1:292
   El Shaddai, 2:177
   nest/Cain, 2:200
   peoples around Moab, 2:197
   Pethor, 2:116
   on Ruel, 1:230
Alden, R. L., 1:276
Alexander, T. D.
   atonement, 2:394
   census figures, 1:107
   kings and kingdom, 2:184
   second Passover, 1:213
   YHWH's judgements, 2:206

Allegro, J. M., 2:176
Allen, R. B., 2:101
   Balaam narrative, 2:100, 2:109, 2:113, 2:116, 2:123, 2:158, 2:164, 2:196
   boundary list, 2:483
   census figures, 1:105
   dispossessing Canaanites, 2:452
   Israel's seed, 2:181
   land distribution, 2:458
   Phinehas episode, 2:230
   rise of a star, 2:195
   wilderness journeys, 2:440
   women, 2:364
   YHWH's message, 2:209
   YHWH's supremacy, 2:193
Allis, O. T., 1:70
   Balaam narrative, 2:100
   census figures, 1:100, 1:102
Alter, R.
   Baal Peor story, 2:212
   Balaam narrative, 2:96, 2:97, 2:168, 2:189
   drink offerings, 2:333
   formula language, 1:217
   Korah's rebellion, 1:402, 1:430
   Levites, 1:464
   'lion' synonyms, 2:168
   roots and water, 2:180
   trumpets, 1:224
Altmann, P., 1:252
Amy-Dressler, J. A., 1:444, 2:20
Anchor Bible Dictionary (ed. Freedman), 1:331
Andersen, Francis I., 2:469
   census figures, 1:107
   clan and kinship, 2:295
   kings of Canaan, 1:348
   land inheritance, 2:305
Anderson, B. A., 2:35, 2:197
Anderson, B. W., 1:225
Anderson, G. A., 1:4
   benediction, 1:166
   burnt offerings, 2:331
   defiant sin, 1:380
   grain offerings, 1:375
   Nazirites, 1:162
   purification rites, 1:196
   on the Tabernacle, 1:5
Anisfeld, M.

Balaam narrative, 2:103, 2:135
   Moses and serpents, 2:67
   water miracle, 2:31
Anthonioz, S., 2:6, 2:27, 2:50
Archer Jr, G. L., 1:71, 1:148
Arden, E.
   Moses, 2:24, 2:47
   water miracle, 2:31
Armgardt, M., 1:70
Artus, O., 1:61
   Joshua and Caleb, 1:342–343
   rebellions, 1:412, 2:407
   water miracle, 2:31
   YHWH's sovereignty, 1:66, 1:280, 1:382
   Zelophehad's daughters, 2:418
Asher, N.
   Aaron's failure, 2:42
   rebellion, 1:338
Asher, Rabbi B. ben, 2:475, 2:481
Ashley, T. R., 1:4, 1:13, 1:61, 1:63, 1:210, 1:235, 1:243
   Amram, 2:275
   army sizes, 1:101
   assembly, 1:409
   'Baal-Meon', 2:418
   Baal Peor, 2:217
   Balaam narrative, 2:127, 2:135
   Balak, 2:114
   benediction, 1:167
   burnt offerings, 2:340, 2:344
   Canaan's description, 1:343
   the censers, 1:434
   census language, 1:84
   cities, 2:271
   cleansing after deaths, 1:499
   crossing Edom, 2:39
   family tombs, 2:41
   Gad and Reuben, 2:406, 2:414, 2:417
   generations in the wilderness, 1:357
   judgement/estimation, 1:143
   kareth penalty, 1:494
   on Kenizzites, 1:326
   kings of Midian, 2:382
   land, 2:456, 2:489
   Levi's tribe, 1:90
   Midianites, 2:376, 2:384
   obedience, 1:218
   Ohad's clan, 2:262, 2:269

Phinehas, 2:222, 2:226
priesthood, 1:451, 1:467, 2:236
public feasts, 2:328
rebellion, 1:341, 1:410, 1:412
sons of Israel, 2:265
staffs, 1:445
trees and the Camp, 2:180
trumpets, 1:228
trust and obedience, 2:71
the unclean person, 1:214
vows and oaths, 2:358
wilderness journeys, 2:432, 2:445
wine, 2:334
Ashlock, R. O., 2:494
Attridge, H. W., 1:381
Auld, A. G.
  cities of reception, 2:465
  tally of tribes, 2:273
Aune, D. E., 1:24
Aurelius, E., 1:244
Averbeck, R. E., 1:373
Avishur, Y., 1:341
  Balaam narrative, 2:133
  formula language, 1:217
  strayed women, 1:144
Avi-Yonah, M., 2:194
Awabdy, M. A., 1:166

Bach, A., 1:55, 1:154
  uncleanness, 1:150
  waters of curses, 1:156
Bachya ben Asher, 1:29, 1:222, 1:255, 1:388
Baden, J. S., 1:402, 2:3, 2:4
  high-handed sin, 1:383
  sacrifices for sin, 1:370
Baentsch, B., 1:68, 1:142, 1:460, 2:212, 2:486
  census figures, 1:100
  land distribution, 2:273
Baigent, M., 1:25
Bailey, L. R., 2:177
Bailey, R., 1:293
Baker, D. W., 2:202
Baker, L. S. K., 1:70
Baldensperger, L., 1:486
Balentine, S. E.
  character of Moses, 1:347
  Moses' crisis, 1:258
  Moses' intercession, 1:350

Balorda, A., 1:60
  covenant of peace, 2:237
  idolatry, 2:215
  jealousy, 2:235–236, 2:239, 2:253–254
  Moabites, 2:216, 2:218
Baltzer, K., 1:300
Bar-Efrat, S., 2:239
Bar-Ilan, M., 1:173
Barker, D., 1:166
Barker, P. A., 1:363
Barnouin, M., 1:25, 1:103
Baron, S. W., 1:100
Barré, M. L.
  Balaam narrative, 2:105, 2:106, 2:204
  Balak's homeland, 2:117
  Pethor, 2:116
Bartelmus, R., 1:142
Barth, L., 1:38
Bartlett, J. R., 2:35
Baruchi-Unna, A.
  penitent weeping, 2:225
  Phineas episode, 2:231
Baskin, J. R., 2:194
Bateman, H. W.
  Balaam narrative, 2:190, 2:196
  David's kingship, 2:206
  Edom, 2:197
  war maces, 2:194
Bauckham, R., 1:276
Baumgarten, A. I., 1:495
Bazak, A., 1:38, 1:54
  Balaam narrative, 2:118
  Balak, 2:112
  Cushite woman, 1:294
  leprosy, 1:305
  Moses' anger, 2:24
  second generation, 2:66
Beale, G. K., 1:21, 1:40
  high priest's breastplate, 1:22
  zodiac and twelve tribes, 1:24–25
Beattie, D. R. G., 1:440, 1:442
Bechara, C. A., 1:60
  Baal Peor, 2:252
  idolatry, 2:250
  Phinehas, 2:254
Beck, J. A., 1:11, 2:20
  the people and the land, 1:329
  spies, 1:325
  the wilderness, 2:7

Beegle, D., 1:260
Begrich, J., 1:492
Beirne, D., 1:243, 1:253
Bekhor Shor, J., 1:295, 1:446
Bellinger, W. H., 1:382
Ben-Barak, Z.
   clan and kinship, 2:294, 2:295, 2:303, 2:487
   land inheritance, 2:288, 2:301, 2:304, 2:305
   marriage and women, 2:368, 2:488
   Zelophehad's daughters, 2:271, 2:283, 2:287, 2:291, 2:491, 2:493
Bendor, S., 2:487
   clan and kinship, 2:294, 2:295
   land tenure, 2:301
Benjamin, D. C., 2:295
Ben-Yosef, E., 2:72
Bergsma, J. S.
   Jubilee, 2:488
   tribal holdings, 2:490
   Zelophehad's daughters, 2:493
Berlin, A., 1:244, 1:404
Berlin, Naftali Zvi Yehud 'Netziv'
   Camp of Israel, 1:27
   The Netziv, 2:270
Berlinerblau, J., 2:358
Berman, J., 1:13, 1:73
   on ark and tablets, 1:190
   holy of holies, 1:90
   source criticism, 1:69
Bernat, D. A.
   Camp experience, 2:494
   Phinehas, 2:226
Bernstein, I.
   wilderness journeys, 2:435
Bertman, S.
   the tassel, 1:388
Bewer, J. A.
   Balaam narrative, 2:99
   taboos and rituals, 1:461
Beyerline, W., 1:168
Bezold, C., 2:120
Biale, D., 1:406
Bibb, B. D., 1:122
Biblia Hebraica Stuttgartensia (BHS), 1:80, 1:113, 1:114, 1:115, 1:180, 1:181, 1:319, 1:368, 1:400–401
   'Ar' the city, 2:198

   'beon', 2:400
   'by day', 1:208
   'Canaan', 2:431
   'cities of' Moab, 2:53
   'fire offering', 1:459
   'hasten', 2:400
   'hunger', 1:242
   'leaders', 2:211
   'majesty', 2:165
   'my bread', 2:325
   'near-offering', 2:325
   Nemuel, 2:262
   purification offerings, 2:325
   'put', 1:243
   'Shephupham', 2:262
   statute of the law, 1:459
   'three days' way', 1:233
   'to take', 1:401
   'trangression against YHWH', 2:374
   'whole burnt offering', 2:325
   a wondrous vow, 1:141
   YHWH commanded, 2:485
   'you will pass through the fire', 2:374
Bick, E., 1:4
   burnt offerings, 2:330
   Levites, 1:444, 1:465
   Midianites, 2:379
   Moses and war, 2:378
   new Eden, 2:277
   purity, 1:146
   wilderness sojourn, 2:376
Biderman, A.
   the veil, 1:35
Biersdorff, K. A., 2:181
Bimson, J. J.
   clan and kinship, 2:295
   harvests, 1:376
   Hebron, 1:331
   land inheritance, 2:302
   land tenure, 2:300
Binns, L. E., 1:68, 1:288
Bin-Nun, Y.
   itinerary in song, 2:483
   Kadesh Barnea, 2:446
   land of Canaan, 2:425
   Midianites, 2:395
   offerings, 2:327
   Wilderness of Paran, 2:445
   Zelophehad's daughters, 2:293

Index of modern authors

Bird, P., 2:215
Birkan, A., 2:88
  bronze serpent, 2:72
  cobra-crest, 2:65
  God's compassion, 2:71
  Moses builds altar, 2:68
  people's grievance, 2:63
  release of serpents, 2:63
Bissell, A. P., 2:471
Black, J., 2:101
Blau, J. L., 1:460
Blenkin, H., 2:332
Blenkinsopp, J., 2:212
  clan and kinship, 2:295
  land inheritance, 2:297, 2:301
  Naboth's vineyard, 2:286
  Phinehas episode, 2:232
Block, D. I., 1:30, 1:32, 1:73
Blum, E., 1:244, 1:249, 1:369
  Moses, 2:22, 2:25
Blumenthal, F., 2:140, 2:190
Bobrick, B., 1:24–25
Bodenheimer, F. S., 1:256
Boer, P. A. H. de, 1:142
Boer, R. de, 1:149, 1:151
Bolger, E. W.
  Balaam narrative, 1:142
  cherubim, 2:138
  Eden and Canaan, 2:179
  good and evil, 1:362, 1:363
Boorer, S., 1:320, 1:321, 1:344, 1:347, 1:351
  decision to ascend, 1:328
  Gad and Reuben's sons, 2:413
  the land, 1:364
  Moses, 1:350, 2:17, 2:27, 2:47
  sin among leaders, 2:4
  YHWH, 1:348, 2:29
Boraas, R. S., 2:69
Borger, R., 2:64
Borowski, O.
  clan and kinship, 2:295
  leprosy, 1:140
Boudreau, G. R., 2:212, 2:214
Bourke, J., 1:275
Bourquin, Y., 1:402, 1:405
Bovati, Pietro, 2:168
Boyce, R. N., 2:47
Boys, T., 1:387
Breland, C. R., 2:489

Brenner, A.
  Cushite woman, 1:293–294
  red heifer, 1:481
Brenton, L. C. L., 1:336
  the censers, 1:434
  messianism, 2:181
Brichto, H. C.
  Balaam narrative, 2:121
  family name, 2:302
  land inheritance, 2:300, 2:304
  Moabite cult, 2:218
  strayed woman, 1:149
Briend, J., 1:261
Briggs, C. A., 1:11
  Balaam narrative, 2:206
  Brown-Driver-Briggs Hebrew and English Lexicon, 1:79
  unfaithfulness, 1:148
Briggs, R. S., 1:55
  Korah's rebellion, 1:402
  'over-spiritualising', 1:158
  uncleanness, 1:150
Brin, G.
  firstborn sons, 1:124, 1:441, 1:472
  inadvertent sin, 1:379
Briscoe, T. V., 1:228
Brodie, T. L., 1:68, 1:436, 1:438, 1:501, 2:240
Bronner, L., 2:272
Broshi, M., 1:101, 1:102
Brown, David, 1:268
Brown, E., 1:308
Brown, F., 1:11, 1:79, 1:148, 2:95
  see also Brown-Driver-Briggs Hebrew and English Lexicon
Brown, K., 2:4, 2:375
  midrash and history, 2:374
  Moses strikes the rock, 2:26
Brown, R., 1:297
Brown-Driver-Briggs Hebrew and English Lexicon, 1:278, 1:373, 1:389
  Aaron's 'please/pray', 1:305
  'Agag', 2:184
  'babbling', 2:364
  'Balak', 2:112
  'beaten' oil, 2:333
  being restrained, 2:343–344
  'belly', 2:229
  'bronze', 2:71

Brown-Driver-Briggs Hebrew and
  English Lexicon (cont.)
  'cling', 2:491
  'contend', 2:13
  'Cozbi', 2:244
  'cutting off', 1:288
  deceit, 2:245
  'destruction', 2:196
  donkey's speech, 2:141
  the elders, 1:264
  'foe', 2:382
  'free from guilt', 2:414
  free of guilt, 2:400
  'furrow', 2:138
  'impale', 2:220
  'impure', 2:382
  innocent women, 2:363
  Israel's seed, 2:181
  judgement/estimation, 1:143
  kings of Midian, 2:382
  'knowledge', 2:193
  land inheritance, 2:296, 2:298
  'liberty', 2:489
  mah, 2:178
  'majesty', 2:313
  manna, 2:62
  Moab and dread, 2:112
  mourning, 1:359
  'murder', 2:465
  'oil' and 'anoint', 1:470
  'parable', 2:152
  penitent weeping, 2:225
  'prison house', 2:359
  'reckoned', 2:156
  'redeem', 1:473
  release of serpents, 2:63
  'scepter', 2:53
  slaughter after battle, 2:381
  smiting, 1:348
  'sorrow', 2:382
  'speaking against', 2:62
  time periods, 1:208
  'to her womb', 2:232
  'trust', 2:29
  unfaithfulness, 1:148
  unripe corn, 2:338
  'Urim and Thummim', 2:314
  'vav of association', 2:265
  'watch', 2:201
'Woe!', 2:201
YHWH's leadership, 2:155
'Zimri', 2:243
Zippor/sparrow, 2:113
'Zur', 2:245
Brueggemann, D. A., 1:200, 1:376
Brueggemann, W.
  Egypt, 1:340
  theology of the land, 1:364
Brumberg-Kraus, J., 1:255
Brütsch, C., 1:40
Buber, M.
  Balaam's narrative, 2:110
  good and evil, 1:363
  the Nazarene, 1:159
Büchler, A., 1:490
Budd, Philip J., 1:61, 1:68, 1:116,
  1:211, 1:225, 1:400, 1:460, 2:326,
  2:401
  Aaron's family, 1:475
  census figures, 1:105, 1:107
  on chapter 36, 2:486
  chieftain names, 1:86
  circumcision, 1:377
  city of Jazer, 2:80
  clapping hands, 2:188
  cleansing after deaths, 1:499
  covenant community, 1:452, 2:264
  the departure, 1:235
  excommunication, 1:215
  firstborn animals, 1:124
  the journey, 1:228
  kingship, 2:166
  Korah's rebellion, 1:401
  land inheritance, 2:302
  Levitical houses, 1:125
  list of journeys, 2:432
  Midianites, 2:376, 2:395–396
  Miriam and Aaron, 2:4, 2:44
  offerings, 1:165, 2:350
  'pate', 2:95
  purification, 1:461, 1:495
  rebellion, 1:342
  red heifer, 1:485
  'rising up', 1:243
  'sanctify' and 'Kadesh', 2:309
  on a 'vow', 1:142
  way of Atharim, 2:56
  Way of the King, 2:38

Index of Modern Authors

Wilderness of Paran, 2:445
women, 2:362
YHWH in Camp, 2:476
YHWH's gift of land, 1:369
Zelophehad's daughters, 2:290
Budge, E. A. W., 2:65
Buell, S. D.
  Aaron and Miriam, 1:306
  Aaron's character, 1:290
Buis, P., 2:25
Bullinger, E. W.
  The Witness of the Stars, 1:24
Burnett, J. S., 2:117, 2:118, 2:123, 2:127, 2:190
Burnham, J. N.
  Baal Peor story, 2:212
  Phinehas, 2:231, 2:254
Burns, R. J., 1:13, 1:281
  deaths of leaders, 2:10
  Korah's rebellion, 1:302
  Miriam, 1:296, 1:303, 1:307, 2:4
  Moses and YHWH, 1:300
Burnside, J. P.
  city dimensions, 2:463
  exclusions, 1:387
  generational conflict, 2:10
  high-handed sin, 1:385
  Moses, 2:23, 2:24, 2:25
  murderers, 2:477
  rebellion against YHWH, 2:46
  Sabbath, 1:384, 1:386
  waters of contention, 2:33
Burrows, E., 1:24
  flowing water, 2:181
  the Zodiac, 2:166
Bush, G., 1:40, 1:49
Butzer, A. G., 2:101

Caine, I., 1:68
Calabro, D., 2:316
Callan, T., 1:221
Calmet, A., 1:29
Calvin, J.
  Aaron's staff, 1:454
  boundaries of Canaan, 2:419
  Moses' crisis, 1:267
  the Nazarene, 1:159
  Nazirites, 1:162
  Zelophehad's daughters, 2:292

Camp, C. V.
  boundary of the Camp, 1:250
  Korah's rebellion, 1:411
  Levites, 1:435
  Miriam and Aaron, 1:305, 1:309
  strangers, 1:89
Canney, M. A., 2:140
Carmichael, C. M., 1:69
Carr, D. M., 1:243
Cartledge, T. W., 2:359
Carvalho, C. L., 2:70
Cassuto, U., 1:70, 1:229–30, 2:123
Castello, G., 2:131
Cathcart, K. J., 2:194
Caulley, T. S., 2:194
Cavasola, A. G. P., 1:103
Cazelles, 1:128
Chavalas, M. W.
  Ashur, 2:201
  Balaam's narrative, 2:108
  Deir 'Alla inscription, 2:116
Chavel, S., 1:215, 1:385
  benediction, 1:166
  development of Sabbath, 1:383
  judicial matters, 2:285
  second Passover, 1:212
  Zelophehad's daughters, 2:287, 2:289
Chen, K., 2:171
Childs, B. S., 1:70
  Korah's pedigree, 1:443
  Moses' divine mission, 2:70
  murmuring language, 2:8
Chinitz, J., 1:181, 2:270
Chizkuni, 2:33, 2:64
Chou, A.
  language for God, 1:38
  the throne-chariot, 1:32, 1:33
Christensen, D. L., 2:75
Claassens, J., 2:284
Clark, I.
  Balaam narrative, 2:99, 2:104, 2:106, 2:126, 2:206
  YHWH's devotion, 2:205
Clark, M., 1:27, 1:270
Clark, R. E. D., 1:104
Clark, T. S.
  covenant relationship, 1:496
  ritual laws, 1:395

Clarke, E. G.
  cities of asylum, 2:470
  Succoth, 2:443
  wilderness journeys, 2:440
Claussen, G., 2:220
Clines, D. J. A.
  authorship of Numbers, 1:69
  on the Tabernacle, 1:9
Coats, G. W., 1:14, 1:48, 1:61, 1:65,
    1:81, 1:143, 1:192, 1:243, 1:402, 2:54
  Balaam narrative, 2:96, 2:101, 2:103,
    2:107, 2:118, 2:205
  character of Moses, 1:298
  divine command, 1:322
  high-handed sin, 1:383
  Israel's Camp, 1:41, 1:43
  on Levites, 1:88, 1:89
  list of journeys, 2:432
  Miriam and Aaron, 1:305
  Moses, 1:258, 1:260, 1:312
  rebellion, 1:341, 1:342, 1:345
  serpents in the desert, 2:64
  strayed woman, 1:153
  tribe placement, 1:93
Cocco, F.
  chieftains, 1:86
  consecration, 1:155
  guiding behaviour, 2:469
  judicial matters, 2:285
  land inheritance, 2:288
  marriage, 2:353
  Moses as mediator, 2:356
  Nazirite vow, 1:374
  strayed woman, 1:144, 1:149, 1:150,
    1:151, 1:153, 1:154, 1:158
  vows and oaths, 2:358
  women, 2:357, 2:365, 2:366, 2:367,
    2:370
  Zelophehad's daughters, 2:287, 2:289,
    2:291, 2:292
Cohen, J. M.
  Aaron's staff, 2:21
  Balaam narrative, 1:145, 2:124–125,
    2:129, 2:130
  daughters of Moab, 2:216
  death of Aaron, 2:42
  failure of Moses and Aaron, 2:10
  leadership, 1:10
  Moses and Cushite wife, 2:227–228

Moses' intercession, 1:346
Phinehas, 2:226
trust, 2:29
Cohen, N., 1:413
Cohn, R. L., 1:499
Cole, R. D., 1:61, 1:66, 1:462
  altar procession, 1:188
  ancient song, 1:210
  apostasy, 2:247
  Balaam's narrative, 2:107, 2:111
  blessedness, 2:170
  Camp's journeys, 2:74
  chieftain names, 1:86
  the Cloud, 1:227
  copper-smelting, 2:72
  to do/make, 1:371
  the Dwelling, 2:165
  Gad and Reuben, 2:409
  Israel's enemies, 2:199
  journey to Canaan, 2:450
  King of Edom, 2:35
  Levites, 1:198
  list of journeys, 2:432
  Midianites and midrash, 2:374
  significance of names, 1:327
  Sinai location, 1:228
  wilderness journeys, 2:441
Colenso, J. W., 1:100
Collins, J. J., 1:292, 2:220
Collins, M. F.
  Balaam narrative, 2:191
  Edom, 2:198
  messianism, 2:181
  rise of a star, 2:194
Condie, K.
  covenant relationship, 1:351
  rebellion, 1:322
Condren, J. C., 1:43, 1:65, 1:68
  atonement, 1:200
  the Cloud, 1:218
  Hobab, 1:230
  Israel's obedience, 1:217
  on Levites, 1:117
  trumpets, 1:223, 1:224
  YHWH's home, 1:192
Conrad, J., 1:263
Cook, S. L., 1:263
Cooper, A. M.
  assembly, 1:427

Korah's rebellion, 1:424
Cornelius, F., 1:70
Cornhill, C. H., 2:6
Cotton, R. D.
  Moses' crisis, 1:258
  Spirit of YHWH, 1:314
Cox, S.
  Balaam narrative, 2:96, 2:100, 2:135
Craigie, P. C., 2:271
  atrocities of war, 2:397
  cherubs and clouds, 1:221
Creach, J. F. D., 1:73
Croatto, J. S., 1:120
Cross, F. M., 1:299
  covenant violations, 2:220
  Cushite woman, 1:292, 1:293
  Phinehas episode, 2:223, 2:229, 2:232
  Wilderness of Paran, 2:445
Crowfoot, G. M., 1:486
Cruzer, H. J., 1:339
Cumming, J. E., 1:36
Currid, J. D., 1:61, 2:4, 2:70
  disputed territory, 2:74
  flagpoles/standards, 2:68–69, 2:71
  food provision, 1:253
  seraphs and serpents, 2:65, 2:66
  Sihon's campaign, 2:81
Curwin, D., 1:374
  good and evil, 1:361, 1:362
  verbal parallels, 1:432

Daiches, S.
  Balaam narrative, 2:107, 2:149, 2:151, 2:160
  divination, 2:171
Darnov, A. M., 2:100
Daube, D., 2:103
Davidson, A. B.
  Midianites, 2:212
  'them'/'their', 2:281
Davidson, R. M., 2:215
Davies, E. W., 1:61, 2:486
  Baal Peor, 2:220
  census figures, 1:100, 1:102, 1:105
  family name, 2:303
  Jubilee, 2:488
  land as *Sheol*, 1:339
  land boundaries, 2:438
  land inheritance, 2:288

Moses, 1:419, 2:6
Nephilim, 1:356
rebellion, 1:342
red heifer law, 1:460–461
the trumpets, 1:223
Davies, G. I., 2:72
  hosting YHWH, 2:480
  wilderness journeys, 2:432, 2:433, 2:441
Davies, J. A., 1:19
  Balaam narrative, 2:157
  consecrated status, 1:449
  Eli and priesthood, 2:238
  Korah's rebellion, 1:410, 1:430, 1:438
  Levites and priests, 1:467
  people's fear, 1:449
  Phinehas episode, 2:235
  staffs, 1:445
  theology of priesthood, 1:451
Davis, J. J., 1:102
Day, J.
  bronze and iron, 2:200
  sons of Sheth, 2:196
Day, P. L., 1:143, 2:136
Day, Q.
  disinheritance, 2:488
  Jubilee, 2:489
Dearman, J. A., 2:79
Delcor, M., 2:116
Delitzsch, F., 1:29, 1:70, 1:129
  Balaam narrative, 2:100, 2:116, 2:118
  food provision, 1:252
  idolatry, 2:215
  Levites, 1:201
  Levitical cities, 2:463
  Moses as foundational, 1:73
  Nazirites and hair, 1:164
  red heifer, 1:484
  spiritual dynamic of Camp, 1:173
  trust and obedience, 2:72
Démare-Lafont, S., 1:157
Demsky, A.
  women in genealogies, 2:272
  Zelophehad's daughters, 2:306
Dentan, R. C., 1:61, 1:68, 1:128, 2:53
Derby, J.
  land distribution, 2:273
  tribal boundaries, 2:488
De Regt, L. J., 1:127, 1:130

DeRouchie, J. S., 1:120, 1:121
  'put out the hand', 2:70
Derrett, J. D. M., 1:410
Destro, A.
  on purity, 1:47
  strayed woman, 1:151
De Vries, S. J., 1:412
Diamond, E.
  Nazirites, 1:160, 1:161, 1:164
  YHWH's glory, 1:174
Díez Macho, A., 2:194
Dijk, H. J. van, 1:459
Dijkstra, M.
  Balaam narrative, 2:148
  with Moab, 2:111
  Sukkoth, 2:115
Dillmann, A., 1:181, 1:207
  census figures, 1:100, 1:102
  land distribution, 2:273
  Levite animals, 1:128
  list of journeys, 2:432
  sacrifices for sin, 1:370
Dobin, J. C., 1:22, 1:23, 1:104
Donner, H., 2:104, 2:122
Dorival, Gilles, 1:262
Douglas, C. E., 1:21, 1:22, 1:23, 1:40, 1:104
Douglas, J. D., 1:291
Douglas, M., 1:42, 1:61, 1:68, 1:95, 1:402
  Balaam narrative, 2:104, 2:105, 2:125, 2:130, 2:157
  disgraced sons, 1:93
  land inheritance, 2:456
  Miriam, 1:303, 1:306, 1:309, 2:11
  ox and lion, 2:166, 2:168
  Phinehas episode, 2:229
  strayed woman, 1:55, 1:157–158
  tribe and family, 1:10, 2:494
  women's vows, 2:369
  Zelophehad's daughters, 2:283
Dozeman, T. B., 1:48, 1:70, 1:143
  on Aaron and Moses, 1:120–121
  Balaam's narrative, 2:103
  the Dwelling, 1:191
  exploring the land, 1:323
  Moses, 1:274, 1:300, 1:311
  promised land, 2:37
  'three days' way', 1:233
  wilderness journey, 1:229, 2:7, 2:77
  Zelophehad, 2:271
Driver, G. R., 2:95
  purification rites, 1:196
  on 'reproof', 1:141
Driver, G. W.
  avengers, 2:469
  high priest, 2:471
  innocent murderer, 2:475
Driver, S. R., 1:11, 1:229, 1:244
  Brown-Driver-Briggs Hebrew and English Lexicon, 1:79
  'end of days', 2:190
  Moses and Aaron, 2:32
  unfaithfulness, 1:148
Dumbrell, W. J.
  history and Midianites, 2:374
  Midianites, 2:383
Durham, J. I.
  benediction, 1:168
  YHWH's presence, 1:171
Dybdahl, J. L., 2:296
  land inheritance, 2:297, 2:298, 2:299–300, 2:304
  pastureland, 2:461

Easton, M. G., 2:226
Eberhart, C., 1:373, 1:375, 2:327, 2:331
Edwards, J. R., 2:3
Ehrlich, A., 1:210, 1:236, 2:53
Ehrlich, C. S., 2:117
Ehrlich, Z. H., 2:306
Eichler, R.
  the ark, 1:114, 1:132
  the Temple, 1:36
  women, 2:368
  YHWH and cherubim, 1:37
Eichrodt, W.
  jealous God, 2:236
  peace, 1:171
  YHWH's leadership, 2:155
Eidelberg, S., 1:156
Eisenstein, J. D., 1:23
Eissfeldt, O.
  Balak's people, 2:116
  water song, 2:77
Elior, R., 1:36
Elitzur, Y.
  census figures, 2:423

Levitical cities, 2:463
wilderness route, 2:432
Zelophehad's daughters, 2:292
Ellicott, Charles, 1:268
Elliger, K. *see Biblia Hebraica Stuttgartensia*
Ellingworth, P., 1:381
Ellul, J., 1:22
Embry, B.
  Balaam narrative, 2:134–135
  Zelophehad's daughters, 2:289, 2:292, 2:490
Emmrich, M.
  generational conflict, 2:10
  rebellion against YHWH, 2:46
  second generation, 2:14
Enns, P.
  'three days' way', 1:233
Erlandsson, S., 2:215
Erlanger, G., 1:22
Etheridge, J. W., 1:29
Etshalom, Y., 2:421
  Gad and Reuben, 2:411
  integrity of tribes, 2:487
  Joshua, 2:318
  sons of Reuben and Gad, 2:405
Ewald, H., 1:322

Fabry, H.-J., 2:69
Fairholm, D. D., 2:29
Farber, Z., 2:77
Farmer, W. R., 2:226
Faulkner, R. O, 2:65
Fauna and Flora of the Bible (United Bible Societies), 1:486
Fausset, A. R., 1:268
Feder, Y.
  atonement, 2:239
  languages and light, 1:170
Fee, G. D., 2:233
Feilchenfeldt, W., 1:70
Feinberg, C. L.
  cities of reception, 2:465
  high priest, 2:471, 2:472
  murder, 2:466
  YHWH as refuge, 2:484
Feinstein, E. L., 1:141
Felder, C. H., 1:293
Feldman, E., 1:146

Feldman, L. H., 1:292, 2:221
Ferguson, S. B., 1:268
Findlay, J., 1:401
Finkelstein, I., 1:102
Fisch, H.
  food provision, 1:271
  spirit *versus* flesh, 1:248
Fischer, E., 2:422
Fischer, I., 1:290
Fishbane, M. A., 1:53, 1:55, 1:145, 1:385, 2:486
  benediction, 1:172
  Jubilee, 2:489
  land inheritance, 2:289
  strayed woman, 1:151, 1:157
  uncleanness, 1:150
  Zelophehad's daughters, 2:287, 2:491
Fisher, L. R., 2:326
Fisk, B. N., 2:50
Fleurant, J.
  Midianites, 2:222
  military campaigns, 2:214
  Phinehas, 2:221
Fokkelman, J. P., 1:404
Forshey, R. O., 2:297
Fouts, D. M., 1:101, 1:105
Fowler, S. W., 1:222
Fox, E., 1:62–63, 1:64, 1:69
  Korah's rebellion, 1:409
  smashed arrows, 2:185
  trumpets, 1:224
Frankel, D., 1:218, 1:326
Franken, H. J., 2:115
Fredricks, C. J., 1:174
Freedman, D. N., 1:53, 1:144, 1:243, 1:299
  benediction, 1:167
  covenant of peace, 2:212
  the departure, 1:235
  'Prolegomenon', 2:153
  Song of the Well, 2:76
Freedman, H., 2:133
Frendo, A. J., 1:102
Fretheim, T. E.
  Egyptian cobra, 2:65
  good and evil, 1:363
  trust in YHWH, 2:69
Frevel, C., 1:13, 1:54, 1:68, 1:123, 2:54
  Aaron's family, 1:471

Frevel, C. (*cont.*)
  Balaam story locations, 2:78
  camps, 1:49, 2:479
  corpses, 1:141, 1:492
  ghosts and death, 1:489
  Israelites and Moabites, 2:55
  leadership, 1:10, 2:436
  on the Levites, 1:115
  logic of the cult, 1:44
  the military, 2:55, 2:311
  murmuring, 2:60, 2:67
  on Nahshon, 1:86
  names, 1:327
  on Numbers 21, 2:53
  Phinehas, 2:228
  promised land, 2:34
  purification and purity, 1:46, 1:141, 1:145, 1:213, 1:215, 1:492, 2:337
  role of priesthood, 2:233
  staff of Aaron, 1:448
  taking of captives, 2:57
  on vows, 1:143
  wilderness journeys, 2:37, 2:72, 2:73, 2:439, 2:449
  YHWH preserves people, 2:86
  Zelophehad's daughters, 2:283
Frick, F. S.
  census figures, 1:102
  red cow ritual, 1:495
Friedman, R. E., 1:246
  Balaam narrative, 2:99, 2:132
  death of Aaron, 2:224
  defeat of Egypt, 2:186
  impurity, 1:152
  Miriam, 1:297
  Moses and Joshua, 1:282, 2:316
  Phinehas episode, 2:229
  priestly services, 1:202
  strayed woman, 1:149, 1:157
  YHWH and Moses, 2:309–310
Frisch, A.
  Balaam narrative, 1:145, 1:146, 2:103, 2:105, 2:118, 2:132
  Balaam's sword, 2:38
Fritz, V., 1:243, 2:432
  wilderness journey, 2:443
Frymer-Kensky, T., 1:55
  corpse pollution, 1:491
  divine justice, 2:240

kareth penalty, 1:382
Miriam's leprosy, 1:308
penalties, 1:133
Phineas episode, 2:230
strayed woman, 1:150, 1:157
transgressions, 2:436–437
unclean, 1:155
waters of curses, 1:156

Gaffin, R. B., 1:268
Galbraith, D., 1:321, 1:338, 1:342
Galil, G., 1:87, 1:98, 1:117, 1:121
Gall, A. F. von, 2:153
Gane, R. E., 1:469, 2:82
  Balaam narrative, 2:135–136, 2:172, 2:175
  corpse contamination, 1:498
  disease, 1:49
  Eleazar, 2:387
  high priest, 2:471
  Korah's rebellion, 1:409, 1:427
  laws, 1:371
  Levites, 1:204, 1:434, 1:463
  Moses and Aaron, 2:41
  Moses' intercession, 1:349
  Nazirites, 1:165
  offerings, 1:381
  people and manna, 2:62
  Phinehas, 2:228, 2:232
  priestly domain, 1:468
  purification, 1:164
  red heifer, 1:484
  sacrifices for sin, 1:370
  sex and idolatry, 2:216
  tribal inheritance, 2:489
  wilderness journeys, 1:373, 1:380, 2:445
  wild ox, 2:167
  women and vows, 2:364
  YHWH's judgements, 1:382, 1:383
  Zelophehad's daughters, 2:285, 2:293
Ganzel, T.
  corpse pollution, 1:501
  purification, 1:490
Gaon, Sa'adia, 2:421
García López, F., 2:111
Garsiel, M., 2:229
Garton, R. E., 2:4
Gaster, M., 1:264

Gaster, T. H., 2:76
Gayford, 2:332
Geikie, C., 2:113
Geller, S. A., 1:375
George, M. K., 1:98
  Camp structure, 1:12, 2:379
  equal access for tribes, 1:202
  hierarchy of congregation, 1:452
  people's complaints, 1:250
  YHWH in the dwelling, 2:455
Gerleman, G., 2:298
Gertel, E. B., 1:63, 1:269, 1:287
Gertz, J. C., 1:69
Gese, H., 2:240
Gesenius Hebrew Grammar, 1:414, 1:449
  'be hostile', 2:212
  'hasten', 2:400
  jussives, 1:142
  prepositional placing of the camp, 1:141
  preposition 'to', 1:208
  'their father', 2:486
  'them'/'their', 2:281
  'three days' way', 1:233
Gevaryahu, G. J., 2:289, 2:489
Gibson, R., 2:256
Gilbert, R. A., 1:24
Gilders, W. K.
  Eleazar's status, 1:482
  red heifer ritual, 1:483, 1:484, 1:488
Gill, John, 1:268
Ginsberg, H. L., 2:491
Ginsburg, C. D., 1:234, 2:95
Ginzberg, L., 1:28
  chieftain names, 1:86
  disease and judgement, 1:52
  failure of Moses and Aaron, 2:10
  Israel's Camp, 1:36
Gispen, W. H., 1:172
  census figures, 1:102
  leadership, 2:312
Godbey, A. H., 2:166
Goldberg, A., 2:110
Goldstein, A., 1:100, 1:103, 1:106
Goldstein, B. R.
  assembly, 1:427
  Korah's rebellion, 1:424
Goldwasser, O., 1:71
Gophna, R., 1:102

Gordley, M. E., 2:195
Gordon, C. H., 1:70
  Balaam narrative, 2:153
  opening prayer, 2:178
Gordon, R. P.
  Korah's rebellion, 1:409, 1:416, 1:427
Görg, M., 2:116
Gorman, F. H.
  annual liturgy, 2:351
  burnt offerings, 2:328, 2:329, 2:330
  Camp divisions, 1:421
  high priest, 2:471
  kareth penalty, 1:382, 1:491
  liturgical order, 2:327
  purity matters, 1:488, 1:492
  red heifer, 1:484–485
  sacred rituals, 1:483
Gottwald, N. K.
  census figures, 1:104
  clan and kinship, 2:295
  intertribal conflict, 2:487
  kings of Canaan, 1:348
Graetz, N., 1:306
Grafius, B. R., 2:220
Granot, T.
  Balaam narrative, 2:190
  divination and enchantment, 2:159
  Edom and Moab, 2:197
  Joshua, 1:353
  journey around Edom, 2:73
  Moses and Canaan, 2:35
  Moses' role, 1:267
Gray, G. B., 1:2, 1:30, 1:46, 1:61, 1:68, 1:142, 1:208, 1:210, 1:243, 1:244, 1:297, 1:320, 1:402, 1:460, 2:325, 2:326, 2:486
  the ark, 1:132
  Balaam narrative, 2:99, 2:101, 2:122, 2:147, 2:153
  Caleb, 1:336
  census, 1:100, 2:270
  chieftains, 2:390
  cultic laws, 1:369
  Cushite woman, 1:292, 1:294
  division of the plunder, 2:394
  'end of days', 2:190
  flowing water, 2:180, 2:181
  free of guilt, 2:400
  Israel's departure, 1:211

Gray, G. B. (*cont.*)
  judicial execution, 1:215
  kings, 2:186
  Korah's rebellion, 1:416
  land boundaries, 2:438
  midrash and history, 2:374
  Mosaic authorship, 1:69
  Moses and water, 2:30
  Moses' sin, 2:6
  Nazirites, 1:160, 1:161
  on offerings, 1:181
  pasturelands, 2:462
  Pethor, 2:116
  salt, 1:475
  scouts' report, 1:338
  sons of Israel, 2:265
  staffs, 1:445, 1:448
  taboos and rituals, 1:461
  tithing, 2:389
  'to annul', 2:365
  tribal arrangement, 1:95
  wilderness journeys, 2:432
Green, W. H., 1:69, 1:70, 1:320, 2:100
Green, Y., 1:390, 1:442
Greenberg, M.
  Camp of Israel, 1:32
  God's own image, 2:474
  high priest, 2:472, 2:478
  impurities, 1:488
  murder and manslaughter, 2:465
  murderers, 2:477
  pasturelands, 2:462
  status of offerings, 1:472
Greenberg, M. A., 1:214, 1:481
Greener, A., 2:72
Greenstein, E. L.
  Book of YHWH's Battles, 2:74
  burnt offerings, 2:329
  water song, 2:77
Greenstone, J. H., 1:114, 1:128
Gregor, Z., 2:82
Greifenhagen, F. V.
  Egypt, 1:340
  people and Egypt, 1:270
Gressmann, H., 1:68, 1:244, 2:121
Grohman, E. D., 2:214
Groningen, G. van
  Balaam narrative, 2:120, 2:191, 2:196
  YHWH's dominion, 2:195, 2:210

Gros Louis, K. R. R., 1:68
Gross, W.
  Balaam narrative, 2:99
  Balak, 2:117
Grossfeld, B., 2:194
Grossman, J., 1:9, 1:14, 1:27, 1:66, 1:185
  accidental murderers, 2:477
  Baal Peor and golden calf, 2:248
  call of Abraham, 1:231
  Camp of Israel, 1:48
  camp structure, 1:31, 1:94
  innocent murder, 2:475
  the journey, 1:8, 1:236, 1:239
  judges of Israel, 2:220
  Korah's rebellion, 1:416
  land distribution, 2:479
  Nazirites, 1:161, 1:164
  rebellion, 1:435
  spies, 1:324
  tainted land, 2:477
  Zimri and Midianites, 2:285
Gruber, M. I., 1:171
Grundke, C. L. K.
  Balaam narrative, 2:100, 2:104
  rise of a star, 2:194
  YHWH's reign, 2:209
Grushcow, L., 1:47, 1:151
Gudme, A. K. de Hemmer
  Nazirites, 1:159, 1:162
Guillaume, A., 2:158
Guillaume, P., 1:27
  Aaron's death, 2:49
  crocodile/serpent, 2:70
Gunneweg, A. H. J., 1:402
  ecstatic behaviour, 1:275
  the elders, 1:274
  food provision, 1:262, 1:271
  Moses, 1:296, 1:300, 1:314
  prophecy, 1:276
Guyot, G. H.
  Balaam narrative, 2:116, 2:118, 2:123
  'end of days', 2:190
  rise of a star, 2:194
  'Seth', 2:197

Habel, N. C.
  Baal of Peor, 2:218
  dust and ashes, 1:493

land inheritance, 2:273, 2:288, 2:297, 2:298, 2:321
Levites, 1:476
theology of the land, 1:364
Haberman, B. D.
jealousy, 1:151
strayed woman, 1:153
Hackett, J. A., 2:115
HaCohen, A., 1:185, 2:463
Halperin, D. J., 1:29, 1:38
Halpern, B, 2:200
Hannah, D. D., 2:194
Hanson, J., 1:292
Hanson, P. D., 2:81
Haran, M., 1:4, 1:122, 1:271
burning incense, 1:413
the censers, 1:434
Korah's rebellion, 1:430
YHWH's light, 1:170
Harrelson, W., 1:12, 1:89
Harrington, H. K., 1:490
Harris, R. L.
atonement, 2:239
unfaithfulness, 1:148
Harris, R. T., 1:495
Harrison, R. K., 1:68, 1:69, 1:370, 1:380
Balaam narrative, 2:100, 2:140
census figures, 1:100–101, 1:106
character of Moses, 1:297
hyssop, 1:486
Israel's seed, 2:181
Levites, 1:201
redemption, 1:128
scribes, 1:265
'Urim and Thummim', 2:314
on use of scribes, 1:71
Harvey, W. Z., 1:392
Hattin, M.
Balaam narrative, 2:127
Gad and Reuben's sons, 2:406
mantic practices, 2:205
second generation, 1:499
tribe of Manasseh, 2:271
Zelophehad, 2:278
Hauge, M. R., 1:219
Hausoul, R. R.
casting lots, 2:273
God's gift, 1:373
land tenure, 2:307

plagues, 1:199
scouts, 1:337
theology of the land, 2:279
YHWH's gift of land, 1:369
Havrelock, R., 1:335
Hawk, L. D.
Balaam narrative, 1:145, 1:146, 2:110, 2:150
Balak, 2:115
Hayes, J. H.
Balaam narrative, 2:121
Moses and YHWH, 1:300
Hayman, H., 2:421
Jepthah, 2:423
Machir and Egypt, 2:422
Hays, J. D.
Cushite woman, 1:291, 1:293, 1:314
on Miriam, 1:309
Phinehas, 2:226
Hayward, R.
Phinehas, 2:226
red heifer, 1:480, 1:481
Healy, M., 1:13
The Hebrew and Aramaic Lexicon of the Old Testament (HALOT), 1:373, 1:389
Caleb's action, 1:336
'Cozbi', 2:244
donkey's speech, 2:141
family and kinship, 2:296
'impale', 2:220
inheritance, 2:296
land inheritance, 2:298
'liberty', 2:489
'looming disaster', 2:164
scribes/officials, 1:265
'to cast down', 1:143
'to her womb', 2:232
Heckl, R., 2:122
Balaam narrative, 2:127
Heifetz, R., 1:257
Heinisch, P.
staffs, 1:445
women, 2:366
Heinzerling, R., 1:103, 1:104
Heiser, M. S., 1:221
Held, S.
Balaam's narrative, 2:104
blossoms and diadem, 1:389

Held, S. (*cont.*)
  Korah's rebellion, 1:410
  Moses' disloyalty, 2:47
Helfgot, N.
  Baal Peor and golden calf, 2:248
  Balaam narrative, 2:119
  chieftains, 2:390
  division of plunder, 2:392, 2:394
  Gad and Reuben, 2:409
  generational difference, 2:18
  lack of water, 2:15
  military battles, 2:387–388
  Moses' leadership, 2:32
  Moses' sin, 2:6
  offerings, 2:394
  scouts and Manassites, 2:420
  second generation, 2:8, 2:85
  sons of Reuben and Gad, 2:404, 2:405
  water miracle, 2:31
Helfmeyer, F. J., 1:14
Hendel, R. S., 2:47–48
Hengel, M., 1:264
Hengstenberg, E. W.
  Balaam narrative, 2:100, 2:116
  Pethor, 2:116
Henrey, K. H., 2:299
Hepner, G.
  Balaam narrative, 1:141, 2:104, 2:134
  serpent in Eden, 2:70
Hertz, J. H., 1:128
  Balaam narrative, 2:156–157
  elder-scribes, 1:276
Hicks, F. C. N., 2:332
Hicks, L., 2:418
Hieke, T., 1:13
  purification offering, 1:493
  red heifer ritual, 1:487
Hiers, R. H.
  land inheritance, 2:302
  Zelophehad's daughters, 2:292, 2:294
Hildebrandt, W.
  Balaam narrative, 2:174
  divine judgement in wind, 1:285
Hill, C., 1:103
Hilliers, D. R.
  the Dwelling, 1:88
Hirsch, S. R., 1:27, 1:79, 1:390
  Aaron's death, 2:43
  almonds, 1:446

'Arad', 2:56
Balaam narrative, 1:143, 2:125, 2:126
benediction, 1:168
blossoms and diadem, 1:389
burnt offerings, 2:330, 2:334, 2:336
Caleb, 1:353
character of Moses, 1:419
cities of reception, 2:465
corpses and personality, 1:141
Day of Atonement, 2:342, 2:343
death and soul, 1:489
divine command, 1:322
divine penalty, 1:468
Edom episode, 2:63
execution of criminals, 2:221
feast of Sukkot, 2:344
flowing water, 2:181
good and evil, 1:363
Israel's mission, 2:345
land boundaries, 2:453
land distribution, 2:274
looking forward, 2:278
meat, 1:270
Midianites, 2:243, 2:378
Moses and water, 2:19
Moses' word, 2:16
names, 1:327
offering procedures, 1:187
the people and the land, 1:329
priestly blessings, 1:53
purification offering, 2:337
purity laws, 1:52
rebellion, 1:345
ritual activity, 1:212
Sanctuary division, 1:186
scouts' report, 1:338
Sea of Sulph, 2:75
shofar, 2:341
snake bites, 2:64
third day of Creation, 1:490
tribes, 1:445, 2:459, 2:487
tribute offerings, 2:333
trumpets, 1:223, 1:224
Way of the King, 2:39
wilderness journeys, 2:7, 2:441
wine, 1:376
women, 2:370
YHWH in Camp, 1:202
'your sheep', 2:414

Zelophehad's daughters, 2:292, 2:294, 2:368
Hobson, G. T., 1:382
Hoegger, M., 1:105
Höflmayer, F., 1:71
Hoftijzer, J., 2:115
Hölscher, G., 2:4
Holzinger, H., 1:68, 1:210, 1:460, 2:212
  census figures, 1:102–103
  cultic laws, 1:369
  Miriam's death, 2:4
  Moses and the water, 2:25
  staffs, 1:445
  taboos and rituals, 1:461
  women, 2:366
Hooke, S. H., 1:124, 2:164
Horbury, W., 1:491
Horn, B.
  inadvertent sin, 1:379
  Moses' intercession, 1:346, 1:350
  spies, 1:388
  YHWH forgives, 1:358
Horst, F., 2:297
Hort, G., 1:426
Hulse, E. V., 1:304
Hulst, A. R., 2:158
Humann, J.
  Camp orientation, 1:483
  cleansing of lepers, 1:487
  corpse pollution, 1:482, 1:489, 1:491, 1:492, 1:495
  dust and ashes, 1:481, 1:493
  guarding the Sanctuary, 1:496
  impurity expulsion, 1:488
  purification, 1:499
  red heifer, 1:482, 1:484, 1:500
  rituals, 1:460, 1:461
  sacrificial offerings, 1:486
  third day of Creation, 1:489–490
Hummelauer, F. de, 2:177
Humphreys, C. J., 1:104
Hundley, M. B., 2:223
Hunt, M. C.
  land inheritance, 2:301
  marriage, 2:491
  Zelophehad's daughters, 2:283, 2:286, 2:287, 2:292
Hurowitz, V. A., 1:174
  Balaam narrative, 2:122

Egyptian serpents, 2:69
Hutchens, K. D., 2:438
Hutton, R. R.
  Moses' character, 1:311
  power struggles, 1:402
Hymes, D., 1:244, 1:264, 1:275, 1:291, 1:299
  character of Moses, 1:297
  Moses and Miriam, 1:312
  Moses' burden, 1:262
  Moses' crisis, 1:258, 1:267
  people and Egypt, 1:270
  the Spirit of YHWH, 1:269, 2:312

Ibn Ezra, A., 1:380, 1:400
  Almon-Diblathaim, 2:449
  Balaam narrative, 1:143, 1:144, 2:128, 2:167, 2:168, 2:174, 2:195
  blue tassels, 1:390
  brothels, 2:224
  burnt offerings, 2:334
  chariot-throne, 1:38
  corpse pollution, 1:486
  covenant of peace, 2:237
  Cushite woman, 1:293
  Da'at Zekenim, 1:235
  Dathan and Abiram, 2:269
  Eagle emblem, 1:28
  execution of criminals, 2:221
  the exodus, 2:200
  the firstborn, 1:408
  idolatry, 2:220
  Jubilee, 2:489
  Korah's rebellion, 1:409, 1:442, 1:443
  land inheritance, 2:490
  Levites, 1:414
  Midianites, 2:113
  Miriam's leprosy, 1:309
  Moses' movement, 2:16
  Mount Nebo, 2:418
  Phinehas episode, 2:232
  seed of Israel, 2:158
  Sefer Yesod Mora, 1:23
  sons of Sheth, 2:196
  spirit of Moses, 1:268
  tassels, 1:392
  tribal leaders, 2:356
  tribal order, 2:266
  water wells, 2:76–77

Ibn Ezra, A. (*cont.*)
  way of explorers, 2:56
  women, 2:366, 2:367, 2:493
  YHWH's plan, 1:351
Ilan, T., 2:285
Imes, C. J.
  blossoms and diadem, 1:389
  cloth prohibitions, 1:393
  priesthood and the Dwelling, 1:411
  YHWH's name, 1:173
Ingalls, A. D., 1:46, 1:56, 1:61, 1:62, 1:68,
    1:142, 1:235, 2:383
Instone-Brewer, D., 2:195
Interpreter's Dictionary of the Bible (ed.
  Butterick), 1:331, 1:376
Isaacs, E., 2:153
Isbell, C. D.
  Balaam narrative, 2:104, 2:120, 2:141,
    2:189
  Balak, 2:112
Israel, A., 1:36

Jacob, B., 2:463
Jacob, E.
  Shaddai, 2:177
  YHWH's leadership, 2:155
Jacobus, Haran R., 1:23
  Chaldean astrology, 1:24
  high priest's breastplate, 1:22
  rise of a star, 2:194
Jamieson, Robert, 1:40, 1:268
Jastrow, M., 1:2
Jensen, I. L., 1:216
Jenson, P. P.
  hierarchy of congregation, 1:452
  high priest's breastplate, 1:21
  incensers, 1:439
  Levites, 1:200
Jeon, J., 1:321
  power struggles, 1:402
  strayed woman, 1:149
Jeremias, J., 1:275
Jeyaraj, B.
  land distribution, 2:274, 2:301, 2:458
  Zelophehad's daughters, 2:289
Jobling, D., 1:257
  arrangement of Camp, 1:244
  Cushite woman, 1:296
  Eldad and Medad, 1:296

food, 1:248, 1:252
Gad and Reuben, 2:406, 2:415, 2:419,
  2:420–421
Hazeroth, 1:290
manna, 1:273
Miriam, 1:305, 1:308, 1:310
Moses, 1:277–278, 1:289, 1:300, 1:311
people's rebellion, 1:249, 1:272
Reuben and Gad's sons, 2:405
topographical codes, 1:247, 1:281
Transjordan land, 2:409
Johnsgard, P. A., 1:286
Johnson, P. J., 1:249
Joines, K. R., 2:65, 2:69
Joosten, J., 2:486
  Camp experience, 2:494
  sojourners, 2:467
Jørstad, M., 1:426

Kahn, A. D., 2:403
Kahn, P., 1:390
  Balaam narrative, 2:134
  impatience for Canaan, 2:15
  Moses' disloyalty, 2:47
Kahn, Y., 1:9, 1:63
  foreigners outside Camp, 1:250
  Miriam and Moses, 1:315
  second generation, 2:264
  wilderness journeys, 2:444, 2:482
Kaiser Jr, W. C.
  Balaam narrative, 2:102, 2:130
  divination, 2:171
  Edom and Moab, 2:197
  Pethor, 2:117
  Phinehas, 2:221
Kalisch, M. M., 2:103
Kallai, Z., 2:438
Kamin, S., 1:296
Kapelrud, A. S., 2:6
Kaplan, M., 2:168
Kaufman, S., 1:307
Kaufmann, Y., 2:101
  Balaam narrative, 2:140–141
  on Kenizzites, 1:326
Kautzsch, E., 1:290, 1:305
Kawashima, R. S., 2:473, 2:477, 2:486
Keddie, G. J., 2:136
Kee, H. C.
  death of Aaron, 2:3

rise of a star, 2:194
Keel, O.
  Egyptian cobra, 2:66
  Mount Hor, 2:41
Keil, C. F., 1:29, 1:70, 1:129
  'Agag', 2:185
  Balaam narrative, 2:100, 2:116, 2:118
  to be cut off, 1:215
  Camp of Israel, 2:158
  firstborn sons, 1:100
  food provision, 1:252
  idolatry, 2:215
  'impale them', 2:220
  Levites, 1:201
  Levitical cities, 2:463
  Nazirites and hair, 1:164
  red heifer, 1:484
  spiritual dynamic of Camp, 1:173
  Tent of Meeting, 1:416
  trust and obedience, 2:72
Kellerman, D., 1:13, 1:52, 1:116, 1:210
Kelly, P. H., 1:8
  the Cloud, 1:220
  on Hobab, 1:230
Kennett, R. H., 2:297, 2:300
Khan, Y., 2:270
Kidner, D., 1:375
Kim, Y., 2:212, 2:231, 2:239
King, P. J.
  avengers, 2:469
  clan and kinship, 2:295
  land tenure, 2:300, 2:301, 2:302, 2:304
Kislev, I., 1:320, 1:344, 2:212, 2:486
  Balaam narrative, 2:123
  clans, 2:263
  execution, 2:467
  high priest, 2:471
  inheritance, 2:274
  Korah's sons, 2:269
  land distribution, 2:273
  tribal boundaries, 2:488
  Zelophehad's daughters, 2:283, 2:287, 2:491
Kitchen, K. A.
  on use of scribes, 1:71
  wilderness route, 2:432
Kitz, A. M.
  Balaam narrative, 2:121, 2:180
  Miriam's leprosy, 1:303

oath ritual, 1:154
  prophecy and divination, 2:118
  strayed woman, 1:154
Kiuchi, N., 1:483, 1:487
Klassen, W., 2:226
Klein, N., 1:103
Klein, S.
  Camp structure, 1:187
  second generation, 2:16
  sin of Moses and Aaron, 2:40
Kleinig, J. W.
  burnt offerings, 1:166, 2:331
  cleansing of lepers, 1:486
Kleinig, V.
  Aaronic blessing, 1:175
  YHWH's light, 1:170
Kline, M. G.
  the Cloud, 1:220
  manifestation of YHWH, 1:30
Knauf, E. A., 2:153, 2:177
Knierim, R. P., 1:14, 1:48, 1:61, 1:65, 1:70, 1:81, 1:143, 1:192, 2:54
  Balaam's narrative, 2:107
  camp formation, 1:94
  divine command, 1:322
  high-handed sin, 1:383
  Israel's Camp, 1:41, 1:43
  Levites, 1:88, 1:89
  rebellion, 1:341, 1:342
  strayed woman, 1:153
  tribe placement, 1:93
  wilderness journeys, 2:435
Knohl, I., 1:380, 1:402
  false oaths, 1:148
  Nazirites, 1:165
  priests and Levites, 1:468
Knoppers, G. N., 2:450
Koch-Westenholz, U., 1:25
Koenig, J., 2:26
Kohata, F., 2:3
Kohler, K., 1:393
Konkel, A. H., 1:216
Kooten, G. H. van, 2:101
Korpel, M. C. A., 1:169
Kosmala, H., 2:153
Kosman, A., 2:82
Krahmalkov, C. R.
  Atharim, 2:56
  Egypt, 2:433

Kraus, H.-J., 2:326
Kselman, J. S., 1:299
Küchler, M., 2:41
Kuenen, A., 1:402
Kugler, R. A., 2:235, 2:257
Kurtz, J. H.
  burnt offerings, 2:332
  corpse pollution, 1:493
  drink offerings, 1:374
  feasts, 2:335
  Nazarites, 1:161
  on offerings, 1:164
  sacrificial gifts, 1:373

Labuschagne, C. J.
  Balaam narrative, 2:157
  defiant sin, 1:381
Lambdin, T. O., 1:303
Landy, F., 1:54, 1:158, 1:166
Lapsley, J. E., 2:127
Largement, R., 2:107
Launderville, D., 1:33
Lawlor, J. I., 1:9, 1:229
Lawrence, P., 1:70
Lawrence, T. E., 2:64
Layton, S. C.
  Balaam narrative, 2:116
  Pethor, 2:116
Leach, E., 2:333
Leder, A. C., 1:62, 1:63, 1:64
  Camp and the land, 2:478
  the journey, 1:309
  YHWH's judgement, 1:303
Lederman, R., 2:64, 2:65
Lee, B. P. Y., 1:61, 1:62
  land inheritance, 2:288, 2:289
  Zelophehad's daughters, 2:293
Lee, W. W., 1:14, 1:210, 2:54
  Aaron's death, 2:49
  assembly before the rock, 2:3
  Balaam narrative, 2:120
  the Cloud, 1:216
  the covenant, 2:30
  lack of water, 2:15
  literary structure, 1:321
  Moses and water, 2:25, 2:28
  Tent of Meeting, 1:91
  water miracle, 2:31
  wilderness, 2:17

LeFebvre, M.
  Aaron's death, 2:448
  generational conflict, 2:9
  Unleavened Bread, 2:338
Lehrman, S. M., 1:28, 1:38
Leibowitz, N., 1:14, 2:88
  attack of serpents, 2:63
  Balaam narrative, 2:128, 2:135, 2:150, 2:257
  covenantal blessing, 2:186
  Edom, 2:39, 2:63
  Gad and Reuben's sons, 2:412–413
  Midianites, 2:382
  Moses' disloyalty, 2:47
  Nazirites, 1:164
  priestly blessings, 1:53
  Reuben and Gad's children, 2:403
  Transjordan lands, 2:406
Leibtag, M.
  good and evil, 1:363
  groups of sacrifices, 2:345
  the journey, 1:192
Leiman, S. Z., 1:234
Lemaire, 2:305
Leonard Jr. A., 2:72
Lerner, E. R., 2:294
Lesko, L. H., 2:65
Leson, M. S.
  Ashur, Kittim and Eber, 2:203
  Balaam narrative, 2:117, 2:137, 2:171
  Midianites, 2:113
  with Moab, 2:111
  wild ox image, 2:165
Leveen, A., 1:475
  Aaron and sons, 1:464
  Baal Peor incident, 2:215
  Camp boundaries, 1:479
  Eleazar at Aaron's death, 2:43
  forms of Israel, 2:11
  guarding the Sanctuary, 1:466
  hardship in wilderness, 1:253
  Levites, 1:463
  vision of future, 2:496
Levias, C., 1:103
Levin, Y.
  Kadesh, 2:454
  land boundaries, 2:438
  Riblah, 2:455

Wilderness of Paran, 2:446
Lévinas, E.
  cities of asylum, 2:470
  high priest, 2:471
Levine, B. A., 1:58, 1:68, 1:115, 1:234, 1:386, 2:212, 2:401
  Arnon River, 2:73
  awe and respect, 2:313
  Balaam narrative, 2:99, 2:103, 2:147, 2:174, 2:272
  borders, 2:455
  bread of the land, 1:378
  burnt offerings, 2:336
  Canaanite victory, 2:56
  captured places, 2:418
  the censers, 1:434
  census, 1:105, 2:278
  cities of reception, 2:465
  clans and kinship, 1:84, 2:266, 2:268, 2:296
  Cushite woman, 1:294
  daughters of Moab, 2:216–17
  death of the valiant, 2:158
  divinations and enchantments, 2:167
  dust and ashes, 1:493
  Egypt, 1:340
  Egyptian serpents, 2:69
  Eldad and Medad, 1:278
  the elders, 1:275, 1:277
  enclosed impurity, 1:492
  evildoers, 2:476
  exploring the land, 1:323
  family, 2:303, 2:307
  food provision, 1:272
  gathered rabble, 1:251
  Hebrew/Eber, 2:202
  'impale', 2:220
  Israel as assembly, 2:114
  Jubilee, 2:489
  land as *Sheol*, 1:339
  land distribution, 2:302, 2:417, 2:458, 2:460, 2:491
  leadership, 2:312
  Levites, 1:123
  livestock, 2:403
  Moses' authority, 1:410
  Moses' sin, 2:310
  Nazirites, 1:165
  offerings, 1:375
  passover, 2:338
  pastureland, 2:462
  Phinehas episode, 2:232
  power struggles, 1:402
  rebellion, 1:357
  red heifer, 1:483
  roots and water, 2:180
  on *ṣābā*, 1:26
  sacrifices, 1:380
  the Sanctuary, 1:468
  scribes, 1:265
  sons of Israel, 2:265
  tabular presentation, 1:188
  Tent of Meeting, 2:224
  'to flee', 2:465
  votive offering, 1:141
  vows and oaths of women, 2:364
  wilderness journeys, 2:440
  women, 2:357, 2:366–367
  YHWH's ascent, 1:360
  YHWH's name, 1:173
  YHWH's people, 2:255
  Zelophehad's daughters, 2:271, 2:289, 2:290, 2:294
Levison, J. R., 1:275, 1:277
Lévi-Strauss, Claude, 1:248
Levy, S.
  Balaam narrative, 2:130, 2:131, 2:137
Lewis, J. P., 2:193
  rise of a star, 2:194
Licht, J., 1:210
  Balaam narrative, 2:99, 2:105
  red heifer, 1:482
Lichtenstein, M., 1:63
  division in Numbers, 1:499
  food provision, 1:250
  Moses' crisis, 1:257, 1:282
  Moses' disloyalty, 2:47
  prophecy, 1:281
Liddell, H. G., 1:262
Liebreich, L., 1:166, 1:167
Lienhard, J. T., 2:194
Lim, J. T. K.
  Aaron and rebellion, 2:42
  Moses and Aaron, 2:47
  Moses' anger, 2:26
  need for water, 2:19
  YHWH's instruction, 2:23
Lincicum, D., 2:234

Lindblom, J.
  Balaam narratives, 2:205
  casting lots, 2:273
  the elders, 1:264
Lipiński, E., 2:297, 2:298, 2:299–300, 2:302
Lipscomb, A. I., 2:120
Liss, H., 1:40
Litke, J.
  land inheritance, 2:288, 2:303
  Moses' anger, 2:24
  'speak'/'command', 2:293
  the wilderness, 2:7
  Zelophehad's daughters, 2:289, 2:290, 2:291, 2:292, 2:294
Liver, J., 1:402
  the censers, 1:434
  Korah's rebellion, 1:407, 1:423, 1:425
  leadership of Moses, 1:406
Lobel, A. D., 1:22
Loewenstamm, S. E., 2:158, 2:401
Lohfink, N.
  scouts, 1:333, 1:358
  water miracle, 2:31
Lohr, M., 2:100
Lucas, A., 1:107
Lund, N. W., 1:387
Lunn, N. P., 1:83, 1:117–119
  tribes, 1:96
  twelve chieftains, 1:80
Lust, J., 2:94, 2:117
Luther, B., 1:225
Luther, B. P., 1:406
Lutzky, H.
  Balaam's narrative, 2:102
  Phineas episode, 2:232
Luzarrage, J., 1:220
Luzzato, M. C. (2016), 1:165
Luzzatto, S. D., 2:46
Lyonnet, S., 2:332

Maarsingh, B., 2:126
Maas, A. J., 2:195
McBride Jr, S. D., 1:73, 1:311
McCarter, P. K., 2:190
McCarthy, B. J., 2:330
Maccoby, H., 1:489
McConville, J. G., 1:19
McCrory Jr, J. H.
  bronze and iron, 2:200
MacDonald, N., 1:54, 1:55
  death and the wilderness, 2:49
  Edomites, 2:37
  fruits, 1:332
  Moses' obedience, 2:22
  red heifer ritual, 1:489
  serpents, 2:71
  strayed woman, 1:158
  YHWH and jealousy, 2:252
MacDonald, W. G., 2:136
McEvenue, S. E., 1:80
  exploring the land, 1:323
  land as *Sheol*, 1:339
  years in the wilderness, 1:356
McGowan, P., 1:286
McIvor, J. S., 1:440, 1:442
McKane, W., 1:151, 1:154
McKenzie, J. L., 1:264
MacKintosh, C. H., 2:187
McNamara, M., 1:29
  Succoth, 2:443
  wilderness journeys, 2:440
McNeile, A. H.
  Nazirites, 1:165
  punishment, 1:215
  staffs, 1:445
  taboos and rituals, 1:461
Madge, S., 1:286
Magness, J., 1:24
Magonet, J.
  Korah's pedigree, 1:443
  Korah's rebellion, 1:406, 1:407, 1:408, 1:409, 1:410, 1:414, 1:419, 1:430, 1:437
  Moses' experience, 1:402
  Numbers theme, 1:12
  scouts' report, 1:338, 1:340
  spiritual harlotry, 2:224
Maier III, W. A., 1:243
  chariot-throne, 1:39
  the Cloud, 1:221, 1:273
  the wilderness Camp, 1:222
Malamat, A.
  land inheritance, 2:297
  Naboth's vineyard, 2:286
  spies, 1:324
Malbim (M. L. ben Jacob)
  Balaam narrative, 2:135

exodus from Egypt, 2:482
Mann, T. W., 1:44, 1:66
　Aaron's staff, 1:454
　Balaam narrative, 2:204
　good and evil, 1:363
　Hobab, 1:230
　Kadesh incident, 2:30
　Korah's rebellion, 1:496
　Levites, 1:466
　Moses' disloyalty, 2:47
　wilderness generation, 1:453
　YHWH's holiness, 2:44
Manoach, C. ben
　dangers in wilderness, 2:64
　Kadesh, 2:33
Marcus, D., 2:105
　Balaam narrative, 2:103, 2:131, 2:132
　eagles, 2:200
　lion image, 2:168
　locusts, 2:119
　wild ox image, 2:166
Marek, L., 2:194
Margaliot, M.
　Aaron, 2:19
　Balaam narrative, 2:100, 2:102, 2:106,
　　2:109, 2:110, 2:125, 2:127, 2:131,
　　2:140, 2:176, 2:190, 2:204
　the covenant, 2:30
　Moses' anger, 2:26, 2:27
　Moses' disloyalty, 2:47
　rebellion, 2:13
　the rock, 2:18
　sin of Moses and Aaron, 2:5
　staff of Aaron, 2:20
　trust, 2:29
　water from a rock, 2:24
　waters of contention, 2:33
Marguerat, D., 1:402, 1:405
Markose, H. M., 1:339
Marquis, L. M., 2:401
　boundaries of Canaan, 2:419
　Gad and Reuben's sons, 2:414
　Manasseh, 2:416
Martinez, F. G., 1:19, 1:20
Mason, H. J. M., 1:28, 1:40
　Camp of Israel, 1:31
　essay on the cherubim, 1:36–37
Mason, S. D.
　Aaron's family, 1:475
　atonement, 1:474
　covenant, 1:466–467, 1:496, 1:497
　Levites, 1:467
　no land principle, 1:477
　perpetual due, 1:473
　Phinehas episode, 2:236, 2:238, 2:239
　protection by priests, 1:468, 2:228
Mathews, K. A. (1996), 1:120
Matthews, V. H.
　Asshurim, 2:201
　clan and kinship, 2:295
Mattingly, K., 2:283
　Joshua, 2:312, 2:315–316, 2:320
Mauchline, J., 2:201
Maunder, E. W., 1:24
May, H. G.
　the crag, 2:20
　many waters, 2:27
Mazar, B., 2:438
Mazor, L., 2:70
Mecklenburg, Yaakov Tzvi, 2:135
Medan, Y., 2:421, 2:422
　Machir, 2:423
　spies, 1:324
Meek, T. J., 1:400
　'becoming rebellious', 1:401
　Korah's rebellion, 1:409
Meer, M. N. van der, 1:320
Meinhold, A., 2:290
Mendenhall, G. E., 2:170
　Baal Peor, 2:215, 2:217
　census figures, 1:104, 1:106–107
　the Cloud, 1:220
　daughters of Moab, 2:216
　Midianites, 2:379
Merrill, E. H., 2:195
Merzbach, Ely, 1:88
Mettinger, T. N. D., 1:26–27, 1:30, 1:243
Meyers, C. L., 2:296
　almonds, 1:447
　clan and kinship, 2:295
　land inheritance, 2:302
　land tenure, 2:300–301
　tree lampstand, 1:193
Michalowski, P., 2:80
Michel, D., 1:488
Miles, J. A., 1:321
Milgrom, Jacob, 1:11, 1:13, 1:53, 1:61,
　1:68, 1.80, 2:490

Milgrom, Jacob (cont.)
  Aaron and Moses, 1:121
  Aaron's family, 1:475, 1:476
  apostasy, 2:243
  the Ark of the Covenant, 1:360
  army like locusts, 2:119
  ashes and dust, 1:488
  astrology, 2:150
  atonement, 2:239, 2:241, 2:242
  Baal Peor, 2:215, 2:217, 2:255
  Balaam narrative, 2:99, 2:103, 2:106–107, 2:119, 2:122, 2:139, 2:147, 2:160, 2:170, 2:173, 2:176, 2:190, 2:191, 2:207
  'barb in the eye', 2:452
  benediction, 1:169
  blame on Moses, 2:23
  burnt offerings, 1:374, 2:333
  on Caleb, 1:326
  Camp structure, 2:389
  Canaan and Edom, 2:37
  census numbers, 1:104
  on chapter 36, 2:486
  character of Moses, 1:297
  on cherubim, 1:35
  chiastic structure, 2:375
  chieftains, 1:86
  cleansing, 1:486, 1:487
  cloth prohibitions, 1:393
  Cloud's movement, 1:217
  copper-smelting, 2:72
  covenant of peace, 2:237
  Cushite woman, 1:294
  David the shepherd, 2:311
  disease and judgement, 1:52
  divine guidance, 1:322, 1:468, 2:315
  donkeys, 2:383
  Edom's refusal, 2:39
  Egypt, 1:340, 1:341
  enclosed impurity, 1:492
  encountering YHWH, 1:271
  the end of its edge, 2:159
  excommunication, 1:215
  family tombs, 2:307
  firstborn, 1:473
  foreign women, 2:231
  Gad and Reuben, 2:419
  gifts to priests, 1:141
  Gilead territory, 2:416
  guarding against defilement, 1:499
  hand-leaning rite, 1:197
  on Hebrew text, 1:74
  Hebron, 1:332
  high-handed sin, 1:381
  Hobab, 1:230, 1:231
  holy objects, 1:464
  idolatry, 2:215
  'impale', 2:220
  impurity expulsion, 1:488
  inadvertent sin, 1:379
  innocent murderer, 2:473–474, 2:475
  iron and metals, 2:467
  Ishmaelites and Midianites, 2:243
  Israel blocked, 1:355
  Israel without fear, 1:343
  Jacob's rule, 2:198
  Jeshimon, 2:78
  key terms of 32, 2:401
  kings and kingdom, 2:184
  Korah's rebellion, 1:412, 1:414, 1:416, 1:423, 1:430
  land inheritance, 2:298–299, 2:305
  leprosy, 1:146
  Levites, 1:115, 1:123, 1:127, 1:194, 1:198, 1:199, 1:411, 1:442, 1:464, 1:466, 1:477
  list of journeys, 2:432
  literary structure, 1:321
  livestock, 2:403
  to make/sacrifice, 1:373
  making atonement, 1:197
  manslayer, 2:465
  marriage covenant, 2:369
  Moses and Phinehas, 2:223
  Moses and YHWH, 1:192
  Moses' authority, 2:436
  Moses' crisis, 1:256, 1:267
  Moses' intercession, 1:350
  Moses' sin, 2:42
  murder/manslaughter, 2:468–469
  nomadic groups, 2:196
  on Numbers 21, 2:53
  oath ritual, 1:154
  offerings, 1:164, 1:165, 1:188, 1:375, 1:470, 1:471, 1:472, 2:355–356
  outline of 11–12, 1:245
  pastureland, 2:461, 2:462
  people and Egypt, 1:270

people's complaints, 1:250
'perish', 2:44
Phinehas, 2:221, 2:222, 2:230, 2:233
placement of tribes, 1:94
pre-Israelite paganism, 1:461
priesthood, 2:236
prophetic intercession, 1:346
public sacrifices, 2:328
purification, 1:162, 1:195, 1:196, 1:380, 1:493, 1:501, 2:337, 2:479
ram of atonement, 1:148
rebellion, 1:342
red cow ritual, 1:495
redemption, 2:465
red heifer, 1:481, 1:482, 1:483, 1:484
Reuben and Gad's sons, 2:406
roots and water, 2:180
salt, 1:475
scouts, 1:330, 1:338, 2:410
shofar, 2:341
'shur'/'wall', 2:443
Sihon's campaign, 2:81
sources, 2:212
speaking against God, 2:62
strange fire, 1:122
strangers, 1:465
strayed women, 1:144, 1:151, 1:152, 1:156, 1:157
tassels, 1:388, 1:389, 1:396
Tent of Meeting, 1:467
tithes, 1:478
'to vow a vow', 2:58
tribal units, 1:84
the trumpets, 1:224, 1:225
'Urim and Thummim', 2:314
vengeance on Midianites, 2:246
vows and oaths, 2:359, 2:363
on waters, 1:195
wilderness journeys, 1:370, 1:391, 2:439, 2:445
women, 2:366, 2:367
YHWH's blessing, 1:171
YHWH's kingship, 2:56
Zelophehad's daughters, 2:285, 2:289, 2:493
Miller, D., 1:156
Miller, J. M., 2:72
  city of Ar, 2:74
  itinerary names, 2:73

mountains of Abarim, 2:449
Miller, P. D., 1:73
  benediction, 1:167, 1:169, 1:170
  YHWH and Moses, 1:422
Miller, R. D., 2:70
Miller, Y. S., 2:220
Mills, W. E., 1:275
Mirguet, F.
  Camp organization, 1:437, 1:452
  Korah's rebellion, 1:410, 1:412, 1:416, 1:420, 1:421, 1:424
  Levites, 1:466
Mitchell, C. W.
  Balaam narrative, 2:127
  benediction, 1:168
Mitchell, D. C., 1:166, 1:427
Mitchell, T. C., 1:230
Moberly, R. W. L.
  Balaam narrative, 2:104, 2:128, 2:129
  Moses and YHWH, 1:312
Mody, R., 2:234
Monroe, L. A. S.
  Moses and Phinehas, 2:223
  Phinehas, 2:222
  plains of Moab, 2:384
  sources, 2:212
  Tent of Meeting, 2:224
  YHWH's order, 2:247
  Zimri, 2:243
Moor, J. C. de
  chieftain names, 1:86
  Shaddai, 2:177
Moore, M. S.
  Balaam narrative, 2:101, 2:103, 2:107, 2:131
Morag, S., 2:180
Morales, L. Michael, 1:6, 1:144, 1:234, 1:268, 1:307, 1:369
  the altar, 1:189, 1:190
  annual festivals, 2:328
  atonement, 1:438
  the atonement lid, 1:191
  Balaam narrative, 2:134, 2:151, 2:195, 2:196
  burnt offerings, 1:166, 1:375, 2:327, 2:329, 2:330, 2:331, 2:332, 2:334, 2:336
  character of Moses, 1:298, 1:419
  covenant formula, 1:393
  David the shepherd, 2:311

Morales, L. Michael (cont.)
  Day of Atonement, 2:342
  descending into Egypt, 1:248
  divine declaration, 1:15
  divine hospitality, 1:271
  Dwelling as Eden, 1:90
  exodus and salvation, 2:165
  fire offerings, 1:473
  gold calf incident, 1:465
  guarding the Sanctuary, 1:496
  hand-leaning rite, 2:312
  heavenly abode, 1:374
  high priest's breastplate, 1:22
  holy and profane, 1:462
  holy of holies, 1:122
  house of God, 1:193
  Jesus and covenant, 2:259
  liturgical calendar, 2:348
  Miriam's leprosy, 1:304
  Nazirites, 1:162, 1:163
  offerings, 1:376, 2:58
  Passover lamb, 2:338
  peace offering, 2:346–347
  purification, 1:196, 2:336
  red heifer, 1:483
  redemption out of Egypt, 2:208
  ritual purity, 1:498
  Sabbath, 1:193, 1:384, 2:335–336
  the Sanctuary, 1:468
  serpent-like Pharaoh, 2:70
  spiritual journeys, 2:443
  submission to YHWH, 2:330
  Tent of Meeting, 1:416
  the throne-chariot, 1:32
  value of gifts, 1:189
  the veil, 1:35
  warfare, 2:397
  water-pouring ritual, 2:344
  YHWH dwelling among people, 2:495
  YHWH's face, 1:98
  YHWH's people, 1:301, 2:321
  YHWH's priesthood, 1:193
Morenz, S., 2:65
Morgan, D. F., 2:327
Morgenstern, J.
  the Cloud, 1:220
  high priest, 2:470, 2:471
  on Ruel, 1:230
  'vaulted tent', 2:229

Moriarty, F. L., 1:68, 2:100
Moriel, 2:24
Morris, L., 1:128–129
Mortensen, B. P., 1:29
Mosser, C., 1:49
Moster, D., 1:332
Motyer, J. A., 1:70
Mowinckel, S.
  the ark, 1:233, 1:235
  Balaam narrative, 2:99, 2:116, 2:153, 2:209
  scepter/star, 2:195
  'tumult', 2:197
Moyer, C. J., 2:105
  Balaam narrative, 1:145, 2:97, 2:104, 2:117, 2:130, 2:157, 2:158
  divination and enchantment, 2:123
  history and oracles, 2:207
  Midianites, 2:114
Müller, H. P., 1:375
Munk, E., 2:422
Myśliwiec, K., 2:65

Nachmanides, M., 1:380
  Aaron's staff, 2:21
  Arba and his sons, 1:331
  atonement, 2:241
  auguries, 2:167
  Balaam narrative, 1:144, 2:109, 2:149–150, 2:160, 2:168, 2:180, 2:191
  Balak, 2:114
  'barb in the eye', 2:452
  Camp of Israel, 1:27–28, 2:158
  chariot-throne, 1:38
  city dimensions, 2:462
  the Cloud, 1:219
  death in the wilderness, 2:277
  defeat of Arad, 2:57
  the elders, 1:264
  fire offering legislation, 2:347
  the four beasts, 2:202
  'great salvation', 2:391
  Jochebed, 2:275
  Kenites, 2:201
  King Amalek, 2:56
  kings, 2:184
  Korah's rebellion, 1:409
  'latter end', 2:159
  long journey, 1:208

Manasseh, 2:417, 2:418
Midianites, 2:113, 2:246
Moab, 2:114
Moses guards, 2:327
Nazirites, 1:54, 1:164
oath-breaking, 2:356
Phinehas episode, 2:244
Reuben and Gad, 2:397
Sarah, 2:272
scouts' report, 1:333, 1:338
strayed woman, 1:158
tribal inheritance, 2:491
vows and oaths, 2:359
water wells, 2:77
way of explorers, 2:56
wine, 2:334
women, 2:367
YHWH in battle, 2:75
YHWH's judgements, 1:383
Zelophehad's daughters, 2:287
Nagen, Y., 2:474
Nahmani, H., 1:407
Nahshoni, Y., 2:5
Najman, H., 1:26
Naylor, P. J., 1:64
   city boundaries, 2:462
   Festival of Booths, 2:346
   God's covenant, 2:120
   Levite distinction, 2:461
   prophecy, 2:208
Nelson, R. D., 2:332–333
Nelson, W. D., 2:482
Neufeld, E.
   family name, 2:302
   land inheritance, 2:301
Neusner, E., 2:366
Neusner, J., 1:311
Newing, E. G.
   kings of Canaan, 1:348
   Moses' intercession, 1:346–347, 1:349
   rebellion, 1:345
   YHWH and Moses, 1:344
Newman, M. L., 1:243
Newton, I., 1:40
Nicholson, E., 1:402
Nicolsky, N. M., 2:472
Niditch, Susan
   Cozbi's name, 2:244
   inner camp, 2:396

Midianite war, 2:385
Nielsen, K., 1:413
Nihan, C.
   number of sacrifices, 2:345
   purification offering, 2:337
Nixon, R. E., 2:296
Noam, V., 1:459
Noonan, B. J.
   failure to enter Canaan, 1:383
   Israel's rebellion, 1:382
   Moses and Aaron, 2:32
   the Sabbath, 1:384, 1:385, 2:495
Noordtzij, A., 1:61
   Balaam narrative, 2:171
   captured places, 2:418
   Gad and Reuben, 2:414
   judicial execution, 1:215
   land inheritance, 2:302, 2:456
   Levites, 1:201
   Reuben, 2:419
   scouts' report, 1:338
   staffs, 1:445
   taboos and rituals, 1:461
North, F. S., 1:208
Notarius, T.
   Balaam narrative, 2:163
   'lion' synonyms, 2:168
   opening exclamation, 2:178
Noth, M., 1:61, 1:68, 1:115, 1:244, 1:400,
   1:460, 2:212, 2:325, 2:326
   the ark, 1:132
   Balaam narrative, 2:103, 2:108, 2:150
   census figures, 1:107
   cultic laws, 1:369
   Cushite woman, 1:292, 1:295
   the elders, 1:264
   food provision, 1:271
   help of God, 1:169
   Israel's power, 2:166
   Jubilee, 2:488
   Korah's rebellion, 1:408, 1:409
   land inheritance, 2:302
   Miriam and Aaron, 1:296
   Miriam's death, 2:4
   Moses and YHWH, 1:301
   Moses' son, 1:124
   on Numbers 21, 2:53
   Phinehas episode, 2:232, 2:238
   taboos and rituals, 1:461

Noth, M. (*cont.*)
  Zelophehad's daughters, 2:286, 2:289, 2:290
Novick, R., 2:132–133
Novick, T.
  the Sabbath, 1:384, 1:386
  in the wilderness, 1:391
Nowell, T.
  itinerary names, 2:73
  water wells, 2:77

O'Connor, M. P., 1:181, 1:217, 1:220, 1:243
Oehler, G. F.
  Korah's rebellion, 1:406
  sons of Reuben, 1:443
Ogden, G. S., 1:82
Olson, D. T., 1:61, 1:62, 1:68, 1:296, 2:349–350
  Aaron and idolatry, 2:228
  Aaron's staff, 1:454
  Baal Peor, 2:234, 2:248
  Balaam story, 2:255
  chieftains, 2:390
  cleansing after deaths, 1:499
  the departure, 1:235
  divine judgement, 2:250
  division of the plunder, 2:394
  land inheritance, 2:456
  Levites' role, 2:476
  Midianites, 2:376
  Miriam and Aaron, 2:44
  Moses' obedience, 2:22
  on Numbers 21, 2:53
  offerings, 1:376, 1:378
  priesthood and tribes, 2:473
  rebellion, 1:436
  red heifer, 1:484
  second generation, 2:411
  wilderness generation, 1:453
  wilderness journeys, 2:68, 2:440, 2:454
  women, 2:357
  YHWH and priests, 1:475
  YHWH's commitment, 1:394
  YHWH's judgements, 1:382
  Zelophehad's daughters, 2:284, 2:486
Olyan, S. M.
  Nazirites, 1:163
  shaving rite, 1:195

Organ, B. E.
  Baal Peor, 2:217
  cultic purity, 2:226
  Midianites, 2:246
  Moses and Phinehas, 2:228
  Phinehas episode, 2:229, 2:231, 2:233
  spiritual harlotry, 2:224
Organ, Barbara, 2:380
Orlinsky, H. M.
  Balaam narrative, 2:107, 2:127
  Zelophehad's daughters, 2:292
Ortiz-Roberts, C. A., 2:492
Ortlund Jr, R. C.
  idolatry, 2:215
  tassel law, 1:392
Osburn, C. D., 2:63
Ottosson, M., 2:277

Pakozdy, L. M. von, 2:100, 2:127
Palmer, M. J., 1:20
Pardes, I., 1:339
Parker, J. D., 1:261, 1:266, 1:287
  arrangement of Camp, 1:244
  food provision, 1:272
  on Mosaic law, 1:72
  Moses' burden, 1:262
  prophecy, 1:275, 1:276
  YHWH and Moses, 1:278
Parr, P. J., 2:246
Paterson, J. A., 1:208, 1:401, 2:400
  'Canaan', 2:431
  clans of Dan, 2:262
  'lift up the head', 2:262
  omission of Eleazar, 2:265
  'sons of Reuben', 2:262
  'them'/'their', 2:281
Paynter, H., 1:152
Pearce, L. E., 1:265
Perdue, L. G., 2:300
Peter, R., 1:197
Peters, M., 2:470
Petersen, D. L., 1:275
Petrie, W. M. F., 1:104, 1:106
Phelps, M. A., 2:113
Philip, J., 1:493–494
Phillips, A., 1:384
Pick, B., 2:194
Pimpinella, D.
  Miriam, 1:291

INDEX OF MODERN AUTHORS   661

Moses and YHWH, 1:300
Plaut, W. G.
  exile, 2:477–478
  Levitical cities, 2:463
  tribes, 2:495
Porten, B., 1:460
Portugali, J., 1:102
Postell, S. D.
  'Agag', 2:184
  Balaam narrative, 2:177, 2:198
  kings, 2:185
  Messiah, 2:187
Powell, T. M.
  Babylonian gods, 2:184–185
  Balaam narrative, 2:100, 2:153, 2:157, 2:161, 2:163, 2:174
  curses, 2:121
  Edom, 2:198
  'glory', 2:165
  Israel's purity and protection, 2:164
  Kenites, 2:201
  peoples around Moab, 2:197
  smashed arrows, 2:186
Press, R., 1:55
  oath ritual, 1:154
  uncleanness, 1:150
Pressler, C.
  Balaam narrative, 2:192
  Israel's obedience, 2:59
  Israel's victories, 2:79
  leadership of YHWH, 2:88
Preuss, H. D., 1:225, 1:226
Price, I. M., 1:375
Price, N., 2:266
Pritchard, J. B., 2:64
Propp, W. H., 2:20
  Aaron, 2:19, 2:21, 2:42
  'crag', 2:18
  Horeb, mountain of God, 2:20
  Israelites at Beer, 2:75
  Miriam's death, 2:4
  new generation, 2:17
  people's complaints, 2:14
  Phinehas, 2:226
Pyschny, K., 1:12, 1:402
  leadership and authority, 1:10
  Tent of Meeting, 1:417

Quesada, J. J., 2:212, 2:223

Rabinowitz, I., 2:74
Rad, G. von
  Balaam narrative, 2:150, 2:152, 2:206, 2:208
  Book of Wars, 2:74
  covenant of peace, 2:237
  land tenure, 2:300
  Phinehas and jealousy, 2:236
Rainey, A. F., 1:189
  burnt offerings, 2:336
  sacrifices, 1:380
Rapp, U., 1:296
Rashbam (Samuel ben Meir), 1:131, 1:250, 1:446, 2:134, 2:358
Rashi, 1:35, 1:44, 1:51, 1:94–95, 1:108, 1:147, 1:198, 1:201
  Aaron and Miriam, 1:302
  Baal Peor plague, 2:233
  Balaam narrative, 2:103, 2:109, 2:118, 2:124, 2:125, 2:130, 2:135, 2:140, 2:148, 2:160, 2:168, 2:171, 2:176, 2:189, 2:190
  Balak's people, 2:116–117
  Caleb, 1:333
  covenant of peace, 2:237
  Cozbi's name, 2:244
  Cushite woman, 1:293
  daughters of Zelophehad, 2:319
  divine command, 1:322
  eighth day, 2:344
  enchantment and divination, 2:166
  the exodus, 2:200
  freewill offerings, 2:347
  Gad and Reuben, 2:415, 2:418
  idolatry, 2:220
  impurity, 1:490
  inheritance, 2:273
  Israel's seed, 2:181
  Israel tests YHWH, 1:352
  Joshua, 2:313, 2:316
  Jubilee, 2:488
  judgement on Moses and Aaron, 2:33
  kings, 2:184
  Korah's rebellion, 1:409
  Midianites, 2:245, 2:377, 2:384–385
  Moab's territory, 2:75
  Moses denied Canaan, 2:309
  Moses' crisis, 1:257, 1:261
  numbers of sacrifices, 2:345
  the people and the land, 1:329

Rashi (cont.)
   plague deaths, 2:272
   purification offering, 2:337
   quail, 1:286
   sacrifices, 2:334
   Sarah, 2:272
   Sea of Suph, 2:61, 2:76
   sets of sacrifices, 2:339
   Sihon and Og, 2:112
   sons of Reuben, 2:417
   sons of Sheth, 2:196
   spies, 1:324
   spirit of Moses, 1:268
   three camps, 2:387
   through Negev, 2:56
   Transjordan inheritance, 2:454
   tribal leaders, 2:356
   tribes and marriage, 2:493
   trust and obedience, 2:71
   vows and oaths, 2:362
   water from the rock, 2:21
   wilderness journeys, 2:7, 2:445–446, 2:448
   YHWH's judgements, 1:383
   Zelophehad's daughters, 2:292, 2:321, 2:488
Reader, W. W., 1:21
Rees, A.
   Midianites, 2:223
   Phinehas, 2:220, 2:230, 2:231
Reif, S. C.
   Phinehas, 2:230, 2:232
   'pour', 1:459
Reis, P. T., 1:244, 1:257
   cutting meat, 1:288
   the elders, 1:274, 1:275, 1:276
   food provision, 1:262, 1:271
   manna, 1:255
   Moses' crisis, 1:246, 1:258–1:259, 1:260, 1:282, 1:289
Reiss, M.
   failure of Moses and Aaron, 2:10
   Miriam, 1:291
Rendsburg, G. A., 1:73, 1:104
   Balaam narrative, 2:119, 2:139, 2:140
   census figures, 1:105
Rendtorff, R., 1:15
Reviv, H., 1:263
Reymond, R. L., 2:136

Richter, G., 1:400
Ridderbos, J., 1:222
Rieder, D., 2:194
Riggans, W., 1:68
Rimon, S., 1.4, 1:27
   Aaron's death, 2:448
   burning incense, 1:413
   Camp of Israel, 1:30, 1:46
   the Cloud, 1:236
   Kadesh-Paran, 2:446
   land inheritance, 2:288
   narratives in census, 2:267–268, 2:269
   Rithmah, 2:446
   wilderness journeys, 2:444
   Wilderness of Paran, 2:445
   Zelophehad's daughters, 2:271, 2:290, 2:494
Ringgren, H.
   fixed law, 1:377
   land inheritance, 2:288
   ritual activities, 1:212
   sacrifical offerings, 1:470
Riskin, S., 1:2
   assemblage, 2:22
   heifer as Israel, 1:500–501
Roberts, B. J., 1:234
Robertson, R. G.
   Cushite woman, 1:292
Robertson Smith, W.
   Korah's rebelllion, 1:302
   sacrificing hair, 1:163
   salt, 1:475
   taboos and rituals, 1:461
Robinson, B. P.
   Cushite woman, 1:294, 1:295
   Miriam and Aaron, 1:297
   Miriam's leprosy, 1:304
   Moses and YHWH, 1:300
   Moses builds altar, 2:68
   Moses' role, 1:312
Robinson, E., 1:101
Robinson, G.
   development of Sabbath, 1:383
   Jubilee, 2:489
Robinson, R. B., 1:120
Robker, J. M.
   Balaam narrative, 2:104, 2:153
   Balak's homeland, 2:117
   Pethor, 2:116

Sukkoth, 2:115
Rofé, A.
   Balaam narrative, 2:103, 2:105, 2:131
   cities of refuge, 2:439
   city dimensions, 2:463
   innocent murderer, 2:477
   Moses and YHWH, 1:300
Rogers, C., 1:297
Rogers, J., 2:77
Rogers, J. H., 1:380
   YHWH's judgements, 1:358
   the zodiac, 1:25
Rolleston, F., 1:23–24
Römer, T., 1:243, 1:247, 1:249, 2:4
   Aaron, 2:11
   Moses and the Torah, 1:311
   Moses' crisis, 1:259
   Moses' role, 1:313
   the Spirit, 1:269
Ron, Z., 1:51
   Moses' disloyalty, 2:47
   Zelophehad's daughters, 2:289
Rosenberg, R. A., 2:195
Rosenblum, J. D., 1:287
Rosen-Zvi, I., 1:47, 1:151
Roskop, A. R., 1:13, 2:72
   list of journeys, 2:432
   on $ṣābā$, 1:27
   wilderness journeys, 2:441
Ross, A. P., 2:288
Ross, J. F., 2:112
Rothenberg, B., 2:72
Rothkoff, A., 1:166
Rouillard, H.
   Balaam narrative, 2:103, 2:104
   Edom, 2:197
Routledge, B., 2:76
Rubenstein, J. L., 2:345
Rudman, D.
   orderly cosmos, 1:425
   waters of separation, 1:494, 1:495
Rudolph, D. J., 1:193, 2:328
Rudolph, J. W., 2:212
Rudolph, W. *see also Biblia Hebraica Stuttartensia*
Ruiten, J. van, 2:101
Runnalls, D., 1:293
Ruppert, L., 1:345

Russaw, K. D.
   land inheritance, 2:305
   Zelophehad's daughters, 2:290
Rütterswörden, U., 1:485

Sabato, M., 1:363
Sabo, P.
   Moses' anger, 2:25
   supply of waters, 2:6
Sabourin, L.
   burnt offerings, 2:332
   the Cloud, 1:220
Sacks, J.
   eighth day, 2:344
   Gad and Reuben, 2:386
   history of redemption, 2:337
   Moses' crisis, 1:257
   Reuben and Gad, 2:370
   shofar, 2:341
   table of nations, 2:345
Sadler Jr, R. S., 1:291, 1:294
Safren, J. D., 2:132
Sailhamer, J. H.
   Balaam oracles, 2:190
   good and evil, 1:363
   laws, 1:371
St Clair, G., 1:23, 1:104
Sakenfeld, K. D., 2:263
   Aaron and Moses, 2:17, 2:23
   Aaron's failure, 2:42
   accusations against Moses, 2:13
   covenant relationship, 1:345
   Jubilee, 2:489
   land inheritance, 2:302
   Moses' intercession, 1:349, 1:350
   Moses' leadership, 2:32
   Moses strikes the rock, 2:25
   red heifer, 1:485
   water miracle, 2:24, 2:31
   Zelophehad's daughters, 2:289, 2:290, 2:492, 2:494
Salomon, J., 1:230
Sals, U., 2:101, 2:131, 2:139, 2:156, 2:204, 2:205
Samet, E., 1:27, 1:67, 1:244, 2:486
   Balaam story, 2:255
   community in the wilderness, 2:7–8
   death outside the land, 2:34
   Gad and Reuben's sons, 2:412

Samet, E. (*cont.*)
    the ground opens, 1:428
    impatience for Canaan, 2:15
    Korah's rebellion, 1:417
    land inheritance, 2:288
    marriage, 2:491
    Midianites, 2:213
    Moses and water, 2:28
    Moses' anger, 2:24
    Moses' burden, 1:262
    Moses' crisis, 1:258, 1:282, 2:47
    Moses' leadership, 2:32
    Phinehas episode, 2:245
    physical and spiritual, 1:328
    Reuben's tribe, 2:268–269
    second generation, 1:499–500
    the Spirit, 1:269
    tribal census, 1:88
    tribal framework, 2:487
    YHWH's commands, 1:359
    YHWH's glory, 2:16
    Zelophehad's daughters, 2:286, 2:289, 2:290
Sanchez, S. H., 2:20
    murmuring language, 2:8
    second generation, 2:13
    YHWH and miracle, 2:29
    YHWH's judgement, 2:17
Sandys-Wunsch, J., 1:61, 1:69
Sargent, A. D., 1:388, 1:390
Sasson, J. M.
    Manasseh, 2:270–271
    waters that curse/bless, 1:141
Savran, G.
    Balaam narrative, 2:136, 2:137, 2:140, 2:179
    roots and water, 2:180
    serpent in Eden, 2:70
    serpents and enchantment, 2:167
Sayce, A. H.
    Balaam narrative, 2:116
    Sheth, 2:197
Saydon, P. P.
    disease and judgement, 1:52
    purification, 1:162–163
Schäfers, K. M., 2:212
    penitent weeping, 2:225
    Phinehas episode, 2:233
    sacred place, 2:223

Schart, A., 1:243, 1:320
    the elders, 1:275
    Kadesh Barnea, 2:446
    mirror narrative, 2:4
    Moses' obedience, 2:22
    spies, 1:325
    the Spirit, 1:269
    'ten times', 1:352
Schechter, S., 1:103
Scheftelowitz, J., 1:461
Schenker, A., 1:381
Schiffman, L. H., 1:19–20
Schmidt, L., 2:54
    Balaam's narrative, 2:103
    wilderness journey, 2:60
Schmidt, P., 1:463, 1:464
Schmitt, H.-C., 2:184
Schmitt, R., 1:153
Schneerson, M. M.
    census figures, 1:106
    Levites, 1:136
Schnittjer, G. E., 1:93
Schwartz, B.
    judgement of YHWH, 1:419
    strayed woman, 1:156
Schwartz, E., 2:106
Schwartz, S., 1:335
    fruit and land, 1:333
    Joshua and Caleb, 1:343
    rebellion, 1:322
    scouts' report, 1:334, 1:337, 1:338, 1:339, 1:340, 1:344
Scolnic, B. E.
    Aaron's death, 2:448
    captured places, 2:418
    census figures, 1:105–106
    itinerary, 2:483
    list of marches, 2:480
    wilderness journeys, 2:435, 2:441, 2:443, 2:445
Scurlock, J., 1:165
Seebass, H., 1:13, 1:46, 1:142, 1:185, 1:243, 2:54, 2:375
    Baal Peor, 2:217, 2:220
    benediction, 1:167
    the Cloud, 1:216
    'impale', 2:220
    light in the tent, 1:192
    Midianite woman, 2:224

'midrash', 2:374
Moses' crisis, 1:259
Moses' role, 1:314
new generation, 2:8–9
Phinehas, 2:213, 2:222
Phinehas episode, 2:232, 2:235
route around Edom, 2:72
the Spirit, 1:269
taboos and rituals, 1:461
vision of God's people, 1:14
YHWH's blessing, 1:171
Seerveld, C. G.
  apostasy, 2:248
  Balaam narrative, 2:104, 2:107, 2:113, 2:154, 2:205
  idolatry, 2:215
  Moab, 2:119
Seevers, B., 1:88
Seforno, O. ben Jacob
  atonement, 2:391
  Baal Peor, 2:250
  land distribution, 2:273
  Transjordan inheritance, 2:453
  Zelophehad's daughters, 2:492
Segal, M. H., 2:418
Seiss, J. A.
  The Gospel in the Stars, 1:24
Seligsohn, M.
  Book of Wars, 2:74
  Midianites, 2:246
Seligson, M., 1:488
Seraphim, The Very Reverend, 2:99
Sergi, O., 2:406
Seybold, K.
  Balaam's oracle, 2:195
  benediction, 1:172
Shamah, M., 1:130, 1:147
  Aaron's priesthood, 1:193
  Balaam narrative, 2:131, 2:229
  bringing Israel to the land, 2:9
  divine guidance, 2:314
  firstborn males, 1:440
  Korah's rebellion, 1:424
  Levitical duties, 1:201
  priests and Levites, 1:464
  on ṣaba, 1:85
  second generation, 2:14
  tassels, 1:389, 1:390
  Tent of Meeting, 1:190

Shanks, H., 2:66
Shapira, H., 2:273
Sharp, C. J., 2:105, 2:123, 2:125, 2:127, 2:176
Shectman, S., 1:157
Shemesh, Y., 2:285, 2:286, 2:287, 2:321, 2:486, 2:492
Shenk, R., 2:103, 2:104, 2:123, 2:126, 2:127, 2:128, 2:134, 2:205
Sherwood, S. K.
  Balaam narrative, 2:124, 2:125, 2:126, 2:147
  Balak, 2:112, 2:119
  'Cozbi', 2:244
  people's fear, 1:449
  red heifer, 1:485
  significance of names, 1:327
Shiloh, Y., 1:101
Shumate, D. R., 1:12, 1:61, 1:135
Sicherman, M.
  Balaam Peor, 2:246
  Midianites, 2:246
Simpson, B. R., 2:178
Sivan, H. Z.
  Moabites, 2:224
  women in Numbers, 2:256
Ska, J. L., 1:61, 1:234
  'dispossessed' and 'dwelt', 2:80
  exploring the land, 1:323–324
Sklar, J., 1:128, 1:381
  atonement, 2:239
  excommunication, 1:384
  expressing apostasy, 1:382
  high-handed sin, 1:383
  holiness and impurity, 1:491
  inadvertent sin, 1:379
  Israel's apostasy, 2:241–242
  penalties, 1:133
  punishment, 1:215
  purification offering, 2:337
  two paths, 1:395
  unclean, 1:155
Slayton, J. C., 2:214
Slotki, J. J., 1:265
  Baal Peor, 2:217
  Balaam narrative, 2:109, 2:125, 2:138
  Balak, 2:114
  burnt offerings, 2:331
  plagues and executions, 2:234

Slotki, J. J. (cont.)
  Reuben and Gad, 2:403
  slandering serpent, 2:70
  wilderness journey, 2:481
  Zelophehad's daughters, 2:284
Smend, R., 2:212
Smick, E. B.
  Balaam narrative, 2:175
  flowing water, 2:181
Smith, H. P.
  red heifer law, 1:460, 1:461
  taboos and rituals, 1:461
Smith, J. Z.
  eating in Eden, 1:256
  narrative reversal, 1:254
Smith, M., 1:352
  benediction, 1:167
  YHWH's light, 1:170
Smith, P. A., 1:220, 1:221
Smoak, J. D., 1:53, 1:145, 1:173
Snaith, N. H., 1:400
  abortion, 1:141
  annual festivals, 2:328
  Balaam narrative, 2:116
  Balak, 2:112
  burnt offerings, 2:330, 2:331
  captured places, 2:418
  census figures, 1:101
  defines 'midrash', 2:374
  land distribution, 2:273
  Moses, 1:297
  offerings, 1:470
  reckless actions, 1:359
  second Passover, 1:213
  trumpets, 1:224
  Zelophehad's daughters, 2:294
Snowden Jr, F. M., 1:293
Soden, W. von, 1:196
Sohn, S.-T.
  Baal and marriage, 2:219
  marriage and covenant, 2:216
Soloveitchik, J. B., 1:243, 1:258, 1:281
Sommer, B. D., 1:71, 1:244
  the elders, 1:263
  Moses and YHWH, 1:266
  Moses' crisis, 1:258, 1:261, 1:267
  Moses' prophecy, 1:311
  Moses' role, 1:313
Sonnet, J.-P., 1:327

Sousek, Z., 2:209
Specht, H., 2:4
Speier, S., 1:471
Speiser, E. A.
  Balaam narrative, 2:120
  chieftains, 1:86
Spencer, J., 1:461
Spencer, J. R., 1:26, 1:216
Sperber, A., 2:194
Sperling, S. D.
  character of Moses, 1:298
  Cushite woman, 1:294
  leprosy, 1:305
  Miriam's role, 1:296
  Moses and YHWH, 1:300
  YHWH's people, 1:301
Spero, S.
  Balaam narrative, 2:100, 2:123, 2:140, 2:141
  Phinehas, 2:251
Spiegelman, M.
  Balaam narrative, 2:166
Spiro, A., 2:226
Spoelstra, J. J.
  almonds, 1:447
  blossoms and diadem, 1:389
  tassels and diadem, 1:393
  YHWH in the Camp, 1:453
Sprinkle, J. M., 1:68, 1:331, 1:335
Spronk, K., 2:171, 2:218
Stager, L. E.
  avengers, 2:469
  clan and kinship, 2:295, 2:306
  land tenure, 2:300, 2:301, 2:302, 2:304
  new Eden, 2:277
Stallman, R. C., 1:271
Staubli, T., 1:378, 2:375
  cherubs and cherubim, 1:39
  on waters, 1:195
Stebbins, R. P., 2:105, 2:115, 2:140
Steele, D., 1:40
Steinberg, P., 2:221, 2:229
Steiner, R. C., 2:53, 2:75
  Book of the Wars, 2:78
  Phinehas episode, 2:230
  water wells, 2:77
Steins, G., 2:177
Steinsaltz, A., 2:341

Stephens, F. J., 1:388, 1:393
Sternberg, M., 2:212
Stigers, H. G., 2:467
Strack, H. L., 2:229
Strauss, G., 1:185
Strawn, B. A.
  Balaam narrative, 2:148
  lions, 2:168–169, 2:186
Štrba, B., 2:309
Strong, J., 2:226
Stronstad, R., 1:314
Stubbs, D. L., 1:53, 1:95, 1:143, 1:145, 1:185, 2:10, 2:208
  Balaam narrative, 2:156
  benediction, 1:167
  blessing of fruitfulness, 2:157
  Camp of Israel, 1:41
  Egyptian serpents, 2:66
  Israel and Eden, 2:180
  kings of Midian, 2:382
  land boundaries, 2:438
  Levites' role, 2:476
  Midianites, 2:374
  Nazirites, 2:58
  patterns in Numbers, 1:69
  purification, 1:496
  Reuben and Gad's sons, 2:408
  salvation, 2:495
  shepherd image, 2:311
  strayed woman, 1:154
  twelve tribes, 1:364
  vows, 2:369
  women, 2:368
  Zelophehad's daughters, 2:289
  'Zimri', 2:243
Sturdy, J., 2:96
  Baal Peor, 2:217
  Balaam narrative, 2:99, 2:103
  'great salvation', 2:391
  midrash, 2:374
  Miriam's death, 2:4
  Phinehas episode, 2:229
  taboos and rituals, 1:461
Sutcliffe, E.
  Balaam narrative, 1:145, 2:104, 2:117
  Balak's people, 2:116
Swanson, K., 2:66
Sweeney, M. A., 1:120
  divine presence in sanctuary, 1:192

firstborn males, 1:440, 1:441
Miriam's death, 2:12–13
Numbers theme, 1:12
Phinehas episode, 2:229

Taggar-Cohen, A.
  Aaron's priesthood, 1:460
  Levites, 1:199, 1:467
  priests' offerings, 1:476
  strangers, 1:465
Talmon, S., 1:210
Taylor, D. J., 1:404, 1:405
  Aaron's staff, 1:444
  Greek text of Numbers, 1:73
  Korah's rebellion, 1:402
Tedford, J. S., 1:154
Tengström, S., 1:120
Tervanotko, H. K., 1:290, 1:291
  Cushite woman, 1:295
  Miriam, 1:308, 2:12
  Passover, 2:9
Theodor, O., 1:256
Theological Dictionary of the Old Testament
  'Cozbi', 2:244
Theological Wordbook of the Old Testament, 1:148
  'inheritance', 2:291
  parable, 2:152
  'Phineas', 2:226
  release of serpents, 2:63
  stone wall, 2:138
  toil, 2:163
Theologisches Handwörterbuch zum Alten Testament, 1:263
Thiessen, M., 2:50
Thomas, M. A.
  firstborn males, 1:441
  toledot narrative, 1:120
Thompson, T., 2:304
Thon, J., 2:226, 2:228, 2:232
Tigay, J. H., 2:271
Török, L., 1:291
Tosato, A., 2:108, 2:153–155, 2:161
Tournay, R., 2:153
Tov, E., 1:73, 1:234, 2:53, 2:283
Trapp, J.
  Balaam narrative, 2:129, 2:173
  Messiah, 2:198

Trevaskis, L. M., 1:146, 1:369, 2:329
Trevett, C., 1:290
Trible, P.
   Cushite woman, 1:295
   Miriam's status, 1:309
Tunyogi, A. C., 1:243
   Moses and YHWH, 1:301
   Moses' character, 1:311
Turnage, M., 2:87
Twersky, G.
   Aaron's death, 2:448
   Balaam narrative, 2:78, 2:81, 2:88, 2:104, 2:138, 2:151, 2:178, 2:186
   narrative sequences, 2:73
   seed of Israel, 2:158
   water wells, 2:77
Twersky, Y., 1:403
   the Dwelling, 1:5
   giving and taking, 1:467
   good and evil, 1:361, 1:363
   Korah's rebellion, 1:418, 1:424
   verbal parallels, 1:432–433
   YHWH's blessing, 1:172

Uehlinger, E., 2:66
Uffenheimer, B., 1:275, 2:487
Ulfgard, H., 2:345
Ullmann, D. W., 2:70, 2:87
Ulrich, D. R.
   Gad and Reuben, 2:410
   losing land, 2:488
   Zelophehad's daughters, 2:486, 2:492

Van Dam, C., 1:437, 1:438
Van der Meer, M.N. *see* Meer, M. N. van der
Van der Toorn, K., 2:493
Van Seters, J., 1:244, 2:72, 2:104
Vasholz, R. I.
   army sizes, 1:101
   census figures, 1:105
   murder and manslaughter, 2:465
Vaughan, P. H., 2:149
Vaulx, J. de, 1:61, 1:69, 1:459, 1:461, 2:95
   Asshurim, 2:201
   the covenant, 1:216
   excommunication, 1:215
   Korah's rebellion, 1:412
   list of journeys, 2:432

Moses strikes the rock, 2:26
Nazirites, 1:159
purification rituals, 1:483
rebellion, 1:342
self-imposed sacrifices, 2:358
strayed woman, 1:149
theology of priesthood, 1:451
wilderness journeys, 2:435
YHWH's dominion, 2:196
Zelophehad's daughters, 2:287
Vaux, R. de
   anti-Exodus, 1:360
   Phinehas episode, 2:229
   scribes, 1:265
Vermes, G., 1:20
   abundant waters, 2:181
   advent of Messiah, 2:195
   Balaam narrative, 2:102, 2:104, 2:190
   rise of a star, 2:194
Viberg, Å., 1:271
Viezel, E., 2:77
Vilensky, Z., 2:56
Vogels, W., 1:193
   annual festivals, 2:328
   spirit of YHWH, 2:312
   wilderness passage, 1:499
Vos, G., 2:36
   authorship of Numbers, 1:69–70
   Balaam narrative, 2:136, 2:195
   eschatology, 2:203
Vriezen, T. C., 1:483
Vulleumier, R., 2:102

Wacholder, B. Z., 1:30, 1:32
Waite, J., 1:104
Wall, L., 1:2
Walsh, C., 1:220
Walsh, J. T.
   list of journeys, 2:432
   Moses' plea, 1:307
Waltke, B. K., 1:181, 1:220, 1:243
   Camp as Paradise, 1:174
   the Cloud, 1:217
   unfaithfulness, 1:148
Walton, J. H., 2:136
Ward Jr, H. D.
   Balaam narrative, 2:96, 2:109, 2:174
   Israel's purity and protection, 2:164
Waters, J. L., 2:212

Phinehas, 2:220
Phinehas episode, 2:230
Watts, J. W.
    burnt offerings, 2:330
    on Mosaic law, 1:72
Waxman, C., 1:27
    Balaam narrative, 2:132, 2:133, 2:134, 2:156
    Divine Presence, 1:41
    Gad and Reuben, 2:420
    heavenly host, 1:37
    livestock, 2:404
    miracles, 1:448
    Moses and water, 2:28
    Moses' anger, 2:24
    Moses' crisis, 1:259
    Moses' disloyalty, 2:47
    the people and the land, 1:330
    Reuben and Gad's sons, 2:408
    Transjordan lands, 2:412
    Wilderness of Paran, 2:11
Way, K. C.
    Balaam narrative, 2:131
    Balak, 2:112
Webb, B. G., 1:55
Wefing, S., 1:461
Weinfeld, M., 1:353
    Balaam narrative, 2:151
    the elders, 1:263
    flying serpents, 2:64
    judges, 2:222
    land distribution, 2:273, 2:274
    marriage and covenant, 2:215–216
    priestly revenues, 1:470
Weingreen, J.
    integrity of tribes, 2:487
    the Sabbath, 1:384
    Zelophehad's daughters, 2:286, 2:291
Weippert, M., 2:115
Weise, U., 2:131, 2:139
Weisman, Z., 1:269
    hierarchy, 1:275
    Moses' crisis, 1:267
Wellhausen, J., 1:70, 2:3
    Balaam narrative, 2:99
    Camp of Israel, 1:46
    food provision, 1:262, 1:271
    Israel's departure, 1:211
    pasturelands, 2:462

priestly blessings, 1:166
    taboos and rituals, 1:461
    YHWH's people, 2:255
Wells, B., 2:65
Wendland, Ernst
    Balaam narrative, 2:138, 2:149, 2:158, 2:175, 2:192
    curse oracles, 2:199
    Korah's rebellion, 1:415, 1:430
    return home, 2:203
    royal imagery, 2:181
Wenham, G. J., 1:11, 1:27, 1:61, 1:68, 1:144, 1:146, 1:154, 1:186, 2:279
    almonds, 1:446
    annual offerings, 2:348, 2:349
    astronomy at the camp, 1:25
    Baal Peor, 2:222, 2:224
    Balaam story, 2:96, 2:97
    to be cut off, 1:215
    burnt offerings, 2:344
    Caleb, 1:337
    cedars in Eden, 2:179–180
    census numbers, 1:102, 1:103, 1:104
    cleansing of lepers, 1:486
    covenant, 2:495
    David's rise, 2:203
    divine judgement, 1:468
    divine speeches, 2:437
    execution, 1:387
    family tombs, 2:41
    food supply, 1:289
    function of Levites, 1:194
    Gad and Reuben, 2:410, 2:418
    God's light, 1:193
    Hazeroth, 1:290
    Hebrews and the church, 1:365
    Hebron, 1:332
    hosting YHWH, 2:480
    idolatry, 2:215
    Israel's arch-enemy, 2:185
    Israel's covenant, 2:218
    judgement of YHWH, 1:418
    kings and kingdom, 2:184
    the lamps, 1:192
    the land, 1:334
    lay assistants to priests, 1:204
    leadership, 2:312
    leaving Sinai, 1:330
    Levites, 1:197

Wenham, G. J. (*cont.*)
    marriage, 2:353
    Midianites, 2:377, 2:383
    Miriam as prophetess, 1:296
    Moses' authority, 1:402–403
    Moses' crisis, 1:259
    on the Nazarites, 1:54
    Passover lambs, 2:335
    protection by priests, 2:228
    purification, 1:493, 1:498, 1:499
    the Sanctuary, 1:468
    second year events, 1:182
    staffs, 1:445, 1:448
    theology of priesthood, 1:451
    tribal land inheritance, 2:491
    uncleanness, 1:150
    vows and oaths, 2:359, 2:361
    YHWH's dominion, 2:196
Wenham, J. W. (1967), 1:100, 1:104
Wenin, A., 2:70
Wenkel, D. H., 1:170
Westbrook, R.
    clan and kinship, 2:295
    family name, 2:303
    Jubilee, 2:489
    land distribution, 2:273, 2:274, 2:288, 2:302
    Zelophehad's daughters, 2:291, 2:493
Westermann, C.
    Balaam narrative, 2:205
    corpses, 1:488
    Cushite woman, 1:291
    the Tent, 1:274
Westminster Shorter Catechism, 2:207
Wevers, J. W., 1:114
    chieftains and idolatry, 2:211
    the elders, 1:263
    Greek text of Numbers, 1:73–74
    tassels, 1:369
Wharton, J. A.
    Balaam narrative, 2:204, 2:205, 2:206
    the Messiah, 2:210
Whitekettle, R.
    innocent murderer, 2:472
    strayed woman, 1:149
Whybray, R. N., 1:69
Widengren, G., 2:181
Widmer, M.
    Caleb and Joseph, 1:354

covenant relationship, 1:351
    Korah's rebellion, 1:416
    Moses' crisis, 1:258
    Moses' intercession, 1:346, 1:350
    psalmist's lament, 1:345
Wiesel, E., 1:278–279
Wifall Jr, W., 2:202
Wiggershaus, B.
    Balaam narrative, 2:107, 2:108–109, 2:122, 2:123, 2:126, 2:127, 2:129, 2:148, 2:149, 2:150, 2:163, 2:167, 2:169, 2:177, 2:188, 2:192
    Balak, 2:112
    covenant community, 2:176
    mantic practices, 2:205
Wijngaards, J., 1:84
Wilch, J. R., 1:226
Wilkinson, John
    census figures, 1:101
    quail, 1:286
Williams, J., 1:304
Williams, R. J., 1:243, 1:320, 2:325
    hope in the wilderness, 1:372
    land inheritance, 2:460
    Midianites, 2:212
    Moses and serpents, 2:67
    recompense, 2:212
    'three days' way', 1:233
Williamson, P. R.
    covenant of peace, 2:237, 2:238
    marriage covenant, 2:369
Wilson, R. R., 1:275
Windsor, G.
    the ark, 1:233–234
    the Cloud, 1:220
Winslow, K. S., 1:247, 1:291
    Cushite woman, 1:295
    Miriam, 1:294
    Miriam and Aaron, 1:296
    Miriam's leprosy, 1:306, 1:308
    Moses' prophecy, 1:311
Wiseman, D. J., 2:65
Wisnefsky, M. Y.
    census figures, 1:106
    Levites, 1:136
Witte, M., 2:153
Wold, D.
    corpse pollution, 1:491
    kareth penalty, 1:382

penalties, 1:133
punishment, 1:215
unclean, 1:155
Wolde, E. J. van, 1:142
   defilement, 2:476
   exile, 2:477
   the land, 2:475
   strayed woman, 1:151, 1:152
Wolf, H., 1:222
Wolf, U., 1:84
Wolff, H. W., 1:488
Wong, K. L., 2:25
Wood, A., 1:37
Wood, L.
   ecstatic behaviour, 1:275
   Holy Spirit, 2:312
Wood, W. P., 1:18
Woods, C. M., 1:380
   water wells, 2:77
   YHWH's judgements, 1:358
Woude, van der, 2:290
Woudstra, M. H.
   the ark, 1:233
Wright, D. P., 1:146, 1:380
   ashes and purity, 1:495
   clan and kinship, 2:295, 2:306
   Holiness School, 1:369
   impurity expulsion, 1:488
   land tenure, 2:299, 2:300, 2:301
   red heifer, 2:387
   on waters, 1:195
Würthwein, E., 1:74, 1:234
Wyatt, N., 2:181

Yadin, Y., 1:13, 1:19, 1:88

Yahuda, A. S., 2:94
   Amau, 2:117
   Balaam narrative, 2:119
Yasur-Landau, A., 1:13, 1:88
Yeung, S. Y. C., 1:287
Yoo, P. Y., 1:290
Young, I. M., 1:71
Young, Robert, 1:232
Youngblood, Gene, 1:69

Zakovitch, Y.
   Edom's refusal, 2:39
   leprosy, 1:305
Zeelander, S.
   Korah's rebellion, 1:430
   people's fear, 1:449
   rebellion, 2:13
Zehnder, M., 2:466
Zenger, E., 1:418
Zertal, A., 2:306
Ziegert, C., 1:104
Ziegler, Y., 1:62, 1:67
   land inheritance, 2:487
   vows and oaths, 2:358
Zimmerli, W., 1:36
   Ezekiel's vision, 1:38
   women, 1:156, 2:368
Zobel, H.-J., 1:224
Zornberg, A. G.
   on the wilderness, 1:2–3
   Zelophehad's daughters, 2:292
Zweig, Y.n., 1:4
Zyl, A. H. van
   Balaam narrative, 2:113
   water wells, 2:77

INDEX OF SUBJECTS

Aaron
  age of, 2:448–449
  anointed with oil, 1:170
  appeals to Moses, 1:245
  atonement and, 2:240
  authority of, 2:44
  blessing of, 1:166, 1:175
  burnt offerings, 2:331
  Camp arrangement, 1:18, 1:91, 1:92–93
  censer, 1:444
  chieftains and, 1:182
  chosen high priest, 1:192
  Cloud of Glory, 2:12, 2:272
  cultic community, 1:225
  death of, 1:123, 1:450, 2:1–2, 2:2, 2:3, 2:40–44, 2:49, 2:56, 2:275, 2:308, 2:426–427
  death of sons, 1:121, 1:122, 2:30
  dissension, 1:227
  duties of, 1:203
  Eleazar replaces, 2:18, 2:33, 2:49, 2:258, 2:264
  end of first generation, 2:14
  envy of, 1:408–409
  Exodus role of, 1:85
  family duties, 1:126, 1:127
  first generation, 2:10
  genealogy of, 1:43, 1:125, 2:261
  golden calf episode, 2:235, 2:251
  holiness of objects, 1:133
  hungry rabble, 1:248
  inner Camp, 1:135
  Judah's tribe and, 1:98
  judgement of, 2:14–15
  Korah's rebellion, 1:302, 1:398–400, 1:406–31
  lampstand and, 1:179, 1:184, 1:185, 1:191, 1:192–194, 1:202
  leadership of, 1:5–6, 1:120, 2:40, 2:441
  Levite duties and, 1:111–113
  Levite genealogy, 2:275
  Levites and, 1:97, 1:109, 1:124, 1:180, 1:199, 1:444–445
  Levites' roles, 1:184–185
  march from Sinai, 1:236
  marries Elisheba, 1:86
  Miriam and, 1:289, 1:306–307
  misrepresents YHWH, 2:3, 2:4, 2:4–34
  on Mt Sinai, 1:109
  passing of a generation, 2:448–449
  passing of first generation, 2:471
  Passover and, 1:205
  penitence, 1:305–306
  place in Camp, 1:127
  priesthood of, 1:42, 1:43–44, 1:50–51, 1:60, 1:66, 1:127, 1:129, 1:134–135, 1:197, 1:202, 1:211, 1:311, 1:398, 1:402, 1:405, 1:406, 1:410, 1:413–414, 1:436, 2:236–237
  priestly blessings, 1:167, 1:171
  punishment of, 1:306–307
  purity laws, 1:52
  rebellion against, 1:341–342
  rebellion at Kadesh, 2:282
  red heifer ritual, 2:387
  represents priests, 2:11
  responsibilities of, 1:463
  sees Miriam's leprosy, 1:303
  sibling of Moses, 1:100
  sins of, 2:40–42, 2:44–48
  slandered, 1:43
  sons of, 1:100, 1:109, 2:261, 2:275–276
  sons transport Ark, 1:92–93
  speaks against Moses, 1:58, 1:290–296, 1:312, 1:315, 2:219, 2:309, 2:357
  staff of, 1:445, 1:446–448, 1:452–455, 2:20–24, 2:26
  stays the plague, 1:403, 1:433–439, 1:450–451, 1:453–455, 2:241
  successor of, 1:11

INDEX OF SUBJECTS 673

tithe contributions, 1:477–478
toledot, 1:117
transgressions of, 1:45
transport of Dwelling, 1:131
tribes and, 1:75–76, 1:77, 1:78, 1:94
vindication of, 1:455
water from the rock, 2:16–29
wilderness and, 1:2
YHWH speaks to, 1:456–459, 1:496
YHWH's anger, 1:242, 1:299
YHWH's command, 1:82
Abarim encampment, 2:51, 2:427, 2:440
Abel, 1:426, 1:440, 2:484
    Cain's banishment, 2:476
    firstborn privilege, 1:440
    Korah parallels, 1:432
Abel-Shittim, 2:434
    Bael Peor, 2:449
    encampment, 2:427, 2:440
    Israel dwells at, 2:210–211
    location and meaning, 2:214
    plague, 2:225
Abidan
    Benjamin chieftain, 1:78
    offerings of, 1:178, 1:183
    setting out on journey, 1:207
    tribe arrangement, 1:76
Abihu, son of Aaron, 1:109, 1:428, 1:430, 1:446
    body carried, 1:214
    death of, 1:122, 1:127, 1:435, 2:30, 2:261, 2:275–276, 2:279
    fate of, 1:155
    genealogy of, 1:125
    no land inheritance, 2:267
    son of Aaron, 1:100
Abimelech, King
    restoration of, 1:305
Abiram, 1:406–408
    census and, 1:107
    complains about land, 1:498, 2:297, 2:307
    family disinheritance, 2:269
    fault Moses, 2:268
    Korah's rebellion, 1:398
    Moses against, 1:262
    rebellion of, 1:443, 2:278, 2:279
    sons die, 2:259
    swallowed into Sheol, 1:403,
        1:424–429, 1:444, 1:449, 1:450, 1:453, 1:455
    YHWH and, 1:417, 1:419, 1:422–425
Abraham
    ancestors and descendants, 2:495
    as astrologer, 1:24
    Balaam and, 2:132–134
    Balaam's oracle and, 2:187
    binding of Isaac, 2:334
    bride for Isaac, 2:363
    burnt offerings, 2:334
    descendants of, 2:208, 2:425, 201
    Hebron and, 1:332, 1:364
    Isaac and, 2:350–351
    Isaac's offering, 1:199
    kings from, 2:184–185
    land for descendants, 2:404
    Lot and, 2:114, 2:403
    multiplying seed of, 1:88
    not to 'see the ground', 2:408
    promise to, 1:98, 1:173, 1:261, 2:450
    Promised Land, 1:238, 2:279
    promises to, 1:42, 1:95
    represented by bulls, 2:339
    returns to his place, 2:203
    Ruth and Naomi, 1:231
    Sarah's potential impurity, 1:151
    sojourners, 1:215
    YHWH's promise, 2:307
    YHWH's promise to, 1:231
Abronah encampment, 2:426, 2:440
Absalom
    kills Amnon, 2:477
Acacia Grove *see* Shittim/Abel-Shittim
Achan, 2:295
Adam, 2:495
    banishment, 2:478
    duties of, 1:90
    in Eden, 1:191
    priesthood of, 1:159
adultery, 1:32
    harlotry in Moab, 1:59
    versus impurity, 1:151–153
    purity laws for women, 1:47
    Reuben and Jacob's concubine, 1:93
Agag, king, 2:184–185, 2:208
Ahiezer
    chieftain for Dan, 1:78
    offerings of, 1:178, 1:183

Ahiezer (cont.)
  setting out on journey, 1:207
  tribe arrangement, 1:76
Ahihud, son of Shelomi
  as chieftain, 2:428, 2:459
Ahira
  Naphtali chieftain, 1:79
  offerings of, 1:178, 1:183
  second census, 2:260
  setting out on journey, 1:207
  tribe arrangement, 1:76
Alalgar of Sumeria, 1:105
alcohol
  grapes in the wilderness, 1:164
  Nazirites and, 1:160–2, 1:165–166
  purity laws, 1:139
  restrictions, 1:55
  sacrifices and, 1:57–58
  'strange fire'?, 1:122
Alexander the Great, 2:202
Almon-Diblathaim encampment, 2:427, 2:440, 2:449
altar
  anointment of, 1:176
  bronze censers, 1:434
  censers and, 2:269
  dedication of, 1:187–190, 1:202, 1:227, 1:229
  fire, 1:190
  gifts for dedication of, 1:186
  heart of the Camp, 1:200
  law of Decalogue, 2:347–348
  life and death, 1:454
  offerings to, 1:176–179, 1:182
  set up, 1:175–176
  transport of, 1:229
Alush encampment, 2:426, 2:444
Amalek, 2:56, 2:201
  end of days, 2:190
  Joshua and, 2:199
  king Agag, 2:184–185
  location, 2:207
Amalekites, 2:199
Ammiel, son of Gemalli, 1:316
  meaning of name, 1:327
Ammon
  Machir and, 2:422
Amnon
  killed by Absalom, 2:477

Amorites
  conquest of, 2:55, 2:80–81
  Israel encounters, 2:204–205
  journey to, 2:50–52
  land, 2:279
  land distribution, 2:399
  land granted, 2:417
  population and, 1:101
  see also Sihon
Amram, son of Kohath, 1:109, 2:261, 2:275
  clan of, 1:126
  genealogy, 1:125
angels
  bring laws to Israel, 1:39
animals
  bird sacrifices, 1:162
  cattle, 1:128
  corpse pollution, 1:213
  firstborn, 1:118, 1:124, 1:128
  ḥayyot/creatures, 1:32
  Levites and, 1:110–111
  livestock, 2:398
  offerings, 1:187–190
  offerings of, 1:176–179
  ram of atonement, 1:138, 1:148
  red heifer ritual, 1:44, 1:60, 1:146, 1:195, 1:210, 1:212
  sacrifice of, 1:129
  unclean, 1:129
  war plunder, 2:383
  see also offerings
Anna, vows of, 2:365
Anu, Mesopotamian god, 1:103
Arad, 2:50, 2:55–56, 2:427
  defeat of, 2:57
  Israel encounters, 2:204–205
  Israel's arrival, 2:449
  land, 2:279
  marker event, 2:434
Ardites
  second census, 2:260
Arelites
  second census, 2:260
Ark of the Covenant
  Cloud and, 1:207
  Decalogue, 1:445
  guarding, 1:126–127
  journey from Sinai, 1:236

Index of Subjects

leads the tribes, 1:65
Levite care of, 1:111–112
locus of revelation, 1:35–36
Moses addresses, 1:207
Moses hears divine voice above, 1:183
procession of, 1:239
rest, 1:240
Sinai to Canaan, 1:233–234
song of, 1:63
transport of, 1:131–134, 1:229
transported of, 1:92–93
veiled, 1:132
YHWH above, 1:190
as YHWH's footstool, 1:233–234
YHWH's presence and, 1:360
YHWH's earthly chariot, 1:36, 1:40
Arodites, 2:260
Aroer, 2:399, 2:417
Asa, 1:103
Asaph, 1:1
Ashbelites, 2:260
Asher, tribe of
  Ahihud as chieftain, 2:428, 2:459–460
  arrangement of Camp, 1:82
  census figures, 1:77, 1:87, 1:93
  change in population, 2:267
  chieftain Pagiel, 1:78
  march from Sinai, 1:236
  offerings of, 1:178, 1:183
  second census, 2:272
  setting out on journey, 1:207
  tribal ordering, 1:96
  zodiacal sign, 1:23
Ashur, 2:200–203, 2:210
Asrielites, 2:260
Assembly, calendar of worship, 2:350
Asshurim, 2:199
astronomy and astrology, 1:25
  ancient astronomy and, 1:25
  in Judaism, 1:23–5
  symbolism in census, 1:103–104
  tribal designations, 1:23–24
asylum cities, 2:462–467, 2:484
  bloodguilt, 2:464
  high priests and, 2:469–473
  logic of, 2:473–479
Ataroth, 2:398, 2:399, 2:406, 2:417
atonement
  atonement lid, 1:188, 1:200

for Baal Peor, 2:392
blood offerings and, 1:187–188
Day of, 1:446
dedication ritual and, 1:195
food and, 1:287
forgiveness and, 1:381
golden calf incident, 2:239
innocent bloodguilt, 2:472–479
innocent murder, 2:484
Israel, 1:188–189
Korah's rebellion, 1:436–439
meaning of, 2:239–240
oath-breakers, 1:47
offerings and, 1:368
Phinehas and, 1:60, 2:235–237, 2:243, 2:258, 2:277
ram of, 1:138, 1:147, 1:148
war plunder offerings, 2:390–391
YHWH's blessing, 1:169–170
Atonement, Day of
  autumn festival, 2:350
  offerings and instructions, 2:328–329, 2:337, 2:342–343, 2:345
  purification, 2:337
  rest, 2:339
Atroth-Shophan, 2:399, 2:417
Ayin spring, 2:428

Baal, 1:45
  Heights of, 2:149
  'husband' meaning, 2:219
  spiritual harlotry, 2:240
Baal Chanan, 2:218
Baal-Meon (Beon), 2:398, 2:399, 2:417
Baal Peor, 1:59, 1:157, 1:199, 2:84
  apostasy, 2:395–396, 2:397
  atonement for, 2:392
  golden calf comparison, 2:248–251
  golden calf episode, 2:233
  Israel settles at, 2:217
  Midian conquest, 2:376
  Midian plunder and, 2:392–398
  Midianite conspiracy and, 2:246–247
  Phinehas incident, 2:212
  plague in, 2:233–234, 2:241–242, 2:252
  spiritual harlotry, 2:369
  straying and, 1:150
  unfaithfulness and, 2:251–254
  vengeance on Midians, 2:377–387

Baal Peor (cont.)
  Zelophehad's character, 2:286–287
Baal-Zephon encampment, 2:440, 2:443
Babylon
  Samson and, 1:417
Balaam, 2:38
  about YHWH, 2:208–210
  Abraham and, 2:132–134
  Baal Peor incident, 2:255
  Balak and, 2:57
  Balak hires, 2:88–89, 2:118–112, 2:204, 2:395
  Balak's rage, 2:187–189
  Balak's second call to, 2:125–130
  blessings and curses, 2:96–99, 2:133–143, 2:163, 2:191–192, 2:204, 2:209
  Camp as paradise, 1:99
  character of, 2:101–110, 2:115–116, 2:143–145
  confesses, 2:144–145
  conspiracy, 2:246, 2:247, 2:257, 2:272, 2:372
  constrained by YHWH, 2:146–149
  contrast with Phinehas, 2:243
  counsels Balak against war, 2:189–191
  Deir 'Alla inscription, 2:123
  divination, 2:151, 2:166–167
  as diviner, 2:108–109, 2:115–116, 2:118–119, 2:121–122, 2:138
  diviner to prophet, 2:205–206
  donkey and, 2:88, 2:98–99, 2:103–106, 2:130, 2:131–146, 2:205, 2:244–245
  eschatology, 2:190–191
  evil and, 2:143–145, 2:146
  final oracles, 2:198–204
  first oracle, 2:149–159, 2:199
  first visit to Moab, 2:121–125
  fourth oracle, 2:192
  future orientation, 2:191–202
  home of, 2:101, 2:116–117
  Israel's blessedness, 1:59
  Judah's tribe and, 2:266
  kingship theme, 2:259
  meets Balak at border, 2:146–149
  messenger from YHWH, 2:88–90, 2:136–146
  messianic prophecy, 1:88, 2:190–196, 2:206, 2:210
  Midianite kings, 2:203

  military force, 1:101
  name of, 2:116
  narrative of, 1:174, 2:57, 2:384
  oracles of, 1:41–42, 2:90–93, 2:97, 2:98
  organization of tribes, 1:92
  Phinehas slays, 2:376, 2:380, 2:382–383, 2:385
  poetic language, 2:152–154, 2:161–162, 2:184–186, 2:190–191
  possible riches, 2:126–128, 2:130, 2:135, 2:147–148
  as prophet, 2:101–102, 2:106–107, 2:133–134, 2:167–168
  returns to his place, 2:203
  role in harlotry, 2:213, 2:229
  second oracle of, 2:244
  sees messenger, 2:174, 2:176–177
  Spirit and, 1:277
  Tell Deir 'Alla inscription, 2:115
  theological aspect, 2:207–208
  third and final oracles of, 2:170–189
  third oracle of, 2:245, 2:496
  tribe of Judah, 2:270
  tribes of Israel, 1:23–24
  unreliability, 2:105
  vengeance upon, 2:394
  vision of Israel, 1:232, 2:204–210, 2:307
  YHWH's anger, 2:134–139, 2:219
  YHWH's angry visit, 2:124–125
Balak, 2:55
  after Balaam, 2:204
  anger with Balaam, 2:139
  Balaam meets, 2:121–125, 2:146–149
  Balaam's oracles, 2:90–93, 2:159–170, 2:170–189
  blessings and curses, 2:96–99, 2:133–143, 2:204
  counselled against war, 2:189–191
  dread of Israel, 2:110–114, 2:118–119
  efforts against Israel, 2:257
  father, Zippor, 1:113, 2:112
  first oracle, 2:151–159
  against Israel, 2:244
  kingship, 2:154, 2:206
  makes offerings, 2:149–151
  offerings of, 2:90–92, 2:99
  Og victory, 2:111
  within the parable, 2:166

INDEX OF SUBJECTS 677

to Peor, 2:170–171
rage at Balaam, 2:187–189
reaction to parables, 2:169
rebuke to, 2:170–171
response to Balaam, 2:159
schemes Israel's demise, 2:204–205
son of Zippor, 2:162
summons Balaam's curse, 2:88–89, 2:113, 2:118–121
wishes to turn YHWH, 2:120–121
Balak, king of Moab
calls on Balaam, 2:57
Bashan
battle at Edrei, 2:52
conquest of, 2:55
land, 2:279, 2:399, 2:407
victory over, 2:82–84
Becherites, 2:260
Beer, 2:449
Bela, son of Benjamin, 2:272
Belaites, 2:260
Bene-Jaakan encampment, 2:426, 2:440, 2:447
Benjamin, tribe of
arrangement of Camp, 1:82
census figures, 1:77, 1:87, 1:93
change in population, 2:267
chieftain Abidan, 1:78
Elidad as chieftain, 2:428, 2:459–460
march from Sinai, 1:236
offerings of, 1:178, 1:183
population drop, 2:272
second census, 2:260, 2:272
setting out on journey, 1:207
tribal ordering, 1:96
tribe arrangement, 1:76
zodiacal sign, 1:23
Beriahites
second census, 2:260
Beth-Haran, 2:399, 2:417
Beth-Jeshimoth encampment, 2:440, 2:449
Beth-Nimrah, 2:399, 2:417
Bezer, asylum city, 2:466
Bilhah, tribal ordering, 1:96
bodily discharge
expulsion for, 1:48, 1:49–50
purity laws, 1:137, 1:142, 1:145–147
wayward women and, 1:52

wilderness and, 1:60
Booths, Feast of
autumn festival, 2:350
burnt offerings, 2:330
instructions and offerings, 2:324–325
life in the wilderness, 2:338
offerings and instructions, 2:326, 2:337, 2:339, 2:343–346
bread
unleavened, 2:326
see also Unleavened Bread Feast
breastplate, high priest's, 1:170
Bukki, son of Jogli
chieftain, 2:428, 2:459

Cain, 1:426, 1:440
and Abel, 2:45
banishment, 2:476–477
firstborn, 1:432
Kenites, 2:200
Korah parallels, 1:432–433
rivalry, 1:440
wanderings, 2:409
Caleb, son of Jephunneh, 1:316
battle of Edrei, 2:82
Canaan and, 1:360
Canaanites' shade removed, 2:271
as chieftain, 2:459
division of land, 2:428
as exception, 2:261, 2:276, 2:279, 2:290
excluded from judgement, 2:32
inhabitants of Canaan and, 1:331, 1:335–337
land granted by YHWH, 2:274
loyalty of, 2:398, 2:408
man of spirit, 2:310
meaning of name, 1:327
scouts and, 1:9, 1:87, 1:330, 1:333–339
spared YHWH's judgement, 1:352–355
spirit of, 2:312
younger generation, 1:326
Camp of
arrangement of, 1:62, 1:80–83
arrangement of tribes, 1:91–99
as 'bride' of YHWH, 1:54–58
census, 1:83–91, 1:100–108
compliance, 1:94
concentric commitments, 1:50–51

Camp of (*cont.*)
  confession to Moses, 1:59
  covenant community, 1:85, 1:97–98
  covenant community and, 1:83
  divine judgement and, 1:61
  Ezekiel's vision and, 1:40–41
  following YHWH's Cloud, 1:94
  generational transition, 1:67–68
  high priest's breastplate, 1:40
  as holy kingdom, 1:40–41
  idolatry, 1:45
  inner and outer' camp, 1:97
  journey of, 1:84
  Levites' arrangement, 1:116
  meaning of arrangement, 1:98–99
  microcosm of creation, 1:41–42
  musters, 1:62
  new generation and, 1:44–46
  order of movement, 1:92–93
  paradigms for community, 1:53–58
  purity laws, 1:46–60
  rebellions, 1:65
  Shekhinah, 1:41–42
  strangers and, 1:89–90
  structure and purity laws, 1:48–53
  theology of, 1:41–42, 1:53–58
  wilderness sojourn, 1:42–45, 1:58–60
  YHWH's earthly entourage, 1:85
Camp of Israel, 1:12–42
  apostasy of second generation, 2:250
  Ark of the Covenant, 31
  arrangement of, 1:18, 1:30–32, 1:36, 1:134–135, 1:137, 1:183, 1:224, 1:228, 1:273, 1:298, 1:315
  in Balaam's oracles, 2:165–166, 2:174, 2:178–179
  burial of the complainers, 1:245, 1:289–290
  Chariot of the *Shekhinah*, 2:270
  community, 1:380–381
  conquests in Canaan, 2:78–88
  covenant community, 1:12–13
  defeats Ammorites, 2:51–52
  delayed progress, 1:247–248
  departure, 1:210
  destruction of Canaanites, 2:54–55
  distribution of war plunder, 2:387–392
  elders/scribes, 1:262–266, 1:271
  encampment, 1:210

excommunication, 1:155
extended Temple, 1:172–173
Ezekiel's vision, 1:19, 1:28–29, 1:30–34
first generation, 1:365, 1:416, 2:28, 2:219
follows Cloud, 2:442, 2:443
foreigners, 2:217
generational shift, 1:378, 1:499, 2:4–5, 2:8, 2:14, 2:26–27, 2:40, 2:85–86
geographical code, 1:247–249
hierarchies of, 1:264
high priest's breastplate, 1:21–25, 1:28, 1:170
as holy community, 1:173–174
hungry complainers, 1:240–242, 1:244–259, 1:307
inner and outer, 1:248, 1:290, 2:6
integration of war captives, 2:387
Jewish interpretation of, 1:27–30
John's vision of, 1:20–21
journey from Hazeroth, 1:308, 1:309–310
journeys out, 1:131–134, 1:183
lack of water, 2:10–16
leaves Sinai, 1:229
lust for flesh, 1:269–272
manna, 2:217
military campaign, 1:13
as model for life in land, 2:265
Moses at centre, 1:249
Moses outside, 1:9
Mt Sinai revelation, 1:14–18
Nazirite parallels, 1:161–162
out of the wilderness, 2:78
outsiders and, 1:314
paradigm of covenant, 1:19–21
penalty for apostasy, 2:222
people's complaints, 2:61–63
place of Moses and Aaron, 1:127
plunder from Midian, 2:383
pollution of harlotry, 2:230–231
possible harms to, 1:169
purity and, 2:215, 2:216
rebellion, 1:311, 1:315–319, 1:340–355, 1:365
redemption and, 1:28
role of elders/scribes, 1:264–266
scouts, 1:258, 1:311
second generation, 1:364, 1:404, 2:255

serpents, 2:50, 2:60–72
setting out on journey, 1:204–240
Sinai theophany, 1:38–40
Spirit in, 1:267–269, 1:278–280
spiritual harlotry, 2:215–219, 2:392
structure of, 1:200–201, 1:203–204,
    1:411–412, 1:452–453, 2:246, 2:458,
    2:483
Tent inside, 1:244
'three days way', 1:233
Throne-chariot, 1:31–34, 1:38, 1:39
transport, 1:13–14
transport of, 1:130–134, 1:181
tribal order of march, 1:236
victory spoils, 2:375
warriors and, 2:396
whoring in Moab, 2:217
YHWH punishes, 1:284–288
YHWH's earthly hosts, 1:25–27
YHWH's judgement on rebellion,
    1:350–362
YHWH's presence in, 1:146–147,
    1:166–173
yhwh ṣĕbā'ôt yōšēb hakkĕrāûbîm,
    1:37–38
zodiac and stars, 1:22–25
Canaan
    anticipation of, 1:65
    boundaries of, 2:430
    Caleb and inhabitants of, 1:335–337
    census for land distribution, 2:263–272
    conquest of, 1:67, 2:278, 2:413
    destruction of Canaanites, 2:54–55
    dispossessing inhabitants, 2:435
    distance from Sinai, 1:232
    east side of Jordan, 2:278
    Eden and, 2:495
    versus Egypt, 1:312
    end of journey, 2:449–450
    idolatry within inhabitants, 2:450–453
    Israel's arrival in, 1:228
    Israel's conquest of, 2:55–59
    Israel's fear of Canaanites, 1:90
    to Jericho, 2:265
    Jordan borders, 2:401
    Joshua and, 1:281
    journey to, 1:238–239
    map of, 2:457
    military force, 1:105
    Moses sees, 2:307
    Moses' hopes for, 1:259
    population and, 1:101
    resting place, 1:234
    Reubenite and Gadite compromise,
        2:410–414
    Reubenite and Gadite pledge,
        2:401–402
    status of Transjordan lands and, 2:419
    tribes hopes for, 1:43
    tribute laws and, 1:373
    vengeance on Midianites, 1:226
    vineyards of Eschol, 1:57
    vows in the land, 2:371
    YHWH defines, 2:427–428, 2:453–456
    YHWH on borders, 2:483
    YHWH's instructions, 2:436
    as YHWH's land, 2:299–301
    YHWH's speech about borders, 2:435
    YHWH gives to Israel, 1:322–323
Carmites, second census, 2:259
censers and incense, 2:269
    corpse pollution and, 2:380
census, first, 1:83–91, 1:182, 1:183, 1:229,
    2:265, 2:272
    calculations of, 1:88
    comparative figures, 1:92
    environmental support, 1:101–102
    evaluating, 1:100
    face value reading, 1:100–102
    families, 1:106
    first generation and, 2:408
    firstborn sons, 1:129
    as hyperbolic, 1:105–106
    land and, 1:66
    Levites, 1:127–130
    meaning of *'elef*, 1:104–105, 1:106–107
    Numbers structure, 1:62
    plague deaths and, 2:233–234
    population in David's era, 1:102
    purpose of, 1:94–95
    symbolism of/gematria, 1:102–104
    taxonomy of holiness, 1:97–98
    totals by encampments, 1:93
    totals of tribes, 1:87–88
    the whole community, 1:106–108
census, second, 2:259–61, 2:263–272,
    2:347
    Baal Peor plague and, 2:264

census, second (*cont.*)
   death in the wilderness, 2:277
   Manasseh tribe, 2:421
   reduced Simeon tribe, 2:246–247
   return of the flock, 2:279
   total count, 2:272
   Zelophehad's daughters and, 2:290
Chaldea
   astrology and, 1:34
Chemosh, 2:122, 2:148–149
   in Moab, 2:216
cherubim
   the Ark and, 1:34–37
   atonement-lid, 1:34–36
   in the Cloud, 1:220–221
   the Dwelling, 1:35, 1:36
   at entrance to Eden, 1:90
   entry to Eden, 1:191
   Ezekiel's vision, 1:30
   heavenly hosts, 1:26
   lead Israel, 1:239
   Mason's essay on, 1:36–37
   ox-like, 1:38
   use of images and, 1:92
   the Veil and, 1:35, 1:36–37
   in the wilderness, 1:34–37
   YHWH's entourage, 1:37–38
   the zodiac and, 1:24
Chinnereth, Sea of, 2:428, 2:455
cities
   of asylum, 2:462–467, 2:484
   Levitical, 2:480
   of refuge, 2:435, 2:439
clothing
   'mixed materials', 1:393
   sandals, 1:155
   tassels, 1:388–394
Cloud of Glory
   ascent of, 1:218, 1:223–224, 1:227, 1:228, 1:237
   cherubim and, 1:220–221
   in the Dwelling, 1:205–206, 1:216–217
   function of, 1:234
   guidance of, 1:205–206, 1:207, 1:209, 1:210–211, 1:216–219, 1:236, 1:237
   movement of, 1:182, 1:183
   sheltering, 1:239–240
   significance of, 1:220–224
corpse pollution, 1:46–47
   animals, 1:213
   cleansing, 1:56
   cleansing Levites, 1:194
   expulsion for, 1:48, 1:49–50
   Midianite conquest and, 2:375–376, 2:380–388, 2:395
   Nazarite vow and, 1:52
   Nazirite vow, 1:237
   Passover and, 1:205, 1:209–210, 1:214, 1:236, 1:279
   purification, 1:461–3, 1:496, 1:498, 1:500
   purity laws, 1:137, 1:142, 1:145–147
   red heifer ritual, 1:212, 1:457–8, 1:479–495, 2:384
   restrictions, 1:55
   souls and, 1:141
   ultimate pollution, 1:490–491
   warriors and, 2:386–387
   waters of separation, 1:492
   wilderness and, 1:60
covenant community, 1:85
   Aaron's priesthood and, 2:242
   ark's guidance, 1:235
   arrangement of Camp, 1:91
   Balaam narrative and, 2:121
   calendar of worship, 2:347–352
   cities and patrimony, 2:303–304
   community of, 1:2, 1:66, 1:83, 1:97, 1:166
   Decalogue, 1:191
   eschatology, 1:98
   journey together, 2:481–482
   lack of water, 2:13
   land and, 2:303–304
   like marriage, 2:495
   Mt Sinai revelation, 1:14–18
   outsiders and, 1:314
   Phinehas saves, 2:242
   Sinai, 1:175
   tested by hunger, 1:260
   testimony and, 1:217
   trumpets and, 1:225
   with YHWH, 1:232
   YHWH within, 1:97–98
   YHWH's blessing, 2:259
   YHWH's jealousy, 2:250
   YHWH's promise to Jacob, 1:194
Cozbi, daughter of Zur, 2:213, 2:284

family and context, 2:243–244
flagrant display, 2:285
harlotry, 2:369–370
harlotry apostasy, 2:222–224
Midianite scheme and, 2:244–245, 2:245–247
Phinehas slays, 1:60, 2:211, 2:220–221, 2:229–230, 2:231–233, 2:258, 2:395
seduction of Zimri, 2:252–253
Zimri and, 1:11, 2:241
Creation
  history and, 1:120
Cush, land of, 1:291
Cush, son of Ham, 1:291
Cushite woman, 1:242
  enigma of, 1:361–362
  identifying, 1:291–296
  Miriam's leprosy and, 1:304
  Moses and, 1:314–315, 2:227
  ritual purity and, 1:309

Dan, tribe of
  arrangement of Camp, 1:82, 1:228
  Bukki as chieftain, 2:428, 2:459–460
  Camp arrangment, 1:18
  census, 1:77, 1:87, 1:92–93, 1:93, 2:267
  chieftain Ahiezer, 1:78
  eagle or serpent emblem, 1:28
  leading tribes, 1:83
  march from Sinai, 1:236
  northern arrangement, 1:92–93
  offerings of, 1:178, 1:183
  order of departure, 1:92
  second census, 2:272
  setting out on journey, 1:207
  standard of, 1:83
  text on standard, 1:29
  tribal arrangement, 1:96
  tribe arrangement, 1:76
  zodiacal sign, 1:23
Daniel, prayer of, 1:167
Dathan, 1:406–408
  census and, 1:107
  complains about land, 1:498, 2:297, 2:307
  family disinheritance, 2:269
  fault Moses, 2:268
  Korah's rebellion, 1:398
  Moses against, 1:262

rebellion, 2:278, 2:279
rebellion of, 1:443
sons die, 2:259
swallowed into Sheol, 1:424–429, 1:444, 1:449, 1:450, 1:453, 1:455
swallowed into *Sheol*, 1:403
YHWH and, 1:417, 1:419, 1:422–425
David, 1:73
  age of Levite service, 1:201
  Balaam's prophecy, 2:194, 2:195
  burnt offerings, 2:330
  chosen by YHWH, 1:87
  covenant, 1:87
  descent from Judah, 1:86
  dynasty of, 1:88
  faithful servant, 1:301
  geneaology of, 2:340
  kills charioteers, 1:100
  kingdom of, 2:206
  leadership, 2:310, 2:311
  Moab and Edom, 2:197
  population of Israel, 1:102
  Psalm 23 and, 1:1
  'raising up' a name, 2:302
  on redemption, 1:129
  rise of, 2:184, 2:203
  Ruth the Moabitess, 2:284
  YHWH as shepherd, 2:279
Day of Atonement, 1:121
  atonement lid, 1:191
  casting of lots, 2:273
  instructions and offerings, 2:323
  Jubilee and, 2:489
  offerings and instructions, 2:326
Decalogue
  with the Ark, 1:445
  ēdut, 1:89
  jealous YHWH, 2:251
  Passover, 2:350
  taking his Name in vain, 2:415
Dibon-Gad, 2:398, 2:399, 2:406, 2:417, 2:427, 2:434
  encampment, 2:449
  given to Reubenites, 2:449
Dibon Gad, 2:440
Dinah, violated by Shechem, 2:227
donkeys
  Abraham's, 2:133
  angel and, 2:137–146

donkeys (*cont.*)
  Balaam's, 2:98–99, 2:103–106, 2:131–146
Dophkah encampment, 2:426, 2:440, 2:444
Doré, Gustave
  'Death of Korah, Dathan and Abiram', 1:430, 1:431
Dwelling of Testimony, 2:242
Dwelling Place
  arrangement around, 1:86
  arrangement of, 1:134–135
  blue, 1:390
  the Camp and, 1:34
  cherubim and, 1:35, 1:36
  Cloud of Glory and, 1:6–8, 1:41, 1:186, 1:189, 1:205–206, 1:216–217
  commands to Moses, 1:72
  consecration of, 1:4–5, 1:182, 1:183
  dust and sandals, 1:155
  Jerusalem and, 1:40
  Levite duties, 1:185
  Levite transport, 1:136
  Levites and, 1:77, 1:89, 2:274–275
  Levites camp around, 1:273
  meaningful arrangement, 1:200–201
  microcosm of creation, 1:41–42
  Moses sets up, 1:175–176
  organizing centre, 1:185
  plunder offerings to, 2:392–398
  priesthood and, 1:411
  purity and, 1:237
  raised and consecrated, 1:227
  sacred vessels of, 1:92
  set up, 1:64
  Shittim wood, 2:214
  as Tent of Meeting, 1:83
  three roles of, 1:8
  transport of, 1:127, 1:130–134, 1:184, 1:186–187, 1:206–207
  YHWH reveals, 1:14
  YHWH's blessing, 1:46
  YHWH's presence, 1:146
  YHWH and, 1:8–9
  see also Tent of Meeting

Eber, 2:202, 2:210
Eden
  Adam and Eve, 1:191
  Balaam's oracle, 2:179
  Canaan and, 1:361–364
  cherubim at entrance of, 1:90
  expulsion from, 1:98
  food and desire, 1:290
  four quadrants and, 1:99
  guarding the Sanctuary, 1:496
  high priest's breastplate, 1:22
  imagery of, 1:194
  serpent of, 2:70
  water provision, 2:20
Edom, 2:2
  Canaan's borders, 2:428, 2:454
  conquest of, 2:204–205, 2:206
  dispossession of, 2:197–198
  journey around, 2:72–76
  judgement of, 2:34
  land, 2:279
  refuses Israel's crossing, 2:34–41, 2:49
  threat to Israel, 2:449
Edrei, 2:52, 2:82
Egypt
  Cushites, 1:291, 1:292–294
  deliverance from, 1:270, 2:86–87
  'descent' to, 1:289
  exodus from, 1:213, 1:236, 1:261, 2:425, 2:439, 2:440–441, 2:443, 2:448
  food of, 1:214, 1:240, 1:248, 1:253–254, 1:270
  generational conflict, 2:15
  Israel plays whore with, 2:215
  Israeli firstborn and, 1:199
  Israel's army and, 1:101
  land and life in, 2:482
  land of 'milk and honey', 1:416
  longing for, 1:241
  Manasseh tribe, 2:421–422
  Medinet Habu, 2:56
  military encampments, 1:88
  Moses recalls to Edom, 2:36
  plagues, 1:199
  Rameses II's military, 1:13
  scribes in, 1:265
  serpents, 2:65–66, 2:85
  shepherding and, 2:404
  subearth, 1:248
  Tanis, 1:331
  wish to return to, 1:340–343

YHWH punishes, 1:285
El, 2:162
  Balaam's oracles, 2:165–166, 2:167, 2:192
  meaning of, 2:155
Eldad, 1:245, 1:247, 1:248, 1:268, 1:296, 1:310, 1:312
  prophesying, 1:241–242, 1:275–284, 1:300
elders and scribes, 1:310, 1:312
  addition to, 1:289
  prophesying and, 1:276
  role of, 1:263
  Spirit in the Tent, 1:241
  in Tent with Spirit, 1:266–269
  Torah and, 1:278
Elealeh, 2:398, 2:399, 2:417
Eleazar
  assumes priesthood, 2:18, 2:33, 2:42–43, 2:49
  corpse pollution, 2:380
  death of, 2:238
  death of Aaron and, 1:450, 2:2
  distribution of plunder, 2:396
  genealogy of, 2:261, 2:275–276
  gold for Levites, 2:391–392
  Joshua's leadership, 2:281, 2:283, 2:311–317
  Midian gold to Tent, 2:375
  oversees land distribution, 2:277
  plunder from Midianites, 2:373
  post-battle rituals, 2:384
  priesthood to Phinehas, 2:258
  red heifer ritual, 1:482–487, 2:258, 2:387
  second census, 2:259, 2:264–265, 2:276, 2:277
  second generation, 1:404
  succeeds Aaron, 2:228, 2:278
  Transjordan requests, 2:405
  Urim and Thummin, 2:273, 2:314–315
  war plunder distribution, 2:388
  YHWH's direct speech to, 2:264
  Zelophehad's daughters and, 2:280, 2:284, 2:320
Eleazar, son of Aaron, 1:109
  Aaron and, 1:11
  Aaron and *toledot*, 1:120–121
  assumes priesthood, 1:44, 1:100, 2:8
  directs sons of Kohath, 1:187
  division of land, 2:428, 2:484
  duties of, 1:127
  genealogy of, 1:125
  guard duties, 1:110
  hierarchy, 1:130
  land distribution, 2:458
  land division, 2:456
  Midian plunder, 2:372
  Moses and, 1:433–434
  priesthood and, 1:135
  role of, 1:119, 1:122–123
  Tent duties, 1:111–112
  transport duties, 1:133
  wilderness and, 1:2
  YHWH names leaders, 2:436
  Zelophehad's daughters, 2:486
Eliab
  chieftain for Zebulun, 1:78
  offerings of, 1:176, 1:183
  second census, 2:259
  setting out on journey, 1:206
  tribe arrangement, 1:76
Eliasaph, son of Lael
  chieftain, 1:126
  duties of, 1:136
  offerings of, 1:177, 1:183
  setting out on journey, 1:206
  tribe arrangement, 1:76
Elidad, son of Chislon
  chieftain, 2:428
  as chieftain, 2:459
Eliezar, son of Moses, 1:100
Elijah
  Elisha and, 1:268–269, 1:277
Elim encampment, 2:426, 2:440
  water and palms, 2:443–444
Elisha
  Elijah and, 1:268–269, 1:277
Elishama
  offerings of, 1:177, 1:183
  setting out on journey, 1:207
  tribe arrangement, 1:76
Elisheba
  priestly sons, 1:86
Elizaphan, son of Parnach
  chieftain, 2:428, 2:459
  leadership, 1:443

Elizaphan, son of Uzziel
  chieftain, 1:126
  duties of, 1:110, 1:136
  genealogy of, 1:125
  leadership, 1:10
Elizsaph, son of Lael
  duties of, 1:110
Elizur
  offerings of, 1:177, 1:183
  offerings to altar, 1:189
  setting out on journey, 1:206
  tribe arrangement, 1:75
Elkanah, 2:354
Elonites, 2:260
Elyon
  Balaam on, 2:192–193
  Balaam's oracle, 2:208
  prophecies of, 2:192–202
  saints of, 2:193
Elzaphan, 1:214
Enoch, son of Cain, 2:268
Enoch, son of Reuben, 2:268
Ephraim, son of Jacob, 1:327
  firstborn, 1:87
Ephraim, son of Joseph
  second son, 2:318, 2:319
Ephraim, tribe of, 2:260
  arrangement of Camp, 1:18, 1:82, 1:228
  census, 1:77, 1:87, 1:93, 2:265–266, 2:267
  chieftain Elishama, 1:78
  Kemuel as chieftain, 2:428, 2:459–460
  leading tribes, 1:83
  march from Sinai, 1:236
  offerings of, 1:177
  ox emblem, 1:28
  perpetuating name, 2:303
  prominence of, 1:86–87
  second census, 2:270
  setting out on journey, 1:206
  standard of, 1:83
  text on standard, 1:29
  tribe arrangement, 1:76
  trumpets and, 1:224
  western arrangement, 1:92–93
  zodiacal sign, 1:23
Epiphanius, 1:2
Er
  death of, 2:260, 2:267, 2:270, 2:279

second census, 2:268
Eranites, 2:260
Erites, 2:260
Esau, 1:440
  Jacob and, 2:35–36, 2:39
  parts from Jacob, 2:403
  Transjordan land, 2:404
eschatology
  Camp arrangement and, 1:98, 1:99
Eschol, 1:332
  grapes and, 1:374
  vineyards of, 1:57
Essenes
  eschatology, 2:194
  Temple plan, 1:19–20
  view of Camp, 1:49
Etham encampment, 2:426
  to Pi-Hahiroth, 2:443
  'Shur', 2:443
Ethiopia
  Moses' wife and, 1:292–293
Evi, Midian king, 2:372, 2:381–382
Exodus, Book of
  ending of, 1:6–8
  Moses and, 1:202
  Mt Sinai revelation, 1:14–18
  redemption of tribes, 1:120
  role of Moses and Aaron, 1:85
  theme of, 1:5
Ezekiel
  Levites and, 1:115
  vision of, 1:23, 1:174
    cherubim, 1:38–39
    divine entourage, 1:30–34
    Shekhinah and, 1:31–32
    temple-city, 1:19, 1:33
    throne-chariot, 1:28–29, 1:31–34, 1:38, 1:39
    YHWH and, 1:259
    YHWH and people, 1:314
Ezion-Geber encampment, 2:426, 2:440, 2:447
Ezra, descendant of Phinehas, 2:226

Feast of Weeks
  Spirit and, 1:314
  Spirit and the people, 1:312–313
Firstfruits, Feast of, 2:338–339
  offerings and instructions, 2:339–340

food
  abib/green corn, 2:338
  atonement and, 1:287
  below the earth, 1:253–254
  divine hospitality, 1:271
  Eden and desire, 1:290
  Egypt and, 1:214, 1:240, 1:248, 1:253–255, 1:270
  evil and, 1:361
  generational differences, 2:15
  grapes, 1:374
  hunger and, 1:240–242
  insatiability, 1:262
  lust for flesh, 1:269–272
  manna, 1:240, 1:244, 1:247, 1:248, 1:249–250, 1:252–253, 1:254–256, 1:270, 1:284, 1:287, 1:307, 1:364, 2:62
  meat-eating, 1:254
  milk and honey, 1:329–330, 1:334, 1:343, 1:416
  monotony, 1:255
  Passover, 1:287
  quail, 1:241–242, 1:244, 1:246–247, 1:248, 1:271–272, 1:284, 1:315
  unleavened bread, 2:323
  in the wilderness, 1:164
  YHWH's punishment, 1:284–288
  see also animals; land; offerings
foreigners
  defined, 2:466
  guarding against, 2:217
  offerings and sacrifices, 1:378

Gabriel, Archangel
  heavenly camp, 1:29
Gad
  livestock plunder, 2:383
  sons of, 2:357, 2:380
  vow to serve, 2:363
Gad, tribe of
  arrangement of Camp, 1:82
  Canaan oath, 2:414–416, 2:425
  Canaan pledge, 2:403–404
  census, 1:76, 1:87, 1:88, 1:93, 2:246–247
  change in population, 2:266–267
  chieftain Eliasaph, 1:78
  cities and sheepfolds of, 2:417
  cities of, 2:399, 2:406
  compromise for land, 2:410–414
  conquest pledge, 2:401
  encamped with Reubenites, 2:405
  land across the Jordan, 1:108
  land granted to, 2:397, 2:415, 2:416–419, 2:458
  march from Sinai, 1:236
  non-ranking, 1:93
  offerings of, 1:177, 1:183
  pledge, 2:370
  pledge to Canaan, 2:406–410
  population decrease, 2:270
  second census, 2:260
  setting out on journey, 1:206
  settlement of, 2:80, 2:88
  settles east of Jordan, 2:271
  status of, 2:418–419
  Transjordan, 1:67
  Transjordan compromise, 2:401–402
  Transjordan land, 2:398–400, 2:423–424, 2:428, 2:455–456
  Transjordan request, 2:401–402, 2:403–10
  tribal ordering, 1:96, 1:97
  tribe arrangement, 1:76
  zodiacal sign, 1:23
Gaddi, son of Susi, 1:316
Gaddiel
  meaning of name, 1:327
  son of Sodi, 1:316
Gamaliel
  Manassah chieftain, 1:78
  offerings of, 1:177–8, 1:183
  setting out on journey, 1:207
  tribe arrangement, 1:76
Gentiles
  Miriam's exile and, 1:303
  Moses' wife, 1:295–296
  sojourners, 1:216
Gershon, 1:84, 1:92
  accounts of, 1:119
  genealogy of, 1:125
  Moses and, 1:124–125
  name of, 1:215
Gershon, son of Levi, 1:92, 1:109, 2:275
Gershon, son of Moses, 1:100, 1:282
Gershon, tribe of, 1:109–110
  clan duties, 1:112, 1:113, 1:116, 1:123

Gershon, tribe of (*cont.*)
  duties of, 1:136, 1:176
  hierarchy, 1:130, 1:134
  Ithamar supervises, 1:187
  march from Sinai, 1:236
  no land inheritance, 2:261
  order of departure, 1:92
  second census, 2:276
  transport and, 1:133–134
  transport duties, 1:186, 1:206, 1:229
  trumpets and, 1:224
Geuel, son of Machi, 1:316
  meaning of name, 1:327
Gidgad, Mount, encampment, 2:426
Gileadites, 2:403
  captured by Manasseh tribe, 2:418
  Gadites and, 2:415
  land granted to, 2:417
  livestock and, 2:398
  Manassite clan, 2:423
  second census, 2:260
  status of, 2:419
  tribe of Manasseh, 2:485
  Zelophehad's daughters, 2:490
  see also Manasseh, tribe of
Girgashites, 1:101
Gog, 2:184
Golan
  asylum city, 2:466
golden calf episode
  Baal Peor and, 2:233–234
  Baal Peor comparison, 2:248–251
  precious material offerings, 2:392, 2:393
  ransom payments, 2:393–394
  at Sinai, 2:444
good and evil
  Eden and Canaan, 1:361–364
Gudgodah encampment, 2:447
Gunites, 2:261

Haggites, 2:260
hair
  Nazirites and, 1:160–166
  as offering, 1:164–165
  shaven Levites, 1:194–195
Ham, 1:291
Hamulites
  second census, 2:260

hand-leaning rite, 1:179, 1:196–197
  Levites, 1:184
handmaid's sons
  arrangement of, 1:93
Hannah
  vow for son, 2:356
Hanniel, son of Ephod
  chieftain, 2:428, 2:459
Hanoch
  see also Enoch
Hanochites
  second census, 2:259
Hansen's disease *see* leprosy
Haradah encampment, 2:426, 2:440
harlotry
  brazen Israelis, 2:225
  brothel near Camp, 230
  Moabite women, 1:11, 1:88, 2:215–219
  Phinehas punishes, 1:90
  spiritual, 1:154, 1:157–158, 2:392
Hashmonah encampment, 2:426
Hattaavah, 1:227
Hazar-Addar
  Canaan's border and, 2:428
Hazar-Enan, 2:455
  Canaan's border and, 2:428
Hazeroth, 1:245, 1:290, 2:426, 2:445
  departure from, 1:242, 1:244, 1:308, 1:309–10
  meaning of, 1:310
Heber, 2:200
Heberites, 2:260
Hebron
  Abraham and, 1:332
  asylum city, 2:466
  clan of, 1:126
  genealogy of, 1:125
  Joseph and, 2:318
  Levite city, 2:297
  scouted out, 1:331–333
Hebron, son of Kohath, 1:109, 1:110
Hebronites
  no land inheritance, 2:261
  third son of Kohath, 2:275
Helekites, 2:260
Hepherites
  Manassite clan, 2:423
  second census, 2:260
  Zelophehad's daughters, 2:271

Heres/Hareseth, 2:434
Heshbon, 2:398, 2:399, 2:406, 2:417
Hezekiah
   Passover and, 1:210
   prayer of, 1:37
Hezronites
   mother's line, 2:304
   second census, 2:259, 2:260
Hittites
   population and, 1:101
Hivites
   population and, 1:101
Hobab, 1:63, 1:254, 2:200
   Moses and, 1:209, 1:236, 1:238–239, 1:295, 1:314
   Moses speaks to, 1:207, 1:230–232
   relation to Moses, 1:229–230
Hoglah (location), 2:305, 2:306
holy of holies
   dedication of altar, 1:192
   lampstand, 1:200
   Mt Sinai and, 1:190
   transporting, 1:131–134
Hor Haggidgad encampment, 2:440
Hor, Mount, 2:50
   Aaron's death and, 2:433
   Canaan's border and, 2:428
   encampment, 2:426–427, 2:440
   from Kadesh, 2:447
Hor, Mount (Lebanese)
   Canaan's borders, 2:454
Hormah, 2:59
   battle of, 2:14
Hosea
   Nazarite vow, 1:56
Hoshea, son of Nun, 1:316
Huphamites
   second census, 2:260
Hur, Midian king, 2:381–382

idolatry
   Baal Peor, 1:199
   Balaam seduces Israel, 2:246–247
   bloodguilt and asylum, 2:464
   within Canaan, 2:450–453
   census and, 1:107
   comparing golden calf and Baal Peor, 2:248–251
   Decalogue and, 2:347–348
   destroying, 2:483
   golden calf, 1:8, 1:9, 1:38, 1:45, 1:90, 1:150, 1:204, 1:260, 1:274, 1:418, 2:48–49
   leprosy and, 1:52
   Levite loyalty and, 2:238
   Moses intercedes, 1:260
   spiritual harlotry, 1:59, 2:215–219
   straying women and, 1:150
   YHWH forgives Israel, 1:192
   YHWH speaks about, 2:427, 2:435, 2:436, 2:438, 2:450–453
   zeal of Levites, 1:121
Igal, son of Joseph, 1:316
   meaning of name, 1:327
Imnahites
   second census, 2:260
incense
   Korah and, 1:399
   non-ritual, 1:413
   priesthood, 1:409
   stays plague, 1:399, 1:433–439
incense and censers
   Korah and, 1:398
   priesthood and, 1:419–420
Ingathering, Feast of, 2:343
inheritance
   daughter to son/husband, 2:293–294
   women and, 2:292–294
Isaac, 1:440
   binding of, 2:334
   not to 'see the ground', 2:408
   offering of, 1:199
   promise to, 1:98, 1:261
   promised Canaan, 1:42
   represented by rams, 2:339
   sacrifice and, 2:350–351
   YHWH's promise, 2:307
Isaiah
   vision of, 1:221
Ishamel, 1:440
Ishar, son of Kohath, 2:275
Ishvites
   second census, 2:260
Israel
   after the exodus, 1:182
   Amalekite victory, 2:269
   approaches Moab, 2:86–88
   Balaam seduces, 2:246

Israel (*cont.*)
  Balaam's blessing, 2:155–159
  Balak's dread of, 2:110–114
  captivity of, 1:171
  change in census, 2:266–272
  change of generation, 2:447–448
  Cloud and obedience, 1:217–219
  community, 1:219
  comparative population, 1:101
  compliance of second generation, 2:401
  concepts of land, 2:296–299
  conquest of enemies, 1:226
  covenant community, 1:2
  death of firstborn, 1:199
  dispossessing Canaan, 2:450–453
  encounters in Promised Land, 2:204–205
  environment of, 1:101–102
  excommunication from, 1:215
  exodus of, 1:202, 1:213, 2:440–441
  failures of two generations, 2:277
  first generation, 2:392–393
  firstborn sons, 1:129, 1:136, 1:184
  as God's 'vine', 1:161
  the golden calf, 1:8, 1:9
  harlotry of, 2:244–245
  history of, 2:207
  intermarriage, 2:227, 2:232
  Jacob and, 2:194, 2:196, 2:197, 2:198
  Jubilee and land, 2:299–301
  judgement on first generation, 2:320
  kinship, 2:294–296
  land for second generation, 2:278
  land inheritance in Canaan, 2:263–272
  land of, 1:66–67
  life and worship in the land, 2:348–352
  like strayed wife, 2:251–254
  lions, 2:198
  marching whole population, 1:101
  Midian victory, 2:264–265
  Midianite women and, 2:395
  Midianites interests, 2:395
  Miriam as representative, 1:309
  Moses as mediator, 1:9
  Moses' parting words, 1:1
  number 42 and, 2:435
  out of bondage, 1:129
  Passover transgressions, 1:215
  Phinehas saves, 2:242–243
  poetic language of journey, 1:217
  promise to Abraham, 1:231
  return from exile, 1:235
  second generation apostasy, 2:234
  second generation census, 2:263–272
  separateness, 2:255–258
  settles at Baal Peor, 2:213
  Sihon victory, 2:111
  Sinai period, 1:232–233
  sinfulness, 1:234
  sojourners, 1:215–216
  Song by the Sea, 2:86–87
  spiritual harlotry, 1:154, 1:157–158, 2:240, 2:248–249, 2:255–256, 2:369
  spiritual shallowness, 1:262
  statutes, 1:225–226
  straying and, 1:149
  theocracy, 1:12
  toledot, 1:121
  tribal leadership, 1:10–12
  unbelief and, 1:312
  use of images, 1:91–92
  vision of Balaam, 2:204–210
  vows in the land, 2:371
  warriors rewarded, 2:388, 2:390
  wilderness experience, 1:1–3
  worship calendar, 2:347–452
  YHWH and firstborn, 1:124
  YHWH forgives, 1:192
  YHWH on journey, 2:439–450
  as YHWH's bride, 1:160
Israel (modern)
  Holocaust and, 1:500–501, 2:332
  Holocaust immigrants, 2:423
  Palestinian Jews, 2:423
Issachar
  between the sheepfolds, 2:274
Issachar, tribe of
  arrangement of Camp, 1:82
  census, 1:76, 1:87, 1:93
  change in population, 2:267
  chieftain Nethanel, 1:78
  march from Sinai, 1:236
  offerings of, 1:176, 1:183
  Paltiel as chieftain, 2:428, 2:459–460
  second census, 2:260
  setting out on journey, 1:206

tribal ordering, 1:75, 1:96
zodiacal sign, 1:23
Ithamar
　genealogy of, 2:261
Ithamar, son of Aaron, 1:100, 1:109, 2:275–276
　directs Levites in transport, 1:187
　genealogy of, 1:125
　role of, 1:122–123
Iye-Abarim encampment, 2:427, 2:449
Iyye-Abarim encampment, 2:440
Iyyim, 2:434
Izhar, 1:443
Izhar, son of Kohath, 1:109
　clan of, 1:126
　genealogy of, 1:125

Jachinites
　second census, 2:259
Jacob, 1:440
　Balaam's parable, 2:154–155
　blessing of sons, 1:91–92
　deathbed blessing, 2:273–274
　drink offering, 2:333
　end of days, 2:190
　Esau and, 2:35–36, 2:39
　Esau parts from, 2:403
　greater younger brother, 2:318–319
　Israel and, 2:196, 2:198
　Joseph's primogeniture and, 2:317
　on Levites, 2:274–275
　Nazirites and, 1:159
　not to 'see the ground', 2:408
　perpetuating name, 2:303
　promise to, 1:98, 1:261
　promised Canaan, 1:42
　represented by lambs, 2:339
　return in peace, 1:171
　sells Joseph, 2:317–318
　sons of, 2:266
　three–generation house, 2:295
　Transjordan land, 2:404
　twelve sons and zodiac, 1:23–22
　twelve sons of, 1:84, 1:85, 1:98, 1:120
　vows, 2:354, 2:358
　YHWH's promise, 2:307
　YHWH's promise to, 1:194
Jael
　the serpent and, 2:196

Jahaz, 2:79–80
Jahleelites
　second census, 2:260
Jahzeelites
　second census, 2:261
Jair (location), 2:399–400
Jair, son of, 2:418
Jair, son of Manasseh, 2:399–400
Jaminites
　second census, 2:259
Jashubites
　second census, 2:260
Jazer, 2:82, 2:399, 2:403, 2:406, 2:417
　livestock and, 2:398
jealousy, 1:32
Jebusites
　population and, 1:101
Jehoshaphat
　symbolic numbers, 1:103
Jephthah
　foolish vow of, 2:356
Jericho, 2:449
　after the plague, 2:278
　encampment near, 2:427
　first conquest, 2:279
　journey to, 2:265
　taking Canaan, 2:428
Jeroboam, 1:226
Jerome
　title of Numbers, 1:2
Jerusalem
　Essenes Temple Scroll, 1:19–20
　holy city, 1:40
　Isaiah's vision, 1:222
　John's vision, 1:20–21
　New, 1:174–175, 1:240
　pilgrim festivals, 1:166
　pilgrimage to, 2:347
　Solomon's Temple, 2:237
　Tabernacle and, 1:40
　trumpets depicted, 1:223
Jerusalem Temple
　YHWH's Name dwells in, 1:172
Jesus Christ, 1:315
　Aaron's staff and, 1:455
　church as bride, 2:256–257
　cup of wrath, 1:154
　Feast of Booths, 2:344
　Good Shepherd, 2:279, 2:311

Jesus Christ (cont.)
  human words, 2:370
  humility of, 1:454–455
  Lamb of God, 2:338
  the light of, 1:170
  the Messiah, 2:207
  Moses and, 1:313
  Moses and the serpent, 2:87
  resurrection, 1:455
  sacrifical death, 1:501
  sacrifice and, 2:351
  salvation, 2:484
  shepherd and sheep, 1:2
  soldiers of God, 2:398
  union with church, 2:234
  vows, 2:361
  waters of Holy Spirit, 2:50
Jethro, 1:63
  Moses and, 1:209, 1:229–230
Jezerites
  second census, 2:261
Jiezerites
  second census, 2:260
Job
  vows, 2:354
Jochebed
  Aaron, Moses and Miriam, 2:275
Jochebed, wife of Amram, 2:261
Joel
  prophecy of, 1:313–314
Jogbehah, 2:399, 2:417
Jonah
  vows, 2:354–355
Jordan
  name of, 2:434
Jordan River, 1:67
  Canaan borders, 2:453
Joseph, son of Jacob, 1:293, 1:306
  brothers conspire against, 2:245
  descendants of, 2:270–271, 2:493
  Egypt and livestock, 2:404
  exile and return, 2:317–320
  firstborn son, 2:405
  Gilead chieftains, 2:490
  Nazirites and, 1:159, 2:319
  scouts narrative and, 2:317–318
  sold for five shekels, 1:129
  son Ephraim, 1:87
  sons of, 2:260

spirit of YHWH, 2:312
  in the wilderness, 2:318
  Zelophehad's daughters, 2:319, 2:320–321
Joseph, tribe of
  census, 1:77–78
  second census, 2:265–266
  tribal ordering, 1:96
  tribe arrangement, 1:76–77
Joshua, son of Nun, 1:66, 1:241
  Amalek battle, 2:315
  against Amalekites, 2:71
  angel with sword, 2:137
  assumed leadership, 2:282
  assumes leadership, 2:311–317, 2:320
  assumes leadership from Moses, 2:280–281
  Baal Peor incident, 2:234
  battle of Edrei, 2:82
  battles Amalek, 2:199
  and Caleb, 1:342–344
  Canaan and, 1:360
  Canaanite's shade removed, 2:271
  chosen new leader, 2:310–313
  compared to Moses, 1:72
  conquests, 1:63, 2:59
  crosses Jordan, 2:214
  descended from Joseph, 2:317
  division of land, 2:428, 2:484
  excepted from judgement, 2:32, 2:276
  exception, 2:261, 2:279, 2:290
  first appearance, 1:261
  good shepherd, 2:322
  identity of, 1:282
  Jacob on younger brother, 2:318
  jealous of Moses, 1:296
  land distribution, 2:458
  land division, 2:456
  land granted by YHWH, 2:274
  leadership, 2:206
  leadership of, 1:11
  loyalty to YHWH, 2:398
  man of spirit, 2:310
  Moses and, 1:281, 1:283
  Moses renames, 1:366
  name from Hoshea, 1:326–327
  not responsible for Midianites, 2:378
  presence in Tent, 1:278
  prophecy about, 1:276

INDEX OF SUBJECTS   691

prophecy of leadership, 1:281
as protégé, 1:357
protests prophesying, 1:245
Rahab's house, 2:295
the rebellion and, 1:343–344
saved by loyalty, 2:408
as scout, 1:9
scout from Ephraim tribe, 1:87
sends spies, 1:324–325, 1:330
shepherd, 1:86
spared YHWH's judgement, 1:353–355
succeeds Moses, 2:278, 2:307–308
transfer to tribe of Ephraim, 2:318
wilderness and, 1:2
YHWH names leaders, 2:436
younger generation, 1:326
Jotbathah encampment, 2:426, 2:440, 2:447
Jubilee
  atonement, 2:473
  Day of Atonement, 2:489
  meaning, 2:489
  Zelophehad's daughters and, 2:488–489
Judah, 2:207
Judah, son of Jacob
  atonement and, 1:87
  sells Joseph, 1:129
Judah, tribe of
  arrangement of Camp, 1:18, 1:82, 1:228
  Balaam's Chronicle, 2:270
  blowing of trumpets, 1:226
  Caleb as chieftain, 2:428, 2:459–460
  census, 1:76, 1:87, 1:92–93
  census figures, 1:93
  change in population, 2:266, 2:267
  David and, 1:98
  eastern arrangement, 1:92–93
  emblem of, 1:29
  first in honour, 1:94
  flag of, 1:29
  inherits southern region, 2:454
  land inheritance, 2:267
  leadership prophecy, 1:95
  leading tribes, 1:83
  Leo zodiacal sign, 1:23–24
  lion figure, 1:91
Lion/Leo emblem, 1:28
march from Sinai, 1:236
Nahshon as chieftain, 1:78
offerings, 1:189
offerings of, 1:176, 1:183
order of departure, 1:92
prominence of, 1:86–87
second census, 2:260, 2:270
setting out on journey, 1:206
standard of, 1:29, 1:83, 1:238
tribal arrangement, 1:75, 1:96
trumpets and, 1:224
Judaism
  Moses and Christianity, 1:313

Kadesh
  disbelief in YHWH, 2:32–34
  encampment, 2:440, 2:444
  encampment in, 2:426
  king of Edom and, 2:2
  Moses rebels, 2:280
  to Mount Hor, 2:447
  rebellion at, 2:407
  sanctified, 2:10, 2:33–4, 2:45–46
  scouts, 2:409–410
  water from rock, 1:16–29, 2:6, 2:45
  Wilderness of Zin, 2:447
  YHWH and leaders, 2:30
Kadesh Barnea, 1:311
  Canaan's border and, 2:428
  Canaan's borders, 2:454
  scouts episode, 2:445
  Wilderness of Paran, 2:445–446
Kedesh
  asylum city, 2:466
Kehelathah encampment, 2:426, 2:440
Kemuel, son of Shiphtan
  chieftain, 2:428, 2:459
Kenath (Nobah), 2:400
Kenites, 2:199, 2:210
  Balaam and, 2:200–201
  location, 2:207
Ketef Hinnom amulets, 1:173
Keturah, wife of Abraham, 1:292
Khothites, 1:452
Kibroth, 1:227
Kibroth-hattaavah, 1:245
Kibroth-hattaavah/Burial of Cravers, 1:242, 1:289, 1:310

Kibroth-Hattaavah encampment, 2:426, 2:440, 2:447
Kimhi
  on *midbar*, 1:2
kingship
  Shofar, 2:341
  theme of Balaam's chronicle, 2:259
kinship and family
  Adam to Zelophehad's daughters, 2:495
  ancient Israel, 2:294–296
  blood avengers, 2:469
  defining, 1:147
  keeping land within, 2:485–495
  Reuben and Gad, 2:405
Kiriathaim, 2:399, 2:417
Kohath, son of Levi, 1:92, 1:109, 2:275
Kohath, tribe of, 1:84, 1:92
  accounts of, 1:119
  assured survival, 2:269
  clan duties, 1:110, 1:111, 1:116
  clan duties at Tent, 1:111–112
  duties, 1:123, 1:126, 1:127, 1:136, 1:176, 1:466
  Eleazar directs, 1:187
  genealogy, 1:125
  Hebronites, 2:275
  hierarchy, 1:130, 1:134
  leadership, 1:10
  march from Sinai, 1:236
  no land inheritance, 2:261
  order of departure, 1:92
  priesthood, 2:275–276
  second census, 2:276
  transport duties, 1:133, 1:206, 1:228, 1:229
  transport holy furnishings, 1:186, 1:187
  trumpets and, 1:224
Korah
  aftermath, 2:230
  approach the Holy One, 1:90
  argument of, 1:402
  Cain and Abel parallels, 1:432–433
  census and, 1:107
  contrast to Zelophehad, 2:285–286
  death of, 1:429–431, 1:453
  disinheritance and, 2:268
  envy, 1:408–409
  judgement on, 1:422–423, 1:435–439, 1:436–439
  Kehelathah encampment, 2:440
  Levites and, 1:406, 2:50
  Moses and Aaron, 2:310
  pedigree of, 1:442
  plague on followers, 1:433–439
  presumption of, 1:404
  pseudo-community, 1:424, 1:427–428, 1:435
  pseudo priesthood, 1:420
  rebellion of, 1:11, 1:43–44, 1:122, 1:187, 1:199, 1:302, 1:397–400, 1:406–431, 1:443, 1:449, 1:496, 2:45, 2:241, 2:278, 2:279, 2:357
  receives no gifts, 1:187
  sons survive, 2:259, 2:267, 2:269
  swallowed into earth, 1:399
  theology of, 1:452
  tribe decreases, 2:266
  Zelophehad not involved with, 2:486
Korahites
  no land inheritance, 2:261
  from son of Izhar, 2:275

Lamech
  avenging Abel's death, 2:477
lampstand
  Aaron attends, 1:192–194
  almond tree and, 1:193–194
  transport of, 1:229
land
  casting lots, 2:273–274
  clan size and, 2:273–274
  compliance with, 2:401
  concepts of, 2:296–299
  covenant community and, 2:303–304
  to daughters, 2:281–282
  daughters and, 2:304–306
  inheritance, 2:347
  inheritance of, 2:397
  keeping in the tribe, 2:485–495
  Moses and, 2:273
  Transjordan, 2:455–456
  worship and, 2:348–352
  YHWH names leaders, 2:428
  YHWH on borders, 2:483
  YHWH's instructions, 2:261
  see also food

INDEX OF SUBJECTS 693

leadership
  Aaron and Moses, 1:120
  Moses, 1:227
  Moses requests spirit in, 2:309–315
  Numbers theme of, 1:10–12
  obedience and, 1:225
  YHWH, 1:12–13
  YHWH and, 1:213
Leah
  Levi and, 1:464
  ranking of sons, 1:93
  Reuben and Gad, 2:405
  son prioritized, 1:95, 1:96
Lebo
  Canaan's border and, 2:428
Lebo-Hamath, 2:455
leprosy
  cleansing, 1:200
  divine punishment, 1:51–52
  expulsion for, 1:48, 1:49–50
  flakes like snow, 1:304
  Hansen's disease, 1:140
  idolatry and, 1:52
  Miriam and, 1:46, 1:58, 1:242, 1:303–308
  Miriam's flakes, 1:293–294
  purification offerings, 1:486
  purification rituals, 1:489
  purity acts and, 1:306, 1:308–309
  purity laws, 1:46, 1:137, 1:142, 1:145–147
  Uzziah and, 1:305
  wilderness and, 1:60
  word-play, 1:51
Levi, son of Jacob
  descendants, 1:109–110
  sons of, 2:275
Levi, tribe of
  covenant of life and peace, 2:238
  genealogy, 1:125
  hierarchy of, 1:134
  kinship structure, 2:296
  see also Levites
Levites
  Aaron and, 1:444
  Aaron's house and, 1:123
  accounts of, 1:119
  age of service, 1:184, 1:200–201
  apart from rebellion, 1:365
  appointment of, 1:182
  asylum cities, 2:462–467
  belong to YHWH, 1:110–111
  Cain and Abel, 1:432–433
  in the Camp, 1:29
  camp around Dwelling, 1:273
  Camp arrangement, 1:18, 1:19, 1:77, 1:78, 1:80–81, 1:82, 1:83
  census, 1:104–105, 1:127–130
  cities of, 2:297, 2:417, 2:435, 2:480
  cities of asylum, 2:480, 2:484
  clans of, 2:261
  cleansing and dedicating, 1:184, 1:185, 1:194–195, 1:200, 1:203–204
  death of Aaron, 2:49
  duties of, 1:84, 1:85, 1:89–91, 1:94, 1:109–113, 1:136, 1:176, 1:192, 1:194–200, 1:204, 1:263, 1:441–442, 1:457, 1:463–468, 2:228
  exclusion of, 1:97
  Feast of Booths, 2:346
  firstborn and, 1:118, 1:134, 1:203
  firstborn story of, 1:440–455
  genealogy of, 1:124–127
  as gift to Aaron, 1:124
  as gift to YHWH, 1:204
  gifts to, 1:182
  given pastureland, 2:461–462
  gold plunder to, 2:391–392
  golden calf, 2:242
  golden calf episode, 1:204
  grades of holiness, 1:97
  granted 48 cities, 2:274–275
  granted cities, 2:460–464
  guard the Tent, 1:94
  guard the Tent of Meeting, 1:497
  hand-leaning, 1:184, 1:196–197
  inheritance of, 1:475–477
  inner camp of, 1:43–44, 1:60, 1:134–135
  installation of, 1:236
  Korah and, 1:402, 1:406
  Korah's rebellion, 1:11, 1:402, 2:50
  leadership, 1:10
  loyalty of, 2:238
  microcosm of creation, 1:41–42
  Midian plunder and, 2:376
  movement of Camp, 1:92
  no land inheritance, 2:269, 2:274–275, 2:297, 2:458

Levites (*cont.*)
  offerings to, 1:496–498
  omission from census, 1:88–89
  pastureland, 2:463
  pastureland and cities for, 2:438
  pastures and cities, 2:435
  in place of firstborn, 1:186
  plunder from Midianites, 2:373
  plunder offerings, 2:392–398
  priesthood and, 1:121, 1:134
  priestly blessings, 1:53
  Psalms of Ascent, 1:166–167
  purification rites, 1:179–180
  refuge cities, 2:435
  release from obligations, 1:204
  replace firstborn, 1:213, 1:198
  responsibilities of, 2:275
  revolt over priesthood, 1:135
  role of, 1:184–185, 1:414–415
  roles and duties, 1:229
  second census, 2:268
  separation of, 1:184, 1:412
  set apart, 1:79, 1:124, 1:129–130, 1:194–200
  special duties of, 1:115–120
  special status, 1:435, 1:436–437
  stand for firstborn, 1:194
  status of, 1:441
  structure of Camp, 1:48–49
  tithes, 1:477–479, 2:275, 2:297, 2:395
  transport duties, 1:130–134
  transport of Tabernacle, 1:200
  transport the Dwelling, 1:4, 1:5
  transportation duties, 1:186
  travel in midst of others, 1:228
  tribal exclusion, 1:96
  vows in marriage, 2:360
  war plunder to, 2:388–389
  YHWH at a distance, 1:92
  YHWH grants cities, 2:484
  YHWH provides pastures and cities, 2:429
  YHWH's instructions, 1:109–113, 1:179–180
  Zimri and Cozbi's intrusion, 2:242
Leviticus, Book of
  bridge from Exodus, 1:18
  end of Exodus, 1:6–8
  Israel's cult, 1:166
  purity laws, 1:146
  role of priesthood, 1:202
  role of priests, 1:121
  Tent of Meeting, 1:120
  theme of, 1:5
Libhnah encampment, 2:426, 2:440, 2:447
Libini, son of Gershon, 1:109
Libnite, tribe of, 1:109
  duties of, 1:126
Libnites
  no land inheritance, 2:261
  from son of Gershon, 2:275
Libweh
  Canaan's borders, 2:454
light
  YHWH's blessing and, 1:170
lions
  Balaam's oracle and, 2:186–187
  Balaam's prophecies, 2:198
livestock
  Midian plunder, 2:373
  plunder distribution, 2:402–403
Lot
  daughters of, 2:216
  descendants in Moab, 2:114, 2:197
  descendants of, 2:57, 2:80
  Transjordan land, 2:403, 2:404, 2:405
  vision of, 2:179
Lot's wife, 1:231
Luke
  laws from angels, 1:39
  on Stephen's speech, 1:73

Machir, clan of
  Egypt and, 2:421–422
  given Gilead, 2:271
  lands granted to, 2:416, 2:417
  second census, 2:260
  Transjordan lands, 2:399
  Zelophehad's daughters, 2:418, 2:423
Machir, son of Manasseh
  Zelophehad's inheritance and, 2:485
Machit
  Hezron and, 2:304
magic
  curses and, 2:120–121
  Israel's resistance to, 2:156
  priests and, 1:156

as whoredom, 2:216
Mahlah (location), 2:305, 2:306
Mahli, son of Merari, 1:109
Mahlite clan, 1:127
Mahlites
  no land inheritance, 2:261
  from sons of Merari, 2:275
Makheloth encampment, 2:426, 2:440
Malachi
  on vows, 2:355
Malchielites
  second census, 2:260
Manasseh
  firstborn of Joseph, 2:405
  granted Gilead, 2:399
  perpetuating name, 2:303
  settlement in Canaan, 2:80
  Transjordan lands, 2:425
Manasseh, son of Joseph
  firstborn, 2:318, 2:319
Manasseh, tribe of
  added to Transjordan settlements, 2:420
  arrangement of Camp, 1:82
  Canaan pledge, 2:403–404
  census, 1:77
  census figures, 1:93
  census total, 1:87
  change in population, 2:267
  chieftain Gamaliel, 1:78
  chieftains of, 1:213
  conquest pledge, 2:401
  Egypt and, 2:421–422
  Gilead and, 2:418
  given Transjordan land, 2:399–400
  half-tribe, 1:67
  Hanniel as chieftain, 2:428, 2:459–460
  Joseph and, 2:318
  land across the Jordan, 1:108
  land inheritance, 2:267
  lands granted to, 2:416–419
  lands to, 2:397
  location names and, 2:305–306
  march from Sinai, 1:236
  offering of, 1:183
  offerings of, 1:177–8
  second census, 2:260, 2:266, 2:270–271, 2:317, 2:317–320, 2:421

setting out on journey, 1:207
settlement, 2:88
settles east of Jordan, 2:271
split Levitical cities, 2:463
Transjordan history, 2:421–424
Transjordan lands, 2:428, 2:455–456
tribal ordering, 1:96, 1:97
tribe arrangement, 1:76
Zelophehad and, 2:289–291
Zelophehad's daughters, 2:291, 2:404–405
Zelophehad's inheritance, 2:485–495
zodiacal sign, 1:23
Manoah
  burnt offering, 2:333
Marah encampment, 1:2, 2:426, 2:440, 2:444
  bitter waters, 1:158, 2:443
marriage
  covenant, 2:369, 2:371
  covenant community and, 2:495
  jealousy and, 1:149–151
  levirate, 2:290
  levirite, 2:321
  levite, 2:301–302
  purity laws and, 1:47, 1:48, 1:54, 1:138–139, 1:148–158
  strayed wife, 2:251–254
  tribe and, 2:487
  wife's vows, 2:363–365
Masoretic Text, 1:73–74
Mattanah, 2:449
Medad, 1:245, 1:247, 1:248, 1:268, 1:296, 1:310, 1:312
  prophesying, 1:241–242, 1:275–84, 1:300
Melah (Salt), 2:434
men
  jealousy and, 1:149–151
  Nazirite vow and, 1:139–140
  paternity of children, 1:152–53
  vows to YHWH, 2:352
  women's vows and, 2:352, 2:357, 2:360–367, 2:367–370
Merari, clan of, 1:84, 1:92, 1:127
  accounts of, 1:119
  clan duties, 1:112–113, 1:116, 1:136, 1:176
  genealogy of, 1:125

Merari, clan of (*cont.*)
  hierarchy, 1:130, 1:134
  Ithamar supervises, 1:187
  march from Sinai, 1:236
  order of departure, 1:92
  second census, 2:276
  son of Levi, 2:275
  transport duties, 1:134, 1:206, 1:229
  transport of Dwelling, 1:186–187
  trumpets and, 1:224
Merari, son of Levi, 1:92, 1:109
  duties of, 1:110
Mesopotamia
  astrology and, 1:25
  symbolic numbers, 1:103
Messiah
  Messianic times, 2:190–191
  prophecies of, 2:35
  Sabbath and, 2:335
  YHWH and, 2:203
Messianism
  arrangement of Camp and, 1:99
  descent from Judah, 1:86
  dynasty of, 1:88
  Nazirites and, 1:159
  prophecy of, 1:45
  Ruth and hope, 2:340
  Simeon Bar Kochba, 2:194
  Spirit and, 1:277
Micaiah ben Imlah, 1:277
Michael, Archangel
  heavenly camp, 1:29
Miciah
  YHWH's throne, 1:221
Midian
  Balaam and, 2:123
  threat to Israel, 2:449
Midianite war
  drama of, 2:397–398
Midianites
  Baal Peor conspiracy, 2:213–214, 2:245–247
  conquest of, 2:371–392
  conspire with Balaam, 2:257
  corpse pollution and, 2:386–387
  Cozbi family and status, 2:243–244
  encounters with, 1:229, 1:231
  fate of captives, 2:384–387, 2:394–395
  Israel's victory over, 2:264–265
  kings slain, 2:372, 2:381–382
  no loss for Israel, 2:396
  plunder from, 2:372–373, 2:387–398
  plunder of, 1:67
  Reuel, 1:207
  seek union with Simeonites, 2:246
  vengeance on, 1:226, 2:375, 2:376, 2:377–384
  war captives, 2:372, 2:373, 2:383, 2:384
  women, 2:55, 2:384–386
  women slain, 2:373
  Zipporah, 1:292
  see also Cozbi
Migdol encampment, 2:426, 2:440, 2:443
Milcah (location), 2:305
military forces
  census and, 1:101
  census figures, 1:88
  symbolic numbers, 1:103
Miriam
  Aaron and, 1:306–307
  Aaron's death and, 2:44
  burial at Kadesh, 2:6, 2:10
  complains, 1:245
  death of, 1:499, 2:1, 2:4, 2:11–12, 2:42, 2:275, 2:448
  delays journey, 1:247–248
  derides Moses, 1:311–312, 1:315
  dissension, 1:227
  divine punishment, 1:51
  exclusion of, 2:4
  exile and return, 1:242, 1:246, 1:249, 1:284, 1:290, 1:303, 1:307–309
  expelled from Camp, 1:46
  family of, 1:308
  first generation, 2:10
  genealogy of, 2:261
  identification of, 1:291
  judgement of, 1:296–297
  leprosy, 1:58, 1:60, 1:246, 1:251, 1:293–294, 1:303–308, 1:310, 2:11
  Levite genealogy, 2:275
  rebellion and, 1:289
  represents Israel, 1:307, 1:310–311
  represents prophets, 2:11
  sibling of Moses, 1:100
  slanders Moses, 1:43, 1:58, 1:290–6
  speaks against Moses, 2:219, 2:357

INDEX OF SUBJECTS   697

water supply, 2:12
YHWH rebukes, 1:299–303
Mishael
  carries Nadab and Abihu, 1:214
Mishnah
  on Mosaic authorship, 1:70
Mithcah encampment, 2:440
Mithkah encampment, 2:426
Moab and Moabites
  Baal of Peor, 2:211
  Balak, 2:57
  camp at, 1:65
  conquest of, 2:206
  daughters of, 2:216, 2:284
  descendants of Lot, 2:114, 2:246
  dispossession of, 2:197–198
  encampment in, 2:427
  harlotry and, 1:11
  Israel and whoring, 2:210–211
  Israel's approach, 2:86–88
  Israel's domination, 2:192
  Israel's harlotry in, 2:215–218
  location, 2:207
  Lot's descendants, 2:57, 2:197
  Machir and, 2:422
  Moabite women, 2:55
  Phinehas slays Cozbi, 2:211
  plains of, 2:267
  threat to Israel, 2:449
  women of, 1:59, 2:215, 2:218, 2:252
  YHWH's anger at whoring, 2:220–221
  see also Balak
Moabite women, 2:57
Molech, 2:216
Moserah/Moseroth
  encampment, 2:426, 2:440, 2:447
Moses
  Aaron and Miriam deride, 1:315
  Aaron petitions, 1:305–306
  Aaron's death and, 2:44
  Aaron's successor and, 1:11
  abuse of office, 2:24–25
  addresses the ark, 1:207
  Amalekite victory altar, 2:269
  appeal for guidance, 1:232
  approach to Edom, 2:53–54
  'Arise, O YHWH!', 1:13, 1:65
  ark in battle, 1:235

  arrangement of Camp, 1:81, 1:91, 1:92
  ascends to Mt Abarim, 2:282
  authority of, 1:41, 1:248, 1:296–297, 1:311, 1:436, 1:438, 2:44–45, 2:415–416
  Baal Peor, 2:234, 2:249
  Balaam's narrative and, 2:60, 2:206
  burden of, 1:262
  burial of the complainers, 1:289–290
  Canaan for remaining tribes, 2:428
  challenge to, 1:296
  character of, 1:282, 2:14, 2:28–30
  character of YHWH, 2:279
  chieftains and, 1:182
  choose Aaron, 1:46
  on the Cloud, 1:221
  compromise on Transjordan, 2:410–414
  consecration of Dwelling, 1:4
  counts firstborn, 1:118
  crises and intercessions, 1:65
  crisis of, 1:257–262, 1:273
  curses on scroll, 1:154
  Cushite wife, 1:297, 1:361–362, 2:227
  Cushite woman, 1:291–296, 1:314–315
  Dathan and Abiram, 2:297
  dealing judgements, 1:215
  death for female captives, 2:394
  death of, 1:66–67, 2:46–48, 2:78, 2:280, 2:306–311, 2:315–317, 2:322, 2:357, 2:376, 2:397
  Decalogue, 1:274
  directs Levites in transport, 1:187
  disobeys YHWH, 2:44–48
  distributes war plunder, 2:387–389
  distribution of plunder, 2:396
  donkeys and, 1:419
  Edom refuses crossing, 2:34–41
  Egyptian education of, 1:71
  Eldad and Medad, 1:275
  elders/scribes, 1:263–264
  Eleazer and, 1:433–434
  entreats for people, 2:66–68
  envy of, 1:408–409
  Exodus role of, 1:85
  farewell speech, 2:371
  feeding the population, 1:108
  final intercession for leader, 2:280
  first census, 2:265

Moses (cont.)
  first generation, 2:10
  forbidden from Canaan, 2:61
  foretaste of conquest, 2:88
  genealogy of, 2:261
  Gershon's name, 1:215
  gold for Levites, 2:391–392
  golden calf and, 1:260, 1:348, 1:418, 2:239, 2:251
  grants Transjordan lands, 2:416
  grumbling against, 1:317–319
  Hobab and, 1:207, 1:209, 1:230–232, 1:236, 1:238–239, 1:295
  humility of, 1:297–298
  hungry complainers, 1:250–258
  hungry people and, 1:240–242
  impending death of, 2:378
  inner Camp, 1:135
  instruction for Camp, 1:228
  intercession with YHWH, 1:366
  interprets YHWH, 2:228
  Jesus and, 1:313
  Jethro's daughters, 2:28
  Joshua and, 1:281, 1:283
  Joshua as protégé, 1:327–328, 1:357
  Joshua succeeds, 2:456, 2:458
  journey to Promised Land, 2:279–280
  judges and, 2:222
  Kadesh rebellion and, 2:424
  Korah and, 1:397–400
  Korah's rebellion, 1:406-31
  land inheritance instructions, 2:261
  leadership, 1:281–284, 1:415–420, 2:40
  leadership goes to Joshua, 2:312–315
  leadership of, 1:10, 1:120, 1:227, 1:247, 1:257, 1:268
  leadership of journey, 2:441
  leadership to Joshua, 2:322
  led by YHWH, 1:239
  leprous hand, 1:51
  Levite genealogy, 2:275
  Levites and, 1:89, 1:109
  lineage of, 1:121
  loss of leadership, 2:32
  manna and, 2:12
  march from Sinai, 1:236
  mediation of, 1:9, 1:214, 1:219, 1:251, 1:256–257, 1:258, 1:269, 1:274, 1:345–355, 1:394, 1:433–439

  Messenger of YHWH, 2:36–37
  Midian gold to Tent, 2:375
  Midianite captives, 2:384–387
  Midianites and, 1:226, 1:229–230
  Miriam and Aaron against, 2:219
  Miriam slanders, 1:58
  misrepresents YHWH, 1:59, 2:1–2, 2:3, 2:4–34
  on Mt Sinai, 1:109
  in the Nile, 2:12
  obedience of, 1:90
  objects to Transjordan land, 2:406–410
  offering laws, 1:372-4
  older generation, 2:234
  orders death of captives, 2:372
  parting words to Israel, 1:1
  Passover and, 1:204–205, 1:213
  patriarch's descendants, 1:88
  place in Camp, 1:127
  pleads for Israel, 1:244
  pleads for Miriam, 1:307
  pleads for people, 1:288
  possible author of Numbers, 1:69–73
  post-battle rituals, 2:384
  prays for new leader, 2:283, 2:307–308, 2:309–315
  preparations for Canaan, 2:434–435, 2:436
  prophecy about, 1:276
  prophecy of death, 1:281
  as prophet, 1:42, 1:44, 1:50, 1:60, 1:66, 1:70, 1:295, 1:296, 1:299–303, 1:310–314, 1:425, 1:435, 2:11, 2:110
  purity laws, 1:52
  rebellions against, 1:340–345, 2:357
  rebellion at Kadesh, 2:282
  rebellion of, 2:308, 2:315, 2:317, 2:320
  refuses Reubenites and Gadites, 2:398, 2:423–424
  registers genealogies, 1:87
  rejects Transjordan request, 2:403–406
  response to Korah, 1:412
  responsibilities of, 1:260–262
  revelation within Tent, 1:97
  role of Levite, 1:184–185
  scouts report to, 1:333–341
  second census, 2:259, 2:276, 2:277
  sees Canaan, 2:307

sends out scouts, 1:316–317, 1:322, 1:323
serpent standard, 2:68–72, 2:87–88, 2:269
serpents, 2:50
sets up the Dwelling, 1:175–176
siblings of, 1:100
slandered, 1:42–43, 1:290–296, 1:299
song about tribes, 1:23
'Song of the Ark', 2:480
Song of the Sea, 2:86–87
sons of, 1:100, 1:124
speaks to YHWH, 1:127, 1:183, 1:185, 1:192, 1:274–275
stunned by harlotry, 2:241
support of Zelophehad, 2:287
Tent of Meeting and, 1:6–8, 1:9, 1:18, 1:212
Tharbis, 1:292
Torah and, 1:300, 1:311
transgressions of, 1:45
Transjordan compromise, 2:398–399, 2:401, 2:404–405, 2:424–425, 2:455–456
Transjordan requests, 2:404–410
tribes and, 1:75, 1:77
trumpets and, 1:206, 1:210
vengeance on Midians, 2:371, 2:377, 2:394
vision of Canaan, 2:483
on vows, 2:352, 2:355, 2:356–357
warned against Moab, 2:114
water from rock, 2:16–29, 2:244, 2:308, 2:315
wife Zipporah, 1:292, 2:112
wilderness and, 1:2
YHWH above the ark, 1:190–192
YHWH and, 1:72–73
YHWH speaks to, 1:75, 1:78, 1:124, 1:137–140, 1:179, 1:202, 1:276, 1:296–297, 1:497
YHWH's command, 1:82
YHWH's commitment, 1:167–168
YHWH's instructions, 1:116
Zelophehad's daughters, 2:280, 2:282, 2:284, 2:291
Zelophehad's inheritance, 2:485–495
murder and manslaughter
asylum cities, 2:429–430, 2:464

blood avengers, 2:469
high priest and, 2:469–473, 2:484
innocent murderer, 2:468–473
intentional and malicious, 2:467–468
logic of asylum cities, 2:473–479
purity of land, 2:484
YHWH on, 2:438
Mushi, son of Merari, 1:109
Mushite tribe, 1:127
no land inheritance, 2:261
from sons of Merari, 2:275

Naamanites
second census, 2:260
Naboth, 2:286
Nadab, son of Aaron, 1:109, 1:428, 1:430, 1:446
body carried, 1:214
death of, 1:122, 1:127, 1:435, 2:30, 2:261, 2:275–276, 2:279
fate of, 1:155
genealogy of, 1:125
no land inheritance, 2:267
son of Aaron, 1:100
Nahaliel, 2:449
Nahbi
meaning of name, 1:327
Nahbi, son of Vophsi, 1:316
Nahshon, son of Amminadab
ancestor of Boaz, 1:86
Judah chieftain, 1:78, 1:180
leadership, 1:10
offerings of, 1:176, 1:183
offerings to altar, 1:189
setting out on journey, 1:206
tribe arrangement, 1:75
Naomi
journeys with Israel, 1:231
Naphtali, tribe of
arrangement of Camp, 1:82
census, 1:77, 1:87, 1:93
change in population, 2:266, 2:267
chieftain Ahira, 1:79
offerings of, 1:178, 1:183
Pedahel as chieftain, 2:428, 2:459–460
second census, 2:272
tribal arrangement, 1:76, 1:96
zodiacal sign, 1:23
Nazirites, 1:312

Nazirites (*cont.*)
  abstentions and purification, 1:160–166
  benediction, 1:174
  cleansing from pollution, 1:237
  corpse pollution and, 1:52, 1:58–59, 1:161–162, 2:9
  food and, 1:252, 1:253
  generational change, 1:500
  grape abstention, 1:160–162
  hair and, 1:160–166
  Hannah's vow and, 2:356
  holiness of Israel and, 1:203
  Joseph and, 2:319
  ordination of priests, 1:164
  origins and meaning of, 1:159–160
  Passover and, 1:210
  Phinehas and, 2:237–238
  purification, 1:162–166
  purity laws and, 1:47–48, 1:139–140, 1:142, 1:144, 1:149
  purity paradigm, 1:54–58
  sacrifice and, 2:351
  separation, 1:162–163
  separation for purity, 2:218
  setback, 1:212
  spiritual harlotry and, 1:158
  transgression, 1:162
  tributes and offerings, 1:374, 1:376
  vow, 1:43, 1:397, 2:58, 2:359, 2:371, 2:396
  waters of impurity, 1:487
  zeal and loyalty, 2:408
Nebo, 2:398, 2:399, 2:417
Nebo encampment, 2:427
Negev, 2:454
  Canaan's border and, 2:428
Nemuel
  second census, 2:259
Nephtali, tribe of
  march from Sinai, 1:236
Nethanel
  chieftain for Issachar tribe, 1:78
  offerings of, 1:176, 1:183
  setting out on journey, 1:206
New Moon
  feast, 2:328–329
Nimrah, 2:398
Nimrod, 1:291

Noah, 2:495
  burnt offerings, 2:330, 2:334
  symbolic age, 1:103
Noah (settlement), 2:305, 2:306
Nobah
  seizes Kenath, 2:418
Nobah (location), 2:400
Nobah, son of Manasseh, 2:400
Numbers, Book of
  authorship of Moses, 1:69–73
  Camp of Israel, 1:64–66
  character of, 1:3
  composition of, 1:68–73
  covenant community, 1:166
  Deuteronomy and, 1:9–12
  Greek translation, 1:73–74
  land of Israel, 1:64, 1:66
  leadership and, 1:10–12
  Masoretic Text of, 1:73–74
  not chronological, 1:63
  origin of title, 1:2
  purity laws, 1:46–60
  theme of, 1:5
  as three books, 1:234
  threefold structure, 1:61–67
  two generations, 1:67–68
  wilderness sojourn, 1:64, 1:66

oaths and oath-breaking
  divine punishment, 1:51–52
  purity laws, 1:47, 1:138, 1:142, 1:143, 1:147–148
  ritual of, 1:154
Obadiah, 2:197
obedience
  the Cloud and, 1:217–219, 1:237
  the Decalogue, 1:393–394
  leadership and, 1:225
Oboth, 2:51
Oboth encampment, 2:427, 2:440, 2:449
offerings
  annual, 2:326, 2:337–338
  from Balak, 2:90–92, 2:99, 2:149–151
  bread, 1:378, 1:394
  burnt, 1:394, 2:346, 2:350
  burnt aroma, 1:375–376
  calendar of worship, 2:322–325
  covenant community, 2:242
  daily, 2:326, 2:329–335

daily worship, 2:322
of elevation, 1:471–472, 1:497
from the fire, 1:470–471, 1:497
firstborn fruits, 1:497
firstborn of the womb, 1:456–457
firstfruits, 1:379
firstfruits of the womb, 1:472–474
food, 1:165
laws and types, 1:366–372
laws for, 1:371
life in the land, 2:348–352
Moabites and, 2:217
monthly, 2:323, 2:326, 2:336–337
Passover, 2:337–339
peace, 2:346
present–/future–oriented, 1:370
for priests, 1:460
to priests and Levites, 1:496–498
Sabbath, 2:322
seven feasts, 2:328–329
sin and, 1:379–380
spoils of war, 2:58
spring and autumn festivals, 2:349–350
summary, 2:346–347
table of, 2:345
tithes, 1:457
tithes to Levites, 1:477–479
tributes/freewill, 1:370–377
types of, 1:371, 1:394
Unleavened Bread, 2:337
vow and freewill, 2:347
vows, 2:354–356, 2:355–356
war plunder, 2:390
weekly, 2:326, 2:335–336
Weeks, 2:337
wine, 1:394, 1:396
YHWH's instructions, 2:326–329
Og, king, 2:52, 2:55, 2:184–185, 2:200, 2:407
conquest of, 2:271, 2:379, 2:397
defeat of, 2:244
threat to Israel, 2:449
victory over, 2:79, 2:82–84, 2:111, 2:308, 2:401, 2:405, 2:411, 2:425
see also Bashan
Ohad, clan of
Zimri and, 2:269–270
On, 1:443
Onan, 1:407

death of, 2:260, 2:267, 2:270, 2:279
second census, 2:268
Oznites
second census, 2:260

Pagiel
offerings of, 1:178, 1:183
tribe arrangement, 1:76
Palluites
second census, 2:259
Palti
meaning of name, 1:327
Palti, son of Raphu, 1:316
Paltiel, son of Azzan
as chieftain, 2:459
Paran, Wilderness of, 1:206, 1:64
encampment in, 1:242
encampments, 2:445–446
journey to, 1:238–239
location of, 1:228
Passover
as beginning, 2:338
celebration of, 1:204–205
corpse pollution, 1:205, 1:209–210, 1:213, 1:214, 1:279
delay of, 1:237
deliverance, 1:117
deliverance of firstborn, 1:43
exodus and, 2:425
feast of departure, 1:236
firstborn sons, 2:448
firstborns, 1:124
food and, 1:287
food of, 1:254
instructions and offerings, 2:323
lamb of God, 2:338
lamb sacrifice, 1:374
lambs, 1:199
lambs instead of sons, 2:334–335
legislation and, 1:212, 1:227, 1:236
offerings and instructions, 2:326
redemption and, 1:128
requests and, 2:404
second year, 1:183, 1:185, 1:203, 1:212–213
spring festival, 2:349–350
theology of, 1:213
time of, 1:208–209, 1:209
YHWH on, 1:204

patriarchy
  covenant community, 2:303–304
  husbands give up patronymy, 2:305
  land distribution, 2:274
  name and patrimony, 2:301–303
  without sons, 2:288–291
Paul
  church as bride, 2:256
  God as 'rock', 2:50
  Jesus union with church, 2:234
  laws from angels, 1:39
  on Moses, 1:301
  on serpents, 2:63
  on the wilderness, 2:278, 2:447
peace
  meaning of, 1:171–172
Pedahel, son of Ammihud
  chieftain, 2:459
  as chieftain, 2:428
Pentateuch
  composition of, 1:69
Peor
  Balaam's final parables, 2:170–189
Perezites
  second census, 2:260
Perizzites
  population and, 1:101
Peter
  speaking ass story, 2:146
Philistines, 2:202, 2:454
  migratory campaigns, 1:88
  reliefs at Medinet Habu, 1:13
Phinehas, 1:43, 2:226
  Aaron and *toledot*, 1:120–121
  atonement, 2:235–237, 2:243, 2:258, 2:277
  atonement and, 2:240–242, 2:383
  atonement for Israel, 1:45
  Baal Peor incident, 2:249–250
  Balaam narrative, 2:100
  battle with Midianites, 1:226
  chief guardian, 1:127
  contrast with Balaam, 2:243
  covenant priesthood, 2:211
  Cush/Nubia, 1:291
  death of, 2:238
  descendants of, 2:238
  different path from Zimri, 2:255
  duties at Tent, 2:228–230
  duties of, 2:220–221, 2:236

  east of Jordan, 2:409
  end of wilderness, 2:243
  everlasting priesthood, 2:230, 2:236–239, 2:242–243
  faithful husband, 2:252
  family context, 2:225–228
  genealogy of, 1:125, 2:276
  guard duties, 2:231–233
  guardian of purity, 2:257
  hatred of idolatry, 2:239
  Israel *versus* Midianite, 2:222
  Israeli–Moab microcosm, 2:224
  jealousy for YHWH, 1:59–60, 1:151
  judgement on, 2:220–221
  Levites and, 2:238
  lineage of, 2:213
  love for YHWH, 2:239
  Midian conquest, 2:393
  name of, 2:226
  Nazirites, 2:237–238
  perpetual priesthood, 2:258
  priesthood and, 1:135
  punishes harlotry, 1:90
  restores Israel, 2:247
  rewarded, 230–231
  role in battle, 2:379, 2:380, 2:381, 2:394, 2:396
  sees brazen harlotry, 2:225
  slays Balaam, 2:380, 2:385
  slays Zimri and Cozbi, 2:211, 2:220–221, 2:229, 2:245, 2:251, 2:258
  spiritual jealousy, 2:252–254
  stays plague, 2:233–234, 2:241
  stopped alternative path, 2:234
  stops spiritual harlotry, 2:369
  sympathy for nation, 2:239
  turns YHWH's fury, 2:235–237
  zeal and loyalty, 2:226, 2:408
Phoenicians, 2:454
Pi Hahiroth encampment, 2:440
pilgrimage
  Jerusalem, 2:347
pillar of cloud/fire, 2:443
Pisgah, Mount
  Balaam's second parable, 2:160
  Moses and, 2:160
plague
  Aaron stays, 1:399, 1:436–439, 1:453, 2:240, 2:241

Index of Subjects

anger at Baal Peor, 2:225
Baal Peor, 2:233, 2:241–242, 2:247, 2:252, 2:272, 2:379, 2:385, 2:483
at Baal Peor, 2:219
David and burnt offerings, 2:330
Korah's rebellion and, 1:433–439
in Moab, 2:228
Ohad clan dies out, 2:269–270
Phinehas stays, 2:277
second census and, 2:264
second census total and, 2:272
second generation and, 2:278
plunder
  distribution of, 2:395–398
  literary context of, 2:392–398
  livestock, 2:398, 2:402–403
  tally of, 2:389–390
prayer
  Lord's prayer, 1:169
  with offerings, 2:348–349
  vows and, 2:354
precious metals and goods
  offerings of, 1:176–179
  offerings to altar, 1:187–190
priesthood
  Aaron and, 1:135, 1:211, 1:311, 1:451
  Aaron to Eleazar, 2:42–43
  atonement and mediation, 1:436–439
  blessings, 1:53, 1:57, 1:143, 1:166–171
  consecration of, 1:185, 1:200
  divine gift, 1:467
  duties of, 1:463–468
  firstborn and, 1:407, 1:440
  as guard duty, 1:127
  high priest's breastplate, 1:21–22, 1:170
  inheritance of, 1:475–477
  instrumentality of, 1:202–203
  Korah's argument, 1:412–415
  Korah's rebellion and, 1:406–431
  leadership, 1:10
  Levites' service to, 1:124
  magic and, 1:156
  Midian plunder and, 2:376
  murderer's asylum, 2:469–473
  Nazirites and, 1:159, 1:164
  offerings to, 1:460, 1:496–498
  ordinations, 1:182

Phinehas, 2:211, 2:229–230, 2:242–243
presence of YHWH, 1:159
purification after battle, 2:384
restrictions, 1:55
revolt over exclusivity, 1:135
roles of, 1:44
sons of Aaron, 1:441
subject to Moses, 1:296
toledot, 1:121
transport of Ark, 1:132
tribes and, 1:202
trumpets and, 1:225, 1:226
washing rituals, 1:487
YHWH gives to, 1:468–477
princes
  division of land, 1:67
  listing of, 1:62
prophecy
  versus divination, 2:108
  Eldad and Medad, 1:275–276, 1:300
  Torah prophets, 1:300
prophets
  Moses' status, 1:301–302
Psalms of Ascent, 1:166–167
Psalter
  vow offerings, 2:355
Punon encampment, 2:427, 2:449
purification, 1:44
  after conquest, 2:374
  asylum cities and, 2:478–479
  Baal Peor and, 2:218
  bitter herbs, 1:205, 1:214
  'blameless', 2:329–330
  bodily discharge, 1:46–47, 1:137, 1:142, 1:145–147
  community legislation, 1:65
  concerns about, 1:237
  corpse pollution, 1:46–47, 1:137, 1:145–147, 1:214, 1:480–491
  covenant community, 2:242
  death penalty for apostasy, 2:222
  dedication ritual, 1:195–196
  expulsion of people, 1:214
  expulsions and, 1:48, 1:49–50, 1:52, 1:142, 1:143, 1:145–147
  generational transition, 1:67–68
  hyssop branch, 1:494
  intermarriage, 2:232

purification *(cont.)*
  leprosy, 1:137, 1:142, 1:145–147, 1:306
    Miriam and, 1:46
  leprosy and, 1:308–309
  Levites, 1:179–180, 1:200
  monthly offerings, 2:336–337
  Nazirite vow and, 1:139–140, 1:142, 1:162–166
  in Numbers, 1:46–60
  oath-breaking, 1:47, 1:138, 1:142, 1:143, 1:147–148
  offerings, 1:164, 1:188–189, 1:379–380
  Passover observance, 1:213–214
  plague on sexual immorality, 2:233
  purification of Midianites, 2:372
  restitution, 1:47
  ritual for women, 1:153–158
  skin disease/leprosy, 1:214
  social, not military, 1:13
  strayed women, 1:48, 1:49–50, 1:142–44, 1:148–158, 2:368–369
  theology of, 1:53–58
  unintentional murder, 2:484
  waters of separation, 1:487, 1:492–495, 1:488–491
  wilderness and, 1:58–60
  YHWH tells Moses, 1:137–140
  see also red heifer ritual
Puvahites
  second census, 2:260

Rachel
  ranking of sons, 1:93
  son prioritized, 1:95, 1:96
Rahab
  Joshua spares house of, 2:295
Ramesses III
  mortuary temple, 1:88
Ramoth
  asylum city, 2:466
Raphael, Archangel
  heavenly camp, 1:29
Reba, Midian king, 2:372, 2:381–382
rebellion
  grumbling against Moses, 1:317–319
  high-handed sin, 1:379, 1:394
rebellions
  Kadesh, 2:407

red heifer ritual, 1:457–458, 2:258
  context of, 1:460–461, 1:498–500
  corpse pollution, 2:386
  instructions and meanings, 1:479–495
  Midianite conquest and, 2:384, 2:395
  rebirth of Israel, 1:501–502
  water and, 2:12
redemption
  covenanted community, 1:98–99
  firstborns, 1:111, 1:116–117, 1:128
  Levites and, 1:111, 1:116–117
  Moses and, 1:118
  Nazirites, 1:163–164
Rekem, Midian king, 2:372, 2:381–382
Rephidim encampment, 2:426, 2:440, 2:444
resurrection
  Sabbath, 2:335
Reuben, son of Jacob
  firstborn of Israel, 1:87
  revolt over priesthood, 1:135
  sells Joseph, 2:317–318
  slept with concubine, 1:93
  sons of, 2:357, 2:380
  vow to serve, 2:363
Reuben, tribe of
  Camp arrangement, 1:18, 1:75, 1:82, 1:96, 1:97, 1:228
  Canaan oath, 2:414–416, 2:425
  Canaan pledge, 2:403–404
  census, 1:76, 1:87, 1:93, 2:246–247
  change in population, 2:267
  cities and sheepfolds, 2:417
  cities of, 2:399
  compromise for land, 2:410–414
  conquest pledge, 2:401
  Elizur as chieftain, 1:78
  encamped with Gadites, 2:405
  flag, men and mandrakes, 1:28
  Korah's rebellion and, 2:266
  land across the Jordan, 1:108
  land distribution, 2:458
  land inheritance, 2:267
  lands granted to, 2:416–419
  lands to, 2:397
  leading tribes, 1:83
  livestock plunder, 2:383
  march from Sinai, 1:236

offerings of, 1:177, 1:183, 1:189
order of departure, 1:92
pledge, 2:370
pledge to Canaan, 2:406–410
requests Transjordan land, 2:398–399, 2:423–424
second census, 2:259, 2:266, 2:268
second in honour, 1:94
setting out on journey, 1:206
settlement in Canaan, 2:80
settlement of, 2:88
settles east of Jordan, 2:271
southern arrangement, 1:92–93
standard of, 1:83
status of, 2:418–419
Transjordan, 1:67
Transjordan compromise, 2:401–402
Transjordan lands, 2:428, 2:455–456
Transjordan request, 2:401–402, 2:403–410
trumpets and, 1:224
zodiacal sign, 1:23
Reuel the Midianite
  Hobab and, 1:207
  Moses and, 1:229–230
Riblah, 2:455
  Canaan's border and, 2:428
Rimmon-Perez encampment, 2:426, 2:440
Rissah encampment, 2:426
Rithmah encampment, 2:426
  Wilderness of Paran, 2:445–446
Rome/'Kittim', 2:202, 2:210
Rosh HaShanah, 2:350
  begins the year, 2:338
  Shofar, 2:341–342
  see also Trumpets, Feast of
Ruth, 2:490
  Feast of Firstfruits, 2:340
  Naomi and, 1:231
Ruth the Moabitess
  exemplary woman, 2:284

Sabbath, 1:172
  annual calendar, 2:350
  breaking, 1:382–387, 2:241
  calendar of worship, 2:323
  Decalogue and, 2:347
  instructions and offerings, 2:322, 2:328–329, 2:345

manna and, 1:256
rest, 2:339
sin and, 1:368
weekly offerings, 2:335–336
sacrifice
  animals, 1:129
  grain and wine, 1:57–58
  Levite duties and, 1:198
  Levites, 1:123
  Nazirites' purification, 1:162
  Passover and, 1:213
  ram of atonement, 1:138, 1:148
  self-, 1:165
  'strange fire'?, 1:122
  war and, 1:226
Salt Sea
  Canaan's border and, 2:428, 2:453, 2:454, 2:455
Samson
  Babylon and, 1:417
  Nazirite vow and, 1:55, 1:159
Samuel
  as Nazirite, 1:159
Samuel, son of Ammihud
  chieftain, 2:428, 2:459
Sanctuary
  Dwelling and altar, 1:186
Sanhedrin
  establishment of, 1:264
Sarah, daughter of Asher
  Isaac's offering, 1:199
  potential impurity, 1:151
  second census, 2:260, 2:268, 2:272
Saul, 2:184
  David and, 2:302
Scorpion's Ascent, 2:454
  Canaan's border and, 2:428
scouts, 1:315–319, 2:424
  Caleb and, 1:333–339
  incident of, 2:420, 2:421
  Joseph parallel, 2:317–318
  Kadesh Barnea, 2:445
  Kadesh rebellion and, 2:409–410
  Levites excluded, 1:356
  mission and report, 1:321–333
  original report, 1:343–344
  report to Moses, 1:333–341, 1:352
  Transjordan lands and, 2:425
Sea of Suph encampment, 2:426

Sea Peoples, 2:202
  migratory campaigns, 1:88
Sebam, 2:398
Seleucids, 2:202
Seredites
  second census, 2:260
serpents, 2:60–72
  bronze standard, 2:85, 2:87–88, 2:269
  in Eden, 2:70
  Egypt, 2:85
Seth
  Sheth and, 2:196–197
Sethur
  meaning of name, 1:327
Sethur, son of Michael, 1:316
sexuality
  pregnancy and, 1:156
  see also bodily discharge; women, strayed
Shaddai, 2:178, 2:208
  Balaam on, 2:193
Shalmaneser I of Sumeria, 1:105
Shammua, 1:316, 1:327
Shaphat, 1:327
Shaphat, son of Hori, 1:316
Shaulites
  second census, 2:259
Shauvot, Feat of, 2:340
Shechem
  asylum city, 2:466
  second census, 2:260
  Simeon cursed for, 1:93
  violates Dinah, 2:227
shekels
  weight and value of, 1:129
Shekhinah, 1:185
  benediction, 1:172
  Camp arrangement, 1:298
  central camp, 1:203
  Chariot of, 2:270
  Cloud of Glory and, 1:222, 1:237
  Ezekiel's vision and, 1:31–32
  grades of holiness, 1:97
  guidance of, 1:280
  holy community, 1:173–174
  Israel's Camp, 1:27–30
  new generation and, 1:44–46
  priestly blessings, 1:53
  purity laws and, 1:48–53

  relation in Camp, 1:175
  YHWH's forgiveness, 1:192
  YHWH's kingship and, 1:166
  YHWH's presence and, 1:218
  see also Israel, Camp of
Shelahites
  second census, 2:260
Shelumiel
  offerings of, 1:177, 1:183
  setting out on journey, 1:206
Shemidaites
  second census, 2:260
Shemini Atzeret, 2:344
Sheol
  the lustful and, 1:289
  meaning of, 1:425–426
Shepham, 2:455
  Canaan's border and, 2:428
Shepher, Mount, encampment, 2:426, 2:440
shepherds
  sheep following, 1:2
Shillemites
  second census, 2:261
Shiloh
  Ephraim tribe hill country, 1:87
Shimei, son of Gershon, 1:109, 2:275
Shimei, tribe of, 1:109
  duties of, 1:126
Shimronites
  second census, 2:260
Shittim see Abel–Shittim
Shofar
  offerings and instructions, 2:340–342
Shunites
  second census, 2:260
Shuphamites
  second census, 2:260, 2:272
Shur, 2:443
Shuthelahites
  second census, 2:260
Sibmah (Sebam), 2:399, 2:417
Sihon, 1:55, 2:34
  battles Israel, 2:51–52
  conquest of, 2:271, 2:379, 2:397
  defeat of, 2:244
  Israel's passage, 2:38
  name of, 2:56
  Shittim and, 2:214

threat to Israel, 2:449
victory over, 2:79–82, 2:111, 2:308, 2:401, 2:405, 2:411, 2:425
Simeon
intermarriage vengeance, 2:227
Simeon Bar Kochba, 2:194
Simeon, son of Jacob
Shechem incident, 1:93
Simeon, tribe of, 2:459–460
arrangement of Camp, 1:82
Baal Peor diminishment, 2:405
census, 1:76, 1:87, 1:93
change in population, 2:267
chieftain Shelumiel, 1:78
land distribution, 2:458
Midianites and, 2:246
offerings of, 1:177, 1:183
population decrease, 2:266, 2:270
Samuel as chieftain, 2:428, 2:459–460
second census, 2:259
setting out on journey, 1:206
tribal ordering, 1:96
tribe arrangement, 1:75
zodiacal sign, 1:23
sin
blasphemy, 1:381
high-handed, 1:381–383, 1:395
lust and, 1:391
offerings and, 1:368, 1:370, 1:379–380
punishment, 1:382–384, 1:387
Sabbath-breaking, 1:382–387
unintentional, 1:379–380
wayward women, 1:395–396
see also idolatry
Sin, Wilderness of, encampment, 2:426, 2:444
Sinai encampment, 2:426
Sinai, Mount
altar miniature, 1:189
assembly of people, 1:225
burnt offerings, 2:330, 2:334
covenant of, 1:175
covenant revealed, 1:65
Day of Atonement and, 2:342–343
departure from, 1:209, 1:249, 1:257, 1:259
the Dwelling and, 1:269

earthly hosts for YHWH, 1:25–26
encampment, 2:440, 2:444
Israel's arrival, 1:227
Jebel Musa site, 1:228
journey to Canaan, 1:232
to Paran wilderness, 1:206
ram's horn and, 1:223
revelation, 1:237
revelation of, 1:14–18
setting out from, 1:238
story of, 1:63
Tent as symbol of, 1:190–191
wilderness of, 1:121–122
YHWH on, 1:218
YHWH's revelation, 1:13
skin disease
purity laws and, 1:214
see also leprosy; purity laws
social relations
purity laws and, 1:48
Solomon, 1:73
dedicatory prayer of, 1:25
Jerusalem Temple, 2:237
kingdom divides, 1:87
rise of, 2:184
YHWH magnifies, 2:313
Song of the Ark, 2:480
sotah ritual, 1:158
Spirit
Feast of Weeks, 1:312–313
versus flesh, 1:312
not flesh, 1:314
prophecy and, 1:277
staffs
Aaron's, 1:452–455, 2:20–24
of Levi, 1:400
symbols, 1:444–445
tribes, 1:451
Stephen
Luke on, 1:73
'strange fire'
possible meanings of, 1:122
strangers
defining, 1:123
guarding against, 1:127
put to death, 1:110, 1:116
Succoth encampment, 2:426, 2:440
to Etham, 2:442
from Ramesses, 2:443

Sumeria
  king-lists, 1:105
Suph, Sea of, encampment, 2:444

Taberah, 1:227
  meaning, 1:310
Taberah encampment, 2:447
Taberah/Place of Burning, 1:302
Tabernacle
  the Cloud and, 1:216
  consecration of, 1:83–84
  function of, 1:185
  lampstand of, 1:192–194
  raised, 1:182, 1:183
  transport of, 1:181, 1:186, 1:200
  see Dwelling Place
Tabernacles
  instructions, 2:329
Tahanites
  second census, 2:260
Tahath encampment, 2:426, 2:440
Talmud
  on Mosaic authorship, 1:70
tassels law, 1:370, 1:388–394, 1:395, 1:447, 2:392, 2:396
  cherubim and, 1:39
  first generation and, 2:250–251
  meanings, 1:57
  priestly calling, 1:410–411
  as reminders, 2:225
  sin of the scouts, 1:363
  YHWH commands, 1:368
Temple
  Essene plan, 1:19–20
  Ezekiel's vision, 1:36
  Tent of Meeting, 1:20
  theology of, 1:25–26
Tent of Meeting, 1:82
  age of Levite service, 1:200–201
  age of service to, 1:130–131
  alcohol and, 1:160
  arrangement of Camp, 1:31, 1:91, 1:93
  bundled contents of, 1:132
  burnt offerings, 2:330, 2:334
  calendar of worship, 2:350
  central in encampment, 1:94
  centre of camp, 1:248
  Cloud of Glory and, 1:6–8, 1:216–217, 1:222
  community and, 1:225
  covenant community and, 1:83
  divine communications, 2:241
  divine-human relationships, 1:48
  Dwelling of the Testimony, 1:89
  eastward entrance, 1:96
  Eden restored, 1:147
  function of, 1:5, 1:18
  furnishings of, 1:126
  God's Dwelling and, 1:4
  guarding, 1:115–116, 1:126–127, 1:131
  harlotry apostasy, 2:222–224
  Korah's rebellion, 1:420–421, 1:422
  lamps in, 1:179
  Levite care of Ark, 1:111–112
  Levite duties and, 1:109–113, 1:115–120, 1:176
  Levite transport, 1:136
  Levites and, 1:44–46, 1:126, 1:127, 1:180
  Levites' dedication rituals, 1:194–196
  Levites guard, 1:456, 1:463–468, 1:497
  Midian gold and, 2:375
  Miriam and Aaron and, 1:298–299
  mobility of, 1:202
  Moses and, 2:16
  Moses' crisis and, 1:273
  offerings and, 2:346
  offerings from plunder, 2:393–394
  Phineas's duties, 2:228–230
  pollution by harlotry, 230–231
  purity laws, 1:46
  rebels devoured in earth, 1:428
  role of Levites, 1:184
  sacred space and objects, 1:465–467
  Spirit and elders/scribes, 1:241
  symbol of Mt Sinai, 1:190–192
  symbolic of the covenant, 1:97–98
  Temple equated with, 1:20
  transporting holy of holies, 1:131–134
  YHWH descends to, 1:247, 1:266–269, 1:299
  YHWH's presence, 1:186, 1:212
  Zimri and Cozbi slain in, 2:211
Tent of the Testimony, 1:216–217, 1:400, 1:456
Terah encampment, 2:426
Terah, father of Abraham, 2:495
Tharbis, wife of Moses, 1:292

throne-chariot
  Revelations and, 1:40–41
Tirzah (city), 2:305, 2:306
Titus, Arch of, 1:223
toledot
  Aaron and, 1:117
  Levites and, 1:120–121
Torah
  elders and, 1:278
  establishment of Sanhedrin, 1:264
  on Mosaic authorship, 1:70
  Moses and, 1:269, 1:300
Transjordan land
  status of, 2:419
treachery and treason
  oath-breaking, 1:147–148
  strayed women and, 1:151
Tree of Knowledge
  Eden, 1:361–363
tribes
  arrangement in Camp, 1:36
  arrangement of, 1:75–83, 1:77–79, 1:91–99
  census figures, 1:76–77, 1:83–91
  chieftains, 1:83, 1:86–87, 1:95–96, 1:99, 1:181–182
  clans and, 1:84–85
  dedication of altar, 1:227
  formation of, 1:84, 1:120
  genealogy and, 1:95
  grades of holiness, 1:97
  high priest's breastplate, 1:28, 1:40
  kinship, 2:294–296
  land division, 2:299–301
  leaders, 1:83
  leaders of, 1:75–76
  listing, 1:62
  matriarchs of, 1:95–96
  microcosm of creation, 1:41–42
  military defeat, 1:43
  Moses and Aaron and, 1:183
  name and patrimony, 2:301–303
  new generation leaders, 2:483
  offerings, 1:183
  offerings to altar, 1:186, 1:187–190
  ordering logic of, 1:95–97
  potential land loss, 2:486–495
  priestly blessings, 1:53
  purity laws and, 1:50
  purpose of census and, 1:94–95
  roles of, 1:185
  setting out, 1:211
  Spirit and, 1:269
  standards/banners, 1:91–92
  symbolic number, 1:104
  tallies of census, 1:87–88
  YHWH's presence, 1:144–145
  zodiac representation of, 1:23
Trumpet Blowing, Day of
  instructions, 2:328–329
trumpets
  calling to congregation, 1:223
  commanded, 1:206, 1:219
  depictions of, 1:223
  functions of, 1:222–223
  manufacture of, 1:211, 1:225, 1:238
  march from Sinai, 1:236
  Midian conquest, 2:376
  Midianite conquest, 2:381
  sound of, 1:211, 1:224
  spiritual engagement, 1:226–227
  uses of, 1:209, 1:210–211, 1:226, 1:238, 1:239
Trumpets, Day of Blast (Shofar)
  offerings and instructions, 2:340–342
Trumpets, Feast of (Shofar)
  autumn festival, 2:350
  offerings, 2:323, 2:337
  offerings and instructions, 2:326, 2:335, 2:345
Tutankhamun
  red chest in tomb of, 1:132

Ugarit Kret epic, 1:105
Unleavened Bread, Feast
  offerings and instructions, 2:328–329, 2:338–339, 2:343, 2:345
  spring festival, 2:350
Uriel, Archangel
  heavenly camp, 1:29
Urim and Thummin, 2:273, 2:381
  Eleazar, 2:314–315
Urim, judgement of, 2:281
Uzziah, son of Kohath
  divine punishment, 1:52
  leprosy, 1:305
Uzziel, Kohath, 1:126
  carries Nadab and Abihu, 1:214

Uzziel, son of Kohath, 1:109, 2:275
  duties of clan, 1:110
  genealogy of, 1:125

vows and oaths
  assertory and promissory, 2:358–359
  breaking, 2:356, 2:367–368
  foolish, 2:356
  legislation for, 2:352–371
  meaning in Israel, 2:354–356
  Moses on, 2:356–357
  Reubenites and Gadites, 2:414–416
  sworn to YHWH, 2:358

Wadi of Egypt, 2:454
  Canaan's border and, 2:428
water
  Balaam's oracle and, 2:180–181
  of contention, 2:280
  lack of, 2:7–16
  Moses rebels, 2:280
  purification, 2:10
  at Rehidim, 2:444
  from rock, 2:3–4, 2:315
  Song of the Well, 2:73–77
  'waters of contention', 2:33, 2:308
  waters of separation, 2:48
  well at Beer, 2:51
  YHWH provides, 2:1–2
  YHWH's abundance of, 2:27–31
  YHWH's kingship, 2:50
Weeks, Feast of, 2:350
  instructions, 2:328–329
  offerings and instructions, 2:326, 2:339–340
wilderness journey
  Aaron's genealogy, 2:258–259
  admonition and humility, 2:278
  around Edom to Moab, 2:72–76
  Beer, 2:75–77
  cherubim in, 1:34–37
  death in, 1:312, 2:277
  divine plan and, 2:409
  Edom's refusal, 2:34–41
  end of, 2:86–87, 2:265
  end of wandering, 2:49
  end of wilderness, 2:78
  ends with Phinehas, 2:243
  food and, 1:214

  forward-looking, 2:15
  generational differences, 2:255
  Israel's camp, 1:14
  Israel's experience of, 1:1–3
  Joseph's return from Egypt, 2:318
  the journey ahead, 1:83
  Kadesh, 2:2
  to Kadesh, 1:316–317
  lack of water, 2:7–15, 2:14–15
  led by YHWH, 1:219
  to Moab, 2:60–72
  no additional offerings and, 2:327
  Paran, 1:227–228, 1:310, 1:325
  Paul speaks of, 2:278
  priestly blessing and, 1:166
  prologue to, 2:17
  purity laws, 1:58–60
  rebellion and, 1:321–361
  rebellions in, 1:453
  scouts, 1:233–234, 1:316–317, 1:321–333
  setting out into, 1:229
  Sinai and, 1:121–122
  sojourn of, 1:42–45
  sojourners and offerings, 1:376–377
  stations of, 2:432–435, 2:440–441, 2:442
  stopping points, 2:425–427
  structure of Numbers, 1:62
  test of, 1:313
  towards the Ammorites, 2:50–52
  weeping, 2:224
  YHWH as shepherd, 1:175
  YHWH outlines, 2:439–450
  YHWH's speech about, 2:435
  YHWH's speech on, 2:479–483
  YHWH and, 1:8–9
wine
  tribute, 1:374
women
  abortions, 1:141
  barren, 2:354
  daughters in patriarchy, 2:289
  execution of Midianites, 2:383
  fate of captives, 2:384–386
  harlots, 1:391, 1:392
  land inheritance rights, 2:282
  loosened hair, 1:153
  menstrual impurity, 1:495

Index of Subjects

menstrual separation, 1:488
Midianite captives, 2:372
Miriam as metaphor, 2:11–12
Nazirite, 1:160
  in patriarchal geneaologies, 2:272
  pregnancy, 1:156
  as 'sons', 2:292–293
  strayed, 2:360, 2:368–369, 2:392
  vow exceptions, 2:357
  vows, 2:371
  vows in marriage, 2:363–365
  vows in relation to men, 2:352, 2:360–367, 2:367–370
  vows of widow or divorcee, 2:365–367
  vows to YHWH, 2:352
  widowed and divorced, 2:352, 2:360
  YHWH on inheritance, 2:292–294
  see also marriage; women, strayed; Zelophehad's daughters
women, strayed, 1:60
  adultery vs impurity, 1:151–153
  bitter waters, 1:141, 1:149, 1:153–156, 1:158, 1:214
  bodily discharge and, 1:52
  harlotry in Moab, 1:59
  idolatry and, 1:150
  Israel and, 1:160
  jealousy and, 1:149–151
  language of, 1:149
  leads to bitterness, 1:174
  paternity of children and, 1:152–153
  purification of, 1:144, 1:149, 1:153–158
  purity and Nazirite vow, 1:54–58
  purity laws, 1:47–48, 1:138–139, 1:143–144, 1:148–158
  spiritual harlotry, 1:154, 1:157–158
  waters of bitterness, 1:138–139

Yam Suph encampment, 2:440
YHWH
  abundant provision of water, 2:6, 2:20, 2:27–31, 2:48–49
  anger at flesh eaters, 1:310
  anger at Midian whoring, 2:211
  anger with Balaam, 2:128–131, 2:134–139
  anger with complainers, 1:287–288
  angry about whoring, 2:211
  angry with complainers, 1:240–242, 1:244–258
  appointing the firstborn, 1:110
  ark as footstool of, 1:233–234
  arrangement of Camp, 1:82, 1:91–99
  on asylum for murders, 2:429–430
  Baal Peor plague, 2:241–242
  Balaam as prophet, 2:101–102
  Balaam's prophecy, 1:59
  Balaam's second parable, 2:163–165
  Balak wishes to turn, 2:120–121
  benevolent plans for Israel, 1:168–170
  blessing of, 1:143, 1:144–145
  burning, 1:251
  calendar of worship, 2:322–325, 2:326–352
  Camp follows Cloud, 1:94
  on Canaan and borders, 2:427–428
  character of, 1:1, 2:279
  chooses David, 1:87
  chosen people, 1:88
  Cloud of Glory, 1:6–8, 1:30, 1:41, 1:89, 1:182, 1:183, 1:186, 1:189, 1:192, 1:202, 1:205–206, 1:210–211, 1:234, 1:237–238, 1:267, 2:272, 2:442
  conquest of Canaanites, 2:58–60
  contributions to Aaron, 1:468–477
  on corpse pollution, 1:205
  covenant with Israel, 1:232
  death of Aaron, 2:40–44
  Decalogue, 2:347–348
  defines Canaan's borders, 2:435
  descends to Tent, 1:299
  descends to elders, 1:273–284
  divine agenda, 1:32, 1:33
  divine hospitality, 1:271
  divine judgement, 1:88
  divine wrath, 1:90
  the Dwelling and, 1:8–9
  dwelling within the community, 1:97–98, 1:127, 1:136
  earthly entourage, 1:85
  earthly hosts in Camp, 1:25–27
  elders/scribes and, 1:263–264
  explains Moses' death, 2:282
  face of, 1:167–168, 1:220
  Feast of Weeks, 1:312–313
  final speeches to Moses, 2:435–438

YHWH (cont.)
   as fire, 1:222
   on firstborn, 1:116
   to flesh cravers, 1:241
   forgiveness, 2:363
   gives inheritance to daughters, 2:280
   glory appears, 1:421–423
   Glory Cloud *see* Cloud of Glory
   grants daughters land rights, 2:282
   grants Levites cities, 2:484
   grants the land, 2:279–280
   guidance through Moses, 1:214
   heavenly king, 1:26–27
   holy city, 1:19
   as host of offerings, 2:346–347
   idolatry, 2:427
   images of God, 2:451
   incident at Baal Peor, 2:213
   instruction for Camp, 1:228
   Israel as 'bride of', 1:54–58
   Israel reunites with, 2:247
   Israel's commitment, 1:50
   Israel's renewed loyalty, 2:397
   Israel's theocracy, 1:12, 1:13
   as jealous, 2:235–236
   as jealous God, 2:216, 2:217
   jealousy of, 2:250, 2:252–254
   Joshua appointed, 2:282–283
   judgement against rebellion, 1:350–362
   judgement on Korah, 1:421–422
   Kadesh rebellion, 2:398
   keeping a distance, 1:92
   as king, 1:40–41
   kingship of, 1:53, 1:175, 2:28
   Korah judgement, 1:436–439
   Korah's rebellion, 1:417
   land grants, 2:407
   leaders to distribute land, 2:428
   leadership of Moses, 1:268
   leadership via Cloud, 1:228
   Levite gift to Aaron, 1:124
   Levite pastures and cities, 2:429
   Levites and, 1:109, 1:128, 1:179–180
   Levitical cities, 2:435
   march from Sinai, 1:236
   mercy, 1:382–383
   mercy of, 2:71–72, 2:483
   messenger to Balaam, 2:88–90, 2:97, 2:99, 2:106, 2:136–146
   Miriam and, 1:296–297
   Miriam's complaint and, 1:294–295
   Moses and, 1:72–73
   Moses and Aaron misrepresent, 2:3
   Moses as agent for, 1:311
   Moses as mediator, 1:345–355
   Moses pleads with, 1:258–262
   Moses speaks for, 1:304–305
   Moses' death, 2:306–311
   Mt Sinai revelation, 1:14–18
   Mt Sinai theophany, 1:38–40
   name of, 1:172–173, 1:175
   names leaders, 2:436, 2:483
   names tribal leaders, 2:456–460
   Nazirites and, 1:159–160, 1:162
   offerings to, 1:366–368
   offerings to altar, 1:188
   orders second census, 2:259
   on Passover, 1:204
   peace offerings to, 1:206
   plague at Baal Peor, 2:233–234
   presence in Camp, 1:146–147, 1:166–173, 1:203, 1:454
   presence in Tent, 1:190–192
   presence of, 1:156, 1:159, 1:186
   priestly blessings and, 1:166–171
   proclaiming name of, 1:167
   promise to Abraham, 1:231, 2:120, 2:307
   promise to Jacob, 1:194
   promises flesh, 1:262
   promises of, 1:261
   promises to Abraham, 1:42
   provides water, 2:51
   punishes complainers, 1:242
   punishes Egypt, 1:285
   punishes flesh cravers, 1:245
   punishes flesh-eaters, 1:315
   punishes meat cravers, 1:284–289
   purpose for humanity, 2:351
   purpose revealed, 2:100
   rebukes Aaron and Miriam, 1:296–299
   releases serpents, 2:50
   return of Israel, 1:235
   Reubenite and Gadite commitment to, 2:412
   revealed only to Moses and Aaron, 2:16
   rewards Phinehas, 2:236–238

Index of subjects 713

sends plague, 2:225
sends serpents, 2:60–72
Shekhinah and, 1:218
as shepherd, 1:219, 2:279, 2:482
shining face of, 1:170–171
significance of Cloud, 1:220–224
sin of Moses and Aaron, 2:4–34
speaks to Aaron, 1:456–459, 1:496
speaks to Eleazar, 2:264
speaks to Moses, 1:116–117, 1:137–140, 1:179, 1:183, 1:185, 1:202, 1:276, 1:296–297
speech defining Canaan, 2:453–456
speech on asylum cities, 2:464–467
speech on Canaan's borders, 2:483
speech on idolatry, 2:450–453
speech on Levitical cities, 2:460–464
Spirit in Camp, 1:278–280
spiritual harlotry, 1:54–57, 2:222–224
Tent of Meeting, 1:18
in Tent with elders, 1:266–269
tribe's inheritance, 2:490
trumpets and, 1:206, 1:226–227
vengeance on Midians, 2:377
visits Balaam, 2:124–125
war plunder distribution, 2:387–389
water from the rock, 2:16–29
in the wilderness, 1:8–9
on wilderness journey, 2:435, 2:470–483
will dwell in Canaan, 2:484
Wind/Spirit, 1:284–286
Zelophehad's daughters, 2:292–294, 2:308

Zadok
descent from Phinehas, 2:237, 2:238
genealogy of, 2:258
Zalmonah encampment, 2:427, 2:440, 2:449
Zebulum, tribe of
change in population, 2:267
Zebulun, tribe of
arrangement of Camp, 1:82
census, 1:76
census figures, 1:93
census total, 1:87
chieftain Eliab, 1:78
dwells by the sea, 2:274
Elizaphan as chieftain, 2:428, 2:459–460
march from Sinai, 1:236
offering of, 1:176, 1:183
second census, 2:260
setting out on journey, 1:206
tribal ordering, 1:96, 1:97
tribe arrangement, 1:75
zodiacal sign, 1:23
Zechariah
YHWH as fire, 1:222
Zedad, 2:455
Canaan's border and, 2:428
Zelophehad
brothers of, 2:304
daughters of *see* Zelophehad's daughters
death in the wilderness, 2:320
death of, 2:420
death of wife, 2:302
of good character, 2:286–288, 2:309
of good name, 2:486
judgement on first generation, 2:320
land inheritance, 2:278
memorial land, 2:290
name preserved, 2:292
second census, 2:260
Zelophehad's daughters, 1:62, 1:65, 1:66, 1:213, 2:11, 2:256
context of, 2:283
counted in census, 2:305
descent from Machir, 2:423
effect of Jubilee, 2:299
faithfulness and character, 2:284–285
genealogy of, 2:285
given inheritance, 2:304–306
inherit land, 2:282
inheritance within clan, 2:485–495
Jubilee and, 2:488–489
land request, 2:404–405
Mahlah, Noah, Hoglah, Milcah and Tirzah, 2:260, 2:280, 2:305–306
marriage and, 2:321
marriage and dowry, 2:290–291
marry cousins, 2:304–305, 2:420, 2:485
memorial land, 2:290
Moses and, 1:215, 2:308
patrimony, 2:301–303
perpetuating name, 2:304

Zelophehad's daughters (*cont.*)
  presentation of case, 2:282
  prominence of, 2:305–306
  pursuit of land, 2:274
  request inheritance right, 2:282, 2:284–291
  request of, 2:320–321
  righteous speech, 2:357
  second census, 2:267, 2:268, 2:270
  in second census, 2:260
  as 'sons', 2:292–293
  Transjordan land, 2:412
  Transjordan request, 2:405
  tribe of Manasseh, 2:317, 2:318, 2:320
  true daughters of Joseph, 2:319, 2:321
  women and vows, 2:368
  YHWH grants land to, 2:298–299
  YHWH's response to, 2:292–294
Zephonites
  second census, 2:260
Zerahites
  second census, 2:259, 2:260
Zilpah
  son prioritized, 1:95, 1:96
Zimri, son of Salu
  alternative path, 2:234, 2:255
  chides Moses, 2:227
  'covenant of peace', 2:237–238
  Cozbi and, 2:241
  family and context, 2:227, 2:243
  flagrant display, 2:285
  harlotry, 1:11, 2:369–370
  harlotry apostasy, 2:222–224
  infidelity of, 2:256
  Midianite scheme and, 2:244–245
  Ohad clan, 2:269–270
  Phinehas slays, 2:211, 2:220–221, 2:229–230, 2:231–233, 2:258
  seduced, 2:252–253
  tribe's death toll, 2:266
Zin, wilderness of, 2:6–7, 2:308, 2:426
  Canaan's borders, 2:428
  Moses rebels, 2:280
  see also Kadesh
Mount Zion, 1:222
  the journey's end, 1:3
Ziphron, 2:455
  Canaan's border and, 2:428
Zippor, 2:154
Zipporah, wife of Moses, 1:292, 1:293, 1:295
zodiac symbols, 1:22–25
Zur, Midian king, 2:243–244, 2:245
  counselled by Balaam, 2:247
  father of Cozbi, 2:382
  slain by Israel, 2:372
  slain in war, 2:376, 2:381–382
Zuriel, son of Abihail, 1:110
  chieftain, 1:127
  duties of, 1:136

Index of Subjects 711

menstrual separation, 1:488
Midianite captives, 2:372
Miriam as metaphor, 2:11–12
Nazirite, 1:160
  in patriarchal geneaologies, 2:272
  pregnancy, 1:156
  as 'sons', 2:292–293
  strayed, 2:360, 2:368–369, 2:392
  vow exceptions, 2:357
  vows, 2:371
  vows in marriage, 2:363–365
  vows in relation to men, 2:352, 2:360–367, 2:367–370
  vows of widow or divorcee, 2:365–367
  vows to YHWH, 2:352
  widowed and divorced, 2:352, 2:360
  YHWH on inheritance, 2:292–294
  see also marriage; women, strayed; Zelophehad's daughters
women, strayed, 1:60
  adultery vs impurity, 1:151–153
  bitter waters, 1:141, 1:149, 1:153–156, 1:158, 1:214
  bodily discharge and, 1:52
  harlotry in Moab, 1:59
  idolatry and, 1:150
  Israel and, 1:160
  jealousy and, 1:149–151
  language of, 1:149
  leads to bitterness, 1:174
  paternity of children and, 1:152–153
  purification of, 1:144, 1:149, 1:153–158
  purity and Nazirite vow, 1:54–58
  purity laws, 1:47–48, 1:138–139, 1:143–144, 1:148–158
  spiritual harlotry, 1:154, 1:157–158
  waters of bitterness, 1:138–139

Yam Suph encampment, 2:440
YHWH
  abundant provision of water, 2:6, 2:20, 2:27–31, 2:48–49
  anger at flesh eaters, 1:310
  anger at Midian whoring, 2:211
  anger with Balaam, 2:128–131, 2:134–139
  anger with complainers, 1:287–288
  angry about whoring, 2:211
  angry with complainers, 1:240–242, 1:244–258
  appointing the firstborn, 1:110
  ark as footstool of, 1:233–234
  arrangement of Camp, 1:82, 1:91–99
  on asylum for murders, 2:429–430
  Baal Peor plague, 2:241–242
  Balaam as prophet, 2:101–102
  Balaam's prophecy, 1:59
  Balaam's second parable, 2:163–165
  Balak wishes to turn, 2:120–121
  benevolent plans for Israel, 1:168–170
  blessing of, 1:143, 1:144–145
  burning, 1:251
  calendar of worship, 2:322–325, 2:326–352
  Camp follows Cloud, 1:94
  on Canaan and borders, 2:427–428
  character of, 1:1, 2:279
  chooses David, 1:87
  chosen people, 1:88
  Cloud of Glory, 1:6–8, 1:30, 1:41, 1:89, 1:182, 1:183, 1:186, 1:189, 1:192, 1:202, 1:205–206, 1:210–211, 1:234, 1:237–238, 1:267, 2:272, 2:442
  conquest of Canaanites, 2:58–60
  contributions to Aaron, 1:468–477
  on corpse pollution, 1:205
  covenant with Israel, 1:232
  death of Aaron, 2:40–44
  Decalogue, 2:347–348
  defines Canaan's borders, 2:435
  descends to Tent, 1:299
  descends to elders, 1:273–284
  divine agenda, 1:32, 1:33
  divine hospitality, 1:271
  divine judgement, 1:88
  divine wrath, 1:90
  the Dwelling and, 1:8–9
  dwelling within the community, 1:97–98, 1:127, 1:136
  earthly entourage, 1:85
  earthly hosts in Camp, 1:25–27
  elders/scribes and, 1:263–264
  explains Moses' death, 2:282
  face of, 1:167–168, 1:220
  Feast of Weeks, 1:312–313
  final speeches to Moses, 2:435–438

YHWH (cont.)
- as fire, 1:222
- on firstborn, 1:116
- to flesh cravers, 1:241
- forgiveness, 2:363
- gives inheritance to daughters, 2:280
- glory appears, 1:421–423
- Glory Cloud *see* Cloud of Glory
- grants daughters land rights, 2:282
- grants Levites cities, 2:484
- grants the land, 2:279–280
- guidance through Moses, 1:214
- heavenly king, 1:26–27
- holy city, 1:19
- as host of offerings, 2:346–347
- idolatry, 2:427
- images of God, 2:451
- incident at Baal Peor, 2:213
- instruction for Camp, 1:228
- Israel as 'bride of', 1:54–58
- Israel reunites with, 2:247
- Israel's commitment, 1:50
- Israel's renewed loyalty, 2:397
- Israel's theocracy, 1:12, 1:13
- as jealous, 2:235–236
- as jealous God, 2:216, 2:217
- jealousy of, 2:250, 2:252–254
- Joshua appointed, 2:282–283
- judgement against rebellion, 1:350–362
- judgement on Korah, 1:421–422
- Kadesh rebellion, 2:398
- keeping a distance, 1:92
- as king, 1:40–41
- kingship of, 1:53, 1:175, 2:28
- Korah judgement, 1:436–439
- Korah's rebellion, 1:417
- land grants, 2:407
- leaders to distribute land, 2:428
- leadership of Moses, 1:268
- leadership via Cloud, 1:228
- Levite gift to Aaron, 1:124
- Levite pastures and cities, 2:429
- Levites and, 1:109, 1:128, 1:179–180
- Levitical cities, 2:435
- march from Sinai, 1:236
- mercy, 1:382–383
- mercy of, 2:71–72, 2:483
- messenger to Balaam, 2:88–90, 2:97, 2:99, 2:106, 2:136–146
- Miriam and, 1:296–297
- Miriam's complaint and, 1:294–295
- Moses and, 1:72–73
- Moses and Aaron misrepresent, 2:3
- Moses as agent for, 1:311
- Moses as mediator, 1:345–355
- Moses pleads with, 1:258–262
- Moses speaks for, 1:304–305
- Moses' death, 2:306–311
- Mt Sinai revelation, 1:14–18
- Mt Sinai theophany, 1:38–40
- name of, 1:172–173, 1:175
- names leaders, 2:436, 2:483
- names tribal leaders, 2:456–460
- Nazirites and, 1:159–160, 1:162
- offerings to, 1:366–368
- offerings to altar, 1:188
- orders second census, 2:259
- on Passover, 1:204
- peace offerings to, 1:206
- plague at Baal Peor, 2:233–234
- presence in Camp, 1:146–147, 1:166–173, 1:203, 1:454
- presence in Tent, 1:190–192
- presence of, 1:156, 1:159, 1:186
- priestly blessings and, 1:166–171
- proclaiming name of, 1:167
- promise to Abraham, 1:231, 2:120, 2:307
- promise to Jacob, 1:194
- promises flesh, 1:262
- promises of, 1:261
- promises to Abraham, 1:42
- provides water, 2:51
- punishes complainers, 1:242
- punishes Egypt, 1:285
- punishes flesh cravers, 1:245
- punishes flesh-eaters, 1:315
- punishes meat cravers, 1:284–289
- purpose for humanity, 2:351
- purpose revealed, 2:100
- rebukes Aaron and Miriam, 1:296–299
- releases serpents, 2:50
- return of Israel, 1:235
- Reubenite and Gadite commitment to, 2:412
- revealed only to Moses and Aaron, 2:16
- rewards Phinehas, 2:236–238

sends plague, 2:225
sends serpents, 2:60–72
Shekhinah and, 1:218
as shepherd, 1:219, 2:279, 2:482
shining face of, 1:170–171
significance of Cloud, 1:220–224
sin of Moses and Aaron, 2:4–34
speaks to Aaron, 1:456–459, 1:496
speaks to Eleazar, 2:264
speaks to Moses, 1:116–117, 1:137–140, 1:179, 1:183, 1:185, 1:202, 1:276, 1:296–297
speech defining Canaan, 2:453–456
speech on asylum cities, 2:464–467
speech on Canaan's borders, 2:483
speech on idolatry, 2:450–453
speech on Levitical cities, 2:460–464
Spirit in Camp, 1:278–280
spiritual harlotry, 1:54–57, 2:222–224
Tent of Meeting, 1:18
in Tent with elders, 1:266–269
tribe's inheritance, 2:490
trumpets and, 1:206, 1:226–227
vengeance on Midians, 2:377
visits Balaam, 2:124–125
war plunder distribution, 2:387–389
water from the rock, 2:16–29
in the wilderness, 1:8–9
on wilderness journey, 2:435, 2:470–483
will dwell in Canaan, 2:484
Wind/Spirit, 1:284–286
Zelophehad's daughters, 2:292–294, 2:308

Zadok
descent from Phinehas, 2:237, 2:238
genealogy of, 2:258
Zalmonah encampment, 2:427, 2:440, 2:449
Zebulum, tribe of
change in population, 2:267
Zebulun, tribe of
arrangement of Camp, 1:82
census, 1:76
census figures, 1:93
census total, 1:87
chieftain Eliab, 1:78
dwells by the sea, 2:274

Elizaphan as chieftain, 2:428, 2:459–460
march from Sinai, 1:236
offering of, 1:176, 1:183
second census, 2:260
setting out on journey, 1:206
tribal ordering, 1:96, 1:97
tribe arrangement, 1:75
zodiacal sign, 1:23
Zechariah
YHWH as fire, 1:222
Zedad, 2:455
Canaan's border and, 2:428
Zelophehad
brothers of, 2:304
daughters of *see* Zelophehad's daughters
death in the wilderness, 2:320
death of, 2:420
death of wife, 2:302
of good character, 2:286–288, 2:309
of good name, 2:486
judgement on first generation, 2:320
land inheritance, 2:278
memorial land, 2:290
name preserved, 2:292
second census, 2:260
Zelophehad's daughters, 1:62, 1:65, 1:66, 1:213, 2:11, 2:256
context of, 2:283
counted in census, 2:305
descent from Machir, 2:423
effect of Jubilee, 2:299
faithfulness and character, 2:284–285
genealogy of, 2:285
given inheritance, 2:304–306
inherit land, 2:282
inheritance within clan, 2:485–495
Jubilee and, 2:488–489
land request, 2:404–405
Mahlah, Noah, Hoglah, Milcah and Tirzah, 2:260, 2:280, 2:305–306
marriage and, 2:321
marriage and dowry, 2:290–291
marry cousins, 2:304–305, 2:420, 2:485
memorial land, 2:290
Moses and, 1:215, 2:308
patrimony, 2:301–303
perpetuating name, 2:304

Zelophehad's daughters (*cont.*)
  presentation of case, 2:282
  prominence of, 2:305–306
  pursuit of land, 2:274
  request inheritance right, 2:282, 2:284–291
  request of, 2:320–321
  righteous speech, 2:357
  second census, 2:267, 2:268, 2:270
  in second census, 2:260
  as 'sons', 2:292–293
  Transjordan land, 2:412
  Transjordan request, 2:405
  tribe of Manasseh, 2:317, 2:318, 2:320
  true daughters of Joseph, 2:319, 2:321
  women and vows, 2:368
  YHWH grants land to, 2:298–299
  YHWH's response to, 2:292–294
Zephonites
  second census, 2:260
Zerahites
  second census, 2:259, 2:260
Zilpah
  son prioritized, 1:95, 1:96
Zimri, son of Salu
  alternative path, 2:234, 2:255
  chides Moses, 2:227
  'covenant of peace', 2:237–238
  Cozbi and, 2:241
  family and context, 2:227, 2:243
  flagrant display, 2:285
  harlotry, 1:11, 2:369–370
  harlotry apostasy, 2:222–224
  infidelity of, 2:256
  Midianite scheme and, 2:244–245
  Ohad clan, 2:269–270
  Phinehas slays, 2:211, 2:220–221, 2:229–230, 2:231–233, 2:258
  seduced, 2:252–253
  tribe's death toll, 2:266
Zin, wilderness of, 2:6–7, 2:308, 2:426
  Canaan's borders, 2:428
  Moses rebels, 2:280
  see also Kadesh
Mount Zion, 1:222
  the journey's end, 1:3
Ziphron, 2:455
  Canaan's border and, 2:428
Zippor, 2:154
Zipporah, wife of Moses, 1:292, 1:293, 1:295
zodiac symbols, 1:22–25
Zur, Midian king, 2:243–244, 2:245
  counselled by Balaam, 2:247
  father of Cozbi, 2:382
  slain by Israel, 2:372
  slain in war, 2:376, 2:381–382
Zuriel, son of Abihail, 1:110
  chieftain, 1:127
  duties of, 1:136